# SOCIAL PROBLEMS:

# PERSISTENT CHALLENGES

# SOCIAL PROBLEMS:
# PERSISTENT CHALLENGES

SECOND EDITION

EDITED BY

**EDWARD C. McDONAGH**
**UNIVERSITY OF ALABAMA**

**JON E. SIMPSON**
**UNIVERSITY OF MASSACHUSETTS**

**HOLT, RINEHART AND WINSTON, INC.**
NEW YORK   CHICAGO   SAN FRANCISCO   ATLANTA
DALLAS   MONTREAL   TORONTO   LONDON   SYDNEY

American society has experienced three great revolutions: the political revolution of the eighteenth century, the industrial revolution of the nineteenth century, and the urban revolution of our time. Each period has had its characteristic problems. For example, during the eighteenth century among the country's great concerns were political tyranny, religious persecution, and an emerging national identity. In the next century Americans became concerned with arduous working conditions and economic exploitation, the termination of slavery, unpredictable economic cycles, and the large number of unassimilated immigrants. The present generation senses some of the same concerns of the two previous centuries, but by this time our society has developed some measure of control over these persistent problems. We now possess the ingenuity to contain and direct, within limits, the effects of a particular social problem once we have identified it.

Students will recognize in the subsequent chapters a host of problems that for the most part have an urban derivation. This is a reflection of what we foresee as the accelerated development of a distinctly urban culture—a society with the capability and motivation to cope with such problems as poverty, minority status, violence, family instability, drug abuse, and population control and distribution. Thus in preparing this collection of readings our goal has been twofold: to provide students with an understanding of the prevailing difficulties of modern man in an urban milieu, with its corollary facets of mass culture and alienation, and at the same time to explore some of the sources of these problems, with a view toward formulating guidelines to relevant and useful solutions to them. In recognition of this latter objective, we have freely incorporated action-oriented selections in the substantive chapters.

Social problems, in the context of our discussion, are viewed as those significant discrepancies between cultural prescriptions and present-day conditions which influential leaders and involved persons believe should be ameliorated by appropriate social action. Our central concern, therefore, is the persistent problems of the twentieth century, not the dramatic problems of panic and disaster. We have avoided treating such major catastrophes as representative social problems because such crises tend to be only occasional and largely unpredictable in occurrence, unique in character, and for the most part not subject to amelioration.

Man seems recently to have learned to avoid two important disasters, economic depression and global war. Our national government has developed economic regulation to the degree that a depression of the scope of that experienced in the 1930s is highly improbable. Too, most nations have joined together politically through the modern media of "hot lines" and the United Nations to limit the possibility of a thermonuclear holocaust. We have thus addressed ourselves to those problems of contemporary man that are largely pervasive and predictable—the chronic problems that by appropriate social action can be made less acute, even if they cannot be altogether eliminated. The persistent challenge is to devise controls that will reduce the impact of these social problems on our lives.

This book is designed as a source of supplementary reading for courses devoted entirely to social problems or for any one of several courses in sociology and other social sciences that have social problems as a central core of their subject matter. For some time there has been a need to bring together selections from the recent social-problems literature published in the journals, books, and paperbacks, which are available to undergraduates in libraries at best only intermittently. A knowledge of primary sources both broadens and deepens the student's appreciation of the subject by exposing him to the original expression of scholars in the field. Students taking the introductory course in sociology will find that this book offers many pragmatic applications of concepts and theories concerning society.

Although the readings reflect a high level of scholarship, they are written with sufficient clarity and precision to place them within the range of this generation of college and university students. The editorial commentaries for each chapter are designed to introduce the selections that follow in a perspective of contemporary sociological thought, to alert the student to some of the historical and institutional characteristics of the problems under analysis, to provide, though in succinct form, an overview of the problem, and finally, to challenge the reader to weigh the evidence presented in the selections and perhaps explore further proofs or solutions.

The principal criteria that guided our selection of readings from the rich store of excellent material have been (1) that the writer be a person of professional competence, (2) that the source be one of acknowledged scholarship, (3) that the selection be a statement of sufficient length to offer a dependable feeling for the author's point of view (hence entire articles are reproduced from periodicals and, if necessary, entire chapters from books and paperbacks), (4) that the selections exhibit a writing style distinguished by readability, and (5) that the article present the type of solid information and lucid organization that will stir the imagination of alert students. Too, we have sought the most recently published statement of the contributor on each topic, and we must express our special gratitude to those writers who voluntarily brought their selections up to date specifically for this book. In brief, it has been our purpose to offer students more readings and fuller statements from among the works of the specialists presently writing on social problems.

In a more theoretical vein, we should perhaps comment that the selection of readings, their organization, and the composition of the editorial commentary have been from the point of view of twentieth-century man in transition from a culture that has been based largely on rural and village standards to an emerging urban culture that seeks to assimilate the diversities of race, social class, and political ideologies. Certainly it seems reasonable to anticipate that this new urban culture will, over the years, begin to provide some of the imperatively sought answers to the dilemmas of modern man. For example, we may expect the nuclear family, bereft of many of its traditional functions, to be supported by auxiliary institutions within the foreseeable future. Among such possibilities are the nursery school, the eleven-month school calendar, the availability in the community of expert counseling service for most family activities, the greater support of health and fringe benefits in industry, and the continued development of functional communities designed to meet the needs of retired persons.

Among the readings in this volume we should like to point out at least three analytical approaches to a perceptive examination of the more specific categories of social problems. First, there is the concept of social change, which is especially useful in reviewing problems related to the dynamics of urbanism and technology. Next, the theories of social disorganization have done much to sort out and bring understanding to problems arising from the breakdown in conventional standards and expectations. Finally, research in deviant behavior has carried forward studies in the individual manifestation of social problems. Of these three approaches, we have perhaps relied the most heavily on social change as a means of classifying problems, with particular emphasis on those problems resulting from social change in an urban setting, since this approach lends itself well to a search for the causes of social problems and their eventual containment.

Significant developments during the past five years have prompted some changes in this edition. More attention is focused on the expressions of discontent by college students, ghetto residents, war resisters, and frightened suburbanites with the slowness of the social and political establishment in providing a creative design for action, if not the vibrant reforms. Special emphasis has been given to materials oriented toward solutions, which comprise one-fourth of this edition. New selections, carefully chosen to maintain continuity with the theme of the previous edition, have been acquired from the latest available sources and include extensive excerpts from the report by the President's Commission on Law Enforcement and Administration of Justice and the Report of the National Advisory Commission on Civil Disorders. Finally, the introductory discussions for each chapter have been updated and expanded.

To help students and instructors correlate individual readings with a variety of course material and basic textbooks, we have provided two cross-reference charts, one keyed to texts on social problems and the other keyed to introductory sociology texts. The Supplemental Readings at the end of each chapter direct the reader to other significant and relevant topics, relate problems in American society to those in other cultures, and in some instances offer a different approach to a problem discussed in the chapter.

We want to express our appreciation to the writers and publishers for permission to reprint their works in this book, even though some selections constitute more than 10 percent of the work in which they were originally published. We acknowledge gratefully the critical comments and constructive recommendations of our former colleagues at the University of Southern California and at other colleges and universities.

*Edward C. McDonagh*
*Jon E. Simpson*

CROSS REFERENCES

TO OTHER TEXTS

# TEXTS IN

# SOCIAL PROBLEMS

Becker, Howard S.: *Social Problems*, New York: John Wiley & Sons, Inc., 1966.

Clinard, Marshall B.: *Sociology of Deviant Behavior*, 3d ed., New York: Holt, Rinehart and Winston, 1968.

Cuber, John F., William F. Kenkel, and Robert A. Harper: *Problems of American Society*, 4th ed., New York: Holt, Rinehart and Winston, 1964.

Dynes, Russell R., Alfred C. Clarke, Simon Dinitz, and Iwao Ishino: *Social Problems*, New York: Oxford University Press, 1964.

Horton, Paul B., and Gerald R. Leslie: *The Sociology of Social Problems*, 3d ed., New York: Appleton-Century-Crofts, Inc., 1965.

Kane, John J.: *Social Problems*, Englewood Cliffs, N.J.: Prentice-Hall, Inc., 1962.

Merton, Robert K., and Robert A. Nisbet: *Contemporary Social Problems*, 2d ed., New York: Harcourt, Brace & Co., 1966.

Raab, Earl, and Gertrude Jaeger Selznick: *Major Social Problems*, 2d ed., New York: Harper & Row, Publishers, 1964.

| CHAPTER IN TEXT | BECKER | CLINARD |
|---|---|---|
| 1 | 11,18,21 27,28 | 9,43 |
| 2 | 22–24 | 21 |
| 3 | 10,13,16 | 1,3–8 |
| 4 | 26 | 2,15,37 |
| 5 | 38–42 | 13,14,32 |
| 6 | 43–47,51 53 | 51 |
| 7 | 29–33,52 | 38–40 |
| 8 | 1,3,4 | 41,42 |
| 9 | 14,15 | 47 |
| 10 | 2 | 45 |
| 11 | 5–8 | 46 |
| 12 | 34–37 | 44 |
| 13 | | |
| 14 | 12,19 | 25,27,28 |
| 15 | | 26 |
| 16 | | 22,30,31 |
| 17 | | 29,33,52 |
| 18 | | 48–50 |
| 19 | | 53 |
| 20 | | |
| 21 | | |
| 23 | | |

| CUBER ET AL. | DYNES ET AL. | HORTON & LESLIE | KANE | MERTON & NISBET | RAAB SELZNICK |
|---|---|---|---|---|---|
| 5,8–10 | 43 | 48 | 43,48,49 | 44,51 | 1,2,4–8,43 48,49 |
| 43 | 9,10,16 | 9,10,43 | 1,2,4,5 | 39,40 | 39,40,50 |
| 48,50 | 2,4 | 50 | 34–37 | 38,41,42 | |
| 13–15 | 25–28 | 32 | | 47,53 | 38,41,42 45–50,53,58 |
| 16 | 11,18,21–24 | 38,41,42 | 44,51 | 46 | 29–31 |
| 1,2,4 | 3 | 39,40 | 26 | 9 | 32,33,52 |
| 34–37 | 48–50 | 25–28 | 39,40 | 45 | 25–28 |
| 25,27,28 | 51 | 3 | 38,42,45 41 | 34–37 | 18,21–24 |
| 21–24 | 5–8 | 34–37 | 47 | 22,29–33, 52 | 14–16 44,51,56 |
| 3 | | 11,18,21–24 | 46 | 25–28 | 3 |
| 6,7 | 29 | 14,15 | 9 | 10,13,16 | 20,34–37 |
| 29–31,33 | 30–33,52 | | 17,29–33, 52 | 14,15 | 9–13,19 |
| | 13,14,17 | 29–31 | 3 | 1–4 | |
| 44,51 | | 33,52 | | 12,20,24 | |
| 26 | 44 | 1,2,4 | 25,27,28 | 43–50 | |
| 38,41,42 | 41–43,38–40 | 5–8 | | | |
| 39,40 | 45–47,53 | 44–47 | 11,18, 21–24 | | |
| 45–47,53 | 41,42 | 51 | | | |
| 11,17–19 32 | | 19 | | | |
| 20 | | 20,49 | | | |
| | | 13 | | | |
| 49 | | | | | |

# TEXTS IN INTRODUCTORY SOCIOLOGY

Bertrand, Alvin L.: *Basic Sociology*, New York: Appleton-Century-Crofts, Inc., 1967.

Bredemeier, Harry C., and Richard M. Stephenson: *The Analysis of Social Systems*, New York: Holt, Rinehart and Winston, 1962.

Broom, Leonard, and Philip Selznick: *Sociology*, 4th ed., New York: Harper & Row, Publishers, 1968.

Chinoy, Ely: *Society*, 2d ed., New York: Random House, Inc, 1967.

Cuber, John F.: *Sociology*, 6th ed., New York: Appleton-Century-Crofts, Inc., 1968.

Horton, Paul B., Chester L. Hunt: *Sociology*, 2d ed., New York: McGraw-Hill Book Company, 1968.

Lundberg, George A., Clarence C. Schrag, and Otto N. Larsen: *Sociology*, 4th ed., New York: Harper & Row, Publishers, 1968.

Mott, Paul C.: *The Organization of Society*, Englewood Cliffs, N.J.: Prentice-Hall, Inc., 1965.

Smelser, Neil: *Sociology*, New York: John Wiley & Sons, Inc., 1967.

Vander Zanden, James W.: *Sociology*, New York: The Ronald Press Company, 1965.

Wilson, Everett K.: *Sociology*, Homewood, Ill.: The Dorsey Press, 1966.

| CHAPTER IN TEXT | BERTRAND | BREDEMEIER & STEPHENSON | BROOM & SELZNICK |
| --- | --- | --- | --- |
| 1 | 48 | 5–8 | 43,48–50 |
| 2 | | 1–4,43 | 9,12 |
| 3 | 30,50 | 9–12 | 5–8 |
| 4 | 9,10,12 | 21–23 | 21,28,44 |
| 5 | 49 | 38–42,44–47 | 3,25–27,30 |
| 6 | 5,8 | 29,32,33,51,53 | 29,31–33 |
| 7 | 6 | 25–28 | 10 |
| 8 | 7,32 | 13–16 | 2,11,17,18 |
| 9 | | 48,49,52 | 34–37 |
| 10 | 28,31,39 | 17,18 | |
| 11 | 17,18 | 30,31 | 22–24 |
| 12 | 20 | 19,20,24 | 38–42,46 |
| 13 | 43–47 | | 1.4 |
| 14 | 38,41–42 | | 13–16 |
| 15 | 2 | | 19,20 |
| 16 | 51–53 | | |
| 17 | 25–27 | | |
| 18 | 11,21–24 | | |
| 19 | 13–16,19 | | |
| 20 | 34–37 | | |
| 21 | 29,33 | | |
| 22 | 1,3,4 | | |
| 23 | | | |
| 24 | | | |
| 25 | | | |
| 26 | | | |
| 27 | | | |
| 28 | | | |

| CHINOY | CUBER | HORTON & HUNT | LUNDBERT ET AL. | MOTT | SMELSER | VANDER ZANDEN | WILSON |
|---|---|---|---|---|---|---|---|
| 48 | 43 | 43 | 49 | 48–50 | 17,32 | 48 | 21,50 |
| 5–8 | 50 | 48,49 | 50 | 2 | 1–3 | 5 | 5,8 |
| 21 | 48,49 | 5–8 | 30 | 21,34,35 | 10,16 | 9,39,43–47 | 6,7 |
| 9,28 | 5–8,10,41 | 29 | 1–4 | 4 | 15,29–31,33 | 8,29 | 24,28 |
| 43 | | 21,44 | 16 | 16 | 13,14 | 16 | 13–15,29,31 |
| | | 27,31 | 46 | | | 13 | 9,23,27 |
| 25–27 | 29 | 9,39–42, 44 46,47 | 17–20 | 36,37 | 21–24 | 6,7 | 1,2,4 |
| 30,31 | | 26 | 7 | | 18–20 | | 34–36 |
| 29,32,33,52 | 21 | 10 | 9,53 | 1,2,5,9 | 25–28 | 21 | 16 |
| | 9,12 | 25,28 | 25–28 | 15,32 | 9,12 | 12,27 | 11,25,26 |
| 1–4 | 22 | 13–15 | 29,31,33 | 13 | 38–47 | 10,26 | 3 |
| 10,13–16 | | 4,22 | 32 | 31 | 48–53 | 40 | 10,19,30 |
| 17–20 | 39,44–47 | 33 | 10 | 14,28,30 | | 30,31 | 38,46,51 |
| | 38 | 11,17,19 | 21–23 | 3 | | 33 | 39,40,43 |
| 2,22–24 | 27,40 | 30,52 | 5,6,8 | 29,33,52 | | 25,28 | 17,18,37,52 |
| 49,50 | 26 | 38 | 11,12 | 38,43 | | 3 | 24,47–49 |
| 34–37 | 16 | 34–37 | 43 | 6–8 | | 14,15 | |
| 12,46,51 | 30,32,33,52 | 1–3 | 39–42,44, 45,47 | 25–27 | | 17,20,32,52 | |
| 38–42,44, 45,47 | 34–37 | 51,53 | | 10 | | 11,22–24 | |
| 53 | 4 | 12,18,32 | 51,52 | 49 | | 1,2,4,34–37 | |
| | 1,2 | | 13–15 | 12,19,24 | | 49–51,53 | |
| | 31 | | 34–47 | 11,17,18 | | | |
| | 13 | | | | | | |
| | 25,28 | | 24,48 | | | | |
| | 14,15 | | | | | | |
| | 17–20 | | | | | | |
| | 13,23,24 | | | | | | |
| | 3 | | | | | | |

# CONTENTS

PART ONE

CONTEMPORARY

SOCIETAL ORIENTATIONS

# URBANISM

## CHAPTER ONE

Contemporary America is an urban society, a society becoming increasingly more urban with the passage of each decade. In 1790 less than 6 percent of the population could be considered urban, whereas today about 75 percent of the American people reside in standard metropolitan areas. Virtually every community in the nation is under the steady urban influence of newspaper, telephone, radio, television, and the proximity of the superhighway. Urbanism is now an established way of life for the majority of Americans. According to urbanologists, the city and its environs contain not only most of the American population, but its major persistent problems. In the city social problems are observed at close range, almost block by block, class by class, and ghetto by ghetto.

The enormous fragmentation of urban populations may well be one of the great challenges of the twentieth century, an observation documented in detail in the selections of Daniel P. Moynihan and the President's Commission on Civil Disorder. Thus for many urban dwellers there are few roots in kinship or lasting friendships. Without the support of family and friends the task of securing social acceptance is difficult. City people are by habit not overtly friendly, and most of their personal contacts tend to be superficial. Hence human relations in the urban area are of the touch-and-go variety. "Urbanism" is coming to mean a collection of unique problems found in our large metropolitan areas. For illustrative purposes a few of these problems are selected to make clear the unique impact of urban living on an increasing number of Americans.

Congestion is perhaps our first impression of a large city. We see people congested on subways, at lunch counters at noon, at sports events, in large department stores, and on the superhighway. This congestion is felt at its worst at the close of the day, when millions of workers quickly empty office buildings and flood the subways and highways leading out of the inner city. Major interchange lanes of major expressways become slow-moving parking lots of automobiles, a truly bumper-to-bumper society of strangers. Without question the automobile has added greatly to urban sprawl; the metropolitan area of Los Angeles, for example, is now larger than 5,000 square miles of congestion. Interestingly, freeway drivers, in the main, steadfastly refuse to

*3*

join motor pools connecting suburbia and the inner city. For literally millions of urban drivers the automobile has become a device for insulating themselves from their families at one end of the trip and bosses at the other. The driver's "reward" for the 37-minute ride home by himself is privacy, a value hard to fulfill in the urban world. More and more Americans are adding to urban congestion by insisting on using their automobiles as a private means of transportation in urban areas. This general tendency is a considerable impediment to attempts to develop efficient means of public transportation and effective reduction of air pollution.

Noise is a strong reminder that much mechanical activity goes on in the city. A person of average sensitivity hears the noises generated by elevated trains, the hum of automobiles, the roar of jet airplanes, the sirens of fire and police vehicles, the clatter of ash cans being emptied with irregular rhythm—all muted by radio music piped into stores, hospitals, and factories. A city without noise would be difficult to imagine. Urbanites become so accustomed to noise that they find it almost impossible to adjust to the lack of noise in chapels, libraries, or soundproof office buildings.

Slums and blighted areas characterize much of the central areas of our large American cities. Slums are largely the result of prolonged neglect by indifferent public officials and citizens. They are the breeding ground for disease, delinquency, and violence. Much of the demand for "law and order on the streets" is directed to the symptoms of the slums, and not at the basic cause of urban violence, the deteriorating inner city. In economic terms, slums are the subsidized areas of cities where taxes fail to support almost half the urban services provided by police, fire, and health departments. Slums continue to be the living areas of the poor, those discriminated against ethnically, the homeless, and the jobless. Businesses such as pawnbrokers' shops, burlesque, and flophouses abound. Slums are emerging faster than planners can eliminate them by urban redevelopment. What was old can be new, but formidable opposition to urban redevelopment seems to be generated by landlords of slum property, "adjusted slum dwellers," and others who oppose government interference in the reduction of human suffering.

The selection "Urban Conditions" by Daniel P. Moynihan, director of the M.I.T.-Harvard Joint Center for Urban Studies, presents an interesting thesis that social scientists are always imagined to be "on the side" of the depressed and disadvantaged. He indicates that when social scientists are critical of the behavior or goals of the disadvantaged they must be prepared to accept the accusation of being described as betrayers. Moynihan raises an interesting question: to what extent are the value system and frame of reference of social scientists significantly different from those of the urban masses? One of the key problems of social scientists is to present social reality accurately and without selective class perception. There is, however, growing evidence that the urban poor do not want their problems described and analyzed by the mass media.

Multicultures of the city represent one of the most intriguing sociological problems of modern times. Man's folkways, mores, and culture were, for the most part, developed in rural settings to solve the needs of a rural society. Man now finds himself living in great metropolitan regions largely without an urban religion, urban philosophy, or urban family patterns. To add to our complications, the urban area is the meeting ground for cultural diversity in religion, race, nationality, and philosophy. Perhaps only the Jews have been able to develop an adequate subculture to survive in the urban environment, and as Fred Massarik points out in "The Jewish Community," there is considerable speculation that the Jews adjust with increasing difficulty to the requirements of the massive urban center. Something more profound than the urban hippie with his sandals and beads is necessary to create a meaningful urban culture; the hippie movement contributes a question about urban culture, not a solution.

In the selection "The Future of the Cities," by the President's Commission on Civil Disorders, some challenging projections are made concerning the increasing segregated status of Negroes. Does the coming of urban apartheid envision a police state to maintain order, or does urban control of the power structure by Negroes anticipate a renaissance in ethnic justice for all minority groups?

Upper-middle-class urban professionals and executives are moving to suburbia as an escape from some of the hard realities of city life. The inner city at night contains a significantly different population than by day. Suburbia, especially in the West, has given some middle-class Americans an opportunity to play a rural role at night and on weekends. Houses are built to affect a "ranch" appearance, rural symbols of wagon wheels become conspicuous parts of the planned landscape, a rail fence encloses the "acreage," and picturesque names of birds, berries, and parts of harness become the identifiers of streets and roads. Horses are often owned or rented for riding, with a strong emphasis placed on learning to ride "Western style." Suburbia offers many symbols of a former rural life, but virtually none of the real advantages of the American frontier. William Dobriner, in "The Natural History of a Reluctant Suburb," analyzes some of the interaction problems encountered by urbanites transplanted to the small community. Taxes for local schools become a great burden, inasmuch as industrial properties are excluded by zoning codes from suburban areas. Suburban life is a poor solution to the problems of urbanization. Perhaps suburban life is best described as a reactive adjustment to urbanism, certainly not as an intelligent solution.

In this chapter four incisive selections touch on some of the most persistent problems urban life offers contemporary man. Daniel P. Moynihan reviews the nature of social indicators necessary to the development of a reliable body of information about urbanism. The President's Commission on Civil Disorder takes a hard look at the present trends in urban areas augmenting ethnic segregation and the long-run implications of an urban world built on ethnic sectors. Fred Massarik discusses the ability of the Jews to create a sense of community in the impersonal city, and William Dobriner presents a critical opinion of the advantages of suburban living in the setting of the long-established American village.

## 1    URBAN CONDITIONS    DANIEL P. MOYNIHAN

A characteristic theme of American politics at this time, and an emerging element of American sensibility, is that of "urban crisis." Shorn of a tendency to overdo, much of this comes down to a common-sense concern with the immediate social and physical environment on the part of a society that has been perhaps overmuch involved with questions of cosmic import—and cosmic inscrutability. This tendency is likely to become more, not less pronounced: the current military involvement in Asia is demonstrating to the nation clearly enough that there are limits to its desire to manage the world, just as there are limits to the world's desire to be managed. Peace is likely to bring a very considerable inward turning, and this is more than likely to be defined in terms of an "attack" (there is no avoiding an excess of aggressiveness in American life) on the problems of cities. Current expositions of the subject, for example, the hearings conducted by Senator Abraham Ribicoff's Subcommittee on Executive Reorganization of the United States Senate Committee on Government Operations, as well as President Johnson's plans for a model cities program, provide the rudiments of a postwar planning program. The proposals will

Reprinted from *The Annals*, vol. 371 (May 1967), pp. 160–177, by permission of the author and The American Academy of Political and Social Science.

be there when, as may be the case, the national government is, of a sudden, looking about for something else to do. Moreover, in a nation that increasingly senses the immense burdens imposed by the racial barriers and hostilities of the present, concern for "urban affairs" is certain to emerge as the most acceptable code word for "Negro" problems—and the white attitudes that give rise to so many of them.

In the familiar pattern, this poses both an opportunity and a problem for the social sciences. Irving Louis Horowitz has put it thus: "The problem of social policy becomes acute precisely to the degree to which social science becomes exact." The demonstrated feasibility of putting social science information and theory to work on social problems imposes a new and special set of strains both on policy-makers and on those who would advise them. To a degree that has not, perhaps, existed since the age of theological certitude, it becomes possible to be "right" or "wrong," and difficult—even impossible—to avoid scrutiny in just these terms. There is no turning back: we have bit this bullet, and had best get on with the slaughter of a good many of those cherished notions which are certain to perish in the first data runs. It will be easy enough to demonstrate what does not work: the job of social science must be to provide some plausible suggestions as to what will work.

## THREE GENERAL PROPOSITIONS

Three general propositions may be made. First of all, it is essential that all concerned with the development of a system of urban social indicators be prepared in advance to find themselves accused of having betrayed some of those very causes with which they have been most allied. Concern about urban affairs derives directly from concern about urban problems: it involves the statement by certain persons that certain things are not as they ought to be, and must be changed for the better. Such attitudes are almost always minority views, at least in the beginning. As a group, however, American social scientists are peculiarly prone to sharing and even to creating such concerns. They are problem-prone and reform-minded, and inevitably come to be seen as allies by those about whose problems they are most concerned. These latter, becoming accustomed to having social scientists on their side, easily come to assume that social science will be. This does not always happen, a fact not easily forgiven. Knowledge is power, and in contemporary society social scientists are often in the position of handing power about in an almost absent-minded way. Professional ethics, at least as ideally defined, can lead them to hand out the very best arguments to those whom they would consider the very worst contenders. This is a dilemma not yet well understood, and certainly not resolved. For the moment, the most that can be done is to be forewarned.[1]

The second proposition is that the way in which urban indicators are developed is likely to have considerable influence on the level of government—and of abstraction—at which the problems are dealt with. Specifically, if urban indicators remain for the most part "national" statistics, a powerful built-in tendency to seek "national" solutions will emerge.

This is no small matter. The economic policies of the federal government over the past two generations—beginning with the New Deal—have been brilliantly successful. But they have concentrated attention on data at the continental, even the global level—"aggregatics" in Bertram Gross's allusive term—to the exclusion, or at very least the neglect, of specific circumstances. Thus, the United States has, quite possibly, the best employment data in the world, but there is no city in the nation that knows what its unemployment rate is. And while the economy of the nation booms, sizzles, and soars, it has somehow become a practice for city workers to riot every summer; after which disturbances, enquiries determine that quite astonishing numbers of them were without work. An impressive number of contradictions have somehow slipped through the interstices of the macropolicy net. We are the richest nation on earth, with some of the worst slums; the most educated, with some of the most marginal school children; and the most mobile, with some of the most rigid caste confinements. One likely source of these contradictions is the reluctance, even the refusal, of many public organizations to report, much less to insist on, the relationship between their activities and concerns with other problems. This must be presumed to be part of the explanation behind Scott Greer's statement that "at a cost of more than three billion dollars, the Urban Renewal Agency has succeeded in materially reducing the supply of low cost housing in American cities." Insisting that one thing has nothing to do with another is likely to have the effect of intensifying rather than moderating the unavoidable interactions.

A third general consideration may be termed a matter of temperament. It has to do with the fact that urban social indicators are almost certainly going to be developed by professors and government executives who will be far more concerned with what is bad about cities than with what is good about them. These men will judge good and bad in terms of their own rather special values acquired in the course of family, religious, educational, and occupational experiences that, by and large, are quite different from those of the urban masses whose condition they will seek to measure. The idea of social indicators, and of an urban subset, is pre-eminently a product of the American intellectual world, although, of course, with a whole European tradition behind it. But the particular quality of the American intellectual—quite distinct from his European counterpart—has been the tendency to view cities with alarm, fear, and distaste, a history which Morton and Lucia White have summed up as "one of adverse metaphysical speculation and bad dreams about urban life, of aesthetic and moral recoil from the American city's ugliness, commercialism, and crime."[2] Surely some measure of the present concern with ugliness, commercialism, and crime is simply an inversion of the earlier views: precisely the same judgment about cities is handed down, with only a gloss of compassion and concern that things might somehow be made otherwise. The view that when one is tired of London one is tired of life is not one that has met much favor on American campuses—nor yet the proposition put to Hennessy by Dooley that while the country might be where the good things in life come from, it is the city that they go *to*. Neither the great Tory nor the Chicago saloonkeeper spoke with the accents of liberal academia: the one too confident, the other too clever for that special world.

The task, then, is to make the most of the special kinds of sensibility that will be brought to bear on cities by this group, including one of its most attractive qualities, the awareness that tastes differ and a willingness to allow, even to encourage, them to do so. A further, almost a defining characteristic of American academics of the present age is the realization that everything has to do with everything else. American professors may be obscure, but they are hardly simple-minded. Their judgment as to what facts are relevant to the urban condition is likely to approach that condition itself in complexity and detail.

## FOUR GUIDELINES

With these considerations in mind, it becomes possible to lay down four general guidelines for a system of urban social indicators, not so much as rules than as principles. It is contended merely that, to the extent information is organized along these principles, it is more likely than not to be useful and to be used.

*First, urban social indicators should be the realm of disaggregation and correlation*

To the greatest possible extent the data should be organized in terms of the Standard Metropolitan Statistical Areas (SMSA's) as defined by the Bureau of Census (there are now 227 SMSA's) and by census tract levels where this is highly significant, as in the case of poverty neighborhoods. Data should be organized in terms of political jurisdictions as well, so that they may be used by government organizations and by political candidates and parties. Moreover, if the relations between different phenomena are to be perceived and responded to in the workaday world of municipal affairs, it is necessary for the indicators to report such relations in the form of correlations and similar mathematical analyses, rather than to await the random initiatives of individual scholars. The relationships of functions such as unemployment to welfare dependency, to use but one example, are matters of fundamental interest to city government, but are rarely known, and even less often commented upon. Social indicators can bring these relations into the open, as it were, making them at once more visible and less threatening.

It will be obvious that some forms of urban indicators, such as air pollution or noise levels, are necessarily defined in terms of specific localities, and will automatically be reported in such terms. Similarly, there are apt to be many topics about which local data would be desirable, but for which survey costs would be greater than the likely return. The point in every instance is simply to collect as much specifically local data as resources permit.

*Second, inasmuch as urban social indicators cannot be apolitical, they must be pan-political*

The very existence of such indicators is a political fact, responding to the desire of a small body of opinion that there should be greater awareness of urban problems—in order that there should be more effective political action in dealing with them. Such information cannot be neutral. The choice of what is to be included, the manner of presenting it, and the interrelations that are sought out will reflect profound political attitudes and interests. They must, therefore, cater to as wide as possible a spectrum of political interests. Ideally, the volume of urban social indicators, should they become a reality, will be found on the desks of the head speech writers for *all* the mayoralty candidates in all the cities that are covered. What applies to the central cities should be equally the case for the surrounding suburbs: the distinction between city and suburb is merely a way of describing one aspect of the urban situation. The greatest danger of the enterprise is that the indicators will be shaped primarily in terms of the political attitudes and social programs of liberal Democrats, for the simple reason that most of the men conceiving the effort and carrying it forward will be of that persuasion. A deliberate effort should be made to include subjects of interest to other parties and more conservative points of view.

Crime is an important instance. It is, and for several generations has been, one of the most important political issues in the nation. There is probably no other issue that is so specifically identified by the public as an "urban" issue and an "urban" problem. It is also a racial problem. For that reason and for a combination of others, liberal academics have tended to ignore or skirt the issue, hoping, perhaps, that it would go away or in some way escape the attention of the public. Nothing of the sort has happened: crime in the streets has become, if anything, a more explosive issue as time has passed. Thus, in his special message proposing the Safe Streets and Crime Control Act of 1967, President Johnson reported that in a recent survey of two of our largest cities: "43 per cent of those interviewed stayed off the streets at night." A survey conducted for the Commission on Law Enforcement and the Administration of Justice showed that crime, after race relations, is clearly thought to be the most important domestic problem.[3] This is the kind of information that can be collected in the present and which can be built into a time series from which important political arguments and deductions can be derived.

Similarly, the racial component of crime must be lived with. The President's Commission on Crime in the District of Columbia has reported that Negro males committed 76 per cent of all serious offenses in the District in the years 1961-1965, and that Negro males and females together accounted for 86 per cent. This represents a rising proportion. In the decade 1950-1960, Negro males committed only 69 per cent of such offenses, while the male-female combination was only 77 per cent. These figures clearly correspond to the impressions of the white community, including the congressional community in the District, and these impressions will not recede simply because such information is not included in a series of urban indicators. If anything, the opposite might be the case: fears are often exaggerated, and will tend to persist for some time after the reality changes. Properly compiled urban crime statistics would probably show stable crime rates in terms of age groups, and will surely pick up declining crime rates well in advance of the popular perception. (Note the wide attention given to the recent announcement by the Bureau of Narcotics that the incidence of Negro drug addiction appears to be declining while that of whites is rising.) At a less heated level of concern is the Republican party's interest in increasing the opportunities of low-income Americans to own their own homes, as recently announced by Congressman Gerald R. Ford and Senator Charles H. Percy. This is a matter easily enough measured, and ought to be included in the housing data on American cities. As time passes, it may abet the Republican cause, or injure it, but in any event the indicators will be relevant to the political world which inspired them.

*Third, urban social indicators should be concerned with the future as well as with the present*

For some reason, government (and, to a lesser degree, business), although they collect and calculate a considerable range of "facts" about the future, are nonetheless curiously hesitant about making them public in any very assertive way. This is surely a mistake. Most public policy proceeds from assumptions as to what the future will be like, and these assumptions can often be significantly influenced by perfectly

**TABLE 1**    *Projections of nonwhite proportion of United States population, 1970–1985*

| Year | High fertility projection, % | Low fertility projection, % |
|------|------------------------------|-----------------------------|
| 1970 | 15.8 | 15.8 |
| 1975 | 16.3 | 15.9 |
| 1980 | 16.7 | 15.9 |
| 1985 | 17.2 | 16.1 |

Source: Derived from "Projections of the White and Non-white Population of the United States, by Age and Sex, to 1985," *Current Population Reports: Population Estimates,* Series P-25, no. 345.

"knowable" information. In areas such as labor-force composition and school enrollment, this can be done with considerable accuracy, and can be used to much greater purpose than has been the case. As an example, current projections of the white and nonwhite population of the United States, when calculated in percentage terms, suggest that the school integration problem will be considerably greater than one might assume from the proposition that "Negroes make up about one-tenth of the population." The nonwhite proportion of the population between ages five and nine over the next twenty years is projected as shown in Table 1. This would suggest, for example, that, in the very near future, upwards of one child in five entering public schools, nationally, will be nonwhite. Obviously, these proportions are much greater in certain central city areas, but, here again, it is possible to forecast with acceptable degrees of probable accuracy.

*Fourth, urban indicators should seek to provide comparisons between local data, average national data, and data corresponding to "best practice" in various fields*

The Council of Economic Advisors' well-established practice of including in their Annual Report an analysis of the "gap" between the actual and the potential gross national product provides an excellent instance of the power of this type of analysis to create pressures for more effective

social and economic policies.[4] A quite startling instance of wide disparities in performance will be found in the Selective Service rejection rates. Thus, in 1965, 48 per cent of the young men called up in South Carolina failed the mental examination, as contrasted with a failure rate of 5 per cent in Iowa. A wide difference in rejection rates exists between whites and nonwhites, and very probably between social class and neighborhood, if the data were available at this level of disaggregation. In 1965, for example, the disqualification rate for white draftees of 14.7 per cent contrasts sharply with a mental disqualification rate for Negroes of 59.6 per cent. With effort, it is likely that a considerable range of national test performance of this kind could be disaggregated to local areas, perhaps health and school districts, with possibly important consequences in terms of local judgments as to the adequacy of community services. In North Carolina, for example, the high rate of Selective Service mental-test rejections has become an issue of considerable concern.

Those things being said, it remains only to assert Bertram Gross's formulation: The object of social indicators should be to report "the condition of man in the metropolitan area" and to do so in three categories: (1) people as individuals, (2) families, and (3) institutions.[5]

## INDIVIDUALS

NUMBERS, DISTRIBUTION, AND DENSITY    The threshold data of any system of urban social indicators should be the direct census counts of individuals by age, sex, race, and any other general categories that may emerge as relevant. This type of information will become increasingly more current and more accurate, but some effort should be made to indicate where the data is presently limited or not accurate. Thus the male-female ratio among nonwhites suggests not only that the information-gathering process is imperfect, but, much more important, that this is so because of a social problem of considerable dimensions (see Table 2).

The distribution of urban population in terms of race and income level is an indispensable set of urban data. Segregation indices, as outlined by Otis Dudley Duncan and Beverly Duncan,[6] should be compiled for every SMSA in the nation, and changes over time should be carefully recorded. Studies such as James Coleman's *Equality of Educational Opportunity* strongly suggest that the stratification of white neighborhoods into homogeneous social and economic groups will have the same impact on those in the lower white strata as does race segregation on lower-status Negroes. This would argue in favor of much more extensive efforts to learn how this kind of "one-class" white neighborhood is developing, particularly in low-density suburbanized areas.

Techniques of computer mapping are advancing rapidly, and are readily adaptable to this type of use. They are similarly available to chart population densities, with perhaps special reference to changes over time and changes during the 24-hour work-day cycle. Since automobiles are an indispensable and an increasingly inseparable adjunct to individuals, some measure of density in this respect ought certainly to be included.

**MOVEMENT** Americans continue to be an immensely mobile, almost a nomadic people, and as Doxiades observes, in the manner of nomads everywhere, lavish considerably more affection on their means of transportation than on their tempo-

**TABLE 2** *Ratio of males per 100 females in the population by color, July 1, 1963*

| Age | Males per 100 females | |
|---|---|---|
| | White | Non-white |
| Under 5 | 104.4 | 100.4 |
| 5-9 years | 103.9 | 100.0 |
| 10-14 years | 104.0 | 100.0 |
| 15-19 years | 103.2 | 99.5 |
| 20-24 years | 101.2 | 95.1 |
| 25-29 years | 100.1 | 89.1 |
| 30-34 years | 99.2 | 86.6 |
| 35-39 years | 97.5 | 86.8 |
| 40-44 years | 96.2 | 89.9 |
| 45-49 years | 96.5 | 90.6 |

Source: *Current Population Reports*, Series P-25, No. 276, Table 1 (total population, including armed forces abroad).

rary abodes. It is clear that this movement responds to the differing levels of economic opportunity in different cities. Movement from the countryside is not likely to be of great significance in the future. Half of the counties in the United States lost population in the 1950's, while the current drop in farm employment suggests that a bottom of sorts is soon to be reached. Hence, most future migration will be from city to city. Because this particularly affects Southern Negroes and, more generally, all low-income groups, it would seem past time that cities began to have some measure of in- and out-migration between SMSA's. Such information would be of particular importance should there develop some effort to provide settling-in services for low-income migrants.

Similarly, a good deal more could be usefully known about movement within metropolitan areas, both the outflow to the suburbs and the reverse flow, or so one hears, of middle-aged couples whose children have established households of their own.

**EMPLOYMENT AND INCOME** There is no single area where disaggregation is more urgently needed than that of employment. Given dependable data on employment and income, it is more than likely that cities and metropolitan areas will be able to respond to opportunities and negotiate hazards with a measure of effectiveness far beyond the contemporary level of campaign promises by mayoralty candidates and *ad hoc* gatherings of concerned corporation executives. Disaggregation must go beyond the labor market area, to the point where something is learned about employment conditions in the deepest slums. A pioneering effort in this direction has been made by the United States Department of Labor in a study of unemployment in the worst slums of twenty major cities, made public in March 1967. The surveys found that "the nonwhite (principally Negro) unemployment rate is about (or more than) three times the white unemployment rate in 8 of these areas, two times as high in 6 or more, half again as high in 2 others."[7] A "subemployment" rate was calculated that ranged as high as 47.4 per cent in

San Antonio. But, just as important, it was found that these rates, while high, concerned small numbers of persons, and the study concluded that "the problem is clearly of manageable proportions." Thus does information reveal both the existence of a social problem and the fact that it is of a size that it can be faced.

Categories of labor-force data of greatest concern to economic and social planning are well known; again it is the disaggregation that is of the essence. Special note might, however, be taken of the increasing signficance in female labor-force participation rates. (In the District of Columbia, nonwhite female labor-force participation reaches as high as 66 per cent.) Similarly, great attention is paid to the prospects for increases or decreases in the overall number of jobs in different occupational categories—that is, manufacturing employment will rise or decline by this per cent or that number. Too little attention is paid to the distribution of job openings that will occur through replacement needs. This source of new job opportunities for individuals is very large indeed, and is often quite at variance with the unemployment elements in the labor force. Similarly, much more close attention needs to be paid to the differentials in income between men and women, between the races, and among men and women of different races. The closing of the white-nonwhite income gap for females is, for example, in dramatic contrast to the persisting gaps for males.

The distribution of job opportunities between low-skill and high-skill occupations has been a traditional concern of economists. Increasingly, city officials are likely also to be concerned with the *locations* of such openings. Thus, there appears to be a powerful long-term trend for new business or new industries to locate outside central cities. In the period of 1954-1965, for example, over 80 per cent of the value of new industrial construction in the Boston, Los Angeles, San Francisco, and Washington, D.C., Standard Metropolitan

TABLE 3  *New private nonresidential building outside the central cities of standard metropolitan statistical areas (SMSA's), 1954–1965\**

| Type of new nonresidential building | Valuation of permits authorized for new nonresidential building, % | | | | | | |
|---|---|---|---|---|---|---|---|
| | United States | Atlanta | Boston | Chicago | Detroit | Indian- apolis | Los Angeles |
| All types† | 49 | 42.5 | 68.0 | 63 | 71.1 | 44.2 | 62 |
| Business | 46 | 40.5 | 69.6 | 61 | 72.5 | 49.5 | 63 |
| Industrial | 63 | 65.9 | 82.0 | 73 | 74.9 | 60.8 | 86 |
| Stores and other mercantile buildings | 53 | 39.5 | 74.2 | 67 | 77.4 | 51.8 | 66 |
| Office buildings | 27 | 21.0 | 51.2 | 39 | 58.3 | 20.8 | 41 |
| Gasoline and service stations | 53 | 60.1 | 82.0 | 59 | 65.0 | 56.3 | 62 |
| Community | 45 | 47.6 | 67.1 | 66 | 70.2 | 40.1 | 63 |
| Educational | 50 | 56.9 | 71.8 | 69 | 79.4 | 45.8 | 59 |
| Hospital and institutional | 36 | 32.2 | 41.0 | 58 | 61.6 | 10.0 | 70 |
| Religious | 54 | 58.9 | 85.6 | 68 | 74.1 | 58.7 | 70 |
| Amusement | 48 | 29.6 | 64.2 | 75 | 43.0 | 51.9 | 50 |

\*Excludes data for 1959, for which comparable information is not available.
†Includes types not shown separately and excludes major additions and alterations for which type of building is not known.

Statistical Areas was located outside the central city. Wendell D. MacDonald, Regional Director of the Bureau of Labor Statistics in the Boston Area, states flatly that this trend is "intensifying the employment problems of the poor, especially Negroes."

**ANTISOCIAL BEHAVIOR**    Crime data have probably been the weakest area of social indicators in recent decades—here as in so many other areas it has not been ignorance that has hurt so much as "knowing all those things that aren't so." The work of the President's Commission provides an important baseline from which it should be possible to move on to a reasonably dependable system of measuring the extent and nature of antisocial behavior.

A much neglected area of police encounters with citizens is that of traffic-law enforcement. The persistent view that somehow a person arrested for a traffic offense has not "really" been arrested suggests that American citizens are getting

used to being arrested: a proposition that Orwell has had something to say about. The incidence of arrest by armed police on the highways is a cause for national concern. Surely there are better ways to regulate a transportation system. In any event, nothing is likely to be done in this area until the true incidence of such events is clearly recorded.

**HEALTH**    Although the disaggregation of health indices would seem to be a rather straightforward affair, there are yet a number of puzzles to be solved. It is possible that careful area studies will show differences of considerable importance that will relate to social and economic issues such as air pollution, slum housing, industrial diseases, and the like; see, for example, Table 3. One potentially important source of localized information would be the medical rejection rate for Selective Service examinations, which could be charted by census tract if the effort were only made. Contrary to general impressions, these rejection rates show an inverse relationship between performance on the mental and the medical examination. Areas with high mental failure rates have low medical failure rates, and vice versa. This is also true, although less strikingly so, of whites and Negroes. This difference has not been explained and, of course, conflicts with what is generally thought to be the case. Mental-test rejection rates are a measure of community success or failure in education, because the test is perfectly uniform and the rates of failure widely divergent. For this reason, mental-test rejection rates have a potential as an indicator of the greatest importance.

**PARTICIPATION RATES**    Participation rates are likely to become the most popular form of urban social indicators. It is here that citizens are most likely to find some measure of their own performance in terms which relate to the populace at large. Because the range of such indices is very considerable, it is, perhaps, not likely that more than a few basic matters can be dealt with at the outset. These should pertain to involvement in basic social institutions: how many persons are in school, at what age group, in which neighborhoods, related

**TABLE 3**    *(continued)*

| | *Valuation of permits authorized for new nonresidential building, %* | | |
| New York | Phila-delphia | San Francisco | Washington, D.C. |
|---|---|---|---|
| 44.0 | 67.3 | 63.1 | 64.3 |
| 43.6 | 69.3 | 63.6 | 62.1 |
| 75.3 | 75.5 | 83.6 | 83.7 |
| 70.6 | 72.1 | 72.4 | 88.6 |
| 18.2 | 51.1 | 37.2 | 47.0 |
| 64.7 | 72.6 | 73.0 | 80.8 |
| 37.8 | 67.6 | 64.1 | 63.8 |
| 33.5 | 72.3 | 73.1 | 57.4 |
| 31.7 | 43.0 | 52.5 | 61.4 |
| 61.1 | 80.4 | 64.8 | 75.2 |
| 32.6 | 71.8 | 55.0 | 94.1 |

Source: Unpublished data of the Bureau of the Census, tabulated at the request of the Bureau of Labor Statistics. Based on a sample of over 3,000 permit-issuing places. Prepared by U.S. Bureau of Labor Statistics, Division of Economic Studies.

in what ways to family income and other correlates; how many persons vote, again in terms of age, sex, race, and neighborhood; how many persons pay taxes of different kinds; how many trade union members are there; and what other organizations have large memberships in the area.

Clearly, it would be of considerable value if objections to public agencies' gathering information on religious affiliation and the actual attendance of religious services could be overcome. At the very least, a system of urban social indicators should include, in additon to public institutions, those private, religious-affiliated institutions that provide the equivalent of public services, and should indicate the relative importance of such private services. Parochial schools, in particular, ought to be thought of as integral elements in the education system and listed as such. Measures such as *de facto* race segregation in schools ought to be applied to private as well as public schools.

Before long it ought to be possible to construct indices on the more organized forms of participation in community affairs, such as the sources of financial contributions to community activities. Harvey M. Sapolsky, for example, has shown that, contrary to what might be the general impression, the per capita level of United Fund contributions in the Chicago area tends to be considerably higher in the working-class communities than in middle-class communities nearby (see Table 4). As James Q. Wilson noted when looking at a similar listing on another occasion, Gary and East Chicago have steel mills and, for citizens, Negroes and Poles,

**TABLE 4**   *Per capita United Fund contributions in the Chicago area*

| Community | Contribution per capita |
| --- | --- |
| Skokie | $0.80 |
| Hammond | 1.21 |
| Des Plaines | 1.66 |
| Oak Ridge/River Forest | 3.83 |
| East Chicago | 4.27 |
| Chicago | 4.50 |
| Gary | 4.70 |

while Skokie and Hammond have shopkeepers and professionals for citizens.

Similarly, a special effort should be made to learn more about the use of cultural facilities such as museums and attendance at theatrical and musical performances in the manner that Baumol and Bowen have recently explored in their book, *The Performing Arts.*[8] Baumol and Bowen have shown that the arts audience is drawn from an extremely narrow segment of the American population. This group is one which is well educated, whose incomes are high, who are predominantly in the professions, and who are in their late youth or early middle age. Obviously, these findings have important implications for those who make policy relating to the arts.

**THE FAMILY**

Expectations perhaps to the contrary, the family remains the basic social unit of American society. For reasons that run deep in the national character, it is a subject that is not easily submitted to public discussion or made an avowed objective of public policy. On the other hand, a considerable range of data relating to family concerns is now more or less routinely collected by the Census Bureau, and, disaggregated to SMSA or neighborhood units, would provide important kinds of information. Family size and structure, income, housing, age distribution, and similar information constitute the base of any information system in this field. Particular attention should be paid to measures of fertility levels, such as adjusted birth rates and total fertility rates, which provide essential information about future social needs and developments, and which will often reveal social problems that are concealed in more familiar social and economic data. Information on illegitimacy trends and infant mortality rates are apt to be similarly revealing, and of direct utility in the allocation, for example, of family-planning services.

A need that is not at present met, however, is that of relating the larger movements of the economy to family welfare (see Table 5). The relation-

TABLE 5    *Quarterly unemployment rates for non-white males aged 20 and over (not seasonally adjusted)*

| Year | | | | | Centered average for three consecutive quarters | | | |
|------|------|------|------|------|------|------|------|------|
| | I | II | III | IV | I | II | III | IV |
| 1950 | 12.7 | 8.1 | 7.4 | 5.6 | | 9.4 | 7.0 | 6.5 |
| 1951 | 6.4 | 3.0 | 3.4 | 3.5 | 5.0 | 4.3 | 3.3 | 4.1 |
| 1952 | 5.5 | 3.5 | 4.5 | 3.3 | 4.2 | 4.5 | 3.8 | 4.1 |
| 1953 | 4.6 | 4.3 | 2.7 | 4.0 | 4.1 | 3.9 | 3.7 | 5.6 |
| 1954 | 10.1 | 8.9 | 8.5 | 8.6 | 7.7 | 9.2 | 8.7 | 9.3 |
| 1955 | 10.9 | 7.7 | 6.4 | 5.9 | 9.1 | 8.3 | 6.7 | 6.8 |
| 1956 | 8.0 | 6.5 | 6.4 | 5.8 | 6.8 | 7.0 | 6.2 | 6.8 |
| 1957 | 8.3 | 7.0 | 6.7 | 8.3 | 7.0 | 7.3 | 7.3 | 9.8 |
| 1958 | 14.4 | 13.5 | 12.1 | 11.0 | 12.1 | 13.3 | 12.2 | 12.3 |
| 1959 | 13.9 | 9.1 | 9.5 | 9.3 | 11.3 | 10.8 | 9.3 | 10.2 |
| 1960 | 11.7 | 8.8 | 8.5 | 9.5 | 9.9 | 9.7 | 8.9 | 10.7 |
| 1961 | 14.0 | 11.6 | 11.1 | 10.1 | 11.7 | 12.2 | 10.9 | 11.2 |
| 1962 | 12.3 | 10.4 | 9.3 | 8.2 | 10.9 | 10.7 | 9.3 | 9.8 |
| 1963 | 11.9 | 8.9 | 7.8 | 8.0 | 9.7 | 9.5 | 8.2 | 8.6 |
| 1964 | 10.1 | 7.3 | 6.8 | 6.4 | 8.5 | 8.1 | 6.8 | 7.3 |
| 1965 | 8.7 | | | | | | | |

ship is direct and obvious, but somehow ignored. Moreover, in certain circumstances it may turn out to be not nearly so obvious as might have been supposed. In any event, there is probably no better way to insist upon the interrelationship of things, as well as to demonstrate the degree to which so many social problems have economic origins, as to insist upon and demonstrate these relationships in a system of urban social indicators.

For example, a striking correlation can be shown to exist between the unemployment rate for nonwhite males aged twenty and over and the per cent of nonwhite married women separated from their husbands (see Table 6). Working back from the separation rate recorded each March, there is, for example, a correlation of .81 at four months (see Table 7).

These very high correlations are for the period 1953-1964, a time of relative peace in the world, but also of intermittent high unemployment, especially for nonwhite males. It is interesting to note from Chart 1 that, with the onset of the 1960's, the strong presumed influence of employment on family structures appears to give out, so that the separation rate begins to rise even when the unemployment rate is falling. The exact implications from such data would be difficult to assess, certainly in the short run, but it is a trend that persons concerned with employment and family welfare would want to keep careful track of. An almost exactly similar phenomenon appears in the relationship between the nonwhite unemployment rate and the number of *new* Aid to Families of Dependent Children (AFDC) cases during this period.

An index of family welfare that is not widely available for the nation, and not at all for different communities, is the incidence rate for children supported by the AFDC program. In June 1965, some 46 children in 1,000 were receiving AFDC support. In 1963, a life-time incidence rate was estimated at 159 per 1,000, with nonwhite children having a recipient-rate incidence approximately six times greater than whites. Given more recent trends, this would suggest that approximately one white child in ten and six nonwhite children in ten live in a family supported by AFDC payments at one time or another during their youth. If these rates could be reduced to area rates, it is likely that important social information would result.[9]

A recent study by the research division of the Teamsters Joint Council No. 16 of New York City has suggested an interesting approach to relating

**TABLE 6** *Actual values, trend values, and deviations from trend*

| Year | Per cent of nonwhite married women separated from their husbands (March data) | | | Unemployment rate for nonwhite males aged 20 and over (9-month average centered in previous November) | | |
|---|---|---|---|---|---|---|
| | Actual | Trend | Deviation | Actual | Trend | Deviation |
| 1950 | 13.9 | 12.3 | +1.6 | | | |
| 1951 | 12.1 | 12.6 | −0.5 | 6.5 | 5.3 | +1.2 |
| 1952 | 12.4 | 12.8 | −0.4 | 4.1 | 5.7 | +1.6 |
| 1953 | 10.6 | 13.0 | −2.4 | 4.1 | 6.2 | −2.1 |
| 1954 | 12.7 | 13.3 | −0.6 | 5.6 | 6.7 | −1.1 |
| 1955 | 15.1 | 13.5 | +1.6 | 9.3 | 7.1 | +2.2 |
| 1956 | 14.2 | 13.7 | +0.5 | 6.8 | 7.6 | −0.8 |
| 1957 | 13.1 | 14.0 | −0.9 | 6.8 | 8.1 | −1.3 |
| 1958 | 16.0 | 14.2 | +1.8 | 9.8 | 8.5 | +1.3 |
| 1959 | 17.6 | 14.4 | +3.2 | 12.3 | 9.0 | +3.3 |
| 1960 | 13.8 | 14.7 | −0.9 | 10.2 | 9.5 | +0.7 |
| 1961 | 14.3 | 14.9 | −0.6 | 10.7 | 9.9 | +0.8 |
| 1962 | 14.9 | 15.1 | −0.2 | 11.2 | 10.4 | +0.8 |
| 1963 | 14.6 | 15.3 | −0.7 | 9.8 | 10.9 | −1.1 |
| 1964 | 14.8 | 15.6 | −0.8 | 8.6 | 11.3 | −2.7 |
| 1965 | 15.3 | 15.8 | −0.5 | 7.3 | 11.8 | −4.5 |

Source: U.S. Bureau of Labor Statistics.

**TABLE 7** *Correlation coefficients for various lags*

| Months from unemployment rate to separation rate | Correlation coefficient, % * |
|---|---|
| 1 | .73 |
| 4 | .81 |
| 7 | .76 |
| 10 | .66 |
| 13 | .49 (not significant at 5 per cent level) |

*Correlation coefficient calculated for the years 1953-1964.

**CHART 1** *Per cent of nonwhite married women separated from their husbands and unemployment rate for nonwhite males 20 and over*

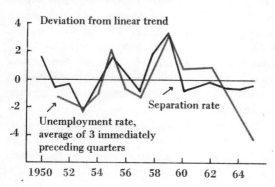

**CHART 2** *Correlation between per cent of nonwhite married women separated from their husbands (deviations from 1958-1964 trend) and unemployment rate of nonwhite males aged 20 and over (deviations from trend) for various time lags*

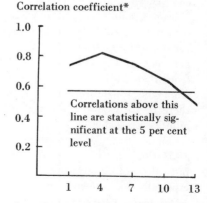

Lag of unemployment rate behind separation status, months

*Correlation coefficient calculated for the years 1953 through 1964.

social and economic data. The study showed that, in 1956, the number of persons in New York City receiving welfare assistance amounted to 8.9 per cent of the nongovernment work force. Ten years later in 1966 this proportion had risen to 17.9 per cent.[10] It is probable also that much information can be gained from special studies such as the "diagnostic surveys" of welfare and medical needs of persons in depressed neighborhoods that are now being sponsored by the Urban Renewal Administration, although it is not clear how well "one-time" studies of this kind would fit in with an ongoing statistical series.

POVERTY NEIGHBORHOODS    From the point of view of urban social indicators, one of the most immediate benefits of the federal government's "war on poverty" are the studies of the "poverty areas" in American cities being carried out by the Bureau of the Census. For the first time, it is possible not only to assess the condition of families in given neighborhoods but to gain some sense of the changing levels of well-being in the neighborhood itself. The ever-present problem of in- and out-migration makes it hazardous to assert that changes in a neighborhood are necessarily changes that occur to the same collection of individuals, but, from the point of view of city government, it is often just as important, and sometimes even more so, to know in which direction a neighborhood is moving.

A recent Census study of Negro families in Cleveland illustrates quite strikingly the interest that such information can have, in this case lending support to the hypothesis that, in recent years, urban Negro communities have shown a tendency to divide between an increasingly prosperous and mobile "middle-class" group and—in relative and even absolute terms—a lower-class group living under steadily deteriorating conditions. The Census study describes nine poverty neighborhoods in Cleveland (of which three have only negligible numbers of Negroes). In 1960, 91 per cent of Cleveland's Negro population, some 228,322 persons, lived in these poverty neighborhoods, while another 22,496, or 9 per cent of the Negro population, lived elsewhere in the city. In

the course of the next five years, the Negro proportion of the population of Cleveland increased from 29 per cent to 34 per cent, and the actual number grew by 25,458. The proportion of the Negro population outside the poverty areas, however, grew to 15 per cent of the total Negro population, amounting now to 41,451 persons.

During this period, the proportion of Negro families living in poverty remained about the same: it was 26.1 per cent in 1959 and 25.4 per cent in 1964. However, the experience of Negro families living outside the poverty area was one of steady improvement, while the conditions of life in the poverty areas grew *worse*.

Among Negro families living outside the poverty area, the incidence of poverty dropped from 17.9 per cent to 9.8 per cent. Median family income rose $1,107 to a total of $7,285 in 1964. The number of female-headed families dropped from 13.9 per cent in 1959, to 9.1 per cent in 1964. The male unemployment rate dropped from 10 per cent in 1960 to 8 per cent in 1965, while the labor-force participation rate rose from 77.6 per cent to 82.2 per cent. This latter contrasts with a 1965 national labor force participation rate of 75.2 per cent (Negro) or 77.6 per cent (over-all).

By contrast, life in the Negro slums was getting worse. The incidence of poverty *rose* from 26.9 per cent to 28.5 per cent. Median family income (1959-1964) increased only $132 to a level of $5,085. The proportion of female-headed families (1959-1964) rose from 20 per cent to 25 per cent. The male unemployment rate (1960-1965) dropped from 13 per cent to 11 per cent, but so also did male labor-force participation, which *declined* from 78.6 per cent to 73.1 per cent.

These over-all rates for the poverty areas conceal even sharper deteriorations in some neighborhoods. Thus, in the Hough section, median family income (1959-1964) declined $766 to $3,966, while in nearby West Central it declined to $2,984. This decline was associated with a significant rise in female-headed families between 1959 and 1964, from 22.5 per cent to 32.1 per cent in Hough, and from 32.6 per cent to 35.1 per cent in West Central. In Hough, three-quarters of female-headed families were living below the poverty line in 1964, and the proportion was not far different elsewhere in the poverty areas. Perhaps significantly, the proportion of families with female heads living below the poverty line outside the poverty areas declined (1959-1964) from 53.5 per cent to 25 per cent, which may suggest that a different type of female-headed household is involved. In an area such as West Central, the male unemployment rate rose to 20.4 per cent in 1965, and the labor-force participation rate dropped to 58.7 per cent. In Hough, the number of children living in poverty increased by one-third.

Whether or not the rioting that occurred in these neighborhoods in 1965 could have been predicted, it will surely be seen that these were areas in which the fabric of social life was deteriorating rapidly and in which increasing numbers of persons were living in conditions of extreme deprivation.

### INSTITUTIONS

Corresponding to the data about individuals and families that is now more or less routinely collected, there needs also to be developed a range of information that might be termed "institutional demography." Cities are organized around institutions, some public, some private, some not quite one or the other. The number, variety, and perhaps also the vigor of these institutions do much to establish the "character" and quality of an urban environment. Washington is one kind of city, Pittsburg another, and the differences are readily to be grasped from the great differences in the types of institutions that characterize the two cities.

*Public service organizations* constitute a familiar category of urban institution, and will be the most readily described. At the same time, considerable art will be required to give some sense of order and hierarchy to the "1400 Governments" that link and overlap to provide the public services of most metropolitan areas. An especially difficult but important task is that of providing some measure of levels of taxation and public expenditure between the different jurisdictions, over time within jurisdictions, and also of intergovernment transfer payments. In a study of thirty-six SMSA's, Alan K. Campbell and Phillip Meranto have, with great force, shown the differences in the revenue structures of central cities in contrast to the surrounding suburbs and the consequences for educational expenditure:

> The cost and number of noneducational governmental services tend to increase with the size and density of a district and to consume a larger proportion of the budget in major cities where many services are provided for nonresidents as well as for residents. It is reasonable to suggest that this "municipal overburden" is supported at the expense of the education function.
>
> The figures . . . show that the central cities were supporting these expenditure levels by taxes that were $23.29 per capita higher than in areas outside the cities. In contrast, the cities received about $5.00 per capita less in total inter-governmental aid and, most importantly, $12.31 less per capita in education aid than did suburban areas, where income was higher. In other words, not only are central cities pressed to support a large array of services by a relatively shrinking tax base, but they tax themselves more heavily to do so and they receive less inter-governmental aid than the more wealthy communities in their metropolitan area.[11]

Whether difficulties of this kind are to be overcome or not is a question to which few would venture an answer, but it is reasonable to suppose that this will not be done until the facts of the disparities involved are clearly and repeatedly set forth in a readily available and authoritative manner.

*Business enterprises* have been and for the time being continue to be the characteristic economic institution of cities. Their number, size, location, growth, or decline are fundamental urban facts, and not nearly so accessible as might be supposed. It is likely that this subject will be particularly plagued by the problem of presenting information in sufficient detail to be of interest to students, while retaining some comprehensibility for general users, as, for example, in distinguishing between locally owned and managed enterprises and those that are branches of larger concerns. As a general rule, it would seem wise to respond to the more general interest, at least in the early stage of any program development.

*Information media* are enterprises of distinct importance and are likely to be of considerable interest to urbanists. The number of newspapers and radio and television stations in an area, and of their audiences, are essential data.

*Educational institutions* if not yet the dominant institutions of the contemporary American city are well on the way to becoming so. In many cities, it is likely that the "education force" has come to outnumber the "work force," and in any event the direct and growing relevance of education to economic activity is now generally acknowledged. Here again, differences in school enrollment and educational institutions vary significantly among the major urban areas. Moreover, the significance of the "learning industry" increasingly lies as much in the amount and kind of employment it provides and generates, as in its more immediate "educational product." Thus, Charles Abrams recently commented that "the loss of a university is much more serious [to a city] than the loss of several industrial institutions," adding that while industries and business are a part of the necessary economic superstructure of a city, universities are part of the very foundation.[12]

*Associational groupings* refers to the great variety of voluntary organizations that characterize any urban setting. The varying patterns of membership in political parties, churches and synagogues, trade unions, fraternal associations, and the like as much as any single factor help to define the distinctive as well as the shared qualities of American cities. Much more could usefully be recorded about their membership. In particular, it is devoutly to be wished that the absurd but reigning fears that prevent the Census Bureau from gathering information on religious affiliation will give way before the great and legitimate interest in this subject on the part of the general public no less than special-

ists—not to mention religious leaders and activists.

Along with the more formal arrangements of institutions, there are patterns of urban life that shape the quality and define the nature of the experience in such ways that they, too, are institutions: organized patterns of behavior. These are the elements that go to make up what might be called the "urban ecology." They are many, diffuse, and often impossible to measure—what is to be said about the ambiance of San Francisco, or the dread sameness of Jersey City? On the other hand, many of these qualities are quantifiable—and are quantified. Air pollution levels, noise levels, and crime levels are all reportable and immensely significant, the more so if followed over time. Moreover, as noted by the recent report by the President's Commission on Law Enforcement and Administration of Justice, there are wide and intriguing variations in rates for different offenses:

> Los Angeles is 1st for rape and 4th for aggravated assault but 20th for murder, with a murder rate less than half that of St. Louis. Chicago has the highest rate for robbery but a relatively low rate for burglary. New York is 5th in larcenies $50 and over, but 54th for larcenies under $50. The risk of auto theft is about 50 per cent greater in Boston than anywhere else in the country, but in Boston the likelihood of other kinds of theft is about the average for cities over 250,000.[13]

It may be hoped that the report of the Crime Commission will have some effect on the quality of crime statistics in the nation's cities, most especially that the practice of recording crime "consumption," that is the incidence of crime victims in the population, will be continued.

Almost a subject to itself in the area of urban ecologies is the matter of densities. The urban condition is at once defined by densities and at certain points spoiled by them: densities of population (66,000 persons per square mile in Central Harlem) and automobiles, land uses in terms of streets, housing, parks, industry, and concentrations of race and social class. Very possibly, in the end we shall come to see that it is not the recorded levels of such measures that determine the quality of urban life so much as our choices as to what it is we shall measure and how widely the meaning of those measures is diffused to the people, who are the city.

Referring once again to Dr. Johnson: to ask what one would care to know about the city is to ask what one needs to know about life. One may begin anywhere, and there is no ending. But given the present range of perceived problems faced by American cities, it is reasonable to concentrate attention on the twin problems of density and poverty, in all their ramifications of congestion, revenue crises, pollution, racial tension, personal disorganization, lagging education, failing public services, and so through the spectrum of issues that at present conceal from us the great human triumphs that are embedded in much of American urban life, and the even greater achievements that could yet come to pass.

## REFERENCES

1  See Daniel P. Moynihan, "Education of the Urban Poor," Address to the Harvard Club and the M.I.T. Alumni Center of New York City, March 1, 1967 (mimeographed).
2  Morton and Lucia White, *The Intellectual versus the City*, Cambridge, Mass.: Harvard University Press and The M.I.T. Press, 1962, p. 75.
3  *The Challenge of Crime in a Free Society*, Report by the President's Commission on Law. Enforcement and Administration of Justice, February 1967, p. 51.
4  See *Economic Report of the President*, Annual Report of the Council of Economic Advisors, January 1967, chart 1, p. 43.
5  Bertram M. Gross, "The City of Man: A Social Systems Reckoning," *Man's Environment: The Next 50 Years*, Bloomington, Ind.: University of Indiana Press, 1967.
6  See Otis Dudley Duncan and Beverly Duncan, "A Methodological Analysis of Segregation Indexes," *American Sociological Review*, vol. 20 (April 1955), pp. 201–217; and Karl Taeuber and A. F. Taeuber, *Negroes in Cities*, Chicago: The University of Chicago Press, 1965.
7  U.S., Department of Labor, "A Sharper Look at Unemployment in U.S. Cities and Slums," Summary Report to the President by the Secretary of Labor, March 1967, p. 1.
8  See William J. Baumol and William G. Bowen, *The Performing Arts: The Economic Dilemma*, New York: Twentieth Century Fund, 1966.
9  See Robert H. Mugge, "Demographic Analysis and Public Assistance," paper prepared for presentation at the Annual Meeting of the Population Association of America, New York City, April 30, 1966 (mimeographed).
10  See press release by the International Brotherhood of Teamsters Joint Council No. 16, New York, Feb. 11, 1967.
11  Alan K. Campbell and Philip Meranto, "The Metropolitan Education Dilemma: Matching Resources to Needs," *Urban Affairs Quarterly*, vol. 2, no. 1 (September 1966), p. 57.
12  See *New York Times*, Feb. 21, 1967.
13  *The Challenge of Crime in a Free Society*, Report by the President's Commission on Law Enforcement and Administration of Justice, Washington, D. C.: U.S. Government Printing Office, 1967, p. 29.

## 2    THE FUTURE OF THE SLUMS
### THE PRESIDENT'S COMMISSION ON CIVIL DISORDERS

We believe action of the kind outlined in preceding pages can contribute substantially to control of

Reprinted by permission from the President's Commission on Civil Disorders, *Report of the National Advisory Commission on Civil Disorders*, New York: Bantam Books, Inc., 1968, pp. 389–408. Copyright ©1968 by The New York Times Company.

disorders in the near future. But there should be no mistake about the long run. The underlying forces continue to gain momentum.

The most basic of these is the accelerating segregation of low-income, disadvantaged Negroes within the ghettos of the largest American cities.

By 1985, the 12.1 million Negroes segregated

within central cities today will have grown to approximately 20.8 million—an increase of 72 percent.

Prospects for domestic peace and for the quality of American life are linked directly to the future of these cities.

Two critical questions must be confronted: Where do present trends now lead? What choices are open to us?

## THE KEY TRENDS

NEGRO POPULATION GROWTH    The size of the Negro population in central cities is closely related to total national Negro population growth. In the past 16 years, about 98 percent of this growth has occurred within metropolitan areas, and 86 percent in the central cities of those areas.

A conservative projection of national Negro population growth indicates continued rapid increases. For the period 1966 to 1985, it will rise to a total of 30.7 million, gaining an average of 484,000 a year, or 7.6 percent more than the increase in each year from 1960 to 1966.

*Central cities*    Further Negro population growth in central cities depends upon two key factors: in-migration from outside metropolitan areas, and patterns of Negro settlement within metropolitan areas.

From 1960 to 1966, the Negro population of all central cities rose 2.4 million, 88.9 percent of total national Negro population growth. We estimate that natural growth accounted for 1.4 million, or 58 percent of this increase, and in-migration accounted for 1 million, or 42 percent.

As of 1966, the Negro population in all central cities totaled 12.1 million. By 1985, we have estimated that it will rise 72 percent to 20.8 million. We believe that natural growth will account for 6 million of this increase and in-migration for 2.7 million.

Without significant Negro out-migration, then, the combined Negro populations of central cities will continue to grow by an average of 316,000 a year through 1985.

This growth would increase the proportion of Negroes to whites in central cities by 1985 from the present 20.6 percent to between an estimated 31 and 35.6 percent.

*Largest central cities*    These, however, are national figures. Much faster increases will occur in the largest central cities where Negro growth has been concentrated in the past two decades. Washington, D.C., and Newark are already over half Negro. A continuation of recent trends would cause the following 11 major cities to become over 50 percent Negro by the indicated dates:

| | | | |
|---|---|---|---|
| New Orleans | 1971 | St. Louis | 1978 |
| Richmond | 1971 | Detroit | 1979 |
| Baltimore | 1972 | Philadelphia | 1981 |
| Jacksonville | 1972 | Oakland | 1983 |
| Gary | 1973 | Chicago | 1984 |
| Cleveland | 1975 | | |

These cities, plus Washington, D.C., (now over 66 percent Negro) and Newark, contained 12.6 million people in 1960, or 22 percent of the total population of all 224 American central cities. All 13 cities undoubtedly will have Negro majorities by 1985, and the suburbs ringing them will remain largely all white, unless there are major changes in Negro fertility rates, in-migration, settlement patterns or public policy.

Experience indicates that Negro school enrollment in these and other cities will exceed 50 percent long before the total population reaches that mark. In fact, Negro students already comprise more than a majority in the public elementary schools of 12 of the 13 cities mentioned above. This occurs because the Negro population in central cities is much younger and because a much higher proportion of white children attend private schools. For example, St. Louis' population was about 36 percent Negro in 1965; its public elementary school enrollment was 63 percent Negro. If present trends continue, many cities in addition to those listed above will have Negro school majorities by 1985, probably including:

| | |
|---|---|
| Dallas | Louisville |
| Pittsburgh | Indianapolis |
| Buffalo | Kansas City, Mo. |
| Cincinnati | Hartford |
| Harrisburg | New Haven |
| Atlanta | |

Thus, continued concentration of future Negro population growth in large central cities will produce significant changes in those cities over the next 20 years. Unless there are sharp changes in the factors influencing Negro settlement patterns within metropolitan areas, there is little doubt that the trend toward Negro majorities will continue. Even a complete cessation of net Negro inmigration to central cities would merely postpone this result for a few years.

GROWTH OF THE YOUNG NEGRO POPULATION We estimate that the nation's white population will grow 16.6 million, or 9.5 percent, from 1966 to 1975, and the Negro population 3.8 million, or 17.7 percent, in the same period. The Negro age group from 15 to 24 years of age, however, will grow much faster than either the Negro population as a whole, or the white population in the same age group.

From 1966 to 1975, the number of Negroes in this age group will rise 1.6 million, or 40.1 percent. The white population aged 15 to 24 will rise 6.6 million, or 23.5 percent.

This rapid increase in the young Negro population has important implications for the country. This group has the highest unemployment rate in the nation, commits a relatively high proportion of all crimes, and plays the most significant role in civil disorders. By the same token, it is a great reservoir of underused human resources which are vital to the nation.

THE LOCATION OF NEW JOBS Most new employment opportunities do not occur in central cities, near all-Negro neighborhoods. They are being created in suburbs and outlying areas—and this trend is likely to continue indefinitely. New office buildings have risen in the downtowns of large cities, often near all-Negro areas. But the out-flow of manufacturing and retailing facilities normally offsets this addition significantly—and in many cases has caused a net loss of jobs in central cities.

Providing employment for the swelling Negro ghetto population will require society to link these potential workers more closely with job locations. This can be done in three ways: by developing incentives to industry to create new employment centers near Negro residential areas; by opening suburban residential areas to Negroes and encouraging them to move closer to industrial centers; or by creating better transportation between ghetto neighborhoods and new job locations.

All three involve large public outlays.

The first method—creating new industries in or near the ghetto—is not likely to occur without government subsidies on a scale which convinces private firms that it will pay them to face the problems involved.

The second method—opening up suburban areas to Negro occupancy—obviously requires effective fair housing laws. It will also require an extensive program of federally-aided, low-cost housing in many suburban areas.

The third approach—improved transportation linking ghettos and suburbs—has received little attention from city planners and municipal officials. A few demonstration projects show promise, but carrying them out on a large scale will be very costly.

Although a high proportion of new jobs will be located in suburbs, there are still millions of jobs in central cities. Turnover in those jobs alone can open up a great many potential positions for Negro central city residents—if employers cease racial discrimination in their hiring and promotion practices.

Nevertheless, as the total number of Negro central city jobseekers continues to rise, the need to link them with emerging new employment in the suburbs will become increasingly urgent.

THE INCREASING COST OF MUNICIPAL SERVICES Local governments have had to bear a particularly heavy financial burden in the two decades since the end of World War II. All United States cities are highly dependent upon property taxes that are relatively unresponsive to changes in income. Consequently, growing municipalities have been hard-pressed for adequate revenues to meet rising demands for services generated by population increase. On the other hand, stable or declining cities have not only been faced with steady cost increases but also with a slow-growing, or even declining, tax base.

As a result of the population shifts of the postwar period, concentrating the more affluent parts of the urban population in residential suburbs while leaving the less affluent in the central cities, the increasing burden of municipal taxes frequently falls upon that part of the urban population least able to pay them.

Increasing concentrations of urban growth have called forth greater expenditures for every kind of public service: education, health, police protection, fire protection, parks, sewage disposal, sanitation, water supply, etc. These expenditures have strikingly outpaced tax revenues. The story is summed up in Table 1.

The fact that the problems of the cities are a national problem is seen in the growth of federal assistance to urban areas under various grant-in-aid programs, which reached the level of $10 billion in the current fiscal year.

Nevertheless, the fiscal plight of many cities is likely to grow even more serious in the future. Local expenditures inevitably will continue to rise steeply as a result of several factors, including the difficulty of increasing productivity in the predominantly service activities of local governments, and the rapid technologically-induced increases in productivity in other economic sectors.

Traditionally, individual productivity has risen faster in the manufacturing, mining, construction, and agricultural sectors than in those involving personal services.

TABLE 1    *Local government revenues, Expenditures and debt (billions of dollars)*

|  | 1950 | 1966 | Increase |
|---|---|---|---|
| Revenues | 11.7 | 41.5 | +29.8 |
| Expenditures | 17.0 | 60.7 | +43.7 |
| Debt outstanding | 18.8 | 77.5 | +58.7 |

However, all sectors compete with each other for talent and personnel. Wages and salaries in the service-dominated sectors generally must keep up, therefore, with those in the capital-dominated sectors. Since productivity in manufacturing has risen about 2.5 percent per year compounded over many decades, and even faster in agriculture, the basis for setting costs in the service-dominated sectors has gone up, too.

In the postwar period, costs of the same units of output have increased very rapidly in certain key activities of local government. For example, education is the single biggest form of expenditure by local governments (including school districts), accounting for about 40 percent of their outlays. From 1947 to 1967, costs per pupil-day in United States public schools rose at a rate of 6.7 percent per year compounded—only slightly less than doubling every ten years.[1] This major cost item is likely to keep on rising rapidly in the future, along with other government services like police, fire, and welfare activities.

Some increases in productivity may occur in these fields, and some economies may be achieved through use of semi-skilled assistants such as police and teachers' aides. Nevertheless, with the need to keep pace with private sector wage scales, local government costs will keep on rising sharply.

This and other future cost increases are important to future relations between central cities and suburbs. Rising costs will inevitably force central cities to demand more and more assistance from the federal government. But the federal government can obtain such funds through the income tax only from other parts of the economy. Suburban governments are, meanwhile, experiencing the same cost increases along with the rising resentment of their constituents.

## CHOICES FOR THE FUTURE

The complexity of American society offers many choices for the future of relations between central cities and suburbs and patterns of white and Negro settlement in metropolitan areas. For practical purposes, however, we see two fundamental questions:

Should future Negro population growth be

concentrated in central cities, as in the past 20 years, and should Negro and white populations become even more residentially segregated?

Should society provide greatly increased special assistance to Negroes and other relatively disadvantaged population groups?

For purposes of analysis, the Commission has defined three basic choices for the future embodying specific answers to these questions:

*The Present Policies Choice* Under this course, the nation would maintain approximately the share of resources now being allocated to programs of assistance for the poor, unemployed and disadvantaged. These programs are likely to grow, given continuing economic growth and rising federal revenues, but they will not grow fast enough to stop, let alone reverse, the already deteriorating quality of life in central-city ghettos.

This choice carries the highest ultimate price, as we will point out.

*The Enrichment Choice* Under this course, the nation would seek to offset the effects of continued Negro segregation and deprivation in large city ghettos. The Enrichment Choice would aim at creating dramatic improvements in the quality of life in disadvantaged central-city neighborhoods—both white and Negro. It would require marked increases in federal spending for education, housing, employment, job training, and social services.

The Enrichment Choice would seek to life poor Negroes and whites above poverty status and thereby give them the capacity to enter the mainstream of American life. But it would not, at least for many years, appreciably affect either the increasing concentration of Negroes in the ghetto or racial segregation in residential areas outside the ghetto.

*The Integration Choice* This choice would be aimed at reversing the movement of the country toward two societies, separate and unequal.

The Integration Choice—like the Enrichment Choice—would call for large-scale improvement in the quality of ghetto life. But it would also involve both creating strong incentives for Negro movement out of central-city ghettos and enlarging freedom of choice concerning housing, employment, and schools.

The result would fall considerably short of full integration. The experience of other ethnic groups indicates that some Negro households would be scattered in largely white residential areas. Others—probably a larger number—would voluntarily cluster together in largely Negro neighborhoods. The Integration Choice would thus produce both integration and segregation. But the segregation would be voluntary.

Articulating these three choices plainly oversimplifies the possibilities open to the country. We believe, however, that they encompass the basic issues—issues which the American public must face if it is serious in its concern not only about civil disorder, but the future of our democratic society.

## THE PRESENT POLICIES CHOICE

Powerful forces of social and political inertia are moving the country steadily along the course of existing policies toward a divided country.

This course may well involve changes in many social and economic programs—but not enough to produce fundamental alterations in the key factors of Negro concentration, racial segregation, and the lack of sufficient enrichment to arrest the decay of deprived neighborhoods.

Some movement towards enrichment can be found in efforts to encourage industries to locate plants in central cities, in increased federal expenditures for education, in the important concepts embodied in the "War on Poverty," and in the Model Cities Program. But so far congressional appropriations for even present federal programs have been so small that they fall short of effective enrichment.

As for challenging concentration and segregation, a national commitment to this purpose has yet to develop. This is seen in the history of national open housing legislation, pending in Congress, which the President has again urged the Congress to enact.

Of the three future courses we have defined, the Present Policies Choice—the choice we are now making—is the course with the most ominous consequences for our society.

## THE PROBABILITY OF FUTURE CIVIL DISORDERS

Under the Present Policies Choice, society would do little more than it is now doing against racial segregation, fundamental poverty, and deprivation. What effect would this have on the potential for major civil disorders?

We believe for two reasons that this choice would lead to a larger number of violent incidents of the kind that have stimulated recent major disorders.

First, the Present Policies Choice does nothing to raise the hopes, absorb the energies, or constructively challenge the talents of the rapidly-growing number of young Negro men in central cities. Therefore, the proportion of unemployed or underemployed among them will remain very high. These young men have contributed disproportionately to crime and violence in cities in the past, and there is danger, obviously, that they will continue to do so.

Second, under these conditions, a rising proportion of Negroes in disadvantaged city areas might come to look upon the deprivation and segregation they suffer as proper justification for violent protest or for extending support to now isolated extremists who advocate civil disruption by guerrilla tactics.

More incidents, however, would not necessarily mean more or worse riots. For the near future, there is substantial likelihood that even an increased number of incidents could be controlled before becoming major disorders. Such control should be possible if society undertakes to improve police and National Guard forces so that they can respond to potential disorders with more prompt and disciplined use of force.

In fact, the likelihood of incidents mushrooming into major disorders would be only slightly higher in the near future under the Present Policies Choice than under the other two possible choices. For no new policies or programs could possibly alter basic ghetto conditions immediately. And the announcement of new programs under the other choices would immediately generate new expectations. Expectations inevitably increase faster than performance: in the short run, they might even increase the level of frustration.

In the long run, however, the Present Policies Choice risks a seriously greater probability of major disorders, worse, possibly, than those already experienced.

If the Negro population as a whole developed even stronger feelings of being wrongly "penned in" and discriminated against, many of its members might come to support not only riots, but the rebellion now being preached by only a handful.

If large-scale violence resulted, white retaliation would follow. This spiral could quite conceivably lead to a kind of urban *apartheid* with semi-martial law in many major cities, enforced residence of Negroes in segregated areas, and a drastic reduction in personal freedom for all Americans, particularly Negroes.

The same distinction is applicable to the cost of the Present Policies Choice. In the short run, its costs—at least its direct cash outlays—would be far less than for the other choices.

Any social and economic programs likely to have significant lasting effect would require very substantial annual appropriations for many years. Their cost would well exceed the direct losses sustained in recent civil disorders. Property damage in all the disorders we investigated, including Detroit and Newark, totalled less than $100 million. The casualty toll was far smaller than that for automobile accidents on an average weekend.

But it would be a tragic mistake to view the Present Policies Choice as cheap. Damage figures measure only a small part of the costs of civil disorder. They cannot measure the costs in terms of the lives lost, injuries suffered, minds and attitudes closed and frozen in prejudice, or the hidden costs of the profound disruption of entire cities.

Ultimately, moreover, the economic and social costs of the Present Policies Choice will far surpass the cost of the alternatives. The rising concentration of impoverished Negroes and other minorities within the urban ghettos will constantly expand public expenditures for welfare, law enforcement, unemployment and other existing programs without reversing the tendency of older city neighborhoods toward decay and the breeding of frustration and discontent. But the most significant item on the balance of accounts will remain largely invisible and incalculable—the toll in human values taken by continued poverty, segregation and inequality of opportunity.

POLARIZATION   Another and equally serious consequence is the fact that this course would lead to the permanent establishment of two societies: one predominantly white and located in the suburbs, in smaller cities, and in outlying areas, and one largely Negro located in central cities.

We are well on the way to just such a divided nation.

This division is veiled by the fact that Negroes do not now dominate many central cities. But they soon will, as we have shown, and the new Negro mayors will be facing even more difficult conditions than now exist.

As Negroes succeed whites in our largest cities, the proportion of low-income residents in those cities will probably increase. This is likely even if both white and Negro incomes continue to rise at recent rates, since Negroes have much lower incomes than whites. Moreover, many of the ills of large central cities spring from their age, their location, and their physical structures. The deterioration and economic decay stemming from these factors have been proceeding for decades and will continue to plague older cities regardless of who resides in them.

These facts underlie the fourfold dilemma of the American city:

Fewer tax dollars come in, as large numbers of middle-income taxpayers move out of central cities and property values and business decline.

More tax dollars are required, to provide essential public services and facilities, and to meet the needs of expanding lower-income groups.

Each tax dollar buys less, because of increasing costs.

Citizen dissatisfaction with municipal services grows as needs, expectations and standards of living increase throughout the community.

These trends already grip many major cities, and their grip is becoming tighter daily.

These are the conditions that would greet the Negro-dominated municipal governments that will gradually come to power in many of our major cities. The Negro electorates in those cities probably would demand basic changes in present policies. Like the present white electorates there, they would have to look for assistance to two basic sources: the private sector and the federal government.

With respect to the private sector, major private capital investment in those cities might have ceased almost altogether if white-dominated firms and industries decided the risks and costs were too great. The withdrawal of private capital is already far advanced in most all-Negro areas of our large cities.

Even if private investment continued, it alone would not suffice. Big cities containing high proportions of low-income Negroes and block after block of deteriorating older property need very substantial assistance from the federal government to meet the demands of their electorates for improved services and living conditions. In fact, all large cities will need such assistance.

By that time, however, it is probable that Congress will be more heavily influenced by representatives of the suburban and outlying city electorate. These areas will comprise 41 percent of our total population by 1985, compared with 33 percent in 1960. Central cities will decline from 31 percent to 27 percent.[2] Without decisive action toward integration, this influential suburban electorate would be over 95 percent white and much more affluent than the central city population.

Yet even the suburbs will be feeling the squeeze of higher local government costs. Hence, Congress might resist providing the extensive assistance which central cities will desperately need. Many big-city mayors are already beseeching the federal government for massive aid.

Thus the Present Policies Choice, if pursued for any length of time, might force simultaneous political and economic polarization in many of our largest metropolitan areas. Such polarization would involve large central cities—mainly Negro, with many poor, and nearly bankrupt—on the one hand, and most suburbs—mainly white, generally affluent, but heavily taxed—on the other hand.

Some areas might avoid political confrontation by shifting to some form of metropolitan government designed to offer regional solutions for pressing urban problems such as property taxation, air and water pollution and refuse disposal, and commuter transport. Yet this would hardly eliminate the basic segregation and relative poverty of the urban Negro population. It might even increase the Negro's sense of frustration and alienation if it operated to prevent Negro political control of central cities.

The acquisition of power by Negro-dominated governments in central cities is surely a legitimate and desirable exercise of political power by a minority group. It is in an American political tradition exemplified by the achievements of the Irish in New York and Boston.

But such Negro political development would also involve virtually complete racial segregation and virtually complete spatial separation. By 1985, the separate Negro society in our central cities would contain almost 21 million citizens. That is about 72 percent larger than the present Negro population of central cities. It is also larger than the current population of every Negro nation in Africa except Nigeria and Ethiopia.

If developing a racially integrated society is extraordinarily difficult today when 12.5 million Negroes live in ghettos, then it is quite clearly going to be virtually impossible in 1985 when almost 21 million Negroes—still much poorer and less educated than most whites—will be living there.

CAN PRESENT POLICIES AVERT EXTREME POLARIZATION? There are at least two possible developments under the Present Policies Choice which might avert such polarization. The first is a faster increase of incomes among Negroes than has occurred in the recent past. This might prevent central cities from becoming even deeper "poverty traps" than they now are. It suggests the importance of effective job programs and higher levels of welfare payments for dependent families.

The second possible development is migration of a growing Negro middle class out of the central

city. This would not prevent competition for federal funds between central cities and outlying areas, but it might diminish the racial undertones of that competition.

There is, however, no evidence that a continuation of present policies would be accompanied by any such movement. There is already a significant Negro middle class. It grew rapidly from 1960 to 1966. Yet in these years, 88.9 percent of the total national growth of Negro population was concentrated in central cities—the highest in history. Indeed, from 1960 to 1966, there was actually a net total in-migration of Negroes from the urban fringes of metropolitan areas into central cities. The Commission believes it unlikely that this trend will suddenly reverse itself without significant changes in private attitudes and public policies.

## THE ENRICHMENT CHOICE

The Present Policies Choice plainly would involve continuation of efforts like Model Cities, manpower programs, and the War on Poverty. These are in fact enrichment programs, designed to improve the quality of life in the ghetto.

Because of their limited scope and funds, however, they constitute only very modest steps toward enrichment—and would continue to do so even if these programs were somewhat enlarged or supplemented.

The premise of the Enrichment Choice is performance. To adopt this choice would require a substantially greater share of national resources—sufficient to make a dramatic, visible impact on life in the urban Negro ghetto.

THE EFFECT OF ENRICHMENT ON CIVIL DISORDERS Effective enrichment policies probably would have three immediate effects on civil disorders.

First, announcement of specific large-scale programs and the demonstration of a strong intent to carry them out might persuade ghetto residents that genuine remedies for their problems were forthcoming, thereby allaying tensions.

Second, such announcements would strongly

stimulate the aspirations and hopes of members of these communities—possibly well beyond the capabilities of society to deliver and to do so promptly. This might increase frustration and discontent, to some extent cancelling the first effect.

Third, if there could be immediate action on meaningful job training and the creation of productive jobs for large numbers of unemployed young people, they would become much less likely to engage in civil disorders.

Such action is difficult now, when there are about 583,000 young Negro men aged 16 to 24 in central cities—of whom 131,000, or 22.5 percent, are unemployed and probably two or three times as many are underemployed. It will not become easier in the future. By 1975, this age group will have grown to nearly 700,000.

Given the size of the present problem, plus the large growth of this age group, creation of sufficient meaningful jobs will require extensive programs, begun rapidly. Even if the nation is willing to embark on such programs, there is no certainty that they can be made effective soon enough.

Consequently, there is no certainty that the Enrichment Choice would do much more in the near future to diminish violent incidents in central cities than would the Present Policies Choice. However, if enrichment programs can succeed in meeting the needs of residents of disadvantaged areas for jobs, education, housing and city services, then over the years this choice is almost certain to reduce both the level and frequency of urban disorder.

**THE NEGRO MIDDLE CLASS**  One objective of the Enrichment Choice would be to help as many disadvantaged Americans as possible—of all races—to enter the mainstream of American prosperity, to progress toward what is often called middle-class status. If the Enrichment Choice were adopted, it could certainly attain this objective to a far greater degree than would the Present Policies Choice. This could significantly change the quality of life in many central city areas.

It can be argued that a rapidly enlarging Negro middle class would promote Negro out-migration,

and thus the Enrichment Choice would open up an escape hatch from the ghetto. This argument, however, has two weaknesses.

The first is experience. Central cities already have sizable and growing numbers of middle-class Negro families. Yet, as noted earlier, only a few have migrated from the central city.

The past pattern of white ethnic groups gradually moving out of central-city areas to middle-class suburbs has not applied to Negroes. Effective open-housing laws will help make this possible. It is probable, however, that other more extensive changes in policies and attitudes will be required—and these would extend beyond the Enrichment Choice.

The second weakness in the argument is time. Even if enlargement of the Negro middle class succeeded in encouraging movement out of the central city, could it do so fast enough to offset the rapid growth of the ghetto? To offset even *half* the growth estimated for the ghetto by 1975 would call for the out-migration from central cities of 217,000 persons a year. This is eight times the annual increase in suburban Negro population—including natural increase—which occurred from 1960 to 1966. Even the most effective enrichment program is not likely to accomplish this.

A corollary problem derives from the continuing migration of poor Negroes from the South to Northern and Western cities.

Adoption of the Enrichment Choice would require large-scale efforts to improve conditions in the South sufficiently to remove the pressure to migrate. It should, however, be recognized that less than a third of the estimated increase in Negro central-city population by 1985 will result from in-migration—2.7 million out of total increase of 8.7 million.

**NEGRO SELF-DEVELOPMENT**  The Enrichment Choice is in line with some of the currents of Negro protest thought that fall under the label of "Black Power." We do not refer to versions of Black Power ideology which promote violence, generate racial hatred, or advocate total separation of the races. Rather, we mean the view which asserts that the American Negro population can assume its proper role in society and overcome its feelings of powerlessness and lack of self-respect only by exerting power over decisions which directly affect its own members. A fully integrated society is not thought possible until the Negro minority within the ghetto has developed political strength—a strong bargaining position in dealing with the rest of society.

In short, this argument would regard predominantly Negro central cities and predominantly white outlying areas not as harmful, but as an advantageous future.

Proponents of these views also focus on the need for the Negro to organize economically and politically, thus tapping new energies for self-development. One of the hardest tasks in improving disadvantaged areas is to discover how deeply deprived residents can develop their own capabilities by participating more fully in decisions and activities which affect them. Such learning-by-doing efforts are a vital part of the process of bringing deprived people into the social mainstream.

**SEPARATE BUT EQUAL SOCIETIES?**    The Enrichment Choice by no means seeks to perpetuate racial segregation. In the end, however, its premise is that disadvantaged Negroes can achieve equality of opportunity with whites while continuing in conditions of nearly complete separation.

This premise has been vigorously advocated by Black Power proponents. While most Negroes originally desired racial integration, many are losing hope of ever achieving it because of seemingly implacable white resistance. Yet they cannot bring themselves to accept the conclusion that most of the millions of Negroes who are forced to live racially segregated lives must therefore be condemned to inferior lives—to inferior educations, or inferior housing, or inferior status.

Rather, they reason, there must be some way to make the quality of life in the ghetto areas just as good. And if equality cannot be achieved through integration then it is not surprising that some Black Power advocates are denouncing integration and claiming that, given the hypocrisy and racism

that pervade white society, life in a black society is, in fact, morally superior. This argument is understandable, but there is a great deal of evidence that it is false.

The economy of the United States and particulary the sources of employment are preponderantly white. In this circumstance, a policy of separate but equal employment could only relegate Negroes permanently to inferior incomes and economic status.

The best evidence regarding education is contained in recent reports of the Office of Education and Civil Rights Commission which suggest that both racial and economic integration are essential to educational equality for Negroes. Yet critics point out that, certainly until integration is achieved, various types of enrichment programs must be tested, and that dramatically different results may be possible from intensive educational enrichment—such as far smaller classes, or greatly expanded pre-school programs, or changes in the home environment of Negro children resulting from steady jobs for fathers.

Still others advocate shifting control over ghetto schools from professional administrators to local residents. This, they say, would improve curricula, give students a greater sense of their own value, and thus raise their morale and educational achievement. These approaches have not yet been tested sufficiently. One conclusion, however, does seem reasonable: any real improvement in the quality of education in low-income, all-Negro areas will cost a great deal more money than is now being spent there—and perhaps more than is being spent per pupil anywhere. Racial and social class integration of schools may produce equal improvement in achievement at less total cost.

Whether or not enrichment in ghetto areas will really work is not yet known, but the Enrichment Choice is based on the yet-unproved premise that it will. Certainly, enrichment programs could significantly improve existing ghetto schools if they impelled major innovations. But "separate but equal" ghetto education cannot meet the long-run fundamental educational needs of the central-city Negro population.

The three basic educational choices are: providing Negro children with quality education in integrated schools; providing them with quality education by enriching ghetto schools; or continuing to provide many Negro children with inferior education in racially segregated school systems, severely limiting their life-time opportunities.

Consciously or not, it is the third choice that the nation is now making, and this choice the Commission rejects totally.

In the field of housing, it is obvious that "separate but equal" does not mean really equal. The Enrichment Choice could greatly improve the quantity, variety, and environment of decent housing available to the ghetto population. It could not provide Negroes with the same freedom and range of choice as whites with equal incomes. Smaller cities and suburban areas together with the central city provide a far greater variety of housing and environmental settings than the central city alone. Programs to provide housing outside central cities, however, extend beyond the bounds of the Enrichment Choice.

In the end, whatever its benefits, the Enrichment Choice might well invite a prospect similar to that of the Present Policies Choice: separate white and black societies.

If enrichment programs were effective, they could greatly narrow the gap in income, education, housing, jobs, and other qualities of life between the ghetto and the mainstream. Hence the chances of harsh polarization—or of disorder—in the next 20 years would be greatly reduced.

Whether they would be reduced far enough depends on the scope of the programs. Even if the gap were narrowed from the present, it still could remain as a strong source of tension. History teaches that men are not necessarily placated even by great absolute progress. The controlling factor is relative progress—whether they still perceive a significant gap between themselves and others whom they regard as no more deserving. Widespread perception of such a gap—and consequent resentment—might well be precisely the situation 20 years from now under the Enrichment Choice,

for it is essentially another way of choosing a permanently divided country.

## THE INTEGRATION CHOICE

The third and last course open to the nation combines enrichment with programs designed to encourage integration of substantial numbers of Negroes into the society outside the ghetto.

Enrichment must be an important adjunct to any integration course. No matter how ambitious or energetic such a program may be, few Negroes now living in central-city ghettos would be quickly integrated. In the meantime, significant improvement in their present environment is essential.

The enrichment aspect of this third choice should, however, be recognized as interim action, during which time expanded and new programs can work to improve education and earning power. The length of the interim period surely would vary. For some it may be long. But in any event, what should be clearly recognized is that enrichment is only a means toward the goal; it is not the goal.

The goal must be achieving freedom for every citizen to live and work according to his capacities and desires, not his color.

We believe there are four important reasons why American society must give this course the most serious consideration. First, future jobs are being created primarily in the suburbs, but the chronically unemployed population is increasingly concentrated in the ghetto. This separation will make it more and more difficult for Negroes to achieve anything like full employment in decent jobs. But if, over time, these residents began to find housing outside central cities, they would be exposed to more knowledge of job opportunities. They would have to make much shorter trips to reach jobs. They would have a far better chance of securing employment on a self-sustaining basis.

Second, in the judgment of this Commission, racial and social-class integration is the most effective way of improving the education of ghetto children.

Third, developing an adequate housing supply

for low-income and middle-income families and true freedom of choice in housing for Negroes of all income levels will require substantial out-movement. We do not believe that such an out-movement will occur spontaneously merely as a result of increasing prosperity among Negroes in central cities. A national fair housing law is essential to begin such movement. In many suburban areas, a program combining positive incentives with the building of new housing will be necessary to carry it out.

Fourth, and by far the most important, integration is the only course which explicitly seeks to achieve a single nation rather than accepting the present movement toward a dual society. This choice would enable us at least to begin reversing the profoundly divisive trend already so evident in our metropolitan areas—before it becomes irreversible.

## CONCLUSIONS

The future of our cities is neither something which will just happen nor something which will be imposed upon us by an inevitable destiny. That future will be shaped to an important degree by choices we make now.

We have attempted to set forth the major choices because we believe it is vital for Americans to understand the consequences of our present failure to choose—and then to have to choose wisely.

Three critical conclusions emerge from this analysis:

**1**  The nation is rapidly moving toward two increasingly separate Americas.

Within two decades, this division could be so deep that it would be almost impossible to unite a white society principally located in suburbs, in smaller central cities, and in the peripheral parts of large central cities; and a Negro society largely concentrated within large central cities. The Negro society will be permanently relegated to its current status, possibly even if we expend great amounts of money and effort in trying to "gild" the ghetto.

**2**  In the long run, continuation and expansion of such a permanent division threatens us with two perils.

The first is the danger of sustained violence in our cities. The timing, scale, nature, and repercussions of such violence cannot be foreseen. But if it occurred, it would further destroy our ability to achieve the basic American promises of liberty, justice, and equality.

The second is the danger of a conclusive repudiation of the traditional American ideals of individual dignity, freedom, and equality of opportunity. We will not be able to espouse these ideals meaningfully to the rest of the world, to ourselves, to our children. They may still recite the Pledge of Allegiance and say "one nation . . . indivisible." But they will be learning cynicism, not patriotism.

**3**  We cannot escape responsibility for choosing the future of our metropolitan areas and the human relations which develop within them. It is a responsibility so critical that even an unconscious choice to continue present policies has the gravest implications.

That we have delayed in choosing or, by delaying, may be making the wrong choice, does not sentence us either to separatism or despair. But we must choose. We will choose. Indeed, we are now choosing.

## REFERENCES AND NOTES

1  It is true that the average pupil-teacher ratio declined from 28 to about 25, and other improvements in teaching quality may have occurred. But they cannot account for anything approaching this rapid increase in costs.

2  Based on Census Bureau Series D projections.

## 3   THE JEWISH COMMUNITY   FRED MASSARIK

The empirical study of the American Jewish community may be at the threshold of a new era. During the last several years (since 1959), a new, more sophisticated tendency has begun to appear in community research designs focusing on Jewish life. And, perhaps most important, beginnings are being made toward the development of a representative nation-wide study of the American Jew. Through the Committee on Jewish Demography of the Council of Jewish Federations and Welfare Funds (the principal national coordinating body of Jewish philanthropic fund raising and community organization), preliminary procedures for design of a national Jewish population sample have been completed. Guide lines to assist local areas in developing comparable studies and research approaches are being devised, hopefully replacing the more haphazard methods of the past. As additional sanguine omens, increasing numbers of competent social researchers have begun to take professional interest in Jewish community inquiry, and an international organization, the World Union of Jewish Studies, has come into being. It may be that we are now in the early stages of a renaissance (or is it simply a birth?) of the systematic, empirical study of contemporary Jewish life.

The present knowledge concerning the Jew in America largely evolves from a mosaic of discrete community studies. This mosaic is not composed of equally lucid pieces that mesh neatly and meaningfully, even though in recent years an increasing number of well-conceived studies have been reported. So far, no nationally representative study

Reprinted with the permission of the author and the publisher from Marvin B. Sussman (ed.), *Community Structure and Analysis*, pp. 238–252. Copyright © 1959 by Thomas Y. Crowell Company.

The introductory statement of this article has been especially revised by the author for this book.

of Jewish population has been conducted, and the individual surveys, often sponsored by private welfare and planning agencies, have utilized a wide variety of questions and classification techniques. Therefore, findings have not always been clearly comparable.

The *American Jewish Yearbook*[1] endeavors annually to compile basic data about American Jewish population. For communities in which no formal surveys are available, population figures are obtained by questioning Jewish community leaders regarding *their* estimates of Jewish community size. The sum total of estimates, as variously derived, suggests that the American Jewish population is somewhere between five and five and one-half million. As even gross population counts are relatively crude, it is no surprise that many further gaps exist in our knowledge concerning characteristics of people and communities composing the population.

### A "TYPICAL" JEWISH COMMUNITY STUDY

The typical Jewish community study is launched by the leadership of the organized Jewish community when plans are underway for a new building or service. In order to obtain a factual basis for the contemplated action, questions must be answered regarding the number and composition of the Jewish population. Sometimes, the study process itself may have certain open and hidden agendas extending beyond the research itself. For instance, a study may provide an opportunity for opposing forces within the Jewish community's leadership to move toward a resolution of the internal conflict.

Some obstacles confront the design of the study. Census data prove of little direct help to the study staff. However, sometimes relatively substantial lists of Jewish households are available, as compiled for purposes of philanthropic fund-raising. It is the word "relatively," however, that from a scientific standpoint gives much trouble, for these lists cannot be assumed to be either representative or exhaustive. Further, the very definition of "Jewishness" is burdened by ambiguity.

Nonetheless, with the fund-raising files as a potential starting point, the study may proceed. Sometimes the so-called "master list" approach is used, especially in small communities; further attempts are made to find additional names not included in the original list. However, if the community is large and highly urbanized, this method frequently falters. The number of names to be added proves to be overwhelming; to find them might very well necessitate a complete door-to-door canvass of great cost and complexity.

Often, supplementary estimates are used to specify the approximate size and distribution of the Jewish population. The various methods, which will not be considered here in detail, include estimates based upon a ratio of "distinctive" Jewish names to names of other Jewish persons, estimates by means of death records, and estimates utilizing data of absences of Jewish children from public schools on Jewish High Holidays. These methods sometimes are used uncritically, other times with some awareness of their limitations and with use of various correction factors.

In order to obtain more detailed information, the typical survey recruits interviewers who are to approach either all households as provided by some basic file or a sample of households. Quite often volunteers are sought for this purpose. With skillful recruitment and supervision, such volunteer interviewers can be utilized effectively. However, in many cases volunteers prove to be inconsistent in the pursuit of their task. It is possible that the use of volunteers in Jewish community research is more feasible in the relatively small community, where the mechanisms of interpersonal social control, resulting from high community cohesion, function more adequately. The experience with volunteer interviewers in Los Angeles, a large heterogeneous urban community has repeatedly been disappointing.

Ultimately, the available data are compiled often without much sophistication, and some attempt is made to utilize the results. All too often, the bridge between research findings and community action is none too firm. Much adequate research lies unused on executives' shelves.

## JEWISH COMMUNITY AS AN URBAN PATTERN

It is an open question as to whether the pundit who said that "Jewish people are like everyone else only more so" deserves to be called perceptive. However, if we still view America as an essentially urban country, there is little doubt that the pattern of Jewish community in the United States meets all the requirements of general urbanism "only more so." It is true that Jewish population is scattered far and wide in virtually every part of the country and in virtually every community of any size. Nonetheless, it is the urban pattern that stands out.

Assuming that the Jewish population in the U.S. is about 5,000,000 we find that some 3,700,000 are concentrated in a dozen major metropolitan centers. As is well known, New York takes the major slice, with a Jewish population of approximately 2,300,000, followed by Los Angeles with about 400,000. Thus, while the 12 largest Jewish communities account for almost *three-quarters* of the Jewish population, the 12 largest metropolitan areas in the U.S., according to the 1950 census, account for only 28 percent of the nation's people.

Within a metropolitan community itself, as for instance in Los Angeles, there is evidence that Jewish population is settled in particularly substantial numbers within the more urban parts of the community. The 1951 Los Angeles Jewish population study[2] (which shall serve as a frequent source of illustrations), found two social planning areas, Beverly-Fairfax and Wilshire-Fairfax, as the areas of greatest Jewish population density.[3] Here, for each one-hundred residents, approximately 63 were Jewish. As measured by an adaptation of the Shevky-Williams index typology, modified by the

Welfare Council of Metropolitan Los Angeles, with the components (1) number of unattached persons, (2) population density per acre, and (3) absence of home ownership,—the urbanization of these two areas is well within the top quartile.[4] The "old" Jewish ghetto-like areas, such as Boyle Heights, scored even higher in urbanization, falling within the upper 15 percent of all Los Angeles planning areas.

However, much as the urban character has been undergoing some transformation in general, so changes are found in the Jewish community. The much publicized movement to suburbia clearly has affected the Jewish population, and other internal migrations have taken place. The impact of these migratory trends has varied considerably from city to city.[5] In some, as for instance in San Francisco, the "old" Jewish community, well integrated within the total pattern, has remained stable, and the suburbs have been fed principally by a mild stream of out-of-state in-migrants. Elsewhere, the traditional areas of Jewish concentration, which at one time resembled the pattern of the ghetto so aptly described by Louis Wirth[6] have disappeared. For example, in Buffalo during the middle 1920's, the east side accounted for some 70 percent of the Jewish population. Today, the movement has been largely away from this section toward the north and toward a general pattern of intermingling with the rest of the population. In Minneapolis 80 percent of the Jewish population once lived on the north side. Recently, the movement has been towards the Park area. Still, in spite of this movement, this section accounts for but 15 percent of the area's Jewish population.

In Newark, the suburbs have become increasingly significant areas of Jewish population settlement. In Los Angeles, it is the east side once more that has gone by the wayside. Here the Jewish population declined from 35,000 in 1940 to less than 10,000 in 1957. Instead a large Jewish population has settled throughout the western part of the city, and a steady and spectacularly large stream of Jewish residents has moved to the various suburbs, most notably to the San Fernando Valley. The latter area's Jewish population has

almost tripled from 1951 to 1957, reaching almost 100,000.

Both conventional urban settlements and the new suburban growth are significant settings for today's American Jewish community. Further, it seems that the days of the classic ghetto are a thing of the past. In many metropolitan centers, Jewish population continues to concentrate in certain major areas, but this concentration is less pronounced and sociologically distinct from the historic ghetto past.

## THE DIMENSIONS OF JEWISH COMMUNITY

Geographical propinquity may be a necessary but not a sufficient condition in a sociologically meaningful definition of community. As a matter of fact the words "Jewish community" are used in widely differing contexts and often communicate diverse meanings. It may be worthwhile therefore to consider a number of dimensions which may be utilized in measuring the "communityness" of Jewish community. These dimensions make no claim for mutual exclusiveness or theoretical purity, but they do reflect some of the approaches that may be made to the Jewish community concept.

THE RELIGIOUS DIMENSION "Jewishness" is often viewed as an ethnic phenomenon. As such, it presumably combines the characteristics of religious and cultural forms of social organization. From a religious standpoint, or indeed from an ethnic standpoint, "Jewishness" can serve only as a generic category. Perhaps most ethnic groups can be differentiated into a number of fairly distinct subcomplexes. However, the more monolithic the pattern of social control, the more homogeneous the resulting cultural complex is likely to be. Many Jewish theologians, philosophers, as well as many Jewish "men of affairs," view the essence Jewishness as a common belief system, rooted in a common heritage, involving a highly flexible but significant "bond of faith" that links Jewish people everywhere. This approach to Jewishness leaves a tremendous amount of room for subcultural variations in ritual, language, and institutions within the Jewish community. There is no official "Jewish dogma" in any way resembling, for instance, a papal encyclical. There is no truly centralized source of religiously derived social control. Indeed, at least three major movements, Reform, Conservative, and Orthodox, coexist on the American Jewish religious scene. In addition, there are specific varieties of religious observances such as those espoused by Sephardic Jewry and the "Reconstructionist" viewpoint that concerns itself with the "organic Jewish community" and the religio-cultural aspects of Jewishness. Any many Jewish people identify as "just Jewish," 31.9 percent according to the 1951 Los Angeles study, while the corresponding percentages for Reform, Conservative, and Orthodox were respectively 29.5 percent, 20.5 percent and 17.1 percent.

The diversity in intra-Jewish religious observance is clearly reflected in the organization of the Jewish community. Individual congregations are essentially autonomous. Coordinating bodies or other confederations tie together internally some of the various movements. There is a bond among Reform congregations through the Union of American Hebrew Congregations, while the Conservative movement is linked through the United Synagogues of America. Less clearly internally related are the Orthodox congregations.

Whatever the state of coordination or confederation, congregation autonomy implies that individual congregations will move in the direction of Jewish population concentration when the local leadership is ready and able to make such a move. Typically, Jewish migration precedes the subsequent shift in organized religious facility. No central power is in a position to dictate where a congregation should locate itself, although persuasion and mild pressure are occasionally applied. Efforts at planning often emerge as by-products of community surveys such as those mentioned previously.

In a community such as Los Angeles tremendous geographic mobility influences the pattern of religious organization. The congregation does not serve as the hub of organized Jewish life as it did years ago. Members often travel great distances and frequently by-pass many nearby congregations for reasons of personal preference linking them to a certain rabbi, or because of a desire to be a member of a high-status congregation.

Economic factors are highly influential in determining congregational membership, but this does not mean that high income and high status congregations are necessarily located directly within the high income and high status ecologic area. For instance, in Los Angeles, two large Reform congregations, many of whose members live in Beverly Hills, Bel-Air, and Brentwood, are located a considerable distance from these areas, and these congregations, in addition, attract other high status membership from elsewhere in the city. Thus, the socio-economic-status nexus replaces the geographic neighborhood—ghetto nexus—as an organizing force in the religious dimension of Jewish community.

Possible exceptions to this trend are the small Orthodox congregations that, because of the prohibition on travel by vehicle or public transportation on holidays, continue to serve a relatively narrowly confined geographic area.

The relative importance of the Reform, Conservative, and Orthodox modes of Jewish identification varies significantly in various cities. Thus, it becomes difficult to generalize the religious pattern without a broadly representative community-by-community investigation.

**THE COMMUNITY INSTITUTION DIMENSION**    Private sectarian philanthropy in the Jewish field has become an increasingly important organizing force of Jewish community; the ideological concept of "taking care of one's own" is of importance historically and currently. The practical outcome of this ideological orientation has been the concentration by significant segments of Jewish community life on the development, maintenance, and use of Jewish community welfare agencies. The United Jewish Appeal, Jewish Welfare Federation campaigns, and the similar federated drives and hospital campaigns are manifestations of the Jewish concern with organized welfare work. In Los Angeles, the

United Jewish Welfare Fund is the second largest philanthropic effort, exceeded in size only by the Community Chest.

Once more the pattern of growth of Jewish welfare agencies has not been the same in all Jewish communities. While its beginnings were rooted in the satisfaction of highly specialized needs—burial societies often were the first Jewish community agencies—today the network of service is comprehensive and complex. The movement of federations and community councils has more recently exerted some coordinating influence upon this involved conglomerate of individual agencies.

The care of the needy and of the ill plays a significant role in Jewish philanthropy, although many of the agencies meeting these needs are also related to the Community Chest movement. The Jewish community centers through the National Jewish Welfare Board and through the individual implementation of recreation programming have come to be an important force. Service to youth through the B'nai B'rith Youth Organization, through youth councils, and through child care agencies functions as another significant cohesive force in the Jewish community. Jewish education, sometimes related to central community bodies but perhaps more frequently tied to the congregations themselves without external influence, provides a long-term guiding influence in perpetuating Jewish observance and ideology.

It is worthy of note, however, that the relative heterogeneity and the lack of tight social control has brought with it some degree of alienation and dissatisfaction. For instance, a study conducted by Salisbury[7] has suggested that the level of satisfaction of Jewish people with their own early religious educational experience typically is considerably below the satisfaction level displayed by Catholic or Protestant church members. The frequency of exposure to religious education and the participation in organized Jewish educational life equally falls below other population segments.

The concept of community council or federation is worthy of attention. While internal diversity is the rule, these bodies often seek to relate informally and by methods of persuasion the various segments of the Jewish community. They provide a meeting ground for some forms of social planning and for the resolution of major conflicts. Various voluntary organizations, including those with national affiliation, such as B'nai B'rith, American Jewish Committee, Hadassah, and the American Jewish Congress, here can find a common meeting ground. Typically, the Community Council and Federation conducts major fund-raising campaigns such as those previously noted. These campaigns often raise money for overseas causes; a single fund-raising campaign sponsored by a single agency accomplishes both purposes and becomes *the* Jewish philanthropic effort. Fund-raising has become a noteworthy device in building Jewish community cohesion. Quite often it manages to substitute concrete communality of action for vague assertions of communal unity.

**THE ECONOMIC DIMENSION** The economic life of the Jewish community is an integral part of the community's total economic process. While not self-contained by any means, certain typical patterns of occupational concentration persist. In general, the greatest portion of the Jewish male labor force is classifiable in the "manager-proprietor" category (36.8 percent in Los Angeles, according to the 1951 study). In many other Jewish communities, the proprietor-manager segment similarly accounts for one-third or more of the Jewish labor force, often followed in size by the professional-technical group, which usually constitutes 10 to 20 percent of the total, 17.6 percent in Los Angeles in 1951. Jewish females in the labor force typically fall within the clerical and sales category, 50.3 percent being so classified by the Los Angeles study.

The findings suggest that the socio-economic level of the Jewish population is somewhat higher than that found in the community generally. While this differential appears to be a common state of affairs, it tells only a part of the story. The very heterogeneity of the Jewish community itself indicates further internal differentiation. This differentiation undoubtedly is linked to a variety of factors, including religious orientation and age. The

Reform group tends to be the most well-to-do (mean household income, Los Angeles, 1951: $7,400), followed by the Conservative group (mean income $6,320), while the Orthodox group is characterized by the relatively lowest economic status (mean income $5,680). Further, the Los Angeles study indicates that the sizeable group of "non-identifying" Jews, Jews who view themselves as "just Jewish" without Reform-Conservative-Orthodox preference, give evidence of an economic level even slightly below that of the Orthodox (mean income $5,560).

Younger people, with an extremely high proportion of college education, tend to move more than ever into the professions, but they extend their scope beyond law and medicine; engineering, accounting, and the sciences seem to be attracting increasing numbers from the youthful Jewish labor force. Also, some "non-traditional" occupations, such as banking and insurance, are beginning to attract a higher proportion of young Jewish workers than was true in the recent past.

In considering the pattern of economic organization within the Jewish community as such, we find that being Jewish often is an asset rather than a handicap. Indeed, anti-Semitism and subtle discrimination in business is not entirely a thing of the past in America. But, the high proportion of proprietorship and managership within the Jewish group offsets internally the external traces of overt and covert discrimination. Sometimes the web of informal social relationships within the Jewish community facilitates the job hunt of the young Jewish entrant into the labor force in such a manner that he can more readily find employment by a Jewish proprietor or manager. In Los Angeles among Jewish young people through age 29, 21.6 percent indicated that being Jewish helped in finding employment, while only 13.5 percent viewed it as a hindrance. No doubt, individual differences in interest and temperament may distinquish the Jewish job applicant who actually makes use of the perceived "assist" in job hunting provided by "Jewishness" from the one who finds employment within the less restrictive range of job opportunities provided by the economy in general. The Jewish employer rarely engages in outright purposeful discrimination against a non-Jewish applicant, so that the firm owned or managed by a Jewish proprietor-manager typically employs a substantial "mix" of Jewish and non-Jewish workers.

## ECOLOGY OF THE JEWISH COMMUNITY

Los Angeles hardly is the "typical" Jewish community in America. Still, in a sense it constitutes a blend of social patterns found elsewhere in the country.

Its growth has been fed by a tremendous stream of in-migration, as well as by a substantial birthrate. The vastness of the in-migration is substantiated by a finding in the 1951 Los Angeles study which showed that 28.3 percent of all Jewish households resident in Los Angeles in 1951 had first settled in the Los Angeles area some time during the five-year interval 1945-1950. In other words, the postwar westward migration within the span of half a decade brought nearly 30,000 Jewish households to the Los Angeles area. Of these in-migrants, nearly half indicated that their last place of residence had been either New York or Chicago.

Above-average fertility ratios, particularly in the suburban sections, are suggestive of the component of growth due to natural increase. For instance, in 1951 in the suburban San Fernando Valley area, there were 239.8 Jewish children under five per 1,000 Jewish persons, 20 to 54, compared to the city-wide average of 153.9

Los Angeles provides illustrations of at least three significant ecological constellations found widely in Jewish communities: (1) the Dense Jewish Urban Area, (2) Jewish Suburbia, and (3) Jewish Population Scatter.

The *Dense Jewish Urban Area* is the contemporary successor of the ghetto. However, as we have mentioned, it clearly is *not* a ghetto in the classical sense. As noted, in Los Angeles, the Beverly-Fairfax and the Wilshire-Fairfax areas are nearly two-thirds Jewish. Some sub-parts are almost entirely inhabited by Jewish residents; others are less densely Jewish. The hub of this high Jewish population concentration accounts for at least 50,000 Jewish persons. It epitomizes the Dense Jewish Urban Area.

The Beverly-Fairfax, Wilshire-Fairfax economic level is essentially near the median for the Los Angeles Jewish population. Here, it is the Conservative religious identification that occurs most frequently (about 30 percent of Jewish households living in area being Conservative), while in contrast the remnants of the more traditional ghetto life (Boyle Heights) are largely Orthodox (nearly 50 percent). The Dense Jewish Urban Area's homes are largely stucco multiple dwellings erected during the mid-twenties and thirties.

Fairfax Avenue, a major thoroughfare, reflects the intense interaction between Jewish culture and the general culture. Here, some stores, following the traditional dietary laws of "kashruth," adjoin establishments reaching for inspiration in their wares to "exotic" foreign countries: Spain, Japan, France, Italy. "Kosher-style" restaurants and delicatessens reflect the "compromise" brought about between tradition and contemporary American convenience. Non-Jewish stores intermingle and sell goods intended primarily for the Jewish customer. American urban values, a cosmopolitan orientation, and Jewish tradition give rise to a new form of social and economic neighborhood organization that is a complex but novel non-ghetto blend.

*Jewish Suburbia* is not so very different from suburbia in general. It does not conform in any traditional sense to the closely patterned, geographically integrated Jewish community of the past. Nor is it very much like the dense Beverly-Fairfax, Wilshire-Fairfax area. The San Fernando Valley, Los Angeles' suburbia *par excellence*, is a sprawling portion to the north of metropolitan Los Angeles. Its principal sociological attribute probably is its home-centered, in contrast to a community-centered or institution-centered, approach to life. The homes themselves have sprung up in fantastic abundance since World War II, but especially during the past few years. The number of dwelling units increased from about 140,000 in

1950 to more than 240,000 in 1957. Whether they are small, boxy tract homes, whether they are the modest "ranch" type, or whether they are elaborate high-prestige dwellings in the Longridge Estates, south of Ventura Blvd., they provide the key focal point of thought and action for their inhabitants. Jewish education for the young children (and they are a large group of the population) becomes an important concern. The development of congregations in Jewish Suburbia often centers about this need, whose roots are in the home, but whose satisfaction requires some reaching out to the sphere of institution and community.

The assumption still is widespread that Jewish Suburbia is a very homogeneous "upward mobile, young couple, tract home" type of community. There are many indications that this assumption is a vast oversimplification. At least San Fernando Valley Suburbia includes within its vast geographic expanse all shadings of the socio-economic spectrum, and it has a wider age diversity than inferred by the usual stereotype of "the Valley." Especially, the impressive Valley-bound immigration of 1950–1956 seems to have expanded the numbers of the upper, more "aged" portions of the area's population.

The Valley's Jewish community, though home-centered, develops its patterns of neighborhood living. There appear to be no highly dense Jewish population clusters of any magnitude. Jewish congregations and other community institutions are fairly well distributed throughout the area, and considerable travel often is necessary to reach them. In contrast, the immediate neighborhood, with its "majority" population of non-Jewish neighbors is the immediate, inescapable locus of activity. Here intergroup relations are developed among Jewish and non-Jewish children; reciprocal baby-sitting patterns emerge and a sense of loose local cohesion grows.

*Jewish Population Scatter*, a third residential pattern, is a catch-all designation for the many areas of the city whose character is basically urban, and whose Jewish population density is relatively low. Here, the rooming house, the large multiple dwelling, the older single-family dwelling provide the typical types of housing. But, once again, one is impressed by the variety in economic level, that ranges from considerably below average (South Boyle Heights, 1951 median family income $2,000), to the very highest (Beverly Hills-Westwood $10,247). Certain areas that once were the neo-ghettos now are but areas of Jewish Population Scatter. The traditional pattern of ecologic succession, with the replacement of one minority group by another, has been clearly operative on the east side (Boyle Heights) and on the near south side (West Adams) as Mexican, Negro, and Japanese populations have taken the place of the earlier Jewish settlers.

In conclusion, a number of trends might be distinguished, though here, the writer's own observation and conjecture, results of research other than those here noted, and, perchance, sheer speculation intermingle. It would seem that the pattern of Jewish community is one of change: decline in the oldest areas of high density, movement toward newer areas of more lofty economic status, and rapid growth of the suburb. Indeed, fundamental change may be taking place within the field of Jewish culture and ideology itself. Herbert J. Gans recently wrote lucidly about the development of a "symbolic Judaism" in America[8]—an approach to Jewish life that substitutes the external symbols of Jewishness for the inevitable and all-encompassing traditions of the past. Jewish youth in America today, in its process of forming the roots of the future's American Jewish community, may be moving into a state of balance with the surrounding non-Jewish community. Being Jewish often appears as a mildly positive value, though not frequently tinged by varying amounts of ambivalence. Mutual acceptance tends to replace intense in-group feeling, but voluntary self-segregation within the Jewish community seems prevalent. The fundamental beliefs of Jewish culture continue to build a strong bond among Jewish people

everywhere. We may expect that the Jewish community some years hence will be increasingly permissive in terms of ritual observance, increasingly related to the larger community, but still very much a definable entity with strong religious and welfare institutions. It will be a community with a broad sense of "togetherness" which, paradoxically will continue to stem from a complex, heterogeneous—perhaps even from a chaotic—network of social and institutional relations.

### REFERENCES AND NOTES

1   See, for instance, American Jewish Committee and Jewish Publication Society of America, *American Jewish Yearbook*, vol. 58 (1957), pp. 65–82, and most prior volumes.
2   Fred Massarik, *A Report on the Jewish Population of Los Angeles*, Los Angeles Community Council, 1953.
3   Planning areas are units of a city composed of one or more census tracts and are delineated by social and welfare community councils for the purpose of describing the population characteristics of the area and for assigning social and welfare services.
4   For a more complete description of the Shevky-Williams index typology, see Marvin B. Sussman (ed.), *Community Structure and Analysis*, New York: Thomas Y. Crowell Company, 1959, see chap. 3.
5   For some observations of recent trends incorporated in this article see mimeographed publication of Jan. 23, 1957 of the Committee on Community Organization, Council of Jewish Federation and Welfare Funds, Inc., 729 Seventh Avenue, New York. See also M. M. Cohen and M. G. Lerner, *The Growth of Suburban Communities*, New York: Council of Jewish Federations and Welfare Funds, 1955.
6   Louis Wirth, *The Ghetto*, Chicago: The University of Chicago Press, 1928 (soft-bound edition published 1956 by Phoenix Books, University of Chicago).
7   W. S. Salisbury, "Some Aspects of the Differential Religious Experience of Catholics, Jews, and Protestants"; paper delivered at the meeting of the American Sociological Society, 1956.
8   See Herbert J. Gans, "American Jewry: Present and Future," *Commentary*, vol. 21 (May 1956), pp. 422–430.

# 4 THE NATURAL HISTORY OF A RELUCTANT SUBURB

WILLIAM M. DOBRINER

One of the most persistent mistakes in the flood of literature about suburbia is the tendency to lump together under the label of "suburban" all sorts of communities caught within the cultural and economic shadow of great cities. But in fact there is an enormous difference between an all-new suburb like a Levittown and an established rural village invaded by suburbanites and turned into a reluctant suburb.

The internal problems of the mass-produced suburb and the sacked village are quite different. A Levittown has to create its institutions—its schools, its churches, its civic organization, shopping centers, "culture" groups, and the like. The invaded village, on the other hand, is a going concern before the suburban assault begins. It has evolved a social system that works for a population of a certain size. There are enough schools, churches, clubs, stores, streets, sewers, sidewalks, parking spaces, etc., to go around. But once the restless city discovers the little village and pumps a stream of suburbanites into its institutions, the social system soon develops a split personality. Where a Levittown is faced with the problem of creating a community from scratch, the sacked village has a community already, but it is soon divided between the pushy, progressive, and plastic world of the newcomers on the one hand, and the accustomed world of the oldtimers—"the villagers" on the other.

Wherever the suburban spearhead is pressing the rural village, the village has little hope of surviving unchanged, because the forces behind metropolitan expansion are irresistible. For a while the village may resist by elaborate zoning requirements or other legal barriers to invasion,

Reprinted from *The Yale Review*, vol. 49 (spring 1960), pp. 399–412, by permission of the authors and *The Yale Review*. Copyright ©Yale University Press.

but these are at best delaying actions. The tides of urbanism may be diverted for a decade or so, but what direct assault has failed to do a fifth column will accomplish. The city will seduce the young people of the village; they will go to urban colleges, take jobs in the metropolis, extend their range of contacts and eventually adopt an urban (suburban) way of life.

What it means for a long-established village to be suburbanized can be seen from the recent history of a community called here, for reasons of tact, "Old Harbor." It is a real place, in the general New England area, off the Atlantic Coast. Over 300 years old, Old Harbor lies at the foot of a curving valley between two green necks of land stretching into the sea. Its history resembles that of many another New England village. In 1662, for example, a "morals committee" of six "respectable" citizens and the minister carefully scrutinized all new settlers who arrived in the community. If the newcomers failed to pass the committee's standards of morality and respectability, they were asked to leave. So Old Harbor's tradition of skepticism and caution as to the worth of recent arrivals is anchored in over 300 years of experience.

In its early years, Old Harbor served as the local nexus of an agrarian and colonial society. Its grist mills ground local grain into flour through the power of the impounded waters of the tide ponds and mill dams. The natural harbor drew shipping from all over the east coast. Whaling ships worked out of the home port, and coastal shipping from ports as far away as the West Indies unloaded hides, rum, cattle, cordwood, charcoal, etc., on Old Harbor's busy wharfs. Over the years the farmers worked the land on the gently rolling slopes leading down to the water. The wheel-wrights turned their wheels, the metal smiths pounded out their pewterware, the shipbuilders sent their vessels splashing into the bay, and the carpenters built the "saltbox" cottages down near the harbor. The village prospered but remained comparatively changeless in some fundamental ways—it continued to be a Yankee village of industrious merchants, seamen, farmers, and craftsmen. Certain family names appear again and again in its records: the Rodgerses, the Platts, the Tituses, the Woodses, the Brushes, the Conklins, the Wickses, the Scudders, the Sopers, the Skidmores. In time more land was cleared, more ships were built, and small but vigorously independent men set up industries and crafts, farms and homes. Yet the essential "ethos" of the village remained constant—Yankee, Protestant, independent, cautious, shrewd, calculating, hard-working, and conservative.

Old Harbor figured in the American Revolution. One of its churches (still standing and functioning) served as headquarters for the local British forces. Eventually, George Washington came to Old Harbor and slept there. By the middle of the nineteenth century, in a society where so many persons, traditions, and things were new, Old Harbor had a lineage of 200 years to look back upon. But change was imminent. In 1867 the railroad came to the village and became a serious competitor with marine transportation, and thereafter the harbor declined as a vital force in the village's economy. Even more ominous was the fact that 36.6 miles from the village lay the border of a city. By today's standards, it was an urban infant, but even then it was showing a capacity for incredible growth and its influence was extending beyond its borders. Though it was still an entity apart and a universe removed from Old Harbor, some of the more perceptive villagers looked to "the city" with something more than casual Yankee curiosity and superiority. In writing to a relative in 1872, one villager noted, "There has been a very curious thing this summer, I must have seen 15 or 20 strangers in town during July and August."

The first invaders of Old Harbor were members of the new industrial aristocracy who emerged in the decades after the Civil War. They were the first outsiders to discover the magical little coves and their verdant overcover, the unspoiled woodlands, the tiny village with so much history, and the green, gentle hills with the spectacular sweep of the sea. By the turn of the century, Old Harbor had become their carefully guarded preserve. They bought old farms and cleared away acres for their summer playgrounds and gigantic estates. They fenced off two and three hundred acre parcels and created separate dukedoms populated by communities of servants and laborers.

On the surface things had not changed much. The rolling hills, the snug harbor, the Yankee village with its saltbox cottages and local crafts, the busy farms, all remained the same. The estates were secluded behind acres of greenery and the new leisure class strove to protect "the colonial charm" of the village and its surroundings. The old inhabitants kept to themselves. They ran the village as they always had, but supplied the estates with provisions, ships, and such services as they were capable of providing. Though there was little basic understanding and compatibility between the "high society" of the nation and the "high society" of the village, the coming of the estates brought a new prosperity to Old Harbor and helped take up the slack left by the decline of the fishing and whaling industries and the harbor in general. By the turn of the century, Old Harbor was passing into another stage of its life. By now the grist mills were great sway-backed structures rotting by the mill dams. The brickkilns, the tannery, and Ezra Prime's thimble factory were alive only in the memories of the very old. Children played sea games in the soft, pungent, peeling hulks of the whalers as they lay beached in the harbor marshes, their masts pointing like splayed fingers against the evening sky. And in the meantime, to the east, the urban goliath was yawning and stretching and looking fitfully about.

By the early 1920's, the township in which Old Harbor is located was undergoing rather intensive immigration from the metropolitan area. The city was going through one of its growth spasms, and the population was spilling over the city limits into the adjacent counties. Old Harbor was one county removed, but this was the decade in which the automobile drastically changed the character of American society and culture. Mass production had made Henry Ford's dream of a low-priced car for every family almost a reality. And a few miles to the south of the Village, in "Old Harbor Station," the railroad terminus, a new and rather singular figure stood on the platform waiting for the 8:05 to the city: the commuter, the classic suburbanite, with his freshly pressed tight trousers, starched white collar, and morning paper folded neatly under his arm.

Now the automobile and the new concrete highways were bringing transient strangers to Old Harbor. The strangers were noisily evident on hot summer nights when a two-hour drive would carry them from the heat and congestion of the city to the beaches and cool valleys of Old Harbor. The character of Old Harbor weekends rudely changed as streams of cranky autos on spindly wheels rattled through the center of town and jammed up at traffic lights. Not only was Main Street becoming a thoroughfare for the beach traffic on weekends, but the city people intruded into the private bathing places along the waterfront. "Private Property" and "No Admittance" signs began to obliterate "the view." The number of both permanent residents and weekend transients, or, as the villagers called them, "shoe boxers," increased.

By the 1930's, the age of the palatial estates, begun seventy-five years earlier, was about over. The huge mansions in English Tudor, Renaissance, Baroque, Spanish, and various combinations had served their purpose. They had proclaimed the grandeur of American industrial growth and had bestowed calculated and lavish honor on those who built them. Now they were in the hands of the third generation or had been sold to second and third buyers, and each time a portion of the land had been sliced off in the transaction. In addition, government action unfriendly to the rich in the New Deal decade was making it difficult to maintain huge houses; income and inheritance

taxes were forcing the estate holders to sell their property or simply to let the palaces go to seed. A few were given to educational institutions and one or two more were turned over to Old Harbor Township as museums or public parks. But there is little contemporary use for a decaying 30-room castle with its entourage of outbuildings, so they waste away in their crabgrass kingdoms, the gargantuan headstones of an excessive age.

After the Second World War population that had been trapped in the city during the war years exploded into the county neighboring Old Harbor. In ten years, the number of people in this "rural" county passed a million and made it one of the most rapidly growing areas in the United States. Large numbers also spilled over into Old Harbor's county, whose sociological border by 1950 was well within the rural-urban fringe. In the ten years from 1945 to 1955, Old Harbor Township doubled its population, and the village itself has now absorbed between two and three times the numbers it had in 1940. In just ten years, a 300-year-old village, with many of the descendants of the original founders still living there, underwent a social shock that wrenched it from whatever remained of the patterns of the past.

As Old Harbor soaks up the steady stream of suburban migrants, it has taken on a physical pattern quite different from the community of twenty years ago. Toward the center of town is the "old village," the nucleus of the "oldtimer" community. There the streets are lined with aging oaks, elms, and maples. The houses are comparatively large and reflect the architectural trends of 150 years—authentic and carefully preserved saltboxes and Cape Cods, two-story clapboard or brick Colonials, straight and angular American Gothics, and prissy, frivolous Victorians. They stand fairly close to each other, but property lines are marked by mature hedges of privet, forsythia, and weigela. Each house proclaims an identity of its own. In front of an occasional Colonial or cottage a small sign will read "1782" or "1712." In the old village, even on a sunny day, there is shade and the scent of many carefully tended flowers.

The sunlight filters through the great overhead branches and throws delicately filigreed shafts of yellow-green light on the clipped lawns, on the small barns and garages tucked behind backyard shrubbery, and on the hulls of old sailboats that will never again put to sea. The sidewalk slates are rippled by the massive roots below. Two elderly ladies, straight and thin, walk by with their market bags. There are few children. There is little noise. You sense that whatever these neighborhoods are now, the best in them has gone before.

Out along the periphery of the old village, up on what were farmlands five years ago, out along the land necks reaching toward the bay, down in the cove valleys, and up among the woody ridges, range the dwellings of suburbia. Here among the asbestos shingle or "hand-split shakes," the plastic and stainless steel, the thermopane and picture window, the two-car garages, and pint-sized dining areas, the weathered wagon wheel and ersatz strawberry barrel, live the suburbanites in their multi-level reconstructions of Colonial America. It is impossible to avoid them. The signs strung along the highways point the way. "Butternut Hill—Turn Right." "This Way to Strawberry Farm Homes." This is no proletarian Levittown. "Peppermill Village" starts with a "minimum" house of "just" seven rooms and two baths for $22,500 and goes on up. But the architectural themes of all of the developments are the same—antiquity, early American, "good taste." The Limited Dream finds a concretized expression of the past's myth in "Authentic Farmhouse Reconstructions" and the "Modernized New England Village."

Where the villagers live in comparative quiet against the steady but increasing hum of Main Street, the suburbanites live in sun and din. The Suburban Sound is a blend of children, dogs, doors, machines, and mothers. The bedlam of children at play is a universal sound, but the constant clatter of small machines and the ever-present yapping of frustrated dogs are uniquely suburban. In the summer months, the machines of suburbia are particularly vocal—the power lawn mowers (the grunt, click, and chug of the reel type serving as bass for the steady, high-powered whine of the rotary), the exhaust fans, the concrete mixers, the post-hole diggers, the tree cutters, the roto-tillers, the flooded-cellar pumpers, the hedge trimmers, and softly, in the distance, the growl and clink of the bulldozer steadily at work making more suburbs. Add to this the shouts of children, the cries of babies, the calls of mothers, and the muted tones of the dual tail pipes on the station wagon headed into the village, and the Suburban Sound is complete.

No longer is there enough space in Old Harbor. You can't park your car on Main Street any more, there may not be room in church if you arrive late on Sunday, class-rooms are "overcrowded", and you have to wait your turn for telephones to be installed in your new house. But these are simply the unsurprising results of sudden growth, and the Old Harborites are on their way to solving many of them. They have built schools and plan more. They are tearing down bits of the old village surrounding Main Street and are putting in parking lots. Some churches are adding wings or erecting entirely new buildings. They have added policemen and fire engines, and have widened the critical streets. The physical problems, in general, are understood and are being coped with realistically.

The fundamental schism between the world of the oldtimers and the world of the newcomers makes a problem that is less obvious but both more important and harder to cope with.

In their occupational characteristics, the old settlers range between the middle and upper-middle class. The majority are employed in Old Harbor as merchants, small manufacturers, and businessmen. They constitute the current rear-guard of the entrepreneurs of the last century. The rest are mostly white collar people of various persuasions who are employed either in Old Harbor or the neighboring, highly suburbanized county. Less than 20 percent commute into the central city.

The average villager is middle-aged, married, and probably has two children either finishing high school or going to college. As a group the old-timer's formal education did not go beyond high school, but they want their children to go to college and they will generally pick one of the better ones. About half of the oldtimers are Protestant, a third are Catholic, and seven percent are Jewish. The Catholic and Jewish populations represent the changes in Old Harbor's ethnic or religious character that began at the turn of the century. The median family income for the oldtimers in 1955 was about $6,700, roughly $2,300 over the national median for that year. Obviously not all oldtimers in Old Harbor are high-school educated, regular church attendants and securely anchored in the white collar occupations, but enough are to justify the image of the oldtimer as localistic, Protestant, economically "comfortable," conservative, and middle-class.

Some of the villagers trace their family lines back ten or twelve generations. Even those who arrived only fifteen or twenty years ago have spent enough time in Old Harbor to have become personally and deeply involved in the community. For them Old Harbor has become a "way of life" and an object of deep affection. When the oldtimer thinks of himself, of his identity as a person, he also thinks of Old Harbor. The community, the social system, the institutions, the organizations, the friendships have become a part of his character. Whatever is the fate of the village has also become each oldtimer's personal fate. An oldtimer merchant put the matter this way: "I have traveled a lot in this country and I've been to Europe a couple of times too. But the biggest thrill in my life was when I got back from Europe and drove over Potter's Hill and saw the spire of Old Christ Church down in the valley. It was the most beautiful sight in the world. I really love this town—Old Harbor is the finest community in the United States."

The suburbanites are another story. They are a high-income group ($9,700 a year) of professional men and executives. Ninety-seven percent arrived in Old Harbor married and almost 94 percent bought house there. They average about two grade-school children per family. Only a fourth are Roman Catholics; the great majority are Protestants, although a few more Jews have entered the community in recent years. Nearly four out of every ten of the newcomers were born outside the state. Two-thirds have been exposed to a college education. Close to half commute to the central city, and another third are employed in the county adjacent to the city.

Though the villagers are economically "comfortable," they are nonetheless rather stationary on the income ladder. They are pretty well frozen into an occupational *cul de sac*. The suburbanites, on the other hand, are upward bound—their jobs pay better and carry more prestige than the villagers'. For them the primary world is the metropolitan area. They work there, play there, and their most intimate friends live there. They tend to see in Old Harbor the familiar culture of the apartment house now spread into one-acre "country estates." To the villager, Old Harbor represents continuity between the generations, stability instead of the city's "chaos," and a place of permanence in a universe of bewildering change. The suburbanite sees in the village a weekend away from the advertising agency or the pilot's compartment. He experiences Old Harbor as a series of isolated, fragmented, unconnected social situations. Old Harbor is the family, a cocktail party, a bathing beach, a movie, a supermarket, a country club, a school, a church, a PTA meeting. It is a one-acre wooded retreat from all of the drive, bureaucracy, and anxiety of the city. But a weekend is enough for the necessary physical and psychological repairs; it's back to the city on Monday.

The temper of the suburbanite "community" may be summarized in the way the suburbanites talk about Old Harbor:

I came to Old Harbor because there is still some green around here and yet I can still get to the airport in 45 minutes. It's a nice place to live— the schools are good, and I like being near the water. It is hard to say how long we'll be here. I would like to be based further south, but as a place to live Old Harbor is fine.

I can't think of Old Harbor as my own town or anything like that. Most of my friends live closer to the city and I work there. I don't have any feeling of living in a small community or anything like that. I guess I sleep more of my time here than anything else, but it's a good place for the kids. I've got a lot of contacts and interests outside.

I have to go pretty much where the company sends me. I was transferred up to the office over a year ago so we bought a place out here in Old Harbor. Probably be here for three or four years then most likely I'll be sent to South America. We like Old Harbor although the way it's building up it will be like the city in no time. Well, it doesn't bother me much; we won't be around here forever.

But an oldtimer says:

They (the suburbanites) don't know what's going on around here. They don't care. But I do; this is my town. I used to fish down at the tide basin. Now they're talking of tearing it down. I went to school here. All my friends live around here. It's crazy what's happening. I can look out of my shop window and can't recognize 49 out of 50 faces I see. There was a time I knew everybody. It used to be our town. I don't know whose it is any more.

For the villagers, Old Harbor is their community and they have a fierce sense of possesion about it. It is a property that they share. And like any valuable property it is cared for and cherished. It must not be profanely or rudely used. This is the real issue that splits the suburbanite and villager communities apart. For the suburbanites, Old Harbor is another commodity; it is a product that can be rationally consumed; it is a means by which they hope to achieve a complex series of personal goals. For the villagers, on the other hand, Old Harbor is not a means to anything; it is simply an end in itself.

The two communities inevitably brush against each other in the course of everyday life. They flow together on the central streets, in the movie houses, on the beaches, at graduation exercises, and in the stores and shops of Main Street. In their economic relationships, villager and suburbanite have struck a symbiotic truce. They need each other, the villager to sell and the suburbanite to buy. Suburbia has brought new prosperity to the villager. Traffic and congestion on Main Street mean crowds of buyers. Parking lots may be expensive, but they also mean customers. On the other hand, there are signs that increasing suburbanization will threaten the retailers of Main Street. The shiny "super shopping centers" to the south of the village, where a couple of thousand cars can park with ease, make the village shops seem dingy and dull. The discount stores and mechanized supermarkets of the shopping centers out along the highway augur a bleaker future along Main Street.

Perhaps the greatest single issue separating villager from suburbanite has been "the school problem." With the tripling of the school population, Old Harbor has been faced with an intensive building program. Since they are essentially realists in their village microcosm, the oldtimers have reluctantly admitted the "need" for more schools. Enough of them have been eventually worn down in public meetings to cast an approving vote for new construction. For many a villager, however, it has seemed to mean money out of his pocket to pay for the schooling of other people's children. But the basic and decisive issue has not been whether to build more schools or not, but what kind of schools to build and what kind of education the children should have.

In their approach to this question, the villagers are traditionalists and conservative. They see a good education as including the basic skills taught by a dedicated but maidenly teacher in a plain school building. The suburbanites, on the other hand, are educational radicals; they are irrepressible spenders and cult-like in their dedication to the cause of modern education. It is an axiom among the oldtimers that the more costly a pending proposition is the more the newcomers will take to it, and they are not entirely wrong. The newcomers appear willing to sacrifice all else to their "children's education" At PTA gatherings and public meetings of the school board, an ecstatic speaker can bring tears to sophisticated suburbanite eyes and justify the most outlandish cause by reminding his audience that "no expense is too great when it comes to our children's welfare. It will just cost the price of a few cartons of cigarettes a year to give our children this new gymnasium. Isn't our children's education, and clean, wholesome recreational facilities worth a few cents more a year? Is there any parent here who can deny their children this? Is there anyone here who will deny their children what America can offer . . . ?"

Everyone will be on his feet applauding, for the side of "the children" has won again, and every villager who voted against the plastic gymnasium or marble swimming pool will have to face the terrible question: "Do I really hate children?"

For the newcomers, anything that is educationally worthwhile must also be very expensive. "After all, you get what you pay for." The villagers, on the other hand, will battle the "frills" and "extravagances" and will turn down "excessive" curricular and building proposals. Eventually a compromise is worked out. But in the suburbias of the upper-middle class, education is the cohesive issue around which a "consciousness of kind" develops for the newcomers. For many, education seems to have taken the place of religion.

While the newcomers have taken over the PTA's and infiltrated the school board, the villagers continue to control the churches. Suburbanites usually join the PTA before they become members of a church, though they swell the numbers of those attending religious services. But even in the ranks of the devout, there have been indications of a schism.

The villagers tend to look upon their churches as something more than formal religious centers. Over the years they have served as rallying points for a good deal of cooperative community activity, and they tend to stand for a morality and a traditionalism highly compatible with villager perspectives. One villager remarked that you can hardly keep from feeling a little possessive about a church you have helped to build. The minister of one Protestant church who rather reluctantly admitted that all was not harmony within his flock, pointed out that the "older residents" had finished paying off the church mortgage sometime around 1947,

and a few years later the church had almost doubled its congregation. As the minister saw it, the villagers were indignant over the invasion of "their" church by "outsiders." They were especially smarting over the fact that, because of the devoted work of the oldtimers, the newcomers had inherited a church free and clear of any financial encumbrance. The villagers felt that the solvency of their church had made it more attractive, and that the enthusiasm the suburbanites showed for it was not without crasser implications. As a consequence, the oldtimers began to champion all church causes that were particularly expensive. It has been the villagers who have stoutly called for a new Sunday School building and finer parish house. The villagers have been on the side of free and easy spending by the church ever since the suburban influx began.

This is not the whole story. A few years back, one of the most fashionable churches of Old Harbor made some sympathetic overtures to a purely newcomer religious group—Jews of the "Reformed" group who were conducting their services in an empty store on Main Street. The minister of this old Protestant church, which traces its origins back to the American Revolution and whose membership consists of the elect of Old Harbor society, offered the facilities of his church to the Jewish newcomers. The Jews happily accepted the offer. This not only brought the two worlds together but the Protestant and localistic villagers and the Jewish, cosmopolitan suburbanites even sponsored joint "functions" together. The differences between the villagers and suburbanites are not insurmountable, nor are the two separated by an impenetrable curtain of prejudice and ignorance.

The newcomers have largely ignored the formal political organizations of Old Harbor. Traditionally the community has been solidly Republican, and the upper-middle-class suburbanites have not threatened the political balance. There are a few more egghead Democrats in Old Harbor in recent years who write books or teach in a college, but they are regarded as odd and harmless, and no one pays much attention to them. This does not mean that the suburbanites are not politically active; they are, but they act outside political parties to do political things. Their means is the civic association. Each development or combination of developments has organized its own. As the Peppermill Village Civic Association, they lobby for sidewalks or against sidewalks, for street lights and sewers, or to keep out the sand and gravel contractor who wants to use the adjacent property for commerical purposes. Through the civic associations, the suburbanites engage in a series of running skirmishes with the villagers over local issues. Usually what they want costs more, so the villagers are against it.

The oldtimers fill almost all the political offices, where they serve to balance the limited and self-interested objectives of the civic associations against the "broader needs" of the village and the township. But in this capacity the oldtimers are more than oldtimers; they are also politicians. Having learned that the suburbanites are amazingly perceptive on the level of neighborhood self-interest, the politicians will throw an occasional sop to the militant civic associations with an eye to the coming elections. Though the suburbanites are circumscribed in their interests, they are nonetheless organized, and can marshal massive political displeasure at the polls. As a consequence, the villager politicians must somehow walk a tightrope, balancing the political expediency of pleasing the newcomers against their own desire to keep the village what it was.

One wonders how many towns like Old Harbor are currently fighting to keep their identities in the industrializing South or in the rapidly growing Far West. How many Old Harbors are there all together? No one can even chance a guess. Each of the 168 great metropolitan centers of the nation is at present consuming a whole series of villages now within its sociological borders. And each village has a different history, a geography of its own and a set of institutions practiced by a population that is the same as nowhere else. Yet beneath the idiosyncratic surface, the villagers look with universal anxiety as the crush of metropolitanization proceeds. Everywhere the spirit of the small village suffers with the encroachment of urban anonymity and transiency. The Levittowns are fresh and naked, yet of a single character. The Old Harbors are split by the struggles of two communities to shape the prevailing character of the whole.

Yet the future lies with the metropolis and not the village. You can see it in the new super expressways that slice through Old Harbor's meadowlands. You sense the shift in internal balance in the village by the domination of the suburbanites at school board meetings. You know it on an autumn's evening, in the crisp sea air, and in the deepening twilight around the mill pond. The great shuddering bulk of the mill squats in the hollow, intimidated by the headlights of the commuters as they race down and through the valley, dreary from the city and hungry for home. Pencils of light search into the gaping slats and crudely intrude upon the embarrassment of the mill's decay—the rusting gears, the splintered shaft, the rotting timbers, and marsh slop heaped up by the last high tide. And then with a rush the auto is gone, driving a little eddy of defiant leaves against the listless doors, leaving the old mill momentarily in shadows, huddled against the lowering sky. Through the empty windows, across the tide basin, and over the harbor, you can see the new shopping center bathed in neon and fluorescent light. There is a busyness about it. Up along the darkening necks the lights are going on in the new split levels and "contemporaries" tucked into the ridges. The lights go on and off as the night rolls in. They seem to be winking at the senile mill as it sits and broods in the gathering darkness.

## SUPPLEMENTAL READINGS

Bogue, Donald J.: *Skidrow in American Cities*, Chicago: Community and Family Study Center, 1964.

Clinard, Marshall B.: *Slums and Community Development*, New York: The Free Press, 1966.

Cox, Harvey: *The Secular City*, New York: The Macmillan Company, 1965.

Duncan, Otis D.: "Optimum Size of Cities," in Paul K. Hatt and Albert J. Reiss, Jr. (eds.), *Cities and Society*, New York: The Free Press, 1957.

Fisher, Webb S.: *Mastery of the Metropolis*, Englewood Cliffs, N. J.: Prentice-Hall, Inc., 1962.

Goldwin, Robert A.: *A Nation of Cities*, Chicago: Rand McNally & Company, 1968.

Hawley, Amos H.: "Power and Urban Renewal Success," *American Journal of Sociology*, vol. 68 (January 1963), pp. 422–431.

Jacobs, Paul: *Prelude to Riot*, New York: Random House, Inc., 1968.

Keller, Suzanne: *The Urban Neighborhood*, New York: Random House, Inc., 1968.

Lewis, Oscar: *A Study of a Slum Culture*, New York: Random House, Inc., 1968.

Minar, David W.: "The Community Basis of Conflict in School System Politics," *American Sociological Review*, vol. 31 (December 1966), pp. 822–834.

Nisbet, Robert A.: *The Quest for Community*, Fairlawn, N. J.: Oxford University Press, 1953.

Reiss, Albert J.: "Rural-Urban Differences in Interpersonal Contacts," *American Journal of Sociology*, vol. 65 (September 1959), pp. 182–195.

Strauss, Anselm L.: *Images of the City*, New York: The Free Press, 1961.

Wilson, James Q.: *City Politics and Public Policy*, New York: John Wiley & Sons, Inc., 1968.

Perceptive writers have long suspected that mass culture is becoming the emblem of twentieth-century man. In a number of ways the major social classes in the United States, because of a shared mass culture, evidence fewer of the distinctive behavior patterns usually associated with specific class backgrounds. It should be no surprise that a mass culture characteristically transmitted to an unseen consumer, the general public, by newspapers, magazines, and radio and television has become an increasing influence in the lives of a majority of the American people.

The American public is continuously bombarded with new information, changing opinions, and prophetic conclusions concerning all problems of society. Radio, television, and newspapers provide almost hourly coverage of news events to millions of Americans. For the most part, the products of mass culture are the work of a small number of idea and opinion makers, news writers, and commentators. However, there seems to be very little effort to ascertain the truth in a controversial issue or story. Magazines such as *Time*, *Newsweek*, and *U.S. News and World Report* interpret the previous week's news with contrived cleverness. Newspapers avoid the responsibility of interpreting the news or social trends by the expedient of providing two or three versions of any issue. Thus the editorial pages of the large metropolitan newspaper will contain several versions of reality described by syndicated editorialists such as Walter Lippmann, Drew Pearson, William Buckley, and James Reston, who comment on social problems with a variety of facts and different political biases. Radio and television, because of rigid time requirements, manifest virtually total indifference to any serious effort to evaluate sources and facts concerning a story, and newscasts tend to the format of a catalog of events that might appropriately be categorized as "what went wrong today."

With such a large amount of information, the public expects trained journalists and radio and television commentators to abstract the salient points and give meaningful conclusions concerning major social trends. The mass media do have the responsibility to search out the facts determinedly in controversial charges and issues; otherwise readers are provided with a meaningless array of information. Newspaper editorials, for example, might render a service by providing a daily analysis of the syndicated columns of the preceding day. As things now stand, the American people are subjected daily to a barrage of unevaluated opinions and snippets of information, plus a strong tendency for the mass media to feature negative occurrences as "news." It is small wonder that a credibility gap has developed between opinion and supporting information.

Mass culture is assumed to be a factor in creating and augmenting some social problems. Television, for example, depicts criminal behavior, and there are a good many people who are certain that there is some causative relationship between the depiction of a social problem and its perpetuation. In fact, some modern societies, such as Sweden, prohibit children under the age of fourteen from seeing motion pictures in which any massive violence is portrayed. It is assumed that to see violence is to develop a tolerance for antisocial ways of settling controversies. In the United States children of all ages are steady consumers of shows of violence. A survey of seven days of network television programs, conducted by the *Christian Science Monitor* six weeks after the assassination of Robert Kennedy, revealed 81 killings in 85½ hours of programming during the prime evening hours and Saturday morning. Some 372 acts of violence or threats of violence were recorded, including 162 on Saturday morning, generally designated as children's hours. The survey disclosed that the most violent evening hours were between 7:30 and 9:00 P.M., when, according to network estimates, more than 25 million children between the ages of two and seventeen watch television. In the early evening there was a murder or killing depicted once every 31 minutes.

Research by behavioral scientists has been unable either to support or to refute the assumption that television and other mass media stimulate violent behavior on the part of children and young adults. The producers of mass media seem convinced that the consumer wants a diet of "gut-level" programs, with crime and violence providing most of the themes. Critics have accused producers of meeting a common demand with the least effort by merely presenting a jumble of "shoot-out scenes." It should be noted, however, that most of the social problems presented by the mass media predate the invention of the media themselves. Various parts of the existing culture may be emphasized by mass media, but it is most difficult to prove that the media actually create a new culture. Thus the mass culture appears to be more a result than a cause of social problems.

The mass media also tend to offer characteristic themes with patterned regularity and emphasis, especially in motion pictures and on television. Americans enjoy themes of the old frontier, where men were able to be autonomous and quick acting. They apparently prefer violence to prolonged conversation between actors; fighting is considered a specific means of communication, with the accurate firing of a revolver the most dramatic way of terminating the dialog. Motion pictures and television series also imply without exception that crime does not pay (although some critics question the realism of a presentation in which there are no perfect crimes, no happy criminals, and none who escape punishment for wrongdoing). In other words, mass media may present extensive episodes of violent behavior as long as the last scene permits society the right to punish the guilty in an appropriate manner.

Mass culture has tended to emphasize informality and "manliness" in social relations. Perhaps the Marlboro advertisement projects as well as any the image of the strong man in all walks of American life. Informality has become a way of life to the extent that people are usually introduced without titles, and often merely by first names. Business and professional clubs have, in the main, adopted informality to such a point that even the first name has given way to initials and nicknames. Informality is an effective method of reducing social distance between people and stressing the value of egalitarianism in human relations, a theme constantly repeated by the collective mass media.

Other themes, presented perhaps with less enthusiasm, are rags to riches, log cabin to White House, or office boy to executive, and the cult of perpetual youth. Women models are "old" by the age of twenty-one; it is the bloom of youth that is worshipped, despite the fact that the bloom years constitute less than 5 percent of the age span of the average person. Past societies traditionally valued the mature years of life, but our present mass culture for the most part disregards the senior citizen. Americans over sixty-five who can afford it are expected to be living in "air-conditioned ghettoes," out of sight and mind. The mass media feature a nation of young people, few over thirty, and then only to advertise a hair rinse that will hide the traces of time.

The titles of the Luce publications vividly capture three important aspects of our new values: *Time* for recency, *Life* for a portrayal of the mass culture, and *Fortune* for maximum profit and success. Although the title of *Playboy* magazine does not accurately reflect its readership, in balancing photography ostensibly aimed at a group of "pleasure-seeking profligates" with articles concerning important issues of the day, it reflects still another aspect of our new mass culture. This is especially apparent in the extension to Playboy Clubs, where hard-working executives entertain other hard-working executives with the help of attractive hostesses in "bunny costumes." Thus work is simulated as play. The other side of this coin is brought to our attention by Lionel S. Lewis and Dennis Brissett in their selection "Sex as Work." Marriage counselors view sex as a serious business, with the subtle implication that it may be fun before marriage but becomes work after marriage.

Perhaps this is a result of the tendency of the mass culture to define anything of importance as work. Golf instructors admonish us to "work harder" on our putts, and tennis instructors urge us to "work" on improving our serves. If we do not work seriously at our play, we may be accused of "just playing around." Although we may not have reached the ultimate in "double-think" language described by George Orwell (war is peace, freedom is slavery, and ignorance is strength), we are surely approaching some of his predictions, as illustrated by an officer in the Vietnam War who declared: "We destroyed the town in order to save it."

Further evidence of the mass-culture trend toward ambiguity may be found in terms that have become the hallmark of the television guest or the panel of a "Meet the Press" discussion. Terms such as "alternative," "coping," "denigrate," "involvement," "hopefully," "meaningful," "sophisticated," and "viable" have become the intellectual dress of modern man. A revealing example of the effect of such trend words in finance and industry is the public response to new companies associated with "technology." According to a survey reported in the *New York Times* (September 24, 1967), the name of a new stock seems to be a greater determinant of public acceptance than its price-earnings ratio. Companies with names ending in "etics" or "onics" or including the words "systems," "data," "instruments," "nuclear," or "computer" are in great demand and tend to appreciate rapidly. Thus, in general, mass culture has defined "blue-chip" holdings as establishment stocks—those held by institutions and retired investors—and favors "youth-oriented" companies with a high potential for future growth. This is perhaps epitomized by the recent remark that "A company paying high dividends is simply one lacking imagination concerning its growth potential."

To what extent, then, is the mass culture an accurate representation of American society? If it is not in fact a reflection of our present way of life, to what extent are we likely to be influenced by the mass media that transmit the new mass culture? Marshall McLuhan, in the selection "Media Hot and Cold," argues that there is a basic difference in effect between "hot" media, those that are highly defined and hence permit little or no observer participation, and "cool" media, those that are low in definition and hence require the observer to participate by inferring the missing details or frame of reference. His argument is often difficult to follow because of the shifting meanings of key terms—and it is interesting that he has chosen the printed word to inform us that the impact of television has transcended that of the printed page. Nevertheless, he provides an analytic framework of some challenge.

The four articles in this chapter delve into a number of assumptions and conclusions concerning the nature and impact of mass culture. Bernard Rosenberg contributes a critical appraisal of the implications of mass culture. André Fontaine discusses the shortcomings of contemporary mass media and some long-range-policy problems that must be faced. McLuhan, an avant-garde authority on the impact of television, develops a comparative framework for the analysis of mass media. Finally, a detailed examination is made by Lewis and Brissett of the leading marriage manuals, which admonish the reader that sex is "work."

## 5   MASS CULTURE IN AMERICA   BERNARD ROSENBERG

The late Morris Raphael Cohen, an extraordinarily gifted teacher, was perhaps best known in and out of the classroom as a superb critic of other philosophers. From time to time students would grumble about his negativism; Cohen tore down whole systems of philosophy without offering an alternative world-view of his own. On one such occasion he is said to have answered this charge as follows: "My first name is an Anglicization from the Hebrew for Moses, and like Moses, I can lead you through the wilderness without bringing you to the Promised Land." The editors of this anthology, whose subject matter is not the universe but only an increasingly significant part of it, feel much as Cohen must have felt when he found himself unable to formulate sweeping answers to every question. Mass culture is not only a wilderness—with oases here and there, to be sure—it is largely uncharted. Indeed, whole parts of it remain to be explored.

Moreover, at the end of this *terra incognita*, even if we wander over its surface for forty years, there may be no Promised Land. One can only have hunches—and of these there is a plethora. But any calculation of what lies before us is premature, especially if it proceeds by extrapolating the imperfectly understood situation that we face today. Our purpose in assembling this formidable selection of readings is rather to present the reader with a guide through what is now known, or thought to be known, about extremely problematic matters.

Mass culture has reached into the Academy both by its pervasive influence and as a subject of serious study. The former, with such spectacular phenomena as audio-visual education, has been more striking than the latter. But, gradually, academicians and detached intellectuals are being drawn into the vortex by a suction force none can resist. They are beginning to ask themselves whether the quality of life has not been decisively altered by mass-circulation magazines, "comic" books, detective fiction, movies, radio, television—with all their meretricious and/or meritorious accompaniments.

Some thoughtful persons are pleased with machine civilization; many more are alarmed by its destructive force. We wish to suggest that this basic division—those who applaud and those who wring their hands over our technological apparatus—explains why there is such a range of differences in the assessment of mass culture. It tells even more than political position, which is also a fairly reliable index. The political lines that have crystallized are approximately these: radicals (Dwight Macdonald, Clement Greenberg, Irving Howe) who, like the arch-conservatives (Ortega y Gasset, T.S. Eliot, Bernard Iddings Bell), although for opposite reasons, are repelled by what they commonly regard as vulgar and exploitative, and the liberals (Gilbert Seldes, David Riesman, Max Lerner) who take a predictable position in the middle. The parallel between left, right, and center in politics and in the "popular arts" is virtually perfect.

Why, then, something still more fundamental? Because, in the mid-twentieth century, political stances and cultural choices are part of a much larger whole. In none of the archeological ages has human society been so thoroughly revolutionary as at present. Consider that man, for the million years since his origin as a distinct species, has had to struggle like every other beast (and like the postgraduate ape he was) for the means of subsistence. Only now, with mechanized agriculture, artificial photosynthesis, use of algae and other foods from the sea, is it possible to speak of a *well-fed* world population much larger than ours. That everyone could enjoy an adequate diet, with relatively little physical exertion to secure it, would have been unimaginable in any earlier age.

As Toynbee's Great West Wind blows all over the world, which quickly gets urbanized and industrialized, as the birth rate declines and the population soars, a certain sameness develops everywhere. Clement Greenberg can meaningfully speak of a universal mass culture (surely something new under the sun) which unites a resident of Johannesburg with his neighbors in San Juan, Hong Kong, Moscow, Paris, Bogota, Sydney and New York. African aborigines, such as those recently described by Richard Wright, leap out of their primitive past—straight into the movie house where, it is feared, they may be mesmerized like the rest of us. First besieged with commodities, post-modern man himself becomes an interchangeable part in the whole culture process. When he is momentarily freed from his own *kitsch*, the Soviet citizen seems to be as titillated as his American counterpart by Tin Pan Alley's products. In our time, the basis for an international sodality of man at his lowest level, as some would say, appears to have been formed.

All this comes at a time when the species' dependence upon nature for a steady food supply has virtually disappeared. Simultaneously, the curse of Adam is being lifted. Frank Lloyd Wright half seriously suggests that we will soon develop a paralysis of all our limbs except the pushbutton finger by whose sweat, rather than the brow's, man may soon live. Utopian philosophers used to speculate about who, in their good society, would do the dirty work. That *someone* had to do it was as clearly an immutable fact as the mortality of man. Now our answer, with imminent automation, and

not for the world of fancy but for that of reality, is, "Nobody." Manual labor is becoming obsolete.

We can do no more than assimilate a fragment of the change before it leads to another innovation whose significance is likewise imponderable. Of this much one can be certain beforehand: no IBM machine, nor yet a Univac, will tell us whether the latest development is for good or ill. Ambiguity is its key characteristic. If men are freed from manual labor and from the struggle with nature, what will they do? Cultivate their minds? Improve their sensibilities? Heighten their understanding? Deepen and broaden themselves? Possibly. The precondition for transfiguring *Homo sapiens* into a higher species begins to exist. When our physical environment has been subdued we may become hypersentient beings. Drudgery, monotony, inanition and brutishness can then be dispelled along with the animal existence we used to lead.

That such a step in human evolution could take place is what makes the likelihood so much more tragic. Before man can transcend himself he is being dehumanized. Before he can elevate his mind, it is being deadened. Freedom is placed before him and snatched away. The rich and varied life he might lead is standardized. This breeds anxiety, and the vicious circle begins anew, for as we are objects of manipulation, our anxiety is exploitable. The mass grows; we are more alike than ever; and feel a deeper sense of entrapment and loneliness. And even if the incubus of hydrogen war could be lifted, these specters would still hover over us.

In short, the postmodern world offers man everything or nothing. Any rational consideration of the probabilities leads to a fear that he will be overtaken by the social furies that already beset him.

There can be no doubt that the mass media present a major threat to man's autonomy. To know that they might also contain some small seeds of freedom only makes a bad situation nearly desperate. No art form, no body of knowledge, no system of ethics is strong enough to withstand vulgarization. A kind of cultural alchemy transforms them all into the same soft currency. Never before have the sacred and profane, the genuine and the specious, the exalted and the debased, been so throughly mixed that they are all but indistinguishable. Who can sort one from the other when they are built into a single slushy compost? Is there anything beyond a debased remnant of theology *or* of psychiatry left in the mind that has been encased in "peace" and whose soul has been similarly laid to rest? But what Norman Vincent Peale, Joshua Liebman and Bishop Sheen do for religion is qualitatively no different from what a horde of popularizers do in absolutely every domain. Nothing remains untouched.

Ernest van den Haag has suggested that there are two assumptions underlying all mass culture: (1) everything is understandable, and (2) everything is remediable. We might add a corollary to the first assumption: "Everything had better be made understandable." The more arcane a subject the less effort it should require for easy absorption. If education and cultivation are gradual, progressive, orderly processes, then popular education is its opposite. For what makes mass culture so tantalizing is the implication of effortlessness. Shakespeare is dumped on the market along with Mickey Spillane, and publishers are rightly confident that their audience will not feel obliged to make any greater preparation for the master of world literature than for its latest lickspittle.

This general phenomenon, although it frightens some and leaves others relatively undisturbed, has seldom been placed at the center of our attention. Now and then an important nineteenth-century figure such as Nietzsche or Tocqueville would express some sense of what lay in store for us. However, it remained for a novelist, Gustave Flaubert, to set the case before his readers in boldest outline. If this were a two-volume selection of readings on mass culture, *Madame Bovary*, saved from the vultures of condensation, would have to be presented in its entirety as a prolegomenon to the understanding of our subject. For Emma and her husband did not simply spring out of Flaubert's mind; they also sprang out of his times. And his times, as he understood them, were a prefiguration of our own.

As they are revealed to us in the novel, Emma's husband, Charles, suffers from an underdeveloped imagination, Emma from an overheated imagination, and neither of them was born or predestined to be that way. Charles is the familiar type of professional man who scarcely "has time to keep up with his medical journals." He has been given a narrow occupational training, and while this vehicle of his social ascent detaches him from the folk, it does not awaken his sensibilities. Charles, like his father, holds culture in small esteem. It cannot be otherwise: this is what his "embourgeoisement" means.

Emma's origins are as humble as her husband's. Her life slides off-center for the same reason, i.e., external forces impinge upon it, as they were soon to impinge upon and engulf the whole Western world. Charles goes to medical school and Emma to finishing school. Charles learns his lessons but remains otherwise unresponsive. Emma, to her mother-in-law's horror, studies dancing, geography, drawing, embroidery and the piano. With sovereign skill Flaubert spells out for us how Emma's mind was debauched, how her emotions were inflamed.

"For six months, Emma, when she was fifteen, battened on the garbage of those out of date 'Libraries of Choice Fiction.' Later on she came to read Walter Scott [This is a prime target of Flaubert's. Still later Emma is thrown into raptures at a production of *Lucie de Lammermoor* which she witnesses with husband and lover.] and got enthusiastic about historical things, forever dreaming of coffers, guardrooms and minstrels." Again, "In the music class, the songs she had to learn were all about little angels with golden pinions, madonnas, lagoons, gondoliers, compositions in which silly words and shoddy music could not conceal the attractive phantasmagoria of their sentimental substratum."

This is the stuff out of which Flaubert forms Emma's character; without it there is no adequate motivation for the behavior he wishes to describe. More, that background, rather than, or set in relief from, the rural milieu, lends a powerful element of inevitability to the drama. Emma, the little villager with her psyche on fire goes quixotically in search of the joy, passion, and intoxication "which had looked so fine to her in books." These are the first drippings of an osmotic process that has only in our day come into its own as full-blown mass culture. Once bathed in them and their deliquescent values, Emma can only be bored to death. She must seek satisfaction in adultery, and failing, seek it again. Any wordly man on the make can have her. She has learned what our mentors in Hollywood now teach us with even greater proficiency, namely, that love is something which

> must come suddenly with a great display of thunder and lightning, descending on one's life like a tempest from above, turning it topsy-turvy, whirling away one's resolutions like leaves and bearing one onward, heart and soul towards the abyss.

Denis de Rougemont, a historian of romantic love, while tracing its medieval lineage, finds the aberrations, as Flaubert did, a particularly virulent one in our day. The romantic complex thrives on inaccessibility in any prototypic representation of the past. Thus Tristan and Iseult or Romeo and Juliet. Consummation, prompted by boredom, brings more of the same in its wake. Emma might have been able to endure her lot if she had only flirted with Leon or merely dreamed of sleeping with Rodolphe. Wish fulfillment intensifies the original discomfort and renders it incurable. Illusions cannot persist when faced with the reality test of actual contact, and as they crumble there is nothing left to sustain their victim. Hence, one lover is discarded for another around whom the same false aura is soon spun. Emma, who could even romanticize Charles—from a distance—is still better at this game with Leon and Rodolphe, only to have each spell broken by prolonged *contact de deux épidermes*.

And in such a crisis, what does the deracinated woman do? "By moonlight in the garden she recited all the love poetry she knew and sighed and sang of love's sweet melancholy. But afterwards she found herself not a whit more calm, and Charles not a whit more amorous or emotional."

Nothing goes more directly to the core of mass culture than this. Any indictment of sleazy fiction, trashy films, and bathetic soap operas, in all their maddening forms, must come to rest finally on Flaubert's prescient insight. Far from dispelling unrest, all the (admittedly slim) evidence now on hand suggests that mass culture exacerbates it. Once understood, this fact cuts the ground from under those who justify organized distraction by claiming that it satisfies a fundamental need. Dwight Macdonald comes much closer to the point when he says that it *exploits* that need.

Contemporary man commonly finds that his life has been emptied of meaning, that it has been trivialized. He is alienated from his past, from his work, from his community, and possibly from himself—although this "self" is hard to locate. At the same time he has an unprecedented amount of time on his hands which, as van den Haag has pointed out, he must kill lest it kill him. Society abhors a vacuum, and quickly fills this one with diversion. Brutes and mimes achieve an apotheosis in these secular surroundings that they seldom enjoyed in the late Roman Empire which, after all, had its more ethereal gods. All this is accepted—and celebrated by a certain percentage of the intelligentsia not altogether unrepresented in our anthology—as a highly desirable kind of public stupefaction. It is widely assumed that the anxiety generated by industrial civilization can be allayed, as the nerves are narcotized, by "historical" novels, radio or television programs, and all the other ooze of our mass media.

It is to be expected that someone will discover hidden virtue in the kind of pin-up magazine catalogued by Goeffrey Wagner, a collector of cultural curiosa. The titles tell us enough: *Cover Girls, Paris Models, Whirl, Laff, Keyhole, Zip, Wham, Stag, Brief, Bare, Eye, Rave, Wink, Titter, Eyeful, Flirt,* etc., etc. Harold Orlans writes, as a contributor to *Dissent* in the winter of 1954, of a situation that has since worsened:

> The postwar flood of pornography shows no signs of abating and, for once, it seems, the dim congressmen, stern churchmen, and stifflaced

ladies are complaining about something real and reckonable . . . . Its recent invasion of the public domain is unmistakable. The most obvious sign is that the two-bit monthlies "glorifying the American girl" which used to be confined to the newsstands around the tracks now overflow the back shelves of the racks in neighborhood drug and candy stores. Six years ago they could not be bought in a dry Southern village, although they were imported from the nearby city to the barber shop, poolroom, and bar. Today they will be found on all the newsstands in a quiet Quaker town—or they were there until a mother, the local editor, and several ministers pounced upon the hapless police chief. They will be back again the day after tomorrow. The magazines are all the same: bosoms and butts, high heels, opera hose, leopard skins, manacles, whips and wrestling ladies. In the back pages, ads for "art photos" sent in plain envelopes via railway express. Was it for this that Peter Zenger stood trial? . . . The bomb is not getting smaller. We have bread. (When do our children die?) On with the circus!

So frightful a juxtaposition of words as "war comics" and "horror comics" may be found in our new lexicon. There is a genre of popular literature —without the written word—that specialized in the representation of lesbians dressed in riding attire with spurs and whips, mercilessly flogging their victims. Yet none of this strikes such terror in the heart as an advertisement Wagner reports having seen for the past few years in *U.S. Camera* side by side with an offer of lewd photographs. This one announces sets of Nazi German atrocity pictures at thirty for two dollars.

Sometimes it seems as if we are overtaking and passing 1984, all unawares. The total obliteration of our privacy is, if not an accomplished fact, one technically easy to accomplish. Here is an illustrative item from *Newsweek* magazine, October 24,1955:

The Calbest Engineering and Electronics Co. announced that by the end of the year it would have perfected a cheatproof device for polling television without the set owners' cooperation or knowledge. Called the "Poll-o-meter," it is a compact portable unit with a directional antenna fitted at the end of a gun-type barrel. The operator drives down a residential street, aims his gadget at passing TV aerials, and pulls a trigger. A sensitive electronic detector picks up each station's characteristic frequency signal and automatically records it.

At its worst, mass culture threatens not merely to cretinize our taste, but to brutalize our senses while paving the way to totalitarianism. And the interlocking media all conspire to that end. Wagner: "So Chop-Chop exclaims, as he wrenches a commie's head off in a *Blackhawk* [comic] book, 'Me study wrestling from television set.'"

But Emma Bovary resorts to the garbage on which she had battened as a girl and feels not a whit more calm—and neither do the rest of us when we follow her example. One feels bad because his life seems to be pointless; he is invited to divert himself, and gladly accepts, only to feel still worse afterwards.

Apart from its ghastliness, which is a matter of taste, mass culture must be indicted for this failure. In an anxious age mass culture builds the tension that it is usually credited with relieving. Meanwhile the electronic wonderworld and the rulers thereof, with a large number of collaborators from every entertainment industry, manage to debar the mass man they have created from any really satisfying experience. A genuine esthetic (or religious or love) experience becomes difficult, if not impossible, whenever *kitsch* pervades the atmosphere. And only the genuine experience, as Flaubert realized, can satisfy us. It presupposes effortful participation. In the arts this may mean no more than a willing suspension of disbelief, an *act* of the imagination which projects the reader or the audience into a state of empathy from which man's fate can be viewed with great understanding. Not everyone can achieve such a state today, and it will be argued that for those who cannot, experiences at a lower level may suffice. But surely those who know there are greater delectations than cultural pap and gruel, which cannot be concocted or appreciated without working at them, should say so.

All this applies with equal force to the pursuit of knowledge. Quite often the most "popular" teachers in our universities are those who simplify their material, make it look simple, and thereby foster the illusion that a challenging body of knowledge can be easily assimilated. This is catch-phrase pedagogy: Plato was an Idealist, Aristotle a Realist, Kant a Dialectician. All you need is a label, and every field has its Will Durant who will retail it for you. No discipline, however exacting, is insusceptible to this treatment. So, though we never really come to grips with philosophy this way, the dangerous belief that we have fully embraced it nevertheless persists. A true teacher will say, "No, there is so much within your reach—only you must stretch yourself to find it." Such an attitude is frequently dismissed as snobbery, an egghead affection, an expression of contempt for the ordinary man. It may be just the opposite, if we say to the *l'homme moyen sensuel*, "Here is what many of you could do. Why settle for so much less? What you consume now may please you for the moment; sub-art and pseudo-knowledge is shoveled down your open mouth; in another moment it will leave you ravenous and restless once again." As *kitsch* is institutionalized and we are robbed of our spontaneity, the likelihood of satisfaction, of tension followed by distension, get to be more and more remote. Culturally, we become hungrier than ever—and our diet, though habit-forming, contains less nourishment than ever.

Success is still the bitch-goddess of American society. The purveyors of mass culture allege that it too can be achieved by passive absorption. Simple rules are set forth in every sphere of activity. This is the significance of what Dwight Macdonald has called "how-to-ism." Surely any of our ancestors would have been bewildered by the library of contemporary books devoted to telling people how they should consummate the sex act—successfully. The *New York Times Magazine* (January 22, 1956) runs a large advertisement for the Salesmen's Book Club of Englewood Cliffs, New Jersey.

The club offers trial members a book for ninety-nine cents ("Take This $4.95 Value") called *The Power of Creative Selling* by Earl Prevette which will do the following things for salesmen who read it attentively. It will tell you:

How to plant YOUR ideas in the prospect's mind.

How to gain the complete attention and interest of every prospect.

How to anticipate your prospect's questions.

How to look behind a prospect's questions.

How to look behind an objection and learn what the prospect is really trying to tell you.

How to use the Law of Repetition.

How to use the Law of Averages.

How to use the Rule of Adaptation.

How to turn your "hunches" into sales—why your instinct is often wiser than your judgment.

How to use "key words" that move your prospect's mind toward a decision to buy.

How to train your imagination to originate a new selling idea, or improve an old one.

How to draw upon an "inner power" to make sales.

All for ninety-nine cents. Here the wedding with Marshall McLuhan's Mechanical Bride is complete. Advertising officiates at the ceremonies, while human engineers, sociologists, public relations executives, and psychologists provide incidental trappings. C. Wright Mills has said that we are all, in some sense, salesmen, and America is an enormous salesroom devoted to the fetishism of commodities. (See *White Collar*.) Some of us are admonished to join the ranks of full-fledged manipulators and achieve success in battering what remains of the American consciousness.

In 1934 three sociologists, George Lundberg, Mirra Komarovsky, and Mary Alice McInerny reported the results of a valuable pioneer study in their book, *Leisure*. It was already obvious to them that, "There are, unhappily, many reasons why mere freedom from vigorous physical toil and long hours of labor will not in itself insure men against heavy and unhappy lives." They used a few random illustrations which have a figurative, as well as a literal, significance: the enforced leisure of the physically handicapped, the blind, the deaf and the convalescent who are usually wretched in their idleness although they may not have economic worries; prisoners whose misery is increased by light work or no work; and millions of the unemployed who find "leisure more burdensome than work ever was"; the many people who "retire" in good health, and find only a debilitating vacuum to replace the old occupation. The authors remind us of Mahatma Ghandi's fear that modern machinery would leave India's millions with "too much leisure."

Twenty-five years ago, Professor L. P. Jacks asked the key (rhetorical) question about people with unprecedented leisure on their hands.

Will they take as the model for their leisure the sort of life now most favored by the "idle rich" and get as much of that sort of thing as their means enable them to procure—display, luxurious feeding, sex excitement, gambling, bridge, golf, globe-trotting and the rest? Or will they spend it in the way the idle poor—by whom I mean the unemployed—are now spending the leisure forced on them by the industrial crisis, which consists for the most part in just stagnating, physically, mentally and morally? Or will it be a mixture of the two—stagnation relieved by whatever doses of external excitement people may have the cash to purchase?

What "they" or "we" will do remains an open question, but one that seems to many of us, and to the majority of "highbrows" represented in this reader, to be closing very rapidly. Maybe not. Any judgment based upon necessarily faulty and partial perception can have only a limited validity. However, a few things do appear to be clear. For instance:

It is necessary to take as holistic a view as possible. No effort to comprehend and evaluate mass culture can start anywhere else than in a large socio-cultural context. From such a standpoint we may clear the air of certain obviously erroneous assumptions:

*Capitalism is responsible for mass culture* Not at all. It flourishes wherever the appropriate technological apparatus emerges, whether slowly or suddenly, and nowhere more so than in Soviet Russia which, whatever else it is, cannot be considered capitalist. A strong case could be made for pinpointing the most malignant features of mass culture where music, art, and ideas are publicly expressed only if they conform with a dictator's infantile conception of music, art, and ideas. In this realm, capitalist America has lost its leadership to the communist world. We are no longer the pacesetters. The view that we are is parochial. A cross-mass-cultural survey would dispel it.

*America is responsible for mass culture* Hardly, and for the same reasons. There is nothing in our national character that makes us peculiarly vulnerable to a condition that is sweeping the earth.

*Democracy is responsible for mass culture* Tocqueville was perhaps the first to make this common mistake. It was shared by democrats who thought that vulgarity through leveling was the price that had to be paid for an otherwise beneficial system, and anti-democrats who thought the price too high.

If one can hazard a single positive formulation (in the form of a hypothesis) it would be that modern technology is the necessary and sufficient cause of mass culture. Neither national character nor the economic arrangement nor the political system has any final bearing on this question. All that really matters is the most recent industrial revolution.

The tentative technological determinism implicit in this formulation may be valid only for the present. *Today*, wherever modern tools are introduced and superimposed on any culture, the mixture seems to be deadly. Differences between backward and advanced countries become attenuated. They meet at the same low level. Maybe at a higher stage of development, society will be "ready" for industrialization, with consequences very different from those we see all around us in the here and now. Meanwhile, change, followed by barbarous accommodation proceeds at an accelerated tempo.

## 6   THE MASS MEDIA: A NEED FOR GREATNESS   ANDRE FONTAINE

Taken as a whole and with all their faults, the mass media in the United States, many authorities agree, are the best mankind has seen. Through newspapers, magazines, and broadcasting, more people are given more information than in any other country in history. Through them, each man's recognition that he is involved in all other men's lives, which is one of history's great change-making ideas, has been vastly expanded. As never before and nowhere else, the mass media have done the job given them by James Madison: "A people who mean to be their own governors, must arm themselves with the power knowledge gives." Government regulation of the media is at a minimum—perhaps too much. Financially, they are in robust health. Through them, diverse and unpopular opinions are expressed and spread, less than idealists wish and more than bigots can abide. They have both contributed to and fostered cultural expression and may even have improved the public taste—*may* have.

Most of the numbers that index the health of the mass media are up and climbing. Although big-city mourners regularly lament the death of newspapers, just about as many daily papers are being born in the suburbs as are dying in the cities. The total number has remained nearly constant for twenty years while the number of readers of daily papers has increased faster than the population. Advertising revenue has nearly quadrupled in the same time and now totals nearly $4.5 billion—more than magazines, radio, and television combined. Profits range from 8 to 20 per cent, according to one official of the American Newspaper Publishers Association, as compared with about 6 per cent for the steel industry. A survey of 1965 figures for the New York State Publishers Associa-

Reprinted from *The Annals*, vol. 371 (May 1967), pp. 73–84, by permission of the author and The American Academy of Political and Social Science.

tion showed that newspaper net profits before taxes ranged from $22,000 for the smallest to $1 million for the largest; the average 20,000–25,000 circulation paper yields 17 per cent of income as profit, before taxes. One index of the financial health of newspapers is that it is becoming almost impossible to find a daily paper for sale at a feasible price today.

Magazines, having passed the crisis in the 1950's that took the lives of many, are back in bursting good health. Circulation of magazines was "increasing faster than the growth of the U.S. adult population," according to the Magazine Publishers Association, while advertising revenue for 1966 was 7 per cent over the previous year.

Broadcasting was equally prosperous. According to the 1967 *Broadcasting Yearbook*, total time sales of both radio and television for 1966 were $2.5 billion, up nearly $200 million from 1965. Some 6,430 radio and television stations broadcast to nearly 55 million homes with television sets and more than 57 million with radios—all figures up from the previous year. And, the National Association of Broadcasters' annual financial report said that the typical television station had a profit margin of 22.65 per cent and the typical radio station, a margin of 7.65 per cent in 1965. Both were up from 1964.

This is fine, because when the mass media are run by private enterprise it is generally true (with exceptions) that the financially healthiest newspapers, magazines, and broadcasters do the best and most responsible jobs. They can afford to; an editor who has a little leeway in his budget is not under quite so much pressure to print only the sure-fire, and usually less responsible, material—if he is truly an editor and not a money-man.

With all their faults, the media are more responsible today than they were half a century ago.

There is less bias in presentation of news, less ve-
nality, broader coverage of national and world affairs, more—but not enough—presentation of complex events in a perspective that makes them
meaningful to readers and viewers. Even television,
which has been the least conscious of its responsibility as an information medium, is showing some
signs of recognizing its obligations. Professor William A. Wood, of Columbia University's Graduate
School of Journalism[1] recently estimated that
about 30 per cent of television and 20 per cent of
radio stations "have reached the point where they
do more than give routine attention to news and
show real responsibility and quality in news services." And in the list of things they are doing he
includes the use of more special-beat reporters by
local stations, more regular hours of news programming, more community service during emergencies,
more local editorials by broadcasters, and more investigative reporting by stations in half the cities in
the country's top fifty markets. Further, both the
Ford Foundation and the Carnegie Commission on
Educational Television had plans which looked toward building a healthier financial base under educational television. The President's Special Message on
Health and Education of February 28, 1967 included elements of each plan and has given some
hope that the medium will be able to discharge its
obligation to keep Americans informed.

In a speech at the University of Pennsylvania,
Dr. Edward M. Glick, director of the American
Institute for Political Communication, said:

Today's press is a far more decent and honor-
able institution than its predecessors of 100 or
even 50 years ago. The media generally—and
the larger newspapers and television stations in
particular—are doing a much more effective job
of disseminating and interpreting the news than
was the case at the turn of the century. And the
federal government has substantially increased
both the scope and quality of its informational
output in the past generation.

"All you have to do to see the change," said
Wade Nichols,[2] editor of *Good Housekeeping* and
one of the most perceptive men in journalism today, "is to go back to the files and compare what
was published years ago with what appears today.
I think, for example, that all mass media have
done an excellent job in handling civil rights issues;
20 years ago all the problems were there, but were
generally ignored."

The growing maturity can be seen in individual
cases, too. *Look* magazine, under the editorship of
the late Daniel Mich, handled more controversial
issues, illuminated more social problems, and spot-
lighted more important trends in United States
society than it ever thought of doing twenty years
ago. Nichols himself transformed *Redbook* from a
frothy, superficial monthly full of boy-meets-girl
fiction into a book that dealt soberly and intelligently with some of the realities of life for American young adults—like mixed marriages, the costs
of medical care, block-busting by real estate operators, and lip-service religion. The *Saturday Evening
Post*, after a brief flirtation with sensationalism
and libel, has steadied down to the kind of responsibility it had under editor Ben Hibbs.

Leading newspapers, too, are responding to the
challenge to make their columns more pertinent to
their readers' lives. The *Wall Street Journal* regularly prints some of the most trenchant and well-
written articles anywhere on subjects which, to the
superficial reader, seem far outside its jurisdiction
(but actually, of course, are not). Ever since a magnificent series on juvenile crime by Harrison E.
Salisbury in the late 1950's, the *New York Times*
has carried hundreds of stories that intelligently
report and appraise current problems and issues.
Newspapers in a dozen leading cities across the
country have recently taken on the job of helping
readers who are trapped in the bureaucracy of government and big business, through columns variously called "Action Line," "Watchem," "Quest."
They act, in fact, as a kind of ombudsman for
their readers.

After the 1964 riots in Watts, the *Los Angeles
Times* ran a series which reported not what some
study commission found, but what the people of
Watts themselves felt and thought about their

quandary. A series by Morton Mintz on the pharmaceutical industry, in the *Washington Post*, became first a book, then the spark for a Congressional investigation.

All this is good; it is not great, and it is not even good enough. The rosy generalities mask a number of failures which, though varying in the different media, apply in some measure to all three. These failures must be repaired if the media are to achieve greatness.

## PEOPLE SIMPLY DO NOT BELIEVE MUCH OF WHAT THE MEDIA TELL THEM

When journalists produce material that their readers reject, they are no longer in the communications business.

Readers do not believe because what they are told contradicts their own experience. Recently the labor editor of *Business Week* opined that, with less than a half-dozen exceptions, there are no labor reporters working for the mass media. Reason: the media ignore labor except when there are strikes, and then their reportage is often anti-labor.

This makes no kind of sense. Some 13.5 million Americans are members of unions; most remain members because the union benefits them. They live through the wrestling over individual grievances, the campaigns for bargaining, and elections of union officers; at union meetings they argue out the endorsement of political candidates and their positions on local issues; they are told about—and often support with money—the struggles of other union members locked in a showdown with management, and some of them know the desperate frustration of being trapped in a racket union where venal leaders and employers conspire to exploit them. Yet they read virtually nothing about this whole aspect of their lives in the mass media. Or else what they read, their experience tells them, is distorted.

In the past few years, Congressional hearings have brought out factual information of close concern to millions—the safety of automobiles, the high cost of drugs, deceptions in packaging, and concealed high interest rates for installment buying. Many people knew of these things through their own experience, but the media had ignored them.

Recently, the publisher of a successful Negro newspaper in Baltimore said on a National Educational Television program that the reason he had been able to start and operate his paper profitably was that Baltimore's big newspapers had ignored Negro news. They were far from the only ones in the country which did, even though Negroes make up 10 per cent of United States population.

People are not stupid; obviously they conclude that the media cannot be trusted. If this distortion goes on too long, or occurs in a controversy that is too bitter, their distrust may spread to everything that the newspaper or magazine prints, and they reject it wholly.

But more often they are selective in their disbelief. They may believe what a newspaper prints on its women's pages, or a magazine in its service section, but be quite untouched by either's political reportage.

People disbelieve because they are better educated today. According to Ben H. Bagdikian in the *Columbia Journalism Review* (Winter 1966):

In 1940 the number of American adults who had gone beyond the eighth grade was 27 million, but in 1964 it was 67 million. . . . The number of white collar, managerial, skilled and professional workers in 1920 was 16 million, in 1965 it was 41 million.

Further, he reported, the sale of books has doubled in the past ten years, and the category with the greatest increase—370 per cent—was in social and economic subjects.

People disbelieve because, under the ceaseless drumfire of advertising and public relations, they are much more sophisticated than media practitioners think. This sophistication enables them to spot a phony message as far as the eye can see, and they detest being fooled. Thus, to the ancient abjuration that journalists must be unbiased for ethical reasons is added the warning that bias simply does not work. You lose your audience.

Recently the Syracuse, New York, papers ran a shrill, one-sided campaign opposing free state medical aid for the indigent. Many of the stories were written by a reporter named Luther Bliven. After some weeks his paper received—and printed—a one-line letter which said "Please keep Mr. Bliven's editorials off the front page." An informal survey of some 300 residents of all socioeconomic levels in the same city at about the same time revealed that the majority thought that the papers were biased and therefore unreliable. One woman said: "I'm a Republican and they're on my side. But still they ought not to be biased."

Lou Schneider, who writes the "Trade Winds" column for the Bell-McClure Syndicate, criticized editors in the October 15, 1966 issue of *Editor & Publisher* for printing too much good news about business. He wrote:

> Editors own stock and also they do not want to upset local department store management and other advertisers. If the story is not bullish, they simply get another story—140 business editors use the PR Wire publicity stories. No one writes the shady side of the street. . . . Yet readers want knowledgeable news they can depend on. There are 21 million investors in New York Stock Exchange stocks alone, and they want straight news about what is happening and what is likely to happen.

When they do not get it, obviously they conclude that the media are not leveling with them.

There is no complete answer to this kind of audience skepticism, simply because no one knows precisely what kind of information people disbelieve or why. The best partial—and too general—answer is found in the old principle of fairness and impartiality. If the people believe a paper or magazine is leveling with them, they accept a good deal of difference of viewpoint without rejecting the entire publication.

The second half of the answer is that editors and writers must know the realities of their readers' concerns, and not let publisher's policy prevent coverage of it.

There is, for example, a general feeling among readers that advertisers determine a medium's policy. Yet scores of editors and writers have said things like: "Never in my 35 years of work has an advertiser influenced anything we have printed." Both are right. The advertiser's influence is subtle and pervasive. Any journalist smart enough to find the right keys on a typewriter quickly learns the taboos, and learns to work within them so surely that he forgets about them. But the readers do not.

If there is an answer, it is probably a lesson that was first learned a quarter-century ago by the *New York Daily News*. A large advertiser objected to something the paper had published and threatened to withdraw its ads. The editor told him to go ahead. The ads were withdrawn, the paper felt the loss, but continued to publish. Within three months, the advertiser asked to come back into the paper and was accepted. The lesson which too many media executives, particularly broadcasters, have not learned is that advertisers need a truly independent publication more than it needs them.

## THERE IS NEITHER ENOUGH NOR THE RIGHT KIND OF INFORMATION IN THE MEDIA

Information, of course, is simply another word for knowledge, and the increase in the sheer bulk of knowledge is one of the revolutionary changes of our time. It has often been said that the total of human knowledge gained since 1940 equals the amount gained in all the years of human history up to 1940. Some specialized areas have far outstripped others; physicists know, for example, that the quantity of new knowledge in their discipline is doubling every decade. And the social sciences generally are among the leaders in the totals of new learning.

As these areas have grown, they have, of course, become more and more specialized, and researchers in them have come to use language that is more and more esoteric and less and less comprehensible to the layman. A major part of the journalist's job is to serve as a communications bridge between the specialists and the average reader. In recent years he has done more of this in all media than ever before, but measured against the skyrocketing totals of knowledge his performance has been a roman candle against a Saturn rocket.

It is trite to point out that television is greatly overbalanced in providing entertainment as against information. Kenneth A. Cox, of the Federal Communications Commission, recently gave this reporter some figures on how much. A report by United Research, Inc., he wrote, found that of 476 television stations nearly two-thirds (62 per cent) devoted between 71 and 80 per cent of their time to it. An earlier study (pre-1962), he added, found that 448 network-affiliated stations spent 78 per cent of their time on entertainment as against 6 per cent for news, 2 per cent for education, and 1.4 per cent for discussion. "I believe," he wrote, "that the proportions [for radio] would be roughly comparable."

Despite a few outstanding exceptions like improved half-hour news programs on the networks and truly distinguished reporters like Walter Cronkite, Edward P. Morgan, and Eric Sevareid, the quality of information programs is superficial and episodic. The magazine *Broadcasting* reported (July 25, 1966) that the Columbia Broadcasting System (CBS) offered to provide three and a half minutes of world and national news to go into late-night local programs to 192 of its affiliates; only 31 were interested, and the offer was dropped. *The Columbia Journalism Review* (spring 1966) likewise pointed out that when local stations were given a chance to reject news material on the Vietnam war they did so "in substantial numbers."

Even Columbia Professor Wood's upbeat report on improvements in radio and television news, cited earlier, found increased responsibility in only 20 and 30 per cent of stations—something less than a majority.

Newspapers have fallen short in both quantity and quality. Editors across the country complain that they have not enough space to print all the information they want. Yet experts agree that the average ratio for all newspapers is 65 per cent of

their space for advertising and 35 per cent for news; individual editions, of course, often carry a much lower ratio of news—sometimes 15 to 20 per cent.

In the *Columbia Journalism Review* article cited earlier, Ben H. Bagdikian found that while

> newspapers today are physically larger than they used to be, an average of 47 pages in 1964 compared with 28 pages in 1925 . . . there has been no significant increase in non-advertising space. . . . The number of non-advertising pages remained at about 17.

Editors frequently complain about the advertising-news ratio; seldom is it changed. It is set in the business office by the owner or publisher who runs the paper, and the editor is given a layout sheet for each page showing a jagged mountain of ads sloping up to the right and leaving a hole which he may fill with news. The priority clearly shows whether advertising or news is considered the more important.

Mass magazines do it differently. In many, perhaps most, the editor, not the business manager, decides on the number of pages each issue will contain. And the advertising-editorial ratio is dramatically different. In a survey of fifty of the largest national magazines for 1965, for example, well over half the space was devoted to editorial content. In some magazines, including some of the largest, the ratio was as high as 70 per cent editorial. Only sixteen had less than 50 per cent and one less than 40 per cent. The figures are not entirely comparable with newspapers since "editorial" on some magazines included fiction, but the percentage of it in most was small, and more than half had none at all.

Such quantitative measurements, however, tell only part of the story, and probably not the most important part. The real measure of any mass medium is its impact on its audience. Do people believe what they see or read? Does it give them new insights and ideas? Does it help them understand themselves or the realities of their lives and world? Does it give them information that is pertinent to the problems they face and the judgments they must make?

In these areas newspapers—with outstanding expectations—have largely failed—many not in all areas, but all in some.

*Newsweek* for November 29, 1965 categorized newspapers as

> smug and, of all things, outdated. . . . they have fallen behind the times technologically, as employers and, most damningly, in the professional tasks of reporting, writing and editing the news.

Chief cause of this is that the ideas of what readers want and can absorb which editors had forty years ago have been passed down almost unchanged. The ideas then and now were that readers might be reasonably intelligent, but had minuscule amounts of information and that they were primarily interested in crime, disaster, death, sports, comics, scandal, and voyeuristic sex. Through the upheavals of the Great Depression, two wars, and what the late Adlai Stevenson called the five revolutions of the midcentury, this formula has remained virtually unchanged.

The same sort of editorial judgment is perpetuated and disseminated nationwide by the Associated Press and United Press International. Here the stories are written and edited in New York (or state capitals) and punched into computer tapes which are sent over wires to local newsrooms where they are set into type automatically so that the very same wording of the very same stories appears on front pages from Nome to Nashville. It is easy and cheap for an editor to fill his paper with these stories if he wants to, and far too many do. Local angles on national news and local editorial evaluations go out the window unless the editor is strong enough and courageous enough to buck the system and then defend his increased budget expenses to his boss. And in newsrooms, as elsewhere in our organizational society, this kind of courage is rare. But it is essential to greatness.

Today's informed, sophisticated reader demands informed, sophisticated writing and editing. The magazines learned this twenty-five years ago, and the best newspapers are now following their lead—but only a few and only the best. The name of the technique is interpretive, or depth, writing. In it a trained and skillful writer examines a complex situation—juvenile crime, slum housing, water pollution, a seemingly senseless murder—studies the background in the library, talks to experts, interviews people involved, and comes up with what, in his judgment, is the essential truth of the situation. Then he writes his story in a way that gets the reader emotionally involved even as he learns the facts. In writing it, he borrows many of the techniques of fiction writing, and even showmanship, but is bound always, of course, by fact.

This is a difficult, highly skilled, creative kind of writing. It takes time and space, and it costs money, but magazines have built multimillion circulations—and millions for their owners—on it, and the newspapers found in anybody's list of the nation's best ten have done likewise. The *Wall Street Journal* was an early innovator, and its offshoot, *The National Observer*, does it consistently today. After the 1965 blackout in the Northeast, for example, the *Observer* reported what New Yorkers did, thought about, and felt like by having Reporter Jane Dowling tell the things that happened to her during the dark hours. Her story was as readable as a whodunit with a touch of poetry.

Speaking at the California Editors Conference recently, Herbert Brucker, editor emeritus of the Hartford *Courant*, said: "Today's news isn't just the geewhiz event that happened a moment ago. It is also the significant fact or trend that is revealed only when dug out by informed professionals who can write."

This kind of editing and writing is the medicine that the media need. For decades, they have been attacked as presenting too much entertainment and not enough information. But nobody ever attacks a story or play for being too entertaining when it gets the reader emotionally involved, causes him to identify deeply with the problem, and finishes by clarifying for him an essential truth about his condition. And this is precisely what the best interpretive writing in magazines, newspapers, and broadcasting does. The criticism of "too much entertainment" is really the criticism of too much superficial entertainment, which makes no point, carries no message, illuminates no corner of the confused and frightening world we all live in.

Most newspaper editors complain that they have not the time, the staff, nor the money for this kind of writing. They do not have the time because they are still shackled by the old idea that a newspaper must be first with the news—in an age when it is impossible for them to beat radio and television with the story. They do not have the staff partly because they do not train their writers to do the job—or have them trained. And they do not have the money because editorial departments on newspapers are traditionally shortchanged in their budgets. Yet it is the editorial department that produces the most important service a newspaper has to offer, and the one which makes the press the only private industry whose freedom is guaranteed by the Constitution. Without it the paper becomes a shopper's guide—which is a perfectly legitimate publication, but is not a newspaper.

Allen H. Neuharth, general manager of the Gannett Newspapers, told a group of editors on June 21, 1966 that "you can increase your editorial costs by 50 per cent and still not increase the overall production cost of the paper." How low editorial costs are in relation to others is shown by an examination of 1965 figures from Inland Daily Press Association.

On papers of 120,000 circulation and over, editorial costs were half (11 per cent) of the cost of the paper they were printed on (23 per cent of the total cost). This disparity gradually decreased as circulations got smaller; at 22,000–27,000 circulation they were about equal and at circulations under 4,000—a very small daily—the editorial department cost twice as much as the newsprint. The lesson is obvious—more money needs to be spent on editorial departments.

## EDITORS NEED MORE POWER WITHIN THEIR OWN ORGANIZATIONS

It is axiomatic that great publications are the product of great editors, not great business or advertising or circulation men. The *Louisville Courier-Journal* became great as the result of a succession of outstanding editors from Barry Bingham and Mark Ethridge through James Pope to Norman Isaacs. It is the editorial genius of Henry Luce and DeWitt Wallace that has built the magazines of Time, Inc., and the *Reader's Digest* into their pre-eminence today. These great editors have possessed the ability to win power for themselves in the organizational jungle. But the great are always too rare. A change in the relative power given editors in the media hierarchy would give the necessary scope to men and women who are first-class editors, but who lack the political skills that are needed to climb the organizational ladder.

To do this will not be easy. It must be done by publishers, and publishers are businessmen who deal in dollars and are under vast pressures to show a profit. Further, at meetings of department heads where policy is set, the advertising and circulation managers also talk in dollars and bring in revenue; the editor talks in terms of ideas and other intangibles, brings in no money, but spends plenty. To rise above the pressures of this imbalance requires a transcendent act of will and understanding of values by the publisher which is not only foreign to his training, but beyond the capacity of many.

Some company managements are clever enough to understand this. As part of the Curtis Publishing Company, for example, the *Saturday Evening Post* became such a vital force in America because, as a matter of company policy, its editor was the ultimate boss of the magazine. Ben Hibbs was not only editor, but also vice-president and a member of the board of directors of the company. And he was the final authority on everything that went into the magazine—advertising as well as editorial. *Holiday* quickly grew to pre-eminence in its field because Ted Patrick had the same authority for his magazine.

But far too few newspaper and magazine editors have this sweeping power. Broadcasting, of course, is just beginning to have editors of any kind. Broadcasting was born out of show business by advertising. It did not have the tradition, as print media did, that the station was an independent entity interposed between the advertiser and the public—an entity called an editor, with opinions, thoughts, and judgments which were imposed on both. This is why broadcasting has been periodically shaken by such upheavals as the recent resignation of Fred W. Friendly, one of the medium's editorial greats, from CBS. It is why broadcasting is far behind print media in the power it gives editors.

If all editors in all media were given the power they need, most would see to it that they got the kind of writing skill the media must have and would give the writers both training and time enough to do the journalistic job that is needed today.

Most would also see to it that young writers are recruited and trained. The media, driven by an annual need of 5,000 new journalists, are just beginning to recruit in the universities; more advanced industries have been doing it for decades. And the media are just beginning to see to it that their best writers get advanced training to equip them for specialized reporting and writing. At that, most of such training is financed by foundations, universities, or the writers themselves. In contrast, most progressive industries have been sending their promising young men back to college at their expense for at least a decade.

### THERE ARE LARGE GAPS IN THE KNOWLEDGE ANYONE HAS ABOUT THE IMPACT THE MEDIA HAVE ON THEIR AUDIENCES

Solid, reliable research is needed in the following areas, among others.

BROADCASTING    There is little disinterested, reliable research data on total audience, how much time that people spend listening or watching what kind of program, the amount of time devoted to commercials per hour, the effect different kinds of programs, and commercials, have on their audience, and similar questions. Much information of this kind is available from commercial research organizations, but its validity is questionable,

especially since the recent congressional hearings concerning the methods. Further, it tries to show how many people are watching a program, but does not measure their reaction. Do they like it? Are they moved by it?

Probably the Federal Communications Commission should provide, and publish periodically, such information both about networks and individual local stations that members of the audience would have reliable yardsticks to judge the stations that they listen to.

PRINT MEDIA    There is no systematic body of knowledge on what techniques of writing, headlining, and graphic presentation are most successful in getting people to read and apprehend the important public issues upon which they must render decisions in the voting booth. Research is both too small in quantity and too superficial in quality.

Recently, Dr. J. B. Haskins, of Newhouse Communications Center, Syracuse University, surveyed existing research on newspapers and found it "primitive." He wrote:

There is a relatively small body of evidence about newspapers (apart from mechanical innovations) that is methodologically sound, deals with important problems, is understandable and is immediately applicable; however, most newspaper people are either unaware of the existence of that evidence or are unwilling to make changes in traditional procedure.

Among the areas Haskins listed as needing research were:

What can newspapers do to attract and keep high-quality editorial personnel?

What is the best education for journalism? (Should not the federal government give greater support to journalism training as part of its effort to improve training for the public service?)

Since broadcasting has replaced newspapers as the major source of news for the majority of people, how should newspapers redefine their primary function? Should they, as suggested herein, devote their pages to putting the day's news in perspective and building bridges of information between the experts and the public?

What is the role of newspapers in formal public education? Can it be one arm of the process?

To what extent can newspaper publishers and editors define their goals? What are they trying to achieve in audience effects? Can they do it? If they can define their goals, are they the right ones?

**ALL MEDIA**    There is little sound knowledge of where people get their information. What there is suggests that the media provide a small percentage of that information. A study by Stanford University of where people first heard of the assassination of President John F. Kennedy, found that nearly half (49 per cent) learned it not from radio or television, not from a newspaper, but from another person.

There is little or no research on precisely how sophisticated the media's audience is and on what kind of information it wants. Present categories in which editors present information—national, crime, sex, sports, and the like—may be outdated. Are they? If so, what new categories should replace them as rules of thumb for editors to apportion the contents of their publications and programs?

There is virtually no reliable information on the effects that the media have on the cities they live in. Does a first-class newspaper or broadcaster give its city a better government? more industry and jobs? a healthier cultural climate? better informed and more active citizens? If so, how?

Probably what is needed is government financing for an *independent* agency in a university or foundation which will provide continuous research on the media and publish it regularly. It must *not* be an industry association, *not* a government agency.

### THE REALLY DIFFICULT QUESTIONS

If these and other gaps in knowledge are filled, if editors use it and are given the power they need, if writers get the time and training they need, then the media may at last begin to face some of the really difficult questions:

*To what extent has newsmen's reportage only of the dramatic distorted their readers' concepts of reality?*

It is an ancient rule of journalism that when nothing happens there is no news. If this was ever true, it is no longer. For decades, Negroes lived in slums with rats and garbage and fear, their men jobless, their children uneducated; it went unreported in the mass media until their desperation drove them to violence.

For decades, police, lawyers, and judges have known that there are two kinds of justice in America, one for the rich and one for the poor; was that not news?

In many communities, for decades, real estate brokers, builders, and contractors have had such control of local government that zoning, building, and sanitation codes were either nonexistent or ignored; the situation and its effects were known and unreported by the media.

For decades, our water and air have been quietly and inexorably polluted; where were the reporters?

The answer that the local Establishment which controlled the press was not interested in these matters is too easy; for there are always journalistic Davids who aspire to giant-killing. But these stories take time and perception and digging and thoughtfulness to get, and, with rare exceptions, the media have not made the requisites available.

Can any editor say with certainty that if these and similar situations had been reported, the people's view of their world would not now be different? or that Watts might never have revolted?

*To what extent has the media's endless exploitation of violence made violence so prevalent in America?*

Last August after Charles Whitman killed fifteen persons in Austin, Texas, Charles Collingwood reported from London that the British were sickened and saddened by their cousins' seemingly incurable addiction to violence. No modern Western nation in the same time span has killed as many of its heads of state while in office as America, according to Professor Carl N. Degler, Vassar historian. Every two minutes some American is killed, beaten, or wounded, said Senator Edward Kennedy recently. Has the endless recitation of crime and death on the front pages, the ceaseless depiction on television of the Old West, where violence is shown as a legitimate means to an end, had nothing to do with this?

*To what extent have the media contributed to the increase in promiscuity and the cheapening of sex?*

Thoughtful observers have pointed out that the rush to end the strictures of puritanism and the constant sexual titillation of the media have led people, particularly the young, to engage in sexual relations as fun and games. But sex without the care and concern and responsibility of love is as shallow and unrewarding an escape as alcoholism or narcotics. In encouraging it, how well have the media served the true human values of our society?

*To what extent have the media contributed to the popularity of extremism and to the devil theory of international relations?*

Any thoughtful review of the McCarthy madness must conclude that if the media did not create McCarthy, they certainly increased his influence. Sober editors wonder, in hindsight, what would have happened to the Senator if they and their colleagues had simply refused to print stories about him. But, in the realities of competition, could they have?

Probably not. But while they reported his demagoguery they could have seen to it their readers also received enough perspective to be able to recognize it for what it was.

McCarthy was a loud and extreme exponent of the devil theory in international affairs—the simplistic idea that everything we do is right, but everything our enemy (currently communism) does is evil. But he was not the only one, either while he was alive or now. Professor Henry Steel Commager, of Amherst, described this well:

What we have here is a deeply ingrained vanity and arrogance . . . fed by isolation, by school histories, by a filiopietistic society which is that we are somehow superior to all other nations, morally and practically, by a thousand editorials, a hundred thousand radio and TV programs which play up the villainy of our enemies—the Russians, the Chinese, the Cubans—and our own morality and nobility.[3]

What editor can say in conscience that he has not contributed to this illusion?

Bernard Kilgore, of the *Wall Street Journal*, has said:

The newspaper editor of tomorrow will be an egghead. . . . the newspaper of the future must become an instrument of educational leadership, an institution of intellectual development —a center of learning.

Speaking May 10, 1966, at the fiftieth anniversary of the Pulitzer Prize awards, James Reston of the *New York Times* said:

Somewhere there is a line where the old skeptical, combative, publish-and-be-damned tradition of the past . . . may converge with the new intelligence and the new duties and responsibilities of this rising and restless generation. I wish I knew how to find it, for it could help both the newspapers and the nation in their present plight, and it would help us believe again, which, in this age of tricks and techniques, may be our greatest need.

This, then, is the challenge: it is the media's job to illuminate the values of American life, both the false and the true, and to use all their skill and technology to instruct and guide and lead the people into a less anxious and more rewarding way of living. Progressively, as they do this they will answer the need for greatness.

**REFERENCES AND NOTES**

1  William A. Wood, "The Sound of Maturity," *Columbia Journalism Review*, vol. 4, no. 4 (winter 1966), p. 7.

2  In an interview, June 1966.

3  In *Current*, January 1964.

## 7 MEDIA HOT AND COLD   MARSHALL McLUHAN

"The rise of the waltz," explained Curt Sachs in the *World History of the Dance*, "was a result of that longing for truth, simplicity, closeness to nature, and primitivism, which the last two-thirds of the eighteenth century fulfilled." In the century of jazz we are likely to overlook the emergence of the waltz as a hot and explosive human expression that broke through the formal feudal barriers of courtly and choral dance styles.

There is a basic principle that distinguishes a hot medium like radio from a cool one like the telephone, or a hot medium like the movie from a cool one like TV. A hot medium is one that extends one single sense in "high definition." High definition is the state of being well filled with data. A photograph is, visually, "high definition." A cartoon is "low definition," simply because very little visual information is provided. Telephone is a cool medium, or one of low definition, because the ear is given a meager amount of information. And speech is a cool medium of low definition, because so little is given and so much has to be filled in by the listener. On the other hand, hot media do not leave so much to be filled in or completed by the audience. Hot media are, therefore, low in participation or completion by the audience. Naturally, therefore, a hot medium like radio has very different effects on the user from a cool medium like the telephone.

A cool medium like hieroglyphic or ideogrammic written characters has very different effects from the hot and explosive medium of the phonetic alphabet. The alphabet, when pushed to a high degree of abstract visual intensity, became

typography. The printed word with its specialist intensity burst the bonds of medieval corporate guilds and monasteries, creating extreme individualist patterns of enterprise and monopoly. But the typical reversal occurred when extremes of monopoly brought back the corporation, with its impersonal empire over many lives. The hotting-up of the medium of writing to repeatable print intensity led to nationalism and the religious wars of the sixteenth century. The heavy and unwieldy media, such as stone, are time binders. Used for writing, they are very cool indeed, and serve to unify the ages; whereas paper is a hot medium that serves to unify spaces horizontally, both in political and entertainment empires.

Any hot medium allows of less participation than a cool one, as a lecture makes for less participation than a seminar, and a book for less than dialogue. With print many earlier forms were excluded from life and art, and many were given strange new intensity. But our own time is crowded with examples of the principle that the hot form excludes, and the cool one includes. When ballerinas began to dance on their toes a century ago, it was felt that the art of the ballet had acquired a new "spirituality." With this new intensity, male figures were excluded from ballet. The role of women had also become fragmented with the advent of industrial specialism and the explosion of home functions into laundries, bakeries, and hospitals on the periphery of the community. Intensity or high definition engenders specialism and fragmentation in living as in entertainment, which explains why any intense experience must be "forgotten," "censored," and reduced to a very cool state before it can be "learned" or assimilated. The Freudian "censor" is less a moral function than an indispensable condition of learning. Were we to accept fully and directly every shock to our various structures of awareness, we would soon be nervous wrecks, doing double-takes and pressing panic buttons every minute. The "censor" protects our central system of values, as it does our physical nervous system by simply cooling off the onset of experience a great deal. For many people, this cooling system brings on a lifelong state of psychic *rigor mortis*, or of somnambulism, particularly observable in periods of new technology.

An example of the disruptive impact of a hot technology succeeding a cool one is given by Robert Theobald in *The Rich and the Poor*. When Australian natives were given steel axes by the missionaries, their culture, based on the stone axe, collapsed. The stone axe had not only been scarce but had always been a basic status symbol of male importance. The missionaries provided quantities of sharp steel axes and gave them to women and children. The men had even to borrow these from the women, causing a collapse of male dignity. A tribal and feudal hierarchy of traditional kind collapses quickly when it meets any hot medium of the mechanical, uniform, and repetitive kind. The medium of money or wheel or writing, or any other form of specialist speedup of exchange and information, will serve to fragment a tribal structure. Similarly, a very much greater speedup, such as occurs with electricity, may serve to restore a tribal pattern of intense involvement such as took place with the introduction of radio in Europe, and is now tending to happen as a result of TV in America. Specialist technologies detribalize. The nonspecialist electric technology retribalizes. The process of upset resulting from a new distribution of skills is accompanied by much culture lag in which people feel compelled to look at new situations as if they were old ones, and come up with ideas of "population explosion" in an age of implosion. Newton, in an age of clocks, managed to present the physical universe in the image of a clock. But poets like Blake were far ahead of Newton in their response to the challenge of the clock. Blake spoke of the need to be delivered "from

single vision and Newton's sleep," knowing very well that Newton's response to the challenge of the new mechanism was itself merely a mechanical repetition of the challenge. Blake saw Newton and Locke and others as hypnotized Narcissus types quite unable to meet the challenge of mechanism. W. B. Yeats gave the full Blakean version of Newton and Locke in a famous epigram:

> Locke sank into a swoon;
> The garden died;
> God took the spinning jenny
> Out of his side.

Yeats presents Locke, the philosopher of mechanical and lineal associationism, as hypnotized by his own image. The "garden" or unified consciousness, ended. Eighteenth-century man got an extension of himself in the form of the spinning machine that Yeats endows with its full sexual significance. Woman, herself, is thus seen as a technological extension of man's being.

Blake's counterstrategy for his age was to meet mechanism with organic myth. Today, deep in the electric age, organic myth is itself a simple and automatic response capable of mathematical formulation and expression, without any of the imaginative perception of Blake about it. Had he encountered the electric age, Blake would not have met its challenge with a mere repetition of electric form. For myth *is* the instant vision of a complex process that ordinarily extends over a long period. Myth is contraction or implosion of any process, and the instant speed of electricity confers the mythic dimension on ordinary industrial and social action today. We *live* mythically but continue to think fragmentarily and on single planes.

Scholars today are acutely aware of a discrepancy between their ways of treating subjects and the subject itself. Scriptural scholars of both the Old and New Testaments frequently say that while their treatment must be linear, the subject is not. The subject treats of the relations between God and man, and between God and the world, and of the relations between man and his neighbor—all these subsist together, and act and react upon one another at the same time. The Hebrew and Eastern mode of thought tackles problem and resolution, at the outset of a discussion, in a way typical of oral societies in general. The entire message is then traced and retraced, again and again, on the rounds of a concentric spiral with seeming redundancy. One can stop anywhere after the first few sentences and have the full message, if one is prepared to "dig" it. This kind of plan seems to have inspired Frank Lloyd Wright in designing the Guggenheim Art Gallery on a spiral, concentric basis. It is a redundant form inevitable to the electric age, in which the concentric pattern is imposed by the instant quality, and overlay in depth, of electric speed. But the concentric with its endless intersection of planes is necessary for insight. In fact, it is the technique of insight, and as such is necessary for media study, since no medium has its meaning or existence alone, but only in constant interplay with other media.

The new electric structuring and configuring of life more and more encounters the old lineal and fragmentary procedures and tools of analysis from the mechanical age. More and more we turn from the content of messages to study total effect. Kenneth Boulding put this matter in *The Image* by saying, "The meaning of a message is the change which it produces in the image." Concern with *effect* rather than *meaning* is a basic change of our electric time, for effect involves the total situation, and not a single level of information movement. Strangely, there is recognition of this matter of effect rather than information in the British idea of libel: "The greater the truth, the greater the libel."

The effect of electric technology had at first been anxiety. Now it appears to create boredom. We have been through the three stages of alarm, resistance, and exhaustion that occur in every disease or stress of life, whether individual or collective. At least, our exhausted slump after the first encounter with the electric has inclined us to expect new problems. However, backward countries that have experienced little permeation with our own mechanical and specialist culture are much better able to confront and to understand electric technology. Not only have backward and nonindustrial cultures no specialist habits to overcome in their encounter with electromagnetism, but they have still much of their traditional oral culture that has the total, unified "field" character of our new electromagnetism. Our old industrialized areas, having eroded their oral traditions automatically, are in the position of having to rediscover them in order to cope with the electric age.

In terms of the theme of media hot and cold, backward countries are cool, and we are hot. The "city slicker" is hot, and the rustic is cool. But in terms of the reversal of procedures and values in the electric age, the past mechanical time was hot, and we of the TV age are cool. The waltz was a hot, fast mechanical dance suited to the industrial time in its moods of pomp and circumstance. In contrast, the Twist is a cool, involved and chatty form of improvised gesture. The jazz of the period of the hot new media of movie and radio was hot jazz. Yet jazz of itself tends to be a casual dialogue form of dance quite lacking in the repetitive and mechanical forms of the waltz. Cool jazz came in quite naturally after the first impact of radio and movie had been absorbed.

In the special Russian issue of *Life* magazine for September 13, 1963, it is mentioned that in Russian restaurants and night clubs, "though the Charleston is tolerated, the Twist is taboo." All this is to say that a country in the process of industrialization is inclined to regard hot jazz as consistent with its developing programs. The cool and involved form of the Twist, on the other hand, would strike such a culture at once as retrograde and incompatible with its new mechanical stress. The Charleston, with its aspect of a mechanical doll agitated by strings appears in Russia as an avant-garde form. We, on the other hand, find the *avant-garde* in the cool and the primitive, with its promise of depth involvement and integral expression.

The "hard" sell and the "hot" line become mere comedy in the TV age, and the death of all the salesmen at one stroke of the TV axe has turned the hot American culture into a cool one that is quite unacquainted with itself. America, in fact, would seem to be living through the reverse process that Margaret Mead described in *Time* magazine (September 4, 1954):

> There are too many complaints about society having to move too fast to keep up with the machine. There is great advantage in moving fast if you move completely, if social, educational, and recreational changes keep pace. You must change the whole pattern at once and the whole group together—and the people themselves must decide to move.

Margaret Mead is thinking here of change as uniform speedup of motion or a uniform hotting-up of temperatures in backward societies. We are certainly coming within conceivable range of a world automatically controlled to the point where we could say, "Six hours less radio in Indonesia next week or there will be a great falling off in literary attention." Or, "We can program twenty more hours of TV in South Africa next week to cool down the tribal temperature raised by radio last week." Whole cultures could now be programmed to keep their emotional climate stable in the same way that we have begun to know something about maintaining equilibrium in the commercial economies of the world.

In the merely personal and private sphere we are often reminded of how changes of tone and attitude are demanded of different times and seasons in order to keep situations in hand. British clubmen, for the sake of companionship and amiability, have long excluded the hot topics of religion and politics from mention inside the highly participational club. In the same vein, W. H. Auden wrote, ". . . this season the man of goodwill will wear his heart up his sleeve, not on it . . . the honest manly style is today suited only to Iago" (Introduction to John Betjeman's *Slick But Not Streamlined*). In the Renaissance, as print technology hotted up the social *milieu* to a very high point, the gentleman and the courtier (Hamlet—Mercutio style) adopted, in contrast, the casual and cool nonchalance of the playful and superior being. The Iago allusion of Auden reminds us that Iago was the *alter ego* and assistant of the intensely earnest and very non-nonchalant General Othello. In imitation of the earnest and forthright general, Iago hotted up his own image and wore his heart on his sleeve, until General Othello read him loud and clear as "honest Iago," a man after his own grimly earnest heart.

Throughout *The City in History*, Lewis Mumford favors the cool or casually structured towns over the hot and intensely filled-in cities. The great period of Athens, he feels, was one during which most of the democratic habits of village life and participation still obtained. Then burst forth the full variety of human expression and exploration such as was later impossible in highly developed urban centers. For the highly developed situation is, by definition, low in opportunities of participation, and rigorous in its demands of specialist fragmentation from those who would control it. For example, what is known as "job enlargement" today in business and in management consists in allowing the employee more freedom to discover and define his function. Likewise, in reading a detective story the reader participates as co-author simply because so much has been left out of the narrative. The open-mesh silk stocking is far more sensuous than the smooth nylon, just because the eye must act as hand in filling in and completing the image, exactly as in the mosaic of the TV image.

Douglas Cater in *The Fourth Branch of Government* tells how the men of the Washington press bureaus delighted to complete or fill in the blank of Calvin Coolidge's personality. Because he was so like a mere cartoon, they felt the urge to complete his image for him and his public. It is instructive that the press applied the word "cool" to Cal. In the very sense of a cool medium, Calvin Coolidge was so lacking in any articulation of data in his public image that there was only one word for him. He was real cool. In the hot 1920's, the hot press medium found Cal very cool and rejoiced in his lack of image, since it compelled the participation of the press in filling in an image of him for the public. By contrast, F.D.R. was a hot press agent, himself a rival of the newspaper medium and one who delighted in scoring off the press on the rival hot medium of radio. Quite in contrast, Jack Paar ran a cool show for the cool TV medium, and became a rival for the patrons of the night spots and their allies in the gossip columns. Jack Paar's war with the gossip columnists was a weird example of clash between a hot and cold medium such as had occurred with the "scandal of the rigged TV quiz shows." The rivalry between the hot press and radio media, on one hand, and TV on the other, for the hot ad buck, served to confuse and to overheat the issues in the affair that pointlessly involved Charles Van Doren.

An Associated Press story from Santa Monica, California, August 9, 1962, reported how

> Nearly 100 traffic violators watched a police traffic accident film today to atone for their violations. Two had to be treated for nausea and shock . . .
>
> Viewers were offered a $5.00 reduction in fines if they agreed to see the movie, *Signal 30*, made by Ohio State police.
>
> It showed twisted wreckage and mangled bodies and recorded the screams of accident victims.

Whether the hot film medium using hot content would cool off the hot drivers is a moot point. But it does concern any understanding of media. The effect of hot media treatment cannot include much empathy or participation at any time. In this connection an insurance ad that featured Dad in an iron lung surrounded by a joyful family group did more to strike terror into the reader than all the warning wisdom in the world. It is a question that arises in connection with capital punishment. Is a severe penalty the best deterrent to serious crime? With regard to the bomb and the cold war, is the threat of massive retaliation the most effective means to peace? Is it not evident in every human situation that is pushed to a point of saturation that some precipitation occurs? When all the available resources and energies have been played up in an organism or in any structure there is some kind of reversal of pattern. The spectacle

of brutality used as deterrent can brutalize. Brutality used in sports may humanize under some conditions, at least. But with regard to the bomb and retaliation as deterrent, it is obvious that numbness is the result of any prolonged terror, a fact that was discovered when the fallout shelter program was broached. The price of eternal vigilance is indifference.

Nevertheless, it makes all the difference whether a hot medium is used in a hot or cool culture. The hot radio medium used in cool or nonliterate cultures has a violent effect, quite unlike its effect, say in England or America, where radio is felt as entertainment. A cool or low literacy culture cannot accept hot media like movies or radio as entertainment. They are, at least, as radically upsetting for them as the cool TV medium has proved to be for our high literacy world.

And as for the cool war and the hot bomb scare, the cultural strategy that is desperately needed is humor and play. It is play that cools off the hot situations of actual life by miming them. Competitive sports between Russia and the West will hardly serve that purpose of relaxation. Such sports are inflammatory, it is plain. And what we consider entertainment or fun in our media inevitably appears as violent political agitation to a cool culture.

One way to spot the basic difference between hot and cold media uses is to compare and contrast a broadcast of a symphony performance with a broadcast of a symphony rehearsal. Two of the finest shows ever released by the CBC were of Glenn Gould's procedure in recording piano recitals, and Igor Stravinsky's rehearsing the Toronto symphony in some of his new work. A cool medium like TV, when really used, demands this involvement in process. The neat tight package is suited to hot media, like radio and gramophone. Francis Bacon never tired of contrasting hot and cool prose. Writing in "methods" or complete packages, he contrasted with writing in aphorisms, or single observations such as "Revenge is a kind of wild justice." The passive consumer wants packages, but those, he suggested, who are concerned in pursuing knowledge and in seeking causes will resort to aphorisms, just because they are incomplete and require participation in depth.

The principle that distinguishes hot and cold media is perfectly embodied in the folk wisdom: "Men seldom make passes at girls who wear glasses." Glasses intensify the outward-going vision, and fill in the feminine image exceedingly, Marion the Librarian notwithstanding. Dark glasses, on the other hand, create the inscrutable and inaccessible image that invites a great deal of participation and completion.

## 8    SEX AS WORK    LIONEL S. LEWIS    DENNIS BRISSET

It is commonly accepted that America is a society of leisure. The society is said to have shifted from one of production to one of consumption.[1] The American of today spends little time working; he has a great deal of time to play.

With this surfeit of leisure, Americans have been called upon to engage in forms of consumption quite unknown to their inner-directed predecessors. There exist extensive opportunities for play, but little knowledge of how to conduct oneself in this play. As Riesman has remarked, "To bring the individual into unfrightening contact with the new range of opportunities in consumption often requires some guides and signposts."[2] Knowing how to play has become problematic; it is something the individual must learn. He must, in a word, be socialized into the art of play.

Faced with this necessary socialization, the consuming American seeks out persons to teach him how to play. Very often this involves engaging the services of avocational counselors. The term avocational counseling ". . . describe[s] the activities undertaken by a number of relatively rapidly growing professions in the United States, including travel agents, hotel men, resort directors, sports teachers and coaches, teachers of the arts, including dancing teachers, and so on."[3] Each of the various counselors supplies the American public with advice on play and leisure. The advice of one such group of counselors is the subject matter of this paper.

Reprinted from *Social Problems*, vol. 15, no. 1, pp. 8–18, by permission of the authors and The Society for the Study of Social Problems.

Quite recently, Nelson Foote has observed that sex, since it is becoming increasingly dissociated from procreation, is becoming more and more a kind of play activity. He states that "the view that sex is fun can . . . hardly be called. the invention of immoralists; it is every man's discovery."[4] The arena of consumption is extended to include the realm of man's sexual activity, and the avocational counselor finds himself a place advising people on the vicissitudes of sex as play.

Concomitant with this increasing amount of leisure time, and the attendant problem of learning how to play, it has been observed that the play of most Americans has become a laborious kind of play. "Fun, in its rather unique American form, is grim resolve. . . We are as determined about the pursuit of fun as a desert-wandering traveler is about the search for water . . . "[5] Consumption, to most Americans, has become a job. Like work, play has become a duty to be performed. This interpretation is supported by the emergence of what Wolfenstein has labeled a "fun morality." Here "play tends to be measured by standards of achievement previously applicable only to work . . . . at play, no less than at work, one asks: 'Am I doing as well as I should?' "[6] Consumption very definitely has become production.

It is the purpose of this article to examine the products of the avocational counselors of marital sex and to inquire as to their depiction of man's sexual behavior. If it is true that play is becoming work in the mass society, it might be necessary to amend Foote's notion of the character of sexual play. In focusing on how marital sex is handled by these avocational counselors, we will show how sex, an area of behavior usually not thought of as involving work, has been treated as such. We will emphasize how general work themes are presented as an essential part of sexual relations, and how the public is advised to prepare for sex just as they are advised to prepare for a job.

## MARRIAGE MANUALS

The avocational counselors of sex with the widest audience are those who write what are frequently referred to as marriage manuals. These manuals are designed to explain all aspects of the sexual side of marriage. Their distribution is wide: many are in paperback and are readily available in drug stores; many can be found in multiple copies in public and university libraries; and some are distributed by facilities which offer services in sex, fertility, and contraception, such as Planned Parenthood clinics.

Fifteen manuals were selected from a listing of almost 50 for analysis in this study. They are listed in the Appendix. The first criterion for using a manual was wide circulation. This was determined by number of printings and number of copies sold. For example, one volume [15] in 1965 was in its forty-fifth printing and had sold more than one-half million copies in the United States; a second [13] was in its forty-eighth printing and had sold almost six hundred thousand; a third [3] was in its thirtieth printing[7] and has "been read by" two million eight hundred thousand;[8] and a fourth [5] advertises on its cover "over a million and a half copies in print." Other criteria were that the book be still read and available. The fifteen volumes ranged from 14-page pamphlets to fullsized, indexed, hard-bound books.

Each manual was read by both authors, and principal themes were recorded. Notes were taken, compared, and classified. Only material about whose meaning both authors agreed was utilized in drawing conclusions about the themes in a book.

## WORKING AT SEX

Marital sex, as depicted by the marriage manuals, is an activity permeated with qualities of work. One need not even read these books, but need only look at the titles or the chapter headings to draw this conclusion. Thus, we have books titled *The Sex Technique in Marriage* [10], *Modern Sex Techniques* [14], *Ideal Marriage: Its Physiology and Technique* [15]. There are also chapters titled "How to Manage the Sex Act" [3], "Principles and Techniques of Intercourse"[7], "The Fourth Key to Soundly Satisfying Sex: A Controlled Sexual Crescendo"[5].

From the outset, as we begin to read the books, we are warned not to treat sex frivolously, indeed not to play at sex:

An ardent spur-of-the-moment tumble sounds very romantic. . . However, ineptly arranged intercourse leaves the clothes you had no chance to shed in a shambles, your plans for the evening shot, your birth control program incomplete, and your future sex play under considerable better-be-careful-or-we'll-wind-up-in-bed-again restraint [5, pp. 34–35].

In other words, marital sex should not be an impromptu performance.

Moreover, sex should not be approached with a casual mien. Rather, we are counseled, sexual relations, at least good sexual relations, are a goal to be laboriously achieved. It is agreed that "satisfactory intercourse is the basis for happy marriage." However, it is added, "It does not occur automatically but must be striven for" [12, p. 39]. In the plain talk of the avocational counselor, "Sexual relations are something to be worked at and developed" [7, p. 6].

This work and its development are portrayed as a taxing kind of endeavor; as behavior involving, indeed requiring, a good deal of effort. That sex involves effort is a pervasive theme in the fifteen manuals. From the start one is advised to direct his effort to satisfying his or her mate so that mutual climax is achieved, sexual activity is continual, and one's partner is not ignored after climax. Thus, we are told, "Remember, *couple* effort for *couple* satisfaction! That's the key to well-paced, harmonious sex play" [5, p. 62].

Certain positions of intercourse are also seen as particularly taxing, in fact so taxing that certain categories of people are advised not to use them. One author, in discussing a particularly laborious position, remarks that "This is no position for a couple of grandparents, no matter how healthy and vigorous they are for their age, for it takes both effort and determination" [4, p. 201]. Quite obviously, certain kinds of marital sex are reserved only for those persons who are "in condition."

The female is particularly cautioned to work at sex, for being naturally sexual seems a trait ascribed only to the male. The affinity of sex to her other work activities is here made clear: "Sex is too important for any wife to give it less call upon her energy than cooking, laundry, and a dozen other activities" [5, p. 36]. To the housewife's burden is added yet another chore.

Even the one manual that takes great pains to depict sex as sport, injects the work theme. It is pointed out that

> You certainly can [strive and strain at having a climax]—just as you can . . . help yourself to focus on a complex musical symphony. . . . Just as you strive to enjoy a party, when you begin by having a dull time at it. Sex is often something to be worked and strained at—as an artist works and strains at his painting or sculpture [6, p. 122].

Sex, then, is considered a kind of work; moreover, a very essential form of labor. Regular sexual activity is said, for instance, to contribute to "physical and mental health" [7, p. 27], and to lead to "*spiritual unity*" [14, frontpiece]. In the majestic functionalist tradition, "A happy, healthy sex life is vital to wholesome family life, which in turn is fundamental to the welfare of the community and of society" [1, xiii]. Marital sex, most assuredly, is the cornerstone of humanity, but not any kind of marital sex—only that which leads to orgasm. "It is the orgasm that is so essential to the

health and happiness of the couple . . ." [10, p. 80].

Indeed it is the orgasm which may be said to be the *product* of marital sexual relations. It is the *raison d'être* for sexual contact, and this orgasm is no mean achievement. In fact,

> Orgasm occasionally may be the movement of ecstasy when two people together soar along a Milky Way among stars all their own. This moment is the high mountaintop of love of which the poets sing, on which the two together become a full orchestra playing a fortissimo of a glorious symphony [4, pp. 182–183].

In masculine, and somewhat more antiseptic terms, "ejaculation is the aim, the summit and the end of the sexual act" [15, p. 133]. Woe be to the couple who fail to produce this state as there are dire consequences for the unsuccessful, particularly for the woman:

> When the wife does not secure an orgasm, she is left at a high peak of sexual tension. If this failure to release tension becomes a regular thing, she may develop an aversion to starting any sex play that might lead to such frustrations. . . . Repeated disappointments may lead to headaches, nervousness, sleeplessness, and other unhappy symptoms of maladjustment [1, p. 65].

So important is it to reach orgasm, to have a product, that all the other sexual activities of marriage are seen as merely prosaic ingredients or decorative packaging of the product.

In fact, orgasm as a product is so essential that its occasion is not necessarily confined to the actual act of intercourse, at least for the women. Numerous counselors indicate that it may be necessary for the man to induce orgasm in the woman during afterplay. "A woman who has built up a head of passion which her husband was unable to requite deserves a further push to climax through intensive genital caress . . ." [5, p. 111]. Particularly in the early years of marriage, before the husband has learned to pace his orgasm, he may have to rely on the knack of digital manipulation. In one author's imagery, "Sometimes it may be necessary for the husband to withdraw and continue the stimulation of his wife by a rhythmic fondling of clitoris and vulva until orgasm is attained" [1, p. 66].

The central importance of experiencing orgasm has led many of the authors to de-emphasize the traditional organs of intercourse. The male penis (member) is particularly belittled. It is considered "only one of the instruments creating sensation in the female, and its greatest value lies as a mental stimulant and organ of reproduction, not as a necessary medium of her sexual pleasure." The same author adds, " . . . the disillusioning fact remains that the forefinger is a most useful asset in man's contact with the opposite sex . . .)" [14, p. 71]. Furthermore, this useful phallic symbol should be directed primarily to the woman's seat of sensation, the clitoris. Only a man who is ignorant of his job directs his digital attention to the vulva, the female organ that permits conventional union.

One must often deny himself immediate pleasure when manufacturing the orgasm. One author, in referring to an efficient technique to attain orgasm, states that: "Unfortunately, some men do not care for this position. This, however, should be of little importance to an adequate lover, since his emotions are the less important of the two" [14, p. 122]. Likewise, the woman may have to force herself in order to reach orgasm, even though she may not desire the activity which precedes it. It is specified that "If you conscientiously work at being available, you may ultimately find the feminine role quite satisfying even in the absence of ardor or desire" [5, p. 38]. The work ethic of the sexual side of marriage, then, is one resting quite elaborately on what has been referred to as the "cult of the orgasm."

Still, one cannot easily perform one's job; its intricacies must first be mastered. After all, ". . . there is considerably more in the sexual relationship than . . . at first thought" [8, p. 136]. "Remember that complete development of couple skills and adaptations takes literally years" [5, p. 206]. There is a great deal to be learned. One author talks of eight steps "in order to facilitate

sexual arousal and lead, finally, to satisfactory orgasm" and of seven "techniques which she and her mate may employ to help her attain full climax" [6, pp. 124–126].

All of this requires a good deal of mastery, a mastery that is necessary if the sex relationship is not to undergo "job turnover." Firstly, in the face of incompetence, the marriage partner may at times, turn to auto-eroticism. One author stipulates that "There cannot be a shadow of a doubt that faulty technique, or a total lack of it on the man's part, drives thousands of wives to masturbation as their sole means of gratification" [3, p. 140]. Moreover, if sexual skills are not acquired, the husband or wife may seek out new partners for sexual activity. The woman is admonished that adequate sexual relations will keep a man from "The Other Woman . . ." [4, pp. 264–265]. The male also must be proficient in sexual encounters for "it is the male's habit of treating . . . [sexual relationships] as such [mechanically] which causes much dissatisfaction and may ultimately drive the wife to someone who takes it more seriously" [14, p. 77].

## LEARNING SEX: PASSIVE AND ACTIVE

Marital sex is said to necessitate a good deal of preparation if it is to be efficiently performed. In one author's words: "This [complete satisfaction] cannot be achieved without study, practice, frank and open discussion . . ." [12, p. 45]. This overall preparation seems to involve both a passive and an active phase. The passive phase seems most related to an acquisition of information previous to engaging in sexual, at least marital sexual, relations. The active phase best refers to the training, one might say on-the-job training, that the married couple receive in the sexual conduct of wedlock.

The matter of passive preparation receives a great deal of attention from the avocational counselors. Thirteen of the fifteen books call attention to the necessity of reading, studying and discussing the various facets of sexual relationships. After listing a number of these activities, one author advises that "If the two of them have through reading acquired a decent vocabulary and a general understanding of the fundamental facts listed above, they will in all likelihood be able to find their way to happiness" [1, p. 20]. Another counselor cites the extreme importance of reciprocal communication by noting that ". . . the vital problem . . . must be solved through intelligent, practical, codified, and instructive discussion . . ." [14, p. 7]. The general purpose of all this learning is, of course, to dispel ignorance, as ignorance is said to lead to "mistakes at work," and such cannot be tolerated. The learning of the other partner's physiology is particularly emphasized, most counselors devoting at least one chapter and a profusion of illustrations to relieve the ignorance of the marriage partners. One author, however, quite obviously feels that words and pictures are insufficient. Presenting a sketch of the woman's genitals, he asserts that "It should be studied; on the bridal night . . . the husband should compare the diagram with his wife's genital region . . ." [14, p. 18].

Together with learning physiology, the various manuals also stress the critical importance of learning the methodology of marital sex. Sexual compatibility seems not a matter of following one's natural proclivities, but rather "The technique of the sexual relation has to be learned in order to develop a satisfactory sex life" [13, p. 172]. One must know one's job if one is to be successful at it. Not surprisingly, to like one's job also requires a learning experience, particularly for the woman. As one book scientifically asserts:

There is a striking consensus of opinion among serious specialists (both men and women) that the average woman of our time and clime must *learn* to develop specific sexual enjoyment, and only gradually attains to the orgasm in coitus. . . . they [women] have to *learn how* to feel both voluptuous pleasure and actual orgasm [15, p. 262].

In summary, then, passive learning involves the mastering of physiology and techniques. By the desexualized female of the marriage manuals, the fine art of emotional experience and expression is also acquired. And the naturally inept male must learn, for "If the husband understands in even a general way the sexual nature and equipment of his wife, he need not give the slightest offense to her through ignorant blundering" [1, p. 20].

This learning process, according to most of the manuals, eventually becomes subject to the actual experience of matrimonial sex. The marriage bed here becomes a "training" and "proving" ground. Again, wives seem particularly disadvantaged: "Their husbands have to be their guides" [3, p. 108]. However, generally the training experience is a mutual activity. As one author suggests in his discussion of the various positions for coitus:

In brief, the position to be used is not dictated by a code of behavior but should be selected as the one most acceptable to you and your mate. To find this you will examine your own tastes and physical conformations. By deliberate application of the trial and error method you will discover for yourselves which is most desirable for you both [11, p. 11].

In training, rigorous testing and practice is a must. In the words of one manual "experimentation will be required to learn the various responses within one's own body as well as those to be expected from one's beloved . . ." [9, p. 7], and also, "After a variable time of practice, husband and wife may both reach climax, and may do so at the same time" [11, p. 10].

Both the husband and wife must engage in a kind of "muscular control" training if the sex act is to be efficiently performed. The woman's plight during intercourse is picturesquely portrayed with the following advice. "You can generally contract these muscles by trying to squeeze with the vagina itself . . . perhaps by pretending that you are trying to pick up marbles with it" [5, p. 97]. Fortunately, the man is able to practice muscular control at times other than during intercourse. Indeed, the man, unlike the woman, is permitted to engage in activities not normally related to sexual behavior while he is training. It is advised that "You can snap the muscles [at the base of the penile shaft] a few times while you are driving your car or sitting in an office or any place you happen to think of it . . ." [5, p. 96]. The practice field, at least for the male, is enlarged.

In general, then, a careful learning and a studied training program are necessary conditions for the proper performance of marital sex. As seems abundantly true of all sectors of work, " 'Nature' is not enough . . . . Man must pay for a higher and more complex nervous system by study, training, and conscious effort . . ." [7, p. 34].

## THE JOB SCHEDULE

As in most work activities, the activity of marital sex is a highly scheduled kind of performance. There is first of all a specification of phases or stages in the actual conduct of the sex act. Although there is disagreement here, some authors indicating four or five distinct phases [15, p. 1], the consensus of the counselors seems to be that "Sexual intercourse, when satisfactorily performed, consists of three stages, only one of which is the sex act proper" [11, p. 7].

The sexual act therefore is a scheduled act and the participants are instructed to follow this schedule. "All three stages have to be fitted into this time. None of them must be missed and none prolonged to the exclusion of others" [8, p. 155]. Practice and study is said to insure the proper passage from one phase to another [12, p. 42]. Moreover, to guarantee that none of the phases will be excluded, it is necessary to engage in relations only when the sexual partners have a sizable amount of time during which they will not be distracted: ". . . husbands and wives should rarely presume to begin love-play that may lead to coitus unless they can have an hour free from interruptions" [1, p. 51]. Even then, however, the couple must be careful, for there is an optimal time to spend on each particular phase. For instance, "Foreplay should never last less than fifteen minutes even though a woman may be sufficiently aroused in five" [14, p. 43]. Likewise, the epilogue to orgasm should be of sufficient duration to permit the proper recession of passion.

Given this schedule of activity, the marriage manuals take great pains to describe the various activities required at each particular phase. It is cautioned, for instance, that "all contact with the female genital region . . . should be kept at an absolute minimum" [14, pp. 42–43] during foreplay. The man is warned furthermore to "refrain from any excessive activity involving the penis" [14, p. 77] if he wishes to sustain foreplay. Regarding afterplay, the advice is the same; the partners must not permit themselves "any further genital stimulation" [15, p. 25].

The "job specification" is most explicit, however, when describing the actual act of intercourse. It is particularly during this stage that the sexual partners must strain to maintain control over their emotions. Innumerable lists of "necessary activities" are found in the various manuals. The adequate lovers should not permit themselves to deviate from these activities. Sometimes, in fact, the male is instructed to pause in midaction, in order to ascertain his relative progress:

> After the penis has been inserted to its full length into the vagina, it is usually best for the husband to rest a bit before allowing himself to make the instinctive in-and-out movements which usually follow. He needs first to make sure that his wife is comfortable, that the penis is not pushing too hard against the rear wall of the vagina, and that she is as ready as he to proceed with these movements [1, p. 61].

## TECHNIQUES

The "labor of love" espoused by the avocational counselors is one whose culmination is importantly based on the proper use of sexual technique. In fact, ". . . *miserable failure results from ignorance of technique*" [3, p. 49]. Indeed "no sex relationship will have permanent value unless technique is mastered . . ." [8, p. 177]. Thirteen of the fifteen books devote considerable space to familiarizing the reader with the techniques of sexual activity. These discussions for the most part involve enumerating the various positions of intercourse, but also include techniques to induce, to prolong, to elevate, and to minimize passion. Many times the depiction of particular coital positions takes on a bizarre, almost geometric, aura. In one such position:

> The woman lies on her back, lifts her legs at right angles to her body from the hips, and rests them on the man's shoulders; thus she is, so to speak, doubly cleft by the man who lies upon her and inserts his phallus; she enfolds both his genital member and his neck and head. At the same time the woman's spine in the lumbar region is flexed at a sharp angle ... [15, p. 218].

Often, however, the mastery of sexual technique seems to involve little more than being able to keep one's legs untangled, ". . . when the woman straightens her right leg the man, leaving his leg between both of hers, puts his left one outside her right, and rolls over onto his left side facing her" [1, p. 58].

At times, in order to make love adequately, it is required of the participants that they supplement their technique with special equipment. Some of this equipment, such as lubricating jellies, pillows, and birth control paraphernalia, is simple and commonplace. Others are as simple but not as common, such as chairs, foot-high stools, and beds with footboards or footrails. Some, like aphrodisiacs, hot cushions, medicated (carbonic acid) baths, and sitz baths, border on the exotic. Still others actually seem to detract from the pleasure of intercourse. In this vein would be the rings of sponge rubber which are slipped over the penis to control depth of penetration and the various devices which make the male less sensitive, such as condoms and a local anesthetic applied to the glans.

This equipment that minimizes stimulation, while not particularly inviting, might be said to give greater pleasure than still other techniques that are suggested to add variety to the sex life. The latter, in fact, seem cruelly painful. For instance, ". . . both partners tend to use their teeth, and in so doing there is naught abnormal, morbid or perverse. Can the same be said of the real love-bite that breaks the skin and draws blood? Up to a certain degree—yes" [15, p. 157]. Indeed, a cer-

tain amount of aggression should be commonplace: ". . . both of them can and do exult in a certain degree of male aggression and dominance. . . . Hence, the sharp gripping and pinching of the woman's arms and nates" [15, p. 159].

At times, the authors seem to go so far as to indicate that the proper performance of the sex act almost requires the use of techniques that create discomfort. The element of irksomeness becomes an almost necessary ingredient of the conduct of marital sex.

## CONCLUDING REMARKS

The kinds of impressions assembled here seem to support the notion that play, at least sexual play in marriage, has indeed been permeated with dimensions of a work ethic. The play of marital sex is presented by the counselors quite definitely as work.

This paradox, play as work, may be said to be an almost logical outcome of the peculiar condition of American society. First of all, it seems that in America, most individuals are faced with the problems of justifying and dignifying their play. In times past, leisure was something earned, a prize that was achieved through work. In the present era, it might be said that leisure is something ascribed or assumed. Indeed, as Riesman and Bloomberg have noted, "leisure, which was once a residual compensation for the tribulations of work, may become what workers recover from at work."[9]

The American must justify his play. It is our thesis that he has done this by transforming his play into work. This is not to say that he has disguised his play as work; it is instead to propose that his play has become work.[10] To consume is, in most cases, to produce. Through this transformation of play, the dignity of consumption is seemingly established; it is now work, and work is felt to carry with it a certain inherent dignity. The individual now is morally free to consume, and moreover free to seek out persons to teach him how to consume, for learning how to play is simply learning how to do one's job in society.

This transformation of play into work has been attended by another phenomenon that is also quite unique to contemporary American society. Given the fact that work has always been valued in American society, a cult of efficiency has developed. As a consequence, the productive forces in America have become very efficient, and an abundance of consumer goods have been created. So that such goods will be consumed, Americans have been socialized into being extremely consumption oriented. As Jules Henry[11] has noted, the impulse controls of most Americans have been destroyed. The achievement of a state of general satisfaction has become a societal goal. To experience pleasure is almost a societal dictum.

Thus there seem to be two antagonistic forces operating in American society. On the one hand, there is an emphasis on work and, on the other hand, there is an emphasis on attaining maximum pleasure. These two themes were recurrent in the fifteen manuals which we read, and as one writer put it, ". . . it may well be that the whole level of sexual enjoyment for both partners can be stepped up and greatly enriched if the man is able to exercise a greater degree of deliberation and management" [1, p. 33]. It was as if the avocational counselors were trying to solve a dilemma for their audience by reminding them to both "let themselves go" while cautioning them that they should "work at this." If sex be play, it most assuredly is a peculiar kind of play.

## APPENDIX

1. Oliver M. Butterfield, Ph.D., *Sexual Harmony in Marriage*, New York: Emerson Books, 1964 (sixth printing).
2. Mary Steichen Calderone, M.D., M.S.P.H., and Phyllis and Robert P. Goldman, *Release from Sexual Tensions*, New York: Random House, 1960.
3. Eustace Chesser, M.D., *Love Without Fear*, New York: The New American Library, 1947 (twenty-ninth printing).
4. Maxine Davis, *Sexual Responsibility in Marriage*, New York: Dial Press, 1963.
5. John E. Eichenlaub, M.D., *The Marriage Art*, New York: Dell Publishing Co., 1961 (fourteenth printing).
6. Albert Ellis, Ph.D., and Robert A. Harper, Ph.D., *The Marriage Bed*, New York: Tower Publications, 1961.
7. Bernard R. Greenblat, B.S., M.D., *A Doctor's Marital Guide for Patients*, Chicago: Budlong Press, 1964.
8. Edward F. Griffith, *A Sex Guide to Happy Marriage*, New York: Emerson Books, 1956.
9. Robert E. Hall, M.D., *Sex and Marriage*, New York: Planned Parenthood-World Population, 1965.
10. Isabel Emslie Hutton, M.D., *The Sex Technique in Marriage*, New York: Emerson Books, 1961 (revised, enlarged, and reset edition following thirty-fifth printing in 1959).
11. Lena Levine, M.D., *The Doctor Talks with the Bride and Groom*, New York: Planned Parenthood Federation, 1950 (reprinted February 1964).
12. S. A. Lewin, M.D., and John Gilmore, Ph.D., *Sex Without Fear*, New York: Medical Research Press, 1957 (fifteenth printing).
13. Hannah M. Stone, M.D., and Abraham Stone, M.D., *A Marriage Manual*, New York: Simon and Schuster, 1953.
14. Robert Street, *Modern Sex Techniques*, New York: Lancer Books, 1959.
15. Th. H. Van de Velde, M.D., *Ideal Marriage: Its Physiology and Technique*, New York: Random House, 1961.

## REFERENCES AND NOTES

1  Leo Lowenthal, "The Triumph of Mass Idols," in *Literature, Popular Culture, and Society*, Englewood Cliffs, N.J.: Prentice-Hall, 1961, pp. 109–140.
2  David Riesman (with Nathan Glazer and Reuel Denney), *The Lonely Crowd*, Garden City, N.Y.: Doubleday Anchor Books, 1953, p. 341.
3  *Ibid.*
4  Nelson Foote, "Sex as Play," in Eric Larrabee and Rolf Meyersohn (eds.), *Mass Leisure*, Glencoe, Ill.: The Free Press, 1958, p. 335.
5  Jules Henry, *Culture Against Man*, New York: Random House, 1963, p. 43.
6  Martha Wolfenstein, "The Emergence of Fun Morality," in Larrabee and Meyersohn, *op. cit.*, p. 93.
7  We were unable to obtain this most recent printing, and our copy was the twenty-ninth printing.
8  These figures were published in *Newsweek*, Oct. 18, 1965, p. 100.
9  David Riesman and Warner Bloomberg, Jr., "Work and Leisure: Tension or Polarity," in Sigmund Nosow and William H. Form (eds.), *Man, Work, and Society*, New York: Basic Books, 1962, p. 39.
10  Many investigators have observed the intertwining of work and play. We are here only interested in one aspect of admixture, the labor of play.
11  Henry, *op. cit.*, pp. 20–21.

SUPPLEMENTAL READINGS

Brucker, H.: "Mass Man and Mass Media," *Saturday Review*, vol. 48 (May 29, 1965), pp. 14-16.

De Fleur, Melvin L.: "Mass Communication and Social Change," *Social Forces*, vol. 44 (March 1966), pp. 314-326.

De Gracia, Sebastian: *Of Time, Work and Leisure*, New York: The Twentieth Century Fund, 1962.

Jarrell, Randall: "A Sad Heart at the Supermarket," *Daedalus*, vol. 89 (spring 1960), pp. 359-368.

Jovanovich, William: "On Purveying Books," *American Scholar*, vol. 34 (fall 1965), pp. 535-543.

Kaplan, Max: *Leisure: A Social Inquiry*, New York: John Wiley & Sons, Inc., 1960.

Klapper, Joseph T.: *The Effects of Mass Communication*, New York: The Free Press, 1960.

McCormack, T.: "Intellectuals and the Mass Media," *American Behavioral Science*, vol. 9 (December 1965), pp. 31-36.

McLeod, J.: "Alienation and Uses of the Mass Media," *Public Opinion Quarterly*, vol. 29 (winter 1965-1966), pp. 583-594.

O'Hara, Robert C.: *Life as the Media See It*, New York: Random House, Inc., 1961.

Pierce, John R.: "Communication," *Daedalus*, vol. 96 (summer 1967), pp. 909-921.

Singer, A.: "Television: Window on Culture or Reflection in the Glass?" *American Scholar*, vol. 35 (spring 1966), pp. 303-309.

Steiner, Gary A.: *The People Look at Television*, New York: Alfred A. Knopf, Inc., 1963.

Tobin, R. L.: "One-world Concept of Mass Communication," *Saturday Review*, vol. 49 (Jan. 8, 1966), pp. 101-102.

Wilensky, Harold L.: "Mass Society and Mass Culture: Interdependence or Independence," *American Sociological Review*, vol. 29 (April 1964), pp. 173-197.

Alienation as a sociological concept refers to man's feelings of estrangement from major beliefs, from established institutions, and from himself. The development of alienated personalities in modern society seems to be associated with a number of current social changes. The processes of urbanization, analyzed in Chapter One, have forced millions of people to live together who do not necessarily share common values and living habits. In accepting "city ways" the newcomer may have given up something of known value. No doubt, a part of the alienation experienced by urbanites is the inability to find a satisfying culture in the city. In fact, some thoughtful critics question the assumption that the city even has a separate and unified culture. In cross section the city is a collection of diverse races, religions, and class ways of behaving; it is therefore a stranger, difficult to understand.

The proximity of strangers and their obvious inability to initiate communication, the inability of city dwellers to change from strangers to friends and their inability to identify with the newly arrived stranger, all seem to augment loneliness. Alienated urbanites are capable of seeing murders committed in the streets and not even telephone the authorities. One of the major obstacles to an effective program of "law and order" in cities is securing the cooperation of citizens in bringing to the attention of police acts of crime and violence. There is good reason to assume that in many instances the failure to cooperate with law-enforcement agencies stems more from indifference and apathy than from fear of possible reprisals.

Industrialization has contributed its share to the alienation of workers. In the preindustrial handicraft period the worker made a pair of shoes, or a kettle, or a harness, and his name was stamped on each article as a matter of personal guarantee and pride. In the modern industrialized society the worker no longer makes products, but parts. Other workers assemble the parts into units of the product, and probably only the consumer sees the total product. Thus workers are more identifed with a component of a product than with the product itself. We find auto workers, for example, more identified with the automatic-transmission division of General Motors than with one of its automobiles. Finally, the industrial union has probably made the worker more job oriented than product centered. As a result, there seems to have been a gradual displacement of the worker from the inner meaning of work, a product well made.

Industrialization has also influenced the white-collar worker's perception of his position as a "rat race." His "race" begins in the morning, when he rides the commuter train or drives the long and congested freeway or expressway to the office. He may spend much of this commuting time brooding over the fact that he is not the prime decision maker in his business or professional operation. He knows he may be moved on short notice to another division of the corporation, transferred to another plant in some distant city, or find his position reclassified by an "outside management team." If he is a "company man," these changes may result in alienation from family and friends; the company must come first, and frequently the price of success is measured in terms of family alienation and value alienation.

Alienation has also been augmented by formal education, and changes in social-class position are especially frequent among those who come from lower socioeconomic backgrounds. Not only does education, especially higher education, provide the student with new occupational opportunities, but the process itself tends to broaden his thinking about a whole spectrum of values. Old beliefs are likely to be shattered by exposure to scientific criteria and facts. The examination of all ideas and beliefs seems to imply that every idea or belief may in part be false. Intellectual testing may weaken the central core of absolute values and beliefs, with all values and beliefs gradually becoming a question of assumption and relative merit. From absolutism the student may drift to relativism, where he becomes absolute only in the conviction that all things are relative. This process of reevaluation may often lead to more feelings of personal estrangement than of inner harmony and satisfaction.

Formal university education usually provides the graduate with a sufficient professional income to live in the typical upper-middle-class neighborhood, where his associates are other "informal" upper-middle-class professionals. Old friends and family members may not be compatible with the new neighbors and colleagues. Thus, in addition to actual estrangement from old relationships, the individual may experience deep guilt and inner doubt about casting off family and friends who have not "succeeded."

Modern man often feels politically alienated from the decision-making processes of intelligent citizenship. All phases of government action seem to have become complicated and the issues more difficult to evaluate. Instead of the town meeting, the citizen today listens to "Meet the Press" or "CBS Reports" with no chance to ask a question. The great questions are implied to be clearly beyond his understanding. An increasing number of television "shows" feature a humorous moderator and three or four controversial guests commenting on selected social problems with considerable levity and frivolity. This jocular treatment by the mass media of poverty, war, divorce, ethnic discrimination, crime, and other related problems certainly further increases the observer's feeling of alienation from society.

Moreover, in our present mass culture the word "politics" is operationally an antonym for "democracy"—a curious measuring of practice and theory. To many the word "politics" suggests a matter of trading favor for votes. Patronage is no longer handed out to groups of deserving individuals, but to selected pressure groups, often as a reward for political support. The alienated, by definition, do not belong to organized groups. One of the early goals of the "war on poverty" was to lessen the feeling of futility on the part of the poor by requiring their "maximum feasible participation" in most programs. The poverty program has floundered largely because of its inability to get the alienated poor involved in their own program—in retrospect, a predictable outcome.

Freedom of choice can be a unique source of frustration—a frustration resulting from having to make too many decisions. A large part of the American public seems almost bewildered by the number of choices concerning products, philosophies, religions, politics, and logical points of view. A potential buyer of stocks and bonds is so confused by the array of listings on the New York Stock Exchange that often the broker's principal job is to reduce the client's choice anxiety by restricting his own recommendations to one or two issues at a time. No doubt, a part of the success of the mutual-fund companies can be attributed to the service of reducing the number of decisions required by investments in common stocks, although the number of mutual funds of varying objectives has proliferated to such an extent that this advantage has been largely lost. The real-estate salesman has also been trained to show a prospective home purchaser only three or four houses to avoid "confusing" the buyer. An affluent society lends itself to the development of product anxiety The conflicting claims of rival advertisers serve to increase confusion over which product is really superior and often even compound this anxiety. For example, although cigarette smokers report that they smoke largely to reduce environmental anxiety, the alleged anxiety reduction is seriously challenged by advertisements for various filter cigarettes purporting to collect the "dangerous tars" that other brands contain. The result is anxiety first over the choice of brand and then over the possible consequences of using any brand of a product sought initially to lessen anxiety.

People may become alienated even from themselves in pondering past "mistakes" and actively questioning former values. Even moderate success at such self-evaluation may cause an individual to define himself in terms leading to self-estrangement. In criticizing and rejecting his "former self," he not only becomes alienated from the "former self," but also develops increasing doubt about the decision-making judgment of the "present self." Another factor contributing to self-alienation is the tendency to reify negative experiences through selective memory.

In this chapter Melvin Seeman analyzes the meaning of the concept "alienation." The special kind of alienation experienced by white-collar workers and middle management is explored by William F. Whyte, who makes an important distinction between the "protestant ethnic" and the "social ethnic." Robert Keniston develops a sympathetic analysis of the problem of the demand of youth for social change to ameliorate persistent human suffering and to lessen participation in legitimized violent behavior. Today's youth, viewed as products of modern parents, are characterized by Keniston as "post-modern youth." Everett C. Hughes, in his selection "Good People and Dirty Work," poses a number of perplexing and soul-searching questions concerning the permissiveness of an advanced people to tolerate the dirty work—the horrors of the concentration camps—being done among, and in a sense by, millions of ordinary, civilized German people.

## 9  ON THE MEANING OF ALIENATION  MELVIN SEEMAN

At the present time, in all the social sciences, the various synonyms of alienation have a foremost place in studies of human relations. Investigations of the "unattached," the "marginal," the "obsessive," the "normless," and the "isolated" individual all testify to the central place occupied by the hypothesis of alienation in contemporary social science.

So writes Robert Nisbet in *The Quest for Commu-*

Reprinted with the permission of the author, the American Sociological Association, and the publisher, from *American Sociological Review*, vol. 24, no. 6 (December 1959), pp. 783–791.

This article is based in part on work done while I was in attendance at the Behavioral Sciences Conference at the University of New Mexico, in the summer of 1958. The conference was supported by the Behavioral Sciences Division, Air Force Office of Scientific Research, under contract AF49(638)-33. The work on alienation was carried out in close conjunction with Julian B. Rotter and Shephard Liverant of The Ohio State University. I gratefully acknowledge their very considerable help, while absolving them of any commitment to the viewpoints herein expressed.

*nity;*[1] and there would seem to be little doubt that his estimate is correct. In one form or another, the concept of alienation dominates both the contemporary literature and the history of sociological thought. It is a central theme in the classics of Marx, Weber, and Durkheim; and in contemporary work, the consequences that have been said to flow from the fact of alienation have been diverse, indeed.

Ethnic prejudice, for example, has been described as a response to alienation—as an ideology which makes an incomprehensible world intelligible by imposing upon that world a simplified and categorical "answer system" (for example, the Jews cause international war).[2] In this examination of the persuasion process in the Kate Smith bond drive, Merton emphasizes the significance of pervasive distrust: "The very same society that produces this sense of alienation and estrangement generates in many a craving for reassurance, an acute need to believe, a flight into faith"[3]—in this case, faith in the sincerity of the persuader. In short, the idea of alienation is a popular vehicle for virtually every kind of analysis, from the prediction of voting behavior to the search for *The Sane Society*.[4] This inclusiveness, in both its historical and its contemporary import, is expressed in Erich Kahler's remark: "The history of man could very well be written as a history of the alienation of man."[5]

A concept that is so central in sociological work, and so clearly laden with value implications, demands special clarity. There are, it seems to me, five basic ways in which the concept of alienation has been used. The purpose of this paper is to examine these logically distinguishable usages, and to propose what seems a workable view of these five meanings of alienation. Thus, the task is a dual one: to make more organized sense of one of the great traditions in sociological thought; and to make the traditional interest in alienation more amenable to sharp empirical statement.[6]

I propose, in what follows, to treat alienation from the personal standpoint of the actor—that is, alienation is here taken from the social-psychological point of view. Presumably, a task for subsequent experimental or analytical research is to determine (1) the social conditions that produce these five variants of alienation, or (2) their behavioral consequences. In each of the five instances, I begin with a review of where and how that usage is found in traditional sociological thought; subsequently, in each case, I seek a more researchable statement of meaning. In these latter statements, I focus chiefly upon the ideas of expectation and value.[7]

## POWERLESSNESS

The first of these uses refers to alienation in the sense of *powerlessness*. This is the notion of alienation as it originated in the Marxian view of the worker's condition in capitalist society: the worker is alienated to the extent that the prerogative and means of decision are expropriated by the ruling entrepreneurs. Marx, to be sure, was interested in other alienative aspects of the industrial system; indeed, one might say that his interest in the powerlessness of the worker flowed from his interest in the consequences of such alienation in the work place—for example, the alienation of man from man, and the degradation of men into commodities.

In Weber's work, we find an extension beyond the industrial sphere of the Marxian notion of powerlessness. Of this extension, Gerth and Mills remark:

> Marx's emphasis upon the wage worker as being 'separated' from the means of production becomes, in Weber's perspective, merely one special case of a universal trend. The modern soldier is equally 'separated' from the means of violence; and the civil servant from the means of administration.[8]

The idea of alienation as powerlessness is, perhaps, the most frequent usage in current literature. The contributors to Gouldner's volume on leadership, for example, make heavy use of this idea; as does the work of C. Wright Mills—and, I suppose, any analysis of the human condition that takes the Marxist tradition with any seriousness. This variant of alienation can be conceived as *the expectancy or probability held by the individual that his own behavior cannot determine the occurrence of the outcomes, or reinforcements, he seeks.*

Let us be clear about what this conception does and does not imply. First, it is a distinctly social-psychological view. It does not treat powerlessness from the standpoint of the objective conditions in society; but this does not mean that these conditions need be ignored in research dealing with this variety of alienation. These objective conditions are relevant, for example, in determining the degree of realism involved in the individual's response to his situation. The objective features of the situations are to be handled like any other situational aspect of behavior—to be analyzed, measured, ignored, experimentally controlled or varied, as the research question demands.

Second, this construction of "powerlessness" clearly departs from the Marxian tradition by removing the critical, polemic element in the idea of alienation. Likewise, this version of powerlessness does not take into account, as a definitional matter, the frustration an individual may feel as a consequence of the discrepancy between the control he may expect and the degree of control that he desires—that is, it takes no direct account of the value of control to the person.

In this version of alienation, then, the individual's expectancy for control of events is clearly distinguished from (1) the *objective* situation of powerlessness as some observer sees it, (2) the observer's *judgment* of that situation against some ethical standard, and (3) the individual's sense of a *discrepancy* between his expectations for control and his desire for control.

The issues in the philosophy of science, or in the history of science, on which these distinctions and decisions touch cannot be debated here. Two remarks must suffice:

1 In any given research, any or all of the elements discussed above—expectancies, objective conditions, deviation from a moral standard, deviation from the actor's standards—may well be involved, and I see little profit in arguing about which is "really" alienation so long as what is going on at each point in the effort is clear. I have chosen to focus on expectancies since I believe that this is consistent with what follows, while it avoids building ethical or adjustmental features into the concept.

2 I do not think that the expectancy usage is as radical a departure from the Marxian legacy as it may appear. No one would deny the editorial character of the Marxian judgment, but it was a judgment about a state of affairs—the elimination of individual freedom and control. My version of alienation refers to the counterpart, in the individual's expectations, of that state of affairs.

Finally, the use of powerlessness as an expectancy means that this version of alienation is very closely related to the notion (developed by Rotter) of "internal *versus* external control of reinforcements." The latter construct refers to the individual's sense of personal control over the reinforcement situation, as contrasted with his view that the occurrence of reinforcements is dependent upon external conditions, such as chance, luck, or the manipulation of others. The congru-

ence in these formulations leaves the way open for the development of a closer bond between two languages of analysis—that of learning theory and that of alienation—that have long histories in psychology and sociology. But the congruence also poses a problem—the problem of recognizing that these two constructs, though intimately related, are not generally used to understand the same things.[9]

In the case of alienation, I would limit the applicability of the concept to expectancies that have to do with the individual's sense of influence over socio-political events (control over the political system, the industrial economy, international affairs, and the like). Accordingly, I would initially limit the applicability of this first meaning of alienation to the arena for which the concept was originally intended, namely, the depiction of man's relation to the larger social order. Whether or not such an operational concept of alienation is related to expectancies for control in more intimate need areas (for example, love and affection; status-recognition) is a matter for empirical determination. The need for the restriction lies in the following convictions: First, the concept of alienation, initially, should not be so global as to make the *generality* of powerlessness a matter of fiat rather than fact. Second, the concept should not be dangerously close to merely an index of personality *adjustment*—equivalent, that is, to a statement that the individual is maladjusted in the sense that he has a generally low expectation that he can, through his own behavior, achieve any of the personal rewards he seeks.[10]

## MEANINGLESSNESS

A second major usage of the alienation concept may be summarized under the idea of *meaninglessness*. The clearest contemporary examples of this usage are found in Adorno's treatment of prejudice; in Cantril's *The Psychology of Social Movements*, in which the "search for meaning" is used as part of the interpretive scheme in analyzing such diverse phenomena as lynchings, the Father Divine movement, and German fascism; and in

Hoffer's portrait of the "true believer" as one who finds, and needs to find, in the doctrines of a mass movement "a master key to all the world's problems."[11]

This variant of alienation is involved in Mannheim's description of the increase of "functional rationality" and the concomitant decline of "substantial rationality." Mannheim argues that as society increasingly organizes its members with reference to the most efficient realization of ends (that is, as functional rationality increases), there is a parallel decline in the "capacity to act intelligently in a given situation on the basis of one's own insight into the interrelations of events."[12]

This second type of alienation, then, refers to the individual's sense of understanding the events in which he is engaged. We may speak of high alienation, in the meaninglessness usage, when *the individual is unclear as to what he ought to believe—when the individual's minimal standards for clarity in decision-making are not met.* Thus, the post-war German situation described by Adorno was "meaningless" in the sense that the individual could not choose with confidence among alternative explanations of the inflationary disasters of the time (and, it is argued, substituted the "Jews" as a simplified solution for this unclarity). In Mannheim's depiction, the individual cannot choose appropriately among alternative interpretations (cannot "act intelligently" or "with insight") because the increase in functional rationality, with its emphasis on specialization and production, makes such choice impossible.

It would seem, for the present at least, a matter of no consequence what the beliefs in question are. They may, as in the above instance, be simply descriptive beliefs (interpretations); or they may be beliefs involving moral standards (norms for behavior). In either case, the individual's choice among alternative beliefs has low "confidence limits": he cannot predict with confidence the consequences of acting on a given belief. One might operationalize this aspect of alienation by focusing upon the fact that it is characterized by a *low expectancy that satisfactory predictions about future outcomes of behavior can be made.* Put

more simply, where the first meaning of alienation refers to the sensed ability to control outcomes, this second meaning refers essentially to the sensed ability to predict behavioral outcomes.

This second version of alienation is logically independent of the first, for, under some circumstances, expectancies for personal control of events may not coincide with the understanding of these events, as in the popular depiction of the alienation of the intellectual.[13] Still, there are obvious connections between these two forms of alienation: in some important degree, the view that one lives in an intelligible world may be a prerequisite to expectancies for control; and the unintelligibility of complex affairs is presumably conducive to the development of high expectancies for external control (that is, high powerlessness).[14]

## NORMLESSNESS

The third variant of the alienation theme is derived from Durkheim's description of "anomie," and refers to a condition of *normlessness*. In the traditional usage, anomie denotes a situation in which the social norms regulating individual conduct have broken down or are no longer effective as rules for behavior. As noted above, Merton emphasizes this kind of rulelessness in his interpretation of the importance of the "sincerity" theme in Kate Smith's war bond drive:

> The emphasis on this theme reflects a social disorder—"anomie" is the sociological term—in which common values have been submerged in the welter of private interests seeking satisfaction by virtually any means which are effective. Drawn from a highly competitive, segmented urban society, our informants live in a climate of reciprocal distrust which, to say the least, is not conducive to stable human relationships. . . . The very same society that produces this sense of alienation and estrangement generates in many a craving for reassurance. . . .[15]

Elsewhere, in his well-known paper "Social Structure and Anomie," Merton describes the "adaptations" (the kinds of conformity and deviance) that may occur where the disciplining effect of collective standards has been weakened. He takes as his case in point the situation in which culturally prescribed goals (in America, the emphasis upon success goals) are not congruent with the available means for their attainment. In such a situation, he argues, anomie or normlessness will develop to the extent that "the technically most effective procedure, whether culturally legitimate or not, becomes typically preferred to institutionally prescribed conduct."[16]

Merton's comments on this kind of anomic situation serve to renew the discussion of the expectancy constructs developed above—the idea of meaninglessness, and the idea of powerlessness or internal-external control. For Merton notes, first, that the anomic situation leads to low predictability in behavior, and second, that the anomic situation may well lead to the belief in luck:

Whatever the sentiments of the reader concerning the moral desirability of coordinating the goals-and-means phases of the social structure, it is clear that imperfect coordination of the two leads to anomie. Insofar as one of the most general functions of the social structure is to provide a basis for predictability and regularity of social behavior, it becomes increasingly limited in effectiveness as these elements of the social structure become dissociated. . . . The victims of this contradiction between the cultural emphasis on pecuniary ambition and the social bars to full opportunity are not always aware of the structural sources of their thwarted aspirations. To be sure, they are typically aware of a discrepancy between individual worth and social rewards. But they do not necessarily see how this comes about. Those who do find its source in the social structure may become alienated from that structure and become ready candidates for Adaptation V [rebellion]. But others, and this appears to include the great majority, may attribute their difficulties to more mystical and less sociological sources. . . . in such a society [a society suffering from anomie] people tend to put stress on

mysticism: the workings of Fortune, Chance, Luck.[17]

It is clear that the general idea of anomie is both an integral part of the alienation literature, and that it bears upon our expectancy notions. What is not so clear is the matter of how precisely to conceptualize the events to which "anomie" is intended to point. Unfortunately, the idea of normlessness has been over-extended to include a wide variety of both social conditions and psychic states: personal disorganization, cultural breakdown, reciprocal distrust, and so on.

Those who employ the anomie version of alienation are chiefly concerned with the elaboration of the "means" emphasis in society—for example, the loss of commonly held standards and consequent individualism, or the development of instrumental, manipulative attitudes. This interest represents our third variant of alienation, the key idea of which, again, may be cast in terms of expectancies. Following Merton's lead, the anomic situation, from the individual point of view, may be defined as one in which there is a *high expectancy that socially unapproved behaviors are required to achieve given goals.* This third meaning of alienation is logically independent of the two versions discussed above. Expectancies concerning unapproved means, presumably, can vary independently of the individual's expectancy that his own behavior will determine his success in reaching a goal (what I have called "powerlessness") or his belief that he operates in an intellectually comprehensible world ("meaninglessness"). Such a view of anomie, to be sure, narrows the evocative character of the concept, but it provides a more likely way of developing its research potential. This view, I believe, makes possible the discovery of the extent to which such expectancies are held, the conditions for their development, and their consequences either for the individual or for a given social system (for example, the generation of widespread distrust).

The foregoing discussion implies that the means and goals in question have to do with such relatively broad social demands as the demand for success or for political ends. However, in his interesting essay, "Alienation from Interaction," Erving Goffman presents a more or less parallel illustration in which the focus is on the smallest of social systems, the simple conversation:

> If we take conjoint spontaneous involvement in a topic of conversation as a point of reference, we shall find that alienation from it is common indeed. Conjoint involvement appears to be a fragile thing, with standard points of weakness and decay, a precarious unsteady state that is likely at any time to lead the individual into some form of alienation. Since we are dealing with obligatory involvement, forms of alienation will constitute *misbehavior of a kind that can be called mis-involvement.*[18]

Goffman describes four such "mis-involvements" (for example, being too self-conscious in interaction), and concludes: "By looking at the ways in which individuals can be thrown out of step with the sociable moment, perhaps we can learn something about the way in which he can become alienated from things that take much more of his time."[19] In speaking of "misbehavior" or "mis-involvement," Goffman is treating the problem of alienation in terms not far removed from the anomic feature I have described, that is, the expectancy for socially unapproved behavior. His analysis of the social microcosm in these terms calls attention once more to the fact that the five variants of alienation discussed here can be applied to as broad or as narrow a range of social behavior as seems useful.

### ISOLATION

The fourth type of alienation refers to *isolation*. This usage is most common in descriptions of the intellectual role, where writers refer to the detachment of the intellectual from popular cultural standards—one who, in Nettler's language, has become estranged from his society and the culture it carries.[20] Clearly, this usage does not refer to isolation as a lack of "social adjustment"—of the warmth, security, or intensity of an individual's social contacts.

In the present context, in which we seek to maintain a consistent focus on the individual's expectations or values, this brand of alienation may be usefully defined in terms of reward values: The alienated in the isolation sense are those who, like the intellectual, *assign low reward value to goals or beliefs that are typically highly valued in the given society*. This, in effect, is the definition of alienation in Nettler's scale, for as a measure of "apartness from society" the scale consists (largely though not exclusively) of items that reflect the individual's degree of commitment to popular culture. Included, for example, is the question "Do you read Reader's Digest?", a magazine that was selected "as a symbol of popular magazine appeal and folkish thoughtways."[21]

The "isolation" version of alienation clearly carries a meaning different from the three versions discussed above. Still, these alternative meanings can be profitably applied in conjunction with one another in the analysis of a given state of affairs. Thus, Merton's paper on social structure and anomie makes use of both "normlessness" and "isolation" in depicting the adaptations that individuals may make to the situation in which goals and means are not well coordinated. One of these adaptations—that of the "innovator"—is the prototype of alienation in the sense of normlessness, in which the individual innovates culturally disapproved means to achieve the goals in question. But another adjustment pattern—that of "rebellion"—more closely approximates what I have called "isolation." "This adaptation [rebellion] leads men outside the environing social structure to envisage and seek to bring into being a new, that is to say, a greatly modified, social structure. It presupposes alienation from reigning goals and standards."[22]

### SELF-ESTRANGEMENT

The final variant distinguishable in the literature is alienation in the sense of *self-estrangement*. The most extended treatment of this version of alienation is found in *The Sane Society*, where Fromm writes:

In the following analysis I have chosen the concept of alienation as the central point from which I am going to develop the analysis of the contemporary social character. . . . By alienation is meant a mode of experience in which the person experiences himself as an alien. He has become, one might say, estranged from himself.[23]

In much the same way, C. Wright Mills comments: "In the normal course of her work, because her personality becomes the instrument of an alien purpose, the salesgirl becomes self-alienated;" and, later, "Men are estranged from one another as each secretly tries to make an instrument of the other, and in time a full circle is made: One makes an instrument of himself and is estranged from It also."[24]

There are two interesting features of this popular doctrine of alienation as self-estrangement. The first of these is the fact that where the usage does not overlap with the other four meanings (and it often does), it is difficult to specify what the alienation is *from*. To speak of "alienation from the self" is after all simply a metaphor, in a way that "alienation from popular culture," for example, need not be. The latter can be reasonably specified, as I have tried to do above; but what is intended when Fromm, Mills, Hoffer, and the others speak of self- estrangement?

Apparently, what is being postulated here is some ideal human condition from which the individual is estranged. This is, perhaps, clearest in Fromm's treatment, for example, in his description of production and consumption excesses in capitalist society: "The *human* way of acquiring would be to make an effort qualitatively commensurate with what I acquire. . . . But our craving for consumption has lost all connection with the real needs of man."[25] To be self-alienated, in the final analysis, means to be something less than one might ideally be if the circumstances in society were otherwise—to be insecure, given to appearances, conformist. Riesman's discussion of other-direction falls within this meaning of alienation; for what is at stake is that the child learns "that

nothing in his character, no possession he owns, no inheritance of name or talent, no work he has done, is valued for itself, but only for its effect on others. . . .[26]

Riesman's comment brings us to the second feature of special interest in the idea of self-alienation. I have noted that this idea invokes some explicit or implicit human ideal. And I have implied that such comparisons of modern man with some idealized human condition should be viewed simply as rhetorical appeals to nature—an important rhetoric for some purposes, though not very useful in the non-analytical form it generally takes. But Riesman's assertion contains, it seems to me, one of the key elements of this rhetoric—one, indeed, that not only reflects the original interest of Marx in alienation but also one that may be specifiable in a language consistent with our other uses of alienation.

I refer to that aspect of self-alienation which is generally characterized as the loss of intrinsic meaning or pride in work, a loss which Marx and others have held to be an essential feature of modern alienation. This notion of the loss of intrinsically meaningful satisfaction is embodied in a number of ways in current discussions of alienation. Glazer, for example, contrasts the alienated society with simpler societies characterized by "spontaneous acts of work and play which were their own reward."[27]

Although this meaning of alienation is difficult to specify, the basic idea contained in the rhetoric of self-estrangement—the idea of instrinsically meaningful activity—can, perhaps, be recast into more manageable social learning terms. One way to state such a meaning is to see alienation as *the degree of dependence of the given behavior upon anticipated future rewards*, that is, upon rewards that lie outside the activity itself. In these terms, the worker who works merely for his salary, the housewife who cooks simply to get it over with, or the other-directed type who acts "only for its effect on others"—all these (at different levels, again) are instances of self-estrangement. In this view, what has been called self-estrangement refers essentially to the inability of the individual to find self-rewarding—or in Dewey's phrase, self-consummatory—activities that engage him.

## CONCLUSION

I am aware that there are unclarities and difficulties of considerable importance in these five varieties of alienation (especially, I believe, in the attempted solution of "self-estrangement" and the idea of "meaninglessness"). But I have attempted, first, to distinguish the meanings that have been given to alienation, and second, to work toward a more useful conception of each of these meanings.

It may seem, at first reading, that the language employed—the language of expectations and rewards—is somewhat strange, if not misguided. But I would urge that the language is more traditional than it may seem. Nathan Glazer certainly is well within that tradition when, in a summary essay on alienation, he speaks of our modern "... sense of the splitting asunder of what was once together, the breaking of the seamless mold in which *values*, *behavior*, and *expectations* were once cast into interlocking forms."[28] These same three concepts—reward value, behavior, and expectancy—are key elements in the theory that underlies the present characterization of alienation. Perhaps, on closer inspection, the reader will find only that initial strangenesss which is often experienced when we translate what was sentimentally understood into a secular question.

## REFERENCES AND NOTES

1  New York: Oxford, 1953, p. 15.
2  T. W. Adorno *et al.*, *The Authoritarian Personality*, New York: Harper, 1950, pp. 617ff.
3  R. K. Merton, *Mass Persuasion*, New York: Harper, 1946, p. 143.
4  Erich Fromm, *The Sane Society*, New York: Rinehart, 1955.
5  *The Tower and the Abyss*, New York: Braziller, 1957, p. 43.
6  An effort in this direction is reported by John P. Clark in "Measuring Alienation within a Social System," *American Sociological Review*, vol. 24 (December 1959), pp. 849–852.
7  The concepts of expectancy and reward, or reinforcement value, are the central elements in J. B. Rotter's "social learning theory"; see *Social Learning and Clinical Psychology*, New York: Prentice-Hall, 1954. My discussion seeks to cast the various meanings of alienation in a form that is roughly consistent with this theory, though not formally expressed in terms of it.
8  H. H. Gerth and C. W. Mills, *From Max Weber: Essays in Sociology*, New York: Oxford, 1946, p. 50.
9  Cf. W. H. James and J. B. Rotter, "Partial and One Hundred Percent Reinforcement under Chance and Skill Conditions," *Journal of Experimental Psychology*, vol. 55 (May 1958), pp. 397–403. Rotter and his students have shown that the distinction between internal and external control (a distinction which is also cast in expectancy terms) has an important bearing on learning theory. The propositions in that theory, they argue, are based too exclusively on experimental studies which simulate conditions of "external control," where the subject "is likely to perceive reinforcements as being beyond his control and primarily contingent upon external conditions" (p. 397). Compare this use of what is essentially a notion of powerlessness with, for example, Norman Podheretz's discussion of the "Beat Generation": "Being apathetic about the Cold War is to admit that you have a sense of utter helplessness in the face of forces apparently beyond the control of man." "Where Is the Beat Generation Going?" *Esquire*, vol. 50 (December 1958), p. 148.
10  It seems best, in regard to the adjustment question, to follow Gwynn Nettler's view. He points out that the concepts of alienation and anomie should not "be equated, as they so often are, with personal disorganization defined as intrapersonal goallessness, or lack of 'internal coherence' . . . [their] bearing on emotional sickness must be independently investigated." "A Measure of Alienation," *American Sociological Review*, vol. 22 (December 1957), p. 672. For a contrasting view, see Nathan Glazer's "The Alienation of Modern Man," *Commentary*, vol. 3 (April 1947), p. 380, in which he comments: "If we approach alienation in this way, it becomes less a description of a single specific symptom than an omnibus of psychological disturbances having a similar root cause—in this case, modern social organization."

With regard to the question of the generality of powerlessness, I assume that high or low expectancies for the control of outcomes through one's own behavior (1) will vary with the behavior involved—e.g., control over academic achievement or grades, as against control over unemployment; and (2) will be differentially realistic in different areas (it is one thing to feel powerless with regard to war and quite another, presumably, to feel powerless in making friends). My chief point is that these are matters that can be empirically rather than conceptually solved; we should not, therefore, build either "generality" or "adjustment" into our concept of alienation. This same view is applied in the discussion of the other four types of alienation.

11    See, respectively, Adorno *et al., op. cit.*; Hadley Cantril, *The Psychology of Social Movements*, New York: Wiley, 1941; and Eric Hoffer, *The True Believer*, New York: Harper, 1950, p. 90.

12    Karl Mannheim, *Man and Society in an Age of Reconstruction*, New York: Harcourt, Brace, 1940, p. 59.

13    C. Wright Mills' description reflects this view: "The intellectual who remains free may continue to learn more and more about modern society, but he finds the centers of political initiative less and less accessible. . . . He comes to feel helpless in the fundamental sense that he cannot control what he is able to foresee." *White Collar*, New York: Oxford, 1951, p. 157. The same distinction is found in F. L. Strodtbeck's empirical comparison of Italian and Jewish values affecting mobility: "For the Jew, there was always the expectation that everything could be understood, if perhaps not controlled." "Family Interaction, Values and Achievement," in D. C. McClelland *et al., Talent and Society*, New York: Van Nostrand, 1958, p. 155.

14    Thorstein Veblen argues the same point, in his own inimitable style, in a discussion of "The Belief in Luck": ". . . the extra-causal propensity or agent has a very high utility as a recourse in perplexity" [providing the individual] "a means of escape from the difficulty of accounting for phenomena in terms of causal sequences." *The Theory of the Leisure Class*, New York: Macmillan, 1899; Modern Library Edition, 1934, p. 386.

15    Merton, *op. cit.*, p. 143.

16    R. K. Merton, *Social Theory and Social Structure*, Glencoe, Ill.: The Free Press, 1949, p. 128.

17    *Ibid.*, pp. 148–149, 138.

18    *Human Relations*, vol. 10 (February 1957), p. 49 (italics added).

19    *Ibid.*, p. 59. Obviously, the distinction (discussed above under "powerlessness") between objective condition and individual expectancy applies in the case of anomie. For a recent treatment of this point, see R. K. Merton, *Social Theory and Social Structure*, rev. ed., Glencoe, Ill.: The Free Press, 1957, pp. 161–194. It is clear that Srole's well-known anomie scale refers to individual experience (and that it embodies a heavy adjustment component). It is not so clear how the metaphorical language of "normative breakdown" and "structural strain" associated with the conception of anomie as a social condition is to be made empirically useful. It may be further noted

that the idea of rulelessness has often been used to refer to situations in which norms are unclear as well as to those in which norms lose their regulative force. I focused on the latter case in this section; but the former aspect of anomie is contained in the idea of "meaninglessness." The idea of meaninglessness, as defined above, surely includes situations involving uncertainty resulting from obscurity of rules, the absence of clear criteria for resolving ambiguities, and the like.

20    Nettler, *op. cit.*, p. 672.

21    *Ibid.*, p. 675. A scale to measure social isolation (as well as powerlessness and meaninglessness) has been developed by Dean, but the meanings are not the same as those given here; the "social isolation" measure, for example, deals with the individual's friendship status (see Dwight Dean, "Alienation and Political Apathy," Ph.D. thesis, Ohio State University, 1956). It seems to me now, however, that this is not a very useful meaning, for two reasons. First, it comes very close to being a statement of either social adjustment or of simple differences in associational styles (i.e., some people are sociable and some are not), and as such seems irrelevant to the root historical notion of alienation. Second, the crucial part of this "social isolation" component in alienation— what Nisbet, for example, calls the "unattached" or the "isolated"—is better captured for analytical purposes, I believe, in the ideas of meaninglessness, normlessness, or isolation, as defined in expectancy or reward terms. That is to say, what remains, after sheer sociability is removed, is the kind of tenuousness of social ties that may be described as value uniqueness (isolation), deviation from approved means (normlessness), or the like.

22    Merton, "Social Structure and Anomie," *op. cit.*, pp. 144–145. Merton is describing a radical estrangement from societal values (often typified in the case of the intellectual)—i.e., the alienation is from reigning *central* features of the society, and what is sought is a "greatly" modified society. Presumably, the "isolation" mode of alienation, like the other versions, can be applied on the intimate or the grand scale, as noted above in the discussion of Goffman's analysis. Clearly, the person who rejects certain commonly held values in a given society, but who values the society's tolerance for such differences, is expressing a fundamental commitment to societal values and in this degree he is not alienated in the isolation sense.

23    Fromm, *op. cit.*, pp. 110, 120.

24    Mills, *op. cit.*, pp. 184, 188.

25    Fromm, *op. cit.*, pp. 131, 134 (italics in original).

26    David Riesman, *The Lonely Crowd*, New Haven, Conn.: Yale University Press, 1950, p. 49. Although

the idea of self-estrangement, when used in the alienation literature, usually carries the notion of a generally applicable human standard, it is sometimes the individual's standard that is at issue: to be alienated

in this sense is to be aware of a discrepancy between one's ideal self and one's actual self-image.

27  Glazer, *op. cit.*, p. 379.
28  Glazer, *op. cit.*, p. 378 (italics added).

## 10  THE ORGANIZATION MAN    WILLIAM H. WHYTE, JR.

Officially, we are a people who hold to the Protestant Ethic. Because of the denominational implications of the term many would deny its relevance to them, but let them eulogize the American Dream, however, and they virtually define the Protestant Ethic. Whatever the embroidery, there is almost always the thought that pursuit of individual salvation through hard work, thrift, and competitive struggle is the heart of the American achievement.

But the harsh facts of organization life simply do not jibe with these precepts. This conflict is certainly not a peculiarly American development. In their own countries such Europeans as Max Weber and Durkheim many years ago foretold the change, and though Europeans now like to see their troubles as an American export, the problems they speak of stem from a bureaucratization of society that has affected every Western country.

It is in America, however, that the contrast between the old ethic and current reality has been most apparent—and most poignant. Of all peoples it is we who have led in the public worship of individualism. One hundred years ago De Tocqueville was noting that though our special genius—and failing—lay in co-operative action, we talked more than others of personal independence and freedom. We kept on, and as late as the twenties, when big organization was long since a fact, affirmed the old faith as if nothing had really changed at all.

Reprinted from *The Organization Man*, pp. 4–24, by permission of the author, Doubleday & Company, Inc., Simon & Schuster, Inc., and Jonathan Cape, Ltd. Copyright © 1956 by William H. Whyte, Jr.

Today many still try, and it is the members of the kind of organization most responsible for the change, the corporation, who try the hardest. It is the corporation man whose institutional ads protest so much that Americans speak up in town meeting, that Americans are the best inventors because Americans don't care that other people scoff, that Americans are the best soldiers because they have so much initiative and native ingenuity, that the boy selling papers on the street corner is the prototype of our business society. Collectivism? He abhors it, and when he makes his ritualistic attack on Welfare Statism, it is in terms of a Protestant Ethic undefiled by change—the sacredness of property, the enervating effect of security, the virtues of thrift, of hard work and independence. Thanks be, he says, that there are some people left—e.g., businessmen—to defend the American Dream.

He is not being hypocritical, only compulsive. He honestly wants to believe he follows the tenets he extols, and if he extols them so frequently it is, perhaps, to shut out a nagging suspicion that he, too, the last defender of the faith, is no longer pure. Only by using the language of individualism to describe the collective can he stave off the thought that he himself is in a collective as pervading as any ever dreamed of by the reformers, the intellectuals, and the utopian visionaries he so regularly warns against.

The older generation may still convince themselves; the younger generation does not. When a young man says that to make a living these days you must do what somebody else wants you to do, he states it not only as a fact of life that must be accepted but as an inherently good proposition. If the American Dream deprecates this for him, it is the American Dream that is going to have to give, whatever its more elderly guardians may think. People grow restive with a mythology that is too distant from the way things actually are, and as more and more lives have been encompassed by the organization way of life, the pressures for an accompanying ideological shift have been mounting. The pressures of the group, the frustrations of individual creativity, the anonymity of achievement: are these defects to struggle against—or are they virtues in disguise? The organization man seeks a redefinition of his place on earth—a faith that will satisfy him that what he must endure has a deeper meaning than appears on the surface. He needs, in short, something that will do for him what the Protestant Ethic did once. And slowly, almost imperceptibly, a body of thought has been coalescing that does that.

I am going to call it a Social Ethic. With reason it could be called an organization ethic, or a bureaucratic ethic; more than anything else it rationalizes the organization's demands for fealty and gives those who offer it wholeheartedly a sense of dedication in doing so—*in extremis*, you might say, it converts what would seem in other times a bill of no rights into a restatement of individualism.

But there is a real moral imperative behind it, and whether one inclines to its beliefs or not he must acknowledge that this moral basis, not mere expediency, is the source of its power. Nor is it simply an opiate for those who must work in big organizations. The search for a secular faith that it represents can be found throughout our society—and among those who swear they would never set foot in a corporation or a government bureau. Though it has its greatest applicability to the organization man, its ideological underpinnings have been provided not by the organization man but by intellectuals he knows little of and toward whom, indeed, he tends to be rather suspicious.

Any groove of abstraction, Whitehead once remarked, is bound to be an inadequate way of describing reality, and so with the concept of the Social Ethic. It is an attempt to illustrate an under-

lying consistency in what in actuality is by no means an orderly system of thought. No one says, "I believe in the social ethic," and though many would subscribe wholeheartedly to the separate ideas that make it up, these ideas have yet to be put together in the final, harmonious synthesis. But the unity is there.

In looking at what might seem dissimilar aspects of organization society, it is this unity I wish to underscore. The "professionalization" of the manager, for example, and the drive for a more practical education are parts of the same phenomenon; just as the student now feels technique more vital than content, so the trainee believes managing an end in itself, an *expertise* relatively independent of the content of what is being managed. And the reasons are the same. So too in other sectors of our society; for all the differences in particulars, dominant is a growing accommodation to the needs of society—and a growing urge to justify it.

Let me now define my terms. By Social Ethic I mean that contemporary body of thought which makes morally legitimate the pressures of society against the individual. Its major propositions are three: a belief in the group as the source of creativity; a belief in "belongingness" as the ultimate need of the individual; and a belief in the application of science to achieve the belongingness.

I will explore these ideas more thoroughly, but for the moment I think the gist can be paraphrased thus: Man exists as a unit of society. Of himself, he is isolated, meaningless; only as he collaborates with others does he become worth while, for by sublimating himself in the group, he helps produce a whole that is greater than the sum of its parts. There should be, then, no conflict between man and society. What we think are conflicts are misunderstandings, breakdowns in communications. By applying the methods of science to human relations we can eliminate these obstacles to consensus and create an equilibrium in which society's needs and the needs of the individual are one and the same.

Essentially, it is a utopian faith. Superficially, it seems dedicated to the practical problems of organization life, and its proponents often use the word *hard* (versus *soft*) to describe their approach. But it is the long-range promise that animates its followers, for it relates techniques to the vision of a finite, achievable harmony. It is quite reminiscent of the beliefs of utopian communities of the 1840's. As in the Owen communities, there is the same idea that man's character is decided, almost irretrievably, by his environment. As in the Fourier communities, there is the same faith that there need be no conflict between the individual's aspirations and the community's wishes, because it is the natural order of things that the two be synonymous.

Like the utopian communities, it interprets society in a fairly narrow, immediate sense. One can believe man has a social obligation and that the individual must ultimately contribute to the community without believing that group harmony is the test of it. In the Social Ethic I am describing, however, man's obligation is in the here and now; his duty is not so much to the community in a broad sense but to the actual, physical one about him, and the idea that in isolation from it—or active rebellion against it—he might eventually discharge the greater service is little considered. In practice, those who most eagerly subscribe to the Social Ethic worry very little over the long-range problems of society. It is not that they don't care but rather that they tend to assume that the ends of organization and morality coincide, and on such matters as social welfare they give their proxy to the organization.

It is possible that I am attaching too much weight to what, after all, is something of a mythology. Those more sanguine than I have argued that this faith is betrayed by reality in some key respects and that because it cannot long hide from organization man that life is still essentially competitive the faith must fall of its own weight. They also maintain that the Social Ethic is only one trend in a society which is a prolific breeder of counter-trends. The farther the pendulum swings, they believe, the more it must eventually swing back.

I am not persuaded. We are indeed a flexible people, but society is not a clock and to stake so much on counter-trends is to put a rather heavy burden on providence. Let me get ahead of my story a bit with two examples of trend vs. counter-trend. One is the long-term swing to the highly vocational business administration courses. Each year for seven years I have collected all the speeches by businessmen, educators, and others on the subject, and invariably each year the gist of them is that this particular pendulum has swung much too far and that there will shortly be a reversal. Similarly sanguine, many academic people have been announcing that they discern the beginnings of a popular swing back to the humanities. Another index is the growth of personality testing. Regularly year after year many social scientists have assured me that this bowdlerization of psychology is a contemporary aberration soon to be laughed out of court.

Meanwhile, the organization world grinds on. Each year the number of business-administration majors has increased over the last year—until, in 1954, they together made up the largest single field of undergraduate instruction outside of the field of education itself. Personality testing? Again, each year the number of people subjected to it has grown, and the criticism has served mainly to make organizations more adept in sugar-coating their purpose. No one can say whether these trends will continue to outpace the counter-trends, but neither can we trust that an equilibrium-minded providence will see to it that excesses will cancel each other out. Counter-trends there are. There always have been, and in the sweep of ideas ineffectual many have proved to be.

It is also true that the Social Ethic is something of a mythology, and there is a great difference between mythology and practice. An individualism as stringent, as selfish as that often preached in the name of the Protestant Ethic would never have been tolerated, and in reality our predecessors co-operated with one another far more skillfully than nineteenth-century oratory would suggest. Something of the obverse is true of the Social Ethic; so complete a denial of individual will won't work either, and even the most willing believers in the group harbor some secret misgivings, some latent antagonism toward the pressures they seek to deify.

But the Social Ethic is no less powerful for that, and though it can never produce the peace of mind it seems to offer, it will help shape the nature of the quest in the years to come. The old dogma of individualism betrayed reality too, yet few would argue, I dare say, that it was not an immensely powerful influence in the time of its dominance. So I argue of the Social Ethic; call it mythology, if you will, but it is becoming the dominant one.

In the first part of this book I wish to go into some of the ideas that have helped produce the Social Ethic. I do not intend an intellectual history; my aim is the more limited one of suggesting how deep are its roots and that it is not a temporary phenomenon triggered by the New Deal or the war or our recent prosperity.

I will then pick up the organization man in college, follow him through his initial indoctrination in organization life, and explore the impact of the group way upon him. While I will speak of the corporation man more than any other, I wish to show the universality of the Social Ethic. I will turn, accordingly, to the research laboratory and academic life and argue that the inclination to the co-operative ideal has had just as important consequences in these areas also. To illustrate further the universality of the Social Ethic, I will take up its expression in popular fiction. This will bring me finally to what I consider the best place to get a preview of the direction the Social Ethic is likely to take in the future.

This is the new suburbia, the packaged villages that have become the dormitory of the new generation of organization men. They are not typical American communities, but because they provide such a cross section of young organization people we can see in bolder relief than elsewhere the kind of world organization man wants and may in time bring about. Here I will go into the tremendous effect transiency has had on the organization people and how their religious life, their politics and the way they take to their neighbors reveal the new kind of rootedness they are looking for. And,

finally, the moral of it all as they explain it to their children—the next generation of organization people.

While the burden of this book is reportorial, I take a position and, in fairness to the reader, I would like to make plain the assumptions on which I base it. To that end, let me first say what I am *not* talking about.

This book is not a plea for nonconformity. Such pleas have an occasional therapeutic value, but as an abstraction, nonconformity is an empty goal, and rebellion against prevailing opinion merely because it is prevailing should no more be praised than acquiescence to it. Indeed, it is often a mask for cowardice, and few are more pathetic than those who flaunt outer differences to expiate their inner surrender.

I am not, accordingly, addressing myself to the surface uniformities of U.S. life. There will be no strictures in this book against "Mass Man"—a person the author has never met—nor will there be any strictures against ranch wagons, or television sets, or gray flannel suits. They are irrelevant to the main problem, and, furthermore, there's no harm in them. I would not wish to go to the other extreme and suggest that these uniformities per se are good, but the spectacle of people following current custom for lack of will or imagination to do anything else is hardly a new failing, and I am not convinced that there has been any significant change in this respect except in the nature of the things we conform to. Unless one believes poverty ennobling, it is difficult to see the three-button suit as more of a strait jacket than overalls, or the ranch-type house than old law tenements.

And how important, really, are these uniformities to the central issue of individualism? We must not let the outward forms deceive us. If individualism involves following one's destiny as one's own conscience directs, it must for most of us be a realizable destiny, and a sensible awareness of the rules of the game can be a condition of individualism as well as a constraint upon it. The man who drives a Buick Special and lives in a ranch-type house just like hundreds of other ranch-type houses can assert himself as effectively and courageously against his particular society as the bohemian against his particular society. He usually does not, it is true, but if he does, the surface uniformities can serve quite well as protective coloration. The organization people who are best able to control their environment rather than be controlled by it are well aware that they are not too easily distinguishable from the others in the outward obeisances paid to the good opinions of others. And that is one of the reasons they do control. They disarm society.

I do not equate the Social Ethic with conformity, nor do I believe those who urge it wish it to be, for most of them believe deeply that their work will help, rather than harm, the individual. I think their ideas are out of joint with the needs of the times they invoke, but it is their ideas, and not their good will, I wish to question. As for the lackeys of organization and the charlatans, they are not worth talking about.

Neither do I intend this book as a censure of the fact of organization society. We have quite enough problems today without muddying the issue with misplaced nostalgia, and in contrasting the old ideology with the new I mean no contrast of paradise with paradise lost, an idyllic eighteenth century with a dehumanized twentieth. Whether or not our own era is worse than former ones in the climate of freedom is a matter that can be left to later historians, but for the purposes of this book I write with the optimistic premise that individualism is as possible in our times as in others.

I speak of individualism *within* organization life. This is not the only kind, and someday it may be that the mystics and philosophers more distant from it may prove the crucial figures. But they are affected too by the center of society, and they can be of no help unless they grasp the nature of the main stream. Intellectual scoldings based on an impossibly lofty ideal may be of some service in upbraiding organization man with his failures, but they can give him no guidance. The organization man may agree that industrialism has destroyed the moral fabric of society and that we need to return to the agrarian virtues, or that business needs to be broken up, and so on. But he will go

his way with his own dilemmas left untouched.

I am going to argue that he should fight the organization. But not self-destructively. He may tell the boss to go to hell, but he is going to have another boss, and, unlike the heroes of popular fiction, he cannot find surcease by leaving the arena to be a husbandman. If he chafes at the pressures of his particular organization, either he must succumb, resist them, try to change them, or move to yet another organization.

Every decision he faces on the problem of the individual versus authority is something of a dilemma. It is not a case of whether he should fight against black tyranny or blaze a new trail against patient stupidity. That would be easy—intellectually, at least. The real issue is far more subtle. For it is not the evils of organization life that puzzle him, *but its very beneficence.* He is imprisoned in brotherhood. Because his area of maneuver seems so small and because the trapping so mundane, his fight lacks the heroic cast, but it is for all this as tough a fight as ever his predecessors had to fight.

Thus to my thesis. I believe the emphasis of the Social Ethic is wrong for him. People do have to work with others, yes; the well-functioning team is a whole greater than the sum of its parts, yes—all this is indeed true. But is it the truth that now needs belaboring? Precisely because it is an age of organization, it is the other side of the coin that needs emphasis. We do need to know how to cooperate with The Organization but, more than ever, so do we need to know how to resist it. Out of context this would be an irresponsible statement. Time and place are critical, and history has taught us that a philosophical individualism can venerate conflict too much and co-operation too little. But what is the context today? The tide has swung far enough the other way, I submit, that we need not worry that a counteremphasis will stimulate people to an excess of individualism.

The energies Americans have devoted to the co-operative, to the social, are not to be demeaned; we would not, after all, have such a problem to discuss unless we had learned to adapt ourselves to an increasingly collective society as well as we have. An ideal of individualism which denies the obligations of man to others is manifestly impossible in a society such as ours, and it is a credit to our wisdom that while we preached it, we never fully practiced it.

But in searching for that elusive middle of the road, we have gone very far afield, and in our attention to making organization work we have come close to deifying it. We are describing its defects as virtues and denying that there is—or should be—a conflict between the individual and organization. This denial is bad for the organization. It is worse for the individual. What it does, in soothing him, is to rob him of the intellectual armor he so badly needs. For the more power organization has over him, the more he needs to recognize the area where he must assert himself against it. And this, almost because we have made organization life so equable, has become excruciatingly difficult.

To say that we must recognize the dilemmas of organization society is not to be inconsistent with the hopeful premise that organization society can be as compatible for the individual as any previous society. We are not hapless beings caught in the grip of forces we can do little about, and wholesale damnations of our society only lend a further mystique to organization. Organization has been made by man; it can be changed by man. It has not been the immutable course of history that has produced such constrictions on the individual as personality tests. It is organization man who has brought them to pass and it is he who can stop them.

The fault is not in organization, in short; it is in our worship of it. It is in our vain quest for a utopian equilibrium, which would be horrible if it ever did come to pass; it is in the soft-minded denial that there is a conflict between the individual and society. There must always be, and it is the price of being an individual that he must face these conflicts. He cannot evade them, and in seeking an ethic that offers a spurious peace of mind, thus does he tyrannize himself.

There are only a few times in organization life when he can wrench his destiny into his own hands—and if he does not fight then, he will make a surrender that will later mock him. But when is that time? Will he know the time when he sees it? By what standards is he to judge? He does feel an obligation to the group; he does sense moral constraints on his free will. If he goes against the group, is he being courageous—or just stubborn? Helpful—or selfish? Is he, as he so often wonders, right after all? It is in the resolution of a multitude of such dilemmas, I submit, that the real issue of individualism lies today.

## THE DECLINE OF THE PROTESTANT ETHIC

Let us go back a moment to the turn of the century. If we pick up the Protestant Ethic as it was then expressed we will find it apparently in full flower. We will also find, however, an ethic that already had been strained by reality. The country had changed. The ethic had not.

Here, in the words of banker Henry Clews as he gave some fatherly advice to Yale students in 1908, is the Protestant Ethic in purest form:[1]

SURVIVAL OF FITTEST  You may start in business, or the professions, with your feet on the bottom rung of the ladder; it rests with you to acquire the strength to climb to the top. You can do so if you have the will and the force to back you. There is always plenty of room at the top. . . . Success comes to the man who tries to compel success to yield to him. Cassius spoke well to Brutus when he said, "The Fault is not in our stars, dear Brutus, that we are underlings, but in our natures."

THRIFT  Form the habit as soon as you become a money-earner, or money-maker, of saving a part of your salary, or profits. Put away one dollar out of every ten you earn. The time will come in your lives when, if you have a little money, you can control circumstances; otherwise circumstances will control you. . . .

Note the use of such active words as *climb*, *force*, *compel*, *control*. As stringently as ever before, the Protestant Ethic still counseled struggle against one's environment—the kind of practical, here and now struggle that paid off in material rewards. And spiritually too. The hard-boiled part of the Protestant Ethic was incomplete, of course, without the companion assurance that such success was moral as well as practical. To continue with Mr. Clews:

Under this free system of government, whereby individuals are free to get a living or to pursue wealth as each chooses, the usual result is competition. Obviously, then, competition really means industrial freedom. Thus, anyone may choose his own trade or profession, or, if he does not like it, he may change. He is free to work hard or not; he may make his own bargains and set his price upon his labor or his products. He is free to acquire property to any extent, or to part with it. By dint of greater effort or superior skill, or by intelligence, if he can make better wages, he is free to live better, just as his neighbor is free to follow his example and to learn to excel him in turn. If anyone has a genius for making and managing money, he is free to exercise his genius, just as another is free to handle his tools. . . . If an individual enjoys his money, gained by energy and successful effort, his neighbors are urged to work the harder, that they and their children may have the same enjoyment.

It was an exuberantly optimistic ethic. If everyone could believe that seeking his self-interest automatically improves the lot of all, then the application of hard work should eventually produce a heaven on earth. Some, like the garrulous Mr. Clews, felt it already had:

America is the true field for the human race. It is the hope and the asylum for the oppressed and downtrodden of every clime. It is the inspiring example of America—peerless among the nations of the earth, the brightest star in the political firmament—that is leavening the hard lump of aristocracy and promoting a democratic spirit throughout the world. It is indeed the gem of the ocean to which the world may well offer homage. Here merit is the sole test.

Birth is nothing. The fittest survive. Merit is the supreme and only qualification essential to success. Intelligence rules worlds and systems of worlds. It is the dread monarch of illimitable space, and in human society, especially in America, it shines as a diadem on the foreheads of those who stand in the foremost ranks of human enterprise. Here only a natural order of nobility is recognized, and its motto, without coat of arms or boast of heraldry, is "Intelligence and integrity."

Without this ethic capitalism would have been impossible. Whether the Protestant Ethic preceded capitalism, as Max Weber argued, or whether it grew up as a consequence, in either event it provided a degree of unity between the way people wanted to behave and the way they thought they *ought* to behave, and without this ideology, society would have been hostile to the entrepreneur. Without the comfort of the Protestant Ethic, he couldn't have gotten away with his acquisitions— not merely because other people wouldn't have allowed him, but because his own conscience would not have. But now he was fortified by the assurance that he was pursuing his obligation to God, and before long, what for centuries had been looked on as the meanest greed, a rising middle class would interpret as the earthly manifestations of God's will.

But the very industrial revolution which this highly serviceable ethic begot in time began to confound it. The inconsistencies were a long while in making themselves apparent. The nineteenth-century inheritors of the ethic were creating an increasingly collective society but steadfastly they denied the implications of it. In current retrospect the turn of the century seems a golden age of individualism, yet by the 1880s the corporation had already shown the eventual bureaucratic direction it was going to take. As institutions grew in size and became more stratified, they made all too apparent inconsistencies which formerly could be ignored. One of the key assumptions of the Protestant Ethic had been that success was due neither to luck nor to the environment but only to one's natural qualities—if men grew rich it was because they deserved to. But the big organization became a standing taunt to this dream of individual success. Quite obviously to anyone who worked in a big organization, those who survived best were not necessarily the fittest but, in more cases than not, those who by birth and personal connections had the breaks.

As organizations continued to expand, the Protestant Ethic became more and more divergent from the reality The Organization was itself creating. The managers steadfastly denied the change, but they, as much as those they led, were affected by it. Today, some still deny the inconsistency or blame it on creeping socialism; for the younger generation of managers however, the inconsistencies have become importuning.

Thrift, for example. How can the organization man be thrifty? Other people are thrifty *for* him. He still buys most of his own life insurance, but for the bulk of his rainy-day saving, he gives his proxy to the financial and personnel departments of his organization. In his professional capacity also thrift is becoming a little un-American. The same man who will quote from Benjamin Franklin on thrift for the house organ would be horrified if consumers took these maxims to heart and started putting more money into savings and less into installment purchases. No longer can he afford the luxury of damning the profligacy of the public; not in public, at any rate. He not only has to persuade people to buy more but persuade them out of any guilt feelings they might have for following his advice. Few talents are more commercially sought today than the knack of describing departures from the Protestant Ethic as reaffirmations of it.[2]

In an advertisement that should go down in social history, the J. Walter Thompson agency has hit the problem of absolution head-on. It quotes Benjamin Franklin on the benefits of spending. "Is not the hope of being one day able to purchase and enjoy luxuries a great spur to labor and industry? . . . May not luxury therefore produce more than it consumes, if, without such a spur, people would be, as they are naturally enough inclined to

be, lazy and indolent?" This thought, the ad says, in a meaningful aside, "appears to be a mature afterthought, qualifying his earlier and more familiar writings on the importance of thrift."

"Hard work?" What price capitalism, the question is now so frequently asked, unless we turn our productivity into more leisure, more of the good life? To the organization man this makes abundant sense, and he is as sensitive to the bogy of overwork and ulcers as his forebears were to the bogy of slothfulness. But he is split. He believes in leisure, but so does he believe in the Puritan insistence on hard, self-denying work—and there are, alas, only twenty-four hours a day. How, then, to be "broad gauge"? The "broad-gauge" model we hear so much about these days is the man who keeps his work separate from leisure and the rest of his life. Any organization man who managed to accomplish this feat wouldn't get very far. He still works hard, in short, but now he has to feel somewhat guilty about it.

*Self-reliance?* The corporation estates have been expanding so dynamically of late that until about now the management man could suppress the thought that he was a bureaucrat—bureaucrats, as every businessman knew, were those people down in Washington who preferred safety to adventure. Just when the recognition began to dawn, no one can say, but since the war the younger generation of management haven't been talking of self-reliance and adventure with quite the straight face of their elders.

That upward path toward the rainbow of achievement leads smack through the conference room. No matter what name the process is called—permissive management, multiple management, the art of administration—the committee way simply can't be equated with the "rugged" individualism that is supposed to be the business of business. Not for lack of ambition do the younger men dream so moderately; what they lack is the illusion that they will carry on in the great entrepreneurial spirit. Although they cannot bring themselves to use the word bureaucrat, the approved term—the "administrator"—is not signally different in its implications. The man of the future, as junior executives see him, is not the individualist but the man who works through others for others.

Let me pause for a moment to emphasize a necessary distinction. Within business there are still many who cling resolutely to the Protestant Ethic, and some with as much rapacity as drove any nineteenth-century buccaneer. But only rarely are they of The Organization. Save for a small, and spectacular, group of financial operators, most who adhere to the old creed are small businessmen, and to group them as part of the "business community," while convenient, implies a degree of ideological kinship with big business that does not exist.

Out of inertia, the small business is praised as the acorn from which a great oak may grow, the shadow of one man that may lengthen into a large enterprise. Examine businesses with fifty or less employees, however, and it becomes apparent the sentimentality obscures some profound differences. You will find some entrepreneurs in the classic sense—men who develop new products, new appetites, or new systems of distribution—and some of these enterprises may mature into self-perpetuating institutions. But very few.

The great majority of small business firms cannot be placed on any continuum with the corporation. For one thing, they are rarely engaged in primary industry; for the most part they are the laundries, the insurance agencies, the restaurants, the drugstores, the bottling plants, the lumber yards, the automobile dealers. They are vital, to be sure, but essentially they service an economy; they do not create new money within their area and they are dependent ultimately on the business and agriculture that does.

In this dependency they react more as antagonists than allies with the corporation. The corporation, it has become clear, is expansionist—a force for change that is forever a threat to the economics of the small businessman. By instinct he inclines to the monopolistic and the restrictive. When the druggists got the "Fair Trade" laws passed it was not only the manufacturers (and customers) they were rebelling against but the whole mass

economy movement of the twentieth century.

The tail wagged the dog in this case and it still often does. That it can, in the face of the growing power of the corporation, illustrates again the dominance mythology can have over reality. Economically, many a small businessman is a counter-revolutionist and the revolution he is fighting is that of the corporation as much as the New or Fair Deal. But the corporation man still clings to the idea that the two are firm allies, and on some particulars, such as fair trade, he often makes policy on this basis when in fact it is against the corporation's interests to do so.

But the revolution is not to be stopped by sentiment. Many anachronisms do remain; in personal income, for example, the corporation man who runs a branch plant on which a whole town depends is lucky to make half the income of the local car dealer or the man with the Coca-Cola franchise. The economy has a way of attending to these discrepancies, however, and the local businessman can smell the future as well as anyone else. The bland young man The Organization sent to town to manage the plant is almost damnably inoffensive; he didn't rent the old place on the hill but a smaller house, he drives an Olds instead of a Caddy, and when he comes to the Thursday luncheons he listens more than he talks. But he's the future just the same.

I have been talking of the impact of organization on the Protestant Ethic; just as important, however, was the intellectual assault. In the great revolt against traditionalism that began around the turn of the century, William James, John Dewey, Charles Beard, Thorstein Veblen, the muckrakers and a host of reformers brought the anachronisms of the Protestant Ethic under relentless fire, and in so doing helped lay the groundwork for the Social Ethic. It would be a long time before organization men would grasp the relevance of these new ideas, and to this day many of the most thoroughgoing pragmatists in business would recoil at being grouped with the intellectuals. (And vice versa.) But the two movements were intimately related. To what degree the intellectuals were a cause of change, or a manifestation, no one can say for certain, but more presciently than those in organization they grasped the antithesis between the old concept of the rational, unbeholden individual and the world one had to live in. They were not rebels against society; what they fought was the denial of society's power, and they provided an intellectual framework that would complement, rather than inhibit, the future growth of big organization.

It is not in the province of this book to go into a diagnosis of the ideas of Dewey and James and the other pragmatists. But there is one point of history I think very much needs making at this time. Many people still look on the decline of the Protestant Ethic as our fall from grace, a detour from Americanism for which we can blame pragmatism, ethical relativism, Freudianism and other such developments. These movements have contributed much to the Social Ethics, and many of their presuppositions are as shaky as those they replaced. To criticize them on this score is in order; to criticize them as having subverted the American temper, however, is highly misleading.

Critics of pragmatism, and followers too, should remember the context of the times in which the pragmatists made their case. The pragmatists' emphasis on social utility may be redundant for today's needs, but when they made their case it was not a time when psychology or adjustment or social living were popular topics but at a time when the weight of conservative opinion denied that there was anything much that needed adjusting. Quite clearly, revolt was in order. The growth of the organization society did demand a recognition that man was not entirely a product of his free will; the country did need an educational plant more responsive to the need of the people. It did need a new breeze, and if there had been no James or no Dewey, some form of pragmatism would probably have been invented anyway. Nonphilosophical Americans sensed that changes were in order too; what the philosophers of pragmatism did was to give them guidance and tell them in intellectually responsible terms that they were right in feeling that way.

Pragmatism's emphasis on the social and the practical, furthermore, was thoroughly in the American tradition. From the beginning, Americans had always been impatient with doctrines and systems; like the Puritans, many came here because and systems; like the Puritans, many came here because of a doctrine, but what they came to was a new environment that required some powerful adapting to, and whenever the doctrine got in the way of practicality, the doctrine lost out. Few people have had such a genius for bending ideals to the demands of the times, and the construction of fundamental theory, theological or scientific, has never excited Americans overmuch. Long before James, *Does it work?* was a respectable question to ask. If impatience at abstract thought was a defect, it was the defect of a virtue, and the virtue, call it what you will, has always been very close to pragmatism as Dewey and James defined it. By defining it they gave it coherence and power at a time when it needed assertion, but the inclination to the practical antedated the philosophy; it was not the product of it.

Reform was everywhere in the air. By the time of the First World War the Protestant Ethic had taken a shellacking from which it would not recover; rugged individualism and hard work had done wonders for the people to whom God in his infinite wisdom, as one put it, had given control of society. But it hadn't done so well for everyone else and now they, as well as the intellectuals, were all too aware of the fact.

The ground, in short, was ready, and though the conservative opinion that drew the fire of the rebels seemed entrenched, the basic temper of the country was so inclined in the other direction that emphasis on the social became the dominant current of U.S. thought. In a great outburst of curiosity, people became fascinated with the discovering of all the environmental pressures on the individual that previous philosophies had denied. As with Freud's discoveries, the findings of such inquiries were deeply disillusioning at first, but with characteristic exuberance Americans found a rainbow. Man might not be perfectible after all, but there was another dream and now at last it seemed practical: the perfectibility of *society.*

**REFERENCES AND NOTES**

1  Henry Clews, *Fifty Years in Wall Street*, New York: Irving Publishing Company, 1908.
2  Helping in this task is what a good part of "motivation research" is all about. Motivation researcher Dr. Ernest Dichter, in a bulletin to business, says, "We are now confronted with the problem of permitting the average American to feel moral even when he is flirt-ing, even when he is spending, even when he is not saving, even when he is taking two vacations a year and buying a second or third car. One of the basic problems of this prosperity, then, is to give people the sanction and justification to enjoy it and to demonstrate that the hedonistic approach to his life is a moral, not an immoral one."

## 11    YOUTH, CHANGE AND VIOLENCE     KENNETH KENISTON

We often feel that today's youth are somehow "different." There is something about today's world that seems to give the young a special restlessness, an increased impatience with the "hypocrisies" of the past, and yet an open gentleness and a searching honesty more intense than that of youth in the past. Much of what we see in today's students and nonstudents is of course familiar: to be young is in one sense always the same. But it is also new and different, as each generation confronts its unique historical position and role.

Yet we find it hard to define the difference. Partly the difficulty derives from the elusive nature of youth itself. Still this generation seems even more elusive than most—and that, too, may be one of the differences. Partly the problem stems from the sheer variety and number of "youth" in a society where youth is often protracted into the mid-twenties. No one characterization can be adequate to the drop-outs and stay-ins, hawks and doves, up-tights and cools, radicals and conservatives, heads and seekers that constitute American youth. But although we understand that the young are as various as the old in our complex society, the sense that they are different persists.

In giving today's American youth this special quality and mood, two movements have played a major role: the New Left and the hippies. Both groups are spontaneous creations of the young; both are in strong reaction to what Paul Goodman

Reprinted from *The American Scholar*, vol. 37 (spring 1968), pp. 227–245, by permission of the author.

calls the Organized System; **both seek alternatives** to the institutions of middle-class life. Radicals and hippies are also different from each other in numerous ways, from psychodynamics to ideology. The hippie has dropped out of a society he considers irredeemable: his attention is riveted on interior change and the expansion of personal consciousness. The radical has not given up on this society: his efforts are aimed at changing and redeeming it. Furthermore, both "movements" together comprise but a few percent of their contemporaries. But, although neither hippies nor New Leftists are "representative" of their generation, together they are helping to give this generation its distinctive mood. By examining the style of these young men and women, we come closer to understanding what makes their generation "different."

### THE STYLE OF POST-MODERN YOUTH

Today's youth is the first generation to grow up with "modern" parents; it is the first "post-modern" generation. This fact alone distinguishes it from previous generations and helps create a mood born out of modernity, affluence, rapid social change and violence. Despite the many pitfalls in the way of any effort to delineate a post-modern style, the effort seems worth making. For not only in America but in other nations, new styles of dissent and unrest have begun to appear, suggesting the slow emergence of youthful style that is a reflection of and reaction to the history of the past two decades.[1]

In emphasizing "style" rather than ideology, program or characteristics, I mean to suggest that the communalities in post-modern youth groups are to be found in the *way* they approach the world, rather than in their actual behavior, ideologies or goals. Indeed, the focus on process rather than program is itself a prime characteristic of the post-modern style, reflecting a world where flux is more obvious than fixed purpose. Post-modern youth, at least in America, is very much in process, unfinished in its development, psychologically open to a historically unpredictable future. In such a world, where ideologies come and go, and where revolutionary change is the rule, a style, a *way* of doing things, is more possible to identify than any fixed goals or constancies of behavior.

FLUIDITY, FLUX, MOVEMENT    Post-modern youth display a special personal and psychological openness, flexibility and unfinishedness. Although many of today's youth have achieved a sense of inner identity, the term "identity" suggests a fixity, stability and "closure" that many of them are not willing to accept: with these young men and women, it is not always possible to speak of the "normal resolution" of identity issues. Our earlier fear of the ominous psychiatric implications of "prolonged adolescence" must now be qualified by an awareness that in post-modern youth many adolescent concerns and qualities persist long past the time when (according to the standards in earlier eras) they should have ended. Increasingly, post-modern youth are tied to social and historical changes that have not occurred, and that may never occur. Thus, psychological "closure," shutting doors and burning bridges, becomes impossible. The concepts of the personal future and the "life work" are ever more hazily defined; the effort to change oneself, redefine oneself or reform oneself does not cease with the arrival of adulthood.

This fluidity and openness extends through all areas of life. Both hippie and New Left movements are nondogmatic, nonideological, and to a large extent hostile to doctrine and formula. In the New Left, the focus is on "tactics"; amongst hippies, on simple direct acts of love and communication. In neither group does one find clear-cut long-range plans, life patterns laid out in advance. The vision of the personal and collective future is blurred and vague: later adulthood is left deliberately open. In neither group is psychological development considered complete; in both groups, identity, like history, is fluid and indeterminate. In one sense, of course, identity development takes place; but, in another sense, identity is always undergoing transformations that parallel the transformations of the historical world.

GENERATIONAL IDENTIFICATION    Post-modern youth views itself primarily as a part of a generation rather than an organization; they identify with their contemporaries as a group, rather than with elders; and they do not have clearly defined leaders and heroes. Their deepest collective identification is to their own group or "Movement"—a term that in its ambiguous meanings points not only to the fluidity and openness of post-modern youth, but to its physical mobility, and the absence of traditional patterns of leadership and emulation. Among young radicals, for example, the absence of heroes or older leaders is impressive: even those five years older are sometimes viewed with mild amusement or suspicion. And although post-modern youth is often widely read in the "literature" of the New Left or that of consciousness-expansion, no one person or set of people is central to their intellectual beliefs. Although they live together in groups, these groups are without clear leaders.

Identification with a generational movement, rather than a cross-generational organization or a nongenerational ideology, distinguishes post-modern youth from its parents and from the "previous" generation. In addition, it also creates "generational" distinctions involving five years and less. Within the New Left, clear lines are drawn between the "old New Left" (approximate age, thirty), the New Left (between twenty-two and twenty-eight) and the "new New Left" or "young kids" (under twenty-two). Generations, then, are separated by a very brief span; and the individual's own phase of youthful usefulness—for example, as an organizer—is limited to a relatively few years. Generations come and go quickly; whatever is to be accomplished must therefore be done soon.

Generational consciousness also entails a feeling of psychological disconnection from previous generations, their life situations and their ideologies. Among young radicals, there is a strong feeling that the older ideologies are exhausted or irrelevant, expressed in detached amusement at the doctrinaire disputes of the "old Left" and impatience with "old liberals." Among hippies, the irrelevance of the parental past is even greater: if there is any source of insight, it is the timeless tradition of the East, not the values of the previous generation in American society. But in both groups, the central values are those created in the present by the "Movement" itself.

**PERSONALISM**    Both groups are highly personalistic in their styles of relationship. Among hippies, personalism usually entails privatism, a withdrawal from efforts to be involved in or to change the wider social world; among young radicals, personalism is joined with efforts to change the world. But despite this difference, both groups care most deeply about the creation of intimate, loving, open and trusting relationships between small groups of people. Writers who condemn the depersonalization of the modern world, who insist on "I-thou" relationships, or who expose the elements of anger, control and sadism in nonreciprocal relationships, find a ready audience in post-modern youth. The ultimate measure of man's life is the quality of his personal relationships; the greatest sin is to be unable to relate to others in a direct, face-to-face, one-to-one relationship.

The obverse of personalism is the discomfort created by any nonpersonal, "objectified," professionalized and, above all, exploitative relationship. Manipulation, power relationships, superordination, control and domination are at violent odds with the I-thou mystique. Failure to treat others as fully human, inability to enter into personal relationships with them, is viewed with dismay in others and with guilt in oneself. Even with opponents the goal is to establish intimate confronta-tions in which the issues can be discussed openly. When opponents refuse to "meet with" young radicals, this produces anger and frequently demonstrations. The reaction of the Harvard Students for a Democratic Society when Secretary McNamara did not meet with them to discuss American foreign policies is a case in point. Equally important, perhaps the most profound source of personal guilt among post-modern youth is the "hangups" that make intimacy and love difficult.

**NONASCETICISM**    Post-modern youth is nonascetic, expressive and sexually free. The sexual openness of the hippie world has been much discussed and criticized in the mass media. One finds a similar sexual and expressive freedom among many young radicals, although it is less provocatively demonstrative. It is of continuing importance to these young men and women to overcome and move beyond inhibition and puritanism to a greater physical expressiveness, sexual freedom, capacity for intimacy, and ability to enjoy life.

In the era of the Pill, then, responsible sexual expression becomes increasingly possible outside of marriage, at the same time that sexuality becomes less laden with guilt, fear and prohibition. As asceticism disappears, so does promiscuity: the personalism of post-modern youth requires that sexual expression must occur in the context of "meaningful" human relationships, of intimacy and mutuality. Marriage is increasingly seen as an institution for having children, but sexual relationships are viewed as the natural concomitant of close relationships between the sexes. What is important is not sexual activity itself, but the context in which it occurs. Sex is right and natural between people who are "good to each other," but sexual exploitation—failure to treat one's partner as a person—is strongly disapproved.

**INCLUSIVENESS**    The search for personal and organizational inclusiveness is still another characteristic of post-modern youth. These young men and women attempt to include both within their personalities and within their movements every opposite, every possibility and every person, no matter how apparently alien. Psychologically, inclusiveness involves an effort to be open to every aspect of one's feelings, impulses and fantasies, to synthesize and integrate rather than repress and dissociate, not to reject or exclude any part of one's personality or potential. Interpersonally, inclusiveness means a capacity for involvement with, identification with and collaboration with those who are superficially alien: the peasant in Vietnam, the poor in America, the nonwhite, the deprived and deformed. Indeed, so great is the pressure to include the alien, especially among hippies, that the apparently alien is often treated more favorably than the superficially similar: thus, the respect afforded to people and ideas that are distant and strange is sometimes not equally afforded those who are similar, be they one's parents or their middle-class values. One way of explaining the reaction of post-modern youth to the war in Vietnam is via the concept of inclusiveness: these young men and women react to events in Southeast Asia much as if they occurred in Newton, Massachusetts, Evanston, Illinois, Harlem, or Berkeley, California: they make little distinction in their reactions to their fellow Americans and those overseas.

One corollary of inclusiveness is intense internationalism. What matters to hippies or young radicals is not where a person comes from, but what kind of relationship is possible with him. The nationality of ideas matters little: Zen Buddhism, American pragmatism, French existentialism, Indian mysticism or Yugoslav communism are accorded equal hearings. Interracialism is another corollary of inclusiveness: racial barriers are minimized or nonexistent, and the ultimate expressions of unity between the races, sexual relationships and marriage, are considered basically natural and normal, whatever the social problems they currently entail. In post-modern youth, then, identity and ideology are no longer parochial or national; increasingly, the reference group is the world, and the artificial subspeciation of the human species is broken down.

**ANTITECHNOLOGISM**   Post-modern youth has grave reservations about many of the technological aspects of the contemporary world. The depersonalization of life, commercialism, careerism and familism, the bureaucratization and complex organization of advanced nations—all seem intolerable to these young men and women, who seek to create new forms of association and action to oppose the technologism of our day. Bigness, impersonality, stratification and hierarchy are rejected, as is any involvement with the furtherance of technological values. In reaction to these values, post-modern youth seeks simplicity, naturalness, personhood and even voluntary poverty.

But a revolt against technologism is only possible, of course, in a technological society; and to be effective, it must inevitably exploit technology to overcome technologism. Thus in post-modern youth, the fruits of technology—synthetic hallucinogens in the hippie subculture, modern technology of communication among young radicals—and the affluence made possible by technological society are a precondition for a post-modern style. The demonstrative poverty of the hippie would be meaningless in a society where poverty is routine; for the radical to work for subsistence wages as a matter of choice is to *have* a choice not available in most parts of the world. Furthermore, to "organize" against the pernicious aspects of the technological era requires high skill in the use of modern technologies of organization: the long-distance telephone, the use of the mass media, high-speed travel, the mimeograph machine and so on. In the end, then, it is not the material but the spiritual consequences of technology that post-modern youth opposes: indeed, in the developing nations, those who exhibit a post-modern style may be in the vanguard of movements toward modernization. What *is* admantly rejected is the contamination of life with the values of technological organization and production. It seems probable that a comparable rejection of the psychological consequences of current technology, coupled with the simultaneous ability to exploit that technology, characterizes all dissenting groups in all epochs.

**PARTICIPATION**     Post-modern youth is committed to a search for new forms of groups, of organizations and of action where decision-making is collective, arguments are resolved by "talking them out," self-examination, interpersonal criticism and group decision-making are fused. The objective is to create new styles of life and new types of organization that humanize rather than dehumanize, that activate and strengthen the participants rather than undermining or weakening them. And the primary vehicle for such participation is the small, face-to-face primary group of peers.

The search for new participatory forms of organization and action can hardly be deemed successful as yet, especially in the New Left, where effectiveness in the wider social and political scene remains to be demonstrated. There are inherent differences between the often task-less, face-to-face group that is the basic form of organization for both hippies and radicals and the task-oriented organization—differences that make it difficult to achieve social effectiveness based solely on small primary groups. But there may yet evolve from the hippie "tribes," small Digger communities, and primary groups of the New Left, new forms of association in which self-criticism, awareness of group interaction, and the accomplishment of social and political goals go hand in hand. The effort to create groups in which individuals grow from their participation in the group extends far beyond the New Left and the hippie world; the same search is seen in the widespread enthusiasm for "sensitivity training" groups and even in the increasing use of groups as a therapeutic instrument. Nor is this solely an American search: one sees a similar focus, for example, in the Communist nations, with their emphasis on small groups that engage in the "struggle" of mutual criticism and self-criticism.

The search for effectiveness combined with participation has also led to the evolution of "new" styles of social and political action. The newness of such forms of political action as parades and demonstrations is open to some question; perhaps what is most new is the *style* in which old forms of social action are carried out. The most consistent effort is to force one's opponent into a personal confrontation with one's own point of view. Sit-ins, freedom rides, insistence upon discussions, silent and nonviolent demonstrations—all have a prime objective to "get through to" the other side, to force reflection, to bear witness to one's own principles, and to impress upon others the validity of these same principles. There is much that is old and familiar about this, although few of today's young radicals or hippies are ideologically committed to Gandhian views of nonviolence. Yet the underlying purpose of many of the emerging forms of social and political action, whether they be "human be-ins," "love-ins," peace marches or "teach-ins," has a new motive—hope that by expressing one's own principles, by "demonstrating" one's convictions, one can through sheer moral force win over one's opponents and lure them as well into participating with one's own values.

**ANTIACADEMICISM**     Among post-modern youth, one finds a virtually unanimous rejection of the "merely academic." This rejection is one manifestation of a wider insistence on the relevance, applicability and personal meaningfulness of knowledge. It would be wrong simply to label this trend "anti-intellectual," for many new radicals and not a few hippies are themselves highly intellectual people. What is demanded is that intelligence be engaged with the world, just as action should be informed by knowledge. In the New Left, at least amongst leaders, there is enormous respect for knowledge and information, and great impatience with those who act without understanding. Even amongst hippies, where the importance of knowledge and information is less stressed, it would be wrong simply to identify the rejection of the academic world and its values with a total rejection of intellect, knowledge and wisdom.

To post-modern youth, then, most of what is taught in schools, colleges and universities is largely irrelevant to living life in the last third of the twentieth century. Many academics are seen as direct or accidental apologists for the Organized System in the United States. Much of what they teach is considered simply unconnected to the experience of post-modern youth. New ways of learning are sought: ways that combine action with reflection upon action, ways that fuse engagement in the world with understanding of it. In an era of rapid change, the accrued wisdom of the past is cast into question, and youth seeks not only new knowledge, but new· ways of learning and knowing.

**NONVIOLENCE**    Finally, post-modern youth of all persuasions meets on the ground of nonviolence. For hippies, the avoidance of and calming of violence is a central objective, symbolized by gifts of flowers to policemen and the slogan, "Make love, not war." And although nonviolence as a philosophical principle has lost most of its power in the New Left, nonviolence as a psychological orientation is a crucial—perhaps *the* crucial—issue. The nonviolence of post-modern youth should not be confused with pacificism: these are not necessarily young men and women who believe in turning the other cheek or who are systematically opposed to fighting for what they believe in. But the basic style of both radicals and hippies is profoundly opposed to warfare, destruction and exploitation of man by man, and to violence whether on an interpersonal or an international scale. Even among those who do not consider nonviolence a good in itself, a psychological inoculation against violence, even a fear of it, is a unifying theme.

## THE CREDIBILITY GAP: PRINCIPLE AND PRACTICE

In creating the style of today's youth, the massive and violent social changes of the past two decades have played a central role. Such social changes are not only distantly perceived by those who are growing up, but are immediately interwoven into the texture of their daily lives as they develop. The social changes of the post-war era affect the young in a variety of ways: in particular, they contribute to a special sensitivity to the discrepancy between principle and practice. For during this era of rapid social change the values most deeply embedded in the parental generation and expressed in their behavior in time of crisis are frequently very different from the more "modern" principles, ideals and values that this generation has professed and attempted to practice in bringing up its children. Filial perception of the discrepancy between practice and principle may help explain the very widespread sensitivity amongst post-modern youth to the "hypocrisy" of the previous generation.

The grandparents of today's twenty-year-olds were generally born at the end of the nineteenth century, and brought up during the pre–World War I years. Heirs of a Victorian tradition as yet unaffected by the value revolutions of the twentieth century, they reared their own children, the parents of today's youth, in families that emphasized respect, the control of impulse, obedience to authority, and the traditional "inner-directed" values of hard work, deferred gratification and self-restraint. Their children, born around the time of the First World War, were thus socialized in families that remained largely Victorian in outlook.

During their lifetimes, however, these parents (and in particular the most intelligent and advantaged among them) were exposed to a great variety of new values that often changed their nominal faiths. During their youths in the 1920's and 1930's, major changes in American behavior and American values took place. For example, the "emancipation of women" in the 1920's, marked by the achievement of suffrage for women, coincided with the last major change in actual sexual behavior in America: during this period, women began to become the equal partners of men, who no longer sought premarital sexual experience solely with women of a lower class. More important, the 1920's and the 1930's were an era when older Victorian values were challenged, attacked and all but discredited, especially in educated middle-class families. Young men and women who went to college during this period (as did most of the parents of those who can be termed "post-modern" today) were influenced outside their families by a variety of "progressive," "liberal," and even psychoanalytic ideas that contrasted sharply with the values of their childhood families. Moreover, during the 1930's, many of the parents of today's upper middle-class youth were exposed to or involved with the ideals of the New Deal, and sometimes to more radical interpretations of man, society and history. Finally, in the 1940's and 1950's, when it came time to rear their own children, the parents of today's elite youth were strongly influenced by "permissive" views of child-rearing that again contrasted sharply with the techniques by which they themselves had been raised. Thus, many middle-class parents moved during their lifetime from the Victorian ethos in which they had been socialized to the less moralistic, more humanitarian, and more "expressive" values of their own adulthoods.

But major changes in values, when they occur in adult life, are likely to be far from complete. To have grown up in a family where unquestioning obedience to parents was expected, but to rear one's own children in an atmosphere of "democratic" permissiveness and self-determination—and never to revert to the practices of one's own childhood—requires a change of values more total and comprehensive than most adults can achieve. Furthermore, behavior that springs from values acquired in adulthood often appears somewhat forced, artificial or insincere to the sensitive observer. Children, clearly the most sensitive observers of their own parents, are likely to sense a discrepancy between their parents' avowed and consciously-held values and their "basic instincts" with regard to child-rearing. Furthermore, the parental tendency to "revert to form" is greatest in times of family crisis, which are of course the times that have the greatest effect upon children. No matter how "genuinely" parents held their "new" values, many of them inevitably found themselves falling back on the lessons of their own childhoods when the chips were down.

In a time of rapid social change, then, a special *credibility gap* is likely to open between the generations. Children are likely to perceive a considerable discrepancy between what their parents avow as their values and the actual assumptions from which parental behavior springs. In many middle-class teen-agers today, for example, the focal issue of adolescent rebellion against parents often seems to be just this discrepancy: the children arguing that their parents' endorsement of independence

and self-determination for their children is "hypocritical" in that it does not correspond with the real behavior of the parents when their children actually seek independence. Similar perceptions of parental "hypocrisy" occur around racial matters: for example, there are many parents who in principle support racial and religious equality, but become violently upset when their children date someone from another race or religion. Around political activity similar issues arise. For example, many of the parents of today's youth espouse in principle the cause of political freedom, but are not involved themselves in politics and oppose their children's involvement lest they "jeopardize their record" or "ruin their later career."

Of course, no society ever fully lives up to its own professed ideals. In every society there is a gap between creedal values and actual practices, and in every society, the recognition of this gap constitutes a powerful motor for social change. But in most societies, especially when social change is slow and institutions are powerful and unchanging, there occurs what can be termed *institutionalization of hypocrisy*. Children and adolescents routinely learn when it is "reasonable" to expect that the values people profess will be implemented in their behavior, and when it is not reasonable. There develops an elaborate system of exegesis and commentary upon the society's creedal values, excluding certain people or situations from the full weight of these values, or "demonstrating" that apparent inconsistencies are not really inconsistencies at all. Thus, in almost all societies, a "sincere" man who "honestly" believes one set of values is frequently allowed to ignore them completely, for example, in the practice of his business, in his interpersonal relationships, in dealings with foreigners, in relationships to his children, and so on—all because these areas have been officially defined as exempt from the application of his creedal values.

In a time of rapid social change and value change, however, the institutionalization of hypocrisy seems to break down. "New" values have been in existence for so brief a period that the exemptions to them have not yet been defined, the situations to be excluded have not yet been determined, and the universal gap between principle and practice appears in all of its nakedness. Thus, the mere fact of a discrepancy between creedal values and practice is not at all unusual. But what is special about the present situation of rapid value change is, first, that parents themselves tend to have two conflicting sets of values, one related to the experience of their early childhood, the other to the ideologies and principles acquired in adulthood; and second, that no stable institutions or rules for defining hypocrisy out of existence have yet been fully evolved. In such a situation, children see the Emperor's nakedness with unusual clarity, recognizing the value conflict within their parents and perceiving clearly the hypocritical gap between creed and behavior.

This argument suggests that the post-modern youth may not be confronted with an "objective" gap between parental preaching and practice any greater than that of most generations. But they are confronted with an unusual internal ambivalance within the parental generation over the values that parents successfuly inculcated in their children, and they are "deprived" of a system of social interpretation that rationalizes the discrepancy between creed and deed. It seems likely, then, that today's youth may simply be able to perceive the universal gulf between principle and practice more clearly than previous generations have done.

This points to one of the central characteristics of post-modern youth: they insist on taking seriously a great variety of political, personal and social principles that "no one in his right mind" ever before thought of attempting to extend to such situations as dealings with strangers, relations between the races, or international politics. For example, peaceable openness has long been a creedal virtue in our society, but it has never been extended to foreigners, particularly with dark skins. Similarly, equality has long been preached, but the "American dilemma" has been resolved by a series of institutionalized hypocrisies that exempted Negroes from the application of this principle. Love has always been a central value in Christian society, but really to love one's enemies—to be

generous to policemen, customers, criminals, servants and foreigners—has been considered folly.

These speculations on the credibility gap between the generations in a time of rapid change may help explain two crucial facts about postmodern youth: first, they frequently come from highly principled families with whose principles they continue to agree; second, that they have the outrageous temerity to insist that individuals and societies live by the values they preach. And these speculations may also explain the frequent feeling of those who have worked intensively with student radicals or hippies that, apart from the "impracticality" of some of their views, these sometimes seem to be the only clear-eyed and sane people in a society and a world where most of us are still systematically blind to the traditional gap between personal principle and practice, national creed and policy, a gap that we may no longer be able to afford.

## VIOLENCE: SADISM AND CATACLYSM

Those who are today in their early twenties were born near the end of World War II, the most violent and barbarous war in world history. The lasting imprint of that war can be summarized in the names of three towns: Auschwitz, Hiroshima and Nuremberg. *Auschwitz* points to the possibility of a "civilized" nation embarking on a systematized, well-organized and scientific plan of exterminating an entire people. *Hiroshima* demonstrated how "clean," easy and impersonal cataclysm could be to those who perpetrate it, and how demonic, sadistic and brutal to those who experience it. And *Nuremberg* summarizes the principle that men have an accountability above obedience to national policy, a responsibility to conscience more primary even than fidelity to national law. These three lessons are the matrix for the growth of post-modern youth.

The terror of violence that has hung over all men and women since the Second World War has especially shaped the outlooks of today's youth. In the first memories of a group of young radicals, for example, one finds the following recollections:

a dim recall of the end of World War II; childhood terror of the atomic bomb; witnessing the aftermath of a violent riot in the United States; being frightened by a picture of a tank riding over rubble; being violently jealous at the birth of a younger brother; taking part in "gruesome" fights in the school yard. Such memories mean many things, but in them, violence-in-the-world finds echo and counterpart in the violence of inner feelings. The term "violence" suggests both of these possibilities: the *psychological* violence of sadism, exploitation and aggression, and the *historical* violence of war, cataclysm and holocaust. In the lives of most of this generation, the threats of inner and outer violence are fused, each activating, exciting and potentiating the other. To summarize a complex thesis into a few words: *the issue of violence is to this generation what the issue of sex was to the Victorian world.*

Stated differently, what is most deeply repressed, rejected, feared, controlled and projected onto others by the post-modern generation is no longer their own sexuality. Sex, for most of this generation, is much freer, more open, less guilt- and anxiety-ridden. But violence, whether in one's self or in others, has assumed new prominence as the prime source of inner and outer terror. That this should be so in the modern world is readily understandable. Over all of us hangs the continual threat of a technological violence more meaningless, absurd, total and unpremeditated than any ever imagined before. Individual life always resonates with historical change; history is not merely the backdrop for development, but its ground. To be grounded in the history of the past two decades is to have stood upon, to have experienced both directly and vicariously, violent upheaval, violent worldwide revolution, and the unrelenting possibility of worldwide destruction. To have been alive and aware in America during the past decade has been to be exposed to the assassination of a President and the televised murder of his murderer, to the well-publicized slaughter of Americans by their fellow countrymen, and to the recent violence in our cities. To have been a middle-class child in the past two decades is to have watched daily the violence of television, both as it reports the bloodshed and turmoil of the American and non-American world, and as it skillfully elaborates and externalizes in repetitive dramas the potential for violence within each of us.

It therefore requires no assumption of an increase in biological aggression to account for the salience of the issue of violence for post-modern youth. The capacity for rage, spite and aggression is part of our endowment as human beings: it is a constant potential of human nature. But during the past two decades—indeed, starting before the Second World War—we have witnessed violence and imagined violence on a scale more frightening than ever before. Like the angry child who fears that his rage will itself destroy those around him, we have become vastly more sensitive to and fearful of our inner angers, for we live in a world where even the mildest irritation, multiplied a billionfold by modern technology, might destroy all civilization. The fact of violent upheaval and the possibility of cataclysm has been literally brought into our living rooms during the past twenty years: it has been interwoven with the development of a whole generation.

It should not surprise us, then, that the issue of violence is a focal concern for those of contemporary youth with the greatest historical consciousness. The hippie slogan "Make love, not war" expresses their sentiment, albeit in a form that the "realist" of previous generations might deem sentimental or romantic. Although few young radicals would agree with the wording of this statement, the underlying sentiment corresponds to their basic psychological orientation. For them, as for many others of their generation, the primary task is to develop new psychological, political and international controls on violence. Indeed, many of the dilemmas of today's young radicals seem related to their extraordinarily zealous efforts to avoid any action or relationship in which inner or outer violence might be evoked. Distaste for violence animates the profound revulsion many of today's youth feel toward the war in Southeast Asia, just as it underlies a similar revulsion against the exploitation or control of man by man. The same psychological nonviolence is related to young radicals' avoidance of traditional leadership lest it lead to domination, to their emphasis on person-to-person participation and "confrontation," and even to their unwillingness to "play the media" in an attempt to gain political effectiveness. Even the search for forms of mass political action that avoid physical violence—a preference severely tested and somewhat undermined by the events of recent months—points to a considerable distaste for the direct expression of aggression.

I do not mean to suggest that post-modern youth contains a disproportionate number of tight-lipped pacifists or rage-filled deniers of their own inner angers. On the contrary, among today's youth, exuberance, passionateness and zest are the rule rather than the exception. Nor are hippies and young radicals incapable of anger, rage and resentment—especially when their principles are violated. But for many of these young men and women, the experiences of early life and the experience of the postwar world are joined in a special sensitivity to the issue of violence, whether in themselves or in others. This confluence of psychological and historical forces helps explain the intensity of their search for new forms of social organization and political action that avoid manipulation, domination and control, just as it contributes to their widespread opposition to warfare of all kinds.

Yet the position of psychologically nonviolent youth in a violent world is difficult and paradoxical. On the one hand, he seeks to minimize violence, but on the other, his efforts often elicit violence from others. At the same time that he attempts to work to actualize his vision of a peaceful world, he must confront more directly and continually than do his peers the fact that the world is neither peaceful nor just. The frustration and discouragement of his work repetitively reawaken his anger, which must forever be rechanneled into peaceful paths. Since he continually confronts destructiveness and exploitation in the world, his own inevitable potential for destructiveness and exploitiveness inevitably arouses in him great guilt. The young men and women who make up the New Left in America, like other post-modern youth,

have far less difficulty in living with their sexual natures than did their parents; but what they continue to find difficult to live with, what they still repress, avoid and counteract is their own potential for violence. It remains to be seen whether, in the movement toward "resistance" and disruption of today's young radicals, their psychological nonviolence will continue to be reflected in their actions.

In pointing to the psychological dimension of the issue of violence, I do not mean to attribute causal primacy either to the experiences of early life or to their residues in adulthood. My thesis is rather that for those of this generation with the greatest historical awareness, the psychological and historical possibility of violence have come to potentiate each other. To repeat: witnessing the acting out of violence on a scale more gigantic than ever before, or imaginatively participating in the possiblity of worldwide holocaust activates the fear of one's own violence; heightened awareness of one's inner potential for rage, anger or destructiveness increases sensitivity to the possibility of violence in the world.

This same process of historical potentiation of inner violence has occurred, I believe, throughout the modern world, and brings with it not only the intensified efforts to curb violence we see in this small segment of post-modern youth, but other more frightening possibilities. Post-modern youth, to an unusual degree, remain open to and aware of their own angers and aggressions, and this awareness creates in them a sufficient understanding of inner violence to enable them to control it in themselves and oppose it in others. Most men and women, young or old, possess less insight: their inner sadism is projected onto others whom they thereafter loathe or abjectly serve; or, more disastrously, historically-heightened inner violence is translated into outer aggression and murderousness, sanctioned by self-righteousness.

Thus, if the issue of violence plagues post-modern youth, it is not because these young men and women are more deeply rage-filled than most. On the contrary, it is because such young men and women have confronted this issue more squarely in themselves and in the world than have any but a handful of their fellows. If they have not yet found solutions, they have at least faced an issue so dangerous that most of us find it too painful even to acknowledge, and they have done so, most remarkably, without identifying with what they oppose. Their still-incomplete lives pose for us all the question on which our survival as individuals and as a world depends: Can we ·create formula-

tions and forms to control historical and psychological violence before their fusion destroys us all?

**NOTE**

1   In the effort to delineate this style, I have been helped and influenced by Robert J. Lifton's concept of Protean Man. For a summary of his views, see *Partisan Review*, winter 1968.

## 12   GOOD PEOPLE AND DIRTY WORK    EVERETT C. HUGHES

... une secte est le *noyau* et le *levain* de toute foule. ... Etudier la foule c'est juger un drame d'après ce qu'on voit sur la scène; étudier la secte c'est le juger d'après ce qu'on voit dans les coulisses.[1]

The National Socialist Government of Germany, with the arm of its fanatical inner sect, the S.S., commonly known as the Black Shirts or Elite Guard, perpetrated and boasted of the most colossal and dramatic piece of social work the world has ever known. Perhaps there are other claimants to the title, but they could not match this one's combination of mass, speed and perverse pride in the deed. Nearly all peoples have plenty of cruelty and death to account for. How many Negro Americans have died by the hands of lynching mobs? How many more from unnecessary disease and lack of food or of knowledge of nutrition? How many Russians died to bring about collectivization of land? And who is to blame if there be starving millions in some parts of the world while wheat molds in the fields of other parts?

I do not revive the case of the Nazi *Endloesung* (final solution) of the Jewish problem in order to condemn the Germans, or make them look worse than other peoples, but to recall to our attention

Reprinted from *Social Problems*, vol. 10, no. 1, pp. 3–11, by permission of the author and The Society for the Study of Social Problems.

dangers which lurk in our midst always. Most of what follows was written after my first postwar visit to Germany in 1948. The impressions were vivid. The facts have not diminished and disappeared with time, as did the stories of alleged German atrocities in Belgium in the first World War. The fuller the record, the worse it gets.[2]

Several millions of people were delivered to the concentration camps, operated under the leadership of Heinrich Himmler with the help of Adolf Eichmann. A few hundred thousand survived in some fashion. Still fewer came out sound of mind and body. A pair of examples, well attested, will show the extreme of perverse cruelty reached by the S.S. guards in charge of the camps. Prisoners were ordered to climb trees; guards whipped them to make them climb faster. Once they were out of reach, other prisoners, also urged by the whip, were put to shaking the trees. When the victims fell, they were kicked to see whether they could rise to their feet. Those too badly injured to get up were shot to death, as useless for work. A not inconsiderable number of prisoners were drowned in pits full of human excrement. These examples are so horrible that your minds will run away from them. You will not, as when you read a slightly salacious novel, imagine the rest. I therefore thrust these examples upon you and insist that the people who thought them up could, and did, improvise others like them, and even worse, from day to day over several years. Many of the victims of the Camps gave up the ghost (this Biblical phrase is the most apt) from a combination of humiliation, starvation, fatigue and physical abuse. In due time, a policy of mass liquidation in the gas chamber was added to individual virtuosity in cruelty.

This program—for it was a program—of cruelty and murder was carried out in the name of racial superiority and racial purity. It was directed mainly, although by no means exclusively, against Jews, Slavs and Gypsies. It was thorough. There are few Jews in the territories which were under the control of the Third German Reich—the two Germanies, Holland, Czechoslovakia, Poland, Austria, Hungary. Many Jewish Frenchmen were destroyed. There were concentration camps even in Tunisia and Algiers under the German occupation.

When, during my 1948 visit to Germany, I became more aware of the reactions of ordinary Germans to the horrors of the concentration camps, I found myself asking not the usual question, "How did racial hatred rise to such a high level?" but this one, "How could such dirty work be done among and, in a sense, *by* the millions of ordinary, civilized German people?" Along with this came related questions. How could these millions of ordinary people live in the midst of such cruelty and murder without a general uprising against it and against the people who did it? How, once freed from the regime that did it, could they be apparently so little concerned about it, so toughly silent about it, not only in talking with outsiders—which is easy to understand—but among themselves? How and where could there be found in a modern civilized country the several hundred thousand men and women capable of such work? How were these people so far released from the inhibitions of civilized life as to be able to imagine, let alone perform, the ferocious, obscene and perverse actions which they did imagine and perform? How could they be kept at such a height of fury through years of having to see daily at close range the human wrecks they made and being often literally spattered with the filth produced and accumulated by their own actions?

You will see that there are here two orders of questions. One set concerns the good people who did not themselves do this work. The other concerns those who did do it. But the two sets are not really separate; for the crucial question concerning the good people is their relation to the people who did the dirty work, with a related one which asks under what circumstances good people let the others get away with such actions.

An easy answer concerning the Germans is that they were not so good after all. We can attribute to them some special inborn or ingrained race consciousness, combined with a penchant for sadistic cruelty and unquestioning acceptance of whatever is done by those who happen to be in authority. Pushed to its extreme, this answer simply makes us, rather than the Germans, the superior race. It is the Nazi tune, put to words of our own.

Now there are deep and stubborn differences between peoples. Their history and culture may make the Germans especially susceptible to the doctrine of their own racial superiority and especially acquiescent to the actions of whoever is in power over them. These are matters deserving of the best study that can be given them. But to say that these things could happen in Germany simply because Germans are different—from us—buttresses their own excuses and lets us off too easily from blame for what happened there and from the question whether it could happen here.

Certainly in their daily practice and expression before the Hitler regime, the Germans showed no more, if as much, hatred of other racial or cultural groups than we did and do. Residential segregation was not marked. Intermarriage was common, and the families of such marriages had an easier social existence than they generally have in America. The racially exclusive club, school and hotel were much less in evidence than here. And I well remember an evening in 1933 when a Montreal business man—a very nice man, too—said in our living room, "Why don't we admit that Hitler is doing to the Jews just what we ought to be doing?" That was not an uncommon sentiment, although it may be said in defense of the people who expressed it, that they probably did not know and would not have believed the full truth about the Nazi program of destroying Jews. The essential underlying sentiments on racial matters in Germany were not different in kind from those prevailing throughout the western, and especially the Anglo-Saxon, countries. But I do not wish to over-emphasize this point. I only want to close one easy way out of serious consideration of the problem of good people and dirty work, by demonstrating that the Germans were and are about as good and about as bad as the rest of us on this matter of racial sentiments and, let us add, their notions of decent human behaviour.

But what was the reaction of ordinary Germans to the persecution of the Jews and to the concentration camp mass torture and murder? A conversation between a German school-teacher, a German architect and myself gives the essentials in a vivid form. It was in the studio of the architect, and the occasion was a rather casual visit, in Frankfurt am Main in 1948.

THE ARCHITECT  "I am ashamed for my people whenever I think of it. But we didn't know about it. We only learned about all that later. You must remember the pressure we were under; we had to join the party. We had to keep our mouths shut and do as we were told. It was a terrible pressure. Still, I am ashamed. But you see, we had lost our colonies, and our national honour was hurt. And these Nazis exploited that feeling. And the Jews, they *were* a problem. They came from the east. You should see them in Poland; the lowest class of people, full of lice, dirty and poor, running about in their Ghettos in filthy caftans. They came here, and got rich by unbelievable methods after the first war. They occupied all the good places. Why, they were in the proportion of ten to one in medicine and law and government posts!"

At this point the architect hesitated and looked confused. He continued: "Where was I? It is the poor food. You see what misery we are in here, Herr Professor. It often happens that I forget what I was talking about. Where was I now? I have completely forgotten."

(His confusion was, I believe, not at all feigned. Many Germans said they suffered losses of memory such as this, and laid it to their lack of food.)

I said firmly: "You were talking about loss of national honour and how the Jews had got hold of everything."

The architect: "Oh, yes! That was it! Well, of course that was no way to settle the Jewish problem. But there *was* a problem and it had to be settled some way."

THE SCHOOL-TEACHER  "Of course, they have Palestine now."

I protested that Palestine would hardly hold them.

THE ARCHITECT  "The professor is right. Palestine can't hold all the Jews. And it was a terrible thing to murder people. But we didn't know it at the time. But I am glad I am alive now. It is an interesting time in men's history. You know, when the Americans came it was like a great release. I really want to see a new ideal in Germany. I like the freedom that lets me talk to you like this. But, unfortunately that is not the general opinion. Most of my friends really hang on to the old ideas. They can't see any hope, so they hang on to the old ideas.

This scrap of talk gives, I believe, the essential elements as well as the flavor of the German reaction. It checks well with formal studies which have been made, and it varies only in detail from other conversations which I myself recorded in 1948.

One of the most obvious points in it is unwillingness to think about the dirty work done. In this case—perhaps by chance, perhaps not—the good man suffered an actual lapse of memory in the middle of this statement. This seems a simple point. But the psychiatrists have shown that it is less simple than it looks. They have done a good deal of work on the complicated mechanisms by which the individual mind keeps unpleasant or intolerable knowledge from consciousness, and have shown how great may, in some cases, be the consequent loss of effectiveness of the personality. But we have taken collective unwillingness to know unpleasant facts more or less for granted. That people can and do keep a silence about things whose open discussion would threaten the group's conception of itself, and hence its solidarity, is common knowledge. It is a mechanism that operates in every family and in every group which has a sense of group reputation. To break such a silence is considered an attack against the group; a sort of treason, if it be a member of the group who breaks the silence. This common silence allows group fictions to grow up; such as, that grandpa was less a scoundrel and more romantic than he really was. And I think it demonstrable that it operates especially against any expression, except in ritual, of collective guilt. The remarkable thing in present-day Germany is not that there is so little reference to something about which people do feel deeply guilty, but that it is talked about at all.

In order to understand this phenomenon we should have to find out who talks about the concentration camp atrocities, in what situations, in what mood, and with what stimulus. On these points I know only my own limited experiences. One of the most moving of these was my first post-war meeting with an elderly professor whom I had known before the Nazi time; he is an heroic soul who did not bow his head during the Nazi time and who keeps it erect now. His first words, spoken with tears in his eyes, were:

"How hard it is to believe that men will be as bad as they say they will. Hitler and his people said: 'Heads will roll,' but how many of us—even of his bitterest opponents—could really believe that they would do it."

This man could and did speak, in 1948, not only to the likes of me, but to his students, his colleagues and to the public which read his articles, in the most natural way about the Nazi atrocities whenever there was occasion to do it in the course of his tireless effort to reorganize and to bring new life into the German universities. He had neither the compulsion to speak, so that he might excuse and defend himself, nor a conscious or unconscious need to keep silent. Such people were rare; how many there were in Germany I do not know.

Occasions of another kind in which the silence was broken were those where, in class, public lecture or in informal meetings with students, I myself had talked frankly of race relations in other parts of the world, including the lynchings which sometimes occur in my own country and the terrible cruelty visited upon natives in South Africa. This took off the lid of defensiveness, so that a few people would talk quite easily of what happened under the Nazi regime. More common were situations like that with the architect, where I threw in some remark about the atrocities in response to Germans' complaint that the world is abusing them. In such cases, there was usually an expression of shame, accompanied by a variety of excuses (including that of having been kept in ignorance), and followed by a quick turning away from the subject.

Somewhere in consideration of this problem of discussion versus silence we must ask what the good (that is, ordinary) people in Germany did know about these things. It is clear that the S.S. kept the more gory details of the concentration camps a close secret. Even high officials of the government, the army and the Nazi party itself were in some measure held in ignorance, although of course they kept the camps supplied with victims. The common people of Germany knew that the camps existed; most knew people who had disappeared into them; some saw the victims, walking skeletons in rags, being transported in trucks or trains, or being herded on the road from station to camp or to work in fields or factories near the camps. Many knew people who had been released from concentration camps; such released persons kept their counsel on pain of death. But secrecy was cultivated and supported by fear and terror. In the absence of a determined and heroic will to know and publish the truth, and in the absence of all the instruments of opposition, the degree of knowledge was undoubtedly low, in spite of the fact that all knew that something both stupendous and horrible was going on; and in spite of the fact that Hitler's *Mein Kampf* and the utterances of his aides said that no fate was too horrible for the

Jews and other wrong-headed or inferior people. This must make us ask under what conditions the will to know and to discuss is strong, determined and effective; this, like most of the important questions I have raised, I leave unanswered except as answers may be contained in the statement of the case.

But to return to our moderately good man, the architect. He insisted over and over again that he did not know, and we may suppose that he knew as much and as little as most Germans. But he also made it quite clear that he wanted something done to the Jews. I have similar statements from people of whom I knew that they had had close Jewish friends before the Nazi time. This raises the whole problem of the extent to which those pariahs who do the dirty work of society are really acting as agents for the rest of us. To talk of this question one must note that, in building up his case, the architect pushed the Jews firmly into an out-group: they were dirty, lousy and unscrupulous (an odd statement from a resident of Frankfurt, the home of old Jewish merchants and intellectual families long identified with those aspects of culture of which Germans are most proud). Having dissociated himself clearly from these people, and having declared them a problem, he apparently was willing to let someone else do to them the dirty work which he himself would not do, and for which he expressed shame. The case is perhaps analogous to our attitude toward those convicted of crime. From time to time, we get wind of cruelty practiced upon the prisoners in penitentiaries or jails; or, it may be, merely a report that they are ill-fed or that hygienic conditions are not good. Perhaps we do not wish that the prisoners should be cruelly treated or badly fed, but our reaction is probably tempered by a notion that they deserve something, because of some dissociation of them from the in-group of good people. If what they get is worse than what we like to think about, it is a little bit too bad. It is a point on which we are ambivalent. Campaigns for reform of prisons are often followed by counter-campaigns against a too high standard of living for prisoners and against

having prisons run by softies. Now the people who run prisons are our agents. Just how far they do or could carry out our wishes is hard to say. The minor prison guard, in boastful justification of some of his more questionable practices, says, in effect: "If those reformers and those big shots upstairs had to live with these birds as I do, they would soon change their fool notions about running a prison." He is suggesting that the good people are either naive or hypocritical. Furthermore, he knows quite well that the wishes of his employers, the public, are by no means unmixed. They are quite as likely to put upon him for being too nice as for being too harsh. And if, as sometimes happens, he is a man disposed to cruelty, there may be some justice in his feeling that he is only doing what others would like to do, if they but dared; and what they would do, if they were in his place.

There are plenty of examples in our own world which I might have picked for comparison with the German attitude toward the concentration camps. For instance, a newspaper in Denver made a great scandal out of the allegation that our Japanese compatriots were too well fed in the camps where they were concentrated during the war. I might have mentioned some feature of the sorry history of the people of Japanese background in Canada. Or it might have been lynching, or some aspect of racial discrimination. But I purposely chose prisoners convicted of crime. For convicts are formally set aside for special handling. They constitute an out-group in all countries. This brings the issue clearly before us, since few people cherish the illusion that the problem of treating criminals can be settled by propaganda designed to prove that there aren't any criminals. Almost everyone agrees that something has to be done about them. The question concerns what is done, who does it, and the nature of the mandate given by the rest of us to those who do it. Perhaps we give them an unconscious mandate to go beyond anything we ourselves would care to do or even to acknowledge. I venture to suggest that the higher and more expert functionaries who act in our behalf represent something of a distillation of what we may consider our public wishes, while some of the others show a sort of concentrate of those impulses of which we are or wish to be less aware.

Now the choice of convicted prisoners brings up another crucial point in inter-group relations. All societies of any great size have in-groups and out-groups; in fact, one of the best ways of describing a society is to consider it a network of smaller and larger in-groups and out-groups. And an in-group is one only because there are out-groups. When I refer to *my* children I obviously imply that they are closer to me than other people's children and that I will make greater efforts to buy oranges and cod-liver oil for them than for others' children. In fact, it may mean that I will give them cod-liver oil if I have to choke them to get it down. We do our own dirty work on those closest to us. The very injunction that I love my neighbor as myself starts with me; if I don't love myself and my nearest, the phrase has a very sour meaning.

Each of us is a center of a network of in and out-groups. Now the distinctions between *in* and *out* may be drawn in various ways, and nothing is more important for both the student of society and the educator than to discover how these lines are made and how they may be redrawn in more just and sensible ways. But to believe that we can do away with the distinction between *in* and *out*, *us* and *them* in social life is complete nonsense. On the positive side, we generally feel a greater obligation to in-groups; hence less obligation to out-groups; and in the case of such groups as convicted criminals, the out-group is definitely given over to the hands of our agents for punishment. That is the extreme case. But there are other out-groups toward which we may have aggressive feelings and dislike, although we give no formal mandate to anyone to deal with them on our behalf, and although we profess to believe that they should not suffer restrictions or disadvantages. The greater their social distance from us, the more we leave in the hands of others a sort of mandate by default to deal with them on our behalf. Whatever effort we put on reconstructing the lines which divide in and out-groups, there remains the eternal problem

of our treatment, direct or delegated, of whatever groups are considered somewhat outside. And here it is that the whole matter of our professed and possible deeper unprofessed wishes comes up for consideration; and the related problem of what we know, can know and want to know about it. In Germany, the agents got out of hand and created such terror that it was best not to know. It is also clear that it was and is easier to the conscience of many Germans not to know. It is, finally, not unjust to say that the agents were at least working in the direction of the wishes of many people, although they may have gone beyond the wishes of most. The same questions can be asked about our own society, and with reference not only to prisoners but also to many other groups upon whom there is no legal or moral stigma. Again I have not the answers. I leave you to search for them.

In considering the question of dirty work we have eventually to think about the people who do it. In Germany, these were the members of the S.S. and of that inner group of the S.S. who operated the concentration camps. Many reports have been made on the social backgrounds and the personalities of these cruel fanatics. Those who have studied them say that a large proportion were *gescheiterte Existenzen*, men or women with a history of failure, of poor adaptation to the demands of work and of the classes of society in which they had been bred. Germany between wars had large numbers of such people. Their adherence to a movement which proclaimed a doctrine of hatred was natural enough. The movement offered something more. It created an inner group which was to be superior to all others, even Germans, in their emancipation from the usual bourgeois morality; people above and beyond the ordinary morality. I dwell on this, not as a doctrine, but as an organizational device. For, as Eugen Kogon, author of the most penetrating analysis of the S.S. and their camps, has said, the Nazis came to power by creating a state within a state; a body with its own counter-morality, and its own counter-law, its courts and its own execution of sentence upon those who did not live up to its orders and standards. Even as a movement, it had inner circles within inner circles; each sworn to secrecy as against the next outer one. The struggle between these inner circles continued after Hitler came to power; Himmler eventually won the day. His S.S. became a state within the Nazi state, just as the Nazi movement had become a state within the Weimar state. One is reminded of the oft quoted but neglected statement of Sighele: "At the center of a crowd look for the sect." He referred, of course, to the political sect; the fanatical inner group of a movement seeking power by revolutionary methods. Once the Nazis were in power, this inner sect, while becoming now the recognized agent of the state and, hence, of the masses of the people, could at the same time dissociate itself more completely from them in action, because of the very fact of having a mandate. It was now beyond all danger of interference and investigation. For it had the instruments of interference and investigation in its own hands. These are also the instruments of secrecy. So the S.S. could and did build up a powerful system in which they had the resources of the state and of the economy of Germany and the conquered countries from which to steal all that was needed to carry out their orgy of cruelty luxuriously as well as with impunity.

Now let us ask, concerning the dirty workers, questions similar to those concerning the good people. Is there a supply of candidates for such work in other societies? It would be easy to say that only Germany could produce such a crop. The question is answered by being put. The problem of people who have run aground (*gescheiterte Existenzen*) is one of the most serious in our modern societies. Any psychiatrist will, I believe, testify that we have a sufficient pool or fund of personalities warped toward perverse punishment and cruelty to do any amount of dirty work that the good people may be inclined to countenance. It would not take a very great turn of events to increase the number of such people, and to bring their discontents to the surface. This is not to suggest that every movement based on discontent with the present state of things will be led by such people. That is obviously untrue; and I emphasize

the point lest my remarks give comfort to those who would damn all who express militant discontent. But I think study of militant social movements does show that these warped people seek a place in them. Specifically, they are likely to become the plotting, secret police of the group. It is one of the problems of militant social movements to keep such people out. It is of course easier to do this if the spirit of the movement is positive, its conception of humanity high and inclusive, and its aims sound. This was not the case of the Nazi movement. As Kogon puts it: "The SS were but the arch-type of the Nazis in general."[3] But such people are sometimes attracted for want of something better, to movements whose aims are contrary to the spirit of cruelty and punishment. I would suggest that all of us look well at the leadership and entourage of movements to which we attach ourselves for signs of a negativistic, punishing attitude. For once such a spirit develops in a movement, punishment of the nearest and easiest victim is likely to become more attractive than striving for the essential goals. And, if the Nazi movement teaches us anything at all, it is that if any shadow of a mandate be given to such people, they will—having compromised us—make it larger and larger. The processes by which they do so are the development of the power and inward discipline of their own group, a progressive dissociation of themselves from the rules of human decency prevalent in their culture, and an ever-growing contempt for the welfare of the masses of people.

The power and inward discipline of the S.S. became such that those who once became members could get out only by death; by suicide, murder or mental breakdown. Orders from the central offices of the S.S. were couched in equivocal terms as a hedge against a possible day of judgment. When it became clear that such a day of judgment would come, the hedging and intrigue became greater; the urge to murder also became greater, because every prisoner became a potential witness.

Again we are dealing with a phenomenon common in all societies. Almost every group which has a specialized social function to perform is in some measure a secret society, with a body of rules developed and enforced by the members and with some power to save its members from outside punishment. And here is one of the paradoxes of social order. A society without smaller, rule-making and disciplining powers would be no society at all. There would be nothing but law and police; and this is what the Nazis strove for, at the expense of family, church, professional groups, parties and other such nuclei of spontaneous control. But apparently the only way to do this, for good as well as for evil ends, is to give power into the hands of some fanatical small group which will have a far greater power of self-discipline and a far greater immunity from outside control than the traditional groups. The problem is, then, not of trying to get rid of all the self-disciplining, protecting groups within society, but one of keeping them integrated with one another and as sensitive as can be to a public opinion which transcends them all. It is a matter of checks and balances, of what we might call the social and moral constitution of society.

Those who are especially devoted to efforts to eradicate from good people, as individuals, all those sentiments which seem to bring about the great and small dirty work of the world, may think that my remarks are something of an attack on their methods. They are right to this extent; that I am insisting that we give a share of our effort to the social mechanisms involved as well as to the individual and those of his sentiments which concern people of other kinds.

## REFERENCES AND NOTES

1 "... a sect is the nucleus and the yeast of every crowd. ... To study a crowd is to judge by what one sees on the stage; to study the sect is to judge by what one sees backstage." S. Sighele, *Psychologie des sectes*, Paris, 1898, pp. 62, 63, 65. These are among the many passages underlined by Robert E. Park in his copy, now in my possession, of Sighele's classic work on political sects. There are a number of references to this work in the Park and Burgess *Introduction to the Science of Sociology*, Chicago, 1921. In fact, there is more attention paid to fanatical political and religious behavior in Park and Burgess than in any later sociological work in this country. Sighele's discussion relates chiefly to the anarchist movement of his time. There have been fanatical movements since. The Secret Army Organization in Algeria is but the latest.

2 The best source easily available at that time was Eugen Kogon's *Der SS-Staat: Das System der Deutschen Konzentration-slager*, Berlin, 1946. Many of my data are from his book. Some years later H. G. Adler, after several years of research, wrote *Theresianstadt, 1941–1945. Das Antlitz einer Zwangsgemeinschaft* (Tuebingen, 1955), and still later published *Die Verheimlichte Wahrheit, Theresienstaedter Dokumente* (Tuebingen, 1958), a book of documents concerning that camp in which Czech and other Jews were concentrated, demoralized and destroyed. Kogon, a Catholic intellectual, and Adler, a Bohemian Jew, both wrote out of personal experience in the Concentration Camps. Both considered it their duty to present the phenomenon objectively to the public. None of their statements has ever been challenged.

3 Kogon, *op. cit.*, p. 316.

## SUPPLEMENTAL READINGS

Aiken, Michael, and Jerald Hage: "Organizational Alienation: A Comparative Analysis," *American Sociological Review*, vol. 31 (August 1966), pp. 497–507.

Cumming, Elaine, and William E. Henry: *Growing Old: The Process of Disengagement*, New York: Basic Books, Inc., Publishers, 1961.

Durkheim, Emile: *Suicide: A Study of Sociology*, New York: The Free Press, 1951.

Fromm, Erich: *Escape from Freedom*, New York: Holt, Rinehart and Winston, Inc., 1941.

Hajda, Jan: "Alienation and Integration of Student Intellectuals," *American Sociological Review*, vol. 26 (October 1961), pp. 758–777.

Heilbroner, Robert L.: "The Impasse of American Optimism," *American Scholar*, vol. 29 (winter 1959–1960), pp. 13–21.

Keniston, Kenneth: "Alienation and the Decline of Utopia," *American Scholar*, vol. 29 (April 1960), pp. 161–200.

Lowenthal, Marjorie Fiske: "Social Isolation and Mental Illness," *American Sociological Review*, vol. 29 (February 1964), pp. 54–70.

Miller, Curtis R., and Edgar W. Butler: "Anomia and Eunomia: A Methodological Evaluation of Srole's Anomia Scale," *American Sociological Review*, vol. 31 (June 1966), pp. 400–405.

Miller, George A.: "Professionals in Bureaucracy: Alienation among Industrial Scientists and Engineers," *American Sociological Review*, vol. 32 (October 1967), pp. 755–767.

Riesman, David, Nathan Glazer, and Reuel Denney: *The Lonely Crowd*, New Haven, Conn.: Yale University Press, pp. 242–260.

Seeman, Melvin: "On the Personal Consequences of Alienation in Work," *American Sociological Review*, vol. 32 (April 1967), pp. 273–385.

Tiryakian, Edward A.: *Sociologism and Existentialism.* Englewood Cliffs, N.J.: Prentice-Hall, Inc., 1962, pp. 151–171.

Todd, Joan F.: *Social Work with the Mentally Subnormal*, New York: Humanities Press, 1967.

Wittenberg, Rudolph M.: *The Troubled Generation: Toward Understanding and Helping the Young Adult*, New York: Association Press, 1967.

PART TWO

# FUNDAMENTAL

# INSTITUTIONAL PROBLEMS

The industrial revolution underlies, in a general sense, all the major problem areas discussed in this book. At this point we examine the impact of industrialization within the economic realm itself, with particular emphasis on the manner in which institutions are interrelated and interdependent. It is almost immediately apparent that the social ramifications of industrialism are not easy to assess because of the conflicting descriptions, interpretations, and evaluations. This has been no less a problem for social scientists. Probably the most widely known scientific explanation of social problems, the "cultural-lag" hypothesis, is still the subject of much controversy. Those who support the lag thesis state that developments in the social structure (family, religion, and the political system) have not kept pace with technological changes; hence there is a strain—a social problem almost by definition— between spheres or parts of the culture. Despite the advantages of this explanation as a theory, investigators have deplored the looseness with which the term "lag" is used and its obvious value connotations; that is, what is a lag for one may not be a lag for another.

From the perspective of the general public, probably the most appropriate example of the lack of consensus on the current nature of the economic system is the ideological battle over the alleged subversion of capitalism, free trade, and private enterprise, with particular stress on the role of government. Many Americans find the term "welfare state" distasteful because of an attachment to ideological positions that are incongruent with present economic trends. In light of the fact that a major part of our population has participated freely in one or more "welfare" programs (veterans' benefits, unemployment compensation, price supports, federal aid to education, and social security) and the many indicators of the unwillingness of business and industry to engage in free competition (restraint of trade, price fixing, patent infringements, oligopolistic tendencies), there may be some question of the gain in perpetuating the laissez-faire myth.

With the increasing complexity of the economic system and, as a consequence, its disruptions from time to time, the federal government has played an increasingly active role, if for no other reason, because of pressures for financial assistance, protection, and regulation from various groups. By now the federal government, as well as state and local governments, are deeply and directly involved in the economic activities of the society as owner, producer, distributor, employer, and consumer. The practices and standards of operation set by government have a significant effect on the rest of the economy. As the ultimate holder of power, the federal government often acts as the final arbiter in conflicts between segments of the economy, such as labor and management, retailers and consumers, and competing firms. Finally, the myriad difficulties associated with the implementation of federally sponsored poverty programs have stimulated key political leaders to recommend greater decentralization in design and administration, including active participation by the private sector. The outcome of conflicting trends in this area may suggest more generally whether there will be any marked change during the 1970s in the nature and degree of involvement by the federal government.

John K. Galbraith and Michael Harrington discuss the contrasting problems of affluence and poverty in contemporary America. Galbraith maintains that our capacity to produce goods and services is substantially higher than our consumption capacity in terms of basic needs and desires, and that we now have to create new demands to keep the economic system in balance. However, because of our preoccupation with production and privately produced goods and services, we are faced with two problems in a peacetime economy: we may have reached a saturation point in the realm of private consumption (anything that can be purchased by an individual), and we have seriously neglected the urgency of public services (educational facilities, hospitals, parks and playgrounds, police services, and roads). Diverting resources to the public services would, according to Galbraith, resolve both problems. In *The Affluent Society* he suggests other techniques to increase consumption: reduction in the length of the workweek, withdrawal of persons from the labor force by increasing the period of formal education and decreasing the age of retirement, and making work more enjoyable.

Michael Harrington grants that the poor in America now have material possessions that would have been regarded as luxuries in the past, and that the poverty of other nations is far more extreme. The fact remains, according to Harrington, that at least 20 percent of the population is entangled in a "culture of poverty" in a society that has the resources to ensure a decent level of living for all its citizens. Family income provides only one of many possible indices of poverty; others include housing, medicine, food, and "opportunities." As another observer has stated, "poverty is a pattern of hopelessness and helplessness, a view of the world and of oneself as static, limited and irredeemably expendable."

The concept of a "poverty line" based on a sliding scale to allow for variations in area of residence and size of family permits us to construct population estimates of the number of Americans subsisting on substandard incomes. On the basis of the current formula of $3,335 a year as the poverty line for an urban family of four as the most typical example (with polar points of $1,180 for a single male on a farm and $7,910 for a city family with eleven or more children), it is estimated that there are 30 million impoverished Americans. Contrary to the impression given by riots and all the other dramatic problems of the slums, Negroes are not the major component of the poor; two out of every three are white. Of the 11 million rural poor, nearly 9 million are white. Nearly half the poor are twenty-one or younger, while one-quarter are fifty-five or older. One-third of all Americans sixty-five or older—over 5 million—are poor. Although Harrington suggests the type of program that is necessary to reduce the culture of poverty, he is not optimistic because of the pervasive indifference to the plight of the poor, many of whom are not covered by welfare provisions. Federal, state, and local governments furnish some type of public assistance to approximately 8 million people, but the remaining 22 million who live below the poverty line defined above are not eligible for public assistance.

After only six years Harrington's recommended action program, which many still regard as the product of an alarmist, is not nearly as far reaching as a guaranteed-income program. Although no specific plan has received widespread support (the "negative income tax" is probably the best known), a growing number of academic, business, and political leaders support the view that some form of universal guaranteed income is the best means of eliminating poverty in the United States. All plans share two basic premises. First, need, as objectively measured by income and family size, should be the only basis for determining the amount of financial assistance to which an individual and/or family is entitled. Second, as an incentive to work and to train for better jobs, payments to families who earn income should be reduced by only a fraction of their earnings. About one-third of the nation's 30 million poor are in families with a full-time breadwinner who earns low wages; incomes in these cases would be supplemented. For the remaining two-thirds, the proponents offer their alternatives to replace the present welfare system, which applies mainly to those who cannot work or cannot work full time.

There are presently two major factors negating implementation of an income-guarantee plan. First, large segments of the general public, who reflect the work-oriented culture, oppose this alternative as just another handout, another way of avoiding work. Second, all plans would be expensive in absolute dollar terms, with estimates ranging from $10 billion to $25 billion a year, in addition to the $8 billion the nation now spends on welfare payments. Balanced against the financial costs, however, is the prospect that "poverty will continue to breed poverty." According to one recent study, more than 70 percent of all poor families have four or more children, in comparison with a national average of 1.35. Although two-thirds of all poor mothers are married and are living with their husbands, half the husbands do not hold regular jobs; the other half have full-time jobs that do not pay enough to lift them above the poverty line.

Unemployment is obviously a central issue. The rates reported by the government are on the high side because anyone who does not have a "job" (for example, housewives, teenagers, and retired persons) is counted as unemployed. However, with a return to a peacetime economy, there is reason for concern in the potential effects of automation and increased mechanization, as well as the continuing impact of the baby boom after World War II. The baby boom alone resulted in the requirement for approximately 50,000 new jobs a week during the 1960s, at least twice the rate for the previous decade. Traditionally, those hardest hit are the unskilled workers, agricultural laborers, minorities, and the aged. With the lower total unemployment rates during the Vietnam period, the key problem has been to fit the available workers to the available jobs. There have been attempts to encourage and train people to fill the presently unmet demand for certain trade, mechanical, and service-repair skills. However, many of the unfilled jobs are at the unskilled level, with the correlates of undesirable hours, unpleasant working conditions, and pay near the statutory minimum ($1.60 an hour). The cost of living in large cities is exceptionally high even without the exploitation of the low-income consumer, detailed by David Caplovitz in the selection from *The Poor Pay More*. In the chapter on population Donald Bogue discusses the effects of the large numbers of unemployed that can be expected with an increasing population even if the rate of unemployment is no higher than 5 to 7 percent.

The extent of consumer debt ties into production and employment. As a consequence of our prevailing philosophy of "buy now, pay later," the average American family is carrying approximately $1,300 in installment obligations, exclusive of home mortgages. Aside from the obvious consequences of personal bankruptcy and foreclosures on home mortgages, overextended consumer debt at any one time tends to dissipate the consumption capacity of society necessary to maintain an expanding economy. Although it is a fascinating and certainly controversial issue, regarded as a social problem of the first order by many, the national debt of the federal government is beyond the scope of this book. Similarly, the more immediate concern about the international financial crises in the latter half of the 1960s, manifested as inflation and a balance-of-payments deficit in the United States, cannot be considered here in detail. However, the budget policies (taxes and spending) and the monetary policies (interest rates and other restrictions on the availability of credit) adopted by the federal government to curb the recent economic boom will be of direct relevance in shaping our capacity to deal with the problems outlined here.

Along with the ideological conflicts, the increasing participation of government, and the problems of affluence and poverty, unemployment, consumer debt, and inflation, another contemporary feature of the American economy is the concentration of resources and power. We now have big business, big unions, and big government. For example, the extent to which economic power is concentrated in a few companies is indicated by the fact that in 1959 the 7,000 corporations with assets over $50 million, comprising 0.2 percent of all corporations, accounted for over 60 percent of all corporate income. The classic single case is AT&T, which controlled gross revenues in 1965 greater in amount than the combined revenues of the three largest state governments of California, New York, and Pennsylvania. In general, a few, usually four or fewer, companies in many industries (such as automobile, tobacco, meat, and aluminum) tend to dominate in terms of capital assets, number of employees, and profits.

The trends indicated by these figures have been intensified recently by a flurry of mergers and the expansion of the conglomerate form of corporation. An associated development is that the control of these large corporations has become concentrated in the hands of management officials, who own very little of the stock. Thus managers, not owners, run the corporations. The power of directors and managers is now being threatened by the officials of large funding institutions such as pension funds and mutual funds, which may hold controlling blocks of shares. Finally, the concentration is reinforced by interlocking directorates, intercorporate stockholding, and reliance upon common servicing firms for financial, legal, advertising, and public-relations assistance. The advantages of large productive units are not denied. The question is what undesirable conditions may occur as a product of the socially approved system.

The same question applies to the developments in labor unions, agriculture, and the professions. With the changing attitude of government in the early 1930s, the strength of unions, both in numbers and in power, has grown tremendously. Unions are now negotiating contracts that cover a wide range of concerns from present income to retirement and work conditions to leisure activities and medical benefits for the entire family. In addition, they influence the selection and election of political candidates, and with increasing frequency they are participating directly with management in establishing company policy. The high costs of modern farming practices and the government-support programs that have favored the large producers are two basic catalysts in the concentration of agriculture. Department of Agriculture estimates indicate that some 650,000 persons a year change from farm to nonfarm residence and that since April 1960 the number of nonwhites living on farms has dropped more than 40 percent. These figures reflect the perpetuation, if not the intensification, of poverty in rural areas, which in turn serves to drive even more people to the cities. Illustrative of the trend toward concentration in the professions is the increasing involvement of the scientist in large-scale team research, the physician in the hospital, and the lawyer in the law firm or "law factory."

It is interesting to note that even the influence of the consumer is less proliferated than in the past, although there has been no sustained effort to organize, despite exploitation by other sectors of the economy. The consumer now has a quasi-protector in giant retailers (mail-order houses and grocery and department-store chains) that buy as cheaply as possible from the producers and sell at a low profit margin to the general public. Recently both federal and state governments have become more active in representing consumer interests through legislative action, advisory councils, and enforcement agencies. Also, in the area of consumer concentration the pivotal role of the government as a consumer is noteworthy. In 1967 approximately 80 percent of the aerospace industry's products and services were absorbed by the federal government. Without reference to level, government spends 20 to 25 percent of the gross national product, that is, the value of all goods and services produced in a year.

Sociologists use the term "bureaucracy" to refer to the pattern of organization that predominates in economic activities, but bureaucracy has also become a prevailing part of all phases of man's social existence because it is well suited to any large-scale association, religious, educational, governmental, or military. Particular bureaucracies vary in the details of their operations, but to a degree they all manifest the following characteristics: (1) rules and regulations to cover every possible contingency, (2) rather elaborate specialization of jobs, (3) a hierarchy of authority with well-established lines of responsibility, (4) selection of personnel on the basis of technical or professional qualifications, and (5) an emphasis on impersonal judgments and evaluations.

Although these ideal characteristics are implemented to facilitate the rational and efficient achievement of the organization's goals, they also cause problems well known to the general public and well documented in the professional literature. Several illustrations must suffice. Evaluation of work performance is made difficult because a person's task may bear on only a minute portion of the total project. The concern with conformity to the rules may slow operations and increase costs, as well as unduly antagonize the customer or client. With the sharp divisions of authority may come avoidance of responsibility, or "buck-passing." A number of observers have stressed the more pervasive consequences, particularly in terms of the value systems and personalities of the participants, as discussed by Whyte in the previous chapter. A theoretical overview that places these problems in perspective is provided by William J. Goode in his article on the protection of the "inept." After examining the processes and patterns that protect the inept as well as limit the effects of their potential destructiveness, Goode defends the hypothesis that "the modern system is more productive because its social structures *utilize the inept more efficiently*, rather than because it gives greater opportunity and reward to the more able."

Future analyses of social problems associated with our economic system will undoubtedly give increasing attention to automation, the nature of work, the employment of married women, and leisure. Automation has significance beyond the problem of declining employment and the redistribution of employment opportunities. Even the controversy about the extent to which unemployment will increase through automation would be substantially resolved by indicators of the extent to which the nation will support programs to reduce poverty, rebuild cities, eliminate pollutants, and develop facilities for leisure activities. New commitments in such areas would offset the potential labor surplus caused by increased productivity through automation and, hopefully, a reduction in our defense economy. Another important aspect of automation is the impact of the computer on decision-making processes, and for that matter, who will participate in the decisions. Will the research scientists, mathematicians, economists, and the managers of the new computer technology replace businessmen and executives as leaders of the economy? Selected implications of a computer technology are dramatically depicted by Alan Westin in "The Snooping Machine," which appears in the next chapter.

The gainful employment of a growing number of married women—approximately one-third of the labor force is female, and most are married—reflects the changing status of all women. Jessie Bernard, whose article is cited in the chapter on the family, has discussed general trends determining the current status of women, particularly in relation to men. More specifically, the high rates of divorce and delinquency imply that ways have not yet been worked out to replace the mother in the home and to readjust the husband-wife relationship. We are even further behind in planning for profitable use of the added leisure as workweeks are shortened with no decrease in income. Perhaps the major requirement is a change in the mores that place a positive value on work and negative connotations on the enjoyment of leisure as an end in itself. But then how will the male who justifies his existence solely on the basis of his vocational endeavors achieve the status of success as work becomes less meaningful? Much of the criticism of existing conditions by both the professional and layman seems to reflect the basic and rapid changes that have taken place in the economic realm within the lifetime of our parents and grandparents. We may speculate over whether our children will feel the same aversion for the concentration of economic power, government controls, bureaucracies, and leisure. Student protests against the establishment suggest that the changeover is not yet a *fait accompli*.

John K. Galbraith leads off this chapter with an overview of his position on the problems of an affluent society. The second selection, by Michael Harrington, serves both as a rebuttal and as a summary of his thesis that a significant segment of our population is enmeshed in poverty. David Caplovitz, in a selection from *The Poor Pay More*, details some of the forces in the merchant-consumer relationship that contribute to the total sensation of being poor. Finally, the process, patterns, and consequences of protecting the inept are examined by William J. Goode.

## 13   ECONOMICS AND THE QUALITY OF LIFE

JOHN KENNETH GALBRAITH

In this article I suggest the social problems, and therewith the political tasks, which become most important with a relatively advanced state of economic development. These tasks are, I believe, of special importance to scientists; their accomplishment places some special responsibility on the scientist.

To see the issues in proper perspective one must have in mind the relation of economic circumstance to social thought and therewith to political action. In the poor society this relationship is powerful and rigid. For various reasons the rich society continues to assume that economic condition must be the dominant influence on social thought and action. This assumption becomes, in turn, a barrier to rational thought and needed action. It is exploited by vested intellectual and pecuniary interests. Let me summarize the matter briefly.[1]

Economic circumstance has a dominant influence on social attitudes in the poor society because, for those who are poor, nothing is so important as their poverty and nothing is so important as its mitigation. In consequence, only religion, with, among other things, its promise of later reward for enduring privation with patience, has had a competitive position. And since for nearly all time nearly all people have lived under the threat

Reprinted from John K. Galbraith, "Economics and the Quality of Life," *Science*, vol. 145 (1964), pp. 117–123, by permission of the author and the American Association for the Advancement of Science. Copyright ©1964 by the American Association for the Advancement of Science.

of economic privation, men of all temperament and views have stressed the controlling and permanent influence of economic need on social attitude. "The modes of production of material life determine the general character of the social, political, and intellectual processes of life."[2] "Here and there the arduor of the military or the artistic spirit has been for a while predominant; but religious and economic influences . . . have nearly always been more important than all others put together."[3]

In the poor society not only do economic considerations dominate social attitudes but they rigidly specify the problems that will be accorded priority. Under conditions of scarcity and human privation there is obvious need to get as much as possible out of the productive resources that are available—to use the labor, capital, natural resources and intelligence of the community with maximum efficiency. Such effort enlarges the supply of goods and thus mitigates the most pressing problem of the society, which is the scarcity of needed things. There is similar concern over who gets the revenues from production and who thus can buy what is produced, for one man's undue advantage will be another man's painful deprivation. Thus the two classical concerns of normative economics—how to increase productive efficiency and how to reconcile this with distributive equity—are the natural consequence of general poverty.

In the past in poor communities those whom feudal prerogative, sanguinary appropriation, personal fortune, exceptional personal accomplishment or military or political success exempted from the common privation quickly became subject to non-economic preoccupations—military adventure, political entrepreneurship, artistic patronage, sexual achievement, social intercourse, horsemanship. Accomplishment in these pursuits and diversions became, indeed, an index of economic emancipation. Increased well-being of people at large also loosens the grip of economics on social attitudes. Improved efficiency no longer mitigates physical pain and privation. The person who gets more does not of necessity impose suffering on the person who gets less. However, economic compulsions continue to have a highly influential bearing on social attitudes and political behavior in the generally affluent community. Although they release their absolute grip, economic goals retain, nonetheless, much of their original prestige.

This is partly for reasons of tradition. Economic goals having so long been considered paramount, they have come to be considered immutable. Economists have also long equated physical with psychic need; for many years none might pass a Ph.D. examination who said that the wish of a poor family for shelter was superior in urgency to the wish of a well-to-do family for a shelter that outshone that of the family next door. To do so was to interpose unscientific judgments and invite immediate discredit. Psychic need being on a parity with physical need, the urgency of increased production, and thus of the economic problem, was not supposed to diminish with increased well-being.

Economics also retains its grip on social attitudes because of compassionate appeal to the problem of the man who is unemployed or, to a lesser but growing extent, a member of a racially less-privileged group. As living standards have risen, consumption has pressed less insistently on income. Failure to offset the resulting savings came to mean unemployment. Against the well-being of the majority had thus to be set the misfortune of those whom increasing affluence left without work and reliable income. And this disadvantage, it has come more recently to be observed, is suffered in special measure by Negroes and other minority groups. So even though improvement in

living standards might be less urgent, improvement in economic performance to provide jobs for the unemployed and the minorities remained of high importance and appeals to this purpose have a high moral content. Increasingly the purpose of the economy has become not the goods it produces but the jobs it provides.

Economic goals are also strongly, if not always visibly, supported by vested interest. The prestige of important groups in the community depends on the priority accorded to their function. If nothing is so important as production no one is as important as the producer—the businessman. If other goals take precedence so do other people. The importance of economic goals for the prestige of the economist needs scarcely to be emphasized.

But economic goals accord even more practical support to vested position. If such goals are paramount, public issues will be decided according to economic tests. These are much more uncomplicated than other tests. A road can be put through a park, a monument replaced by an earning asset, a greenbelt turned over to industry or housing, a change in work rules resisted, a welfare measure rejected on a simple showing of economic effect. This is a great advantage to those identified with economic activity. Different goals would lead to a different—and also less predictable—decision with different benefits and other beneficiaries.

Finally economic goals remain important for the vacuum they fill. A society must have a purpose. The most obvious and tangible purpose is to produce goods for private consumption. The annual increase in this production can then be a measure of national vigor. That is the measure we now employ.

We are allowed occasional doubts about our present measures of national achievement. And there are anomalies that are a trifle embarrassing. As more basic requirements are filled, expansion naturally occurs in less urgent items. There is diminished emphasis on steel or bread grains (these, or the capacity for producing them, may even be redundant) and more on electric golf carts and electric toothbrushes. Questions may arise—as I have noted on other occasions—whether national vigor is to be measured by ability to have dental hygiene without muscular effort or athletic endeavor while sitting down. Economic growth is a measure of stern devotion to national goals. Growth consists increasingly of items of luxury consumption. Thus we perform the considerable feat of converting the enjoyment of luxury into an index of national virtue. This arouses at least some doubts.

We are allowed concern, also, as to whether all of the important tasks of the society, economic and non-economic, are being equally well-performed. The contrast between public penury and private affluence is increasingly remarked. Finally a few may have speculated as to why individuals, as they achieve higher levels of well-being, should escape from economic preoccupations while a nation, passing upward along the same path, must remain under the spell of economic compulsion. Why, if individuals turn to non-economic preoccupations, must a nation remain resolutely Philistine?

But, in general, we remain subject to economic preoccupations. Economic goals are paramount. The guidance of economists on how to achieve them is accepted as a matter of course. There are, I believe, serious dangers in this delegation. This we see if we look more closely at the sociology and the mystique of economics. We then see how this most developed and influential of the social sciences can be influential also in misguidance when the society is subject to change and when the social problem has ceased to be primarily economic.

## CHANGE IN ECONOMICS

Unlike the natural sciences, which have long been viewed as the behavioral norm by economists, economics is subject to two types of change. The first is in the interpretation of given phenomena. The second is in needed accommodation to change in economic behavior or institutions. The development of the social accounts (national income, gross national product, and their components) in the thirties, the evolution of the input-output matrix in the forties, the analysis of money flows, the development of operations analysis, and the application of computer techniques to economic data in the fifties and sixties are all examples of the first type of change. The accommodation of economic theory to the rise of the trade union or the development of the large corporation or to changing behavior resulting from transition of the average person from comparative privation to, by past standards, comparative well-being are examples of the second type of change.

Economics is progressive as regards the first type of change—conceptual advances or innovations in interpretive apparatus are frequent, promptly examined and, where useful, willingly adopted. From index numbers through the social accounts to modern quantitative methods, these developments have contributed greatly to the guidance of the American economy and the conduct of business. Modern public and business administration are deeply dependent on them.

By contrast, economics is rigorously conservative in accommodating interpretation to underlying change. Until quite recently, wage theory was not accommodated to the existence of the unions. Their existence and even their importance was not denied. But, by an agreeable convention, one was allowed in pedagogy and scientific discourse to assume away the effect of such inconvenient change. "Let us suppose there are no unions or other impediments in the labor market." The modern corporation has not yet been assimilated to economic theory, although the corporate system is all but coterminous with mining, communications, public utilities and manufacturing—in short, the largest part of economic life. The theory of the firm makes no distinction between a Wisconsin dairy farm and General Motors Corporation except to the extent that the latter may be thought more likely to have some of the technical aspects of monopoly.[4] All economists agree that there has been a revolutionary increase in popular well-being in the past thirty years. Most textbooks have yet to concede that this has altered economic calculation or affected economic motivation. It is not supposed that the shape of the economic problem is changed by being solved.

The reasons for reluctance to admit to the effects of underlying change are three: again there is tendency to protect vested interest; there is the old and familiar phenomenon of the imitative scientism of the social sciences which is, perhaps, carried farther in economics than in any other discipline; and there is the natural wish of the scholar to avoid rowdiness and controversy.

On vested interest there need be little comment. We all have a lively stake in what we understand. Moreover, much underlying change, especially the movement to higher levels of well-being, diminishes the urgency and scope of economic judgment and diminishes, in some degree, the importance of the discipline. Unions and corporations introduce social theories of organization which replace the economists' market theory; well-being reduces the importance of economic choice and therewith of economic advice based on economic calculation. So, like cavalrymen, locomotive firemen and fundamentalist pastors, economists find it tempting to deny what it is professionally disadvantageous to concede.

The natural sciences are not subject to underlying institutional or behavioral change. In consequence, economics seems more scientific if it is deemed to have a similar immutability. This explains, in turn, the considerable scientific self-righteousness with which sophisticated scholars avow the irrelevance of, say, the advent of modern advertising for the theory of demand. It is a libel on the subject to suppose that its scientific verities are affected by such superficial change. Moreover, the first steps to bring institutional changes within the framework of economic analysis are invariably tentative, oral rather than mathematical and lacking the elegance of a methodological innovation. Hence they are readily dismissed by the men of scientific reputation or pretension as rather sloppy.[5] Thus does scientism sublimate the progressive instincts of the profession away from institutional accommodation and into methodological advance. It does so with the blessing of presumptively scientific attitude, method and conscience.

But an instinct to caution also plays a role.

Methodological change rarely has implications for public policy; if it does, they are likely to be minor. Assimilation to change, by contrast, may have large and radical policy implications. Economists who have been associated with such changes and the related policy—the late Lord Keynes in Britain, Alvin Hansen in the United States—have led a highly controversial existence. This is not to the taste of all. I do not suggest that economists are craven. Other disciplines have far less experience with controversy because they are not under attack at all. But it seems certain that many economists do find harmony agreeable. At the present time, having just come through the accommodation to underlying change now denoted as the Keynesian Revolution, and having discovered that the critics who once dissented are acquiescent and may indeed be sensing a common ground with economists on the conservative consequences of according priority to economic goals, there may well be a special reluctance to look for new trouble. In the intellectual backwaters the name of Keynes still strikes a radical note. Surely it is possible to bask a bit longer in the reputation for living dangerously that his name thus invokes.[6]

### ACCOMMODATION TO CHANGE

This reluctance to accommodate to underlying change is not new. Its consequence is that in time of change the practical advice which reflects the accepted economic view will often and perhaps usually be in error. The advice will relate to previous and not to the present institutions; but, needless to say, action must be related to the reality. If it is not it will be in some degree damaging.

The danger here can be illustrated by reference to the last great change in underlying behavior and institution and the related watershed in economic decision. In this century, as I have observed, unemployment—the failure to use resources—replaced the problem of efficiency in resource use. In the autumn of 1929, when unemployment began to grow rapidly, President Hoover's first instinct was to cut taxes, which he promptly recommended, and to urge corporations to maintain purchasing power by not reducing wages. This was completely in conflict with accepted economic views. These continued to respond to the belief that efficient production, not unemployment, was the central need. In accordance with these views there should be no interference with the labor market. Business confidence, also important for efficiency, required adherence to the gold standard and a balanced federal budget. This advice was of no value for preventing unemployment; nearly all economists would now agree that measures so inspired would make matters worse. In time, it might be added, Mr. Hoover surrendered to the accepted economic view. The subsequent reversal of the approved policies by President Roosevelt in 1933 was viewed at a minimum with skepticism and at a maximum with hostility by most economists of acknowledged reputation.[7] This outcome was to be expected. There had been extensive underlying change leading to change in the problem to be solved. Accommodation was, as usual, slow. Prescription was, accordingly, for the wrong problem. As a matter of prudence, this tendency of economists must be expected in any time of change.

## UNEMPLOYMENT

The preoccupation of economists continues to be with unemployment and with the immediately related question of the volume of output of goods and services which is the remedy for unemployment. As noted this is reinforced by moral sentiment. Only the heartless would countenance any other concern. Once again underlying change has made the preoccupation partially obsolete; as a result the recommendations are once again either irrelevant or damaging. I have used the phrase "partially obsolete." The problem is complicated by the tendency of institutional change to introduce new preoccupations without entirely dispensing with the old ones. In the 1930's, though unemployment became the central problem, inefficiency did not become unimportant. Economy in the use of resources remained desirable both in the interest of domestic users and the competitive position of the country. A high level of employ-

ment and an adequate rate of economic growth remain important now. The need is to prescribe first for the most important problems. If there is inconsistency in prescription for the primary and secondary (or other subordinate) problems, priority must go to the primary problem.

It will be agreed that, as unemployment declines from the (perhaps) 25 percent of the labor force which is reached as a maximum during the thirties to the 2 or 3 percent which is the practical minimum, concern should gradually shift to other issues. Some such transfer of attention should presumably have occurred when unemployment had reached the present level of around 6 percent. Failure so to shift attention will reflect some irrationally stubborn insistence on unemployment as *the* problem. A shift in attention will be even more certainly in order if there are obvious shortcomings in the lives of those who are employed—if education is deficient, regional development is unequal, slums persist, health care is inadequate, cultural opportunities unequal, entertainment meretricious, or racial equality imperfect. And the need for prior concern for education, slum abatement, improved health, regional development, or racial equality would be even more clear if these could be shown to be the cause of unemployment and retarded economic growth. In fact all of the conditions for a shift from the primary preoccupation with unemployment and growth do exist. The primary prescription must henceforth be for what may broadly be called the quality of life. This is now the primary goal.

Reference to the quality of life will be thought replete with value judgments; the condemnation of value judgments is one of the devices by which scientism enforces adherence to traditional preoccupations.[8] But there should be no major quarrel even by economists with a social goal which accords the individual the opportunity of providing for all of his needs, not merely for a part of them. And there will, one imagines, be a considerable measure of agreement that the individual is the end in himself and not the instrument of the organization, public or private, which was created to serve him. There are now recognizable imperfections in both of these areas. They follow from the priority accorded economic goals and the considerable power of the machinery we have created to pursue these goals.

## ECONOMIC GOALS

There is first the continuing imbalance in meeting of needs. We identify economic performance with the production of goods and services, and such production is the task of the private sector of the economy. As a result privately produced goods and services, even of the most frivolous sort, enjoy a moral sanction not accorded to any public services except defense. Desire for private goods is subject to active cultivation—a point to which I will return. And the equation of psychic with physical need excludes any notion of satiety. It is a mark of an enfeebled imagination to suggest (say) that two automobiles to a family is some kind of limit. Public services, by contrast, are the subject of no similar promotion; that there are severe limits to what should be expended for such services is, of course, assumed.

The consequence of this differential attitude is a sharp discrimination in favor of one and against another class of needs. Meanwhile a series of changes in the society increases the pressure for public services. Increasing population and increasing density of population increase the friction of person upon person and the outlay that is necessary for social harmony. And it is reasonable to suppose that growing proportion of the requirements of an increasingly civilized community—schools, colleges, libraries, museums, hospitals, recreational facilities—are by their nature in the public domain.

Finally increasing private production itself increases the urgency of public services. The automobile makes obvious demands in its requirements for streets and highways, for traffic control, control of air pollution and investment in public order. From the pressure of mining, fishing, lumbering and other resource industries on public agencies responsible for conservation to the pressure of the exploding container industry on trash removal,

the effect is similar.

It should also be observed that if appropriate attention is not accorded all needs, the private sector itself will suffer in technical performance. As Francis M. Bator has pointed out, "modern science has made public the very activity of producing inventions."[9] And modern industry has come to require its own type of man. One significant consequence is that a major part of the unemployment with which we are preoccupied is of people whose location, family characteristics, youthful environment or race denied them access in their youth to normal opportunities for education and training.[10] The same is true of individuals and families which fall below the poverty line.[11] Thus it comes about that the remedy for unemployment and individual privation depends to a very considerable degree on the balance between public and private services—or, more generally, on measures to improve the quality of life.

I have dealt with a number of these concerns before; I do not wish further to risk the rebuke that accrues to the scholar who repeats his own work and that of other people. But there is a new danger in this area which is now urgent.

If unemployment is deemed to be the dominant problem, and if, as in the past, expansion of the economy is deemed a complete remedy, it will not matter much how this is achieved. Tax reduction and an acceleration of the expansion in demand for the output of the private sector will be entirely appropriate. Even some reduction in public services if offset by a larger increase in private outlays will be sound policy. However, if the problem is the quality of the society, it will matter a great deal how the expansion of demand is managed. Improvement in needed public services, given the tendency to imbalance, improves the quality of the society. Expansion of private services without expansion of public services brings *prima facie* no similar improvement. It could lead to distortions that would mean a reduction in the quality of life. And plainly an expansion of the private sector which is won at the expense of the public sector is intolerable. It provides what we least need at the expense of what we most need. And since the ultimate remedy for much unemployment depends on public sector investment in the unemployed (or their children), the policy may fail in even its avowed purpose.

There may be times when tax reduction will be a legitimate measure for securing improved economic performance. Defense expenditures are a large share of all public outlays and also are protected by a different set of attitudes. Should it be possible and practical to reduce these, it would be possible and perhaps necessary to reduce taxes— even while improving other services.

It is possible also that prior to the recent tax cut, the tax system, with its highly progressive impact on increased personal and corporate income, took an undue amount of income from the economy when this was at or near full employment. As a result, with lower taxes there could be a higher rate of growth, higher public revenues and better provision for public services. This case was vigorously made. While I was less confident of the calculations than some of my friends—a recession arising from then current levels of tax collections was firmly predicted for mid-1963—one could not entirely reject the argument. But it is the only case that had merit. The Keynesian argument, which was and remains the more common case for tax reduction, is that any source of spending is acceptable that expands the economy. By bringing unbalanced expansion it misses opportunity for improvement in the quality of life. And since expansion and increased unemployment require improved public services, it may even be self-defeating. It also unites an undiscriminating and obsolete Keynesianism with those who argue for lower taxes and less government. This could be a formidable and damaging coalition.[12]

## SUBORDINATION OF THE INDIVIDUAL

The quality of life will also suffer if the individual is not an end in himself but an instrument of some purpose that is not his own. This too is inherent in our situation. We have developed an economic system of considerable power. We have reason to be grateful for its achievements. But it has its

purposes; it seeks naturally to accommodate society to these purposes. If economic goals are preoccupying we will accept the accommodation of society to the needs of economic organization as an economic imperative. We will regret our surrender but we will reconcile ourselves to the inevitable. If we have economic goals in proper perspective we will see that no such subordination is necessary.

One part of this subordination, that of the individual to specific organization, most notably the corporation, has been much discussed.[13] There can be little doubt as to the tendency. The corporation requires its own type of man; he must be willing to subordinate his own goals to those of the organization. And it is necessary that he do so if the organization is to succeed. Such subordination, in some form or other, makes possible group performance of tasks. This merges experience, knowledge or technical skills for a result superior in content and reliability to that of the individual. It is a functional necessity of modern organization. Such suppression of individuality in modern organization is not lessened by the contemporaneous espousal, as regularly happens, of a muscular creed of individualism.

We must keep this part of the problem in perspective. The competitive market also has its *type*, and it is not so clear that the wary, uncompassionate, self-regarding, wit-matching trader, in whom both deviousness and cupidity may have been as often rewarded as penalized, would have been kept in the Temple in competition with the Organization Man. The corporation executive commits himself voluntarily to what Mr. Whyte has called the social ethic of the corporation.[14] He can readily escape if he is willing to forego the compensation which purchases his conformity.

The most serious problem is not the discipline imposed by organization on its members and accepted by them. The problem is the discipline such organization seeks to impose on society to make the latter accord better with its needs. The behavior and beliefs of society are in fact subject to extensive management to accord with economic need and convenience. Not even scientific truth, much as our culture presumes to canonize it, is at all exempt. Thus the tobacco industry does not conceal its discontent with scientists who, on the basis of rather impressive evidence aver that cigarettes are a cause not only of lung cancer but a disconcerting assortment of other fatal or disabling maladies. The economic well-being of the industry requires the active and energetic recruitment of new customers. This need is paramount. So there is no alternative to impeaching the scientists and their evidence.[15] We should notice that the freedom of the individual to smoke and contract cancer is not at issue here. That fundamental liberty is not in question.

Similarly, and in conceivably a more dangerous area, we have come to assume that our defense strategy, and even in some degree our foreign policy, will be accommodated to the needs of the industries serving the defense establishment. Before leaving office, President Eisenhower issued his notable warning on the rise of the civilian-military complex, a concern which had previously been pressed somewhat less influentially by the late C. Wright Mills.[16] The Eisenhower-Mills contention was, in essence, that defense budgets and procurement were being influenced not by national need but by what served the economic interests of suppliers. Similar consideration, as distinct from national need, has manifested itself on behalf of manned bombers, Skybolt, Dyna-Soar and other weapons including some where it met with success. The resistance in 1963 to the partial nuclear test ban by organizations closely identifed with the manufacture of weapon delivery systems was motivated not by a unique view of national interest but by industrial need and the preferences of the Air Force.

However, these are only extreme cases; they highlight an effort that is pervasive and inherent. No producer, in our present state of economic development, would be so naive as to launch a new product without appropriately reconstructing the pattern of consumer wants to include the innovation. He cannot be sure of succeeding. But he would never be forgiven if he failed to try. Nor does any commercially viable producer leave the

consumer to unpersuaded choice among existing products. The management of consumption in accordance with economic interest has become one of the advanced arts of our time. The participants urge their virtuosity in uninhibited terms save, perhaps, when it becomes a subject for scientific discussion. At this stage it becomes a bland though indispensable exercise in providing public information.

In a well-to-do community we cannot be much concerned over what people are persuaded to buy. The marginal utility of money is low; were it otherwise people would not be open to persuasion. The more serious problem lies in a conflict with the truth and esthetics. The meretriciousness associated with the shaping of popular taste to economic need is by way of becoming one of the hallmarks of the culture. There is little that can be said about most economic goods. A toothbrush does little but clean teeth. Aspirin does little but dull pain. Alcohol is overwhelmingly important only as an intoxicant. An automobile can take one reliably to a destination and return him and its further features are of small consequence as compared with the traffic encountered. There being so little to be said, much must be invented. Social distinction must be associated with a house or automobile, sexual fulfillment with an automobile or shaving lotion, social acceptance with a hair oil or mouthwash, improved health with a cigarette or a purgative. We live surrounded by a systematic appeal to a dream world which all mature, scientific reality would reject. We, quite literally, advertise our commitment to immaturity, mendacity, and profound gulibility. We justify it by saying that it is economically indispensable.

The conflict with esthetics is even more serious and much more general. As the economic problem is resolved, people can be expected to become increasingly concerned about the beauty of their environment. The natural priorities of a society proceed from the getting of the goods to getting the surroundings in which they can be enjoyed. But, at least in the short run, there is no necessary harmony between economic and esthetic accomplishment. On the contrary, short-run conflict must be assumed.

With rare and probably accidental exceptions, an esthetically attractive environment requires development within an overall framework. Thus agreeable urban communities are invariably those in which law or fashion allow of variant treatments within a larger and symmetrical framework. Such communities must be related to properly protected open space, for parks and countryside lose their meaning if they are invaded at random by habitation, traffic, industry, or advertising. Some segregation of industry and commerce from living space is essential if the latter is to be agreeable—neither a steel mill nor a service station is an esthetically rewarding neighbor. In a different area good theatre and good music require the protection of a mood; they cannot be successfully juxtaposed to rhymed jingles on behalf of a laxative.

## ECONOMIC PRIORITY

All of this is in conflict with short-run economic priority.[17] The latter will seek the greatest possible freedom for uninhibited use and dissonance; it is the essence of esthetics that there be some framework and hence some control. Those who sense the need for such control surrender to the assumed economic necessity. For its part economic organization strongly affirms its need for freedom. Proposals for control are pictured as subversive; concern for beauty is pictured as effete. Purely as a matter of tactics this makes sense. It is an elementary precaution in a conflict of this kind to identify the enemy with bolshevism or pederasty.

We see, however, that this need not necessarily be accepted. The priority of economics will continue to be defended—and with enhanced vigor that derives partly from the sense of increasing obsolescence and the need to resist it. But we can have the social planning that erases grime and squalor and which preserves and enhances beauty. A price in industrial efficiency may be necessary. Indeed it should be assumed. Economic development enables us to pay the price; it is why we have development. We do not have development in order to make our surroundings more hideous, our

culture more meretricious or our lives less complete.

Nor, as scholars and scientists, should we be detained for a moment by the protest that this is a highbrow view and that people want what they want. This is the standard defense of economic priority. Those who most insist that this is what people really want are those who most fear that, given the opportunity, people would make a different choice--one that involves a greater measure of social control of environment.

It will be sensed that these are controversial matters—much more controversial than the questions surrounding economic growth and full employment. Important questions of social policy inevitably arouse passion. A consenses is readily reached on those that are unimportant or on their way to solution. There could be no better test that economics is now solving the wrong problem.

Escape from the commitment to economic priority has, it will be clear, a broadly emancipating role. It enables us to consider a range of new tasks from the beautification of our cities, the cleaning up of roadside commerce and advertising, the enlargement of cultural opportunity, the redemption of mass communications to the suppression of the influence of weapons makers on foreign policy. The political and social power that is available for these tasks is not negligible. Scientists, humane scholars, teachers, artists, and the community that is identified with these preoccupations have been asserting themselves with increasing influence and self-confidence. Given a clear view of the issue and need and given release from the assumption of economic priority, that influence will surely deepen and expand. Nothing is more to be wished, welcomed and urged.

## REFERENCES AND NOTES

1   I have discussed the matter at some length in *The Affluent Society*, Boston: Houghton-Mifflin, 1958, chap. 2.

2   Karl Marx, preface to *Critique of Political Economy*, 1859.

3   A. Marshall, *Principles of Economics*, 5th ed., London: The Macmillan Company, 1907, p. 1.

4   ". . . the functioning of the modern corporate sys-

tem has not to date been adequately explained or, if certain explanations are accepted as adequate, it seems difficult to justify." E. S. Mason, *The Corporation and Modern Society*, Cambridge, Mass.: Harvard University Press, 1959, p. 4.

5  One thinks here of Adolf Berle's efforts to bring the corporation within the framework of economic analysis. Though it has many shortcomings it has had much greater relevance to the behavior of the firm than theoretical models which ignore questions of size and corporate structure. But among the economic cognoscenti the work has enjoyed very little standing.

6  I should like to stress again that in discussing the reluctance of economists to accommodate to underlying change my motive is not criticism but to isolate a fact of some contemporary consequence. And while I am identified with the notion that increased well-being has had a profound effect on economic behavior, I am not entering a personal complaint of neglect. On the contrary, it is the view of important economies that these contentions have received too much attention. Thus in a recent article George Stigler, the present president of the American Economic Association, expresses "shock" that so many more Americans have read *The Affluent Society* than *The Wealth of Nations* ("The Intellectual and the Market Place," *University of Chicago Graduate School of Business, Selected Papers No. 3*, 1963). I am reluctant to reply to Professor Stigler, for I could seem to be urging the claims of my book against those of a very great classic. And I should conceivably be missing the deeper cause of Professor Stigler's sorrow, which may be not that so many read Galbraith and so few read Smith, but that hardly anyone reads Stigler at all.

7  The Roosevelt economists were largely without professional prestige. None of them—Rexford G. Tugwell, Gardiner C. Means, Mordecai Ezekiel, Lauchlin Currie—ever fully survived the premature identification with policies that nearly all economists now consider right. They were righteously excluded from professional honors. Nor were they the only ones. In 1936 the Harvard Department of Economics dismissed as eccentric a suggestion that John Maynard Keynes, the prophet of the policies related to unemployment, be numbered among the leading economists of the day who were being endowed with an honorary degree at the tercentenary celebrations in that year. Honors went to men who, in general, urged wrong but reputable policies.

Compare for example, *The Economics of the Recovery Program*, by seven Harvard economists, New York: Whittlesey House, McGraw-Hill Book Co., 1933.

8  It is held that the provision of an expanding volume of consumer goods, among which the consumer exercises a sovereign choice, involves no value judgments. This might be approximately true if everything the consumer needs were available from the market and if no attempt were made to manage his choice. Conservatives instinctively but wisely insist that almost all important needs can be provided by the market, and that management of the consumer is of negligible importance. This enables them to rest their case on an impersonal manifestation of individual choice. It is also evident that the preconditions for their case are far from being met.

9  F. M. Bator, *The Question of Government Spending*, New York: Harper & Row, Publishers, 1950, p. 107.

10  In March 1962, 40 percent of the unemployed had 8 years of schooling or less. This educational group accounted for only 30 percent of the total labor force. At a time when national unemployment was 6 percent among males aged 18 and over, it was 10.4 percent of those with 4 years of schooling or less and 8.5 percent among those with 5 to 7 years of schooling. Unemployment dropped to 4 percent among those with 13 to 15 years of schooling and to 1.4 percent of those with college training. Testimony of Charles Killingsworth, "Automation, Jobs and Manpower," Subcommittee on Employment and Manpower, U.S. Senate (The Clark Committee), Sept. 20, 1963.

11  In 1956, 13 percent of families had incomes of less than $2000. Of those with 8 or fewer years of education, 33.2 percent had incomes of less than $2000. Among all unattached individuals 54.1 percent had incomes of under $2000. Of those with 8 or fewer years of education, 80.3 percent had incomes under $2000. National Policy Committee on Pockets of Poverty, Washington, D.C., Dec. 6, 1963 (mimeographed).

12  "There is mounting realization of the injury to incentives and economic growth arising out of the magnitude of taxation. From this has come increasing determination to do something about it. This is all to the good. There is also a rising realization that there is something wrong about reducing taxes unless something also is done about curbing expenditures to avoid the need for big deficits in budgets. This also is good. But the general insistence on reducing expenditures falls short of that on reducing taxes. This failure to place equal emphasis on expenditure reduction can mean a danger of continuing big deficits." "Important Trends in Our Economy," *United States Steel Corporation, 1963 Annual Report*, p. 38.

13  W. H. Whyte, Jr., *The Organization Man*, New York:

Simon and Schuster, 1956. Whyte relates this subordination is rationalized by ". . . that contemporary body of thought which makes morally legitimate the pressures of society against the individual" (p. 7).

14 *Ibid.*

15 On March 31 of this year, Zach Toms, president of Liggett & Myers Tobacco Company, said of the Surgeon General's report: "we think . . . [it] went beyond the limits of the problem as now understood by other qualified scientists." At the same time the president of the American Tobacco Company, Robert B. Walker, dismissed the scientific evidence as ". . . first of all the frustrations of those who are unable to explain certain ailments that have accompanied our lengthening span of life on earth and who see in tobacco a convenient scapegoat." On April 14, Joseph F. Cullman, III, of Philip Morris, Inc., said that his advisers "do not feel the prime conclusion is justified on the basis of available scientific knowledge and evidence."

16 C. W. Mills, *The Power Elite*, New York: Oxford University Press, 1956.

17 Given the self-destructive character of much unplanned investment, the longer-run conflict is not so clear.

## 14 THE OTHER AMERICA MICHAEL HARRINGTON

The United States in the sixties contains an affluent society within its borders. Millions and tens of millions enjoy the highest standard of life the world has ever known. This blessing is mixed. It is built upon a peculiarly distorted economy, one that often proliferates pseudo-needs rather than satisfying human needs. For some, it has resulted in a sense of spiritual emptiness, of alienation. Yet a man would be a fool to prefer hunger to satiety, and the material gains at least open up the possibility of a rich and full existence.

At the same time, the United States contains an underdeveloped nation, a culture of poverty. Its inhabitants do not suffer the extreme privation of the peasants of Asia or the tribesmen of Africa, yet the mechanism of the misery is similar. They are beyond history, beyond progress, sunk in a paralyzing, maiming routine.

The new nations, however, have one advantage: poverty is so general and so extreme that it is the passion of the entire society to obliterate it. Every resource, every policy, is measured by its effect on the lowest and most impoverished. There is a gigantic mobilization of the spirit of the society:

aspiration becomes a national purpose that penetrates to every village and motivates a historic transformation.

But this country seems to be caught in a paradox. Because its poverty is not so deadly, because so many are enjoying a decent standard of life, there are indifference and blindness to the plight of the poor. There are even those who deny that the culture of poverty exists. It is as if Disraeli's famous remark about the two nations of the rich and the poor had come true in a fantastic fashion. At precisely that moment in history where for the first time a people have the material ability to end poverty, they lack the will to do so. They cannot see; they cannot act. The consciences of the well-off are the victims of affluence; the lives of the poor are the victims of a physical and spiritual misery.

The problem, then, is to a great extent one of vision. The nation of the well-off must be able to see through the wall of affluence and recognize the alien citizens on the other side. And there must be vision in the sense of purpose, of aspiration: if the word does not grate upon the ears of a gentile America, there must be a passion to end poverty, for nothing less than that will do.

In this summary chapter, I hope I can supply at least some of the material for such a vision. Let us try to understand the other America as a whole, to see its perspective for the future if it is left alone, to realize the responsibility and the potential for ending this nation in our midst.

But, when all is said and done, the decisive moment occurs after all the sociology and the description is in. There is really no such thing as "the material for a vision." After one reads the facts, either there are anger and shame, or there are not. And, as usual, the fate of the poor hangs upon the decision of the better-off. If this anger and shame are not forthcoming, someone can write a book about the other America a generation from now and it will be the same, or worse.

Perhaps the most important analytic point to have emerged in this description of the other America is the fact that poverty in America forms a culture, a way of life and feeling, that it makes a whole. It is crucial to generalize this idea, for it profoundly affects how one moves to destroy poverty.

The most obvious aspect of this interrelatedness is in the way in which the various subcultures of the other America feed into one another. This is clearest with the aged. There the poverty of the declining years is, for some millions of human beings, a function of the poverty of the earlier years. If there were adequate medical care for everyone in the United States, there would be less misery for old people. It is as simple as that. Or there is the relation between the poor farmers and the unskilled workers. When a man is driven off the land because of the impoverishment worked by technological progress, he leaves one part of the culture of poverty and joins another. If something were done about the low-income farmer, that would immediately tell in the statistics of urban unemployment and the economic underworld. The same is true of the Negroes. Any gain for America's minorities will immediately be translated into an advance for all the unskilled workers. One cannot raise the bottom of a society without benefiting everyone above.

Indeed, there is a curious advantage in the wholeness of poverty. Since the other America forms a distinct system within the United States, effective action at any one decisive point will have a "multiplier" effect; it will ramify through the entire culture of misery and ultimately through the entire society.

Then, poverty is a culture in the sense that the mechanism of impoverishment is fundamentally the same in every part of the system. The vicious circle is a basic pattern. It takes different forms for the unskilled workers, for the aged, for the Negroes, for the agricultural workers, but in each case the principle is the same. There are people in the affluent society who are poor because they are poor; and who stay poor because they are poor.

To realize this is to see that there are some tens of millions of Americans who are beyond the welfare state. Some of them are simply not covered by social legislation: they are omitted from Social Security and from minimum wage. Others are covered, but since they are so poor they do not know how to take advantage of the opportunities, or else their coverage is so inadequate as not to make a difference.

The welfare state was designed during that great burst of social creativity that took place in the 1930's. As previously noted its structure corresponds to the needs of those who played the most important role in building it: the middle third, the organized workers, the forces of urban liberalism, and so on. At the worst, there is "socialism for the rich and free enterprise for the poor," as when the huge corporation farms are the main beneficiaries of the farm program while the poor farmers get practically nothing; or when public funds are directed to aid in the construction of luxury housing while the slums are left to themselves (or become more dense as space is created for the well-off).

So there is the fundamental paradox of the welfare state: that it is not built for the desperate, but for those who are already capable of helping themselves. As long as the illusion persists that the poor are merrily freeloading on the public dole, so long will the other America continue unthreatened. The truth, it must be understood, is the exact opposite. The poor get less out of the welfare state than any group in America.

This is, of course, related to the most distinguishing mark of the other America: its common sense of hopelessness. For even when there are programs designed to help the other Americans, the poor are held back by their own pessimism.

On one level this fact has been described in this book as a matter of "aspiration." Like the Asian peasant, the impoverished American tends to see life as a fate, an endless cycle from which there is no deliverance. Lacking hope (and he is realistic to feel this way in many cases), that famous solution to all problems—let us educate the poor—becomes less and less meaningful. A person has to feel that education will do something for him if he is to gain from it. Placing a magnificent school with a fine faculty in the middle of a slum is, I suppose, better than having a run-down building staffed by incompetents. But it will not really make a difference so long as the environment of the tenement, the family, and the street counsels the children to leave as soon as they can and to disregard schooling.

On another level, the emotions of the other America are even more profoundly disturbed. Here it is not lack of aspiration and of hope; it is a matter of personal chaos. The drunkenness, the unstable marriages, the violence of the other America are not simply facts about individuals. They are the description of an entire group in the society who react this way because of the conditions under which they live.

In short, being poor is not one aspect of a person's life in this country, it is his life. Taken as a whole, poverty is a culture. Taken on the family level, it has the same quality. These are people who lack education and skill, who have bad health, poor housing, low levels of aspiration and high levels of mental distress. They are, in the language of sociology, "multiproblem" families. Each disability is the more intense because it exists within a web of disabilities. And if one problem is solved, and the others are left constant, there is little gain.

One might translate these facts into the moralistic language so dear to those who would condemn the poor for their faults. The other Americans are those who live at a level of life beneath moral choice, who are so submerged in their pover-

ty that one cannot begin to talk about free choice. The point is not to make them wards of the state. Rather, society must help them before they can help themselves.

There is another view about the culture of poverty in America: that by the end of the seventies it will have been halved.

It is important to deal in some detail with this theory. To begin with, it is not offered by reactionaries. The real die-hards in the United States do not even know the poor exist. As soon as someone begins to talk on the subject, that stamps him as a humanitarian. And this is indeed the case with those who look to a relatively automatic improvement in the lot of the other America during the next twenty years or so.

The second reason why this view deserves careful consideration is that it rests, to a considerable extent, upon the projection of inevitable and automatic change. Its proponents are for social legislation and for speeding up and deepening this process. But their very arguments could be used to justify a comfortable, complacent inaction.

So, does poverty have a future in the United States?

One of the most reasonable and sincere statements of the theme that poverty is coming to an end in America is made by Robert Lampman in the Joint Committee Study Paper "The Low-Income Population and Economic Growth." Lampman estimates that around 20 percent of the nation, some 32,000,000 people, are poor. (My disagreements with his count are stated in the Appendix.) And he writes, "By 1977-87 we would expect about 10 percent of the population to have low income status as compared to about 20 percent now."

The main point in Lampman's relatively optimistic argument is that poverty will decline naturally with a continuing rate of economic growth. As the sixties begin, however, this assumption is not a simple one. In the postwar period, growth increased until about the mid-fifties. Then a falling off occurred. In each of the postwar recessions, the recovery left a larger reservoir of "normal" prosperity unemployment. Also, long-term unemployment became more and more of a factor among the jobless. There were more people out of work, and they stayed out of work longer.

In the first period of the Kennedy Administration, various economists presented figures as to what kind of Government action was necessary so as really to attack the problem of depressed areas and low-income occupations. There were differences, of course, but the significant fact is that the legislation finally proposed was usually only a percentage of the need as described by the Administration itself. There is no point now in becoming an economic prophet. Suffice it to say that serious and responsible economists feel that the response of the society has been inadequate.

This has led to a paradoxical situation, one that became quite obvious when economic recovery from the recession began in the spring of 1961. The business indicators were all pointing upward: production and productivity were on the increase. Yet the human indexes of recession showed a tenacity despite the industrial gain. Unemployment remained at high levels. An extreme form of the "class unemployment" described earlier seemed to be built into the economy.

At any rate, one can say that if this problem is not solved the other America will not only persist; it will grow. Thus, the first point of the optimistic thesis strikes me as somewhat ambiguous, for it too quickly assumes that the society will make the needed response.

But even if one makes the assumption that there will be steady economic growth, that will not necessarily lead to the automatic elimination of poverty in the United States. J. K. Galbraith, it will be remembered, has argued that the "new" poverty demonstrates a certain immunity to progress. In making his projection of the abolition of half of the culture of poverty within the next generation, Lampman deals with this point, and it is important to follow his argument.

Lampman rejects the idea that insular (or depressed-areas) poverty will really drag the poor down in the long run. As an example of this point, he cites the fact that the number of rural farm families with incomes of under $2,000 fell during the 1947-1957 period from 3.3 million to 2.4 million because of a movement off the farm.

This point illustrates the problem of dealing with simple statistics. A movement from the farm to the city, that is, from rural poverty to urban poverty, will show an upward movement in money income. This is true, among other reasons, because the money income of the urban poor is higher than that of the country poor. But this same change does not necessarily mean that a human being has actually improved his status, that he has escaped from the culture of poverty. As was noted in the chapter on the agricultural poor, these people who are literally driven off the land are utterly unprepared for city life. They come to the metropolis in a time of rising skill requirements and relatively high levels of unemployment. They will often enter the economic underworld. Statistically, they can be recorded as a gain, because they have more money. Socially, they have simply transferred from one part of the culture of poverty to another.

At the same time, it should be noted that although there has been this tremendous exodus of the rural poor, the proportion of impoverished farms in America's agriculture has remained roughly the same.

Then Lampman deals with Galbraith's theory of "case poverty," of those who have certain disabilities that keep them down in the culture of poverty. Here it should be noted again that Galbraith himself is somewhat optimistic about case poverty. He tends to regard the bad health of the poor, physical as well as mental, as being facts about them that are individual and personal. If this book is right, particularly in the discussion of the twisted spirit within the culture of poverty, that is not the case. The personal ills of the poor are a social consequence, not a bit of biography about them. They will continue as long as the environment of poverty persists.

But Lampman's optimism goes beyond that of Galbraith. He believes that disabilities of case poverty ("mental deficiency, bad health, inability to adapt to the discipline of modern economic life, excessive procreation, alcohol, insufficient education") are "moderated over time." And he takes as his main case in point education. "For example, average educational attainment levels will rise in future years simply because younger people presently have better education than older people. Hence, as the current generation of old people pass from the scene, the percent of persons with low educational attainment will fall."

This is true, yet it is misleading if it is not placed in the context of the changes in the society as a whole. It is much more possible today to be poor with a couple of years of high school than it was a generation ago. As I have pointed out earlier, the skill level of the economy has been changing, and educational deficiency, if anything, becomes an even greater burden as a result. In this case, saying that people will have more education is not saying that they will escape the culture of poverty. It could have a much more ironic meaning: that America will have the most literate poor the world has ever known.

Lampman himself concedes that the aged are "immune" to economic growth. If this is the case, and in the absence of ranging and comprehensive social problems, the increase in the number and percentage of the poor within the next generation will actually increase the size of the other America. Lampman also concedes that families with female heads are immune to a general prosperity, and this is another point of resistance for the culture of poverty.

Finally, Lampman is much more optimistic about "nonwhite" progress than the discussion in this book would justify. I will not repeat the argument that has already been given. Let me simply state the point baldly: the present rate of economic progress among the minorities is agonizingly slow, and one cannot look for dramatic gains from this direction.

Thus, I would agree with Galbraith that poverty in the sixties has qualities that give it a hardiness in the face of affluence heretofore unknown. As documented and described in this book, there are many special factors keeping the unskilled workers, the minorities, the agricultural poor, and the

aged in the culture of poverty. If there is to be a way out, it will come from human action, from political change, not from automatic processes.

But finally, let us suppose that Lampman is correct on every point. In that case a generation of economic growth coupled with some social legislation would find America in 1987 with "only" 10 percent of the nation impoverished. If, on the other hand, a vast and comprehensive program attacking the culture of poverty could speed up this whole development, and perhaps even abolish poverty within a generation, what is the reason for holding back? This suffering is such an abomination in a society where it is needless that anything that can be done should be done.

In all this, I do not want to depict Robert Lampman as an enemy of the poor. In all seriousness, the very fact that he writes about the subject does him credit: he has social eyes, which is more than one can say for quite a few people in the society. And second, Lampman puts forward "A Program to Hasten the Reduction of Poverty" because of his genuine concern for the poor. My argument with him is not over motive or dedication. It is only that I believe that his theory makes the reduction of poverty too easy a thing, that he has not properly appreciated how deeply and strongly entrenched the other America is.

In any case, and from any point of view, the moral obligation is plain: there must be a crusade against this poverty in our midst.

If this research makes it clear that a basic attack upon poverty is necessary, it also suggests the kind of program the nation needs.

First and foremost, any attempt to abolish poverty in the United States must seek to destroy the pessimism and fatalism that flourish in the other America. In part, this can be done by offering real opportunities to these people, by changing the social reality that gives rise to their sense of hopelessness. But beyond that (these fears of the poor have a life of their own and are not simply rooted in analyses of employment chances), there should be a spirit, an élan, that communicates itself to the entire society.

If the nation comes into the other America grudgingly, with the mentality of an administrator, and says, "All right, we'll help you people," then there will be gains, but they will be kept to the minimum; a dollar spent will return a dollar. But if there is an attitude that society is gaining by eradicating poverty, if there is a positive attempt to bring these millions of the poor to the point where they can make their contribution to the United States, that will make a huge difference. The spirit of a campaign against poverty does not cost a single cent. It is a matter of vision, of sensitivity.

Let me give an example to make this point palpable. During the Montgomery bus boycott, there was only one aim in the Negro community of that city: to integrate the buses. There were no speeches on crime or juvenile delinquency. And yet it is reported that the crime rate among Negroes in Montgomery declined. Thousands of people had been given a sense of purpose, of their own worth and dignity. On their own, and without any special urging, they began to change their personal lives; they became a different people. If the same élan could invade the other America, there would be similar results.

Second, this book is based upon the proposition that poverty forms a culture, an interdependent system. In case after case, it has been documented that one cannot deal with the various components of poverty in isolation, changing this or that condition but leaving the basic structure intact. Consequently, a campaign against the misery of the poor should be comprehensive. It should think, not in terms of this or that aspect of poverty, but along the lines of establishing new communities, of substituting a human environment for the inhuman one that now exists.

Here, housing is probably the basic point of departure. If there were the funds and imagination for a campaign to end slums in the United States, most of the other steps needed to deal with poverty could be integrated with it. The vision should be the one described in the previous chapter: the political, economic, and social integration of the poor with the rest of the society. The second nation in our midst, the other America, must be brought into the Union.

In order to do this, there is a need for planning. It is literally incredible that this nation knows so much about poverty, that it has made so many inventories of misery, and that it has done so little. The material for a comprehensive program is already available. It exists in congressional reports and the statistics of Government agencies. What is needed is that the society make use of its knowledge in a rational and systematic way. As this book is being written, there are proposals for a Department of Urban Affairs in the Cabinet (and it will probably be a reality by the time these words are published). Such an agency could be the coordinating center for a crusade against the other America. In any case, if there is not planning, any attempt to deal with the problem of poverty will fail, at least in part.

Then there are some relatively simple things that could be done, involving the expansion of existing institutions and programs. Every American should be brought under the coverage of social security, and the payments should be enough to support a dignified old age. The principle already exists. Now it must be extended to those who need help the most. The same is true with minimum wage. The spectacle of excluding the most desperate from coverage must come to an end. If it did, there would be a giant step toward the elimination of poverty itself.

In every subculture of the other America, sickness and disease are the most important agencies of continuing misery. The *New York Times* publishes a list of the "neediest cases" each Christmas. In 1960 the descriptions of personal tragedy that ran along with this appeal involved in the majority of cases the want of those who had been struck down by illness. If there were adequate medical care, this charity would be unnecessary.

Today the debate on medical care centers on the aged. And indeed, these are the people who are in the most desperate straits. Yet it would be an error of the first magnitude to think that society's responsibility begins with those sixty-five years of age. As has been pointed out several times, the ills of the elderly are often the inheritance of the earlier years. A comprehensive medical program, guaranteeing decent care to every American, would actually reduce the cost of caring for the aged. That, of course, is only the hardheaded argument for such an approach. More importantly, such a program would make possible a human kind of existence for everyone in the society.

And finally, it must be remembered that none of these objectives can be accomplished if racial prejudice is to continue in the United States. Negroes and other minorities constitute only 25 percent of the poor, yet their degradation is an important element in maintaining the entire culture of poverty. As long as there is a reservoir of cheap Negro labor, there is a means of keeping the poor whites down. In this sense, civil-rights legislation is an absolutely essential component in any campaign to end poverty in the United States.

In short, the welfare provisions of American society that now help the upper two-thirds must be extended to the poor. This can be done if the other Americans are motivated to take advantage of the opportunities before them, if they are invited into the society. It can be done if there is a comprehensive program that attacks the culture of poverty at every one of its strong points.

But who will carry out this campaign?

There is only one institution in the society capable of acting to abolish poverty. That is the Federal Government. In saying this, I do not rejoice, for centralization can lead to an impersonal and bureaucratic program, one that will be lacking in the very human quality so essential in an approach to the poor. In saying this, I am only recording the facts of political and social life in the United States.

The cities are not now capable of dealing with poverty, and each day they become even less capable. As the middle class flees the central urban area, as various industries decentralize, the tax base of the American metropolis shrinks. At the same time, the social and economic problems with which the city must deal are on the rise. Thus, there is not a major city in the United States that is today capable of attacking poverty on its own.

On the contrary, the high cost of poverty is dragging the cities down.

The state governments in this country have a political peculiarity that renders them incapable of dealing with the problem of poverty. They are, for the most part, dominated by conservative rural elements. In every state with a big industrial population, the gerrymander has given the forces of rural conservatism two or three votes per person. So it is that the state legislatures usually take more money out of the problem areas than they put back into them. So it is that state governments are notoriously weighted in the direction of caution, pinchpenny economics, and indifference to the plight of the urban millions.

The various private agencies of the society simply do not have the funds to deal with the other America. And even the "fringe benefits" negotiated by unions do not really get to the heart of the problem. In the first place, they extend to organized workers in a strong bargaining position, not to the poor. And second, they are inadequate even to the needs of those who are covered.

It is a noble sentiment to argue that private moral responsibility expressing itself through charitable contributions should be the main instrument of attacking poverty. The only problem is that such an approach does not work.

So, by process of elimination, there is no place to look except toward the Federal Government. And indeed, even if there were alternate choices, Washington would have to play an important role, if only because of the need for a comprehensive program and for national planning. But in any case there is no argument, for there is only one realistic possibility: only the Federal Government has the power to abolish poverty.

In saying this, it is not necessary to advocate complete central control of such a campaign. Far from it. Washington is essential in a double sense: as a source of the considerable funds needed to mount a campaign against the other America, and as a place for coordination, for planning, and the establishment of national standards. The actual implementation of a program to abolish poverty can be carried out through myriad institutions, and the closer they are to the specific local area, the better the results. There are, as has been pointed out already, housing administrators, welfare workers, and city planners with dedication and vision. They are working on the local level, and their main frustration is the lack of funds. They could be trusted actually to carry through on a national program. What they lack now is money and the support of the American people.

There is no point in attempting to blueprint or detail the mechanisms and institutions of a war on poverty in the United States. There is information enough for action. All that is lacking is political will.

Thus the difficult, hardheaded question about poverty that one must answer is this: Where is the political will coming from? The other America is systematically underrepresented in the Government of the United States. It cannot really speak for itself. The poor, even in politics, must always be the object of charity (with the major exception of the Negroes, who, in recent times, have made tremendous strides forward in organization).

As a result of this situation, there is no realistic hope for the abolition of poverty in the United States until there is a vast social movement, a new period of political creativity. In times of slow change or of stalemate, it is always the poor who are expendable in the halls of Congress. In 1961, for instance, the laundry workers were dropped out of the minimum wage as part of a deal with the conservatives. Precisely because they are so poor and cruelly exploited, no one had to fear their political wrath. They, and others from the culture of poverty, will achieve the protection of the welfare state when there is a movement in this land so dynamic and irresistible that it need not make concessions.

For that matter, it is much easier to catalogue the enemies of the poor than it is to recite their friends.

All the forces of conservatism in this society are ranged against the needs of the other America. The ideologues are opposed to helping the poor because this can be accomplished only through an expansion of the welfare state. The small businessmen have an immediate self-interest in maintaining the economic underworld. The powerful agencies of the corporate farms want a continuation of an agricultural program that aids the rich and does nothing for the poor.

And now the South is becoming increasingly against the poor. In the days of the New Deal, the Southern Democrats tended to vote for various kinds of social legislation. One of the most outspoken champions of public housing, Burnet Maybank, was a senator from South Carolina. For one thing, there is a Southern tradition of being against Wall Street and big business; it is part of the farmers' hostility to the railroads and the Babylons of the city. For another, the New Deal legislation did not constitute a challenge to the system of racial segregation in the South.

But in the postwar period, this situation began to change. As industrialization came to the South, there was a growing political opposition to laws like minimum wage, to unions, and to other aspects of social change. The leaders of this area saw their depressed condition as an advantage. They could lure business with the promise of cheap, unorganized labor. They were interested in exploiting their backwardness.

The result was the strengthening of the coalition of Southern Democrats and conservative Northern Republicans. The Northern conservatives went along with opposition to Civil Rights legislation. The Southerners threw their votes into the struggle against social advance. It was this powerful coalition that exacted such a price in the first period of the Kennedy Administration. Many of the proposals that would have benefited the poor were omitted from bills in the first place, and other concessions were made in the course of the legislative battle. Thus poverty in the United States is supported by forces with great political and economic power.

On the other side, the friends of the poor are to be found in the American labor movement and among the middle-class liberals. The unions in the postwar period lost much of the élan that had characterized them in the thirties. Yet on questions of social legislation they remained the most powerful mass force committed to change in general, and to bettering the lot of the poor in particular. On issues like housing, medical care, minimum wage, and social security, the labor movement provided the strongest voice stating the cause of the poor.

Yet labor and the liberals were caught in the irrationalities of the American party system, and this was an enormous disadvantage to the other America. The unionists and their liberal allies are united in the Democratic party with the Southern conservatives. A Democratic victory was usually achieved by appealing to those who were concerned for social change. But at the same time it brought the forces of conservatism powerful positions on the standing committees of the Congress.

Indeed, part of the invisibility of poverty in American life is a result of this party structure. Since each major party contained differences within itself greater than the differences between it and the other party, politics in the fifties and early sixties tended to have an issueless character. And where issues were not discussed, the poor did not have a chance. They could benefit only if elections were designed to bring new information to the people, to wake up the nation, to challenge, and to call to action.

In all probability there will not be a real attack on the culture of poverty so long as this situation persists. For the other America cannot be abolished through concessions and compromises that are almost inevitably made at the expense of the poor. The spirit, the vision that are required if the nation is to penetrate the wall of pessimism and despair that surrounds the impoverished millions cannot be produced under such circumstances.

What is needed if poverty is to be abolished is a return of political debate, a restructuring of the party system so that there can be clear choices, a new mood of social idealism.

These, then, are the strangest poor in the history of mankind.

They exist within the most powerful and rich society the world has ever known. Their misery has continued while the majority of the nation talked of itself as being "affluent" and worried about neuroses in the suburbs. In this way tens of millions of human beings became invisible. They dropped out of sight and out of mind; they were without their own political voice.

Yet this need not be. The means are at hand to fulfill the age-old dream: poverty can now be abolished. How long shall we ignore this underdeveloped nation in our midst? How long shall we look the other way while our fellow human beings suffer? How long?

---

## 15  THE POOR PAY MORE  DAVID CAPLOVITZ

The visitor to East Harlem cannot fail to notice the sixty or so furniture and appliance stores that mark the area, mostly around Third Avenue and 125th Street. At first this may seem surprising. After all, this is obviously a low-income area. Many of the residents are on relief. Many are em-

Reprinted with permission of The Macmillan Company from *The Poor Pay More*, by David Caplovitz. Copyright © 1963 by The Free Press, a Division of The Macmillan Company.

This article is based in part on an unpublished research report by Wolfram Arendt and Murray Caylay.

ployed in seasonal work and in marginal industries, such as the garment industry, which are the first to feel the effects of a recession in the economy. On the face of it, residents of the area would seem unable to afford the merchandise offered for sale in these stores.

That merchants nevertheless find it profitable to locate in these areas attests to a commonly overlooked fact: low-income families, like those of higher income, are consumers of many major durables. The popular image of the American as striving for the material possessions which bestow upon him both comfort and prestige in the eyes of his fellows does not hold only for the ever-increasing middle class. The cultural pressures to buy major durables reach low- as well as middle-income families. In some ways, consumption may take on even more significance for low-income families than for those in higher classes. Since many have small prospect of greatly improving their low social standing through occupational mobility, they are apt to turn to consumption as at least one sphere in which they can make some progress toward the American dream of success. If the upper strata that were observed by Veblen engaged in conspicuous consumption to symbolize their social superiority, it might be said that the lower classes today are apt to engage in *compensatory consumption*. Appliances, automobiles, and the dream of a home of their own can become compensations for blocked social mobility.[1]

The dilemma of the low-income consumer lies in these facts. He is trained by society (and his position in it) to want the symbols and appurtenances of the "good life" at the same time that he lacks the means needed to fulfill these socially induced wants. People with small incomes lack not only the ready cash for consuming major durables but are also poorly qualified for that growing substitute for available cash—credit. Their low income, their negligible savings, their job insecurity all contribute to their being poor credit risks. Moreover, many low-income families in New York City are fairly recent migrants from the South or from Puerto Rico and so do not have other requisites of good credit, such as long-term residence at the same address and friends who meet the credit requirements and are willing to vouch for them.[2]

Not having enough cash and credit would seem to create a sufficient problem for low-income consumers. But they have other limitations as well. They tend to lack the information and training needed to be effective consumers in a bureaucratic society. Partly because of their limited education and partly because as migrants from more traditional societies they are unfamiliar with urban culture, they are not apt to follow the announcements of sales in the newspapers, to engage in comparative shopping, to know their way around the major department stores and bargain centers, to know how to evaluate the advice of salesmen—practices necessary for some degree of sophistication in the realm of consumption. The institution of credit introduces special complex requirements for intelligent consumption. Because of the diverse and frequently misleading ways in which charges for credit are stated, even the highly-educated consumer has difficulty knowing which set of terms is most economical.[3]

These characteristics of the low-income consumer—his socially supported want for major durables, his small funds, his poor credit position, his lack of shopping sophistication—constitute the conditions under which durables are marketed in low-income areas. To understand the paradox set by the many stores selling high-cost durables in these areas it is necessary to know how the merchants adapt to these conditions. Clearly the normal marketing arrangements, based on a model of the "adequate" consumer (the consumer with funds, credit, and shopping sophistication), cannot prevail if these merchants are to stay in business.

On the basis of interviews with fourteen of these merchants, the broad outlines of this marketing system can be described. This picture, in turn, provides a backdrop for the more detailed examination in later chapters of the marketing relationship from the viewpoint of the consumer.

## MERCHANDISING IN A LOW-INCOME AREA

The key to the marketing system in low-income areas lies in special adaptations of the institution of credit. The many merchants who locate in these areas and find it profitable to do so are prepared to offer credit in spite of the high risks involved. Moreover, their credit is tailored to the particular needs of the low-income consumer. All kinds of durable goods can be obtained in this market at terms not too different from the slogan, "a dollar down, a dollar a week." The consumer can buy furniture, a TV set, a stereophonic phonograph, or, if he is so minded, a combination phonograph-TV set, if not for a dollar a week then for only a few dollars a week. In practically every one of these stores, the availability of "easy credit" is announced to the customer in both English and Spanish by large signs in the windows and sometimes by neon signs over the doorways. Of the fourteen merchants interviewed, twelve claimed that from 75 to 90 per cent of their business consisted of credit and the other two said that credit made up half their business. That these merchants extend credit to their customers does not, of course, explain how they stay in business. They still face the problem of dealing with their risks.

## THE MARKUP AND QUALITY OF GOODS

It might at first seem that the merchant would solve his problem by charging high rates of interest on the credit he extends. But the law in New York State now regulates the amount that can be charged for credit, and most of these merchants claim they use installment contracts which conform to the law. The fact is that they do not always use these contracts. Some merchants will give customers only a card on which payments are noted. In these transactions the cost of credit and the cash price are not specified as the law requires. The customer peddlers, whom we shall soon meet, seldom use installment contracts. In all these cases the consumer has no idea of how much he is paying for credit, for the cost of credit is not differentiated from the cost of the product.

Although credit charges are now regulated by law, no law regulates the merchant's markup on his goods. East Harlem is known to the merchants of furniture and appliances in New York City as the area in which pricing is done by "numbers." We first heard of the "number" system from a woman who had been employed as a bookkeeper in such a store. She illustrated a "one number" item by writing down a hypothetical wholesale price and then adding the same figure to it, a 100 per cent markup. Her frequent references to "two number" and "three number" prices indicated that prices are never less than "one number," and are often more.

The system of pricing in the low-income market differs from that in the bureaucratic market of the downtown stores in another respect: in East Harlem there are hardly any "one price" stores. In keeping with a multi-price policy, price tags are conspicuously absent from the merchandise. The customer has to ask, "how much?," and the answer he gets will depend on several things. If the merchant considers him a poor risk, if he thinks the customer is naive, or if the customer was referred to him by another merchant or a peddler to whom he must pay a commission, the price will be higher. The fact that prices can be affected by "referrals" calls attention to another peculiarity of the low-income market, what the merchants call the "T.O." system.

Anyone closely familiar with sales practices in a large retailing establishment probably understands the meaning of "T.O." When a salesman is confronted with a customer who is not responding to the "sales pitch," he will call over another salesman, signal the nature of the situation by whispering, "this is a T.O.," and then introduce him to the customer as the "assistant manager."[4] In East Harlem, as the interviewers learned, T.O.s extend beyond the store. When a merchant finds himself with a customer who seems to be a greater risk than he is prepared to accept, he does not send the customer away. Instead, he will tell the customer that he happens to be out of the item he wants, but that it can be obtained at the store of his "friend" or "cousin," just a few blocks away. The merchant will then take the customer to a storekeeper with a less conservative credit policy.[5] The second merchant fully understands that his colleague expects a commission and takes this into account in fixing the price.[6] As a result, the customer who happens to walk into the "wrong" store ends up paying more. In essence, he is being charged for the service of having his credit potential matched with the risk policy of a merchant.

As for the merchandise sold in these stores, the interviewers noticed that the furniture on display was of obviously poor quality. Most of all, they were struck by the absence of well-known brands of appliances in most of the stores. To find out about the sales of better-known brands, they initially asked about the volume of sales of "high-*price* lines." But this question had little meaning for the merchants, because high prices were being charged for the low-quality goods in evidence. The question had to be rephrased in terms of "high *quality*" merchandise or, as the merchants themselves refer to such goods, "custom lines." To quote from the report of these interviews:

It became apparent that the question raised a problem of communication. We were familiar with the prices generally charged for high quality lines and began to notice that the same prices were charged for much lower quality merchandise. The markup was obviously quite different from that in other areas. The local merchants said that the sale of "custom" merchandise was limited by a slow turnover. In fact, a comparable markup on the higher quality lines would make the final price so prohibitively high that they could not be moved at all. A lower markup would be inconsistent with the risk and would result in such small profits that the business could not be continued.

The high markup on low-quality goods is thus a major device used by the merchants to protect themselves against the risks of their credit business. This policy represents a marked departure from the "normal" marketing situation. In the "normal" market, competition between merchants results in a pricing policy roughly commensurate with the quality of the goods. It is apparent, then, that these merchants do not see themselves competing with stores outside the neighborhood. This results in the irony that the people who can least afford the goods they buy are required to pay high prices relative to quality, thus receiving a comparatively low return for their consumer dollar.

In large part, these merchants have a "captive" market because their customers do not meet the economic requirements of consumers in the larger, bureaucratic marketplace. But also, they can sell inferior goods at high prices because, in their own words, the customers are not "price and quality conscious." Interviews found that the merchants perceive their customers as unsophisticated shoppers. One merchant rather cynically explained that the amount of goods sold a customer depends not on the customer but on the merchant's willingness to extend him credit. If the merchant is willing to accept great risk, he can sell the customer almost as much as he cares to. Another merchant, commenting on the buying habits of the customer, said, "People do not shop in this area. Each person who comes into the store wants to buy something and is a potential customer. It is just up to who catches him."

The notion of "who catches him" is rather important in this economy. Merchants compete not so much in price or quality, but in getting customers to the store on other grounds. (Some of these gathering techniques will shortly be described.)

Another merchant commented rather grudgingly that the Negroes were beginning to show signs of greater sophistication by "shopping around." Presumably this practice is not followed by the newer migrants to the area.

But although the merchants are ready to exploit the naivete of their traditionalistic customers, it is important to point out that they also cater to the customer's traditionalism. As a result of the heavy influx of Puerto Ricans into the area, many of these stores now employ Puerto Rican salesmen. The customers who enter these stores need not be concerned about possible embarrassment because of their broken English or their poor dress. On the contrary, these merchants are adept at making the customer feel at ease, as a personal experience will testify.

Visiting the area and stopping occasionally to read the ads in the windows, I happened to pause before an appliance store. A salesman promptly emerged and said, "I know, I bet you're looking for a nice TV set. Come inside. We've got lots of nice ones." Finding myself thrust into the role of customer, I followed him into the store and listened to his sales-pitch. Part way through his talk, he asked my name. I hesitated a moment and then provided him with a fictitious last name, at which point he said, "No, no—no last names. What's your first name? . . . Ah, Dave; I'm Irv. We only care about first names here." When I was ready to leave after making some excuse about having to think things over, he handed me his card. Like most business cards of employees, this one had the name and address of the enterprise in large type and in small type the name of the salesman. But instead of his full name, there appeared only the amiable "Irv."

As this episode indicates, the merchants in this low-income area are ready to personalize their services. To consumers from a more traditional society, unaccustomed to the impersonality of the bureaucratic market, this may be no small matter.

So far, we have reviewed the elements of the system of exchange that comprise the low-income market. For the consumer, these are the availability of merchandise, the "easy" installments, and the reassurance of dealing with merchants who make them feel at home. In return, the merchant reserves for himself the right to sell low-quality merchandise at exorbitant prices.

But the high markup on goods does not insure that the business will be profitable. No matter what he charges, the merchant can remain in business only if customers actually pay. In this market, the customer's intention and ability to pay—the assumptions underlying any credit system—cannot be taken for granted. Techniques for insuring continuity of payments are a fundamental part of this distinctive economy.

**FORMAL CONTROLS** When the merchant uses an installment contract, he has recourse to legal controls over his customers. But as we shall see, legal controls are not sufficient to cope with the merchant's problem and they are seldom used.

*Repossession* The merchant who offers credit can always repossess his merchandise should the the customer default on payments. But repossession, according to the merchants, is rare. They claim that the merchandise receives such heavy use as to become practically worthless in a short time. And no doubt the shoddy merchandise will not

stand much use, heavy or light. One merchant said that he will occasionally repossess an item, not to regain his equity, but to punish a customer he feels is trying to cheat him.

*Liens against property and wages* The merchant can, of course, sue the defaulting customer. By winning a court judgment, he can have the customer's property attached. Should this fail to satisfy the debt, he can take the further step of having the customer's salary garnisheed.[7] But these devices are not fully adequate for several reasons. Not all customers have property of value or regular jobs. Furthermore, their employers will not hesitate to fire them rather than submit to the nuisance of a garnishment. But since the customer knows he may lose his job if he is garnisheed, the mere threat of garnishment is sometimes enough to insure regularity of payments.[8] The main limitation with legal controls, however, is that the merchant who uses them repeatedly runs the risk of forfeiting good will in the neighborhood.

*Discounting paper* The concern with good will places a limitation on the use of another legal practice open to merchants for minimizing their risk: the sale of their contracts to a credit agency at a discount. By selling his contracts to one of the licensed finance companies, the merchant can realize an immediate return on his investment. The problem with this technique is that the merchant loses control over his customer. As an impersonal, bureaucratic organization, the credit agency has recourse only to legal controls. Should the customer miss a payment, the credit agency will take the matter to court. But in the customer's mind, his contract exists with the merchant, not with the credit agency. Consequently, the legal actions taken against him reflect upon the merchant, and so good will is not preserved after all.

For this reason, the merchant is reluctant to "sell his paper," particularly if he has reason to believe that the customer will miss some payments. When he does sell some of his contracts at a discount, his motive is not to reduce risk, but rather to obtain working capital. Since so much of his capital is tied up in credit transactions, he frequently finds it necessary to make such sales. Oddly enough, he is apt to sell his better "paper," that is, the contracts of customers who pay regularly, for he wants to avoid incurring the ill will of customers. This practice also has its drawbacks for the merchant. Competitors can find out from the credit agencies which customers pay regularly and then try to lure them away from the original merchant. Some merchants reported that in order to retain control over their customers, they will buy back contracts from credit agencies they suspect are giving information to competitors.[9]

*Credit association ratings*  All credit merchants report their bad debtors to the credit association to which they belong. The merchants interviewed said that they always consult the "skip lists" of their association before extending credit to a new customer.[10] In this way they can avoid at least the customers known to be bad risks. This form of control tends to be effective in the long run because the customers find that they are unable to obtain credit until they have made good on their past debts. During the interviews with them, some consumers mentioned this need to restore their credit rating as the reason why they were paying off debts in spite of their belief that they had been cheated.

But these various formal techniques of control are not sufficient to cope with the merchant's problem of risk. He also depends heavily on informal and personal techniques of control.

INFORMAL CONTROLS    The merchant starts from the premise that most of his customers are honest people who intend to pay but have difficulty managing their money. Missed payments are seen as more often due to poor management and to emergencies than to dishonesty. The merchants anticipate that their customers will miss some payments and they rely on informal controls to insure that payments are eventually made.

All the merchants described their credit business as operating on a "fifteen-month year." This means that they expect the customer to miss about one of every four payments and they compute the markup accordingly. Unlike the credit companies, which insist upon regular payments

and add service charges for late payments, the neighborhood merchant is prepared to extend "flexible" credit. Should the customer miss an occasional payment or should he be short on another, the merchant considers this a normal part of his business.

To insure the close personal control necessary for this system of credit, the merchant frequently draws up a contract calling for weekly payments which the customer usually brings to the store. This serves several functions for the merchant. To begin with, the sum of money represented by a weekly payment is relatively small and so helps to create the illusion of "easy credit." Customers are apt to think more of the size of the payments than of the cost of the item or the length of the contract.

More importantly, the frequent contact of a weekly-payment system enables the merchant to get to know his customer. He learns when the customer receives his pay check, when his rent is due, who his friends are, when job layoffs, illnesses, and other emergencies occur—in short, all sorts of information which allow him to interpret the reason for a missed payment. Some merchants reported that when they know the customer has missed a payment for a legitimate reason such as illness or a job layoff, they will send a sympathetic note and offer the customer a gift (an inexpensive lamp or wall picture) when payments are resumed. This procedure, they say, frequently brings the customer back with his missed payments.

The short interval between payments also functions to give the merchant an early warning when something is amiss. His chances of locating the delinquent customer are that much greater. Furthermore, the merchant can keep tabs on a delinquent customer through his knowledge of the latter's friends, relatives, neighbors, and associates, who are also apt to be customers of his. In this way, still another informal device, the existing network of social relations, is utilized by the neighborhood merchant in conducting his business.[11]

The weekly-payment system also provides the merchant with the opportunity to sell other items to the customer. When the first purchase is almost paid for, the merchant will try to persuade the customer to make another. Having the customer in the store, where he can look at the merchandise, makes the next sale that much easier. This system of successive sales is, of course, an ideal arrangement—for the merchant. As a result, the customer remains continuously in debt to him. The pattern is somewhat reminiscent of the Southern sharecropper's relation to the company store. And since a number of customers grew up in more traditional environments with just such economies, they may find the arrangement acceptable. The practice of buying from peddlers, found to be common in these low-income areas, also involves the principle of continuous indebtedness. The urban low-income economy, then, is in some respects like the sharecropper system; it might almost be called an "urban sharecropper system."[12]

### THE CUSTOMER PEDDLERS

Characteristic of the comparatively traditional and personal form of the low-income economy is the important role played in it by the door-to-door credit salesman, the customer peddler. The study of merchants found that these peddlers are not necessarily competitors of the store-owners. Almost all merchants make use of peddlers in the great competition for customers. The merchants tend to regard peddlers as necessary evils who add greatly to the final cost of purchases. But they need them because in their view, customers are too ignorant, frightened, or lazy to come to the stores themselves. Thus, the merchants' apparent contempt for peddlers does not bar them from employing outdoor salesman (or "canvassers," as they describe the peddlers who work for one store or another). Even the merchants who are themselves reluctant to hire canvassers find they must do so in order to meet the competition. The peddler's main function for the merchant, then, is getting the customer to the store, and if he will not come, getting the store to the customer. But this is not his only function.

Much more than the storekeeper, the peddler operates on the basis of a personal relationship with the customer. By going to the customer's home, he gets to know the entire family; he sees the condition of the home and he comes to know the family's habits and wants. From this vantage point he is better able than the merchant to evaluate the customer as a credit risk. Since many of the merchant's potential customers lack the standard credentials of credit, such as having a permanent job, the merchant needs some other basis for discriminating between good and bad risks. If the peddler, who has come to know the family, is ready to vouch for the customer, the merchant will be ready to make the transaction. In short, the peddler acts as a fiduciary agent, a Dun and Bradstreet for the poor, telling the merchant which family is likely to meet its obligations and which is not.

Not all peddlers are employed by stores. Many are independent enterprisers (who may have started as canvassers for stores).[13] A number of the independent peddlers have accumulated enough capital to supply their customers with major durables. These are the elite peddlers, known as "dealers," who buy appliances and furniture from local merchants at a "wholesale" price, and then sell them on credit to their customers. In these transactions, the peddler either takes the customer to the store or sends the customer to the store with his card on which he has written some such message as "Please give Mr. Jones a TV set."[14] The merchant then sells the customer the TV set at a price much higher than he would ordinarily charge. The "dealer" is generally given two months to pay the merchant the "wholesale" price, and meanwhile he takes over the responsibility of collecting from his customer. Some "dealers" are so successful that they employ canvassers in their own right.[15] And some merchants do so much business with "dealers" that they come to think of themselves as "wholesalers" even though they are fully prepared to do their own retail business.

Independent peddlers without much capital also have economic relations with local merchants. They act as brokers, directing their customers to neighborhood stores that will extend them credit. And for this service they of course receive a commission. In these transactions, it is the merchant who accepts the risks and assumes the responsibility for collecting payments. The peddler who acts as a broker performs the same function as the merchant in the T.O. system. He knows which merchants will accept great risk and which will not, and directs his customers accordingly.

There are, then, three kinds of customer peddlers operating in these low-income neighborhoods who cooperate with local merchants: the canvassers who are employed directly by the stores; the small entrepreneurs who act as brokers; and the more successful entrepreneurs who operate as "dealers." A fourth type of peddler consists of salesmen representing large companies not necessarily located in the neighborhood. These men are, for the most part, canvassers for firms specializing in a particular commodity, e.g., encyclopedias, vacuum cleaners, or pots and pans. They differ from the other peddlers by specializing in what they sell and by depending more on contracts and legal controls. They are also less interested in developing continuous relationships with their customers.

Peddlers thus aid the local merchants by finding customers, evaluating them as credit risks, and helping in the collection of payments. And as the merchants themselves point out, these services add greatly to the cost of the goods. One storekeeper said that peddlers are apt to charge five and six times the amount the store charges for relatively inexpensive purchases. Pointing to a religious picture which he sells for $5, he maintained that peddlers sell it for as much as $30. And he estimated that the peddler adds 30 to 50 per cent to the final sales price of appliances and furniture.

## UNETHICAL AND ILLEGAL PRACTICES

The interviewers uncovered some evidence that some local merchants engage in the illegal practice of selling reconditioned furniture and appliances as new. Of course, no merchant would admit that he did this himself, but five of them hinted that their competitors engaged in this practice.[16] As we shall see, several of the consumers we interviewed were

quite certain that they had been victimized in this way.

One unethical, if not illegal, activity widely practiced by stores is "bait" advertising with its concomitant, the "switch sale." In the competition for customers, merchants depend heavily upon advertising displays in their windows which announce furniture or appliances at unusually low prices. The customer may enter the store assuming that the low offer in the window signifies a reasonably low price line. Under severe pressure, the storekeeper may even be prepared to sell the merchandise at the advertised price, for not to do so would be against the law. What most often happens, however, is that the unsuspecting customer is convinced by the salesman that he doesn't really want the goods advertised in the window and is then persuaded to buy a smaller amount of more expensive goods. Generally, not much persuasion is necessary. The most popular "bait ad" is the announcement of three rooms of furniture for "only $149" or "only $199." The customer who inquires about this bargain is shown a bedroom set consisting of two cheap and (sometimes deliberately) chipped bureaus and one bed frame. He learns that the spring and mattress are not included in the advertised price, but can be had for another $75 or $100. The living-room set in these "specials" consists of a fragile-looking sofa and one unmatching chair.[17]

The frequent success of this kind of exploitation, known in the trade as the "switch sale," is reflected in this comment by one merchant: "I don't know how they do it. They advertise three rooms of furniture for $149 and the customers swarm in. *They end up buying a $400 bedroom set for $600 and none of us can believe how easy it is to make these sales.*"

In sum, a fairly intricate system of sales-and-credit has evolved in response to the distinctive situation of the low-income consumer and the local merchant. It is a system heavily slanted in the direction of a traditional economy in which informal, personal ties play a major part in the transaction. At the same time it is connected to impersonal bureaucratic agencies through the instrument of the installment contract. Should the informal system break down, credit companies, courts of law, and agencies of law enforcement come to play a part.

The system is not only different from the larger, more formal economy; in some respects it is a *deviant* system in which practices that violate prevailing moral standards are commonplace. As Merton has pointed out in his analysis of the political machine, the persistence of deviant social structures can only be understood when their social functions (as well as dysfunctions) are taken into account.[18] The basic function of the low-income marketing system is to provide consumer goods to people who fail to meet the requirements of the more legitimate, bureaucratic market, or who choose to exclude themselves from the larger market because they do not feel comfortable in it. As we have seen, the system is extraordinarily flexible. Almost no one—however great a risk—is turned away. Various mechanisms sift and sort customers according to their credit risk and match them with merchants ready to sell them the goods they want. Even the family on welfare is permitted to maintain its self-respect by consuming in much the same way as do its social peers who happen not to be on welfare. Whether the system, with its patently exploitative features, can be seriously altered without the emergence of more legitimate institutions to perform its functions, is a question to be considered at length in the concluding chapter of this book.

In the following chapters, certain themes running through this account of the low-income market will be systematically examined from the viewpoint of the consumers. It appears, for example, that there are enough consumers of these goods to support the many stores. But to what extent are low-income families oriented toward major durables? Which types of families are heavy consumers and which are not? What proportions of low-income families buy from neighborhood stores and from peddlers? How do the families with broader shopping horizons differ from those who buy only in the neighborhood? What prices do low-income families pay for their appliances and how do their shopping decisions affect the prices they pay? Since credit is the mainstay of the neighborhood merchant, which types of families make use of credit? And how do the consumers experience the pressures exerted upon them by the merchants? What sales gimmicks have resulted in the purchase of initially unwanted goods, and which families are particularly vulnerable to these gimmicks? What do low-income families do when they get into trouble as consumers? To what extent are they aware of community agencies that can help them with their problems as consumers, and how often do they make use of them? In short, we must still find out how the system of sales-and-credit is experienced by the consumers.

**REFERENCES AND NOTES**

1   I am indebted to Robert K. Merton for suggesting the apt phrase, "compensatory consumption." The idea expressed by this term figures prominently in the writings of Robert S. Lynd. Observing the workers in Middletown, Lynd noted that their declining opportunities for occupational advancement and even the depression did not make them class-conscious. Instead, their aspirations shifted to the realm of consumption: "Fascinated by a rising standard of living offered them on every hand on the installment plan, they [the working class] do not readily segregate themselves from the rest of the city. They want what Middletown wants, so long as it gives them their great symbol of advancement—an automobile. Car ownership stands to them for a large share of the 'American dream'; they cling to it as they cling to self respect, and it was not unusual to see a family drive up to the relief commissary in 1935 to stand in line for its four or five dollar weekly food dole." The Lynds go on to quote a union official: "It's easy to see why our workers don't think much about joining unions. So long as they have a car and can borrow or steal a gallon of gas, they'll ride around and pay no attention to labor organization. . . ." Robert S. Lynd and Helen Merrill Lynd, *Middletown in Transition*, New York: Harcourt, Brace and Co., 1937, p. 26; see also pp. 447–448.

It should be noted that the Lynds identify the installment plan as the mechanism through which workers are able to realize their consumption aspirations. Similar observations are to be found in *Knowledge for What?* Princeton University Press, 1939, pp. 91, 198. Lynd's student Eli Chinoy also makes use of the idea of compensatory consumption in his study of automobile workers. He found that when confronted with the impossibility of rising to the ranks of management, workers shifted their aspirations from the occupational to the consumption sphere. "With their wants constantly stimulated by high-powered advertising, they measure their success by what they are able to buy." Eli Chinoy, "Aspirations of Automobile Workers," *American Journal of Sociology*, vol. 57 (1952), pp. 453–459. For further discussion of the political implications of this process, see Daniel Bell, "Work and its Discontents" in *The End of Ideology*, New York: The Free Press, 1960, pp. 246 ff.

2 A frequent practice in extending credit to poor risks is to have cosigners who will make good the debt should the original borrower default. The new arrivals are apt to be disadvantaged by their greater difficulty in finding cosigners.

3 Professor Samuel S. Myers of Morgan State College has studied the credit terms of major department stores and appliance outlets in Baltimore. Visiting the ten most popular stores, he priced the same model of TV set and gathered information on down payments and credit terms. He found that the cash price was practically the same in the various stores, but that there were wide variations in the credit terms, leading to sizable differences in the final cost to the consumer. (Based on personal communication with Professor Myers.)

In his statement to the Douglas Committee considering the "Truth in Interest" bill, George Katona presented findings from the consumer surveys carried out by the Survey Research Center of the University of Michigan. These studies show that people with high income and substantial education are no better informed about the costs of credit than people of low income and little education. See *Consumer Credit Labeling Bill, op. cit.*, p. 806.

4 The initials stand for "turn over." The "assistant manager" is ready to make a small concession to the customer, who is usually so flattered by this gesture that he offers no further resistance to the sale. For further descriptions of the "T.O.," see Cecil L. French, "Correlates of Success in Retail Selling," *American Journal of Sociology*, vol. 66 (September 1960), pp. 128–134; and Erving Goffman, *Presentation of Self in Everyday Life*, New York: Doubleday & Co., Anchor Books, 1959, pp. 178–180.

5 The interviewers found that the stores closer to the main shopping area of 125th Street generally had more conservative credit policies than those somewhat farther away. This was indicated by the percentage of credit sales the merchants reported as defaults. The higher-rental stores near 125th Street reported default rates of 5 and 6 per cent, those six or seven blocks away, as high as 20 per cent.

6 The referring merchant does not receive his commission right away. Whether he gets it at all depends upon the customer's payment record. He will keep a record of his referrals and check on them after several months. When the merchant who has made the sale has received a certain percentage of the payments, he will give the referring merchant his commission.

7 It is of some interest that the low-income families we interviewed were all familiar with the word "garnishee." This may well be one word in the language that the poorly educated are more likely to know than the better educated.

8 Welfare families cannot, of course, be garnisheed, and more than half the merchants reported that they sell to them. But the merchants can threaten to disclose the credit purchase to the welfare authorities. Since recipients of welfare funds are not supposed to buy on credit, this threat exerts powerful pressure on the family.

9 Not all merchants are particularly concerned with good will. A few specialize in extending credit to the worst risks, customers turned away by most other merchants. These men will try to collect as much as they can on their accounts during the year and then will sell all their outstanding accounts to a finance company. As a result, the most inadequate consumers are apt to meet with the bureaucratic controls employed by the finance company. For a description of how bill collectors operate, see Hillel Black, *Buy Now, Pay Later*, New York: William Morrow and Co., 1961, chap. 4.

10 See *ibid.*, chap. 3, for a description of the world's largest credit association, the one serving most of the stores in the New York City area.

11 The merchant's access to these networks of social relations is not entirely independent of economic considerations. Just as merchants who refer customers receive commissions, so customers who recommend others are often given commissions. Frequently, this is why a customer will urge his friends to deal with a particular merchant.

12 The local merchants are not the only ones promoting continuous debt. The coupon books issued by banks and finance companies which underwrite installment contracts contain notices in the middle announcing that the consumer can, if he wishes, refinance the loan. The consumer is told, in effect, that he is a good risk because presumably he has regularly paid half the installments and that he need not wait until he has made the last payment before borrowing more money.

13 A systematic study of local merchants and peddlers would probably find that a typical career pattern is to start as a canvasser, become a self-employed peddler, and finally a storekeeper.

14 According to a former customer peddler, now in the furniture business, the peddlers' message will either read "Please *give* Mr. Jones . . ." or "Please let Mr. Jones *pick out* . . ." In the former case, the customer is given the merchandise right away; in the latter, it is set aside for him until the peddler says that it is all right to let the customer have it. The peddler uses the second form when his customer is already heavily in debt to him and he wants to be certain that the customer will agree to the higher weekly payments that will be necessary.

15 One tiny store in the area, with little merchandise in evidence, is reported to employ over a hundred canvassers. The owner would not consent to an interview, but the student-observers did notice that this apparently small merchant kept some four or five bookkeepers at work in a back room. The owner is obviously a "dealer" whose store is his office. As a "dealer," he has no interest in maintaining stock and displays for street trade.

16 Events are sometimes more telling than words. During an interview with a merchant, the interviewer volunteered to help several men who were carrying bed frames into the store. The owner excitedly told him not to help because he might get paint on his hands.

17 In one store in which I inspected this special offer, I was told by the salesman that he would find a chair that was a "fairly close match."

18 Robert K. Merton, *Social Theory and Social Structure*, rev. ed., New York: The Free Press of Glencoe, 1957, pp. 71–82.

---

## 16   THE PROTECTION OF THE INEPT   WILLIAM J. GOODE

The dissident have throughout history voiced a suspicion that the highly placed have not earned their mace, orb, and scepter. Plato designed a city in which the ablest would rule, but this was accomplished only in his imagination. Leaders in the Wat Tyler Rebellion expressed their doubts that lords were of finer quality than the peasants they ruled. Against the grandiloquent assertion of kings that they were divinely appointed, both court jesters and the masses have sometimes laughed, and asked, where were their virtue and wisdom? In more recent times, this skepticism about their merit has culminated in the dethronement or weakening of practically every ascriptive ruler in the world.

Nor has the end of kings by birth stifled this doubt that the elite are indeed the ablest, that the inept may be protected in high position. Jefferson spoke of a "natural aristocracy," but he did not suppose the members of the ruling class necessarily belonged to it. In our less heroic epoch, we are assured that we live in an achievement-oriented society, and the norm is to place individuals in their occupations by merit. Nevertheless, the inquiries of sociologists and psychologists demonstrate that as the child passes through the successive gateways to higher position, the cumulative effect of class, race, sex, and other readily ascribed traits grows rather than lessens. For example, lower class or Negro children who could perform well by comparison with their more advantaged peers in the first few grades drop farther and farther behind. The gap between them widens.

Of course, not all talent at any class level would be transmuted into skill, even in the best of *possible* worlds. However the privileged (at all levels of privilege) do try systematically to prevent the talent of the less privileged from being recognized

Reprinted with the permission of the author, the American Sociological Association, and the publisher from *American Sociological Review*, vol. 32 (February 1967), pp. 5–19.

The 1965 MacIver Award lecture, delivered at the annual meetings of the Pacific Sociological Association, April 1966, in Vancouver. For aid in preparing this paper the author is indebted to Gresham Sykes, Florence Kluckhohn, Melville Dalton, Amitai Etzioni, Alvin W. Gouldner, Peter McHugh, Robert K. Merton, Walter Goldfrank, Seymour M. Lipset, Yehudi Cohen, Nicholas Tavochis and Marshall Childs. This paper was prepared with the support of NIMH Grant No. NH 11389–01.

or developed. And though analysts of stratification assume that social mobility is an index of open competition, ample if unsystematic evidence suggests that both the able and the inept may move into high position.

These comments should not be interpreted as the jaundiced complaints of the misanthrope, or as a call for destruction of the stratification system. Such common observations from Ecclesiastes (". . . the race is not to the swift . . .") and Plato onward describe arrangements which every social system exhibits, and which cope with a universal *system problem*: How to utilize the services of the less able?

The social responses to this problem are the resultant of two sets of factors in tension: protection *of* the inept; and protection of the group *from* the inept. In almost all collectivities, for reasons to be explored later, the arrangements for protecting the less able seem to be more pervasive, common, and effective than those for protecting the group from ineptitude. Industrial society is highly effective at production not so much because it allows the most able to assume positions of high leadership, but because it has developed two great techniques (bureaucracy and machinery) for both using the inept and limiting the range of their potential destructiveness.[2]

Adequate proof of this rather laconic theoretical statement, and a full exposition of its implications, is not possible within the brief compass of a single paper. In subsequent sections we shall consider these issues:

1 Does the evidence suggest there is a widespread pattern of protecting the less competent?

2 In supposedly achievement-oriented societies, is this protection merely an evasion of widely accepted achievement norms, i.e., is it "real," as contrasted with "ideal," behavior, or do people in fact accept many norms contrary to achievement?

3 What are the specific or general processes and patterns protecting the less able?

4 Presumably, different social structures handle the problem of ineptitude differently.

5 What consequences flow from these differences?

One can at least imagine, even if one will never find, a society in which the division of labor in every type of group allots tasks and rewards entirely on the basis of achievement, or one in which those allotments are made without regard for achievement. All societies fall between these two extremes. Leaders within industrial societies assert, in part as a defense of the system they lead, that the lowly able will rise, and that the highly placed deserve their rank. Even if such statements are classified as exhortations or hopes, evidence can be adduced to show that on the average the successful are more talented or skilled than the less successful, e.g., the research productivity of Nobel Prize winners *vs.* that of nonwinners.[3]

Yet such averages are, after all, derived from *distributions*. These distributions always reveal that *some* of the less successful seem equal or superior to the more successful. Far more important for our present inquiry, all such individuals live and work in *groups*, so that the relevant comparison is not with all other individuals in the same aggregate, such as all full professors, but with other members of the same group, such as the *department*. The protection of the inept is a *group* phenomenon, an aspect of a collectivity.

Let us, then, consider briefly some of the wide array of evidence that groups do not typically expose or expel their members for lesser achievement or talent. The following findings are only a reminder of how widespread our research has shown such social arrangements to be.

Almost every inquiry into the productivity of workers has shown that the informal work group protects its members by setting a standard which everyone can meet, and they develop techniques for preventing a supervisor from measuring accurately the output of each man.[4] Higher level management has for the most part evaded such scrutiny, but industrial sociologists have reported comparable behavior there, too.[5] The protection of one another by lower-level workers might be due to less commitment; the fact that higher-level men do the same suggests the need for a more general explanation.

All professions, while claiming to be the sole

competent judges of their members' skills, and the guardians of their clients' welfare, refuse to divulge information about how competent any of them are, and under most circumstances their rules assert it is unethical to criticize the work of fellow members to laymen.[6] Wall Street law firms try to find good positions in other firms for those employees they decide are not partnership material.[7] When a new profession is organized, grandfather clauses permit older practitioners with less training to continue in practice without being tested. When hospitals begin to demand a higher performance standard from those who enjoy staff privileges, inevitably rejecting some, both patients and physicians object.[8] One study of a group of physicians showed that there was little relationship between an M.D.'s income and the quality of medical care he gave to his patients.[9]

Wherever unions are strong, foremen know that promotion by merit rather than by seniority is unwise, and in any event unusual.[10] Many corporations do not fire their managers; they find or create other posts for them.[11] Employees are close students of promotion behavior, and are "notoriously suspicious and cynical" about management claims that promotion is through merit.[12] Many are not convinced the best men are at the top.[13] More generally, members of what Goffman calls "teams" (army officers, parents, policemen, managers, nurses, and so forth) protect each other from any exposure of their errors.[14]

In all societies—if present psychological testing may be extrapolated—there are more talented, in absolute numbers, born into the lower social strata than into the upper; every detailed study of a class system describes how the upper strata prevent the lower from acquiring the skills appropriate for higher level jobs. This effort alone is a good indicator that the upper strata include many who are less talented. For example, the Southerner as well as the Northerner would not even *need* to discriminate against the Negro child or man, if in fact he were always untalented; performance alone would demonstrate his inferiority. The same proposition holds for the poor generally, for Jews (as in bank-

ing or heavy industry), for women, and (in some circles) for Catholics.[15]

Few are fired for incompetence, especially if they last long enough to become members of their work group. One consequence is that, in craft or white collar jobs, higher standards are set for obtaining a job than for performance. The result is that a high level of formal education is often necessary for jobs that any average eighth-grader could learn to perform rather quickly. Once the person enters his work group, however, the social arrangements do not permit much overt discrimination between the less able and the rest. Thus we observe the irony in our generation that the middle classes, with their greater access to education, continue to have the advantage in getting jobs, though the standards, i.e., formal education, are ostensibly universalistic and achievement-based.

As Galbraith has pointed out, the greatest source of insecurity for both individuals and companies has been competition; business men "have addressed themselves to the elimination or mitigation of this source of insecurity."[16] Cartels, price and production agreements, tariffs, price fixing by law, and quiet understandings are among the techniques used to prevent the less able from being pushed to the wall. The "development of the modern business enterprise can be understood only as a comprehensive effort to reduce risk . . . (and) in no other terms."[17]

Analysts have reported such behavior most often from work groups, but similar patterns are observable if we look instead at the operation of any type of collectivity. All groups are creating *some* type of output, whether the socialization of a child or sheer entertainment. On the other hand, as we shall note later, the *degree* of protection may vary from one type of activity to another.

In examining the protection of ineptitude, we are considering the division of labor from a different perspective. For our limited purposes, the inept are made up of two classes of people in any collectivity: (1) with reference to one or more tasks, some are likely to be less skilled than others who do not enjoy the rewards of membership in that group; (2) in addition, some in that collectivity will be considerably less skilled than others. Clearly the group does not typically expel these less competent members. Instead, in each collectivity there are structures or processes which protect them.

## ACHIEVEMENT NORMS VS. BEHAVIOR

Even so brief a selection from the evidence confirms the impression from daily experience that some social behavior protects the less able from open competition. Is this, however, simply one more instance of action counter to a norm? Perhaps all these cases are only violations of the well-accepted norm of achievement. Let us, then, examine the possibility that people are only partially committed to the criterion of achievement as the basis for reward, and also accept other opposing norms.

The current sociological tradition, following Linton and Parsons, views industrial society as achievement-based, i.e., stratified by achievement criteria, in contrast to most other social systems, in which statuses are mostly ascribed.[18] However, we may question such descriptions, and assert instead that people in our own type of society feel committed to many criteria of ranking that run counter to achievement, and that in the so-called ascriptive societies the principle of placement by birth is in turn qualified a good deal by achievement norms. That is, let us consider whether both behavior and norms in all societies prevent the exposure of the less competent and productive.

I have not been able to locate an adequate empirical study of even the American population—the one most studied by sociologists—concerning its commitment to the notion of ranking by achievement, but I shall venture several armchair descriptions of some value patterns that I believe are now observable.

In the so-called achievement societies—the most conspicuous being traditional China and the industrial West—the norm of free competition has been accepted for other people's sons, but most parents have believed their own sons deserved somewhat better than that. On the other hand, I doubt that

even a majority of people in ascriptive societies (Western or not) have believed it was right for those *above* them to have been placed there by birth, although of course a majority might have affirmed their right by birth to be *above* others.[19]

Even in relatively "ascriptive" societies, the norm is that those who inherit their place should also validate it by both training and later adequate performance, e.g., knighthood. Almost never is there a norm denying any importance to achievement. Similarly, myths and legends recount with approval the ascent of the lowly to high position through merit.

In our presumably achievement-based society, few whites will fail to sense a twinge of the injustice of it all, when a superior Negro is made their boss. Few men believe that a woman should be promoted over them, even if by the criterion of merit she has earned it. Men with seniority believe it should count for more than achievement; and so on. Note, I am not stating merely that they are resentful, but that their value affirmations are in favor of other norms than performance when by those other norms they can lay claim to preferment.

Similarly, not only do the analyses of class membership, kinship, or friendship ties show the advantages or disadvantages of these non-achievement factors, but most individuals will, if pressed, admit they believe these factors should be used as norms, too. At a minimum, for example, if kinship or friendship is rejected in favor of merit as a norm, most will feel they are obliged either to give an additional justification of such a decision (thus demonstrating their lack of strong belief in the norm of achievement itself), or perhaps to help their role partner in some other way.

In an ongoing work group, both supervisors and members affirm a wide variety of other norms than achievement—seniority, the man's need, loyalty,—to justify the retention of all but the most flagrantly inept and non-contributing members.

In all industrial countries, and perhaps especially in the Communist countries, whether industrial or industrializing, the *rhetoric* of placement by achievement is insistent. It has a strong political appeal. It is like a handful of other such normative positions as hard work, opposition to sin, or an open mind: people do not publicly deny their worth, but they do believe they are much better when used to measure the worth of the other fellow.

The appeal of this rhetoric is illustrated well by the vociferous objection in the 1870's and 1880's to the introduction of merit placement in the United States Civil Service. People did not, after all, argue much against merit itself. On the other hand, they did introduce different standards, e.g., humanistic and anti-intellectual ones,[20] so as to avoid asserting that jobs should be given to the less able. In short, even in a society which is widely described as adhering to the rule of placement by achievement, not only does this norm not determine action consistently, but the commitment itself is highly qualified or weakened by belief in a wide range of other criteria as bases for rewards. Doubtless, one may argue nevertheless that members of an industrial society are somewhat more committed to this norm than are members of most other societies, but the contrast does not seem so great as contemporary sociology has asserted.

So persistent a phenomenon, even in a society whose rhetoric is permeated by achievement norms, cannot be interpreted as simply the usual failure of any society to implement its own values fully; in fact, people are committed to competing values as well.

The social arrangements (both behavioral and normative) that I have labeled "the protection of the inept" comprise a range of answers to a universal resource problem, which grows from the tension between the challenges of the external environment and the internal resources of the social system. Specifically, these arrangements comprise a partial answer to the question of what to do with that inevitable segment of a group that is relatively less productive or competent? How can the group utilize them, how gain from them that smaller, but measurable, amount of marginal productivity the group believes their efforts can contribute?

More generally, given the existence of the rela-tively inept in nearly all groups, what are the patterns or processes which will on the one hand protect them from the rigors of untrammeled competition (and thus gain their support and contribution), and on the other hand protect the group from the potentially destructive consequences of their ineptitude? Needless to say, there is no evidence that the social arrangements now observable are the most productive possible, whether of material goods or human satisfaction.

Having broadly reviewed some of the widespread evidence that such protective patterns exist, and that the norms in favor of reward by achievement are not unchallenged, let us now examine more closely the factors that create or support such patterns.[21]

## FACTORS THAT INCREASE OR DECREASE THE PROTECTION OF INEPTITUDE

These factors can be classified by whether they are *mainly* generated in the outside environment, as high or low demands are made on the collectivity for its output; or whether they largely originate in connection with internal social processes of the collectivity.

**EXTERNAL FACTORS** Perhaps the simplest formulation is that when there is a very high demand for a given type of group output or performance, the pressures on the group to fire, expel, or downgrade a member will be low. That is, the collectivity prospers in such an environment without demanding a higher performance from its members, or without recruiting more effective members. This principle is perhaps most clearly illustrated by the extraordinary current expansion of the college and university system in this and several other countries, and particularly by the expansion of graduate education. We do not create high-level men merely by announcing that a department will henceforth grant graduate degrees. Similarly, the increasing contemporary demand in business and government for expertise in a wide range of subjects offers new and increased rewards, and will doubtless eventually produce more skilled men.

However, at present the expansion of opportunities occurs faster than that of skills, with the consequent protection of ineptitude in many places.[22]

We may also derive from this relation a secondary formulation, that, when the supply of services, outputs, or candidates is relatively low, a similar result is produced: a higher tolerance of ineptitude.[23] The best illustrations can be found at the lower job levels, where few people actively *want* that kind of work. However, at such levels those who hire cannot easily find substitutes, such as machines, or a new source of labor. This type of work is ranked as socially necessary but not important. Thus, though the demand may not be high, it will not drop to meet a low supply. The typical result in most societies seems to be the same: people decide they would rather pay little and tolerate ineptitude than pay good wages and thus be able to demand a high level of performance.

This formulation applies to most slave labor, to domestic work in almost all countries past or present, to nearly all dirty, unskilled tasks, to K.P. in the armed services, and of course by and large to the performance of family role obligations.

By a structural peculiarity of the recruitment process this principle may be observed in the academic world—though instances in other spheres are doubtless to be uncovered. Here the administrative jobs pay relatively well, but the most desirable recruits are likely to be professors who rank that type of job as somewhat of a comedown. Thus, there is a relatively low supply of the highly competent, with the same result, a greater protection of ineptitude than would otherwise occur. This type of recruitment may also be observed in the selection of administrative personnel in foundations.

Third, demand may be *deliberately* kept low by the sociopolitical structure. Here again there is little pressure on the group or collectivity to expose or punish the less productive. It is especially in government that one may locate such sub-units, although perhaps they are common in all organizations large enough to confront the whole society

on many fronts, e.g., General Motors or the Catholic Church.

In the recent past, examples have included such agencies as the Office of Civil Defense, numerous antidiscrimination units, vice squads and gambling squads, agencies to reduce or prevent water and air pollution, or to beautify and develop parks and highways, and so on. Safety research in the automobile industry is another such instance. A high level of performance by this type of sub-unit would produce strong political opposition. As a consequence, a fairly low, often ritual, level of output is tolerated, and thus there are few pressures to evaluate the personnel by reference to the supposed target performance.

In general, of course, where clients do not demand high quality in performance, whether in Civil Defense or American cooking, the inept are relatively better protected than in other types of situations.

A fourth variant formulation of the basic supply-demand relation is that there will be less or more protection of ineptitude, depending on its consequences for the power or prestige of the person who heads the collectivity. For example, if the subordinate's ineptitude reduces the chief's power, the latter is unlikely to tolerate low competence. This type of case may occur when the subordinate's action is highly visible, or has a public dimension, e.g., the messenger boys of the House of Representatives. An employee whose function it is to move between social systems or sub-systems will be under greater pressure to perform well, if a poor performance would reduce the authority of his chief.

**INTERNAL PROCESSES**    Of course, such environmental factors can operate only through group processes, but the collectivity also generates protective measures because of its own internal needs as well. Among these, the following may be noted. The first is that the inept create a "floor," a lowest permissible level of competence. To fire them is to raise that level, so that those who are now comfortably above it might be threatened. To some degree, the mediocre "need" the really inept. The Southern White, in this sense, has needed the

Negro. Consequently, in perhaps most collectivities the thoroughgoing application of achievement criteria would be viewed as a threat.

Second, even the less competent have powers of bargaining, resources, pelf, contracts to give. Or they can make their fellow members feel guilty of inhumane conduct, thus invoking an alternate set of standards. In any given set of performance measurements, the costs of firing or downgrading the less able, or replacing them by better men, are weighted against the costs of permitting them to remain in the collectivity. This is simply another application of the general theory of role bargaining.[24]

Third, collectivities also assent to patterned exemptions from role obligations,[25] by which inevitable dips in performance are tolerated. These dips may be of short duration or not. Some permit the relaxing of standards because of another role obligation of high urgency or priority, e.g., the child of a working mother is ill, accidents, death in the family, and so on. Others express the tolerance of the group for individual fluctuations in personal integration, e.g., a man is going through a difficult marital crisis, has a work block, or becomes a heavy drinker for a while.

Another rule recognizes with compassion that the individual has entered on the normal declining curve in productivity with advancing age. What that age is will depend on the kind of activity the man performs. It is low among physical scientists, perhaps highest in politics and the law. In the occupational world, various structural solutions for this problem have been found, such as transferring a man to an essentially honorary or symbolic position, giving him easy physical work in a factory, handing over tasks of an essentially "human relations" type, or making him a representative of the organization in dealing with outside groups. More often, no formal changes are made, but less production is expected of him.[26]

A fourth internal factor is the complex problem of evaluation. That shrewd contemporary social analyst, Peter Ustinov, has noted that if the Secretary of State were to pass himself off as a comic, the observer would know within a few minutes that this is not his *métier*, but if a comic were to become Secretary of State, we would not at once discern any failure. The performance of the university president is especially difficult to measure, because of the complex relations between what the president does and the responses of his professors. Rewards are paid to the effective professor himself, but the prestige of professors may also be used as a measure of the president's achievement (at the levels where presidents are evaluated) even if in fact he has hindered their work. That is, the professor is motivated to work hard for himself, but his achievement may be viewed as proof of the president's competence. By contrast, the president of a municipal university may be given a lower evaluation because he fails to attract creative professors, when it is the low achievement of the tenured men which makes the university unattractive to potential recruits.

In any event, the less able are protected more in those types of performances that are difficult to evaluate. Parenthood, religious behavior, and administration are conspicuous examples. When war included hand-to-hand combat, performance could of course be evaluated much more easily than it is today. Similarly, sports offer an especially clear set of standards by which to evaluate performance, though here too some protection of weaker members by their teams can be observed. To some degree, the adversary system in Anglo-Saxon law tests competence in a public way. The higher levels of basic research constitute another area in which the less able are more likely to be exposed, and their lower performance made known.

These instances are notable because they *do* permit ready evaluation of performance. Granted that measurement is difficult, the interesting sociological question remains: Why do people (who after all constantly measure each other as individuals) not create group techniques for evaluating and making known the individual's performance level? Throughout this analysis, I am, of course suggesting that, in spite of some achievement rhetoric, people do not really want such a measurement system built into the social structure. We can, however, take note of several main *types* of answers to the measurement problem.

Perhaps the most difficult performances to measure are those of interpersonal skills or personal interaction. It is especially in such activities and occupations that the less able have a greater chance of avoiding exposure and—as social commentators have reminded us for centuries—of obtaining a desired post. Of course, people do weigh one another with respect to these skills. However, the individual who can create a friendly atmosphere about himself may be able to escape any exposure of his inability to elicit a high performance from his subordinates, or to execute a bureaucratic task skillfully. He may make friends, but contribute little to the main task or target performance.

In such tasks, one common pattern of avoiding open competiton is to assume that the problem of measurement can be skirted by refusing the position to people in low-ranking statuses, such as Negroes, Jews, and women, even when these traits are not important for the task, and some available candidates with those characteristics might conceivably manage the job well.

This pattern of "insulation" protects the less able by preventing competition with all but a limited number of pre-selected people. Essentially, then, the group selects an *irrelevant* trait, which can be a status or a performance that makes little or no contribution to the main task. The collectivity may alternatively focus instead on only *part* of the target performance. For example, a man may elicit loyalty among his crew, but cannot persuade them to work hard; the group ranks him by the loyalty of his crew.

A focus on the irrelevant status may combine with insulation to produce a lower skill level among those whose competition might otherwise be feared. If the group or stratum can command the *gateways* to training, insulating their own sons from open competition, then the *ultimate* result is that their own sons can indeed outperform those who were kept from acquiring those skills. The protection of ineptitude, then, begins much earlier, so that at the end point those who receive the

training may well be superior. This complex process may be observed among the lower social strata, Negroes, Mexican-American, women, and so on.

This pattern is most strikingly illustrated in music. The less able can be less easily protected when a conspicuously inborn talent makes a difference, i.e., when measurement is easier. Thus, a goodly number of Negroes have achieved great success in popular music, though they were nearly autodidacts. By contrast, concert performance of standard music requires both high talent and a long and costly training. It is notable, but to be expected, that Negroes are rare in the latter field.[27]

These "answers" to the problem of measurement—focusing on an irrelevant trait, seizing on an irrelevant performance, insulating members from outside competition, barring the gateways to training—protect the less talented or less skillful. That evaluation of performance may be difficult goes without saying, but it is equally noteworthy that collectivities make few sustained moves toward solving the problem in the direction of rewarding on the basis of achievement. The work of a clergyman is especially hard to measure, in part because there has been little agreement on what the performance ought to achieve. However, both his superiors and clients are more likely to measure his work by, say, an increase in church attendance rather than by the parishioners' increased rejection of sin.

## CONSEQUENCES OF PROTECTING THE LESS ABLE

Although we have by implication considered some of the consequences of these forms of protection, let us now examine them directly. One question must be faced at the outset. Does the protection of the less productive result in much ineffeciency, so that the sub-system or collectivity (family, church, sports team) might fall or be destroyed?

Three important theoretical principles bear on this question. First, if I am correct in arguing that nearly all groups have social arrangements for protecting their inept, then that fact alone would not necessarily handicap any particular group. The soldier or sailor, observing the general disorganization, unwise recruitment, and misapplication of personnel resources during a war, may suppose that his side is bound to lose. However, since the opposing forces are similarly crippled, it is likely that other factors than the protection of the inept will decide the war. In blunt terms, most organizations and individuals do not have to perform at peak capacity in order to survive, because the competition is not doing so either.

At a somewhat broader level of generality, as I have elsewhere argued, social systems can operate with considerable anomie and incompetence.[28] This is especially true for societies. Except in the case of war, which measures only one kind of performance, the threat of the environment is almost never so great as to destroy the advantages of human intelligence and organization.[29] Nearly always there is a sufficient surplus of manpower and resources to absorb almost any attack from the environment.

A second principle to be considered, in weighing the costs of protecting the less able, is that in fact some collectivities probably do go under because they protect their members too well. Organizations and sub-units compete primarily with others performing the same type of task, rather than with other social units in general. Upper-class families, for example, face their harshest competition for the available power, pelf, and prestige from other families in their own stratum, not from families at lower social ranks. For several generations their margin of safety may be great, but eventually they may fail. Other upper-class families are a more direct political threat. They are eligible for all the lucrative posts any given elite family possesses. Until the advent of the mass army, the elite fought each other in war.

The irony of the universal family pattern of protecting the less able children from open competition is that to the very extent that they succeed in this effort, they risk the diminution of their own family rank, because the next generation will be unable to survive the *intra*-elite contest—or even, possibly, the threat from men who rise from still lower ranks. Moreover, there is some evidence that the chances of revolution increase when a set of elite families succeeds too well in excluding the able who seek to rise.

## CONSEQUENCES OF NOT PROTECTING THE LESS ABLE

At a still deeper level of theoretical analysis, even for maximum efficiency the system-needs of any social unit *require* some protection of the inept, no matter what the goals of the group are, from the socialization of the child to the manufacture of transistor radios. The rigorous application of the norm of performance to the actions of all members of a collectivity would under most circumstances destroy both its social structure and its productivity.

It is, however, rare that any measurement of this kind has been carried out. Two of my first inquiries in the sociology of work ascertained: (1) that when sales performance was measured by individual success with the customer, salesmen engaged in several kinds of behavior that lowered *group* totals—holding customers who might have been waited on by others, refusing to replenish stock, and so on; and (2) that when management could prevent the formation of a genuine group, workers might have low morale but high individual productivity.[30] Also Blau outlined the consequences of the objective appraisal of performance in a clerical agency, some of which included falsifying records, undermining of the supervisor's authority, inconveniencing clients, and so on.[31] More recently, people doing industrial research have questioned the general assumption that an objective appraisal process would increase individual production.[32]

The sociological view is that placement, or punishment and reward, on the basis of performance alone, would essentially create a Hobbesian jungle, the undermining of group structure, the loss of the usual benefits of organization and cooperation, and the dissolution of group loyalties. Gouldner expresses this theoretical position effectively in his analysis of the contest system in Athenian society.[33] That system, he argues, "disposes individuals to make decisions that are often at variance with the needs and interests of the group." The type of open competition represented by the Greek contest system leads to bitterness, lowers the individual's commitment to group cooperation, creates strains in interpersonal relations, reduces conformity to established morality, and undermines the stability of the *polis*. The failure to protect the inept would also, then, lower the output of the group.

Needless to say, I am omitting from this sketch the primarily psychodynamic consequences of appraisal by merit. These may include feelings of being threatened, responses of distrust and hostility toward those doing the appraising, aversion of superiors to communicate those appraisals to their subordinates, resistance mechanisms of individuals who receive low appraisals, lowering of the individual's performance because of his diminished esteem after receiving a low appraisal, and so on.[34]

### STRUCTURES WITH LESS PROTECTION OF INEPTITUDE

The laconic assertion that not protecting the inept would lower group output needs further analysis, since clearly there are types of activities and groups in which a close approximation of appraisal and reward by merit occurs, without a destructive outcome. Perhaps the closest approximations, as noted earlier, are sports and the basic scientific research in a university department or corporation. The cases may be instructive.

The relevant relationships can be sketched briefly. On a sports team, when an individual does very well, the system of measurement makes this known, but the rewards of the less able are *increased*, while their work load is decreased. This is also true of the basic research team, though less so. In the university department engaged in scientific research, this relationship is somewhat weaker—because what one individual first discovers, another cannot. Nevertheless: (1) if the more able do reduce their work output, this will not raise the relative standing of the less able, since performance is measured by reference to achievement in the field as a whole; (2) in addition, men in the same department usually work on different problems; and

(3) if all reduce their production in order to protect the less able, all individuals lose somewhat because the prestige of their department drops,[35] and work becomes less fun for the participants.

### COOPERATION AND OUTPUT

These relationships do not hold in most work situations, although the more skilled corporation managers try to achieve such a structure where possible. If an individual does his best, knowing that achievement criteria alone will determine his advancement, the less able will drop relatively in the esteem of their supervisors, and possibly the level of required production from each member will rise. The less able members may, in fact, be squeezed out because they do not meet the new standard. Moreover, if each individual is rewarded only for his own performance, then in effect the group has given him nothing; whether his achievement level is high or low, he will feel no loyalty to the group.

If, as is now generally true of work systems, production does in fact partly depend on the efficiency of group organization and cooperation, the end result is likely to be less output, not more. By contrast, if the individual knows that when he needs it he will be protected somewhat by the group, he enjoys his personal relations with its members more, feels more securely identified with them, protects himself less from them, and is willing for the sake of the group to cooperate even when it will not raise his individual standing on the achievement scale.

Of course the professions, for all their emphasis on the rhetoric of individualism and achievement, illustrate the structural pattern common to most work situations, especially those with a strong union: the loss to all members would be greater, if the organizational structure failed, than would be the gain to a few highly able individuals if unrestricted public measurement of skill and effectiveness were permitted.[36]

Even the actual combat situation in war illustrates once more the dependence of organizational effectiveness on some protection of the inept. Without it, the competent will be killed along with the incompetent, for the former need the firepower and the loyalty of the latter. Such loyalty would not be so freely given if the inept could not count on being protected themselves. As implied earlier, the treatment of the demoted in management is an index of the judgment that the less able must be protected, to increase the effectiveness of the larger group.[37]

### UTILIZATION OF THE INEPT UNDER INDUSTRIALIZATION

The preceding relationships merit further testing, but it is also worthwhile here to consider how they should be qualified on theoretical grounds. For even if all societies, and nearly all collectivities do protect the less able, and even if failure to protect them will usually reduce output, it is equally clear that the protection of ineptitude can also *reduce* the effectiveness of the group. Certainly the evidence from societies with a high protection of the inept, such as caste or feudal systems, suggests that a high degree of protection is typically associated with low production. How does the utilization of the inept affect output?

The earlier sections of this paper anticipated that question by offering the hypothesis that social structures embody a tension between two factors, the protection *of* the inept and the protection of the group *from* the inept. At the psychological level this may be viewed as a tension between the frustration of the more able, and the degradation of the less able. Social structures vary in their solutions to this tension. For example, as noted earlier, family systems are far toward the extreme of placing little emphasis on achievement in ranking people, while sports (especially individual competition) fall toward the opposite extreme.

Social analysts have noted these differences, and have generally asserted that, for psychological integration, the individual cannot operate solely in activities whose criteria for reward are mainly those of performance. Everyone must at times retreat to other areas, such as friendship or the family, or perhaps religion and recreation, in which people are somewhat more protected from group downgrading or expulsion by a relatively lower frequency of public rankings, and the lack of refined ranks.[38]

This paper has focused, however, on the social structures which support nonachievement behavior *and* values even in groups or organizations whose rhetoric emphasizes achievement criteria. Some of the resulting protection of the inept is necessary if the collectivity is to produce effectively.

Yet such a hypothesis does not answer the question of how *much* protection of the inept is necessary for the highest efficiency or output. It is obvious, however, as a partial answer, that the modern industrial system outproduces all prior social systems. Is this the result, as so many have claimed, of giving freer scope to the highest talent and skill, and from rewarding more by merit than other societies have done?

That possibility cannot now be rejected, but I wish to suggest an alternative hypothesis, which emerges from the basic focus of this inquiry—how social structures handle the problem of what to do with the less competent. My alternative hypothesis is that the modern system is more productive because its social structures *utilize the inept more efficiently*, rather than because it gives greater opportunity and reward to the more able.

At one level this alternative explanation is merely self-evident. The two most significant tools of industrial society are the rationalized bureaucracy and the factory; their relation to ineptitude is the same. Both are based on a high division of labor, with fairly precise definitions of the task. As a consequence, a wide range of talent can acquire the skill necessary to carry out most jobs. Within any job level, some people will be much less competent than others, or than others whose job levels are lower, but they *can* do the job. Both the machine and the bureaucratic system lower the chances of catastrophic individual failure by the inept. They embody a control system which diminishes the range of possible error on the part of the individual worker. And, as so many essayists have noted, they also diminish the advantages that high talent would create, by narrowing the scope of free action. Then too, modern egalitarian ideology encourages men to feel valued as persons, providing motivation to all.

By contrast, the caste or feudal society gave great scope to talent, but only if the talented man was born to high position. Relying on placement by birth, such societies gave much protection to the inept, but gained little from it. Their productive technology was not organized into sub-tasks or sub-units or carefully articulated job assignments, which would maximize the productivity of the less able. The less competent in high places could do more damage, and the inept in lower positions could not contribute as much, as in modern society.

**VARIATION WITHIN INDUSTRIAL SOCIETY**    Evidently societies vary in their solutions to this problem, as do smaller units (sports teams, churches, and so forth) within each society. However, even with similar types of work organizations some variation is observable. In the French bureaucracy, for example, very little freedom of action is given to the outstanding, or for that matter even to the chief, and the lower echelons are still more controlled. On the other hand, from time to time an imaginative new organizational system is evolved by the very top men in the bureaucracy.[39]

In the Japanese system, entrance is granted to those who do well in competitive examinations, but of course that success is strongly determined by ascriptive criteria. Belonging to the right families guarantees better training for the tests.[40] Once hired, they move upward by seniority rather than merit, and people are rarely fired. However, the supervisor of a work unit gets credit for any ideas generated by people in his group, and precisely for that reason he need not attempt to stifle good ideas. Granted, the more able man receives little advantage in promotion, but he does receive group esteem and some of his talent is put to use. Individuals are protected, and there is a correspondingly high degree of group loyalty. One result is that the organization as a whole is much more productive and creative than the United States observer would predict from the simple statement that nonachievement factors play a large role in the Japanese factory and bureaucracy.

In the American bureaucracy, perhaps the worker can obtain more individual credit for his contribution than would be likely under the Japanese system. Both factory and bureaucracy in the United States seem to change more easily than in France. The American system has become more decentralized, and more autonomous at the lower levels, than either the Japanese or the French. Superiors consult more easily with subordinates in the United States than in the other two countries. This pattern may increase somewhat the chances of obtaining an advantage from the contributions of the more able, but also yields less protection to the less competent.

## CONCLUSION

So brisk a set of comparisons does not aim at a full answer to the question of optimum production or efficiency, but rather serves to illustrate the fact that apparently similar types of structure may give more or less protection to the inept, and more or less protection *from* the inept. The answer, if we were able to obtain it over the next few decades, would yield a still more useful by-product: how to create sets of social structures in different areas of action, to correspond more closely with our own values. In these relations, as in much of our social life, we may *will* some of the proximate social patterns without approving their ultimate result. If we knew better the full consequences of given arrangements for protecting the inept, we might decide to change these structures.

With reference to such values, I have ignored a number of issues that would have to be faced in a more extensive analysis. One, of course, is whether a society can or should reward equally those who are known to be less productive.[41] On a different level of values, though we may feel the less able performer ought not to be given more rewards, some of us may also assert that the performances properly to be rewarded are not those of automobile production and billboards, or even moon-rockets, but the far less easily measurable performances of warmth and loving, truth—note that the problem here is not one of ineptitude but simply a total lack of demand—beauty and taste, laughter, compassion, courage, generosity, or the support of variety in men and women.

We would, at the last, also have to examine not only our own values about the equality of opportunity, and the degradation of those who would inevitably fall behind,[42] but the more complex consequences for every sector or sub-system of the society. In doing so, we might have to take on a significant but nearly neglected task of an imaginative theory of society, the analysis and creation of utopias,[43] based on our widening and deepening knowledge of how social systems really operate. What kinds of societies are in fact possible, other than those which have existed?

Perhaps, by ascertaining both our values and the possible organizations for achieving them, we might learn that the costs of many contemporary patterns are too great. I do not agree with the many critics in sociology who hold that our dominant theory is merely an extended Panglossian commentary, providing this is the best of all possible worlds. Doubtless, whatever is, is possible, and whatever is may have had to be, but we can, I believe, go beyond those powerful laws and demonstrate, as other sciences have before us, that many desirable but presently nonexistent arrangements *are* also possible.

## REFERENCES AND NOTES

1   Allen H. Barton and David E. Wilder, "Research and Practice in the Teaching of Reading: A Progress Report," in Matthew B. Miles (ed.), *Innovation in Education*, New York: Columbia University, Teachers College, 1964, pp. 361–398.

2   More cautiously, the chances that the chief of a bureaucracy may be able to act irresponsibly and destructively are probably reduced. However, (1) the bureaucracy itself generates power, so that his usually limited range of action may nevertheless be more destructive than that of a feudal chieftain could be; and (2) in the event that the chief (Stalin, Hitler) *can* really capture the bureaucracy, his range of destructiveness is multiplied greatly.

3   See Harriet Zuckerman, "Nobel Laureates in Science: Patterns of Productivity, Collaboration, and Authorship," presented at the 61st Annual Meeting of the American Sociological Association, Aug. 31,

1966, especially the comments on the "uncrowned Laureates."

4   As a contrary case, because its members did not form a real group, see William J. Goode and Irving Fowler, "Incentive Factors in a Low Morale Plant," *American Sociological Review*, vol. 14 (October 1949), pp. 618–624.

5   For one such comment, see Julius A. Roth, "Hired Hand Research," *American Sociologist*, vol. 1 (August 1966), pp. 192–193. See also Melville Dalton, *Men Who Manage*, New York: John Wiley & Sons, Inc., 1959, chaps. 7–9. Most analyses of management make such comments implicitly or explicitly.

6   It is noteworthy that, when such ratings are made, it is typically "outsiders" who make them. See, for example, the Teamsters' study of hospital care in New York City: *The Quantity, Quality and Costs of Medical and Hospital Care Secured by a Sample of Teamster Families in the New York Area*, Columbia University School of Public Health and Administrative Medicine, n.d.

7   Erwin O. Smigel, *The Wall Street Lawyer: Professional Organization Man?*, New York: The Free Press, 1964, chap. 4.

8   For related comments, see Jules Henry, "The GI Syndrome," *Trans-Action*, vol. 1 (May 1964), pp. 8–9, 30; and Eliot Freidson, "The Professional Mystique," *ibid.*, pp. 18–20. For a broader analysis, see my "Community within a Community: The Professions," *American Sociological Review*, vol. 22 (April 1957), pp. 195–200; and "Encroachment, Charlatanism, and the Emerging Profession: Psychology, Sociology, and Medicine," *American Sociological Review*, vol. 25 (December 1960), pp. 902–914.

9   O. L. Peterson *et al.*, "An Analytical Study of North Carolina General Practice," *Journal of Medical Education*, vol. 31 (1956), p. 130.

10  Ely Chinoy, "The Tradition of Opportunity and the Aspirations of Automobile Workers," in Philip Olson (ed.), *America as a Mass Society*, New York: The Free Press, 1963, pp. 506, 508, 512 and especially n. 17; John W. Gardner, *Excellence*, New York: Harper & Row, Publishers, 1961, p. 110; Melville Dalton, *op. cit.*, pp. 5–6, 128; and his "Economic Incentives and Human Relations," in *Industrial Productivity*, Publication 7 of Industrial Relations Research Association, Madison Wisc., 1951, pp. 130–145; as well as Michel Crozier, *The Bureaucratic Phenomenon*, Chicago: University of Chicago Press, 1964, chap. 3.

11  For example, see the revealing article in the *Wall Street Journal*, Jan. 24, 1966, "Obsolete Executives," as well as Fred Goldner, "Demotion in Industrial Management," *American Sociological Review*, vol. 30 (October 1965), pp. 714–724. Consider, too,

the perceptive essay by one of our more imaginative social theorists, C. Northcote Parkinson, "Pension Point or the Age of Retirement," in his *Parkinson's Law*, Boston: Houghton Mifflin, 1962, pp. 101–113.

12  James G. March and Herbert A. Simon, *Organizations*, New York: John Wiley & Sons, Inc., 1963, p. 62.

13  For some evidence that they are right, see Dalton, *op. cit.*, chap. 6, and his "Unofficial Union-Management Relations," *American Sociological Review*, vol. 15 (October 1950), especially p. 615.

14  Erving Goffman, *The Presentation of Self in Everyday Life*, New York: Doubleday & Co., Anchor edition, 1959, chap. 2.

15  It is hardly necessary here to cite from the voluminous literature on discrimination of various types. See, however, E. Digby Baltzell, *The Protestant Establishment*, New York: Random House, Inc., 1964; Melvin M. Tumin, *Inventory and Appraisal of Research on American Anti-Semitism*, New York: B'nai Brith, 1961; C. Northcote Parkinson should not be overlooked: "The Short List or Principles of Selection," *op. cit.*, pp. 45–48; and George E. Simpson and J. Milton Yinger, *Racial and Cultural Minorities*, 3rd ed., New York: Harper & Row, Publishers, 1965.

16  John K. Galbraith, *The Affluent Society*, Harmondsworth: Penguin Books, Inc., 1965, pp. 90–91.

17  *Ibid.*, p. 91.

18  See, for example, Ralph Linton, *The Study of Man*, New York: Appleton-Century-Crofts, Inc., 1936, pp. 115, 127–129; Talcott Parsons, *The Social System*, Glencoe, Ill.: The Free Press, 1951, pp. 151–200; Leonard Broom and Philip Selznick, *Sociology*, 2d ed., White Plains, N.Y.: Row, Peterson, 1959, p. 191.

19  Joseph W. Elder found that 44 percent of the Mill Elite and 58 percent of the Brahmins believed that lower caste persons in that status were there because of sins committed in a previous life. "Industrialization in Hindu Society," Ph.D. dissertation, Harvard University, 1959, pp. 411, 415, 439.

20  Richard Hofstadter, *Anti-intellectualism in American Life*, New York: Alfred A. Knopf, Inc., 1963, especially pp. 181ff.

21  As will be seen, several of these have been adapted from H. M. Blalock, "Occupational Discrimination: Some Theoretical Propositions," *Social Problems*, vol. 9 (winter 1962), pp. 240–247.

22  Though numerically less important, it should not be forgotten, on the other hand, that jobs in this environment may be given to *some* talented and skilled men who would in a tighter market be classified by personnel men as "inept," i.e., "socially unacceptable," or too innovative or deviant, and so on.

23  Space does not permit me to go into the matter, but there are technical and theoretical reasons for considering high demand and low supply separately. Although occupational and other outputs do operate through market processes, I believe that a wide variety of such demands—such as love, emotional support, household and "dirty" types of work—have a high inelasticity, especially at the lower demand levels. At a cautious minimum, there are some obvious sociological factors that limit the *range* within which both supply and demand *can* respond swiftly.

24  See William J. Goode, "A Theory of Role Strain," *American Sociological Review*, vol. 25 (August 1960), pp. 483–496; and Peter M. Blau, *Exchange and Power in Social Life*, New York: John Wiley & Sons, Inc., 1964, especially chap. 4.

25  Robert K. Merton, *Social Theory and Social Structure*, rev. ed., Glencoe, Ill.: The Free Press, 1957, pp. 368–384.

26  See Goldner, *op. cit.*, pp. 714–724.

27  Perhaps the popular stereotype that "Negroes have rhythm" and are "musical" arose in part because it is one of the few areas in which it would be difficult to overlook a great talent. Until recently in the South, Whites sometimes visited Negro churches to listen to their choirs. One result was that a handful of Negro female singers *did* get the long and expensive education necessary to become concert performers of the standard repertoire.

28  See especially my "Illegitimacy, Anomie, and Cultural Penetration," *American Sociological Review*, vol. 26 (December 1961), pp. 910–925; and also "Social Mobility and Revolution," Camelot Conference, Airlee House, Virginia, June 4–6, 1965; and "Family Patterns and Human Rights," *International Social Science Journal*, vol. 18, no. 1 (1966), pp. 41–54.

29  This is one reason for the sterility of the search for the "requisites for the continuation of a society." Far too few societies have totally failed at all, and perhaps none has failed because it lacked any of these requisites. Lacking negative cases, it is difficult to test such requisites, and they are therefore to be viewed as a way of defining a society.

30  Nicholas Babchuk and William J. Goode, "Work Incentives in a Self-determined Group," *American Sociological Review*, vol. 16 (October 1951), pp. 679–687; and Goode and Fowler, *op. cit.* In the latter case, fortunately for the manager-owner, productivity depended very little on the maintenance of a group structure.

31  Peter M. Blau, *The Dynamics of Bureaucracy*, Chicago: University of Chicago Press, 1955, pp. 44–47, 162–167, 208–213.

32  Alvin Zander (ed.), *Performance Appraisals*, Ann

Arbor, Mich.: The Foundation for Research on Human Behavior, 1963.

33 Alvin W. Gouldner, *Enter Plato*, New York: Basic Books, 1965, pp. 52ff.

34 Most of these are noted by Alvin Zander, in "Research on Self-evaluation, Feedback and Threats to Self-esteem," in Zander, *op. cit.*, pp. 5–17. See also T. Whisler and S. Harper (eds.), *Performance Appraisal: Research and Practice*, New York: Holt, Rinehart and Winston, 1962; and Arthur R. Cohen, "Situational Structure, Self-esteem and Threat-oriented Reactions to Power," in Dorwin Cartwright (ed.), *Studies in Social Power*, Ann Arbor, Mich.: Institute for Social Research, 1959.

35 That individuals gain from being in the more successful departments is shown by Diane Crane, "Scientists at Major and Minor Universities," *American Sociological Review*, vol. 30 (1965), pp. 699–714.

36 This is pointed out in my two articles, "Community within a Community: The Professions," *op. cit.*, and "Encroachment, Charlatanism, and the Emerging Profession: Psychology, Sociology, and Medicine," *op. cit.*; and in more detail in William J. Goode, Mary Jean Huntington, and Robert K. Merton, "Code of Ethics," *The Professions in Modern Society*, Russell Sage Foundation, 1956 (mimeographed).

37 Fred H. Goldner interprets the varied solutions to this problem as ways of avoiding the "dysfunctions" of demotion, in his "Demotion in Industrial Management," *op. cit.* He also introduces the useful fact that demotion is psychologically easier for some, because the costs of high responsibility are thought to be great: weighed against these costs, demotion can sometimes be palatable.

38 In Talcott Parsons' formulation, each sub-system must go through the "latency phase" of the AGIL sequence from time to time, but other sub-systems (notably the family) may have as a *primary* activity (its "output") the latency function, thus restoring the individual to a healthier state for further effective participation in, say, an "instrumental" system such as the factory. See "An Outline of the Social System," in Talcott Parsons *et al.* (eds.), *Theories of Society*, New York: The Free Press, 1961, vol. 1, pp. 30–79.

39 Crozier, *op. cit.*, pp. 40ff, 282ff.

40 See Herbert Passin, *Society and Education in Japan*, New York: Columbia University Teachers College, 1965, especially chap. 6; and Ezra F. Vogel, *Japan's New Middle Class: The Salary Man and his Family in a Tokyo Suburb*, Berkeley, Calif.: University of California Press, 1963.

41 For an examination of some relevant arguments about this matter, see Melvin M. Tumin, "Some Unapplauded Consequences of Social Mobility in a Mass Society," *Social Forces*, vol. 36 (October 1957), pp. 32–37; and "Some Disfunctions of Institutional Imbalance," *Behavioral Science*, vol. 1 (July 1956), pp. 218–223; as well as "Rewards and Task Orientations," *American Sociological Review*, vol. 20 (August 1955), pp. 419–423.

42 Michael Young, *The Rise of the Meritocracy, 1872–1933*, London: Pelican Books, 1963, implies that a pure system by merit could be inaugurated, and the principle of merit really accepted by the lower social strata. The dissidence that develops in his satire, comes primarily from the proposal to return to placement by inheritance.

43 Wilbert E. Moore, "The Utility of Utopias," *American Sociological Review*, vol. 31 (December 1966), pp. 765–772.

## SUPPLEMENTAL READINGS

Allen, Frederick: *Only Yesterday*, New York: Bantam Books, Inc., 1959.

Beck, Bernard: "Bedbugs, Stench, Dampness, and Immorality: A Review Essay on Recent Literature about Poverty," *Social Problems*, vol. 15 (summer 1967), pp. 101–114.

Blauner, Robert: *Alienation and Freedom: The Factory Worker and His Industry*, Chicago: University of Chicago Press, 1966.

Boguslaw, Robert: *The New Utopians: A Study of System Design and Social Change*, Englewood Cliffs, N.J.: Prentice–Hall, Inc., 1965.

Carson, Rachel: *Silent Spring*, Boston: Houghton-Mifflin Company, 1962.

Faunce, William A.: "Automation in the Automobile Industry," *American Sociological Review*, vol. 23 (August 1958), pp. 401–407.

Hughes, Everett C.: *Men and Their Work*, New York: The Free Press, 1958.

James, Ralph C., and Estelle James: *Hoffa and the Teamsters: A Study of Union Power*, Princeton, N.J.: D. Van Nostrand Company, Inc., 1965.

Michael, Donald N.: *Cybernation: The Silent Conquest*, Santa Barbara, Calif.: Fund for the Republic, Inc., 1962.

Orshansky, Mollie: "Counting the Poor: Another Look at the Poverty Profile," *Social Security Bulletin*, Washington, D.C.: U.S. Social Security Administration, January 1965, pp. 3–29.

Porter, John: "The Future of Upward Mobility," *American Sociological Review*, vol. 33 (February 1968), pp. 5–20.

Presthus, Robert: *The Organizational Society*, New York: Alfred A. Knopf, Inc., 1962.

Shostak, Arthur B., and William Gomberg, (eds.): *Blue-collar World*, Englewood Cliffs, N.J.: Prentice-Hall, Inc., 1964.

Smigel, Erwin O. (ed.): *Work and Leisure*, New Haven, Conn.: College and University Press Services, Inc., 1963.

Veblen, Thorstein: *The Theory of the Leisure Class*, New York: New American Library of World Literature, Inc., 1953.

Wilensky, Harold L., and Charles N. Lebeaux: *Industrial Society and Social Welfare*, New York: The Free Press, 1965.

Although other institutions have played dominant roles in the control and direction of society at various times in history, most thoughtful observers would agree that today in advanced technological societies, characterized by urban concentration of great populations, government has assumed the predominant role. Government is generally the institution to which people turn when great problems arise. If the economy manifests serious symptoms of weakness, the typical citizen reacts immediately with an outcry that the government "ought to do something about it." The Johnson administration, for example, was quick to turn to commission reports on crime, riots, and violence as manifest evidence of "doing something about it." Congress' answer to the people is usually to hold extended hearings on critical issues for the purpose of developing enabling legislation and to make known to the people via television that "something is being done about it."

A significant number of citizens have expressed real concern that there may be too much government involvement in the operation and control of other institutions. There may be disagreement on the extent to which government should be involved, but most people acknowledge that it is involved and is generally pervasive in modern society.

The United States has the oldest representative republican government in the world. It is a federal government predicated on the acceptance of orderly change through appropriate legislation and constitutional amendment. Its three branches are organized into the executive, the legislative, and the judiciary. A similar pattern is followed at the state level. Federal and state governments both have a number of exclusive powers and rights, detailed in the Constitution and interpreted periodically by the United States Supreme Court and lower courts. Problems of jurisdiction often arise between the federal government and state governments, and at present we seem to be in a period of renewed claims by state governments of the federal government's encroachment on their "rights" and responsibilities. The federal government has seized the initiative on many fronts by the simple device of enacting funding legislation with the proviso that state governments match these grants, and state governments that do not cooperate with the federal government in matching the grants simply lose them. However, all regulations concerning the expenditure of the grant money for programs, facilities, and personnel are set by federal legislation.

New York is one of the few states that has had enough autonomy to develop its own programs and facilities somewhat independently of the federal government, largely on the premise that the costs would be lower if they were determined locally. The Governor of New York has observed on numerous occasions that he receives from the federal government only 5 cents on every dollar of taxes sent to Washington. However, for the most part, states have come to heel when federal grants were involved and have informally accepted their junior position to the federal government, a major status change from the model of the original federation of states. Perhaps some state will have the imagination to offer to appropriate a specific sum of money for a major local need, provided the federal government matches the grant.

Formal legislative and executive representation is based on a multi-party system, although in realistic terms there are only two parties. For more than 100 years the Democrats and the Republicans have represented a wide spectrum of political beliefs and policies. In general the Democrats have become more liberal and the Republicans more conservative, almost a reversal of their respective positions a century ago. Today the Democrats are the majority party, with a strong welfare orientation and with great support from urban areas, the Eastern Seaboard, and minority groups. Republicans range from progressives to extreme conservatives. The presidential races of 1964 and 1968 saw the Republicans contesting the Democrats in the "solid South."

One of the chief critics of the functioning of our political system was the late C. Wright Mills, who argued that the American society was in fact controlled by three elite groups—the political leaders, the military generals, and the business executives—whose enormous coordinated power enabled them to shape the destinies of all citizens. These elite are, in Mills' view, the makers of wars, depressions, and peace agreements; in short, they are the real history makers. Mills assumed that virtually all members of the power elite have the same interests and thus a ready-made faculty for agreement. Other students of American society feel that this hypothesis is overstated as an explanation of day-to-day decision making. It may have great validity during periods of national disaster and crises, but then during such periods all groups in society, including feuding neighbors, will tend to pull together as a matter of immediate survival.

Most social scientists agree that the government of the United States is an institution with the ability to accommodate the needs of many conflicting interests and groups. In reality it is difficult to imagine Mills' power elite agreeing on any important decision without serious conflict and lengthy discussion of alternative programs. In the past even the military establishment was not monolithic, and national defense was weakened by interservice bickering and jealousy. The Department of Defense was developed as a progressive effort to coordinate the Army, Navy, and Air Force and restrict their divisive in-fighting. Within the business community there is certainly intense competition and in-fighting for consumer markets, government contracts, product ideas, and productive personnel. The term "trade secret" symbolizes the intensity of this competition.

Carey McWilliams, in the selection "Protest, Power and the Future of Politics," brings to our attention the concentration of political power in the executive branch of the federal government. McWilliams believes that the dominant power over industry, the military, and Congress and the judiciary now lies, not with an elite in Mills' sense, but with the executive branch of the government. Americans, he feels, are becoming aware of their helplessness to govern their own lives effectively. If this trend of concentration of power in the executive branch continues, it is not difficult to predict an increasing alienation of the American people from their government. Much of the problem seems to stem from the fact that administrative decision making has become dominant through the executive branch of the government, and Congress and the judiciary have failed to exercise independent power to the same degree; in fact, the executive branch exercises more control over the lives of the American people than the congressional and judicial branches combined.

McWilliams goes a step further than Mills and identifies the military, industrial, and academic complex as subordinate to the executive branch of the federal government. For example, even though the hostilities in Vietnam have never been formally defined by Congress as a war, the Tonkin Resolution of August 7, 1964, gave the President power to "take all necessary measures to repel any armed attack against the forces of the United States and to prevent further aggressions." The military view of our involvement in Vietnam, of course, is evident in General William C. Westmoreland's statement on November 19, 1967, that "We are winning a war of attrition," and within two years or less we may be able to "phase down the level of our military effort." In passing the Tonkin Resolution, Congress simply transferred its power to define war to the executive branch. One of the key men behind this resolution was Senator J. William Fulbright, who in the spring of 1968 admitted that it was a "mistake," particularly in view of the confused military action surrounding the destroyers *U.S.S. Maddox* and *U.S.S. C. Turner Joy* on August 2–4, 1964. It appears that the role of the military as a functioning element of the executive branch is particularly highlighted when "police actions" are a vital aspect of foreign policy McWilliams raises some interesting questions concerning the weakness of bipartisan foreign policy and the need to extend evidences of direct democracy when representative democracy becomes indifferent to consensus opinion.

With the increased concern for national defense, the matter of internal security has become prominent. Persons who might weaken the government must not be permitted to occupy responsible positions in government service or have access to classified information. Thus all applicants for government positions must undergo an intensive security check. Neighbors, employers, and former teachers are usually questioned about wide areas of an applicant's behavior. The information they supply is not evaluated by an intelligence agency, but is merely forwarded to the security board or officer making the final decision. There have been complaints that this procedure provides an opportunity for the exercise of deliberate malice in providing false information or misinformation about an applicant's behavior or beliefs.

Alan Westin projects as an allegory the life of Roger M. Smith, 2734-2124-4806, in the year 1975, when all personal and business activities will be monitored by computers. He presents some startling possibilities of an economy operating entirely on a credit basis, with each consumer's rating evaluated hourly, and takes a hard look at some evidences of the "snooping-machine" operation in our daily lives. No doubt, many Americans are beginning to realize that their social-security numbers are being requested on state and federal income-tax forms, college and university registration applications, and dividend reports to various government agencies, and even the military service is beginning to substitute social-security numbers for serial numbers. With a single identification number for each citizen it is now possible to collect quickly vast amounts of information about anyone. It also becomes convenient for various agencies of federal and state government to exchange information of common interest. Some Western European governments now make public all kinds of data on income, wealth, educational status, and marital status (including legitimacy).

It is becoming clear that as the political establishment becomes more proficient in the science of monitoring the behavior of private citizens thoughtful students are going to question both the goals and methods of such surveillance. Many Americans find something inconsistent in a secret watch on the behavior of a free people. Students around the world, representing both right- and left-wing governments, are beginning to protest the erosion of freedom. Seymour Lipset, in his selection "Students and Politics," documents the extensiveness of student activism in specific countries. The "new left" or the "new right" invariably turns out to be the young left or the young right, indicating that young people are now welding idealism with political action. Critical students are going to continue to examine the assumptions of man, his government, and his basic institutions.

The selections that follow analyze a number of important political problems of the present day. McWilliams comments on the twin forces of protest and power in politics. Westin describes the enormous potential for the invasion of privacy by government agencies and the development of monitoring devices. Lipset discusses political action by students in a comparative perspective. Charles E. Osgood takes a look at national-security policies as assumptions rather than as national-security principles.

## 17    PROTEST, POWER AND THE FUTURE OF POLITICS

CAREY McWILLIAMS

A preoccupation with power—black power, student power, flower power, poor power, "the power structure"—is the most striking aspect of the American political scene at the moment. Oddly enough, obsession with power goes hand in hand with a fear of power. Some of the New Left groups that talk the toughest about power are extremely reluctant to see power operate in institutional form; within their own organizations, they shun "hierarchies" and formally structured relations of authority. What the preoccupation with power reflects, essentially, is a deep-seated, pervasive feeling of powerlessness. The feeling is not restricted to particular groups; most citizens, a majority perhaps, are bedeviled by it. "A feeling of having no choice," Mary McCarthy has noticed, "is becoming more and more widespread in American life."

So intense is the feeling of powerlessness that it has given rise to "anti-movements" and "anti-politics." Instead of building new, strong, viable organizations through which to exercise political power, the tendency—at least on the Left—has been to move in the reverse direction, that is, to reject the instruments of politics. Discussion has been superseded by "uproar," debate by demonstrations, dialogue by confrontation, civil disobedience by overt resistance. Often in the past, young voters have bade "farewell to reform" and then turned to radical politics; this time they have swung toward no politics at all. The idea of government by and through elected representatives is seriously questioned by some and indignantly rejected by others. The very process of politics has come under direct attack from young and old alike.

Apart from increasing evidence of this active

Reprinted with the permission of the author and the publisher from *The Nation*, vol. 206 (Jan. 15, 1968), pp. 71–77.

disaffection, there is among those who have by no means despaired of politics a widespread anxiety about what Walter Lippmann has called "the rot of the American political system." On November 10, NBC presented an analysis of voter attitudes on the 1968 election, and found that most voters had little faith that any major candidate for the Presidency could master either of the two major problems we face (war and race), and worse, seemed to feel that the electorate was being denied live options on most issues. The survey indicated "a stunning lack of confidence in the President and in his political opponents." A mountain of supporting evidence might be cited. Yet despite the active disaffection and the mounting general concern, little attention has been focused on what it is that accounts basically for the malfunctioning of the political system. The problem has two aspects. Power has been concentrated in our society in such a way, and to such a degree, that normal political processes are perhaps no longer able to cope with it. But one can't be sure of that because if certain specific weaknesses in the political system not directly related to the concentration of power, were remedied (at the moment they are not widely recognized, much less discussed) the reform might go far to remove the "rot" from the system.

On the first aspect, that of power, Thomas C. Cochran, the economic historian, has reminded us that "the modern centralized, militarized, and welfare-directed state" did not come into being overnight; it is the result of a complex internal evolution. Not consciously planned, it is a response to fears: first of internal economic collapse; second of external dangers and "enemies." The New Deal, a war against impending economic collapse, was fought as any war is fought. Emergency agencies, with extraordinary powers, came into being overnight; crash programs were rushed into motion; executive decisions took precedence over cumbersome legislative processes; and more and more power was vested in the Presidency. At the same time, and as part of the same process, economic power was increasingly concentrated. On the eve of World War II, a study made by a group including six members of President Roosevelt's Cabinet ("The Structure of the American Economy," 1939), expressed, even then, growing alarm at the political consequences of tightly held economic power.

The concentration of power became much tighter after we entered World War II. Under the stress of rapid mobilization, a remarkable fusion of economic and political power took place; more accurately, perhaps, a fusion of economic and administrative or Executive power. This had been true also in World War I, but unlike the procedure after 1918, the war-making machine of World War II was never fully dismantled. The swift onset of the cold war, then the fighting in Korea and Vietnam, set the pattern for a permanent war economy. The rapid pace of military technology, which began to diverge sharply from civilian advances, created a political rationale for continuous research and improvement in weapons systems and the like. Nuclear weapons and virtually instantaneous delivery systems authorized an ever-larger permanent military establishment; in any future war, it was said, there would be "no time to mobilize." In the past, industries had "converted" to war production and then "reconverted" to peacetime production. After 1945 new defense industries came into being specifically to manufacture military hardware. At the same time the magnitude of the military budget revolutionized government finance. Defense-related expenditures will this year probably exceed $100 billion. In a recent survey, the AP referred to the Pentagon as wielding "the mightiest concentration of economic power in the world today."

In his famous farewell address, General Eisenhower expressed misgivings about our ability to control "the military-industrial complex" by normal political processes. More recently, the same concern has been more specifically voiced by others. "The huge size of military budgets," said Dr. Arthur F. Burns, "and incomplete disclosure concerning their management, carry with them the dangers of political abuse"—as by building military stockpiles of certain raw materials to maintain price levels during periods of overproduction or of stepping up defense spending as an offset to declining employment. Dr. Charles J. Hitch, an expert on defense planning, now president of the University of California, has made a similar observation: "Certainly the defense budget is a large and powerful tool for the government, and one is tempted to seek its uses to solve an array of problems. . . . Defense spending has become a substantial and more or less normal factor in the economic reckoning of many American businesses."

Senator Fullbright spoke most soberly on this point in the Senate on December 13:

> More and more our economy, our government and our universities are adapting themselves to the requirements of continuing war—total war, limited war and cold war. The struggle against militarism into which we were drawn twenty-six years ago has become permanent, and for the sake of conducting it, we are making ourselves into a militarized society. . . . For all the inadvertency of its creation and the innocent intentions of its participants, it [the military-industrial-academic complex] has become a powerful new force for the perpetuation of foreign military commitments, for the introduction and expansion of expensive weapons systems and, as a result, for the militarization of large segments of our national life. Most interest groups are counterbalanced by other interest groups, but the defense complex is so much larger than any other that there is no effective counterweight to it except concern as to its impact on the part of some of our citizens and a few of our leaders, none of whom have material incentive to offer.

For this reason, the defense complex has not been challenged by either party; in fact both have been about equally responsible for it. But it is doubtful that the growth of the complex could have been arrested even if one of the major parties had been willing to incur the risk of such a stand. And it is doubtful today that the Republican Party can bring itself to challenge the disastrous course of present policies, not because it is blind to the dangers or fails to appreciate the political possibilities in capitalizing on the existing discontent, but because power is now so bipartisan in structure that the opposition party cannot, apparently, muster the resources or the will to make the effort. James Reston notes, moreover, that the powerful Eastern Establishment in the GOP is by no means unanimously displeased with Johnson and his policies.

As the militarization of the society has proceeded, the power of the Congress relative to the Presidency has steadily declined. The recent report of the Senate Foreign Relations Committee on "National Commitments" (November 20) points out that the last twenty years have seen a nearly complete reversal of the positions of the Executive and legislative branches in the area of foreign affairs. Dr. Ruhl Bartlett, of the Fletcher School of Law and Diplomacy, told the committee that "the greatest danger to democracy in the United States and to the freedom of its people and to their welfare—as far as foreign affairs are concerned—is the erosion of legislative authority and oversight and the growth of a vast pyramid of centralized power in the Executive branch of the government." Dr. Edgar Eugene Robinson of Stanford suggested in a recent speech that the acquisition by the President of immense power over foreign affairs during the last twenty years means that the Constitution is outdated. "There is no possibility," he says, "of real change in the President's foreign policy except by removal . . . by death, resignation, impeachment or defeat at the polls." What in his view makes this development particularly dangerous is the dexterity with which the President can fuse two constitutional functions: his role as commander in chief and his responsibility for the conduct of foreign affairs. Once war has become an instrument of national policy, it is hard to tell which role a President is playing. If his foreign policy is

challenged, he can always assert his powers as commander in chief, and these powers are almost unlimited. (See, also, Sen. Frank Church's speech, October 29, on "President and Congress in Foreign Policy: The Threat to Constitutional Government.")

The process by which political and economic power have been concentrated through expansion of the war-making machine has been hastened by a series of postwar "revolutions": the organizational revolution, the scientific and technological revolution, the cybernetic revolution and, most notably, the communications revolution. As Dr. Robinson also pointed out, the communications revolution has made it possible for a new Presidential order, decision or proclamation to be carried instantaneously by radio and television. "Consequently, the effectiveness of that action is amplified millions of times by the miracle of swift communication."

Over the past twenty years the power of appropriation, which is supposed to be the bedrock of Congressional control, has been seriously eroded. A study of how the military budget has been handled in successive Congresses since the end of World War II would demonstrate that it is now firmly controlled by the Executive. And the military budget is today so immense, particularly if expenditures for NASA and the AEC are included, that the power to manipulate it conveys, as a side effect, power to shape the whole national budget.

The fallacy in the guns-and-butter proposition, as Dr. Burns has pointed out, is that "Financial transactions and the price system are merely mechanisms for putting a nation's resources to work and for distributing what is produced among people and their government. The resources that we devote to national defense are not available for making consumer goods or for adding to the stock of industrial equipment or for public uses in the sphere of education, health, or urban development. To the extent that we allocate labor, materials, and capital to national defense, we cannot satisfy our desires for other things. . . . Bombs or missiles add nothing to a nation's capacity to produce, while new equipment serves to augment production in the future. The real cost of the defense sector consists, therefore, not only of the civilian goods and services that are currently foregone on its account; it includes also an element of growth that could have been achieved through larger investment in human or business capital." In fact a former member of President Eisenhower's Council of Economic Advisers, Dr. Paul McCracken, has expressed the opinion that the Executive's seizure of decision-making has resulted in a federal budget whose expenditures, in the technical sense, are now out of control.

Any erosion of the power of Congress is an erosion of the power of the people. Given a society in which for a period of twenty years—almost the span of a generation—the real power of decision has been increasingly ceded to the President, it is not hard to account for the prevalent sense of "powerlessness." Just as the ghetto dweller feels that he lives in "occupied territory," so many people come to feel that they have been "displaced" from their role as electors. A force which they cannot control or directly influence has taken charge of their lives and destinies. "There are many signs," writes A. H. Halsey (*New Society*, October 26), "from love-ins in the Haight-Ashbury district of San Francisco to the 'privitization' of affluent workers . . . that a theory of the impotence of politics is being accepted." If the country has in fact been "occupied" by a power not sanctioned by the Constitution, then it must be "liberated." But given the degree to which power has been concentrated, can the direction of policy be reversed by conventional political means? In such a situation, public protests become increasingly directed against the symbols of power, and that has the effect of diverting energies from the political process and, at the same time, discrediting it.

In the nature of things, it is difficult for "anti-movements" to cooperate with movements—of any kind. The objectives, the sense of tactics, the style of action, are different or divergent. That some of the "anti-movements" share with the infinitely larger movement of "concerned" and "dissatisfied" citizens the short-term objective of stopping the war does not mean that they see the war in the same terms or that they agree on other objectives. The "anti-movement" of Negro nationalists does not even share the short-term objective of stopping the war (at least, it is not for them a priority objective). And, to complicate matters, the larger movement is itself not well organized and lacks sufficient program.

By and large, "anti-movements" are not elated when a dove defeats a hawk; they have lost confidence in the political process as it now exists—not without reason—and they want to discredit it, the better, no doubt, to fill the political vacuum with a new politics. If the "anti-movements" openly espoused revolutionary objectives, then a measure of "parallel" politics might be possible (it may still be, depending on developments). But as of now, the Black Nationalists and the New Activists, as William Appleman Williams has observed, "have no vision of a Socialist commonwealth, let alone even the beginnings of serious proposals to create and govern such a society." They seem less concerned with the concentration of power, and the growing political vacuum which could set the stage for an American fascism, than with the hateful discrepancy between liberal ideals and liberal practice. They give little thought to the possibility that something about the functioning of a capitalist economy may lead to the concentration of power. The heroes of the "anti-movements" are Debray and Che Guevara, not Gramsci who thought that the proper place to find those who aspired to lead revolutionary movements was in the reading rooms of public libraries. Because they are not really concerned with the *political* consequences of particular protests and demonstrations, they discount polls which show that certain recent demonstrations have stimulated a reaction and strengthened the President's hand. This, of course, is a logical attitude for those who have lost confidence in the political process. But it carries a distressing echo of the "social fascism" line that the Communist Party pursued in the early 1930s.

However, the "anti-movements" have had some highly desirable political consequences. The stress on personal commitment, on values, on life styles, the exposure of liberal pretense, have released new energies, focused attention on particular issues, and pointed up the relation between morality and politics. One of the only means whereby individuals can make what they think and feel relevant in a society in which power is highly concentrated is to stress the morality—or immorality—of public policies. But it is precisely in such a period that as Iris Murdoch has noted, "political moralizing comes to be thought of as an idle idealism, a sort of utopianizing which is just a relief from looking at unpleasant facts." This was the position into which many cold-war liberals were driven, or into which they retreated, when they decided that there was little point in attempting to bring moral judgments to bear in the field of foreign policy. Today many of these same individuals have recoiled in horror from the consequences of the "crackpot realism" of Dulles and Acheson and Rusk. For this shift in attitude, the "anti-movements" are entitled to some credit. But if we are to answer the cynic in ourselves, moral judgments, as Miss Murdoch stresses, must be *realistic enough* to be political judgments as well. For the ultimate cynicism is to conclude that politics is a futile game. Such a conclusion severs the relation between morality and politics. To stress the immorality of the war in Vietnam, while rejecting the possibility of stopping it *by political means*, is self-defeating. Before anyone declared politics obsolete, he should at least try to identify the rot which has brought such discredit upon the institution.

Perhaps the most important single cause of the rot has been adherence to a bipartisan foreign policy. Politics does *not* stop at the water's edge. In today's world, one might well say that it begins there. The American party system had its origins in a dispute over foreign policy. The bipartisan concept dates from Roosevelt's determination to secure ratification of the UN charter by obtaining Republican support in advance. But the cold war came along almost before the Charter had been ratified, and what had been projected as a temporary expedient crystallized as a national dogma. The policy that resulted has been one of preserving the *status quo*, of pushing American economic expansion throughout the world under cover of a

rigid "anti-Communist" ideology. At the same time the fear of communism—in part real, in part concocted—made it relatively easy to wrest cold-war appropriations from Congress, particularly military appropriations. Since the major interest groups all benefited directly or indirectly—if not evenly—they became adherents to bipartisan cold-war policies and the country, enjoying the prolonged boom, acquiesced.

Given the generally conservative cast of successive postwar Congresses, the emphasis on military spending in support of mostly reactionary cold-war policies won majority bipartisan support. For one thing, it was a way of keeping domestic spending for welfare and other purposes under control. Then, as military spending increased, the influence of the military on foreign policy also increased, as did the power of the President. The public hearings which the Senate Foreign Relations Committee staged in 1966 are generally conceded to represent the first significant attempt by that committee in the postwar period to regain some of the power it once possessed. Not to debate foreign policy assumptions and alternatives was, in today's world, to forgo significant debate on domestic issues as well. It was as though both parties had agreed to a twenty-year moratorium on significant politics. Today the rot that this moratorium produced is all too evident.

But there are signs—and they are multiplying—that the bipartisan consensus is breaking up. Senator Morton's dramatic announcement last summer —"I was wrong. Our country has been painted into a corner out there. There's going to have to be a change"—was an event of major political importance. Since then, as Don Oberdorfer points out in *The New York Times Magazine* (December 17), the "wobble" on Capitol Hill has become increasingly evident. "The summer and fall of 1967 have been a time of switching . . . a scurrying in many directions, in search of a stance that took account of the growing distaste for the war." The splendid spadework on Vietnam undertaken by a 29-year-old freshman Republican, Rep. Donald W. Riegle, Jr., and some of his colleagues is a sign that the twenty-year infatuation with bipartisan cold-war policies is beginning to lose its appeal to Republicans. Never before have so many dissenting voices begun to link foreign affairs with domestic politics (Dr. Martin Luther King is an example), which suggests that in the end the crisis in domestic affairs will force a reconsideration of foreign policy. But even as the ferment spreads, efforts are made to reimpose the "consensus," to choke off partisan debate before it gets started. General Eisenhower has said that any Republican who departs from the official line on Vietnam "will have me to contend with. . . . That's one of the few things that would start me off on a series of stump speeches across the nation"—a statement not calculated to encourage the Republicans to offer an alternative policy and program. However, increasing numbers of Republicans continue to "wobble."

Adherence to a bipartisan foreign policy was made all the easier when the Left collapsed after World War II. By Left, I mean all those elements that might have been disposed to challenge the assumptions on which the cold-war policy rested. Twenty years of systematic redbaiting, conducted not by private but by government agencies, and financed by public funds, gravely distorted the political spectrum; it shifted the center of gravity in both parties well to the right. The Left, in the European sense, was never strong here; during the McCarthy phase it ceased to exist. Nor was this merely a matter of disrupting certain organizations; currents of "undesirable" critical opinion were driven underground, individuals censored their own thoughts, organizations purged their own ranks.

The collapse of the old Left in the postwar period meant that the liberals of the Democratic Party were subject to no pressure or competition except from conservative or right-wing sources (much the same state of affairs prevailed in the trade union movement). The official liberalism of the Democratic Party, which was really "the new conservatism," lived off the store of ideas that had been developed in the 1930s. It responded to new issues and new problems by offering "more of the same," that is, extending the programs of the New Deal.

More important, the collapse of the Left has deprived us all of a comprehensive critique of American society, its values, its direction, its performance. The New Deal was not based on any carefully thought-out assumptions; its programs were mostly improvisations. The continued failure of the liberal Democrats to provide a serious alternative to the "reformism" of the early progressive movement had the effect of minimizing ideological differences of all kinds, including those between Democrats and Republicans. Both parties professed the same values, the same purposes, essentially the same policies. Both parties have accepted the ideology of "free enterprise," joined in the "American celebration," and endorsed the objectives of an expansionist foreign policy. Both have pushed the new American imperium. No partisan challenge has been offered to the Administration's assertion of a right of unilateral military intervention wherever it feels that vital "interests" have been threatened.

The collapse of the Left is an essential key to explaining the rot because the absence of ideological differences has been the historic weakness of American politics. Not only has the American Left contributed to this weakness; the lack of a consistent ideological drive explains the feebleness of the Left itself. "The American Left," as Michael Davie points out, "has always been more eccentric than effective. In Europe, men have had to battle for the establishment of their basic rights, and have needed a theory of drastic social change to go to war with." But not here. As Tom Hayden, one of the leaders of the New Left observes: "How *do* you act as a revolutionary against a nation-state that celebrates your values while betraying their substance?" Even in the fiercest American struggles, everyone of major political importance has believed in the same basic things. "The mainstream of the American political tradition," to quote Davie again, "thus flows between firm banks (though it is not yet clear whether they can contain the Negro revolution) and features a steady belief in the sanctity of private property, the importance of economic individualism, and the unifying influence of greed. . . . Outside Portugal, Marx has had less influence in the United States than on any country in the Western world. . . . The most wretched victims of the American system [are kept] safely in the mainstream of the American political tradition—convinced that only luck or geography, never the system itself, stand between them and all-American prosperity." Al Capone once said to Claud Cockburn that "This American system of ours . . . gives to each and every one of us a great opportunity if we only seize it with both hands and make the most of it." Capone's view is still shared by most Americans. That it was never really true Indians and Negroes and others can testify, but it seemed to be true until fairly recent times. In the past, a debilitated American Left tried to mount a critique of the prevailing ideology, but the collapse of the Left in the postwar period silenced this type of criticism precisely when it was most needed.

The abdication of the Left in the postwar period, and the failure of the New Left thus far to fill the vacuum, have meant that the idea of a radical politics and the function it can serve in our kind of political system has been forgotten. Radical political pressures played a role in bringing the Republican Party into being. Radical political pressures also helped to shape the New Deal. Radical politics revivified the labor movement in the 1930s. Recently J. H. Plumb reviewed a collection of papers by American planners on environmental problems. In not one of these papers, he noted, had thought been given to the kind of politics that would be needed if any of the plans were to win a fair hearing. What he said has direct relevance to the rot in the political system:

> Environment problems get too easily abstracted from social problems, and social problems from their historical roots.
>
> How can planning work in a society which has sharp social divisions due to disparity in wealth as well as differences in color? How can planning work in a society in which profit, personal or corporate, must be a more urgent motive than control or conservation?
>
> So long as society is structured as it is there

will be slums. . . . No amount of thinking about environment, no amount of planning the optimum space and minimal communal facilities can be effective without political action, and that means political action of a radical nature.

> The history of the last hundred years shouts that fact aloud. Human beings are like carrion crows, not Christians. They will not give up what they have to the poor, they have to be scared before they will disgorge.

A radical politics, whether organized as a party or as a movement, is needed today—as it has always been needed—to goad the two major parties, to offer a general critique of the society, and to give *political* expression to the discontents that can gain a hearing in neither major party. The New Left may meet this need; it has not done so to date.

A secondary but relevant explanation of the rot is that the major parties are hopelessly old-fashioned. On essential matters they have changed little in the last century. At the *national* level they are loosely organized. They spend a pittance on research and planning, and even less on education. They rally briefly during national elections but for the rest of the time are "demobilized" and lethargic. This slackness of organization mirrors the attitude of most voters, who are content to limit their political enterprise to the ritual act of voting every two years—when they bother to vote. The professionals who run the parties do not encourage any greater activity. The parties engage the active support of perhaps not more than 3 to 5 per cent of the membership. There was a time when various organizations and interest groups participated directly in political decision-making, but this pluralistic pattern has almost vanished, and today most of the interest groups are long since "integrated" into the power structure, i.e., they are more dependent on the party in power than it is on them. The New Left groups, therefore, quite properly attempt to build new bases of local power which may eventually acquire enough votes or enough "disruptive" power to engage the major parties and particular state and local administrations in meaningful bargaining. Even if this were to occur, however, national political decisions would still need to be made, national priorities established, and for that purpose well-organized national parties are indispensable.

At the national level, both major parties are still loosely organized coalitions formed for the purpose of conducting campaigns. The Republican coalition, established at the time of the Civil War, was ascendant until the successful New Deal coalition was put together in 1932. Since then, the Republicans have been unable or unwilling to form a new coalition and the New Deal coalition is now disintegrating. At the moment it would be difficult to say which party is the more sharply divided internally. Neither seems able to confront the new issues (too risky) or appeal to the new constituencies which have emerged since 1932 (to do so, just now, would endanger what is left of the old coalition). Yet recent polls show that a large—perhaps a third or more—and steadily increasing percentage of the electorate is dissatisfied with the candidates and programs and styles of both parties and therefore disinclined to participate actively in politics.

Instead of addressing themselves to the new issues and the new constituencies, both parties evade their responsibilities by resort to excessive "personality politics," TV-style (with the result that rising campaign costs threaten to make the Senate once more the "millionaire's club" that it was in the 1890s). The effect of all this is to encourage the feeling of "powerlessness" and enforce the conviction that political action is futile. It needs to be stressed that whereas at one time national coalition parties functioned reasonably well, today's problems are much more complex, the resistances to be overcome are much greater and the concentration of power is formidable. To make politics alive once more, national parties must be coherently and purposefully organized, and they must command enough energy, not merely to secure adoption of new programs but to make certain that they are properly administered. Neither party today is so qualified.

A related cause of the rot is the failure of the Republican Party to function as an opposition party. Since 1932 it has been obvious that the two-party system was endangered by the failure of the GOP to offer effective opposition by urging alternative programs and policies. It was generally assumed in 1952 that President Eisenhower would reorganize the party which had been, even then, much too long out of power. He had the prestige and the power, but he showed not the slightest interest in the problem, and a great opportunity was lost. The Goldwater explosion of 1964 was the logical consequence of failure to renovate the party and, judging by recent events, the need is still there.

The party system has been further weakened by a new situation. A combination of factors, with heavy emphasis on the mass media, has made a measure of "direct democracy" possible. Representative government is at best slow, cumbersome, exasperating. Nowadays many decisions must be made quickly if they are to be effective. Let's say that the mayor announces the immediate closing of a city hospital. There isn't time to distribute leaflets, interview officials, petition the parties, organize a campaign. So those opposing the closure chain themselves to the office furniture, after first giving the TV news rooms notice of time and place. A vast audience is immediately alerted, with little effort, at minimal expense.

In a sense, *the new media become a substitute for the party.* Often official reaction is swift and responsive; whereas when petitioners go through channels, elected officials can stall, appoint commissions, order investigations, etc. A pamphlet by John Morris on "Direct Democracy," published recently in London, explains the theory. The universal defect of representative democracy, so the argument goes, is the formation of controlling elites. Such government lets the people vote periodically for politicians or for parties, but seldom for policies. This, of course, merely echoes Michels' cynical comment: "The one right which the people reserve is the ridiculous privilege of choosing from time to time a new set of masters." Representative government was once a necessity; people had to *send* representatives to the capital. But modern communications have made a degree of direct democracy possible and people are beginning to like it. Polls have somewhat replaced primaries as a means of registering voter preference. Experiments are being made to test the possibility of "instant" opinion polls by the use of computer techniques. Up to a point, there is much to be said for direct democracy and we shall see more of it; but it cannot substitute for partisan debate on significant issues, much less for representative government which extends and clarifies the partisan debate and, in the end, should resolve it. Direct democracy can stimulate and supplement representative government; it can never replace it.

Given the extent of the rot that currently besets the American political system—and given the degree to which power is concentrated—it is not surprising that many people feel powerless, or that they have lost confidence in politics or are voicing doubts about representative government and liberal political institutions. Nor is it surprising that many young people have turned to "anti-movements" of one kind or another and taken to the streets to air their grievances and express their frustrations. What *is* surprising, given these factors, is the way in which "concerned" and "dissatisfied" citizens have tried to find new but democratic ways of expressing their judgments and preferences, with no aid and little encouragement from either party. It was not until the President began to escalate the war in 1965 that serious misgivings about it arose. Until then it had seemed merely another "police action" in furtherance of cold-war policies which had been pursued by both parties for twenty years without serious question or opposition. But once Mr. Johnson suggested the need for an increase in taxes, once it became clear that the war had been "Americanized," once the manpower requirements and the casualties began to increase, public dismay mounted rapidly. It took a quantum leap early in the summer. Between July and September, the percentage of the public supporting the war dropped 14 points; between September and October it declined a further 11 per cent.

Now, in part as a reaction to certain recent demonstrations, opinion seems to be shifting back a bit in support of the Administration. But during the last two years, there has been a sharp increase in concern and it has found expression through a variety of ingenious devices and forms *in spite of* the political rot. Most of these forms had to be improvised. Abhorrence of the war has found expression in advertisements, petitions, pamphlets, art exhibits, poetry readings, sit-ins, teach-ins, pray-ins, and all manner of protests and demonstrations. Criticism has been voiced in newspaper polls, and in informal referenda, Students have been polled; professional organizations have canvassed their members; faculties have done the same. In Cambridge, Mass., and San Francisco, the issue has been forced on the ballot with results that under the circumstances have been truly impressive. What this rising protest lacked, until recently, was any semblance of national political leadership; and what it still lacks, in general, is a sustained political emphasis. In a way, it represents a kind of "anti-politics" since neither political party has, to date, seen fit to respond to it.

All the same, the prospects for a reversal of policy, for a redirection of American power, are not nearly as bleak as they have been pictured. An enormous volatility, as yet unexpressed, just might ignite in 1968. In any case, it would be a sad mistake to write off the political prospects as unrealistic and improvise a kind of guerrilla "anti-politics" until an attempt was made to overcome the rot in the political system and to infuse it with an energy equivalent to what now finds expression in demonstrations and protests, many of which lack direct political relevance. It may be impossible, in the end, to cope with the concentration of power that exists today by normal political processes, but we shall never know until we give the system a chance to function. It is not a question of either/or but of both, a great deal more of both. Action protests can be combined with radical politics; action protests can also be combined with conventional politics. But action protests without politics will not stop the war, much less reverse the direction of American policy, much less open the structural changes needed by American society. The task of those who are concerned with these objectives, then, is to concentrate, for a chance, on the political problems.

18   STUDENTS AND POLITICS   SEYMOUR MARTIN LIPSET

Ten years ago, hardly anyone devoted himself to research on students and politics. Today hundreds of scholars are analyzing student political movements, behavior, and attitudes. It is evident that student activism and the importance of students in politics long antedates the current interest. Students were a key element in the Revolutions of 1848 in Germany and Austria, and student activism stimulated the "Professors' Parliament," which almost succeeded in toppling several monarchs. In Czarist Russia, students spearheaded various revolutionary movements, and the university campus was a major center of revolutionary activity. In the East European countries, where education was limited to a small proportion of the population, students were often the carriers of modern ideas of liberty, socialism, industrialization, and equality of opportunity.

The important role of students in the movements for national independence in the developing areas also goes back a half century or more. In Imperial China, students were crucial to the

Reprinted with the permission of the author and the publisher from *Daedalus*, Journal of The American Academy of Arts and Sciences, Boston, vol. 97 (winter 1968), pp. 1–20.
This article is a condensation of an effort to sum up the various issues presented in the analysis of student politics that have arisen in the work of the Comparative Student Politics Project of the Harvard Center for International Affairs. I have drawn on various papers delivered at the San Juan Conference on Students and Politics, many of which are included in this issue of *Daedalus*. Papers reported on in San Juan which deal with Latin America are published in a special issue of *Aportes*, no. 5 (July 1967). Other publications of the project which contain articles and materials referred to here are S. M. Lipset (ed.), *Student Politics*, New York, 1967, and S. M. Lipset and Aldo Solari (eds.), *Elites in Latin America*, New York, 1967. A detailed bibliography of articles, books, and theses is Philip G. Altbach, *Select Bibliography on Students, Politics, and Higher Education*, Cambridge, Mass., 1967.

Imperial effort at modernization, but at the same time spread republican and radical ideas throughout the society. Students helped overthrow the dynasty in 1911, and were thereafter one of the elements continually pushing China toward modernization and radical ideologies. In other Asian and African countries, students were often a central element in anticolonial struggles. Particularly important were the "returned students"— those individuals who had lived and studied abroad, mostly in Europe, and returned home with ideas of modernization and Marxism, socialism and struggle. International student meetings were held as early as the 1920's, and such men as Nehru of India and Hatta of Indonesia were profoundly influenced by these student organizations and movements.

Scholars in the past paid relatively little attention to the rather major role students played in reform and radical movements, in part because student movements are quite transitory in character and have left fewer records than adult organizations. Moreover, to stress the role of youth and students, rather than that of the social classes or religion, seemed in a sense to underemphasize the seriousness and significance of the happenings and to turn them into "children's crusades."

Then, too, from the Marxist perspective, intellectuals and students are not significant independent social forces. Rather, they have been viewed as vacillating, unreliable, "*petit-bourgeois* elements" who are inclined to shift with the prevailing ideological winds. Although students have played a rather major role in supporting various Communist movements at different times, the Party has tended to deprecate their role.

The greater willingness to recognize the political role of students stems, in part, from the awareness by many on the left that other social forces are not always available for support. The organized workers of the developed countries of Europe and America, for example, have become a conservative force, as C. Wright Mills has pointed out. Trade unions and labor-based parties have been integrated into an institutional system of representation and collective bargaining. As such, they are not concerned with policies and programs that may upset the political pattern. The orthodox (pro-Russian) Communist Parties in many countries have also become part of the regular system of representation and no longer advocate use of extralegal and extraparliamentary tactics. In Latin America, they oppose the guerrilla tactics fostered by Castroites and Maoists.

Mills saw in the intellectuals and students a major potential mass base for new revolutionary movements. They have *remained* a source of new radical leadership and mass support, while other elements of society have not. Thus, more attention is being focused on the American student movement at present than occurred during the 1930's, even though the movement was larger in both absolute and proportionate terms in the thirties. But beyond the emergence of an intellectual concern with the politics of students, well-publicized events of the past decade have illustrated the significance of student politics. Student demonstrations and movements played a considerable role in the overthrow of Péron in Argentina in 1955; the downfall of Pérez Jiménez in Venezuela in 1958; the successful resistance to Diem in Vietnam in 1963; the massive riots against the Japan-U.S. Security Treaty in Japan in 1960 which forced the resignation of the Kishi government; the anti-Sukarno movement in Indonesia in 1966; the October demonstrations for greater freedom in Poland in 1956; and the 1956 Hungarian Revolution. It is important to note, however, that although students may be catalysts for political action, they can seldom bring a revolutionary movement to fruition. In Korea, students began the movement that succeeded in toppling the Rhee government in 1960, but they relied on popular pressure and the army to make their movement successful.

Although much of the recent writing on student politics has focused on leftist activist groups,

it is also important to analyze the strength and activities of traditional and conservative groups as well. Opinion data for various countries assembled by Glaucio Soáres indicate that the left-wing students are in a minority, often very small, even in countries where leftist demonstrations have made international headlines. Even though university campuses provide a significant proportion of the future radical leadership, as well as the mass base for antigovernment demonstrations, most students are not involved in such activities. In most countries, the vast majority of students are apolitical and tend to endorse the moderate or even conservative parties. In the United States today, the largest campus political groups are the Young Democrats and Young Republicans, which have a total combined membership of under 250,000 members, as contrasted to 7,000 members of the new-left Students for a Democratic Society (SDS). A recent (1967) U. S. survey of American college students reports that a plurality favors the Republicans for the 1968 Presidential Election. Four national surveys conducted during 1965 and 1966 found that from two thirds to three quarters of American students support the Vietnamese war.

Influences derivative from university experiences are, of course, not the sole or even primary determinants of student political beliefs. Family perspectives often influence students' orientations. The high correlation between the political stance of students and that of their parents would imply that the children of poorer families should be more leftist than those of the more well-to-do, since socio-economic class and political choice are generally related in this way. Although research in various countries tends to validate the generalization, it does not, for a number of reasons, apply this simply to student populations. Students from relatively poor families tend to come from that minority within the lower strata which is strongly oriented toward upward mobility and the values of the privileged. Hence, their parents are often among the more politically conservative of their class. Moreover, upwardly mobile students who represent the first generation of their family attending university tend to be vocationally oriented. They are more likely to be found in fields that lead to professions. This strong concentration on careerist professional objectives, plus the need to have a job during the school term, results in these students being less available for political or other extracurricular activities than those from more privileged backgrounds.

In Scandinavia, a student of working-class origins is likely to shift from a Social Democratic family orientation to a conservative one. There is less probability that a student from a conservative middle-class background will shift to left-wing parties. Recent American data suggest the reverse finding. Attendance at university is stronger in pressing well-to-do students to a position to the left of their parents, than in moving those from less-privileged Democratic and liberal families to the right. Such findings should be subjected to more precise specification as to type of school attended and academic discipline studied. The greater shift to liberalism among the more well-to-do in the United States may reflect the high proportion attending the better universities, which characteristically have the most creative, intellectually oriented, and liberal faculties. Conservative students on such campuses experience a political atmosphere hostile to their family political beliefs.

Well-to-do parents are also among the better educated. Particularly is this so among professionals. Increased education is associated in most underdeveloped countries with approval of modern, as contrasted with traditional, values and in the developed societies with belief in "noneconomic liberalism"—support for civil liberties for unpopular minorities, internationalism, and so forth. These orientations are generally fostered by the more liberal or leftist campus groups. Matters related to economic class are less salient sources of campus politics than noneconomic ones. Students in the United States, for example, are much more concerned with civil rights for Negroes or political rights on campus and in the larger society, than with the power of trade unions or the consequences of different systems of taxation on economic growth.

Many of those who experience a tension between the political atmosphere of the university and their family tradition escape the choice by abstaining from politics, by accepting the doctrine that school and politics do not mix. Most students from conservative backgrounds remain in this tradition. In countries where there is a visible difference in the dominant political orientation of universities, continuity in family political orientations may be facilitated by the process of conscious selection of universities because of their political reputations. In Latin America, conservative privileged families will often send their children to schools with a conservative or apolitical reputation, such as the Catholic or other private universities. Unfortunately, there is little reliable information on this subject.

American research findings suggest that there is congruence between the characteristic political orientation of different disciplines and the political beliefs of entering students who plan to major in them. Conservatives are more likely to study engineering or business, and liberals the humanities or social sciences. Such selection reflects the extent to which varying political orientations influence students to opt for different career goals. Leftists, particularly those from well-to-do and well-educated families, are inclined to favor academic fields concerned with social and political issues or careers in the arts, social work, scholarship, and public service.

Academic ecology, the social environment in which a student happens to find himself by virtue of his choice of university or academic field, tends to be more important than his class background in affecting his opinions. The faculty within which students are enrolled seems more predictive of their political stance than class origins. In various Latin American countries, the differences among universities in their modal political choice are greater than the social-class variation within them. Nevertheless, those who bring strong traditionalist values with them to the university are more likely to remain conservative and apolitical than others. This may be seen most strongly in the role of religion. In the Catholic countries of Latin America and Europe, practicing Catholic students are much more conservative than nonbelievers. Thus, reported differences in family religious practices are highly predictive in this respect. Similar findings have been reported for India. In the United States, Catholics and evangelical Protestants are also among the most conservative groups in the university.

Minority-majority social status also seems more important than economic class background in affecting student propensity for action. In Germany and Austria, for example, students from minority groups (Jews and Slavs) and from the lower-middle class spearheaded the Revolution of 1848. Students from minority ethnic backgrounds were also active in the pre-revolutionary Russian student movement as well. Today in the United States, Britain, and Argentina, Jews contribute heavily to the membership and support of activist left groups.

In many of the developing countries and in nations like Belgium and Canada, there are often deep cleavages that prevent a sense of community among the students. Religious divisions, regional, linguistic, caste, racial, and tribal differences often severely inhibit the growth of national student movements devoted to societal objectives, or even to university reform. In a number of countries, divergent student groupings based on such variations are locked in conflict. In India, students have taken to the streets because of religious or linguistic differences. In Indonesia, student groups are often organized on the basis of religious or regional affiliation.

The varying demands that universities make on students also affect the possibilities for political participation and the political climate on the campus. The examination system used is a key factor in determining student political activism In the American system, for example, students are generally required to take examinations at regular intervals and to maintain at least minimal academic standards to stay in school. They may take part in extracurricular activities, political or other, but these are at the expense of their studies. In Latin America, where examinations are not so important or may be postponed, such sanctions do not exist.

In many countries, it is possible to predict accurately the cycle of student activism on the basis of examination schedules. In India, students do not generally study until a month before the annual examinations. Thus, most students have a very substantial amount of free time during the year. In Latin America, many student leaders are able to maintain their status within the university for years by postponing their examinations and devoting themselves full-time to political activity.

Entrance requirements to a university may also affect political reactions. The Japanese and American patterns place great emphasis on getting into the best universities and require high-school students to work long hours under considerable psychic pressure. These patterns clearly affect the way some students behave after they are admitted to the university A great deal of Japanese and American student activism is concentrated in the freshmen and sophomore years, which may reflect the students' reaction to being released from the pressures of entrance anxiety. Upperclassmen tend to be more liberal in their attitudes than lower-division groups, but to give less time to politics. Presumably years of university attendance are associated both with greater liberalism and more concern with preparing for jobs or admission into good graduate schools.

The greater activism of lowerclassmen may also reflect the liberating influences of the university. Students often express their newly found freedom by engaging in various forms of "nonconformist" behavior. Regardless of class in school, students living away from home, either in dormitories or in private accommodations, are more likely to participate in activist politics than those commuting from home. Moreover, Berkeley data suggest that "new" students—whether freshmen, juniors, or graduate students—are more likely to be activists than students who have been in residence for some time. In other words, recent transfer students contribute disproportionately to the activist core. This raises a general question about transferring from one campus to another. A campus is not always a community in which students remain for the entire period of their education and in which they are gradually socialized into the community norms. Frank Pinner suggests that young people, particularly students, join organizations or integrated collectivites because they have just left their families, their home town, or friends and are anxious, disoriented, and lonely. They find in organizational life—particularly in movements that have a sense of commitment, purpose, and high intimacy—a kind of replacement for the collectivity they have just left. This factor, which would apply more to the new than to older students, would also vary by country and university system. It would depend, in part, on what proportion of students live at home or close to home.

Opinions as to the place of politics in the university are inherently related to feelings about the larger society. Those—whether of the extreme left or right—who believe that drastic changes are necessary, that major evils exist, or that the basic verities are under attack will feel that students and faculty ought to be deeply involved in politics. Conversely, moderate conservatives and liberals are more likely to accept President Benitez's formula that a university is a "house of study," rather than a "house of politics." Conservatives, as believers in the *status quo*, will generally be even less active politically than liberals or moderate leftists. Glaucio Soares's Brazilian data indicate that conservative students not only are not interested in politics, but often "perceive student politics as an undue interference with their studies." The leftists, on the other hand, feel that they have a duty to be politically engaged and that the university should be an agency of modernization and radical change. As Soares puts it, conservatives argue that the political and academic roles should be compartmentalized, while leftists seek to integrate the two. This means, of course, that under current conditions in most countries, the student left will mobilize a much greater proportion of its potential strength for politics than will the moderates or the rightists.

Most of the recent writing on student activism tends to ignore the phenomenon of rightist activism. Indeed, although many students are conservatives, there has been little rightist campus activism since the 1930's. As a result, little material has been published concerning the activities of the extreme rightist student groups of the 1920's and 1930's in much of Europe. German and Austrian students were on the left during the early-nineteenth century, but many turned to rightist nationalism in the late-nineteenth and early-twentieth centuries. Anti-Semitism and extreme nationalism were characteristic of many of the more politically sophisticated German fraternities, and Nazism had great appeal in the universities in the 1930's. French Fascism, strong during the interwar period, received considerable support from university students. Many of the student groups active during the 1930's in Latin America had strong Fascist views, due mainly to the influence from Spain and Italy, while German Nazi influence was strong in some Arab movements. In the colonial areas, nationalist movements often looked with favor on Hitler and Mussolini because of their opposition to the imperialist powers of Western Europe. Although ideological issues were confused, university students tended to accept some aspects of Fascist ideology, particularly the stress on militant nationalism and race pride and the concern with militaristic thinking.

From a functional point of view, such "rightist" behavior is quite similar to contemporary left-wing styles of politics. Rightist students were nationalistic, anti-authority, and concerned with the seeming inferiority of their nation within the world community. The subtleties of ideology were not meaningful to the rightist student movements of the 1930's. There was often a mixture of rightist and Marxist rhetoric, which combined notions of racialism with ideas of "proletarian" and exploited nations.

As Frank Pinner suggests, student organizations may, for analytical purposes, be divided into two categories: *transgressive* groups, which are directed mainly against the authority structures of their societies, and *traditional* groups, which socialize their members into their role as conventional citizens of the society. A similar distinction can be made in the role of the university itself. On the one hand, universities are centers of innovation where scholars are expected to challenge the traditional truths of their fields and receive the highest rewards for work which is sharply innovative. On the other, they are schools with faculties of teachers and, thereby, part of the socialization process of their society. Universities and the subdivisions within them vary in the extent to which they emphasize these functions. Many parts of the university, particularly the professional schools, are essentially concerned with a socialization function—training students in socially useful skills. The so-called liberal-arts subjects, on the other hand, tend to value scholarly innovation and competence in research more highly. Thus, transgressive student groups are more likely to be found among liberal-arts students than among those in professional schools, such as engineering, education, or business. In Latin America and other countries, universities that are affiliated to religious bodies tend to have little student activism. In Japan and the United States, the most important centers of scholarship tend also to be the strongholds of transgressive student movements.

It is possible to differentiate further among transgressive social movements: Some are concerned with changes in basic social *values* (ultimate ends or conceptions about basic social institutions) and others with affecting *norms* (means to attain agreed upon social values).

Movements concerned with value change are more prevalent and stronger in the underdeveloped countries than in the developed ones. Talcott Parsons and S. N. Eisenstadt have suggested the need to look at the magnitude of the differences between the values of the adult and youth generations in varying types of societies. They indicate that generational conflict is caused, at least in part, by sharp value differences among generations, and that such cleavages—particularly between the better educated (younger on the average) and the uneducated (older)—are great in modernizing societies, but relatively minor in the developed societies.

Similarly, the difference between the values of the university and those of society is considerable in backward societies and small in developed societies. Michio Nagai has argued, for example, that the university is basically universalistic and meritocratic, even in societies that are neither universalistic nor meritocratic. On the one hand, the university judges people, events, and research on the basis of objective achievement criteria, and, on the other, it values freedom of inquiry and discussion. Thus, when we speak of a university anywhere in the world, we have a similar model in mind, no matter how far reality may deviate from that model. The norm of academic freedom is basic to the idea of the university. The tension between university and society will, therefore, be great in authoritarian societies, considerable in emerging and developing nations, which are normally quite particularistic, and relatively small in the developed democratic societies. Faculty and students will reflect the depth of these tensions in their behavior. One should expect *value* conflicts (differences about ends) between student movements and the society in emerging or authoritarian nations and more normative conflicts in developed societies. Education, particularly university education, is inherently a modernizing force, and hence in underdeveloped countries it will be in conflict with those elements seeking to maintain traditional values and institutions. In the democratic developed states, the society more generally accepts the values of universalism, achievement, and freedom.

These distinctions help to account for the varying emphases on ideology among student movements. In general, ideological concerns have declined among student activists in advanced industrialized countries during the postwar period, as compared to the 1930's, but have remained important in many of the developing countries. Nationalism, which involves a concern for modernizing and industrializing, is also particularly important in developing countries. Even such relatively non-leftist groupings as the Philippine student movement and the militant KAMI organization of Indonesia are extremely nationalistic. The ideological concerns of student groups in the emerging nations reflect their interest in value change in the larger society. They are at odds with any forces that support traditional values or stand in the way of rapid economic growth.

In the West, however, where the tension between social values and the political concerns of students is less manifest, even the relatively small radical student movements do not show a strong attachment to formal ideologies. Thus, pragmatism and a preoccupation with specific issues characterize its student politics. This obtains even in Eastern Europe, perhaps because ideologies would be difficult to voice. Students there have been a key element in demanding liberalization in the name of the manifest socialist values and have argued for a nondogmatic approach to society and politics. Even the French Communist students have been in the forefront of revolt against the ideological commitments of the parent Party. Scandinavian students have campaigned for individual freedom and an end to social regulations, particularly those related to sex.

In many countries, one may find some version of the maxim: "Anyone under twenty who is not a radical [socialist, Communist, anarchist] does not have a heart; anyone over forty who still is one does not have a head." There is a notion that it is normal, appropriate, and morally correct for young people to be radicals or revolutionaries. Indeed, many societies treat radical youth, particularly students, as if they believed this maxim. They permit students a degree of political freedom, even license, to violate the norms and laws of society without being punished, or with less punishment than is generally meted out to others. Thus, Berkeley students who surrounded a police car and held it captive for thirty hours were neither arrested nor otherwise sanctioned. Even in authoritarian countries like Czarist Russia, Communist Poland, or Franco Spain, student oppositionists have been treated more lightly by the authorities than have other organized opponents. Sentences against student revolutionaries are usually mild compared to those given non-students.

This tolerance reflects, in part, the fact that university students are often the children of the "elite." The vast majority of the offspring of the privileged strata go to university. This elite finds it difficult to employ stringent measures against its own children. In Cuba, the Batista regime was undermined, in part, because some of the young people with Castro in the mountains were the children of Cuban upper-class families. Members of the Havana elite exerted tremendous pressure on Batista to quit because they wanted their children back from the mountains alive. In recent years, many of the trials of student activists in Spain have involved at least one son of an important family. In this context, the Spanish courts have been faced by two conflicting forces: the particularism of the society, which requires that an offender who belongs to a privileged family be treated lightly, and the universalism of the law, which implies that all those who commit similar offenses be treated in the same way. Most of the punishments of Spanish students have, therefore, been relatively mild.

Nations may also be differentiated by their varying conceptions of youth. Revolutionary ideologies are generally positive toward youth. Hence, the vitality of revolutionary ideologies may be measured by the extent to which they still identify virtue with youth. One of the best pieces of evidence that the American revolutionary tradition is still viable is the prevalent belief in youth, which interestingly the Russians no longer have. The United States is very much a youth culture; it stresses the truism that the young will inherit the world and are probably on the side of justice and progress, as opposed to adults. Many adults thus feel youth should be encouraged in their disdain for the old, in their advocacy of progress and change. Older people consequently lack assurance when debating with youth. It is significant that the Soviet Union has sharply modified the belief in youth that prevailed immediately after the Revolution. Stalin eliminated the notion that youth is right in its conflicts against the older elements, and his successors have not reinstated it. Mao Tse-tung, in his seventies, however, is attempting to emphasize the role of youth as the main source of support for a continuing revolutionary ideology in China.

Authoritarian systems like Fascist Italy or Communist Cuba have, however, been interested not in encouraging students to be critical of the system, but in using "youth" as a social base to support a supposedly "revolutionary" regime against conservative adults. They have hoped to inhibit adult opponents by impressing on them the idea that they represent a historic anachronism. A stress on the worth of youth politics in a democracy may bring to reform movements the support and encouragement of students and other youth. Conversely, it may inhibit some adults who disagree from strongly resisting the proposals of activist students.

Michio Nagai has suggested that as societies "modernize," their universities necessarily move from a diffuse to a specific relationship with both the state and religion. The growth of the scholarly and research function has required universities to separate themselves from the clergy and the politicians. The university must be free to find and teach what is scientifically "true," without concern for the reactions of religious or political establishments. The norm of academic freedom assumes that these outside bodies will leave the university alone. Conversely, if the university insists on freedom from external interference, from being criticized or coerced by those not involved in scholarly pursuits, the norm implies that it must abstain as a university community from attacking others.

The extent to which universities have differentiated themselves from society will, of course, differ. The Confucian ethic stresses the linkages between scholarship and the state. Chinese, Japanese, and Korean scholars were civil servants and supporters of the state. They maintained a relationship with the state similar to that between the religious scholars and the church in the West. In more recent times, universities in the East, particularly state universities, have been expected to be agents of state purposes. Nagai concludes that the considerable involvement of students in the political life of these countries is to some extent linked to the continued strength of Confucian values.

Similarly, in many developing countries the national emphasis on economic development and

modernization overrides the idea of the completely autonomous university. Various sections of the governing elite, as well as many faculty members and students, believe that the university should serve the national interest of fostering development. They do not think the nation can afford the "luxury" of supporting pure scholarship which is not related to development objectives, nor can students or faculty isolate themselves from active involvement in politics. These are, of course, highly debated issues in many of the countries, but insofar as the university is perceived as serving political objectives, it necessarily becomes a source of political stimulation.

The effort to separate the university from extramural influences has been most successful in the developed countries of Western Europe and the English-speaking world. The university gradually freed itself from political and religious interference in the late-nineteenth and twentieth centuries. In recent decades, however, the growing role of the university as the key center of research and development for the public sector has necessarily involved it in political controversy. Governments and scholars have broken down the barriers between politics and science by using academics as temporary government officials or as consultants. Scientists have not been able to escape taking responsibility for the social and political uses of their discoveries. Physicists have had to take a position on the various controversies concerning the military uses of atomic energy, academic economists have been called on to take part in the debates on national economic policy, and sociologists and psychologists are involved in issues concerning race relations, education, and the culture of poverty.

Seemingly, the process that brought about increased differentiation between the academy and other institutions has been reversed. The growing complexity of modern society has challenged the effort to segregate the university as an "ivory tower," seeking primarily to serve scholarly ends. As the university in the West becomes a "multiversity," to use Clark Kerr's term, it will continue to be a center of political agitation, as those who favor or disagree with specific endeavors seek to use or attack it. The growing involvement of the Western university as the research arm of the governing elite has, for example, led some critics to view it as a "tool" of the establishment. Universities have nevertheless generally remained as major sources of criticism, despite their growing ties to government. In France, where all universities are state controlled, faculty and students were in the forefront of the opposition to the Algerian war. In the United States many have been the principal centers of support for the Negro struggle for equality and an important source of protest against the Vietnam war.

Student politics is also affected to a considerable degree by the social position and political values of the country's intellectual community. The position of the English intellectuals vis-à-vis power in the political establishment differs from that of the French or the American intellectual. The English have been included in effective political life; the French are outside it. In the United States, intellectuals have great power as experts, but there is no intellectual political community comparable to that in Britain. In many ways, the "nonexpert" American intellectual, similar to the French, has high status but little power and views himself as alienated from the power structure, while the American academic "expert," like the English, has considerable status and power and is more likely to identify with the political-decision makers.

The attitudes of intellectuals and of students toward the national *status quo* are, moreover, not simply a function of their position within the society. More than any other group, intellectuals tend to have an international reference group. To use Merton's distinction between "cosmopolitans" (oriented to outside groups for standards of comparison) and "locals" (concerned with the evaluations of the community within which one resides), intellectuals are clearly more likely to be cosmopolitans. As such, they will be aware of the shortcomings of their nation compared with the standards of the leading countries. The intellectuals and academics of the underdeveloped countries gener-

ally realize that they are at the summits of nations or university systems that are considered "backward." This awareness heightens their desire to foster change within their own society and increases their resentment against local or foreign groups that inhibit modernization. The intellectuals in Central and Eastern Europe in the nineteenth century regarded their countries as backward compared to France and Britain, and many of them supported radical political movements.

Intellectuals who are resentful of their society often stimulate rebellious "apprentice intellectuals"—students. In many countries professors see themselves as a deprived stratum, one which is not given the rewards of working conditions appropriate to their role. This sense of resentment will vary, of course, both within nations and among them. Students, particularly in the better universities, are more prone to rebel when the faculty are relatively incompetent in their teaching and show authoritarian tendencies. Student indiscipline in India has been linked with the low salaries, long hours, and bad working conditions of the faculty. The historic pattern of the "part-time" professor in Latin America is a crucial factor in the lack of commitment to scholarly endeavors and values by many students. The very bad faculty-student ratio of French universities and the low salaries of Japanese professors, which require them to find other sources of remuneration, have been cited as factors lowering the educational level of the institutions of higher education and encouraging protest movements.

Student political patterns are also determined, in part, by variations in political institutions. As Robert Scott points out, the lack of political stability in much of Latin America has stimulated student activism, since the possibility of successful agitation has been substantial, and students have occasionally been able to exert political leverage on weak governments. In Scandinavia, on the other hand, as Erik Allardt and Richard Tomasson indicate, the stability and legitimacy of the established political structures have discouraged student activism, and national politics is not generally seen as a legitimate domain of student concern. The same pattern can be seen in other politically stable nations.

Confrontation politics is characteristic of politics in which students, and other groups as well, lack legitimate channels of communication to authority. Clark Kerr has observed that political groups turn to activist demonstrations when they find themselves ignored by the adult power structure. Nevertheless, the existence of student militancy, in and of itself, does not necessarily indicate that such channels do not exist. Youth generally lack a long time-perspective; they tend to become quickly frustrated if their demands are not met immediately. Hence, even in countries with reasonably good channels of political communication, students may turn to confrontation politics if their political idealism has been activated by a major moral issue. For example, American students concerned with civil rights for Negroes or with ending the Vietnam war have not been satisfied with communicating with authority. Whether such alienation becomes pervasive and long-term will be related to the reality of the democratic institutions. In stable democracies, student unrest tends to be a temporary phenomenon.

The pressures on higher educational institutions to expand have been tremendous, but countries have responded to them differently. The military government of Burma has used severe repressive measures to keep the university population limited. In other nations—notably, the Philippines, Korea, India, the United States, and Japan—rapid educational expansion has caused substantial strains on the educational system and may be a factor in student unrest. The arts and law faculties, which rely on lectures and do not need laboratories, can expand most rapidly. Classes are simply enlarged. The effect of expansion has varied considerably within university systems. Educational standards have fallen most rapidly in the liberal arts, as have elite occupational opportunities. In many countries, students in the sciences are often able to obtain remunerative jobs in expanding technological fields, while liberal-arts graduates face an oversupply, which has led to educated unemployment and political unrest.

There is no clear-cut simple relationship between size or rate of expansion of the student body and patterns of political behavior. The emergence of large student populations on one campus or within given cities, particularly national capitals, has facilitated student activism. It has become relatively easy to mobilize a visibly large protest demonstration. A small minority of the students in Buenos Aires, Mexico City, Berkeley, Calcutta, Tokyo, or Paris can constitute an impressive protest in absolute numbers. The creation of "University Cities" in places like Caracas or Paris has increased the potential for mass student action. On the other hand, in nations in which there is only one university and the student body is small and homogeneous, a small group of activists can have an impact on the ideological climate of the national student body and on political events. This was true in the Congo after independence in 1960. The growth of the student population increases the size of the minority available for activist protest and makes for a more heterogeneous student body, one which may sustain competing campus political groupings.

In many countries, the university system is completely state-financed; in others, both in the developed and underdeveloped world, the universities are divided among public, private, and religious schools. Such differences permit substantial variation in quality among institutions. Universities with religious affiliations not only tend to recruit from the most traditionalist sectors of society, but their administrations and faculties are more likely to ban politics than are those in secular universities. Nippon University, the largest private university in Japan, prohibits participation in the *Zengakuren*, the national student union. Other private universities like Waseda, which have a history of student activism, were originally established as a means of training opposition to the governmental elite educated in the University of Tokyo. In the Philippines, the extensive system of private colleges includes many "diploma mills" designed to get students, often from less-well-to-do families, through a nominal university education as quickly and easily as possible. As might be expected, there is little student politics in these institutions.

"Statistically significant" relationships found in one country need not hold up in others. There are, for example, interesting variations concerning the effects of different disciplines on politics. Disciplines tend to be identified with student activism and leftist ideas in some countries, but not in others. Medicine has a leftist aura in various Latin countries in the Americas and Europe, but is traditionally quite conservative in most of nothern Europe and the Anglophonic world. In the Catholic world, this orientation seems to stem from the historic conflict between science and the church, a tension relatively absent from the politics of most Protestant countries. Where economics is taught as an extremely technical, mathematically based subject, those who concentrate in the field are less radical than where it remains concerned with qualitative and historical institutional analysis. Similarly, in some countries "law" means a pre-professional discipline or a professional field as it does in the United States; in other places, it denotes a broad social-science or philosophical training. Consequently, the behavior of law students may vary considerably from country to country.

One may also differentiate between subjects that lead to explicit role models and those which involve diffuse objectives. (Pre-professional subjects have explicit role models, while some of the humanities and social-science subjects have diffuse postgraduate role expectations.) Glaucio Soares has distinguished between students whose role image is that of the intellectual as against those who conceive of themselves as scientists or professionals. These images are highly predictive of political orientations. Those with an intellectual role identity are much more leftist and activist than those who identify as scientists or professionals.

This difference is, of course, a subjective one. In every discipline, those who think of themselves as intellectuals rather than professionals are more politically activist. It also works out objectively, in terms of the types of disciplines. Those disciplines that are thought of as "intellectual"—the humanities and most of the social sciences—are more

activist and leftist than those that are oriented toward the professional or scientific world. In Puerto Rico, almost all the supporters of the radical and nationalist FUPI (pro-independence) movement have come from the social sciences and have seen themselves primarily as intellectuals, with strong ambitions toward writing and journalism. Chile and Argentina have demonstrated similar patterns. Most of the activists in the Indian and Indonesian student movements, particularly during the nationalist periods, came from the liberal arts. In the United States, the activists in groups like the Students for a Democratic Society tend to be in the social sciences and humanities and to see themselves as intellectuals rather than as professionals.

Thus, differences in the political behavior of students in different universities or countries may be linked to variations in the fields in which they specialize. Certain schools deal primarily with liberal arts subjects; others, like the University of Moscow, are essentially institutes for technology and science. Most underdeveloped countries, particularly in Latin America, tend to have proportionally fewer students enrolled in technical and vocational subjects. (In some, however, like Israel and Nigeria, the proportion is quite high.) The Communist countries rank highest in proportions of students engaged in vocational and professional training, which may contribute to the relative political passivity of their student bodies.

The political orientations of professors and their students do not necessarily vary in the same way. There is a congruence in some fields. In such professional schools as engineering, education, or business, faculty and students are both relatively conservative. In other areas, such as mathematics or molecular biology, they tend to be relatively leftist. In still others, particularly sociology or political science and especially in the better universities, the students tend to be to the left of the faculty. Where discrepancies between faculty and student orientations exist, the student and the faculty often differ in their conceptions of the subject. Thus, students view some of the social sciences as fields concerned with remedying "social problems." As scholarly disciplines, however, they are essentially concerned with the elaboration of knowledge within scientifically rigorous conceptual frameworks and methodology. Since social scientists see crucial political questions as having complex causes and different solutions, they tend to refrain from endorsing simple solutions. Thus, political concerns motivate many students to major in the social sciences, while the canons of scholarship press social scientists to refrain from taking public political positions. Natural scientists or humanists, on the other hand, may take political positions without reference to their special roles as scholars. Politically motivated students who hold to an "ethic of ultimate ends," which requires a total commitment to furthering politically desirable goals, will not understand nor sympathize with Max Weber's insistence that introducing one's personal values into scientific analysis undermines the ability to understand the facts. Accepting Weber's position often places social scientists in conflict with their best students, who see any faculty reluctance to link scholarly and political roles as cowardly.

These are some of the issues with which any analysis of the role of students in politics and higher education must deal. The university is premised on the belief that "knowledge will make man free" and will increase his ability to control and to better his environment. Those interested in the role of students in politics are obligated to avoid using their special competencies and knowledge as weapons in ongoing campus politics. To separate one's role as scholar and citizen is often difficult. In this case, it is almost impossible.

## 19    THE SNOOPING MACHINE    ALAN WESTIN

The year is 1975. The place is a suburb in the United States. The setting is a record-control society that could make George Orwell's Oceania almost look like a haven of privacy.

At seven A.M., our typical citizen, an engineer named Roger M. Smith, wakes up, dresses, has breakfast and gets ready to commute by car to his office in Central City. Already, heat, light and water records fed directly from his home to the Central City Utility Corporation (for purposes of billing and use analysis) provide data that can establish when Smith got up and just how he moved through his house.

Smith takes his car out of the garage and drives onto the turnpike, heading downtown. As he reaches the tollgate, his license plate is automatically scanned by a television camera and his number is sent instantaneously to an on-line computer containing lists of wanted persons, stolen cars and traffic-ticket violators. If Smith's plate registers a positive response, police stationed 100 yards along the turnpike will have the signal before Smith's car reaches their position.

As he stops at the tollgate, Smith gives the initial performance of what will be a ritual repeated many times during the day. He places his right thumb in front of a scanning camera. At the same time, he recites into the unit's microphone, "Smith, Roger M., 2734-2124-4806." Roger has just used his thumbprint, voiceprint and personal identification number to carry out his first financial transaction of the day.

Roger's inputs are carried swiftly by data line to the Downtown National Bank, the central depository of Roger's financial account. Though he may have accounts in other banks throughout the country, these are all registered and monitored by the bank in Smith's place of residence or work. When the thumbprint and voiceprint recorded at the tollgate are compared with the bank's master prints, establishing that it is really "Smith, Roger M., 2734-2124-4806," the bank's computer posts a 75-cent charge to his account and flashes a 75-cent credit to the bank holding the Turnpike Authority account.

Throughout his typical day, when he parks at the Triangle Garage, is registered in and out of the company office for payroll verification, has lunch at Jimmy's East, makes purchases at Macy's, goes to Central City Stadium for a ball game, places a bet on the daily double, buys plane tickets, settles his hotel bill or buys 500 shares of Electronic Computers Unlimited, Roger Smith will use no cash. Money has been eliminated, except for pocket-change transactions.

Of course, all of Roger's regular, continuing obligations are paid automatically from his account —his mortgage installments, insurance premiums, magazine subscriptions, organizational membership dues, etc. Those continuing accounts that fluctuate monthly are also verified and paid automatically—medical bills, psychiatrist's fees, gasoline charges, telephone bills, pay-TV account, book-club purchases, etc. All financial credits to Roger's account, each carefully identified as to the source and classified as to the basis for payment, go directly to the bank, not to Roger. Roger's various Federal, state and local tax obligations are determined by computer analysis and are automatically paid when due.

This is a superb system—efficient, practical and far cheaper than the money economy with which mankind fumbled along for so long. But one by-product of the cashless society is that every significant movement and transaction of Roger Smith's life has produced a permanent record in the computer memory system. As he spends, uses and travels, he leaves an intransmutable and centralized documentary trail behind him. To those with access to his financial account, Roger Smith's life is an open tape.

But the daily denuding of Roger Smith has only begun. For every person in the United States in 1975, there are four master files. His complete educational record, from preschool nursery to postgraduate evening course in motorboat eco-

nomics, is in an educational dossier, including the results of all intelligence, aptitude and personality tests he's taken, ratings by instructors and peers and computer analyses of his projected educational capacities.

Roger's complete employment record contains entries for every job he has held, with rate of pay, supervisors' evaluations, psychometric test results, recommendations, outside interests, family milieu and a computer-analyzed, up-to-date job-security profile. All of this is available for instant print-out when an employer wants to consider Roger for a job or a promotion.

Roger's financial file is probably the largest. It contains a selected history of his financial transactions, from his earliest entry into the computerized economy to his latest expenditure for a new Carramba-35 sports car. His patterns of earnings, fixed expenditures, discretionary spending, computer-projected earning capacity and similar items are all kept ready, so that decisions involving loans, mortgages, insurance and other credit-line transactions for Roger Smith are made with full knowledge of his fiscal history.

Finally, there is Roger's national citizenship file. This is a unified Federal-state-local dossier that contains all of Roger's life history that is "of relevance" to Government. In 1975, that is quite a broad category. It includes his birth facts and permanent identification number, his educational file in full (after all, it was either public education or publicly assisted), his military service, all the information from his license applications, income-tax records and Social Security data and, if he now works or worked in the past as a Government employee, consultant or contractor, his public employment record and assorted security clearances. If Roger was ever arrested for a crime other than a minor traffic violation, a special public-offender intelligence file is opened on Roger Smith that includes a large base of information relating to his educational, employment, military, family and civic activity. Citizenship files also include a personal-health category, developed to aid public-health measures and to assist individuals caught in health crises away from their home physicians.

This contains a complete medical dossier from birth condition and psychosexual development to reports of last week's immunization shot, cardiogram flutter or extended-depression check-up. Most important of all these four master files on education, employment, finances and citizenship can be put together into one unified print-out whenever a Government agency with subpoena power chooses to do so.

For purposes of economic forecasting, demographic studies and behavioral prediction, the data base such a dossier society has created provides unequaled opportunities for research and policy analysis. For enforcement of public programs—educational reforms, integration rules, crime control, mental health—the national file system brings unparalleled advantages. But crucial elements of privacy in a free society, such as the partial anonymity of life, limited circulation of personal information and preservation of confidence in certain intimate relationships, are the bleeding casualties of a dossier society. For the Roger Smiths of 1975, life is by, on and for the record.

How does the record net work? For Roger Smith, who started work as an engineer at Consolidated Technics in the "old personnel system" days of 1965, the flash of understanding came when he was considered for the key promotion of his career, a possible move from engineering supervisor at Consolidated Technics to deputy vice-president for engineering at General Space, Incorporated. As Roger sat in the office of the information-system analyst (formerly personnel director) of General Space, he found himself staring at a print-out that had just been handed to him. It was titled "Inconsistent Items for Personal Explanation at Assessment Interview." As he scanned the list, he found these items:

**HIGH SCHOOL PERSONALITY-TEST PROFILE**
High score on the Fosdick Artistic and Literary Interest Inventory; technical career rated "doubtful."

**CRIMINAL RECORD**  Disturbing-the-peace conviction, Daytona Beach, Florida, age 18. Speeding tickets, New Jersey Turnpike, 1973, 1974.

**CIVIC ACTIVITY**  Signed antidraft petition circulated by Colgate University chapter, Make Love Not War Society. Door registers showed attendance at campus lecture by George Lincoln Rockwell, age 20.

**INCOME-MANAGEMENT RATING**  Average annual personal loan held during past five years—$3000 to $5000. Balance in savings account on April 1, $217.41.

"If you have studied this long enough," the information-system analyst broke in, "let me briefly explain our procedure here to you. You are one of four men being considered for this position. We want you to take as much time as you need to write out an explanation of these items in your record. Your answers should be in terms of how these items might affect a possible career for you here at General Space, Incorporated. Keep in mind that we do seventy-five percent of our work for the Federal Space Voyage Program, and that involves classified information. The explanations you give us will become part of your general personnel files, of course, including the disposition we make of your employment review.

"Since this is the first time you seem to have applied for a job under the new computerized career-analysis system, let me reassure you that this is not an unusually large number of inconsistent items to be presented with. Your complete file runs close to two hundred and fifty pages, which is about the average length for a man of your age. However, I think it is only fair to tell you that two of the men being evaluated for the position have no inconsistencies to comment on as part of their personal interviews. After you have done this on several occasions, you will probably get used to it. . . ."

At this point, Rod Serling should appear on the television screen, grin his raffish grin and say, "Portrait of life in a fish bowl, somewhere in the Twilight Zone." We should all be able to smile appreciatively at his superb science-fiction imagination and then check the late movie on channel two. The trouble is that Roger Smith's dilemma is closer to reality than we think, both technologically and as a matter of social trends in America.

Consider first the question of technological feasibility. The average person knows that computers can collect and store vast amounts of data, search this with great swiftness, make comparisons and collations and engage in machine-to-machine exchanges of data, all at quite reasonable cost per bit of information. Despite this general awareness, there is still a common tendency to believe that "technological limitations" make it impossible to collect information for a dossier system of the detail described for Roger Smith.

Such a belief is simply nonsense. To illustrate this fact, we need only look at one data memory process recently developed by the Precision Instrument Company of Palo Alto, California. This system uses a one-watt, continuous-wave argon laser to burn minute "pits" in the opaque coating of plastic computer tape. The laser is so precise and can be focused so intensely that each pit is only one micron, or .000039 inch in size. Where normal recording has been about 5600 bits of information on an inch of magnetic tape, the new laser process can put *645,000,000* bits in microscopic parallel rows on each inch. And the recording process achieves speeds of 12,000,000 bits per second.

Once recorded, the information is permanently available for use. To read the data, a lower-powered laser beam examines the tape as it flies past at high velocity, translating the light that shines through the pits into an electrical pulse that is sent to a print-out machine or a computer for further use.

In terms of a dossier society, the laser memory system means that a single 4800-foot reel of one-inch tape could contain about 20 double-spaced typed pages of data on every person in the United States—man, woman and child. It would take only four minutes to retrieve a person's dossier under such a system. With 100 reels of tape, stored in a room no larger than 15 feet by 20 feet, 2000 pages of data could be maintained on every American. Allowing extra time to locate the particular reel on which a subject's file was stored, his entire 2000-page dossier could be retrieved in about ten minutes.

The cashless society lies equally within technological reach. Enough computers could easily be produced to handle the volume of transactions that would be generated by an automatic economy. Remote-point inquiries and inputs from small desktop units to a central computer are in common use today in airline- and hotel-reservation systems. New types of telephone instruments, such as the Bell Touch Tone card-dialing system, allow bills to be paid from the home and permit merchants to verify availability of funds before releasing products to purchasers. Vending machines have been developed that use optical scanners to accept credit cards. Though there are still some problems in achieving unique identification of each individual by single fingerprint or voiceprint, simultaneous use of these techniques could now prevent all but the most elaborately conceived frauds. Any losses of this kind would probably be far less than those currently sustained by check forgery and stolen credit cards. Technologically, then, we now have the capability of installing a computerized economic system.

Even though both the dossier network and the automated economy are technologically possible, this does not mean that American society has to use its capabilities in this way. Why shouldn't we dismiss this prospect as something that Government and private organizations would never think of adopting? The answer is that several basic social trends in American life have been moving us in precisely such a direction during the past two decades.

The first of these trends is the enormous expansion of information gathering and record keeping in our society. Partly, this stems from factors such as the increasing complexity of our industrial system, the expansion of regulatory, welfare and security functions by Government and the growth of large-scale bureaucracies in our corporations, universities, unions and churches. Partly, the growth in record collection stems from the breakdown of traditional, face-to-face techniques for personal evaluation of individuals by authorities.

In an age of increased personal mobility, nationalization of culture and standardized mass education, when so many people within each socioeconomic group look, talk and think alike, "the file" becomes the Government's instrument for distinguishing among them.

Similarly, the turn of social science from rational or interest-seeking models of human motivation to heavily psychological and sociological explanations of human behavior means that masses of highly personal data must be collected to analyze events "scientifically" and make wise choices in public policy. Self-disclosure by individuals, then, becomes an obligation of good citizenship in the modern age, as well as an act of faith in "science."

Thus, when each American today reaches the gatekeepers of public and private authority, the official's basic response is to open a file on him, ask for extensive self-revelation, conduct independent investigations and share information with other certified file managers of our society. If anyone thinks this is an exaggerated portrait, just stop and think for one moment: How many Government forms and reports on yourself or your family did you fill out during the past year? How many questionnaires did you answer about yourself? How many progress reports on your activities did you file with financial, employment and organizational authorities? How many investigations of yourself do you think were conducted without your knowledge? How many investigators asked you about other people's lives? How many evaluations of others did you contribute to the permanent files? Did you ever refuse to answer questions about others or yourself? Do you know anyone who did?

This growth of investigations, dossiers and information sharing has been, of course, enormously accelerated by the advent of the computer. Now, private and public organizations can process 10, 50, 100 times as much personal information about their employees, clients or wards than was ever possible in the eras of print, paper and analysis by eyes and ears. The older barriers of too much cost, not enough time and too much error that once protected privacy of personal transactions have been overcome by the computer in just the same way the barriers of closed rooms or open spaces that once protected privacy of conversation have been swept away by new electronic eavesdropping devices.

The impact of the computer is not just economic, however. Its real force is on the mental processes of our society, in the way we think we should make decisions once we have machines that are capable of accepting, storing and processing so much information. When machines can store so much data, and so many questions that we once thought beyond our capacities to resolve can be answered factually and logically, our society comes to expect that decisions of business, government and science ought to be based on analysis of all the data. Anyone who advocates withholding the necessary data from the information systems in the name of fragile values such as privacy or liberty may be seen as blocking man's most promising opportunity in history—to know himself and to make more rational, more predictable decisions about human affairs.

These technological capabilities and social pressures became a tangible issue for the American public with current proposals to create a national data center. For years, computer-industry leaders, Government data collectors and social scientists had been exchanging wistful memos on the need to bring together the statistical data gathered and held separately by various public agencies. Though this was felt to have great value for statistical research, it was generally believed that cost factors, technical problems and an "unready" public opinion made such a data center something for the future.

In 1965, a committee of the Social Science Research Council recommended that the Federal Bureau of the Budget create a national center for "socio-economic" data. The S.S.R.C. is one of the leading private sponsors of academic research, and the Budget Bureau is the President's chief coordinating instrument for Executive agencies. The report pointed out that bureaus within 21 major Federal agencies had accumulated more than 600 bodies of statistical data on 30,000 computer tapes and 100,000,000 punch cards, that there was a risk of destruction for some of this data and that what was kept was not being coordinated effectively for analytical use.

The Budget Bureau responded by hiring a management consultant named Edgar S. Dunn, Jr., to study the issue. Late in 1965, he reported that the data-center idea was excellent. Computer technology, he noted, now made possible statistical aids to public policy analysis that had never been possible before. At the same time, important new Federal responsibilities for urban renewal, health, antipoverty, education and civil rights programs made amalgamation of statistical data essential. Dunn observed that the nucleus of the center could be some 9000 tapes that had been identified as the most important of the Federal data pool. These would be drawn from housing and current population data held by the Census Bureau, consumer-expenditure surveys and industry-labor data from the Bureau of Labor Statistics, Social Security data and Internal Revenue Service records.

The Dunn report recommended that the Budget Bureau ask Congress for a small appropriation in 1967 to preserve the 9000 key tapes and to start design of the data center. The proposal seemed to be gaining momentum when the Budget Bureau named a task force in December 1965 to make over-all recommendations for more effective utilization of Federal data. This committee, chaired by Professor Carl Kaysen, an economist who had served with the Kennedy Administration and is now chairman of the Institute for Advanced Study at Princeton, was expected to give the data-center proposal warm endorsement. About the same time, the press reported that another Federal Executive commission had urged the creation of a computerized national employment service; this would contain personnel files on persons seeking employment and would be used to match prospective employees with new job openings. Yet another Federal study group reported in 1965 that a national citizens' medical data bank would be desirable and would probably be established "in the next decade."

To those familiar with the Washington political process, it looked as though the full Executive "softening-up process" was at work. Prestigious private groups had called on the Executive branch to move forward with a badly needed program. Executive task forces had affirmed the necessity and feasibility of the proposal. If no Congressional authorization had been needed to go ahead with this "technical program" and if existing funds could have been used for the early design studies, the national data center might well have been launched.

But 1966 was a year too full of public alarms over Big Brother technology for this proposal to slide by unnoticed. In early 1966, two Congressional subcommittees that had specialized in probing invasions of privacy by Executive agencies—one under Congressman Cornelius Gallagher of New Jersey and the other chaired by Senator Edward V. Long of Missouri (see "Big Brother in America," *Playboy*, January 1967)—began studying the proposed data center, and with serious initial reservations. While they were doing so, the Washington press corps learned of the idea: a series of sharp attacks on the Dunn report appeared in leading national magazines and newspapers during May and June 1966. The liberal *Washington Post* headlined its story, "CENTER FOR DATA ON EVERYBODY RECOMMENDED." "Apparently no secrets would be kept from the data center," the *Post* concluded. The conservative *U.S. News & World Report* was even more alarmed. In "A GOVERNMENT WATCH ON 200,000,000 AMERICANS," *U.S. News* warned its readers: "Your life story may be on file with the Government before long, subject to official scrutiny at the push of a button." In addition, several articles were written about the millions of investigative files, or dossiers, that were being collected regularly on American citizens by Government agencies and private credit bureaus. The public began to realize just how much personal information was going into public and private information files.

Though Senator Long held a two-day hearing that explored the Dunn report, the full-dress confrontation on the national data center came in July 1966, when the Gallagher subcommittee called Executive agency officials in to testify. The principal witnesses were Edgar Dunn and Raymond T. Bowman, Assistant Director for Statistical Standards of the Budget Bureau. Both explained that the data center was only a tentative idea in development stage, not a finished "decision." They also acknowledged that the S.S.R.C. report and the Dunn report had not been "careful enough in their wording" and had been faulty in failing to discuss in detail the problem of safeguarding privacy. As their testimony proceeded, they stressed that only statistical socioeconomic data would go into the center, not "personal" matters such as educational or court records, psychological test results, etc., and that the data would be used solely for statistical analysis. Information about named individuals would not be used for regulatory or law-enforcement purposes; this was to be a statistical and not an intelligence system.

As for the need to create such a data center, the Executive spokesmen noted that hundreds of millions of dollars of Federal money were being spent for socioeconomic programs about which the Administration, Congress and the public had inadequate or, sometimes, no significant data on which to plan or judge policy alternatives. Finally, the witnesses explained that everyone associated with the data-center idea had simply assumed that statutory provisions would be enacted to limit the uses of the data to statistical purposes and forbid all regulatory or prosecutive use and that administrative rules would have been set to enforce anti-disclosure and confidentiality laws. The model they had taken for granted was the Census Bureau, which has a tight statute, strict rules and no known instances of misuse of its data since it began operations at the start of the American republic.

However persuasive this Executive case for the data center might seem when summarized here, it was completely shot down in flames at the Gallagher hearings. The first missiles came from several computer specialists, particularly Paul Baran of the RAND Corporation. These witnesses informed the Congressmen that, as long as the identities of individuals were kept attached to the data

put into the center, there was always the possibility that those managing the center or those obtaining access to it could convert it into an intelligence system and obtain a comprehensive print-out of all the information about a target individual. They also showed how much personal and potentially damaging information about individuals and businesses could be extracted by trained intelligence personnel from the kinds of data that would be going into the proposed center.

When pressed by Congressman Gallagher about these problems, the Executive officials admitted that they could not separate identities from data. The center had to have the name, the Social Security number or some personal identification system permanently linked to the data so that the income-tax files of Roger Smith could be linked to his Social Security and Census files and so that the progress of identified individuals could be traced through time. Thus, even though the identities would not appear on any of the statistics drawn, the very nature of the system made it impossible to prevent intelligence files from being obtained on particular individuals. Though several computer specialists indicated that elaborate safeguards against outside intrusion and many types of inside misuse had been developed for national-security computer systems, none of these technological safeguards had been considered as yet by the data-center proponents. In fact, they displayed considerable ignorance about design and machine techniques for assuring privacy.

The other attack on the data center came from legal and civil-liberty experts testifying before the subcommittee. Congressman Gallagher and his colleagues drew from the Executive witnesses damning admissions that they had not thought through the constitutional and legal protections that ought to be attached to personal information given to the Government for one purpose and then compiled into a centralized data pool for other uses. The legal specialists showed that the system could have enormous potential effects on the citizen's privacy and could lead to a major increase of power in the hands of Federal officials who might use the data for intelligence purposes. Given these possibilities, Congressman Gallagher argued that thorough analysis of the full range of problems was called for in advance of any decision to start a center. Yet the Gallagher subcommittee established that no committee or advisory group had been called in to consider the technological, psychological, constitutional and political implications of the data center, despite the availability of experts on all of these matters.

The Gallagher hearings ended with a promise by the Budget Bureau spokesmen that no start on the data center would be made without seeking approval from Congress. Publications as diverse as the *Nation*, *The Wall Street Journal*, *The New York Times* and the *NAM* (National Association of Manufacturers) *Reports* applauded the Gallagher subcommittee for its work in halting the "computerized garbage pail" and "biggest Big Brother." Several publications, noting the weakness of the Executive presentations, predicted that the proposal was probably dead.

This was one of the most premature obituaries in history. In October 1966, the Kaysen committee issued its report recommending establishment of the data center. Having been warned by the Congressional hearings and press attacks, the men who wrote the report included an appendix discussing means that should and would be taken to guarantee privacy. While far more informed and thoughtful than the Dunn report or the Bowman testimony on this issue, the Kaysen discussion of privacy still left the issues of design safeguards and legal standards disturbingly vague. Congressman Gallagher published an angry letter he had written to the director of the Budget Bureau expressing dissatisfaction with the Kaysen report and insisting that a clearer showing of the need for one central facility, a concrete description of what was going into it and advance planning by computer specialists and constitutional experts were all prerequisites for any further action.

In March 1967, Senator Long's subcommittee held further hearings on the data center, questioning Kaysen and Executive-agency proponents and hearing civil-liberties objections from a law professor and the Washington director of the American Civil Liberties Union. Throughout the rest of 1967, the data center was debated at national meetings of groups from the American Bar Association to the Joint Computer Conference, and dozens of newspaper articles and magazine pieces explored its implications.

In January 1968, the Long subcommittee held hearings at which it published a comprehensive survey of the information about individuals that is presently collected by each Federal agency. The survey found that many Federal agencies were collecting more personal and intrusive information than even the most charitable concept of their legitimate needs or missions could justify. Furthermore, the Long-subcommittee survey found that a substantial segment of these records was not presently protected by legal guarantees of confidentiality against disclosure. The Long hearings also went into the rapid growth of other kinds of computer data centers—credit-bureau computer systems, employment data banks, law-enforcement systems and a host of other burgeoning data pools, some private and totally unregulated, some governmental with careful privacy safeguards and others lacking such measures.

As of this writing, there is no national data center. There has been talk by Budget Bureau officials of attempting a small (two-percent) sample of the various data that would go into the full center, in order to design the system, see how it might operate and demonstrate it for Congressional review. There has also been talk of creating an advisory panel of constitutional lawyers, Executive officials, Congressmen, social scientists and computer specialists to help the Budget Bureau devise the package of necessary safeguards—a thorough statute, administrative regulations and audit-review procedures. Some original advocates of the center now talk of concentrating on the design of a limited data pool to provide statistical analyses in a few of the most pressing areas of national socioeconomic policy, such as poverty programs or Medicare, and build slowly outward from there.

Whether any of these plans go forward is now a White House decision. The costs of starting another furor in Congress may not have high appeal in an election year, and many Washington observers expect the national data center problem to be deferred until after 1968.

Ironically, much more attention was given by Congress and the press to possible misuse of this statistical system than to the quiet initiation by the FBI of its National Crime Information Center in 1967. This uses a central computer to collect and distribute national, state and local information on stolen cars, stolen property and certain wanted persons. While the system is presently narrow in scope, the plans are to expand it in the future to collect much more intelligence information. Which names will go into files and what information about them will be collected remains to be seen. What safeguards will control the FBI operation has not been aired in the press or questioned in Congress. The Congressional committees that went after Budget Bureau and Census Bureau officials with sharp inquiries have shown no desire to put questions to J. Edgar Hoover.

Looking at the national data center debates of 1966–1967, we can see three distinctly different approaches to the problem of new computer technology and privacy. The first position, reflected in the initial thinking of most of the Executive-agency officials, computer manufacturers and behavioral scientists, assumed that a modest adaptation of traditional administrative and legal safeguards, plus the expected self-restraint of officials who would manage any statistical system, would be enough to protect the citizen's privacy. The more reflective spokesmen in this group would add that our society is requiring greater visibility of certain individual and group activities, in order to carry out rationally important socioeconomic programs that have the deep support of the American public. Since privacy has never been an absolute value, they reason, we should accept certain minimal risks to privacy as part of the balancing of values in a free society.

The second position, reflected by the initial views of most newspaper editorials, civil-liberties groups and Congressional spokesmen, is to oppose creation of a data center completely. The need of Government officials and behavioral scientists to have better statistics for policy analysis is seen as simply inadequate when weighed against the increase in Federal power that such a system might bring and the fears of depersonalization and loss of privacy that it could generate among citizens. The only situation that would satisfy these critics would be a "tamper-proof" system in which all identities were removed from the data.

The third position is the one that seems most persuasive and that may be the ground on which the two initial positions will meet, now that the privacy considerations have been thoroughly aired. This sees the added threats to privacy from centralized data systems as requiring a new legal and technical approach to sensitive-information management by Government. While this approach would be applied differently, according to the type of data center involved—statistical, social-service or law-enforcement—it is the statistical center that concerns us here.

At the outset, we must recognize that the individual's right to limit the circulation of personal information about himself is a vital part of his right to privacy that should not be infringed upon without showing strong social need and satisfying requirements as to protective safeguards. When Government takes information from an individual for one purpose, such as income taxation, census enumeration or Social Security records, and uses it to influence, regulate or prosecute the individual on unrelated matters, this strikes a blow at the individual's autonomy and violates the confidence under which the information was originally given.

Following this view, a statistical data center must have both "machine system" safeguards to limit the opportunities for misuse, and legal controls to cover those human abuses that cannot be averted by technology itself. At the system level, we should realize that storing data in computers allows us—if we want to—to create far more protection for sensitive information than is possible when written files are available for physical inspection. Information bits in the memory banks can be locked so that only one or several persons with special passwords can get them out. Computers can be programed to reject requests for statistical data about groups that are really designed to get data on specific individuals or business firms. (For example: "All the records on elected Federal officials from New York State who are under 45 and served in the President's Cabinet in the past ten years.") Furthermore, a data system can be set up so that a permanent record is made of all inquiries. Such an "audit trail" can be reviewed annually by the management of the center, Congressional committees and an independent "watchdog" commission of public officials and private citizens set up for that purpose.

Though many additional ways of guarding a data center from outside intrusion or inside misuse could be outlined, one clear fact remains. The system can still be beaten by those in charge of it, from the programmers who run it and the mechanics who repair breakdowns to those who are in charge of the enterprise and know all the passwords. This means that a package of legal controls is absolutely essential. For example, a Federal statute could specify that the data were to be used solely for statistical purposes; could forbid all other uses to influence, regulate or prosecute, making such use a crime and excluding all such

data from use as evidence in courts; and could forbid all persons other than data-center employees from access to the data-center files. The data could be specifically exempted from subpoena. An inspector general or Ombudsman type of official could be set up to hear individual complaints of alleged misuse, and judicial review of the decisions in such cases could be provided.

What this all boils down to is the fact that American society wants both statistical data *and* privacy. Ever since the Constitution was written, our efforts to secure both order and liberty have been successful when we have found ways to grant authority to Government but to control it with the standards, operating procedures and review mechanisms that protect individual rights. Such a balance of powers is possible with a data center, if both the fears of the critics and the enthusiasm of technical proponents can be turned to constructive measures. For the Roger Smiths, 1975 demands effective Government as well as freedom from a data-file Big Brother. A free society should not have to choose between these values if we apply our talents for democratic government.

## 20    ASSUMPTIONS ABOUT NATIONAL SECURITY

CHARLES E. OSGOOD

There are many contributions the intellectual, academic or otherwise, can make to public policy. As a professional specialist he can orient his research and scholarship toward unwrangling some of the admittedly complicated but critical issues underlying policy. In doing so he may have to relax somewhat the level of confidence he usually applies to his own work, realizing that people in

Reprinted with permission of the author and the publisher from "Questioning Some Unquestioned Assumptions about National Security," *Social Problems*, vol. 11, no. 1 (summer 1963), pp. 6–13.

The ideas expressed in this paper are the author's and do not necessarily represent those of any organization to which he belongs.

government have to make decisions regardless of the certainty of the evidence at hand. He can try to inject the viewpoint of his discipline into the decision-making process. In doing so he may find, as I have, that the view of man that he and his colleagues take more or less for granted is quite novel—sometimes refreshing, sometimes threatening—to many people in government. Another role he can play is that of Devil's Advocate: he can make explicit some of the fundamental assumptions underlying public policy that usually remain implicit.

It is this last role I wish to play here. I want to question some assumptions about national security that usually remain unquestioned. Precisely because they are not recognized *as assumptions*, open to debate, these implicit rules form the most rigid framework of national policy, and there is often resistance to even considering them. Nevertheless, they must be questioned and debated—because in doing so we may open some new areas for flexibility and social innovation we didn't realize existed. Even though it may be true that some of these assumptions are questioned *in private* by our decision-makers, if they espouse them in public as obvious facts it really makes little difference as far as the value of publicly questioning them is concerned.

## ABOUT THE NATURE OF POLITICAL MAN

*Assumption 1    That national decision-making is predictable from models that assume rationality*

Men can behave rationally, and often do; men can also behave irrationally, and often do With a few exceptions, writers on national decision-making and researchers using game theory and other methods for simulating international relations have assumed that political man behaves rationally, regardless of what ordinary man may do. If our national policies are in fact based on this assumption, and it turns out to be wrong, we may be in for some grim surprises.

Psychologists are familiar with the fact that, as emotional stress increases beyond some optimum level, certain non-rational mechanisms in human thinking become more prevalent. Faced with an overwhelming threat over which he feels he has no control, the human individual typically denies the reality of the danger rather than keeping it in mind and trying to cope with it. This is particularly the case when the very language used to talk about the threatening situation is remote from his own experience—as are "megatons," "intercontinental ballistic missiles," and "fifty million casualties." The greater the stress under which he is operating, the more likely he is naively to project his own norms and values onto others; having done so, he easily condemns others as deliberately lying when they claim to see things differently than he does.

Striving to simplify this complicated and dangerous world, he typically substitutes psycho-logic for logic, applying double standards of morality to the WE's and the THEY's and distorting facts so as to maintain a TV-Western view of the world in which everything is absolutely black or absolutely white. Driven by exacerbated hopes and fears, he becomes prone to deciding in terms of mere possibilities rather than reasonable probabilities—like the paranoid psychotic. Under stress, his thinking and his behavior become more stereotyped; his perspective narrows to the immediately here and now, the range of alternatives he can conceive of narrows to this or that, and thus, paradoxically, he becomes least capable of solving problems when solutions are most urgently needed.

Is all this in any way relevant? Do men become purely rational when they join in groups or become members of the decision-making elite? Or would our war and peace games provide a better mirror of reality if we played them under more realistic conditions of stress? I do not know the answer to this question, but I think we should find out. Robert C. North's recent analysis of decision-making in past crises, like the build-up to World War I, clearly suggests that these irrational factors operate on leadership elites as well as the rest of us. Certainly, when such fundamental policy notions as the feasibility of "stabilized deterrence" depend upon the answer, we should try to find out whether political man is always rational—and if not, when not.

*Assumption 2    That the primary motive of the opponent is aggression, not fear*

Psycho-logic encourages us to believe that our motives are always defensive and theirs are always offensive. When WE arm ourselves ever more impressively, when WE conduct a new series of nuclear tests, it is because the enemy leaves us no choice. But when THEY arm themselves ever more threateningly, when THEY conduct yet another series of nuclear tests, it is because they want to destroy us and make the world over in the communist model. Since we assume that the opponent shares our own image of ourselves as primarily peaceful in intent, we are unable to explain his behavior as being based on fear. And yet if there is anything certain in this uncertain world, it is that the Soviets are just as fearful of us as we are of them. All one need do is look objectively at the way Khrushchev justified their newest series of nuclear tests and he will see that it matched, almost word for word, the way Kennedy justified our tests.

If both sides could fully accept the fact that their motives are symmetrical, not asymmetrical, that both are impelled primarily by fear and only secondarily by a desire to eradicate the other's way of life, I think this one insight would breathe fresh hope across the world. But is this the case? One would suppose that on a matter so critical there would be solid evidence, but instead he finds a mountain of opinion floating on a sea of ambiguity.

One difficulty with research in this area arises from what I call *the relativity of credibility*—which, again, is a special instance of psycho-logic. Soviet communications to us are complex, diverse and often contradictory—as are ours to them. Unfortunately, it is always easier to believe aggressive statements from an opponent (like "We'll bury you!") than conciliatory statements (like "We can co-exist peacefully"); this is because, psychologically, it is consistent for Bad Guys to make threats and inconsistent for them to make friends. But surely the scholar, aware of this built-in bias, can search for objective evidence on Soviet motivation—in his internal communications, in his justifications for actions, and in his actions themselves.

### ABOUT THE NATURE OF DETERRENCE

*Assumption 3    That we must maintain military superiority*
This assumption is an extension of our traditional policy of "peace through military strength" into the nuclear age. In this age, where the weapons are primarily offensive as well as incredibly destructive—and where the two polar powers are apparently committed to the same assumption—this traditional policy becomes "peace through fear of

mutual annihilation." The hope is that this mutual fear of reprisal will somehow preserve a stable, if uneasy, peace. Is this hope justified? I do not think so. It is becoming abundantly clear that the same fear that deters also drives an arms race, and, because the arms *are* essentially offensive rather than defensive, our real security is decreasing as our military capabilities increase.

It is necessary to distinguish between two different philosophies about armaments: the deterrent philosophy and the superiority philosophy. The *deterrent philosophy* assumes that there is some minimum degree of retaliatory destructive capacity that is near-maximal in its deterrent effect; we do not need more than this, as long as our intent is to deter. It says, in effect, that to be able to destroy the opponent's civilization once, but good, probably deters him almost as much as to be able to do it ten or even one hundred times over. The *superiority philosophy* assumes that the deterrent effect on an opponent increases linearly with the ratio of our capability to his, regardless of the absolute level of destructiveness.

It is clear that when two opponents share the superiority philosophy, an arms race is the inevitable result. It is also clear that if the two opponents shared the deterrent philosophy, the arms race would peter out at some level where the degree of potential mutual destruction became unacceptable. What is *not* clear—and therefore invites research—is how a shift from one philosophy to the other could be accomplished. Is it possible for one party to induce a deterrent posture from the other by assuming it himself? I do not know the answer to this question, but if the motives of the opponents are really symmetrical, based on mutual fear, then I suspect the answer is "yes."

*Assumption 4    That an invulnerable nuclear retaliatory capability is nothing more than a deterrent*
Here we have a magnificent, and dangerous, example of the Tyranny of Words. We refer to our capacity to deliver devastating destruction to the opponent as our "deterrent"—a threat which, as long as he is rational, inhibits him from attacking

us. We worry about the credibility of our "deterrent" to the opponent and about the stability of a system of mutual "deterrence." And here, caught in the grasp of a term, most strategic thinking seems to stop. I think that the entire pattern of our strategy might have been quite different had we gotten into the habit of calling the same nuclear retaliatory system our "security base" instead of our "deterrent"—for it is equally both. To the extent that this system does deter, does make an opponent cautious about aggression, then to that extent it also provides its possessor with security.

Security for what? Security that enables us to take the initiative, gives us room for calculated risk-taking. The problem is to utilize the small margin for risk-taking provided by this security base in such a way as to gradually broaden it. This can be done *if* we emphasize the second-strike or retaliatory nature of the deterrent (and thus reduce reciprocal fears of surprise attack), *if* we use the risk-taking potential to reduce and control international tensions rather than increase them, and *if* we communicate this intent effectively to the opponent—which leads directly into the next assumption.

*Assumption 5   That maintaining the credibility of our deterrent requires a hostile image of ourselves in the eyes of the opponent*

The usual rationale goes something like this: We believe that the Soviets want to destroy us and are kept from attacking only by their fear of our retaliation; the best way to convince them of our will to retaliate is to demonstrate by word and deed that we are implacably hostile; any word or deed of a conciliatory nature will be interpreted by the opponent as a sign of weakness and thus will encourage him to attack. Of course, since the opponent reasons the same way, he also behaves like an implacably hostile enemy, which confirms our expectations about him—and vice versa.

How can such a vicious, self-fulfilling cycle be interrupted and reversed? The first step, I think, is to recognize that there are two types of credibility and two kinds of behavior to be deterred.

*Credibility type 1   The implacably hostile enemy image A* behaves in such a way as to convince *B* that he is unalterably hostile and is liable to attack *B* regardless of what *B* does. *A* creates the impression of irrationality by behaving unpredictably, by not practicing what he preaches, and generally by keeping *B* uncertain and anxious. *B* is convinced that *A would* attack if given an opportunity. This is the kind of credibility employed by rival gangs of teenagers in our city slums.

*Credibility type 2   The firm but potentially cooperative image A* behaves in such a way as to convince *B* that he is potentially cooperative and will only attack if *B* breaks certain prescribed rules. *A* creates the impression of rationality by behaving predictably, by making his words and deeds consistent with each other, and generally by making *B* feel less threatened. *B* is convinced that *A* would attack under the prescribed conditions but not otherwise (since, after all, *A* is rational and predictable and always does what he says he will do). This is the kind of credibility a wise father tries to create; it is the kind of credibility that police officers have found to be most effective in deterring criminal behavior, as well as in encouraging socially constructive behavior.

What kinds of behavior on the part of the Soviet Union do we wish to deter?

*Behavior type A   All-out nuclear or conventional attack* We want to deter the Soviets from launching a full-scale nuclear attack—which because of the obvious advantage of first-strike, would necessarily be a surprise attack that would make Pearl Harbor look like a tea party in slow motion. We also want to deter the Communists from starting the type of large-scale conventional attack that would probably, because of its locus and significance, escalate into all-out nuclear war.

*Behavior type B   Limited and sublimited aggression.* We would like to deter the Communists from all use of aggression and force as means to their ends, and this includes limited actions like the Korean War as well as the constant guerrilla nibbling around the perimeter of the Non-Communist World. It seems perfectly obvious that to employ Credibility Type 1 (implacable hostile image) as a means of deterring both Behaviors Type *A* and *B* creates a highly volatile and dangerous international environment. It is one in which the likelihood of *unintended* war is high—because accidents, miscalculations, and errors of judgment are much more likely to be interpreted as having deliberate aggressive intent when mutual hostile images exist. The extreme of this posture was John Foster Dulles' concept of massive retaliation—which might be likened to a man threatening to use dynamite to get rid of mice in his house! It also seems fairly obvious that to use Credibility Type 2 (firm but potentially cooperative image) to deter Behavior Type *A* (all-out attack), while relying on conventional, non-nuclear means to deter Behavior Type *B* (limited and sublimited aggression), would maximize stability and encourage a general easing of tensions. The problem, of course, is *how*. How can we create in Soviet eyes the image of a nation that is potentially cooperative and yet firm in its resolve to resist aggression? To answer this question we must inquire into some other assumption.

## ABOUT THE NATURE OF NON-VIOLENT ALTERNATIVES

*Assumption 6    That prior commitment from both sides is necessary before either can undertake any tension-reducing action*

The traditional non-violent means of resolving conflict between groups is negotiation. If successful, both sides proceed to act as agreed, each feeling secure in the prior commitment from the other. This procedure appeals to the legal mind, but it is not the only means of resolving human conflicts. As a matter of fact, in most sub-national forms of conflict (e.g., marriage relations, parent-child relations, intra-committee relations, and intra-government relations) negotiated agreement is neither the most frequent nor the most effective means. Nevertheless, nations seem to operate on the assumption that prior commitment from the opponent is an absolute prerequisite for any tension-reducing action—otherwise it might be perceived as a sign of weakness. In effect, each side is providing the other with a veto over its own freedom of initiative in this direction.

Let me begin my advocacy of the converse by questioning the notion that prior commitment really guarantees an agreement will be kept. Even though a formal agreement does carry the weights of private morality and public opinion, when these are put in balance with a nation's "vital interests," the commitment is usually evaded in some way. Capacity for rationalization at the level of the nation-state is unbounded. At least, this seems to be the lesson of history. But, more than this, the prospects for even achieving prior commitments of any significance in the present atmosphere of tension and distrust seem very remote. This is another lesson of history.

Once the assumption that prior commitment is a prerequisite is questioned, an array of new strategies appears. The arms race itself provides a model for one kind of interdependent behavior between nations that does not require prior commitment. We do not wait upon agreements with the Soviets before producing a new weapons system or conducting a new series of tests—we do it on our own initiative. But the fact that we *have* done it creates pressures on the Soviets to reciprocate by making further tests and developing more effective weapons systems of their own. In other words, in an arms race a kind of *post commitment* (the reciprocation) is substituted for prior commitment.

Can the notion of post commitment be substituted for the requirement of prior commitment in formulating a type of conflict-resolving behavior? I think it can. This notion is the essence of a policy proposal I have elaborated in some detail elsewhere,[1] bearing the complicated but accurately descriptive title, *Graduated and Reciprocated Initiative in Tension-reduction*.

The essence of the idea is that this country should take the initiative by unilaterally executing steps of a tension reducing and controlling nature across a broad spectrum (e.g., cultural, economic, diplomatic, and scientific actions as well as arms control, disengagement and disarmament). These steps would be designed, executed and communicated about in such a way as to maximize the pressure upon the opponent to reciprocate with tension-reducing steps of his own. Such reciprocation would constitute the post commitment that makes it possible for the process to continue and develop momentum. Each side would graduate its own actions in terms of its own evaluation of what the other side has been doing, and each would maintain adequate national security by retaining capacity to deliver unacceptably devastating nuclear retaliation should it be taken advantage of in any serious way. This deterrent is the security base which makes such graduated risk-taking possible. By combining (1) persistent tension-reducing steps across the global board with (2) firm resistance to encroachments, wherever they may occur, we should be able to create and maintain the kind of credibility (Type 2) required for maintaining security without provocation.

*Assumption 7  Inspection is prerequisite to any disarmament*

Inspection has assumed the proportions of a Sacred Cow on both sides of the fence. Since the Soviets are the weaker contestant in a strictly military sense, but have a closed and controlled society, secrecy about military missile and production sites becomes a primary defense for them and perhaps feasible. As the stronger contestant in a military sense, the main danger perceived by the U.S. is that of being duped and then subjected to surprise attack after honestly disarming. Of course, "fool-proof" inspection is technically and humanly impossible in any case, yet psycho-logic dictates that if THEY *can* cheat, then, being evil and always seeking an advantage, THEY *will* cheat. Is there any way out of this impasse?

First, let us look at some of the points where the Americans and Soviets agree.

1 They agree roughly on the phased ordering of disarmament—beginning with nuclear weapons and ending with a world disarmed except for national forces of sufficient strength to maintain internal order.

2 They agree that the greater the degree of disarmament achieved, the more intensive must be the degree of inspection—the argument here being

that in a largely disarmed world, the possessor of even a few nuclear weapons should be able to blackmail his opponent into submission.

3 They agree that inspection and regulation must be by "the other" rather than by "the self" —although here the Soviet position is not as clear as the American.

What about the "nuclears first, pop-guns last" order of disarmament? This order is consistent with public concern but it may be inconsistent with the political and psychological realities of our present world situation. The nuclear powers see their security as resting primarily in the deterrence provided by their ultimate weapons, and when mutual tensions are high it is difficult to imagine them seriously negotiating these weapons. A "pop-guns first, nuclears last" ordering of disarmament would begin with actions of a non-military nature designed to reduce the tension atmosphere; it would proceed to political and military adjustments designed to disengage the opponents and neutralize the regions between them; it would then move into negotiated agreements to reduce conventional forces and transfer policing authority and power to international bodies; and it would finally proceed to the dismantling of the nuclear deterrent systems themselves, by negotiation in a much less tense atmosphere. Note that retaining nuclear retaliatory capabilities until late in the process provides the degree of security which permits limited risk-taking in the early phases.

What about the felt need for inspection? It seems likely that it is inversely related to mutual trust. We feel no need to inspect Canada for concealed nuclear weapons, although they *could* be there in large numbers and prepared for use against us. We trust the Canadians. If this inverse relation holds, then techniques which increase mutual trust can be substituted for techniques of inspection in maintaining equal degrees of felt security. Furthermore, it seems hardly conceivable that mutual disarmament steps could be taken without increasing mutual trust. Therefore, rather than requiring legions of inspectors crawling over the globe, an increasingly disarmed world should demand less and less inspection.

I will make the further assertion, as a basis for debate and research, that "self" regulation is psychologically more acceptable and more stable than "other" regulation. As every parent, teacher, employer or leader soon discovers—often to his deep dismay—distrust breeds counterdistrust and is the rationalization for cheating. If the same rule applies to international relations, as I suspect it does, then in a fundamental sense *insistence on "other" inspection is self-defeating.* It maintains the very mutual distrust it is supposed to alleviate, and it encourages evasion.

But what if the Russians really are *not* trustworthy? (Or for that matter, what if we are not?) I submit that, even if this were the case, retaining invulnerable nuclear second-strike capability makes it possible for both sides to take limited disarmament risks without requiring any more direct inspection than present techniques permit. Rather than insisting on "other" inspection, we could take the initiative in providing *demonstrations* of our own internal compliance, thereby setting powerful precedents for the opponent to follow. Would the Soviet communal ethic support "self" regulation as effectively as the Western individual ethic would, once the commitment to disarm had been accepted? This is yet another important area for research.

Questioning these assumptions about national security has revealed their interlocking nature. It has also, I think, directed attention toward some pivotal issues of policy to which behavioral and social science research could contribute significantly. Advocacy of the converse has enlivened some fresh alternatives. If, like ourselves, our opponent behaves irrationally under stress and is motivated more by fear than by aggression, then a deterrent weapons philosophy offers us more security in the long run than a weapons superiority philosophy. If we fully committed ourselves to a deterrent philosophy and used our deterrent as a security base from which to take calculated risks in the interest of tension-reduction, thereby creating credibility for being firm but potentially cooperative, we should be able to get out of the inspection/disarmament dilemma and take the initiative in moving gradually toward a more peaceful world.

**NOTE**

1  C. E. Osgood, *An Alternative to War or Surrender*, University of Illinois Press, Urbana, Ill.: 1962.

## SUPPLEMENTAL READINGS

Banfield, Edward C., and James Q. Wilson: *City Politics*, Cambridge, Mass.: Harvard University Press, 1963.

Berman, Ronald: *America in the Sixties*, New York: The Free Press, 1968.

Carmichael, Stokely, and Charles V. Hamilton: *Black Power*, New York: Random House, Inc., 1967.

Domhoff, G. William: *Who Rules America?* Englewood Cliffs, N.J.: Prentice-Hall, Inc., 1967.

Etzioni, Amitai: *The Active Society*, New York: The Free Press, 1968.

Gamson, William A.: *Power and Discontent*, Homewood, Ill.: The Dorsey Press, 1968.

Greer, Scott: *Governing the Metropolis*, New York: John Wiley & Sons, Inc., 1962.

Gusfield, Joseph R.: "Mass Society and Extremist Politics," *American*

*Sociological Review*, vol. 27 (February 1962), pp. 19–30.

Hall, Richard H.: "Professionalization and Bureaucratization," *American Sociological Review*, vol. 33 (February 1968), pp. 92–103.

Haurek, Edward W., and John P. Clark: "Variants of Integration of Social Control Agencies," *Social Problems*, vol. 15 (summer 1967), pp. 46–60.

Hess, Robert D., and Judith V. Torney: *The Development of Political Attitudes in Children*, Chicago: Aldine Publishing Co., 1967.

Horton, John E., and Wayne E. Thompson: "Powerlessness and Political Negativism," *American Journal of Sociology*, vol. 67 (March 1962), pp. 485–493.

Hunter, Floyd: *Community Power Structure*, Chapel Hill, N.C.: University of North Carolina Press, 1953.

Lane, Robert E.: *Political Life*, New York: The Free Press, 1959.

Lipset, Seymour M.: "The Value Patterns of Democracy," *American Sociological Review*, vol. 28 (August 1963), pp. 515–532.

Lockard, Duane: *Toward Equal Opportunity*, New York: The Macmillan Company, 1968.

Morgenthau, Hans M.: "Paradoxes of Nuclear Strategy," *American Political Science Review*, vol. 63 (March 1964), pp. 23–35.

Rose, Arnold: *The Power Structure*, Fairlawn, N.J.: Oxford University Press, 1967.

Schur, Edwin M.: *Law and Society*, New York: Random House, Inc., 1968.

Westin, Alan F.: "The Deadly Parallels: Radical Right and Radical Left," *Harper's Magazine*, vol. 224 (April 1962), pp. 25–33.

## CHAPTER SIX

Americans exhibit a generally uncritical faith in the efficacy of education, particularly public education, to solve a wide variety of personal and social problems of contemporary man. Education has become the pragmatic synonym for the word "solution." The patent answer by political and economic leaders to a difficult problem is likely to be a program of "education," or if existing educational programs are not satisfactory, to suggest "more education." Education has thus become the dominant American secular belief, with 40 million pupils attending public schools and about 2 million teachers employed. Nevertheless, education, like religion, develops areas of serious internal conflict when specifics of philosophy, method, or auspices are examined carefully.

Maintaining a balance between academic freedom and academic responsibility is not easy. Since teachers may serve as adult models to impressionable young minds, the teacher's views on political and social issues may become a matter of community interest and concern. A minority of citizens have argued that the school should not discuss any controversial problems. Others have argued that to refrain from discussing controversial issues gives young people no framework for judging such issues when they become adults. On American college campuses much discussion has been generated on the topic of permitting known Communists to speak to students, with some arguing that the college library has all the literature necessary to provide knowledge about communism or any other political ideology. Because some large metropolitan areas are lacking in available Communist speakers, the task of presenting the Communist viewpoint to college students has fallen on one or two persons willing to take on an interested college audience in a question-and-answer period, a necessary format when only one side of an issue is aired. If propaganda presents one side of an issue, education strives to present all sides of an issue and let the student make up his own mind.

In 1954 the United States Supreme Court, in the famous case *Brown v. Board of Education*, ruled that planned school segregation on the basis of race is unconstitutional. It is not surprising in a country with several centuries of prejudicial conditioning on the issue of race that the high court's momentous decision has brought forth a number of reactional tactics both in the North and in the South. The South, with varying degrees of willingness, has accepted on a token basis the necessity of desegregating its schools. However, in the urban North a new problem has become manifest, *de facto* school segregation, a condition resulting from residential housing patterns. The Supreme Court has not ruled that *de facto*, or unplanned, school segregation is unconstitutional, but the matter troubles the social conscience of thoughtful Americans.

In Northern cities a number of plans are under way to lessen the impact of *de facto* school segregation. School boundaries are redrawn to improve ethnic balance; usually the boundaries are enlarged to achieve a greater representation of all ethnic groups. Parents may ask on a voluntary basis that their children be transferred to a school that is more or less homogeneous in ethnic population. In Princeton, New Jersey, all children attend the first three grades of elementary school in a Negro neighborhood and all children later attend the next three grades in a school located in a white neighborhood. A number of smaller communities have developed modifications of the "Princeton Plan." School boards have attempted to locate new schools in fringe areas to achieve ethnic balance. In a few school districts the "all-Negro school" has been closed, and Negro children have been transferred to other schools. In New York City compulsory transfer of both white and Negro pupils to various schools to achieve ethnic balance is under way.

In schools serving ethnic minorities a special effort is being made to develop a number of programs of compensatory education, including remedial reading and mathematics, special tutorial services sponsored primarily by college students, area exchange programs in which a student enrolled in a given secondary high school may take a specialized class in another high school, and novel programs of scholarships. Negroes have not been able to compete on even terms with other students for academic scholarships, particularly the National Merit Scholarships. To remedy this situation the Ford Foundation has awarded $7 million to the National Merit Scholarship Corporation to fund 200 scholarships each year only to Negro students. Henry T. Heald, president of the Ford Foundation, observed that the eventual goal "might be defined as the day when Negroes can win academic recognition in parity with other young people, and actually no longer need special scholarship programs." Some criticism has been directed to the action of the Ford Foundation in giving exclusive support to the Negro child and doing nothing for Mexican-Americans, American Indians, and others, all of whom have serious language "handicaps" in the usual testing situation.

The most important legal action on the assumed unfairness of *de facto* school segregation was the United States district case of *Hobson v. Hansen*, in which Judge James Skelly Wright (June 1967) ordered that the School Board of Washington, D.C., must bus volunteers from the overcrowded Negro schools to the less crowded white schools. He insisted that faculties must represent more integration in staffing and assignment and was opposed to any grouping of children in "tracks" of bright, average, or dull groups: "Even in concept the track system is undemocratic and discriminatory. . . . Its creator admits it is designed to prepare some children for white-collar, and other children for blue-collar jobs. Considering the tests used to determine which children should receive the blue-collar special, and which the white, the danger of children wearing the wrong collar is far too great for this democracy to tolerate." Critics of this decision have challenged its social significance on two grounds: (1) Since more than 90 per cent of the pupils in Washington, D.C., are Negro, it is impossible to integrate the schools in any real sense. (2) If both the bright and the dull Negro child are to be taught in the same grade as a result of his ruling against the track system and the tests available, there is a serious danger that both will be frustrated and that the teacher will be unable to cope with such wide individual differences in learning. If Judge Wright's decision is extended to higher education, there would be serious question about the CEEB, GRE, and admission tests used in the professional schools.

The "academic" advantages of integration have not been settled by sound and scholarly experiments. In one experiment in Hartford, Connecticut, it was found that Negroes from slum schools who were sent to suburban elementary schools manifested some improvement in IQ and achievement scores. The director of Project Concern, Thomas W. Mahan, Jr., observed that the minority children developed a "better self-image" and were motivated to achieve in the suburban school settings of Hartford. He reported that there were encouraging but not miraculous differences in performance between the children bussed to schools in four suburbs—Manchester, Farmington, Simsbury and South Windsor—and the control group of 300 children who remained in the inner-city schools of Hartford. However, no significant differences were found between those who stayed in Hartford and those who were bussed to the fifth suburb, West Hartford. West Hartford was not supplied with extra teachers, as were the other four suburban towns. Director Mahan concluded: "I was surprised by the West Hartford results. They point toward the possibility that bussing alone does not provide adequate help; that without supportive and remedial help, it does not make much difference simply to put a child in a different school."

Recently another complication has developed in a number of communities attempting to integrate white and Negro students. Some Negro leaders are beginning to request that children not be bussed to white middle-class schools, but that more Negro teachers and administrators be employed and that the curriculum include a study of the cultural history of the achievements of the Negro in America and Africa. The black nationalists are demanding a school environment that builds ethnic morale by having black teachers and leaders who are symbols of success. Thus after the many legal battles to break down separate schools, there appears to be developing a demand for separate Negro schools with specialized curricula. Sociologists have traditionally held that middle-class values will become the dominant culture of America regardless of ethnic background. However, the Anglo middle-class school is no longer accepted as the model for ethnic minorities, and we can expect considerable demand for special schools and subject matter for the larger ethnic minorities in urban America.

State and federal support of the 11 million Catholic children attending parochial schools has not been settled. Indirect support of parochial schools is provided by nontaxation of properties, bus service in a number of states, and state textbooks in a number of jurisdictions. American public education emerged as a symbol of religious freedom, protected from the domination by sectarianism that characterized schools in Europe. However, after the Civil War Catholic groups in the United States could not accept the idea of a secular school totally divorced from any religious foundation. In all fairness, it must be admitted that the public school was mainly an extension of the protestant point of view, with a school board almost, and sometimes literally, a replication of the board of deacons in the Protestant neighborhood church.

Current problems arising from a dual system of public and parochial education are an obvious duplication of physical facilities in the same neighborhood, a tendency for each type of school to claim an unproved superiority, and the promotion of a form of Protestant and Catholic segregated snobbery. No doubt, both types of schools do a superior job of education when there is proximity of schools and a competition for excellence—a side effect that is probably more positive than negative.

The issue of religion in the public schools has been the subject of a number of Supreme Court decisions. In general, the high court has opposed devotional religious services in the public schools, not the study of religion as a part of Western culture. The First Amendment to the Constitution states that Congress shall make no law respecting an establishment of religion or prohibiting the free exercise thereof, and the courts have favored the interpretation that the word "Congress" extends to all governmental and public agencies, including the public schools. Some critics of the high court's interpretation have claimed that "God is being taken out of the public schools of America." However, it is difficult to find a statement of prayer or sacred text that a pluralistic society will consider suitably nondenominational. The antecedents of our religious groupings are the personification of homogeneity—Sweden is 98 percent Lutheran, Italy is 98 percent Catholic. In Sweden and Italy intellectuals may be anticlerical but are not likely to be in conflict about denominational differences. In the United States, although there is virtually no organized anticlerical movement, there is strong competition for position among the various denominations, with direct implications for schools.

The freedom—or, to some critics, the anarchy—of American education has also become a subject of some serious concern. Free choice of subject matter, especially at the secondary level, has been criticized as merely placing an institution at the mercy of immature minds. Others have purported that as a result of such a system American students tend to omit the difficult subjects from their schedules. Perhaps the sharpest criticism of American education has been leveled at the development of so-called educational "frills"—an epithet applied to life-adjustment courses, courses in driver education, health habits, dancing, consumer economics, and so forth. No doubt, a major part of the conflict between those who stress the "fundamentals" and educators who argue for the "frills" lies in a basic disagreement over the relative importance of present and deferred values. The former want evidence of academic competence now, whereas the latter tend to judge the product of the schools in terms of mature adult personalities and perceive the schools as involved in social engineering as well as the teaching of skills.

At the university level a split has developed between the academic and vocational (science and applied) areas. During the last decade there has been an undermining of the "professional" status of medicine, law, engineering, and dentistry. The graduate science and liberal-arts faculties have dubbed many of their colleagues in professional schools "vocationally oriented" appliers of knowledge. Professional schools have reacted vigorously to this implication of second-class status by increasing the number of full-time professors engaged in basic research. The swing of the pendulum toward research activities has perhaps overcorrected the charges of vocationalism, so that thoughtful people are questioning the technical competence of the new physicians, attorneys, engineers, and dentists. The consumer of professional services is more concerned with the curative or practical skills of these professions than with their scientific foundations or methods. It appears, however, that the professional schools, because of the power of the university community over curricula and research training, have the greater say in this matter.

In this chapter four selections highlight important problems of American education. Bruce Eckland states that the tendency of sociologists to dismiss any discussion of the hereditary in the development of intelligence is a discipline bias and presents some data that make it most difficult to discuss the hereditary factors as meaningless in the formation of intelligence. In a subtle way he ridicules the extreme environmentalist position that "anyone can learn anything." Joseph Alsop's critical essay concerns the efforts to desegregate the nation's schools and the possibility of improving the ghetto schools. Today about 1.5 million Negro children attend ghetto schools, and the thrust of his statement is in terms of doing something now about the reality of *de facto* segregation in schools. John Harp and Philip Taietz examine the relationship between cheating in the writing of term papers and factors of intellectual ability, fraternity and nonfraternity membership, attendence in liberal arts and professional schools, and intellectual and nonintellectual orientation of college students. In the final selection Irving Louis Horowitz discusses the involvement of social scientists in the applied areas of "classified" research of the Department of Defense. He evaluates the findings of the *Report of the Panel on Defense, Social, and Behavioral Sciences* sponsored by the Defense Science Board of the National Academy of Sciences and describes in detail the "high-payoff" concerns of the Department of Defense in research on selected areas of human behavior.

## 21    GENETICS AND SOCIOLOGY    BRUCE K. ECKLAND

Ever since Mendel discovered that the cross-fertilization of a smooth-surfaced pea and a wrinkled pea had a predictable outcome, the ensuing issue of "nature versus nurture" in the development of human behavior has remained unresolved. Associated with the failure of the biological and social sciences to reach a resolution has been a general neglect of the *interaction* between genetic and social processes. Rather than considering our being as a product of nature *and* nurture, until recently the separate disciplines have seldom moved beyond their gainless attempts to attribute some specified amount of the observed variability to one source or the other.

Explanations of measured intelligence, for example, usually either followed the behaviorist's optimism, which denied any major role to heredity, or followed the equally extreme position of hereditarians who have consistently maintained that the influence of environment is quite small. In areas other than intelligence, the situation has been much the same. With few "moderate" spokesmen, the logical ties between genetics and the social sciences slowly deteriorated and nearly were buried.[1]

Moreover, as we shall note, sociologists have been far more resistant to any synthesis or work-

ing arrangement between the biological and social sciences than have other investigators in these areas, including the geneticists themselves. It appears, in fact, that the last major sociological work published in the United States that gave serious attention to the interdependence of heredity and environment was Sorokin's essay in 1927 on social mobility.[2]

We will argue for the advancement of a theory of the organization of social and genetic processes.[3] Not only under specified conditions can both environment and genetic variabilities be demonstrated, but geneticists, anthropologists, and psychologists have begun to articulate the connections between heredity and environment in new ways. Many of their concerns, moreover, do not deal strictly with genes, culture, or the individual, but with the traditional subject matter of sociology.

The discussion to follow centers on mental ability or 'intelligence."[4] Although many of our conclusions may apply to other behavioral traits, our choice is a simple one. Some of the crucial issues in the evolution of modern societies concern the allocation of status, social mobility and the like; in this process the identification, development, and utilization of talent have become increasingly familiar elements. Probably few readers would disagree. Perhaps unclear, in light of this, is just how genetic and sociological principles may be brought

Reprinted with the permission of the author, The American Sociological Association, and the publisher from *American Sociological Review*, vol. 32 (April 1967), pp. 173–194.

together to produce a more adequate conceptualization and understanding of essentially sociological issues. The greater part of this paper will be devoted to this problem, with special reference to population genetics, the family, education, and social mobility.

Our objectives, then, are three-fold: (1) To review some of the conditions that have brought us to our present posture on the subject of genetics; (2) To suggest a number of reasons why we, as sociologists, should re-examine our posture; and (3) To describe four "sociological" problems in which the integration of genetic and social processes is especially relevant.

## OUR PRESENT POSTURE

First, as our discipline has developed, we have had a vested interest in establishing a strong environmentalist approach to the study of human behavior. Moreover, we have been moderately successful in doing so. One of our favorite targets, for example, has been educational testing, especially IQ testing. There appear to be so many subtle ways in which environmental factors may contribute to inter-individual differences on these tests that some observers are nearly convinced that, except for a small number of mental defectives, no genetic component is involved whatsoever, at least in terms of what is being measured. Besides the early development of verbal skills, there is evidence that achievement motivation, formal academic training, and the immediate conditions of the test-taking situation itself all may differentially influence an individual's test performance.[5]

It should not be forgotten, too, that the sociologist's posture has been reinforced substantially in the past by many cultural anthropologists, some of whom still hold to the view that the biological evolution of man has run its course and cultural evolution has long since taken over. At one time, we not only gained the impression from them that man is no longer evolving in any genetic sense but that the genetic base of man is uniform everywhere. Carried one step farther, this often has been taken to mean that all observed variations in human behavior both within and between Mendelian populations are the sole result of cultural determinants.

Yet, have some cultural determinists and other ardent environmentalists carried their argument too far? Is the plasticity of man so unlimited? Is the genetic basis of man so uniform and, therefore, inconsequential? We will return to these questions in a moment.

A second condition that has led us to disregard the work of behavior geneticists seems to involve the utility of our own perspective. There have been few, if any, simple means for applying genetic principles in such a way as to produce a significant change in the cultural or social arrangements of human societies. Not only are technical problems involved but the very idea of controlling genetic processes brings forth the sinister and repugnant image of the "Brave New World." Perhaps for this reason even those who agree with the proposition that genetically "all men are *not* born equal" often overlook its significance.

In contrast, social arrangements can be altered by manipulating the environment with much greater convenience, with less resistance, and, to a large extent, without regard to genetic processes. This seems to be the position of many sociologists, like Faris, and others who have suggested that the present limits of our nation's supply of mental ability are not set by genetic factors but very appreciably by the environment.[6] We agree that there is considerable room for improvement in the training and utilization of our collective manpower. It also is easy to agree with Faris' conviction that "immense potentialities of human abilities are being smothered by systematic social influences." On the other hand, we cannot share his renewed optimism that "anybody can learn anything."[7]

Certainly, except for a small proportion of the population, it may be appropriate for some purposes to assume that all human beings are born with the potentiality to act intelligently. But what do we mean by acting intelligently? Does this include everything from the normal conduct of man's affairs to the kinds of decisions that might be involved in dropping the next atomic bomb? Is there no important genetic variability in human functioning beyond certain minimal (and, we believe, arbitrary) structural prerequisites, as some have suggested? This is a static concept of man and society. It also is a concept insensitive to the joint effects of the biological and social processes that undoubtedly are involved in the development of intelligence.[8]

Lastly, we would be amiss not to mention one other condition that has brought us to our present posture. This involves the traditional values which the social scientist, and the sociologist in particular, has held and still holds. On this and most other controversial issues he is a "liberal" or at least believes in a free, equalitarian society. However, fortunately or not, it is quite easy for this ideology, or any ideology, to influence the manner in which the scientist approaches his subject matter. A statement by a British psychometrician, P. E. Vernon, aptly describes what we mean:

> Those with left-wing opinions dislike the assumption that anyone born from an upper- or middle-class family has some innate superiority over those of less privileged birth, and believe that social reform and improved education will rectify such divergencies. Whereas the view often expressed in the nineteenth century, and still occasionally heard, is that the poor cannot benefit from, and do not deserve, as good an environment and education as the rich. Communist theory so strongly emphasizes the modifiability of genetic constitution that for a time Mendelian principles were rejected in Soviet Russia, and intelligence testing is still regarded merely as a ruse to perpetuate social-class and educational differences. The most extreme hereditarians were the Nazi racial theorists of the 1930s, who ascribed all the desirable human traits and abilities to people of Nordic descent, all the undesirable ones to Jews.[9]

There should be no forced choice here, since neither position, of course, is consistent with the evidence. On the other hand, even if neither of these positions could be rejected on presentation of a scientific argument, we, as sociologists, still would have no license to dismiss unpopular theories simply because they are inconsistent with popular ideologies.

## WHY CHANGE?

"Inheritance of intelligence" does not mean that one's wits are decided and fixed at conception or at birth; it only means that with uniform upbringing and education people's wits would continue to be variable.[10]

Only in *quantity*, never in *fact*, has the contribution of heredity to the observed variability of human behavior ever been effectively challenged. Although environmental components are easily identified, they typically "explain" only a relatively small amount of the total variance in test (IQ) performance.[11] This does not prove the case for genetics any more than it disproves the case for environment, since the "unexplained" variance may involve a certain amount of measurement error, plus whatever environmental *and* genetic factors we may have neglected to consider.

First, in theory, geneticists do have a straightforward estimate of the mean proportion of genes that one has in common with any particular relative. Whether in reference to intelligence or other continuous traits, like height, the coefficients are exactly the same.[12] For example, between a parent and child or between ordinary siblings (including fraternal twins), roughly 50 percent of the genes are held in common.[13] Interestingly, the observed parent-child and sib-sib correlations on intelligence are quite orderly and generally obtain the theoretical value. When all genes are held in common, as in the case of identical twins, again the observed correlations in all studies have been generally in line with the theoretical value. The similarity in test performance of identical twins reared together, about 0.87, is nearly as high as the intra-individual reliabilites of the tests employed, i.e., the correlation between two parallel tests for the same individual.[14] While this contrasts with a lower correlation of about 0.75 in studies of identical twins reared apart, note how much higher even this latter figure is than the 0.23 correlation usually found for unrelated persons reared together.[15]

These comparisons illustrate what Dobzhansky meant when he observed that "whenever the matter has been studied, both genetic and environmental components of the variability have usually come to light."[16] As a result, behavioral geneticists have made a useful and important distinction between the concepts of genotype and phenotype. Whereas genotype refers to the presumably unalterable genetic make-up of an individual, phenotype refers to the observable physical and social characteristics that result from the interaction of the individual's genotype with his environment. Owing to environmental differences, it is often the case, as Gottesman notes, that "different genotypes may have the same phenotypes, and different phenotypes may be displayed by the same genotypes."[17] In other words, even though the theoretical genotypic similarity and observed phenotypic similarity are very close on mental tests, two individuals with the same IQ scores may have quite different genotypes, while another two individuals with quite different scores may, in fact, have very similar genotypes.[18] The phenotypic expression of intelligence, therefore, is always a relative and flexible matter; the genotype is not.

Although the related genotype(s) probably cannot be clearly identified by any phenotypic (behavioral) measure of intelligence, the genetic component nevertheless has been demonstrated rather convincingly in the twin studies. Most common have been comparisons between identical and fraternal twins.[19] In this situation it is presumed that because the trait-relevant environments are about the same for all twins who are reared together in the same family, the genetic component can be inferred from the greater similarity of performance between identical twins than between fraternal twins. An alternative, though less frequent, approach has been to compare identical twins who have been reared together with those who have been reared apart. Thus the same genotypes are studied in different environments, rather than different genotypes in the same environment.

In both types of studies, roughly 70 percent of the variance within families in intelligence has been attributed to genetic heredity. Moreover, the findings have been remarkably consistent despite differences in the methods used to construct the heritability coefficients, differences in the types of intelligence tests, differences in the age structure, ethnic composition, or socioeconomic character of the samples, differences in the regions studied, i.e., whether local, national, or foreign samples, and differences in sample size, which have been unusually large in some cases, such as the 631 twins in a recent Swedish investigation[20] and the 1169 twins in a study reported recently by the National Merit Scholarship Corporation.[21]

Given, however, the somewhat tenuous assumptions that all twin studies are required to make, the size of the heritability component perhaps has been exaggerated. Nevertheless, even allowing for some measurement error and questionable controls, the estimated variance attributed to heredity on these tests probably would remain very high. The factual evidence really is not in dispute.

In addition to the twin studies and the orderliness of other correlations between family members of varying degrees of relationship, the presence of a genetic component in conventional IQ tests has been demonstrated in studies of foster and adopted children. If intelligence is determined primarily by environment, it is argued, then the IQs of children removed from their biological parents as infants certainly should correlate more closely with the IQs of their foster parents than their biological parents. The inverse, however, is true.[22]

Again let us stress the point that inter-individual differences in test performance are not due solely to variations in heredity. We agree that most, if not all, intelligence tests consistently favor children reared in a stimulating and instructive environment. Yet, no research has demonstrated that the cultural component in these tests "explains" as much as 50 percent of the inter-individual variance; while, at the same time, no research has ever found that the genetic component "explains" less than 50 percent of the variance.

On the other hand, the evidence must be interpreted cautiously, not because it is wrong but because to ask how much behavior is determined by heredity and how much by environment is not a very sensible approach. Heredity and environment should not be set against each other in this way; as we shall note, the problem is far more complex. We merely wish to emphasize here that the acceptance of one set of evidence does not require us to reject the other. Rather, we should accept both, and once having done so, begin to move on to the more important work of developing a common framework for understanding the connections between the biological and cultural evolution of human societies.

There are also other reasons for re-examining our posture with regard to the nature-nurture question. One of these reasons stems from a marked change in the orientations of behavior geneticists and anthropologists to the problem. Geneticists, for example, have all but given up the question of how much a behavioral trait is due to heredity and how much to environment. Rather, many are now concerned with such questions as how modifiable by systematic manipulation of the environment is the phenotypic expression of a trait and how heredity interacts with the environment to produce phenotypic variations.[23] One approach to these questions is to think of heredity as determining a norm of reaction. Gottesman explains the approach in this manner:

> Within this framework a genotype determines an indefinite but circumscribed assortment of phenotypes, each of which corresponds to one of the possible environments to which the genotype may be exposed. *If* and *when* the effort is expended to change radically the natural environment of a known genotype, e.g., maze bright and maze dull rat strains, there is a complete masking of the genotypic expectation and the two strains cannot be differentiated from their behavior . . . It is the plasticity of such a phenotypic character as human behavior in a heterogeneous environment and its invariance in a homogeneous environment which has led extremists to lose their perspective about the situations in which nature is more important than nurture and vice versa.[24]

Moreover, behavior geneticists, like sociologists, are interested in exploring the complexities of human behavior in such areas as child socialization, educational attainment, fertility, and social mobility. Their vantage point warrants our attention.

Many anthropologists, in dealing with evolutionary theories, also have changed their perspective. The "critical point" theory, which only ten years ago had stifled any real synthesis between physical and cultural anthropology, is being redressed in some quarters. The theory had held that the biological evolution of man proceeded up to a "critical point" when suddenly man became a culture-bearing animal. Having reached this "point," any further development of man's physical being became inconsequential as his accumulation of ingenious devices (culture) extended his pre-existing capacities like a "superorganic cake of custom."[25] The recent progress, however, of archeologists and paleontologists in their efforts to piece together the evolutionary record of man through human fossils and cultural artifacts has led to quite a different perspective. Rather than sequential, the biological and cultural evolution of man appears to have occurred in a slow synchronous (reciprocal) manner. In other words, the development of man's innate capacity was itself dependent upon the gradual development of culture.[26] This not only suggests that man's cultural environment probably will continue to shape his future physical development but that heredity and environment involve inseparable processes.

Finally, if for no other reason, we must begin to take note of genetic principles because, whether or not we or other social scientists accept them, their generally popular acceptance has very real consequences for social arrangements. Let us explain. Technological advancement, especially in a competitive world society, has stimulated us to utilize all human resources more effectively and to seek solutions to the problems that now obstruct their full development. Moreover, against an existing normative backdrop of equalitarian values, this force is translated into the ideology of a meritocracy.[27] While allowing for such contingencies as differences in individual performance, a complex division of labor, and differences in social rewards, the meritocracy is a society in which positions are allocated on the basis of "talent" (plus "effort") rather than class or social advantage. A rational utilization of talent, however, requires some degree of control over ongoing practices which, to be effective, in turn requires special knowledge about the distribution of talent and the mechanisms that enhance or impede its development. Thus, the "Great Society" has geared itself to achieve the fullest (and fastest) development of each individual *according to his capacities*, and, as the search for talent goes on, mass programs in mental testing become part of the establishment.

A basic and often explicit assumption is, of course, that the intellectual "endowments" of individuals *do* differ and that, owing to these differences, not everyone *can* learn anything. Furthermore, it is generally presumed, at least by those whose decisions are most likely to affect current practices, that attempting to act as if everyone *were* equal, as in uniform educational programs, is inefficient, impedes the development of the brighter student, and places unreasonable expectations on the probable achievement of the slow learner.

The significant questions then become: To what extent are mental tests actually used, for what purposes are they used, what do people believe the tests measure, and is their use generally accepted? Later we will elaborate on the answers to these questions. It suffices, for the moment, simply to note that students, teachers, and parents typically believe that the standardized tests now in use measure, at least to some extent, the traits with which a person is born. In addition, the general acceptance and use of these tests has become so widespread in recent years that it is inconceivable that their continued use will not have a very profound impact on the structure of the American society in the years ahead. Goslin, one of the principal investigators of this particular problem, has summarized the situation in the following manner:

For the first time in the history of the world, a conscientious attempt is being made to measure objectively the intellectual abilities of human beings and to make it possible for those individuals having the greatest abilities to rise to positions of high status. Although many other characteristics of individuals still play an important role in the assignment of status in western society, objective estimates of ability are fast becoming of crucial importance as a result of the development of standardized ability tests.[28]

In the remainder of this article, we will present four brief but specific illustrations of the manner in which genetic and social processes, if taken together, could provide the basis for framing an essentially sociological investigation. As we have need for them, genetic principles will be introduced, including those dealing with breeding populations, regression toward the mean, and random genetic drift.

## CLASS, FERTILITY, AND INTELLIGENCE

In the classical treatment of social classes as Mendelian or "breeding" populations, attention has focused on conceivable alterations in man's genetic character due to a combination of differential fertility rates (favoring the lower class) and assortative mating, i.e., marriages between phenotypically, and therefore presumably genotypically, similar individuals.

A breeding population simply is an aggregate of individuals who are statistically distinct from other aggregates with respect to some gene frequencies as a result of assortative mating and other processes. Although the observed differences in IQ tests of children born of parents from different classes admittedly are attributable in part to cultural variations, the findings are at least equally predictable from a genetic theory of intelligence. It should be no surprise, therefore, that correlations between spouses are found to range between 0.3 and 0.6 in most studies, in terms of both measured intelligence and various socioeconomic characteristics.[29] Assortative mating then *does* occur.

Furthermore, although no direct evidence is available, assortative mating with respect to intelligence probably is increasing, owing to the growth of a mass system of higher education in which mental abilities are the main criterion for selection, as we will note, and where sex ratios are beginning to approach equality.[30] Social classes, most likely, have always been breeding populations; and today, to the extent that intelligence has a genetic base and social positions are allocated according to ability, assortative breeding between genetically similar adults tends to favor the reproduction of genetically similar children in any given stratum. As in Young's meritocracy, talented adults rise to the top of the social hierarchy and the dull fall or remain at the bottom. Therefore, as the system strives to achieve full equality of opportunity, the observed within-class variance among children tends to diminish while the between-class variance tends to increase on the selective traits associated with genetic differences.[31]

Yet the system never reaches full circle, or to the point where mobility ceases, because no parent ever reproduces an exact replica of himself. Human variability is just as much a law of nature as is human heritability. Without the former, the entire process of evolution (natural selection) is impossible; without the latter, no species, *qua species* could survive.

In viewing social classes as breeding populations, we hesitate to speculate upon the many sociological implications. Yet in the area of fertility and population studies, there are some rather firm and interesting data.[32] Differential fertility by socioeconomic status has been observed for centuries,[33] and until lately, the low fertility of high-status groups frequently has been referred to by sociologists as one factor that accounts for vertical mobility.[34] With the advent of intelligence testing, moreover, a similar inverse correlation has been found between family size and the IQ of children.[35] As a result, a number of writers several years ago predicted that the collective intelligence of the population would gradually decline at a rate of one to four IQ points each generation.[36] There was nothing especially complicated about their reasoning. If the least intelligent adults of the lower classes were producing proportionately more children, as they thought, and if living conditions

had substantially improved life expectancies and, therefore, the reproductive capacities of the children of the lower-classes, then the total forces of selection were favoring lower intelligence.

Yet longitudinal data in Scotland,[37] England,[38] New Zealand,[39] and the United States,[40] while covering only about one generation, have shown no decline. The paradox finally was resolved when it was recognized that fertility and family size do not correlate with intelligence in the same manner.[41] Previous studies, it is noted, had surveyed children only and thereby excluded the unmarried and infertile adults. Accordingly, a number of studies recently have demonstrated that these adults have the lowest intelligence and, when taken into account, no simple linear correlation between fertility and intelligence exists.[42] In other words, although the least intelligent groups produce more children within marriage, they are the least likely to marry.

While these findings, along with a number of equally cogent arguments,[43] may temporarily put aside the ominous thesis that selective forces have been operating in an unfavorable direction for the species, they set forth another interesting question. If social class and intelligence are positively related and fertility and intelligence are *un*related, how do we explain the negative correlation between fertility and social class? What might be suggested is either that the high-ability, high-status adults have more children than the high-ability, low-status adults or that the low-ability, high-status adults have more children than the low-ability, low-status adults.[44]

Either hypothesis appears defensible. For example, young intelligent adults of childbearing age and from lower or lower-middle class backgrounds may anticipate upward mobility or at least recognize the utility of family planning and therefore limit their family size. On the other hand, family size probably does not especially restrict the opportunities of adults from higher socioeconomic groups.[45] In regard to the alternative hypothesis, dull, and especially retarded adults from lower socioeconomic families tend to be less fertile in part because, as we already have noted, they tend not to marry. In contrast, it is perhaps by no means unusual for an upper or upper-middle class family to encourage the marriage and fertility of a moderately dull offspring, while taking, in the process, whatever precautions necessary (especially in the case of a son) to ensure the "selection" of an "intelligent" mate. These hypotheses suggest some new directions for research.

## THE FAMILY AND THE "REGRESSION TOWARD THE MEAN"

This illustration deals with the nuclear family in urban industrial societies. As an extension of the genetic and sociological principles already discussed, our hypothesis is that a basic contradiction exists between the institutionalization of child-rearing practices in the nuclear family and the parent-child nexus. By fortuitous circumstances, the family does not and cannot effectively perform its most primary societal function. The point certainly could be argued using the dialectics of a model of class, race, or sex discrimination. For purposes here, however, we will argue essentially from the standpoint of genetics, though no geneticist (or sociologist) would necessarily agree with our hypotheses.

The irreconcilable predicament of the modern family, from this standpoint, is the genetic variability of man about which we previously spoke. This variability has two important consequences here. It produces a standard regression toward the mean; and on the other hand, in large breeding populations, it produces a broad range of genotypes that even within a uniform environment could conceivably produce almost any known phenotypic trait.

In regard to the first point, the standard regression toward the mean undoubtedly is, in part, a statistical artifact that should be expected to occur when there is any chance for measurement error. That is, whether the same individuals are being re-tested or whether two groups of individuals are being compared, such as the IQs of parents and children, the scores that are being matched against persons who initially were placed high or low on the scale will tend to be closer to the mean. More important to our argument, however, is that regression toward the mean also occurs because this is the manner in which probabilities in genetics actually work.[46] In other words, although a parent who is above average in intelligence is likely to have children also above average, the "native" intelligence of these children, on the whole, will be lower than that of the parent—that is to say, toward the mean of the total adult population. The inverse, of course, is also true. The chances are greater for a dull parent to produce a brighter than a duller child; but usually the child will still be somewhat below average.[47]

In regard to the second point, the range of possible hereditary traits that are transmitted in any particular mating is limited only statistically. The overlap or variability in measured intelligence between breeding populations has always been a remarkable discovery, and certainly not easily explained from other than a genetic standpoint. How else *can* one explain the perhaps more than occasional exceptions of a bright child born of dull lower-class parents or a subnormal child born of bright middle-class parents? Although, again, some of the exceptions probably can be explained by "environment," we seriously doubt that all or even most exceptions can be explained in this manner. Even under the most restricted environment, it is possible for dull parents to produce a bright child, and vice versa. Moreover, it is entirely plausible that there are far more exceptions than actually observed, since culturally-induced responses probably mask *both* the brightness of some children and the subnormality of others. Interestingly, while most observers are quick to concur that a restricted environment may disguise the native intelligence of some lower-class children, we seldom inspect the reverse situation. That is, it is equally probable that an enriched environment, especially one which accentuates "social" skills, may tend to disguise the subnormal intelligence of some middle- or upper-class children.[48]

How then does genetic variability put some modern families in a predicament? The task of rearing a particular child is the "culturally-induced" responsibility of the parents who are directly related to the child but whose genetic endowments may be too poorly matched (to the child) to succeed.

If our national ideals include equality of opportunity and a full utilization of all human resources and if to pursue these goals the structure of the family is so designed that children eventually must be emancipated from their families of orientation, then the obligation of parents to rear a child on account of the accident of birth is an obviously obsolete (or at least contradictory) feature of a modern society.[49] Differential advantages and handicaps are rooted in the nature of the parent-child relationship. Obviously, we are speaking here of cultural deprivation. However, rather than the common discriminatory class barriers we usually think of, the source of deprivation is tied to the variable mental capacities of parents to provide an appropriate environment for a particular child to develop according to *his* capacities.

Without discussing the full ramifications of this problem, we only raise the question: How is it possible for two dull parents to stimulate a potentially bright child, to be aware of his personal problems, and to effectively guide his development? It is not possible, and, apparently, it is partly for this reason that through crash poverty and educational programs we have intruded upon the social structure of the lower-class family. Because we believe it is both an "equitable" and "efficient" utilization of human resources, we physically and emotionally remove the child from his parents, in some instances, in order to give him opportunities more commensurate with his abilities.

One might wonder, however, just when we will begin to apply the same logic to the "equitable" and "efficient" treatment of the subnormal child of normal, middle-class parents. Do well-meaning intelligent parents, for example, have the "right" to attempt to push their children to a level of performance the achievement of which would place them under excessive emotional strain? Are children, instead, sometimes pushed into delinquent or other marginal roles?[50] How apropos is

Conant's first point in the summarization of his observations of the American high school:

> The main problem in wealthy suburban schools is to guide the parent whose college ambitions outrun his child's abilities toward a realistic picture of the kind of college his child is suited for.[51]

## EDUCATIONAL TESTING AND GENOTYPIC VARIABILITY

The variability in intelligence is a phenomenon closely linked to but usually evaded in current discussions on transformations in mass education in this country. Our discussion here will not be directly concerned with the (intergenerational) source of this variability, which was at the root of the preceding problem. Rather, we will be concerned with a basic dilemma that arises as attempts are made to institutionalize a system of educational selection based upon the variability itself when, in fact, we cannot perfectly identify the genotypic variation of intelligence but only its phenotypic expression (what the tests measure). Before elaborating upon this issue, let us look at one of the important elements involved, i.e., educational testing.

The development of standardized tests of ability has been closely associated with and partly a response to the growth of secondary education prior to World War II and, more recently, the growth of higher education. Beginning in the primary grades and continuing through college, standardized tests are now being employed as the primary basis for sorting and selection among a very diverse student population for placement in a very diverse range of programs. The extent of this development is itself quite remarkable. Below, we have summarized some of the most relevant findings from recent studies by the Russell Sage Foundation[52] and Project Talent[53] on testing in the nation's elementary and secondary schools.

1 Virtually all schools now use standardized tests. Moreover, a large majority of the secondary schools in this country plan to expand their testing programs in the near future.

2 Standardized tests are used to assess the potential learning ability of students, in order to provide individualized instruction, and to guide students in their decisions about school curricula, going to college, and jobs. A fairly large majority of the nation's youth actually are being placed into homogeneous classes on the basis of these tests, either by establishing completely separate programs of instruction for different students ("tracking") or by assigning students to different sections of the same course ("grouping").

3 A majority of both students and adults believe that standardized tests measure the intelligence a person is born with; although most, at the same time, recognize that learning makes an important difference. Students and parents alike believe that the tests are basically accurate. While teachers essentially agree with the students and parents on these points, they also tend to believe that the tests are their best single index of a student's intellectual ability.

4 Although public acceptance of standardized testing seems to depend largely upon the specific purposes for which the tests are used, a majority of the students believe that these tests are and should be important, especially in terms of deciding who should go to college.

This is only part of the story. For the college-going aspirants, the first two major hurdles—Educational Testing Service's Preliminary Scholastic Aptitude Test (PSAT) and National Merit Scholarship Corporation's Qualifying Test—usually come in the eleventh grade. Scores on the PSAT are not used to decide *who* goes to college, since that decision presumably was made some years earlier. Rather, one of the primary purposes of the test is to help decide who goes *where* to college by giving each student an early estimate of the probabilities of being admitted to any particular school.[54] The National Merit examination, on the other hand, is designed to select among the uppermost two percent of the country's students those who will receive special commendation and awards.[55] While in competition with other programs, the growth of the PSAT and National Merit programs in the past ten years has been so phenomenal that both are

being administered today in roughly three-fourths of the nation's high schools.[56]

The next major, and perhaps most important, challenge comes about a year later—the college admissions tests and, for those in accelerated programs, the Advanced Placement examinations. Whether administered nationally or locally, tests are being used today by most colleges in their admissions process or for placement. Indeed, the proportion of high-scoring students that a college can attract has become the most objective criterion available for ranking the colleges themselves.[55] In addition, many secondary schools and colleges are participating in the Advanced Placement Program of the College Entrance Examination Board. Although presently involving fewer students and schools, its growth has closely paralleled that of the National Merit program.[57]

As the student progresses further, the significance of educational testing does not diminish. Upon completion of most undergraduate programs, admission to nearly any reputable graduate or professional school is fast becoming dependent, in part, upon the student's sophistication on such nationally administered tests as the Graduate Record Examination, the Admission Test for Graduate Study in Business, or the Law School Admissions Test. Likewise, entry into a particular field direct from a four-year undergraduate program sometimes requires additional testing, such as the National Teachers Examination or the Foreign Service Examination. Even the Peace Corps requires the Peace Corps Entrance Tests.[58]

Now, the basic issue in educational testing and selection, we believe, involves two competing sets of forces. On the one hand, the pressures *to* test appear irreversible.[59] It is generally recognized by most observers that individual capacities to learn vary rather markedly, especially when it comes to complex subject matter for any given grade level. Because it is both "equitable" (see conclusions) and "efficient" (as noted earlier), we test. We do so, too, and perhaps more importantly, because enrollment pressures have forced our colleges to become more selective, especially since the postwar babies "came of age."[60] This, in turn, has pushed testing and selection down the grades to a point where now a student, or really his parents and teachers, probably must decide sometime before he leaves the eighth grade whether or not he is going on to college.

We therefore institutionalize programs for the separate and individualized treatment of the slow learners, the average, and the "gifted." Homogeneous grouping or tracking within a school, differentiated programs between the various units of a school system,[61] or even the differentiation between the "public" and "private" sectors[62] of American education, all add up to the same thing. The use of standardized tests and differential treatment can be found at nearly every point in the educational system. Moreover, there is constant pressure, as noted, to introduce mental tests into the selection process at an increasingly early point in the child's life in order that the development of his capacities will not be left to circumstance.[63]

On the other hand, there are obvious dangers in the use of standardized tests which lead their users to proceed cautiously. These dangers, in part, directly involve the size and nature of the discrepancy between innate intelligence (the genotypes) and what the tests measure (phenotypes). In early childhood and infancy, when intelligence tests are least blurred by culturally-induced responses, they are least reliable (temporally unstable) owing presumably to the slow development of the neurological structures related to intelligence.[64] Yet in later childhood and adolescence, when the tests are more reliable (stable), they are less valid in the sense that the phenotypic expression of intelligence at later age levels is far more sensitive to culturally-induced responses.

The "resolution" of the problem (no real solution is presently possible nor teleological explanation intended here) has been to seek a balance between testing programs that are introduced neither too early nor too late. If premature, the determination of status rests on arbitrary (unreliable) data; if postponed, the advantages of individualized treatment are neglected, and, moreover, depressing environmental influences become firmly established and are all too conspicuous.[65]

Some educational programs appear to compensate for the "mistakes" that occur. One of the objectives of the open door junior college, for example, is to give the slow learners and culturally deprived a realistic opportunity to recoup their losses and, if it should exist, demonstrate their capability to do college work.[66] However, perhaps with the exception of innovations like Head Start, most of the established programs unfortunately attack the problem at a point when few of the even capable students can be retrieved from the involuntary course upon which they have been set. Thus, despite all efforts to keep the doors open, to keep the dropouts in, and to keep the testers out, "sponsored mobility" is more a part of the American scene than most observers probably have thought.[67]

We believe that more sociologists should put aside their aversion to mental testing and strive to understand and disentangle the problems set forth here.[68] If not, we may soon find, if it is not already true, that about half of the children by age seven (the current figure in England and Wales)[69] have already been "tracked" on ability lines. We do not mean to suggest that the "professional" opinions of social scientists or even politicians would matter very much, at the moment, since certainly the feelings of the educators and school teachers are far more likely to determine just what goes on in the classroom anyway. But perhaps this is because, in contrast to the teachers who claim to "know better," we continue to insist that "all kids are alike," except, of course, our own or except those who get to college where *we* can observe them and readily "explain" the observed variations on the basis of the diverse educational experiences they already have encountered.[70]

## THE CONCEPT OF "PERFECT MOBILITY"

Our final illustration of the importance of genetic processes to the sociologist deals with the manner in which we typically conceptualize vertical mobility. Nearly all studies in this area have taken person-to-person comparisons of the social stratum occupied by fathers and sons as the unit of analysis, and then assessed the openness of the class structure either directly from these comparisons or by various kinds of indices of association (and dissociation).[71] Essentially, once having accounted for "forced" mobility, i.e., mobility which is caused by changes in stratum composition or size, the remaining movement or degree of association is taken as an estimate of "pure" mobility, or "equality of opportunity." For instance, in the standard mobility matrix, "inequality" is signified when the occupational distributions of the sons born of fathers in different strata do not match. Conversely, in the ideal model, a system of full equality is perceived as one in which identical proportions of sons from all strata eventually will enter any given occupation.

What is basically wrong with this model? Although individual differences in ability are acknowledged, at least implicitly, and although the model permits migration from one stratum to another on the basis of these differences, it assumes that ability is randomly distributed at birth and that any differences observed among the children of different strata are solely a matter of environmental conditioning. Any genetic basis for these differences is dismissed as irrelevant. To dismiss the genetic factor, however, we would have to accept the unrealistic idea that, biologically, there is no more resemblance between a child and his parent than between a child and a total stranger.

If, on the other hand, an important part of the observed variations in intelligence between children from different social classes actually can be attributed to assortative mating and genetic processes, our model of "perfect" mobility requires a fundamental revision. That is, as mental functioning is made the principal criterion for the ascription of status, a model that specifies that full equality is achieved only when the same proportions of children from each class are assigned to any given status is not exactly appropriate. The matter-of-fact reason is that it apparently is becoming increasingly unlikely that the same proportions of children from each class have equal capacities to take advantage of their opportunities. The tendency for elites to replace themselves (intergen-

erationally) is somewhat ensured by the nature of any system in which intelligence is a dynamic factor affecting status placement.[72] Note that this particular restriction on mobility is conceptually distinct from all cultural barriers that may otherwise limit the channels of mobility and with which "equal opportunity" models are more properly concerned.

Lest the preceding discussion should be misunderstood, let us make firm the equally important point that genetic variability guarantees a relatively substantial pool of very bright children from lower-class backgrounds, which is sufficient reason, in both utilitarian and ideological terms, for social policies that emphasize the importance of this "overlap." Moreover, when entire groups of children from these backgrounds are systematically deprived of the same opportunities for development as other children, as presently persists, then the size of this pool is larger than that which otherwise might be estimated on the basis of heritability coefficients alone.

For instance, consider a hypothetical model of a simple bipartite structure in a moderately fluid system which has a one-to-three ratio between the size of the upper and lower classes. Although the upper class might produce the largest relative proportion of children with high intelligence, the greatest absolute number probably would come from the lower class.[73] This does not, however, dislodge our previous point; that is to say, the distribution of intelligence is by no means random and any mathematical or other model that purports to estimate the "openness" of a class structure should make adequate allowance for genetically-based inequalities.[74] These inequalities are not the same as the moral or political inequalities with which contemporary theories of stratification have generally been concerned.[75] Moreover, we question whether they should be, since equality of opportunity neither presupposes nor promotes equality of ability.

### A NOTE ON RACE

Before concluding, we are obligated to regard the relevance of some of the foregoing to the observed differences in intelligence between racial groups, lest again we are misunderstood. We fully agree with the environmentalist's position here that it is doubtful that the observed differences can be attributed to genetic differences. Our explanation, however, is not the same as the one usually given by sociologists and others who have come to this conclusion, since we must explain just how it is possible to claim that differences in measured intelligence between *social classes* but not *races* are due, in part, to heredity. The answer perhaps is not self-evident.

Both social classes and races *can* be treated as Mendelian populations. On the other hand, when describing, as we have, the selecting and sorting mechanisms that increase the between-group variance in intelligence, whites and Negroes cannot be thought of as being joined in this selection process. For all practical purposes, the fact persists that the American Negro, owing to discriminatory practices, is part of an adjacent but clearly separate structure which makes any comparisons of phenotypic traits between Negroes and whites especially tenuous, except for skin color. (This is not true for social classes within either structure.)

Races are breeding populations which differ significantly from each other in the frequency of one or more genes.[76] Twenty years ago the usual explanation offered for these differences involved something about the adaptive quality of the selective traits in a natural or social environment. An explanation gaining acceptance today, however, is that many racial differences represent random variations that (like eufunctions) can become part of the stable characteristics of any population that remains relatively isolated over a period of time, as long as the trait or traits, of course, are not *maladaptive*.[77] This process is known as "genetic drift," and has no necessary correspondence to the theory of natural selection or, more precisely, "climatic or social adaptation." Moreover, it appears that the theory could explain a majority of the observed variations between racial groups. This suggests that few, if any, of the observed differences can be taken as badges of inferiority or superiority, since no "adaptive" quality is necessary for them to develop or persist. It suggests, too, that the biological study of races actually involves the flow and admixture of specific traits rather than discrete (and distorted) taxonomies.[78]

It is true that whites differ from the American Negro in gene frequencies related to a number of traits. However, whether the *origins* of these differences once involved genetic drift, climatic adaptation, or both, is somewhat irrelevant. Also somewhat irrelevant is the possibility that minor hereditary variations in intelligence might have existed at one time. The primary trait today that selectively sets whites and Negroes apart is skin color. If no genes other than those associated with the color of one's skin are the basis for selective breeding, then, for the most part, it must be presumed that most other genes, including those associated with intelligence, simply "drift" across these populations. At least in the United States, there is ample evidence to believe (on the basis of traits far more clearly associated with heredity than intelligence) that the amount of gene flow has been so marked as to "wash out" many of the differences that, at one time, may have existed.

There is no contradiction, therefore, in our claim that the observed phenotypic variations in intelligence between social classes represent, to some extent, actual genetic differences, but that the observed variations between races probably do not. As breeding populations, only social classes, not races, tend to remain isolated by virtue of assortative mating based on intelligence.

## SUMMARY AND CONCLUSIONS

It appears that sociologists have tended to pass over some perfectly reasonable ties between their discipline and behavior genetics. They have done so, in part, because sociology, as a natural point of order, has had first to establish and articulate an environmental theory of behavior. At this, it not only has been successful, but there is reason to believe that its ideas can be and have been put into practice. Furthermore, sociological theories, intentionally or not, have been consistent with liberal-democratic values whereas genetic theories, in the past, have aroused far more suspicion.

We have argued, however, that the dichotomy between genetically and environmentally determined intelligence can no longer be permitted to dominate our thinking, since both really are parts of an interacting system. Our review of some of the recent evidence should begin to convince us that both heredity and environment are important and that neither agent alone can produce intelligence. Moreover, we noted that scientists in allied fields have a more balanced view of the question than do sociologists. Others appear willing to accord ample weight to environmental influences, but not to the exclusion of the genetic materials which, in important ways, regulate the adaptation of the human organism to its social environment, and vice versa.

To illustrate these connections, we presented four specific ways in which genetic processes are sociologically relevant. Although there are no simple solutions to the problems we outlined, it was suggested that we should be more sensitive to the work of behavior geneticists and avoid systems models, such as those in our current treatment of vertical mobility, that assume a uniform or random genetic base. We cannot opt for a biologically based model of social structure; on the other hand, we should not be so shortsighted as to continue to insist that "all men are created equal." While "inequality" is essentially a social phenomenon, it is nevertheless dependent upon the necessities of both social and genetic differentiation.

In concluding, we also can offer no special methodological tools for estimating the "norm of reaction" of the genotypes associated with intelligence. There are, of course, no means presently available for doing so.[79] Yet we need not wait for geneticists or others to provide more accurate instruments. Our present testing devices, including IQ, aptitude, or even achievement tests could be used, if cautiously, quite profitably in sociological investigations, and certainly far more than they are presently. Even though they do not isolate innate ability, individual and (sometimes) group differences on these tests do, in fact, measure it. Regard-

less, performance on these tests is swiftly becoming one of the most, if not *the* most important single criterion for the allocation of status.

All sociological investigations and commentaries, of course, have not neglected the treatment of intelligence. In addition to Anderson, Clark, Faris, and Rogoff, whose activities we already have noted, there are other sociologists who have dealt with the problem in a serious way. Of more than cursory interest are:

1 Cicourel and Kitsuse's study of the professionalization of the role of the guidance counselors who administer the school's testing program and, owing to moral and bureaucratic imperatives, must "do something" when the academic performance of students falls below their predicted grade-point averages[80]

2 Goslin's continuing work on the social and psychological consequences of educational testing, and especially his interpretation of causal patterns of this form, the dissemination of test information→self-concepts of ability→achievement motivation[81]

3 Sewell's several studies on the interrelationships between neighborhood context, intelligence, and social mobility, one of which very recently engaged him (and Armer) in an important controversy in this journal when Turner, Boyle, and Michael all refused to accept the causal priority of intelligence when estimating the effects of neighborhood on educational aspirations[82]

4 Duncan's current working papers on how intelligence might be represented in a formal model of the process of achievement, and, more precisely, on how intelligence and "environment" might interact in this process when two separate estimates of the correlates of "early" and "later" intelligence are available[83]

5 Farber's re-analysis of Burt's data using a procedure based on the Pascal triangle for identifying different effects of social class on intellectual development at the upper and lower IQ ranges, which indicates that the relationship between social class and intelligence is nonlinear, and suggesting that we must proceed cautiously when attempting to explain the interaction between hered-

ity and environment.[84]

Also, in concluding, there is one point with which perhaps we should have begun, since it may help clarify the firm resistance of some sociologists who hold that any biological interpretation of human behavior is simply specious reasoning. We have in mind the "voluntarism" found in Linton's classic distinction between achieved and ascribed status[85] and its extension in the sometimes "soft" determinism of modern sociology.[86] In the meritocracy, as within any truly "deterministic" framework, Linton's distinction tends to break down, at least in terms of what we believe its most common usage to be.

Contrasted with "ascription," "achievement" generally refers to the allocation of status on the basis of properties not assigned by birth, such as class, sex, or race, but ones over which the individual presumably has some control and, therefore, "merits." In other words, the individual's *private* capacities are involved. But do not the individual's few capacities depend to more than a trivial degree upon the genetic material with which he enters the social contest, and over which he has no more control than his race or his sex? And, therefore, is not the allocation of status according to ability actually just as much an "ascribed" criterion as the more traditional assignment of positions based on "social" heredity?

If one of the major social issues facing contemporary societies, as we have suggested, involves a basic confrontation between the principles of social heredity and the meritocracy, then which mode of selection is more equitable? Which is more "just" if volition is involved in neither the mental capacities that an individual inherits nor the social advantages conferred upon him by his parents?

Although one mode is perhaps no more equitable than the other, *one* does appear to be more rational. Here, we would agree with Linton's position, and others, that social heredity, while not "dysfunctional" in simpler societies, no longer meets the demands of a complex technology. To the extent that the survival of our present technology (and social order) depends upon the effective utilization of human resources, then the identification, sorting, and development of talent will continue to be persuasive arguments.

## REFERENCES AND NOTES

1 This article is directed particularly to those who believe that the ties between sociology and genetics either "have been" or "should be" buried. For others, it is an attempt to illustrate the manner in which genetic principles might find their way into the sociologist's repertoire.

2 Pitirim A. Sorokin, *Social and Cultural Mobility*, New York: The Free Press of Glencoe, 1964.

3 Fuller once advocated a similar position with respect to the subject matter of psychology, but he failed to illustrate how any synthesis between the hereditarians' and environmentalists' positions might be brought about. See John L. Fuller, *Nature and Nurture: A Modern Synthesis*, New York: Doubleday & Co., 1954.

4 The term "intelligence" has no precise meaning. Although most psychometricians probably do not subscribe to Spearman's single-factor theory, only a few have begun to identify any of the conceptually distinct abilities that may be involved. The only distinction employed in this paper is between "innate" intelligence and that which intelligence tests generally measure, or, to be explained later, the genotypes and phenotypes of intelligence. The meaning, hopefully in all instances, will be clear by the context in which the term is used.

5 Goslin, for example, has developed an interesting paradigm for studying the interrelationships of the influencing factors. See David Goslin, *The Search for Ability*, New York: Russell Sage Foundation, 1963, pp. 130–132. A classical review of the original research on intelligence as related to socioeconomic differences may be found in Kenneth Eells, Allison Davis, *et al.*, *Intelligence and Cultural Differences: A Study of Cultural Learning and Problem-solving*, Chicago: The University of Chicago Press, 1951. These and other correlates of intelligence, such as basal metabolism rates, EEG alpha frequency, etc., are reviewed by both Anastasi and Tyler; see Anne Anastasi, *Differential Psychology*, New York: The Macmillan Company, 1958; and Leona E. Tyler, *The Psychology of Human Differences*, New York: Appleton-Century-Crofts, Inc., 1965.

6 In his presidential address in 1961 before the American Sociological Association, Faris gave this interesting analogy: "If it appears illogical to claim that physiological differences exist, but do not produce differences in performance, consider the rates of

speed of automobiles on crowded metropolitan streets. The vehicles differ in horsepower, and in observed speeds, but the speeds may depend entirely on factors other than the horsepower—openness of the way ahead, urgency of the trip, nerves of the driver, and disposition of back-seat passengers." See Robert E. L. Faris, "The Ability Dimension in Human Society," *American Sociological Review*, vol. 26 (December 1961), p. 838, n. 7.

Faris later admits, however, that if the way ahead were open, if the trip were urgent, and if the driver and backseat passengers were similarly disposed, then the variability of the automobiles' horsepower has to be taken into account. Now in respect to the relationship between *genetic* horsepower and *human* performance, it does, in fact, appear that the structure of opportunities or "the way ahead" is becoming increasingly open, that achieving maximum performance is a goal which is being pursued with considerable urgency, and that the dispositions of everyone in the contest, although occasionally irregular, do not differ markedly in the sense that most want to "get ahead." If generally true, then it would also appear that the observed variability in performance has become increasingly dependent upon individual differences in the mental capacities that unavoidably handicap the slow learners and, just as unavoidably, favor the really fast ones.

7    *Ibid.*, p. 838. This optimism is as groundless as that of J. B. Watson, in the 1920's the leader of the school of behaviorism in psychology. K. B. Clark more recently has argued, too, that IQ scores indicate almost nothing about the ceiling of what an individual can learn but rather the rate of learning and the amount of effort that learning will require; see Kenneth B. Clark, "Educational Stimulation of Racially Disadvantaged Children," in A. Harry Passow (ed.), *Education in Depressed Areas*, New York: Columbia University Press, 1963.

For the bulk of the formal subject matter in most elementary and secondary schools, Clark perhaps is right. His remarks, however, were made primarily in reference to group differences in IQ by race, and it is uncertain that he would carry this argument to the point of suggesting that with unlimited time and effort almost anyone can learn anything. Even if this were true, the rate of learning itself is a variable probably just as significant to the issues set forth in this paper as any inter-individual differences in the limits of learning. Just as the value of a computer depends largely upon the speed at which it can function, so too it would seem that human performance is closely associated with the rate of learning. In strictly economic terms, moreover, since the productive years of the life of any individual are biologi-

cally limited, there is far more return on the educational investment if it takes (only) 30 years, rather than 35, 40, or more, to train a scientist to perform at a minimum level of proficiency. Besides, limiting performance to any particular set of standards is hardly consistent with the rising and continuously changing demands of a modern technology.

8    While insisting that intelligence is neither fixed nor predetermined by heredity (with which we agree), after Hunt's very comprehensive review of the evidence he nevertheless insists that the genes prescribe basic directions in intellectual growth and set irrevocable limits on the range of capacities that can be developed (with which we also agree); see J. McVicker Hunt, *Intelligence and Experience*, New York: Ronald Press, 1961.

9    P. E. Vernon, *Intelligence and Attainment Tests*, London: University of London Press, 1960, p. 138. *Cf.* Sorokin, *op. cit.*, p. 330, nearly thirty-five years earlier; and John W. Gardner, *Excellence*, New York: Harper & Row, Publishers, 1961, p. 56.

10   Theodosius Dobzhansky, *Mankind Evolving*, New Haven, Conn.: Yale University Press, 1962, p. 86.

11   Occasionally, quite striking improvements or rises on IQ tests have been noted when retarded children or others whose background has been extremely adverse are placed in an "enriched" environment. Usually, however, the results are rather small, especially for any substantial batch of cases. Moreover, changes in test results under controlled conditions do not substantially reduce the variability of test performance, but only tend to move the entire range of scores upward. Obviously, these changes demonstrate that the environment is an important determinant; they do not, however, demonstrate that it is the only or necessarily even the most important determinant. Even Bloom, who in many ways is a leading proponent of the environmentalist view, after a careful review of the relevant materials, regarded (only) 20 IQ points as a fair estimate of any long-term effects that extreme environments might have on intellectual growth (although occasionally some of the "observed" changes exceed this figure). See Benjamin S. Bloom, *Stability and Change in Human Characteristics*, New York: John Wiley & Sons, Inc., 1964, p. 71.

12   David Krech and Richard S. Crutchfield, *Elements of Psychology*, New York: Alfred A. Knopf, Inc., 1958, p. 576.

13   The theoretical additive parent-offspring and sib-sib correlations actually are 0.5 plus the quotient of the assortative mating coefficient divided by 2, and not 0.5 as commonly reported in the literature. See R. Stanton, "Filial and Fraternal Correlations in Successive Generations," *Annals of Eugenics*, vol. 13

(1946), pp. 18–24. I wish to thank zoologist Carl Jay Bajema for drawing my attention to this point.

14    Although preschool-age IQ tests are notably unreliable, later correlations normally are quite stable over time. One twenty-five year longitudinal study of 111 individuals obtained the following correlations between test and re-test: preschool and adolescence (a ten-year span), 0.65; preschool and adulthood (a twenty-five year span), 0.59; and adolescence and adulthood (a fifteen-year span), 0.85, which again is nearly as high as the reliability of these tests. See Katherine P. Bradway and Clare W. Thompson, "Intelligence at Adulthood: A Twenty-five Year Follow-up," *Journal of Educational Psychology*, vol. 53 (February 1962), pp. 1–14.

15    The three statistics reported above are based on Erlenmeyer-Kimling and Jarvik's comprehensive review of this literature, covering over 50 studies and, in total, yielding over 30,000 correlational pairings. See L. Erlenmeyer-Kimling and Lissy F. Jarvik, "Genetics and Intelligence: A Review," *Science*, vol. 142 (Dec. 13, 1963), pp. 1477–1479.

16    Dobzhansky, *op. cit.*, p. 322.

17    Irving I. Gottesman, "Bio-genetic Perspectives," Duetch and Jenson, *Race, Class, and Psychological Development*, New York: Holt, Rinehart and Winston, in press. Environment is taken here not only to refer to the social milieu but to a host of prenatal or molecular factors between the embryonic cells. See C. H. Waddington, *The Strategy of Genes*, New York: The Macmillan Company, 1957; and W. W. Meissner, "Functional and Adaptive Aspects of Cellular Regulatory Mechanisms," *Psychological Bulletin*, vol. 64 (September 1965), pp. 206–216.

18    Writers do not agree about the nature of the genotypes involved in intelligence. For example, Hayes provides a cogent argument that the hereditary basis of intelligence consists of motivational drives, rather than any specific or general abilities, as such. See Keith J. Hayes, "Genes, Drives, and Intellect," *Psychological Reports*, vol. 10 (April 1962), pp. 299–342. While I have not done so elsewhere, I will intentionally avoid, where possible, any specific discussion of motivation or values in this paper which, in contrast to Meissner's view, may be treated simply as part of the environment or social milieu. See Bruce K. Eckland, "Social Class and College Graduation: Some Misconceptions Corrected," *American Journal of Sociology*, vol. 70 (July 1964), pp. 36–50, and "College Dropouts Who Came Back," *Harvard Educational Review*, vol. 34 (summer 1964), pp. 402–420.

19    Identical or "monozygotic" twins are produced from the division of a single fertilized egg, while fraternal or "dizygotic" twins arise from the fertilization of two separate ova. The latter are no more genetically alike than ordinary siblings. Thus, the chances are about even, for example, that fraternal twins will be of the same or opposite sex, whereas identical twins are always of the same sex. Most, although not all, identical twins can be diagnosed on the basis of appearance. In fact, recent cross-validation studies (against the more precise method of blood typing) have found that this approach is about 93 percent accurate. See Robert C. Nichols, "The National Merit Twin Study," in Steven Vanderberg (ed.), *Methods and Goals in Human Behavior Genetics*, New York: Academic Press, 1965. The point is noteworthy, since one of the most frequent criticisms of the early twin studies was the questionable validity of similarity of appearance as a method for diagnosing zygosity.

20    T. Husen, *Psychological Twin Research*, vol. 1, Stockholm: Almqvist and Wiksell, 1959.

21    Nichols, *op. cit.*

22    Marie Skodak and Harold M. Skeels, "A Final Follow-up Study of One Hundred Adopted Children," *Journal of Genetic Psychology*, vol. 75 (September 1949), pp. 85–125. Again, the evidence is subject to criticism, but mainly in terms of interpreting the relative strength of the genetic component, not its presence. For critical reviews, see R. S. Woodworth, "Heredity and Environment: A Critical Survey of Recently Published Material on Twins and Foster Children," *Social Science Research Council Bulletin 47*, 1941; and Anastasi, *op. cit.*

23    An introduction to the complexities of these questions can be found in the writings of the behavior geneticists, such as J. Fuller and W. Thompson, *Behavior Genetics*, New York: John Wiley & Sons, Inc., 1960; Irving I. Gottesman, "Genetic Aspects of Intellectual Behavior," in Norman Ellis (ed.), *Handbook of Mental Deficiency: Psychological Theory and Research*, New York: McGraw-Hill Book Co., 1963, pp. 253–296; J. Hirsch, "Individual Differences in Behavior and Their Genetic Basis," in E. Bliss (ed.), *Roots of Behavior*, New York: Harper & Row Publishers, 1962, pp. 3–23; and G. E. McClearn, "Genetics and Behavior Development," in M. L. and Lois W. Hoffman, (eds.), *Review of Child Development Research*, vol. 1, New York: Russell Sage Foundation, 1964, pp. 433–480.

24    Gottesman, *op. cit.*

25    Clifford Gertz, "The Growth of Culture and the Evolution of Mind," in Jordon M. Scher (ed.), *Theories of the Mind*, New York: The Free Press, 1962, pp. 713–740.

26    For a recent and sensitive discussion by a zoologist on the convergence of organic and cultural evolution in the foundation of human societies, see Alfred E.

Emerson, "Human Cultural Evolution and Its Relation to Organic Evolution of Insect Societies," University of Chicago, unpublished manuscript.

27  Michael Young, *The Rise of Meritocracy*, London: Thames and Hudson, 1958.

28  Goslin, *op. cit.*, p. 189.

29  For an extensive review of the literature on assortative mating, see J. N. Spuhler, "Empirical Studies on Quantitative Human Genetics," in *The Use of Vital and Health Statistics for Genetics and Radiation Studies*, United Nations and World Health Organization, 1962, pp. 241–252. Although Burt's interpretation of his own data is subject to criticism, he is, no doubt, one of the leading proponents of the idea that class differences in intelligence are largely due to genetic variation. See Cyril Burt, "Class Differences in General Intelligence: III," *British Journal of Statistical Psychology*, vol. 12 (May 1959), pp. 15–33; and Cyril Burt, "Intelligence and Social Mobility," *British Journal of Statistical Psychology*, vol. 14 (May 1961), pp. 3–24. Also see Bernard Berelson and Gary A. Steiner, *Human Behavior: An Inventory of Scientific Findings*, New York: Harcourt, Brace & Company, 1964, p. 309. For general reviews on the relationship between social class and intelligence, see John B. Miner, *Intelligence in the United States*, New York: Springer, 1957; B. G. Stacey, "Some Psychological Aspects of Inter-generation Occupational Mobility," *British Journal of Social and Clinical Psychology*, vol. 4 (December 1965), pp. 275–286; and Fuller, *op. cit.*

30  I base this proposition largely on the fact, too, that the education of two spouses accounts for far more of the variance in mate selection (and has for at least 30 or 40 years) than any other known factor. See Bruce L. Warren, "Multiple Variable Approach to the Assortative Mating Phenomenon," *Eugenics Quarterly*, in press.

31  Dobzhansky, *op. cit.*, p. 244.

32  While dealing with these materials only in an introductory fashion here, more complete coverage can be found in Anne Anastasi, "Intelligence and Family Size," *Psychological Bulletin*, vol. 53 (May 1956), pp. 187–209; Anne Anastasi, "Differentiating Effect of Intelligence and Social Status," *Eugenics Quarterly*, vol. 6 (June 1959), pp. 84–91; Cyril Burt, *Intelligence and Fertility: The Effect of the Differential Birth Rate on Inborn Mental Characteristics*, London: The Eugenics Society and Cassell, 1952; and J. N. Spuhler, "The Scope for Natural Selection in Man," in W. J. Schull (ed.), *Genetic Selection in Man*, Ann Arbor, Mich.: University of Michigan, 1963, pp. 1–111.

33  See Frank W. Notestein, "Class Differences in Fertility," *Annals of the American Academy of Political and Social Science* (November 1936), pp. 1–11, for a review of this subject.

34  The data no longer suggest today that the upper classes are not reproducing themselves.

35  The correlations cluster around −0.3; see Anastasi, *op. cit.* It should be noted, too, that the correlations persist when occupational class is controlled.

36  For references, see Gottesman, *op. cit.*, and Vernon, *op. cit.*

37  Scottish Council for Research in Education, *The Trend of Scottish Intelligence*, London: University of London Press, 1949.

38  Raymond B. Cattell, "The Fate of National Intelligence: Test of a Thirteen-year Prediction," *Eugenics Review*, vol. 42 (October 1950), pp. 136–148; and W. G. Emmett, "The Trend of Intelligence in Certain Districts of England," *Population Studies*, vol. 3 (March 1950), pp. 324–337.

39  Betty M. Giles-Bernardelli, "The Decline of Intelligence in New Zealand," *Population Studies*, vol. 4 (September 1950), pp. 200–208.

40  R. D. Tuddenham, "Soldier Intelligence in World Wars I and II," *American Psychologist*, vol. 3 (1948), pp. 54–56.

41  With limited data at hand, Penrose appears to be the first to have recognized the possibility that persons of extremely low intelligence, whom he found more likely to be infertile, could balance out the decline attributable to their larger numbers. See L. S. Penrose, "Genetical Influences on the Intelligence Level of the Population," *The British Journal of Psychology, General Section*, vol. 15 (March 1950), pp. 128-136.

42  The results actually indicate a slight bimodal or curvilinear relationship, wherein low fertility is associated with both low and high (but not average) intelligence. See J. Higgins, Elizabeth W. Reed, and S. C. Reed, "Intelligence and Family Size: A Paradox Resolved," *Eugenics Quarterly*, vol. 9 (June 1962), pp. 84–90; and Carl Jay Bajema, "Estimation of the Direction and Intensity of Natural Selection in Relation to Human Intelligence by Means of the Intrinsic Rate of Natural Increase," *Eugenics Quarterly*, vol. 10 (December 1963), pp. 175–187.

43  Otis Dudley Duncan, "Is the Intelligence of the General Population Declining?" *American Sociological Review*, vol. 17 (August 1952), pp. 401–407; and Hunt, *op. cit.*, pp. 337–343.

44  Or perhaps, much more simply, the solution for this problem is quite the same as for the original paradox. That is, just as the low fertility of adults of very low intelligence was obscured in earlier studies, the low fertility of very low socioeconomic (including institutionalized) adults may have been obscured in studies purporting to demonstrate the relationship between fertility and social class.

45 There is evidence, for example, of a negative correlation between upward intergenerational mobility and family size. See Dudley Kirk, "The Fertility of a Gifted Group: A Study of the Number of Children of Men in *Who's Who*," in Proceedings of the 1956 Annual Conference of the Milbank Memorial Fund, *The Nature and Transmission of the Genetic and Cultural Characteristics of Human Populations*, Milbank Memorial Fund, 1957, pp. 78–98; and especially Richard F. Tomasson, "Social Mobility and Family Size in Two High-status Populations," *Eugenics Quarterly*, vol. 13 (June 1966), pp. 113–121. Also, there is evidence that the negative association of fertility with general socioeconomic status masks its positive association with income, so that when other background characteristics like education (and we might venture to substitute intelligence here) are controlled, income appears to enhance fertility. See Deborah S. Freedman, "The Relation of Economic Status to Fertility," *American Economic Review*, vol. 53 (June 1963), pp. 414–426; and Otis Dudley Duncan, "Marital Fertility as a Career Contingency," April 12, 1966, unpublished manuscript.

46 There is no contradiction here between the "regression toward the mean" and the principles of "evolution." For instance, students frequently ask how the giraffe's long neck could have evolved to its present length if the offspring of exceptionally long-necked adults were shorter on the average than their parents. The answer is simple: the regression is toward the mean of the *total* adult population of the *parent's* generation. If, owing to some selection process, the exceptionally long-necked giraffes were more fertile than others in a particular generation, a new mean would be established for the offspring. Although the necks of the offspring of the long-necked adults would tend to be somewhat shorter than those of their parents, the new mean would nevertheless be higher than the old mean of the previous generation. Also, the necks of some offspring would probably exceed the longest of any adults in the previous generation. Evolution is slow, but certain. Furthermore, there is no reason to believe that the genotypes associated with intelligence do not operate in precisely the same manner.

47 It is possible that part of the regression toward the parental mean, in terms of the phenotypic range of intelligence, is also due to environmental variation, but only to the extent that the trait-relevant environments are not positively related to the genotypes associated with higher intelligence.

48 Certainly it may be hard to convince any intelligent middle-class parent that the chances are that the "native" intelligence of any one of his children probably is less than his own and perhaps not much better than average. The parent, however, is hardly in any position to judge.

49 Barrington Moore, Jr., *Political Power and Social Theory*, Cambridge, Mass.: Harvard University Press, 1958, p. 163. Also, note one of Lipset and Bendix' concluding remarks: "There can be no doubt . . . that the discrepancy between the distribution of intelligence in a given generation of youth and the distribution of social positions in the parental generation is a major dynamic factor affecting mobility in all societies in which educational achievement or other qualities associated with intelligence play an important role in status placement." See Seymour Martin Lipset and Reinhard Bendix, *Social Mobility in Industrial Society*, Berkeley, Calif.: University of California Press, 1959, p. 236.

The statement, of course, would be more applicable to my argument if we were to substitute the term "intelligence" for "social position" in their phrase "the distribution of social position in the parental generation." To the extent that "qualities associated with intelligence play an important role in status placement," the substitution does not appear inappropriate.

50 Readers may recognize the obvious linkages here to the large body of literature on deviant behavior that has developed from Merton's "means-ends" paradigm. However, no research, to my knowledge, has attempted to explain either lower- or middle-class delinquency in terms of Merton's model by taking into account the discrepancies between the parents' and child's intelligence, or even between the parents' status and the child's intelligence. Are not these discrepancies probably just as much a part of the "structure of opportunities" as those that are culturally prescribed? John A. Clausen has raised a similar question in a recent (1966) unpublished manuscript "The Organism and Socialization."

51 James Bryant Conant, *Slums and Suburbs*, New York: McGraw-Hill Book Co., 1961, p. 144.

52 David Goslin, Roberta R. Epstein, and Barbara A. Hallock, *The Use of Standardized Tests in Elementary Schools*, New York: Russell Sage Foundation, 1965; Orville G. Brim, Jr., David A. Goslin, David C. Glass, and Isadore Goldberg, *The Use of Standardized Ability Tests in American Secondary Schools and Their Impact on Students, Teachers, and Administrators*, New York: Russell Sage Foundation, 1965; and Orville G. Brim, John Neulinger, and David C. Glass, *Experience and Attitudes of American Adults Concerning Standardized Intelligence Tests*, New York: Russell Sage Foundation, 1965.

53 Clearly one of the largest and most comprehensive (and costly) surveys ever undertaken in this country,

I nevertheless have found few sociologists who are any more than vaguely familiar with Project Talent. Baseline data were gathered in 1960 when a two-day battery of psychometric tests and biographical questionnaires were administered to nearly one-half million 9th through 12th grade students in roughly 1,000 public and private high schools. Adding to these auspicious beginnings, long-range plans call for a series of follow-ups one, five, ten, and 25 years after each class graduates. It is, indeed, unfortunate that sociologists have not been more aware of this "data bank" and its potential applications. Among the several monographs published to date, segments of the above findings were reported in John C. Flanagan, John T. Dailey, Marion F. Shaycoft, David B. Orr, and Isadore Goldberg, *Studies of the American High School*, Pittsburgh: University of Pittsburgh Project Talent Office, 1962.

54   Owing to their similarity in content, some schools, no doubt, use the PSAT, too, as a "practice" test for the SAT (the most widely used of the college admissions tests) which generally is administered the following year.

55   Inadvertently, the National Merit examinations also are being used as a basis for ranking both the high schools and the colleges. On the one hand, the absolute number of "finalists" has become a mark of considerable prestige among the secondary schools. (Sociologists and others should be warned, however, that the "prestige" accorded any school on the basis of these awards is not relative to any set of national norms, but relative only to other schools in the same state. The reason is that different cutting points on the National Merit examination are established for each state in order that equal proportions of their enrollments are eligible for the awards.) In regard to ranking the colleges, the attempts of most researchers have been frustrated either because different colleges use tests which are not always comparable (even though the College Board's SAT holds a pre-eminent position) or because published scores are not available. In lieu of these problems, Astin recently devised a "selectivity" scale for nearly all colleges in the country on the basis of the "choices" indicated by the National Merit semi-finalists and recipients of its Letter of Commendation in 1961. (The "choices" are regularly obtained since the size of the stipends they award are based, in part, on tuition fees.) An influential work, particularly among the pre-college guidance counselors, is Alexander W. Astin's *Who Goes Where to College?*, Chicago: Science Research Associates, 1965.

56   In regard to the National Merit examination, see the *Annual Report*, Evanston, Ill.: National Merit Scholarship Corporation, 1965. Of special interest to sociologists should be the fact that NMSC has been obtaining socioeconomic data along with the administration of its tests. As these data continue to accumulate in the years ahead, we should have a rather good historical record of the interrelationships between ability, social class, and college choice.

57   For example, whereas in 1955–56 only 1,229 students who entered 130 colleges from 104 secondary schools took the Advanced Placement examinations, the respective figures for the year 1963–64 were 28,874 students entering 885 colleges from 2,086 secondary schools. See *College Decisions on Advanced Placement* (a CEEB Research and Development Report), Princeton, N.J.: Educational Testing Service, January 1966. Associated with the growth of both the APP and the NMSC, the number of honors programs in American colleges tripled between 1957 and 1965. Moreover, it generally is recognized that the basic fundamental of honors work is an insistence that each student fulfills his potential; see Joseph W. Cohen (ed.), *The Superior Student in American Higher Education*, New York: McGraw-Hill Book Co., 1966.

58   I have only touched on some of the highlights in the development of educational testing. Furthermore, I have neglected almost entirely any consideration of the use of standardized tests in business, government, and the military service. For a more complete overview of ability testing today, see Goslin, *The Search . . ., op. cit.*

59   It is doubtful that the controversy related to "invasion of privacy" that came to a climax in the 1965 congressional investigations will, in the long run, stem the tide. Nor is it likely that the more recent threats of legislative intervention, even if they materialize, will significantly restrict the actual administration of tests or other instruments in our schools. For a thorough review of testing and public policy, see the November 1965 issue of the *American Psychologist*, vol. 20.

60   It is difficult to generalize about the privately endowed schools, some of which flourish (expand) in response to the demand for higher education, while others hold their size and simply become more selective. Most of the state-supported schools, on the other hand, appear to respond in very much the same two ways, both of which require these schools to employ some device, like testing, to decide who should go to college and where.

One factor is that before a state-supported school can expand its faculties or facilities it must provide the state legislature with appropriate evidence that its requests are warranted. Since "projected" enrollment figures probably are not too convincing, the only acceptable evidence seems to be the number of "qualified" students who had to be "turned away last year." There is, therefore, a constant lag between demand and supply which requires the colleges and universities to make an "acceptable" choice between who should and who should not be admitted.

The second factor involves the differentiation in purpose and function of different colleges within the same system. As increasingly larger segments of the college-age population look for some form of post-secondary education, the major institutions of higher learning seek to protect their standards in new ways. At one time, it was acceptable to admit anyone and then simply "weed out" the poorer students during the freshman year. However, the method probably was devastating to both the students and the faculty. Nevertheless, as enrollment pressures have mounted, the practice could not survive without making administrative "monsters" out of the schools whose immense size already creates far too many problems. As a result, we are witnessing the proliferation of the junior and community colleges and the remarkable transformation of the teacher's colleges and "cow" colleges into liberal arts schools, accompanied by the establishment of formal criteria, including testing, to decide who goes where.

61 I have in mind here something in addition to the more traditional separation of the "academic" and "vocational" schools. In a number of large public school systems around the country, entire units have been set aside in recent years not just as preparatory schools for the college aspirants but specifically for the "gifted" students. For example, the student bodies at Bronx High and Hunter High in New York City, as a whole, rank in the 99th percentile on standardized tests. See Cohen, op. cit., p. 226. (Roughly three-fourths of them, too, win recognition on the National Merit examinations.)

62 To a limited extent, selection into the private sector occurs across all socioeconomic classes. For example, highly selective independent schools like Exeter and Andover "sponsor" a "fair" number of students from lower socioeconomic backgrounds. (The author, along with Richard E. Peterson at Educational Testing Service, is currently involved in a study of all living alumni from the "Exeter community.")

63 In addition to the eventual determination of college plans, formal evaluation takes place early in order to identify both children with very exceptional abilities and those who, owing to their deficiencies, require special attention. See David A. Goslin, The School in Contemporary Society, Chicago: Scott, Foresman and Company, 1965, p. 110.

64 Vernon, op. cit., p. 143. It should not be surprising that, in a physiological sense, the brain centers asso-

ciated with intelligence are slow to mature. This seems to be characteristic of the human child as a whole. With a few exceptions, like the sucking reflex, the human infant enters the world exceedingly ill-equipped, for some time, to deal with his environment. See Weston LaBarre, The Human Animal, Chicago: The University of Chicago Press, 1960.

65 These forces also appear to explain what kinds of tests are administered and when. Whereas IQ tests generally are used as screening devices in the early primary grades when specific kinds of learnings or experiences are perhaps somewhat less likely to invalidate the tests, aptitude and achievement tests are more often used later when little or no pretense is required concerning what the tests actually measure. Psychometricians freely admit that achievement tests are bound to specific kinds of subject matter, since this is the purpose for which they are designed. Most, however, are much less willing to admit that their aptitude tests are "subject-bound."

66 Burton R. Clark, The Open Door College, New York: McGraw-Hill Book Co., 1960. In addition to the "cooling-out" function that Clark so aptly describes, another "compensatory factor" involves the repeated use of standardized tests of various forms and at various points in the educational process. For example, some observers believe that the PSAT (see note 53) which usually is administered during the eleventh grade and just a year before the college entrance examinations is an unnecessary proliferation of tests. They argue that the accumulated scores from other tests administered throughout the primary and earlier secondary grades are sufficient both to predict how well most students will do on the entrance examinations and to "narrow down" the choice of a college. Certainly, for predicting how any "group" of students will do, these observers probably are correct. On the other hand, multiple testing nevertheless makes it possible to detect and take into account the uneven inter-individual patterns of intellectual growth (plus changes in motivation and error terms) that undoubtedly affect every student's test performance.

67 Ralph H. Turner, "Sponsored and Contest Mobility in the School System," American Sociological Review, vol. 25 (December 1960), pp. 855–867. While Turner suggested that the United States has been moving toward a system of sponsorship, the proliferation of testing in this country really was just beginning when he wrote this article.

68 In my judgment, the best complete text on the sociology of education that has appeared so far, Corwin's discussion of the "talent hunt" nevertheless strongly reflects the biases of the environmentalists. See Ronald G. Corwin, A Sociology of Education,

New York: Appleton-Century-Crofts, Inc., 1965, especially pp. 191–207.

69  Brian Jackson, *Streaming: An Education System in Miniature*, London: Routledge & Kegan Paul, 1964.

70  Not only is our own "field of vision" restricted by pre-college attrition and selection, it is largely limited to the relatively narrow range of aptitudes that characterizes the student body at any particular college or university. Owing to increased diversity and selectivity in higher education, the inter-institutional differences in intelligence (or scholastic aptitude) are usually about as great as, and often greater than, the intra-institutional differences. See, for example, T. R. McConnell and Paul Heist, "The Diverse College Student Population," in Nevitt Sanford (ed.), *The American College*, New York: John Wiley & Sons, Inc., 1962, pp. 225–252.

71  For example, see David Glass, *Social Mobility in Britain*, London: Routledge & Kegan Paul, 1954; Natalie Rogoff, *Recent Trends in Occupational Mobility*, New York: The Free Press, 1953; Gosta Carlsson, *Social Mobility and Class Structure*, Lund: C.W.K. Gleerup, 1958; and W. Lloyd Warner, *et al.*, *The American Federal Executive*, New Haven, Conn.: Yale University Press, 1963.

72  In a quite different context, Rogoff discusses this problem with reference to predicting the rate of college-going among persons of different ability and different class origins. See Natalie Rogoff, "American Public Schools and Equality of Opportunity," in A. H. Halsey, Jean Floud, and C. Arnold Anderson (eds.), *Education, Economy, and Society*, New York: The Free Press, 1961, pp. 140–147.

73  A. H. Halsey, "Genetics, Social Structure and Intelligence," *The British Journal of Sociology*, vol. 9 (1958), pp. 15–28; and J. L. Gray and P. Moshinski, *The Nation's Intelligence*, Watts, 1936.

74  Both Burt and Anderson have used models that estimate the difference between the expected and observed frequencies of mobility on the basis of class differentials in the distribution of intelligence. In Anderson's model, for example, "ideal" mobility is defined as the perfect correspondence between intelligence and occupation whereby the degree of departure from the "ideal" is taken essentially as an index of inequality. While this model avoids the trappings I described above, it has the objectionable weakness of making no allowance for culturally-induced variations in measured intelligence. Anderson recognizes this objection and freely admits that the model is simply based on the "efficiency" goal of economic theory. Burt, on the other hand, is much less sensitive to the problem. See Cyril Burt, *op. cit.*; and C. Arnold Anderson, James C. Brown, and Mary Jean Bowman, "Intelligence and Occupational Mobility,"

*Journal of Political Economy*, vol. 60 (June 1952), pp. 218–239.

75  For an excellent discussion of the kinds of "discriminatory imparities" I have in mind, and with which we *should* be concerned, see C. Arnold Anderson and Philip J. Foster, "Discrimination and Inequality in Education," *Sociology of Education*, vol. 38 (fall 1964), pp. 1–18.

76  W. Boyd, *Genetics and the Races of Man*, Boston: Little, Brown, and Company, 1950. In terms of this definition, note that as breeding populations races and social classes do not differ, nor should they.

77  In small breeding populations, as certainly must have typified the early evolution of man, "chance" fluctuations in the genetic character of the populations can easily become stabilized over a "relatively" few generations of inbreeding and then without having to be "adaptive" to the environment, gradually "drift" through outbreeding with contiguous populations. See LaBarre, *op. cit.*, and Dobzhansky, *op. cit.*, especially pp. 279–283. Each trait has then its own geographic center of origin, or quite probably several such centers. The pattern of drift, like Burgess's cities, tends to conform to concentric circles, occasionally broken by natural or social barriers and with lower gene frequencies in the outer rings.

78  S. L. Washburn, "The Study of Race," *American Anthropologist*, vol. 65 (June 1963), pp. 521–531; Paul R. Ehrlich and Richard W. Holm, "A Biological View of Race," in Ashley Montague (ed.), *The Concept of Race*, New York: The Free Press, 1964, pp. 153–179; and Jean Robert Laurent Hiernaux, "The Concept of Race and the Taxonomy of Mankind," in Montague, *op. cit.*, pp. 29–45.

79  Some writers, such as Cattell, believe they have come close to one, however. In Cattell's case, a "culture-fair" test has been developed that purportedly measures an individual's ability to adapt to new situations and in which his "crystallized" (learned) skills are of no particular advantage. In comparison with other measures of intelligence, he maintains that this test has about twice the normal standard deviation, is more stable with changes in age or culture, and, therefore, is more biologically determined. See Raymond B. Cattell, "Theory of Fluid and Crystallized Intelligence," *Journal of Educational Psychology*, vol. 54 (February 1963), pp. 1–22. My own belief is that the most significant advances in this regard are not likely to be made by psychometricians. The idea of a completely "culture-fair" test is, as others have suggested, probably absurd. Rather, any new breakthroughs are likely to be the work of biochemists. Since the chemical structure of the genetic "alphabet" has been discovered, one can only agree with Dobzhansky that "the day may not be too far away

when the sequences of the genetic 'letters' in the various genes in man and in other organisms may become known." See Theodosius Dobzhansky, *Heredity and the Nature of Man*, New York: Harcourt, Brace & Co., 1964, p. 37.

80  Aaron V. Cicourel and John I. Kitsuse; *The Educational Decision-makers*, New York: Bobbs-Merrill Company, Inc., 1963. Nearly as extraordinary as the recent growth in educational testing has been the establishment of formal guidance programs. It is estimated that nearly 90 percent of the nation's high schools have trained guidance counselors today, as against about 36 percent in 1955. See Project Talent, *op. cit.*, chap. 3, p. 38.

81  In addition to his work previously noted, see David A. Goslin, "The Social Consequences of Predictive Testing in Education" (1965), and "The Social Impact of Testing in Guidance" (1966), both unpublished manuscripts.

82  William H. Sewell and J. Michael Armer, "Neighborhood Context and College Plans," *American Sociological Review*, vol. 31 (April 1966), pp. 159–168; and commentaries by Ralph Turner, Richard Boyle, John Michael, William Sewell, and J. Michael Armer, *American Sociological Review*, vol. 31 (October 1966), pp. 698–707. In Sewell's defense, I wish to note that the evidence from several longitudinal studies clearly indicates that during adolescence the intra-individual (test-retest) correlations on IQ across this age range are very stable under normal conditions, i.e., about as high as the reliabilities of the tests employed. Moreover, the small *gains* that can be isolated from one point in time to another appear to be correlated with the earlier level of ability, despite either Benjamin Bloom's (*op. cit.*) or Robert Thorndike's ["Intellectual Status and Intellectual Growth," *Journal of Educational Psychology*, vol. 57 (June 1966), pp. 121–127] pessimism.

The best evidence is yet unpublished but comes from the "Growth Study" at Educational Testing Service. In a closely administered eight-year program involving the repeated use of the same or equated tests in 23 schools, early results indicate that the children who show rapid intellectual growth over one period of time tend to be the same children who had a prior history of rapid growth. If this is the case, there perhaps is less room for "neighborhood context" than previously thought, especially after socioeconomic (family) status has been partialed out. Nevertheless, the possibility still exists that a *small* part of the association between intelligence and neighborhood can be attributed to the effect of the latter on the former, and, to this extent, Sewell and Armer probably should have been more cautious.

83  Otis Dudley Duncan, "Intelligence and Achievement: Preliminary Results," April 22, 1966, and "Intelligence and Achievement: Further Calculations," July 20, 1966, both unpublished manuscripts. Duncan's data tentatively suggest that while intelligence has a significant effect on occupation apart from its correlation with family background, all or nearly all of its effects operate within the context of the school system and therefore do not add to the "explained" variance in occupation that can be accounted for by family background and education alone.

84  Bernard Farber, "Social Class and Intelligence," *Social Forces*, vol. 44 (December 1965), pp. 215–225.

85  Ralph Linton, *The Study of Man*, New York: Appleton-Century-Crofts, Inc., 1936.

86  For example, see David Matza, *Delinquency and Drift*, New York: John Wiley & Sons, Inc., 1964.

## 22   GHETTO EDUCATION   JOSEPH ALSOP

It is time to stop talking nonsense about Negro education. It is time to start dealing with the hard, cruel facts of the problem of the ghetto schools, which is in turn the very core of the race problem in the United States. Above all it is time to cease

Reprinted with the permission of the author and the publisher from *The New Republic*, vol. 157 (July 22, 1967), pp. 18–23. Copyright ©1967 by Harrison-Blaine of New Jersey, Inc.

repeating, "End *de facto* segregation!" as though this virtuous incantation were a magical spell. For school desegregation must always be a central and essential goal; but sad experience has proved that desegregation is very far from being an instant remedy.

For any practical-minded man, who holds that putting an end to racial injustice is the highest and most urgent task of this country at this time, the foregoing are the only possible comments on Judge James Skelly Wright's much-publicized decision concerning the District of Columbia's schools. The school system of the capital is sordid and shameful, and Judge Wright's moral indignation is only too well founded, as *The New Republic's* Alexander M. Bickel pointed out in these pages two weeks ago. Yet this decision can even be described as wicked; for it is always wicked to hold out false hopes and offer fake panaceas to those in desperate need of hope and help. And that, in essence, is precisely what Judge Wright's decision has done to the people of Washington—a city which has gradually become no more than a gigantic Negro ghetto thinly concealed behind a pompous white federal facade.

In justice to Judge Wright, it must be said at once that his evident good intentions were by no means the only good features of his decision. His condemnation of the discriminatory "track system" was fully justified. His comparison between the District's school expenditure—near to the lowest per pupil of any big city in this country—and the District's police expenditure—the nation's highest *per capita*—was both pointed and valuable. It was useful to emphasize, too, that per-pupil outlays in the District's few remaining white and quasi-white schools exceed the outlays in the deep ghetto schools by over a third. But it must be noted also, in this connection, that Judge Wright was here unknowingly putting his finger on one of the greatest deficiences in the extremely deficient Coleman report (which seems to have influenced him greatly). For the Coleman report, as Samuel Bowles and Henry M. Levin have noted in an important paper, never tested its conclusions about "equal" education by exploring the widespread existence of differential, per pupil outlays *within* school districts, as here in Washington.

But all this sinks into insignificance, as compared with the main thrust of Judge Wright's decision, which was to put forward more desegregation as the solution for the ghetto school problem in Washington, and presumably, as the solution in all the other American big cities where the same problem is festering and growing more inflamed with

every passing year. In Washington, to begin with, serious school desegregation is such an obvious impossibility that it is plain silly to talk about it. Officially, any school that is more than half Negro is defined as segregated. But in the District of Columbia, the primary and elementary schools are 93 percent Negro, and even the high schools are pushing up toward 90 percent. Therefore, total, forcible homogenization of the entire school system would still leave Washington with overwhelmingly segregated schools. Indeed, this kind of forcible homogenization would quite certainly result in even greater segregation; for the predictable consequence would be an increase in the Negro percentage in the primary and elementary schools from 93 percent to 98 or 99 percent.

*Unprepared* desegregation in a grossly underfinanced school system has in fact been one of the two main causes of this city's transformation into an urban super-ghetto—a kind of near-Watts on a metropolitan scale. Since the war, every one of the great urban centers above the Mason-Dixon line has received countless thousands of Negro immigrants from the South. From this cause alone, Washington's Negro population has grown very greatly; but Negro immigration has been only one aspect of the two-sided demographic movement that has now produced a city two-thirds Negro and one-third white. The other aspect, equally important, has been white emigration to the affluent suburbs. And the crucial role of the schools in this white emigration can in turn be clearly seen, if you merely look at those who have fled and those who have stayed behind. Those who have stayed behind number close to 250,000; yet this white population of about a quarter of a million includes only 13,000 children of school age! Of the District's 13,000 white children of school age, furthermore, rather more than 5,000 attend parochial or other private schools. The conclusion is inescapable that Washington's remaining white population is almost exclusively composed of (1) old people, (2) single people, (3) couples without children of school age, and (4) couples who can afford to send their children to parochial or private schools or who live in the few neighborhoods where the schools are still mainly white. No such demographic result as that shown above could conceivably have been produced in the normal course of events. It means, beyond question, that just about every white couple outside the above-listed categories has moved to the suburbs, at least as soon as it came time to send the children to school.

The available statistics are grossly inadequate, but enough is known to show that precisely the same kind of two-sided demographic movement is tending to produce much the same sort of result in a good many other American urban centers. Washington, which has been treated as an exceptional case, is merely an *advanced* case. The best figures I have got thus far are for last year. Taking the percentages of Negro children in the primary and elementary schools as the gauge, one can then show how far six other major cities have traveled to date, along the road that has made the nation's capital into a concealed super-ghetto. Here is the picture:

Baltimore, schools 64 percent Negro, equals Washington in 1954–55.

Chicago, schools 56 percent Negro, equals Washington in 1952–53.

Cleveland, schools 53 percent Negro, equals Washington in 1951–52.

Detroit, schools 57 percent Negro, equals Washington in 1953–54.

Philadelphia, schools 60 percent Negro, nearly equals Washington in 1954–55.

St. Louis, schools 64 percent Negro, equals Washington in 1954–55.

Two fundamental problems are revealed by these figures. The first is what may be called the progressive ghettoization of a whole series of America's great urban conglomerations. In the fairly near future, this phenomenon can too easily produce social and economic consequences that hardly bear thinking about. Ghetto city centers, from which even commerce, banking and industry will have fled to the fatly affluent white suburbs, are not an attractive prospect, either for the wretched ghetto-denizens, or for anyone else. But this is not the problem to which I have been trying to address myself. I have been trying to show,

rather, that in almost all cases, the practical result of *unprepared* desegregation is *an enlarged ghetto with a greater number of segregated schools than there were in the first instance*. This has in truth been the experience in every major Northern city known to me. Furthermore, it has been the experience in a good many cases in which the ugly influence of racial prejudice can be effectively ruled out. In the first flush of civil rights enthusiasm, for example, the parents of a liberal-Jewish neighborhood in Brooklyn voted all but unanimously to pair their school with a nearby ghetto school. The New York Board of Education promised special support (which took the ludicrously inadequate form of a general patch-up of the school buildings). PS 7 and PS 8 were then merged, wholly on the motion of the white parents. But within a very short time, two segregated schools had come into being where there had been one before. The pairing caused school quality to go to Hell in a hack; and the white parents, seeing their children's education in jeopardy, either sent them to private schools or moved to the suburbs. And these were the very same parents, mind you, who had sponsored the pairing.

## WHEN THE BURDEN BECOMES TOO MUCH

This is only one item of evidence—there is a mass of it, for instance, in the supporting studies behind the Watts report—to show that school quality is a far more important factor than racial feeling, in this white flight from desegregated schools that has made such a mockery of the good intentions of people like Judge Wright. When a middle-class school receives a massive infusion of children of extremely deprived background—whether Puerto Rican, or Mexican-American, or Appalachian white, or Negro—there are only two possible results. Either the added burden of the disadvantaged, educationally retarded children becomes too much for the teaching staff, whereupon school quality promptly and shockingly deteriorates and middle-class emigration quickly begins. Or the local school authorities take all the special measures that are needed to maintain school quality, in which case—thus far an almost unheard-of case—there is an excellent chance that most of the emigration can be averted.

Nor is this the end of the grim story. If we are honest with ourselves, the overwhelming majority of the children of the ghettos are going to be educated exclusively in ghetto schools; and this is going to go on happening for many years to come, no matter how much poulticing and patching and court-ordering we may do. Free busing can and should be offered. Gerrymandered white school districts can and should be condemned (while due preparation is also made to maintain school quality). More integrated housing patterns can and should be promoted by every means possible. But these measures (strengthened, if you please, by every other measure you may happen to fancy) can never do more than fray the fringes of the ghetto school problem in cities with school populations 50 percent Negro and above. It is scandalous—it is indeed a bitter indictment of the large group in the American intellectual community that has concerned itself with the matter—that so few have been willing to face the distasteful, inescapable truth, which has been glaringly visible for years. The truth is that whatever else we may do, the problem of the ghetto schools must be mainly solved *inside the ghetto schools*, at any rate for a long time to come.

## THE UNIQUE NON-REMEDY

As an example of the scandal, consider the recent Civil Rights Commission report on "Racial Isolation in the Public Schools." It shows that America's schools are just about as segregated as they ever were, despite all the court orders that have been issued since 1954, and all the attempts, more or less sincere, to comply with those court orders. It says nothing of the white emigration that has played such a huge role in making a nonsense of the court orders. Using evidence chosen with suspicious selectivity (and misusing it gravely at that, if the Philadelphia data are any guide), the report further seeks to discredit school improvement inside the ghettos. By implication, it takes the

shocking though fashionable liberal educators' view once so bitterly but accurately summarized by Floyd McKissick in this journal's pages, that if you "put Negro with Negro, you get stupidity." And having established school desegregation as the unique remedy, the report finally proposes busing on a massive scale as the best means to secure desegregation. Yet the report is datelined Washington, where no amount of busing would make the school system anything but segregated—short of a constitutional amendment permitting forcible imposition of wholly different living and schooling patterns in the District, Maryland and Virginia. Are we then to conclude that more than 90,000 Negro schoolchildren in Washington are to be forever condemned to defeat and despair? Or are we to conclude that this report, like so many other very similar documents, is the product of the kind of self-serving reasoning that must too often be expected, alas, from virtuous academics with a personal vested interest in a badly researched theory?

The answer is, of course, that it is not only viciously heartless and socially disastrous, but also wholly needless, to accept the viewpoint of the Civil Rights Commission and Judge Wright. There is something arrogant, there is even something disgusting, in this strange view that ghetto children can never be rescued, can never be educated, unless they are subjected to the benign classroom influence of white middle-class children. Ghetto children have all the potential of any other children; but in their background of poverty and deprivation, they have a heavy handicap. What is needed, therefore, is to overcome the handicap, by those special measures I have already mentioned as useful and needful to prepare for school desegregation, wherever desegregation is feasible. This means taking a series of steps of the most ABC simplicity. First, the children's school experience must begin early, at least in pre-kindergarten. For the inability to speak common English, which afflicts so many children of the ghettos, can only be overcome by catching them very young. Second, they must be taught in small classes—not more than 15 in pre-kindergarten and kindergarten, and not more than 22 or so in grades one through six.

Otherwise, *teaching* will cease and keeping order will become the sole aim. For ghetto children mainly come from homes wholly unoriented to learning and to books. Gaining and holding their learning-attention (which is the right way to maintain sound discipline) is therefore the most difficult feat for every teacher in every ghetto school. And only reduced classes permit good, average teachers to accomplish this feat. Third, a certain number of backup teachers are needed—one extra for each three or four classes—so that when Billy and Sally, Victor and Jane begin to fall behind, these laggards can be promptly gathered into still smaller classes, for more concentrated work until they catch up again. Fourth, all the obvious extras in the way of remedial reading, health care, psychiatric care, etc., also have to be provided. These are, in fact, the principal features of the More Effective Schools program, that has been under way in New York City for three years. One wonders why this program was not chosen for study by the authors of the Civil Rights Commission's report. Perhaps the answer is that in the More Effective Schools, all children have shown a very great average improvement, and those children who have begun in pre-kindergarten and continued on from there are actually performing, on average, *at grade level or above*. If this program had been chosen for analysis, it would have sadly undermined the thesis of the authors of the Civil Rights Commission report; but it is nonetheless quite wonderful news, which should be published in Mao-style Big Character Posters in the corridors of every university where educational theorists flourish.

That it should be news at all, is a considerable showup of the ways of thinking and working and dealing with facts of all too many American white liberal intellectuals. In this instance, it goes without saying that properly prepared school desegregation is the ideal solution of the educational problem of America's Negro minority. It goes without saying, too, that wherever desegregation can be successfully accomplished, the moral and social duty to accomplish it must never be dodged or ducked, even if the needed preparations for successful desegregation are difficult, time-consuming

and costly. But a good many of our liberal intellectuals never appear to have heard the rule, *"Le mieux est l'ennemi du bien"*; it never appears to occur to them, in fact, that exclusive pursuit of the ideal solution can prevent the practical solution; and few of them seem to have bothered to do the tedious homework, on urban demographic patterns, for instance, that would have shown them how far the ideal solution is out of reach for most ghetto children at present. Their performance would be less unadmirable, I must add, if they had been content to urge their ideal solution, despite its unreality for all but a small minority of ghetto children. But they have not been content. A good many of the liberal educators and sociologists have done everything possible to discredit and to block the practical solution of the educational problem of our Negro minority, which is radical school improvement inside the ghetto. These people seem to have taken the attitude, in fact, that if they could not get desegregation, nothing else would do—and to hell with the millions of Negro children who have little hope of entering integrated schools!

## QUALITY ON THE CHEAP

This has been a main reason, one suspects, for the extraordinary belatedness and extreme paucity of the serious attempts to help these children, and for the almost universal failure to defend and support those attempts when they have been made. In New York in 1957, for instance, the Demonstration School Project produced excellent results at the high school level, at a cost of about $200 per pupil above the normal outlay. Whereupon the New York Board of Education, by an automatic reflex, tried to get the same results at about one-third the extra cost, in the Higher Horizons program, which was a flat bust. But did anyone protest the debasement of the Demonstration School Project into Higher Horizons? Almost no one did; and meanwhile a chorus of progressive educators has ever since been heard, proclaiming that Higher Horizons' wholly predictable failure was final proof of the uselessness of improved education in ghetto schools. In the same fashion, the More Effective

Schools program, which has an extra per-pupil cost of about $430 a year, is beginning to be nibbled to death by the economy-ducks on the Board of Education; but no one has sprung to its defense except this writer and, far more importantly, the United Federation of Teachers, whose leaders largely devised the program. And this program, launched in 1964–65, is literally the first to produce clear test results showing that ghetto children can be given a fully adequate education in ghetto schools. For when the testers say that the children who were caught young enough by the More Effective Schools are performing, on average, *at grade level and above*, they merely mean that these children are performing just as well as white middle-class children. And this is the first case of complete victory over that terrible educational lag that is the curse of America's Negro minority.

For economic and social reasons, because of injustice and discrimination, above all, because of the circumstances in which this heedless, ruthless society condemns them to live, Negro children normally enter the first grade considerably behind white children; and worse still, they generally fall further and further behind, the longer they stay in school. On average, those who stay through high school are by then three and a half years below grade level, which means that the *average Negro high school graduate only has a slightly better than eighth grade education.* "Stay through high school" is in fact the right phrase, rather than "go through high school." Since the average is at the level of eighth-grade-plus, it is not surprising that the military draft tests have revealed a shockingly high proportion of functional illiterates, even among Negro high school graduates. Add the two-thirds and more of Negro boys and girls who drop out before finishing high school, and you have a frightening result.

Briefly, 400,000-plus eighteen-year-old Negroes are annually injected into this country's socio-economic bloodstream; but of these 400,000-plus, hardly 10 percent have the true equivalent of a normal white middle-class high-school education—which means no more than an ordinary *blue-collar education*! In other words, we annually add to the

American body politic no less than 360,000 Negroes of both sexes who are wholly unequipped to get or hold any job in which grossly deficient schooling is a handicap—and that means, more and more with every passing year, just about any job at all! If a malevolent and astute racist were asked to design a system guaranteed to prevent Negro achievement, to promote bitterness, frustration and violence, to perpetuate and even to intensify discrimination, this is the system that he would surely come up with. To reform this system, any outlay, any sacrifice, any effort, however great and however painful, is not merely a moral imperative; it is also a political and social imperative of the most pressing and urgent character. And the system is not going to be reformed, alas, by more desegregation orders.

## WHAT WILL IT ALL COST?

The outlays for adequate reform will be enormous indeed, when and if we make up our minds to pursue desegregation by all means possible, but also, and above all at this stage, to insure quality education in the ghetto schools that are beyond practical reach of early desegregation. The job can only be done by the federal government, for the cities and states are already overstrained; and it will cost billions—how many billions, no one has figured out, but certainly quite a number.

There are two points to make in this connection. First of all, anyone who discovered a reasonably reliable cancer cure, and then withheld it because of its expense, would be treated as a monster. And in effect, we are talking, here, about a social-political-economic cancer that is approaching the terminal stage. Secondly, however, the proof by the More Effective Schools that improved schools really can cure the cancer is by no means a proof that the MES program is the ideal cure. There may be other, better, perhaps cheaper ways to get comparable results. Since what is required is positive discrimination—by which I mean very much heavier investment per pupil in ghetto and other deprived neighborhoods—it is obvious that the discrimination should be no greater than is absolutely necessary. (In New York there is already resentment of the MES program, even within the ghettos, among parents of children whose neighborhood schools have not been included in the program—and since there are only 21 More Effective Schools, and expansion of the program has been halted by the duck-nibblers, that means, potentially, resentment by something like nine-tenths of the ghetto parents in New York.) Thus a systematic and unbiased effort should be inaugurated, to see whether comparable results can be attained in more economical ways. Such an effort should center in New York City, for the test-background of MES, though so brief, is unique and therefore essential for comparative purposes. Instead of unsystematic nibbling, such as the Board of Education has now begun, expansion of the MES program should clearly be resumed. A follow-on program should equally clearly be adopted, in particular in the relevant junior high schools. Otherwise many of the MES children will experience the kind of disheartening setback on entering jungle-junior-high, that the Head Start children have experienced when they have entered unimproved primary schools. But these supportive measures should also be combined with experiments to discover whether altering this or that expensive feature—using one back-up teacher for every four classes, instead of one for every three as at present, for example—will produce satisfactory results.

The only point on which there should be no compromise is the schoolchildren performing *at grade level*. And if even larger investments are shown to be required—for example, in recreational and para-education activities after normal schools hours, in the schools of the very most tragic neighborhoods—then there should be no nasty nonsense about this being "too expensive," to quote the mole-sighted new chairman of the New York Board of Education, Albert Giardino. When you are talking about cancer cures, "too expensive" is an impermissible phrase. And of course, in this systematic experimental effort, due attention should also be given to the other efforts of school improvement much more recently launched under Title I of the Education Act, which will surely be

remembered as the greatest domestic achievement of the Johnson Administration. If one or another of these show, when the tests have all been made, that there is another, cheaper or better way to get the ghetto children to perform *at grade level*, that will be the system to back wholeheartedly.

In this business, there are only three rules. First, face the facts as they are, and deal with them as they are. Second, spend no more than is needed for the children to perform, on average, at grade level; for this is the outside limit of positive discrimination that other people are likely to tolerate. But, third, invest until it hurts cruelly, if need be, so that the average performance of the children of the ghettos reaches grade level or above; for there is no other cure for the cancer that threatens American urban life.

I am not so foolish as to suppose that the hoary, furtive vice of racial prejudice can be abruptly overcome by this long-range cure, any more than I suppose that *prepared* school desegregation can do more than greatly soften the effects of racial prejudice. But I submit, the white people of goodwill in America, and above all our well-intended liberal intellectuals, have been almost inconceivably unrealistic, flabbly-minded and lazy about learning the facts concerning this cardinal American problem. Take a minority differentiated by skin color. Tolerate a national school system that gives nine-tenths of this minority an education very widely inferior to the normal education of blue collar workers, let alone persons of higher achievement. How, then, can you expect or hope for an end to discrimination and racial prejudice?

Or if you want the other side of the medal, look at the few areas in American life, in which prejudice and discrimination have been, if not absolutely banished, at least minimized in recent years to the point where there is no grave problem. Too few people recall that in the lifetimes of a good many of us, Marian Anderson and Joe Lewis were, in some sense, nine day wonders as well as precursors. And too few people are even aware that real integration of the armed services only began in the line in Korea. (I can still remember AWOL Negro soldiers from the segregated logistical units, and even from the unhappy 24th Regiment, coming up to the hottest parts of the line—one or two, or three or four, or even 10 or 12 a day—to ask whether there was any place for them in battalions in combat; and I remember, too, how they were warmly welcomed, though the battalion commanders always knew they were AWOL, simply because the line was stretched so thin in those first months of the war!) Yet in the arts—not just jazz, but all the arts and throughout show business—and sports and the armed services, discrimination has now been so largely overcome. And what has so largely overcome discrimination in these tragically few departments of our national life? Brilliant Negro achievements is the answer. And what has permitted this achievement in these special areas? Again, the answer is the relative easiness of achievement in these few areas, despite deficient schooling, for those with aptitude and ambition and courage.

## MORAL CART BEFORE THE PRACTICAL HORSE

Once again, I am not so foolish as to suppose that high achievement in every area of national life would be immediately guaranteed, even if every one of the 400,000-plus Negroes who become 18 each year were assured of a first-rate high school education, with the university to follow, of course, for the abler boys and girls. Prejudice is an ugly reality. The tentacles of custom, born of prejudice, are also ugly realities. Yet those same tentacles had the armed forces in their grip less than two decades ago, and had the world of sports in their grip hardly more than three decades ago. And what has lopped off the tentacles? Negro achievement, and nothing but Negro achievement. For no amount of enforced desegregation would have ended discrimination in the hard-bitten army and harder-bitten professional sports teams, if Negroes had not pegged even, and often much better than even, with their white fellow soldiers and fellow athletes. Yet in most areas of our national life, conspicuous Negro achievement is all but impossible, simply because so few American Negroes as yet

receive normally decent schooling. Give them the needed education. At the outset, it may be, only seven in 20 will break through the barriers of prejudice and custom. But those few will surely inspire the next generation to say, "If *they* could do it, *we* can do it." And by the same token, white prejudice will surely be eroded, in every area where Negroes are enabled to achieve highly.

The truth is that in our approach to almost every aspect of the race problem—whether segregation, or discrimination, or Negro poverty, or whatever it may be—we have persistently been placing the moral cart before the practical horse. Education is the key to the whole problem, because education leads to jobs; jobs lead to achievement; and achievement reduces discrimination. That is the common-sense formula, which puts the horse ahead of the cart. And if we do not get the moral cart moving at long last—if we cannot provide good education and decent jobs for our Negro fellow citizens, and if these first steps do not begin to erode discrimination and open ever wider doors of opportunity—then this country can too soon become a place in which none will wish to live, who still care much about the things that America is supposed to stand for.

Some may say: "But if many white Americans have always cared so much about these things America is supposed to stand for, why this belated sense of urgency? Why did not Franklin Roosevelt, for instance, begin pressing for serious civil rights legislation nearly 40 years ago?" In the abstract, those who say this will be dead right. But the sad truth is that any national problem that is highly controversial, very difficult, yet possible to shove under the rug, invariably ends by getting shoved under the rug with extreme firmness. While the race problem in America was mainly a rural Southern problem, it could still be shoved under the rug. But in the last two decades and more, our race problem has more and more become a Northern urban problem, as well as a more and more urban problem even in the South, where the major cities show the same pattern of demographic change already traced above. In this new guise, the race problem cannot any longer be shoved under the rug. Justice must be done at last, or we must expect a gradual decline toward the sort of country that will choose a new President Verwoerd. Those are, literally, the choices before us. For my own part, I am confident that justice can and will be done, at no matter what cost to the budget and the taxpayer, if only we can manage to look at the problem in common-sense terms.

## 23  CHEATING AMONG COLLEGE STUDENTS

JOHN HARP    PHILIP TAIETZ

Without norms of academic integrity the stability and continuity of the academic system could not be maintained. Educators view any violation of the norms of academic integrity both as an ethical problem and as a negation of one of the objectives of education, i.e., the development of independent critical thinking. Students themselves regard cheating as morally wrong. Yet cheating is a common phenomenon on American college campuses, as a number of studies have shown. In 1952 a study conducted in eleven colleges found that nearly two-fifths of the students polled admitted cheating. A recently completed nationwide study reports that 49 percent of the students cheat. Another study reveals the following incidence of cheating reported by seniors: 26 percent at Columbia, 30 percent at Cornell, 52 percent at Fordham, and 54 percent at Notre Dame.[1]

Colleges vary in the formal and informal means they use to communicate the norms of academic integrity and the associated sanctions. It is quite possible that the norms may be vague and variously interpreted in regard to specific items of behavior. Furthermore, the norms of academic integrity do not have the same salience for all subgroups in the academic system. For example, studies[2] have shown that the incidence of reported cheating is higher among fraternity members than among independents.

A revision of an article by John Harp and Philip Taietz entitled "Academic Integrity and Social Structure: A Study of Cheating Among College Students," which first appeared in *Social Problems*, vol. 13 (spring 1966), pp. 365–373. Reprinted with the permission of the authors and the publisher.

### CHEATING AS A FORM OF DEVIANCY

Cheating on term papers and examinations by college students is conceptualized as a form of deviance. A sociological conception of deviance involves a consideration of the norms to which the members of the system are oriented and subsequent deviation from the expectations of others. Support for this kind of conception is found in student-conduct codes and other statements which reflect the attitudes of faculty and administration toward cheating.[3] A recent nationwide study reported on student definitions of cheating. Both faculty and students considered "copying on a term paper or other assignment" as a form of cheating. It is evident that both parties regard cheating as a contravention of legitimate rules governing academic integrity.[4] It should be pointed out, however, that the concept legitimacy as used in the sociological literature implies a moral validity. It is worthy of mention, therefore, that data from two previous studies involving a number of universities show that a majority of students regard cheating as "morally wrong" or believe that "students are morally obliged not to cheat." The latter results leave little chance for disparity between the legal and moral aspects of legitimacy as described by Cloward and Ohlin.[5] The legal aspects of legitimacy are therefore given a strong moral reinforcement.

Following the perspective offered by Merton's paradigm, cheating may be conceived as a form of deviancy, and more specifically an adaptive type of behavior resulting from an acceptance of the institutionalized goals but not the institutionalized means.[6] The question as to why some students choose to reject legitimate means while accepting the goals is not answered by this earlier formulation of the problem. Nevertheless, several sources of explanation have been identified and refer in general to criteria originating within the social structure, including inadequate or inappropriate socialization to the institutionalized norms and those common to the personality system. It is the former category which is most relevant to a sociological analysis of the problem. One might reason that as a result of earlier socialization the norms governing academic integrity may not be as salient for some students as for others, or there may exist a differential individual capacity to comply with the norms in question.[7]

The present analysis will emphasize the more immediate social environment, the social situations that give rise to patterns of behavior representing a contravention of norms governing academic integrity. Are students socialized to a covert norm of cheating as they progress through college, and are there certain structures which facilitate this socialization process and provide solutions for students with particular adaptive problems?[8] These are the principal questions which will serve to guide our analysis.

Various measures of cheating were developed for a stratified random sample of male students enrolled in the three largest colleges of an Ive League university. Two forms of cheating essentially agreed upon by faculty and students as comprising a class of acts which violate norms of academic integrity were selected. They were "cheating on tests and final exams" and "cheating on term papers and reports." Contrary to the results of a recent study, the two measures were not found to be intercorrelated. Nor were similar patterns of relationships found with external variables.[9] A small amount of variation for the cheating-on-exams variable may partially explain our low correlations. Continuing the search for additional measures of deviancy, which cover a great range of behaviors, led us to explore the relationships among cheating, cutting classes, and tardiness in submitting class assignments. They were not related, nor was a scale of deviant acts of the order cited obtainable from the present data.[10]

Cheating on term papers was chosen as the indicator for intensive analysis since (1) a much higher incidence was reported than was true for the other variables—40 percent of all students reported cheating on term papers—and (2) it represents a type of behavior which requires some semblance of organization.

## STRUCTURAL SOURCES OF DEVIANCY

Beginning with the largest organizational units within the university, the various colleges, one observes that they may reflect differences in curriculum, such as emphasis on vocational objectives, as well as differences in individual characteristics resulting from variations in admissions procedures. Both these influences are operative for the three colleges included in the sample, Arts and Sciences, Agriculture, and Engineering. The latter two are considerably more vocational than Arts and Sciences and differ significantly with respect to their students' verbal SAT scores.[11]

**TABLE 1**    *Incidence of ever copying on term papers or assignments by college and year in college*

| College | Freshmen | Sophomore | Junior | Senior |
|---|---|---|---|---|
| Agriculture | 18.4 (142) | 42.4 (140) | 54.9 (144) | 55.7 (116) |
| Arts and Sciences | 12.3 (205) | 27.4 (198) | 36.6 (203) | 29.9 (155) |
| Engineering* | 26.1 (238) | 58.6 (164) | 70.9 (110) | 59.7 (114) |
| All colleges | 19.4 (585) | 41.8 (502) | 50.7 (457) | 49.5 (385) |

*113 fifth-year Engineering students not included.

Following the freshman year a significant difference in the incidence of cheating on term papers is found for the three colleges. Forty-two and 50 percent of the students in Agriculture and Engineering reported cheating, compared with 26 percent for Arts and Sciences. For all colleges the incidence of cheating is highest during the junior and senior years (see Table 1). Past studies have also reported a larger amount of cheating for students in the more vocationally oriented colleges than for those whose curricula do not share this emphasis.[12]

A structural source of deviancy may also be present in certain major social groupings on university campuses, such as the residence unit. The distribution of living arrangements for our sample places one-third of the students in fraternities, one-third in university dormitories, and the balance in off-campus housing. Previous studies have reported a higher incidence of cheating for fraternity members than for independents. Explanations after the fact have invariably emphasized the anti-intellectual theme within the fraternity system.[13] Our results support the empirical hypothesis, which continues to hold when controls for college affiliation are employed. Some additional data concerning the intellectual character of fraternities is relevant and concerns the students' self-concept. Although only 20 percent of the students regarded themselves as intellectuals, 42 percent of these intellectuals resided in fraternities. Further evidence obtained on cumulative grade averages and verbal SAT scores for fraternity members compared with nonfraternity members is considerably less supportive of any intellectual orientation for these residence units. One must recognize, of course, that differences do exist among houses, but our data will not permit analysis of variations within the fraternity system.

Suffice it to say that a higher incidence of cheating is reported by fraternity members in all three colleges than for nonfraternity members. There is, however, a significant difference among colleges in the incidence of cheating by fraternity members, with the highest incidence reported by the more vocational colleges. Both college affiliation and fraternity membership appear to be exercising an influence on student conduct.[14]

## OPPORTUNITY STRUCTURES AND DEVIANCY

A more adequate explanation for the higher incidence of cheating on term papers for fraternity members (see Table 2) would view the organizations as opportunity structures in the sense of providing both the physical facilities necessary for the behavior and the requisite normative support.[15] Parsons notes this duality of opportunity by referring to "a concrete resource aspect on the one hand, a normatively controlled 'mechanism' or standard aspect on the other."[16] The availability of illegitimate means is controlled, as Cloward points out, by various criteria and in the same manner as conventional means.[17] One must be concerned with both differentials in access and differentials in fulfillment. Cloward comments on this as follows:

TABLE 2    *Incidence of cheating according to college affiliation and fraternity membership*

| | | |
|---|---|---|
| Agriculture | | |
| Fraternity | 64 (164) | $\chi^2 = 45.781$ |
| Nonfraternity | 33 (373) | $P < 0.01$ |
| Arts and Sciences | | |
| Fraternity | 38 (365) | $\chi^2 = 50.599$ |
| Nonfraternity | 15 (392) | $P < 0.01$ |
| Engineering | | |
| Fraternity | 67 (371) | $\chi^2 = 82.209$ |
| Nonfraternity | 33 (365) | $P < 0.01$ |

**TABLE 3**  *Incidence of cheating according to college affiliation, within college verbal SAT score groupings and fraternity membership*

| | |
|---|---|
| Agriculture | 41.8 (541) |
| Low SAT | 54.5 (167) |
| Fraternity | 76.7 (60) |
| Nonfraternity | 42.1 (107) |
| Medium SAT | 36.7 (166) |
| Fraternity | 72.1 (43) |
| Nonfraternity | 24.4 (123) |
| High SAT | 30.7 (166) |
| Fraternity | 43.8 (48) |
| Nonfraternity | 25.4 (118) |
| Arts and Sciences | 26.1 (762) |
| Low SAT | 32.2 (242) |
| Fraternity | 43.4 (136) |
| Nonfraternity | 17.9 (106) |
| Medium SAT | 24.3 (247) |
| Fraternity | 36.2 (116) |
| Nonfraternity | 13.7 (131) |
| High SAT | 22.5 (249) |
| Fraternity | 33.3 (102) |
| Nonfraternity | 15.0 (147) |
| Engineering | 50.1 (739) |
| Low SAT | 51.5 (235) |
| Fraternity | 63.6 (121) |
| Nonfraternity | 38.6 (114) |
| Medium SAT | 53.8 (240) |
| Fraternity | 69.5 (128) |
| Nonfraternity | 35.7 (112) |
| High SAT | 44.8 (232) |
| Fraternity | 63.6 (107) |
| Nonfraternity | 28.8 (125) |
| SAT unavailable | 45.9 (98) |
| Total | 38.9 (2042) |
| Fraternity | 54.4 (904) |
| Nonfraternity | 26.7 (1138) |

Some occupations afford abundant opportunities to engage in illegitimate activity; others offer virtually none. The businessman, for example, not only has at his disposal the means to do so, but, as some studies have shown, is under persistent pressure to employ illegitimate means, if only to maintain a competitive advantage in the market place.[18]

The competitive nature of higher education in the United States may offer a parallel to the business world in this respect.

Although the presence of an opportunity structure may serve as a necessary antecedent for the adaptive behavior described as cheating on term papers, it is not sufficient to explain why all members of these social groups do not cheat. Having identified certain environmental influences, we must also explain why they are not completely successful, and to do so requires that we juxtapose the parts played by individual and group influences on deviant behavior. Proceeding in this way should also enable us to identify more closely the functions performed by the opportunity structure in question. Access to legitimate means was described by Merton as a function of one's position in the social structure. It is our contention that a more relevant source of variation with respect to accessibility of legitimate means rests with the individual's ability or capacity to comply with them. The question is, therefore: Is there any evidence to indicate that structures of this kind facilitate the adaptive response of cheating for students who lack the ability to follow the more legitimate course?

First, we observe that the adequacy of role capacity or ability as measured by verbal SAT scores and cumulative averages is negatively associated with the adaptive response indexed by cheating on term papers. However, as the results reported in Tables 3 and 4 show, with the exception of students in the College of Engineering, students whose ability and performance are relatively low and who belong to fraternities comprise a significantly higher proportion of deviants than those members who placed higher on ability and performance. Stated another way, our evidence suggests the fraternity system viewed as an opportunity structure may provide illegitimate adaptive solutions for students who score low on ability and performance.

### INTERVENING VARIABLES

An examination of the effect of social psychological variables such as self-concept, attitudes, and aspirations will provide a basis for further contextual analyses. Reference was made to the self-

**TABLE 4**   *Incidence of cheating by cumulative-average groupings and fraternity membership**

|  | *Low* | *Medium* | *High* | *NA* |
|---|---|---|---|---|
| Total | 41.1 (618) | 43.4 (703) | 34.1 (663) | 12.1 (58) |
| Fraternity | 62.3 (239) | 55.6 (356) | 47.7 (302) | 0.0 (0) |
| Nonfraternity | 27.7 (379) | 31.1 (347) | 23.8 (361) | 12.1 (58) |

Term-paper cheating $(f)$ Cumulative average supported, $\chi^2 = 13.604$, $P < 0.01$.
Term-paper cheating $(f)$ Cumulative average for fraternity members, $\chi^2 = 11.222$, $P < 0.01$.
Term-paper cheating $(f)$ Cumulative average for nonfraternity members, $\chi^2 = 6.126$, $P < 0.05$.

*Cumulative average is as reported by the students. The low, medium, and high groups were formed by breaking at points that would yield nearest equality of group sizes. The groups are low 74 and below, $N = 618$; medium 75–79, $N = 703$; high 80 and above, $N = 663$. Fifty-eight of the students filling out questionnaires did not indicate their grade averages. Grade average is used as a rough measure of ability. The same measure is used by William J. Bowers in his report, "Student Dishonesty and Its Control in College," New York: Columbia University Bureau of Applied Social Research, 1964.

concept of "intellectual" in earlier discussions of the fraternity system. It is used in this instance as an individual attribute rather than to describe any particular social unit. The term "intellectual" was defined for students as ". . . one given to study, reflection, and speculation especially concerning profound or abstract issues," and the relationship with cheating was in the expected direction.[19] Cheating was reported by 31 percent of the intellectually oriented students, compared with 41 percent of the students who did not share this self-concept $(P < 0.01)$.

However controlling for intellectual orientation, fraternity members continue to cheat more than nonmembers. The results are given in Table 5, and once again the social environment appears to be exercising a dominant influence over the students' choice of a solution to his problem of adjustment.

Reference was made earlier in the discussion to a general acceptance of educational goals by students, at least regarding a desire to complete their education.[20] However, an increasing number of students gave evidence of educational aspirations which included enrolling in graduate school upon completion of their undergraduate program.[21]

Acceptance of the so-called goal-internalization

**TABLE 5**   *Incidence of cheating according to self-concept as intellectual and membership in fraternity and college*

| College | Intellectual | | Not Intellectual | |
|---|---|---|---|---|
| **Agriculture** | | | | |
| Fraternity | 62 (16) | $\chi^2 = 5.104$ | 64 (148) | $\chi^2 = 40.550$ |
| Nonfraternity | 30 (43) | $P < 0.05$ | 33 (330) | $P < 0.01$ |
| **Arts and Sciences** | | | | |
| Fraternity | 35 (102) | $\chi^2 = 13.275$ | 39 (262) | $\chi^2 = 35.892$ |
| Nonfraternity | 15 (139) | $P < 0.01$ | 16 (250) | $P < 0.01$ |
| **Engineering** | | | | |
| Fraternity | 63 (57) | $\chi^2 = 17.860$ | 67 (313) | $\chi^2 = 63.518$ |
| Nonfraternity | 25 (61) | $P < 0.01$ | 35 (303) | $P < 0.01$ |
| **All colleges** | | | | |
| Fraternity | 47 (175) | $\chi^2 = 33.686$ | 57 (723) | $\chi^2 = 125.666$ |
| Nonfraternity | 20 (243) | $P < 0.01$ | 29 (883) | $P < 0.01$ |

TABLE 6    *Incidence of cheating according to plans for graduate school and self-concept as intellectual*

|  | Intellectual | | Not Intellectual | |
|---|---|---|---|---|
| Plans for graduate school | 29 (338) | | 38 (941) | $\chi^2$ = 11.43 |
| No plans for graduate school | 37 (83) | $P > 0.05$ | 46 (672) | $P > 0.01$ |

hypothesis could lead one to predict a higher incidence of cheating for those with graduate plans. The results are not supportive of this relationship, and indeed the opposite is found to hold. Students who aspire to graduate school cheat significantly less than those who do not (35 percent, compared with 45 percent, $P < 0.01$). What is lacking is a control for the intellectual orientation of the student. It would seem more logical to suggest that students who plan to attend graduate school but do not approach the decision with an intellectual orientation would be more inclined to cheat (i.e., adopt illegitimate means to achieve this goal) than those with similar orientations who have no graduate-school plans.

Although there is no support for the goal-internalization hypothesis, as shown in Table 6, the question remains as to the relative strength of this variable when it is examined in a context of fraternity membership. The results of such an analysis, reported in Table 7, show that regardless of an individual student's orientation and goals, a higher incidence of cheating is reported by fraternity members than by independents. Examining fraternity members as a class, however, it may be seen that a significantly higher incidence of cheating is reported by members with a nonintellectual orien-

tation who plan graduate school than by those with an intellectual orientation who have similar plans. Similarly, for fraternity members with no graduate plans nonintellectuals report a higher incidence of cheating than intellectuals.

Returning to our overall comparison, the results reaffirm the dominant influence of the social milieu and offer further evidence of the existence of a type of opportunity structure, the fraternity system.[22]

### REFERENCES AND NOTES

1    A few pertinent studies are H. Hartshorn and M. A. May, *Studies in Deceit*, New York: The Macmillan Company, 1928; Robert J. McNamara, "The Interplay of Intellectual and Religious Values," unpublished Ph.D. dissertation, Cornell University, 1963; Rose Goldsen, Morris Rosenberg, Robin M. Williams, Jr., and Edward A. Suchman, *What College Students Think*, Princeton, N.J.: D. Van Nostrand, 1960; William J. Bowers, *Student Dishonesty and Its Control in College*, New York: Columbia University Bureau of Applied Social Research, 1964. Studies may be classified as experimental or survey in design, and the latter type is more often encountered in the literature. A wide range of sophistication in methodology and design is found, however, and ranges from the classic studies of Hartshorn and May to purely descriptive accounts of the problem.

TABLE 7    *Incidence of cheating on term paper according to self-concept as intellectual, plans for graduate school, and fraternity membership*

|  | Intellectual | | Not Intellectual | |
|---|---|---|---|---|
| Graduate plans |  | | | |
| Fraternity | 43.9 (139) | $\chi^2$ = 23.612 | 51.1 (437) | $\chi^2$ = 63.288 |
| Nonfraternity | 19.1 (197) | $P < 0.01$ | 25.0 (500) | $P < 0.01$ |
| No graduate plans |  | | | |
| Fraternity | 56.8 (36) | $\chi^2$ = 10.971 | 63.9 (283) | $\chi^2$ = 64.990 |
| Nonfraternity | 21.7 (45) | $P < 0.01$ | 32.6 (384) | $P < 0.01$ |

2   See Goldsen *et al.*, *op. cit.*

3   The university at which the study was conducted has published a brochure defining plagiarism for the students and describing other types of cheating as violations of the student code. All were described as forms of academic dishonesty.

4   Bowers, *op. cit.*

5   Cloward and Ohlin discuss the implications of this interpretation of legitimacy for delinquent subcultures. Richard A. Cloward and Lloyd E. Ohlin, *Delinquency and Opportunity*, New York: The Free Press, 1963, pp. 16–18.

6   Robert K. Merton, *Social Theory and Social Structure*, New York: The Free Press, 1957, pp. 357–368. This is not to be confused with the popular usage of the term, and the authors readily concede that cheating is in no sense new, but does represent a contravention of norms concerning academic integrity. Merton testifies as to the historical continuity of this type of response in American society as follows: "The history of great American fortunes is threaded with strains toward institutionally dubious innovation, as is attested by many tributes to the Robber Barons. . . . This is no new phenomenon." *Ibid.*, pp. 141–142. Merton comments further that ". . . it is necessary to reiterate that the typology of deviant behavior is far from being confined to the behavior which is ordinarily described as criminal or delinquent." *Ibid.*, p. 181.

7   Merton cites both sources: "Owing to their objectively *disadvantaged* position in the group as well as to distinctive *personality configurations*, some individuals are subjected more than others to the strains arising from the discrepancies between cultural goals and effective access to their realization. They are consequently more vulnerable to deviant behavior." *Ibid.*, pp. 179–180.

8   Cloward and Ohlin, *op. cit.* Cloward and Ohlin offer an interpretation which rests on a general acceptance of middle-class values by lower-class boys. They hypothesize that individuals who find the legitimate paths for obtaining the goals blocked turn to illegitimate means. See also Richard A. Cloward, "Illegitimate Means, Anomie, and Deviant Behavior," *American Sociological Review*, vol. 24 (1959), pp. 164–176.

9   For example, significant differences were found among colleges in cheating on term papers but not in cheating on tests and final exams.

10  A recent study of eleven colleges and universities by the Columbia Bureau of Applied Research did find a relationship between copying an answer from someone else during an exam and submitting another student's work as one's own. Bowers discusses the relationship as follows: "They are highly related to each other, being more or less inclusive measures of the same phenomenon. For purposes of analysis, it would make little difference which one we use to classify students." Bowers, *op. cit.*, p. 65.

A recent study of scholastic dishonesty in two large Southern universities utilized an index of the following six items:

1. Seeking information about a final exam from students who had already taken it
2. Copying from another student's paper during a quiz
3. Collusion in a take-home assignment
4. Lying about an absence
5. Bringing written information into an examination and using it
6. Purchasing a final exam from a bootlegger

It was further reported that the items scaled and acceptable coefficients of reproducibility and scalability were obtained. See Charles M. Bonjean and Reece McGee, "Scholastic Dishonesty among Undergraduates in Differing Systems of Social Control," *Sociology of Education*, vol. 38 (winter 1965), p. 130.

11  The median SAT verbal scores for the entering class of 1962, given in descending order, are Arts and Sciences 630, Engineering 605, and Agriculture 559.

12  Bowers interprets a similar finding in this fashion: "Students in the most clearly career-oriented fields, business, engineering and education, are much more likely to cheat than students majoring in history, the humanities, or languages." A commitment to the intellectual life is, in Bowers' interpretation, more characteristic of the latter group, thereby predisposing them to cheat less. Bowers, *op. cit.*, p. 105.

13  Goldsen *et al.*, *op. cit.*

14  The pervasive influence of fraternities on the total environment of the university is described by Bowers as follows: "The more closely students are associated with a fraternity or sorority, the more likely they are to cheat. Interestingly enough this principle extends even to nonmembers, for the students who are at schools that have no fraternities or sororities are less prone to cheat than those who do not belong but attend schools that do have Greek letter societies." Bowers, *op. cit.*, pp. 109–110.

15  With regard to essential physical facilities in this case, Bowers and others have reported the common practice in fraternities of keeping files of old term papers, which are made available to the members: "Some fraternities and sororities have old term papers and exams on file, which serve as temptations for some and opportunities for others to engage in academic dishonesty." (*Ibid.*, p. 109).

16  Talcott Parsons, "Some Considerations on the The-

ory of Social Change," *Rural Sociology*, vol. 26 (September 1961), p. 230.

17  Cloward, *op. cit.*

18  *Ibid.*, p. 173. Cloward and Ohlin discuss the new insights to be gained by conceiving of delinquent subcultures as illegitimate opportunity structures. For example: "Delinquent subcultures are not simply the aggregates of impulsive, egoistic, individualistic, and selfish persons. The capacities of participants to conform to the norms of their subcultures seem to be neither less nor greater than the abilities of other persons in our society to conform to the dictates of the groups to which they belong." Cloward and Ohlin, *op. cit.*, p. 37.

   Palmore and Hammond have also suggested that the degree of deviance is dependent upon (1) barriers to legitimate opportunities and (2) the degree of exposure to illegitimate opportunities. Erdman Palmore and Philip E. Hammond, "Interacting Factors in Juvenile Delinquency," *American Sociological Review*, vol. 29 (December 1964), pp. 848–854.

19  Similar findings are reported by Bowers, who states that "Academic dishonesty is most prevalent among those who place high value on the social criteria and low value on the intellectual criteria; it is least prevalent among those who emphasize intellectual and de-emphasize social values." Bowers, *op. cit.*, p. 101.

20  Cloward and Ohlin discuss the applicability of the goal internalization hypothesis for delinquent subcultures and conclude: "The disparity between what lower-class youth are led to want and what is actually available to them is the source of a major problem of adjustment. Adolescents who form delinquent subcultures have internalized an emphasis upon conventional goals. Faced with limitations on legitimate avenues of access to these goals, and unable to revise their aspirations downward, they experience intense frustrations; the exploration of nonconformist alternatives may be the result." Cloward and Ohlin, *op. cit.*, p. 86.

21  For the present study 80 percent of the students enrolled in the college of Arts and Sciences indicated plans to attend graduate school, while approximately one-half of those in the colleges of Agriculture and Engineering had similar plans.

22  Bonjean and McGee report that fraternity-sorority membership yields the highest relationship with self-reported cheating, as measured by their six-item scale. The authors choose to conceptualize fraternity membership as a personal-background characteristic and treat as situational variables or collective properties perceptions of friends' attitudes, perception of formal norms, and similar dimensions.

---

## 24    SOCIAL SCIENCE YOGIS AND MILITARY COMMISSARS
### IRVING LOUIS HOROWITZ

"The bonds between the government and the universities are . . . an arrangement of convenience, providing the government with politically usable knowledge and the university with badly needed funds." The speaker of these words, Senator J. William Fulbright, went on to warn that such alliances may endanger the universities, may bring about "the surrender of independence, the neglect of teaching, and the distortion of scholarship." Many other distinguished Americans are worried by the growing number of alliances between the military and the university.

Reprinted with the permission of the author and the publisher from *Trans-Action* magazine, vol. 5 (May 1968), pp. 29–38. Copyright ©1968 by Washington University, St. Louis, Mo.

Instead of the expected disclaimers and denials from university officials, however, in recent months these men—from both the administrative and academic sides—have rushed to take up any slack in doing secret research on campus, asking that the number of projects they are already handling be increased. Arwin A. Dougal, assistant director of the Pentagon's office for research and engineering, has indicated that while some major universities are gravely concerned about academic research for military ends, most universities realize how important "classified research" is to the national security. Indeed, Dougal has said that many professors involved in secret research actually try to retain their security clearances when their projects are completed. Rather than disengaging themselves, they, like many university leaders, are eager to participate to an even greater extent.

Symptomatic of the ever-tightening bond between the military and the social scientist is a "confidential," 53-page document entitled *Report of the Panel on Defense Social and Behavioral Sciences.* It was the offspring of a summer 1967 meeting, in Williamstown, Mass., of members of the Defense Science Board of the National Academy of Sciences. This board is the highest-ranking science advisory group of the Defense Department. The meeting's purpose: to discuss which social-science research could be of most use to the Department of Defense (DoD).

## THE SETTING

The DoD is the most sought-after and frequently-found sponsor of social-science research. And the DoD is sought and found by the social scientists, not, as is often imagined, the other way around. Customarily, military men provide only grudging acceptance of any need for behavioral research.

There are four distinct reasons why the DoD is sponsoring more and more social-science research.

First, money. In fiscal 1968, Congressional appropriations for research and development amount to the monumental sum of $14,971.4 million. Of this, an incredible $13,243.0 million, or about 85 percent, is distributed among three agencies whose primary concern is the military system: the Atomic Energy Commission, the National Aeronautics and Space Administration, and the DoD. The figure for the DoD alone is $6680.0 million. This means that a single federal agency commands nearly two-fifths of the government research dollar. So it is easy to see why so much effort and energy is expended by social scientists trying to capture some of the monies the DoD can experiment with. As bees flock to honey, men flock to money—particularly in an era when costly data-processing and data-gathering strain the conventional sources of financing.

Second, the protection that research has when done for the DoD. I am referring to the blanket and indiscriminate way in which Congressional appropriations are made for both basic and applied research. Policy-linked social scientists operate under an umbrella of the secrecy established by the DoD's research agencies. Reasons of security ward off harassment by Congressional committees. Attacks over supposed misallocation of funds and resources—undergone by the National Institutes of Health at the hands of the committee headed by Rep. L. H. Fountain of North Carolina—are spared those academics with Defense Department funding.

This dispensation is strikingly illustrated by the fact that DoD allocations for research and development are not itemized the way allocations are for Health, Education, and Welfare. This auditing cover allows for even more experimenting in DoD spending than its already swollen funds might indicate. Such a *carte blanche* situation probably places far less of a strain on social scientists than would be the case if they worked for other agencies. In the world of research, power provides the illusion of freedom.

Third, the relatively blank-check Congressional approach to DoD funds, and the security umbrella of the auditing system, provide social scientists with unlimited resources. DoD allocations are not broken down into sub-agencies, nor are any of their specialized activities or services checked—unlike the usual scrutiny directed at other agencies.

That this fact has not gone entirely unnoticed is shown by the Congressional demand that as of 1968 the DoD be called to account on an appropriation budget.

Fourth, the DoD's connection with the "national security"—which protects the DoD and those who work for it—offers great temptations to social researchers interested in the "big news." For it enables the DoD not only to outspend such agencies as the National Science Foundation in university-based activities, but to penetrate areas of non-Defense research that are central only to the social-science researcher. Programs to support juvenile-delinquency research (Project 100,000) and others to upgrade academic institutions (Project Themis) are sponsored by the DoD rather than by the Office of Economic Opportunity, and not simply because of their disproportionate fundings. Just as important is the legitimation the DoD can provide for policy-oriented researchers in sensitive areas.

These are the main reasons why many social-science researchers are now enlisting the support of the DoD in their activities—despite the negative publicity surrounding Project Camelot and other such fallen angels.

*The Report of the Panel on Defense Social and Behavioral Sciences* throws a good deal of light on current relations between the national government and the social sciences. Unlike Project Camelot, the abortive academic-military project to investigate counterinsurgency potentials in the Third World, this Report was not inspired by government contractual requests. It is the work of leading social scientists who have been closely connected with federal research. Unlike *Report from Iron Mountain*, this Report can hardly be described as a humanistic hoax. The authors are known, the purpose of the Report explicit, and the consequences clearly appreciated by all concerned. What we have in this Report is a collective statement by eminent social scientists, a statement that can easily be read as the ominous conversion of social science into a service industry of the Pentagon.

Most of the scholars who prepared this Report have one striking similarity—they have powerful and simultaneous academic and government linkages. They move casually and easily from university to federal affiliation—and back again to the university.

The panel's chairman, S. Rains Wallace, the exception, is president of the American Institutes of Research, a nonprofit organization that does research under contract for government agencies, including the DoD.

Gene M. Lyons, who is executive secretary of the Advisory Committee on Government Programs in the Behavioral Sciences of the National Research Council (affiliated with the National Academy of Sciences), is also a professor at Dartmouth College. (He maintains, however, that he attended only one day of the meeting, and as an observer only.)

Peter Dorner, functioning through the Executive Office of the President on the Council of Economic Advisers, is also a professor of economics at the Land Tenure Center of the University of Wisconsin.

Eugene Webb, listed as a professor at Stanford University, is now serving a term as a member of the Institute for Defense Analysis, specifically, its science and technology division.

Other panel members—Harold Guetzkow of Northwestern University; Michael Pearce of the RAND Corporation; anthropologist A. Kimball Romney of Harvard University; and Roger Russell, formerly of Indiana University and now Vice-Chancellor for Academic Affairs at the University of California (Irvine)—also shift back and forth between the polity and the academy. It is plain, then, that these men have penetrated the political world more deeply than members of past project-dominated research activities.

In addition to this similarity, nearly all of these social scientists have had overseas experience, and are intimately connected with federal use of social science for foreign-area research. Yet, as in the case of Camelot, this common experience does not seem to produce any strong ideological unanimity. The men range from relatively conservative political theorists to avowed pacifists. This underscores the fact that patriotism and professional purpose tend to supersede the political viewpoints or credos these men may adhere to.

## THE REPORT

The Report closely follows the memorandum that John S. Foster Jr., director of Defense Research and Engineering of the Department of Defense, issued to the chairman of the panel. Foster's marching orders to the panel members requested that they consider basically four topics: "high-payoff" areas in research and development—"areas of social and behavioral science research in which it would be reasonable to expect great payoffs over the next three to ten years"; research to solve manpower problems; Project Themis, a DoD project for upgrading the scientific and engineering capabilities of various academic institutions so they can do better research for the Defense Department; and, finally, broad-ranging government-university relationships.

Before commenting on the Report, let me provide a summary of its findings and recommendations.

To begin with, the Report urges increased effort and funding for research on manpower, in all its aspects; for research on organization studies; for research on decision-making; for increasing the understanding of problems in foreign areas; and for research on man and his physical environment. Under "Manpower," we read, among other things:

> In order to make full use of the opportunities provided by Project 100,000 [to make soldiers out of rehabilitated juvenile delinquents] both for the military and for the national economy, we recommend that fully adequate funds be invested to cover all aspects of the military and subsequent civilian experience of the individuals involved.

Under "Organization Studies":

> Research on style of leadership and improved methods of training for leadership should be revitalized.

Under "Decision-Making":

> Techniques for the improvement of items which might assist in forecasting alliances, neutralities, hostile activities, etc., and for use in tactical decision-making need to be expanded, applied, and tested in the real world.

Under "Understanding of Operational Problems in Foreign Areas":

> Despite the difficulties attendant upon research in foreign areas, it must be explicitly recognized that the missions of the DoD cannot be successfully performed in the absence of information on (a) sociocultural patterns in various areas including beliefs, values, motivations, etc.; (b) the social organization of troops, including political, religious, and economic; (c) the effect of change and innovation upon socio-cultural pat-

terns and socio-cultural organization of groups; (d) study and evaluation of action programs initiated by U.S. or foreign agencies in underdeveloped countries.

> Solid, precise, comparative, and current empirical data developed in a programmatic rather than diffuse and opportunistic fashion are urgently needed for many areas of the world. This goal should be pursued by: (a) multidisciplinary research teams; (b) series of field studies in relevant countries; (c) strong representation of quantitative and analytic skills; (d) a broad empirical data base.

Under "Man and His Physical Environment":

> Continuing and additional research are needed on the effect of special physical and psychological environments upon performance and on possibilities for the enhancement of performance through a better understanding of man's sensory and motor output mechanisms, the development of artificial systems which will aid performance, and the search for drugs or foods which may enhance it.

Under "Methodology":

> We recommend increased emphasis upon research in behavioral-science methodology. While this is basic to all of the areas listed above, it needs to be recognized as worthy of investment in its own right. The systematic observation of the many quasi-experimental situations which occur in everyday military activities must be made possible if we are to learn from experience. We recommend that a capability be established in one or more suitable in-house laboratories to address the question of how the logistical problems of such observation can be solved.

On government-university relations:

> There is disagreement concerning the involvement of first-rate academic groups in behavioral science research relevant to long-term DoD needs. The task statement implies that DoD has not been successful in enlisting the interest and service of an eminent group of behavioral scientists in most of the areas relevant to it. This

panel does not concur. We therefore recommend that the [National Academy of Sciences] Panel on Behavioral and Social Sciences be asked to address this problem and to determine whether, in fact, an acceptable proportion of first-rate academic workers are involved in DoD behavioral-science research.

More high-quality scientists could probably be interested in DoD problems if DoD would more frequently state its research needs in terms which are meaningful to the investigator rather than to the military. . . . Publicity concerning the distinguished behavioral scientists who have long-term commitments to the DoD should be disseminated as a way of reassuring younger scientists and improving our research image.

### THE PANELISTS

Why did these distinguished social scientists accept the assignment from the DoD? Most of them seemed particularly intrigued by the chance to address important issues. They view the work done by the DoD in such areas as racially segregated housing, or the rehabilitation of juvenile delinquents through military participation, as fascinating illustrations of how social science can settle social issues. It is curious how this thirst for the application of social science led the panelists to ignore the *prima facie* fact that the DoD is in the defense business, and that therefore it inevitably tends to assign high priority to military potential and effectiveness. Further, the question of what is important is continually linked to matters of relevance to the DoD. In this way, the question of professional autonomy is transformed into one of patriotic responsibility.

In general, the idealism of social scientists participating in DoD-sponsored research stems from their profound belief in the rectifiability of federal shortcomings, as well as in the perfectibility of society through the use of social science. Despite the obviousness of the point, what these social scientists forget is that the federal government as well as its agencies is limited by historical and geopolitical circumstances. It is committed to managing cumbersome, overgrown committees and data-gathering agencies. It is committed to a status quo merely for the sake of rational functioning. It can only tinker with innovating ideas. Thus federal agencies will limit investigation simply to what is immediately useful not out of choice, but from necessity.

The social scientist often imagines he is a policy formulator, and innovating designer. Because of the cumbersome operations of government, he will be frustrated in realizing this self-image and be reduced to one more instrumental agent. His designing mentality, his strain toward perfecting, will appear unrealistic in the light of what he can do. He gets caught up in theoryless applications to immediacy, surrenders the value of confronting men with an image of what *can be*, and simply accepts what others declare *must be*. Thus, what the social scientist knows comes down to what the Defense Department under present circumstances can use.

Although the initiative for this Report came from the social scientists, the DoD provided the structure and direction of its content. To a remarkable degree, the study group accepted DoD premises.

For example, the two major assumptions that influenced its thinking are stated baldly. First, since the DoD's job now embraces new responsibilities, its proper role becomes as much to wage "peacefare" as warfare. Peacefare is spelled out as pacification of total populations, as well as a role in the ideological battle between East and West. Toward such ends, it is maintained, social science can play a vital part.

Nowhere in the document is the possibility considered that the DoD ought not to be in many of these activities—that perhaps the division of labor has placed too great an emphasis upon this one agency of government at the expense of all others. Nor is it anywhere made clear that similar types of educational and anti-poverty programs the DoD is engaged in are already under way in other branches of government—that DoD activities might be duplicating and needlessly multiplying the efforts of the Department of Health, Education and Welfare or the National Science Foundation.

The second explicit assumption the group makes is that hardware alone will not win modern wars; Manpower is needed, too. Here the panelists see social science as providing data on the dynamics of cultural change and a framework for the needs and attitudes of other people.

But here, too, there is a remarkable absence of any consideration of the sort of "manpower" deployed in foreign environments; or of the differing responses of overseas peoples to such manpower. The foreign role of the U.S. Defense Department is simply taken as a given, a datum to be exploited for the display of social science information. In this sense, U.S. difficulties with foreign military activities can be interpreted as a mere misunderstanding of the nature of a problem. Expertise and objectivity can then be called upon where a policy design is lacking or failing. Thus even the DoD can mask policy shortcomings behind the fact of a previously inadequate supply of data. In this way, the credibility gap gets converted into a mechanical informational gap. Which is exactly what is done in the Report. All efforts, in other words, are bent to maximizing social science participation rather than to minimizing international conflict.

Still a third assumption of the panel participants—one that is not acknowledged—is that their professional autonomy will not be seriously jeopardized by the very fact of their dependence upon the DoD. Indeed, many scholars seem to have abandoned their primary research interests for the secondary ones that can be funded. And the main responsibility for this shift lies not with the DoD but with the social-science professions and the scholarly community at large.

As one panel member ironically noted, in response to my questionnaire, the position of the DoD is an unhappy reflection of university demands that individual scholars and university presidents pay for expanding university overhead and enlarge graduate programs—rather than any insistence by federal agencies that the nature of social science be transformed. Another panel member indicated that, whatever dishonor may exist in the present relationships between social science and the DoD, the main charge would have to be leveled at the professoriat, rather than at the funding agencies. And while this assignment of priorities in terms of who is responsible for the present era of ill will and mistrust can be easily overdone, and lead to a form of higher apologetics in which there is mutual accusation by the social scientists and government policy-makers, it does seem clear that the simplistic idea that the evil government corrupts the good social scientist is not only an exaggeration but, more often, a deliberate misrepresentation.

## THE FINDINGS

Reexamining the specific findings of first section of the Report, "High Payoff Research in Development Areas," leaves no doubt that the panelists mean by "high payoff" those potential rewards to be netted by the DoD, rather than advantages to be gained by social scientists. This is made explicit in the section on "Manpower," in which the main issues are contended to concern problems of improving the performance of soldiers equipped with high-level technology. It is in this connection that the panelists heartily approve of Project 100,000. Although (with the exception of two panelists) there is a special cloudiness as to the nature of Project 100,000, the panelists have no doubt that the employment of delinquents in this fashion makes the best use of marginal manpower for a "tremendous payoff" for the future efficiency of the defense establishment.

A number of the Report's recommendations amount to little more than the repetition of basic organizational shibboleths. But even at this level, special problems seem to arise. There is confusion in the minds of the panelists, or at least throughout the Report that they prepared, about what constitutes internal DoD functions as opposed to those belonging to general military functions. The phrase "military establishment" functions as an umbrella disguising this ambiguity. Not only is the relationship between a civilian-led DoD and a "military establishment" unresolved, but beyond that the panelists appear willing to discount the organizational intermingling of the DoD with other governmental agencies—such as the Census Bureau, the Department of Labor, and the Department of Health, Education, and Welfare.

This leads to a tacit acceptance of DoD organizational colonialism. Not only is the DoD urged to be on the lookout for other agencies' collecting similar data and doing similar sorts of analyses, but also an explicit request that the DoD exert a special effort to use the work of outside agencies is included. On behalf of "cooperation," there exists the risk of invasion of privacy, and other dangers encountered when any single department functions as a total system incorporating the findings of other sub-units.

The Report contends that those parts of the armed services responsible for developing basic knowledge about decision-making have done their work well. It is interesting that no examples are given. Moreover, the military and civilian personnel who provide support for decision-making within the military establishment are said to have a rare opportunity to contribute to this steadily-improving use of sound decision-making models for areas like material procurement for front-line battle medical services. Nothing is said about the nature of the conflict to be resolved, or the values employed in such decisions.

While several members of the panel, in response to the questionnaire of mine, indicated that they held this Report to be an indirect resolution of problems raised by Project Camelot, the formulations used in this Report are similar to those used in the Camelot study concerning overseas research.

The Report states: "Comparative organizational work should not be done only within civilian groups such as large-scale building and construction consortia and worldwide airlines systems, but also within foreign military establishments." In Project Camelot, the same desire for military information was paramount. Curiously, no attention is given to whether, in fact, this is a high-payoff research area; or if it is, how this work is to be done without threatening the sovereignty of other nations. In other words, although the Report superficially is dedicated to the principle of maximum use of social science, this principle is not brought into play at the critical point. The ambiguities and doubts raised by previous DoD incursions into the area of foreign social research remain intact and are in no way even partially resolved.

The panelists are dedicated to the principle of high-payoff research, but appear to be disquietingly convinced that this is equivalent to whatever the members of the panel themselves are doing, or whatever their professional specialties are. Thus a high-payoff research area becomes the study of isolation upon individual and group behavior; or the area of simulation of field experiences that the military may encounter; or the study of behavior under conditions of ionizing radiation. It is not incidental that in each instance the panelists themselves have been largely engaged in such kinds of work. One is left with the distinct impression that a larger number of panelists would have yielded only a larger number of "high-payoff" areas, rather than an integrated framework of needs. This leads to a general suspicion that the Report is much more self-serving than a simple review of its propositions indicates.

The references to methodology again raise the specter of Camelot, since it is evident that no general methodology is demonstrated in the Report itself and no genuine innovations are formulated for future methodological directions. There is no discussion of the kind of methodology likely to yield meaningful prediction. Instead, the DoD is simply notified of the correctness of its own biases. We are told that "predictive indicators of a conflict or revolutionary overthrow are examples of the type of data which can gain from control applications." No illustrations of the success of such predictors is given. The purpose turns out to be not so much prediction as control of revolutionary outbreaks. This, then, constitutes the core methodological message of the Report.

## PROJECT THEMIS

As for Project Themis, designed to upgrade scientific and engineering performances at colleges and universities for the benefit of the Defense Department, the project titles at the institutions already selected do not furnish enough information to assess the actual nature of the research. A proposal of more than $1.1 million for research into "chemical compounds containing highly electro-negative elements" was turned down by the dean of faculties at Portland State College. Said he: "I know what the proposal was talking about. It could very easily be interpreted as a proposal involving biological warfare. The proposal could be construed as committing the university to biological warfare."

Among the universities now contracted for Project Themis work is the University of Utah, with the project title "Chemistry of Combustion." Newspaper accounts during the summer of 1967 indicated clearly that this project was aimed at improving missile fuels. Additional illustrations could be given, but the point is clear: Project Themis is what it claims to be, a program to involve universities in research useful to the Defense Department.

The panelists assure us that "DoD has been singularly successful at enlisting the interest and services of an eminent group of behavioral scientists in most of the areas relevant to it." They go on to say that, indeed, "the management of behavioral science research in the military department should be complimented for long-term success in building the image of DoD as a good and challenging environment in which to do both basic and applied research." No names are cited to indicate that there are eminent clusters of behavioral scientists working in the DoD. Nor is there an indication whether "the eminent men" connected with DoD are in fact remotely connected as part-time consultants (like the panelists themselves) or intimately connected with basic work for the government. And even though Foster's letter indicates that there is a problem of recruitment and government-university relations, the panel simply dismisses this as insignificant. Yet members go on to note that the DoD image is perhaps more tarnished than they would like to think; that, for example, the Civil Service Commission discriminates against the behavioral scientist with respect to appointments,

and that it is hard to persuade behavioral scientists that the DoD provides a supportive environment for them. Despite the censure of the Civil Service Commission, it is claimed that the DoD has not been as attractive and as successful in social-science recruitment as we were earlier led to believe.

More damaging, perhaps, is the allegation of the panelists that quality control of research at universities is not in any way superior to that exercised within other research sources, such as the DoD. They tend to see "quality control" as something unrelated to university autonomy and its implications for objectivity. Lest there be any ambiguity on this point, they go on to indicate in an extraordinary series of unsupported allegations that the difficulty is not one of social-science autonomy versus the political requirements of any agency of government, but rather one of bad public relations—which is in turn mostly blamed on "Representatives of Civilian Professional Organizations" who lack a clear picture of DoD requirements and yet testify before Congressional committees, which in turn are backed up by social and behavioral scientists who regard such DoD activities as a threat to academic freedom and scientific integrity, and who "are usually ignorant of the work actually being performed under DoD's aegis."

The specific committee hearings referred to are nowhere indicated. Certainly, the various hearings on such proposed measures as a national social science foundation, or on social accounting, do exhibit the highest amount of professional integrity and concern. It might be that DoD intellectuals are concerned precisely over the non-policy research features of such proposed legislation.

Finally, the panelists offer a gentle slap on the wrist to defense research managers who allegedly lack the time to address themselves to these kinds of problems. In short and in sum, the Report ignores questions having to do with social science autonomy as if these were products of misperceptions to be resolved by good will and better public relations between the DoD and the Academy. That such conclusions should be reached by a set of panelists, half of whom are highly placed in academic life, indicates the degree to which closing the gap between the academy and the polity has paradoxically broken down the political capabilities of social science by weakening its autonomous basis.

The panelists have enough firmness of mind to make two unsolicited comments. But the nature of the comments reveals the flabbiness that results from the tendency of social scientists to conceive of their sciences as service activities rather than as scientific activities. They urge, first, that more work be done in the area of potential high-payoff fields of investigation that might have been overlooked in their own Report, given the short time they had available in preparing it. They further urge the establishment of a continuous group with time to examine other areas in greater depth and to discuss them more deliberately, so that high-payoff areas can be teased out and presented for cost considerations. In other words, the unsolicited comments suggest mechanisms for improving these kinds of recommendations and making them permanent. They do not consider whether the nature of social science requirements might be unfit for the bureaucratic specifications of Foster's originating letter.

### ADVISE AND DISSENT

In some ways, the very tension between social scientists and policy-makers provided each group with a reality test against which basic ideas could be formulated about policy issues. But the very demand for a coalescence of the two, whether in the name of "significant" research or as a straight patriotic obligation, has the effect of corrupting social science and impoverishing policy options.

The question that the Report raises with terrible forcefulness is not so much about the relationship between pure and applied research, but about what the character of application is to be. Applied research is clearly here to stay and is probably the most forceful, singular novel element in American social science in contrast to its European background. What is at stake, however, is a highly refined concept of application that removes theoretical considerations of the character and balance of social forces and private interests from the purview of application. The design of the future replaces the analysis of the present in our "new utopian" world.

The panelists simply do not entertain the possibility that the social world is a behavioral "field" in which decisions have to be made between political goals no less than means. Reports cannot "depoliticize" social action to such an extent that consequences do not follow and implicit choices are not favored. Innovation without a political goal simply assumes that operations leading to a change from one state to another are a value. The Report does not raise, much less favor, significant political changes in the operations of the DoD; and its innovative efforts are circumscribed to improving rather than to changing. However, efficiency is a limited use of applicability because it assumes rather than tests the adequacy of the social system.

The era of good feelings between the federal government and social science, which characterized the period between the outbreak of World War II and extended through the assassination of President John F. Kennedy, no longer exists. In its place seems to be the era of tight money. The future of "nonprofit" research corporations tied to the DoD is being severely impeded from both sides. Universities such as Pennsylvania, the University of California, and Princeton have taken a hard look at academic involvement in classified research for the Pentagon. Princeton, with its huge stake in international-relations programming, is even considering cancelling its sponsorship of a key research arm, the Institute for Defense Analysis. On the other side, many of the "hard" engineering types have continued to press their doubts as to the usefulness of software research. And this barrage of criticism finds welcome support among high military officers who would just as soon cancel social science projects as carry out their implications.

With respect to the panelists, it must be said that a number of them have indicated their own doubts about the Report. One of the participants has correctly pointed out that the Report has not yet been accepted by the DoD, nor have the findings or the recommendations been endorsed by the National Academy of Sciences. Another member claimed that his main reason for accepting the invitation to serve on the panel was to argue against the Defense Department's involving universities in operations such as Project Camelot. He went on to point out that his mission was unsuccessful, since he obviously did not influence the other panelists.

A third panelist points out that the Camelot type of issue was not, to his recollection at least, a criterion in any discussion of the topics. Yet he strongly disclaims his own participation as well as membership in the National Academy of Science Advisory Committee on Government Programs in the Behavioral Sciences. He also indicates that his panel had nothing but an administrative connection with the National Academy of Sciences, and he, too, seems to indicate that he had an ancillary advisory role rather than an integrated preparatory role.

Trying to gauge the accuracy with which the final Report represented a true consensus of the panelists proved most difficult. While most panelists, with hedging qualifications, agreed that the Report reflected an accurate appraisal of their own views, the question of the actual writeup of the document brought forth a far from consistent response. One panelist claims that "all members contributed to the basic draft of the Report. Each assumed responsibility for composing a section, all of which were then reviewed by the panel as a whole." Another panelist declared his participation only "as an observer," and that he was not involved in any final writeup. Yet a third panelist disclaimed any connection with preparing the Report.

A final, and still different, version was stated as follows:

> The report was written by members of the committee and the overall editing and bringing-together responsibility was undertaken by Rains Wallace. One or two members of the committee were assigned to specific topics and drafts were prepared at Williamstown. These went to Wallace, who organized them, did some editing, and sent them back to us. Each person responded and the final version was then prepared by Wallace.

In other words, the actual authorship of a document that was released "in confidence" over the names of some of America's most distinguished social scientists is either the work of all and the responsibility of none, or perhaps—as is more likely the case—the work of one or two people and the responsibility of all.

## FAR vs DoD

The issuance, even in semi-private form, of this Report reveals the existence of a wide gap between the thinking of the two chief departments involved in sensitive research and in research in foreign areas—namely, the Department of Defense and the Department of State. Indeed, the issuance of this Report is likely to exacerbate the feelings of high officials in the State Department that the Defense Department position represents an encroachment.

The memorandum issued in December 1967 by the Department of State's Foreign Area Research Coordination group (FAR), in which it set forth foreign-area research guidelines, represents a direct rebuke or, at the very least, a serious challenge to the orientation that the Report of the Defense Science Board represents. It is a high point in federal recognition that real problems do exist.

The FAR Report is broken into two different sections with seven propositions in each section. First, under Guidelines for Research Contract Relations Between Government and Universities, are the following:

1 The government has the responsibility for avoiding actions that would call into question the integrity of American academic institutions as centers of independent teaching and research.

2 Government research support should always be acknowledged by sponsor, university, and researcher.

3 Government-supported contract research should, in process and results, ideally be unclassi-

fied, but given the practical needs of the nation in the modern world, some portion may be subject to classification. In this case the balance between making work public or classified should lean whenever possible toward making it public.

4 Agencies should encourage open publication of contract research results.

5 Government agencies that contract with university researchers should consider designing their projects so as to advance knowledge as well as to meet the immediate policy or action needs.

6 Government agencies have the obligation of informing the potential researcher of the needs that the research should help meet, and of any special conditions associated with the research contract, and generally of the agency's expectations concerning the research and the researcher.

7 The government should continue to seek research of the highest possible quality in its contract program.

A second set of seven recommendations is listed under Guidelines for the Conduct of Foreign Area Research Under Government Contract, and these too bear very directly on the panel Report and do so most critically and tellingly.

1 The government should take special steps to ensure that the parties with which it contracts have the highest qualifications for carrying out research overseas.

2 The government should work to avert or minimize adverse foreign reactions to its contract research programs conducted overseas.

3 When a project involves research abroad, it is particularly important that both the supporting agency and the researcher openly acknowledge the auspices and financing of research projects.

4 The government should under certain circumstances ascertain that the research is acceptable to the host government before proceeding on the research.

5 The government should encourage cooperation with foreign scholars in its contract research program.

6 Government agencies should continue to coordinate their foreign-area research programs to eliminate duplication and overloading of any one geographical area.

7 Government agencies should cooperate with academic associations on problems of foreign-area research.

This set of recommendations (with allowances made for the circumstances of their issuance) unquestionably represents the most enlightened position yet taken by a federal agency on the question of the relationship between social science and practical politics. These sets of recommendations not only stand as ethical criteria for the federal government's relationship to social scientists, but —even more decisively—represent a rebuke to precisely the sort of militarization of social science implicit in the panel Report. The reassertion by a major federal policy-making agency of the worth to the government of social science autonomy represented the first significant recognition by a federal agency that Project Camelot was the consequence, not the cause, of the present strains in social science-federal bureaucracy relationships.

## SUPPLEMENTAL READINGS

Alsop, Joseph: "Ghetto Education," *New Republic*, vol. 157 (Nov. 18, 1967), pp. 18–23.

Astin, Alexander W.: *Who Goes to College?* Chicago: Science Research Associates, 1965.

Ballinger, Stanley: "Social Studies and Social Controversy," *School Review*, vol. 71 (spring 1963), pp. 97–111.

Brameld, Theodore: *Education for the Emerging Age*, New York: Harper & Row, Publishers, 1961.

Caplow, Theodore, and Reece J. McGee: *The Academic Marketplace*, New York: John Wiley & Sons, Inc., 1961.

Coleman, James S.: "The Adolescent Subculture and Academic Achievement," *American Journal of Sociology*, vol. 65 (May 1960), pp. 337–347.

Conant, James E.: *The Education of American Teachers*, New York: McGraw-Hill Book Company, 1964.

Dreeben, Robert: *On What Is Learned in School*, Reading, Mass.: Addison-Wesley Publishing Co., Inc., 1968.

Greely, Andrew M., and Peter Rossi: *The Education of Catholic Americans*, Chicago: Aldine Publishing Co., 1966.

Jencks, Christopher, and David Riesman: *The Academic Revolution*, Garden City, N.Y.: Doubleday & Company, Inc., 1968.

Kelley, Dean M.: "Protestant and Parochial Schools," *Commonweal*, vol. 79 (Jan. 31, 1964), pp. 520–524.

Kerr, Clark: *The Uses of the University*, Cambridge, Mass.: Harvard University Press, 1963.

McCreary, Anne: "Intergroup Relations in the Elementary School," *Journal of Teacher Education*, vol. 14 (March 1963), pp. 74–79.

Pelz, Donald C., and Frank M. Andrews: *Scientists in Organization*, New York: John Wiley & Sons, Inc., 1966.

Sanford, Nevitt: *The American College*, New York: John Wiley & Sons, Inc., 1962.

Scott, John Finley: "The American College Sorority: Its Role in Class and Ethnic Endogamy," *American Sociological Review*, vol. 30 (June 1965), pp. 514–527.

Schwartz, Robert, Thomas Pettegrew, and Marshall Smith: "Fake Panaceas for Ghetto Education," *New Republic*, vol. 157 (Sept. 23, 1967), pp. 16–19.

Sewell, William H.: "Community Residence and College Plans," *American Sociological Review*, vol. 26 (February 1964), pp. 24–37.

Turner, Ralph H.: *The Social Context of Ambition*, San Francisco: Chandler Publishing Company, 1964.

Most of the problems discussed in this book may be seen at close range in the family group. Although the family unit is still the primary institution of influence and responsibility, its relative power has been lessened during the last five or six decades. The family's inability to adapt satisfactorily to social change has been the subject of much attention by both behavioral scientists and the general public. The family and the school are institutions that most Americans feel competent to discuss with authority, with personal experience substituted for hard facts and replicated research findings.

Important functions of the family have been lost or greatly curtailed. Families formerly *made* a living together; today individual members of the family are likely to be *earning* a living. Prior to the industrial and urbanization periods family members shared the labor of planting and harvesting crops and caring for the livestock. During the handicraft period household articles such as shoes, clothes, and utensils were actually manufactured in the home, with each family member contributing in some way to the completed product. Formerly the family enjoyed a sense of group identity associated with its farm, its product, or its way of working. Today very few families are economic units in the sense of group economic participation. Father and mother may be working, but at different jobs, and probably at different places and times of employment. The children are in school and are thus largely removed from the labor market. These significant changes have had a major impact on the American family.

The traditional roles of men and women have changed dramatically. Formerly most women were homemakers as a permanent calling. Today the task of maintaining the home is frequently restricted to the early years of marriage, with the cooperative help of the husband. Women were formerly second-class citizens and were not able to vote, serve on juries, or own property. In most states women now enjoy "approximately equal" rights—and in some states with community-property laws some men believe women have "more than equal" rights. Increasing evidence points to the favorable effect of Title VII of the Civil Rights Act of 1964, banning employment discrimination on the basis of race, religion, or sex. On August 5, 1968, the Equal Employment Commission ruled that it was illegal for employers to fill most positions through separate "male" and "female" help-wanted advertisements. The commission did not list what jobs and positions would qualify for exemption; it did express the opinion that the burden of proof that a particular sex was preferable was on the employer running such an advertisement. Sonia Pressman, a commission attorney, observed that the board had granted exceptions in the cases of actors and models, and she believed that the commission would permit exceptions where there was a "traditional element of sex appeal," such as with Playboy Club "bunnies." A few days later, on August 9, 1968, the Equal Employment Commission ruled that an airline stewardess may not be dismissed when she passes her thirty-third birthday or when she marries. The commission, in an earlier ruling, had pointed out that sex could not be a qualification for the job of airline cabin attendant. An interesting question may arise when some male applicant for the position of air steward is turned down on the basis of "sex appeal." Thus much attention has centered in the conflict between family and careers for women. With ever-increasing opportunities for higher education and high-paying professional positions, more able women are confused about the proper sequence of these two roles: family first and then career, or career first and then family, or both simultaneously.

Considerable discussion has been directed to the increase in divorce, from a low of 3 in 100 marriages in 1870 to about 1 in 4 marriages today in urban America. Marriages were formerly believed to be lifelong religious or civil relationships broken only by death. Family elders assumed the role of bringing young people together for the purpose of marriage, and practical considerations of health and finance of prospective mates loomed large. However, with the post-Reformation a period of romanticism developed, confined at first to upper-class feudal society. With romance as the chief uniting factor, any marked disenchantment between the couple seriously weakened the objective of the marriage. Many marriages today seem to be entered into not "for better or for worse," but merely "for better." The revolution in attitudes toward marriage as a relationship is certain to be a disorganizing experience for many couples.

Divorce seems to occur more frequently among childless couples, those married less than ten years, teenage marriages, urban marriages, couples with a short acquaintance before marriage, couples whose kin and friends disapproved strongly of the marriage, and couples of less, rather than more, formal education. Divorce has become so common in our society that the stigma of divorce now seems to be minimal; in fact, a divorced woman of forty probably has more status than a woman of the same age who has never been married. Some sociologists have argued that the status of marriage has forced many young women into marginal marriages rather than risk the chance of never marrying. Others are inclined to see the day coming when women will express considerably more independence and autonomy concerning the status of marriage. There is a general consensus that later marriages would probably be more enduring.

State laws permit a variety of grounds for divorce, but these laws frequently do not represent the real reasons that couples seek separation through the courts. No state permits a divorce because the husband and wife hate each other. No state permits a divorce for mutual agreement of general unhappiness. And further, no two states have the same marriage and divorce laws. In general, most states consider as legal grounds for divorce adultery, desertion, sterility, cruelty, nonsupport by the husband, and conviction for a felony. In fact, marriage and divorce laws vary so much that middle-class couples can shop around for states to get married in and others to get divorced in, with Nevada being able to accommodate the largest number. The increase in the number of grounds for divorce in several states is an acknowledgement of the discrepancy between state laws on divorce and the real reasons for divorce. Until very recently New York granted divorces only for adultery; its new law permits divorce on grounds of adultery, cruelty, desertion, and conviction for a felony.

Desertion is often the easiest ground for divorce. The husband simply leaves the home for a stipulated time, and the wife may then use this "desertion" as a suitable legal ground. Desertion has thus become a mutual arrangement that provides an ideal ground for divorce; inasmuch as the "deserter" is not present in the court, there is no contest of plaintiff and defendant and, more important, no airing of marital difficulties to increase bitterness or be exposed to the public. Until the courts are able to consider the real reasons for divorce, we may expect continuing use of spurious grounds as an effective subterfuge for resolving domestic unhappiness.

One of the demographic factors rarely discussed in connection with the increase in divorce is the declining death rate. More married persons are living into their late-middle and retirement ages. Today divorce rather than death is likely to separate many couples with children. In fact, with proper correction for the increase in life expectancy, there may even be fewer broken homes than there were a century ago. As simple logic, the longer couples survive, the greater chance that they will be separated by divorce rather than death.

With the general increase in divorce a new problem has emerged, that of remarriage, especially as it relates to children. Children of a divorced couple are usually assigned by the courts to their mother, and when she remarries her children have the task of adjusting to a new "father." There are predictable complications when the real father comes to visit his children in their new family setting. The old quip of "your children, my children, and our children" is becoming a more common description of many remarriages. Some parents prefer to avoid subjecting their children to this strain by placing them in boarding schools, and this solution, of course, carries its own problems.

Family problems vary significantly in terms of social-class requirements. William H. Sewell and Vimal P. Shah document the influence of parents in encouraging their children to attend college. Their study reveals the relationship of educational aspirations to intelligence and to parental encouragement, and of intelligence to socioeconomic status. On the one hand, middle-class children are under all kinds of parental pressure to realize the importance of "getting ahead" and "keeping ahead." In order to achieve a place in society, they are expected to defer marriage, to defer employment, and to defer impulse gratification. On the other hand, lower-class families tend to permit their children to engage in "impulse following" rather than expecting them to defer gratification. In general lower-class children are more often permitted to engage in fighting, to indulge more freely in sexual experience, and to terminate schooling earlier. Part of the current "war on poverty" is aimed at giving the lower-class child a sense of achievement, making him a "go-getter," and helping him to avoid the low aspirations of his family. Schools are viewed as "compensatory institutions" to bridge the gap between the lower-class family and the middle-class expectation of achievement. Interestingly enough, some lower-class parents have challenged the schools' middle-class bias on the matter of language, protesting, for example, that they do not want their children told that the word "ain't" may not be used in school conversation. Some groups view the middle-class bias of the school as a direct challenge to their emerging ethnic morale.

In this chapter four important selections survey some basic problems of the modern family. Otto Pollak examines the impact of government, standardization, and professionalism on the American family. Robert F. Winch and Scott A. Greer analyze the relationship between ethnicity and extended familism in an urban-rural continuum. Erwin O. Smigel and Rita Seiden describe the heterosexual behavior of young people in the United States over a period of four decades. Finally, an impressive study by William H. Sewell and Vimal P. Shah reports on the social class, parental encouragement, and educational aspirations of a randomly selected group of 10,318 Wisconsin high school seniors.

## 25   THE OUTLOOK FOR THE AMERICAN FAMILY   OTTO POLLAK

The various dimensions of governmental impact upon family life analyzed in the preceding chapters must impress the reader of this issue with optimism and also with apprehension. Governmental support seems to be associated with governmental control inseparably. It has been part of the sociological tradition to notice with regret that the government is taking over functions previously performed by the family,[1] and Clark Vincent has done us a great service in questioning this tradition.[2] It should be emphasized that this sociological tradition has not yet paid sufficient attention to the advances in medicine, in technology, in the natural sciences, and in the standard of living. The family may have had educational functions among illiterate people, but it may safely be assumed that together with literacy the school master made his entrance into the educational domain. A farmer may have taught his son how to sow and harvest; his wife may have taught her daughter how to milk, cook, and make butter; but it is probably a fallacy to assume that the family and the family alone ever taught its children the three R's. When literacy and compulsory education became a pattern in our civilization, fathers and mothers were not expelled from an educational function which they formerly had. They were asked by the school system to become "assistant teachers" after school hours, supervising homework and helping with it. In many instances this was an impossible task, because in immigrant families the children usually spoke the language better than their parents and were introduced to a level of education foreign to their parents. In recent years the new mathematics and phonetic spelling, nuclear physics, aerodynamics, and computer techniques have left parents stranded in educational obsolescence, making assistance in homework an impossible assignment.

Even in the field of nutrition one can identify governmental impact on family function as supplementation rather than as substitution. The school lunch for children from poor homes is not a lunch which they would have had from their mothers; it is a better lunch. The medical examination which children receive at school is not a medical examination for which, in the past, their parents arranged privately; it is a measure of health care formerly unavailable to children. "Case finding" was not done by the family, because the medical orientation did not exist and the necessary instrumentation was not invented; the necessary skills require professional or paraprofessional training. The accusation of invasion into the family domain which is repetitively made against the government ignores the change in living conditions which has made governmental intervention and provision of services a necessity rather than an imposition.

It is true, however, that these governmental services have imposed upon the family new interactors and new decision makers which have produced complexities, feelings of inadequacy and guilt. Experts in the fields of health, welfare, and education have brought, along with governmental service, standards against which family members cannot help but feel wanting. The mental health accusations against mothers and fathers charging them, with never-varying monotony, of being failures in providing models of masculinity and femininity are a case in point.[3] Educators are frequently tempted to blame failure of children in school

Reprinted with the permission of the author and the publisher from *Journal of Marriage and the Family*, vol. 29 (February 1967), pp. 193–206.

This article was prepared upon request for the *Journal of Marriage and the Family* and was supported by a grant from the Russell Sage Foundation.

on their parents. The juvenile courts blame and sometimes punish parents for the delinquencies of their children. Visiting nurses imply by their instruction that the women of the household don't know how to feed, clean, and nurse their children; and public welfare regulations make benefits dependent on a code of conduct which welfare recipients frequently do not have and do not consider desirable.

## INVASIONS INTO FAMILY LIFE

The function which truly has been taken away from the family by other institutions is not education, health care, or homemaking, but the autonomy of setting its own standards. This autonomy may always have been limited. It certainly was limited by religion. It probably was limited by the feudal relationship between lord and serf, but against these earlier models the nineteenth century model was one of great freedom in decision making. In that perspective, the twentieth century model presents a loss of autonomy, a being put on the defensive, a position of cultural lag, a being exposed to the demands of the new standards set by experts who are equipped with the power to render service which the family wants but which, without compliance with these standards, the family cannot have.

Here is a new issue for family life in modern times: the defense of its own power against the expert, the emotional security necessary to protect itself against becoming a dependent variable of changing opinions in the fields of education, health care, and public welfare. The discovery that all experts can make mistakes, that one may have the right to be poor, and the right to be sick is one of the challenges of the future for the American family, confronted by experts who can and do change their opinions as a matter of normal professional development.

One very important invasion of family life produced by governmental services is the invasion of family time in association and development. The American middle-class child is notoriously overscheduled; with school hours, dancing lessons, music lessons, and paraeducational experiences such as newspaper routes, baby-sitting, and lawn-cutting, the American youngster of middle-class parents has little time to be with them and to acquire intergenerational competence. With governmental services via education and health care reaching the children of the poor, a similar invasion of family time may well occur in the near future for these population groups. The same is true for developmental time. The wisdom of past generations has kept children at home for the first six years of their lives to give the developing personality anchor points in outside demands.[4] School reform and the therapeutic culture of our time have pushed the separation of a child from his home through kindergarten and nursery school into earlier and earlier developmental phases. In view of the emotional demands which particularly the oedipal phase of development makes upon children in the fourth and fifth years of life, nursery schools represent an experiment in socialization which has not yet been sufficiently linked with later difficulties in development.

From this point of view, projects such as Head Start and Get Set represent a preparation for grade school which in turn will demand a price in human development which families will have to pay. The involvement of parents in these projects, even if successful, will present in turn a new invasion of family time. It would be an interesting empirical study to compute the time demands of modern educational standards and health care standards together with the time demands of making a living or a home, to see whether the natural framework of a 12-hour day can accommodate them all. Such items as travel time to clinics and schools, waiting time in health care facilities, and chauffeuring children to different extra-curricular activities may assume threatening proportions for mothers with several children.

This is frequently overlooked in the prescriptions that doctors and nurses give for the body management of patients who are not hospitalized. Other claims for time and attention may well account for many failures to carry out a medical regimen which undoubtedly would benefit the patient. These conflicting time demands present the modern family with the problem of setting its own priorities, for which no professional expert advice is available. The power of the government and the opinion of these experts, however, produce new elements of culture which have ethical impact and over time will change priorities among different uses of time.

## NEW RESPONSIBILITIES

The modern model of medicine requires regular health checkups which must be performed by various experts assisted by technicians. Under the old model of medicine, one used to see a single practitioner when one felt sick and did not want to be stoic about it. Now one has to see not one doctor but several doctors. When one is ill, he has no right to neglect his own health. This obligation to check on one's health, similar to the obligation to check the condition of one's automobile or the engines of an airplane, has introduced into the life of the American family a whole new pattern of anxieties. Cancerophobia is a case in point; it renews itself for people over 40 years of age every six months, and they are anxious not only for themselves but also for their marriage partners. The checkup by an ophthalmologist renews in one-year intervals fear of glaucoma and cataracts. A visit to the dentist for a checkup on dental health raises apprehensions about unexpected expenditures which cannot be fitted into the normal budget. Even the civic duty of entering an ambulatory station for a chest X ray may leave one with days of anxiety over the possibility of having tuberculosis. The increase in the life span, in individual instances, has brought about decades and decades of fears of dying, of anticipation of morbidity, and of the experience of prolonged chronic illness for which the only hope is not cure but postponement of death.

These psychological side effects of modern health care are creating another new issue for modern family life: the problem of fortitude concerning the outcome of health examinations for oneself and other family members and the marshalling of energy in coping with the findings.

In caring for the aged economically and medically, and now also—through supported housing—residentially, the government seems to have truly taken over and incidentally vastly improved the performance of an old family function. As mentioned before, it should not be forgotten, however, that many people live out a fuller life span as a result of modern health care than they did before. A family which formerly may have had to support one grandparent may easily now have to support four. Thus the government may seem to have stepped into a family role which has become too burdensome a responsibility. However, problem solution means problem creation; relief of economic, medical, and residential responsibility does not mean relief from emotional responsibility. Adult sons and daughters now will have to spend decades in interactions with aging parents and inlaws and thus have to develop a new type of interpersonal competence, the competence of positively interacting with a person who stimulates by his very existence and development one's own anxieties about dying. Interestingly enough, the advocacy of home care for chronic patients interferes with one of the traditional defenses against having one's anxieties so stimulated, namely, with the separation from such stimuli by long-term hospitalization of the patient.

Here again we may have a phenomenon of social change which extends the time impact of a traditional family obligation to such a degree as to create a new family responsibility. The old philosophical problem of the point at which a change in quantity creates a change in quality makes its appearance here. Home care of an aging family member probably was much more limited in the historical model than it is now. Undetected cancers, incarcerated hernias, untreated diabetes, and uncontrolled hypertension may frequently have put an early time limit upon home care. With the modern armamentarium of illness detection and illness management, this time limit may be extended beyond the levels of tolerance previously demanded of family members. Under such conditions, physicians and medical social workers will encounter family opposition to home care arrangements probably less as an expression of emotional alienation between aging parents and their adult children than as a realistic assessment of the dimensions of care which medical advance has given to old filial responsibility. Where, however, responsibility is accepted, new emotional complications are likely to occur. Repressed death wishes may be invited to return into consciousness or may be created on the conscious level simply as a form of psychological coping with burdensome reality. The resulting conflict with our still-operative ethical system may result either in poor performance of the home care function or in compensatory mechanisms such as flight into illness by the adult son or daughter in charge of home care. At least it may result in feelings of guilt for which psychoanalytically oriented therapy does not offer outlets as compatible with a person's wish for growth and development as the identification of wishes for gratification due to unresolved conflicts of early childhood. Incestuous wishes and fears of punishment related to such wishes may be recognized as infantile and restructured. There is nothing in our Judeo-Christian tradition which would interfere with this restructuring, in the perspective of adulthood. Death wishes against an aging parent, however, cannot be accommodated within such an orientation. This tension between life maintenance under modern health care and the limits of tolerance within which filial responsibility was formerly meant to operate will probably create a new mental health culture orchestrated with a replacement of filial responsibility by public responsibility.

It is, however, not only the aged who, due to government-supported medical services, are now returned home for long spans of time without expectation of getting well. Family members in other age groups, middle-aged and adolescents and in the future probably also children, who were formerly thought of as requiring custodial care, will—under the impact of governmental pressure for community psychiatry—return home in increasing numbers. There again they will represent home-care problems that are new in historical perspective. In these instances, families will be asked to assume not only caretaker functions but also therapeutic functions. In relatively favorable situations, family members—particularly parents—will be asked to serve as treatment aides by doctors and social workers. In less favorable situations, they will be asked to join the patient as co-patients and undergo treatment on their own in order to make it possible for him to benefit from home care.

## FAMILY FUNCTION AND FAMILY PATHOLOGY

This tendency to see the family of a patient as a treatment resource or at least as a reception station for a patient whom doctors have despaired of helping in hospitals or institutions presents not only a new function for the family; it probably is also therapeutically counter-indicated. It is by now fairly well established in dynamically oriented psychiatry and diagnostically oriented casework that it is almost impossible for one family member to be mentally sick and for the other family members to be well. Mental disturbance in one marriage partner is usually found in interaction with mental disturbance in the spouse. The relationship between a punishing, masochistic wife and an orally dependent alcoholic husband comes to mind in this respect.[5] The impact of parental pathology upon the pathology of children is textbook material, and so is the impact of sibling rivalry upon personality development. The appearance of health versus disease within one family group is frequently the result of family pathology itself. "Scapegoating" one family member into the role of the "sick" occurs frequently in families with one schizophrenic son or daughter.[6] Sometimes the pathology of one person appears like virtue in the traditional value system. The martyrdom of "wife and mother" vis-à-vis dependent husband and children lends to a psychological exploitation the appearance and dignity of sacrifice.[7] A masochistic assumption of being alone guilty and the cause of all dissatisfactions in a marital relationship can give to the other marriage partner an appearance of health and victimization which he does not deserve.[8] In consequence, it will frequently happen that under the pressure of community psychiatry, a patient will be returned to a family setting which was the cause or at least one of the causes, of his disturbance. Where this will be recognized, family treatment will have to become the treatment of choice. Where it will not be recognized, relapses of the patient or outbreak of overt pathology in other family members is likely to result.

This has become fairly established doctrine in the mental-health-serving disciplines. There is, however, the possibility that similar phenomena and similar relationships of interlocking physical pathologies will be found to operate in families. As far as hypertension, ulcers, and obesity are concerned, the relationship between interpsychic, interpersonal, and physiological factors is apparently taken for granted by specialists in internal medicine and psychiatrists alike, but the reactions of organically oriented physicians seem to take a direction opposed to those of psychiatrists and social workers. Under the modern model of health care, doctors frequently see and treat only one member of a family. This is particularly so in group health plans under which family members may not even be eligible.[9] Specialization works in the same direction. Where, however, only one family member is treated, lasting success is unlikely to result. It is therefore possible and likely that patients would be physiologically rehabilitated in hospital care and released to families where all conditions conducive to hypertension, ulcers, and obesity will continue to operate.

Since every trend, however, has a countertrend creating feedback, it is very likely that in the not-too-distant future and particularly under the stimulus of government-supported research, organically oriented medicine will recapture the methods of family health care which were used by the solo practitioner of the old health-care model on an impressionistic basis.[10]

In summary, it would appear that the emphasis on home care and on community psychiatry will make family therapy a preferred treatment form in the organic as well as in the psychiatric specialties. Again, this will mean a claim on family time and a new health care morality for the family which will have to be integrated with other claims on family time and priorities resulting from other systems of family values. This integration task, however, will have to be done by a family which is ill prepared for rendering sick-care functions and frequently unwilling to assume the self-conception of a sick family system.[11] Medical services will have an uphill fight in bringing family members to an acceptance of this concept. They will, however, be strengthened in this task by the increasing recognition on the part of the general public that government agencies have tended to tackle health problems that were not effectively solved under the traditional model of private health care.

In this respect, one is reminded of the "expediter"[12] suggested by sociologists active in the war against poverty as an indigenous service agent who helps poor families to gather in the various strands of welfare services available in metropolitan centers and to "expedite" the rendering of these services. In many ways the American family and the service professions stand here at a crossroad. With governmental services in health, education, and welfare offering higher standards of care in so many dimensions through so many organizations and so frequently limited to only one or the other member of a family, it may well become a function of the modern family to integrate these services and to develop expertise in their use and orchestration. This family function is unprecedented and would represent a new expression of our changing society. On the other hand, the idea of the "expediter" may be picked up by one of the existing health and welfare serving professions and may be extended from service confined to poor families to service available to all families. It might well become a new form and content of community organization far exceeding the usefulness and potential of community organization in the traditional meaning of the term. The time has arrived when the bureaucratic jungle of governmental offerings of service in the fields of health, education, and welfare will either produce its professional scouts or force the family to develop these scouting skills in its own membership. From this viewpoint it may be much more important for a father to take his children to a district health office, to a department of welfare, to a large city clinic, to the school board, to the campus of a state university, to a community health center, and to an office of the Social Security Administration than to take him fishing or camping. The fun may not be quite so obvious, the air not so fresh, the father's skill not quite so obviously superior, but the growth in coping capacity and the relevance of information and orientation to our world derived from such expeditions are likely to be considerably greater.

## THE FAMILY AND BUREAUCRACY

It has been part and parcel of the American tradition that the schools educate the children away from the parents, providing them with information, language skills, and an orientation to the world which the parents do not possess. In the private school system, particularly of a denominational or class specificity, the parents usually got, and are still getting, some compensation for this alienation of their children through education from the fact that this was the education chosen by them for their children. The maintenance of the denominational tie or the maintenance of class status provides educational benefits which parents can consider as a perpetuation of their own self-concepts in their children and thus provides significant compensation for the adaptive superiority with which the school systems separate the children from them. As far as the public school system is concerned, such compensation did not exist and does not exist now. The antagonism of parents against the school system is codetermined by the widespread antagonism of parents to authority and particularly to governmental authority. Shostak has pointed out that currently the school system forces parents into a confrontation with the issues of racial integration.[13] This, of course, cannot help but increase parental antagonism to the school system in many instances. A perhaps not so clearly perceived reason for conflict between school and family lies in the fact that school personnel tend to blame family conditions and particularly parental behavior for the school failure of the children.

With all these reasons for an antagonistic attitude toward education, parents cannot afford to assume a fighting stance. The ever-increasing standards for employment, the demands of our technology for manpower with developed mathematical ability, and the communication explosion which makes it difficult to find relevant teaching material without organizational guidance leave many parents who are concerned about the future of their children without an alternative to government-supported school systems. There is, of course, in many instances a difference in standards between public and private schools, but the economic situation of many parents makes the use of the public school system not only an obligation but also the only available opportunity to attain for their children the educational qualifications required by the employment standards in our society.

This presents for the modern American family an interesting psychological challenge, the challenge of not letting one's own resentments and conflicts interfere with one's children's use of the school system. Frequently it has been found that the parents of children with school difficulties are persons in conflict with authority who need professional help to protect their children against becoming the battlefield of their parents' fight with the school.[14] Due to the availability of professional help, the increasing importance of school counselors in the educational system, and the referral relationships between school systems and child-guidance clinics, situations of conflict between parents and schools are by no means doomed to permanence. The pervasiveness of our growing mental health culture promises to bring increasing awareness of childrearing problems to both school personnel and families. On the basis of such shared understanding, the conflicts between family and school may well become smaller than they are today. Having the monopoly of education, the schools will, of course, try to impose the behavioral standards of their experts upon the families; but, as the American family of all classes increasingly accepts the mental health principles from which these standards are developed, the experience of friction will tend to become smaller. He who agrees with authority feels free.[15]

In all areas so far covered, the services of the government can be obtained only at the price of dealing .with bureaucracy; and the school system has been accused of preparing America's children for effectiveness in such dealings and generally for an acceptance of such bureaucratic arrangements not only in governmental services but also in employment and other institutional expressions of mass culture. This accusation is probably true in fact. It would be difficult to imagine a bureaucratic system which would train people for a non-bureaucratic way of life. Even if that were possible, however, one would wonder whether young persons so trained would be served by their education. Our stage of civilization is, for better or for worse, geared to corporate organization, in which the individual must be replaceable and therefore a conformist and in which he must be willing to be transferred from location to location and therefore cannot afford to have deep emotional ties outside the family circle. There are no alternatives, given the stage of our technology and our standards of living. It should be noted that the people who take exception to this education[16] operate within its framework and have to give their own anger and rebellion an organizational frame of reference with mass communication, coordination of effort, and bureaucratic avenues to effectiveness.

There is only one counterpoint to bureaucratic adaptation, and this release from bureaucratic restraints can be found in the modern American family. It is, perhaps, in modern times the family's most important function. In a civilization of large organizations, even the extended family is a small one. Nobody in it is really replaceable, and nobody is expected to be. Even as objects of hostility, its members are secure in their individuality. As a matter of fact, the family may be that spot in bureaucratic civilizations in which the need to express hostility may yet be gratified without irreparable consequences. School relationships, employment relationships, health care relationships, and welfare relationships punish antagonism severely and often destructively. In family relation-

ships, hostility can frequently be tolerated; although currently there is still the risk of starting vicious cycles of response. In the family of the future, however, the need to express hostility may even be accepted as one of the release functions which a family must render its members. In all probability, it will become less destructive with the shared increase in understanding of dynamic principles of interaction. It has been observed in modern times that people know more about one another than they used to know. A general awareness of psychodynamics is in the process of development. Such concepts as hostility, displacement, and projection begin to become part of a framework of interpersonal orientation. In the century of "psychological man,"[17] the understanding which follows from familiarity with these concepts is likely to grow. It is probable that with such understanding will come greater acceptance of the function of emotional release for the family than would have been thought possible 100 years ago. Since understanding means adequacy, the human targets of aggression within the family will be less vulnerable than they were when human understanding had not yet encompassed interpersonal dynamics.

In a bureaucratic organization one never knows all his opponents and enemies, and one must be opponent and enemy of many persons whom he does not even know. For this reason the organization man is an anxious and frequently angry man. Not to know one's enemies is invariably associated with feelings of inadequacy, and these in turn are accompanied by feelings of anger and rage. One can hardly be in school or in employment, in a hospital or in a welfare agency, without having these experiences of inadequacy and anger, and it is the greatest burden of this situation that these feelings cannot be expressed in the setting in which they were generated. Sinc cathartic experiences have the advantage of immediacy, although not of permanency, in giving relief, no society of bureaucratic organization can avoid explosions without institutions which furnish such an outlet. In our time the family has the making of such an institution. The more women enter the labor force and participate in our educational system, the more they will understand the displaced anger of their husbands. It may be startling to see this function delineated for an institution which is supposed to be based on love, but this is a problem of gestalt rather than a problem of motivation. Hostility in the family looks out of place if one views families as organizations based on feelings of love. If one considers them as organizations of freedom of expression in a world of constraints, hostility appears in place.

In a wider frame of reference, the family of the future should be visualized as a place of intimacy in a world of loose and depersonalized relationships. "Intimacy" means closeness but closeness in other than purely physiological dimensions. The Latin root of the term signifies fear. We find it in the words "timid" and "timorous" still. If we extend the meaning of the Latin root, "intimacy" means a relationship in which one enters the fears of the partner. In our society where one comes more and more to realize to what degree his destiny is determined by impersonal and unpredictable forces such as atomic warfare, occupational obsolescence, and simply bureaucratic career mishap, the need for family members' willingness to enter into one's fears will become urgent and demanding. It will probably be one of the most important functions of the family in our time. In the past the ministry met such needs to a degree. In our time psychiatrists and social workers have met it. But no manpower extension in the helping professions is likely to ever attain coverage in meeting these needs. It is the family which is available and may increasingly be ready to do so.

In such a family in which husband and wife, parents and child will have to fulfill the relief function with psychological understanding, power relationships between parents and older children are likely to appear absurd; for in the realm of intimacy there are only equals. In a child who understands the displaced anger of his father and in a husband who understands the anger of his domineering wife, the target quality of hostility disappears and is replaced by that of a recipient of a meaningful emotional communication. The family becomes a community of sufferers who understand one another and an organization of self-help and regeneration for the battles of bureaucratic existence.

## A MODEL OF FAMILY FUNCTIONS

In the article "Mental Health and the Family," Clark Vincent has suggested that one of the areas least explored by family sociologists is the marital relationship in its various dimensions.[18] The author of this concluding chapter should like to add to this complaint by pointing out that the field of sibling relationship has remained similarly unexplored and that the area of relationship between parents and children has been much more adequately covered in terms of what parents do for and to their children than in terms of the reverse phenomenon of what children do for and to their parents. Furthermore, the relationship between parents and children has been frequently perceived as one covering the phases of development from infancy to adolescence and has taken little note of the much longer part of the life span between young adulthood and senescence. It may be a useful closure of this chapter on the outlook for American family life to propose a model of family functions in which the governmental impact on family life would be seen as imbedded in the wider frame of reference of the family under the impact of social change.

The complexity of family life, even within the limited membership of the nuclear family, can be conveniently analyzed by visualizing it as the orchestration of three systems of interpersonal relationships. The word "system," according to its Greek derivation, implies a single topic or issue around which the activities and feelings of a plurality of human beings are coordinated. Due to the biological facts of growth and decay, of heterosexuality and generational difference, one can say that the family is a small organization of people related to one another by age and sex for purposes of life maintenance in the here and now and preparation for the future. It may be noted that the expectation on the basis of which most modern

American families are created, the expectation of happiness, is not included in the definition. Happiness is an evaluation of the degree to which life maintenance in the present and preparation for the future are met by the interactions among the family members. Similarly, love and hate are emotional assessments of satisfactions rendered or not rendered by family members to one another. They will invariably accompany family experiences, but they are emotional evaluations of family performances rather than functional assignments to be met in family life.

It pertains to the nature of a system that change in one member or one part will produce change in the other members or the other parts. In families, dyadic relationships can never operate without a transactional effect upon the overtly nonparticipating members. A fight between brothers and sisters will affect the parents; a fight between a parent and a child will affect the other parent and the other siblings; and a fight between the parents will affect the children. Every fight between family members invites those not directly involved to offer substitute gratifications. Wives, disappointed in their marriages, turn to their sons for emotional gratification. Disappointed husbands turn, similarly, to their daughters. On the other hand, every relationship of closeness excludes, to a degree, those who are not direct partners. It may be shocking to some to face the proposition that a close marital relationship keeps the children at a distance and that a close parent-child relationship leaves the other parent and the other children emotionally outside, thus inviting them to form compensatory alliances. It follows that any shift in one of these relationships must bring about shifts in the others and that improvement in one is frequently accompanied by deterioration in another. Problem solution in one family relationship can therefore frequently give the impression of problem creation in another.[19] The proposition taken in this paper, however, does not consider problem creation through problem solution as malfunctioning in family life but as the normal price to be paid for human development. The same principle holds for the evaluation of the impact of govern-ment upon family life discussed in this issue. Governmental services may solve family problems in health, education, and welfare; it is unavoidable that by doing so they also create problems. In consequence, the family functions that will be presented in the concluding part of this chapter will be presented as problem solving and problem creating within the general framework of unavoidable social and developmental costs.

## THE MARITAL RELATIONSHIP

In the marital relationship itself, our society in its present stage of historical development presents the marriage partners with the following functions: (1) interpersonal reorientation, (2) inter-institutional orchestration, (3) community organization, (4) sexual synchronization, (5) economic coordination, (6) outlet and rescue, (7) ego-support in the defensive and executive areas of the ego, and (8) therapeutic cooperation with the health care services. One of the first functions in marriage is the provision of one's spouse with a new and age-appropriate anchor of close interpersonal association. Such an anchor is provided in childhood by parents and in some aspects by siblings; in adolescence it is provided by peers.[20] In marriage these earlier anchors of close interpersonal association have to be replaced. The need for doing so becomes apparent when a young wife responding to a conflict with her husband packs up and returns to mother. It becomes less obvious, but equally significant, if a young husband in conflict with his wife or simply under stress returns to the street-corner gang. In smooth and rough weather it is the function of a marriage in our society to provide the partners with a new key person and focus for interpersonal closeness. In the development of the marriage relationship, this interpersonal reorientation is not left to remain undisturbed. The arrival of children creates a new function for the marriage partners, namely, giving emotional permission for the other to find additional anchor points for close interpersonal relationships in sons and daughters. At a later stage, with the departure of children from the home, the marital relationship requires from the spouses yet other permissions, namely, the permission to feel loss over the departure of children and the permission to express such loss. At the same time it requires readiness of the spouses to offer each other a renewed anchor for interpersonal closeness. Ultimately, the likelihood or possibility of survival puts upon marriage partners the function of helping one another to search for new stimuli of interpersonal reorientation. This is probably one of the most difficult functions implied in the marriage relationship. In marriages which have worked out well, life tends to appear inconceivable without the other marriage partner. The need for a positive self-concept tempts the marriage partners to draw upon their learning experience with one another in an ever-renewed effort of making themselves indispensable to one another. In the perspective of time, this apparent perfection of the marriage relationship may well conceal extreme egotistical cruelty. To leave the other person without at least a potential of interpersonal reorientation borders on marital exploitation in the cloak of marital love.

Equally important in our time is the function of furnishing a counterpoint to bureaucratic depersonalization and standardization. Throughout this issue we have been alerted to the human price of governmental services. Meeting eligibility requirements, relating one's self-concept to categorization, and meeting standards prescribed by governmental experts who can combine frequently changing opinions with the claim of authority at all stages of their professional development make demands upon our need for an individualized self-concept which cry out for compensation. It is this compensation which ultimately only a marriage partner can provide. The closeness and intimacy of marital association make depersonalization an impossibility; and if it were possible, it would not be wanted. The exclusiveness of monogamy and the ideology of romantic love assume, in the context of interplay with bureaucratic forces, a new meaning of counterpoint and relief. One may not be happy in a marriage, but one is not easily replaceable. One has accepted the assignment of uniqueness, and it is almost impossible to fail in fulfilling the assignment. A divorce may prove that one may have failed to be the right individual or to have chosen the right individual, but it does not prove that one has not been an individual, and it sets one free to look for another individual. However pathological,[21] the search will always be for an individual.

In this respect it is interesting to point out that a marriage is usually also the basis for individualized surroundings. The standardization of large-scale organization always implies the denial of this extension of the ego. One hospital room is like the other; one office is like the other; we lie in standard beds; we sit at standard desks; we work with standard equipment; we go to standard cafeterias for our lunch; we get help in standardized offices of social workers; we are interviewed in standard offices; even as graduate students we study in standard classrooms. In this respect, the consumption function of the marriage performs a true function of individualization. The standardization of mass production notwithstanding, every room in a private home is an island of individualism. It is a miracle of marriage that, at least in the perception of the inhabitants, nobody has a room which duplicates his own.

Some reference has been made to the fact that the proliferation of governmental services available to the family presents an intricate task or organization. Education and health services have to be integrated with welfare services. The goals of prevention have to be pursued by checkups in many areas. Parents have to remain in touch with the school and to respond to report cards in appropriate fashion; mothers have to bring their babies to the well-baby clinic; parents are informed by the school of the results of the health examination of their children and are expected to take appropriate action. It should be noted in passing that even the Social Security Administration advises employees to check their Social Security status every three years. The concern with checkups in so many different areas, the new morality of having to respond to the findings with appropriate immediate action, the limitations of time and the demands of our paper world with its application forms and report forms represent a task for the marriage partners which is only dimly perceived. The tasks of organizing the available services and of providing, storing, and retrieving information represent functions in which the marriage partners almost with necessity have to cooperate with one another. It is a fair proposition that no long income tax form can be answered correctly without the cooperation between husband and wife and that this cooperation has to start on the first day of the calendar year. Similarly, no intake interview with a social worker in a family service agency can produce sufficient information unless both marriage partners cooperate in providing it. The same would be true in a conference with a school counselor or pediatrician. As a consequence, it can be postulated that the high standard of services provided by our various governmental agencies has produced a complex of needed information and a task of organization, a task of assigning priorities under the impact of limited time, and a task of resource-finding which reflects the complexity of modern bureaucratic life.

In recent months the work of Masters and Johnson[22] has brought into the awareness of the American reading public the extension of sexual life associated with the increasing number of people who live out the life span of 70 years or more. In the model of nineteenth century family life, sexual gratification in marriage was supposed to be limited by menopause and climacteric. Apprehension about its impending cessation was noted linguistically as the "dangerous years." While the sexual experience as such is being extended under the impact of improved health care, its reproductive aspect is experiencing governmental impact as well. Recently the state government of Pennsylvania attempted to authorize birth control information for married women if they requested it, an interesting categorization of those eligible for an educational service. On the national scene, the war against poverty is very likely to produce similar educational efforts assisted by the expectation of a change in the official Catholic position. In both dimensions, then—interactional and reproductive—the marital partners are faced with the function of changing their sex habits in response to indirect and direct governmental impact. Implied in these changes are changes in the ideology of sex which are likely to separate it increasingly from the reproductive function both through extension beyond the period of childbearing life and through a wider spread of birth control.

It is by no means facetious to say that the true social security system of the United States is provided by the entrance of the American woman into the labor force. This makes possible not only an extension of the portion of time which her husband can still devote to education; it relieves the family also of dependence on one earner. It raises the standard of living; it provides two claims to Social Security in the legal sense; and it provides for true social equality between the sexes. In an economic sense, the social security of a marriage and the resulting family unit appear therefore vastly enhanced. Again, however, the solution of this problem creates another one, and this is the conflict about sexual identification in a world in which division of labor between the sexes is disappearing. As long as provision of the income was the task of the male and the making of the home was the task of the female, self-concepts related to biological destiny found social support from the assumption of a sex-associated competence in social roles. Males were supposed to be superior earners; females were supposed to be superior homemakers. Adequacy in a social sphere assigned to cultivation by the other sex was considered a flaw in personality development. With the gap of earning power between the sexes narrowing perceptively and with equal participation of men and women an accomplished fact in education, governmental authority in concert with technological change has brought about a situation where neither husband nor wife can find satisfaction or security in a division of labor between the sexes.

It becomes then a task of marital interaction to give the spouses an opportunity to find ego-support in their sexual identity. This appears to be a field for interpersonal experimentation in marriage which again will have to stress individuality rather than categorization. It implies, however, the risk of a distribution of power in decision-making according to the actual distribution of ability and concern between the spouses. This is a great risk, because it is likely to contradict traditional models and self-concepts related to sex. All men encounter femininity at first in the form of motherhood. Under patriarchal arrangements they learn to overcome the original association between femininity and superior power through the encounter with social arrangements favoring the male sex. In our times the opportunities for such encounters come only rarely and, if at all, relatively late in life. Actually our young girls are entrusted with limit-setting on dates and thus meet their potential husbands with a stance of maternity from the start. The absence of the husband from the home leaves decision-making power in the daily affairs of living with the wife. This produces a tendency toward permanent boyhood in the male and toward permanent adulthood in the female. Since this denies both sexes equality in development, as a general principle one might suggest that it would be the task of the wife to make it possible for her husband to overcome the tendency to see a mother-figure in all women. Correspondingly, it might be the task of the husband to help his wife free herself from her eternal stance of maternity toward all men. In its simplest form a modern marital relationship can be visualized as presenting to the woman the task of letting her husband "grow up" and to a man the task of letting his wife be "young."

Ego-support in marriage, however, has a wider field to cover. The legal concept of incompatibility highlights the necessity of this function in marriage. One person, without any hostility, aggression, or intent to hurt—merely through the expression of his existence—may be damaging for another. The phenomenon of developmental arrest may have occurred on different levels in two marriage partners. To use psychoanalytic terminology, an oral character in the wife and an anal character in the husband defy marital coexistence. A woman who has to spend and a husband who has to save cannot maintain their self-concepts in marriage without hurting the self-concept of the other. A husband whose anxieties require business success as a defense cannot help but turn the life of a wife who suffers from separation anxiety into a living hell. Examples could be presented in a never-ending stream, but the essence of the constellation is highlighted. Where the character structures of husband and wife or their defenses against the return of repressed material interfere with one another, failure to perform a basic marriage function has occurred. This function is support for the defenses of the other as long as they are not socially maladaptive.

In the conflict-free sphere of the ego, i.e., in the area of adaptation to outer reality without interfering unconscious factors,[23] support in marital interaction is also required. The fast pace of social change makes it impossible for husbands and wives to go through life without having to learn new techniques, new social roles, and new methods of coping. Learning is one experience which in the fantasies of people is always expected to be terminable. One hopes from step to step of learning that no future learning will be necessary. When rapid social change ever again through life destroys this fantasy, marital support and adaptation become a necessity. In modern America, wives must support their husbands in fighting occupational obsolescence, and husbands of working wives must do the same. The development of governmental services and their utilization similarly require ever-new learning. To give only a recent example, elderly marriage partners have now to learn how to use Medicare, a study assignment which few of them have yet completed. Their adult sons and daughters have to learn how to advise their parents on maintaining supplementary Blue Cross and Blue Shield benefits and whether to maintain major medical insurance from private insurance companies. The mothers of children in Head Start and Get Set programs will have to learn how to participate in these educational enterprises. The parents of adolescents who want to join the Peace Corps or VISTA will have to learn how to change their earlier notions of a career sequence for their children. All this can hardly be done without spouse support, and such support is a function which in itself has to be learned. In sum, it may be said that marriage is not only a counterpoint to organizational life in a bureaucratic world, but it is also a rehabilitative institution which generates new coping power in the encounter of modern man with social change and thus enables him to use what our world has to offer.

In the history of medicine the focus of therapeutic intervention has been predominantly and persistently the body of one individual. Under the impact of recent developments and particularly under the influence of psychoanalysis and its predecessors, the focus of attack has been extended to comprise the working of the mind. Only after decades of disappointment with therapeutic efforts which confine their area of impact to one human being, has a system approach led psychiatrists to consider the family system as the patient. This development has been strengthened by the tradition of social workers to claim the family as the unit of their concern and by the association of sociologists with the helping professions who have claimed the importance of the family members not seen in interventive practice for the outcome of the intervention.[24] With the proliferation of governmental services in the field of health, education, and welfare, the family has also become the focus of governmental concern and has been variously claimed as the patient or the potentially collaborating organization for the interventive effort. In consequence, marriage partners are frequently approached as either noxious agents who have caused developmental mishaps in their children and therefore are obligated to offer themselves as patients, or as therapeutic agents who can aid doctor and social worker and therefore are obligated to do so.

Marriage partners are faced therefore with the function of viewing one another as co-patients, caught in a web of maladaptive interactions which they must attempt to change in the interest of their children as well as in their own self-interest. Alternatively, they must view one another as "indigenous" therapists who must join the professional in a team relationship, associating professional and laymen committed to a process of helpful intervention.

This dichotomy probably conceals a homogeneity of functions. Ever since Freud questioned the separation of illness from health, the separation of therapist from patient has become questionable. In the realms of emotions and interpersonal dynamics, helpfulness originates with the suffering of the helper. Suffering ultimately does not allow for a distinction between professionals and laymen. The imposition of patient roles is balanced by the invocation of therapeutic roles which the culture of our time addresses to the family. From a long-range point of view, this augurs well for an ideological reorientation of families toward a healing civilization, in turn a counterpoint represented by the family in relation to the destructiveness operative in intergroup relationships and on the international scene.

## THE RELATIONSHIP BETWEEN PARENTS AND CHILDREN

Parent-child relationships conventionally have been discussed in terms of children and young adults. The functional side of this relationship has been specified by and large in terms of what parents do for their children in a one-way passage. Children have been perceived as recipients rather than as reciprocators of parental functions. It has been taken for granted rather than analyzed as a contribution that children by their very existence give to their parents the status of parenthood, new thought content, and, new feelings to their interaction as a married couple as well as justification of their adulthood. Similarly, it has been disregarded that children divert parents from questioning the purpose of self, that they give a promise of emotional and economic security in old age, and that to parents conflicted over sex they give an absolution of their sexuality and help them renew the experience of positive responses through body language. In a democracy it may not sound good to state theoretically what most people know experientially—that children, at least in their early years, give their parents a feeling of power such as our society does not otherwise provide. Although this network of reciprocation would be a proper subject for much more detailed analysis, its brief indication above may suffice for introducing a major change in the parent-child relationship due to governmental intervention in the fields of health care and welfare. Adult sons and daughters are called upon to perform much more frequently and for much longer periods of time than formerly as the emotional nurturants of their parents. Governmental housing policy, as has been pointed out by Nathan Glazer in one of the preceding articles,[25] may increasingly provide residential separation from their grown-up children for aging parents. Social Security may relieve adult sons and daughters of the financial aspects of filial obligations, but the obligation of emotional care, of catering to dependency legitimated by age, has been vastly extended. The resulting emotional burdens of anxiety and guilt over death wishes have been discussed before. It should be pointed out, however, that this in turn generates a function on the part of the aging parent, namely, so to age as not to create aging anxiety in his adult sons and daughters. This is a mental health function of the first order in a civilization in which many people are facing death without the comforts of religion and the goal structure of a life after death.

## SIBLING RELATIONSHIPS

As far as the sibling relationship is concerned, life in a bureaucratic society offers many stimuli for transference from the family experience to the organizational experience. The phenomenon of transference of feelings generated in the parent-child relationships to the relationships between subordinate and superior is well known and verified by the wisdom of the language. In monarchies, particularly, the association between king and father has always been noted. The same is true in the church, where priests are called "fathers" and the administrator of a convent is called "Mother Superior." In large-scale organizations such as the army, we encounter the transference of sibling feelings to organizational associates. We speak of "brother officers." The same is true for unions,

where the membership claims "brotherhood." It is frequently overlooked that, in a family, brothers and sisters furnish one another with a feeling of strength that comes from numbers. One child faced by the challenge of living with two adults has resort to little but fantasy in his need for compenstory power experiences. If fantasy fails him, he must "close the system" and become independent and self-reliant at the price of alienating people who reach out toward him and at the risk of claiming monopoly in human relations when he breaks out of his confinement in self. Since in a bureaucratic society, more than in any other, interdependence is encountered in many places and monopoly in human relations is inadmissible, personalities which have closed their systems are likely to be unusable or unused. There is no better training ground than sibling rivalry and mutual sibling support for organizational life.

Siblings teach one another that emotional scarcity is part of the human condition, that to claim a person completely is likely to be abortive, and that self-reliance is unnecessary as well as expensive. The claim for parental time which the wide array of governmental services offered for children makes upon a mother of several sons and daughters in itself has the impact of bringing home the lesson that to be a sibling means sharing and giving up for gaining. At the same time it teaches that governmental intervention is invariably in the service of large numbers and that the lonely person has no social strength.

In a final sense the impact of government upon the family is the impact of large-scale organization upon small-scale organization, the impact of standardization upon autonomy, the impact of security upon risk, and the impact of the professional upon the layman. From the vantage point of the past, this appears to be invasion and limitation. From the vantage point of the future, the following reformulation may be in order: In the ups and downs of social change, the impact of government upon the family is followed by the impact of the family on the government. Seen in this light it is the impact of autonomy upon standardization, the impact of courage upon security, and the impact of individualism upon depersonalization in a maintained state of point and counterpoint.

## REFERENCES

1  William F. Ogburn and Meyer F. Nimkoff, *Sociology*, Boston: Houghton Mifflin Co., 1958, pp. 750–751.
2  Clark E. Vincent, "Mental Health and the Family," *Journal of Marriage and the Family*, vol. 29, no. 1 (February 1967).
3  Erik Erikson, *Childhood and Society*, New York: W. W. Norton and Co., 1950, p. 247.
4  Berta Bornstein, "Analysis of the Phobic Child," *The Psychoanalytic Study of the Child*, vol. 3/4 (1949), pp. 220–221.
5  Samuel Futterman, "Personality Trends in Wives of Alcoholics," *Journal of Psychiatric Social Work*, vol. 23 (1953), pp. 37–41.
6  Nathan W. Ackerman, *The Psychodynamics of Family Life*, New York: Basic Books, Inc., 1958, pp. 103–104, 106.
7  Mark Zborowski and Elizabeth Herzog, *Life Is with People*, New York: International Universities Press, Inc., 1952.
8  Futterman, *op. cit.*
9  R. E. Weinerman, "As Patients See Us," *Proceedings of the Group Health Association 13th Annual Institute*, Detroit, 1963.
10  Elliot Freidson, *Patient's Views of Medical Practice*, Russell Sage Foundation, New York, 1961.
11  Talcott Parsons and Rene Fox, "Illness, Therapy, and the Modern Urban Family," *Journal of Social Issues*, vol. 8 (1952), pp. 31–44.
12  Robert Reiff and Frank Riessman, "The Indigenous Non-professional," *National Institute of Labor Education Report* 3, pp. 17–28.
13  Arthur Shostak, "Education and the Family," *Journal of Marriage and the Family*, vol. 29, no. 1 (February 1967).
14  Gertrude K. Pollak, "New Uses of a Family Life Education Program by the Community," *Social Casework*, vol. 44, no. 6 (June 1963), pp. 335–342.
15  Robert Waelder, "Authoritarianism and Totalitarianism," in George B. Wilbur and Warner Muensterberger (eds.), *Psychoanalysis and Culture*, New York: International Universities Press, Inc., 1951.
16  Paul Goodman, *Growing Up Absurd*, New York: Random House, Inc., 1960.
17  Phillip Rieff, *Freud: The Mind of the Moralist*, Garden City, N.Y.: Doubleday & Company, Anchor edition, 1961, pp. 361–392.
18  Vincent, *op. cit.*
19  Mildred Burgum, "The Father Gets Worse: A Child Guidance Problem," *American Journal of Orthopsychiatry*, vol. 12 (July 1942), p. 474.
20  Otto Pollak, "Sociological and Psychoanalytic Concepts in Family Diagnosis," in Bernard L. Greene (ed.), *The Psychotherapies of Marital Disharmony*, New York: The Free Press, 1965, pp. 15–26.
21  Edmund Bergler, *Divorce Won't Help*, New York: Harper & Brothers, 1948.
22  William H. Masters and Virginia E. Johnson, *Human Sexual Response*, Boston: Little, Brown, and Company, 1966.
23  Heinz Hartmann, *Ego Psychology and the Problem of Adaptation*, New York: International Universities Press, Inc., 1958, p. 121.
24  Otto Pollak, *Integrating Sociological and Psychoanalytic Concepts*, New York: Russell Sage Foundation, 1956.
25  Nathan Glazer, "Housing Policy and the Family," *Journal of Marriage and the Family*, vol. 29, no. 1 (February 1967).

# 26    URBANISM AND EXTENDED FAMILISM

ROBERT F. WINCH        SCOTT A. GREER

## FAMILISM AND THE URBAN-RURAL CONTINUUM

There was a time when it seemed that everyone knew—or at least we sociologists knew—that there were in our country a rural family form and an urban family form. According to that view the rural family was large, highly functional, and had much interaction with extended kin. We also knew that the urban family was small, showed few, if any, functions, and was adrift in a sea of urban anonymity with the result that it was thought to have no contact with kinsmen and thus to be a detached social system. Furthermore, since we also knew that our society was rapidly becoming urban, it followed that the family was rapidly becoming small, detached, and functionless.

The general explanation for rural-urban differences in familial form was, simply, the better fit between a small nuclear family and a society that was mobile and individually oriented. In such a society, so the argument ran, commitment to extended kin restricted mobility; at the same time, the increasing development of formal, commercial enterprises for various goods and services replaced the kin group as a source of exchange and security. And with the increasing socioeconomic status of the population, particularly increasing disposable income (which has more than doubled in the last 60 years), the cash nexus could easily substitute for the older exchange system. To telescope the argument: the nature of large-scale society encouraged, and indeed demanded, spatial and social mobility; extended kinship hindered mobility; market organization of goods and services substituted for the positive functions of kin and thus allowed the mobility to occur with displacement of functions of both the nuclear and the extended family. .

More recently, beginning in the 1950's, some sociologists, who were following our tribal custom of disbelieving and criticizing our elders, began studies of the family in urban settings. From these studies it developed that the nuclear family was not usually detached from its kin but interacted with them and exchanged services with them.

To some it seemed that this spate of studies showed the earlier writers to have been generally wrong in their view of the difference between the

Reprinted with the permission of the authors and the publisher from "Urbanism, Ethnicity, and Extended Familism," *Journal of Marriage and the Family*, vol. 30 (February 1968), pp. 40–45.

The authors are happy to acknowledge the financial support of this study provided by the Center for Metropolitan Studies of Northwestern University. Data for the paper come from a survey carried out in the fall of 1964. The authors also wish to thank Joyce Sween for programming the statistical analysis and Rae Lesser Blumberg for a critical review of the statistical analysis.

rural and the urban family in America. To us it seems the time has come to examine the question by the simple device of cross-tabulating measures of extended familism and an index of urbanism-ruralism.

Our data come from a survey based on a statewide probability sample carried out in Wisconsin in the fall of 1964.[1]

We have four measures of extended familism that we call *extensity* of the presence of kin, *intensity* of the presence of kin, *interaction* with kin, and the *functionality* of the interaction with kin. Extensity of presence is based on the respondent's answer to the question: how many households of kin do you and your spouse have in this community? Intensity has to do with degree of kin of both respondent and respondent's spouse. A distinction is drawn between those of the respondent's kin who have been or are now in his family of orientation and of procreation—parents, siblings, and offspring, spoken of as "nuclear" kin—and all other relatives, characterized as "extended" kin. "High" intensity signifies that the respondent reports having in the community households of both nuclear and extended kin and that the respondent also reports that his or her spouse has households of both nuclear and extended kin in the community. "None" denotes that neither spouse has a household of kin of any degree in the community; "other" indicates the presence of one or more households of kin of respondent and/or spouse but not enough of the appropriate degrees on both sides of the house to qualify as "high." Interaction has to do with the number of categories of households of kin with which some member of the respondent's household interacts at least monthly.[2] Functionality concerns the instrumental value of the interaction as revealed in the giving and/or receiving of goods and services.

To get the purest possible measure of urbanism, we classify Milwaukee, Madison, Wauwatosa, and West Allis as urban; our rural category consists of all unincorporated territory not in any SMSA. The remaining area is labelled "other" and is regarded as of intermediate urbanism-ruralism.

Table 1 shows that two of our four measures of extended familism—interaction and functionality—

**TABLE 1**    *Percentage distribution of respondents by ecological type and by level of extended familism, for four measures of extended familism*

| Measure and level of extended familism* | Ecology† | | | | Gamma |
|---|---|---|---|---|---|
| | Metropolitan N = 115 | Other N = 286 | Rural N = 112 | Total N = 513 | |
| **Extensity of presence** | | | | | |
| None | 17.4 | 14.0 | 10.7 | 14.0 | |
| Some | 40.0 | 48.6 | 38.4 | 44.4 | .10 |
| High | 42.6 | 37.4 | 50.9 | 41.5 | |
| **Intensity of presence** | | | | | |
| None | 17.4 | 14.0 | 10.7 | 14.0 | |
| Some | 60.9 | 64.0 | 64.3 | 63.4 | .09 |
| High | 21.7 | 22.0 | 25.0 | 22.6 | |
| **Interaction** | | | | | |
| None | 7.8 | 7.7 | 7.1 | 7.6 | |
| Some | 55.7 | 49.7 | 35.7 | 48.0 | .20** |
| High | 36.5 | 42.7 | 57.1 | 44.4 | |
| **Functionality** | | | | | |
| None | 20.0 | 12.6 | 7.1 | 13.1 | |
| Some | 59.1 | 52.8 | 47.3 | 53.0 | .30** |
| High | 20.9 | 34.6 | 45.5 | 33.9 | |

*Extensity of presence* refers to the number of households of kin in the community: "some" = 1-8; "high" = 9+. *Intensity of presence* refers to the degree of kin present in the community. In the following categories, a nuclear kinsman is a member of the respondent's family of orientation or of procreation. "None" means neither the respondent nor spouse reports any household of kin in the community; "high" means both respondent and spouse report having households of both nuclear and extended kin in the community; and "some" signifies the presence of kin but not satisfying the conditions of the "high" category. *Interaction* refers to the number of categories of households of kin with which some member of the respondent's household has been in contact (face to face, phone, or mail) at least monthly. "Some" = 1-3; "high" = 4-6. *Functionality* refers to the number of categories of service given to and/or received from some kinsman. "Some" = 1-2; "high" = 3+.

†The three ecological types are
Metropolitan: Milwaukee, Madison, West Allis, and Wauwatosa
Rural: unincorporated territory outside any SMSA
Other: residual territory—small cities, suburbs, etc.

**The gammas so marked are significant at the .01 level; the others are not significant at the .05 level. Although the data in this and subsequent tables are reported as percentages, the measures of association and tests of significance have been conducted on the frequencies.

are significantly and monotonically related to urbanism-ruralism with ruralism at the highly familistic end. Neither extensity nor intensity of presence correlates significantly with urbanism-ruralism. We conclude, therefore, that although there is little variation in the number of households of kin as we move from the country through the small towns and suburbs to the city, there is appreciable variation in both interaction and functionality. To state it more fully, on the average, rural households interact more with their kin than do urban households and

that interaction tends to be more functional.

Having found some degree of association between ruralism-urbanism and certain measures of extended familism, one is entitled to inquire about third variables that might account for the association. Socioeconomic status and migratory status are two that seem especially to warrant our attention. It turns out that, when socioeconomic status is used as a control variable, the correlations between the rural-urban dimension and extended familism (as measured by interaction and functionality) remain generally unaffected.[3]

When migratory status was used as a control variable, the correlations between ecology and the two measures of familism disappeared where neither spouse was a migrant but held up otherwise.[4] In other words, in couples where one or both spouses are migrants, there is more interaction and more functional interaction with kin among rural families than among urban. An understanding of how migratory status is associated with extended familism can be obtained from Table 2, where it is seen that only where both spouses are migrants is there any appreciable proportion with no kin in the local community.

## EXTENDED FAMILISM AND ETHNICITY

In earlier studies we have found separately and jointly that in our American samples Jewish families are more familistic than are Christian families.[5] A more recent paper has investigated a proposed explanation of Jewish familism. This involved the idea that Jews were more concentrated in less migratory occupations than non-Jews and that Jews were more familistic because their lower migration permitted them to be. The data were interpreted, however, as indicating that the Jews were less migratory because they were more familistic rather than the other way about. Among the Christians the Catholics were a bit more familistic than the Protestants, a bit less so than the Jews.[6]

Since the data underlying the above-stated conclusions (see Table 3) came from an upper-middle-class suburb, the authors were interested in determining whether or not similar relationships would obtain in the broader social space afforded by the state-wide probability sample of Wisconsin. This sample offered a considerably broader range with respect to socioeconomic status and urban-rural residence, but it lacked the full ethnic spectrum represented in the United States, and in particular it had too few Jews and Negroes to permit their being used as statistical categories.

In the earlier study we regarded the classification of respondents into Jewish and non-Jewish as a dimension of ethnicity rather than of religion, because we were interested in values and behavior pertaining to the family rather than in theology. In the present study the same reasoning led us to look for what we thought of as ethnicity in our data on religious affiliation. Two large denominations, accounting for slightly more than two-thirds of the sample, were Roman Catholic and Lutheran. We decided to use these two categories and, anticipating that Lutherans would be more familistic than most other Protestant denominations, we decided to add a third category of "other Protestants" that would also include the "none" and "don't know" responses to the query about religious affiliation.[7]

We were intrigued to see whether, with our highly familistic Jews absent from the analysis, we should still find that ethnicity correlated with extended familism. Table 3 shows a pattern that is

**TABLE 2** *Percentage distribution of migratory statuses, by intensity of presence of kin*

| Intensity of presence of kinship* | Migratory status | | | | Gamma |
|---|---|---|---|---|---|
| | Both migrants N = 230 | One migrant N = 150 | Neither migrant N = 124 | Total N = 504 | |
| None | 29.1 | 1.3 | 1.6 | 14.1 | |
| Some | 60.4 | 76.0 | 51.6 | 62.9 | .67† |
| High | 10.4 | 22.7 | 46.8 | 23.0 | |

*These categories are explained in the footnotes to Table 1.
†Significant at the .01 level.

TABLE 3    *Percentage distribution of respondents by ethnic category and by level of extended familism, for four measures of extended familism*

| Measure and level of extended familism* | Ethnicity | | | | Gamma |
|---|---|---|---|---|---|
| | Catholic N = 197 | Lutheran N = 177 | Other Protestant N = 138 | N = 512 | |
| **Extensity of presence** | | | | | |
| None | 9.1 | 13.0 | 21.7 | 13.9 | |
| Some | 40.6 | 45.8 | 48.6 | 44.5 | −.26† |
| High | 50.3 | 41.2 | 49.7 | 41.6 | |
| **Intensity of presence** | | | | | |
| None | 9.1 | 13.0 | 21.7 | 13.9 | |
| Some | 64.0 | 62.1 | 64.5 | 63.5 | −.25† |
| High | 26.9 | 24.9 | 13.8 | 22.7 | |
| **Interaction** | | | | | |
| None | 4.1 | 6.2 | 13.8 | 7.4 | |
| Some | 49.7 | 42.4 | 52.9 | 48.0 | −.17† |
| High | 46.2 | 51.4 | 33.3 | 44.5 | |
| **Functionality** | | | | | |
| None | 15.2 | 9.0 | 15.2 | 13.1 | |
| Some | 49.2 | 58.2 | 51.4 | 52.9 | −.02 |
| High | 35.5 | 32.8 | 33.3 | 34.0 | |

*These indexes and categories are explained in the footnotes to Table 1.
†Significant at the .01 level.

similar to, but markedly weaker than, that found in the suburban study—the interaction and two presence measures producing larger gammas than functionality.[8] With respect to extensity and intensity of presence, Catholics are most familistic, Lutherans intermediate, and other Protestants least. In the case of interaction, Lutherans are a bit more familistic than Catholics, and the gamma would be larger if these two categories were reversed.

When the two indexes of socioeconomic status were employed as control variables, it was found that at the high level of SES all six correlations between ethnicity and the three measures of extended familism (with which it correlated significantly) remained significant and in the same direction. At the lower socioeconomic level, however, the four following correlations became nonsignificant: with income as the index, the correlations with interaction and extensity;[9] with education as

the index, the correlations with interaction and intensity. These results indicate that the order of ethnic categories with respect to extended familism—Catholics most familistic, Lutherans intermediate, and other Protestants least familistic—is operative at the upper socioeconomic level, but at the lower level, especially with respect to interaction, there is some tendency for ethnic differences to wash out.

When migratory status is introduced as a control variable, the correlation between ethnicity and extended familism remains for the "both migrant" category but disappears for the other two migratory statuses. When one or both spouses are nonmigrants, then the data indicate that Catholics and Lutherans are not significantly more familistic than other Protestants.

Since both socioeconomic status and migratory status affect the correlation between ethnicity and extended familism, it is of interest to see what happens when they are introduced simultaneously as control variables. The result is that most of the correlations between ethnicity and extended familism shrink to nonsignificance. Of the 36 gammas computed, only six remained significant.[10] Of these six, three combined the both-migrant status with high socioeconomic status; of the other three, two combined the both-migrant and low socioeconomic statuses, and the sixth combined one-spouse-migrant with high SES.

If the foregoing reasoning is correct, it should follow that the correlations between the three categories of ethnicity and the three measures of extended familism with which it correlates significantly are higher in metropolitan areas, where the proportion of migrants and the average SES are relatively high, than in rural areas, where they are low. As Table 4 indicates, such a relationship is supported by the data, which also show the relationship in small towns and suburbs (the "other" ecological level) to be much like that in metropolitan areas.

Taking into account that there is an ethnic gradient of migration such that the proportion of migrants is lowest among Catholics and highest among other Protestants,[11] these results seem to indicate that for the most part the correlation between ethnicity and extended familism prevails where both spouses are migrants and their socioeconomic status is relatively high and that this familism consists in interacting with more households of kin and, to some extent, having more households of kin to interact with. In other words, when neither spouse is a migrant, there is no significant difference among ethnic categories with respect to extended familism, but when both spouses are migrants, the correlation of ethnicity with familism prevails.

## SUMMARY AND CONCLUSIONS

This article has sought to illuminate the dependent variable of extended familism, which has been operationalized by means of four indexes: extensity (number of households of kin in the local community), intensity (degree of kinship of these households on both husband's and wife's sides), interaction (number of categories of households of kin interacted with), and functionality (instrumental value of that interaction).

No matter how we operationalize extended familism—whether as extensity or intensity of presence of kin, as categories of kin interacted with, or as the functionality of that interaction—the overwhelming majority of our respondents report involvement with kin. Indeed, this is the case with even the least familistic subcategories of our respondents.

Ruralism correlates significantly with extended familism as indexed by functionality and interaction, but there is little difference between rural and urban couples in the number of households of kin or the degree of kinship of these households. The ruralism-familism correlation is not related

**TABLE 4**    *Measures of association (gammas) between ethnicity and three measures of extended familism, within ecological level*

| Measure of extended familism | Ecology | | | Total |
| --- | --- | --- | --- | --- |
| | Metropolitan N = 115 | Other N = 286 | Rural N = 112 | N = 513 |
| Extensity of presence | −.31* | −.30† | −.14 | −.26† |
| Intensity of presence | −.35* | −.26† | −.15 | −.25* |
| Interaction | −.24 | −.23† | −.07 | −.17* |

*Significant at the .05 level.
†Significant at the .01 level.

to socioeconomic status, but it is to migratory status. That is, the correlation stands up where one or both spouses are migrants and disappears where neither is a migrant. Stated differently, non-migrant urban couples are as familistic, on the average, as non-migrant rural couples, but migrant urban couples are less familistic than migrant rural couples. (It should be kept in mind, of course, that the dimension of ruralism-urbanism is being investigated within Wisconsin.)

Ethnicity—represented here as Catholic, Lutheran, and other Protestants—correlates significantly with extended familism in that Catholics and Lutherans are more familistic than other Protestants with respect to extensity, intensity, and interaction, but there is little difference among ethnic categories with respect to functionality. With respect to our control variables, this correlation tends to hold up for migratory couples of relatively high SES and those in urban areas; conversely, there is little correlation between ethnicity and familism in couples of low SES, where one or both spouses are non-migrants, and in rural areas.

In this sample, then, the extended familism associated with ruralism consists largely of functionality and of interaction, and this familism tends to occur differentially in ecological categories where one or both spouses are migrants. The extended familism associated with the levels of ethnicity considered here consists largely of the presence and degree of households of kin (extensity and intensity), and to some extent it consists of interaction with these households; the interethnic difference is most evident in both-migrant couples of high socioeconomic status and those of urban residence.

Thus the argument stated in brief at the beginning of this paper gains some plausibility. Non-migration is associated with the maintenance of extended kin networks, and part of the greater familism of rural areas is due to the greater stability of the population. But part of it is associated with the greater familism of migrants in rural areas. Perhaps the rural, and, to a less extent, small-town and suburban, areas are more conducive, culturally or ecologically, to using whatever

kin system is present. In this case we have an interaction of individual attributes (migratory status) and situational attributes (the general level of kin interaction and functionality in the community).[12]

With respect to ethnicity, we note that it makes a difference in interaction but not in functionality. Furthermore, it holds only for migrant couples of higher status. Thus one suspects it is most important for "phatic" interaction[13] rather than mutual aid and, conceivably, is related to the greater resources for visiting in general, and therefore visiting of relatives, among those with more money, time, and education.

### REFERENCES AND NOTES

1   This survey is based upon a multistage area probability sample design that gives each housing unit in the state an equal chance of being selected for interviewing. The procedure begins with a sample of the state's counties and moves to a sample of U.S. Census enumeration districts within counties. From the enumeration district is made a sample of chunks (geographical areas containing approximately 30 housing units each). From each chunk is drawn a sampling segment (a small geographical area containing approximately four housing units). This procedure identifies for the interviewer the housing unit within which he or she is to make the call. Finally, there is a random procedure for selecting the person to be interviewed among the persons in the household who have passed their twenty-first birthdays. In the two largest cities of Wisconsin—Milwaukee and Madison—a somewhat different procedure is followed: a sample of addresses is drawn from the annually revised city directory, and coverage of addresses not appearing in the directories is obtained through the use of area samples of city blocks. No substitutions are permitted for sample housing units or for respondents. Four or more calls are made by the interviewers, if necessary, in order to interview the randomly specified respondent. A sample of 702 people was interviewed—322 men and 380 women. As of 1960, about 48 percent of the population of Wisconsin over the age of 19 was male; in the sample the proportion male was 46 percent. We wish to thank Harry Sharp, Director, and the Wisconsin Sample Survey Laboratory for making these data available to us.

Because of our interest in having a standard basis for estimating the opportunity of a household to engage in familistic behavior, we based our study on married couples. (It is reasonable to assume that the number of households of kin available to a married couple is different from the number available to a single person.) Accordingly, we eliminated from the sample all respondents who were not either married male heads of households or wives of heads. Presently it will be seen that we were also interested in the religious affiliation of respondents. Because they represented categories too differentiated from others to be combined with them and too small for separate analysis, Jews and eastern rite Catholics were omitted. The number of nonwhites was also too small for statistical analysis. After these exclusions were made, the sample of 702 shrank to 513. Of these there was an absence of information with respect to migratory status on nine individuals and with respect to religious affiliation on one.

2    The measure of interaction in this study differs from that in our suburban study (*cf.* note 6 below). In this study it is based on the number of categories of kin households with which someone in the respondent's household has at least monthly contact. The categories are respondent's (1) siblings, (2) parents, and (3) other kin, as well as (4) to (6) the same categories of the respondent's spouse's kin.

3    Family income and education of head of household were the two indexes used for socioeconomic status. Each was dichotomized as near the median as possible, and gammas were computed between the ecological (rural-urban) variable and the two familistic variables showing significant gammas in Table 1. Of the eight resulting gammas, only one became nonsignificant: in the low-income category the correlation between ecology and interaction was of the same sign as before but dipped below the significance level.

Generally speaking, extended familism is not correlated with membership in voluntary organizations. Only at the lower level of SES and in the rural ecological category do significant correlations appear. Indeed, in the low-SES-rural category the more familistic are the greater joiners as is reflected by a gamma of .60, $P < .01$.

4    A person was classed as a non-migrant if he or she had been born in the community where interviewed or if brought there before turning 18. Migratory status was trichotomized: both migrants, one spouse migrant, and neither spouse migrant. The interaction-ecology correlation for the both-migrant category was .20, very slightly below the two-sided .05 level of significance; for the one-migrant category, it was .29, significant at the .05 level. The functionality-ecology gammas were .30 and .49, respectively, both significant at the .01 level.

5    Scott Greer, unpublished tabulation from the Metro-politan St. Louis Survey, 1957; Robert F. Winch, *Identification and Its Familial Determinants*, Indianapolis: Bobbs-Merrill Company, Inc., 1962, table 7, p. 122; Robert F. Winch and Scott A. Greer, "The Uncertain Relation between Early Marriage and Marital Stability: A Quest for Relevant Data," *Acta Sociologica*, vol. 8 (1964), pp. 83–97.

6    Robert F. Winch, Scott Greer, and Rae Lesser Blumberg, "Ethnicity and Extended Familism in an Upper-middle-class Suburb," *American Sociological Review*, vol. 32 (1967), pp. 265–272.

7    An ethnic category is an aggregate of people sharing, and therefore participating in, a common culture. Since our interest is in culture rather than attitudes toward or beliefs about a supernatural being, we speak of this variable as ethnicity rather than religion. It is realized that within each of the three above categories there is considerable variation in national origins and that for this reason the reader may decline to attribute cultural homogeneity to them. A study is now under way to investigate the cultural homogeneity of the Lutheran category. The authors believe there is some homogeneity within each category with respect to attitudes about the family, but no harm will be done if the reader disagrees and simply prefers to regard these as categories of religious affiliation. Because we expected that Lutherans would be intermediate between other Protestants and Catholics with respect to familism, we chose the ordinal measure of association, gamma.

8    In the suburban study the gammas between ethnicity (Jewish, Catholic, Protestant) and extended familism (extensity, intensity, interaction, functionality) were .81, .68, .74, and .29, respectively, all significant at the .01 level. See *ibid.*

9    This correlation was marginal, however, the pattern of association being the same and the gamma being just slightly below that required for the .05 level of significance.

10    The 36 gammas represent three indexes of extended familism (extensity, intensity, interaction), three levels of migration, two indexes of socioeconomic status, each at two levels, and 3×3×2×2=36.

11    Gamma = .21, significant at the .01 level.

12    Peter Blau, "Structural Effects," *American Sociological Review*, vol. 25 (1960), pp. 178–193; and James A. Davis, Joe L. Spaeth, and Carolyn Huson, "A Technique for Analyzing the Effects of Group Composition," *American Sociological Review*, vol. 26 (1961), pp. 215–225.

13    In phatic discourse the words mean "nothing excepting as a device to avoid silence and signify social solidarity." Gordon W. Allport, *The Nature of Prejudice*, Garden City, N.Y.: Doubleday & Company, Inc., Anchor Books, 1958, p. 273.

# 27     THE DECLINE AND FALL OF THE DOUBLE STANDARD

ERWIN O. SMIGEL     RITA SEIDEN

To find meaningful correlations,[1] especially in a pluralistic society, between the multitude of social forces and sexual behavior is difficult; to determine these correlations accurately, when appropriate data on sexual behavior are not available, is impossible. Nonetheless, it is our assignment to examine these social forces in order to see what effect they have had on sexual behavior and attitudes—specifically on sexual behavior and attitudes of unmarried heterosexuals of college age and younger in the United States.

Most recent examinations of sexual behavior still cite Kinsey's data[2] (1938–1949) and/or Terman's[3] (1934–1935). No one has published a Kinsey-type study for the United States in the 1960's. However, a few limited studies[4] on premarital sexual behavior have been completed since Kinsey published *The Human Male* in 1948. The various studies of college students show percentages of premarital coitus for males and females which range from 54:35 in 1929;[5] 51:25 in 1938;[6] to 56:25 in 1951;[7] and, in 1953, 68:47, 41:9, or 63:14, depending on whose figures are accepted.[8] The most recent examination of sexual behavior puts the rate of college female premarital experience at 22 per cent.[9] This is consistent with Kinsey's findings that 20 per cent of all college women had had premarital intercourse.[10]

Most of the studies of sex completed after Kinsey's main works appeared have been limited to collecting statistics on attitudes. The most extensive of these studies, for which data was collected through 1963, was conducted by Ira Reiss, on sexual permissiveness.[11] Reiss's findings point to a coming together of sexual prac-

Reprinted from *The Annals*, vol. 376 (March 1968), pp. 7–17, by permission of the authors and The American Academy of Political and Social Science.

tices, and, for the young at least, of attitudes about sex. He found definite movement away from the orthodox double standard toward a standard of permissiveness with affection (shorthand for "premarital sex is acceptable when there is mutual affection between the partners").

The earlier statistics of Kinsey and Terman point up important differences in sexual behavior between the generation of women born before 1900 and the generation born in the following decade. Kinsey found that 73.4 per cent of women born before 1900 had had no premarital intercourse, but among those born between 1900 and 1909, only 48.7 per cent had been virgins at marriage. The figures for those born in the 1920–1929 generation are the same—48.8 per cent.[12] Terman's findings are essentially in agreement. The statistics for both the Kinsey and Terman studies referred to here are for women of all ages, and not just for college women.[13] Terman found that 74 per cent of the females born between 1890 and 1899 had had no premarital intercourse, whereas among those born between 1900 and 1909, the percentage of virgin brides had dropped to 51.2. His figures reveal that this trend also held for men: of those interviewees born between 1890 and 1899, 41.9 per cent had had no premarital coitus, whereas of the interviewees born in the next generation, 32.6 per cent had had no such premarital experience.[14] Clearly, the major change in sex practices occurred in the generation born in the decade 1900–1909, which came to sexual age during or immediately after World War I, a period characterized by marked social change and innovation.

It may well be true that changes in sexual behavior and attitudes are related to the social changes which began in the late nineteenth century and accelerated rapidly over the past 67 years. It is not as clear, except perhaps for the post-World War I years, exactly what the effects of these social changes have been on sexual behavior. Reiss argues that, despite popular belief to the contrary, "the sexual revolution [is] a myth and the only basic change [is] a trend toward more equality between the sexes. . . . There has been less change than [is] popularly believed between modern American males and their Victorian grandfathers."[15]

It is generally thought, however, that the late-nineteenth-century break with Victorian morality was a tangential result of the Industrial Revolution, urban migration, war, the feminist movement, and the scientific study of once-taboo topics. Wilbert Moore, a leading authority on social change, credited industrialization with certain effects on the social structure;[16] and it is our opinion that industrialization affected sex attitudes and behavior as well. He specified increased social and geographic mobility; growth of industrial centers with concomitant concentration of population in urban areas; emphasis on rationality as a necessary part of an industrialized society (for example, a lessening of the influence of religion); transition from extended (rurally located) families to nuclear (urban) families; emphasis on individualism resulting from the breakdown[17] of the extended kinship system; decreased family size accompanied by a decline in the economic significance of the family unit as the unit of survival; and, finally, increased education.

Each of these general effects of social change can be shown, at least theoretically, to have potential impact on sexual behavior and attitudes. As the population moves from small towns and intimate personal relationships to urban centers, old forms of social control break down. This disintegration and the accompanying anonymity is speeded by new and faster forms of transportation which further increase the possibilities of anonymity and independence. A rational society affects the individual's world view, and he tends to see his own life in terms of more rational standards. As the extended kinship system dissolves or loses its

importance, mate-selection processes become a more personal responsibility, and increase the importance of peer group norms, which take precedence over family norms. In the evolving industrial society, women take a new and larger part in the working world, thereby securing greater independence for themselves and increased equality in male-female relationships. The general increase in education has made possible widespread dissemination of sex information to the public.

In sum, the family has declined in importance as the unit upon which or around which society is organized, and individualism, in relationship to the family, is in the ascendency. As individualism has grown, sexual behavior has become more a personal matter and is less exclusively influenced by family and procreational considerations.

The complex social changes discussed have been gradual, but the impact of war can be immediate and abrupt. This is clearly indicated in the data on sexual behavior during and immediately after World War I. In any war, the mores governing family life tend to decay. Removed from some of the responsibilities, restrictions, and supports of the family, removed from the all-seeing eye of the small town or the neighborhood, soldiers are suddenly subject only to the mostly approving observations of their fellow soldiers. In the face of death or the possibility of being severely wounded, hedonism becomes the prevailing attitude. This attitude appears to be contagious and spreads to the civilian population. In World War I, it particularly affected the young women who were working in factories, taking on roles and responsibilities that had once belonged exclusively to men, often for the first time living alone in relative anonymity, and in many instances emotionally involved with men who were scheduled to be sent overseas. (This same hedonistic philosophy may be held by contemporary young people who are faced with the dangers of limited wars and the always present possibility of extinction by nuclear explosion.)

Many soldiers had contact with prostitutes and contracted venereal diseases. The United States Interdepartmental Social Hygiene Board reports: "Between September, 1917, and February 14,

1919, there were over 222,000 cases of venereal disease in the army and there were over 60,000 in the navy."[18] Venereal disease and the prostitute taught the soldier more about sex in his relatively short career in the armed services than he might normally have learned. The incidence of venereal disease was so high that it became a matter of both private and official army talk. The consequence was that most soldiers left the service knowing not only the protective effects but also the birth control uses of prophylactic sheaths. This kind of sex education became a standard part of the army curriculum.

The soldier who went abroad had new sexual experiences and came in contact with women whose behavior derived from different and more permissive sex norms; the returned veteran brought back with him sexual attitudes shaped by these new norms. Although they were not consciously intended for his mother, sister, wife, or wife-to-be, they tended to affect them as well.

War also tends to spread industrialization and to extend the need for women in industry, and, in turn, to increase their economic independence. The war and wartime experiences intensified the gradual way in which industrialization was changing the social structure.

War, industrialization, and an increase in political democracy seem to have led to the struggle for equal rights for women. The nineteenth-century feminists, who fought for financial and social rights and by 1920 had been enfranchised, were now also demanding more sexual freedom. Margaret Sanger, an American housewife, was a leader in this war. She waged a courageous battle for the control of pregnancy, and she was brought to trial for making birth control information available to interested persons. It was the trial, the wide publicity she received, and her persistence which helped to acquaint the public with the possibilities of birth control. She and other fighters for female sexual freedom were supported by a backdrop of the new norms of the returning soldiers, the effects of economic gains for women, and an increase in the scientific study of sex.

Although Krafft-Ebing,[19] Havelock Ellis,[20]

and others were writing about sex pathology and sexuality, Freud's writings about the unconscious and the effect of sex on personality had the most influence upon American behavior and attitudes. Although *Studies in Hysteria*, written by Freud and Breuer, which made these ideas available to the public, was published in 1895, "it was not until after the war that the Freudian gospel began to circulate to a marked extent among the American reading public."[21] No one can estimate what popularization of psychoanalytic theory has done to free individuals—particularly women—from the puritan anxieties about sex. The fact of its influence, however, cannot be doubted. These studies by the sexologists and those by the sociologists, anthropologists, and psychologists studying and writing in the late 1920's and early 1930's provided the setting for the public acceptance of Kinsey's impressive work—which may in turn have had great influence on a society already impatient with Victorian sex mores. In any event, studies of sex were being undertaken, and they provided information about taboo topics which helped to free the average individual from the restraint against serious discussion of sexual behavior. Each generation of sex researchers has extended the study and broadened the understanding of sex, from Kinsey's counting of sexual outlets in the 1940's to Masters and Johnson's detailed study of human sexual response[22] in the early 1960's.

In addition to those factors already described, which have affected so many aspects of the social structure, other elements, although less powerful forces for general change, have also contributed to the alteration of sexual mores in a more immediate sense. Cultural interchange resulting from wartime contact since World War I and from the great increase in travel has led to a broadened participation with other societies. Furthermore, the disappearance of the chaperon undoubtedly created opportunities for sexual freedom which are not subject to the social sanctions of one's own society. The availability of the automobile, the affluent society which permits young people to live apart from their parents, and the growth of community size made privacy much more accessible. There has been a virtual removal of "fear-evoking" deterrents with the development of effective contraceptive devices.

All of these factors seem to be related to the change in sexual practices and to the apparent liberalization of sexual standards reflected in Reiss's data.[23] Since these social forces are still operating in the same direction, we should also expect to see changes in the direction of permissive sexual attitudes and behavior to continue.

The data we have on sexual behavior are limited; but more data are available on attitudes.

The research statistics are analyzed in Tables 1, 2, 3, and 4.[24]

Reiss's later data, collected in 1959 and 1963,[25] confirm the trends evidenced in the findings of the earlier studies (see Table 2).

We can probably safely conclude from these data:

1 Abstinence and permissiveness with affection are the favored standards for both males and females.

2 There has been a rise in female approval of permissiveness with affection and a decline in approval of the abstinence standard.

3 Permissiveness without affection, if we consider it comparable to a blanket endorsement of

**TABLE 2**   *Percentage accepting each standard, 1959\**

| Standard | Male | Female | Total |
|---|---|---|---|
| Permissiveness with affection | 24 | 15 | 19 |
| Permissiveness without affection | 13 | 2 | 7 |
| Abstinence | 28 | 55 | 42 |
| Orthodox double standard | 9 | 13 | 11 |
| Transitional double standard† | 18 | 10 | 14 |
| N | (386) | (435) | (821) |

\* The sample was drawn from the student populations of five schools: two Virginia colleges (one Negro, one white); two Virginia high schools (one Negro, one white); and one New York college. Percentages of adherents to the reversed double standard have been omitted. Therefore totals do not equal 100 per cent.

†Transitional double standard means that sex relations are considered all right for men under any condition, but are acceptable for women only if they are in love.

casual sex relations for both, is apparently on the decline—even more sharply for men than for women.

4 The orthodox double standard is also on the decline if we compare the Table 1 data (sex rela-

**TABLE 1**   *Attitudes toward premarital intercourse, percent*

| Approve of | Cornell, 1940* | | | Michigan State University, 1947† | | | 11 Colleges, 1952–1955† | | | University of Florida, 1958†* | | |
|---|---|---|---|---|---|---|---|---|---|---|---|---|
| | M | F | Total | M | F | Total | M | F | Total | M | F | Total |
| Sex relations for both | 15 | 6 | 9 | 16 | 2 | | 20 | 5 | | 42 | 7 | 25 |
| Abstinence | 49 | 76 | 65 | 59 | 76 | | 52 | 65 | | 20 | 86 | 52 |
| Sex relations for men only | 23 | 11 | 16 | 10 | 15 | | 12 | 23 | | 33 | 0 | 17 |
| Sex relations for engaged/ in love | 11 | 6 | 8 | 15 | 7 | | 16 | 7 | | 5 | 7 | 6 |
| N | (73) | (100) | (173) | | | (2000) | | | (3000) | (45) | (42) | (87) |

\*Percentages are based on N of 173, but 3 per cent (1 per cent male, 2 per cent female) did not answer the question. The total per cent appearing in Reiss is 101; therefore, ours totals 98.

†Separate N's for the male and female samples were not given; therefore, it was not possible to compute total percentage advocating each standard.

\*\*Total percentages were not shown by Reiss and were computed by the authors of this article.

tions for men only) with the Table 2 data (ortho-dox double standard).

5 The percentage of men who favor permissiveness with affection has increased markedly while the female endorsement remains about the same. The redistribution of women's attitudes seems to be away from abstinence and the orthodox double standard toward greater endorsement of the transitional double standard—coitus is all right for men under any condition, but is acceptable for women only if they are in love. Therefore, while women still endorse abstinence more highly than other standards, they are coming to favor sexual relations in the context of affection. Reiss's 1963 data support the 1959 evidence which indicates an increasingly favorable attitude on the part of females[26] toward sex with affection. Eighteen per cent favor permissiveness with affection; one per cent endorse permissiveness without affection; 56 per cent support abstinence. The percentage endorsing the transitional double standard was not given.[27]

6 Succinctly: The percentage of both men and women who accept increased permissiveness with affection as their standard has increased (see Table 3).

Since the 1947, 1952–1955, and 1959 studies used the largest number of subjects and employed somewhat more rigorous sampling techniques, they are probably more reliable indicators of the trend in these attitudes. They strongly support the assumption that there has been an important change in attitudes toward sex in the direction of permissiveness.

**TABLE 3** *Percentage accepting the standard of sex relations for engaged/in love\**

| 1940 | | 1947 | | 1952-1955 | | 1958 | | 1959 | | 1963† | |
|---|---|---|---|---|---|---|---|---|---|---|---|
| M | F | M | F | M | F | M | F | M | F | M | F |
| 11 | 6 | 15 | 7 | 16 | 7 | 5 | 7 | 24 | 15 | | 18 |

\*We are considering Reiss's "permissiveness with affection" as equivalent to "sex relations for engaged/in love."

†Figure for men has been omitted as total number of male interviews is a small proportion of the total sample.

In explaining the differences between statistics on sexual behavior and statistics on attitudes (namely, that behavior seems to have changed little since the 1920's, but attitudes have become more liberal), Reiss suggests that we are seeing a "consolidation process" taking place, that is, "a change in attitudes to match the change in behavior" is occurring.[28] Nelson Foote cites a variety of evidence which, he claims, indicates the decline of the double standard: decline in prostitution, increasingly equal sexual opportunities and experiences for women, increase in orgasm in marital sex relations, "the steady approach to equivalence of male and female premarital petting and marital sex play techniques," the increase of extramarital coitus, decreasing insistence on virginity in females at marriage, and "some decline in frequency of marital coitus implying more mutual consent and less unilateral demand."[29]

Finally, in line with both Reiss's and Foote's arguments that there is a trend toward a new single standard of permissiveness with affection, Robert Bell suggests that for young adults, sex becomes acceptable today when the couple feels they are in love. Peer group members accept and approve of sex without marriage, but not of sex without love.[30]

For the unmarried, there is an increasing tendency to reject marriage as the arbitrary dividing line between "socially approved and socially disapproved sexual intimacy."[31] And in the same way that male and female roles have become more equal in other areas of life, greater equality has come to the area of sexual relations: "fair play has been replacing chastity as the badge of honor in the interpersonal relations of the sexes."[32]

The results of the various studies of attitudes show two particularly interesting and possibly related findings:

First, there has been an increase in permissive attitudes toward sex since the 1940's. This may be due to the accumulating reforming influence of those social factors which was operating in the twentieth century. Certainly, the changed attitude shows itself sharply in the increase in sexual content of movies, the candid use of sexual lures in advertising, an increasing social sanctioning (if not precisely approval) of sexual material in popular literature, and a generally freer atmosphere which permits open talk about sex. But the new standard for coital involvement insists on permissiveness with affection.

Second, the parent generation (sampled in 1963 by Reiss) is far more conservative than the younger generation—and is apparently more conservative than it was when it was the younger generation. In Reiss's 1963 adult sample, only 17 per cent endorsed permissiveness with affection for males and only 5 per cent endorsed this standard for females.[33]

Apparently, the conservative parent generation refuse to endorse for their children standards of behavior in which members of their generation, and perhaps they themselves, engaged. What appears to be a "generation gap," however, is probably a manifestation of a change in role.[34] Reiss's data on his adult sample give a concise picture of the relationship between role position and attitudes (see Table 4).

Permissiveness evidently reaches its highest point on one curve (for the college student) while it reaches its lowest point on another curve (for the parents of the college student). What the data describe, then, are changes which occur as individuals come to occupy parental role positions, and they are not descriptive of differences between individuals of the post-World War II generation and their parents' generation.

In part, this information suggests that parents try to modify behavior in their children in which they themselves participated as young adults. This reaction may portend how the current young adult generation will feel when they are parents themselves. However, the qualification to be noted here is that the generation which came to maturity in the 1920's broke with previous generations in terms of behavior. The following generations continued in the same kind of practices but gradually came to express more liberal attitudes. The new liberalism of the younger generation may very well contribute to a shift in expressed adult values for the parent generations of the late 1960's and 1970's.

We know that sexual attitudes have changed and that sexual standards appear to be in a period of transition. "What was done by a female in 1925 acting as a rebel and a deviant can be done by a female in 1965 as a conformist."[35]

Data based on a large sample are available on sex behavior up to 1949 and on attitudes up to 1963. We do not know what has happened during the last five years or what is happening now. The general public impression is that there has been a very recent sexual revolution and that it is still going on. Most researchers do not believe that this is the case. The authors of this article, as social observers and recent reviewers of the literature on sexual behavior and attitudes toward sex, will attempt to "crystal ball" what has occurred during the last five years and what is occurring now. What follows, then, is not fact, but guess.

Past trends in social change, in behavior, and in attitudes toward sex are continuing. What seems to be taking place (except for pockets of our society) is a growing tendency toward more sexual permissiveness among the young unmarried. Sex with affection appears to be increasingly accepted. More and more this norm is based on personal choice, and it manifests itself for middle-class college youth in the form of trial marriage, for the girl, and for the boy at least as a stable, monogamous relationship, to the point of setting up house-

**TABLE 4**   *Marital and family status and permissiveness in the adult sample*

| Marital and family status | Per cent permissive | N |
|---|---|---|
| Single | 44 | (108) |
| Married | | |
|    No children | 23 | (124) |
|    All preteen | 22 | (384) |
|    Preteen and older | 17 | (218) |
|    All teen and older | 13 | (376) |

Source: Ira L. Reiss, *The Social Context of Premarital Sexual Permissiveness*, New York: Holt, Rinehart and Winston, 1967, p. 142, table 9.2 (some data omitted).

keeping. Increasingly, this happens with parental knowledge though not necessarily with parental approval. If Kinsey repeated his study today, he would probably find premarital virginity slightly lower and figures for those who have had premarital intercourse only with their spouse, a circumstance which was already on the increase in 1947 (born before 1900, 10.4 per cent; born 1920–1929, 27.3 per cent),[36] somewhat higher.

Promiscuity, a word objected to by many young people, probably has lessened. Certainly the use of prostitutes has diminished. If we are correct in believing that more young people are living monogamously together, and if marriage for both men and women (the figures are: median age of first marriages in 1890 for brides was 22.0 and for grooms was 26.1;[37] for 1966, the median age for brides was 20.5 and for grooms 22.8[38]) is occurring at earlier ages, then the statistical probabilities of premarital promiscuity have lessened, except when it is a reflection of mental illness. Today, except for the "hippies," who, according to the press, indulge in group sex, promiscuity as a form of rebellion is significantly on the decline.

We are living in a much more permissive society, and we are much more vocal about sex. As Walter Lippman put it, even as early as 1929: "It was impossible to know whether increased openness about sex reflected more promiscuity or less hypocrisy."[39] While we do not have much new evidence concerning sexual behavior, we do have nonsystematic overt indications about attitudes. It is seen in advertisements which are much more suggestive than they used to be. At one time, an advertiser would indicate to a male reader that, if he used a certain product, a pretty girl would kiss him. Now the ads suggest that she will have intercourse with him: "When an Avis girl winks at you she means business," and as Chateau Martin asks, leering only slightly, "Had any lately?" Movies have become less suggestive and more obvious; nudity as well as intercourse have become not uncommon sights. The Scandinavian picture *I, A Woman* for example, consists of a number of seductions with a number of different men. Perhaps what is more significant is that censorship boards,

the courts, and power groups in this country have sharply amended their definitions of obscenity. The theater has, for some time, been more open about sex and its various ramifications, and four-letter words are becoming a theatrical cliché.

Another indicator of this generation's expressed attitudes toward sex are the omnipresent buttons, which express not only political, but also sexual opinions. The buttons are designed for fun and shock, and for public declaration for sexual freedom. Sold in large cities all over this country, they range from simple position-statements such as "Make Love Not War," "I'm For Sexual Freedom," or "Equality for Homosexuals," to invitations which read "Roommate Wanted," "Join the Sexual Revolution—Come Home With Me Tonight," to such shock jokes as "Phallic Symbols Arise," "Stand Up For S-X," and "Come Together."

More sophisticated young people feel that the dirty-word movements or the shock words no longer have any impact. In the October 26, 1967, *Washington Square Journal*, a New York University publication, the student reviewer of an off-Broadway production, *The Beard*, which freely uses four-letter words and ends with an act of cunnilingus on stage, says: "Unfortunately the force of the play rests on the anticipated violation of social taboo, and violating social taboos just isn't what it used to be."

Except for the rediscovered poor, the United States is a society of unprecedented abundance. Upper- and middle-class white Americans pamper their children, give them cars and money, send them to college and abroad, and set them up in their own apartments while they are going to school. These young people have leisure and the wherewithal to use it in amusing themselves—only the war is real, which gives a special significance to college as a way of avoiding the war. This abundance means that college-age men and women can travel together, live together, and have a sex life encouraged by their peers, whose opinions they have now come to value more than those of their elders.

Abundance for the young unmarrieds in the

city has made it possible to meet other young un-married in new ways. Apartment houses are being built for them; clubs are formed for them, but perhaps the most significant of all the develop-ments is the use of bars, now often called pubs, which serve as meeting places where singles can meet without prejudice. A girl who visits the pub is under no obligation to "go to bed" with the man whom she meets and with whom she may leave. These pubs (and they begin to specialize in different kinds of singles), in a sense, institutional-ize a system of bringing together like-minded peo-ple; they speed the dating and the trial-and-error process, for they offer this particular group of af-fluent young people a wide variety of partners to choose from, and they can choose quickly, inde-pendently, and frequently.[40]

Many observers of the current scene consider the "pill" the most significant single force for in-creased sexual freedom. A count of the articles listed in the *Reader's Guide to Periodical Litera-ture* reveals that more articles were published about birth control in the period March 1965 to February 1966 than were listed in a ten-year sam-pling starting with 1925 and ending with 1957. The sampling yielded 89 titles. But we doubt that the pill has added materially to the increase in the number of young adults or adolescents who have had premarital sex. Effective techniques of birth control existed, and were used, before the pill. True, the pill makes birth control easier to manage (except for the memory requirement), but roman-tic love is still important; it makes taking the pill, when no definite partner is available, undesirable. What the pill does is to give sexual freedom to those who are having steady sexual relationships, for then the use of the pill adds to romantic love by making elaborate preparations unnecessary.

According to our crystal ball, which, of course, may be clouded, we have not had a recent or cur-rent sexual revolution in terms of behavior. How-ever, there probably has been some increase in the proportion of women who have had premarital in-tercourse. It is our guess that the increase has oc-curred largely among women who have had pre-marital sex only with their spouses-to-be. If there

has been a sexual revolution (similar to the 1920's but ideologically different[41]), it is in terms of frankness about sex and the freedom to discuss it. Women have demanded and have achieved more education, more independence, and more social rights; one of these is the right to choose a partner for sex. Men are accepting many of these changes in the status of women and are tempering their insistence on what have generally been considered male prerogatives, for example, the right to de-mand that a bride be a virgin. Young men today are probably less promiscuous and more monoga-mous, and their relationships tend to be more sta-ble. Both sexes are approaching a single standard based on sex with affection. We are still in a stage of transition. Despite the title of this article, the only indisputable conclusion which we can draw from the current scene is that we are witnessing the decline, but not yet the fall, of the double standard.

## REFERENCES AND NOTES

1   It is understood that even if it were possible to deter-mine these correlations accurately, we would not have an explanation of causation.

2   Alfred C. Kinsey, Wardell B. Pomeroy, Clyde E. Mar-tin, Paul Gebhard, *et al., Sexual Behavior in the Hu-man Female*, Philadelphia: W. B. Saunders, 1953. The data on the female subjects were collected from 1938 through 1949. Alfred C. Kinsey, Wardell B. Pomeroy, and Clyde E. Martin, *Sexual Behavior in the Human Male*, Philadelphia: W. B. Saunders, 1948. Data on the male subjects were collected from 1938 to 1947.

3   Lewis M. Terman *et al., Psychological Factors in Marital Happiness*, New York: McGraw-Hill Book Co., 1938.

4   Gilbert Youth Research, "How Wild Are College Stu-dents?," *Pageant*, vol. 7 (1951), pp. 10–21; Ernest W. Burgess and Paul Wallin, *Engagement and Mar-riage*, Chicago: J. P. Lippincott, 1953; Judson T. Landis and Mary Landis, *Building a Successful Mar-riage*, 3d ed., Englewood Cliffs, N.J.: Prentice-Hall, Inc., 1957; Winston Ehrmann, *Premarital Dating Be-havior*, New York: Holt, Rinehart and Winston, 1959; Mervin B. Freedman, "The Sexual Behavior of American College Women: An Empirical Study and an Historical Study," *Merrill-Palmer Quarterly*, vol. 2 (1965), pp. 33–48; Ira L. Reiss, *The Social Context*

*of Premarital Sexual Permissiveness*, New York: Holt, Rinehart and Winston, 1967, chap. VII. Reiss's primary purpose was not to examine behavior (at least not in this latest presentation); he was interested in attitudes. He asked 268 students (42 of them males) in an Iowa college about their behavior. What he did was to correlate expressed feelings of guilt with behavior, and found relationships with age and behavior and relationships between expressed standards and behavior. The Institute for Sex Research at Indiana University conducted a 1967 study of sex behavior among college students, but the final results have not yet been published.

5 Gilbert V. Hamilton, *A Research in Marriage*, 2d ed., New York: Lear, 1948, p. 348.

6 D. D. Bromley and F. H. Britten, *Youth and Sex*, New York: Harper & Brothers, 1938, p. 36.

7 Gilbert Youth Research *op. cit.*, p. 15.

8 Burgess and Wallin, *op. cit.*, p. 330; Landis and Landis, *op. cit.*, pp. 216 and 212; Ehrmann, *op. cit.*, pp. 33–34 and 46.

9 Freedman, *op. cit.*, p. 47.

10 Kinsey, *The Human Female*, p. 288.

11 Reiss, *op. cit.*

12 Ira L. Reiss, "Standards of Sexual Behavior," in Albert Ellis and Albert Abarbanel (eds.), *Encyclopedia of Sex*, New York: Hawthorne Books, 1961, p. 999. "These data were based on Kinsey (1953), but were especially prepared for [Reiss's] paper . . . [by] Drs. Gebhard and Martin of the Institute of Sex Research. These were based on 2,479 women who either were or had been married by the time of the interview."

13 Confirming this change are data reported by K. B. Davis, *Factors in the Sex Life of Twenty-two Hundred Women*, New York: Harper & Brothers, 1929, p. 232. Of those women who attended college in the early 1900's (that is, were born before 1900), only 7 per cent had premarital intercourse. According to Bromely and Britten, *loc. cit.*, 25 per cent of the college women of the 1930's had premarital intercourse. And according to Freedman (*op. cit.*, p. 45), "the rate of premarital nonvirginity tripled from 1900 to 1930."

14 Terman, *op. cit.*, p. 321; Kinsey, *The Human Male*, *op. cit.*, p. 395. Kinsey noted generational differences within his male sample; but the "generations" were formed by dividing his subjects into "younger" (under 33 years of age at the time of the interview) and "older" (over 33 years of age at the time interviewed) groups. He did not compare them by decade of birth as he did the women. The median age of the younger group was 21.2 years, that is, born approximately between 1917 and 1926. The median age of the older group was 43.1 years, that is, born approxi-

mately between 1895 and 1904 (Kinsey, *The Human Female*, *op. cit.*, chap. VII). Information is provided here that premarital petting had increased with each generation since 1920 even though incidence of premarital coitus had not. One of the possible explanations for the continued relatively high number of virgins is that heavy petting is now very common, so that there are a large number of "technical" virgins who engage in almost everything except coitus.

15 "Iowa Sociologist Calls Sex Revolution a Myth," *New York Times*, Oct. 22, 1967, sec. I, p. 80.

16 Wilbert E. Moore, *Social Change*, Englewood Cliffs, N.J.: Prentice-Hall, Inc., 1963, pp. 100–103.

17 In a recent article, Thomas K. Burch casts doubt on whether there has indeed been a breakdown of the extended family or a decline in the size of the family because of urbanization. See Thomas K. Burch, "The Size and Structure of Families: A Comparative Analysis of Census Data," *American Sociological Review*, vol. 32 (1967), pp. 347–363. We feel, however, that there can be little doubt about the relation between urbanization and changes in function and meaning of the family.

18 T. A. Storey, *The Work of the United States Interdepartmental Social Hygiene Board*, New York: United States Interdepartmental Social Hygiene Board, 1920, p. 6.

19 *Psychopathia Sexualis*, the best known work of Krafft-Ebing, was originally published in German in 1886. The first English translation was published shortly thereafter.

20 *The Psychology of Sex*, which represents Ellis' main body of work, was published in English in six separate volumes from 1900 to 1910 by F. A. Davis, Philadelphia. Volumes I and II had appeared in French (1897) before they appeared in English.

21 Frederick Lewis Allen, *Only Yesterday: An Informal History of the Nineteen-twenties*, New York: Blue Ribbon Books, 1932, p. 98.

22 William H. Masters and Virginia E. Johnson, *Human Sexual Response*, Boston: Little, Brown, and Company, 1966.

23 Ira L. Reiss, *Premarital Sexual Standards in America*, New York: The Free Press, 1960, pp. 219–221.

24 These tables are rearranged in chronological order and condensed for our purposes from the ones appearing in Reiss, *The Social Context of Premarital Sexual Permissiveness*, *op. cit.*, pp. 16–18. The categories used by L. Rockwood and M. Ford in their (1940) study of Cornell students, *Youth, Marriage, and Parenthood*, New York: John Wiley & Sons, Inc., 1945, p. 40, were used for classifying the data of the other studies. The 1947 and 1952–1955 studies were made by J. T. Landis and M. Landis and reported in *Building a Successful Marriage*, p. 215.

Their categories were "Sexual Relations: For both, None for either, For men only, Between engaged only." The 1958 study by Ehrmann, *op. cit.*, p. 189, used the standards: "Double (comparable to Sex Relations for men only), Conservative single (Abstinence), General liberal single (Sex Relations for both), and Lover liberal single (Sex Relations for those engaged or in love)" as categories.

25  Reiss, *The Social Context of Premarital Sexual Permissiveness*, *op. cit.*, tables 2.5, 2.6, and 2.7, pp. 25–27. The reverse double standard category has been omitted, for Reiss says that this "response is almost certainly an error." For his discussion of this point, see *ibid.*, p. 24. Reverse double standard adherents are understood to believe that women should have greater sexual freedom than men. Percentage accepting this standard were: 1959–9 per cent male, 6 per cent female, 7 per cent total; 1963–0 per cent male, 5 per cent female, 4 per cent total.

26  *Ibid.*, p. 128. The data for males have not been utilized because the men represent only a small percentage of the total number of cases in the sample.

27  Reiss reported 20 per cent of the females endorsing the double standard, but did not break down the figure to show the percentage accepting the orthodox standard nor the percentage accepting the traditional standard.

28  Reiss, *Premarital Sexual Permissiveness in America*, *op. cit.*, p. 233.

29  Nelson N. Foote, "Sex as Play," *Social Problems*, vol. 1 (1964), p. 161.

30  Robert Bell, "Parent-Child Conflict in Sexual Values," *Journal of Social Issues*, vol. 22 (1966), pp. 38–39.

31  *Ibid.*, p. 43.

32  Foote, *op. cit.*, p. 161.

33  Reiss, *The Social Context of Premarital Sexual Permissiveness*, *op. cit.*, table 2.7, p. 142.

34  *Ibid.*, pp. 140–143; and Bell, *op. cit.*, pp. 38–39.

35  Ira L. Reiss, "The Sexual Renaissance: A Summary and Analysis," *Journal of Social Issues*, vol. 22 (1966), p. 126.

36  Reiss, "Standards of Sexual Behavior," *loc. cit.*

37  U.S. Department of Health, Education, and Welfare, *Vital Statistics: National Summaries*, vol. 50, no. 28 (November 1959). Source: U.S. Bureau of the Census, "Population Characteristics," *Current Population Reports*, Series P–20, 105–3.

38  U.S. Bureau of the Census, *Statistical Abstracts of the United States, 1967*, 88th ed., Washington, D.C.: U.S. Government Printing Office, 1967, table 75: "Median Age at First Marriage, by Sex: 1920–1966." Source: U.S. Bureau of the Census, *Current Population Reports*. Series P–20, No. 159;

39  Walter Lippman, *A Preface to Morals* New York: The Macmillan Company, 1960, p. 228.

40  For an interesting comment on this phenomenon see "The Pleasures and Pain of the Single Life," *Time*, Sept. 15, 1967, pp. 26–27.

41  See Bennett M. Berger, "The New Morality," paper read at the Plenary Session of the Society for the Study of Social Problems, Aug. 27, 1967.

# 28  PARENTAL ENCOURAGEMENT AND EDUCATIONAL ASPIRATIONS
### WILLIAM H. SEWELL    VIMAL P. SHAH

It is a sociological truism, evidenced by a number

Reprinted from *The American Journal of Sociology*, vol. 73 (March 1968), pp. 559–572. by permission of the authors and The University of Chicago Press. Copyright © 1968 by The University of Chicago Press.

Paper presented at the 62d annual meeting of the American Sociological Association, San Francisco, August 1967. The research reported was financed by a grant from the National Institutes of Health, U.S. Public Health Service (M-6275). The authors acknowledge the services of the University of Wisconsin Computing Center and wish to thank Otis Dudley Duncan and Warren Hagstrom for their helpful comments on an earlier draft.

of studies, that children of higher social class origins are more likely to aspire to high educational and occupational goals than are children of lower social class origins.[1] This is true despite wide differences among the studies in the nature of their samples, the age level of their subjects, their measurement procedures, and the particular cutting points used to categorize the variables.[2] Even when other variables known to be related to both social class origins and aspirations—such as sex, intelligence, high school achievement, value orientations, and contextual variables such as neighborhood and community of residence—have been controlled, social class origins have been found to have an independent influence on educational and occupational aspirations. The question is often raised as to what it is about social class that accounts for this relationship and through what intervening variables this relationship may be further explained. In other words, the need is emphasized for specifying the variables by which the social class characteristics of individuals are translated into differences in aspiration and subsequently into achievement.[3] One factor which has come in for considerable emphasis is the degree to which the child perceives his parents as encouraging or even pressuring him to have high educational and occupational goals.

Kahl first suggested the importance of parental encouragement in his study of the educational and occupational aspirations of "common-man" boys. After finding that intelligence and social class position accounted for the major variations in college aspirations of boys of common-man or working-class origins, he noted that the attitude of the parents regarding the importance of occupational success for personal happiness was the critical factor.[4]

Kahl's findings, although based on a very small sample of twenty-four common-man boys, have led many social scientists to emphasize the importance of parental encouragement and other social-psychological variables in explaining the relation of social stratification to aspirations. For example, in a critique of social structure and American education, Gross observes the following:

> It is frequently assumed that because children come from backgrounds, similar on such criteria as education, occupation, and religion of parents that these children experience similar influences. However, as Kahl's paper suggests, in a setting of highly similar social status dimensions, quite disparate sociological and psychological influence, in this case parental pressure, may be operative on the child. This suggests that to type children simply on the basis of the characteristics of their socioeconomic environment or "social class" may provide an extremely inaccurate picture of the crucial influences affecting them. Social class typing of children, in short, may obscure more than it may reveal regarding influences operative on children.

Bordua, in a study of 1,529 ninth through twelfth graders in two cities of Massachusetts, found that socioeconomic status was related positively to college plans at all school-year levels in both sexes and in Catholic, Protestant, and Jewish religious affiliations.[6] Since parental stress on college was positively and linearly related to college plans when sex and school year were controlled, Bordua asked whether these relationships were due to differential stress on college by the parents of boys as opposed to girls, to high socioeconomic status levels as opposed to low, and to Jews as opposed to Protestants and Catholics. He, therefore, controlled for parental stress on college and found that the effects of religious affiliation and socioeconomic status on college aspirations were reduced but not eliminated. Also, parental stress on college was related about equally to college plans whether or not socioeconomic status was controlled. However, Bordua's findings should be viewed with certain reservations because he did not control for all variables simultaneously, and particularly because he did not control for intelligence which has been found consistently related to both socioeconomic status and college plans. Similar limitations of methodology and data are characteristic also of Simpson's study of 743 boys in white high schools in two southern cities, in which it was concluded that "parental advice is a much better predictor of high ambition than is the boy's social class."[7]

In a study of 2,852 male sophomores in secondary schools in six middle-sized Pennsylvania cities, Rehberg and Westby found that the father's education and occupation influence educational expectancy both through parental encouragement and independent of it. Further, they found that the larger the family the greater the reduction not only in the frequency with which the parents encourage their children to continue their education beyond high school but also in the effectiveness of any given frequency level of parental educational encouragement.[8] Although family size was used as an additional control variable in their study, in the absence of data on intelligence Rehberg and Westby were unable to partial out the influence of ability on either parental encouragement or educational expectancy of the students. Further, they may have overstated the influence of parental encouragement in their top social status category when they suggested that "parental encouragement comes to being a *necessary* condition for the continuation of education beyond the high school level in *all* strata and not just in the lower classes."[9]

A critical review of these and other studies of the influence of parents' attitudes on youths' aspirations indicates not only major limitations of past studies but also the need for a clear formulation of a series of research questions. The purpose of this paper is to determine: (1) whether or not observed social class differences in the college plans of youth can be explained in terms of the differences in the level of perceived parental encouragement when intelligence is taken into account; (2) and if not, what additional influence parental encouragement has on college plans over and above the influence of social class and intelligence; (3) the direct and indirect influences that social class, intelligence, and parental encouragement have on college plans; (4) and, finally, whether or not there are any subpopulations of sex, intelligence, and parental encouragement in which social class differences in college plans might be eliminated.

### THE DATA

The data for the present study come from a survey of graduating seniors in all public, private, and parochial schools in Wisconsin.[10] Information was obtained from the respondents, school authorities, and a statewide testing program on a number of matters, including the student's educational and occupational plans, the student's percentile rank in measured intelligence, the socioeconomic status of his family, his rank in his high school class, his course of study, and the educational attitudes of

the student and his family. The analysis reported in this paper is based on 10,318 seniors who constituted about a one-third random sample of all 1957 seniors in Wisconsin.

The variable *socioeconomic status* ($X_1$) of the student's family is based on a weighted combination of father's occupation, father's formal educational level, mother's formal educational level, an estimate of the funds the family could provide if the student were to attend college, the degree of sacrifice this would entail for the family, and the approximate wealth and income status of the student's family. The sample was divided into four roughly equal groups, labeled "High," "Upper Middle," "Lower Middle," and "Low" in socioeconomic status.[11]

The variable *intelligence* ($X_2$) is based on scores on the Henmon-Nelson Test of Mental Ability, which is administered annually to all high school juniors in Wisconsin.[12] The categories used represent the division of the sample into approximately equal fourths in measured intelligence, according to established statewide norms, labeled "High," "Upper Middle," "Lower Middle," and "Low" in intelligence.

The variable *paternal encouragement* ($X_3$) is based on the student's response to four statements intended to record his perception of his parents' attitude toward his college plans. The students were asked to check *any one* of the following four statements: (1) My parents want me to go to college; (2) My parents do not want me to go; (3) My parents do not care whether I go; and (4) My parents will not let me go. For the purposes of this study, the students responding to the first statement are considered to have perceived positive parental encouragement to plan on college, while the students responding to the other three statements are considered not to have perceived positive parental encouragement to plan on college. The variable is dichotomized accordingly into high and low parental encouragement categories.

The variable *college plans* ($X_4$) is based on a statement by the student that he definitely plans to enrol in a degree-granting college or university (or one whose credits are acceptable for advanced standing by the University of Wisconsin). That these statements reflect realistic rather than vague hopes is supported by the fact that 87.3 per cent of the boys and 86.7 per cent of the girls who had stated that they planned on college actually attended college. [13]

## STATISTICAL PROCEDURE

The principal purpose of this paper is to examine the relationship between socioeconomic status and college plans. The strategy followed is to partial out the influence of intelligence and parental encouragement prior to determining the relationship between socioeconomic status and college plans. Also, separate analysis is made for males and females because of known differences in their propensity to pursue higher education as well as likely differences in the influence of socioeconomic status, intelligence, and parental encouragement on their college plans. Various statistical techniques are used to achieve the purpose of this study.

First, the gross relationships of socioeconomic status, intelligence, and parental encouragement to college plans and to one another are determined from their zero-order correlation coefficients. Second, the relationship of socioeconomic status to college plans, controlling for intelligence and parental encouragement, is determined by means of first- and second-order partial correlation coefficients. Third, the additional contribution of parental encouragement in predicting college plans, over and above the contribution of socioeconomic status and intelligence, is determined by means of stepwise multiple correlation coefficients. Fourth, the relative direct and indirect effects of socioeconomic status, intelligence, and parental encouragement on college plans are determined by using the method of path analysis. [14] And fifth, a multivariate cross-tabular analysis of the data is made to demarcate the differential influence of socioeconomic status on the college plans of various subgroups which differ by sex, intelligence, and degree of parental encouragement. The statistical significance of the relationships examined throughout the analysis is determined by appropriate tests using the .05 probability level.

## RESULTS

The gross relationships of socioeconomic status, intelligence, and parental encouragement to college plans can be examined from the zero-order correlations given in the intercorrelation matrix of Table 1. The zero-order correlation coefficients of socioeconomic status, intelligence, and parental encouragement with college plans are all positive and statistically significant for males as well as for females. For males, socioeconomic status and intelligence each explains about 18 per cent of the variance in college plans. For females, socioeconomic status explains 22.9 per cent of the variance in college plans while intelligence explains only 12.6 per cent. Parental encouragement explains about one-fourth of the variance in the college plans of boys and about one-third of the variance

**TABLE 1** *Intercorrelation matrix*

| Variable | $X_1$ | $X_2$ | $X_3$ | $X_4$ |
|---|---|---|---|---|
| **Males** | | | | |
| $X_1$ (socioeconomic status) | | .30 | .40 | .43 |
| $X_2$ (measured intelligence) | | | .35 | .42 |
| $X_3$ (perceived parental encouragement) | | | | .51 |
| $X_4$ (college plans) | | | | |
| **Females** | | | | |
| $X_1$ (socioeconomic status) | | .32 | .44 | .48 |
| $X_2$ (measured intelligence) | | | .29 | .36 |
| $X_3$ (perceived parental encouragement) | | | | .57 |
| $X_4$ (college plans) | | | | |

in the college plans of girls. Thus, the zero-order correlation coefficients indicate that the relationship of parental encouragement to college plans is stronger than that of either socioeconomic status or intelligence to college plans and that the relationship of parental encouragement to college plans is stronger for females than for males. Socioeconomic status and intelligence have an equally strong relationship to the college plans of males, but socioeconomic status has a considerably stronger relationship to the college plans of females than does intelligence.

The stronger relationships of socioeconomic status and parental encouragement to the college plans of females than to those of males seem to reflect the differential pattern of role expectations from adult males and females in our society. College education is considered as desirable and increasingly necessary for fulfilling male occupational roles, but for females the situation is doubtless complicated by marital roles and economic considerations. Presumably, therefore, the family resources exert stronger influence on the college plans of females than on those of males, while ability exerts stronger influence on the college plans of males than on those of females.

Although the examination of various factors determining different levels of parental encouragement is outside the scope of this paper, the socioeconomic status of the family and the ability level of the children seem to be two of the most pertinent factors. Consequently, the relationship of parental encouragement to socioeconomic status and intelligence is examined.

Judging from the zero-order correlation coefficients, for both males and females socioeconomic status indicates a stronger relationship with parental encouragement than does intelligence. Socioeconomic status explains about one-sixth of the variance in perceived parental encouragement for males and about one-fifth of the variance in perceived parental encouragement for females. But, intelligence explains about one-eighth of the variance in perceived parental encouragement for males and only about one-twelfth of the variance for females. Thus, as in the case of college plans, socioeconomic status is more strongly related to perceived parental encouragement for females than for males, but intelligence is more strongly related to perceived parental encouragement for males than for females.

An examination of the intercorrelation between socioeconomic status, intelligence, and parental encouragement indicates that these variables are related not only to college plans but also to each other and that their relationships are different for males and females. Consequently, intelligence and parental encouragement should be controlled while the relationship of socioeconomic status to college plans is examined.

From the first-order partial correlation coefficients of socioeconomic status to college plans (Table 2), it is clear that when either intelligence or parental encouragement is controlled, the relationship between socioeconomic status and college plans of both males and females is reduced but not eliminated. When controlled for intelligence, socioeconomic status explains 12.0 per cent of the variance in the college plans of males, but it explains 17.0 per cent of the variance in the college plans of females. Similarly, when controlled for parental encouragement, socioeconomic status explains 8.0 per cent of the variance in the college plans of males, but it explains 9.4 per cent of the variance in the college plans of females. It should be noted that controlling for parental encouragement makes a greater reduction in the relationship of socioeconomic status to college plans than the reduction made in the relationship when intelligence is controlled. In either case, however, the relationship continues to be substantial and statistically significant. Also, the stronger relationship of socioeconomic status to the college plans of females than to those of males is evident when either intelligence or parental encouragement is controlled.

When intelligence and parental encouragement are both controlled in the second-order partial correlation coefficients (Table 2), the relationship of socioeconomic status to college plans is further reduced, but socioeconomic status still explains 5.8 per cent of the variance in the college plans of males and 7.2 per cent of the variance in the col-

**TABLE 2**    *First-order and second-order partial correlation coefficients of socioeconomic status with college plans, separately for males and females*

| Independent variable | Dependent variable | Control variable(s) | Males | | Females | |
|---|---|---|---|---|---|---|
| | | | Partial r | Variance explained, % | Partial r | Variance explained, % |
| Socioeconomic status | College plans | Intelligence | .346 | 12.0 | .412 | 17.0 |
| Socioeconomic status | College plans | Perceived parental encouragement | .283 | 8.0 | .307 | 9.4 |
| Socioeconomic status | College plans | Intelligence and perceived parental encouragement | .240 | 5.8 | .268 | 7.2 |

lege plans of females. Thus, even after partialing out the effects of intelligence and parental encouragement, the relationship of socioeconomic status to college plans continues to be substantial and statistically significant.

The zero-order and partial correlation coefficients indicate that there is a positive and statistically significant relationship between socioeconomic status and the college plans of both males and females, with or without controls for intelligence and parental encouragement, which are themselves related to each other and to both socioeconomic status and college plans. The analysis thus far demonstrates the independent relationship of socioeconomic status to college plans. The strength of parental encouragement for predicting college plans

over and above the strength of socioeconomic status and intelligence will be determined by examining the multiple correlation coefficients.

The multiple correlation coefficient of socioeconomic status and intelligence to college plans is the same for both males and females ($R = .524$—Table 3); together they explain a little over one-fourth of the variance in college plans. This suggests that although socioeconomic status has a stronger relationship to the college plans of girls than of boys, and although intelligence has a stronger relationship to the college plans of boys than of girls, their combined strength is the same for both sexes.

From Table 3, in addition to the variance explained by socioeconomic status, intelligence ex-

**TABLE 3**    *Stepwise multiple correlation coefficients of socioeconomic status, measured intelligence, and perceived parental encouragement with college plans, separately for males and females*

| Independent variable(s) | Dependent variable | Males | | Females | |
|---|---|---|---|---|---|
| | | r/R | Variance explained, % | r/R | Variance explained, % |
| Socioeconomic status | College plans | .426 | 18.2 | .478 | 22.9 |
| Socioeconomic status and measured intelligence | College plans | .524 | 27.5 | .524 | 27.5 |
| Socioeconomic status and perceived parental encouragement | College plans | .567 | 32.2 | .620 | 38.4 |
| Socioeconomic status, measured intelligence, and perceived parental encouragement | College plans | .607 | 36.8 | .638 | 40.7 |

plains 9.3 (27.5 − 18.2) per cent of the variance in the college plans of males and 4.6 (27.5 − 22.9) per cent of the variance in the college plans of females, but parental encouragement explains 14.0 (32.2 − 18.2) per cent of the variance in the college plans of males and 15.5 (38.4 − 22.9) per cent of the variance in the college plans of females over and above that explained by socioeconomic status. Thus, both intelligence and parental encouragement add substantially to the variance explained by socioeconomic status, but the additional variance explained by parental encouragement is greater than the additional variance explained by intelligence. It should also be noted that the additional variance explained by parental encouragement is almost equal for males and females. Finally, socioeconomic status, intelligence, and parental encouragement together explain 36.8 per cent of the variance in college plans for males and 40.7 per cent of the variance for females. Parental encouragement explains 9.3 (36.8 − 27.5) per cent of the variance in the college plans of males and 13.2 (40.7 − 27.5) per cent of the variance for females over and above that explained by both socioeconomic status and intelligence. In short, parental encouragement adds very substantially to the explained variance in the college plans of both males and females over and above that explained by socioeconomic status and intelligence.

In summarizing the correlational analysis, it is evident that social class differences in the college plans of Wisconsin high school seniors are not

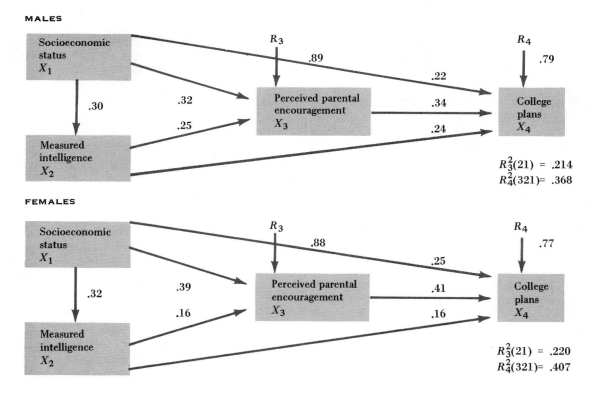

**FIGURE 1** *Path diagrams showing the influence of socioeconomic status, measured intelligence, and perceived parental encouragement on college plans (by sex).*

completely accounted for either by the level of students' intelligence or by perceived parental encouragement, or both. Also, the relationship of parental encouragement to college plans is not simply an additive combination of the relationships of socioeconomic status and intelligence to parental encouragement. Its added independent contribution to the explained variance in the college plans of males as well as females is substantial. This demonstrates the usefulness of parental encouragement as an explanatory variable without undermining the importance of socioeconomic status and intelligence as explanatory variables. It is possible to determine and compare the direct and indirect effects of these variables on college plans by following the method of path analysis.

It is assumed in the path diagrams shown in Figure 1 that parental encouragement is determined by socioeconomic status and intelligence and that all three in turn determine college plans. The relationship between socioeconomic status and intelligence is not analyzed, and, consequently, no assumption is made regarding the causal link between them. The $R_3$ and $R_4$ indicate the residual factors determining parental encouragement and college plans, respectively. Although the path analysis generally corroborates the findings of the correlational analysis, several observations should be made from the path coefficients indicated in this figure.

First, neither parental encouragement nor college plans are completely accounted for by the variables explicitly included in this study. The magnitude of the effect of the residual factors on these variables is very large. Substantial proportions of the variance in parental encouragement (78.6 per cent for boys and 78.0 per cent for girls) cannot be accounted for by socioeconomic status and intelligence. Similar proportions of the variance in the college plans of males and females are not accounted for by socioeconomic status, intelligence, and parental encouragement—63.2 per cent and 59.3 per cent, respectively. These large residuals indicate the need for bringing additional variables into the system.

Second, for both boys and girls the contribu-

tion of socioeconomic status to parental encouragement is greater than that of intelligence. But, while the effect of socioeconomic status on parental encouragement is greater for girls than for boys, the effect of intelligence on parental encouragement is greater for boys than for girls.

Third, the direct effect of parental encouragement on the college plans of boys as well as girls is greater than that of either socioeconomic status or intelligence. It should be noted in this connection that both socioeconomic status and intelligence also exert some indirect effect on college plans through their effect on parental encouragement. The direct effects of socioeconomic status and intelligence on the college plans of boys are almost equal, but the direct effect of socioeconomic status on the college plans of girls is much greater than the direct effect of intelligence on their college plans.

Finally, for boys as well as girls, while the direct effects of intelligence on parental encouragement and on college plans are almost equal, the direct effect of socioeconomic status on parental encouragement is much greater than its direct effect on college plans.

In summary, the correlational and the path analyses indicate very clearly that while there is some common component in socioeconomic status, intelligence, and parental encouragement which accounts for their relationship to college plans, all three variables have substantial independent relationships of their own to college plans. With particular reference to the major purpose of this study, neither intelligence nor parental encouragement, individually or jointly, can completely account for the social class differences in the college plans of either males or females. This conclusion leads to the examination of a final question in this paper, namely, whether or not there are specific subpopulations of sex, intelligence, and parental encouragement in which social class differences in college plans are eliminated.

The multivariate cross-tabular data presented in Table 4 give the percentages of males and females planning on college, by socioeconomic status, intelligence, and parental encouragement. The

**TABLE 4**   *Percentages of students who planned on college, by socioeconomic status, measured intelligence, and perceived parental encouragement, separately for males and females*

| Socioeconomic status | Perceived parental encouragement | | | | | | | | | | | |
|---|---|---|---|---|---|---|---|---|---|---|---|---|
| | Males | | | | | | Females | | | | | |
| | Low* | | High* | | Total* | | Low* | | High | | Total* | |
| Low intelligence | % | N | % | N | % | N | % | N | % | N | % | N |
| Low | 1.1 | 353 | 16.8 | 77 | 4.0 | 430 | 1.1 | 459 | 17.0 | 53 | 2.7 | 512 |
| Lower middle | 0.8 | 234 | 24.3 | 111 | 8.4 | 345 | 3.7 | 296 | 32.2 | 90 | 10.4 | 386 |
| Upper middle | 4.6 | 174 | 34.1 | 138 | 17.6 | 312 | 4.1 | 170 | 33.3 | 108 | 15.5 | 278 |
| High | 7.6 | 52 | 40.6 | 96 | 29.0 | 148 | 10.7 | 56 | 38.3 | 94 | 28.0 | 150 |
| Total | 2.2 | 813 | 29.8 | 422 | 11.7 | 1,235 | 3.0 | 981 | 31.8 | 345 | 10.5 | 1,326 |
| **Lower middle intelligence** | | | | | | | | | | | | |
| Low | 4.2 | 216 | 31.4 | 105 | 13.0 | 321 | 1.6 | 317 | 23.0 | 71 | 5.0 | 378 |
| Lower middle | 3.4 | 208 | 40.3 | 159 | 19.4 | 367 | 7.5 | 255 | 34.8 | 135 | 16.9 | 390 |
| Upper middle | 4.8 | 126 | 40.2 | 184 | 25.8 | 310 | 6.3 | 206 | 45.4 | 165 | 23.7 | 371 |
| High | 9.6 | 52 | 57.8 | 218 | 48.3 | 265 | 6.6 | 75 | 59.1 | 186 | 44.0 | 261 |
| Total | 4.4 | 602 | 44.5 | 661 | 25.4 | 1,263 | 4.9 | 853 | 45.0 | 547 | 20.6 | 1,400 |
| **Upper middle intelligence** | | | | | | | | | | | | |
| Low | 8.7 | 138 | 41.3 | 92 | 21.7 | 230 | 3.6 | 224 | 36.4 | 55 | 10.0 | 279 |
| Lower middle | 9.4 | 127 | 50.2 | 185 | 33.6 | 312 | 6.8 | 176 | 42.2 | 147 | 22.9 | 323 |
| Upper middle | 15.6 | 109 | 59.6 | 248 | 46.2 | 357 | 6.4 | 186 | 47.6 | 191 | 27.3 | 377 |
| High | 18.0 | 50 | 77.5 | 289 | 68.7 | 339 | 21.6 | 60 | 74.0 | 311 | 65.5 | 371 |
| Total | 11.8 | 424 | 61.8 | 814 | 44.7 | 1,238 | 7.0 | 646 | 57.2 | 704 | 33.2 | 1,350 |
| **High intelligence** | | | | | | | | | | | | |
| Low | 13.0 | 77 | 53.2 | 92 | 34.9 | 169 | 11.9 | 109 | 53.8 | 52 | 25.4 | 161 |
| Lower middle | 17.7 | 96 | 66.8 | 178 | 49.6 | 274 | 11.7 | 128 | 59.0 | 122 | 34.8 | 250 |
| Upper middle | 12.5 | 48 | 73.0 | 271 | 64.0 | 319 | 19.8 | 101 | 64.8 | 219 | 50.6 | 320 |
| High | 32.0 | 25 | 88.4 | 468 | 85.6 | 493 | 21.0 | 62 | 78.6 | 458 | 71.7 | 520 |
| Total | 16.6 | 246 | 77.3 | 1,009 | 65.4 | 1,255 | 15.2 | 400 | 70.7 | 851 | 53.0 | 1,251 |
| **Total** | | | | | | | | | | | | |
| Low | 4.4 | 784 | 36.3 | 366 | 14.6 | 1,150 | 2.8 | 1,109 | 32.1 | 221 | 7.7 | 1,330 |
| Lower middle | 5.7 | 665 | 47.9 | 633 | 26.3 | 1,298 | 6.6 | 855 | 42.5 | 494 | 19.8 | 1,349 |
| Upper middle | 8.1 | 457 | 55.5 | 841 | 38.8 | 1,298 | 7.8 | 663 | 50.4 | 683 | 29.4 | 1,346 |
| High | 14.5 | 179 | 75.0 | 1,066 | 66.4 | 1,245 | 14.6 | 253 | 70.2 | 1,049 | 59.4 | 1,302 |
| Total | 6.5 | 2,085 | 58.6 | 2,906 | 36.9 | 4,991 | 6.2 | 2,880 | 55.6 | 2,447 | 28.9 | 5,327 |

*The $\chi^2$ for each column designated is significant beyond the .05 level

separate relationships of socioeconomic status, intelligence, and parental encouragement to college plans can be examined from the marginals in this table. Each of these relationships is positive, monotonic, and statistically significant. The relationship of socioeconomic status to college plans controlling only for intelligence, can be examined from the columns marked "Total" under the four intelligence categories. The control for intelligence reduces but does not eliminate the social class differences in the college plans of males and females in each category of intelligence. Similarly, from the bottom part of Table 4, the relationship of socioeconomic status to college plans continues to be positive, monotonic, and statistically significant when only parental encouragement is controlled. However, since the purpose of this multivariate cross-tabular analysis is to specify the subgroups in which the influence of social class on college plans is either markedly pronounced or markedly reduced, only the columns showing a simultaneous cross-tabulation of socioeconomic status, intelligence, and parental encouragement will be discussed here. Several observations can be made from these data.

First, the dictum that the higher the level of socioeconomic status the higher the level of educational aspirations is generally true, even after sex, intelligence, and parental encouragement are controlled. Except for some slight reversals in the two middle categories of socioeconomic status, the relationship between socioeconomic status and college plans is generally positive and monotonic. While only about 1 per cent of males and females with low intelligence and low parental encouragement from the low socioeconomic status category planned on college, 88.4 per cent of the males and 78.6 per cent of the females with high intelligence and high parental encouragement from the high socioeconomic status category planned on college. The proportions planning on college in the remaining socioeconomic status categories, by intelligence and parental encouragement, fall within this range. However, the difference in the percentage of students planning on college from the bottom and the top socioeconomic status categories of

these subgroups varies over a wide range—from a minimum of 5 per cent to over 35 per cent.

Second, the socioeconomic status differences in the college plans of the seniors are almost four times as great for those who perceived parental encouragement as for those who did not. Further, these differences are generally greater for those who are in the two upper categories of intelligence than for those in the two lower categories of intelligence. Thus, differences in the levels of both intelligence and parental encouragement seem to increase the socioeconomic status differences in the college plans of youth. In other words, the socioeconomic status differences in college plans of youth are greater among the most able and the most encouraged than among the least able and the least encouraged.

Third, in most categories of socioeconomic status, intelligence, and parental encouragement, the proportion of students planning on college is greater for males than for females. This indicates the important influence of sex-role expectations on the college plans of youth. However, sex-role expectations seem to bear more heavily on those who are high in intelligence than on those who are low in intelligence. The greater proportions of females than of males planning on college in some of the subgroups within the two lower categories of intelligence support this conclusion.

Fourth, the socioeconomic status differences in college plans of the seniors in both categories of parental encouragement are greater among those who are most intelligent than among those who are least intelligent. On the one hand, among those who did not perceive parental encouragement and who are least able, only about 1 per cent of males and females from the low socioeconomic status category planned on college as against 7.6 per cent of males and 10.7 per cent of females from the high socioeconomic status category. On the other hand, among those who did not perceive parental encouragement but who are most able, 13.0 per cent of males and 11.9 per cent of females from the low socioeconomic status category planned on college as against 32.0 per cent of males and 21.0 per cent of females from the high socioeconomic status category. Similarly, among those who perceived parental encouragement and who are least able, about 17 per cent of both males and females from the low socioeconomic status category planned on college as against 40.6 per cent of males and 38.3 per cent of females from the high socioeconomic status category. Among those who perceived parental encouragement and who are most able, about 53 per cent of males and females from the low socioeconomic status category planned on college as against 88.4 per cent of males and 78.6 per cent of females from the high socioeconomic status category. Thus, ability continues to accentuate the social class differences in aspirations of both males and females, regardless of whether or not they perceive parental encouragement to plan on college.

Finally, in each category of socioeconomic status and intelligence, the proportion of males and females planning on college is greater among those who perceived parental encouragement than among those who did not. In particular, in all categories of intelligence, the proportion of males and females planning on college is greater among the low socioeconomic status seniors who perceived parental encouragement than among the high socioeconomic status seniors who did not perceive parental encouragement. Consequently, parental encouragement seems to be a powerful factor in encouraging seniors who are low in socioeconomic status but high in ability to plan on college. In general, however, parental encouragement appears to have its strongest effect on the college plans of males and females who score relatively high on intelligence and come from families occupying relatively high socioeconomic positions.

In addition to providing the reader with an opportunity to see the effects of the several variables on college plans in familiar percentage terms, the multiple cross-tabular analysis tends mainly to emphasize and reinforce what was already known from the correlation analysis; namely, that (1) there are large differences between the socioeconomic status categories in college plans; (2) even though these differences are reduced when sex, intelligence, and parental encouragement are controlled, there are still large and important socioeconomic status differences in college plans, especially in the top two intelligence groups where college plans are most relevant in any case; (3) where parental encouragement is low, relatively few students, regardless of their intelligence or socioeconomic status levels, plan on college (even highly intelligent students with high social class origins who are not encouraged by their parents are not likely to plan on college); (4) where parental encouragement is high, the proportion of students planning on college is also high, even when socioeconomic status and intelligence levels are relatively low. Thus, it may be concluded that while social class differences cannot be entirely explained by differences in parental encouragement (or intelligence) among the various socioeconomic classes, parental encouragement makes an independent contribution to social class differences in college plans of both males and females; (5) the effects of sex-role expectations are such that girls' educational aspirations are generally lower than those of boys and are somewhat more sensitive to socioeconomic background than to ability or parental encouragement.

## CONCLUSIONS

The correlational, causal, and cross-tabular analyses in this study substantiate, on the whole, the claim made by other investigators using less rigorous methods and less representative samples that parental encouragement is a powerful intervening variable between socioeconomic class background and intelligence of the child and his educational aspirations. While parental encouragement does not "explain" social class differences in aspirations, it contributes to the explanation of these differences. Because parental encouragement is a social-psychological variable, it is presumably subject to modification by means of programs of counseling directed at parents or parents and children, whereas the child's intelligence and family socioeconomic status are likely to be more difficult to influence at this point in the child's development.

At the same time there is still a good deal of variance in college plans of the socioeconomic classes that is not explained either individually or jointly by parental encouragement and intelligence. This leads to the question of what other factors may help to explain social class differences. Within the complex which is subsumed under socioeconomic status, the economic resources available for the support of college education must be an important determinant, and none of the studies reported to date have adequately assessed this aspect of socioeconomic level. Information regarding the economic resources of the families of the seniors under study is being currently collected from public sources which will make such an analysis possible. Other variables that should be considered include the student's knowledge of available opportunities for scholarships, loans, and jobs, and the student's self-conceptions—including his assessment of his chances for success in college, his reference groups, and various contextual influences such as the value climate and the opportunity structures of his school and community. All of these factors are in need of further study for increasing and strengthening the knowledge of the factors involved in social class differences in educational aspiration and for understanding more fully the contribution of nonintellectual factors to educational aspiration.

### REFERENCES AND NOTES

1   There is a vast literature in this regard. References to these studies are given in William H. Sewell, Archibald O. Haller, and Murray A. Straus, "Social Status and Educational and Occupational Aspiration," *American Sociological Review*, vol. 22 (February 1957), pp. 67–73; William H. Sewell, "Community of Residence and College Plans," *American Sociological Review*, vol. 29 (February 1964), pp. 24–38; William H. Sewell and Alan M. Orenstein, "Community of Residence and Occupational Choice," *American Journal of Sociology*, vol. 70 (March 1965), pp. 551–63; William H. Sewell and Archibald O. Haller, "Educational and Occupational Perspectives of Farm and Rural Youth," in Lee G. Burchinal (ed.), *Rural Youth in Crisis*, U.S. Department of Health, Education, and Welfare, Washington, D.C.: U.S. Government Printing Office, 1965, pp. 149–69; William H. Sewell and J. Michael Armer, "Neighborhood Context and College Plans," *American Sociological Review*, vol. 31 (April 1966), pp. 159–168; and William H. Sewell and Vimal P. Shah, "Socioeconomic Status, Intelligence, and the Attainment of Higher Education," *Sociology of Education*, vol. 40 (winter 1967), pp. 1–23.

2   Interesting evidence is provided by Haller and Miller, who attempted to test the hypothesis of a positive correlation between the level of occupational aspiration and social class status, race, parents' willingness to contribute financial support to help the youth, and posteducational work experience. They examined data from several published and unpublished studies. The hypothesis was confirmed in twenty-three instances, and the authors were somewhat doubtful about the validity of all of the remaining instances classified by them as contrary to the hypothesis. Archibald O. Haller and Irwin W. Miller, *The Occupational Aspiration Scale: Theory, Structure and Correlates*, East Lansing, Mich.: Michigan State University Agricultural Experiment Station, 1963, pp. 28–55.

3   For example, Peter Rossi, "Social Factors in Academic Achievement," in E. H. Halsey, Jean Floud, and C. Arnold Anderson (eds.), *Education, Economy and Society*, Glencoe, Ill.: The Free Press, 1961, p. 269, in surveying the researches on social factors affecting the achievement of students in American elementary and high schools, observed that "it is characteristic of past researches on individual differences that they have not gone much beyond measuring the association between characteristics of individual students and their achievement scores, to specify the processes by which these characteristics are translated into differences in achievement."

4   Kahl selected twenty-four subjects for his study from a larger sample of 3,971 boys in public high schools in eight towns of the Boston metropolitan area. These twenty-four boys had intelligence scores in the top three deciles of their schools and therefore were considered intelligent enough to succeed in college. While most upper-status boys aimed toward college as a matter of course, most lower-status boys tended to be uninterested in college. Consequently, working-class boys who aimed high were exceptions, and Kahl's intensive study of this group was designed to discover the source of their higher aspirations. See Joseph A. Kahl, "Educational and Occupational Aspirations of 'Common-Man' Boys," *Harvard Educational Review*, vol. 23 (summer 1953), pp. 186–203.

5   Neal Gross, "A Critique of Social Class Structure and American Education," *Harvard Educational Review*, vol. 23 (fall 1953), pp. 298–329.

6   David J. Bordua, "Educational Aspirations and Parental Stress on College," *Social Forces*, vol. 38 (March 1960), pp. 262–269.

7   Richard L. Simpson, "Parental Influence, Anticipatory Socialization, and Social Mobility," *American Sociological Review*, vol. 27 (August 1962), pp. 517–522.

8   Richard A. Rehberg and David L. Westby, "Parental Encouragement, Occupation, Education and Family Size: Artifactual or Independent Determinants of Adolescent Educational Expectations?" *Social Forces*, vol. 45 (March 1967), pp. 362–374.

9   *Ibid.*, p. 371.

10  The over-all results of this survey are given in J. Kenneth Little, *A Statewide Inquiry into Decisions of Youth about Education beyond High School*, Madison, Wisc.: University of Wisconsin School of Education, 1958.

11  These six indicators of family socioeconomic status were factor analyzed using the principal-components method and were orthogonally rotated according to the verimax criterion. This produced a three-factor structure composed of a factor on which the three economic items were most heavily loaded, a factor on which the two educational items were most heavily loaded, and a factor on which the occupational item was most heavily loaded. The composite socioeconomic status index was developed by squaring the loadings of the principal items on each factor as weights, then multiplying students' scores on the items by the respective weights, and, finally, summing the weighted scores of the principal items on each factor. The three factors were combined into a composite socioeconomic status score after multiplying the scores of all students by certain constants which would produce approximately equal variances for each status dimension. The resulting sum of the weighted scores was then multiplied by a constant to produce a theoretical range of scores between 0 and 99.

12  V. A. C. Henmon and M. J. Nelson, *The Henmon-Nelson Test of Mental Ability*, Boston: Houghton Mifflin Co., 1942.

13  A follow-up survey was conducted by means of mailed questionnaires and telephone interviews, and responses were obtained from 9,007, or 87.2 per cent, of the students in the original one-third sample. For further information on the follow-up, see Sewell and Shah, *op. cit.*, pp. 6–7.

14  Path analysis provides a convenient and efficient method for determining the direct and indirect effects of each of the independent variables in a causal chain composed of standardized variables in a closed system. These effects are expressed in path coefficients which are the $\beta$ weights of all of the preceding independent variables on the successive dependent variables in the system. For a brief summary of the method of path analysis, see Otis Dudley Duncan "Path Analysis: Sociological Examples," *American Journal of Sociology*, vol. 72 (July 1966), pp. 1–6.

## SUPPLEMENTAL READINGS

Adams, Bert N.: *Kinship in an Urban Setting*, Chicago: Markham Publishing Company, 1968.

Bardis, Panos D.: *The Family in a Changing Civilization*, New York: Simon & Schuster, Inc., 1967.

Benson, Leonard: *Fatherhood*, New York: Random House, Inc., 1968.

Blood, Robert O., Jr.: *Love Match and Arranged Marriage*, New York: The Free Press, 1967.

Burgess, Ernest W.: *Aging in Western Societies*, Chicago: The University of Chicago Press, 1960.

Burney, Elizabeth: *Housing on Trial*, Fairlawn, N.J.: Oxford University Press, 1968.

Christensen, Harold T.: "Child Spacing Analysis via Record Linkage," *Journal of Marriage and Family Living*, vol. 25 (August 1963), pp. 272–281.

Elder, Glen H., Jr.: "Family Structure and Educational Attainment," *American Sociological Review*, vol. 30 (February 1965), pp. 81–96.

Goode, William J.: *World Revolution and Family Patterns*, New York: The Free Press, 1963.

Lewis, Oscar: *The Children of Sanchez*, New York: Random House, Inc., 1961.

Lovibond, S. H.: "The Effect of Media Stressing Crime and Violence upon Children's Attitudes," *Social Problems*, vol. 15 (summer 1967), pp. 91–100.

Reiss, Ira: *The Social Context of Premarital Sexual Permissiveness*, New York: Holt, Rinehart and Winston, Inc., 1967.

Rosow, Irving: *Social Integration of the Aged*, New York: The Free Press, 1967.

Sklare, Marshall: "Intermarriage and the Jewish Future," *Commentary*, vol. 37 (April 1964), pp. 46–52.

Udry, J. Richard: *The Social Context of Marriage*, Philadelphia: J. B. Lippincott Company, 1966.

Williamson, Robert: *Marriage and Family Relations*, New York: John Wiley & Sons, Inc., 1966.

PART THREE

SELECTED

CRITICAL PROBLEMS

Although the basic conclusion of the National Advisory Commission on Civil Disorders that "our nation is moving toward two societies, one black, one white—separate and unequal" has been disputed by many, its observation that Negro-white relations are currently our most grave and perplexing domestic problem is hardly open to qualification. In probing for the common elements of the riot process, the investigators found that the disorders during the summer of 1967 were not the result of a single precipitating incident. The triggering incident was, in itself, frequently routine or trivial. Instead, the riots were generated out of an increasingly disturbed social atmosphere, in which typically a series of tension-heightening events over a period of weeks or months became associated in the minds of many in the Negro community with a shared network of underlying grievances. The importance of specific grievances varied somewhat from city to city, but the commission identified and ranked by level of intensity at least twelve deeply held grievances. The first, and the greatest, level of concern was expressed toward police practices, unemployment and underemployment, and inadequate housing. The second level comprised reactions to inadequate educational opportunities, poor recreation facilities and programs, and ineffective political structures and grievance mechanisms. The third level included perceptions of disrespectful white attitudes, discriminatory practices in administration of justice, inadequate federal programs, limited municipal services, discriminatory consumers' and credit practices, and inadequate welfare programs.

The results of the broad range of studies undertaken by the commission give substance to the argument that the race problem is chiefly a consequence of social definitions and interpretations. The term "race" refers literally to a large number of persons who possess a distinguishable combination of inherited physical characteristics. For analytic purposes, however, the term has only limited value, because it is nearly impossible to isolate a substantial number of persons who manifest all the designated physical traits for a given racial category without also finding many .others who possess one or more of the same characteristics in a somewhat different combination. More significantly, the physical traits that are used to delimit racial categories (hair texture, skin color, stature, and nose form) are nonadaptive and of little survival value. Yet, as a consequence of social prerequisites, many still believe that some races have superior innate mental abilities and, in general, a more favorable biological endowment than others, and that differences in temperament and morality are linked inherently to racial traits. The extent to which social criteria take precedence over biological criteria is pinpointed in the lay definition of a "Negro" as any person who has any known Negro ancestry, no matter how distant.

In recognition of this social definition, specialists in the field often substitute the term "minority" to stress the point that racial traits typically become the symbols around which differential status is ascribed. Louis Wirth defines a minority as a group of people who are singled out for differential and unequal treatment on the basis of their physical or cultural characteristics and who therefore define themselves as the object of collective discrimination. To distinguish arbitrarily between minorities identified by cultural rather than physical criteria, an ethnic group is a number of people who share loyalty to a distinctive set of cultural traits (values, food preferences, tastes in art and music, and child-rearing practices).

The dynamics of race relations are subsumed within the concepts of prejudice and discrimination. We may think of "prejudice" as a hostile and rigid attitude toward the members of a racial or ethnic group and "discrimination" as the differential treatment of an individual because he is a member of a particular racial or ethnic group. Thus prejudice represents a predisposition or tendency to act, while discrimination incorporates the actual overt behavior. Although the concepts are closely related, they should not be equated; a person may discriminate even though he is not prejudiced, or he may be prejudiced and yet not discriminate. For example, a fraternity member may oppose an affidavit of nondiscrimination because of social pressure from his peers even though he feels no antipathy toward those subject to exclusion. Or a white teacher with at least moderate prejudices may refrain from discrimination against black students because of an even stronger emotional commitment to his professional standards, or simply to avoid the possible sanctions of school officials and the community. As will be noted in the discussion of action programs, the distinction between prejudice and discrimination is particularly significant in the consideration of strategies to alleviate the race problem.

Social scientists have been relatively successful in identifying the causes of discrimination and prejudice. This does not mean that a neat formula now exists, but increased attention has been focused on the interaction of three sets of variables: personality needs, group conflict, and cultural traditions. Within the realm of personality factors, contemporary explanations stress the displacement of hostility resulting from frustrated goal seeking, crises or chronic problems, or pressures to conform to cultural prescriptions. Prejudice may also be an outgrowth of more specific personality needs, such as the need to enhance self-esteem or to ensure social acceptance. In essence, the group-conflict theme rests on the premise that the dominant group seeks to improve or maintain its favorable competitive position with respect to political power, economic resources, and prestige at the expense of minority groups. Anti-immigration legislation, restricted-housing practices, differential wages and employment opportunities, political disfranchisement, and laws against intermarriage are all important antecedents of contemporary majority-minority group relations in the United States. That the devices used in group conflict are in a state of flux can be seen in the breakdown of some of the more overt forms. Recent modification of the immigration laws has eliminated the national-origins quota system instituted in 1929, which means that increasing numbers of Italians, Greeks, Portuguese, Chinese, and Filipinos will replace declining numbers of English, Irish, Dutch, and German immigrants. The Supreme Court has invalidated state laws restricting intermarriage. Additional examples appear in the review of current developments in areas such as employment, education, and housing.

Since not all potential minority groups are objects of discrimination, we must examine the cultural traditions to understand why certain groups are selected as targets while others are ignored, and sometimes positively valued. Even in the absence of the personality and conflict variables, people may acquire prejudices simply by virtue of learning folkways. However, as previously noted, these variables usually do not operate independently, as illustrated by the process in which the prevailing cultural traditions facilitate displacement of hostility onto certain minority groups and such acts in turn reinforce the normative system.

Turning from the causes to the consequences of discrimination and prejudice, the costs borne by the dominant segments of society, although not as obvious or as subvertive as those suffered by the minorities themselves, can no longer be ignored. The alleged advantages gained through discrimination are more than offset by such representative costs as reduction in the buying power of a significant portion of the population; the absolute expenses resulting from riots and the additional financial burden assumed by a "garrison state" in anticipation of periodic disorder; duplication of expenditures for segregated facilities; higher costs of public services in slum areas inhabited by minorities; fears and anxieties that minorities will rebel by means of sexual aggression, disloyalty, or physical violence, or that they will take over jobs, schools, and neighborhoods; confusion and guilt over the marked discrepancy between the "American Creed" and the actual discriminatory treatment of minorities; paralysis in the face of growing problems in education, urban renewal, and medical care because the appropriate solutions might alter the existing system of race relations; and the dissipation of efforts to gain the support of the so-called "uncommitted" nations as a result of the projected image of hypocrisy stimulated by the contrast between our professed democratic way of life and our treatment of minorities.

In addition to the summary of grievances prepared by the National Advisory Commission on Civil Disorders, the selections in this chapter entitled "Men and Jobs" and "The Negro Middle Class" and the selection from the Riot Commission's report "The Future of the Slums" in the chapter on urbanism suggest the descriptive material available concerning the impact of discrimination on minorities. The differentials in "life chances" (staying alive, being arrested, going to college, obtaining skilled or professional employment, and owning a home) are well documented in any standard problems textbook. Space limits us here to only a few examples of recent developments that have substantial implications for the status of minorities.

Within the economic institutions there is little evidence of major gains by minorities, although the growing involvement of big business and the passage of a national riot-insurance program are hopeful signs. The median Negro family income is still less than 60 percent of median white family income; most craft unions remain highly segregated, and the percentages of Negroes in white-collar, professional, and technical jobs have increased only slightly during the past 10 to 15 years; ghetto residents pay premium prices (particularly when inflated by credit charges) for marginal goods and services. The new insurance law should end mass cancellations of insurance covering ghetto properties and should make it easier, and perhaps cheaper in some cases, to obtain necessary protection. Without insurance, banks and other financial institutions are unable to make loans, new businesses cannot be started, and existing businesses cannot expand or even survive. "Communities without insurance are communities without hope."

The Supreme Court's decision in June 1968 holding that a civil-rights law of 1866 prohibits racial discrimination in the sale and rental of *all* real estate was probably the single most dramatic event in the area of housing in recent years. However, as J. Milton Yinger stresses in his review of recent developments in race relations, cited in the Supplemental Readings, there are at least five distinct types of housing arrangements for which the causes and consequences are not identical: "(1) segregated, nonwhite ghettos . . . largely characterized by poverty, overcrowding, and discrimination, (2) public housing, some integrated, some segregated, (3) the occasional purchase of a home by a nonwhite family in an established middle- or upper-class white neighborhood, (4) new communities, established by private contractors, working within limits set by the capital and mortgage markets, public attitudes, and legal possibilities; and (5) nonwhite suburbs. . . ." According to Yinger, the past five years show trends both toward dispersal and toward integration, which should make the last four patterns increasingly important.

It no longer appears feasible to achieve balanced integration in the public schools of either the North or the South, since most Negro children in many cities are enrolled in schools in which they constitute a majority of the study body. The running controversy over whether efforts to integrate should be dropped in favor of programs to improve educational opportunities in the segregated ghetto schools is reflected in the statement by Joseph Alsop, reviewed in the chapter on education. Unfortunately, those who stress the advantages of integration have been unable to devise methods that are likely to receive widespread public support for stemming the flight of whites to the suburbs and to private schools. At the college level the growing black militancy seems to reflect a combination of several forces: the black-power movement in the society at large, which asserts the value of "blackness" rather than integration; the student-power movement, which is challenging the anachronistic practices of administrations and faculties; and the age-old identity crisis that characterizes nearly all youth but may be especially acute for young members of minority groups. Many whites find it extremely difficult to empathize with the goals and procedures of militant black students, but then no explanation or vicarious experience can adequately convey the despair and humiliation of second-class citizenship. It is doubtful that those who have not had to ask a question such as "Do you cut colored boys' hair?" can develop more than a superficial sensitivity to the nature of minority status.

The reactions of minority group members to prejudice and discrimination fall within the range circumscribed by three basic types of adjustment: aggression, avoidance, and acceptance. The specific form of reaction varies with individual factors, such as age, sex, color, personality type, and socioeconomic status, and group characteristics, such as cohesiveness, size, and cultural traditions. Thus withdrawal from the minority group through assimilation or by "passing," as a subtype of avoidance, is open only to those who possess the physical and cultural traits of the majority. A less obvious illustration is the differential sense of urgency to become a part of the mainstream of American life which is implicit in the different adjustment patterns adopted by Mexican-Americans and Negroes. This may be explained in part by the fact that Mexican-Americans share a distinctive set of cultural traditions that provides an alternative reward system, while Negroes have been, until the past few years, fully committed to and dependent upon the goal values of the dominant system. As Negroes in America become more cognizant of their own heritage and develop pride in their own traditions, while later generations of Mexican-Americans are no longer exposed to the traditions and patterns of the Latin cultures, the relative motivation of these two groups to integrate may even become reversed.

In his monumental work *An American Dilemma* Gunnar Myrdal introduced the concept of the "vicious circle" to describe the difficulties encountered in changing patterns of prejudice and discrimination. Robert K. Merton's concept of the "self-fulfilling prophecy," which rests on similar premises, is based on the theory that public definitions of a situation become an integral part of the situation and thus affect subsequent efforts to reduce the present racial conflict in America. According to Merton's analysis, "the self-fulfilling prophecy is, in the beginning, a *false* definition of the situation evoking a new behavior which makes the originally false conception come *true*." As a starting point, discrimination results in lower standards of living, less formal education, poorer health practices, and so forth, which in turn reinforce dominant-group prejudices and rationalizations for further discrimination. As indicated by Myrdal and Merton, the chain can be broken either by a decrease in discrimination or by an improvement in the achievements of minorities.

Current action programs recognize both sides of this equation, but despite the opportunity and poverty programs, greater attention is still given to the direct reduction of discrimination, particularly through legislative and judicial action. Certainly it is impossible to legislate attitudes, values, or "preferences." Those who place their faith in the legal approach feel that changes in behavior representing a decrease in discrimination (fair-employment practices, nondiscrimination in public facilities, and equal justice in the courts) will facilitate a concomitant decrease in prejudice. However, the so-called "white backlash" is indicative of the potential risks entailed in instituting changes if they have little public support. An excellent analysis of the contemporary forms of white backlash may be found in *The Impossible Revolution?* by Lewis M. Killian. Killian argues that token desegregation has become respectable among whites, but that the backlash "consists of a reluctance to accept those *intermediate* steps that are necessary to make equality a reality for the many Negroes who are in no way prepared to live according to white middle-class standards."

"Black power" has become a key issue in the rhetoric about techniques by which to improve the lot of minorities. As Charles V. Hamilton has stated the moderate version of the case for black power, "black people will gain only as much as they can win through their ability to organize independent bases of economic and political power—through boycotts, electoral activity, rent strikes, work stoppages, pressure-group bargaining." Francis Fox Piven and Richard A. Cloward, in the selection "What Chance for Black Power?" are not optimistic about the prospects for black power in view of the continuing centralization of corporate and federal power over the city.

A related issue is the extent to which the rights of the majority may be subverted in the haste to rectify the situation of minorities. A brief discussion of *de facto* segregation in some public schools in Northern urban centers may clarify this point. Since the racial composition of student bodies often reflects the effects of segregated housing patterns, a number of school districts have sought to achieve integration by transporting students to schools outside their local neighborhoods. With the even greater concentrations of minorities expected in our central cities in the near future, the only way integration is likely to take place is through development of large scale "educational plazas." In the process of providing more favorable educational opportunities to minorities, children of the majority group may be placed in a disadvantageous position by school assignments based solely on the criterion of race. Milton M. Gordon provides a considered evaluation of the issues in moving from segregation to desegregation to integration within the context of current sociological realities and our democratic value system. He gives special attention to the role of government in guiding and stimulating the various transitional stages.

An introductory discussion of race relations must necessarily neglect many issues worthy of detailed analysis. The race problem is unique in that each day brings new developments, incidents, and decisions that affect the conditions of majority-minority interaction. As a result, we can only speculate on the answers to a number of questions: What impact will a "war on poverty," or any similar federal program, have in breaking the "vicious circle." What is required to change an image of police brutality that may in part be a reflection of special law-enforcement problems in a minority area? Will extremism in the form of calls for violence by nationalistic movements and white-supremacy organizations become an increasing impediment to responsible efforts to find long-term solutions? Will the intensity of conflict continue to increase as limited gains by minority groups become, in turn, the basis for new unmet aspirations? Certainly by the time the answers to these questions become more apparent, other issues will have come to the fore as a result of the constant state of flux that characterizes this problem. Although the discussion in this chapter is keyed to generic facets of the minority-majority problem, the emphasis is explicitly on the contemporary primacy of black-white conflicts.

The selection by Robert K. Merton introduces the concept of "the self-fulfilling prophecy" to highlight the importance of invalid perceptions in creating and perpetuating race problems. In the selection from *Tally's Corner*, Elliott Liebow conveys a sensitive portrait of employment experiences as one segment of the lower-class Negro male's struggle for both survival and a sense of dignity. The selection by E. Franklin Frazier vividly discusses the point that the impact of discrimination reaches far beyond the issues of housing, employment, and civil rights by focusing on the reactions and adaptations of middle-class blacks. The last two articles deal with selected questions about current efforts to reduce prejudice and discrimination. Piven and Cloward suggest that the black-power movement is a necessary catalyst for improvement in the status of Negroes, but they anticipate that the black middle class will be "absorbed" into the dominant structures, while the black masses will not gain substantial political or economic advancement. A more general assessment of the prospects for inter-group relations is presented by Gordon, with special stress on the principles that should be implemented in programs designed to achieve integration. The article in the final chapter by Charles C. Moskos, Jr., on the results of racial desegregation in the armed forces indicates what we might expect in a racially integrated America.

## 29   THE SELF-FULFILLING PROPHECY   ROBERT K. MERTON

In a series of works seldom consulted outside the academic fraternity, W. I. Thomas, the dean of American sociologists, set forth a theorem basic to the social sciences: "If men define situations as real, they are real in their consequences." Were the Thomas theorem and its implications more widely known more men would understand more of the workings of our society. Though it lacks the sweep and precision of a Newtonian theorem, it possesses the same gift of relevance, being instructively applicable to many, if indeed not most, social processes.

"If men define situations as real, they are real in their consequences," wrote Professor Thomas. The suspicion that he was driving at a crucial point becomes all the more insistent when we note that essentially the same theorem had been repeatedly set forth by disciplined and observant minds long before Thomas.

When we find such otherwise discrepant minds as the redoubtable Bishop Bousset in his passionate seventeenth-century defense of Catholic orthodoxy; the ironic Mandeville in his eighteenth-century allegory honeycombed with observations on the paradoxes of human society; the irascible genius Marx in his revision of Hegel's theory of historical change; the seminal Freud in works which have perhaps gone further than any others of his day toward modifying man's outlook on man; and the erudite, dogmatic, and occasionally

Reprinted with the permission of the author and the publisher from *Antioch Review*, vol. 8, no. 2 (summer 1948), pp. 193–210.

sound Yale professor, William Graham Sumner, who lives on as the Karl Marx of the middle classes—when we find this mixed company (and I select from a longer if less distinguished list) agreeing on the truth and the pertinence of what is substantially the Thomas theorem, we may conclude that perhaps it's worth our attention as well.

To what, then, are Thomas and Bousset, Mandeville, Marx, Freud and Sumner directing our attention?

The first part of the theorem provides an unceasing reminder that men respond not only to the objective features of a situation, but also, and at times primarily, to the meaning this situation has for them. And once they have assigned some meaning to the situation, their consequent behavior and some of the consequences of that behavior are determined by the ascribed meaning. But this is still rather abstract, and abstractions have a way of becoming unintelligible if they are not occasionally tied to concrete data. What is a case in point?

It is the year 1932. The Last National Bank is a flourishing institution. A large part of its resources is liquid without being watered. Cartwright Millingville has ample reason to be proud of the banking institution over which he presides. Until Black Wednesday. As he enters his bank, he notices that business is unusually brisk. A little odd, that, since the men at the A.M.O.K. steel plant and the K.O.M.A. mattress factory are not usually paid until Saturday. Yet here are two dozen men, obviously from the factories, queued up in front of the tellers' cages. As he turns into his private office, the president muses rather compassionately: "Hope they haven't been laid off in midweek. They should be in the shop at this hour."

But speculations of this sort have never made for a thriving bank, and Millingville turns to the pile of documents upon his desk. His precise signature is affixed to fewer than a score of papers when he is disturbed by the absence of something familiar and the intrusion of something alien. The low discreet hum of bank business has given way to a strange and annoying stridency of many voices. A situation has been defined as real. And that is the beginning of what ends as Black Wednesday—the last Wednesday, it might be noted, of the Last National Bank.

Cartwright Millingville had never heard of the Thomas theorem. But he had no difficulty in recognizing its workings. He knew that, despite the comparative liquidity of the bank's assets, a rumor of insolvency, once believed by enough depositors, would result in the insolvency of the bank. And by the close of Black Wednesday—and Blacker Thursday—when the long lines of anxious depositors, each frantically seeking to salvage his own, grew to longer lines of even more anxious depositors, it turned out that he was right.

The stable financial structure of the bank had depended upon one set of definitions of the situation: belief in the validity of the interlocking system of economic promises men live by. Once depositors had defined the situation otherwise, once they questioned the possibility of having these promises fulfilled, the consequences of this unreal definition was real enough.

A familiar type-case, this, and one doesn't need the Thomas theorem to understand how it happened—not, at least, if one is old enough to have voted for Franklin Roosevelt in 1932. But with the aid of the theorem the tragic history of Millingville's bank can perhaps be converted into a sociological parable which may help us understand not only what happened to hundreds of banks in the '30's but also what happens to the relations between Negro and white, between Protestant and Catholic and Jew in these days.

The parable tells us that public definitions of a situation (prophecies or predictions) become an integral part of the situation and thus affect subsequent developments. This is peculiar to human affairs. It is not found in the world of nature. Predictions of the return of Halley's comet do not influence its orbit. But the rumored insolvency of Millingville's bank did affect the actual outcome. The prophecy of collapse led to its own fulfillment.

So common is the pattern of the self-fulfilling prophecy that each of us has his favored specimen. Consider the case of the examination neurosis. Convinced that he is destined to fail, the anxious student devotes more time to worry than to study and then turns in a poor examination. The initially fallacious anxiety is transformed into an entirely justified fear. Or it is believed that war between two nations is "inevitable." Actuated by this conviction, representatives of the two nations become progressively alienated, apprehensively countering each "offensive" move of the other with a "defensive" move of their own. Stockpiles of armaments, raw materials, and armed men grow larger; eventually the anticipation of war helps create the actuality.

The self-fulfilling prophecy is, in the beginning, a *false* definition of the situation evoking a new behavior which makes the originally false conception come *true*. The specious validity of the self-fulfilling prophecy perpetuates a reign of terror. For the prophet will cite the actual course of events as proof that he was right from the very beginning. (Yet we know that Millingville's bank was solvent, that it would have survived for many years had not the misleading rumor *created* the very conditions of its own fulfillment.) Such are the perversities of social logic.

It is the self-fulfilling prophecy which goes far toward explaining the dynamics of ethnic and racial conflict in the America of today. That this is the case, at least for relations between Negroes and whites, may be gathered from the fifteen hundred pages which make up Gunnar Myrdal's *An American Dilemma*. That the self-fulfilling prophecy may have even more general bearing upon the relations between ethnic groups than Myrdal has indicated is the thesis of the considerably briefer discussion which follows.[1]

As a result of their failure to comprehend the operation of the self-fulfilling prophecy, many Americans of good will are (sometimes reluctantly) brought to retain enduring ethnic and racial prejudices. They experience these beliefs, not as prejudices, not as prejudgments, but as irresistible products of their own observation. "The facts of the case" permit them no other conclusion.

Thus our fair-minded white citizen strongly supports a policy of excluding Negroes from his labor union. His views are, of course, based not upon prejudice, but upon the cold hard facts. And the facts seem clear enough. Negroes, "lately from the nonindustrial South, are undisciplined in traditions of trade unionism and the art of collective bargaining." The Negro is a strikebreaker. The Negro, with his "low standard of living," rushes in to take jobs at less than prevailing wages. The Negro is, in short, "a traitor to the working class," and should manifestly be excluded from union organizations. So run the facts of the case as seen by our tolerant but hard-headed union member, innocent of any understanding of the self-fulfilling prophecy as a basic process of society.

Our unionist fails to see, of course, that he and his kind have produced the very "facts" which he observes. For by defining the situation as one in which Negroes are held to be incorrigibly at odds with principles of unionism and by excluding Negroes from unions, he invited a series of consequences which indeed made it difficult if not impossible for many Negroes to avoid the role of scab. Out of work after World War I, and kept out of unions, thousands of Negroes could not resist strikebound employers who held a door invitingly open upon a world of jobs from which they were otherwise excluded.

History creates its own test of the theory of self-fulfilling prophecies. That Negroes were excluded from unions (and from a large range of jobs) rather than excluded because they were strikebreakers can be seen from the virtual disappearance of Negroes as scabs in industries where they have gained admission to unions in the last decades.

The application of the Thomas theorem also suggests how the tragic, often vicious, circle of self-fulfilling prophecies can be broken. The initial definition of the situation which has set the circle in motion must be abandoned. Only when the original assumption is questioned and a new definition of the situation introduced, does the consequent flow of events give the lie to the assumption. Only then does the belief no longer father the reality.

But to question these deep-rooted definitions of the situation is no simple act of the will. The will, or, for that matter, good will, cannot be turned on and off like a faucet. Social intelligence and good will are themselves *products* of distinct social forces. They are not brought into being by mass propaganda and mass education, in the usual sense of these terms so dear to the sociological panaceans. In the social realm, no more than in the psychological realm, do false ideas quietly vanish when confronted with the truth. One does not expect a paranoiac to abandon his hard-won distortions and delusions upon being informed that they are altogether groundless. If psychic ills could be cured merely by the dissemination of truth, the psychiatrists of this country would be suffering from technological unemployment rather than from overwork. Nor will a continuing "educational campaign" itself destroy racial prejudice and discrimination.

This is not a particularly popular position. The appeal to "education" as a cure-all for the most varied social problems is rooted deep in the mores of America. Yet it is nonetheless illusory for all that. For how would this program of racial education proceed? Who is to do the educating? The teachers in our communities? But, in some measure like many other Americans, the teachers share the very prejudices they are being urged to combat. And when they don't, aren't they being asked to serve as conscientious martyrs in the cause of educational utopianism? How long would be the tenure of an elementary school teacher in Alabama or Mississippi or Georgia who attempted meticulously to disabuse his young pupils of the racial beliefs they acquired at home? Education may serve as an operational adjunct but not as the chief basis for any but excruciatingly slow change in the prevailing patterns of race relations.

To understand further why educational campaigns cannot be counted on to eliminate prevailing ethnic hostilities, we must examine the operation of "in-groups" and "out-groups" in our society. Ethnic out-groups, to adopt Sumner's useful bit of sociological jargon, consist of all those who are believed to differ significantly from "ourselves" in terms of nationality, race, or religion. Counterpart of the ethnic out-group is of course the ethnic in-group, constituted by those who "belong." There is nothing fixed or eternal about the lines separating the in-group from out-groups. As situations change, the lines of separation change. For a large number of white Americans, Joe Louis is a member of an out-group—when the situation is defined in racial terms. On another occasion, when Louis defeated the nazified Schmeling, many of these same white Americans acclaimed him as a member of the (national) in-group. National loyalty took precedence over racial separatism. These abrupt shifts in group boundaries sometimes prove embarrassing. Thus, when Negro-Americans ran away with the honors in the Olympic games held in Berlin, the Nazis, pointing to the second-class citizenship assigned Negroes in various regions of this country, denied that the United States had really won the games, since the Negro athletes were by our own admission "not full-fledged" Americans. And what could Bilbo or Rankin say to that?

Under the benevolent guidance of the dominant in-group, ethnic out-groups are continuously subjected to a lively process of prejudice which I think goes far toward vitiating mass education and mass propaganda for ethnic tolerance. This is the process whereby "in-group virtues become out-group vices," to paraphrase a remark by the sociologist Donald Young. Or, more colloquially and perhaps more instructively, it may be called the "damned-if-you-do" and "damned-if-you-don't" process in ethnic and racial relations.

To discover that ethnic out-groups are damned if

they do embrace the values of white Protestant society and damned if they don't, we have only to turn to one of the in-group culture heroes, examine the qualities with which he is endowed by biographers and popular belief, and thus distill the qualities of mind and action and character which are generally regarded as altogether admirable.

Periodic public opinion polls are not needed to justify the selection of Abe Lincoln as the culture hero who most fully embodies the cardinal American virtues. As the Lynds point out in *Middletown*, the people of that typical small city allow George Washington alone to join Lincoln as the greatest of Americans. He is claimed as their very own by almost as many well-to-do Republicans as by less well-to-do Democrats.

Even the inevitable schoolboy knows that Lincoln was thrifty, hard-working, eager for knowledge, ambitious, devoted to the rights of the average man, and eminently successful in climbing the ladder of opportunity from the lowermost rung of laborer to the respectable heights of merchant and lawyer. (We need follow his dizzying ascent no further.)

If one did not know that these attributes and achievements are numbered high among the values of middle-class America, one would soon discover it by glancing through the Lynds' account of "The Middletown Spirit." For there we find the image of the Great Emancipator fully reflected in the values in which Middletown believes. And since these are their values, it is not surprising to find the Middletowns of America condemning and disparaging those individuals and groups who fail, presumably, to exhibit these virtues. If it appears to the white in-group that Negroes are *not* educated in the same measure as themselves, that they have an "unduly" high proportion of unskilled workers and an "unduly" low proportion of successful business and professional men, that they are thriftless, and so on through the catalogue of middle-class virtue and sin, it is not difficult to understand the charge that the Negro is "inferior" to the white.

Sensitized to the workings of the self-fulfilling prophecy, we should be prepared to find that the anti-Negro charges which are not patently false are only speciously true. The allegations are "true" in the Pickwickian sense that we have found self-fulfilling prophecies in general to be true. Thus, if the dominant in-group believes that Negroes are inferior, and sees to it that funds for education are not "wasted on these incompetents" and then proclaims as final evidence of this inferiority that Negroes have proportionately "only" one-fifth as many college graduates as whites, one can scarcely be amazed by this transparent bit of social legerdemain. Having seen the rabbit carefully though not too adroitly placed in the hat, we can only look askance at the triumphant air with which it is finally produced. (In fact, it is a little embarrassing to note that a larger proportion of Negro than of white high school graduates go on to college; obviously, the Negroes who are hardy enough to scale the high walls of discrimination represent an even more highly selected group than the run-of-the-high-school white population.)

So, too, when the gentleman from Mississippi (a state which spends five times as much on the average white pupil as on the average Negro pupil) proclaims the essential inferiority of the Negro by pointing to the per capita ratio of physicians among Negroes as less than one-fourth that of whites, we are impressed more by his scrambled logic than by his profound prejudices. So plain is the mechanism of the self-fulfilling prophecy in these instances that only those forever devoted to the victory of sentiment over fact can take these specious evidences seriously. Yet the spurious evidence often creates a genuine belief. Self-hypnosis through one's own propaganda is a not infrequent phase of the self-fulfilling prophecy.

So much for out-groups being damned if they don't (apparently) manifest in-group virtues. It is a tasteless bit of ethnocentrism, seasoned with self-interest. But what of the second phase of this process? Can one seriously mean that out-groups are also damned if they *do* possess these virtues? Precisely.

Through a faultlessly bisymmetrical prejudice, ethnic and racial out-groups get it coming and going. The systematic condemnation of the out-grouper continues largely *irrespective of what he does*. More: through a freakish exercise of capricious judicial logic, the victim is punished for the crime. Superficial appearances notwithstanding, prejudice and discrimination aimed at the out-group are not a result of what the out-group does, but are rooted deep in the structure of our society and the social psychology of its members.

To understand how this happens, we must examine the moral alchemy through which the in-group readily transmutes virtue into vice and vice into virtue, as the occasion may demand. Our studies will proceed by the case-method.

We begin with the engagingly simple formula of moral alchemy: the same behavior must be differently evaluated according to the person who exhibits it. For example, the proficient alchemist will at once know that the word "firm" is properly declined as follows:

I am firm,
Thou art obstinate,
He is pigheaded.

There are some, unversed in the skills of this science, who will tell you that one and the same term should be applied to all three instances of identical behavior. Such unalchemical nonsense should simply be ignored.

With this experiment in mind, we are prepared to observe how the very same behavior undergoes a complete change of evaluation in its transition from the in-group Abe Lincoln to the out-group Abe Cohen or Abe Kurokawa. We proceed systematically. Did Lincoln work far into the night? This testifies that he was industrious, resolute, perseverant, and eager to realize his capacities to the full. Do the out-group Jews or Japanese keep these same hours? This only bears witness to their sweatshop mentality, their ruthless undercutting of American standards, their unfair competitive practices. Is the in-group hero frugal, thrifty, and sparing? Then the out-group villain is stingy, miserly and penny-pinching. All honor is due the in-group Abe for his having been smart, shrewd, and intelligent and, by the same token, all contempt is owing the out-group Abes for their being sharp, cunning, crafty, and too clever by far. Did the indomitable Lincoln refuse to remain content with a life of work with the hands? Did he prefer to make use of his brain? Then, all praise for his plucky climb up the shaky ladder of opportunity. But, of course, the eschewing of manual work for brain work among the merchants and lawyers of the out-group deserves nothing but censure for a parasitic way of life. Was Abe Lincoln eager to learn the accumulated wisdom of the ages by unending study? The trouble with the Jew is that he's a greasy grind, with his head always in a book, while decent people are going to a show or a ball game. Was the resolute Lincoln unwilling to limit his standards to those of his provincial community? That is what we should expect of a man of vision. And if the out-groupers criticize the vulnerable areas in our society, then send 'em back where they came from. Did Lincoln, rising high above his origins, never forget the rights of the common man and applaud the right of workers to strike? This testifies only that, like all real Americans, this greatest of Americans was deathlessly devoted to the cause of freedom. But, as you examine the recent statistics on strikes, remember that these un-American practices are the result of out-groupers pursuing their evil agitation among otherwise contented workers.

Once stated, the classical formula of moral alchemy is clear enough. Through the adroit use of these rich vocabularies of encomium and opprobrium, the in-group readily transmutes its own virtues into others' vices. But why do so many in-groupers qualify as moral alchemists? Why are so many in the dominant in-group so fully devoted to this continuing experiment in moral transmutation?

An explanation may be found by putting ourselves at some distance from this country and following the anthropologist Malinowski to the Trobriand Islands. For there we find an instructively similar pattern. Among the Trobrianders, to a degree which Americans, despite Hollywood and the confession magazines, have apparently not yet approximated, success with women confers honor and prestige on a man. Sexual prowess is a positive value, a moral virtue. But if a rank-and-file Trobriander has "too much" sexual success, if he achieves "too many" triumphs of the heart, an achievement which should of course be limited to the elite, the chiefs or men of power, then this glorious record becomes a scandal and an abomination. The chiefs are quick *to resent any personal achievement not warranted by social position*. The moral virtues remain virtues only so long as they are jealously confined to the proper in-group. The right activity by the wrong people becomes a thing of contempt, not of honor. For clearly, only in this way, by holding these virtues exclusively to themselves, can the men of power retain their distinction, their prestige, and their power. No wiser procedure could be devised to hold intact a system of social stratification and social power.

The Trobrianders can teach us more. For it seems clear that the chiefs have not calculatingly devised this program of entrenchment. Their behavior is spontaneous, unthinking, and immediate. Their resentment of "too much" ambition or "too much" success in the ordinary Trobriander is not contrived, it is genuine. It just happens that this prompt emotional response to the "misplaced" manifestation of in-group virtues also serves the useful expedient of reinforcing the chiefs' special claims to the good things of Trobriand life. Nothing could be more remote from the truth and more distorted a reading of the facts than to assume that this conversion of in-group virtues into out-group vices is part of a calculated, deliberate plot of Trobriand chiefs to keep Trobriand commoners in their place. It is merely that the chiefs have been indoctrinated with an appreciation of the proper order of things, and see it as their heavy burden to enforce the mediocrity of others.

Nor, in quick revulsion from the culpabilities of the moral alchemists, need we succumb to the equivalent error of simply upending the moral status of the in-group and the out-groups. It is not that Jews and Negroes are one and all angelic while Gentiles and whites are one and all fiendish. It is not that individual virtue will now be found exclusively on the wrong side of the ethnic-racial tracks and individual viciousness on the right side. It is conceivable even that there are as many corrupt and vicious men and women among Negroes and Jews as among Gentile whites. It is only that the ugly fence which encloses the in-group happens to exclude the people who make up the out-groups from being treated with the decency ordinarily accorded human beings.

We have only to look at the consequences of this peculiar moral alchemy to see that there is no paradox at all in damning out-groupers if they do and if they don't exhibit in-group virtues. Condemnation on these two scores perform one and the same social function. Seeming opposites coalesce. When Negroes are tagged as incorrigibly inferior because they (apparently) don't manifest these virtues, this confirms the natural rightness of their being assigned an inferior status in society. And when Jews or Japanese are tagged as having too many of the in-group values, it becomes plain that they must be securely controlled by the high walls of discrimination. In both cases, the special status assigned the several out-groups can be seen to be eminently reasonable.

Yet this distinctly reasonable arrangement persists in having most unreasonable consequences, both logical and social. Consider only a few of these.

In some contexts, the limitations enforced upon the out-group—say, rationing the number of Jews permitted to enter colleges and professional schools—logically imply a fear of the alleged superiority of the out-group. Were it otherwise, no discrimination need be practiced. The unyielding, impersonal forces of academic competition would soon trim down the number of Jewish (or Japanese or Negro) students to an "appropriate" size.

This implied belief in the superiority of the out-group seems premature. There is simply not enough scientific evidence to demonstrate Jewish or Japanese or Negro superiority. The effort of the in-group discriminator to supplant the myth of Aryan superiority with the myth of non-Aryan superiority is condemned to failure by science. Moreover, such myths are ill-advised. Eventually, life in a world of myth must collide with fact in the world of reality. As a matter of simple self-interest and social therapy, therefore, it might be wise for the in-group to abandon the myth and cling to the reality.

The pattern of being damned-if-you-do and damned-if-you-don't has further consequences—among the out-groups themselves. The response to alleged deficiencies is as clear as it is predictable. If one is repeatedly told that one is inferior, that one lacks any positive accomplishments, it is all too human to seize upon every bit of evidence to the contrary. The in-group definitions force upon the allegedly inferior out-group a defensive tendency to magnify and exalt "race accomplishments." As the distinguished Negro sociologist, Franklin Frazier, has noted, the Negro newspapers are "intensely race conscious and exhibit considerable pride in the achievements of the Negro, most of which are meagre performances as measured by broader standards." Self-glorification, found in some measure among all groups, becomes a frequent counter-response to persistent belittlement from without.

It is the damnation of out-groups for "excessive achievement," however, which gives rise to truly bizarre behavior. For, after a time and often as a matter of self-defense, these out-groups become persuaded that their virtues really are vices. And this provides the final episode in a tragicomedy of inverted values.

Let us try to follow the plot through its intricate maze of self-contradictions. Respectful admiration for the arduous climb from office boy to president is rooted deep in American culture. This long and strenuous ascent carries with it a two-fold testimonial: it testifies that careers are abundantly open to genuine talent in American society and it testifies to the worth of the man who has distinguished himself by his heroic rise. It would be invidious to choose among the many stalwart figures who have fought their way up, against all odds, until they have reached the pinnacle, there to sit at the head of the long conference table in the longer conference room of The Board. Taken at random, the saga of Frederick H. Ecker, chairman of the board of one of the largest privately managed corporations in the world, the Metropolitan Life

Insurance Company, will suffice as the prototype. From a menial and poorly paid job, he rose to a position of eminence. Appropriately enough, an unceasing flow of honors has come to this man of large power and large achievement. It so happens, though it is a matter personal to this eminent man of finance, that Mr. Ecker is a Presbyterian. Yet at last report, no elder of the Presbyterian church has risen publicly to announce that Mr. Ecker's successful career should not be taken too seriously, that, after all, relatively few Presbyterians have risen from rags to riches and that Presbyterians do not actually "control" the world of finance—or life insurance, or investment housing. Rather, one would suppose, Presbyterian elders join with other Americans imbued with middle-class standards of success to felicitate the eminently successful Mr. Ecker and to acclaim other sons of the faith who have risen to almost equal heights. Secure with their in-group status, they point the finger of pride rather than the finger of dismay at individual success.

Prompted by the practice of moral alchemy, noteworthy achievements by out-groupers elicit other responses. Patently, if achievement is a vice, the achievement must be disclaimed—or at least, discounted. Under these conditions, what is an occasion for Presbyterian pride must become an occasion for Jewish dismay. If the Jew is condemned for his educational or professional or scientific or economic success, then, understandably enough, many Jews will come to feel that these accomplishments must be minimized in simple self-defense. Thus is the circle of paradox closed by out-groupers busily engaged in assuring the powerful in-group that they have not, in fact, been guilty of inordinate contributions to science, the professions, the arts, the government, and the economy.

In a society which ordinarily looks upon wealth as a warrant of ability, an out-group is compelled by the inverted attitudes of the dominant in-group to deny that many men of wealth are among its members. "Among the 200 largest nonbanking corporations . . . only ten have a Jew as president or chairman of the board." Is this an observation of an anti-Semite, intent on proving the incapacity

and inferiority of Jews who have done so little "to build the corporations which have built America"? No; it is a retort of the Anti-Defamation League of B'Nai Brith to anti-Semitic propaganda.

In a society where, as a recent survey by the National Opinion Research Center has shown, the profession of medicine ranks higher in social prestige than any other of ninety occupations (save that of United States Supreme Court Justice), we find some Jewish spokesmen manoeuvred by the attacking in-group into the fantastic position of announcing their "deep concern" over the number of Jews in medical practice, which is "disproportionate to the number of Jews in other occupations." In a nation suffering from a notorious undersupply of physicians, the Jewish doctor becomes a deplorable occasion for deep concern, rather than receiving applause for his hard-won acquisition of knowledge and skills and for his social utility. Only when the New York Yankees publicly announce deep concern over their eleven World Series titles, so disproportionate to the number of triumphs achieved by other major league teams, will this self-abnegation seem part of the normal order of things.

In a culture which consistently judges the professionals higher in social value than even the most skilled hewers of wood and drawers of water, the out-group finds itself in the anomalous position of pointing with defensive relief to the large number of Jewish painters and paper hangers, plasterers and electricians, plumbers and sheet-metal workers.

But the ultimate reversal of values is yet to be noted. Each succeeding census finds more and more Americans in the city and its suburbs. Americans have travelled the road to urbanization until less than one-fifth of the nation's population live on farms. Plainly, it is high time for the Methodist and the Catholic, the Baptist and the Episcopalian to recognize the iniquity of this trek of their core-ligionists to the city. For, as is well known, one of the central accusations levelled against the Jew is his heinous tendency to live in cities. Jewish leaders, therefore, find themselves in the incredible position of defensively urging their people to move into the very farm areas being hastily vacated by city-bound hordes of Christians. Perhaps this is not altogether necessary. As the Jewish crime of urbanism becomes ever more popular among the in-group, it may be reshaped into transcendent virtue. But, admittedly, one can't be certain. For in this draft confusion of inverted values, it soon becomes impossible to determine when virtue is sin and sin, moral perfection.

Amid this confusion, one fact remains unambiguous. The Jews, like other peoples, have made distinguished contributions to world culture. Consider only an abbreviated catalogue. In the field of creative literature (and with acknowledgment of large variations in the calibre of achievement), Jewish authors include Heine, Karl Kraus, Börne, Hofmannsthal, Schnitzler, Kafka. In the realm of musical composition, there are Meyerbeer, Felix Mendelssohn, Offenbach, Mahler, and Schönberg. Among the musical virtuosi, consider only Rosenthal, Schnabel, Godowsky, Pachmann, Kreisler, Hubermann, Milstein, Elman, Heifetz, Joachim, and Menuhin. And among scientists of a stature sufficient to merit the Nobel prize, examine the familiar list which includes Beranyi, Mayerhof, Ehrlich, Michelson, Lippmann, Haber, Willstätter, and Einstein. Or in the esoteric and imaginative universe of mathematical invention, take note only of Kronecker, the creator of the modern theory of numbers; Hermann Minkowski,[2] who supplied the mathematical foundations of the special theory of relativity; or Jacobi, with his basic work in the theory of elliptical functions. And so through each special province of cultural achievement, we are supplied with a list of pre-eminent men and women who happened to be Jews.

And who is thus busily engaged in singing the praises of the Jews? Who has so assiduously compiled the list of many hundreds of distinguished Jews who contributed so notably to science, literature and the arts—a list from which these few cases were excerpted? A philo-Semite, eager to demonstrate that his people have contributed their due share to world culture? No, by now we should know better than that. The complete list will be found in the thirty-sixth edition of an anti-Semitic handbook by the racist Fritsch. In accord with the alchemical formula for transmuting in-group virtues into out-group vices, he presents this as a roll call of sinister spirits who have usurped the accomplishments properly owing the Aryan in-group.

Once we comprehend the predominant role of the in-group in defining the situation, the further paradox of the seemingly opposed behavior of the Negro out-group and the Jewish out-group falls away. The behavior of both minority groups is in response to the majority-group allegations.

If the Negroes are accused of inferiority, and their alleged failure to contribute to world culture is cited in support of this accusation, the human urge for self-respect and a concern for security leads them *defensively* often to magnify each and every achievement by members of the race. If Jews are accused of "excessive" achievements and "excessive" ambitions, and lists of pre-eminent Jews are compiled in support of this counter-accusation, then the urge for security leads them *defensively* to minimize the actual achievements of members of the group. Apparently opposed types of behavior have the same psychological and social functions. Self-assertion and self-effacement become the devices for seeking to cope with condemnation for alleged group deficiency and condemnation for alleged group excesses, respectively. And with a fine sense of moral superiority, the secure in-group looks on these curious performances by the out-groups with mingled derision and contempt.

Will this desolate tragicomedy run on and on, marked only by minor changes in the cast? Not necessarily.

Were moral scruples and a sense of decency the only bases for bringing the play to an end, one would indeed expect it to continue an indefinitely long run. In and of themselves, moral sentiments are not much more effective in curing social ills than in curing physical ills. Moral sentiments no doubt help to motivate efforts for change, but they are no substitute for hard-headed instrumentalities for achieving the objective, as the thickly populated graveyard of soft-headed utopias bears witness.

There are ample indications that a deliberate and planned halt can be put to the workings of the self-fulfilling prophecy and the vicious circle in society. The sequel to our sociological parable of the Last National Bank provides one clue to the way in which this can be achieved. During the fabulous '20's, when Coolidge undoubtedly caused a Republican era of lush prosperity, an average of 635 banks a year quietly suspended operations. And during the four years immediately before and after The Crash, when Hoover undoubtedly did not cause a Republican era of sluggish depression, this zoomed to the more spectacular average of 2,276 bank suspensions annually. But, interestingly enough, in the twelve years following the establishment of the Federal Deposit Insurance Corporation and the enactment of other banking legislation while Roosevelt presided over Democratic depression and revival, recession and boom, bank suspensions dropped to a niggardly average of 28 a year. Perhaps money panics have not been institutionally exorcized by legislation. Nevertheless, millions of depositors no longer have occasion to give way to panic-motivated runs on banks simply because deliberate institutional change has removed the grounds for panic. Occasions for racial hostility are no more inborn psychological constants than are occasions for panic. Despite the teachings of amateur psychologists, blind panic and racial aggression are not rooted in "human nature." These patterns of human behavior are largely a product of the modifiable structure of society.

For a further clue, return to our instance of widespread hostility of white unionists toward the Negro strikebreakers brought into industry by employers after the close of the very first World War. Once the initial definition of Negroes as not deserving of union membership had largely broken down, the Negro, with a wider range of work opportunities, no longer found it necessary to enter industry through the doors held open by strikebound employers. Again, appropriate institutional change broke through the tragic circle of the self-fulfilling prophecy. Deliberate social change gave the lie to the firm conviction that "it just ain't in the nature of the nigra" to join co-operatively with his white fellows in trade unions.

A final instance is drawn from a study of a bi-racial housing project which I have been conducting with Patricia J. Salter, under a grant from the Lavanburg Foundation. Located in Pittsburgh, this community of Hilltown is made up of fifty percent Negro families and fifty percent white. It is not a twentieth-century utopia. There is some interpersonal friction here, as elsewhere. But in a community made up of equal numbers of the two races, fewer than a fifth of the whites and less than a third of the Negroes report that this friction occurs between members of *different* races. By their own testimony, it is very largely confined to disagreements *within* each racial group. Yet only one in every twenty-five whites initially *expected* relations between the races in this community to run smoothly, whereas five times as many expected serious trouble, the remainder anticipating a tolerable, if not altogether pleasant, situation. So much for expectations. Upon reviewing their actual experience, three of every four of the most apprehensive whites subsequently found that the "races get along fairly well," after all. This is not the place to report the findings of the Lavanburg study in detail, but substantially these demonstrate anew that under *appropriate institutional and administrative conditions*, the experience of interracial amity can supplant the fear of interracial conflict.

These changes, and others of the same kind, do not occur automatically. *The self-fulfilling prophecy, whereby fears are translated into reality, operates only in the absence of deliberate institutional controls.* And it is only with the rejection of social fatalism implied in the notion of unchangeable human nature that the tragic circle of fear, social disaster, reinforced fear can be broken.

Ethnic prejudices do die—but slowly. They can be helped over the threshold of oblivion, not by insisting that it is unreasonable and unworthy of them to survive, but by cutting off their sustenance now provided by certain institutions of our society.

If we find ourselves doubting man's capacity to

control man and his society, if we persist in our tendency to find in the patterns of the past the chart of the future, it is perhaps time to take up anew the wisdom of Tocqueville's 112-year-old apothegm: "What we call necessary institutions are often no more than institutions to which we have grown accustomed."

Nor can widespread, even typical, failures in planning human relations between ethnic groups be cited as evidence for pessimism. In the world laboratory of the sociologist, as in the more secluded laboratories of the physicist and chemist, it is the successful experiment which is decisive and not the thousand-and-one failures which preceded it. More is learned from the single success than from the multiple failures. A single success proves it can be done. Thereafter, it is necessary only to learn what made it work. This, at least, is what I take to be the sociological sense of those revealing words of Thomas Love Peacock: "Whatever is, is possible."

**REFERENCES AND NOTES**

1   The counterpart of the self-fulfilling prophecy is the "suicidal prophecy" which so alters human behavior from what would have been its course had the prophecy not been made, that it *fails* to be borne out. The prophecy destroys itself. This important type is not considered here. For examples of both types of social prophecy, see R. M. MacIver, *The More Perfect Union* New York: The Macmillan Company, 1948; for a general statement, see R. K. Merton, "The Unanticipated Consequences of Purposive Social Action," *American Sociological Review*, vol. 1 (1936), pp. 894–904.

2   Obviously, the forename must be explicitly mentioned here, else Hermann Minkowski the mathematician may be confused with Eugen Minkowsky, who contributed so notably to our knowledge of schizophrenia, or with Mieczyslaw Minkowski, high in the ranks of brain anatomists, or even with Oskar Minkowski, discoverer of pancreatic diabetes.

## 30   TALLY'S CORNER   ELLIOTT LIEBOW

A pickup truck drives slowly down the street. The truck stops as it comes abreast of a man sitting on a cast-iron porch and the white driver calls out, asking if the man wants a day's work. The man shakes his head and the truck moves on up the block, stopping again whenever idling men come within calling distance of the driver. At the Carry-out corner, five men debate the question briefly and shake their heads no to the truck. The truck turns the corner and repeats the same performance up the next street. In the distance, one can see one man, then another, climb into the back of the truck and sit down. In starts and stops, the truck finally disappears.

What is it we have witnessed here? A labor scavenger rebuffed by his would-be prey? Lazy, irresponsible men turning down an honest day's pay

for an honest day's work? Or a more complex phenomenon marking the intersection of economic forces, social values and individual states of mind and body?

Let us look again at the driver of the truck. He has been able to recruit only two or three men from each twenty or fifty he contacts. To him, it is clear that the others simply do not choose to work. Singly or in groups, belly-empty or belly-full, sullen or gregarious, drunk or sober, they confirm what he has read, heard and knows from his own experience: these men wouldn't take a job if it were handed to them on a platter.[1]

Quite apart from the question of whether or not this is true of some of the men he sees on the street, it is clearly not true of all of them. If it were, he would not have come here in the first place; or having come, he would have left with an empty truck. It is not even true of most of them, for most of the men he sees on the street this weekday morning do, in fact, have jobs. But since, at the moment, they are neither working nor sleeping, and since they hate the depressing room or apartment they live in, or because there is nothing to do there,[2] or because they want to get away from their wives or anyone else living there, they are out on the street, indistinguishable from those who do not have jobs or do not want them. Some, like Boley, a member of a trash-collection crew in a suburban housing development, work Saturdays and are off on this weekday. Some, like Sweets, work nights cleaning up middle-class trash, dirt, dishes and garbage, and mopping the floors of the office buildings, hotels, restaurants, toilets and other public places dirtied during the day. Some men work for retail businesses such as liquor stores which do not begin the day until ten o'clock. Some laborers, like Tally, have already come back from the job because the ground was too wet for pick and shovel or because the weather was too cold for pouring concrete. Other employed men stayed off the job today for personal reasons: Clarence to go to a funeral at eleven this morning and Sea Cat to answer a subpoena as a witness in a criminal proceeding.

Also on the street, unwitting contributors to the impression taken away by the truck driver, are the halt and the lame. The man on the cast-iron steps strokes one gnarled arthritic hand with the other and says he doesn't know whether or not he'll live long enough to be eligible for Social Security. He pauses, then adds matter-of-factly, "Most times, I don't care whether I do or don't." Stoopy's left leg was polio-withered in childhood. Raymond, who looks as if he could tear out a fire hydrant, coughs up blood if he bends or moves suddenly. The quiet man who hangs out in front of the Saratoga apartments has a steel hook strapped onto his left elbow. And had the man in the truck been able to look into the wine-clouded eyes of the man in the green cap, he would have realized that the man did not even understand he was being offered a day's work.

Others, having had jobs and been laid off, are drawing unemployment compensation (up to $44 per week) and have nothing to gain by accepting work which pays little more than this and frequently less.

Still others, like Bumdoodle the numbers man, are working hard at illegal ways of making money, hustlers who are on the street to turn a dollar any way they can: buying and selling sex, liquor, narcotics, stolen goods, or anything else that turns up.

Only a handful remains unaccounted for. There is Tonk, who cannot bring himself to take a job away from the corner, because, according to the other men, he suspects his wife will be unfaithful if given the opportunity. There is Stanton, who has not reported to work for four days now, not since Bernice disappeared. He bought a brand new knife against her return. She had done this twice before, he said, but not for so long and not without warning, and he had forgiven her. But this time, "I ain't got it in me to forgive her again." His rage and shame are there for all to see as he paces the Carry-out and the corner, day and night, hoping to catch a glimpse of her.

And finally, there are those like Arthur, able-bodied men who have no visible means of support, legal or illegal, who neither have jobs nor want them. The truck driver, among others, believes the Arthurs to be representative of all the men he sees idling on the street during his own working hours. They are not, but they cannot be dismissed simply because they are a small minority. It is not enough to explain them away as being lazy or irresponsible or both because an able-bodied man with responsibilities who refuses work is, by the truck driver's definition, lazy and irresponsible. Such an answer begs the question. It is descriptive of the facts; it does not explain them.

Moreover, despite their small numbers, the don't-work-and-don't-want-to-work minority is especially significant because they represent the strongest and clearest expression of those values and attitudes associated with making a living which, to varying degrees, are found throughout the streetcorner world. These men differ from the others in degree rather than in kind, the principal difference being that they are carrying out the implications of their values and experiences to their logical, inevitable conclusions. In this sense, the others have yet to come to terms with themselves and the world they live in.

Putting aside, for the moment, what the men say and feel, and looking at what they actually do and the choices they make, getting a job, keeping a job, and doing well at it is clearly of low priority. Arthur will not take a job at all. Leroy is supposed to be on his job at 4:00 P.M. but it is already 4:10 and he still cannot bring himself to leave the free games he has accumulated on the pinball machine in the Carry-out. Tonk started a construction job on Wednesday, worked Thursday and Friday, then didn't go back again. On the same kind of job, Sea Cat quit in the second week. Sweets had been working three months as a busboy in a restaurant, then quit without notice, not sure himself why he did so. A real estate agent, saying he was more interested in getting the job done than in the cost, asked Richard to give him an estimate on repairing and painting the inside of a house, but Richard, after looking over the job, somehow never got around to submitting an estimate. During one period, Tonk would not leave the corner to take a job because his wife might prove unfaithful; Stanton would not take a job because his woman had been unfaithful.

Thus, the man-job relationship is a tenuous one. At any given moment, a job may occupy a relatively low position on the streetcorner scale of real values. Getting a job may be subordinated to relations with women or to other non-job considerations; the commitment to a job one already has is frequently shallow and tentative.

The reasons are many. Some are objective and reside principally in the job; some are subjective and reside principally in the man. The line between them, however, is not a clear one. Behind the man's refusal to take a job or his decision to quit one is not a simple impulse or value choice but a complex combination of assessments of objective reality on the one hand, and values, attitudes and beliefs drawn from different levels of his experience on the other.

Objective economic considerations are frequently a controlling factor in a man's refusal to take a job. How much the job pays is a crucial question but seldom asked. He knows how much it pays. Working as a stock clerk, a delivery boy, or even behind the counter of liquor stores, drug stores and other retail businesses pays one dollar an hour. So, too, do most busboy, car-wash, janitorial and other jobs available to him. Some jobs, such as dishwasher, may dip as low as eighty cents an hour and others, such as elevator operator or work in a junk yard, may offer $1.15 or $1.25. Take-home pay for jobs such as these ranges from $35 to $50 a week, but a take-home pay of over $45 for a five-day week is the exception rather than the rule.

One of the principal advantages of these kinds of jobs is that they offer fairly regular work. Most of them involve essential services and are therefore somewhat less responsive to business conditions than are some higher paying, less menial jobs. Most of them are also inside jobs not dependent on the weather, as are construction jobs and other higher-paying outside work.

Another seemingly important advantage of working in hotels, restaurants, office and apartment buildings and retail establishments is that they frequently offer an opportunity for stealing on the job. But stealing can be a two-edged sword. Apart from increasing the cost of the goods or services to the general public, a less obvious result is that the practice usually acts as a depressant on the employee's own wage level. Owners of small retail establishments and other employers frequently anticipate employee stealing and adjust the wage rate accordingly. Tonk's employer explained why he was paying Tonk $35 for a 55-60 hour workweek. These men will all steal, he said. Although he keeps close watch on Tonk, he estimates that Tonk steals from $35 to $40 a week.[3] What he steals, when added to his regular earnings, brings his take-home pay to $70 or $75 per week. The employer said he did not mind this because Tonk is worth that much to the business. But if he were to pay Tonk outright the full value of his labor, Tonk would still be stealing $35-$40 per week and this, he said, the business simply would not support.

This wage arrangement, with stealing built-in,

was satisfactory to both parties, with each one independently expressing his satisfaction. Such a wage-theft system, however, is not as balanced and equitable as it appears. Since the wage level rests on the premise that the employee will steal the unpaid value of his labor, the man who does not steal on the job is penalized. And furthermore, even if he does not steal, no one would believe him; the employer and others believe he steals because the system presumes it.

Nor is the man who steals, as he is expected to, as well off as he believes himself to be. The employer may occasionally close his eyes to the worker's stealing but not often and not for long. He is, after all, a businessman and cannot always find it within himself to let a man steal from him, even if the man is stealing his own wages. Moreover, it is only by keeping close watch on the worker that the employer can control how much is stolen and thereby protect himself against the employee's stealing more than he is worth. From this viewpoint, then, the employer is not in wage-theft collusion with the employee. In the case of Tonk, for instance, the employer was not actively abetting the theft. His estimate of how much Tonk was stealing was based on what he thought Tonk was able to steal despite his own best efforts to prevent him from stealing anything at all. Were he to have caught Tonk in the act of stealing, he would, of course, have fired him from the job and perhaps called the police as well. Thus, in an actual if not in a legal sense, all the elements of entrapment are present. The employer knowingly provides the conditions which entice (force) the employee to steal the unpaid value of his labor, but at the same time he punishes him for theft if he catches him doing so.

Other consequences of the wage-theft system are even more damaging to the employee. Let us, for argument's sake, say that Tonk is in no danger of entrapment; that his employer is willing to wink at the stealing and that Tonk, for his part, is perfectly willing to earn a little, steal a little. Let us say, too, that he is paid $35 a week and allowed to steal $35. His money income—as measured by the goods and services he can purchase with it—is, of course, $70. But not all of his income is available to him for all purposes. He cannot draw on what he steals to build his self-respect or to measure his self-worth. For this, he can draw only on his earnings—the amount given him publicly and voluntarily in exchange for his labor. His "respect" and "self-worth" income remains at $35—only half that of the man who also receives $70 but all of it in the form of wages. His earnings publicly measure the worth of his labor to his employer, and they are important to others and to himself in taking the measure of his worth as a man.[4]

With or without stealing, and quite apart from any interior processes going on in the man who refuses such a job or quits it casually and without apparent reason, the objective fact is that menial jobs in retailing or in the service trades simply do not pay enough to support a man and his family. This is not to say that the worker is underpaid; this may or may not be true. Whether he is or not, the plain fact is that, in such a job, he cannot make a living. Nor can he take much comfort in the fact that these jobs tend to offer more regular, steadier work. If he cannot live on the $45 or $50 he makes in one week, the longer he works, the longer he cannot live on what he makes.[5]

Construction work, even for unskilled laborers, usually pays better, with the hourly rate ranging from $1.50 to $2.60 an hour.[6] Importantly, too, good references, a good driving record, a tenth grade (or any high school) education, previous experience, the ability to "bring police clearance with you" are not normally required of laborers as they frequently are for some of the jobs in retailing or in the service trades.

Construction work, however, has its own objective disadvantages. It is, first of all, seasonal work for the great bulk of the laborers, beginning early in the spring and tapering off as winter weather sets in.[7] And even during the season the work is frequently irregular. Early or late in the season, snow or temperatures too low for concrete frequently sends the laborers back home, and during late spring or summer, a heavy rain on Tuesday or Wednesday, leaving a lot of water and mud behind it, can mean a two or three day workweek for the pick-and-shovel men and other unskilled laborers.[8]

The elements are not the only hazard. As the project moves from one construction stage to another, laborers—usually without warning—are laid off, sometimes permanently or sometimes for weeks at a time. The more fortunate or the better workers are told periodically to "take a walk for two, three days."

Both getting the construction job and getting to it are also relatively more difficult than is the case for the menial jobs in retailing and the service trades. Job competition is always fierce. In the city, the large construction projects are unionized. One has to have ready cash to get into the union to become eligible to work on these projects and, being eligible, one has to find an opening. Unless one "knows somebody," say a foreman or a laborer who knows the day before that they are going to take on new men in the morning, this can be a difficult and disheartening search.

Many of the nonunion jobs are in suburban Maryland or Virginia. The newspaper ads say, "Report ready to work to the trailer at the intersection of Rte. 11 and Old Bridge Rd., Bunston, Virginia (or Maryland)," but this location may be ten, fifteen, or even twenty-five miles from the Carry-out. Public transportation would require two or more hours to get there, if it services the area at all. Without access to a car or to a car-pool arrangement, it is not worthwhile reading the ad. So the men do not. Jobs such as these are usually filled by word of mouth information, beginning with someone who knows someone or who is himself working there and looking for a paying rider. Furthermore, nonunion jobs in outlying areas tend to be smaller projects of relatively short duration and to pay somewhat less than scale.

Still another objective factor is the work itself. For some men, whether the job be digging, mixing mortar, pushing a wheelbarrow, unloading materials, carrying and placing steel rods for reinforcing concrete, or building or laying concrete forms, the work is simply too hard. Men such as Tally and Wee Tom can make such work look like child's play; some of the older work-hardened men, such as Budder and Stanton, can do it too, although not

without showing unmistakable signs of strain and weariness at the end of the workday. But those who lack the robustness of a Tally or the time-inured immunity of a Budder must either forego jobs such as these or pay a heavy toll to keep them. For Leroy, in his early twenties, almost six feet tall but weighing under 140 pounds, it would be as difficult to push a loaded wheelbarrow, or to unload and stack 96-pound bags of cement all day long, as it would be for Stoopy with his withered leg.

Heavy, backbreaking labor of the kind that used to be regularly associated with bull gangs or concrete gangs is no longer characteristic of laboring jobs, especially those with the larger, well-equipped construction companies. Brute strength is still required from time to time, as on smaller jobs where it is not economical to bring in heavy equipment or where the small, undercapitalized contractor has none to bring in. In many cases, however, the conveyor belt has replaced the wheelbarrow or the Georgia buggy, mechanized forklifts have eliminated heavy, manual lifting, and a variety of digging machines have replaced the pick and shovel. The result is fewer jobs for unskilled laborers and, in many cases, a work speed-up for those who do have jobs. Machines now set the pace formerly set by men. Formerly, a laborer pushed a wheelbarrow of wet cement to a particular spot, dumped it, and returned for another load. Another laborer, in hip boots, pushed the wet concrete around with a shovel or a hoe, getting it roughly level in preparation for the skilled finishers. He had relatively small loads to contend with and had only to keep up with the men pushing the wheelbarrows. Now, the job for the man pushing the wheelbarrow is gone and the wet concrete comes rushing down a chute at the man in the hip boots who must "spread it quick or drown."

Men who have been running an elevator, washing dishes, or "pulling trash" cannot easily move into laboring jobs. They lack the basic skills for "unskilled" construction labor, familiarity with tools and materials, and tricks of the trade without which hard jobs are made harder. Previously unused or untrained muscles rebel in pain against the new and insistent demands made upon them, seriously compromising the man's performance and testing his willingness to see the job through.

A healthy, sturdy, active man of good intelligence requires from two to four weeks to break in on a construction job.[9] Even if he is willing somehow to bull his way through the first few weeks, it frequently happens that his foreman or the craftsman he services with materials and general assistance is not willing to wait that long for him to get into condition or to learn at a glance the difference in size between a rough 2″ X 8″ and a finished 2″ X 10″. The foreman and the craftsman are themselves "under the gun" and cannot "carry" the man when other men, who are already used to the work and who know the tools and materials, are lined up to take the job.

Sea Cat was "healthy, sturdy, active and of good intelligence." When a judge gave him six weeks in which to pay his wife $200 in back child-support payments, he left his grocery-store job in order to take a higher-paying job as a laborer, arranged for him by a foreman friend. During the first week the weather was bad and he worked only Wednesday and Friday, cursing the elements all the while for cheating him out of the money he could have made. The second week, the weather was fair but he quit at the end of the fourth day, saying frankly that the work was too hard for him. He went back to his job at the grocery store and took a second job working nights as a dishwasher in a restaurant,[10] earning little if any more at the two jobs than he would have earned as a laborer, and keeping at both of them until he had paid off his debts.

Tonk did not last as long as Sea Cat. No one made any predictions when he got a job in a parking lot, but when the men on the corner learned he was to start on a road construction job, estimates of how long he would last ranged from one to three weeks. Wednesday was his first day. He spent that evening and night at home. He did the same on Thursday. He worked Friday and spent Friday evening and part of Saturday draped over the mailbox on the corner. Sunday afternoon, Tonk decided he was not going to report on the job the next morning. He explained that after working

three days, he knew enough about the job to know that it was too hard for him. He knew he wouldn't be able to keep up and he'd just as soon quit now as get fired later.

Logan was a tall, two-hundred-pound man in his late twenties. His back used to hurt him only on the job, he said, but now he can't straighten up for increasingly longer periods of time. He said he had traced this to the awkward walk he was forced to adopt by the loaded wheelbarrows which pull him down into a half-stoop. He's going to quit, he said, as soon as he can find another job. If he can't find one real soon, he guesses he'll quit anyway. It's not worth it, having to walk bent over and leaning to one side.

Sometimes, the strain and effort is greater than the man is willing to admit, even to himself. In the early summer of 1963, Richard was rooming at Nancy's place. His wife and children were "in the country" (his grandmother's home in Carolina), waiting for him to save up enough money so that he could bring them back to Washington and start over again after a disastrous attempt to "make it" in Philadelphia. Richard had gotten a job with a fence company in Virginia. It paid $1.60 an hour. The first few evenings, when he came home from work, he looked ill from exhaustion and the heat. Stanton said Richard would have to quit, "he's too small [thin] for that kind of work." Richard said he was doing O.K. and would stick with the job.

At Nancy's one night, when Richard had been working about two weeks, Nancy and three or four others were sitting around talking, drinking, and listening to music. Someone asked Nancy when was Richard going to bring his wife and children up from the country. Nancy said she didn't know, but it probably depended on how long it would take him to save up enough money. She said she didn't think he could stay with the fence job much longer. This morning, she said, the man Richard rode to work with knocked on the door and Richard didn't answer. She looked in his room. Richard was still asleep. Nancy tried to shake him awake. "No more digging!" Richard cried out. "No more digging! I can't do no more God-damn digging!" When Nancy finally managed to wake him, he dressed quickly and went to work.

Richard stayed on the job two more weeks, then suddenly quit, ostensibly because his pay check was three dollars less than what he thought it should have been.

In summary of objective job considerations, then, the most important fact is that a man who is able and willing to work cannot earn enough money to support himself, his wife, and one or more children. A man's chances for working regularly are good only if he is willing to work for less than he can live on, and sometimes not even then. On some jobs, the wage rate is deceptively higher than on others, but the higher the wage rate, the more difficult it is to get the job, and the less the job security. Higher-paying construction work tends to be seasonal and, during the season, the amount of work available is highly sensitive to business and weather conditions and to the changing requirements of individual projects.[11] Moreover, high-paying construction jobs are frequently beyond the physical capacity of some of the men, and some of the low-paying jobs are scaled down even lower in accordance with the self-fulfilling assumption that the man will steal part of his wages on the job.[12]

Bernard assesses the objective job situation dispassionately over a cup of coffee, sometimes poking at the coffee with his spoon, sometimes starting at it as if, like a crystal ball, it holds tomorrow's secrets. He is twenty-seven years old. He and the woman with whom he lives have a baby son, and she has another child by another man. Bernard does odd jobs—mostly painting—but here it is the end of January, and his last job was with the Post Office during the Christmas mail rush. He would like postal work as a steady job, he says. It pays well (about $2.00 an hour) but he has twice failed the Post Office examination (he graduated from a Washington high school) and has given up the idea as an impractical one. He is supposed to see a man tonight about a job as a parking attendant for a large apartment house. The man told him to bring his birth certificate and driver's license, but his license was suspended because of a backlog of

unpaid traffic fines. A friend promised to lend him some money this evening. If he gets it, he will pay the fines tomorrow morning and have his license reinstated. He hopes the man with the job will wait till tomorrow night.

A "security job" is what he really wants, he said. He would like to save up money for a taxicab. (But having twice failed the postal examination and having a bad driving record as well, it is highly doubtful that he could meet the qualifications or pass the written test.) That would be "a good life." He can always get a job in a restaurant or as a clerk in a drugstore but they don't pay enough, he said. He needs to take home at least $50 to $55 a week. He thinks he can get that much driving a truck somewhere. . . . Sometimes he wishes he had stayed in the army. . . . A security job, that's what he wants most of all, a real security job. . . .

## REFERENCES AND NOTES

1   By different methods, perhaps, some social scientists have also located the problem in the men themselves, in their unwillingness or lack of desire to work: "To improve the underprivileged worker's performance, one must help him to learn to *want* . . . higher social goals for himself and his children. . . . The problem of changing the work habits and motivation of [lower class] people . . . is a problem of changing the goals, the ambitions, and the level of cultural and occupational aspiration of the underprivileged worker." (Emphasis in original.) Allison Davis, "The Motivation of the Underprivileged Worker," p. 90.

2   The comparison of sitting at home alone with being in jail is commonplace.

3   Exactly the same estimate as the one made by Tonk himself. On the basis of personal knowledge of the stealing routine employed by Tonk, however, I suspect the actual amount is considerably smaller.

4   Some public credit may accrue to the clever thief but not respect.

5   It might be profitable to compare, as Howard S. Becker suggests, gross aspects of income and housing costs in this particular area with those reported by Herbert Gans for the low-income working class in Boston's West End. In 1958, Gans reports, median income for the West Enders was just under $70 a week, a level considerably higher than that enjoyed by the people in the Carry-out neighborhood five

years later. Gans himself rented a six-room apartment in the West End for $46 a month, about $10 more than the going rate for long-time residents. In the Carry-out neighborhood, rooms that could accommodate more than a cot and a miniature dresser —that is, rooms that qualified for family living— rented for $12 to $22 a week.

Ignoring differences that really can't be ignored— the privacy and self-contained efficiency of the multi-room apartment as against the fragmented, public living of the rooming-house "apartment," with a public toilet on a floor always different from the one your room is on (no matter, it probably doesn't work, anyway)—and assuming comparable states of disrepair, the West Enders were paying $6 or $7 a month for a room that cost the Carry-outers at least $50 a month, and frequently more. Looking at housing costs as a percentage of income—and again ignoring what cannot be ignored: that what goes by the name of "housing" in the two areas is not at all the same thing—the median income West Ender could get a six-room apartment for about 12 percent of his income, while his 1963 Carry-out counterpart, with a weekly income of $60 (to choose a figure from the upper end of the income range), often paid 20-33 percent of his income for one room. See Herbert J. Gans, *The Urban Villagers*, pp. 10–13.

6   The higher amount is 1962 union scale for building laborers. According to the Wage Agreement Contract for Heavy Construction Laborers (Washington, D.C., and vicinity) covering the period from May 1, 1963 to April 30, 1966, minimum hourly wage for heavy construction laborers was to go from $2.75 (May 1963) by annual increments to $2.92, effective November 1, 1965.

7   "Open-sky" work, such as building overpasses, highways, etc., in which the workers and materials are directly exposed to the elements, traditionally begins in March and ends around Thanksgiving. The same is true for much of the street repair work and the laying of sewer, electric, gas, and telephone lines by the city and public utilities, all important employers of laborers. Between Thanksgiving and March, they retain only skeleton crews selected from their best, most reliable men.

8   In a recent year, the crime rate in Washington for the month of August jumped 18 percent over the preceding month. A veteran police officer explained the increase to David L. Bazelon, Chief Judge, U.S. Court of Appeals for the District of Columbia: "It's quite simple. . . . You see, August was a very wet month. . . . These people wait on the street corner each morning around 6:00 or 6:30 for a truck to pick them up and take them to a construction site. If it's raining, that truck doesn't come, and the men are going to be idle that day. If the bad weather keeps up for three days . . . we know we are going to have trouble on our hands—and sure enough, there invariably follows a rash of purse-snatchings, house-breakings and the like. . . . These people have to eat like the rest of us, you know." David L. Bazelon, Address to the Federal Bar Association, p. 3.

9   Estimate of Francis Greenfield, President of the International Hod Carriers, Building and Common Laborers' District Council of Washington, D.C., and Vicinity. I am indebted to Mr. Greenfield for several points in these paragraphs dealing with construction laborers.

10   Not a sinecure, even by streetcorner standards.

11   The overall result is that, in the long run, a Negro laborer's earnings are not substantially greater—and may be less—than those of the busboy, janitor, or stock clerk. Herman P. Miller, for example, reports that in 1960, 40 percent of all jobs held by Negro men were as laborers or in the service trades. The average annual wage for nonwhite nonfarm laborers was $2,400. The average earning of nonwhite service workers was $2,500 (*Rich Man, Poor Man*, p. 90). Francis Greenfield estimates that in the Washington vicinity, the 1965 earnings of the union laborer who works whenever work is available will be about $3,200. Even this figure is high for the man on the streetcorner. Union men in heavy construction are the aristocrats of the laborers. Casual day labor and jobs with small firms in the building and construction trades, or with firms in other industries, pay considerably less.

12   For an excellent discussion of the self-fulfilling assumption (or prophecy) as a social force, see "The Self-fulfilling Prophecy," chap. XI, in Robert K. Merton's *Social Theory and Social Structure*.

## 31 THE NEGRO MIDDLE CLASS    E. FRANKLIN FRAZIER

Since the black bourgeoisie live largely in a world of make-believe, the masks which they wear to play their sorry roles conceal the feelings of inferiority and of insecurity and the frustrations that haunt their inner lives. Despite their attempt to escape from real identification with the masses of Negroes, they can not escape the mark of oppression any more than their less favored kinsmen. In attempting to escape identification with the black masses, they have developed a self-hatred that reveals itself in their deprecation of the physical and social characteristics of Negroes. Likewise, their feelings of inferiority and insecurity are revealed in their pathological struggle for status within the isolated Negro world and craving for recognition in the white world. Their escape into a world of make-believe with its sham "society" leaves them with a feeling of emptiness and futility which causes them to constantly seek an escape in new delusions.

### THE MARK OF OPPRESSION

There is an attempt on the part of the parents in middle-class families to shield their children against racial discrimination and the contempt of whites for colored people. Sometimes the parents go to fantastic extremes, such as prohibiting the use of the words "Negro" or "colored" in the presence of their children.[1] They sometimes try to prevent their children from knowing that they can not enter restaurants or other public places because they are Negroes, or even that the schools they attend are segregated schools for Negroes. Despite such efforts to insulate their children against a hostile white world, the children of the black bourgeoisie can

not escape the mark of oppression. This is strikingly revealed in the statement of a seventeen-year-old middle-class Negro youth. When asked if he felt inferior in the presence of white people, he gave the following answer—which was somewhat unusual for its frankness but typical of the attitude of the black bourgeoisie:

> Off-hand, I'd say no, but actually knowing all these things that are thrown up to you about white people being superior—that they look more or less down upon all Negroes—that we have to look to them for everything we get—that they'd rather think of us as mice than men—I don't believe I or any other Negro can help but feel inferior. My father says that it isn't so—that we feel only inferior to those whom we feel are superior. But I don't believe we can feel otherwise. Around white people until I know them a while I feel definitely out of place. Once I played a ping-pong match with a white boy whose play I know wasn't as good as mine, and boys he managed to beat I beat with ease, but I just couldn't get it out of my mind that I was playing a white boy. Sort of an Indian sign on me, you know.[2]

The statement of this youth reveals how deep-seated is the feeling of inferiority, from which even the most favored elements among Negroes can not escape. However much some middle-class Negroes may seek to soothe their feeling of inferiority in an attitude which they often express in the adage, "it is better to reign in hell than serve in heaven," they are still conscious of their inferior status in American society. They may say, as did a bewildered middle-class youth, that they are proud of being a Negro or proud of being a member of the upper stratum in the Negro community and feel sorry for the Negro masses "stuck in the mud," but they often confess, as did this youth:

However, knowing that there are difficulties that confront us all as Negroes, if I could be born again and had my choice I'd really want to be a white boy—I mean white or my color, providing I could occupy the same racial and economic level I now enjoy. I am glad I am this color—I'm frequently taken for a foreigner. I wouldn't care to be lighter or darker and be a Negro. I am the darkest one in the family due to my constant outdoor activities. I realize of course that there are places where I can't go despite my family or money just because I happen to be a Negro. With my present education, family background, and so forth, if I was only white I could go places in life. A white face holds supreme over a black one despite its economic and social status. Frankly, it leaves me bewildered.[3]

Not all middle-class Negroes consciously desire, as this youth, to be white in order to escape from their feelings of inferiority. In fact, the majority of middle-class Negroes would deny having the desire to be white, since this would be an admission of their feeling of inferiority. Within an intimate circle of friends some middle-class Negroes may admit that they desire to be white, but publicly they would deny any such wish. The black bourgeoisie constantly boast of their pride in their identification as Negroes. But when one studies the attitude of this class in regard to the physical traits or the social characteristics of Negroes, it becomes clear that the black bourgeoisie do not really wish to be identified with Negroes.

### INSECURITIES AND FRUSTRATIONS

Since the black bourgeoisie can not escape identification with Negroes, they experience certain feelings of insecurity because of their feeling of inferiority. Their feeling of inferiority is revealed in their fear of competition with whites. There is first a fear of competition with whites for jobs. Notwithstanding the fact that middle-class Negroes are the most vociferous in demanding the right to compete on equal terms with whites, many of them still fear such competition. They prefer the security afforded by their monopoly of certain occupations within the segregated Negro community. For example, middle-class Negroes demand that the two Negro medical schools be reserved for Negro students and that a quota be set for white students, though Negro students are admitted to "white" medical schools. Since the Supreme Court of the United States has ruled against segregated public schools, many Negro teachers, even those who are well-prepared, fear that they cannot compete with whites for teaching positions. Although this fear stems principally from a feeling of inferiority which is experienced generally by Negroes, it has other causes.

The majority of the black bourgeoisie fear competition with whites partly because such competition would mean that whites were taking them seriously, and consequently they would have to assume a more serious and responsible attitude towards their work. Middle-class Negroes, who are notorious for their inefficiency in the management of various Negro institutions, excuse their inefficiency on the grounds that Negroes are a "young race" and, therefore, will require time to attain the efficiency of the white man. The writer has heard a Negro college president, who has constantly demanded that Negroes have equality in American life, declare before white people in extenuation of the shortcomings of his own administration, that Negroes were a "child race" and that they had "to crawl before they could walk." Such declarations, while flattering to the whites, are revealing in that they manifest the black bourgeoisie's contempt for the Negro masses, while excusing its own deficiencies by attributing them to the latter. Yet it is clear that the black workers who must gain a living in a white man's mill or factory and in competition with white workers cannot offer any such excuse for his inefficiency.

The fear of competition with whites is probably responsible for the black bourgeoisie's fear of competence and first-rate performance within its own ranks. When a Negro is competent and insists upon first-rate work it appears to this class that he is trying to be a white man, or that he is insisting that Negroes measure up to white standards. This is especially true where the approval of whites is taken as a mark of competence and first-rate performance. In such cases the black bourgeoisie reveal their ambivalent attitudes toward the white world. They slavishly accept the estimate which almost any white man places upon a Negro or his work, but at the same time they fear and reject white standards. For example, when a group of Negro doctors were being shown the modern equipment and techniques of a white clinic, one of them remarked to a Negro professor in a medical school, "This is the white man's medicine. I never bother with it and still I make $30,000 a year." Negroes who adopt the standards of the white world create among the black bourgeoisie a feeling of insecurity and often become the object of both the envy and hatred of this class.

Among the women of the black bourgeoisie there is an intense fear of the competition of white women for Negro men. They often attempt to rationalize their fear by saying that the Negro man always occupies an inferior position in relation to the white woman or that he marries much below his "social" status. They come nearer to the source of their fear when they confess that there are not many eligible Negro men and that these few should marry Negro women. That such rationalizations conceal deep-seated feelings of insecurity is revealed by the fact that generally they have no objection to the marriage of white men to Negro women, especially if the white man is reputed to be wealthy. In fact, they take pride in the fact and attribute these marriages to the "peculiar" charms of Negro women. In fact, the middle-class Negro woman's fear of the competition of white women is based often upon the fact that she senses her own inadequacies and shortcomings. Her position in Negro "society" and in the larger Negro community is often due to some adventitious factor, such as a light complexion or a meager education, which has pushed her to the top of the social pyramid. The middle-class white woman not only has a white skin and straight hair, but she is generally more sophisticated and interesting because she has read more widely and has a larger view of the world. The middle-class Negro woman may make fun of the "plainness" of her white competitor and the latter's lack of "wealth" and interest in "society"; nevertheless she still feels insecure when white women appear as even potential competitors.

Both men and women among the black bourgeoisie have a feeling of insecurity because of their constant fear of the loss of status. Since they have no status in the larger American society, the intense struggle for status among middle-class Negroes is, as we have seen, an attempt to compensate for the contempt and low esteem of the whites. Great value is, therefore, placed upon all kinds of status symbols. Academic degrees, both real and honorary, are sought in order to secure status. Usually the symbols are of a material nature implying wealth and conspicuous consumption. Sometimes Negro doctors do not attend what are supposedly scientific meetings because they do not have a Cadillac or some other expensive automobile. School teachers wear mink coats and maintain homes beyond their income for fear that they may lose status. The extravagance in "social" life generally is due to an effort not to lose status. But in attempting to overcome their fear of loss of status they are often beset by new feelings of insecurity. In spite of their pretended wealth, they are aware that their incomes are insignificant and that they must struggle to maintain their mortgaged homes and the show of "wealth" in lavish "social" affairs. Moreover, they are beset by a feeling of insecurity because of their struggles to maintain a show of wealth through illegal means. From time to time "wealthy" Negro doctors are arrested for selling narcotics and performing abortions. The life of many a "wealthy" Negro doctor is shortened by the struggle to provide diamonds, minks, and an expensive home for his wife.

There is much frustration among the black bourgeoisie despite their privileged position within the segregated Negro world. Their "wealth" and "social" position can not erase the fact that they are generally segregated and rejected by the white world. Their incomes and occupations may enable them to escape the cruder manifestations of racial prejudice, but they can not insulate themselves against the more subtle forms of racial discrimination. These discriminations cause frustrations in Negro men because they are not allowed to play the "masculine role" as defined by American culture. They can not assert themselves or exercise power as white men do. When they protest against racial discrimination there is always the threat that they will be punished by the white world. In spite of the movement toward the wider integration of the Negro into the general stream of American life, middle-class Negroes are still threatened with the loss of positions and earning power if they insist upon their rights.[4] After the Supreme Court of the United States ruled that segregation in public education was illegal, Negro teachers in some parts of the South were dismissed because they would not sign statements supporting racial segregation in education.

As one of the results of not being able to play the "masculine role," middle-class Negro males have tended to cultivate their "personalities,"[5] which enable them to exercise considerable influence among whites and achieve distinction in the Negro world. Among Negroes they have been noted for their glamour.[6] In this respect they resemble women who use their "personalities" to compensate for their inferior status in relation to men. This fact would seem to support the observation of an American sociologist that the Negro was "the lady among the races," if he had restricted his observation to middle-class males among American Negroes.[7]

In the South the middle-class Negro male is not only prevented from playing a masculine role, but generally he must let Negro women assume leadership in any show of militancy. This reacts upon his status in the home where the tradition of female dominance, which is widely established among Negroes, has tended to assign a subordinate role to the male. In fact, in middle-class families, especially if the husband has risen in social status through his own efforts and married a member of an "old" family or a "society" woman, the husband is likely to play a pitiful role. The greatest compliment that can be paid such a husband is

that he "worships his wife," which means that he is her slave and supports all her extravagances and vanities. But, of course, many husbands in such positions escape from their frustrations by having extra-marital sex relations. Yet the conservative and conventional middle-class husband presents a pathetic picture. He often sits at home alone, impotent physically and socially, and complains that his wife has gone crazy about poker and "society" and constantly demands money for gambling and expenditures which he can not afford. Sometimes he enjoys the sympathy of a son or daughter who has not become a "socialite." Such children often say that they had a happy family life until "mamma took to poker."

Preoccupation with poker on the part of the middle-class woman is often an attempt to escape from a frustrated life. Her frustration may be bound up with her unsatisfactory sexual life. She may be married to a "glamorous" male who neglects her for other women. For among the black bourgeoisie, the glamour of the male is often associated with his sexual activities. The frustration of many Negro women has a sexual origin.[8] Even those who have sought an escape from frustration in sexual promiscuity may, because of satiety or deep psychological reasons, become obsessed with poker in order to escape from their frustrations. One "society" woman, in justification of her obsession with poker remarked that it had taken the place of her former preoccupation with sex. Another said that to win at poker was similar to a sexual orgasm.

The frustration of the majority of the women among the black bourgeoisie is probably due to the idle or ineffectual lives which they lead. Those who do not work devote their time to the frivolities of Negro "society." When they devote their time to "charity" or worthwhile causes, it is generally a form of play or striving for "social" recognition. They are constantly forming clubs which ostensibly have a serious purpose, but in reality are formed in order to consolidate their position in "society" or to provide additional occasions for playing poker. The idle, overfed women among the black bourgeoisie are generally, to use their language "dripping with diamonds." They are forever dieting and reducing only to put on more weight (which is usually the result of the food that they consume at their club meetings). Even the women among the black bourgeoisie who work exhibit the same frustrations. Generally, they have no real interest in their work and only engage in it in order to be able to provide the conspicuous consumption demanded by "society." As we have indicated, the women as well as the men among the black bourgeoisie read very little and have no interest in music, art or the theater. They are constantly restless and do not know how to relax. They are generally dull people and only become animated when "social" matters are discussed, especially poker games. They are afraid to be alone and constantly seek to be surrounded by their friends, who enable them to escape from their boredom.

The frustrated lives of the black bourgeoisie are reflected in the attitudes of parents towards their children. Middle-class Negro families as a whole have few children, while among the families that constitute Negro "society" there are many childless couples.[9] One finds today, as an American observed over forty years ago, that "where the children are few, they are usually spoiled" in middle-class Negro families.[10] There is often not only a deep devotion to their one or two children, but a subservience to them. It is not uncommon for the only son to be called and treated as the "boss" in the family. Parents cater to the transient wishes of their children and often rationalize their behavior towards them on the grounds that children should not be "inhibited." They spend large sums of money on their children for toys and especially for clothes. They provide their children with automobiles when they go to college. All of this is done in order that the children may maintain the status of the parents and be eligible to enter the "social" set in Negro colleges. When they send their children to northern "white" colleges they often spend more time in preparing them for what they imagine will be their "social" life than in preparing them for the academic requirements of these institutions.

In their fierce devotion to their children, which generally results in spoiling them, middle-class Negro parents are seemingly striving at times to establish a human relationship that will compensate for their own frustrations in the realm of human relationships. Devotion to their children often becomes the one human tie that is sincere and free from the competition and artificiality of the make-believe world in which they live. Sometimes they may project upon their children their own frustrated professional ambitions. But usually, even when they send their children to northern "white" universities as a part of their "social" striving within the Negro community, they seem to hope that their children will have an acceptance in the white world which has been denied them.

## SELF-HATRED AND GUILT FEELINGS

One of the chief frustrations of the middle-class Negro is that he can not escape identification with the Negro race and consequently is subject to the contempt of whites.[11] Despite his "wealth" in which he has placed so much faith as a solvent of racial discrimination, he is still subject to daily insults and is excluded from participation in white American society. Middle-class Negroes do not express their resentment against discrimination and insults in violent outbreaks, as lower-class Negroes often do. They constantly repress their hostility toward whites and seek to soothe their hurt self-esteem in all kinds of rationalizations. They may boast of their wealth and culture as compared with the condition of the poor whites. Most often they will resort to any kind of subterfuge in order to avoid contact with whites. For example, in the South they often pay their bills by mail rather than risk unpleasant contacts with representatives of white firms.[12] The daily repression of resentment and the constant resort to means of avoiding contacts with whites do not relieve them of their hostility toward whites. Even middle-class Negroes who gain a reputation for exhibiting "objectivity" and a "statesman-like" attitude on racial discrimination harbor deep-seated hostilities toward whites. A Negro college president who has been considered such an inter-racial "statesman" once confessed to the writer that some day he was going to "break loose" and tell white people what he really thought. However, it is unlikely that a middle-class Negro of his standing will ever "break loose." Middle-class Negroes generally express their aggressions against whites by other means, such as deceiving whites and utilizing them for their own advantage.

Because middle-class Negroes are unable to indulge in aggressions against whites as such, they will sometimes make other minority groups the object of their hostilities. For example, they may show hostility against Italians, who are also subject to discrimination. But more often middle-class Negroes, especially those who are engaged in a mad scramble to accumulate money, will direct their hostilities against Jews. They are constantly expressing their anti-semitism within Negro circles, while pretending publicly to be free from prejudice. They blame the Jew for the poverty of Negroes and for their own failures and inefficiencies in their business undertakings. In expressing their hostility towards Jews, they are attempting at the same time to identify with the white American majority.

The repressed hostilities of middle-class Negroes to whites are not only directed towards other minority groups but inward toward themselves. This results in self-hatred, which may appear from their behavior to be directed towards the Negro masses but which in reality is directed against themselves.[13] While pretending to be proud of being a Negro, they ridicule Negroid physical characteristics and seek to modify or efface them as much as possible. Within their own groups they constantly proclaim that "niggers" make them sick. The very use of the term "nigger," which they claim to resent, indicates that they want to disassociate themselves from the Negro masses. They talk condescendingly of Africans and of African culture, often even objecting to African sculpture in their homes. They are insulted if they are identified with Africans. They refuse to join organizations that are interested in Africa. If they are of mixed ancestry, they may boast of the fact that they have Indian ancestry. When making compliments concerning the beauty of Negroes of mixed ancestry, they generally say, for example, "She is beautiful; she looks like an Indian." On the other hand, if a black woman has European features, they will remark condescendingly, "Although she is black, you must admit that she is good looking." Some middle-class Negroes of mixed ancestry like to wear Hindu costumes— while they laugh at the idea of wearing an African costume. When middle-class Negroes travel, they studiously avoid association with other Negroes, especially if they themselves have received the slightest recognition by whites. Even when they can not "pass" for white they fear that they will lose this recognition if they are identified as Negroes. Therefore, nothing pleases them more than to be mistaken for a Puerto Rican, Philippino, Egyptian or Arab or any ethnic group other than Negro.

The self-hatred of middle-class Negroes is often revealed in the keen competition which exists among them for status and recognition. This keen competition is the result of the frustrations which they experience in attempting to obtain acceptance and recognition by whites. Middle-class Negroes are constantly criticizing and belittling Negroes who achieve some recognition or who acquire a status above them. They prefer to submit to the authority of whites than to be subordinate to other Negroes. For example, Negro scholars generally refuse to seek the advice and criticism of competent Negro scholars and prefer to turn to white scholars for such co-operation. In fact, it is difficult for middle-class Negroes to co-operate in any field of endeavor. This failure in social relations is, as indicated in an important study, because "in every Negro he encounters his own self-contempt."[14] It is as if he said, "You are only a Negro like myself; so why should you be in a position above me?"

This self-hatred often results in guilt feelings on the part of the Negro who succeeds in elevating himself above his fellows.[15] He feels unconsciously that in rising above other Negroes he is committing an act of aggression which will result in hatred and revenge on their part. The act of aggression may be imagined, but very often it is real. This is the case when middle-class Negroes oppose the economic and social welfare of Negroes because of their own interests. In some American cities, it has been the black bourgeoisie and not the whites who have opposed the building of low-cost public housing for Negro workers. In one city two wealthy Negro doctors, who have successfully opposed public housing projects for Negro workers, own some of the worst slums in the United States. While their wives, who wear mink coats, "drip with diamonds" and are written up in the "society" columns of Negro newspapers, ride in Cadillacs, their Negro tenants sleep on the dirt floors of hovels unfit for human habitation. The guilt feelings of the middle-class Negro are not always unconscious. For example, take the case of the Negro leader who proclaimed over the radio in a national broadcast that the Negro did not want social equity. He was conscious of his guilt feelings and his self-hatred in playing such a role, for he sent word privately to the writer that he never hated so much to do anything in his life, but that it was necessary because of his position as head of a state college which was under white supervision. The self-hatred of the middle-class Negro arises, then, not only from the fact that he does not want to be a Negro but also because of his sorry role in American society.

## ESCAPE INTO DELUSIONS

The black bourgeoisie, as we have seen, has created a world of make-believe to shield itself from the harsh economic and social realities of American life. This world of make-believe is created out of the myth of Negro business, the reports of the Negro press on the achievements and wealth of Negroes, the recognition accorded them by whites, and the fabulous life of Negro "society." Some of the middle-class Negro intellectuals are not deceived by the world of make-believe. They will have nothing to do with Negro "society" and refuse to waste their time in frivolities. They take their work seriously and live in relative obscurity

so far as the Negro world is concerned. Others seek an escape from their frustrations by developing, for example, a serious interest in Negro music—which the respectable bourgeoisie often pretend to despise. In this way these intellectuals achieve some identification with the Negro masses and with the traditions of Negro life. But many more middle-class Negroes, who are satisfied to live in the world of make-believe but must find a solution to the real economic and social problems which they face, seek an escape in delusions.

They seek an escape in delusions involving wealth. This is facilitated by the fact that they have had little experience with the real meaning of wealth and that they lack a tradition of saving and accumulation. Wealth to them means spending money without any reference to its source. Hence, their behavior generally reflects the worst qualities of the gentleman and peasant from whom their only vital traditions spring. Therefore, their small accumulations of capital and the income which they receive from professional services within the Negro community make them appear wealthy in comparison with the low economic status of the majority of Negroes. The delusion of wealth is supported by the myth of Negro business. Moreover, the attraction of the delusion of wealth is enhanced by the belief that wealth will gain them acceptance in American life. In seeking an escape in the delusion of wealth, middle-class Negroes make a fetish of material things or physical possessions. They are constantly buying things—houses, automobiles, furniture and all sorts of gadgets, not to mention clothes. Many of the furnishings and gadgets which they acquire are never used; nevertheless they continue to accumulate things. The homes of many middle-class Negroes have the appearance of museums for the exhibition of American manufactures and spurious art objects. The objects which they are constantly buying are always on display. Negro school teachers who devote their lives to "society" like to display twenty to thirty pairs of shoes, the majority of which they never wear. Negro professional men proudly speak of the two automobiles which they have acquired when they need only one. The acquisition of objects which are not used or needed seems to be an attempt to fill some void in their lives.

The delusion of power also appears to provide an escape for middle-class Negroes from the world of reality which pierces through the world of make-believe of the black bourgeoisie. The positions of power which they occupy in the Negro world often enable them to act autocratically towards other Negroes, especially when they have the support of the white community. In such cases the delusion of power may provide an escape from their frustrations. It is generally, however, when middle-class Negroes hold positions enabling them to participate in the white community that they seek in the delusion of power an escape from their frustrations. Although their position may be only a "token" of the integration of the Negro into American life, they will speak and act as if they were a part of the power structure of American society. Negro advisers who are called into counsel by whites to give advice about Negroes are especially likely to find an escape from their feelings of inferiority in the delusion of power. Negro social workers, who are dependent upon white philanthropy, have often gained the reputation, with the support of the Negro press, of being powerful persons in American communities.

However, the majority of the black bourgeoisie who seek an escape from their frustrations in delusions seemingly have not been able to find it in the delusion of wealth or power. They have found it in magic or chance, and in sex and alcohol. Excessive drinking and sex seem to provide a means for narcotizing the middle-class Negro against a frustrating existence. A "social" function is hardly ever considered a success unless a goodly number of the participants "pass out." But gambling, especially poker, which has become an obsession among many middle-class Negroes, offers the chief escape into delusion. Among the black bourgeoisie it is not simply a device for winning money. It appears to be a magical device for enhancing their self-esteem through overcoming fate.[15] Although it often involves a waste of money which many middle-class Negroes cannot afford, it has an irresistible attraction which they often confess

they can not overcome.

Despite the tinsel, glitter and gaiety of the world of make-believe in which middle-class Negroes take refuge, they are still beset by feelings of insecurity, frustration and guilt. As a consequence, the free and easy life which they appear to lead is a mask for their unhappy existence.

## REFERENCES AND NOTES

1   E. Franklin Frazier, *Negro Youth at the Crossways*, Washington, D.C.: American Council on Education, 1940, p. 62.

2   *Ibid.*, p. 67.

3   *Ibid.*, p. 66.

4   See, for example, the article "YMCA Secretary in Virginia Fired for Equality Fight," *Washington Afro-American* August 1954, p. 20.

5   One cannot determine to what extent homosexuality among Negro males is due to the fact that they can not play a "masculine role."

6   See *Ebony*, July 1949, where it is claimed that a poll on the most exciting Negro men in the United States reveals that the heyday of the "glamour boy" is gone and achievement rather than a handsome face and husky physique is the chief factor in making Negro men exciting to women.

7   See Robert E. Park and Ernest W. Burgess, *Introduction to the Science of Sociology*, Chicago: University of Chicago Press, 1924, p. 139.

8   See Kardiner and Ovesey, *op. cit.*, pp. 312ff. concerning this point.

9   See Frazier, *The Negro Family in the United States*, pp. 440–443.

10  Robert E. Park, "Negro Home Life and Standards of Living," in *The Negro's Progress in Fifty Years*, Philadelphia: American Academy of Political and Social Science, 1913, p. 163.

11  A Middle-class mulatto woman, a former school teacher, who was fearful of the impact of this book on European readers and southern detractors of "The Race," concluded her review of the original French edition with these words: "Isn't it about time our sociologists and specialists on the 'race problem' in America began to discuss and consider middle class Negroes as middle class Americans, or better, *all* U.S. Negroes as *Americans* with three hundred unbroken years of American tradition, way of life, cultural and spiritual contacts behind them— influences which have moulded them as they have moulded all others who are considered, even when not treated completely so, as members of the American community? Isn't it time to stop thinking of and

talking about Negroes as a separate and distinct entity in the general scheme of things? And above all, isn't it time to realize that the melting pot has melted truly and fused together all the myriad (albeit conflicting) racial, cultural, educational, spiritual and social elements which have combined in such peculiar fashion to produce the American Negro of our time?" *Journal of Negro Education*, vol. 25, p. 141.

12  See Charles S. Johnson, *Patterns of Negro Segregation*, New York: Harper & Brothers, 1943, chaps. XII–XIV, which describe the ways in which Negroes in various classes deal with racial discrimination.

13  See Kardiner and Ovesey, *op. cit.*, pp. 190, 282, 297.

14  *Ibid.*, p. 177.

15  *Ibid.*, p. 203.

## 32   WHAT CHANCE FOR BLACK POWER?

### FRANCES FOX PIVEN    RICHARD A. CLOWARD

If there is a lesson in America's pluralistic history, it is that the ability of an outcaste minority to advance in the face of majority prejudices partly depends on its ability to develop countervailing power. It is extraordinary that so conventional an idea has evoked so bitter a controversy in the civil rights community. For, stripped of rhetoric, the idea of "black power" merely emphasizes the need to augment Negro influence by developing separatist institutions, ranging from economic enterprise to political organization.

Older civil rights organizations take umbrage at the separatist impulse because it appears to repudiate the principle of integration. Considering that ethnic labor unions, ethnic political machines and other ethnic institutions have been essential to the rise of various minorities, it is puzzling to hear it said that Negroes must restrain themselves from following the same course. Indeed, those institutions in the black community which are "integrated"—whether political organizations, the rackets, or social welfare agencies—actually contribute to black impotence, for they are integrated only in the sense that they are dominated by whites and serve white interests.

Those who are dismayed by the separatist position also fear that it will alienate liberal and labor

Reprinted with the permission of the authors and the publisher from *The New Republic*, vol. 158 (March 30, 1968), pp. 19–23. Copyright ©1968 by Harrison-Blaine of New Jersey, Inc.

allies. Blacks are a minority, to be sure, and cannot go it alone. But neither will they ever be more than a nominal participant in coalitions unless they are better organized; rather, their leaders will serve mostly to legitimize programs from which others' benefit. An organized group need not sit about debating the pros and cons of seeking allies; it will be sought out by others, and offered genuine concessions because it has strength to bring to any alliance. Those who now urge color-blind coalition are unable to show why the black poor would have more effective leverage in future alliances than they have had in the past.

Before damning black power for its principles or dooming it for its strategy, one should look at what the Negro has so far achieved without power, and what the future holds if his powerlessness persists.

The upheavals which are sometimes called "the Negro revolution"—the civil rights protests, the spreading violence in the cities, and the controversy over black power—are reflections of economic changes. When old patterns are rapidly undermined, dislocating masses of people, disorder often follows.

No group has been more acutely affected by technological change than the Negro, although the middle class and the poor have been affected quite differently. Educated Negroes are in demand in professional, scientific, and technical occupations because of the growing need for skilled manpower.

Since the end of World War II, the proportion of Negro families earning between $5,000 and $7,000 (in 1965 dollars adjusted for price changes) almost trebled and now approximates the proportion of whites in that income class. The proportion earning between $7,000 and $10,000 did treble and is now about two-thirds of the proportion of whites in that income group.

It was this rising class that launched the civil rights movement, especially the young of a newly arriving Southern bourgeoisie. As is often the case, ascending economic fortunes had themselves generated expectations which outpaced the actual rate of advance. Thus Negro colleges, once training grounds for a segregated elite, suddenly disgorged cadres to lead boycotts, freedom rides and sit-ins. Nor was this economic discrepancy the only source of discontent. A segregated society also deprived them of the symbols of prestige which normally accompany higher economic status. Spurred by these status discrepancies, the movement focused much of its energy on desegregating lunch counters and public accommodations.

Much of what was aspired to has been achieved —the legal and symbolic representations that American institutions were made "for whites only" are crumbling. That these features of our social life are collapsing so quickly (as these things go) is a mark of the extent to which they had become outmoded as a result of economic changes.

For the mass of black poor, however, the technological revolution has had less happy consequences. Although the proportion of poor families has dropped considerably in the past two decades, more than half of the black families in America still have incomes of less than $5,000, and one in four subsists on less than $3,000. Furthermore, apparent increases in income are often offset by the forced migration to the cities, where it costs more to live. Most ominous, the technological advances which made old patterns of segregation obsolete are also making a substantial segment of the black poor obsolete. Southern Negro sharecroppers, driven off the land by machines, can now eat at a desegregated lunch counter, take a desegregated interstate bus North, and arrive in a city with a fair employment ordinance—but no jobs. The mechanization of the farms they left is matched in the cities by the automation and decentralization of industry. Wherever black people are concentrated, North or South, true rates of unemployment (both those looking for work and those who have given up) range from 20 to 50 percent.

In the rural South, the more fortunate among the unemployed barely subsist on federal surplus commodities; the less fortunate starve. If they could get on the welfare rolls, people would have a bit of money, but they are kept off by a tangle of exclusionary laws, bureaucratic obstacles, and just plain illegal rejections. Feared at the polls and no longer needed in the fields, they are told to go North. As it happens, the women and children are more likely to get on welfare rolls in the North, provided that their men "desert" them first. And so unemployed husbands and fathers stand about "in hiding" on every ghetto street-corner. Meanwhile welfare administrators and politicians curry public favor by promoting job training for welfare mothers—but not for their men. At that, the women are trained for jobs that don't exist, or won't for long. The work they do get is in low-paid, dead-end jobs: in 1966, Negroes composed 42 percent of the private household work force and 25 percent of nonfarm laborers. Poor blacks, in brief, are being shut out of the economic system. They have progressed from slave labor to cheap labor to no labor at all.

The violence in the cities is the response of the black poor to their new social and economic condition, just as the civil rights protests were the response of the black middle class to their changing condition. It is not that poverty or unemployment produces mass discontent and violence, for if this were so no society could be stable. Rather, massive economic *displacement* may have a reverberative effect on other institutions, weakening their capacity to regulate sentiments and behavior, and culminating finally in violence.

The most obvious reverberation is the shift of populations from rural to urban areas. Blacks have become an urban people in just two or three decades, and this has set them loose from existing structures of social control. Although a repressive, feudalistic system persists in the South, a great many Negroes have been liberated from it just by no longer being there. Nor have they been absorbed by the main regulatory institutions of the city, especially the economic system. Ghetto institutions, such as churches and political machines, have also not incorporated them. Furthermore, the press of numbers is disrupting traditional accommodations upon which racial peace depends: the boundaries of previously sacrosanct white neighborhoods and schools are being breached, and white political power in city halls is threatened. When tensions rise as institutional controls weaken, the eruption of violence should not be surprising.

The splintering off of a segment of the civil rights movement—symbolized by the raised black fist and the cry of "black power"—is also a response to these upheavals. New conditions of life, by altering mass attitudes, undercut old patterns of leadership. Traditional Negro elites who have maintained their hegemony by serving as the agents of white power and resources are being challenged by new aspirants to leadership whose insistent nationalism reflects the current mood of discontent. And whatever else may be said of its rhetoric—the language of violence and the allusions to revolution—black power, by calling on people to be, feel, think and act black, is fostering a new sense of community in the ghetto, especially among the young. This is a hopeful trend, for solidarity is one prerequisite to the political power without which the mass of black poor cannot advance economically.

There is no doubt that major governmental action will be taken to deal with disruptions in the cities. Corporation executives and mayors, union officials and presidential aspirants—men whose interests are in one way or another threatened by urban disorder—are agreed in demanding federal programs to stem rising municipal costs, "crime in the streets" and riots. But while this "urban coalition" wants to ease urban trouble, the groups it includes have interests quite at odds with those of the black poor. And experience shows that the poor have good reason to be apprehensive about programs formed in their name by the powerful.

To appreciate the grounds for apprehension, look at the differences between government programs for the organized and unorganized poor. In response to the crisis in the thirties, the federal government proclaimed its responsibility for the poor but promulgated legislation favoring those of the urban poor who, already partly organized in unions and political machines, were important to the newly formed Democratic coalition. Political leaders pressed through a series of social welfare measures designed to protect the urban worker—unemployment compensation, old age and survivors insurance, and housing subsidies for those with moderate incomes. More important, workers got concessions that nourished their organizations, especially the Wagner Act, which gave them the right to bargain collectively and thus made the growth and stabilization of unions possible—membership expanded from three million in 1930 to 14 million in 1945. In this way, the working classes were able to make gains in the economic system, and to guard governmental programs designed for them.

The poor who lacked political power were left behind. The worst poverty still exists among those who did not win collective bargaining rights by legislation, such as agricultural laborers. In the cities, the still unorganized black masses continue to be victimized by programs ostensibly intended for their benefit. Consider, for example, the public welfare programs enacted in 1935 which promised decent subsistence for everyone; three decades later, the average family of four on ADC (Aid to Dependent Children) gets only $1,800 a year. The Public Housing Act of 1937 proclaimed the goal of providing decent housing for the poor; today there are about 10 million substandard dwelling units in the country, for only 600,000 units of public housing have been constructed. Our national policy of full employment, enunciated by legislation in 1946, has proved to be meaningless rhetoric.

Worse yet, manifestly egalitarian measures have been turned against the poor. Federal agricultural subsidies, established to aid all farmers, actually helped to bankrupt small ones and enrich large ones. The Housing Act of 1949 asserted the right of every American to "a decent and standard dwelling unit," but initiated the Urban Renewal Program that destroyed 350,000 low-rental housing units in the course of reclaiming slum neighborhoods for commercial facilities and better-off residents. Several hundred thousand more low-rental homes were demolished during the same period by public works and federal highway construction—programs also put forward under the banner of improving the urban environment. Indeed, these programs "for the community as a whole" have succeeded in destroying more low-rental units than government has constructed since the Public Housing Act was passed.

Finally, what concessions the unorganized poor did get actually inhibited their capacity for political action. This is especially true of public welfare and public housing programs in which benefits are made conditional on compliant behavior by recipients. The poor, dealt with as supplicants by functionaries who can evict them or cut off their checks at will, are rendered more helpless in exchange for the benefits they receive.

New proclamations about action to help the poor are now being made, and new programs discussed. But what reason is there to suppose that these measures will not also be tokenistic, or turned to serve the interests of other groups, or designed to intimidate the recipients still more? For the simple truth is that governmental action has not worked for the unorganized poor and is not likely to work for them in the future unless they become a political force in initiating and shaping it.

If the history of past programs is not fully convincing, consider the major proposal now being advanced to ease violence in the cities—namely, that public subsidies be used to spur investments by national corporations in ghetto housing and employment. This plan is being promoted by alliances of corporation executives and political leaders,

with representatives of organized labor and civil rights bringing up the flank.

The corporate interest in these proposals reflects more than a response to the promise of subsidized profit-making. Violence in the cities results in the wholesale destruction of property. And the spreading disorder, threatening to pit racial groups against each other in armed conflict, undermines the civic stability on which large-scale enterprise depends.

Moreover, corporate enterprise can now take a benevolent stance toward blacks because it no longer has a major stake in domestic racism. At an earlier stage of production, racism helped to depress the cost of labor by ensuring a supply of cheap black workers as well as a supply of scabs to inhibit union organizing among whites. But labor costs are now a less important factor in profits, and union organization has turned out to be an advantage in stabilizing and regulating the work force. Racism is no longer an economic asset; by threatening social stability, it has become a liability.

Corporate investments will result in quick improvements in the ghetto. But what pressure will there be for continuing and expanding investments once order is restored? Other markets are more profitable, and national political leaders can derive greater political advantage by turning subsidies to larger or more influential groups—such as suburbanites. Furthermore, if national corporations absorb the subsidies for programs ranging from manpower training to redevelopment, no black enterprise will emerge. The ghetto will merely become a subsidized market to be exploited by white enterprise; once again, it will be weakened by a coalition acting in its name. There is, in short, good reason for poor blacks to beware of corporate representatives bearing tax-deductible gifts.

How, then, are the black poor to develop greater political influence? Some observers point to the fact that the growing concentration of blacks in the central cities is making them a substantial electoral force. Earlier groups of the poor, it is noted, exploited the resources and powers of municipal government to aid their rise in the economic order; why not blacks as well? The parallel is far from exact, as we shall show. For the moment, however, let us assume that the black community is not weaker than earlier ethnic communities, and that city government is as important in the federal system as it once was.

First, as majorities in the cities, or even as large voting blocs, blacks would have the means to prevent the recurrent incursions on the ghetto by urban renewal, highway construction, and public works programs. At the same time, funds now being spent on others could be directed to improving ghetto services and facilities. Municipal power might also be used to force private enterprise and unions to admit Negroes. Public officials have numerous sources of leverage: they fix budget allocations for services and projects, approve private construction plans, and decide whether to pass on requests for state and federal grants. Each of these decisions is an occasion to exact concessions from other groups. Employers who want city contracts can be induced to hire and promote blacks. Similarly, unions can be opened to Negroes by blocking approvals for new construction or by threatening to reform archaic building codes on which their jobs partly depend.

These powers also offer a way for blacks to gain access to the more desirable neighborhoods now occupied by the white working and middle classes. Black government can override resistance to public housing in white areas and enforce bans on discrimination in the rental and sale of housing. Where public officials are elected on a precinct basis, the spread of blacks would entrench their political control by assuring majorities in each district.

Acquiring access to white institutions is one way to advance; developing black instutional relationships to the society is another and more important way. Separatist institutional development will not take place quickly, but in the long run its effects could be profound, for nothing about the Negro community is more conspicuous than the absence of its own institutions. In part, this condition is a heritage of slavery and of laws passed in

the wake of Reconstruction which prohibited free assembly and the formation of assocations among Negroes. The traditional isolation of most blacks in rural and feudalistic settings has also inhibited the formation of institutions, especially of a kind that would be viable in the city.

The need for communal institutions is one of the major themes of black power advocates. And municipal control could be the key. Where else is the money to come from to foster such a development? The black poor are very poor, indeed, and they confront an economy dominated by large-scale corporations, in which the would-be entrepreneur has far less likelihood of success than in the more open economy of the past. Nor can much be expected of efforts to unionize blacks, for many of them, if they work at all, are in occupations too marginal and dispersed to be organized effectively (e.g., domestic service). Moreover, the black middle classes will not lead a separatist development; they have been absorbed into white institutions and cannot be enticed back unless substantial occupational rewards are available. To overcome these obstacles, blacks need the resources controlled by municipal officials—contracts for all manner of projects and services to nurture new enterprises, as well as the leverage over white economic interests to induce them to deal with black enterprises. In these ways urban power might in time enable the black community to develop the infra-structure which has served other groups so well, especially black economic enterprise and black labor unions to organize the workers in the resulting jobs.

Finally, greater black influence in national politics depends on strong local organization capable of promoting electoral participation and assuring discipline. To build organization, black leaders need the platform of municipal office to reward their followers. For all these reasons, many now see the city as the hope for the Negro.

But the prospects for black urban power, as we have just defined them, rest on the erroneous assumption that American politics are formed by voting numbers alone. The conventions of electoral politics are regularly subverted in many ways. Those already holding power will not yield the spoils of office quickly or easily to new majorities. Even when official representation is achieved, responsiveness by government requires a constituency capable of watching over and pressuring officials. To be sure, blacks will assume nominal power in the cities because of the sheer weight of their numbers; but compared to earlier groups, blacks have few organizational ropes to keep rein on their leaders. Black officials will find themselves confronted by a variety of well-organized white groups—such as unions of public employees—who have the power to obstruct the business of government. They will be pressed to defer to these white interests, and an unorganized black constituency will give them the slack to do it. Although it may be too soon to draw conclusions, the first statements and appointments of Cleveland's newly elected black mayor suggest just such conciliation of whites.

Moreover, local government has been greatly weakened since the heyday of the ethnic urban machine. Localities now collect a mere seven percent of tax revenues, while the federal government collects two-thirds. This fiscal weakness underlies the great vulnerability of local government to national centralized power, reflected both in the schemes for intervention by national corporations discussed earlier, and in new encroachments by the federal government under the guise of metropolitan planning.

The national government is using its multitude of existing programs for localities to form a new system of metropolitan-wide bureaucracies. This new level of government will impose federal policies on localities in the course of channeling grants-in-aid to them.

The need for metro administration is commonly justified on the ground that the concentration of people in sprawling urban areas has produced a host of problems—transportation, water supply, pollution control—which transcend narrow municipal boundaries. The solution of these problems is said to require programs planned and implemented on a metropolitan basis. For some problems, per-

haps so; however, many urban problems remain unsolved, not for lack of area-wide planning, but for lack of political will. That communities do not apply for federal funds to build public housing needs no explanation beyond local reluctance to house the poor and black. Nevertheless, metro bureaucracies are emerging, and they will supersede the cities just as blacks come to power.

Whose interests will the federal metro agencies reflect? It takes no special acumen to see the answer. Their policies will be formed in deference to the inner-city and suburban whites who are an overwhelming majority in the metro region. Thus programs for the inner city will be designed to protect and ease the ethnic working classes, the residual middle class, and corporate groups with heavy property investment in the core. And there will be suburban services and facilities to meet the needs of decentralizing industry and white residents, whose electoral power now exceeds that of inner-city populations. Judging from the past, programs for blacks will be designed to treat their presumed deficiencies—to engender "good work habits and incentives," strengthen family life, improve mental health.

If the black middle class has so far benefited from technological change, it will prosper even more from the corporate-metro solutions to the urban crisis. To smooth the path of intervention, the black middle class will be absorbed into white corporate and metropolitan agencies. It should not be surprising, therefore, that these new approaches are already being hailed by Negro elites. The rationale given is that they will further integration—metropolitanism is said to be the way to breach the wall between ghetto and suburb in housing and education, and corporate programs the way to promote economic integration. But as metropolitan administrations take control, they are not likely to promote the dispersal of blacks to white neighborhoods in the face of resistance by an area-wide majority; meanwhile, white corporate control will be extended to the ghetto. Thus these new systems will enable whites, even as the ideal of integration is invoked, to maintain political and economic hegemony over the black masses.

The black poor, then, have few prospects for political or economic advancement. Because of the current disruptions, they will get a few concessions to restore tranquillity. But once the cities are tranquillized, what then? As we have said, the main chance for black power is in the cities, but the odds are lengthening. If there is a question to be debated, it is not whether the idea of black power is desirable; it is whether the power of this idea can prevail in the face of the continuing centralization of corporate and federal power over the city.

## 33 ASSIMILATION IN AMERICAN LIFE  MILTON M. GORDON

We are now ready to assess the meaning of the foregoing analysis for the field of intergroup relations. As noted on the opening page of this volume, we are concerned ultimately with problems of prejudice and discrimination; however, our study has focused directly not on individual psychological states and activities related to ethnically prejudiced behavior, but rather on the nature and structure of group life itself in the United States. We have pursued this line of analysis not out of a conviction that individual psychological states are unimportant in explaining the phenomena under consideration but rather because of a firm belief that group life and social structure constitute the matrix in which cumulative psychological states are embedded, that the latter cannot be thoroughly understood without reference to the former, and that social structure and group life have been relatively neglected as dynamic factors in etiological analysis of racial and cultural prejudice.

To put the matter in another way, one may consider racial and cultural prejudice in America in two different contexts. One is to think of 190 million American individuals, some of whom happen to be white Protestant, some white Catholic, some Jewish, some Negro, etc. We then ask why some of these individuals are ethnically prejudiced

and others not, or only partly so, and then concentrate on studying the personality syndromes (and their etiological roots) of the various types along the prejudice continuum. Much valuable research has been carried out along these lines. Our inquiry has been substantially different, although the two approaches can be considered complementary rather than competing or mutually exclusive. We have chosen to focus on the nature of group life itself in the United States as constituting the social setting in which relationships among persons of differing race, religion, and national origin take place. For these 190 million Americans are not just individuals with psychological characteristics. They belong to groups: primary groups and secondary groups, family groups, social cliques, associations or formal organizations, networks of associations, racial, religious, and national origins groups, and social classes. And the nature of these groups and their interrelationships has a profound impact upon the way in which people of different ethnic backgrounds regard and relate to one another.

In particular, we have called attention to the nature of the ethnic group itself as a large subsociety, criss-crossed by social class, and containing its own primary groups of families, cliques, and associations—its own network of organizations and institutions—in other words, as a highly structured community within the boundaries of which an individual may, if he wishes, carry out most of his more meaningful life activities from the cradle to the grave. We have pointed to the considerable body of evidence which suggests that the various ethnic varieties of Americans, excepting the intellectuals, tend to remain within their own ethnic group and social class for most of their intimate, primary group relationships, interacting with other ethnic and class varieties of Americans largely in impersonal secondary group relationships. The United States, we have argued, is a multiple melting pot in which acculturation for all groups beyond the first generation of immigrants, without eliminating all value conflict, has been massive and decisive, but in which structural separation on the basis of race and religion—structural pluralism, as we have called it—emerges as the dominant sociological condition. The implications of this analytical description of American group life for intergroup relations will now occupy our attention. The following remarks will vary considerably in the generality of their theme and the specificity of their conclusions and recommendations. Furthermore, they will, from time to time, call into play certain ideological premises which will at such times be carefully identified. With these considerations in mind we are ready to proceed to a discussion of the implications of our analysis seriatim.

## STRUCTURAL SEPARATION, FUNCTIONAL CONSEQUENCES, AND PREJUDICE

Recent studies have pointed to the role of intimate equal-status contact between members of majority and minority groups in reducing prejudice.[1] Structural separation, by definition, denotes a situation in which primary group contacts between members of various ethnic groups are held to a minimum, even though secondary contacts on the job, on the civic scene, and in other areas of impersonal contact may abound. In view of the tendency of human beings to categorize in their psychic perceptions and reactions and to form in-groups and, frequently, out-groups on the basis of familiar experiences and contacts,[2] it may be plausibly argued that just as intimate primary group relations tend to reduce prejudice, a lack of such contacts tends to promote ethnically hostile attitudes. It should be carefully noted that we are not thereby

concluding that prejudice and discrimination cannot be reduced under conditions of structural pluralism; nor, indeed, that structural pluralism is necessarily undesirable from a philosophical point of view. Obviously, even from a sociological viewpoint, the matter is one of degree and should be discussed in that context.

On the one hand, structural separation of ethnic groups, brought about in part by the prejudices of the majority and in part by the desire of most such groups to maintain their own communal identity and subculture, can proceed to a point which is dysfunctional both for the creation of desirable attitudes and relations between the groups and for the workable operation of the society itself. The operation of modern urbanized industrial society is predicated upon the assurance of the easy interchangeability and mobility of individuals according to occupational specialization and needs. The fulfillment of occupational roles, the assignment of living space, the selection of political leaders, and the effective functioning of the educational process, among others, demand that universalistic criteria of competence and training, rather than considerations based on racial, religious, or nationality background, be utilized. The subversion of this principle by ethnic considerations would appear bound to produce, in the long run, confusion, conflict, and mediocrity. American society has not moved as far in this direction of "compartmentalization" or "columnization" as have certain other countries such as Holland and Lebanon,[3] but a trend toward this type of structural organization in America may well be in the making. As Lenski has cautioned, after surveying the data from his study of socio-religious groups in Detroit:

Currently we seem merely to be drifting into a type of social arrangement which Americans of all faiths might well reject if they became fully aware of all it entails.

This problem should be of special concern to religious leaders. Our current drift toward a "compartmentalized society" could easily produce a situation where individuals developed a heightened sense of religious group loyalty combined with a minimal sense of responsibility for those outside their own group. In a more compartmentalized society there is good reason to fear a weakening of the ethical and spiritual elements in religion and a heightening of the ever dangerous political elements. Such a development would be a serious departure from the basic ideals of all of the major faiths in America, sharing as they do in the Biblical tradition. Hence, on both religious and political grounds, Americans might do well to study more critically than they yet have the arguments advanced by advocates of pluralistic society.[4]

With regard to prejudice itself, it would seem reasonable to conclude that excessive compartmentalization or structural separation, since it prevents the formation of those bonds of intimacy and friendship which bind human beings together in the most meaningful moments of life and serve as a guard-wall against the formation of disruptive stereotypes, sets up the conditions under which ethnic prejudice will grow and flourish. It is possible that even a modest degree of structural separation will tend always to have as a sociological concomitant a low, endemic degree of prejudice among the various ethnic groups (varying considerably, of course, for individuals). This is by no means a counsel of despair and is in no way meant to discourage the attempts to combat prejudice and discrimination by those standard means currently being used by various agencies, private and public. At the very least, however, it suggests that one may not be able to eat *all* of one's cake and have it too, and it puts high on the agenda the carrying out of research focused on the causal relationship between degrees and types of structural separation and the holding of ethnically prejudiced attitudes. It makes mandatory, too, careful consideration by those ethnic agencies, institutions, and officials (of whatever religion, race, or nationality) of the desirability of program and policy measures calculated to produce a heightening of the level of structural separation now existing among the various ethnic groups in America. Furthermore, it raises questions about the ultimate desirability of the acquiescence by manifestly community-wide

civic agencies and programs (of which the Boy Scouts and Girl Scouts are salient examples) in organizational segregation at the local level according to religion, as a result of the stipulations of religious communal leaders and officials.

The characteristic disclaimer by denominational communal leaders that "We want our people to participate actively in *both* denominational organizations and activities *and* community-wide organizations and affairs" must be measured against the simple reality that people's time and energy are not infinite in extent and, in fact, are bounded by substantial limitations. If the ordinary citizen is continually exhorted by his ethnic leaders to participate unreservedly in the ever-expanding array of ethnic-enclosed communal institutions springing up at all age levels, he will, in fact, have little or no resources of time and energy left to participate in those agencies and activities of the broader community that through their broader perspective and membership bind the religious, racial, and nationality groups of America into a viable nation—a nation that for reasons of both sociological health and traditional political ideals must strive to be substantially more than an instrumental federation of mutually suspicious ethnic groups.

## STRUCTURAL AND CULTURAL PLURALISM: LEGITIMATION AND RELATIONSHIP TO DEMOCRATIC VALUES

Although we have just finished warning of the dangers of an excessive degree of structural pluralism, our second point calls attention to the overwhelming reality of this form of social organization in America, to the extreme unlikelihood that its essential outlines will be changed in the foreseeable future, and to the need for demonstrating to the public consciousness that structural and cultural pluralism in moderate degree are not incompatible with American democratic ideals. The evidence we have examined indicates that, apart from the subsociety of the intellectuals, intimate primary group relations between members of different racial and religious groups in the United States remain at a minimal level. This structural separation provides for the preservation of the communal nature of the ethnic group, and, in the case of the major religious denominations, makes for the retention of a core of differentiated religious beliefs, values, and historical symbols important to the loyal members of the faith. To this extent, one is entitled to say that structural pluralism in America is accompanied by a moderate degree of cultural pluralism as well. There is certainly nothing in the democratic value-complex shared by most Americans and anchored in the country's historical traditions which dictates that these differentiated historico-religious values and their cultural concomitants should perforce be merged into one over-all religious system, or that Catholics and Jews should abandon their religion and convert to Protestantism. Nor does the American democratic value-creed imply that the citizens of this land do not have the right to choose their intimate friends and their organizational affiliations on the basis of whatever criteria of likeness and congeniality they find it convenient and desirable to utilize. To put it another way, subsocietal affiliation and participation in America, so far as the state is concerned, are voluntary matters (notwithstanding the fact that informal social pressures ascribe such affiliation on the basis of birth—that is, on the basis of the parents' affiliation), and the voluntary selection of structural and subsocietal affiliations, within functional limits, is well within the area of personal choice provided for by democratic values.

This position, of course, in no way justifies the use of racial or religious criteria in employment, housing, education, access to public facilities, or any other area in which functional benefits crucial to the fulfillment of human personality and the general welfare are concerned. In other words, it does not justify *discrimination*. But it does reserve the matter of choice in intimate primary group relationships for personal decision on whatever grounds the individual may elect to use. By the same token, it enjoins the state or any private citizen or group of citizens from interfering with those individuals who wish to form primary group relationships *across* racial or religious lines. There is no justification, for instance, in the value system of either political democracy or the Hebraic-Christian religious tradition for state or municipal laws forbidding social relationships between whites and Negroes (or other racial groups) up to and including the marriage relationship.

Finally, then, if a moderate degree of structural and cultural pluralism are legitimated by the American Creed, legitimation should be made salient in the public consciousness. For to legitimate and explain the system as it actually operates is to justify it and help to draw away the animus that many Americans have toward minority groups which, in their minds, do not "assimilate" or "melt"—in other words, do not merge into the white Protestant population, give up their communal identity, and relinquish their cultural differences in crucial areas of belief and practice. As we have indicated, for those who do not wish to "merge" to this extent, ample justification in the American value system exists. The legitimation of pluralism and the projection into the public consciousness of its justification and its reality on the American scene would also help to dispel the erroneous conclusion that it is only this group or that group that desires to maintain communal separation. In this respect, the Jews have frequently been singled out as a "separatist" minority; "clannish" is the adjective often applied. As our study has shown, although they do not succeed with the intellectuals, all of the major religious faiths—Jews, Catholics, and Protestants—operate functionally so as to perpetuate ethnic communality in the general population. The Protestants are least aware of the process since their majority status and historical precedence in America tend to make them unaware of the Protestant assumptions and criteria operative in many of the institutions which are labeled as "American" and "community-wide." Being the majority group, numerically, also tends to lessen objectively the possibility of the erosion of Protestant ethnic communality and cultural values through the process of intermarriage and other types of interethnic primary relationships. Thus Protestants have less to lose in encouraging ethnic mixture.

Our point, in sum, is not that interethnic primary group contacts are undesirable. Quite the contrary. It is rather that since many, perhaps most, members of the major faiths (and, among racial groups, notably the American Indians) basically desire some form of ethnic communality and subcultural preservation, both the reality of the system and its justification in the American value creed should be clearly brought home to the American population as a whole.

## PLURALISM AND ASSIMILATION: GUIDELINES FOR AGENCIES CONCERNED WITH ORIENTING THE IMMIGRANT TO AMERICAN LIFE

The analysis which we have made of the assimilation process, the factoring out of the various subtypes of assimilation, and the discussion of the interaction of these subtypes, theoretically and empirically on the American scene, suggest a number of guidelines for those agencies and institutions concerned with the adjustment of immigrants and their descendants to American life and culture. These may be listed as follows:

1 Structural assimilation of immigrants to the United States (that is, the first generation arriving as adults), who enter the country in numbers substantial enough to make feasible a communal life of their own, is both impossible of attainment in most cases and undesirable as a goal toward which pressure on the immigrant might conceivably be exercised. While exceptional individuals will occasionally assimilate structurally into a native American subsociety—in many cases, the community of intellectuals—the great majority of newcomers to the country will need and prefer the security of a communal life made up of their fellow-immigrants from the homeland. This generalization is particularly applicable to immigrants of peasant, working-class, and lower-middle-class backgrounds, whose perspectives and orientations, on a statistical basis, will be inevitably narrow; however, it encompasses the great majority of immigrants of higher class origins, as well, who, in any case, are less likely to arrive in large numbers. Thus, efforts, however well-intentioned, to force structural assimilation

on the immigrant are likely to be both futile and tension-producing. The newcomer needs the comfortable sociological and psychological milieu which the communality of his own group provides. Even those individuals who eventually will make major structural contact with native subsocieties can profitably use the communal base of their own group to make their initial adjustment and to fall back upon if their tentative interethnic primary group contacts prove unsatisfactory. Immigrant-adjustment agencies, then, should not waste their time and energy in attempting to promote structural assimilation on a massive scale but should accept the functional desirability of immigrant communal life with good grace. In this area, they might well limit their efforts to making significant opportunities for primary group contacts with native Americans available as alternatives on a thoroughly voluntary basis for that relatively small minority of immigrants who wish to and can meaningfully make use of such opportunities for broadening their communal life.

2 The major efforts of immigrant-adjustment agencies, then, should be directed toward acculturation, or cultural assimilation, and even here in modest degree and in selected areas. The basic goal should be the adjustment of the immigrant to American culture and institutions in those areas of secondary group and institutional contact which permit him to obtain and keep a job commensurate with his potential and training, to receive appropriate retraining and education where necessary, to perform adequately his role as a potential future citizen of both the nation and the local community, and to raise his children in ways which will neither do emotional violence to the traditions of the homeland nor subvert the family socialization process congenial to child-rearing in a basically middle-class American culture. This places the emphasis on the provision of instrumental skills: adequate use of the English language not at the expense of (nor denigration of) but in addition to the native tongue, occupational training, orientation to standard technological devices, knowledge of how to make use of the vast array of

American educational opportunities, sophistication in citizenship adjustment, voting behavior, and participation in the political process generally. The functional goal would be the successful relationship of the immigrant, both culturally and structurally, to the secondary groups and instrumental institutional areas of American life. Changing the direction or nature of his intimate, primary group communal life would be excluded as a feasible or desirable product of directed effort.

3 The institutional and subcultural life of the immigrant community should be regarded not only as a necessary concession to the sociological and psychological health of the new American but as providing a positive and effective means of enabling such a degree of acculturation as is posited as desirable and feasible in the paragraph above. The forms and devices of the immigrant community face two ways. On the one hand, providing the indispensable comfortable milieu, they continue the newcomer's orientation to the culture of the old country and the old locality, to its familiar ways of doing things, to its current history and its current gossip. On the other hand, they gradually incorporate elements of the American culture, interpret that culture to the newcomer in ways which he can understand, and sift its elements and bring them to his attention in a degree and at a pace which muffles and makes bearable the shock of cultural collision. The immigrant's burial and insurance societies, his indigenous church, his "foreign language" press, his favorite cafés and coffee houses, his old-style theatrical entertainments, his network of social cliques and "nationality" organizations, his ceremonies and folk dances, are never created or recreated simply as replicas of old country elements; they always progressively reflect the influence of American conditions and American events, serving as a sturdy bridge between the old and the new. In a word, the immigrant subsociety mediates between the native culture of the immigrant and the American culture. The recognition of this fact is the indispensable prerequisite for effective use of the communication channels and influence networks of the immigrant's communal life to aid and encourage the achievement of worth-while acculturation goals.

4 The American-born children of immigrants, the second generation, with exceptions based on the existence of a few rigidly enclosed enclaves, should be realistically viewed as a generation irreversibly on its way to virtually complete acculturation (although not necessarily structural assimilation) to native American cultural values at selected class levels. Exposed to the overwhelming acculturative powers of the public school and the mass communications media, the immigrants' children will proffer their unhesitating allegiance to those aspects of the American cultural system which are visible to them in their particular portion of the socio-economic structure. The feasible and necessary task of the immigrant-adjustment agencies, in this area, is to aid in making this acculturative transition as smooth as possible, in view of the many potential difficulties, for both the children and their parents.

The tendency will be for native-born children to become alienated from their immigrant parents and the culture they represent, as they respond affirmatively to the higher status American cultural values. The challenge for social welfare agencies and institutions in the immigration field is, without mounting a doomed effort to stem the inevitable tide of American acculturation, to aid the second-generation child to gain a realistic degree of positive regard for the cultural values of his ethnic background, which will hardly retard the acculturation process, but which will give the child a healthier psychological base for his confrontation with American culture and for his sense of identification with and response to his parents. Such an effort should not preclude, of course, the encouragement of the development of effective English language skills, since this development is indispensable to adequate adjustment to American life. Nor do these counsels obviate the need to deal with the interconnected problems that the second-generation child traditionally faces as a member of a minority group, subject to some degree of prejudice and discrimination, and as a person being socialized in the lower and underprivileged sector of the socio-economic environment.

## DESEGREGATION, INTEGRATION, AND THE ROLE OF GOVERNMENT

Our sociological focus on the phenomenon of ethnic communality in the United States suggests certain important implications for the current controversies surrounding the attempts to eliminate racial discrimination by law—a series of events launched into full motion by the Supreme Court school desegregation decision of 1954.

The basic theoretical distinction which it is necessary to make in the types of processes involved in these turbulent happenings has been well delineated by Kenneth Clark, who points to the differences between *desegregation* and *integration*.[5] Desegregation refers to the elimination of racial criteria in the operation of public or quasi-public facilities, services, and institutions, which the individual is entitled to as a functioning citizen of the local or national community, equal in legal status to all other citizens. It is the achievement in full of what is usually referred to as his "civil rights." Integration, however, embraces the idea of the removal of prejudice as well as civic discrimination and therefore refers to much more. In Clark's words, "Integration, as a subjective and individual process, involves attitudinal changes and the removal of fears, hatreds, suspicions, stereotypes, and superstitions. Integration involves problems of personal choice, personal readiness, and personal stability. Its achievement necessarily requires a longer period of time. It cannot come about 'overnight.' It requires education and deals poignantly with the problems of changing men's hearts and minds."[6] To which we would add that, in social structural terms, integration presupposes the elimination of hard and fast barriers in the primary group relations and communal life of the various ethnic groups of the nation. It involves easy and fluid mixture of people of diverse racial, religious, and nationality backgrounds in social cliques, families (i.e., intermarriage), private organizations, and intimate friendships. From this basic distinction

between desegregation and integration, and the relation of this distinction to both sociological realities and the American democratic value system, a number of conclusions follow:

1 Desegregation—the process of eliminating racial discrimination in the operation of public and quasi-public institutional facilities—will not lead *immediately* or, in the intermediate future, *necessarily* to integration in the sense of the dissolution of ethnic communality and the formation of large-scale primary group relationships across racial and religious lines. The tendency toward ethnic communality, as we have demonstrated, is a powerful force in American life and is supported, once the ethnic subsociety is formed, by the principles of psychological inertia, comfortable social immersion, and vested interests. Even if all southern public schools and other public facilities were to be immediately desegregated, there is no reason to suppose that the Negro and the white subcommunities would merge into one another or that the traditional barriers to intimate friendships and relationships between Negroes and white would at once come tumbling down. Certainly there is no basis for the belief that Negroes and whites, respectively encapsulated in their own subcommunity and subculture, would rush to marry each other. This sociological insight, it will be noted, is offered here in a spirit of scientific neutrality and not as a conclusion which is either good or bad from the point of view of some particular value system. I have already pointed out that, on the basis of traditional American democratic values, Negroes and whites should have the right to make close friendships and to marry across racial lines at their pleasure. But sociological realities do not indicate that these phenomena would be likely to take place in significant volume in the immediate future, even if all public and institutional discrimination were to be eliminated. If die-hard segregationists who now bitterly oppose the granting of full civic equality to Negroes could be made to understand this fact, it is possible that the debate over desegregation could be carried out in a less emotional and a more rational climate of discus-

sion and action. It is necessary to repeat that this point is not a concession to any *right* of segregationists to bar interracial primary group relationships; it is a statement of sociological probabilities which, if correctly understood, might clear the way for more rapid and effective action in such areas as public education, public transportation, public recreation, jobs, housing, and the operation of ordinary institutional facilities which belong to all Americans on an equal basis.

2 The proper role of government in racial and ethnic matters, under the American democratic system, can be defined in three steps:

1 It is the responsibility of the government to effect desegregation—that is, to eliminate racial criteria—in the operation of all of its facilities and services at all levels, national, state, and local. The American democratic value system and the specific constitutional expression of these values in the Fifth Amendment and the three Civil War Amendments to the Federal Constitution, particularly the Fourteenth, with its clause enjoining the state from depriving any person of the "equal protection of the laws," provide the legal mandate for such a ban, and the execution of this mandate demands action (some of which, it should be noted, has already been taken) in the form of legislation, court orders, or executive orders, in such areas as jobs, housing, voting, education, service in the armed forces, and access to public facilities. Since the national government, through grants, loans, and purchasing, now has a hand in so many types of activities which were once exclusively private or, if public, purely within the scope of states and municipalities, the way is opened for entirely legitimate pressure to be exerted by the national government on recalcitrant or hesitant local governments, businesses, institutions, and individuals who still want to preserve the old segregated pattern but are reluctant to dispense with federal largesse. There will inevitably be some areas of activity where the question of whether there actually is governmental participation of sufficient scope to warrant a judgment that "state action" applies will be unclear;[7] these matters can only be decided by

subsequent judicial decision. Nevertheless, the major goal of getting the government—the focal expression of the will and welfare of all the people of the country—out of the business of supporting racial discrimination, either directly or indirectly, remains both clear and irreproachable.

2 It is neither the responsibility nor the prerogative of the government to attempt to impose integration, as here defined—that is, to take official notice of personal attitudes and preferences (beyond the ordinary teaching process in the public schools where standard facts and interpretations underlie the curriculum), and to interfere in any way with those personal choices in primary group relationships and organizational affiliations which make either for ethnic communality or interethnic mixture, as the case may be. I except here specific incitations to violence and, of course, paramilitary operations which threaten law and order. In short, the ordinary processes of communality, whether intra-ethnic or interethnic are beyond the scope of governmental interference or concern.

3 It is neither the responsibility nor the prerogative of the government to use racial criteria positively in order to impose desegregation upon public facilities in an institutional area where such segregation is not a function of racial discrimination directly but results from discrimination operating in another institutional area, or from other causes. If institutional area *A* is *de facto* segregated not because of the direct use of racial criteria but because institutional area *B* is segregated and because there is a relationship between institutional areas *A* and *B*, then the place to fight discrimination is not *A* but *B*. The obvious case in point is the operation of the public school system. The attempt by well-meaning "race liberals" in a number of northern communities to desegregate public schools by overturning the principle of neighborhood assignment—that is, to positively promote Negro-white intermixture by means of racial assignment across neighborhood lines—is, in my opinion, misguided. It is misguided because it does exactly what is in principle wrong, regardless of how laudable the goal. It puts the government in the business of using race as a criterion for opera-

ting one of its facilities. This is precisely what the government should not be doing, either negatively or positively. The genius of the American political tradition, in its best sense, in relation to race is that it dictates that racial criteria are *not* legitimate in the operation of governmental facilities and should be rigorously eschewed. To bring racial criteria in by the front door, so to speak, even before throwing them out the back, represents, in my opinion, no real gain for the body politic and has potentially dangerous implications for the future. If racial criteria are legitimate criteria for government consideration (which I firmly argue they are not), then the way is left open for many ominous disputes as to the merits of any particular racial clause in governmental operations.

It should be understood that I am making no specific plea here for the particular merits of the principle of neighborhood assignment to public schools. This is a matter which the educationists can debate among themselves. Furthermore, where inferior facilities in a school in a predominantly Negro area exist, or Negroes or members of any ethnic group are not appointed to teaching positions on the basis of individual qualifications, then we are in the presence of legitimate cases of racial discrimination which call for effective remedy.[8] My basic point, however, is that if *de facto* segregation of public schools in many northern cities exists because of segregation in housing (which, of course, it does), the place to fight the battle of civil rights is housing, not the public school system, and the way to fight it is to eliminate racial criteria from the routes of access to housing space, not to inject them into the operation of the educational system.

It is unwise and unjustifiable for the government to create programs labeled and reserved for the benefit of any special racial group, or to set up racial quotas in any area of activity such as employment, as is currently demanded by some civil rights proponents. It is undeniable that the burden of unemployment bears most heavily at present on Negroes, as a result of the cumulation of past discriminatory events. However, there are white, Indian, and Oriental unemployed workers who need

aid, also, and any government program designed to retrain or upgrade the job skills of occupationally disadvantaged Americans should include them as well. In other words, it should be set up as an all-inclusive "functional" rather than an exclusive racial program. It goes without saying that job hiring and promotion at all levels should be made on the basis of individual merit, not racial quotas, however "benignly" the latter may be motivated. Present wrongs do not solve the problems created by past injustices and only assure that the underlying social evil will further plague the future. We do not want "see-saw discrimination" in American life; we want the dismantling of the discriminatory apparatus.

In sum, the proper role of government is to deal equitably with all persons under its jurisdiction without taking into consideration their racial background for any purpose.

## DESEGREGATION, INTEGRATION, AND PRIVATE INSTITUTIONS

The distinction between the processes of desegregation and integration is not nearly so vital for assessing the role of private institutions and organizations in racial and ethnic matters. For one thing, in many types of private social institutions—for instance, fraternities and social clubs—desegregation automatically implies integration because of the kind of social relationship implicit in the operation of the institution. In other private institutions of larger scope, as, for instance, the private university, college, or academy, desegregation may or may not lead to integration depending upon particular factors associated with the life of the institution such as size and the presence or absence of segregated or self-segregated subgroups. Moreover, the arguments surrounding the choices of segregation, self-segregation, or desegregation are more varied, more complex, and more conflicting than in the case of government. However, several insights and guide-lines to action are suggested by the direction and scope of our previous analysis:

Some types of private organizations are those for whose goals and operation ethnic background is functional and centrally relevant. Quite obviously, a Methodist mission society, a Catholic sodality, a Jewish Temple sisterhood, or a club instituted to insure social welfare benefits for Polish immigrants and their descendants cannot reasonably be expected to throw open its membership to persons of other faiths or nationalities, as the case may be. Here one can confidently assert that there is no discrimination but simply a functionally relevant definition of membership.

Private organizations and institutions which serve a more general purpose, while they may be, under some circumstances, technically free to restrict membership on an ethnic basis, must face a series of crucial queries. Do they receive any assistance from the public treasury either in the form of grants or exemption from the payment of taxes? Can they justify an exclusionary policy on the basis of major functional relevance to the goals of the organization? Do they claim to operate under the general principles of American democracy, Hebraic-Christian brotherhood, and fair play? Do they perform a quasi-public function such as providing general education? If, in many cases, the answers to these questions should suggest the inappropriateness of an exclusionary policy, then the way is certainly left open for efforts to institute a policy which is nondiscriminatory. If such efforts by concerned members make the segregationists in the organization unhappy, it must be pointed out that initiating change in the policy of a voluntary organization at the will of a majority of its members is a thoroughly democratic procedure. Thus the ethnic practices of private organizations can frequently be settled by the dynamics of policy-making in a democratic setting where traditional procedures are subject to current examination in a changing society.

### THE BUILT-IN TENSION BETWEEN THE GOALS OF ETHNIC COMMUNALITY AND DESEGREGATION

Earlier in this chapter we stated that desegregation in public and quasi-public facilities was unlikely to lead to the rapid breakdown of barriers between the primary group communal life of the various ethnic groups in America, and that the fears in this area of the segregationists, however unworthy, were thus unfounded. Here we examine a point which may appear at first to repudiate the above conclusion, but which, in fact, does not, but only qualifies it.

Desegregation—or, put positively, the achievement in full of civil rights for all groups—creates situations on the job, in the neighborhood, in the school, and in the civic arena, which place persons of different ethnic background into secondary, frequently equal-status, contacts with each other. These secondary contacts will not necessarily lead to primary group relationships, such as clique friendships, common membership in small organizations, dating, and intermarriage, and in the immediate or intermediate future will probably not seriously disturb the basic outlines of ethnic communality which have been shown to exist in America. However, over a sufficiently extended period of time, these new secondary group relationships between people of diverse ethnic backgrounds will presumably lead to an increase in warm, personal friendships across ethnic lines, a broadening of cultural perspective, an appreciation of diverse values, and in some degree a rise in the rate of interethnic marriage. All of these last-named developments run counter to the sociological requirements, whether realized or admitted, of ethnic closure and ethnic communality. Here, then, is another major area of social reality where the advocates of cultural pluralism (and, by implication, structural pluralism) cannot eat their cake and have it, too. There are built-in tensions between the simultaneously desired goals of ethnic communality and full civic equality, and these tensions create for the cultural pluralists a poignant dilemma. The dilemma is particularly acute for the two large minority religious groups—the Jews and the Catholics—who do not wish to see their young people "lost" to the numerically and culturally dominant Protestant subsociety or to the community of intellectuals and yet who ardently support the fight to secure full civic equality for all persons in American society. The racial groups approach the problem somewhat differently: the Negroes, apart from the new crop of "black nationalists," have never been ideologically committed to racial communality, however much they have been forced to create it; however, those whites who desire the full complement of civil rights for all, but who are reluctant to support the idea of racial intermarriage, must wrestle with the possibility that the rate of racial intermarriage will eventually increase under conditions of full equality. The nationality groups which still hope for subcultural survival are fighting such a rear-guard and eventually futile action that the dillemma for them has less realistic overtones.

There is, I believe, no clear course of action which neatly resolves this dilemma to the complete satisfaction of all parties concerned. My point, in this section, has simply been to make the conflicting considerations apparent. It is a dilemma which is certainly close to the center of the social problems attendant upon the presence of groups of diverse cultural origins and background in a modern industrial society. I shall leave my own "solution" of it for the concluding remarks of my analysis.

### REFERENCES AND NOTES

1    Samuel A. Stouffer, Edward A. Suchman, Leland C. DeVinney, Shirley A. Star, and Robin M. Williams, Jr., *The American Soldier: Adjustment during Army Life*, Princeton, N.J.: Princeton University Press, 1949, pp. 586–595; Morton Deutsch and Mary Evans Collins, *Interracial Housing*, Minneapolis, Minn.: University of Minnesota Press, 1951; John Harding (ed.), "Intergroup Contact and Racial Attitudes," *Journal of Social Issues*, vol. 8, no. 1 (1952); Gordon W. Allport, *The Nature of Prejudice*, Cambridge, Mass.: Addison-Wesley Publishing Co., 1954, pp. 261–282;

Daniel M. Wilner, Rosabelle Price Walkley, and Stuart W. Cook, *Human Relations in Interracial Housing: A Study of the Contact Hypothesis*, Minneapolis, Minn.: University of Minnesota Press, 1955; George E. Simpson and J. Milton Yinger, *Racial and Cultural Minorities*, rev. ed., New York: Harper and Brothers, 1958, pp. 751–757.

2    Allport, *op. cit.*, pp. 17–67.

3    Gerhard Lenski, *The Religious Factor, op. cit.*, pp. 326–330. On the question of dysfunctional consequences of excessive pluralism in the Netherlands, see David O. Moberg, "Social Differentiation in the Netherlands," *Social Forces*, vol. 39, no. 4 (May 1961), pp. 333–337. The following quotation is instructive: "Community solidarity and efficiency [in the Netherlands] are diminished. Not only is group set against group in political affairs, but even when there are community-wide activities with cooperative planning there must nearly always be representation from all major confessional groupings of the community. As a result, incompetence is often evident; considerations of religious politics are placed above competence in the appointment or selection of personnel for community organizations and committees. Even when federated activity cuts across the religious columns, actual association of persons with different religious views takes place only among the small proportion of the population which holds positions of leadership. 'Water-tight' partitions separate the rank-and-file members." (Moberg, *op. cit.*, p. 336.)

4    Lenski, *op. cit.*, pp. 329–330.

5    Kenneth B. Clark, "Desegregation: The Role of the Social Sciences," *Teachers College Record*, vol. 62, no. 1 (October 1960), pp. 16–17.

6    *Ibid.*, p. 16.

7    For a discussion of one interesting case where the definition of "state action" was crucial and controversial, see Milton M. Gordon, "The Girard College Case: Resolution and Social Significance," *Social Problems*, vol. 7, no. 1 (summer 1959), pp. 15–27.

8    Another qualification is necessary here. If school districts were gerrymandered originally for the sake of instituting all or predominantly Negro schools, then this initial act of discrimination should be fought and redress should be demanded.

## SUPPLEMENTAL READINGS

Allport, Gordon W.: *The Nature of Prejudice*, Reading, Mass.: Addison-Wesley Publishing Co., Inc., 1954.

Baldwin, James: *Notes of a Native Son*, Boston: Beacon Press, 1955.

Brown, Claude: *Manchild in the Promised Land*, New York: The Macmillan Company, 1965.

Clark, Kenneth: *Dark Ghetto*, New York: Harper & Row, Publishers, 1965.

"Color and Race," *Daedalus*, vol. 96 (spring 1967).

Horowitz, Irving, and Louis and Martin Lieboweitz: "Social Deviance and Political Marginality: Toward a Redefinition of the Relation between Sociology and Politics," *Social Problems*, vol. 15 (winter 1968), pp. 280–296.

Hutchinson, E. P. (ed.): "The New Immigration," *The Annals*, vol. 367 (September 1966).

Killian, Lewis M.: *The Impossible Revolution?* New York: Random House, Inc., 1968.

Kozol, Jonathan: *Death at an Early Age*, New York: Bantam Books, Inc., 1968.

Lewis, Oscar: *La Vida*, New York: Random House, Inc., 1966.

Marx, Gary: *Protest and Prejudice*, New York: Harper & Row, Publishers, Incorporated, 1967.

Moynihan, Daniel P., *et al.: The Negro Family: The Case for National Action*, The Moynihan Report, Washington, D.C.: U.S. Government Printing Office, 1965.

Nelson, Harold A.: "The Defenders: A Case Study of an Informal Police Organization," *Social Problems*, vol. 15 (fall 1967), pp. 127–147.

Penalosa, Fernando, and Edward C. McDonagh: "Social Mobility in a Mexican-American Community," *Social Forces*, vol. 44 (June 1966), pp. 498–505.

Pettigrew, Thomas F.: *Profile of the Negro American*, Princeton, N.J.: D. Van Nostrand Company, Inc., 1964.

Sklare, Marshall: "Intermarriage and the Jewish Future," *Commentary*, vol. 37 (April 1964), pp. 46–52.

Taeuber, Karl, and Alma Taeuber: *Negroes in Cities*, Chicago: Aldine Publishing Co., 1965.

Westie, Frank R.: "The American Dilemma: An Empirical Test," *American Sociological Review*, vol. 30 (August 1965), pp. 527–538.

Williams, Robin M., Jr., *et al.: Strangers Next Door*, Englewood Cliffs, N.J.: Prentice-Hall, Inc., 1964.

Wirth, Louis: *The Ghetto*, Chicago: University of Chicago Press, 1928.

Yinger, J. Milton: "Recent Developments in Minority and Race Relations," *The Annals*, vol. 378 (July 1968), pp. 130–145.

Social scientists have an excellent understanding of the key variables that have created a population explosion in recent decades with potential consequences second only to those of a nuclear war—yet nearly 2.5 million babies were born last week somewhere in the world. Present estimates indicate a total world population of more than 6 billion by the turn of the century, in comparison with 3.4 billion in 1968. Americans tend to associate dramatic population growth and its attendant problems only with the underdeveloped countries and to ignore the fact that although our annual rate of population growth is comparatively low, the total population of the United States has increased greatly. We do not face the prospects of malnutrition and starvation, the most immediate concerns of one-half to two-thirds of the world's present population. Nevertheless, the reality of the population dilemma in this country has already been felt in such forms as severe strains on public schools, a rapidly expanding labor force, and higher taxes to extend community facilities.

The many warnings of impending disaster have gone virtually unheeded until recently, chiefly because high birth rates have historically been offset by high death rates, so that the rate of population increase, if any, was always minimal. Between 1900 and 1960, however, the increase alone was greater than the total world population for 1850 and almost equalled the 1900 population of 1.6 billion; that is, in 60 years the world population almost doubled. An accelerated rate of growth was first experienced in countries such as the United States, those of Northwest Europe, and Japan, where the effect of an increasing standard of living and gains in public sanitation and medical science reduced mortality rates more rapidly than birth rates (which also decreased as a reflection of industrialization and urbanization). At present the United States is expected to maintain birth and death rates that will result in a stable annual growth rate of less than 1.7 percent. Any decrease depends almost entirely on changes in the birth rate, as the mortality rate is not likely to decline substantially below the present level.

The countries that are least able to cope with an expanding population are now manifesting increases almost twice as great as the more affluent societies (that is, their populations double in 20 to 25 years, compared with the estimate of 40 years for the United States).

*381*

Mortality rates in the underdeveloped countries have been reduced dramatically since the end of World War II by widespread application of the latest medical discoveries and the most advanced techniques to improve public sanitation. These programs have been initiated and supported primarily by organizations from the outside, such as the World Health Organization, and high birth rates continue to prevail because no essential changes in the way of life of the receiving countries have been stimulated. Since the nonindustrialized countries now comprise about two-thirds of the world's population, the problems related to a rapidly expanding population will not be reconciled until their birth rates are reduced markedly. The importance of economic development and its concomitant changes is underscored by recent reports indicating that the "big difference between high and low birth rate nations is not whether they are Catholic, but whether they are economically underdeveloped." That is, analyses involving comparisons between countries, as well as population segments within a single nation, show that levels of income and education are better predictors of family size than the prevailing religion. Also, in the developing countries the infrequent use of contraceptive methods has been associated with lack of knowledge and availability rather than with religious beliefs.

The strongest evidence against these propositions is represented by Latin America, where Roman Catholicism coincides with high birth rates; however, the two countries with the lowest birth rates, Argentina and Uruguay, also have the highest literacy rates. Moreover, all gross population rates may conceal or distort many of the contributing influences, as illustrated by the situation in Uruguay. The lower birth rates may be attributed in part to the higher literacy rates, but an even greater factor is the abortion rate, estimated at three for every live birth. According to surveys sponsored by the United Nations and Cornell University in six Latin American cities, devout Catholic women have a slightly smaller number of children than women who are only nominally Catholic. In fact, the annual birth rate of 18.1 per 1,000 for all the Catholic countries of Europe is almost identical to the rate of 18.0 per 1,000 for the non-Catholic countries of Europe. Parenthetically, since the females who will enter the childbearing ages during the next two decades have already been born, a substantial reduction in crude birth rates—assuming that it occurs—would only partially offset the influence of the increased number of women available for childbearing. This point is discussed in detail in the selection by Donald J. Bogue.

The consequences of a burgeoning population pose additional problems for the underdeveloped countries. They face the dilemma of a mandatory diversion of substantial portions of their national resources to long-range capital investment just to meet the needs of an increasing population, with no surplus available for this purpose because of the immediate survival requirements of the present population. Efforts to raise the standard of living require long-term commitments for economic development which similarly are subject to dissipation by a spurting population. Sharp reductions in mortality result in an even higher proportion of children and adolescents in these countries, because the impact of health measures is most pronounced at the younger ages. When 40 percent or more of a country's population is under the age of fifteen, as is common throughout Latin America, Asia, and Africa, the added burdens are not difficult to identify: a further drain on capital resources, pressures for new educational facilities and trained teachers, and ultimately a requirement for expanded employment opportunities in a "static" agrarian economy.

All these factors undermine efforts to improve the prevailing standard of living, and this may be the most serious problem in the near future. People in underdeveloped countries are becoming increasingly aware of the standard of living enjoyed by the industrialized societies. The political repercussions may be particularly serious if the new aspirations are not matched by periodic evidence of improvement or if it is suggested that the underdeveloped countries must permanently settle for less. For a discussion of this point see the selection by Philip M. Hauser.

The events of recent years make it patently clear that any discussion of the consequences of the population problem for the developed countries, with emphasis on the United States, must include the political and economic difficulties of the agrarian nations. Economic assistance and dissemination of birth-control information to foreign countries and intervention in the internal affairs of the "new" nations represent only a cross section of the controversial issues that are currently debated and that are directly related to population pressures. Our unique problems fall into two broad categories: congestion, and continuation of the present high standard of living, with special requirements to incorporate the large segment of the poor. As indicated by Bogue, at the present rate of natural increase the United States can expect a population of approximately 1 billion persons within the next century. Even if the annual growth rate were to stabilize at 0.8 percent, the lowest ever experienced by this country, we would have a population of more than 400 million by the year 2070.

The importance of increases in what is called "fertility potential" is well illustrated by current estimates for the next decade, which confirm Bogue's data. The number of women in the most fertile ages of childbearing, twenty to twenty-nine, will increase from 14 million in 1967 to 20 million in 1980. If American women were to have an average of four children instead of three, then within 30 years the population increase would have doubled our present population. Since there is a concomitant trend toward concentration of the population in metropolitan areas, problems of congestion may soon override the advantages of an urban system. It is impossible to calculate the psychic and financial costs of commuting, decaying central areas, polluted air and watersheds, and required public facilities and services. Decentralization of the urban complex is not the answer, as the almost immediate outcome is simply more congestion with each outward extension of the city.

The rapid population growth of the United States poses a serious threat to the existing high standard of living and impedes efforts to extend the benefits of an affluent society to a broader base of the population. Bogue details the sequence of difficulties now unfolding as a result of the baby boom in 1946. Crises in the form of double-shift and oversize classes have already occurred in the primary school level; attendance at the high school level increased by 50 percent during the 1960s, and even now colleges and universities are facing strong enrollment pressures because of the higher proportion of students who go on to college and remain for postgraduate training. Similar problems are anticipated in the areas of housing, public facilities, and employment opportunities for an enlarged labor force. Certainly it can be argued that the economy is stimulated by the consumption requirements (food, clothing, housing, cars, and so forth) of an increased population. However, the dependency status of the baby-boom children creates a severe drain on the resources available to maintain the prevailing standard of living and to encompass those now at marginal levels.

Sharp opposition to the alarmist tenor of the preceding discussion is provided by (1) those who believe that the detrimental aspects are overdramatized, (2) those who argue that in the near future there will be an "automatic" decrease in birth rate in both the agrarian and the industrial nations, and (3) those who deny that the undesired conditions are caused by rapid population growth. The first position rests on the premise that the standard of living of most of the world's population has continued to improve during the period of rapid growth and the expectation that the findings of science will enable the support of many additional billions of people. The second point of view predicts that as urbanization takes place and levels of education are increased in the underdeveloped countries the birth rates will fall naturally; also as population pressures become unmanageable in the industrial nations, people will voluntarily implement greater fertility control. Finally, the leaders of the Communist world have consistently stated that overpopulation is a myth created to distract attention from the failures of capitalism, which are the actual causes of poverty, hunger, unemployment, and war. The influence of this last approach has hindered the work of the United Nations and its associated agencies, which have spearheaded the ameliorative efforts throughout the world.

Perhaps some phases of the population problem are debatable, but it is yet to be demonstrated that a higher standard of living is a derivative of uncontrolled population growth. On the contrary, unless something is done the poorer nations are condemning themselves to perennial poverty, and the prosperous nations will suffer accordingly. Thus increasing numbers of experts are expressing the view that the United States should take the lead in actively supporting the establishment of birth-control programs. What are the obstacles? J. Mayone Stycos, whose article is cited in the Supplemental Readings, provides an excellent point of departure through an analysis of the reasons that the governments of underdeveloped countries have been reluctant to introduce fertility-control programs. Among the conditions he stresses are a growing wave of nationalism which fosters pride in a large population and views an act of intervention as a reimposition of Western imperialism, a naive faith in the "magic of economic development," and a host of erroneous conceptions about the causes of high fertility (for example, that the people want many children and that the lower economic classes have more intense sexual drives and fewer inhibitions). Demographers have reported significant changes in the attitudes of government leaders over the past five years. Apparently there has been a growing understanding of the problems forced on them by runaway population growth.

Religious opposition is generally assumed to be the major deterrent. In reality the Roman Catholic concern with individual obligations for procreation and parental responsibility presents the only major theological obstacle to population control. Pope Paul's encyclical of 1968 reaffirming the prohibition against birth control by techniques other than the "rhythm method" will be the subject of much debate in coming years. Theologians who are considered liberals in the church support the position that the Pope can only recommend a stance on a particular moral issue, as any papal ruling dealing with human wisdom, rather than divine revelation, cannot be imposed as infallible teaching. This interpretation allows the conclusion that "spouses may responsibly decide according to their conscience that artificial contraception in some circumstances is permissible and indeed necessary to preserve and foster the values and sacredness of marriage."

There is considerable doubt that the papal declaration will have substantial impact in modifying the behavior of the growing segment of Catholic women throughout the world who had previously adopted some form of artificial means of contraception. However, in view of the statement's strong position against government-sponsored birth-control programs, the potential consequences for international and national efforts to reduce population growth are obvious. Certainly the leadership position of the United Nations may be further impaired. The United State's food-for-peace program may be revised to eliminate several basic provisions designed to encourage nations to adopt birth-control programs. In Latin America and in other Catholic countries the declaration not only raises the prospect of political controversy over continued public support of family-planning programs, but it also increases the likelihood that the professionals (physicians and social workers), many of whom are Catholic, will not be available in sufficient numbers to maintain effective programs.

Inertia, outmoded customs, illiteracy, and problems of communication are serious handicaps. In addition, fertility programs require reasonably well-developed health and community services that may not exist. Finally, because of the lag in impact of such programs, it is not unusual to have the effects nullified by a concurrent increase in the population.

That the prospects are not hopeless is made explicit by Dudley Kirk in the selection on recent changes in the underdeveloped world. Kirk's optimism rests on the increasingly favorable climate of opinion regarding family planning, the invention of new methods of contraception which offer a wider choice of procedures, and the adoption of national family-planning programs. The success of a national program instituted by Japan furnishes a specific example. Initially, abortions probably contributed as much to Japan's declining birth rate as contraception, but it is anticipated that as contraception is more widely practiced the felt need for abortions will diminish. A peak population in Japan of 108 million is forecast for 1990, with a reduction to 99 million in 2015 and a growth rate thereafter less than half the rate of increase as recently as 1947. As described by Kirk, the recent developments in most other countries, although impressive, are not occurring rapidly enough "to forestall massive population growth and continuing critical problems of population at least through the next decade." Even with the papal encyclical on birth control, changes in Catholic doctrine during this century, as illustrated by the endorsement of periodic continence or the rhythm method and the growing support by priests and lay leaders of the liberal position favoring selective use of contraceptive devices, form the basis for increased fertility control.

Although economic development does not represent a cure-all, it would be misleading to deny its significance. For example, food production can be raised dramatically by the use of more fertilizers, improved seed, better irrigation, crop rotation, and other agricultural techniques. Incredibly, more than 70 percent of the world's farmers are still dependent upon a hoe or a wooden plow. And the hypothesis of a natural decrease in birth rates as a correlate of economic development has merit. The fact remains, however, that further delay in taking massive action may have disastrous consequences. One more generation of the current trends may set in motion forces that will change the basic nature of human existence. Certainly we stand at the crossroads, since population as much as anything else will determine the future course of history.

Dennis H. Wrong presents an overview of the issues in the contemporary population debate, with special attention to Malthus' theory of population. Bogue provides detailed coverage of the patterns of population growth and distribution in the United States and uses these patterns to draw out the implications for our present standard of living. Similarly, Philip Hauser analyzes the relationship of the impact of the population explosion in underdeveloped countries to world political problems. Kirk's concluding article deals with the prospects for reductions in birth rates in the less industrialized countries by reviewing the population policies and programs sponsored by governments in Asia, Africa, and Latin America.

## 34    THE MALTHUSIAN PROBLEM     DENNIS H. WRONG

### MALTHUS' PRINCIPLE OF POPULATION

Thomas Robert Malthus, an early nineteenth-century economist, is generally considered to be the father of population study as a field of scholarship. Since the publication in 1798 of the first edition of his *An Essay on the Principle of Population*, his views have been the subject of heated controversy. Few students of population today accept his theory of population in the form in which it was originally stated, yet many modern writers advance views which may, without doing them undue violence, be described as neo-Malthusian. There have been able theorists on population before and after Malthus, but he alone succeeded in making his name almost synonymous with the field of population study, at least among those who are not professional population specialists. "His true claim to fame," James A. Field observes, "rests not on the originality of his ideas but rather on the fact that people listened to what he said."[1]

In essence, Malthus' theory was that human populations tend to increase at a more rapid rate than the food supply needed to sustain them. Malthus based this conclusion on several postulates about man's material needs, sexual instincts, and reproductive capacities. He believed that sexual passion was a powerful, virtually uncontrollable, and unchanging component of human nature. Thus gratification of sexual desires carries with it the risk of producing children for whom the means of support are unavailable. Man's biological need for food and his sexual impulses are inescapably in conflict.

Malthus' principle of population can best be stat-

ed in his own words. In the second edition of his famous *Essay* he reduced it to three propositions:

> (1) Population is necessarily limited by the means of subsistence. (2) Population invariably increases where the means of subsistence increase, unless prevented by some very powerful and obvious checks. (3) These checks, and the checks which repress the superior power of population, and keep its effects on a level with the means of subsistence, are all resolvable into moral restraint, vice, and misery.[2]

Malthus believed that he had discovered an impregnable argument against the optimistic views of social progress advanced by William Godwin and other liberal reformers of the eighteenth century. If population always increases to the point where any further increase is checked by the limits of the food supply, obviously material progress can produce no lasting improvement in the living conditions of mankind. Instead of permitting the existing population to lead a more comfortable life, increases in food production will merely allow a larger population to subsist at the same low levels that prevailed before the rise in food output. Thus, Malthus asserted, the hopes of the Godwinian believers in progress were vain; they defied the "natural law" of population growth.

The checks imposed on population growth by the means of subsistence were, Malthus held in his third proposition, all "resolvable into moral restraint, vice, and misery." Those conditions which produce vice and misery he called *positive checks*; moral restraint he labeled the *preventive check*. Wars, infanticide, plagues, and famine constitute the major positive checks; some of these, like plagues and famines, "appear to arise unavoidably from the laws of nature and may be called exclusively misery." Others, such as wars and infanticide, "we obviously bring upon ourselves," but "they are brought upon us by vice, and their consequences are misery."[3] By moral restraint, the sole preventive check to population increase Malthus recognized, he meant the prudential postponement of marriage for the purpose of avoiding reproduction when the individual is unable to support children.

The positive checks, in short, are those which limit population growth by raising the death rate, while the preventive check achieves the same effect by lowering the birth rate. Clearly there are other means of lowering the birth rate than postponing marriage, notably voluntary birth control, which has in fact been the means chiefly responsible for reducing fertility in Western countries. But Malthus refused to countenance birth control and classed it with vice. "A promiscuous intercourse to such a degree as to prevent the birth of children," he wrote, "seems to lower, in the most marked manner, the dignity of human nature."[4] Malthus' disapproval of birth control stemmed less from moral objections to sexual pleasure freed from procreative aims than from his conviction that man was naturally indolent and needed the fear of inability to support his children to goad him into efforts to improve his economic situation; if sexual gratification could be achieved without the risk of conception, human progress, Malthus thought, would come to a standstill.[5]

Thus the postponement of marriage until a man is able to support a wife and at least six children, in conjunction with total premarital sexual abstinence, was the only preventive check Malthus admitted and dignified with the name moral restraint. Since he doubted the capacity of mankind, in particular the lower classes, to exercise this restraint, he was inclined to believe that human society would always be threatened by the positive checks of starvation, disease, and war. In his later years he became more hopeful, but his fundamental pessimism earned for economics the title of "the dismal science."

## MAJOR CRITICISMS OF MALTHUS

The first and purely logical objection to Malthus' principle is the ambiguity with which it is often stated. Malthus spoke of population as having a constant *tendency to increase* at a rate faster than the means of subsistence. Sometimes it is unclear whether he meant that population *does in fact* increase more rapidly than the means of subsistence or merely that it *could do so if not checked*. Except for short periods in societies where the average standard of life is well above the minimum subsistence level, the former is clearly an impossibility. As Kingsley Davis argues:

> The very fact that numbers are increasing indicates that the means to support them is increasing too. Otherwise mortality would have risen and the population would never have grown to its present size. To think of the world's population as "outrunning" its normal food supply is like thinking of the hind feet of a horse outrunning its front feet.[6]

At times Malthus so qualified his law that he appeared to be claiming merely that population has the *capacity* to increase more rapidly than food production. This is undeniable, but it leaves entirely open the question of the degree to which at a given time the capacity is actually being realized. As Ian Bowen has pointed out, the principle is irrefutable when stated in this way, for whenever a case is found in which the means of subsistence are abundant and population growth falls short of Malthus' maximum rate, *by definition* the checks are at work preventing a more rapid increase.[7]

There are also empirical objections to Malthus' law. His gloomy insistence on the ever-present pressure of numbers on subsistence has scarcely been justified by the history of the Western world since his day. He had the misfortune—from the standpoint of the plausibility of his theory—of writing on the eve of the industrial revolution in England and of the opening up to cultivation of the grassy plains of North America. The resulting increase in wealth was attended by rapid population growth, which, in contrast to expectations derived from the Malthusian theory, failed to prevent the occurrence of a general rise in the standard of living that has continued almost unabated to the present day.

As Malthus himself conceded in later versions of his theory, he had underestimated the extent to which what he called fresh starts in agriculture might enable the means of subsistence to increase more rapidly than population, for at least limited periods of time. Yet the technological revolution in agriculture still continuing today has made it possible "to grow two blades of grass when only one grew before" on a scale never imagined by Malthus. He tended to identify the limits of food production with the limits of cultivable land area and minimized the possibility of great improvements in agricultural technique. Nor did he foresee the extent to which England would be able to support a growing population on food imports from sparsely settled areas overseas.

Nevertheless, the great increases in agricultural productivity of the past century and a half may have simply temporarily defeated Malthus' law, although they clearly invalidate his oft-expressed view that there was a *constant* short-run pressure of numbers on resources. The decline of the birth rate is a more serious empirical contradiction of his theory. As we have seen, the practice of birth control after marriage, largely by means of contraceptive techniques, has been responsible for the decline in fertility that has checked Western population growth. Only one Western nation, Catholic Ireland, has followed Malthus' advice and controlled fertility primarily by marrying late rather than by practicing birth control after marriage. Considering Malthus' disapproval of birth control, it is ironic that his name is almost inseparably linked in the popular mind with the birth control movement. The early propagandists for birth control used Malthusian arguments, and to this day proponents of birth control have called themselves neo-Malthusians, the "neo" symbolizing their recognition that Malthus himself did not approve of birth control as a preventive check to population growth.

Clearly Westerners have not elected to limit the size of their families in order to prevent an otherwise inevitable operation of the eliminative checks of starvation and disease. Unless Malthus' term "means of subsistence" is taken to mean not only the sheer minimum necessary for physical survival but also all of the diverse and culturally variable material wants of modern populations, it cannot be concluded that limited means of subsistence have been the chief factor preventing fertility from realizing its maximum biological potential. The desire for a high standard of living which has arisen in advanced urban-industrial societies underlies the trend towards smaller families.

Actually, it is one of Malthus' inconsistencies that he often recognized this himself, observing that "a decided taste for the conveniences and comforts of life" does not "operate as an encouragement to early marriages" but often has the reverse effect.[8] One would expect, therefore, that as more and more people were raised above subsistence level, their desire to maintain their "conveniences and comforts" would encourage them to avoid excessive childbearing. And this is precisely what has happened in industrial societies, although the means of avoiding childbearing has been birth control rather than the postponement of marriage favored by Malthus.

Although the Malthusian law no longer threatens Western societies, many people maintain that it still applies to overcrowded, underdeveloped countries such as India and China, and that it was applicable to most human societies before the modern era. If by the Malthusian law one means simply the pressure of numbers on resources, this is indisputably true. Malthus' great contribution to social thought was to call attention to population pressure as a major source of human suffering. Yet Malthus' view of human nature was that of a biological determinist. Even in overcrowded societies living close to the bare subsistence level there are, as we saw in Chapter 4, social and cultural restrictions on fertility unrelated to population pressure. Conceding the rigor of Malthus' thought, the correctness of his insistence that human numbers cannot go on increasing indefinitely, and the relevance of population pressure to the social and economic plight of contemporary underdeveloped nations, the conception of an unchanging, biologically fixed human nature from which he derived his law has long since been rejected by social scientists.

## THE CONTEMPORARY POPULATION DEBATE

Since World War II there has been a resurgence of fear that world population is increasing at a rate which threatens low-income areas with mass famine and malnutrition, and high-income areas with a reduction of living standards. The increased responsibilities of the United States as a world power have forced Americans to become more aware of the problems of poverty-stricken and over-crowded parts of the world. This awareness and the postwar rise of the birth rate in Western nations themselves have led to renewed concern with the world population-food ratio, in contrast to the 1930's when the possible dangers of underpopulation were more widely publicized.

But it is not merely professional population students who have become concerned over the rapid increase in world population. The world problems created by population growth have become a matter of public debate as well. Students of population who have long been concerned with the relation between the increase of numbers and the availability of resources to support them, find their subject at last receiving the attention its importance merits. Public discussion is unquestionably preferable to indifference, but it must be admitted that many current pronouncements on the "population explosion" reveal more about the passions and doctrinal beliefs of the speaker than about the realities of the problem. No doubt this is inevitable where moral and religious convictions regarding the family, sex, childbearing, the role of women, and the responsibilities of the rich to-

wards the poor—always emotion-laden topics—are at the very heart of the matter. "Population studies," as one writer has observed, "are basically concerned with primitive instincts—so primitive, so remote and fierce, and yet so near to consciousness, that the objectivity of any human . . . observer must always be in doubt unless he is content to describe facts."[9]

The facts of world population growth and the distribution of world resources are not subject to controversy. The desirability of the attainment of a higher standard of living by the overcrowded, underdeveloped countries by means that avoid war or the risk of war is also generally acknowledged. Disagreement centers on rival interpretations of the facts, interpretations which clash on the questions of whether population growth is an aid or an obstacle to economic development and on what the effects of limiting growth by encouraging the spread of birth control are likely to be. These differences are usually rooted in political ideologies or in religious convictions concerning the morality of various methods of birth control. Both official Communist doctrine and the Catholic church have, for different reasons, adopted positions that can loosely be characterized as "anti-Malthusian" in the sense that they deny the relevance of population pressure to the economic and social problems of the underdeveloped countries and oppose governmental efforts to reduce the rate of population growth in these countries by encouraging the spread of family limitation by contraceptive means.[10]

On the other hand, the neo-Malthusian writers call attention to the fact that birth rates remain high in many parts of the world, death rates are falling rapidly, few new lands open to settlement remain, and the exploitive use of land already under cultivation has reduced its productivity and led to widespread erosion of valuable topsoil.[11] The neo-Malthusians paint horrendous pictures of a future world in which, if present population growth rates continue, people will be packed together shoulder to shoulder covering every square foot of space on earth. The inference is drawn, or at least suggested, that unless the present rate of increase falls we are likely to end up living in such a sardine-can world.

Too often the whole subject is discussed as if only two points of view in direct conflict with one another existed: that of those who wish to limit population growth by means of birth control on the one hand, and that of those who favor an all-out effort to raise food production on the other. Yet most professional students of the problem refuse to see these as mutually exclusive alternatives and advocate a joint program of encouraging both birth control and economic development. Moreover, they favor an economic development plan that is designed to increase the production of all goods and services rather than merely of food alone. The governments of several underdeveloped countries, most notably India, are already committed to promoting the voluntary practice of birth control as part of the general objective of modernizing their economies and raising the standard of living.

Since what we loosely call the standard of living of a country is determined by the relation between the size of its population and its total economic output, it makes obvious sense, if we wish to raise that standard, to try to influence both sides of the numbers-output equation. More accurately, it makes sense to try to control population growth as well as to increase output *if* the population is already so large and so dense that additional people will have no room to spread out onto unsettled land and *if* additions to the population will not increase the productivity of labor by making possible greater occupational specialization. These conditions are clearly present in India, Pakistan, China, and Egypt, and they are just as clearly absent in Canada, Australia, and the larger South American countries. Thus the high rates of growth in the latter nations provide little cause for anxiety, while the somewhat lower growth rates of the former are a major cause of concern.

The opponents of the neo-Malthusians, who might be called neo-Godwinians, are likely to counter alarmism over the world population explosion with glowing estimates of the purely technical possibilities of increasing world agricultural output.[12] They point to new lands in the tropics which might be brought into production, to the higher yields obtainable by using improved farming methods in underdeveloped countries, to economic reorganizations that promise to increase productivity, and to unrealized possibilities of growing food plants in water tanks, farming the ocean floor, and synthesizing foodstuffs from wood and even from inorganic materials. If all, or even some, of these things were done, they insist, the earth could support a far larger population that at present. And there remains the prospect of space travel to alleviate the continued pressure of growing numbers by permitting emigration to other planets, so the sky is literally no limit.[13]

While these contentions are undeniably true, the fact that the obstacles to creating a "world economy of abundance" are political, economic, and social, that is, rooted in social institutions and belief systems created by man, does not make the problem of balancing population and resources any easier to solve. It is a mistake to equate what is *technically* possible with what has a reasonable probability of happening in a world of competing national sovereignties, wars, revolutions, and ideological and racial antagonisms.[14] The herculean effort required to maintain a rate of economic growth high enough to keep perpetually ahead of uncontrolled population growth is just not likely to be forthcoming. Social institutions and attitudes have their own inertia and intractability to change, which often prove to be as formidable obstacles to increasing economic production as biological and geographic barriers. Moreover, glowing estimates of future advances in productivity usually concentrate on possible gains in food production, ignoring the fact that human beings, however well-fed, also need *space*. Never-ending population growth would ultimately lead to a shortage of space even if the problem of food supply were solved.

The advocates of birth control as a check to population growth believe on good evidence that reduced growth will make possible more rapid economic progress to eliminate the terrible poverty afflicting the majority of the inhabitants of the world's underdeveloped countries.[15] They fear that without a slowing up of population increase these countries may simply end up supporting more people at the same low standard of living, whereas a successful program combining fertility control with economic development would enable a smaller total population to achieve what we in the West consider to be minimum standards for human decency and dignity. The accusation often made that the proponents of birth control are misanthropes who want fewer people in the world and lack faith in the ability of science and technology to raise the standard of living is, therefore, absurd.

Sometimes, it is true, those who voice alarm over world population growth resort to scare statistics which obscure the real reasons for alarm. The point about the imaginary sardine-can world they describe is not that such a world is a real and unpleasant possibility, but rather that it is inconceivable. Long before we were confined to standing room only on the earth's surface, population growth would fall as a result of a rise in mortality. The population *cannot* go on increasing indefinitely; it *must* eventually reach a point of stability. This is the core of truth in Malthus' often contradictory formulations and it is evaded with amazing persistence by the neo-Godwinians who do not wish to face up to the eventual necessity of population control. While it is possible for the world to support a population a good deal larger than the present one, the fundamental choice we face is between achieving population stability by lowering the birth rate as opposed to achieving it by allowing the death rate to rise. Those who object to birth control ought to be prepared to declare themselves in favor of higher mortality instead. The world's present population problems could be solved for a long time by a few mass famines, a world-wide repetition of the Great Plagues of medieval Europe, or, for that matter, by several well-placed thermonuclear bombs. Are we prepared to see them solved in this way?

But it is by no means certain that mass genocide, demographically motivated wars, or even the milder policy of holding back death control measures could finally "solve" the population problem.

A temporary rise in mortality might facilitate rapid economic development, which would then lead to the adoption of family planning. But more probably, the result would be a cycle of wars, civil strife, mass bitterness and apathy that would themselves retard or prevent economic development. It is sometimes argued that the Black Death, which carried away from one-third to one-half of the population of Europe in the 14th century, was a necessary condition for the later occurrence of the Industrial Revolution. But here again we are probably dealing with a confusion between short- and long-run considerations. Even though the Black Death was not a man-made disaster, two centuries of disorder, violence, and cultural lag intervened between its ravages and the immense releases of human energy we call the Renaissance and the Reformation. And most historians agree that the troubles of this period, "the waning of the Middle Ages," stemmed directly from the trauma of mass death by plague and famine. Would man-made holocausts have a lesser effect?

In the first round of debate on the issue of population and food supply in modern Western history, William Godwin answered Thomas Robert Malthus with the prediction that the day would come when mankind would be able to grow its entire food supply in a single flowerpot. Godwin may prove to be ultimately right; he was clearly right in stressing the inventiveness and creativity of human beings as against Malthus' insistence on ineluctable, unchanging laws of nature. And certainly the hysterical insistence of some contemporary neo-Malthusians that science not only is incapable of saving us but even aggravates our problems is not convincing,[16] nor is their contention that although Westerners have achieved a state of demographic grace by adopting birth control, the peoples of Asia and Africa are incapable of learning from their experience. Let us assume, however, that the marvels of science and technology do succeed in creating a world in which productivity rises at unprecedented rates. Those who talk blithely of algae out of the sea and rockets to Mars rarely pause to ask themselves whether we really want to live in a world where population pressure compels us to rely on such expedients, leaving us no choice. Even if other planets are habitable, astronomers doubt whether they would be very pleasant places to live. And even though a sardine-can world is a fantasy and a larger world population can in principle be comfortably supported, are we utterly indifferent to considerations of space and density? Do we care nothing if the world resembles a rabbit warren so long as people get enough to eat?[17] It is curious that those who oppose the universal adoption of birth control should so often think of themselves as conservatives, as upholders of tradition, for the transformation of our way of life required to support a vastly larger population would be far greater than that resulting from the world-wide practice of birth control.

We need have no difficulty in imagining what a world in which birth control is universally practiced would be like. For, as we have seen in Chapters 4 and 5, birth control is *already* widely practiced in the major countries of Western civilization. The belief that the mass use of contraceptive birth control is an untried, new-fangled notion amounting to an unprecedented departure from the wisdom and restraint of the past is without rational foundation. The West has already rejected uncontrolled human fertility with the result that her population growth is able flexibly to adjust itself to changing economic and social trends. This is the goal the developing nations of the "Third World" must now achieve under far more difficult conditions. It will undoubtedly be difficult to persuade tradition-minded peasants in underdeveloped areas to adopt effective methods of birth control—even if a new, simpler method such as a pill is invented in time—before they have experienced the social and economic transformations that created the desire for small families in the West. But the chances of doing so are far better than the chances of winning a never-ending race between economic growth and population increase.

Those who do not approve of birth control would do better to base their opposition on religious or absolutist moral grounds alone. These are, of course, the real grounds for opposition in most cases, but their upholders invariably seek additional support by advancing questionable arguments about the purely secular problem of the relation between population growth and economic progress. Even those who do not share it can respect the integrity of a genuine religious position, if not the dogmatism of an erroneous social and economic theory such as Communist anti-Malthusianism. But instead of hiding behind shaky arguments, such a position should be stated forthrightly even when it can only make the ancient demand, unacceptable to many of us, that justice be done though the world perish.

## POPULATION AND ECONOMIC DEVELOPMENT

Whatever measures of economic well-being one selects, the contrast between the nations of Western civilization and the rest of the world, containing over half of the earth's total population, stands out.[18] The non-Western countries are poorer in per capita income, their per capita food consumption is lower and nutritionally less adequate,[19] their agriculture is less productive, and their social institutions encourage high fertility which in combination with declining mortality makes possible explosive population growth threatening to intensify the pressure of population on resources and condemn ever-increasing numbers of people to poverty and malnutrition. Kingsley Davis has ably described the vicious circle in which the Indian peasant is caught, a description that is applicable to peasant cultivators in other densely populated Asian countries.[20] The peasant must devote all his efforts to wresting a meager subsistence from his small plot of ground; his poverty is so great that he cannot afford to apply capital such as machine-made implements or commercial fertilizers to his land in order to increase its productivity and check the ravages of erosion and declining soil fertility. To obtain the maximum yield from it he can only apply manpower, so he is motivated to raise large families, thus creating more mouths to be fed from the land's limited produce. He is constantly in the position of trying to raise himself by his own bootstraps to break out of this vicious circle. Nor can the pile-up of people on the land be alleviated by migration to cities so long as capital investment in transportation and manufacturing is lagging. The continuation of rapid population increase perpetuates this lag by requiring the constant diversion of capital and manpower to agriculture in order to increase the food supply in circumstances where there is little room for expansion of crop acreage.[21]

If we assume that industrialization would, as it has in the Western world, "automatically" create the social conditions favoring smaller families and thus of itself cut back the rate of population growth, we need to remind ourselves that it was in the early stages of industrialization that the greatest population increases took place in the West. And the underdeveloped Asian countries with few exceptions already have far larger and denser populations than western Europe at the beginning of the industrial revolution. The same is true of several Latin-American countries, although, in common with Africa south of the Sahara, the larger continental South American countries are relatively thinly populated and can more readily support additional numbers than can underdeveloped Asia and North Africa. In the larger countries of the latter group, India, China, and Indonesia, even a low rate of natural increase adds colossal absolute numbers to a base population already pressing heavily on resources.

Economic development cannot, therefore, be undertaken in the densely settled underdeveloped areas without considering how it will affect and be affected by demographic trends. In contrast to the past experience of the West and the possible future experience of Africa and South America,[22] Asia cannot await the automatic transition to low fertility that has invariably followed industrialization elsewhere. A population policy designed to reduce fertility must be an integral part of development schemes if the gains of higher productivity are not to be used merely to support a larger population whose further growth will eventually wipe out the very achievements in mortality control and improved living conditions that have already been won. The government of India has realized this

and become the second nation to adopt an official anti-natalist policy of encouraging birth control (Japan was the first), and even the doctrinally anti-Malthusian government of Communist China has given uncertain signs of recognizing it.[23]

Some means of fertility control have seemed almost as offensive to Western sensibilities as would a policy of deliberately increasing the death rate. Western social scientists and medical specialists have generally favored the voluntary use of chemical or mechanical contraceptives by individual married couples. But it is beginning to appear that sterilization and abortion may have greater appeal to some peoples as forms of birth control than the advanced techniques favored to Western advisors.[24] Nor is it clear that an improved oral contraceptive or the new intra-uterine devices that have recently loomed large in discussions of population control would necessarily have greater appeal. Since the goal of anti-natalist policies in the underdeveloped world must be to achieve fertility decline *before* rather than after the achievement of full social and economic modernization, it ill behooves Westerners to frown on the encouragement of methods like sterilization and abortion. The underdeveloped countries simply cannot afford to delay fertility reduction until after they have attained the benefits of modernization, and perhaps contraceptive birth control will itself have to be viewed as one of those benefits.

The gap between the economic have and have-not nations has been widening since World War II. The dangers this poses for international peace should be apparent. Even in the absence of the cold war between the Communist and Western blocs of nations, population pressure might eventually induce the larger Asian countries to invade their more thinly settled neighbors in search of additional resources.[25] The attractions of Communist totalitarianism as a drastic short-cut to economic modernization and national power may very well increase, although, as G. L. Arnold and others have argued, its appeal is likely to be greatest not to the peasant masses but to military, bureaucratic, and intellectual elites whose aspirations are blocked by traditional social structures and attitudes.[26] For these reasons the political and economic transformation of the non-Western world, a transformation that will be profoundly affected by their demographic situation, is the central issue of contemporary history.

## REFERENCES AND NOTES

1  James A. Field, *Essays on Population and Other Papers*, Chicago: University of Chicago Press, 1931, p. 250.

2  T. R. Malthus, *An Essay on Population*, 2 vols., London: J. M. Dent and Sons, New York: E. P. Dutton and Co. (Everyman's Library, no. 692), 1914, vol. I, pp. 18–19.

3  *Ibid.*, p. 14.

4  *Ibid.*, p. 13.

5  See especially his argument in *ibid.*, vol. II, pp. 157–159.

6  Kingsley Davis, *Human Society*, New York: The Macmillan Company, 1949, p. 612.

7  Ian Bowen, *Population*, London: James Nisbet and Co., Cambridge: Cambridge University Press (Cambridge Economic Handbooks), 1954, p. 105.

8  Malthus, *op. cit.*, vol. II, p. 140. See the analysis of Malthus' ambiguities on the subject of the standard of living and fertility by D. E. C. Eversley, *Social Theories of Fertility and the Malthusian Dabate*, Oxford: The Clarendon Press, 1959, pp. 249–257.

9  Eversley, *op. cit.*, p. 279.

10  For the Catholic position, see William J. Gibbons, "The Catholic Value System in Relation to Human Fertility," in George F. Mair (ed.), *Studies in Population*, Princeton, N.J.: Princeton University Press, 1949, pp. 108–134; for a general account of Christian and Jewish attitudes towards the family and fertility, see Richard Fagley, *The Population Explosion and Christian Responsibility*, New York: Oxford University Press, 1960; for the Communist position, see Frank Lorimer, "Population Policy and Politics in the Communist World," in Philip M. Hauser (ed.), *Population and World Politics*, Glencoe, Ill.: The Free Press, 1958, pp. 214–236.

11  For two extreme statements of the neo-Malthusian viewpoint, see William Vogt, *Road to Survival*, New York: William Sloane Associates, 1948; and Robert C. Cook, *Human Fertility: the Modern Dilemma,,* New York: William Sloane Associates, 1951.

12  Two doctrinaire statements of the neo-Godwinian position are Josué de Castro, *The Geography of Hunger*, Boston: Little, Brown and Co., 1952; and Jacob Oser, *Must Men Starve?* New York: Abelard-Schuman, 1957.

13  Actually, interplanetary migration as a solution to overpopulation is both economically and sociologically impossible. See Lincoln and Alice Day, *Too Many Americans*, Boston: Houghton Mifflin Co., 1964, pp. 168–170.

14  One of the few broad, nontechnical books on the subject which carefully distinguishes between what is *possible* and what is *probable* is Harrison Brown's valuable *The Challenge of Man's Future*, New York: The Viking Press, 1954, chap. 7.

15  Their point of view is well represented by Joseph J. Spengler, "The Population Obstacle to Economic Betterment," in Joseph J. Spengler and Otis Dudley Duncan (eds.), *Population Theory and Policy: Selected Readings*, Glencoe, Ill.: The Free Press, 1956, pp. 305–316; and Kingsley Davis, "Population and the Further Spread of Industrial Society," in Spengler and Duncan, *op. cit.*, pp. 317–333. See also *The Determinants and Consequences of Population Trends*, New York: United Nations, 1953, pp. 282–284.

16  See, for example, Vogt, *op. cit.*; and Fairfield Osborn, *Our Plundered Planet*, Boston: Little, Brown and Co., 1950, chap. 5.

17  Joseph J. Spengler, "The Aesthetics of Population," *Population Bulletin*, vol. 13 (June 1957), pp. 61–75.

18  See Simon Kuznets, "Regional Economic Trends and Levels of Living," in Hauser, *op. cit.*, pp. 79–117; and Everett Hagen, "World Economic Trends and Living Standards," in Hauser, *op. cit.*, pp. 118–136; *The Determinants and Consequences of Population Trends*, *op. cit.*, chap. 15.

19  Kuznets, *op. cit.*, pp. 87–91.

20  Kingsley Davis, *The Population of India and Pakistan*, Princeton: Princeton University Press, 1951, chap. 21.

21  Ansley J. Coale and Edgar M. Hoover have shown that at present rates of economic growth, per capita income in India would increase by nearly 40 per cent if the birth rate fell by half in one generation. See Coale and Hoover, *Population Growth and Economic Development in Low-Income Countries,* Princeton, N.J.: Princeton University Press, 1958, p. 272.

22  Puerto Rico has already experienced a sharp decline in fertility, which may be a harbinger of the future of other Latin-American countries. See Christopher Tietze, "Human Fertility in Latin America," *The Annals*, vol. 316 (March 1958), pp. 84–93.

23  Irene B. Taeuber, "Population Policies in Communist China," *Population Index*, vol. 22 (October 1956), pp. 261–273.

24  See J. Mayone Stycos, "A Critique of the Traditional Planned Parenthood Approach in Underdeveloped Areas," in Clyde V. Kiser (ed.), *Research in Family*

*Planning*, Princeton, N.J.: Princeton University Press, 1962, pp. 477–501.

25  This is one of the major themes of Warren S. Thompson's *Population and Progress in the Far East*, Chicago: University of Chicago Press, 1959.

26  G. L. Arnold, *The Pattern of World Conflict*, New York: The Dial Press, 1955, pp. 202–227; see also

Morris Watnick, "The Appeal of Communism to the Peoples of Underdeveloped Areas," in Reinhard Bendix and Seymour Martin Lipset (eds.), *Class, Status and Power: A Reader in Social Stratification*, 2d ed., Glencoe, Ill.: The Free Press, 1966, pp. 428–436.

## 35  POPULATION GROWTH IN THE UNITED STATES

DONALD J. BOGUE

When the topic of overpopulation is introduced, one often gets the impression that Americans tend to heave a sigh of relief that here, at least, is one thing about which we need not worry. Uncle Sam is paying farmers not to grow food. Billions of dollars of food surpluses are stored in little crib cities throughout the agricultural regions. Although it is true that starvation from overpopulation is a remote possibility here, whereas it is an emergent reality in other parts of the world, the United States has its population problems too. Our lives may not be at stake, but our way of life and standard of living are imperiled. Just as overrapid population growth threatens to eat up the social and economic gains for which the nations of Asia, Africa and Latin America are working, so it threatens to devour many of the social and economic gains which the United States has gained, and to which it still aspires. Here and in other economically advanced nations, therefore, rapid population growth is a threat less to subsistence than to living. Since 1946 our rate of population growth has been so high as to lead some experts to call it, also, a "population explosion."

Such growth has a high social and economic cost, which merits full consideration. We have not

Reprinted from Donald J. Bogue, "Population Growth in the United States," in Philip M. Hauser (ed.), *The Population Dilemma*, by permission of Prentice-Hall, Inc., Englewood Cliffs, N.J., and the author. Copyright ©1963 by The American Assembly, Columbia University, New York.

yet become fully aware of our increased growth since 1946. Some of the more serious effects will begin to be felt quite strongly by 1965, for after this date the population count will mount higher and higher in amounts that will make the building of subdivisions in one year to provide housing for the growth of a half-dozen average-sized metropolitan areas the equivalent of the entire settlement of the West.

These are strong assertions. Let us examine the facts of present and prospective growth on which they are based, and then search for their implications.

### CURRENT AND PROSPECTIVE GROWTH

The population of the United States is the fourth largest in the world. Only China, India, and the USSR have larger populations. On July 1, 1963, we numbered about 190 million persons, which is one sixteenth of all of the earth's population. Thus we comprise only a comparatively small proportion of the earth's human creatures. But in proportion to land area, we have our share (the United States land area is about six percent of the earth's total land).

Our population is now increasing at the rate of three million persons per year. Never before in the nation's history has the population growth been so great as in recent years. Our actual growth of thirty million from April 1953 to April 1963 was equal to the entire net growth of the territory which is now the United States during the two and a third centuries from the landing of the pilgrims to the Civil War (1620 to 1860). It is equal to nearly twice the growth of the nation during any decade since the nation was established.

Despite this tremendous volume of growth, the *rate* of growth expressed in percentage terms does not seem impressively high. It is only 1.63 percent per year (for 1960–61). Among the nations of the world this is about an average rate of growth, or even a little below average. Most of the nations of Europe are growing more slowly than this, while most of Asia and Latin America are growing more rapidly. In Europe, a growth rate of 0.5 to 0.75 percent is about average, while in Asia and Latin America the average growth rate is about 2.5 percent per year. But 1.63 percent of 190 million is equal to 3.1 million persons.

The fact that the population is able to grow by such large amounts with what appears to be only a small rate has a very important implication: as the population size increases, if the rate remains the same, the amount of annual increase will become larger and larger. The annual increments ultimately become so large that numbers which look impossibly high are obtained. For example, if our current population of 190 million persons continues to grow for only one century at its present rate, the population of the United States would be about one billion persons. This is equivalent to one-third of the world's present inhabitants, and would be roughly equivalent to moving all of the population of Europe, Latin America and Africa into the territory of the fifty states. Table 1 reports what the population of the United States would be at each census for the next century if it continues to grow at the rate of 1960–61; Figure 1 charts the trend population growth would take.

During the depth of the economic depression, the growth rate sank to a record low of 0.8 percent for the year 1933. The population has never grown more slowly than this in the nation's history. If we returned to this level instantaneously, we would still have a very large population by 2065, as Table 1 shows. Projecting the curve for only a few decades beyond one hundred years

leads to numbers which quickly become fantastically high, even at the slow rate of growth.

What does this mean for America? It means that although we are not yet aware we have a population problem, we nevertheless have all the ingredients of a very serious one which could reach very critical proportions in only a generation from now. If present rates continue, our children born today, if they live to retire at age sixty-five, will be living in a nation nearly *three times* as populous as at present. Thus, the intolerable impact of runaway population growth is not a spectre that can be banished to far-away places like India and China. It is lurking in the background here, and could blight the lives of our children and grandchildren already born or to be born from now on.

These calculations are straightforward and simple. They are based on an expected birth rate of 23.6 per thousand population and a death rate of 9.3 and a very limited amount of immigration. Applying the annual rate of 1.63 to the 1960 population, using the compound interest formula, yields the results just cited. The picture is rendered even more dismal by the realization that the population of almost every nation on earth outside Europe is racing toward a level that is of even greater magnitude than that of the United States.

THE BOOM BABIES GROW UP   The prolonged "baby boom" of 1946–1963 emerged as a surprise to most demographers after the low and falling birth rates during the 1930's (see Figure 2). During the period 1926 to 1941, in fact, the number of births actually fell below those of earlier years, and the nation seemed headed toward a leveling off in total population size, and perhaps even a decline.

If Figure 2 is studied carefully, the nature of the problem becomes clearer.

1 From 1920 to 1933 the birth *rate* fell steadily and by a substantial number of points. It declined from 27.7 in 1920 to 18.4 in 1933 (a decline of 35 percent). Meanwhile, the annual *number* of births declined much more slowly. There was no decline at all to speak of until 1926–27, but the rate fell so sharply after 1926 that the number of births declined. But the decline in birth

**TABLE 1**    *Projected population for the United States at each census, 1970–2060, on the assumptions that the population continues to grow at the rate of 1.63 percent per year and at the rate of 0.8 percent per year*

| Year | Annual rate 1.63 | | Annual rate 0.8 | |
|---|---|---|---|---|
| | Estimated population, millions | Estimated increase during preceding decade, millions | Estimated population, millions | Estimated increase during preceding decade, millions |
| 1960 | 180 | 28 | 180 | 28 |
| 1970 | 212 | 32 | 195 | 15 |
| 1980 | 249 | 37 | 211 | 16 |
| 1990 | 292 | 43 | 229 | 18 |
| 2000 | 344 | 51 | 248 | 19 |
| 2010 | 404 | 61 | 268 | 20 |
| 2020 | 475 | 71 | 290 | 22 |
| 2030 | 558 | 83 | 314 | 24 |
| 2040 | 656 | 98 | 341 | 27 |
| 2050 | 771 | 115 | 369 | 28 |
| 2060 | 907 | 137 | 399 | 30 |
| 2065 | 1,000 | . . . | 416 | . . . |

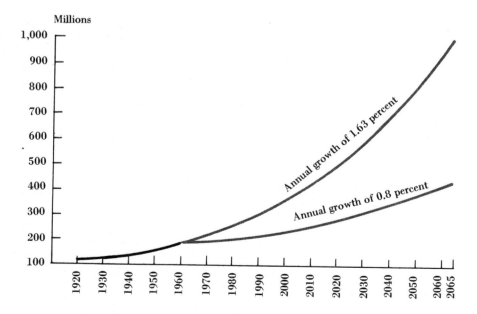

**FIGURE 1**    *Projected growth of U.S. population on the assumption that it continues to grow (a) at the 1961–1962 rate of 1.63 percent per year and (b) at the minimal rate of 0.8 percent per year.*

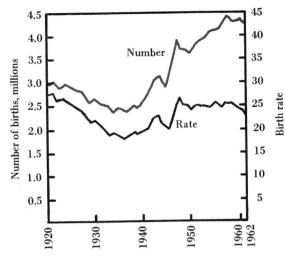

**FIGURE 2**    *Trend in the number of live births and in the crude birth rate, 1920–1962.*

numbers was much less than in the birth rate. This happened because the declining rate was applied to a base of women of childbearing age still growing.

2 When the birth rate rose in the 1940's, there was a very substantial increase in the annual number of births. Between 1946 and 1951 the *increase* amounted to more than one million births per year. During these years the moderately high rate of about twenty-five per thousand was applied to the rather large group of women born during the years 1916 to 1924, when the birth rate was also moderately high about twenty-seven per thousand.

3 Figure 2 shows that the onset of the baby boom came just as the first of the smaller cohorts born between 1925 and 1945 (idem) grew up, married, and began to produce children. *Since 1945 our corps of childbearers has been comprised of a shrinking number of women of prime childbearing age.* As of 1963, the last of the undersized cohorts had entered the reporductive age, and hereafter the number of women of childbearing age will increase rapidly. From now on birth rates must fall by a substantial amount just to keep the number of births constant at about four and one-half million.

But what has happened to the birth rate in the last few years? Figure 2 shows that since 1957 it has been declining steadily. But we must remember that this is the *crude* birth rate (births per 1,000 population), and includes in the denominator the large and increasing number of children born since 1946. A more refined way of measuring the fertility rate is to observe the rate for each age group and then to compute an age-standardized general fertility rate based upon women of childbearing age only. Demographers are generally agreed that this is the best single measure of fertility level.

Table 2 reports the age specific fertility rate of the United States population for 1950 and 1960,

**TABLE 2**    *Age specific fertility rates and summary rates of fertility for the white and nonwhite populations of the United States, 1950–1960*

| Fertility measures | White | | | Nonwhite | | |
|---|---|---|---|---|---|---|
| | 1960 | 1950 | % change 1950–1960 | 1960 | 1950 | % change 1950–1960 |
| Age specific rates, years | | | | | | |
| 15–19 | 79.8 | 70.3 | +13.5 | 163.4 | 169.0 | −3.4 |
| 20–24 | 252.8 | 190.4 | +32.8 | 294.2 | 242.6 | +21.3 |
| 25–29 | 194.9 | 165.1 | +18.0 | 214.6 | 173.8 | +23.5 |
| 30–34 | 109.6 | 102.6 | +6.8 | 135.6 | 112.6 | +20.4 |
| 35–39 | 54.0 | 51.4 | +5.1 | 74.2 | 64.3 | +15.4 |
| 40–44 | 14.7 | 14.5 | +1.4 | 22.0 | 21.2 | +3.8 |
| 45–49 | 0.8 | 1.0 | −20.0 | 1.7 | 2.6 | −52.9 |
| Summary rates | | | | | | |
| Crude birth rate | 22.7 | 23.0 | −1.3 | 32.1 | 33.3 | −3.7 |
| General fertility rate (births per 1,000 women 15–44) | 113.2 | 102.3 | +10.7 | 153.6 | 137.3 | +11.9 |
| Standardized fertility rate | 105.8 | 89.2 | +18.8 | 139.7 | 120.9 | +15.6 |
| Total fertility rate (15–44) | 3,533.0 | 2,976.0 | +18.7 | 4,528.0 | 3,929.0 | +15.2 |

and the age standardized general fertility rates—with percent change in the measures. The data are reported separately for the white and nonwhite population in order that we may make comparisons later. From this table emerges a most surprising finding: American fertility *increased* sharply between 1950 and 1960, despite the fact that the crude birth rates were falling. For the white population the standardized general fertility rate rose from 84.2 to 109.5, an increase of twenty-three percent. For the nonwhite population, it increased by fifteen percent. The table shows that the greatest increases occurred in the age group 20–29 for whites and 20–34 for nonwhites.

The explanation for this apparent contradiction lies, of course, in the smaller number of women available for childbearing between 1950 and 1960. The "baby boom" was created by an unusually small cohort of women of childbearing age who have been bearing children at a rapid rate, a rate that has been rising.

Lay observers have been noting the fall in the *crude* birth rate and are beginning to conclude that the "baby boom" is over. This is a great oversimplification and may be far from the truth. Instead, we possibly are facing a sudden spurt in population growth that could make the baby boom of 1946 look small. In fact, the only way it can be averted is for birth rates for women of all ages to decline by fifteen to twenty-five percent.

The reason for this is that we are moving into an era when the number of women of childbearing age will be increasing rapidly. Table 3 gives the picture of the number of women of childbearing age (fifteen to forty-four years of age) at each

**TABLE 3**  *Number of women of childbearing age, in millions*

| Year | Age 15–44 | Age 20–29 |
|------|-----------|-----------|
| 1930 | 29 | 11 |
| 1940 | 32 | 12 |
| 1950 | 34 | 12 |
| 1960 | 36 | 11 |
| 1970 | 43 | 15 |
| 1980 | 54 | 20 |
| 1990 | 70 | 22 |

census 1930–60, and the projected number to 1990.

These are actual population counts or official population projections of the U.S. Bureau of Census, and there is very little guess work in them. For all but an insignificant portion of the population of 1980, they represent persons who were already born in 1960, and who will be merely growing up to enter the reproductive ages. A look at these figures shows how the number of women of childbearing ages (and especially in the peak years of childbearing, 20–29) has remained nearly constant for the past twenty to thirty years, but how it will undergo a phenomenal increase during the present decade. No matter what the birth rates are during the next two decades, they will apply to a population of childbearers that will double between 1960 and 1990. It will take a most dramatic fall in birth rates to avoid extremely rapid population growth in the next twenty years. It *is* possible for this decrease to occur. The American population knows how to use contraception effectively if it so desires. There is some evidence that as of 1962 it was beginning to take some action to reduce the fertility rates. The big question is, "Will the reduction be big enough and fast enough to avert serious social and economic dislocation?"

A careful study of the incomplete statistics at hand suggests that *perhaps* in 1961 or 1962 there was a *start* toward reduction in fertility. Applying the age-specific fertility rates of 1960 to the number of women of childbearing age estimated for 1962 yields an estimate of the number of births expected in 1962 if there had been no change in fertility levels. Extrapolating the preliminary data for January to October of 1962 population (the last month for which data are available), it appears that the 1962 population failed to achieve this expected amount by 2.5 percent. In other words, when the factors of age and race are held constant, the American birth rate seems to have declined by 2.5 percent in the last two years. This may very well be the beginning of a major readjustment to demographic reality. But so far the extent of this curtailment is much too small to offset the very great impact of the increased number of childbearers who will replace the small cohorts of depression childbearers just now passing out of the picture. At least one-half of the recent decline in the crude birth rate is due to the rapidly changing age composition of the childbearing force of women. Thus, as the baby boom babies grow up, they threaten to initiate another round of population growth, simply because the number of childbearers will be greatly increased. They will also have other effects, which we will now examine.

## THE NEXT 25 YEARS

America's population problem has more dimensions than that which relates to the attempt to reduce fertility under conditions of a rising number of childbearers. Even if we could by some magical trick lower fertility today to a point where it would level off and not rise above 4.5 million births per year, we would still be faced with population problems of a thorny nature. In 1963 there was an unprecedented number of infants and children up to seventeen years old, born after the onset of the baby boom in 1946. These children have caused some inconvenience and public concern because of the demands they have made upon the economy. We have had to build grammar schools at a pace so rapid that only federal intervention has managed to prevent a catastrophe in many communities. Even so, double-shift classes have become commonplace, and teachers have been burdened with oversize classes. There have been other inconveniences: the station wagon has become stylish; the much more expensive four-bedroom house or apartment has come into demand again after a quarter-century of declining popularity. Juvenile delinquency has been on the increase in badly overcrowded slum areas; television and other mass media have been accused of catering to the tremendous juvenile audience rather than to the much smaller adult audience.

But these changes and inconveniences are probably minor in comparison with those in store in the next 25 years. Beginning in June 1964, and in every June thereafter, our high schools will spew out a graduating class of students that will be, on the average, one million students larger than the previous level. For each three graduates in 1960 there will be four graduates after 1965.

The current flurry over "school drop-outs" is just an out-of-focus example of the forthcoming problem. The *rate* of school drop-outs has *not* risen. In fact, it has declined. But the number of children now in the upper grades who are exposed to the possibility of dropping out has increased so much that a new and serious problem has been created. During the quarter century 1965 to 1990 a whole series of population problems of this type will unfold. The foundations for each one have already been laid, because the actors have already joined the cast and are only awaiting their cue to enter on stage at the appropriate moment of the life cycle. We will discuss some of these problems.

HIGH SCHOOL ENROLLMENT    The baby boom cohorts are just now beginning to have their impact upon the high schools. By January 1, 1965, the entire high school system will consist of baby boom enrollees. Thereafter, the high school enrollment will continue to rise at a steady rate of about three percent per year until 1980, as babies already born grow up to enter high school. Projections prepared by the Bureau of Census indicate an expected enrollment of 15.1 million students in high schools in 1970 in comparison with 10.1 in 1960. In the decade 1960—70, the enrollment in grammar school will remain about stationary, while high school enrollment will jump by fifty percent.

What happens to the high school enrollment after 1980 depends, of course, upon the course of the birth rate after 1960—62. We might add, parenthetically, that the peak of the expansion in grammar school enrollment seems to have been reached. During the years 1963 to 1970 it will remain stationary. This is due to the fact that the number of births has remained comparatively steady for the past eight to ten years.

The cost of providing education at the high school level is greater per pupil-year, because of the much greater number, variety and complexity of the facilities required. For this reason, public

TABLE 4    *Estimated college enrollment*

| Year | Millions of students |
|------|----------------------|
| 1960 | 4 |
| 1965 | 6 |
| 1970 | 8 |
| 1975 | 10 |
| 1980 | 12 |

TABLE 5    *Estimated increase in employment*

| Year | Labor force, millions | Increase per year, millions |
|------|-----------------------|-----------------------------|
| 1960 | 73 | 1.0 |
| 1965 | 79 | 1.2 |
| 1970 | 87 | 1.5 |
| 1975 | 94 | 1.4 |
| 1980 | 100 | 1.3 |

reaction to the rising expenditures for secondary public schools may be much stronger than for elementary schools. Unless facilities are provided, the quality of training given can fall precipitously.

COLLEGE ENROLLMENT    The college enrollment picture is similar to that for high schools except that it is complicated by two additional factors: (1) the rapidly rising rate of college attendance, as an increasing proportion of students leaving high school go on to college; and (2) the prolongation of college education with a growing emphasis upon post-graduate training.

Projections of the college enrollment have been made to 1980 by the United States Bureau of Census. A near doubling of college enrollments is forecast for the decade 1960–70 and a fifty percent increase for the decade 1970–80. From the calculations made it appears that within the twenty years from 1960 to 1980 college and professional enrollment will treble in size. The estimated college enrollment by years is shown in Table 4.

A few of the very first of the baby boom babies enrolled as college freshmen in the autumn of 1962. This trickle is destined to become a flood, so that by 1965 the enrollment will be about 1.7 million above the four million of 1960. Since college and especially graduate training require far more elaborate and costly facilities than high school, it is clear that the task of educating the children of the baby boom at a high level will be most expensive. The problem of maintaining quality in teaching and standards of excellence in student performance under these conditions may be very serious in the next two decades.

THE EXPLODING LABOR MARKET    The same enlarged cohorts of young persons who will be invading colleges will also be seeking jobs. Consequently, the labor force is beginning to experience an explosion of growth at the present time, and will continue to do so for at least the next twenty-five years. This expansion has already begun because many of the boom babies have already passed the minimum fourteen-year age limit, and have begun to work instead of continuing in school. Table 5, prepared from projections of the United States Census Bureau, shows what future employment levels will probably be like.

We are currently adding a net of more than one million new workers each year. By 1970 this will have been stepped up to a 1.5 million increase in workers per year. Such expansion will result, by 1980, in a labor force of about one hundred million persons. This estimate is very likely to materialize, because all but an insignificant fraction of the workers-to-be have already been born; the process of maturation will bring them into the labor force, barring a national calamity or war. The trend of labor force participation rates is also relatively stable and reasonably predictable. Never in its history has the nation been faced with such an expansion in the work force. Labor is a commodity which must go to market as it is produced by the nation's school systems. What effect such a large supply will have upon wages or prices is not clear. It remains to be seen whether the economy can absorb new workers at this rate without gradually building up a large volume of hard core unemployment. Some economists see labor force expansion as an important spur to the economy because these young workers will bring with them a vast demand for additional production—automobiles, houses, and all of the purchases that accompany the establishment of a new household.

A point which needs to be considered is that with an expanded labor market it will be possible to develop a large caste of unemployed persons under the guise of "business normality." Even if unemployment levels of five to seven percent remain in effect, by 1980 this will mean a total of five to seven million unemployed on a routine basis. This represents a total *volume* of human misery on a *routine basis* more than half as great as was experienced during the great economic depression of 1931–40. A really severe recession could send the number of unemployed skyrocketing to over fifteen million. The potentialities for the quantity of human suffering that can now emanate from even moderate business recessions are becoming immense.

There is evidence already that this problem is beginning to plague us, and create a drag on our economic progress. Until recently, urban poverty in the United States has had almost a hundred percent turnover from generation to generation; the children of the poor in one generation almost all climbed into the middle income bracket and were replaced by a fresh wave of in-migrants from rural areas. Now there is mounting evidence that this process is slowing down, so that in our slums the poor are begetting children destined to remain poor. We are hearing more and more of families and individuals on relief whose parents also were on relief, and of the emergence of a "culture of dependency." The recent book *National Income and Welfare* by Morgen, David, *et al.*, provides statistical evidence that this actually is occurring, and is not just a nightmare conjured up by sociologists. That Negro citizens are being singled out to comprise this caste of professional public dependents makes it an even more worrisome population problem.

FUTURE HOUSEHOLDS    An average household at the present time contains 3.4 persons. It is clear that there will be a vast increase in the number of households—roughly one million per year from 1965 to 1975 and even greater thereafter. This is roughly equivalent to building one complete Chicago during each year in the foreseeable future merely to keep abreast of population growth—without replacing housing already built.

A very large quantity of housing built in the 1920's and earlier is becoming obsolete and in need of replacement. By 1980 much of this will have become substandard. In order to clear and replace it a large program of renewal will be required. Whether this can be done at a time when such vast amounts of housing are needed merely to keep abreast of population growth will depend upon the level of prosperity and purchasing power of the population. If the labor force succeeds in absorbing the new cohorts as they emerge, the housing needed may be produced as a simple matter of keeping up with the market. If, however, purchasing power lags, there may be a serious housing problem.

In 1958 the U.S. Bureau of Census prepared projections of future trends in the number of households; and these are still reasonably precise estimations of what we may expect. The census in 1960 counted 53.0 million households instead of the 51.9 million households projected, but the *trends* envisaged would be roughly the same. Table 6 summarizes these trends.

It is clear that under almost any set of assumptions, the nation is faced with the need for a major

TABLE 6    *Estimated increase in number of households*

| Year | Increase in households during the year |
|------|----------------------------------------|
| 1960 | 701 |
| 1961 | 482 |
| 1962 | 730 |
| 1963 | 857 |
| 1964 | 878 |
| 1965 | 750 |
| 1966 | 776 |
| 1967 | 867 |
| 1968 | 1,019 |
| 1969 | 830 |
| 1970 | 886 |

house-building program to handle its population growth.

FUTURE EXPENDITURES FOR COMMUNITY FACILITIES    Within the next two decades, population growth will require a substantial extension of community facilities. Despite the fact that they have constructed numerous, costly and elaborate freeways, a majority of metropolitan areas have serious traffic problems that can be solved only by additional public outlays for more freeways, or by the construction of subway systems. The problem of water supply is becoming extremely serious in many metropolitan areas, and one that can be solved only by the construction of new systems that tap new supplies—often hundreds of miles away. Population growth has caused the flow of sewage to mount to such proportions that not only is its disposal a problem, but it also complicates greatly the problem of water supply elsewhere. High densities of great populations are bringing problems of smog and air pollution. As our population grows, present parks and other recreation facilities are becoming badly overloaded, and the taxpayer is asked to approve bond issues for acquisition of new areas, in addition to the bonds for subways, water purification systems, sewage disposal systems, etc.

Many economists would maintain that each new unit of population brings with it the added earning power (and hence tax-paying power) to repay the community for the added facilities it must build. Others point out that cities, increasing in size and complexity, eventually reach a point where additional units have a more-than-proportional cost, and that the modern metropolis is reaching or has reached this point. In the future, population growth may impose costly financial burdens which fiscally weakened municipalities will be ill prepared to bear.

Irrespective of which of these two views is correct, the next three decades are going to require extensive expansion in community facilities, and the funds for providing them must be raised either from current or deferred taxes. The full impact of this demand will be felt after 1965, as the pace of

new family formation picks up. The amount of public expenditure required to provide streets, sidewalks, street lights, police and fire protection, and all other community facilities to new households far outweighs the amount of public expenditure required to maintain new pupils in elementary school or high school. It is this latter, much greater expenditure which the baby boom will be generating henceforth.

SUMMARY    From whatever perspective we care to view the next twenty-five years, it is clear that the baby boom children, now becoming adults, will create an impact of major proportions. It must be reemphasized that this impact is predicated upon people already born, and is completely independent of the prospects for longer-run growth. These are the dimly foreseen consequences of fertility upsurge. In our renewed enthusiasm for childbearing and having children, we may have unwittingly created a situation which will cause those children to live at a substantially lower level of comfort and security than was enjoyed by the people who bore them.

It is quite possible that the unmistakable, but as yet small-scale, reduction in fertility that has set in since 1962 may be a mass reaction to the rather unrestrained fertility of the period 1946–60.

The questions we have itemized as public population problems are now being faced in millions of individual households throughout the land, in the form of voting on bonds for high school construction; seeing the rising college tuition rates; having two or three children simultaneously searching for work; needing a larger house that one cannot afford; paying state as well as federal income taxes to build public facilities. Unfortunately for all concerned, the full force of the blow lags about fifteen to eighteen years behind the blessed events that caused it.

## POPULATION DISTRIBUTION

Concurrently with its growth the American population has been undergoing a dramatic geographic redistribution. The following shifts are among the most outstanding:

1 Migration from rural (especially rural-farm) areas has been taking place rapidly.

2 There has been heavy movement of population toward metropolitan areas.

3 There has been extensive outward movement from low-income areas to higher income areas of greater economic opportunity.

4 There has been a flow of middle- and upper-income population from the North and East to the South (especially Florida and the Gulf Coast) and the Southwest.

5 There has been heavy migration to the Pacific Coast of persons from all strata and from all regions.

6 There has been massive out-movement of population from the densely settled core of metropolitan areas to the suburban fringe. This movement has become so extensive that the metropolitan areas are beginning to merge one with another, to form extensive chains of megalopolitan proportions, or "conurbations" as the British call them.

7 There has been a concentration of the Negro population into ghetto-like deteriorated portions of our largest metropolises.

None of these trends is new; all began several decades ago. However, each one has now proceeded to a point where at least some observers are beginning to inquire whether the process has not gone too far or is going too fast. The writer holds no firm opinion about the pattern by which population ought to be distributed for maximal well-being of the nation. It is important, however, to be familiar with the facts and issues, because during the next few decades there will undoubtedly be much discussion of each of these distributional trends.

In presenting the statistical facts about each of these trends, it is necessary to compare one region of the nation with another. A comparatively recent system of regional classification, the system of Economic Regions, has been employed by the Census Bureau and others for more precisely portraying differences in growth patterns from one section of the country to another. The boundaries of these regions are shown in Fig. 3. Table 7 reports the population and growth rates for each of the thirteen economic regions.

DEPOPULATION OF RURAL AREAS     Between 1950 and 1960 the urban population of the nation increased by twenty-nine percent, while the rural population declined slightly (one percent). During this decade, when the nation as a whole was undergoing the greatest population growth in its history, almost one-half (forty-nine percent) of the 3,134 counties actually *lost* population. These are rural counties and especially counties with large farm populations. Thus, the rural (and especially rural-farm) areas of the nation are in the grip of a great depopulation. This same phenomenon took place in the 1940's, so that in the past two decades many parts of the nation have lost one-fourth to one-half of their 1940 population. The movement has been to cities. At the time of the 1960 census more than seventy percent of the population was urban and only thirty percent rural. This phenomenally rapid growth of the urban population has three sources. First, there has been a very great out-migration of people from rural to urban areas, as described above. Second, the urban people have had moderately high birth rates, and have contributed a great deal to their own growth. Finally, small towns grow to a size where they are defined by the census as urban, and subdivisions on the edges of cities are gradually built up solidly enough to be included as a part of the urban population. Between 1950 and 1960 the equivalent of the total migration loss to the rural population, from all sources, seems to have been drawn from the farm population. In 1960 the farm population numbered only 13.4 million, or 7.5 percent of the total. The exact amount of the loss of farm population between 1950 and 1960 cannot be determined because of a change in the definition of the farm population, but it probably was about six million, or roughly one-fourth of the farm population as of 1950.

How many farmers should we have? Some economists say we still have too many, that the nation's food could be grown on far fewer, more factory-like farms managed by experts using the

**TABLE 7**  *Distribution of population by economic provinces and economic regions, 1950 and 1960, with measures of distributional change, 1950–1960*

| Province and region | Population, 1960, millions | Economic region | Total population, % 1960 | 1950 |
|---|---|---|---|---|
| Total | 179.0 | | 100.0 | 100.0 |
| A    Atlantic Metropolitan Belt Province | 36.5 | . . . | 20.3 | 20.5 |
|     Atlantic Metropolitan Belt Region | 36.5 | I | 20.5 | 20.5 |
| B    The Great Lakes and Northeastern Province | 41.1 | . . . | 22.9 | 23.5 |
|     Eastern Great Lakes and Northeastern Upland Region | 10.1 | II | 5.6 | 6.1 |
|     Lower Great Lakes Region | 25.2 | III | 14.1 | 14.1 |
|     Upper Great Lakes Region | 5.8 | IV | 3.2 | 3.3 |
| C    The Midwestern Province | 23.2 | . . . | 13.0 | 13.5 |
|     North Center (Corn Belt) Region | 17.2 | V | 9.6 | 10.1 |
|     Central Plains Region | 6.0 | VI | 3.4 | 3.4 |
| D    The Southern Province | 52.1 | . . . | 29.0 | 30.0 |
|     Central and Eastern Upland Region | 14.9 | VII | 8.3 | 9.4 |
|     Southeast Coastal Plains Region | 16.4 | VIII | 9.1 | 9.9 |
|     Atlantic Flatwoods and Gulf Coast Region | 11.8 | IX | 6.6 | 5.3 |
|     South Center and Southwest Plains Region | 9.0 | X | 5.0 | 5.5 |
| E    The Western Province | 26.5 | . . . | 14.8 | 12.5 |
|     Rocky Mountain and Intermountain Region | 4.6 | XI | 2.6 | 2.4 |
|     Pacific Northwest Region | 4.9 | XII | 2.7 | 2.7 |
|     Pacific Southwest Region | 17.0 | XIII | 9.5 | 7.5 |

Source: Donald J. Bogue and Calvin L. Beale, *Economic Areas of the United States*, New York: The Free Press, 1961, table A, part I.

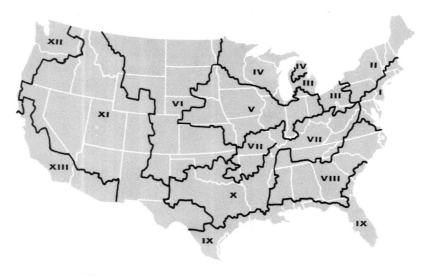

**FIGURE 3**  *Economic regions of the United States. (U.S. Department of Agriculture.)*

**TABLE 7**    *(Continued)*

| Percentage point change | Population increase, %, 1950–1960 | Urban, %, 1960 | Rural, %, 1960 |
|---|---|---|---|
| 0.0 | 18.5 | 69.9 | 30.1 |
| –0.2 | 17.5 | 86.6 | 13.4 |
| –0.2 | 17.5 | 86.6 | 13.4 |
| –0.6 | 15.7 | 72.5 | 27.5 |
| | | | |
| –0.5 | 9.7 | 60.2 | 39.8 |
| +0.1 | 18.6 | 80.7 | 19.3 |
| –0.1 | 14.5 | 58.3 | 41.7 |
| –0.5 | 13.6 | 58.5 | 41.5 |
| –0.5 | 12.6 | 57.9 | 42.1 |
| 0.0 | 16.4 | 60.0 | 40.0 |
| –1.0 | 14.7 | 49.9 | 50.1 |
| –1.1 | 5.1 | 49.9 | 50.1 |
| –0.8 | 9.6 | 47.5 | 52.5 |
| +1.3 | 48.1 | 76.0 | 24.0 |
| –0.5 | 8.3 | 60.4 | 39.6 |
| +2.3 | 39.6 | 78.2 | 21.8 |
| +0.2 | 26.7 | 59.7 | 40.3 |
| 0.0 | 21.7 | 64.4 | 35.6 |
| +2.0 | 50.1 | 87.1 | 12.9 |

most scientific methods. Others say we have too few farmers, that the family-size farm is a social institution that we must not abandon. The farm community is reputed to produce wholesome and earnest citizens who suffer less than urban-reared persons from the various personality diseases and, as adults, are more resistant to the disorganizing influences of the big city. Those who hold this philosophy feel that we should preserve the family-farm as a wholesome childrearing as well as a nation-feeding institution. The wholesale consolidation of family size farms into fewer but larger, more economically "efficient" units has another important side-effect. As the number of farmers decreases, it causes the small town trade centers that served farmers' needs to shrivel up and disappear, so that the whole fabric of rural and small-town social organization is disappearing throughout the rural Midwest, West, and South.

Farmers' children must now be hauled dozens of miles on buses to schools, and the farm community is now so dispersed as to be almost nonexistent in many parts of the land. Is it good to have population density in the rural areas decline to a point where community life disappears—especially when the empty rural areas are contrasted with over-full metropolises in which two-hour-long commuting journeys are a part of the daily routine? Do we want somehow to distribute the economy over the land so that we can use our environment for more enjoyable living and reap the personal benefits of freedom and space to be found in a less confined semi-urban location? Has the time come to try to control the urbanward trend in order to preserve some of the culture, character traits, and physical vitality of rural dwellers? These are questions that are being asked by more and more people.

As we become more prosperous as a nation, can we now afford to give greater priority to desirable residential factors in locating the population and less priority to the factors of plant-location and a central concentration of business executives? A perfectly uniform distribution of the population over the land is obviously an impractical and probably undesirable goal. The question of how concentrated the population should be is not simple, yet it obviously poses problems for future discussion.

**THE METROPOLITAN SHIFT**    For several decades there has been a steady shifting of population to form large urban aggregates that have come to be called "metropolitan areas." The federal government in 1960 recognized 212 of these super-agglomerations as "standard metropolitan statistical areas." Together, these places comprise only a small fraction of the total land area, yet between 1950 and 1960 they hogged eighty-four percent of the total population increase in the nation. The vast nonmetropolitan territory grew only very slowly. This metropolitanization took place in all regions. Thus, the traditionally rural South is now not only urbanized, but is also metropolitanizing rapidly as several of its leading cities accumulate large populations.

This tight agglomeration of the nation's people into a comparatively few very large centers also raises the question of the best location for dwellings in terms of welfare and desirable community life. The present pattern is forcing a larger and larger share of the work force to travel long distances to work each day. Billions of dollars are being spent on expressways and freeways to get people to work in the morning and home at night. Almost as quickly as such expensive systems are built, they seem to become clogged with an overcapacity load. It is ironic that only a few miles outside many of these arteriosclerotic metropolises there are many small and medium-size cities languishing for want of new industrial and commercial life. On the one hand, the farm population that once formed a part of their economic base has been decimated by the new enclosure movement in agriculture. On the other hand, the recent wave of corporate mergers and consolidations has killed off many small plants that were started as local community enterprises but which became obsolete in the new era of automated industry. City planners are wondering whether, in the light of our prospective continued growth, we should not strive to create a national system of many more small metropolises, more systematically spaced to maximize community living and minimize congestion, air pollution, problems of water and sewage, and social problems of crime, delinquency, and social disorganization.

EXODUS FROM DEPRESSED AREAS The delineation of the nation into economic regions (Figure 3) recognized a "Central and Eastern Upland Region," comprised of the mountainous portions of the southern states. This region is one of widespread economic hardship and chronic un- and underemployment. It has comparatively few metropolitan centers, and many of its industries are depressed. Under the combined impact of the pull of large metropolitan centers in all directions outside, this area has suffered a very severe out-migration. Despite the fact that its birth rates are very high, between 1950 and 1960 it grew at the rate of only 5.1 percent, the slowest growth rate for any of the economic regions.

From one point of view, this outmovement may be regarded as a national gain, since it removes population from a point where it is unable to earn a livelihood to points where the chances are much improved. But again a question may be raised: might not the long-run interests of less concentrated distribution be better served by undertaking to develop the region by new industry, better transportation systems, and improved income distribution than by encouraging the draining off of population, leaving only limited human resources behind?

In previous decades, another economic region, the Central Plains Region (Region VI), was denuded of population because of outmigration in the face of prolonged drought, mechanization of wheat farming, and farm consolidation. Much of Region IV, the Upper Great Lakes Region, is a wasteland abandoned after the forests and minerals were exploited. The same is true of Region II, the Eastern Great Lakes and Northeastern Upland Region. The rural areas of Region VIII, the Southeast Coastal Plains and Piedmont Region, are also in a state of chronic depression because of erosion and soil depletion, and the competition of new cotton lands opened up in the West. All of these regions have been suffering severe population losses to the more prosperous regions.

The solution to the problems of the economically depressed Regions II, IV, VI, VII, and VIII is a topic for major national concern. Together they comprise almost one half of the total land area of the nation. Is it wise to permit or encourage the more prosperous regions to drain them of their population, or should we try to hold the population there and raise its prosperity by some sort of "economic development" of the type we are promoting in Asia, Latin America, and Africa? If we can jar metropolitan Naples,

Düsseldorf, and Tokyo out of a state of chronic depression into greater prosperity through selective encouragement of industry, can we do the same for Cairo, Illinois; Charleston, West Virginia; Bangor, Maine; Scranton, Pennsylvania; Pueblo, Colorado; and others?

THE IN-MOVEMENT TO THE GULF COAST     One region of the South, the Gulf Coast and Atlantic Flatwoods (Region IX), grew at the phenomenally rapid rate of nearly fifty percent between 1950 and 1960. It was equalled only by the growth of the Pacific Coast. This sudden build-up along the Gulf Coast has many different components. A part of it is recreation and retirement migration of people seeking to escape the rigors of the northern cold (and with modern air conditioning, to cool them in summer). A part of it is industrial and is based upon growing economic ties with Latin America. A part of it is due to military installations. Most of this flow toward the South is one of middle-income and upper-income groups. The impact upon the economic, political, and social life of the states involved is profound, and this impact has not yet exerted its full force. It has already subverted the old-South political system of Texas and Florida, and may be expected to have similar effects upon Louisiana, Mississippi, Alabama, Georgia and South Carolina. As the coastal development matures, its effect will spread further inland to encompass the lower one-half of each of the states bordering on the Gulf or Atlantic Coast.

This population development is reported not as a "problem" about which we should worry but as a very healthful growth which will help to solve a variety of old population problems. This boom in the Gulf South offers a very important lever for wiping out the last vestiges of the archaic, slavery-based social system. Most of the new Gulf industry is of an inter-state variety. Most of the new employment is of a type which elsewhere is highly unionized. In almost every segment the federal government is the big spender providing much of the impetus. The newly arriving migrants from the North have a lower level of race prejudice. All of these things conjoined could lead, under a long-range policy of nondiscrimination in employment, to an elimination of the caste status for Negroes in the South. Already this development has weakened that system greatly. Just as our economic aid to the nations of Asia, Latin America, and Africa is promoting the development of a democratic society in those nations, our economic development of the South, and especially the Gulf Coast, can be used to accomplish the same objectives there.

THE IN-MOVEMENT TO THE PACIFIC COAST     Region XIII, the Pacific Southwest Region, grew by fifty percent in the short space of ten years, 1950 to 1960. The entire region from San Francisco and Sacramento in California down the coast and around the southern one-third of Arizona has mushroomed in a most spectacular fashion. The growth is no longer based upon taking advantage of the region's raw resources—gold, agricultural land, and forests. The growth is now entirely urban and metropolitan. Los Angeles is now the nation's second largest metropolis. The State of California has already taken the place of New York as the most populous state of the Union. This dramatic growth has brought problems. The problems of smog and water supply are well known. Less well known and less well appreciated are the problems of economic base. Has this growth been so rapid that it is built upon an economic base that is highly vulnerable to business fluctuations? In the event of a major economic recession would the interior of the nation be flooded with drifting "Cali's" looking for a subsistence in the same way that California was once invaded by "Okies" from the Dust Bowl? The problem is difficult to answer, but it is quite possible that the industrial base of the Pacific Southwest is more vulnerable to the vagaries of the business cycle, the Congressional budget, and technological change than that of any other region in the nation.

THE DYING CENTRAL CITY     Almost all of the phenomenal growth that metropolitan areas have been enjoying has been concentrated around their suburban edges. The central cities themselves have grown only very slowly, and almost all of what net growth they achieved between 1950 and 1960 was through annexation. Since the fertility rates in central cities have been moderately high, the failure to grow can indicate only what is well known: the middle class and more well-to-do population have been fleeing to the suburbs in search of more space, more privacy, modern housing, pure air, less delinquency and crime, and neighbors of their own choosing.

This move has created a tremendous building boom in the suburbs. But it has had a most depressing effect upon the central cities themselves. For at least three decades the central cities have been receiving a disproportionately small share of the investments in plants and equipment, new retail ventures, and the construction of residences. As the demand for housing of good quality has eased off, residential properties have been allowed to sink into slum use, with subdivision of living quarters into smaller units, less building maintenance, and less neighborhood upkeep.

Many real estate economists and housing officials actively engaged in "urban renewal" fail to see the direct connection between slum formation and population decline. They tend to blame the influx of low-income incoming migrants. But the fact is that the volume of in-migration is far smaller than the volume of suburbanward out-migration. The phenomenon of community deterioration is everywhere evident, as fine old residential communities which formerly had a high level of community spirit and community integration now degenerate into unorganized masses of obsolescent and under-maintained housing.

**THE URBANIZATION OF NEGROES** For more than a century the rural South has struggled with the problem of Negro-white accommodation following a long era of slave-master arrangements. Suddenly, within the short space of only two

decades, the problem has been handed over to urban areas (and particularly the big metropolitan centers) to solve. As recently as 1940 less than one-half of the Negro population was living in cities; a large share was living on farms as sharecroppers or tenants. By 1960, almost three-quarters of the Negro population was urban, and a huge migratory flood of refugees from the collapse of the sharecropper system is continuing to pour into cities—both in the South and the North. Much of this migration has turned westward, so that California and the entire Mountain Region also have large and growing urban Negro populations.

For a very high percentage of Negroes, the movement out of the rural South is advantageous. A substantial share realize a big rise in real income, acquire better housing, have better health and medical care, and can send their children to better schools.

But this population shift has its problematic aspects too. Residential segregation, job discrimination, and differential treatment by community institutions are widely prevalent in the North. Huge Negro ghettos are springing up in our metropolises, and some are beginning to despair that the urban North will be no more successful than the rural South in solving the problem of racial equality. Businesses have capitalized on this race tension, so that Negroes are forced to pay a 10 to 25 percent "color tax" for housing and many other commodities and services. Often they pay the conventional or established price for goods or services of inferior quality. This seems to be especially true of medical, dental, legal, and other professional services. This is not unlike the exploitation of the sharecropper system.

Yet this shifting of the Negro population from a rural to an urban setting may eventually prove to be the critical event that leads to a resolution of race tension. At the present moment, it is greatly complicating the problem of urban renewal and slum clearance. Under present conditions, the massive arrival of the rural Negroes from the

South, bringing with them very high birth rates and a low level of skills for the metropolitan labor market, makes more difficult and more massive the task of rehabilitating the central portions of our cities.

SUMMARY Quite independently of the problem of total population size, these problems of population distribution pose some very fundamental questions for policy. It should be pointed out that all of these population movements seem to be intimately connected to industrial development, for counterparts of them are found throughout Europe, and are also topics of concern there. The problem has been described in many ways. Perhaps the most general and abstract formulation would be that in all of these economies, prime importance is given to the location and distribution of productive enterprises, and citizens are expected to adjust their residences as best they can to conform to the pattern dictated by the location of jobs.

Recent research has shown that there is very great flexibility in the location of manufacturing and other basic activities. Instead of location being a highly critical consideration, there is a wide range which provides a viable site. Intensive research into the full implications of this fundamental proposition, coupled with imaginative planning, may lead to a national program of population distribution which may give us all of the benefits of our modern technology and yet permit us to live in more pleasant environments and in neighborhoods that afford more rewarding living off-the-job.

## CONCLUSION

When the demographic facts for the United States are assembled, they suggest that instead of smugly patting ourselves on the back for escaping the impact of the population explosion, we must realize that we are participants. At present we are on a collision course that could lead us to catastrophe, timed to arrive only a very few decades after our sister nations (if they too do not alter their growth rates) have crashed on the Malthusian reefs. There is growing agreement among demographers of the world that rapid population growth does have its costs—wherever it occurs. In the United States it makes it more difficult to make progress, and may lead to a decline in well-being for a substantial share of the population. The fertility holiday in which the United States has indulged herself in the past fifteen years will profoundly affect all aspects of our national life in the next quarter century.

If this unwanted and excessive growth is to be avoided, the fertility limitations needed to stop it must be accepted by the children of today (who are ten years of age and under) when they grow to adulthood and by all future generations of children. Fertility levels are greatly influenced by the family values inherited by children from parents and religious leaders. The time to begin the program of education and guidance which these children need in order to live in the demographic world of the twenty-first century is not the year 2000, but *now*. The drastic change in thinking needed to prepare for this situation on the part of both political and religious leaders should already have been made. The fact that we are only now beginning the process may be a serious matter.

If one accepts these premises, then it is difficult to escape the conclusion that voluntary family limitation with each couple utilizing means that it finds acceptable on religious, aesthetic and physical grounds, is the alternative to some much more radical choices only a few years from now.

In discussions of actions to be taken, one point should be kept clearly in mind: a full solution of the nation's problems of population size can be achieved without requiring dramatic acts of self-restraint or self-denial of the population. A state of zero population growth can be achieved if every person marries and each couple has approximately two children, to replace themselves when they die.

## 36   DEMOGRAPHIC DIMENSIONS OF WORLD POLITICS

PHILIP M. HAUSER

Politics in general, as well as world politics, is a branch of engineering—social engineering—not of science. Yet the consideration of the demographic aspects of world politics is not an inappropriate subject for a scientific journal. It is the purpose of this article to point to ways in which the findings of the science of demography illuminate various aspects of the world political scene.

There are various ways in which this subject can be developed, but I have arbitrarily chosen to discuss population factors in relation to politics, broadly conceived, on the global and on the international levels, respectively. By "global" problems I mean those that concern the earth as a whole; by "international" problems I mean those that arise among the various political subdivisions of the globe.

### GLOBAL CONSIDERATIONS

There is no world government charged with the task of achieving world order and performing other civil governmental functions for the earth as a whole. This, however, does not mean that there are no political problems of a global, as distinguished from an international, character. Some such global problems are in fact dealt with by the United Nations and its specialized agencies, which are, of course, organizations of individual sovereign nations rather than organs of world government. Examples of global problems—problems which transcend and cannot be contained within national boundaries—include health, weather, fallout, and the newly emergent problems of outer space. It is easy to

Reprinted from *Science*, vol. 131 (1960), pp. 1641–1647, by permission of the author and the American Association for the Advancement of Science. Copyright © 1960 by the American Association for the Advancement of Science.

demonstrate that the contemporary rate of world population growth also constitutes a global problem—one which would be of great concern to a world government if we had one, and one which is of increasing concern to various organs of the United Nations and the specialized agencies.

Although the first complete census of mankind has yet to be taken, it is possible to reconstruct, with reasonable accuracy, the history of world population growth. This history may be encapsulated in the following estimates of the population of the earth: at the end of the Neolithic period in Europe (8000 to 7000 B.C.),[1] 10 million; at the beginning of the Christian era, 200 to 300 million; at the beginning of the modern era (1650), 500 million; in 1950, 2.5 billion.

These four numbers constitute a measurement of one of the most dramatic aspects of man's existence on the globe, and they explain the purple language of the demographer in describing the changes in rates of population growth during the modern era as a "demographic revolution" or "population explosion."[2]

The basis for the demographer's emotionally surcharged language may be summarized as follows:

1 The present population of the world could be produced from an initial population of two dozen individuals increasing at the rate of 0.02 percent per year over a period of 100,000 years, and man has been on the earth for at least 200,000 to 1 million years.

2 The rate of population growth has increased enormously over the three centuries of the modern era (1650–1950), during which time it averaged about 0.5 percent per year. Over this period the rate of growth increased from about 0.3 percent per year between 1650 and 1750 to 0.9 percent per year between 1900 and 1950. World

population growth averaged 1 percent per year between 1930 and 1940.

Now, a 1 percent return per year, even compounded, would by our standards represent a meager return on investment. But it constitutes a fantastically rapid rate of population increase. One hundred persons multiplying at 1 percent per year, not over the period of 200,000 to 1 million years of man's occupancy of this globe but merely for the 5000 years of human history, would have produced a contemporary population of 2.7 billion persons per square foot of land surface of the earth! Such an exercise in arithmetic, although admittedly dramatic and propagandistic, is also a conclusive way of demonstrating that a 1 percent per year increase in world population could not have taken place for very long in the past; nor can it continue for very long into the future.

The demographer's concern is not based only on considerations of the past. It is even more justified by postwar developments in population growth.

Since the end of World War II the rate of population increase has continued to accelerate and has reached a level of about 1.7 percent per year. There is justification, indeed, for pointing to a new population explosion in the wake of World War II of a greater magnitude than that previously observed. At the rate of world population increase for the period 1800–1850, for example, the present population would double in 135 years; at the 1900–1950 rate, in 67 years; and at the post-war rate, in only 42 years.

Projection of the post-World War II rate of increase gives a population of one person per square foot of the land surface of the earth in less than 800 years. It gives a population of 50 billions (the highest estimate of the population-carrying capacity of the globe ever calculated by a responsible scholar) in less than 200 years! This estimate, by geochemist Harrison Brown,[3] is based on the assumptions that developments in the capturing of solar or nuclear energy will produce energy at a cost so low that it would be

feasible to obtain all the "things" we need from rock, sea, and air, and that mankind would be content to subsist largely on food products from "algae farms and yeast factories"!

Moreover, the United Nations estimates of future world population indicate even further acceleration in the rate of world population growth during the remainder of this century. Between 1950 and 1975 the average annual percentage of increase, according to the United Nations "medium" assumptions, may be 2.1 percent, and between 1975 and 2000, almost 2.6 percent.[4] Such rates of increase would double the population about every 33 and 27 years, respectively.

It is considerations of this type that would make it necessary for a world government to exercise forethought and planning, which constitute rational decision making, in facing the future. This, of course, is the purpose of the projections. The figures do not show what the future population of the world will be—for the world could not support such populations. They do demonstrate that man, as a culture-building animal, has created an environment in which the rhythm of his own reproduction has been modified in such a manner as to point to crisis possibilities.

### CRISIS POSSIBILITIES

The crisis possibilities are of several forms, each posing major world political problems. The first, we may note, is the ultimate crisis, which would result from the fact that the globe is finite[5] and that living space would be exhausted. Unless one is prepared to argue that future technological developments will enable man to colonize other globes,[6] it is clear that present rates of population increase must come to a halt by reason of lack of space. No facts or hopes as to man's ability to increase his food production and to increase other types of goods and services can indefinitely increase man's *lebensraum* (or could do so even if we accept the absurd assumption that man, at terrific cost, could burrow into the earth, live in man-made layers above it, or live on the seas).

In the short run, let us say to 1975 or to 2000, world population will be confined to much more manageable numbers. The United Nations projects, on the basis of its medium assumptions, a world population of about 3.8 billion by 1975 and 6.3 billion by 2000.[7]

In the short run there is no problem of exhausting the space on the globe, nor is there reason to fear serious decreases in world per capita food supply, as is evidenced by projections of The Food and Agricultural Organization and others concerning foodstuffs.[8] But there is great reason to be pessimistic about the possibility of greatly increasing the average world level of living during the remainder of this century.

In 1950, world per capita income was estimated at $223.[9] In North America, per capita income was $1100. Had each person on the globe enjoyed the North American level of living in 1950, as measured by per capita income, the aggregate world product in 1950 would have supported only 500 million persons, as contrasted with the actual world population of 2.5 billion. For average world income to have matched income in North America, aggregate income would have had to be increased about fivefold. To bring world per capita income by 1975 to the level enjoyed in North America in 1950 would require about a 7.5-fold increase of the 1950 level in 25 years. To do the same by 2000 would require a 12-fold increase in the 1950 world income within 50 years.

Even if the more modest income level of Europe ($380 per capita in 1950) were set as the target, great increases in productivity would be necessary, because of prospective rates of population increase, to raise average world income to the required level by 1975 or 2000. To achieve this goal by 1975, world income would have to be increased 2.5-fold over the 1950 level, and to achieve it by 2000, the required increase would be greater than fourfold. A decline in the rate of world population growth to that of the period 1800 to 1850—namely, to 0.5 percent—would decrease by three-fourths and four-fifths, respectively, the projected world-income requirements for attaining this goal by 1975 or 2000.

These considerations not only show the enormous difficulty of materially increasing the world level of living on the basis of present rates of population increase but indicate, also, the weakness of the argument that a solution to the population problem is to be found in more equitable distribution of the world's food supply or of goods and services in general.[10] The equitable distribution of world income in 1950 would, to be sure, have raised the per capita income of Latin America by 31 percent; of Africa, almost threefold, and of Asia, four- to fivefold, but it would still have produced a per capita income per annum of $223, only one-fifth that in North America and only three-fifths that in Europe (exclusive of the U.S.S.R.). The miserably low level of living of most of the world's population is attributable not so much to maldistribution as to low aggregate product, the result of the low productivity of most of the world's peoples.

These political problems of a global character may perhaps be better understood through consideration of their international aspects, special attention being given to the plight of the two-thirds of the world's population resident in the underdeveloped areas of the world, in Asia, Africa, and Latin America.

## INTERNATIONAL CONSIDERATIONS

The short-run implications of present rates of world population growth are manifest in specific forms and in varying degrees of intensity among the various regional and national subdivisions of the globe. The distribution of the world's population and of the world's utilized resources, manifest in differentials in levels of living, is the result, of course, of millenia of human history. The demographic dimensions of international politics may best be comprehended

TABLE 1    *Population, income, and energy consumed per capita, by continent, about 1950*

| Area | Total population | | Aggregate income | | Per capita income, $ | Energy consumed per capita, KW-HR† |
|------|------------------|---|------------------|---|---------------------|-----------------------------------|
| | No., thousands | % | million* | % | | |
| World | 2497 | 100.0 | 556 | 100.0 | 223 | 1,676 |
| Africa | 199 | 8.0 | 15 | 2.7 | 75 | 686 |
| North America | 219 | 8.8 | 241 | 43.3 | 1100 | 10,074 |
| South America | 112 | 4.5 | 19 | 3.4 | 170 | 741 |
| Asia | 1380 | 55.3 | 69 | 12.4 | 50 | 286 |
| Europe (exclusive of U.S.S.R.) | 393 | 15.7 | 149 | 26.8 | 380 | 3,117 |
| U.S.S.R. | 181 | 7.2 | 56 | 10.1 | 310 | 1,873 |
| Oceania | 13 | 0.5 | 7 | 1.3 | 560 | 3,543 |

*See note 8.

†Data are based on J.J. Spengler, *Proceedings of The American Philosophical Society*, vol. 95 (1951) p. 53; original data (for 1937) from *Energy Resources of the World*, Washington, D.C.: U.S. Government Printing Office, 1949, p. 102ff.

Source: United Nations data, except as indicated.

against the background of differences among peoples in levels of living and the significance of these differences at this juncture in world history[11] (see Table 1).

To note the extremes, North America in 1950, with about 16 percent of the earth's land surface, contained less than 9 percent of the world's population but about 43 percent of the world's income. Asia, in contrast, with about the same proportion of the world's land surface (18 percent), had 55 percent of the world's population but only 12 percent of the world's income. Per capita income in Asia was at a level of about $50 per year as contrasted with a level of $1100 in North America. Despite the fact that such comparisons are subject to considerable error,[12] there is no doubt that a tremendous difference in per capita income existed, of a magnitude perhaps as great as 20 to 1.

The major factor underlying this difference is indicated by the contrast in the difference in nonhuman energy consumed in North America and Asia, respectively—over 10,000 kilowatt-hours per capita per year for the former in contrast to less than 300 for the latter. The availability of nonhuman energy for the production of goods and services is perhaps the best single measurement available of differences in capital investment, know-how, and technology which account for the great differences in productivity and, consequently, in the size of the aggregate product available for distribution.

The other relatively underdeveloped continents of the world also had relatively low shares of world income as compared with their proportions of world population. Africa, with a per capita income of about $75 per year, and South America, with $170, were also well below not only the level for North America ($1100) but also the levels for Europe (exclusive of the U.S.S.R.) ($380), the U.S.S.R. ($310), and Oceania ($560). There is a high correlation among these areas between per capita income and amount of nonhuman energy consumed (Table 1).

These differences in levels of living, as it turns out, are in general inversely related to present and prospective rates of population increase. The populations of the relatively under-

**TABLE 2**    *Estimated population and population increases, by continent, 1900–2000*

| Area | Population, *millions* | | | | | Av. annual increase, %* | | | |
|---|---|---|---|---|---|---|---|---|---|
| | 1900 | 1925 | 1950 | 1975 | 2000 | 1900–1925 | 1925–1950 | 1950–1975 | 1975–2000 |
| World | 1550 | 1907 | 2497 | 3828 | 6267 | 0.9 | 1.2 | 2.1 | 2.6 |
| Africa | 120 | 147 | 199 | 303 | 517 | 0.9 | 1.4 | 2.1 | 2.8 |
| Northern America | 81 | 126 | 168 | 240 | 312 | 2.2 | 1.3 | 1.7 | 1.2 |
| Latin America | 63 | 99 | 163 | 303 | 592 | 2.3 | 2.6 | 3.4 | 3.8 |
| Asia | 857 | 1020 | 1380 | 2210 | 3870 | 0.8 | 1.4 | 2.4 | 3.0 |
| Europe (including U.S.S.R.) | 423 | 505 | 574 | 751 | 947 | 0.8 | 0.6 | 1.2 | 1.0 |
| Oceania | 6 | 10 | 13 | 21 | 29 | 2.3 | 1.4 | 2.4 | 1.6 |

*Arithmetic mean of percentage of increase for 25-year periods.

Source: *The Future Growth of World Population*, New York: United Nations, 1953.

developed continents of the world are increasing at a more rapid rate than those of the economically advanced continents[13] (Table 2). Between 1950 and 1975, to use the medium projections of the United Nations, while the population of Northern America is increasing at an average annual rate of 1.7 percent and that of Europe, at 1.2 percent, that of Asia will be growing at an average annual rate of 2.4 percent, that of Africa at 2.1 percent, and that of Latin America at 3.4 percent. Between 1975 and 2000, while the rate of increase for Northern America will average 1.2 percent per year and that for Europe, 1.0 percent, the rate for Asia will be 3.0 percent, that for Africa 2.8 percent, and that for Latin America 3.8 percent, a rate at which the population would double about every 18 years.

As I have indicated above, rapid increase in world population imposes a severe burden on efforts to raise levels of living. It is easy to demonstrate that the burden would become an impossible one for the economically underdeveloped areas should their rates of population increase follow the trends indicated in the United Nations projections.

For example, Asia, merely to maintain her present low level of living, must increase her aggregate product by 60 percent between 1950 and 1975, and by an additional 75 percent between 1975 and 2000. To raise her per capita income to the European level for 1950 while continuing to experience her rapid population growth, Asia would have to increase her 1950 aggregate income 12-fold by 1975 and 21-fold by 2000. Africa, to do the same, must increase her aggregate income eight-fold by 1975 and 13-fold by 2000, and Latin America would have to increase her aggregate income fourfold by 1975 and eight-fold by 2000.[14]

To achieve a per capita income equal to that of Northern America in 1950 while experiencing the projected population growth, Asia would have to increase her aggregate income 35-fold by 1975 and 62-fold by 2000. Africa, to achieve a similar goal, would require 22-fold and 38-fold increases, respectively, in aggregate income, and Latin America, 12-fold and 23-fold increases.

These considerations provide additional justification for the use by the demographer of the phrase *population explosion*; and they certainly indicate the hopeless task which confronts the underdeveloped areas in their efforts to achieve higher levels of living while experiencing rapid population growth. The control of rates of population growth would unquestionably decrease the magnitude of the task of achieving higher levels of living in the underdeveloped areas, especially in those with populations that are large relative to resources.[15]

Increasingly large proportions of the population in the underdeveloped areas of the world are becoming concentrated in urban places. The continued acceleration in the rate of world urbanization during the first half of this century was mainly attributable to urbanization in the underdeveloped areas, which proceeded at a pace considerably above that in the developed areas.[16] I have had occasion to make projections of the urban population of the world and of Asia to 1975; these are presented in Table 3 as illustrative of what is in prospect in the underdeveloped areas of the globe.[17] For the rate of urbanization in Latin America and Africa is, also, accelerating.

The projections for Asia indicate that in the 25 years between 1950 and 1975, in cities either of 100,000 and over or of 20,000 and over, urban population will increase by at least two-thirds and may perhaps triple. The lower projection is based on the assumption that the proportion of urban population in Asia will be the same in 1975 as it was in 1950. Under this assumption the projected increase would result from total population growth alone. But if it is assumed that the rate of urbanization in Asia will increase as it did between 1900 and 1950 while the total population continues to grow at the rate projected by the United Nations, then tripling of Asia's urban population is indicated.

Thus, while the nations of Asia are attempting to improve their miserable urban living conditions, their urban populations will continue to increase explosively—perhaps to triple within a period of less than one generation.

In the economically more advanced nations of the world, urbanization is both an antecedent and a consequent of technological advance and of a high level of living—a symbol of man's mastery over nature. In the underdeveloped nations, however, urbanization represents instead the transfer of rural poverty from an overpopulated and unsettled countryside to a mass urban setting. In the economically underdeveloped areas of the world, urbanization is outpacing economic development and the city is more a symbol of mass misery and political

**TABLE 3**    *Summary of projections of urban population for the world and for Asia, 1975\**

| Cities, category | Projected population, millions, 1975 | | | Estimated increase in population, 1950–1975, millions | | Estimated increase in population, 1950–1975, % | | Projected proportion of total population in cities | |
|---|---|---|---|---|---|---|---|---|---|
| | 1950 | Upper | Lower | Upper | Lower | Upper | Lower | 1950 | 1975* |
| **World** | | | | | | | | | |
| 100,000 and over | 314 | 745 | 488 | 431 | 174 | 138 | 55 | 13 | 19 |
| 20,000 and over | 502 | 1155 | 779 | 653 | 277 | 130 | 55 | 21 | 30 |
| Asia | | | | | | | | | |
| 100,000 and over | 106 | 340 | 176 | 234 | 70 | 222 | 66 | 8 | 15 |
| 20,000 and over | 170 | 544 | 283 | 374 | 113 | 220 | 66 | 13 | 25 |

*Figures are based on the "upper" projection, which assumes urbanization of an increasing proportion of the population.

Source: P. M. Hansen, "Implications of Population Trends for Regional and Urban Planning in Asia," *UNESCO Working Paper 2*, U.N. Seminar on Regional Planning, Tokyo, 1958.

instability than of man's conquest of nature.[18]

The prospect for individual nations, while variable, is in general the same—one of explosive growth. Between 1955 and 1975, according to the United Nations medium projections, the population of China will increase by 294 million persons and that of India, by 177 million.[19] That of Pakistan will increase by 45 million persons, and that of Indonesia, by 40 million, in these 20 years. Japan, although she has now greatly slowed down her rate of population growth, will, despite her already great population pressure, increase by an additional 27 million. To confine our attention to the Far East for the moment, smaller countries with the most explosive increases include South Korea, Taiwan, and Ceylon. Each of these nations is faced with a task of tremendous proportions merely to maintain her present level of living, let alone to greatly increase it while continuing to grow at the projected rates.

## POLITICAL INSTABILITY

What will happen if the underdeveloped areas in Asia are frustrated in their efforts to attain a higher standard of living?

Warren S. Thompson devotes his latest book to providing an answer to this question.[20] The larger of these nations are not apt to remain hungry and frustrated without noting the relatively sparsely settled areas in their vicinities— the nations in the South-East Asian peninsula: Burma, Thailand, and the newly formed free countries of Indochina, Laos, Cambodia, and Vietnam. (Vietminh, that is North Vietnam, is already engulfed by Communist China.) Even parts of thinly settled Africa may be subject to the aggressive action of the larger and hungrier nations as feelings of population pressure mount. Moreover, Communist China, the largest nation in the world by far, faced with the greatest absolute population increases to add to her already heavy burdens in striving for eco-

nomic development, may not confine her attention only to the smaller nations within her reach. Her present actions relative to her boundaries with India and possible tensions over her boundaries with the U.S.S.R. contain explosive possibilities.

It is Thompson's conclusion that the larger nations in the Far East, including Japan, India, and Pakistan as well as China, may resort to force to achieve access to additional resources under sufficient population pressure. The smaller countries may not be able to resort to force but are almost certain to require outside aid to prevent chaos. Furthermore, while neither Indonesia nor the Philippines is in a position to be aggressive or is easily accessible to aggressors, both, under mounting population pressures, are likely to continue to experience growing internal political instability.

Population pressure as a factor in political instability is not confined to the Far East. Populations of the Middle East and North Africa—the Muslim area (exclusive of Pakistan)—may increase from 119 million in 1955 to 192 million by 1975, an increase of 73 million or 61 percent in 20 years.[21] As Irene Taeuber has noted, this is an area "where internal instabilities and conflicts of religious and ethnic groups create recurrent crises for the region and world." Taeuber observes that the immediate political instabilities in this area are attributable more to "diversities among the peoples and the nations than to population pressure or population growth."[22] But she points to the importance, in the decades that lie ahead, of economic advances to lessen tension in this region and to the barrier that rapid population growth may contribute to that development.

Latin America, although in large part still a sparsely settled area of the world, is already experiencing problems associated with rapid population growth which give promise of worsening. For Latin America, as has been reported above, is faced with a population increase of 86 percent between 1950 and 1975 and of 95 percent, almost a doubling, between 1975 and 2000.[23] Especially difficult in Latin America are the problems posed by accelerating rates of urbanization. Recent measurements of rate of urban growth in Latin America indicated that of 15 countries for which data were available, urban population in one, Venezuela, was increasing at 7 percent per year, a rate which produces a doubling about every 10 years; seven had growth rates which would double their population in less than 18 years; and only two (Chile and Bolivia) had rates of urban growth of less than 1 percent per year.[24] Growth rates (total and urban) of the magnitude which Latin America is experiencing are likely to add appreciably to the difficulty of raising living levels and are likely to worsen already existent political instabilities that threaten internal order and may affect world peace.

Finally, a fourth region of political instability to which the population factor is a contributing element, and one where it will be increasingly manifest, is sub-Saharan Africa.[25] Middle Africa is sparsely settled, but increasing knowledge about the area indicates high birth rates, decreasing death rates, and explosive growth. The United Nations projections indicate a population increase from 154 million in 1955 to about 202 million in 1975, or an increase of 31 percent. The familiar syndrome of underdeveloped areas—malnutrition, disease, and urban and rural squalor on the one hand and aspirations for independence and economic developments on the other—are now emergent in this most primitive continent of the globe. And here, as in the other underdeveloped areas, rapid population growth is likely to intensify political unrest.

In southern Africa another type of population problem is also a major element in a political problem that has grave implications for world order as well as for the stability of the Union of South Africa. This is the problem arising from the conflict between the indigenous people and European settlers manifest in apartheid. Rapid and differential rates of growth of native and European populations are likely to intensify rather than to allay conflict in southern Africa.

The tensions and political instabilities generated by explosive population growth in the economically underdeveloped nations have a special significance in the contemporary world, characterized by the bipolar conflict between the Free and Communist blocs and the effort on the part of each to win the allegiance of the uncommitted nations of the world. This conflict has several demographic dimensions of importance.

### THE FREE AND COMMUNIST BLOCS

The first of these dimensions is evident in the way in which population is distributed among the three political blocs into which the world is divided. For in 1955, each of these political groups—the free nations, the Communist nations, and the uncommitted nations—had approximately the same population. The Free and the Communist blocs, respectively, each have much to gain in the struggle to win the allegiance of the uncommitted third of the world's people. This titanic competition is focused primarily on South and Southeast Asia at the present time, because the bulk of the world's politically uncommitted population is located there.

In this war for men's minds, the competition between free-world and Communist ideologies, each of the contestants has powerful weapons. Apart from military power, which I will leave out on the assumption that a nuclear stalemate exists, the key weapons of the Communists, as is daily attested to by their propaganda, are the exploitation of the wide gap between the levels of living of the "have" and "have-not" nations and the attribution of blame for the misery of the "have-not" nations on the imperialistic and colonial practices of the "have" powers. Needless to say, the fire of this propaganda is effectively fed by the frustration of the underdeveloped areas in their efforts to advance their levels of living, or in their efforts to win independence from imperial powers, where this is not yet accomplished.

The Communist bloc, with relatively little, but with increasing, surplus product, is attempting more and more to help the uncommitted nations in economic development. The U.S.S.R. may perhaps be departing from its postwar cold-war policy of trying to persuade uncommitted nations to accept its ideology by means either of internal coups or direct external aggression.

The chief weapon of the free nations, apart from the example of their free way of life, is, undoubtedly, the provision of assistance to the underdeveloped nations to help them achieve their economic goals.

Thus, the success or failure of underdeveloped areas to raise their levels of living has the most profound world political implications. The most important immediate international political question is the question of whether the free-world approach or the Communist approach is the more effective one for achieving economic development.

It is to be emphasized that this is not a rhetorical or hypothetical question. It is being answered by the course of events, the definitive test of achievement. It is being answered by what may be regarded as the most important experiments of all time—experiments under way in each of the three blocs of nations. A great race is on among the economically underprivileged nations to attain higher living levels—some by relatively free, and some by totalitarian and Communist, methods. The contests involve nations within each of the great political blocs, for within each of them both economically advanced and underdeveloped areas are to be found.[26]

The greatest single race under way is undoubtedly the race between the leaders of the Free and Communist blocs, respectively—that is, the United States and the U.S.S.R. The U.S.S.R. has certainly served notice that, by its methods, it hopes to surpass the level of living attained by the United States, and in the not too distant future. Overshadowed only by the direct contest between the United States and the U.S.S.R. is the race between India and Communist China,[27] a race of special and direct immediate interest to the underdeveloped areas. For these mammoth nations, the two largest in the world, are bending every effort to achieve higher living standards—one through the Communist approach and the other by democratic methods. The outcome of this race will be of great interest not only to the underdeveloped nations in the uncommitted bloc but also to those in the Free bloc—the underdeveloped nations in Latin America as well as those committed to the Free bloc in Asia and in Africa.

The international political situation, then as described above, gives a special significance to explosive population growth. For present and future rates of population growth may, indeed, prevent underdeveloped nations from raising their levels of living. Simon Kuznets' examination of the evidence indicates that the gap between "have" and "have-not" nations is increasing rather than decreasing.[28] To the extent that underdeveloped nations are frustrated in their efforts to advance their living standards, they will, it may be presumed, be more open to the blandishments of the Communist bloc. Furthermore, if the underdeveloped Communist nations demonstrate that they can achieve more rapid economic progress than the underdeveloped free nations, the free way of life may well be doomed. Success or failure in this fateful contest may well hinge on the ability of the nations involved to decrease their rates of population growth.[29]

## THE ALTERNATIVES

The "why" of the population increase, in an immediate sense, is readily identifiable. It is to be found in the great increase in "natural increase"—in the gap between fertility and mortality.[30] Quite apart from the precise timing of changes in the relations between mortality and fertility, it is clear that explosive growth can be dampened only by decreasing natural increase. This is true for the world as a whole in the ultimate sense, with differences in timing for different parts of the world. For suggested solutions to the problems of present and prospective rates of population growth in the various subdivisions of the world through migration, foreign trade, redistribution of wealth, and similar means hold forth little promise, if any, even in the short run.[31]

There are only three ways to decrease natural increase: (1) by increasing the death rate; (2) by decreasing the birth rate; and (3) by some combination of the two.

Although it is true that decreased death rates were largely responsible for the population explosion in the past and are foreseen to be a large factor in the future, the adoption of a policy to increase mortality, or to diminish efforts to increase longevity, is unthinkable. Unless one is prepared to debate this, two of the three ways of decreasing natural increase are ruled out. For two of them involve an increase in death rates.

If longevity gains are to be retained, then, the only way to reduce explosive population growth is to decrease the birth rate. That is, the "death control" mankind has achieved can be retained only if it is accompanied by birth control. This proposition, even though it flows directly from the demographic facts of life, in view of prevalent value systems provokes heated debate of the type manifest in the press. Birth control has recently, indeed, made the front pages of the world press.

What is important about the value controversy under way is that it definitely affects global and international policy and action on matters of population and, therefore, on the crucial political problems involved. The most significant thing about all the available methods of birth control—a fact mainly obscured in the present public controversy—is that they are by no means adequate to the task of slowing down explosive world population increase, especially that in the underdeveloped areas. The great mass of mankind in the economically less advanced nations which are faced with accelerating rates of growth fail to limit their birth rates not because of the factors at issue in the controversy we are witnessing but because they do not have the desire, the know-how, or the means to do so. The desire to control fertility, arising from recognition of the problem, is, however, increasing. Japan is already well down the road to controlling its birth rate, although by methods which are not enthusiastically endorsed either by the Japanese themselves or by other peoples. China, India, Pakistan, and Egypt[32] have population limitation programs under way or under serious consideration, and other underdeveloped areas are showing increasing interest in this problem.[33] The changes in value systems which will create mass motivation to adopt methods of family limitation are not easily brought about,[34] but they are at least under way.

Birth control methods in use in the economically more advanced nations are not, in the main well adapted for use in the underdeveloped areas. But the results of increased research and experimentation with oral contraceptives are encouraging,[35] and there may soon be a breakthrough on obtaining adequate means for the task of limiting population growth in the underdeveloped areas.

## CONCLUSION

The demographer and the increasing number of his allies, in directing attention to the implications of world population growth, are in fact pointing to major global and internation political problems—problems that cannot be ignored. Needless to say, the solution to the problems is not to be found in appeals to the traditions of the past, sacred or secular. The solution is to be found in the policies and actions which man himself, as a rational animal, must work out and implement. The mind of man, which has conceived remarkable methods for increasing life expectancy, is probably ingenious enough to devise methods by which the population explosion can be controlled within the framework of man's diverse value systems.

## REFERENCES AND NOTES

1   *Determinants and Consequences of Population Trends*, New York: United Nations, 1953, chap. 2.
2   See the objection to this phrase in "Statement by Roman Catholic Bishops of U.S. on Birth Control," *New York Times*, Nov. 26, 1959.
3   H. Brown, *The Challenge of Man's Future*, New York: Viking, 1954.
4   *The Future Growth of World Population*, New York: United Nations, 1958.
5   This fact is ignored by Roman Catholic bishops (see note 2) and by the Pope (see "Pope Denounces Birth Limitation," *New York Times*, Dec. 15, 1959).
6   The impracticability of colonizing other planets is considered by G. Hardin, *J. Heredity*, vol. 50 (1959), p. 2.
7   *Determinants and Consequences of Population Trends, op. cit.*, p. 123.
8   W. H. Leonard, *Sci. Monthly*, vol. 85 (1957), p. 113.
9   *National and Per Capita Income of 70 Countries in 1949*, U.N. Statistical Papers, Series E, No. 1, New York: United Nations, 1950. The calculations were made by using United Nations per capita income figures for each continent applied to revised United Nations estimates of 1950 population of continents to obtain revised aggregate income by continent and for the world, as shown in Table 1. A new world per capita figure of $223 was obtained, as compared with the published figure of $230.
10   For the Communist position see F. Lorimer, "Population Policies and Politics in the Communist World," in P. M. Hauser (ed.), *Population and World Politics*, Glencoe, Ill.: The Free Press, 1958; for the Catholic position see "Pope denounces Birth Limitation," *op. cit.*; for the Socialist position see J. D. Bernal, "Population Growth Is No Threat for a Free Society," *National Guardian*, Dec. 7, 1959 (extract from J. D. Bernal, *Science in History*).
11   *National and Per Capita Income of 70 Countries in 1949, op. cit.*; W. S. Woytinsky and E. S. Woytinsky, *World Population and Production*, New York: Twentieth Century Fund, 1953; and S. Kuznets, "Regional Economic Trends and Levels of Living," in Hauser, *op. cit.*
12   *Report on International Definition and Measurement of Standards and Levels of Living*, New York: United Nations, 1954.

13   Brown, *op. cit.* Note the different definition of area in Tables 1 and 2. In Table 2, which gives population projections to 1975 and 2000, "Northern America" includes only North America north of the Rio Grande; "Latin America" includes South America, Central America, and North America south of the Rio Grande. For the rough comparisons made, no adjustment of the data was necessary.
14   Calculations were based on revised data, as explained in note 9. For Latin America the calculations were based on a comparison of estimated aggregate income for "Latin America" in 1950, per capita income for "South America" being used.
15   The "population problem" differs for areas with different ratios of population to resources; for example, see "Political and Economic Planning," in *World Population and Resources*, Fairlawn, N.J.: Essential Books, 1955.
16   P. M. Hauser, "World and Urbanization in Relation to Economic Development and Social Change," *Urbanization in Asia and Far East*, Calcutta: UNESCO, 1957, p. 57, based on work of K. Davis and H. Hertz.
17   P. M. Hauser, "Implications of Population Trends for Regional and Urban Planning in Asia," *UNESCO Working Paper 2*, U.N. Seminar on Regional Planning, Tokyo, 1958.
18   P. M. Hauser (ed.), *Urbanization in Latin America*, New York: UNESCO, in press.
19   *The Future Growth of World Population, op. cit.*; "The Population of South East Asia (Including Ceylon and China: Taiwan) 1950–1980," *U.N. Report 3 on Future Population Estimates by Sex and Age*, New York: United Nations, 1958.
20   W. S. Thompson, *Population and Progress in the Far East*, Chicago: University of Chicago Press, 1959.
21   *The Future Growth of World Population, op. cit.*
22   I. B. Taeuber, "Population and Political Instabilities in Underdeveloped Areas," in Hauser, *Population and World Politics, op. cit.*
23   *The Future Growth of World Population, op. cit.*; "The Population of Central America (Including Mexico), 1950–1980," *U.N. Report 1 on Future Population-Estimates by Sex and Age*, New York: United Nations, 1954; "The Population of South America, 1950–1980," *U.N. Report 2 on Future Population Estimates by Sex and Age*, New York: United Nations, 1955.
24   "The Population of South East Asia," *op. cit.*; "Demographic Aspects of Urbanization in Latin America," UNESCO Seminar on Urbanization Problems in Latin America, Santiago, Chile, 1959.
25   Taeuber, *op. cit.*; *Social Implications of Industrialization in Africa South of the Sahara*, London: UNESCO, 1956.

26  K. Davis, "Population and Power in the Free World," in Hauser, *Population and World Politics, op. cit.*

27  W. Lippman, "China is No. 1 Problem," *Chicago Sun-Times*, Dec. 14, 1959; "To Live India Must Change Its Way of Life. . . ," *Chicago Sun-Times*, Dec. 15, 1959.

28  Kuznets, *op. cit.*

29  Nor is population a factor in political instability only in the underdeveloped areas. There are many other demographic dimensions of world politics which cannot be treated here because of limitations of space. The authors of a recent symposium volume which it was my privilege to edit include further considerations of population as a factor in world politics. Especially pertinent are the articles by Kingsley Davis, Frank Lorimer, Irene Taeuber, and Quincy Wright, from which I have drawn material for this discussion.

30  *Determinants and Consequences of Population Trends, op. cit.*

31  Thompson, *op. cit.*, chap. 18.

32  "Japan's Population Miracle," *Population Bulletin*, vol. 15, no. 7 (1959); "The Race between People and Resources in the ECAFE Region. part 1," *Population Bulletin*, vol. 15, no. 5 (1959), p. 89.

33  *Asia and the Far East: Seminar on Population*, New York: (United Nations, 1957).

34  F. W. Notestein, "Knowledge, Action, People," *University: A Princeton magazine*, vol. 2 (1959); P. Streit and P. Streit, "New Light on India's Worry," *New York Times Magazine*, March 13, 1960.

35  See, for example, G. Pincus *et al.*, *Science*, vol. 130 (1959), p. 81; and G. Pincus *et. al.*, "Field Trials with Norethnyodrel as an Oral Contraceptive," Shrewsbury, Mass.: Worcester Foundation for Experimental Biology, in preparation.

## 37    POPULATION CONTROL IN THE UNDERDEVELOPED WORLD
### DUDLEY KIRK

Two-thirds of the world's people live in its "developing" or less industrialized countries.[1] The populations of these countries are growing at an accelerating pace in the so-called "population explosion," thanks to welcome gains in reducing mortality.

The present imbalance between birth and death rates in the developing world is generally recognized. Current rates of population growth cannot continue for any long historical period. Already the growth rate in many developing countries exceeds 3 per cent per year, a rate at which numbers double in twenty-three years and increase twentyfold in the course of a century. From the mathematics of compound interest, it is clear that in the not too distant future, birth rates must come down or death rates must go up.

Of more immediate concern is the fact that the present and emerging rates of population growth seriously handicap socioeconomic advance in many of the developing countries. In some it has

Reprinted from *The Annals*, vol. 369 (January 1967), pp. 49–60, by permission of the author and The American Academy of Political and Social Science.

created food shortages and even the threat of famine. A lower rate of growth (that is, a lower birth rate) would facilitate their development.

With continuing decline in death rates throughout the world, the modal European birth rates of some seventeen or eighteen births per thousand population would seem to be a reasonable target for the world as a whole by the end of the century. This is what has been achieved in Japan, and this is probably a factor in the spectacular economic success of that country. As in Europe and Japan today, such birth rates would still leave a margin of population growth.

Birth rates in the developing areas still average 40 to 45 per 1,000 population. To bring these rates down to a reasonable balance of natality and mortality (that is, the European level) involves a drop of some 25 points, or more than 50 per cent from the current level. With a present population of 2.3 billion in the underdeveloped world, such a reduction implies the prevention of well over 50 million births per annum at this time. These are the dimensions of the problem of reducing natality in the underdeveloped world.

Fortunately, there are grounds for optimism that birth rates can be brought down in time to avert a rise in death rates, barring some catastrophe such as nuclear war. The prospect for reductions in the birth rate in the less industrialized countries has never been more hopeful than it is today.

1   Foremost perhaps is the rapid change in climate of opinion regarding family planning. To appreciate the significance of this change it is important to note that the European demographic transition occurred in an atmosphere of overt and covert institutional hostility toward birth control. The European population learned to limit family size, but the process was gradual and stemmed from private decisions made *in spite of* restrictive legislation, religious opposition (Protestant as well as Catholic), and public denunciation of birth control practices in what was generally a "conspiracy of silence" on sexual matters and human reproduction. The prevailing middle-class morality prevented free public discussion, and public authorities harassed militant fringe groups that advocated birth control. With the growing understanding of the impact of high rates of population growth on economic development, the hitherto restrictive atmosphere is rapidly yielding to a climate of public approval and sponsorship of family planning programs which can be expected to accelerate the adoption of contraceptive practice.

2   In the developing world, except for Latin America, religious doctrine does not oppose family planning. Religions other than the Catholic and the Orthodox do not have clear doctrinal positions that ban the use of contraceptives, and their views on abortion are often more permissive; for example, the Moslem doctrine forbids abortion after the quickening, but it is far less clear on earlier abortions. This is not to suggest that religion does not play a part in natality differentials in the developing countries; it does, but not in the sense of formal opposition to family planning.

3   New methods of contraception, derived by intensive research, now offer a wider choice of methods and already include some that seem applicable in poor and peasant cultures. The two major new developments are the oral contraceptives and the intra-uterine devices (IUD's). Even better methods are on the way.

In the Western experience, the decline in the birth rate resulted from later age at marriage; from male methods of contraception, especially *coitus interruptus* and the condom; and from the female method of abortion. These are still much the most common methods of family limitation in the world. The "conventional" chemical and mechanical methods have probably not been of major importance in controlling Western fertility, and seem unsuited to the peoples of the developing world. Continued research will almost certainly produce even more effective, simple, inexpensive, and safe methods, unrelated to the sex act. Not to be overlooked are better techniques of abortion and the general availability and acceptance of abortion in many countries.

4   The rapid decline of the death rate in today's developing countries is itself an important factor in changing motivations in favor of family limitation. With more children surviving, the pressure of larger families, especially in the context of growing aspirations for the children, is more quickly evident. The change from low to moderate and even high survival rates within a single generation has an impact on parents and grandparents that favors considerably more rapid acceptance of family planning than occurred in the West, where slowly declining death rates were followed by a gradual decline in births.

5   The traditional view that birth rates and population growth are a "given" not amenable to deliberate social and governmental influence is no longer tenable. Today it is increasingly appreciated among all cultures and strata of people that, within nature's limits, man can control his destiny over births as well as deaths. Numerous surveys in many

developing countries on knowledge, attitudes, and practice (the so-called KAP surveys) have shown that the general public, rural as well as urban, is interested in controlling family size. Very few now think it necessary to have as many children "as God wills." On the contrary, almost everywhere there is a substantial "market" for contraceptive knowledge, materials, and services, provided these are made available in a form appropriate to local conditions.

6   A final point concerns the relationship between population growth and economic progress. Despite impressive aggregate economic gain in many developing countries in recent years (of the order of 4 per cent to 6 per cent per year on growth of real gross domestic product),[2] per capita gains have often been trivial and even negative. In the matter of food and agricultural production, world output since 1958 has grown at about the same rate as world population, but only because the developed world has compensated for deficiencies in per capita output in the developing countries.[3] Although primarily agricultural, the developing countries, with over two-thirds of the world's people, account for less than 45 per cent of the world's agricultural output.[4]

### POPULATION POLICIES

Confronted with these realities and the failure of their economic development plans to materialize in per capita terms, responsible leaders in developing countries are increasingly concerned with the handicaps of rapid population growth to social and economic progress. Their growing realization that people want and presumably will use available contraceptive information and services has precipitated and reinforced a novel view: that governments can and should do something about high rates of population growth.

The pressures for the adoption of policy are more than a quinquennial affair related to drawing up five-year economic development plans. They are experienced daily in many forms: shrinking plots of land as numerous children inherit their parents' holdings, as in India; in the formidable task of providing schooling for a child population that exceeds 40 per cent of the total population; in crowded urban slums, as rural people migrate to cities to seek escape from the poverty of the countryside; in large numbers of unemployed and many more underemployed; and in growing resort to induced abortion, as in Latin America, where one-fourth of the beds of the major maternity hospitals are occupied by women with complications arising out of illegal abortions.

In response to these and similar forces, population policy has become an accepted part of development programs. By now more than half the people in the developing world live under governments that favor family planning.[5]

ASIA   A review of government family planning programs appropriately begins with Asia. In numbers it is the principal home of mankind; it has the most visible population problems; the four largest countries in the developing world are on that continent; and it is the region where national family planning programs under governmental auspices began.

INDIA, NEPAL, AND PAKISTAN   The first country to adopt a national policy to control population growth was India. The beginnings, in the mid-1950's, were modest. Major bottlenecks were lack of an administrative structure to reach India's enormous rural population, and acute shortages of medical personnel, especially of women doctors. Except for financial subsidies, authority rests with the individual states. Organization in the Ministry of Health has moved slowly, and the government has been slow to adopt the newer methods of contraception. Nevertheless, the program has gained momentum as indicated by the data on expenditures in Table 1.

Annual expenditures have risen from 13.8 million rupees in 1961-1962 to 60.5 in 1964-1965 and to an estimated 120 in 1965-1966.[6] The last two represent per capita expenditures of about

**TABLE 1**  *India's family planning expenditures, 1951–1971*

| Five year plan | Expenditures, millions of rupees |
|---|---|
| First    (1951–1956) | 1.5 |
| Second (1956–1961) | 21.6 |
| Third   (1961–1966) | 261.0 |
| Fourth (1966–1971), allocation | 950.0 |

two and four cents. The Fourth Plan allocation implies an annual expenditure of $25.4 million or about five cents per person. Food shortages have made India's efforts more urgent. Symbolic of this is the change in name from Ministry of Health to Ministry of Health and Family Planning.

The Indian program has relied chiefly on clinics, which numbered 15,808 in July 1965. Although rhythm and conventional mechanical and chemical methods were first offered, IUD's were introduced in 1965, with one million inserted by mid-1966. Since 1963 over 100,000 male and female sterilizations have been performed per year in "sterilization camps" temporarily set up for this purpose. The cumulative total of sterilizations is soon expected to exceed one million. Oral contraceptives have not yet been approved for general use in India.

Impressive as these recent achievements are, they have not had any measurable influence on the Indian birth rate, except perhaps in the largest Indian cities, where family planning seems to be spreading in the population (but probably as much through private as through government services). The object of the program is to reduce the annual birth rate from over 40 to 25 per thousand population "as soon as possible." Targets rise annually to 1971 when it is hoped to have 19.7 million IUD users, 4.5 million sterilizations, and 4.7 million condom users.[7] Success in this magnitude is indeed necessary for a major impact on the Indian birth rate. India is a country of almost 500 million people, with some 100 million women in the reproductive ages and some 20 million births annually.

Interested in these developments in India, Nepal inforporated a family planning program in its Third Plan, 1965-1970, but it has yet to be implemented.

Pakistan formulated a population control program in the late 1950's which was allocated 30.5 million rupees in the Second Five Year Plan (1960-1965). The objective is to supply family planning services through the existing health services in hospitals, dispensaries and rural clinics for voluntary participation of couples in limiting family size and spacing of children.

These efforts encountered many of the problems noted in India. In the first four years only 9.4 million rupees[8] of the budgeted expenditures of 24.7 million were actually used.[9] The problems related more to administration and organization than lack of funds. The plan for reaching 1.2 million women as contraceptive users and the targets for distribution of contraceptives, specifically condoms and foam tablets, were met only at the level of 17 per cent and 15 per cent, respectively.[10]

In July 1965 the Family Planning Directorate was upgraded to one of the most ambitious in the world today. Its five-year budget of 300 million ruppees represents an average annual budget of about 12 cents per person. A major innovation is to be the insertion of IUD's by midwives, under medical supervision. These midwives will receive incentive payments for referrals and insertions. By 1970 no less than 50,000 village midwives are to be recruited and given a five-week training course.[11]

**KOREA AND TAIWAN**  More immediate success has been achieved in two smaller Asian countries, South Korea and Taiwan. South Korea's Supreme Council for National Reconstruction adopted a national family planning policy in 1961 as an integral part of the development plan. The targets were more specific than in most countries as regards training, use of contraceptives and effects on the rate of growth. By April 1965 some 2,200 full-time field workers had been recruited and trained, one for each 2,500 women in the childbearing ages.[12] Main reliance of the program is now on the

IUD. Insertions were 112,000 in 1964, and 233,000 in 1965,[13] against targets of 100,000 and 200,000, respectively. The latter is estimated to be about 15 per cent of the target women, that is, those exposed to the risk of unwanted pregnancy. IUD's and conventional contraceptives are being manufactured in Korea.

The official objective is to reduce the rate of population growth from a current estimate of 2.9 per cent per year to 1.8 per cent in 1971. The Economic Planning Board estimates that by 1980 full implementation of the family planning program will bring down the rate of growth to 1.16 per cent compared to 3.15 without a reduction in the birth rates. The difference in growth rates will mean a per capita income 36 per cent higher in 1980 than would be the case in the absence of a fertility decline.

These ambitious objectives would sound unrealistic were it not for the fact that the government program is clearly "swimming with the tide" of social change. Attitude surveys show an overwhelming approval of family planning in Korean population and a rapid increase in contraception and abortion,[14] the latter perhaps because of Japanese influence. Though not yet approved by the government, a bill is currently before the Korean Assembly to legalize induced abortion.

In the absence of accurate vital statistics, it is difficult to measure year-to-year changes in the birth rate. An indirect measure, ratios of children under five to women in the childbearing ages, does strongly suggest a recent rapid decline in the birth rate, especially in 1965. Although this decline was already in process, the greater rate of decline in 1965 might reflect the effects of the government program in 1964, when it first reached mass proportions.

Taiwan does not have an official population policy, but family planning services are now provided throughout the island by the Provincial Department of Health. Impetus for the island-wide program stemmed from the mass action research program in the city of Taichung[15] (in which it was first established that the IUD would be widely accepted in a mass campaign) and from experimental projects begun in 1959 under the euphemistically-called "Prepregnancy Health Program." This term paid tribute to the sensitivities of the United States Agency for International Development (AID), which was providing indirect assistance to the health services. The expanded action program for the island as a whole was initiated in 1964, and in 1965 the program effectively achieved the target of inserting 100,000 IUD's.[16]

The principal feature of the Taiwan plan is insertion of 600,000 IUD's within five years.[17] Were there no removals or expulsions this would mean a loop for one-third of the married women of childbearing age, including those marrying in the interim. Since a substantial percentage of the IUD's are not retained, the net effect will probably be less. Oral contraceptives are being introduced on an experimental basis to provide an alternative method for women who cannot or do not wish to use the IUD.

In contrast with most developing countries Taiwan has excellent vital statistics and other methods of evaluating program success. It can be seen on the basis of the information in Table 2 that the birth rate in Taiwan has been falling precipitously.

The government program could not have initiated this decline, but the especially large drop in 1964 and 1965 is to be noted. Rising age at marriage, an increase of about two months per year, is known to be a factor. In addition to its direct effects, the government program may operate indirectly to stimulate greater interest in family planning and in induced abortion. Since abortions

TABLE 2    *Crude birth rate for Taiwan*

| Year | Rate |
|------|------|
| 1959 | 41.2 |
| 1960 | 39.5 |
| 1961 | 38.3 |
| 1962 | 37.4 |
| 1963 | 36.3 |
| 1964 | 34.5 |
| 1965 | 32.7 |

Source: United Nations, *Demographic yearbook, 1965*, table 12.

are illegal, their number is not known. The real tests of the effectiveness of the government program still lies in the future.

**SOUTHEAST ASIA** In Hong Kong, Singapore, and Malaysia, family planning programs were initiated under private auspices and with government subsidies. The private Family Planning Associations in these areas have been among the most successful in the world. In Singapore the government took over the private family planning services in January 1966. These services may well have been a factor in the rapid decline of the birth rate in Singapore from 45.4 per 1000 in 1952 to 29.9 in 1965, although rising age at marriage and changes in age structure were important elements.

Malaysia incorporated a family planning policy in its First Malaysia Plan 1966-1970, adopted in 1965. Voluntary organizations, government departments, and mass communications are to be used for education in and promotion of family planning. The birth rate in Malaysia has been declining, especially among the population of Chinese ancestry. While the role of the private Family Planning Association may have been important in popularizing birth control, its direct services were numerically insufficient to have affected the birth rate.

In Ceylon, the government's national family planning program is being introduced by stages into different sections of the country, first in the Colombo area.[18] Ceylon is a kind of Ireland of Asia—its high age at marriage has led to a lower birth rate than in neighboring India. Swedish technical assistance supports the Ceylon program.

Thailand does not have a population policy, but pilot projects in family planning have been strikingly successful, and family planning is now being introduced as an integral part of health services in major hospitals and in the health units of the northeastern region.

**MAINLAND CHINA** Government interest in family planning in Mainland China goes back to 1956 and 1957 when a birth control campaign was initiated by the government and services were provided in government health clinics. In 1958 a change of policy slowed the campaign to very low gear, but by 1972 renewed governmental interest became evident. In January of that year import regulations were revised to admit contraceptives duty-free. The government advocated later age at marriage. Japanese doctors visiting China in 1964 and 1965 reported that family planning was being advocated as part of maternal and child health programs and that all methods of contraception, including sterilization and abortion, were available. Oral contraceptives and IUD's manufactured in China were apparently becoming increasingly popular.

According to Premier Chou:

> Our present target is to reduce population growth to below 2 per cent; for the future we aim at an even lower rate. . . . However, I do not believe it will be possible to equal the Japanese rate (of about one per cent) as early as 1970. . . . We do believe in planned parenthood, but it is not easy to introduce all at once in China. . . . The first thing is to encourage late marriages.[19]

Many of the 17 million Communist party members and 25 million Young Communists have received birth control instruction, and they, in turn, are expected to become models and teachers. One son and one daughter are now considered an ideal family size.[20]

Far too little is known about the Chinese program, but it may well be the most important national program in the world, if for no other reason than the tremendous numbers involved. The Chinese population may now be as high as 800 million, equal to about one-fourth of the human race.

**MIDDLE EAST AND AFRICA** Four countries in the Middle East and North Africa have adopted national family planning programs. In the United Arab Republic (UAR) the government's interest goes back to 1953, when a National Population Commission was established and a few clinics were opened. Government policy dates from the May 1962 draft of the National Charter, in which President Nasser declared:

Population increase constitutes the most dangerous obstacle that faces the Egyptian people in their drive towards raising the standard of production. . . . Attempts at family planning deserve the most sincere efforts supported by modern scientific methods.[21]

However, a substantial program was not initiated until February 1966, when the government launched a widespread campaign using oral contraceptives.

In Tunisia an experimental program to develop a practical family planning service with IUD's was started in 1964. The success of this experiment led to a national campaign with a goal of 120,000 IUD's.[22] An unusually interesting feature of the Tunisian program has been the use of Destour party members as a major source of information and publicity. The program may have been set back by President Bourguiba's speech on Woman's Day, August 12, 1966, against celibacy and in favor of a young vigorous population.

In April 1965 Turkey repealed an old law against contraception and provided the legal framework and financial basis for a nationwide family planning program.[23] Full-time family planning personnel are to be trained and added to the Health Ministry, and supplies are to be offered free or at cost. Interesting features of the Turkish program are plans for an informational campaign on birth control in the armed forces (to provide a "ripple" effect when the conscripts return to civilian life) and incorporation of demographic and biological aspects of population into the school curriculum.

Morocco decided in 1966 to adopt a national family program to be introduced by stages through the public health clinics in the various parts of the country. A national sample survey of attitudes on family planning has been started by the government.

Although Algeria has no population policy or program, Dr. Ahmed Taleb, Minister of National Education, stated on the opening of the school year (fall 1966):
. . . we have to fight an extremely high birth rate. If nothing is done to stop this growth rate through birth control, the problem of educating all the Algerian children will remain unsolved.[24]

TROPICAL AFRICA    Although no formal population policies have yet been adopted by countries in Africa south of the Sahara, considerable interest was expressed in population matters at the First African Population Conference held at the University of Ibadan, Nigeria, in January 1966.[25]

Kenya's 1966-1970 Development Plan includes "measures to promote family planning education" through the establishment of a Family Planning Council and by providing services in government hospitals and health centers. In Mauritius the 1966 budget provides funds for family planning services.

LATIN AMERICA    Latin America has the most rapid rate of population growth of any major region of the world. This has not generally been a matter of much public concern, partly because of the traditional position of the Catholic Church and partly because Latin-American countries have a historical image of themselves as underpopulated.

Two forces are rapidly changing this disinterest. One is the growing recognition that high growth rates are obstacles to achieving planning goals. In many countries population is growing faster than food supply; the difficulties in providing public education, health services, and other facilities are formidable; and the intrusive problem of unemployment and underemployment has serious political as well as economic implications as people flock into the cities. A second element is the growing concern, especially in the medical profession, over the problem of induced abortion. The possibility of family planning appears to be gaining favorable attention both among responsible leaders, and among large segments of the population, according to sample attitude surveys in eight Latin-American capitals (coordinated by the United Nations Latin-American Demographic Center in Santiago, Chile).[26]

Latin-American countries may be less likely to adopt formal population policies than other parts of the underdeveloped world owing to the influence of the Church. However, natality regulation has been approved for the public health service in Chile, and several major birth control projects using public health facilities exist in Santiago. In Honduras the Minister of Health recently announced that family planning is to be an integral part of preventive medical services. In Jamaica a Family Planning Unit has been established within the Ministry of Health with administrative costs provided by AID. In Colombia the private Association of Medical Faculties has established a Population Division, which has organized a nationwide program for training health officers in family planning. In October 1966 AID authorized the use of counterpart funds to finance this program. In Peru a government-sponsored population studies center was established to "formulate programs of action with which to face the problems of population and socio-economic development." Barbados has had an official policy favoring family planning since 1954, expressed chiefly by subsidy of the private Family Planning Association.

## EVALUATION OF FAMILY PLANNING PROGRAMS

Most government family planning programs are very new, and it would be unfair to expect major results so soon. Their very existence in so short a time is in itself remarkable. Operating through the existing health network, generally under the Health Ministry, most programs are still largely clinic-oriented despite the common experience that other means may be more effective. Problems of organization; administration; production, distribution and supply of contraceptives; and shortage of skilled personnel are more serious than the question of finance.

Partly because of their newness, the programs have tended to place great emphasis on the magic of the new contraceptive methods. They all have shied away from abortion, which has been a major factor in reducing birth rates in large populations as in Japan, the Soviet Union, and eastern Europe. The present female-oriented programs minimize the role of male participation, which, if not for

presently recommended methods, is nevertheless important for information and motivation. Few of the programs have thus far made use of mass communication, and Ministries of Information and Education have yet to be effectively involved.

National programs may be evaluated at different levels: in-service statistics, as, for example, success in reaching targets in number of clinics, patients, contraceptive users, and the like; more broadly in their effects on knowledge, attitudes, and practices of the general population (measured by the so-called KAP students); and, for the present purpose, the effects on the birth rate, the ultimate test of a population control program.

Since very few of the countries of the underdeveloped world have sufficiently accurate vital statistics to measure year-to-year changes in the birth rate, other means must be sought. Censuses can be used to measure natality changes, but these occur too infrequently for the purpose at hand. In the absence of official data, sample registration and periodic sample population surveys are conducted to provide data for measuring year-to-year changes. These have come to be known as Population Growth Estimate (PGE) Studies. Experimental projects of this type are going forward in Pakistan, Turkey, and Thailand.

As programs accelerate, the deficiency in accurate vital data will become increasingly important. In-service data can give good measures of the scope of the programs and their success in achieving targets. However, the number of contraceptive "users," as measured by accepters, can be very deceptive, since failure of the method and, even more important, failure of couples to use methods as required, can significantly reduce "use-effectiveness." This is true of IUD's as well as other effective methods such as oral contraceptives and condoms. Many women do not retain the IUD's, or have them removed. In the national program in Taiwan 62 per cent of the women still had the IUD in place at the end of twelve months, 52 per cent at the end of eighteen months. Experience elsewhere has been better, up to 80 per cent retention at the end of a year. In all methods there is substantial shrinkage between ideal use and actual effectiveness in preventing pregnancy.

It should also be noted that family planning programs are most likely to succeed rapidly in countries of greatest socioeconomic advance, where realization of the smaller family ideal has already made some progress. The success of a program in countries like Korea and Taiwan chiefly reflects rapid progress in other ways. In such countries mass acceptance of government services is not an equivalent gain in family planning practice, since many of the couples concerned were already practicing family planning (perhaps by less effective methods or abortion) or would have done so regardless of a government program. In these countries the government program may accelerate a trend already in existence. Indeed, in some countries, the influence of the program on couples to use private sources of supply, methods not requiring supplies, and abortion may well surpass the effect of the direct services offered. Yet this indirect effect is least susceptible to measurement.

## SUMMARY AND CONCLUSIONS

By now at least twenty-three nations in the underdeveloped world have explicit official population policies. One is struck by the recency and rapidity with which these programs have come into being. In some instances there is policy, but little if any program; in others, program, but no policy. In most cases neither policy nor program has yet had much opportunity to produce a measurable effect on the national birth rate. Even in those countries with most marked successes, such as Korea and Taiwan, the reduction of the birth rate so far is surely much more the result of general social change than of public policy.

The newness and frailties of family planning programs reflect the tentative approach of governments to their population problems. Thus far, they have involved very small material investments in relation both to economic development plans and to potential economic gains. Some have argued that the "normal" tendency of the birth rate to decline in the course of socioeconomic development will bring about a resolution of present population problems. Government family planning programs now seem to be part of this "normal" development.

With knowledge rapidly becoming available for individual couples to exercise voluntary control over births, fortified by governmental approval and assistance in supplies and medical services, it is quite possible that family planning may progress more rapidly than some other forms of socioeconomic advance. Several non-European areas of different cultures and relatively low per capita incomes (notably Taiwan, Korea, Singapore, and Hong Kong; Soviet Asia and the western provinces of Turkey; and Argentina and Uruguay) already give clear evidence of reductions in birth rates. Given the favorable attitudes found in the KAP surveys, family planning may be easier to implement than major advances in education or the economy, which require large structural and institutional changes in the society as a whole.

The most rapid progress will come in East Asia where the normal demographic transition is already well advanced. While the evidence is scant, family planning may also move ahead rapidly in Mainland China despite its low level of socioeconomic development. The Communist regime has done much to disrupt the ancient pattern of Chinese family life, which, in any case, based on the experience of Chinese outside Mainland China, is less a barrier to the small family norm than had been supposed.

In India, many cultural practices restrain freedom of sexual expression. Widespread acceptance of sterilization (vasectomy), while not yet sufficient to affect the birth rate, is, nevertheless, surprising evidence of a greater concern for family size among men than might have been supposed. Although ten years old, the Indian family planning program has reached significant proportions only in the last year or so. If present trends continue, both in the national program and in independent individual initiative in contraceptive practice, one may expect a sufficient escalation of family planning to produce a decline in the birth rate. That it will achieve the goal of a birth rate of only 25 per 1,000 population by 1971 seems doubtful, but I venture to predict a perceptible drop from the present level of over 40. At the same time, however, the death rate will probably have dropped below 15 so that to reach the target growth rate of one per cent will require still further reductions in the birth rate.

In Moslem society, family planning is making headway among the upper classes and among populations closest to European influence, as in Albania, Turkey, and the Central Asia Republics of the Soviet Union. Several Moslem countries have population policies (Turkey, Tunisia, the United Arab Republic, Morocco), but other things being equal, family planning is likely to gain slower popular acceptance among Moslems than among most other cultural groups.[27]

As measured by most indices of socio-economic advance, tropical Africa would not seem ready for widespread family planning practice. Nevertheless, Africans gladly seize on cultural innovation, and a surprising interest has already been shown. One can scarcely expect any measurable effect on the birth rate in a tropical African country in ten years; but in twenty years I would expect this to have occurred.

In Latin America, urban-rural fertility differentials are not so large as in other parts of the world, partly because of the heavy immigration into the urban shanty towns of rural people who have yet to become integrated into urban life. Nevertheless, studies reveal widespread interest in family planning (at least in the large capital cities), and abortion has become very common. A shift in the position of the Catholic Church toward permissive policies, if not outright acceptance of family planning, will accelerate what is already a major social trend.

In several, perhaps most, Latin-American countries I would anticipate a measurable reduction in their very high birth rates within the next ten years. Within twenty years, growth rates should be markedly reduced despite a continuing decline in mortality. Present fertility plus the inertia of age structure, however, will probably double the population of Latin America by the end of the century.

The picture that emerges is a range in birth rates of 20 to 25 per 1,000 population within a decade in the most progressive parts of East and Southeast Asia, and possibly within two decades in India and Mainland China if those countries avoid war, disaster, and social chaos. By that time, one can expect important reductions in the birth rate in all of the larger developing countries in Asia, in the Middle East and North Africa, and in Latin America. Taking the underdeveloped world as a whole, within two decades I expect to see the solution well in sight, though not yet fully achieved.

These conclusions imply great efforts and accomplishments in the face of cultural resistance and inertia. The achievements will not be easily won, nor will they forestall the massive population growth that, in the absence of catastrophe, will be with us at least through the 1970's. The critical problem of world population growth will remain, though in the longer run there is now real hope for its solution.

## REFERENCES AND NOTES

1   Africa, Asia excluding Japan and the Soviet Union, and Latin America excluding Argentina and Uruguay.
2   United Nations, *Statistical Yearbook*, 1965, tables 183, 184.
3   *Ibid.*, table 6.
4   *Ibid.*, table 4.
5   For official statements of governmental policy on population, see *Studies in Family Planning*, no. 16, New York: Population Council, in press.
6   B. L. Raina, "India," in Bernard Berelson *et al.* (eds.), *Family Planning and Population Programs: A Review of World Developments*, Chicago: University of Chicago Press, 1966.
7   *Ibid.*, p. 119.
8   One Pakistan rupee equals 21 cents.
9   E. Adil, "Pakistan," in Berelson *et al., op. cit.*, p. 127.
10  *Ibid.*, p. 128.
11  *Family Planning Scheme for Pakistan during the Third Five Year Plan Period, 1965-1970*, Government of Pakistan, pp. 3, 10.
12  *Korea, Summary of First Five-Year Economic Plan*, Government of Korea, 1962-1966.
13  *Monthly Report on IUD Insertions*, Government of Korea, Ministry of Health and Social Welfare (mimeographed).

14  According to a survey made in 1964, one out of three pregnancies among married women in Seoul is terminated by induced abortion. See S. B. Hong, *Induced Abortion in Seoul, Korea*, Seoul: Dong-A Publishing Company, 1966, p. 78.

15  This is fully described in Bernard Berelson and Ronald Freedman, "A Study in Fertility Control," *Scientific American*, vol. 210, no. 5 (May 1964), pp. 3–11.

16  *Family Planning in Taiwan, Republic of China, 1965-1966*, Government of Taiwan, 1966, p. iii.

17  *Taiwan, Ten Year Health Program, 1966-1975*, Government of Taiwan.

18  *Provisional Scheme for a Nationwide Family Planning Programme in Ceylon, 1966–1976*, Government of Ceylon.

19  As reported by Edgar Snow in *The New York Times*, Feb. 3, 1964.

20  *The Sunday Times* (London), Jan. 23, 1966.

21  *The Charter* draft presented by President Nasser on May 21, 1962, UAR Information Department p. 53.

22  A. Daly, "Tunisia," in Berelson *et al., op. cit.*, p. 160.

23  T. Metiner, "Turkey," in Berelson *et al., op. cit.*, p. 136.

24  Translation from *La Presse*, Tunis, Sept. 30, 1966.

25  Proceedings to be published in 1967. Also see J. C. Caldwell, "Africa," in Berelson *et al., op. cit.*

26  C. A. Miro and F. Rath, "Preliminary Findings of Comparative Fertility Surveys in Three Latin-American Cities, Part 2" *Milbank Memorial Fund Quarterly*, vol. 43, no. 4 (October 1965), pp. 36–68.

27  D. Kirk, "Factors Affecting Moslem Natality," in Berelson, *et al., op. cit.*

## SUPPLEMENTAL READINGS

Bakol, Carl: "The Mathematics of Hunger," *Saturday Review*, vol. 46 (April 28, 1963), pp. 16–19.

Bogue, Donald J.: "The End of the Population Explosion," *Public Interest*, vol. 7 (spring 1967), pp. 11–20.

Carr-Saunders, A. M.: *World Population*, Oxford: Clarendon Press, 1936.

Davis, Kingsley: "The Urbanization of the Human Population," *Scientific American*, vol. 213 (September 1965), pp. 40–53.

Easterlin, Richard A.: "Effectis of Population Growth on the Economic Development of Developing Countries," *The Annals*, vol. 369 (January 1967), pp. 98–108.

Freedman, Ronald (ed.): *Population: The Vital Revolution*, Garden City, N.Y.: Anchor Books, Doubleday & Company, Inc., 1964.

Hill, Reuben, *et al.: The Family and Population Control*, Chapel Hill, N.C.: University of North Carolina Press, 1959.

Osborn, Fairfield: *Our Crowded Planet*, Garden City, N.Y.: Doubleday & Company, Inc., 1962.

Rainwater, Lee: *And the Poor Get Children*, Chicago: Quadrangle Books, 1960.

Ryder, Norman B.: "The Character of Modern Fertility," *The Annals*, vol. 369 (January 1967), pp. 27–36.

Stycos, J. Mayone: "Obstacles to Programs of Population Control," *Journal of Marriage and the Family*, vol. 25 (February 1963), pp. 5–13.

Taeuber, Irene B.: *Population in Japan*, Princeton, N.J.: Princeton University Press, 1958.

Taeuber, Irene B.: "Population and Society," in Robert E. L. Faris (ed.), *Handbook of Modern Sociology*, Chicago: Rand McNally & Company, 1964, pp. 83–126.

Thomlinson, Ralph: *Population Dynamics*, New York: Random House, Inc., 1965.

Thomlinson, Ralph: *Demographic Problems*, Belmont, Calif.: Dickenson Publishing Company, Inc., 1967.

Westoff, Charles F., *et al.: Family Growth in Metropolitan American*, Princeton, N.J.: Princeton University Press, 1961.

Whelpton, Pascal K., *et al.: Fertility and Family Planning in the United States*, Princeton, N.J.: Princeton University Press, 1966.

In seeking to understand the nature of crime and delinquency as a social problem, several factors should be stressed. First, the great public concern about the crime problem, which was a central issue in the national elections of 1968, is not unique to the present period in our history, but instead has been a constantly recurring theme (for expanded coverage of this point see the selection from the report of the President's Crime Commission dealing with public attitudes toward crime and law enforcement). Further, the attitudes of most people about the serious forms of crime are derived largely from vicarious sources rather than from direct personal involvement, especially as a victim. The Crime Commission report clearly advocates that the public be informed about the nature and extent of criminal and delinquent violations, although there is some contention that the disproportionate fear resulting from overdramatization may restrict the scope of social and cultural activities, further decrease confidence in public officials, and add to the public's sense of indifference toward those in trouble.

Even with the significant gains in new information realized from the Crime Commission report, there are still serious limitations in the available statistics, which is a second feature worthy of special comment. Although the general impression fostered by public officials and held by the lay public is that the crime rate has expanded geometrically in recent years, so many variables influence the information on the extent of crime and delinquency that it is not possible objectively to support or refute sensational evaluations. For instance, since only the very serious offenses are reported to legal authorities, the preponderance of violations are lost for purposes of calculating crime rates. Also, the variability in definition, identification, prosecution, and reporting among jurisdictions and within a single jurisdiction over time negates valid comparisons. Finally, the amount of crime sensitively reflects the degree of concern by the public and the police. To illustrate this point, a chronically high crime rate or a great increase in the number of violations may result in strong pressure for an increase in law-enforcement personnel and resources, with the intent of deterring criminal or delinquent acts through tighter surveillance. An equally probable outcome, however, is that the number of known violations, that is, the crime rate, may be further increased simply because the additional attention brings more of them to light.

A third dimension is that the current concepts of crime and delinquency are often vague and ambiguous. Some professionally trained specialists as well as members of the general public apply these terms to any behavior that violates the law, without consideration of seriousness, intent, adjudication, and possible contribution of the victim. The more legalistically oriented observer does not consider any act a crime unless and until the offender has been found guilty by a court. Still another approach suggests that these terms should incorporate all antisocial behavior, that is, acts that have negative consequences for society, regardless of whether they are prohibited by law. Finally, academic criminologists have often defined crime operationally as those violations of the criminal codes, rather than the civil codes, that come to the attention of an official agency, usually the police. This lack of consensus concerning the criteria for identifying criminal and delinquent populations is manifest in evaluating all aspects of the problem, such as the number of violators, the construction of "causal" explanations, and treatment or punishment proposals.

The fourth basic issue follows from this last point. Even under the most restrictive of the above definitions, the legalistic viewpoint, the extremely broad range in types of behavior and offender characteristics requires further delimitation in terms of more homogeneous categories. Such legally defined criminal acts as traffic violations, sale of narcotics, and income-tax evasion have little in common with each other and the multitude of the remaining offenses, other than that they are legally defined as violations of the criminal codes. Thus the present classificatory systems should be examined with the knowledge that the variations within each category may be as great as those between categories in terms of the social and psychological characteristics of the offenders, probability of recidivism, effectiveness of punishment as a deterrent, and amenability to rehabilitation.

The most common offender *types* can be classified as follows:

1   Situational offenders, persons who use an illegal device to extricate themselves from a pressing situation or who respond eruptively and irrationally to a disturbing situation that represents the breaking point after an extended period of tension-provoking experiences. Within the broad range of behaviors comprising this category would be such varied offenses as hit-and-run, unpremeditated murder of spouse, naive check forgery, and use of an invalid passport.

2   Violent offenders, well characterized by two of the categories Don Gibbons has used in constructing criminal typologies, the "psychopathic" assaultist, "who engages in robbery-assaults in which his coercive and violent actions are essentially 'senseless,' " and the violent sex offender, who employs extreme forms of aggression against female victims which are ostensibly sexual in character.

3    Career offenders, a category that includes the ordinary, professional, and organized criminals, all of whom engage in property crimes, usually without actual violence but with the threat often at least implicit, as their major source of economic support.

4    White-collar violators, persons of high socioeconomic status who in the course of their legitimate occupations commit criminal violations, such as embezzlement, antitrust violations, unlawful sale of narcotics, bribery of public officials, and income-tax evasion.

5    Public-order offenders, those whose repetitive law-violating actions are essentially a reflection of social welfare, medical, or psychiatric problems which are difficult to control and to treat by traditional legal processes (hence the discussion of alcoholism, drug addiction, prostitution, and homosexuality is included in the following chapter covering personality deviations).

A fifth aspect that has particular implications for efforts to reduce the scale of the problem is the stance of the American public with respect to law violations. Although the general public is periodically aroused to a high emotional pitch by vivid accounts of a dramatic criminal act or series of acts in the mass media and pronouncements on the increase in crime and delinquency rates by public officials, indifference or apathy has been the more characteristic posture until the past several years. Several American traditions, which Walter C. Reckless has succinctly noted, help to explain this orientation. On the one hand, major segments of our heterogeneous population subscribe to conflicting value systems without a compensating commitment to an arbitrary set of guidelines, such as the legal codes. The lack of public consensus about the crime problem is compounded by divisions between and within the white and black communities on the more general theme of the implications of racial conflict for the preservation of law and order. On the other hand, our society has sought to maintain a minimum amount of control over the individual by the police and courts. In addition, as individuals, we take special pride in demonstrating that the implementation of the law can be manipulated in our favor. Finally, as reported in the second half of the selection on public attitudes, most people simply do not believe that they as individuals can do anything about crime, even in their own neighborhoods.

With these points in mind let us now turn to the main issues upon which the sociologist focuses in studying crime and delinquency: causation, prevention, control, treatment, and the unique aspects of delinquency and its relationship to adult crime. Past failures in constructing monistic formulations have not noticeably dampened the search for causal explanations of criminal and delinquent behavior. Contemporary theories of criminology tend to draw from one rather than some combination of three frames of reference: the biological, psychological, or sociological. Proponents of the biological factor argue that genetically determined characteristics have an important bearing on behavior. Modern criminologists have discarded the earlier belief that the criminal is a distinct physical type manifesting the characteristics of an earlier form of animal life, or the somewhat updated version that criminal behavior results from the exposure of inherently inferior organisms to the adversities and temptations of their social environment. However, the more recent statements, of which the work of Sheldon and Eleanor Glueck is best known, have attempted to relate physique and assorted temperament and mental traits to criminal behavior. According to this position, the mesomorph (athletic physique), who tends to be aggressive, hostile, and adventurous, has a higher potential for illegal behavior than the other physical types, with their concomitant personality patterns. There has also been some recent research on the relation of number of chromosomes to criminal behavior.

The psychological theories are predicated on the position that behavior is dependent upon mental or emotional processes, and mental subnormality, mental illness (such as neuroses and psychoses), and certain personality-trait syndromes have been advanced as causal antecedents. Not much success has been achieved with these variables because empirical investigations have tended to show similar distributions, in frequency and degree, for samples of criminals and the general population. Notable exceptions are the new exploratory investigations of the relationship between sociopathy and criminal or delinquent behavior and the work of Bandura and Walters, which has sought to trace the development of antisocial aggressiveness to impaired dependency relationships. The psychiatric approach has had more general impact. The relevant theories stress one of two themes—that criminal and delinquent behavior is the product of an underdeveloped superego that fails to contain the expression of innate drives, or that it results from an overinternalization of society's norms, with punishment for the illegal act unconsciously intended to expiate guilt feelings over the desire to express innate drives.

The lack-of-containment thesis has also been supported by sociologists, who are usually more directly concerned with the nature of social relationships and cultural patterns. The containment theorists (as illustrated by the Reckless and Dinitz selection) suggest that the probability of delinquent behavior is high in the absence of personal-control variables (high frustration tolerance, sense of responsibility, and positive self-concept) and/or social-control variables (reasonable and consistent role expectations for adolescents, effective supervision, and consistent standards of morality). The "drift hypothesis" of David Matza is an imaginative variation of this approach. Matza's formulation places special emphasis on the techniques by which delinquents accept the conventional norms but are able to rationalize both their own deviations ("neutralization" of the dominant normative system) and the "subterranean" values (search for excitement or "kicks," emphasis on leisure in place of work, and the taste for violence) shared generally by all levels of society.

Volkman and Cressey, whose selection appears in the chapter on solutions, review the key dimensions of a second major approach widely adopted by sociologists, the differential-association hypothesis, which in essence is that criminal behavior is most likely to occur when there is significant and consistent association with others who transmit the techniques and the supporting attitudes, motives, and aspirations for engaging in illegal endeavors. Finally, many of the contributions during the past decade, of which the research report by James F. Short, Jr., and his associates is one, pertain to delinquency among the lower classes. Although the specific theories diverge at numerous points, the central premise is that the lower-class male is inadequately prepared to compete for socially approved ends in a socially acceptable manner, and that delinquency represents for him a means of obtaining such social goals as status, material possessions, or self-respect. Short *et al.* outline the best known of the contemporary formulations, "opportunity-structure theory," and seek to evaluate some of its postulates in terms of empirical data. Their conclusions bear special attention because the position taken combines two levels of causal explanation, the social-structure and the personality levels.

The newer theoretical statements focused on lower-class youth may have wider application than is apparent at present; however, the desirability of isolating homogeneous types of violations or offenders becomes patently clear from a review of the unsuccessful search for an all-encompassing causal explanation. Multiple-factor approaches have been almost equally unsatisfactory; thus they are not a practical substitute for developing restricted theories for specific types of offenders.

With the very divergent viewpoints defended by competent authorities, within as well as between disciplines, it appears that the issue of etiology will not be easily unraveled in the near future. Meanwhile strong pressure from officials and the public requires that something be done to reduce the scale and impact of the problem. The concepts of prevention, control, and treatment cover the entire spectrum of proposals and programs directed toward this end.

Prevention refers to the measures designed to eliminate or reduce the prospects that an individual who has not previously had frequent or serious encounters with law-enforcement agencies will engage in behavior that may eventuate in his being labeled and processed as a delinquent or criminal. Since prevention, by definition, entails action taken in anticipation of future violations, the most appropriate illustrations are programs that seek to reach youth with a high potential for future delinquency. Almost every imaginable technique has been advocated, if not actually tried, to prevent delinquency, without demonstrable success. Among the better-known programs are boys' clubs, mental-hygiene clinics, neighborhood-improvement associations, gang workers, family counseling, and youth-opportunity boards (the latter are an outgrowth, in large part, of the Cloward and Ohlin theory, which is the subject of the selection by Short *et al.* Walter C. Reckless and Simon Dinitz present a fairly detailed discussion of an action program that has been initiated in response to their research findings on the apparent "insulating" effects of a positive (middle-class-oriented) self-concept. Prevention efforts are severely handicapped by the present inability to pinpoint the essential catalysts of delinquency. Too many of the programs are conducted in "closed" or "protected" environments that are not representative of the conditions and pressures faced by the subject at home and in the streets. Finally, the limited resources are often dissipated because of the failure to identify and concentrate on the most vulnerable children or those for whom a specific program will have the greatest positive impact.

The essential objectives of the control emphasis are to keep the level of crime and delinquency at a minimum and to neutralize its effects on the society as a whole. Thus control measures, oriented in terms of the individual offender, are designed to contain or eliminate continued misbehavior, without direct efforts to rehabilitate. Maximum control depends primarily upon effective police and court systems and adequate laws. A delicate balance exists between the requirements to protect the rights of both the individual violator and society. The article on public attitudes toward law enforcement indicates that the general public tends to be flexible and issue-oriented in establishing the balance of rights—seemingly in contrast to those who have decried the trends in recent Supreme Court decisions and any additional restraints on police surveillance.

There is now greater agreement among interested specialists on the revisions needed to assure control without jeopardizing individual liberties. For example, the degree to which a law is enforced may be more significant than its provisions. Application of the nominal penalties associated with white-collar offenses would undoubtedly have a marked deterrent value, whereas it remains to be demonstrated that capital punishment exerts an independent deterrent effect. The requirement for basic changes in the role of police within the urban ghettos has been made patently clear by frequent civil disorders, but the necessity for change can also be supported all too often in the daily exchanges between the police and ghetto residents. As the President's Crime Commission concludes, "While community relations units, neighborhood advisory committees, and fair procedures for processing citizen complaints are essential for reducing existing friction between the police and the community, these programs will have little enduring effect if persons are not treated justly in their contacts with police officers."

The myriad consequences that follow from "plea bargaining" merit special study by the serious student of law-enforcement systems. Approximately 90 percent of the convictions for serious charges, and as much as 95 percent for the less serious misdemeanor cases, are based on the defendant's admission of guilt by a plea in court. The most frequently used form of the plea bargain is an arrangement between the prosecutor and the defendant or his lawyer whereby the defendant agrees to plead guilty, and in return the prosecutor agrees to press a charge less serious (lower potential maximum sentence) than that warranted by the evidence. A recent article by Arthur Rosett, cited in the Supplemental Readings, proposes a number of modifications to eliminate the existing plea-bargaining practices that are characterized by "fears of unfairness and corruption and an air of hypocrisy," while retaining the operational advantages required to dispose of large numbers of cases.

There is also the matter of inherent conflicts in the juvenile-court program as a result of the combined objectives of intervening in behalf of the child and enforcing the provisions of legal codes. Two landmark decisions, *Kent v. United States* (1966) and *In re Gault* (1967), have served to alter the previous pattern in which a juvenile could be removed from the custody of his parents and committed to a state institution at the virtually unlimited discretion of a juvenile court. The *Kent* decision permitted a waiver of the jurisdiction of a juvenile court to allow trial of a juvenile in an adult criminal court, and the *Gault* opinion dealt with denial of notice of the charges, right to counsel, right to confrontation and cross examination, privilege against self-incrimination, right to a transcript of the proceedings, and right to appellate review. The issues suggested by these illustrations are resolvable. However, the general public's ambivalence regarding law enforcement, created by conflicting concerns with the alleged increase in crime and delinquency and the desire to perpetuate a weak enforcement system that can be manipulated, act as impediments to changes that might enhance the programs oriented toward the control aspect.

On the premise that basic long-term modifications of the social environment, though perhaps the key to rehabilitation, are difficult to achieve, most treatment programs seek instead to prepare the offender to cope with his situation in a socially acceptable manner. In addition to the prevention programs mentioned above, which, with appropriate modifications, have been used in treatment, the institutional programs, as well as probation and parole, merit special attention. Group-interaction techniques (guidance and therapy), both within the institution and in the community, have been widely explored in recent years. LaMar Empey and Jerome Rabow furnish a detailed description of such a program in an article cited in the Supplemental Readings. The key to this approach is the use of the peer group (which may comprise delinquents, addicts, murderers, or others) as the principal treatment mechanism. The action program worked out in connection with the Reckless and Dinitz project also warrants attention in this regard. Of particular importance in any treatment program located within an institution are the procedures by which the individual is released to the community. "Halfway houses" represent a popular device to reduce the impact of such transitional difficulties as employment, family reactions, exposure to opportunities for legal violations, and restrictions of parole.

Probation and parole are aimed at supervision, and in some instances treatment, within the community as a substitute for incarceration. Probation is suspension of the penal sentence, with no time served in an institution. The specific implications for rehabilitation are that the treatment process takes place within the setting to which the offender must ultimately adjust, employment and family ties can be maintained if desirable, and the negative influences of institutional life are avoided. Parole, which takes place after an offender has served part of his sentence in an institution, is intended to facilitate his reentry into the community. Contrary to the widely held view that delinquents and criminals are not likely to modify illegal behavior patterns, many instances of recidivism shortly after a period of confinement can be traced directly to inadequate preparation for the change from a highly controlled environment to the less ordered life in the community and to the pressures resulting from the public stigma of parole.

Thus far we have made no formal distinction between delinquency and crime. However, this is not intended to lend support to the invalid assumption that delinquents are underaged criminals, and that the criminal population consists primarily of previous delinquents. Not only are the offense distributions for juveniles and adults quite different, but there is increasing evidence that a substantial proportion of the adult offenders, especially those who commit crimes against the person, were never officially processed as delinquents. The variation in offense distributions reflects the fact that juveniles may come to the attention of the courts for a host of misbehaviors (truancy, promiscuous sexual relations, or definace of parents) that have no legal relevance for adults. Also, much delinquency represents the particular problems of adolescence, as most dramatically illustrated by auto theft and vandalism. In 1966, 63 percent of all persons arrested for auto theft were under the age of eighteen, and 17 percent were under fifteen. Persons under twenty-one comprised 80 percent of the total. The figures for all persons arrested for vandalism in 1966 were 77 percent under eighteen (with 51 percent under fifteen) and 86 percent under twenty-one. There are strong arguments for encouraging greater public tolerance toward all but a small number of juvenile offenses (Ruth Shonle Cavan presents arguments in support of this position in her article, cited in the Supplemental Readings). Yet the view that punishment is the most effective deterrent continues to receive support from the mass media, public officials, and the police. This approach fails to recognize that the problems of delinquency and crime mirror the character of urban life and point clearly to the need for new perspectives that match the realities of mass society.

The first selection, prepared by the staff of the President's Commission on Law Enforcement and Administration of Justice, summarizes special survey data on the public's attitudes toward selected crime issues. The next two selections focus on causation from the sociological point of view. Short and his colleagues report on their efforts to test the hypothesis that delinquency in the lower class stems from the basic discrepancies between aspirations and the possibilities of achieving them by legitimate means. They conclude that social-structure theories can explain variations in delinquency rates manifested by different segments of the society but are not appropriate to account for "individual episodes or degrees of involvement in delinquency." As an alternative to the structure theories, Reckless and Dinitz outline and defend the usefulness of one variation of the containment approach. Their contribution also demonstrates how a theoretical position can be implemented in an action program. Finally, to give explicit recognition to the differences in types of criminal behavior, overviews of the unique features of organized crime and white-collar crime are presented, respectively, by Thomas C. Schelling and the late Edwin H. Sutherland.

## 38     PUBLIC ATTITUDES TOWARD CRIME     THE PRESIDENT'S COMMISSION ON LAW ENFORCEMENT AND ADMINISTRATION OF JUSTICE

At various periods in history, there are surges of public alarm about crime, such as the national concern about gangland crime in the nineteen-twenties. More frequently, however, alarm about "crime waves" has been localized. A few cases of terrible offenses can terrorize an entire metropolis and rising crime rates in once safe areas can arouse new fears and anxieties. At other times in the past, however, some of these crises have been synthetic ones, manufactured as circulation-building devices by the "yellow press." Lincoln Steffens, for example, recounts how he created crime waves by giving dramatic banner headline play to crimes that were actually ordinary occurrences in the metropolis.[1]

Although it is not possible to identify all the factors that affect the rise and fall in public alarm

Reprinted from *Task Force Report: Crime and Its Impact—An Assessment*, President's Commission on Law Enforcement and Administration of Justice, Washington, D.C.: U.S. Government Printing Office, 1967, pp. 85–95.

about crime, it is a constantly recurring public theme.[2] A legal scholar recently took a look over the literature of the past 50 years and noted that each and every decade produced prominent articles about the need for strong measures to meet the then-current crisis in crime.[3] Periodically throughout the century, there have been investigating committees of the Congress, of the State legislatures, and special commissions of cities to deal with the particular crime problem of the time. It may be that there has always been a crime crisis, insofar as public perception is concerned.

### CRIME AS A NATIONAL ISSUE

Many circumstances now conspire to call greater attention to crime as a national, rather than a purely local, problem. Concern with crime is more typically an urban than a rural phenomena and the rural population of the country is declining. At one time, for a majority of the population, reports of crime waves related only to those remote and not quite moral people who inhabited cities.

Now, also, more people are informed by nationally oriented communications media and receive crime reports from a much wider territorial base. In recent years news of the violent and fearful mass killing of 8 nurses in a Chicago apartment, 5 patrons of a beauty shop in Mesa, Ariz., and 13 passersby on the University of Texas campus in Austin received detailed coverage throughout the country. The fear of the people of Boston in 1966 of the brutal attacks of the "Boston Strangler" must have been sympathetically shared and understood in many homes across the land. Some part of the public fear of crime today is undoubtedly due to the fact that the reports of violent crime we receive daily are drawn from a larger pool of crime-incident reports than ever before. But perhaps most important has been the steady stream of reports of rising crime rates in both large and small communities across the Nation. From all this has emerged a sense of crisis in regard to the safety of both person and property.

HEIGHTENED CONCERN ABOUT CRIME AS A PUBLIC PROBLEM  The national public opinion polls provide evidence of the heightened concern today about the crime problem.[4] International problems have invariably been at the top whenever open ended questions were asked by the Gallup poll about the problems facing the Nation. Crime problems were not mentioned as an important problem by enough people to appear among the list. When the National Opinion Research Center conducted a national survey for the Commission during the summer of 1966, interviewers asked citizens to pick from a list of six major domestic problems facing the country the one to which they had been paying most attention recently.[5] Crime was second most frequently picked from among the list of domestic problems; only race relations was selected by more people. (Lower income nonwhites placed more emphasis on education than crime.)

In a consideration of local rather than national problems people rank juvenile delinquency higher

on the scale than almost any other issue, including adult crime. Gallup polls reported in 1963 that when persons were asked to name the top problems in their community from a list of 39, juvenile delinquency was second in frequency of selection —exceeded only by complaints about local real estate taxes. The third most frequently mentioned problem was a not completely unrelated matter in the public's perception—the need for more recreation areas.

Whether more concerned about adult or juvenile crime, most people think the crime situation in their own community is getting worse, and, while substantial numbers think the situation is staying about the same, hardly anyone sees improvement. A Gallup survey in April 1965, showed this pessimistic perception of the problem prevailed among men and women, well educated and less well educated, and among all age, regional, income, and city size groupings.

SOURCES OF PUBLIC ATTITUDES ABOUT CRIME  From analysis of the results of its surveys of the public, the Commission tried to determine to what extent this increased public concern about crime was a reflection of personal experience as a victim, or vicarious impressions received from acquaint-

TABLE 1  *Most important domestic problem, by race and income*

| Domestic problem | White, % | | Nonwhite, % | |
|---|---|---|---|---|
| | Under $6,000 | Over $6,000 | Under $6,000 | Over $6,000 |
| Poverty | 9 | 5 | 7 | 8 |
| Inflation | 15 | 17 | 4 | 4 |
| Education | 12 | 19 | 23 | 21 |
| Crime | 27 | 22 | 19 | 22 |
| Race relations | 29 | 34 | 32 | 38 |
| Unemployment | 8 | 3 | 15 | 7 |
| Number | (3,925) | (6,461) | (1,033) | (462) |

Source: Philip H. Ennis, "Attitudes toward Crime," Interim Report to the President's Commission on Law Enforcement and Administration of Justice, 1966 (mimeographed).

ances, the mass media, or other sources. Although it was not possible to answer this question fully, the available data indicate that for most people, attitudes about serious crimes and crime trends come largely from vicarious sources. This is especially the case with the crimes of violence which, although the focus of the public's concern, are relatively rare.

Very few incidents in which citizens have been victimized by crime were of such great significance in their lives as to be readily remembered for any length of time. This conclusion is one of the findings from the intensive methodological work undertaken for the Commission by the Bureau of Social Science Research in Washington, D.C., in preparation for surveys of the public regarding victimization.[6] This was first observed in pretest interviewing that showed extremely pronounced "recency effects"; that is, the bulk of such incidents as respondents did report were incidents that had occurred within the very recent past—in the space of just the last few months. A very steep decline occurred when the number of cases of victimization were plotted by month of occurrence from the present into the past—even for as short a period as 1 year. While the investigators were ultimately able to achieve far greater exhaustiveness of reporting through methods that facilitated recall and led their respondents to give more time and effort to the task of remembering, even these revised methods showed pronounced effects of forgetting.

This effect is even very evident in the dates victimized citizens gave for crimes mentioned in response to questions about the worst crime that had ever happened to them or to any member of their household. Taking the most remote of any incidents of victimization mentioned by each respondent, over half had occurred during the previous 18-month period and 60 percent in the past 2 years. Only 21 percent of all incidents described as "the worst ever" were said to have happened more than 5 years ago.[7]

The seriousness of most crimes reported by the citizens interviewed by BSSR also led to the inference that people generally do not readily remember minor incidents of victimization, though relatively trivial criminal acts, such as vandalism and petty larcenies from automobiles and of bicycles, are undoubtedly much more prevalent than are more serious offenses.[8]

These observations may help explain why the surveys of citizens conducted for the Commission found little statistical relationship between having been directly victimized by crime and attitudes toward most aspects of the crime problem. Undoubtedly, if there had been sufficient cases to relate reliably the personal experiences and attitudes of persons suffering victimization from the most serious crimes of rape, aggravated assault, robbery, etc., a direct relationship would have been found in such cases. However, for all victims as a group in contrast to nonvictims, having been personally victimized did not influence perceptions of whether crime was increasing or not, or the degree of a person's concern with the crime problem in most instances. The NORC national survey did show that victims tended to have somewhat more worry about burglary or robbery. This was true for both males and females as can be seen in Table 2, though females, whether they had been

**TABLE 2**  *Concern of victims and nonvictims about burglary or robbery*

| Worry about burglary or robbery | Victim, % | Nonvictim, % |
|---|---|---|
| **Males** | | |
| Worried | 69 | 59 |
| Not worried | 31 | 41 |
| Number | (1,456) | (3,930) |
| **Females** | | |
| Worried | 84 | 77 |
| Not worried | 16 | 23 |
| Number | (2,399) | (6,189) |

Source: Philip H. Ennis, *Criminal Victimization in the United States: A Report of a National Survey*, Field Survey II, President's Commission on Law Enforcement and Administration of Justice, Washington, D.C.: U.S. Government Printing Office, 1967, adapted from tables 48 and 50, pp. 77–79.

victimized or not, were more concerned about their safety than males. However, other data from the NORC survey show that recent experience of being a victim of crime did not seem to increase behavior designed to protect the home. Almost identical proportions, 57 percent of victims and 58 percent of nonvictims, took strong household security measures.[9]

In its Washington study BSSR found similar results. An index of exposure to crime was developed based on having personally witnessed offenses or on whether one's self or one's friends had been victimized. Scores on this index, in general, were not associated with responses to a variety of questions on attitudes toward crime and toward law enforcement that respondents were asked. Nor did exposure to crime appear to determine the anxiety about crime manifested in the interviews. The one exception appeared in the case of the Negro male. Negro men showed a tendency to be influenced in their attitudes and behavior according to whether they had been victims of some type of crime or not.[10]

In addition, the BSSR study found that the average level of concern with crime in a predominantly Negro police precinct that had one of the highest rates of crime in the city, according to police data, was lower than it was in another Negro precinct that had a low rate, relative to the first.[11]

All of these observations suggest that people's perception of the incidence and nature of crime and even to some extent their concern about it may be formed in large part by what they read or hear about from others. This does not mean, of course, that what people learn to think and feel about the crime problem in this way is any less valid or important as grounds for launching renewed efforts at crime control and prevention, or that either the extent of the crime problem or people's fears about it should be minimized. It does indicate the need for a greater public responsiblity to insure that people have a chance to learn facts about crime that are not only accurate and trustworthy but also most relevant to the situations in which they live and work. It also means,

because of the apparent importance of vicarious impressions in forming public attitudes about crime, that we need many more intensive studies to determine what it is that most influences people's views and feelings about crime.

A further indication of the importance of vicarious impressions in forming the public's perceptions of crime is that a majority of citizens almost everywhere think that the situation right where they live is not so bad. While the predominant opinion is that the crime situation is terrible and getting worse, most people tend to think of the situation as one that characterizes places other than their own immediate neighborhood. In the nationwide NORC study for the Commission, 60 percent of those questioned compared their own neighborhood favorably to other parts of the community in which they lived with regard to the likelihood that their home would be broken into, while only 14 percent thought their area presented a greater hazard.[12] This is the case even in areas that are regarded as very crime-ridden by the police. In the BSSR survey of residents of areas in Washington, D.C., that have average to high crime rates, only one out of five of those interviewed thought his neighborhood was less safe than most in the city.[13] Surveys conducted for the Commission by the Survey Research Center of the University of Michigan concerning public attitudes about crime in four medium to high crime rate police precincts in Boston and Chicago found that 73 percent of the respondents thought their own neighborhoods were very safe or average compared to other neighborhoods in relation to the chances of getting robbed, threatened, beaten up, or anything of that sort.[14]

Almost half of the nationwide sample contacted by the NORC survey said there was no place in the city in which they lived (or suburb or county for those not living in cities) where they would feel unsafe. Two-thirds of the respondents say they feel safe walking alone when it is dark if they are in their own neighborhood. Responses to the questions: "How likely is it that a person walking around here at night might be held up or attacked—very likely, somewhat likely, somewhat unlikely or very unlikely?" were very heavily weighted toward the "unlikely" direction.

PERSONAL FEAR OF CRIME    The core of public anxiety about the crime problem involves a concern for personal safety and to a somewhat lesser extent the fear that personal property will be taken. Perhaps the most intense concern about crime is the fear of being attacked by a stranger when out alone. According to the NORC survey, while two-thirds of the American public feel safe about walking alone at night in their own neighborhoods, the remaining one-third do not. In Table 2, as noted above, women worry more than men about the risk of burglary or robbery. According to an April 1965 Gallup survey, the percentage of people feeling unsafe at night on the street is higher in large cities than in smaller ones and higher in cities than in rural areas.

Recently studies have been undertaken to develop an index of delinquency based on the seriousness of different offenses.[15] They have shown that there is widespread public consensus on the relative seriousness of different types of crimes and these rankings furnish useful indicators of the types of crime that the public is most concerned about. Offenses involving physical assaults against the person are the most feared crimes and the greatest concern is expressed about those in which a weapon is used.

Fear of crime makes many people want to move their homes. In the four police precincts surveyed for the Commission in Boston and Chicago, 20 percent of the citizens wanted to move because of the crime in their neighborhoods, and as many as 30 percent wanted to move out of the highest crime rate district in Boston.[16]

Fear of crime shows variations by race and income. In the survey in Washington, the Bureau of Social Science Research put together an index of anxiety about crime. It found that Negro women had the highest average score, followed by Negro men, white women, and white men. Anxiety scores were lower at the higher income levels for both Negroes and whites.[17]

The NORC survey asked people whether there

have been times recently when they wanted to go somewhere in town but stayed at home instead, because they thought it would be unsafe to go there. Sixteen percent of the respondents said that they had stayed home under these conditions. This type of reaction showed marked variation with race; one out of every three Negro respondents had stayed home as contrasted with one in eight whites.[18]

People also take special measures at home because of the fear of unwanted intruders. The national survey showed that 82 percent of the respondents always kept their doors locked at night and 25 percent always kept their doors locked even in the daytime when the family members were at home. Twenty-eight percent kept watchdogs and 37 percent said they kept firearms in the house for protection, among other reasons.[19]

The special city surveys disclosed that a substantial number of people take other measures to protect themselves from crime. In Boston and Chicago 28 percent had put new locks on their doors primarily, as one might expect, because they had been victimized or were worried about the high crime rate in the area. Another 10 percent had put locks or bars on their windows; this occurred primarily in the highest crime rate areas. Nine percent said they carried weapons, usually knives, when they went out, and this figure rose to 19 percent in the highest crime rate district in Boston.[20]

The close relationship between worry about crime and the taking of strong precautionary measures is further demonstrated by the results from the national survey. Respondents were asked how much they worried about being victimized by robbery or burglary and their responses were related to their tendency to take strong household security measures. Persons worried about both burglary and robbery are most likely to take such precautions, about 50 percent more likely than those who are worried about neither.[21]

Perhaps the most revealing findings on the impact of fear of crime on people's lives were the changes people reported in their regular habits of life. In the high-crime districts surveyed in Boston and Chicago, for example, five out of every eight respondents reported changes in their habits because of fear of crime, some as many as four or five major changes. Forty-three percent reported they stayed off the streets at night altogether. Another 21 percent said they always used cars or taxis at night. Thirty-five percent said they would not talk to strangers any more.[22]

CONCLUSIONS ABOUT THE PUBLIC'S FEAR OF CRIME   The Task Force cannot say that the public's fear of crime is exaggerated. It is not prepared to tell the people how fearful they should be; that is something each person must decide for himself. People's fears must be respected; certainly they cannot be legislated. Some people are willing to run risks that terrify others. However, it is possible to draw some general conclusions from the findings of the surveys.

The first is that the public fears the most the crimes that occur the least—crimes of violence. People are much more tolerant of crimes against property, which constitute most of the crimes that are committed against persons or households or businesses. Actually, the average citizen probably suffers the greatest economic loss from crimes against business establishments and public institutions, which pass their losses on to him in the form of increased prices and taxes. Nevertheless, most shoplifters never get to court; they are released by the store managers with warnings. Most employees caught stealing are either warned or discharged, according to the reports of businesses and organizations in the Task Force's survey in three cities.[23]

Second, the fear of crimes of violence is not a simple fear of injury or death or even of all crimes of violence, but, at bottom, a fear of strangers. The personal injury that Americans risk daily from sources other than crime are enormously greater. The annual rate of all Index offenses involving either violence or the threat of violence is 1.8 per 1,000 Americans.[24] This is minute relative to the total accidental injuries calling for medical attention or restricted activity of 1 day or more, as reported by the Public Health Service.[25] A recent study of emergency medical care found the qual-

ity, numbers, and distribution of ambulances and other emergency services severely deficient, and estimated that as many as 20,000 Americans die unnecessarily each year as a result of improper emergency care.[26] The means necessary for correcting this situation are very clear and would probably yield greater immediate return in reducing death than would expenditures for reducing the incidence of crimes of violence. But a different personal significance is attached to deaths due to the willful acts of felons as compared to the incompetence or poor equipment of emergency medical personnel.

Furthermore, as noted in chapter 2, most murders and assaults are committed by persons known to the victim, by relatives, friends, or acquaintances. Indeed on a straight statistical basis, the closer the relationship the greater the hazard. In one sense the greatest threat to anyone is himself, since suicides are more than twice as common as homicides.

Third, this fear of strangers has greatly impoverished the lives of many Americans, especially those who live in high-crime neighborhoods in large cities. People stay behind the locked doors of their homes rather than risk walking in the streets at night. Poor people spend money on taxis because they are afraid to walk or use public transportation. Sociable people are afraid to talk to those they do not know. In short, society is to an increasing extent suffering from what economists call "opportunity costs" as the result of fear of crime. For example, administrators and officials interviewed for the Commission by the University of Michigan survey team, report that library use is decreasing because borrowers are afraid to come out at night. School officials told of parents not daring to attend PTA meetings in the evening, and park administrators pointed to unused recreation facilities.[27] When many persons stay home, they are not availing themselves of the opportunities for pleasure and cultural enrichment offered in their communities, and they are not visiting their friends as frequently as they might. The general level of social interaction in the society is reduced.

When fear of crime becomes fear of the stranger, the social order is further damaged. As the level of sociability and mutual trust is reduced, streets and public places can indeed become more dangerous. Not only will there be fewer people abroad but those who are abroad will manifest a fear of and a lack of concern for each other. The reported incidents of bystanders indifferent to cries for help are the logical consequence of a reduced sociability, mutual distrust and withdrawal.

However, the most dangerous aspect of a fear of strangers is its implication that the moral and social order of society are of doubtful trustworthiness and stability. Everyone is dependent on this order to instill in all members of society a respect for the persons and possessions of others. When it appears that there are more and more people who do not have this respect, the security that comes from living in an orderly and trustworthy society is undermined. The tendency of many people to think of crime in terms of increasing moral deterioration is an indication that they are losing their faith in their society. And so the costs of the fear of crime to the social order may ultimately be even greater than its psychological or economic costs to individuals.

Fourth, the fear of crime may not be as strongly influenced by the actual incidence of crime as it is by other experiences with the crime problem generally. For example, the mass media and overly zealous or opportunistic crime fighters may play a role in raising fears of crime by associating the idea of "crime" with a few sensational and terrifying criminal acts.[28] Past research on the mass media's connection with crime has concentrated primarily on depictions and accounts of violence in the mass media as possible causes of delinquency and crime. Little attention has thus far been given to what may be a far more direct and costly effect—the creation of distorted perceptions of the risk of crime and exaggerated fears of victimization.

The greatest danger of an exaggerated fear of crime may well reside in the tendency to use the violent crime as a stereotype for crimes in general. For example, there may be a significant interplay between violence, the mass media, and the reporting of general crime figures. Publicity about total crime figures without distinguishing between the trends for property crime and those for crimes against persons may create mistaken ideas about what is actually happening. If burglaries and larcenies increase sharply while violent crimes decrease or remain stable, the total figures will follow the property crime figures, since crimes against property are more than four-fifths of the total. Yet under these conditions people may interpret the increases in terms of the dominant stereotype of crimes of violence, thus needlessly increasing their fears. They may not only restrict their activities out of an exaggerated fear of violence but may fail to protect themselves against the more probable crimes. The fact is that most people experience crime vicariously through the daily press, periodicals, novels, radio and television, and often the reported experiences of other persons. Their fear of crime may be more directly related to the quality and the amount of this vicarious experience than it is to the actual risks of victimization.

The Task Force believes that there is a clear public responsibility to keep citizens fully informed of the facts about crime so that they will have facts to go on when they decide what the risks are and what kinds and amounts of precautionary measures they should take. Furthermore, without an accurate understanding of the facts, they cannot judge whether the interference with individual liberties which strong crime control measures may involve is a price worth paying. The public obligation to citizens is to provide this information regularly and accurately. And if practices for disseminating information give wrong impressions, resources should be committed to developing more accurate methods.

## ATTITUDES TOWARD CAUSES AND CURES

Attitude surveys involving questions on the causes of crime and measures for remedying the situation yield results reflecting differences in fundamental beliefs regarding man and society. Some regard punitive and repressive measures as the best means for coping with the problem while others prefer measures of social uplift. Some see inherent and immutable differences between the character of those who commit crimes, on the one hand, and the ordinary citizen on the other. Others see criminal tendencies as modifiable by instruction or changes in environmental circumstances. Some view many current social changes as leading toward a progressively more law-abiding citizenry; others see in them the undermining of moral beliefs and constraints which keep men law-abiding.

While there undoubtedly are some persons whose views fit neatly into this liberal versus conservative polarity this is by no means universally so. The lack of a rigid polarity is evidenced by conflicting poll and survey results, especially between notions of causes and cures, and between ideas of appropriate actions in general or in concrete cases.

A Gallup poll in August 1965 asked people what they thought was responsible for the increase in crime in this country. The major share of the reasons people mentioned were things having directly to do with the social or moral character of the population, rather than changes in objective circumstances or in law enforcement. Gallup classified more than half of all the answers given under the category "Family, poor parental guidance." About 6 percent of the answers gave breakdown in moral standards as the reason for increased crime. A variety of other directly moral causes were given in addition, such as: people expect too much, people want something for nothing, and communism. Relatively few (12 percent) of the responses were in terms of objective conditions such as unemployment, poverty, the automobile, or the population explosion. Inadequate laws and the leniency of the courts were mentioned by 7 percent and not enough police protection by only 3 percent.

The responses to a query by Harris the same year were classified differently but a similar pattern emerges. Disturbed and restless teenagers was mentioned by more persons than any other cause and poor police departments by very few.

Harris later asked specifically why people become criminal rather than the reasons for an increase in crime. Most respondents attributed criminality to environmental and developmental factors rather than inborn characteristics, emphasizing such factors as poor training and companions, sometimes simply bad environment.

Although a majority of persons queried tended to think of inadequate moral training rather than inherent weaknesses when asked about the cause of crime, their response concerning the best way to cope with the problem tended to depend upon how the issue was phrased. For example, the BSSR survey in Washington asked citizens what they thought was the most important thing that could be done to cut down crime in the city.[29] Their responses were classified as to whether a repressive measure, a measure of social amelioration, or one of moral inculcation was being advocated. (Repressive measures included such things as more police, police dogs, stiffer sentences, cracking down on teenagers. Social amelioration included advocacy of such things as more jobs, recreation and youth programs, better housing, and improved po-

**TABLE 3**    *Why people become criminals*

| Factor | Total public, %* |
|---|---|
| Upbringing | 38 |
| Bad environment | 30 |
| Mentally ill | 16 |
| Wrong companions | 14 |
| No education | 14 |
| Broken homes | 13 |
| Greed, easy money | 13 |
| Too much money around | 11 |
| Not enough money in home | 10 |
| Liquor, dope | 10 |
| Laziness | 9 |
| For kicks | 8 |
| No religion | 8 |
| No job | 8 |
| No chance by society | 7 |
| Born bad | 5 |
| Feeling of hopelessness | 4 |
| Moral breakdown of society | 3 |
| Degeneracy, sex | 2 |
| Failure of police | 2 |

*Percentages add to more than 100 because people volunteered more than 1 cause.

Source: Harris poll, conducted in 1965 and reported in 1966.

lice-community relations. Moral measures were better child training, religious training and revival, community leadership, and, most simply, teach discipline.) Sixty percent of the respondents recommended repressive measures, as compared with 40 percent who suggested social and amelioration or moral inculcation.

Further, evidence of this tendency to think of repressive measures as the way to deal with some aspects of the crime problems is contained in the answers to the question. "In general, do you think the courts in this area deal too harshly or not harshly enough with criminals?" asked in a 1965 Gallup survey. The majority of responses was not harshly enough; only 2 percent said too harshly. The BSSR study in Washington avoided the use of the word criminal by asking whether the sentences given by courts in Washington were generally too lenient or too harsh. Again, most respondents, including Negroes, thought the courts too lenient.[30]

However, when survey items pose alternatives rather than general open ended questions, they have yielded somewhat different results. The NORC national study asked people whether the main concern of the police should be with preventing crimes from happening or with catching criminals. All but 6 percent of those asked felt they could make a choice between these two emphases—61 percent chose preventing crimes and 31 percent catching criminals.[31]

Another question by the Harris poll in 1966 posed these alternatives:

Leading authorities on crime feel there are two ways to reduce crime. One way is to head off crime by working with young people to show them that nothing can be gained through a life of crime. Another way is to strengthen our law enforcement agencies to make it hard for criminals to get away with crime. While both ways might be desirable, if you had to choose, which one would you favor: trying to stop criminals before they begin or strengthening the police force to crack down on crime?

More than three-fourths of respondents chose "work with young people," only 16 percent

"strengthen police." There were 8 percent who were not sure which was preferable.

A nonpunitive approach was also evident in a third question in the same survey which asked people to choose between corrective and punitive goals for prisons. Again, over three-fourths of the respondents choose correction as the alternative, only 11 percent punishment. Apparently, when the alternatives are put sharply enough, especially in dealing with the misbehavior of young people, the general preference of the public for preventive or rehabilitative rather than repressive measures emerges.

The tendency to be nonpunitive and repressive when considering the handling of youthful offenders is strikingly illustrated by the results of a 1963 Gallup survey. A sample was drawn from 171 communities across the Nation to sit in judgment on a hypothetical case. The respondents were asked how they would deal with a 17-year-old high school student from their own community who was caught stealing an automobile. They were told he had no previous record. Fewer than 10 percent recommended confinement of any sort: the largest number said they would give him another chance (Table 4).

These survey results indicate the existence of public attitudes endorsing current trends in the criminal justice field that would increase the effectiveness of law enforcement and at the same time greatly expand preventive and rehabilitative efforts, particularly with young people. Though at first glance public attitudes toward the causes and cures for crime might appear contradictory, a more careful analysis suggests that the public

**TABLE 4**  *How public would deal with youth caught stealing a car, rank order of answers*

1  Give him another chance, be lenient.
2  Put him on probation; give him a suspended sentence.
3  Put him under care of psychiatrist or social worker.
4  Put him in an institution: jail, reformatory, etc.
5  Release him in the custody of his parents.
6  Punish his parents; fine them.

Source: Gallup polls, 1963.

assumes different attitudes toward different aspects of the crime problem. This provides potential support for many different types of action programs ranging all the way from increased police powers and more severe penalties for crime to the benign types of treatment and prevention programs.

### CITIZEN INVOLVEMENT IN CRIME PREVENTION

Public concern about crime can be a powerful force for action. However, making it one will not be easy. The Washington survey asked people whether they had ever "gotten together with other people around here or has any group or organization you belong to met and discussed the problem of crime or taken some sort of action to combat crime?"[32] Only 12 percent answered affirmatively, although the question was quite broad and included any kind of group meeting or discussion. Neither did most persons believe that they as individuals could do anything about the crime in their own neighborhoods. Just over 17 percent thought that they could do something about the situation.

The question of what could be done to reduce crime was put to administrators and officials of public and quasi-public organizations in three cities.[33] These officials suggested ameliorative measures, such as greater equality of opportunity, rehabilitative, recreational and youth programs more frequently than did the sample of the general population. These citizens in positions of responsibility also relied to a great extent on the police; almost as many suggested improved and augmented police forces as suggested the social measures. There was, however, much greater emphasis on improvement in the moral fiber and discipline of the population than was true of the sample of the general population. Administrators of parks, libraries, utility companies, housing projects frequently stressed greater respect for property, for persons, or for the police; they believed that education could inculcate these values in the population. As these officials were responsible for organizations which suffered considerable loss through vandalism, it seemed reasonable to them that greater respect for property would solve much of the crime

problem. School officials proposed more alternative activities for youth while park and traffic officials emphasized more police activity and better police-community relations, reflecting their own perceived need for more patrolling.

These administrators and officials who were interviewed also acknowledged a number of ways in which they might help to reduce crime. Some suggested that they might cooperate with the police in ways calculated to make law enforcement easier. Others thought that they might cooperate in neighborhood and community programs, particularly by donating money for youth activities. The largest number of suggestions, however, involved what might be termed extension of the organizations' services. Electric companies considered more and brighter street lights, park officials more parks and recreational programs, and school principals more youth programs and adult education. Another category of responses by officials concerned participation in activities directed toward community goals. They thought that integration of work crews and the support of community relations programs might be helpful. Interestingly, some of these suggestions were not offered until the officials were specifically asked what their organizations might do. Park officials, for example, did not suggest recreational and other alternative activities as a means of reducing crime until asked what park departments might do. Nonetheless, these administrators and officials did see the potential of their own organizations as useful in reducing crime, creating the possibility that they might do something other than rely on the police. They also take a broader view of crime prevention than does the general public. Understandably, they might as citizens and organizations feel more competent to participate effectively in these broader programs while other segments of the public are more likely to believe that control and prevention is not within their province.

### AMBIVALENCE REGARDING POLICE PRACTICES AND LAW ENFORCEMENT

The public surveys show that there is a considerable willingness to permit practices the police and law enforcement agencies consider important—but not an unqualified willingness. The complexity of the feelings about the relative rights of the police and the accused person is apparent in the responses of persons questioned by the BSSR in Washington and also in the results of the national study.

As one might expect, a substantial majority of the respondents in Washington, 73 percent, agreed that the police ought to have leeway to act tough when they have to.[34] In addition, more than half—56 percent—agreed that there should be more use of police dogs, while less than one-third (31 percent) disagreed. However, the person who takes a strong position on one question may refuse to do so on another. Further, there is little consistency between a general respect and sympathy for police and willingness to enlarge police powers. Table 5 shows that there is some tendency for those with high police support scores to be willing to give the police greater power, but that there are also many who regard the police favorably who would restrict their power. The public's attitudes seem to be more responsive to particular issues than to anything which might be called a generalized high or low attitude toward supporting the police.

A similar ambivalence was observed in the results of the national survey conducted for the Commission.[35] There were four questions concerned with the power of the police. Forty-five percent favored civilian review boards (35 percent opposed them, 20 percent had no opinion or were indifferent); 52 percent believed that the police should have more power; 42 percent that police should risk arresting an innocent person rather than risk missing a criminal; and 65 percent favored the ruling that police may not question a suspect without his lawyer being present or the suspect's consent to be questioned without counsel. These percentages indicate that individuals vary considerably from one issue to the next as to the desirability of enlarging or restricting police powers.

To test this motion, the answers of each respondent were combined to form a scale of restrictiveness or permissiveness regarding law enforcement policy (Table 6). Those consistently in favor of expanding police powers would score 0 and those most restrictive of police power would score 8. The distribution of scores in Table 6 illustrates the variations in attitudes about different law enforcement policies or issues. Only 11 percent of the respondents show extreme scores advocating expansion of police power and 15 percent show extreme restrictive scores. Many give restrictive

**TABLE 5**  *Attitudes toward supporting police and approval of certain police practices*

|  | Agree | | Disagree | |
|---|---|---|---|---|
|  | No. | % | No. | % |
| "The police should have leeway to act tough when they have to." | | | | |
|     Low police support score* | 136 | 36.5 | 59 | 53.6 |
|     High police support score | 237 | 63.5 | 51 | 46.4 |
| Total | 373 | 100.0 | 110 | 100.0 |
| "There should be more use of police dogs." | | | | |
|     Low police support score | 100 | 35.1 | 86 | 53.4 |
|     High police support score | 185 | 64.9 | 75 | 46.6 |
| Total | 285 | 100.0 | 161 | 100.0 |

*A police support score was assigned each respondent depending on whether he gave a positive or negative response to six statements about the police.

Source: Albert D. Biderman, Louise A. Johnson, Jennie McIntyre, and Adrianne W. Weir, *Report on a Pilot Study in District of Columbia on Victimization and Attitudes toward Law Enforcement*, Field Survey I, President's Commission on Law Enforcement and Administration of Justice, Washington, D.C.: U.S. Government Printing Office, 1967. Hereinafter referred to as the BSSR study.

**TABLE 6**    *Attitudes toward law enforcement policies*

|  | | Score Value | Percent |
|---|---|---|---|
| Recently some cities have added civilian review boards to their police departments. Some people say such boards offer the public needed protection against the police, and others say these boards are unnecessary and would interfere with good police work and morale. In general, would you be in favor of civilian review boards or opposed to them? | 2 | In favor | 45 |
|  | 0 | Opposed | 35 |
|  | 1 | Don't know | 20 |
|  |  | N | (14,366) |
| Do you favor giving the police more power to question people, do you think they have enough power already, or would you like to see some of their power to question people curtailed? | 0 | Police should have more power | 52 |
|  | 1 | Have enough power already | 43 |
|  | 2 | Should curtail power | 5 |
|  |  | N | (13,190) |
| The police sometimes have a hard time deciding if there is enough evidence to arrest a suspect. In general, do you think it is better for them to risk arresting an innocent person rather than letting the criminal get away, or is it better for them to be really sure they are getting the right person before they make an arrest? | 0 | Risk arresting innocent | 42 |
|  | 2 | Be really sure | 58 |
|  |  | N | (13,488) |
| The Supreme Court has recently ruled that in criminal cases the police may not question a suspect without his lawyer being present, unless the suspect agrees to be questioned without a lawyer. Are you in favor of this Supreme Court decision or opposed to it? | 2 | In favor | 65 |
|  | 0 | Opposed | 35 |
|  |  | N | (12,994) |

Source: Adapted from Philip H. Ennis, *Criminal Victimization in the United States: A Report of a National Survey*, Field Survey II, President's Commission on Law Enforcement and Administration of Justice, Washington, D.C.: U.S. Government Printing Office, 1967. Hereinafter referred to as the NORC study, pp. 64–65.

answers to some questions and permissive answers to others.

The public surveys also show that most people believe that the police do not discriminate in the way they treat members of different groups. About half of the Negro and 20 percent of the white citizens interviewed in Washington thought that Negroes get no worse treatment than other people. Among the comments of those respondents who do believe the police discriminate were that the police pick on Negroes more, they are rude to Negroes, use brutality and physical force, or else ignore Negroes more than other people. Half of the Washington respondents believed that people who have money for lawyers don't have to worry about police.[36] Somewhat fewer but nonetheless almost half of the respondents in Boston and Chicago said that the way police treat you depends on who you are.[37] In these cities, 35 percent saw rich and respectable persons as being favored by the police while 38 percent said that being a Negro makes a difference.[38] In the predominantly Negro districts in each of these cities, more persons thought that Negroes receive less than equitable treatment while in the predominantly white areas more persons spoke of favorable treatment of rich persons.[39]

The single most outstanding finding of the survey in Washington, however, was not the differences between groups but rather the generally high regard for the police among all groups, including Negro men. Although the BSSR survey found that more than half of the Negro men believed that many policemen enjoy giving people a hard time, 79 percent said that the police deserve more thanks than they get. And 74 percent thought that there are just a few policemen who are responsible for the bad publicity that the police force sometimes gets.[40] It is not so surprising to find this potential for good will toward the police when it is remembered that Negroes expressed the most worry about being the victims of crime and a general reliance on the police to prevent and control crime. This was the case even among Negro men who are not well educated and who live in the poorer areas of the city with relatively high rates of crime.

In general, the surveys found public concern for safeguarding individual rights. Only 38 percent of the respondents agreed that too much attention is paid to the rights of persons who get in trouble with the police, when that question was asked in Washington, Boston, and Chicago.[41] The questions which comprised the law enforcement policy scale in the national survey also were concerned with various aspects of the relative rights of the accused and the police.[42] When asked several questions in which various extensions of police powers were posited against protections of individual rights, in only one case did a majority favor the enlargement of police power.[43] Barely more than half, 52 percent, thought that police should have more power to question people. A pronounced concern with the rights of citizens is particularly apparent when the rights issue is very explicit. It also is apparent that most persons do not perceive this concern with rights of citizens as being derogatory toward the police. Of those persons questioned in Washington who took a prorights position, more than half indicated strong respect and sympathy for the police.[44]

Negroes were somewhat more likely to take the rights position than white respondents but the differences were not great. The survey in Washington found that 49 percent of the Negroes and 46 percent of the white respondents did not think that too much attention was being paid to the rights of people who get into trouble with the police.[45] The same question was asked in Boston and Chicago; in both cities there were more prorights replies in the districts which were predominantly Negro than in those which were predominantly white. In Boston the proportions of prorights replies were 46 percent in the predominantly Negro district and 20 percent in the predominantly white area. In Chicago it was 40 and 33 percent in predominantly Negro and white areas respectively.[46] The differences between the mean scores on the police policy index also reflected more concern with the rights of citizens on the part of nonwhite than white persons in the national sample.[47]

Another form of concern with the rights of citizens in recent years has been the question of allowing political and civil rights demonstrations. People who were questioned in the national study were asked whether such demonstrations should be allowed no matter what, should be allowed only if the demonstrators remain peaceful, or should not be allowed at all.[48] A majority of both whites and nonwhites would allow the demonstrations, most with the proviso that they remain peaceful. Among white persons there was a relationship between income and tolerance toward demonstrations. Those persons with higher incomes would more frequently allow demonstrations if they were peaceful and less frequently prohibit all demonstrations. Nonwhites tended to be more permissive regarding demonstrations regardless of income level. The upper income nonwhites, however, more often qualified their tolerance by requiring that demonstrations be peaceful. The tolerance of demonstrations as an indication of concern for rights was far from synonymous with a desire to restrict police powers as they related to the rights

**TABLE 7**   *Police policy index*

| Index value* | Percent |
|---|---|
| 0 | 7.5 |
| 1 | 3.6 |
| 2 | 16.4 |
| 3 | 10.7 |
| 4 | 16.9 |
| 5 | 17.1 |
| 6 | 12.5 |
| 7 | 13.1 |
| 8 | 2.2 |
| N | (11,742) |

*0, most in favor of increasing police powers, to 8, most in favor of restricting police power.

of citizens, however. More than 50 percent of the white respondents who would allow demonstrations would also enlarge police powers. (More of the nonwhites would restrict police powers.)

The national survey also found a strong preponderance of favorable opinion toward the Supreme Court's decision regarding right of counsel.[49] Almost three-quarters of the persons questioned approved the decision that the State must provide a lawyer to suspects who want one but cannot afford to pay the lawyer's fee. Not only does a strong majority approve the decision but no income, sex, or racial group opposes it.

## NONREPORTING OF CRIMES TO THE POLICE

Americans believe that the crime problem is a matter for police rather than citizen action. They nevertheless frequently fail to take the one essential action that they as citizens must take if the police are to intervene in any particular criminal instance. Fewer than half of the incidents of victimization uncovered by NORC in the national survey conducted for the Commission had been reported while the residents of Washington had notified the police of only 65 percent of the incidents they disclosed to BSSR interviewers.[50] NORC found considerable variation by type of crime.[51] Generally the more serious the crime the more likely the police were called. A higher percentage of grand than petty larcenies and of aggravated than simple assaults were reported, for example. Except for the more serious crimes against the person, however, crimes which were completed were reported no more frequently than the attempted crimes. It is apparent that the simple desire to recover losses or damages is not the only factor in a victim's decision for or against police notification. This study did not find that any racial or income group was any more likely than another to report or decline to report crimes.[52]

The victim's or witness' reluctance to get involved was one of the most frequently cited reasons for nonreporting.[53] Sometimes he did not want to take the time to call the police and present evidence, perhaps spending time in court and away from his work. Some persons who said they had witnessed incidents which might have been crimes did not feel it was their responsibility to intervene, that it was not their business to call the police or take any other action. A few persons expressed this sentiment by stating to the interviewers, "I am not my brother's keeper."

Others said they did not think the victim would want the police to be notified or they indicated a concern for the offender. Victims, too, were sometimes reluctant to cause trouble for the offender. In half the cases of family crimes or sex offenses (other than forcible rape) reported to NORC interviewers the police were not notified and the reason most frequently given was that it was a private rather than a police matter.[54] Similarly for all classes of offenses except serious crimes against the person, the police were less likely to be called if the offender were personally known to the victim than if he were a stranger.

The fear of reprisal or other unfortunate consequences sometimes deterred victims or witnesses from notifying the police of an incident. Some feared personal harm might come from the offender or his friends. Some feared that they themselves would become the subject of police inquiry or action. In the case of property offenses the fear of increased insurance rates or even of cancellation of insurance was more likely to be the reason. Businessmen often refrained from reporting burglaries, believing that it was less expensive to absorb some of these losses than to pay more for their insurance.[55]

The most frequently cited reason for not reporting an incident to the police is the belief in police ineffectiveness; 55 percent of the reasons given for nonreporting by respondent in the national study fell in this category. This does not necessarily constitute evidence of a pervasive cynicism regarding police. The victim may instead have simply accepted that the damage had been done, there were no clues and the police could not be expected to apprehend the offender or undo the damage. For example, in malicious mischief where it is unlikely the offender will be caught, police ineffectiveness is the preponderant reason for nonreporting.

For similar reasons, businessmen interviewed by the University of Michigan survey team said that they rarely called the police to handle cases of employee dishonesty. In 46 percent of the cases where the police were not called, the reason given questions the capability of the police to do anything in the situation.[56] They do not question that the police will respond to their call but doubt whether the police would or could accept the kind of evidence they have, or they do not feel that the courts would accept the evidence even if the police formally made an arrest. These businessmen also frequently responded in terms of not wanting to get involved and preferring to handle the matter themselves. Dismissal of the employee apparently requires less time and effort than referral of the matter to the police. Their feeling that it was not worthwhile to call the police then did not always indicate a negative evaluation of the police. Ironically, many of these same businessmen who do not report instances of employee dishonesty use police records as a screening device for selecting potential employees.[57]

Another factor which may be operating here is the relationship between the employer and employee. The employer has in a sense taken some responsibility for the relationship by engaging the employee; what happens then is seen as a matter between himself and the person he has hired. Similarly, when a businessman agrees to cash a customer's check he infrequently calls the police when the check is returned for insufficient funds or other reasons. Only 19 percent of the owners and managers said they called police when they are given a bad check and another 8 percent said they would do so if they could not collect.[58] By far the most frequent response is to request that the offender make good. This is also the most frequent response in the case of shoplifting but here there is a greater willingness to call the police. Nonetheless only 37 percent say they call the police and another 5 percent will call them if they cannot make the offender pay for the goods. Half of them try to make the offender pay for the goods.[59] There is, of course, greater reliance on law enforcement agencies than is apparent in these figures on nonre-

porting. Some businessmen suggested that they could threaten to call the police if the offender did not make restitution; in other instances the threat would be implicit.

## CONCLUSION

Analysis of the findings of public opinion polls and surveys of the measures citizens take to cope with the threat of crime shows an increased concern about the crime problem and greatly aroused fears of being victimized, especially from the violent acts of strangers. This fear leads many people to give up activities they would normally undertake particularly when it may involve going out on the streets or into parks and other public places at night. The costs of this fear are not only economic, though a burdensome price may be paid by many poor people in high crime rate areas who feel compelled to purchase protective locks, bars, and alarms, who reject an attractive night job because of fear of traversing the streets or who pay the expense of taxi transportation under the same circumstances. In the long run more damaging than costs are the loss of opportunities for pleasure and cultural enrichment, the reduction of the level of sociability and mutual trust, and perhaps even more important, the possibility that people will come to lose faith in the trustworthiness and stability of the social and moral order of the society.

At the same time most people seem to feel that the effort to reduce crime is a responsibility of the police, the courts, and other public or private agencies engaged in the tasks of crime prevention and control. Though the people generally see little they can do as individuals, they are prepared to endorse a variety of programs to remedy the situation. These range all the way from stricter policies of law enforcement to expensive crime prevention and treatment programs for offenders. Public attitudes about various programs or policies reflect both a desire for a better system of protection against crime and an interest in protecting individual rights and freedom. For this reason the pattern of public attitudes is complex and varies considerably from one issue to another. Thus, a majority of citizens believe the police should have more power to question people; but a somewhat greater majority favor the Supreme Court ruling regarding access to legal counsel as a precondition to police questioning following arrest. A majority feel that courts are too lenient in sentencing criminals, and yet they overwhelmingly prefer rehabilitative rather than punitive goals in corrections, and in the case of a young first offender the largest number would give him another chance.

Much more should be known about these public attitudes, how they vary from issue to issue, and how they differ for various social, economic, ethnic, and other groupings of the population. Nevertheless, it seems reasonable to conclude that there is substantial public support for a vigorous program of law enforcement, for more intensive use of rehabilitative treatment methods, and for broad programs of social, educational, and economic reforms that will help prevent youth from becoming enmeshed in delinquent and criminal careers.

## REFERENCES AND NOTES

1   Lincoln Steffens, *The Autobiography of Lincoln Steffens*, New York: Harcourt, Brace & Globe, 1931, pp. 285–291.

2   E.g., Daniel Bell, "The Myth of Crime Waves," in *The End of Ideology*, 2d ed., New York: Collier Books, 1962, pp. 151–174.

3   Yale Kamisar, "When the Cops Were Not 'Handcuffed,'" *New York Times Magazine*, Nov. 7, 1965.

4   Surveys by George Gallup, director, American Institute of Public Opinion, Princeton, N.J., will be referred to as Gallup polls. Those by Louis Harris, public opinion analyst, will be cited as Harris surveys.

5   Philip H. Ennis, *Criminal Victimization in the United States: A Report of a National Survey*, Field Survey II, President's Commission on Law Enforcement and Administration of Justice, Washington, D.C.: U.S. Government Printing Office, 1967. Hereinafter referred to as the NORC study.

6   Albert D. Biderman, Louise A. Johnson, Jennie McIntyre, and Adrianne W. Weir, *Report on a Pilot Study in the District of Columbia on Victimization and Attitudes toward Law Enforcement*, Field Survey I, President's Commission on Law Enforcement and Administration of Justice, Washington, D.C.:

U.S. Government Printing Office, 1967. Hereinafter referred to as the BSSR study.

7   *Ibid.*, p. 40.

8   *Ibid.*, p. 33.

9   Philip H. Ennis, "Attitudes toward Crime," Interim Report to the President's Commission on Law Enforcement and Administration of Justice, 1966 (mimeographed).

10  BSSR study, *op. cit.*, p. 127.

11  *Ibid.*, p. 125.

12  NORC study, *op. cit.*, table 47, p. 76.

13  BSSR study, *op. cit.*, p. 121.

14  Albert J. Reiss, Jr., *Studies in Crime and Law Enforcement in Major Metropolitan Areas*, Field Survey III, President's Commission on Law Enforcement and Administration of Justice, Washington, D.C.: U.S. Government Printing Office, 1967, vol. 1, sec. 2, p. 30. Hereinafter referred to as the Reiss studies.

15  Thorsten Sellin and Marvin E. Wolfgang, *The Measurement of Delinquency*, New York: John Wiley & Sons, Inc., 1964, table 69, p. 289.

16  Reiss studies, *op. cit.*, p. 31.

17  BSSR study, *op. cit.*, p. 124.

18  NORC study, *op. cit.*, table 44, p. 74.

19  Ennis, *op. cit.*

20  Reiss studies, *op. cit.*, pp. 103–106.

21  NORC study, *op. cit.*, table 48, p. 77.

22  Reiss studies, *op. cit.*, p. 103.

23  Donald J. Black and Albert J. Reiss, Jr., "Problems and Practices for Protection Against Crime Among Businesses and Organizations," report to the President's Commission on Law Enforcement and Administration of Justice, Ann Arbor, Mich.: University of Michigan Department of Sociology, 1966 (mimeographed).

24  "UCR, 1965," p. 3.

25  Accident Facts, Chicago: National Safety Council, 1966, p. 2.

26  Data obtained by interview from American College of Surgeons, Washington, D.C., 1966.

27  Stephen Cutler and Albert J. Reiss, Jr., "Crimes Against Public and Quasi-public Organizations in Boston, Chicago and Washington, D.C.," report to the President's Commission on Law Enforcement and Administration of Justice, Ann Arbor, Mich.: University of Michigan Department of Sociology, 1966 (mimeographed).

28  It is also possible at the same time that overexposure of the public to accounts of violent crime creates a dullness and indifference to the crime problem that only news of the most violent crimes can penetrate. For a discussion of this possible effect and a review of studies of crime and the mass media see Edwin H. Sutherland and Donald R. Cressey, *Principles of Criminology*, 7th ed., New York: J. P. Lippincott Company, 1966, pp. 257–265.

29  BSSR study, *op. cit.*, p. 134.
30  *Ibid.*, p. 135.
31  NORC study, *op. cit.*, p. 59.
32  BSSR study, *op. cit.*, unpublished supplement.
33  Cutler and Reiss, *op. cit.*
34  BSSR study, *op. cit.*, p. 146.
35  NORC study, *op. cit.*, pp. 64–72.
36  BSSR study, *op. cit.*, p. 144.
37  Reiss studies, *op. cit.*, p. 42.
38  *Ibid.*, pp. 43–47.
39  *Ibid.*, pp. 42–47.
40  BSSR study, *op. cit.*, p. 137.
41  BSSR study, *op. cit.*, p. 149; and Reiss studies, *op. cit.*, p. 82.
42  For a description of the police policy index see NORC study, *op. cit.*, pp. 64–65.
43  NORC study, *op. cit.*, p. 64.

44  BSSR study, *op. cit.*, p. 150.
45  *Ibid.*, p. 149.
46  Reiss studies, *op. cit.*, p. 82.
47  NORC study, *op. cit.*, p. 68.
48  *Ibid.*, table 36, p. 63.
49  *Ibid.*, table 40, p. 70.
50  NORC study, *op. cit.*, p. 42, and BSSR study, *op. cit.*, p. 40.
51  See table 5 in chap. 2.
52  NORC study, *op. cit.*, table 27, p. 46.
53  *Ibid.*, table 24, p. 44.
54  *Ibid.*, table 26, p. 46.
55  Black and Reiss, *op. cit.*
56  *Ibid.*
57  *Ibid.*
58  *Ibid.*
59  *Ibid.*

## 39   PERCEIVED OPPORTUNITIES AND DELINQUENCY

### JAMES F. SHORT, JR.    RAMON RIVERA    RAY A. TENNYSON

Not since the advent of psychoanalysis has a theory had such impact on institutionalized delinquency control as the theory, explicit or implied, in *Delinquency and Opportunity*.[1] Given the impetus of major foundation and federal support, the theory has been extensively adopted as a rationale

Reprinted with the permission of the American Sociological Association and the publisher from *American Sociological Review*, vol. 30 (February 1965), pp. 56–67.

This research is supported by grants from the Behavior Science Study Section of the National Institute of Mental Health (M-3301 and MH-07158); the Office of Juvenile Delinquency and Youth Development, Welfare Administration, U.S. Department of Health, Education, and Welfare in cooperation with the President's Committee on Juvenile Delinquency and Youth Crime (#62220); the Ford Foundation; and the Research Committee of Washington State University. We are grateful for this support and for the support and encouragement of staff members at the University of Chicago, Washington State University, and the Program for Detached Workers of the YMCA of Metropolitan Chicago, whose wholehearted cooperation makes the entire enterprise such an exciting "opportunity." An earlier version of this paper was read at the annual meetings of the Pacific Sociological Association, 1963.

for action programs in many areas of the country. There is some danger that, like psychoanalysis, "opportunity structure theory" may be rationalized and elaborated so rapidly and extensively as to discourage, if not render impossible, empirical testing, pragmatic validation, or demonstration of worth by any other criterion of "good theory." *Delinquency and Opportunity* has been widely praised for its theoretical integration, e.g., as "a logically sound deductive system that is rich in its implications for delinquency causation and control," but the same critic also notes that "examined in terms of its logical, operational, and empirical adequacy, the theory poses a number of questions concerning the accuracy of some of its postulates and theorems."[2] Our paper will bring data to bear on certain aspects of the opportunity structure paradigm as we operationalized it in a study of delinquent gangs in Chicago.

Table 1 reproduces in paradigm form the principal elements of "opportunity structure theory" concerning *criminal* and *conflict* subcultures. It subdivides the "Innovation" category of Merton's deviance paradigm, referring to acceptance (internalization) of culturally prescribed success goals and rejection (incomplete internalization) of institutional norms or culturally prescribed means, by those for whom legitimate means to success goals are restricted.[3] To this the paradigm adds Cloward's four sets of defining conditions for the relative availability of illegitimate means to success goals,[4] and the two hypothesized types of "collective response among delinquents" produced by the preceding conditions.[5]

In our research in Chicago we have attempted to measure variables specified in this paradigm and to investigate their interrelations. For this purpose we have studied lower-class "delinquent gangs" involved in a "detached worker" program of the YMCA of Metropolitan Chicago, control groups of lower-class nongang boys from the same neighborhoods as the gang boys, and middle-class nongang boys.[6] Elements of the paradigm were operationalized in terms of the *perceptions* reported by the boys studied.[7] In this paper we direct attention to

**TABLE 1**  *Social context and modes of delinquent behavior: a paradigm*

| *Structural Features* | *Type of subculture* | |
|---|---|---|
| | Criminal (integrated areas) | Conflict (unintegrated areas) |
| **I Independent variable** | | |
| A. Culturally prescribed success goals | Internalized | Internalized |
| B. Availability of legitimate means to success goals | Limited; hence intense pressures toward deviant behavior | Limited; hence intense pressures toward deviant behavior |
| **II Intervening variables** | | |
| A. Institutional norms | Incomplete internalization | Incomplete internalization |
| B. Availability of illegal means to success goals | Available | Unavailable |
| 1. Relations between adult carriers of conventional and criminal values | Accommodative; each participates in value system of other | Conflicted; neither group well organized; value systems implicit, and opposed to one another |
| 2. Criminal learning structure | Available; offenders at different age levels integrated | Unavailable; attenuated relations between offenders at different age levels |
| 3. Criminal opportunity structure | Stable sets of criminal roles graded for different ages and levels of competence; continuous income; protection from detection and prosecution | Unarticulated opportunity structure; individual rather than organized crime; sporadic income; little protection from detection and prosecution |
| 4. Social control | Strong controls originate in *both* legitimate and illegal structures | Diminished social control; "weak" relations between adults and adolescents |
| **III Dependent variable** | | |
| A. Expected type of collective response among delinquents | Pressures toward deviance originate in limited accessibility to success goals by legitimate means, but are ameliorated by opportunities for access by illegal means. Hence, delinquent behavior is rational, disciplined, and crime-oriented | Pressures toward deviance originate in blocked opportunity by *any* institutionalized system of means. Hence, delinquent behavior displays expressive conflict patterns |

perceptions of legitimate and illegitimate opportunities by Negro and white lower-class gang and nongang boys and middle-class boys of both races, and to the relations among these perceptions. Detailed discussion of the relation of perceived opportunities and patterns of behavior derived from self-reports and, for gang boys only, from detached-worker ratings, is deferred for later presentation.[8]

Data reported elsewhere establish different levels of aspiration among the boys studied, but they show that regardless of race, class, or gang membership, mean levels of both occupational and educational aspirations considerably exceed fathers' achieved levels of occupation and education.[9] In this sense the independent variable—internalization of culturally prescribed success goals—may be said to have a positive value among all the boys studied. For the first intervening variable in the paradigm, however—internalization of institutional norms—our gang members are less positive than the other boys studied. With "values" data from semantic differential scales, we established the fact that all groups assign equally high value and degree of legitimacy to such "middle-class" images as "Someone who works for good grades at school" and "Someone who likes to read good books" —again indicating that certain values are common to all groups—but gang boys of both races hold more positive attitudes toward *deviant* images than do the other boys.[10] These deviant images represented hypothesized "delinquent subcultures;" e.g., conflict ("Someone who is a good fighter with a tough reputation"), criminal ("Someone who knows where to sell what he steals" and "Someone who has good connections to avoid trouble with the law"), and retreatist ("Someone who makes easy money by pimping and other illegal hustles" and "Someone who gets his kicks by using drugs"). Middle-class boys generally attribute to these deviant images a lower value and less legitimacy, as we expected.

This article is concerned with other elements in the paradigm, based on data from one part of an extensive interview schedule administered by specially trained interviewers to more than 500 boys in the six categories (race by class status and gang membership) under study. Respondents were instructed to indicate whether each of a series of statements was true of the "area where your group hangs out." In this way we hoped to measure perceptions of relatively specific legitimate and illegal opportunities. Perceptions of legitimate means to success goals, for example, were sampled by a series of statements concerning the *educational* and *occupational* orientations, abilities, and prospects for "guys in our area." We hoped by the impersonal referent to avoid the personalized ambitions and expectations which were the subject of inquiry in another part of the interview and thus to obtain measures referring to the boys' perceptions of general opportunities for legitimate and illegal achievement in their respective areas.

Aspects of the availability of illegal means to success goals to which attention was directed concerned the relative integration of the carriers of criminal and noncriminal values (in terms of the respectability of persons making money illegally and the orientation of local police toward law violation); adult "connections" and opportunities for learning and abetting criminal activities; the availability of criminal role models; and the probability of successful criminal enterprise in the area. Finally, because Cloward and Ohlin stress the importance of these matters for social control, perceptions of appropriate adult role models and their interest and sincerity concerning the problems of adolescents were also covered. The list of statements is in Table 2, together with the percentage of boys in each group answering "true."[11]

In most cases responses to the statements concerning open legitimate opportunities and adult helpfulness form a gradient: gang boys are least likely to answer "true," followed by nongang and then by middle-class boys of each race. For negatively stated legitimate opportunity questions, and for the two negative adult power ("clout") statements, this gradient is reversed.[12] White gang boys generally are more sanguine than Negro gang boys about occupational opportunities and adult "clout," while Negroes tend to be slightly more

**TABLE 2** *Percentage of boys answering "true" to opportunity structure questions, by race, class, and gang status*

| Interviewer: "Once again I want you to think about the area where your group hangs out. I'm going to read a few statements to you, and all you have to do is say 'true' or 'false' after each statement. If you think the statement is true about the area, say 'true'; if you don't think it's true, say 'false.'" | Negro | | | White | | |
|---|---|---|---|---|---|---|
| | Lower class gang N = 206 | Lower class nongang N = 89 | Middle class N = 26 | Lower class gang N = 90 | Lower class nongang N = 79 | Middle class N = 53 |
| **Legitimate educational opportunities** | | | | | | |
| 1 In our area it's hard for a young guy to stay in school. (−)* | 48.5 | 28.1 | 7.7 | 52.2 | 21.5 | 0.0 |
| 2 Most kids in our area like school. (+) | 43.2 | 49.4 | 80.8 | 32.2 | 60.8 | 94.3 |
| 3 Most of the guys in our area will graduate from high school. (+) | 30.6 | 44.9 | 96.2 | 32.2 | 65.8 | 100.0 |
| 4 In our area, there are a lot of guys who want to go to college. (+) | 37.4 | 47.2 | 84.6 | 16.7 | 44.3 | 98.1 |
| 5 College is too expensive for most of the guys in the area. (−) | 75.7 | 76.4 | 53.8 | 80.0 | 65.8 | 7.5 |
| 6 As far as grades are concerned, most of the guys in our area could get through college without too much trouble. (+) | 46.6 | 43.8 | 50.0 | 43.3 | 40.5 | 73.6 |
| **Legitimate occupational opportunities** | | | | | | |
| 7 It's hard for a young guy in our area to get a good paying honest job. (−) | 77.2 | 62.9 | 46.2 | 56.7 | 31.6 | 9.4 |
| 8 Most of the guys in the area will probably get good paying honest jobs when they grow up. (+) | 51.9 | 59.6 | 61.5 | 65.6 | 79.7 | 92.5 |
| 9 For guys in this area honest jobs don't pay very well. (−) | 56.3 | 47.2 | 26.9 | 40.0 | 22.8 | 3.8 |
| 10 Guys in this area have to have connections to get good paying jobs. (−) | 53.9 | 51.7 | 30.8 | 56.7 | 44.3 | 22.6 |
| 11 In this area it's hard to make much money without doing something illegal. (−) | 54.9 | 38.2 | 23.1 | 37.8 | 13.9 | 0.0 |
| **Integration of the carriers of criminal and non-criminal values** | | | | | | |
| 12 Some of the most respectable people in our area make their money illegally. (+) | 44.2 | 19.1 | 15.4 | 24.4 | 10.1 | 3.8 |
| 13 The police in this area get paid off for letting things happen that are against the law. (+) | 51.5 | 37.1 | 30.8 | 42.2 | 36.7 | 20.8 |
| **Criminal learning structures** | | | | | | |
| 14 There are connections in this area for a guy who wants to make good money illegally. (+) | 57.8 | 49.4 | 38.5 | 47.8 | 35.4 | 5.7 |

*Signs in parentheses indicate the "valence" of a "true" answer relative to the opportunity structure area indicated.

TABLE 2   *Continued*

| Interviewer: "Once again I want you to think about the area where your group hangs out. I'm going to read a few statements to you, and all you have to do is say 'true' or 'false' after each statement. If you think the statement is true about the area, say 'true'; if you don't think it's true, say 'false.'" | Negro | | | White | | |
|---|---|---|---|---|---|---|
| | Lower class gang N = 206 | Lower class nongang N = 89 | Middle class N = 26 | Lower class gang N = 90 | Lower class nongang N = 79 | Middle class N = 53 |
| 15 Young guys can learn a lot about crime from older people in the area. (+) | 75.2 | 66.3 | 34.6 | 52.2 | 35.4 | 11.3 |
| 16 There are adults in this area who help young guys make money illegally. (+) | 59.2 | 49.4 | 30.8 | 42.2 | 26.6 | 15.1 |
| Visibility of criminal careers | | | | | | |
| 17 In this area there are some people who make their living by doing things that are against the law. (+) | 83.0 | 73.0 | 69.2 | 70.0 | 60.8 | 30.2 |
| 18 Some of the young guys in our area will be making a living someday by doing things that are against the law. (+) | 83.0 | 79.8 | 73.1 | 75.6 | 59.5 | 39.6 |
| Elite ciminal opportunities | | | | | | |
| 17 A lot of these guys who make money illegally do not operate alone. They have to answer to people above them who are calling the shots. (−) | 62.6 | 62.9 | 65.4 | 45.6 | 40.5 | 18.9 |
| 18 A lot of these guys won't be operating alone either. They'll have to answer to people above them who'll be calling the shots. (−) | 70.4 | 70.8 | 65.4 | 62.2 | 53.2 | 30.2 |
| 19 A guy from this area has a chance of really making it big in the rackets. (+) | 45.1 | 30.3 | 34.6 | 35.6 | 24.1 | 3.8 |
| 20 None of the people who make big money in the rackets live in this area. (−) | 54.4 | 66.3 | 38.5 | 56.7 | 75.9 | 60.4 |
| Adult "clout" | | | | | | |
| 21 Not many really successful people live in this area. (−) | 63.6 | 59.6 | 19.2 | 42.2 | 26.6 | 0.0 |
| 22 Adults in this area haven't much clout (pull). (−) | 55.3 | 42.7 | 23.1 | 48.9 | 48.1 | 13.2 |
| Adult helpfulness | | | | | | |
| 23 There are adults in this area who help young guys get jobs. (+) | 82.5 | 93.3 | 92.3 | 78.9 | 89.9 | 94.3 |
| 24 Adults in the area do a lot to help young guys keep out of trouble. (−) | 67.0 | 91.0 | 61.5 | 50.0 | 73.4 | 88.7 |

optimistic concerning education and adult helpfulness. For all these areas, white middle-class boys
have the most *open* view of "opportunities."

Conversely, gang boys are more likely to perceive illegitimate opportunities as open than are
other boys, and these perceptions are held by
more Negro than white boys in each stratum. The
latter finding is somewhat surprising, in view of
the acknowledged white domination of organized
crime in Chicago. Informal observation suggests
that vice organized on a large scale does flourish in
Negro communities, and that "independent entrepreneurship" in such forms as small (and large)
policy wheels, marijuana peddling, street-walking
prostitutes, pool sharks, professional burglars and
robbers, and the like, is more common in lower-
class Negro than in lower-class white communities.[13] In any case, illegitimate opportunities appeared to be open to more Negro than white boys.

To reduce these data further, we assigned an
opportunity structure score to each item. Except
for items 17(A) and 18(A) answers were scored 2,
1, or 0, with 2 assigned to *open* opportunity perceptions, whether legitimate or illegitimate. Thus,
for questions in Table 2 followed by (−), a "true"
answer received a 0, "Don't know," a 1, and
"False," a 2. The reverse procedure was applied to
questions followed by (+).

Statements 17(A) and 18(A) are difficult to
score. At first we assumed that a positive response
to these questions indicated that illegitimate opportunities were perceived as closed. Boys were
asked these questions only if they had already responded positively to questions 17 and 18. Thus, a
"true" response to the statement that "A lot of
these guys who make money illegally do not operate alone. They have to answer to people above
them who are calling the shots," was taken to
mean that the "really big" hoodlums were not
available as role models; hence, to this extent illegitimate opportunities for "making it big" were
perceived as closed. On the other hand, a boy
might answer *"false"* to this statement on the
grounds that those who were making money illegally were involved in such petty pursuits as not to
warrant concern or control by the syndicate, or,

particularly in the case of middle-class white boys,
illegal pursuits might be in the nature of white-
collar crime and so not subject to syndicate control. In the latter case, a "false" answer still would
be consistent with an *open* perception of opportunity, while in the former it would not. Answers
to "elite criminal opportunities" questions are the
only exceptions to the observed gradient for perceptions of illegitimate opportunities, suggesting
that boys within each class of respondents may
have interpreted these questions less uniformly
than they did the others.

Before answers to these questions are dismissed
as invalid, however, they should be examined more
carefully. Note that responses to questions 17(A)
and 18(A) follow a pattern: more Negro than
white boys say that people in their areas who
make money illegally have to "answer to people
above them." Unfortunately the question did not
specify where these "higher ups" lived or whether
they were visible to the boys. We may infer, however, that a higher proportion of persons making
money illegitimately in the white areas were
among the "higher ups" in organized crime than
was the case in Negro neighborhoods.

The middle-class boys' answers to the entire set
of four "elite" questions are especially interesting.
Negro middle-class boys are far more likely to indicate that local area people have "a chance of really
making it big in the rackets" and far less likely to
say that locals do not "make big money in the
rackets." Drake and Cayton[14] and Frazier[15] have
described important criminal and otherwise
"shady" elements in the Negro middle class. Frazier, in particular, indicates that influential segments of the "black bourgeoisie" are "recruited
from the successful underworld Negroes, who have
gained their money from gambling, prostitution,
bootlegging, and the 'numbers.' "[16] Frazier attributes the flashy consumption patterns of the new
Negro middle class to the influence of these elements and contrasts this way of life with that of
the old upper and middle classes who "erected an
impenetrable barrier between themselves and Negroes who represented the 'sporting' and criminal
world."[17] The white middle-class boys, who were

chosen precisely because they were the "cream" of YMCA Hi-Y clubs, are very unlikely to be exposed to this sort of community influence. Such differences as these, if they are real, should find expression in other data from these subjects.[18]

These ambiguities in interpretation led us to score "elite" criminal opportunities in two ways—with and without questions 17(A) and 18(A). When they were included, we followed our original assumptions, adjusting the scoring so that if either question was not asked, implying closed opportunities, the boy was scored zero for the question; if the question was asked and a "true" answer recorded, a score of 1 was given; "undecided" was scored 2, and "false," 3.

Table 3 presents mean opportunity structure scores, by race, class, and gang status of respondents. The trends apparent in Table 1 appear here, also.

In addition, it is clear that for *legitimate* opportunities, gang-nongang and middle-class differences *within* racial categories are greater than the Negro-white differences for each of the three gang and class strata. For *illegitimate* opportunities, differences between races are greater than within-race differences.

### PERCEIVED OPPORTUNITIES AND AN OFFICIAL DELINQUENCY RATE

In Table 4, ranking on each of the summary opportunity scores is compared with the official delinquency rates of the six race-by-class-by-gang-status groups.[19] As far as the *ordering* of the six groups is concerned, perception of *legitimate* opportunities is more strongly associated with delinquency rates than is perception of illegitimate opportunities. This is consistent with the assumption

**TABLE 3**   *Mean opportunity structure scores, by race, class, and gang status*

| Aspect of opportunity structure* | Negro | | | White | | |
|---|---|---|---|---|---|---|
| | Lower class gang $N = 206$† | Lower class nongang $N = 89$ | Middle class $N = 26$ | Lower class gang $N = 89$ | Lower class nongang $N = 75$ | Middle class $N = 53$ |
| Legitimate educational (0–12) | 4.8 | 5.7 | 9.0 | 3.8 | 6.4 | 11.2 |
| Legitimate occupational (0–10) | 4.2 | 5.2 | 6.6 | 5.4 | 7.3 | 9.1 |
| Integration of carriers of criminal and noncriminal values (0–4) | 2.1 | 1.4 | 1.2 | 1.5 | 1.0 | 0.5 |
| Criminal learning structures (0–6) | 4.0 | 3.6 | 2.3 | 3.0 | 2.2 | 0.7 |
| Visibility of criminal careers (0–4) | 3.4 | 3.2 | 3.0 | 3.0 | 2.5 | 1.4 |
| Criminal opportunities (0–10) | 4.7 | 4.0 | 4.6 | 4.7 | 4.3 | 4.6 |
| Adult "*clout*" (0–4) | 1.5 | 1.9 | 3.0 | 2.0 | 2.4 | 3.7 |
| Adult helpfulness (0–4) | 3.0 | 3.7 | 3.2 | 2.6 | 3.2 | 3.7 |
| Criminal opportunities (0–4) | 1.8 | 1.2 | 1.8 | 1.5 | 1.0 | 0.9 |
| Summary scores | | | | | | |
| Legitimate educational and occupational opportunities (0–22) | 9.0 | 11.0 | 15.6 | 9.3 | 13.7 | 20.2 |
| Illegitimate opportunities (0–24) | 14.3 | 12.3 | 11.0 | 12.1 | 10.0 | 7.2 |
| Illegitimate opportunities less inclusive (0–18) | 11.4 | 9.5 | 8.2 | 9.0 | 6.7 | 3.5 |
| Adult power and helpfulness (0–8) | 4.5 | 5.6 | 6.2 | 4.7 | 5.6 | 7.4 |

*Figures in parentheses indicate the possible range for each score.
†*N*'s vary slightly for some scores, due to nonresponse. Scores are based in each case on the number of boys who actually gave meaningful responses.

**TABLE 4**    *Mean opportunity structure scores known to the police, by race, class, and gang status*\*

| Legitimate educational and occupational opportunities (0–22) | Perception of illegitimate opportunities (less inclusive) (0–18) | Perception of adult power and helpfulness (0–8) | Total opportunities score (–18–30)† | Mean number of offenses known to police, per boy |
|---|---|---|---|---|
| NG    9.0 | NG   11.4 | NG   4.5 | NG    2.1 | NG   3.14 |
| WG    9.3 | NLC   9.5 | WG   4.7 | WG    5.0 | WG   2.73 |
| NLC  11.0 | WG    9.0 | NLC  5.6 | NLC   7.1 | NLC  0.47 |
| WLC  13.7 | NMC   8.2 | WLC  5.6 | WLC  12.6 | WLC  0.31 |
| NMC  15.6 | WLC   6.7 | NMC  6.2 | NMC  13.6 | NMC  0.06 |
| WMC  20.2 | WMC   3.5 | WMC  7.4 | WMC  24.1 | WMC  0.02 |

\*NG stands for Negro gang members, NLC for Negro lower-class boys, and so on.

†Total opportunities score is designed to reflect both legitimate and illegitimate pressures toward delinquency. It is obtained by adding together legitimate educational and occupational opportunities and adult power and helpfulness scores, and from this sum subtracting illegitimate opportunity scores. Hence it should be negatively correlated with delinquency.

that perceived legitimate opportunities are independent variables, while perceived illegitimate opportunities intervene, after legitimate opportunities have been appraised and found wanting. Legitimate achievement tends to be the universal standard in our culture, highly valued even by very deviant individuals.[20] Note, however, that *within* racial categories, perception of illegitimate opportunities does order the groups according to official delinquency rates.

Official delinquency rates measure the hypothesized dependent variables only in a very gross sense. The gang-nongang distinction probably measures participation in delinquent subcultural activity, and adding the middle-class—lower-class division permits a test of the theory in terms somewhat broader than it was originally set forth. Here the theory holds up well: gang boys of both races perceive greater restrictions on legitimate opportunities than do nongang boys in the same neighborhoods or middle-class boys. Thus, the *negative* pressure toward deviance is greater for gang boys. Within each racial group, gang boys perceive better illegitimate opportunities; hence the greater "pull" toward deviance. While perceived adult power and

helpfulness, combined, rank the groups very much as do official delinquency rates, adult power alone turns out, as predicted, to be negatively related to delinquency, while helpfulness, which may be exercised by carriers of criminal as well as noncriminal values, is related inconsistently to delinquency among Negro boys.

Adult power and helpfulness are both hypothesized by Cloward and Ohlin to be negatively related to the emergence and maintenance of conflict subcultures. "The term that the bopper uses most frequently to characterize his relationships with adults is 'weak'. . . . He views himself as isolated and the adult world as indifferent. The commitments of adults are to their own interests and not to his. Their explanations of why he should behave differently are 'weak,' as are their efforts to help him."[21] This description holds up well with respect to "clout." Gang boys score lower than the others and Negro gang boys—by far our most conflict oriented[22]—score lowest of all. But helpfulness scores are comparatively high for all groups, and they are lowest for the less conflict-oriented white gang boys.[23]

Differences between nongang and gang boys on

both scores are sufficient to suggest that these factors are important in selection for gang membership, though their relation to a particular type of delinquent subculture—conflict—is inconsistent with the theory. The previously noted higher illegitimate opportunity scores registered by the Negro boys are also inconsistent, but the greater visibility and availability of petty criminal activities in lower-class Negro communities may account for this. Similarly, the comparatively low Negro middle-class scores on clout and helpfulness are consistent with Frazier's descriptions of the superficial show put on by Negro middle-class "society," which he regards as a somewhat futile attempt to compensate for status insecurities relative to whites.[24]

The hypothesis that perceived adult power is inversely related to gang conflict is essentially a social control argument. But helpfulness, when exercised by illegitimate adults, may be conducive to involvement in a criminal subculture. To investigate this possibility, we examined the relations *between* perceptions of various types of opportunities.

### THE RELATION BETWEEN LEGITIMATE AND ILLEGITIMATE OPPORTUNITIES

The product-moment correlations between opportunity scores, for all boys and for gang boys only, by race, are in Table 5. Legitimate opportunity scores tend to be positively correlated with one another, as are illegitimate opportunity scores, and between legitimate and illegitimate scores correlations are negative. There are exceptions to this general pattern, however; for example, perceptions of legitimate educational and occupational opportunities are significantly correlated for all groups except white gang boys. The low correlation in the latter group suggests that perceptions of legitimate educational and occupational opportunities often are not mutually reinforcing.

The relation between adult power and perceived illegitimate opportunities suggests greater "integration" of the carriers of criminal and conventional values in white neighborhoods: the correlations are low but *positive* among white boys, and *negative* among Negroes. For both races, adult helpfulness is negatively correlated with illegitimate opportunities.

Correlations between perceived illegitimate opportunities are higher for white boys, particularly those involving the criminal *elite* measures. Thus, while white boys perceive illegitimate opportunities as less available than do Negro boys, "integration" as we have operationalized it is actually more characteristic of white than Negro gang areas. Negro gang boys perceive illegitimate opportunities as relatively open, but they tend to perceive illegitimate adults as neither powerful nor helpful. White gang boys, however, tend to perceive illegitimate adults as powerful but not very helpful. A similar pattern occurs in data from another section of the interview, in which boys were asked to indicate four characteristics of several adult roles in their local areas. Among Negro gang boys, 38 per cent, compared with 53 per cent of white gang boys, felt that adults making money illegally have "a lot of clout," while only about one boy in five in both racial groups felt that such adults are "interested in the problem of teen-agers." Lower-class nongang boys consistently rated legitimate adult roles higher than gang boys did on scales reflecting their interest in and degree of contact with teen-agers, their "clout," and the extent to which they are considered "right guys."[25]

In the present analysis, the relations between various opportunity scores reveal no significant or consistent differences that explain behavioral differences between gang and nongang lower-class boys. The most striking differences are between middle-class Negro boys and all other groups in the correlation between adult helpfulness and perceived elite criminal opportunities. This correlation is positive for both elite scores (.34 for the more inclusive measure, .20 for the less inclusive measure) among Negro middle-class boys, but both correlations are negative in all other groups. Adult clout was also correlated positively with the two elite criminal opportunity scores among Negro middle-class boys (.22 and .30), and among white

**TABLE 5**  *Correlations among opportunity structure scores, by race**

| | Legitimate educational | | Legitimate occupational | | Adult "clout" | | Adult helpfulness | | Criminal, noncriminal integration | | Criminal learning opportunities | | Visibility of criminal careers | | Criminal opportunities, elite (less inclusive) | | Criminal opportunities, elite (inclusive) | |
|---|---|---|---|---|---|---|---|---|---|---|---|---|---|---|---|---|---|---|
| | W† | N** | W | N | W | N | W | N | W | N | W | N | W | N | W | N | W | N |
| Legitimate educational | 1.00 | | .48 | .38 | .45 | .34 | .35 | .27 | −.36 | −.17 | −.49 | −.22 | −.42 | −.23 | −.27 | −.13 | −.06 | −.03 |
| Legitimate occupational | .13 | .34 | 1.00 | | .42 | .35 | .28 | .28 | −.26 | −.32 | −.31 | −.37 | −.26 | −.30 | −.25 | −.23 | −.10 | −.08 |
| Adult "clout" | .10 | .22 | .28 | .37 | 1.00 | | .29 | .29 | −.14 | −.25 | −.13 | −.23 | −.19 | −.23 | .04 | −.01 | .10 | .05 |
| Adult helpfulness | .23 | .32 | .23 | .35 | .19 | .32 | 1.00 | | −.23 | −.26 | −.19 | −.15 | −.26 | −.14 | −.27 | −.21 | −.19 | −.13 |
| Criminal, noncriminal integration | −.26 | −.19 | −.18 | −.33 | .05 | −.23 | −.27 | −.29 | 1.00 | | .49 | .51 | .37 | .32 | .46 | .32 | .20 | .14 |
| Criminal learning opportunities | −.26 | −.20 | −.15 | −.31 | .16 | −.22 | −.20 | −.19 | .59 | .52 | 1.00 | | .54 | .43 | .52 | .27 | .19 | −.02 |
| Visibility of criminal careers | −.28 | −.27 | −.17 | −.39 | .10 | −.22 | −.34 | −.16 | .37 | .34 | .46 | .37 | 1.00 | | .38 | .21 | .00 | −.14 |
| Criminal opportunities, elite (less inclusive) | −.21 | −.18 | −.24 | −.25 | −.04 | .24 | −.32 | −.24 | .60 | .31 | .64 | .29 | .49 | .23 | 1.00 | | .73 | .70 |
| Criminal opportunities, elite (inclusive) | −.03 | −.05 | −.15 | −.07 | .01 | .19 | −.23 | −.15 | .32 | .08 | .41 | −.03 | .16 | −.10 | .74 | .66 | 1.00 | |

*Italicized coefficients below the diagonal represent gang boys only; coefficients above the diagonal represent all boys, including gang members.

†White: p <.05 = .13 (all boys) and .21 (gang boys); p <.01 = .18 (all boys) and .27 (gang boys).

**Negro: p <.05 = .11 (all boys) and .14 (gang boys); p <.01 = .14 (all boys) and .18 (gang boys).

gang members, but negatively in the other groups. Again, reference to Frazier's perceptive analysis is pertinent.[26]

## SUMMARY

Legitimate occupational opportunities are perceived as available less often by gang than by nongang boys, and most often by middle-class boys. White boys are more likely than Negro boys to perceive such opportunities as available, in each of the strata examined. With respect to legitimate educational opportunities, the same pattern occurs, except that the racial difference does not occur among gang boys. Race and class-by-gang-status gradients are both present concerning adult clout, but not perceived adult helpfulness, among lower-class boys. These data are consistent with the apparently greater *protest* orientation of white as compared with Negro gang boys.[27] Gradients within racial groups are consistent with inferences from the Cloward and Ohlin theory.

Differences in perceptions of illegitimate opportunities reverse most of those found for legitimate opportunities, as expected. These differences are inconsistent with the greater conflict orientation of Negro gang boys, but when adult clout is correlated with criminal opportunity scores, and other data are introduced, "integration" of criminal opportunities and between criminal and legitimate opportunities is greater for white than for Negro boys. Even for white gang boys, however, the negative correlations between adult helpfulness and criminal opportunity scores, and their small positive correlations with adult clout suggest a low degree of "integration" between the carriers of criminal and conventional values.[28]

The logic of the theory clearly presumes that perceptions of opportunities *precede* involvement in delinquency, while our data reflect perceptions "after the fact." We cannot fully resolve this problem. Evidence concerning the relation of *individual* gang boys' perceptions of opportunities to their behavior as individuals, is relevant, however, and its mention permits brief discussion of the somewhat different causal model that has emerged from
the larger study of which this paper is a partial report. Correlations between opportunity scores and theoretically relevant behavior scores for individual gang boys are low. For example, *conflict factor scores*, consisting of a combination of individual and gang fighting (with and without weapons), assault, and carrying concealed weapons, are not systematically related to perceptions of either legitimate or illegitimate opportunity scores. That is, boys with high scores do not have lower opportunity scores.[29] It seems unlikely, therefore, that data reported in this paper reflect the boys' efforts to rationalize delinquent behavior by "blaming" the lack of opportunity. Although this does not solve the problem of temporal order, it is presumptive evidence against an alternative interpretation based on the assumption of "after-the-fact" (of delinquency or gang membership) influences on perception.

Our argument is not that the latter are unimportant. Other data from our study suggest that social structure influences the development of ethnic, class, life-cycle, and perhaps "delinquent" subcultures with relatively distinctive content. Social structural theories are therefore appropriately applied to the social distribution of many phenomena—to delinquency "rates" rather than to individual episodes or degrees of involvement in delinquency. It is to the question of "rates" or the social distribution of delinquent subcultures, that the Cloward and Ohlin theory is addressed—appropriately. To account for selection into subcultures —into gang membership, for example—from the youngsters available, and for individual behavior within the context of a subculture, requires reference to "levels" of explanation other than social structure.[30] We have found it necessary to invoke personality level variables, as Inkeles suggested,[31] and *group process* considerations, to explain delinquent behavior *within* our gangs.[32] The give and take of interaction among gang boys, and between gang boys and others; a variety of role relations within the gang and status considerations related to these roles and to opportunities present in situations of the moment—these are prime determinants of what happens in the gang, of who becomes involved in what type of behavior, and with whom.[33] This *level* of explanation "washes out" variations in perceptions of opportunities related to social structure as a major determinant of individuals' behavior in the gang context.

## REFERENCES AND NOTES

1  Richard A. Cloward and Lloyd E. Ohlin, *Delinquency and Opportunity: A Theory of Delinquent Gangs*, New York: The Free Press of Glencoe, 1960.

2  Clarence Schrag, "Delinquency and Opportunity: Analysis of a Theory," *Sociology and Social Research*, vol. 46 (January 1962), pp. 167–175.

3  Robert K. Merton, *Social Theory and Social Structure*, New York: The Free Press of Glencoe, 1958, chap. 4.

4  Richard A. Cloward, "Illegitimate Means, Anomie, and Deviant Behavior," *American Sociological Review*, vol. 24 (April 1959), pp. 164–176.

5  Cloward and Ohlin use a different theoretical rationale to explain "retreatist" subcultures, but our data are not relevant specifically to this aspect of the theory. See Cloward and Ohlin, *op. cit.*, pp. 25–27, 178ff.

6  Selection and description of study populations and other characteristics of the research program are described in previous publications and in greatest detail in a forthcoming book. See, for example, James F. Short, Jr., Fred L. Strodtbeck, and Desmond Cartwright, "A Strategy for Utilizing Research Dilemmas: A Case from the Study of Parenthood in a Street Corner Gang," *Sociological Inquiry*, vol. 32 (spring 1962), pp. 185–202; James F. Short, Jr., "Street Corner Groups and Patterns of Delinquency: A Progress Report," *American Catholic Sociological Review*, vol. 24 (spring 1963), pp. 13–32; and James F. Short, Jr., and Fred L. Strodtbeck, *Group Process and Gang Delinquency*, Chicago: The University of Chicago Press, in press, especially chap. 1.

7  Cloward and Ohlin refer to "common perceptions" of opportunities, and Schrag explains that one of the basic postulates of the theory is that "perceived disadvantage, regardless of the accuracy of the perception, is for lower-class youth the functional equivalent of objectively verified disadvantage in that it has the same effect on overt behavior." (Schrag, *op cit.*, p. 168.) This is not to deny the importance of *objective* opportunities, legitimate and illegitimate. The former can be demonstrated to be greater for whites than Negroes, and for middle- than for lower-class persons. It is more difficult to demonstrate gang-nongang differences except in terms of the cumula-tive *effects*—school performance, relations with the police, etc.—which favor nongang boys. Differences in objective illegitimate opportunities are similarly difficult to demonstrate, though the illegal enterprises are more likely to be present in a lower-class than in a middle-class environment.

8  Behavior factors based on detached-worker ratings of gang boys are reported in James F. Short, Jr., Ray A. Tennyson, and Kenneth I. Howard, "Behavior Dimensions of Gang Delinquency," *American Sociological Review*, vol. 28 (June 1963), pp. 411–428. Self-reported behavior factors are presented in Short and Strodtbeck, *op. cit.*, chap. 7.

9  See James F. Short, Jr., "Gang Delinquency and Anomie," in Marshall B. Clinard (ed.), *Deviant Behavior and Anomie*, New York: The Free Press of Glencoe, 1964; see also Jonathan Freedman and Ramon Rivera, "Education, Social Class, and Patterns of Delinquency," paper read at the Annual Meeting of the American Sociological Association, 1962. Elliott's study of "200 delinquent and nondelinquent boys attending two adjoining high schools in a large West Coast city" supports these findings. See Delbert S. Elliott, "Delinquency and Perceived Opportunity," *Sociological Inquiry*, vol. 32 (spring 1962), pp. 216–227.

10  The data are reported in Robert A. Gordon, James F. Short, Jr., Desmond S. Cartwright, and Fred L. Strodtbeck, "Values and Gang Delinquency: A Study of Street Corner Groups," *American Journal of Sociology*, vol. 69 (September 1963), pp. 109–128.

11  In the interview schedule the statements were not labeled according to which "opportunity structures" were being studied, and they were arranged in different order.

12  Elliott, *op. cit.*, finds that deliquents consistently perceive lower opportunities for education and occupational "success" than do nondelinquents. For evidence of other gradients among boys in the present study, see Gordon *et. al.*, *op. cit.*, and Short and Strodtbeck, *op. cit.*

13  See Short and Strodtbeck, *op. cit.*, especially chap. 5, "Racial Differentials in Gang Behavior."

14  St. Clair Drake and Horace R. Cayton, *Black Metropolis: A Study of Negro Life in a Northern City*, New York: Harper and Row Publishers, 1962, vol. II.

15  E. Franklin Frazier, *Black Bourgeoisie*, New York: Collier Books, 1962.

16  *Ibid.*, p. 109.

17  *Ibid.*, pp. 109–110.

18  We were first alerted to differences between our Negro and white middle-class boys when they came to our offices for testing, and later by analysis of semantic differential data. See Gordon *et al.*, *op. cit.* It

should be emphasized that primary data for this paper represent perceptions rather than objective measures of opportunities or of the communities in which these boys live. Other investigators have emphasized the extent to which middle-class Negroes are like their white counterparts in terms of the character and stability of their institutions and their community leadership, and in interracial situations. Life styles, interaction patterns with whites, and leadership among middle-class Negroes vary greatly, however. See, for example, the discussion in Robin M. Williams, Jr., *et al., Strangers Next Door: Ethnic Relations in American Communities*, New York: Prentice-Hall Inc, 1964, especially chaps. 7–10; see also James Q. Wilson, *Negro Politics: The Search for Leadership*, New York: The Free Press of Glencoe, 1960.

19    These rates refer to the mean number of offenses known to the police, per boy, in each group. Data are based on John M. Wise, "A Comparison of Sources of Data as Indexes of Delinquent Behavior," M.A. thesis, University of Chicago, 1962.

20    See Gordon *et al., op. cit.*

21    Cloward and Ohlin, *op. cit.*, pp. 24–25.

22    For documentation, see Short, *et al., op. cit.*, and Short and Strodtbeck, *op. cit.*, especially chaps. 1, 5, and 9. It was in large part because they were involved in gang fighting that most of the Negro gangs received the attention of newspapers, police, and the Program for Detached Workers with which this research program was associated. Close observation of the gangs over periods ranging from several months to more than three years suggests that nearly all the Negro gangs had at one time been more involved in "conflict subcultures" than had any of the white gangs. Finally, detailed analysis of behavior ratings by detached workers indicates greater conflict involvement by Negro than white gangs.

23    These findings are consistent with boys' ratings of a series of adult roles in the same interview. See James F. Short, Jr., Ramon Rivera, and Harvey Marshall, "Adult-Adolescent Relations and Gang Delinquency: An Empirical Report," *Pacific Sociological Review*, fall, 1964.

24    Frazier, *op. cit.*

25    A more detailed report of these data is in Short *et al., op. cit.*

26    Frazier, *op. cit.*

27    See Short *et al., op. cit.*, and Short and Strodtbeck, *op. cit.*, chap. 5.

28    This, perhaps, explains why we had such difficulty locating criminal gangs. See Short and Strodtbeck, *op. cit.*, chaps. 1 and 9.

29    Derivation of the scores is detailed in Short *et al., op. cit.* Full presentation of the data concerning individual opportunity perception and behavior is beyond the scope of this paper.

30    See David Bordua's critique of social structural theories in this regard. David Bordua, "Delinquent Subcultures: Sociological Interpretations of Gang Delinquency," *Annals of the American Academy of Political and Social Science*, vol. 338 (November 1961); and David Bordua, "Sociological Theories and Their Implications for Juvenile Delinquency," Children's Bureau *Juvenile Delinquency: Facts and Facets 2*, Washington, D.C.: U.S. Government Printing Office, 1960. See also Short and Strodtbeck, *op. cit.*; and James F. Short, Jr., "Social Structure and Group Process in Explanations of Gang Delinquency," paper read at the Fifth Social Psychology Symposium, University of Oklahoma, 1964, to be published in the symposium volume.

31    Alex Inkeles, "Personality and Social Structure," in Robert K. Merton, Leonard Broom, and Leonard S. Cottrell, Jr., (eds.), *Sociology Today*, New York: Basic Books, 1959. From the present study, see Robert A. Gordon and James F. Short, Jr., "Social Level, Social Disability, and Gang Interaction," in Short and Strodtbeck, *op. cit.*

32    See, especially, Short, "Gang Delinquency and Anomie," *op. cit.*; Short and Strodtbeck, *op. cit.*; James F. Short, Jr., and Fred L. Strodtbeck, "The Response of Gang Leaders to Status Threats: An Observation on Group Process and Delinquent Behavior," *American Journal of Sociology*, vol. 68 (March 1963), pp. 571–579; James F. Short, Jr., and Fred L. Strodtbeck, "Why Gangs Fight," *Trans-Action*, vol. 1 (September-October 1964), pp. 25–29; and Fred L. Strodtbeck and James F. Short, Jr., "Aleatory Risks v. Short-run Hedonism in Explanation of Gang Action," *Social Problems*, fall 1964.

33    The point is made in more general theoretical terms in Albert K. Cohen, "The Sociology of the Deviant Act: Anomie Theory and Beyond," *American Sociological Review*, vol. 30 (February 1965).

## 40 SELF-CONCEPT AND DELINQUENCY

### WALTER C. RECKLESS     SIMON DINITZ

This paper presents a retrospective assessment of a pioneering line of research on the self-concept as an insulator against delinquency. The authors were in search of a clue—a possible self-factor—which might shed light on what it is that steers youths in high delinquency areas of a large city away from involvement in delinquency. Certainly, criminologists and sociologists are well aware of the simple fact that a large percentage of adolescents in high delinquency areas manage to keep out of official trouble with the law, walk around the street-corner gang and avoid its so-called "subculture", stay in school rather than drop out, identify with the norms and values of the dominant society, and turn their backs on the availability of illegitimate means to ends in their neighborhood environment. What, then, are the components which enable adolescents to develop and maintain non-delinquent patterns of conduct despite the adversities of family, class position, and neighborhood?

It was decided that the best subjects for an initial inquiry would be the sixth-grade boys in high delinquency areas. Attention was focused on white sixth-grade boys, so as not to complicate the research design with race and sex variables. One might well ask: why sixth-grade boys? The answer is that they are approximately 12 years of age and are at the threshold of adolescence as well as the threshold of officially complained-upon delinquency. Complaints on boys for delinquency begin to increase at this age and keep on increasing through the succeeding years of adolescence. In addition, it begins to be feasible to interview a child, at the age of 12, about himself and his world as he sees it. Attempts to obtain, by verbal interviews or pencil and paper inventories, subjective data from young children about themselves run into difficulty. This does not mean, however, that one cannot procure objective data from preadolescent children.

As a start, the authors in 1955 gained permission to ask sixth-grade teachers in predominantly white elementary schools in high delinquency areas of Columbus, Ohio—teachers who interact with their pupils the entire school day for an entire school year—to indicate from among the white boys in their classes those who would never get into trouble with the law. Despite the fact that most of the teachers were middle-class females, the authors maintain—and we think very rightly so—that they have a sense of the direction in which their pupils are going. Kvaraceus' work in developing a delinquency proneness measure certainly bears out our contention that teachers' behavior ratings, evaluations, or prognostications are quite accurate.

### A CLOSE LOOK AT SAMPLING AND PROCEDURE

Thirty sixth-grade teachers nominated 192 white boys in their classes who in their opinion would not experience police or juvenile court contact. The range was from 15 to 100 percent of the white boys in the 30 classes and the average per class was 6.4 boys.

The teachers at the time of making their nominations of the so-called "good boys" were asked to give their reasons for each nomination. They mentioned 1,033 reasons or 5.4 reasons per boy; 45 percent represented favorable personal characteristics, attitudes, and interests; 27 percent, one or more aspects of favorable home situations; 20 percent, participation in character-building

Reprinted with the permission of the authors and the publisher from *The Journal of Criminal Law, Criminology and Police Science*, vol. 58 (December 1967), pp. 515–523.

youth organizations, religious activities, conforming in-school behavior, after-school employment; 7 percent, negative evaluations such as being excessively timid, naive, or overprotected so as to preclude involvement in delinquent behavior.

Sixteen of the 192 "good boys", constituting 8.3 percent of the teachers' nominees, turned out to have had, after clearance was made, previous contact with the police or the juvenile court. In 13 of the 16 cases, one or more members of the family had also had contact with the courts. Members of 42 additional families also had court contact, although the boys were not involved.

The authors eliminated these 16 boys, who already had contact with the law, from their "good boy" sample. In addition, when interviewers tried to locate the remaining 176 boys (out of the original 192), they could not find 51 boys, probably due in small part to wrong address, but in most part to removal of the family from the community in the interim of the several months between the teachers' nominations and the field follow-up. The project was left with a sample of 125 (192 minus 16 minus 51).[2]

A schedule was developed to be administered on an individual basis to each of the 125 good boys in their own homes. Among other formal scales and inventories included in the schedule were 50 items which attempted to assess the boy's perception of himself in relation to his family, friends, school, and possible involvement with the law. We called these items self-concept items, because the responses represented the boy's perception of himself in reference to the significant others in his immediate world.

Two research interviewers contacted the mother at home and obtained permission to interview her and her son. The one interviewer administered the schedule to the boy in one room; the other interviewer administered a specially prepared schedule to the mother in another room simultaneously.

The following school year, namely 1956, the authors returned to the same 30 sixth-grade classrooms and asked the teachers, most of whom were the same ones they interviewed in 1955, to nominate the white boys in their rooms, who would, in their opinion, almost certainly experience police or juvenile-court contact in the future.

The teachers named 108 white boys, constituting about 25 percent of the eligible boys. Twenty-four of the 108 nominated "bad boys" (23 percent) had already had contact with the police and juvenile court (as against 8.3 percent of the "good boy" nominees). In view of a much shorter time span between teacher nomination and home interview, we only lost 7 boys in the "bad boy" sample, reducing it to 101 cases. The interview schedules for the boy and the mother were the same in the 1956 101-bad-boy sample as in the 125-good-boy sample of the previous year.

The scores on the two directionally-oriented scales of the California Psychological Inventory (*De* scale and *Re* scale), which were included in the schedule administered to each boy, were different in the expected directions: significantly more favorable for the good-boys than for the bad-boys or more unfavorable for the bad-boys than the good-boys. Because the *De* scale of the CPI (now called the Socialization scale, measuring directionality toward and away from delinquency) and the *Re* scale of the CPI (measuring directionality toward social responsibility) are standardized scales, with national and even some international norms, the authors felt that the convincingly and significantly more favorable showing of the good, and the more unfavorable showing of the bad-boy sample, tended to validate the teacher's nominations. Likewise, these scale scores provided corroboration for the more favorable answers on the self-concept items received from the good than from the bad boys. In addition to these associations, the answers of the mothers to questions about their sons, paralleling virtually all of the questions used in the self-concept inventory for the boys, also added an additional dimension of validation. Thus, the teachers, the mothers, the *De* and *Re* Scales, and the boys' responses to the self-concept questions were highly consistent.

## FOLLOW-UP FOUR YEARS LATER

Four years after initial contact (1959 for the good and 1960 for the bad boys), the authors set about determining how many of the boys were known to the juvenile court. Out of the total of 125 in the 1955 sample of good boys, they were able to locate and assess 103; out of the 101 in the 1956 sample of bad boys, 70. Incidentally, attrition was not related to scale scores or self-concept responses in either cohort. Those who remained in the community had scored neither better nor worse on the *De* and *Re* scales or on the self-concept responses than those who left.

Twenty-seven of the 70 bad boys (39 percent) had contact with the juvenile court for delinquency in the four year follow-up period—not including the court contacts in the instance of 24 out of the original 101 sample, prior to our study. Each of the twenty-seven out of the traceable 70 bad-boys averaged over 3 contacts with the juvenile court throughout the four-year period or from the time the boys were approximately 12 to the time they were 16 years of age.

In contrast, just four out of the 101 good boys who were followed had a one-time record in the juvenile court in the ensuing four-year period of follow-up—and only for very minor offenses. Ninety-nine of the 103 good boys were still in school, although half of them had passed legal age for drop-out. Of the 99 still in school, all but four impressed their teachers as unlikely to get into future difficulty. Their responses to the re-administered self-concept items were quite favorable, just as favorable as they were four years previously and the mothers' evaluations were just as favorable as four years earlier.

There was a remarkable four-year cohort stability on all of the directional indicators in both the good- and bad-boy samples: self concept projections, teachers' prognostications, mothers' evaluations, scores on the *De* and *Re* scales of the CPI.

Furthermore, the authors were able to compare the traceable 103 good, and the 70 bad-boys, on the Nye-Short self-reporting delinquency check list (using 7 of the original Nye-Short items) and they found that the latter scored more unfavorably than the former. (This self-reporting check list was not available to us in 1955 and 1956.) Hence, "professed" involvement corroborated reported involvement in delinquency as well as the direction of the self-concept responses, and the teachers' expectations.

At this point it is important to duplicate the theoretical underpinning of our quest to discover what insulates a boy in the high delinquency areas against involvement in delinquency.

In our quest to discover what insulates a boy against delinquency in a high delinquency area, we believe we have some tangible evidence that a good self concept, undoubtedly a product of favorable socialization, veers slum boys away from delinquency, while a poor self concept, a product of unfavorable socialization, gives the slum boy no resistance to deviancy, delinquent companions, or delinquent sub-culture. We feel that components of the self strength, such as a favorable concept of self, act as an inner buffer or inner containment against deviancy, distraction, lure, and pressures. Our operational assumptions are that a good self concept is indicative of a residual favorable socialization and a strong inner self, which in turn steers the person away from bad companions and street corner society, toward middle class values, and to awareness of possibility of upward movement in the opportunity structure. Conversely, the poor concept of self is indicative of a residual unfavorable socialization (by 12 years of age probably not the result of participation in delinquency subculture) and indicative of weak inner direction (self or ego), which in turn does not deflect the boy from bad companions and street corner society, does not enable him to embrace middle class values, and gives him an awareness of being cut off from upward movement in the legitimate opportunity system.

We feel that the selective operation of the self element is not specified in the response to the models of behavior presented to the person by his associates in differential association theory (Sutherland) and is even less specified in delinquency subculture theory (Cohen), as well as "opportunity structure" theory (Cloward and Ohlin).[3]

## CROSS-SECTIONAL STUDIES

In 1957, the authors administered 717 schedules to sixth-grade children in 24 classes in eleven elementary schools of Columbus, Ohio, chosen according to census tract indexes of socio-economic status as well as high and low delinquency. Eight of the schools (with 17 sixth-grade classes) served disadvantaged areas with high delinquency rates, while 3 served middle-class areas where delinquency rates were low. All the sixth-grade pupils present in class on the appointed day were administered a schedule. The schedule consisted of 46 items from the *De* scale, 38 items from the *Re* scale (both from the California Psychological Inventory which is a factor-analyzed version of the Minnesota Multiphasic Inventory), 56 self concept items, plus certain social background items. During the administration of the inventories, the sixth-grade room teacher was interviewed elsewhere by a research assistant. With her cumulative record cards before her, the teacher rated each child in her class as either headed for trouble with the law, not sure, or not headed for trouble with the law.

Since the schedule was administered in school, a standard introductory statement requesting cooperation and allaying fears was used. On the front page of the schedule the following statement appeared in bold type: *Remember this is not a test. We simply want to know how you feel about things. There are no right or wrong answers. The right answer for you is how you feel about things.* Dr. Dinitz read aloud each question, reminding the pupils of the response pattern: true or false; yes or no.

Dr. Ernest Donald analyzed 354 boys' schedules from among the total of 717. Because the teachers nominated too few girls as headed for trouble with the law to warrant comparison, the Donald analysis applied only to white and colored sixth-grade boys in both the high and low delinquency areas of Columbus, Ohio in 1957.[4] The various subgroups in the 1957 sample of 354

sixth-grade boys consisted of the subgroups shown in Table 1.

It was possible to relate the favorable and unfavorable responses on each of the 56 self-concept items with the dichotomous nominations of the sixth-grade teachers (headed for trouble with the law, including not sure, versus not headed for trouble with the law). Table 2 lists 16 of the 56 self-concept items, used in the 1957 schedule, which were found to be differentiated by teacher nomination at the .05 level of confidence and beyond (9 items at the .001; 3, at the .01; 1, at the .02; and 3, at the .05 level of confidence). Note that the items through number 39 were answered by yes or no; items 42 and 46 were answered by a response format of often, sometimes, never; item

**TABLE 1**    *The sample of sixth grade boys, by subgroups, Columbus, Ohio, 1957*

| Subgroup | Number |
|---|---|
| Teacher's nomination | |
|   Not headed for trouble (good) | 222 |
|   Headed for trouble* (bad) | 132 |
| Race | |
|   White | 234 |
|   Negro | 120 |
| Area | |
|   Low delinquency (good) | 125 |
|   High delinquency (bad) | 229 |
| Nomination by race | |
|   Good white | 155 |
|   Good Negro | 67 |
|   Bad white | 79 |
|   Bad Negro | 53 |
| Nomination by race by area | |
|   Good white (good) | 86 |
|   Good white (poor) | 69 |
|   Good Negro (poor) | 67 |
|   Bad white (good) | 39 |
|   Bad white (bad) | 40 |
|   Bad Negro (bad) | 53 |

*Including the teacher's evaluation of "not sure." The teacher rated each boy in terms of whether she thought he was headed for trouble with the law, not sure, or not headed for trouble with the law.

Source: Donald and Dinitz, "Self Concept and Delinquency Proneness" in Reckless and Newman (eds.), *Interdisciplinary Problems of Criminology: Papers of the American Society of Criminology*, 1965, p. 50.

50, as will be seen on inspection, was answered by checking one out of three possibilities.

When the favorable and unfavorable responses on these 16 self-concept items were related to high and low scores on the *De* scale of the California Psychological Inventory (which also measures direction toward or away from delinquency), all but one item (number 25) reached the minimum .05 level of statistical significance. Certainly, there is

**TABLE 2**    *Significant self-concept items according to teacher nomination, associated with high and low scores on the De scale of the California Psychological Inventory*

| Original schedule no. | Self-concept items |
|---|---|
| 1 | Will you probably be taken to juvenile court sometime? |
| 2 | Will you probably have to go to jail sometime? |
| 6 | If you found that a friend was leading you into trouble, would you continue to run around with him or her? |
| 11 | Do you plan to finish high school? |
| 12 | Do you think you'll stay out of trouble in the future? |
| 17 | Are grown-ups usually against you? |
| 21 | If you could get permission to work at 14 would you quit school? |
| 23 | Are you a big shot with your pals? |
| 24 | Do you think your teacher thinks you will ever get into trouble with the law? |
| 25 | Do you think your mother thinks you will ever get into trouble with the law? |
| 26 | Do you think if you were to get into trouble with the law, it would be bad for you in the future? |
| 27 | Have you ever been told that you were headed for trouble with the law? |
| 39 | Have most of your friends been in trouble with the law? |
| 42 | Do you confide in your father? |
| 46 | Do your parents punish you? |
| 50 | Do you think you are quiet _____ average _____ active _____. |

Source: Donald and Dinitz, "Self Concept and Delinquency Proneness," in Reckless and Newman (eds.), *Interdisciplinary Problems of Criminology: Papers of the American Society of Criminology*, 1965, p. 50.

corroboration here; teacher nomination, response to self-concept items, and scores on the *De* scale are going in the same direction.

Five of the 16 significant self-concept items according to teachers' nomination, as presented in Table 2, were discriminated by the race of the sixth-grade (1957) Columbus boys (items 2, 12, 23, 39, 52); seven, by high and low delinquency area (items 1, 2, 12, 25, 26, 27, and 39); 6, by I.Q. level, 94 and above, 93 and below (items 2, 17, 23, 27, 30, and 42); 1, by reading achievement (item 17); and 7 by arithmetic achievement (1, 2, 11, 12, 24, 26, and 29).

After having spotted the 16 significant self-concept items, it was possible to obtain a total self-concept score on the 16. High total scores were in the unfavorable (delinquency) direction. When the mean (total) scores on the 16 self-concept items were computed for various subgroups of the sixth-grade boy sample (1957), the difference in the means for white and colored boys was (*a*) slight (although significant statistically); (*b*) somewhat larger for boys by type of area (again statistically significant); (*c*) not significant for white boys in high and in low delinquency areas; (*d*) significant for white boys in good areas and colored boys in bad areas; and (*e*) not significant for white boys and Negro boys (both) in areas of high delinquency.

By way of comparison, the mean self-concept score for boys with high *De* scores and that for boys with low *De* scores differed most of all and at a significance level of .00001.[5] In commenting on these findings relative to self-concept scores by various subgroups of the sixth-grade Columbus boys, Donald had this to say:

One is almost ready to hazard the guess that race and type of neighborhood, whatever they may signify in the accumulated socialization of 12-year-old boys, are relatively unimportant in determining self concepts. On the other hand, a large mean score difference on the self-concept items is found when the sixth-grade boys are divided by favorable and unfavorable direction of socialization as measured by the scores on the *De* scale. Evidently the big thing which determines the boy's self-concept orientation is something other than race and neighborhood. Might we say that it is the quality of family interaction and impact, apart from class and race, plus the impact of other supplementary relationships found within the child's world?[6]

Further details on the entire 717 (1957) "big run," giving the mean scores for girls as well as boys on the *De* and *Re* scales, IQ, Reading Achievement, and Arithmetic Achievement, by sex, race, type of area, and teacher nomination were presented in a special article, published in 1958.[7] In addition, an analysis of 400 of the 717 (1957) sixth-grade children, girls as well as boys, all from high delinquency areas, was published in 1960.[8]

## SOUNDINGS IN BROOKLYN AND AKRON

Prior to Donald's 1963 item analysis of the authors' self-concept items, using 354 schedules of sixth-grade boys in the 1957 Columbus, Ohio sample, and establishing 16 discriminating items which could be summated into a total score, the authors received permission in 1959 to administer a schedule to 697 sixth-grade children in six elementary schools of Brooklyn, serving high, medium, and low delinquency areas. The object here was to determine whether the trends noted in Columbus applied to the more complex, heterogeneous, urban environment of New York.

The Brooklyn schedule consisted of 46 items of the *De* scale; 34 self-concept items, including 9 which deal with a general view that the child has of himself, 7 with his view of his home and parents, and 8 with his view of how his father deals with him (a sort of father rejection assessment), and 10 with his projection about getting into trouble with the law; and 7 items taken from the Nye-Short inventory of self-reported delinquency involvement. However, it was not possible to obtain the sixth-grade teachers' prognostications of delinquency vulnerability in the Brooklyn project.

The findings on the Brooklyn study were never published. It was expected, however, that the sixth-grade males would test more unfavorably than the sixth-grade females, Negro more than white, high-delinquency area more than low-delinquency area pupils, Puerto Rican sixth graders about the same as Negro sixth graders, on all or most of the measures in the schedule. The greatest over-all differences between the various subgroups among the 1959 Brooklyn sixth-grade pupils occurred in mean scores on the *De* scale, which measures direction toward and away from delinquency. The 10 self-concept items dealing with projected involvement with the law made less sharp distinctions than the *De* scale between the various subgroups, although practically all differences between the means scores were significant. The mean subgroup scores on the self-concept items which focused on the father's rejection of the child were not significant, while most of the mean scores on the child's view of his home and parents did not distinguish the various subgroups in Brooklyn. The mean scores on the Nye-Short self-reported involvement in delinquency, likewise, for the most part did not differentiate the various subgroups. The authors wished that they could have gone into Brooklyn with a self-concept scale based on the 16 discriminating items which Donald analyzed and with more sophisticated measures of self-reported involvement.

The authors received considerable encouragement from the results of a 1959 Akron, Ohio study made by Dr. Edwin L. Lively.[9] Lively administered the authors' Brooklyn schedule to 1171 pupils, boys and girls, in Akron: 192 in sixth-grade, 324 in seventh-grade, 325 in eight-grade, and 300 in ninth-grade rooms, divided among schools serving lower and middle class neighborhoods as well as high and low delinquency areas. It was possible in this study to tell whether the mean scores by various subgroups (sex, race, high-low delinquency area, and teacher prognostication) had stability with increasing age in adolescence (roughly 12 through 15).

The mean scores on the *De* scale (now called the Socialization scale) of the CPI, the 10 self-concept items projecting involvement with the law, and the 7 items dealing with the child's view of his home, were quite stable throughout the four age samples (sixth, seventh, eighth, and ninth graders). The scores on the 8 items dealing with the child's view of his relations with his father (mostly rejection items) were not stable for the subgroups of the four age levels. The mean scores on the 7 self-reported involvements in delinquency increased with age (which trend seems logical).

Very interesting, as far as directional corroboration is concerned, is the fact that scores on the five instruments analyzed in the Akron study (*De* scale—now called Socialization scale, home items, law involvement items, father rejection items and self-reported delinquency) intercorrelated very well indeed ranging from +.27 to +.65, and at about the same levels of intercorrelation for each age sample: sixth, seventh, eighth and ninth grade.[10] (One should remind himself that if the coefficients of correlation had been in the high seventies, eighties, or nineties, he should suspect that any two measures which highly correlated would be assessing the same component of self.) This directional corroboration plus the corroboration of stability with age gave re-assurance to the authors that a self factor seems to be involved in vulnerability toward or insulation against delinquency.

A disconcerting note, however, needs to be inserted at this point. The authors attempted to administer the Brooklyn schedule in representative sixth, seventh, eighth, and ninth grades of two large metropolitan school systems after the excellent results in Akron. But they were turned down in both instances, due to the political dynamite which could be caused by administering schedules to children. And just recently a new National Institute of Mental Health regulation requires that the principal investigators of research projects obtain parental permission before administering scales and inventories to school children.

## APPLICATION TO PREVENTION

In 1959, the authors were asked by the Columbus, Ohio school system, to attempt some practical application of their findings. A demonstration on a very limited scale was undertaken to determine the feasibility of presenting appropriate models of behavior to sixth-grade boys, selected by teachers as headed for trouble. (Parental permission was obtained and the program occupied the last school period plus a half hour over school-closing time each day.) The main thrust of this demonstration was directed toward helping the vulnerable sixth-grade boy internalize effective models of behavior, thus building-up or strengthening his self concept. The worker in charge of the model-building sessions was also trained to be a most significant other (adult) in the lives of the participants.

Three years of such limited demonstration projects led to the formulation of a large demonstration-research project, supported by grants from the National Institute of Mental Health, to discover whether appropriate presentation of realistic models of behavior in the classroom could "beef up" a vulnerable boy's self. The design followed the theory and procedures of our original work on the self concept as the insulating agent against trends toward delinquency.

The authors selected eight junior high schools of the inner city of Columbus, Ohio, which served disadvantaged and high delinquency neighborhoods. These 8 junior high schools were fed pupils by 44 elementary schools. In May of 1963, the authors, after having received the go-ahead signal from the granting agency, asked the sixth-grade teachers of the 44 elementary schools to nominate the boys in their classes who, in their opinion were likely to get into trouble with the law and likely to drop out of school as well as the boys who were likely not to get into trouble with the law and likely to stay in school. In each school, the principal reviewed and confirmed the sixth-grade teacher's rating.

The over-all average was about 75 percent good; 25 percent bad boys. The following September when the boys reached the eight junior high schools, the nominated vulnerable ("bad") boys were randomly divided into two groups: an experimental, and a control group. The project also called for a continuing follow-up of a sample of 15 percent of the so-called "good" boys.

Preliminary data on the validity of these teacher-nominations of their students as vulnerable, doubtfully vulnerable or not vulnerable to later involvement with the law have been obtained. These data tend to support the contention that teacher-nominations are reasonably valid indicators of case outcomes of the 176 boys nominated as "good" (not vulnerable) in May, 1963; 154 or 87.5% had no contact with the police as of August, 1966. Of the unsure nominees, 69.4% avoided police contact in the comparable 3-year period, while just 53.7% of the nominated "bad" (vulnerable) boys were free of contact in the same three and one-fourth year time period.

The Columbus junior high schools at the time of the intervention demonstration operated "self contained classes," which ran for three consecutive school periods (of forty minutes each) with the same teacher. In these self-contained classes, world geography, Ohio history, and English were taught in mixed groups, boys as well as girls. The project called for placing the experimental group (randomly split half of the vulnerable boys) into an all-boy self-contained class of approximately 25 boys. It called also for retaining the other half of the vulnerable boys as well as the nonvulnerable boys in the regular mixed self-contained classes.

Permission was obtained from parents to gather the experimental group into a special all-boy section. When the boys and parents asked why, our reply was that Mr. Jones, the teacher, wanted Joe in his class and wanted an all-boy section.

Four male seventh-grade project teachers were selected by the authors (the principal investigators). They were specially trained to present "model" materials, as a youth development supplement to the regular diet of world geography, Ohio history, and English. They were trained also to play the role of the most significant adult in the lives of these boys in the experimental classes. They were involved in a summer tooling-up program, met with the project's research director each day after school, and with the project's consulting child psychiatrist each Saturday morning as a group.

Each of the four project teachers had two experimental self-contained classes: one in the morning at one junior high school and one in the after-noon at another junior high school. Thus, there was one experimental all-boy self-contained class in each of the 8 junior high schools serving children from disadvantaged, high-delinquency areas. The four project teachers worked with the research director in developing appropriate "lesson plans" to get on target of presenting models of behavior in an effective way. In addition, the project teachers, as a result of their Saturday morning discussions with the project's consulting psychiatrist, developed a class-room climate or atmosphere conducive to internalization of the regular class fare and the project's supplementation. The experimental group was found, on an average, to be reading at the fourth-grade level. Consequently, the project used seventh-grade materials written at a fourth-grade comprehension level and it availed itself of various reading-therapy procedures.

The youth-development supplementation (presentation of models of behavior) was fed into the experimental all-boy classes at the same time, in all eight groups—feeding in the same lesson plans— such as finding out something about the man on your city block who has the reputation of being the best worker so as to put on the board (on such and such day). During the first year of operation (1963–1964), the project teachers worked valiantly to develop lesson plans which had possibility of model takeover. These plans were standardized and used in the same way, to supplement the regular school fare, in two successive years, namely 1964–1965 and 1965–1966. During the last two years of the project, it was possible for the project teachers to use their after-school over-time for making home visits.

The demonstration-research design consisted of an experimental group and two control groups, in three cohorts, 1963–1964, 1964–1965, and 1965–1966. Standard information was accumulated on each boy. Certain inventories were administered to the three groups in September and again in May of each year, at the close of the school year. Available school information on reading and arithmetic achievement, absences, conduct, school performance, is being collected for the file. Yearly clearance (every year until 1970) of all three subgroups (the experimental group and the two control groups) is made through school records and through the files of the juvenile bureau of the police department in the summer of each follow-up year, to record truancy, non-attendance, and complaints for delinquency. Each yearly cohort will have four yearly clearances and by the time of the fourth clearance each boy will have passed his sixteenth birthday and will have had the legal opportunity to quit school and go to work.

Is the youth development supplement, in terms of presentation of appropriate models of behavior, strong enough preventive medicine? Does it reach the adolescent boy and presumably his self? Will the teacher-nominated vulnerable boys, who received Dr. Reckless and Dinitz's vitamins do better over a four-year period than their untreated firstcousins (also vulnerable boys) and even the teacher-nominated "good boys"? This is the question. The authors will have some answers in the fall of 1970.

## CONCLUSION

It is no longer sufficient for sociologists who study criminal and delinquent behavior to call attention to the possible impact of disorganized and disadvantaged neighborhoods, family tensions and insufficiencies, bad companions and street-corner gangs, and the availability of illegitimate means to ends. Who responds to carriers of patterns of delinquency and crime? Who resists and goes the other way? We live in a society of alternates, where the self has more and more opportunities for acceptance or rejection of available confrontations. Consequently, sociologists as criminologists must join the search for the self-factors which determine direction of behavior or choice among alternates and in this endeavor they must work with their colleagues in psychology and psychiatry in an effort to discover what self factors actually determine the direction of behavior and how they can be controlled.

The proposal herein has been to explore the self-concept as one important self-factor which controls the direction of the person. There is certainly some preliminary evidence in the authors'

work to date, to indicate that the self-concept might be one of the important self-factors in determining the "drift" toward or away from delinquency and crime. The authors do not presume that such a self-factor would operate in instances of deep character and emotional disturbances. But for the large majority of unofficial and official offenders as well as effective conformers to the dominant norms of a democratic, industrial, urban, mobile society, it is certainly feasible to operate on the hypothesis that self-factors determine direction of behavior toward or away from delinquency and deviance in general.

The authors feel they uncovered some corroborating evidence, namely that the self-concept of early adolescent might be one of the self-factors which controls directionality. Certainly, teachers' prognostications of sixth-grade boys—even the mothers' evaluations—plus the *De* scale (now called Socialization scale) indicate that directionality, toward or away from delinquent behavior, can be sensed and assessed. If, in the future, effective assessment of self-reported delinquency can be made, sociologists as well as behavioral-science researchers will have another effective instrument to gauge directionality of the youth.

It seems to the authors that these indicators of directionality toward or away from deviance point to the strong possibility of a favorable-to-unfavorable self concept in the young person, which is acting as the controlling agent. Our large crosssectional study in 1957 certainly indicated that self-concept factors, the teachers' prognostication of direction of the youth, the *De* scale's assessment of direction were interrelated. And the authors, if they might be spared glibness, do not think it is the subtle "rub-off" of the teacher's sense of the individual youth's direction which causes an internalization of a favorable image of himself (although this might happen in rare instances). And in the 1955 and 1956 samples, when the mother's projections of direction in which the son was travelling were obtained, the authors did not feel that in the overwhelming majority of instances the mother's faith or lack of faith in the directional outcome of her boy was the "looking glass" which gave the boy his image (although this might happen in more instances than in the impact of the sixth-grade teacher's sense of direction on the boy). The authors believe that a youth in American society obtains his self-concepts from many experiential sources, inside and outside the home and school.

The findings from the Akron study point to stability of direction as assessed by teacher's nomination and other instruments of assessment. Here again, the authors' interpretation is that directional stability in comparable samples of the sixth, seventh, eighth and ninth grades reflects the operation of a self factor. However, this is not as convincing evidence as if the same sample of children could be tested during four successive years of adolescence. Nevertheless, the authors felt they received indications of longitudinal stability in the operation of a self factor in the four-year follow-up of the 1955 good-boy sample and the 1956 bad-boy sample.

Undoubtedly, there is a need for the development of an effective self-concept measure which can assess the direction toward or away from delinquency or deviant behavior generally. There is need also to develop measures of other self factors which control directionality. When such factors are uncovered and when they are effectively measured, then it should be possible to chart workable programs to prevent delinquency and to re-enforce the components of self which enable the youth to be an effective conformer.

Certainly, the authors' experience in Brooklyn indicates that it is necessary to use much more discriminating instruments than the ones they used and it could very well be that much more sensitive instruments are needed to record differences in self development among sixth graders in high, medium, and low delinquency areas as well as white, colored, and Puerto Rican sixth graders than among sixth-grade white and colored adolescents in different areas of Columbus and Akron, Ohio.

In the meantime, more faith can be placed in the sixth-grade teacher's evaluations or her assessments of the directionality of her male pupils. Sophisticated studies could be made of the predictive efficacy of her ratings. More use could be made of her ratings, say in May of each year after 35 weeks of daily contact, for designing preventive programs or attempting individualized corrective therapy. More sophisticated effort should also be expended on attempting to develop improved measures of self-reported delinquency.

One of the most difficult tasks would be to follow a large stratified sample of children who were evaluated at the first-grade level by the Gluecks' family-factor prediction instrument, to obtain teacher's prognostication, a self-reported delinquency measure, and an assessment of self concept at the sixth-grade level, and to make an official delinquency clearance on each youth in the sample at 18 years of age, no matter how many times he may have changed residence.

## REFERENCES AND NOTES

1 Kvaraceus, *Anxious Youth: Dynamics of Delinquency*, 1966, pp. 102–108.

2 Reckless, Dinitz, and Murray, "Teacher Nominations and Evaluations of 'Good' Boys in High-delinquency Areas," *Elementary School Journal*, vol. 57 (1957), p. 221.

3 Dinitz, Scarpetti, and Reckless, "Delinquency Vulnerability: A Cross Group and Longitudinal Analysis," *American Sociological Review*, vol. 27 (1962), p. 517.

4 Donald and Dinitz, "Self Concept and Delinquency Proneness," in Reckless and Newman (eds.), *Interdisciplinary Problems of Criminology: Papers of the American Society of Criminology, 1964*, 1965, pp. 49–59.

5 *Ibid.*, pp. 52–53.

6 *Ibid.*, p. 54.

7 Dinitz, Kay, and Reckless, "Group Gradients in Delinquency Potential and Achievement Scores of Sixth Graders," *American Journal of Orthopsychiatry*, vol. 33 (1958), p. 598.

8 Simpson, Dinitz, Kay, and Reckless, "Delinquency Potential in Pre-adolescents in High Delinquency Areas," *British Journal of Delinquency*, vol. 10 (1960), p. 211.

9 Lively, Dinitz, and Reckless, "Self Concept as a Predictor of Juvenile Delinquency," *American Journal of Orthopsychiatry*, vol. 32 (1962), p. 1.

10 Lively, "A Study of Teen-age Socialization and Delinquency Insulation by Grade Levels," Ph.D dissertation, Ohio State University, 1959, pp. 70–71.

## 41   THE ECONOMICS OF ORGANIZED CRIME

THOMAS C. SCHELLING

At the level of national policy, if not always of local practice, the dominant approach to organized crime is through indictment and conviction. This is in striking contrast to the enforcement of anti-trust or food-and-drug laws, or the policing of public utilities, which work through regulation, accommodation, and the restructuring of markets. For some decades, anti-trust problems have received the sustained professional attention of economists concerned with the structure of markets, the organization of business enterprise, and the incentives toward collusion or price-cutting. Racketeering and the provision of illegal goods (like gambling) have been conspicuously neglected by economists. (There exists no analysis of the liquor industry under prohibition that begins to compare with the best available studies of the aluminum or steel industries, air transport, milk distribution, or public-utility pricing.) Yet a good many economic and business principles that operate in the "upperworld" must, with suitable modification for change in environment, operate in the underworld as well—just as a good many economic principles that operate in an advanced competitive economy operate as well in a socialist or a primitive economy.

In addition to the sheer satisfaction of curiosity, there are good policy reasons for encouraging a "strategic" analysis of the criminal underworld. Such an analysis, in contrast to "tactical" intelligence aimed at the apprehension of individual criminals, could help in identifying the incentives and disincentives to organize crime, in evaluating the costs and losses due to criminal enterprises, and in restructuring laws and programs to minimize the costs, wastes, and injustices that crime entails.

What market characteristics determine whether a criminal activity becomes "organized"? Gambling, by all accounts, invites organization; abortion, by all accounts, does not. In the upperworld, automobile manufacture is characterized by large firms, but not machine-tool production; collusive price-fixing occurs in the electrical-machinery industry, but not in the distribution of fruits and vegetables. The reasons for these differences are not entirely understood, but they are amenable to study. The same should not be impossible for gambling, extortion, and contraband cigarettes.

How much does organized crime depend on at least one major market in which the advantages of large scale are great enough to support a dominant monopoly firm or cartel? Not all businesses lend themselves to centralized organization; some do, and these may provide the nucleus of capital and entrepreneurial talent for extension into other businesses that would not, alone, support or give rise to an organized monopoly or cartel. Do a few "core" criminal markets provide the organizational stimulus for organized crime? If the answer turns out to be yes, then a critical question is whether the particular market so essential for the "economic development" of the underworld is a "black market," whose existence is dependent on the prohibition of legal competition, or instead is an inherently criminal activity. Black markets always offer to the policy maker, in principle, the option of restructuring the market—of increasing legal competition, of compromising the original prohibition, of selectively relaxing either the law itself or the way it is enforced. If, alternatively, that central criminal enterprise is one that rests on violence, relaxation of the law is likely to be both ineffectual and unappealing.

Reprinted from Thomas C. Schelling, "Economics and Criminal Enterprise," in *The Public Interest*, vol. 7 (spring 1967), pp. 61–78, by permission of the author and *The Public Interest*. Copyright © 1967 by National Affairs Inc.

Since one of the interesting questions is why some underworld business becomes organized and some not, and another, what *kinds* of organization should be expected, a classification of these enterprises has to cover more than just "organized crime" and to distinguish types of organization. A tentative typology of underworld business might be as follows.

BLACK MARKETS    A large part of organized crime is the selling of commodities and services contrary to law. In what we usually consider the underworld this includes dope, prostitution, gambling, liquor (under prohibition), abortions, pornography, and contraband or stolen goods. Most of these are consumer goods.

In what is not usually considered the underworld, black markets include gold, contraceptives in some states, rationed commodities and coupons in wartime, loans and rentals above controlled prices, theater tickets in New York, and a good many similar commodities that, though not illegal per se, are handled outside legitimate markets or diverted from subsidized uses.

In some cases (gambling) the law bans the commodity from all consumers; in others (cigarettes), some consumers are legitimate and some (minors) not. In some cases what is illegal is that the tax or duty has not been paid; in some, it is the price of the transaction that makes it illegal. In some (child labor, illegal immigrant labor), it is buying the commodity, not selling it, that is proscribed.

RACKETEERING    Racketeering includes two kinds of business, both based on intimidation. One is *criminal monopoly*, the other *extortion*.

"Criminal monopoly" means the use of criminal means to destroy competition. Whether a competitor is actually destroyed or merely threatened with violence to make him go out of business, the object is to get protection from competition when the law will not provide it (by franchise or tariff protection) and when it cannot be legally achieved (through price wars, control of patents, or preclusive contracts).

We can distinguish altogether three kinds of "monopoly": those achieved through legal means, those achieved through means that are illegal only because of anti-trust and other laws intended to make monopoly difficult, and monopolies achieved through means that are criminal by any standards—means that would be criminal whether or not they were aimed at monopolizing a business. It is also useful to distinguish between firms that, in an excess of zeal or deficiency of scruple, engage when necessary in ruthless and illegal competition, and the more strictly "racketeering" firms whose profitable monopoly rests entirely on criminal violence. The object of law enforcement in the former case is not to destroy the firm but to curtail its illegal practices. If the whole basis of success in business, though, is strong-arm methods that keep competition destroyed or scare it away, it is a pure "racket."

"Extortion" means living off somebody else's business by the threat of violence or of criminal competition. A protection racket lives off its victims, letting them operate and pay tribute. If one establishes a chain of restaurants and destroys competitors or scares them out of business, that is "monopoly"; if he merely threatens to destroy people's restaurant business, taking part of their profits as the price for leaving them alone, he is an extortionist and likes to see them prosper so that his share will be greater.

For several reasons it is difficult to distinguish "extortion" that, like a parasite, wants a healthy host, from "criminal monopoly" that is dedicated to the elimination of competitors. First, one means of extortion is to threaten to cut off the supply of a monopolized commodity—labor on a construction site, trucking, or some illegal commodity provided through the black market. That is to say, one can use a monopoly at one stage for extortionate leverage at the next. Second, extortion itself can be used to secure a monopoly privilege: instead of taking tribute in cash, for example, a victim signs a contract for the high-priced delivery of beer or linen supplies. The result looks like monopoly, but arose out of extortion.

It is evident that extortion can be organized or

not, but in important cases it has to be. Vulnerable victims, after all, have to be protected from other extortionists. A monopolistic laundry service, deriving from a threat to harm the business that does not subscribe, has to destroy or to intimidate not only competing legitimate laundry services but other racketeers who would muscle in on the same victim. Thus, while criminal monopoly may not depend on extortion, organized extortion always needs an element of monopoly.

**BLACK-MARKET MONOPOLY**    Any successful black marketeer enjoys a "protected" market in the way a domestic industry is protected by a tariff, or butter is protected by a law against margarine. The black marketeer gets protection from the law against all competitors unwilling to pursue a criminal career. But there is a difference between a "protected industry" and a "monopolized industry." Abortion is a black market commodity but not a monopoly; a labor racket is a local monopoly but not a black-market one; a monopoly in dope has both elements—it is a "black-market monopoly."

**CARTEL**    A "conspiracy in restraint of trade" that does not lead to single-firm monopoly but to collusive price-fixing, and that maintains itself by criminal action, gives rise to a cartel that is not in, but depends on, the underworld. If the garment trade eliminates competition by an agreement on prices and wages, hiring thugs to enforce the agreement, it is different from the monopoly racket discussed above. If the government would make such agreements legally enforceable (as it does with retail-price-maintenance laws in some states), the business would be in no need of criminally enforcing discipline on itself. Similarly, a labor union can use criminal means to discipline its members, even to the presumed benefit of its members, who may be better off working as a bloc rather than as competing individuals. If the law permits enforceable closed-shop agreements, the criminal means become unnecessary.

**ORGANIZED CRIMINAL SERVICES**    A characteristic of the businesses listed above is that they usually involve relations between the underworld and the upperworld. But as businesses in the upperworld need legal services, financial advice, credit, enforcement of contract, places to conduct their business, and communication facilities, so in the underworld there has to be a variety of business services that are "domestic" to the underworld itself. These can be organized or unorganized. They are *in* the underworld, but not because they exploit the underworld as the underworld exploits the legitimate world.

**THE INCENTIVES TO CRIMINAL ORGANIZATION** The simplest explanation of a large-scale firm, in the underworld or anywhere else, is high overhead costs or some other element of technology that makes small-scale operation more costly than large-scale. The need to keep equipment or specialized personnel fully utilized often explains at least the lower limit to the size of the firm.

A second explanation is the prospect of monopolistic prices. If most of the business can be cornered by a single firm, it can raise the price at which it sells its illegal services. Like any business, it does this at some sacrifice in size of the market; but if the demand is inelastic, the increase in profit margin will more than compensate for the reduction in output. Of course, decentralized individual firms would have as much to gain by pushing up the price, but without discipline it will not work; each will undercut its competitors. Where entry can be denied to newcomers, centralized price-setting will yield monopoly rewards to whoever can organize the market. With discipline, a cartel can do it; in the absence of discipline a merger may do it; but intimidation, too, can lead to the elimination of competition and the conquest of a monopoly position by a single firm.

Third, the larger the firm, and especially the larger its share of the whole market, the more will formerly "external" costs become costs internal to the firm. "External costs" are those that fall on competitors, customers, bystanders, and others outside the firm itself. Collection of all the business within a single firm causes the costs that individual firms used to inflict on each other to show up as costs (or losses) to the larger centralized firm now doing the business. This is an advantage. The costs were originally there but disregarded; now there is an incentive to take them into account.

Violence is one such external cost. Racketeers have a collective interest in restricting violence, so as to avoid trouble with the public and the police—but the individual racketeer has little or no incentive to reduce the violence connected with his own crime. There is an analogy here with the whaling industry, which has a collective interest in not killing off the whales although an individual whaler has no incentive to consider what he is doing to the future of the industry when he maximizes his own catch. A large organization can afford to impose discipline, holding down violence if the business is crime, holding down the slaughter of females if the business is whaling.

There are also "external economies" that can become internalized, to the advantage of the centralized firm. Lobbying has this character, as does cultivating relations with the police. No small bookie can afford to spend money to influence gambling legislation, but an organized trade association or monopoly among those who live off illegal gambling can. Similarly with labor discipline; the small firm cannot afford to teach a lesson to the labor force of the industry, since most of the lesson is lost on other people's employees, but a single large firm can expect the full benefit of its labor policy. Similarly with cultivating the market; if one cultivates the market for dope, by hooking some customers, or cultivates a market for gambling in a territory where the demand is still latent, he cannot expect much of a return on his investment if opportunistic competitors will take advantage of the market he creates. Anything that requires a long investment in cultivating a consumer interest, a labor market, ancillary institutions, or relations with the police, can be undertaken only by a fairly large firm that has reason to expect that it can enjoy most of the market and get a satisfactory return on the investment.

Finally, there is the attraction of not only monopolizing a market but achieving a dominant position in the underworld itself, and participating in its governing. To the extent that large criminal business firms provide a governmental structure to the underworld, helping to maintain peace, setting rules, arbitrating disputes, and enforcing discipline, they are in a position to set up their own businesses and exclude competition. Constituting a "corporate state," they can give themselves the franchise for various "state-sponsored monopolies." They can do this either by denying the benefits of underworld government to their competitors or by using the equivalent of their "police power" to prevent competition.

**MARKET STRUCTURE**     In evaluating crime, an accounting approach gives at best a benchmark as to magnitudes, and not even that for the distribution of economic and social gains and losses. The problem is like that of estimating the comparative incidence of profits taxes and excise taxes, or the impact of a minimum-wage law on wage differentials. Especially if we want to know who bears the cost, or to compare the costs to society with the gains to the criminals, an analysis of *market adjustments* is required. Even the pricing practices of organized crime need to be studied.

Consider the illegal wire-service syndicate in Miami that received attention from Senator Kefauver's committee. The magnitude that received explicit attention was the loss of state revenues due to the diversion of gambling from legal race tracks, which were taxable, to illegal bookmakers, whose turnover was not taxable. No accounting approach would yield this magnitude; it depended (as was pointed out in testimony) on what economists call the "elasticity of substitution" between the two services—on the fraction of potential race track business that patronized bookmakers.

Similar analysis is required to determine *at whose expense* the syndicate operated, or what the economic consequences of the syndicate's removal would have been. The provision of wire-service was of small economic significance. It accounted, on a cost basis, for less than 5% of the net income of bookmakers (of which the syndicate took approximately 50%). And cheaper wire service to the bookies might have been available in the absence of the syndicate, whose function was not to provide wire service but to eliminate wire-service competitors.

The essential business of the syndicate was to practice *extortion against bookmakers*. It demanded half their earnings, against the threat of reprisals. The syndicate operated like a taxing authority (as well as providing some reinsurance on large bets); it apparently did not limit the number of bookmakers so long as they paid their "taxes".

How much of this tax was passed along to the customer (on the analogy of a gasoline or a sales tax) and how much was borne by the bookie (on the analogy of an income or profits tax) is hard to determine. If we assume (1) that bookmakers' earnings are approximately proportionate to the volume of turnover, (2) that their customers, though sensitive to the comparative odds of different bookmakers, are not sensitive to the profit margin, (3) that they tend, consciously or implicitly, to budget their total bets and not their rate of loss, we can conclude that the tax is substantially passed along to the customer. In that case the bookmaker, though nominally the victim of extortion, is victimized only into raising the price to his customers, somewhat like a filling station that must pay a tax on every gallon sold. The bookmaker is thus an intermediary between an extortionate syndicate and a customer who pays his tribute voluntarily on the price he is willing to pay for his bets.

The syndicate in Miami relied on the police as their favorite instrument of intimidation. It could have been the other way around, with the police using the syndicate as their agency to negotiate and collect from the bookmakers, and if the police had been organized and disciplined as a monopoly, it would have been the police, not the syndicate, that we should put at the top of our organizational pyramid. From the testimony, though, it is evident that the initiative and entrepreneurship came from the syndicate, which had the talent and organization for this kind of business, and that the police lacked the centralized authority for exploiting to their own benefit the power they had over the bookmakers. Presumably—though there were few hints of this in the hearings—the syndicate could have mobilized other techniques for intimidating the bookmakers; the police were the chosen instrument only so long as the police's share in the proceeds was competitive with alternative executors of the intimidating threats.

Any attempt to estimate the long-term effect on police salaries would have to take into account how widespread and non-discriminatory the police particpation was, especially by rank and seniority in service. Recruiting would be unaffected if police recruits were unaware of the illegal earnings that might accrue to them; senior members of the force who might otherwise have quit the service, or lobbied harder for pay increases, would agitate less vigorously for high wages if their salaries were augmented by the racket. One cannot easily infer that part of the "tax" paid by the bookmaker's customer subsidized the police force to the benefit of non-betting taxpayers; mainly they supported a more discriminatory and irregular earnings pattern among the police—besides contributing, unwittingly, to a demoralization of the police that would have made it a bad bargain for the taxpayer anyway.

This is just a sketch, based on the skimpy evidence available, of the rather complex structure of "organized gambling" in one city. (It is not, of course, the gambling that is organized; the organization is an extortionate monopoly that nominally provides a wire-service but actually imposes a tribute on middlemen who pass most of the cost along to their voluntary customers.) Similar analysis would be required to identify the incidence of costs and losses (and gains, of course) of protection rackets everywhere (e.g., monopoly-priced beer deliveries to bars or restaurants, vending machines installed in bars and restaurants under pain of damage or nuisance, etc.).

**INSTITUTIONAL PRACTICES** Institutional practices in the underworld need to be better understood. What, for example, is the effect of the tax laws on extortion? Why does an extortionist put cigarette machines in a restaurant or provide linen service? Do the tax laws make it difficult to disguise the payment of tribute in cash but easy to disguise it (and make it tax deductible) if the tribute takes the form of a concession or the purchase of high-priced services? Why does a gambling syndicate bother to provide "wire service" when evidently its primary economic function is to shake down bookies by the threat of hurting their businesses or their persons, possibly with the collusion of the police?

The Kefauver hearings indicate that the wire-service syndicate in Miami took a standard 50% from the bookies. The symmetry of the 50% figure is itself remarkable. Equally remarkable is that the figure was uniform. But most remarkable of all is that the syndicate went through the motions of providing a wire service when it perfectly well could have taken cash tribute instead. There is an analogy here with the car salesman who refuses to negotiate the price of a new car, but is willing to negotiate quite freely the "allowance" on the used car that one turns in. The underworld seems to need institutions, conventions, traditions, and recognizable standard practices much like the upper-world of business. A better understanding of these practices might lead not only to a better evaluation of crime itself but also to a better understanding of the role of tax laws and regulatory laws on the operation of criminal business.

The role of vending machines, for example, appears to be that they provide a tax-deductible, non-discriminatory, and "respectable" way of paying tribute. Pinball and slot machines installed by a gang in somebody's small store may be only half characterized when identified as "illegal gambling"; they are equally a conventionalized medium for the exaction of tribute from the store owner. Effective enforcement of a ban on the machines will take care of the "gambling" part of the enterprise; what happens to the extortion racket depends then on how readily some other lucrative concession, some exclusive delivery contract, or some direct cash tribute can be imposed on the store owner.

Even the resistance to crime would be affected by measures designed to change the cost structure. Economists make an important distinction between a lump-sum tax, a profits tax, and a specific or ad valorum tax on the commodity an enterprise sells. The manner in which a criminal monopolist or extortionist prices his service, or demands his tribute, should have a good deal to do with whether the cost is borne by the victim or passed along by the customer. The "tax" levied by the racketeer uniformly on all his customers—monopoly-priced beer or linen supplies—may merely be passed along in turn to their customers, with little loss to the immediate victims, if the demand in their own market is inelastic. A bar that has to pay an extortionate price for its beer can seek relief in either of two ways. It can try to avoid paying the extortionate or monopolized price; alternatively, it can insist that its supplier achieve similar concessions from all competing bars, to avoid a competitive disadvantage. An individual bar suffers little if the price of wholesale beer goes up; it suffers when competitors' prices do not go up.

Similarly, legal arrangements that make it difficult to disguise illegal transactions, and that make it a punishable offense to pay tribute, might help to change the incentives. In a few cases, the deliberate stimulation of competing enterprises could be in the public interest: loan-sharking, for example, might be somewhat mitigated by the deliberate creation of new and specialized lending enterprises. Loan-sharking appears to involve several elements, only one of which is the somewhat outmoded notion—outmoded by a few centuries—that people so much in need of cash that they'd pay high interest rates should be protected from "usury" even if it means merely that they are protected by being denied any access to credit at all. A second element is that, now that debtors' prison has been liberally abolished, people who cannot post collateral have no ready way to assure their own motivation to repay—attachment of wages has also been liberally made illegal—so that those without assets who need cash must pledge life and limb in the underworld. Thus when the law has no way of enforcing contract, the underworld provides it: a man submits to the prospect of personal violence as the last resort in contract enforcement. Finally, the borrower whose prospects of repayment are so poor that even the threat of violence cannot hold him to repayment is enticed into an arrangement that makes him a victim of perpetual extortion, one who cannot go to the law because he is already party to a criminal transaction. Evidently there is some part of this racket that thrives on a void in our legal and financial institutions.

**EVALUATING COSTS AND LOSSES** Crime is bad, as cancer is bad; but even for cancer, one can distinguish among death, pain, anxiety, the cost of treatment, the loss of earnings, the effects on the victim and the effects on his family. Similarly with crime. It is offensive to society that the law be violated. But crime can involve a transfer of wealth from the victim to the criminal, a net social loss due to the inefficient mode of transfer, the creation of fear and anxiety, violence from which nobody profits, the corruption of the police and other public officials, costs of law enforcement and private protection, high prices to customers, unfairness of competition, loss of revenue to the state, and even loss of earnings to the criminals themselves who in some cases may be ill-suited to their trade.

There are important "trade-offs" among these different costs and losses due to crime, and in the different ways that government can approach the problem of crime. There will be choices between reducing the incidence of crime and reducing the consequences of crime, and other choices that require a more explicit indentification and evaluation of the magnitude and distribution of the gains and losses.

If there were but one way to wage war against crime, and the only question how vigorously to do it, there would be no need to identify the different objectives (costs and consequences) in devising the campaign. But if this is a continual campaign to cope with some pretty definite evils, without any real expectation of "total victory" or "unconditional surrender," resources have to be allocated and deployed in a way that maximizes the value of a compromise.

In the black markets it is especially hard to identify just what the evils are. In the first place, a law-abiding citizen is not obliged to consider the procurement and consumption of illegal commodities inherently sinful. We have constitutional procedures for legislating prohibitions; the out-voted minority is bound to abide by the law but not necessarily to agree with it, and can even campaign to become a majority and legalize liquor after a decade of prohibition, or legalize contraceptives in states where they have been prohibited. Even those who vote to ban gambling or saloons or dope can do so, not because they consider the consumption sinful, but because *some* of the consequences are bad; and if it is infeasible to prohibit the sale of alcohol only to alcoholics, or gambling only to minors, we have to forbid all of it to forbid the part we want to forbid.

The only reason for rehearsing these arguments is to remind ourselves that the evil of gambling, drinking, or dope, is not necessarily proportionate to how much of it goes on. The evil can be greater or less than suggested by any such figure. One might, for example, conclude that the consumption of narcotics that actually occurs is precisely the consumption that one wanted to prevent, and that it is the more harmless consumption that has been eliminated; or one might conclude that the gambling laws eliminate the worst of gambling, that what filters through the laws is fairly innocuous (or would be, if its being illegal per se were not harmful to society), and that gambling laws thus serve the purpose of selective discrimination in their enforcement if not in their enactment.

The evils of abortion are particularly difficult to evaluate, especially because it is everybody's privilege to attach his own moral value to the commodity. Are the disgust, anxiety, humiliation, and physical danger incurred by the abortionists' customers part of the "net cost" to society, or are they positively valued as punishment for the wicked? If a woman gets an abortion, do we prefer she pay a high price or a low one? Is the black-market price a cost to society, a proper penalty inflicted on the woman, or merely an economic waste? If a woman gets a safe cheap abortion abroad, is this a legitimate bit of "international trade," raising the national income like any gainful trade, or is it even worse than her getting an expensive, more disagreeable, more dangerous abortion at home, because she evaded the punishment and the sense of guilt?

These are not academic questions. There are issues of policy in identifying what it is we dislike about criminal activity, especially in deciding where and how to compromise. The case of prostitution is a familiar example. Granting the illegality of prostitution, and efforts to enforce the law against it, one may still discover that one particular evil of prostitution is a hazard to health—the spread of venereal disease, a spread that is not confined to the customers but transmitted even to those who had no connection with the illicit commodity. Yet there is some incompatibility between a campaign to eradicate venereal disease and a campaign to eradicate prostitution, and one may prefer to legislate a public health service for prostitutes and their customers even at the expense of "diplomatic recognition" of the enemy. The point is that a hard choice can arise and ideology gives no answer. If two of the primary evils connected with a criminal activity are negatively correlated, one has to distinguish them, separately evaluate them, and then make up one's mind.

Similarly with abortion. At the very least, one can propose clinical help to women seeking abortion for the limited purpose of eliminating from the market those who are actually *not* pregnant, providing them the diagnosis that an abortionist might have neglected or preferred to withhold. Going a step further, one may want to provide reliable advice about post-abortion symptoms to women who may become infected or who may hemorrhage or otherwise suffer from ignorance. Still a step further, one may like to provide even abortionists with a degree of immunity so that if a woman needs emergency treatment he can call for it without danger of self-incrimination. None of these suggestions compromises the principle of illegality; they merely apply to abortion some of the principles that would ordinarily be applied to hit-and-run driving or to an armed robber who inadvertently hurt his victim and preferred to call an ambulance.

One has to go a step further, though, on the analogy with contraception, and ask about the positive or negative value of scientific discovery, or research and development, in the field of abortion itself. Cheap, safe and reliable contraceptives are now considered a stupendous boon to mankind. What is the worth of a cheap, safe and reliable technique of abortion, one that involves no surgery, no harmful or addicting drugs, no infection, and preferably not even reliance on a professional abortionist? Suppose some of the new techniques developed in Eastern Europe and elsewhere for performing safer and more convenient abortions become technically available to abortionists in this country, with the consequence that fewer patients suffer—but also with the consequence that more abortions are procured? How do we weigh these consequences against each other? Each of us may have his own answer, and a political or judicial decision is required if we want an official answer. But the questions cannot be ignored.

The same questions arise in the field of firearm technology. Do we hope that non-lethal weapons become available to criminals, so that they kill and damage fewer victims, or would we deplore it on grounds that any technological improvement available to criminal enterprise is against the public interest? Do we hope to see less damaging narcotics become available, perhaps cheaply available through production and marketing techniques that do not lend themselves to criminal monopoly, to compete with the criminally monopolized and more deleterious narcotics? Or is this a "compromise" with crime itself?

**SHOULD CRIME BE ORGANIZED OR DISORGANIZED?** It is usually implied, if not asserted, that organized crime is a menace and has to be fought. But if the alternative is "disorganized crime"—if the criminals and their opportunities will remain, with merely a lesser degree of organization than before—the choice is not an easy one.

There is one argument for favoring the "organization" of crime. It is that organization would "internalize" some of the costs that fall on the underworld itself but go unnoticed, or ignored, if criminal activity is decentralized. The individual hijacker may be tempted to kill a truck driver to destroy a potential witness—to the dismay of the underworld, which suffers from public outrage and the heightened activity of the police. A monopoly or a trade association could impose discipline. This is not a decisive argument, nor does it apply to all criminal industries if it applies to a few; but it is important.

If abortion, for example, will not be legalized and cannot be eliminated, one can wish it were better organized. A large organization could not afford to mutilate so many women. It could impose higher standards. It would have an interest in quality control and the protection of its "goodwill" that the petty abortionist is unlikely to have. As it is, the costs external to the enterprise—the costs that fall not on the abortionist but on the customer or on the reputation of other abortionists—are of little concern to him and he has no incentive to minimize them. By all accounts, criminal abortion is conducted more incompetently and more irresponsibly than illegal gambling.

### COMPROMISING WITH ORGANIZED CRIME

It is customary to deplore the "accommodation" that the underworld reaches, sometimes, with the forces of law and order, with the police, with the prosecutors, with the courts. Undoubtedly there is corruption of public officials, bad not only because it frustrates justice but also because it lowers standards of morality. On the other hand, officials concerned with law enforcement are inevitably in the front line of diplomacy between the legitimate world and the underworld. Aside from the approved negotiations by which criminals are induced to testify, to plead guilty, to surrender themselves, or to tip off the police, there is always a degree of accommodation between the police and the criminals—tacit or explicit understandings analogous to what in military affairs would be called the limitation of war, the control of armament, and the delineation of spheres of influence.

In criminal activity by legitimate firms—such as conspiracy in restraint of trade, tax evasion, illegal labor practices, or the marketing of dangerous drugs—regulatory agencies can deal specifically with the harmful practices. One does not have to declare war on the industry itself, only on the illegal practices. Regulation, even negotiation, are recognized techniques for coping with those practices. But when the business itself is criminal, it is harder to have an acknowledged policy of regulation and negotiation. For this involves a kind of "diplomatic recognition."

In the international field, one can cold-bloodedly limit warfare and come to an understanding about the kinds of violence that will be resisted or punished, the activities that will be considered non-aggressive, and the areas within the other side's sphere of influence. Maybe the same approach is necessary in dealing with crime itself. And if we cannot acknowledge it at the legislative level, it may have to be accomplished in an unauthorized or unacknowledged way by the people whose business—law enforcement—requires it of them.

### THE RELATION OF ORGANIZED CRIME TO ENFORCEMENT

We have to distinguish the "black market monopolies," dealing in forbidden goods—gambling, dope, smuggling, prostitution—from the racketeering enterprises. It is the black market monopolies that depend on the law itself. Without the law and some degree of enforcement, there is no presumption that the organization can survive competition—or, if it could survive competition once it is established, that the organization could have arisen in the first place in the face of competition.

There must be an "optimum degree of enforcement" from the point of view of the criminal monopoly. With no enforcement—either because enforcement is not attempted or because enforcement is not feasible—the black market could not be profitable enough to invite criminal monopoly (at least not any more than any other market, legitimate or criminal). With wholly effective enforcement, and no collusion with the police, the business would be destroyed. Between these extremes, there may be an attractive black market profitable enough to invite monopoly.

Organized crime could not, for example, possibly corner the market on cigarette sales to minors. Every 21-year-old is a potential source of supply.

No organization, legal or illegal, could keep a multitude of 21-year-olds from buying cigarettes and passing them along to persons under 21. No black market price differential, great enough to make organized sale to minors profitable, could survive the competition. And no organization, legal or illegal, could so intimidate every adult that he would not be a source of supply to the youngsters. Without there being any way to enforce the law, organized crime would get no more out of selling cigarettes to children than out of selling them soft drinks.

The same is true of contraceptives in those states where their sale is nominally illegal. If the law is not enforced, there is no scarcity out of which to make profits. And if one is going to try to intimidate every drugstore that sells contraceptives, in the hope of monopolizing the business, he may as well monopolize toothpaste, which would be more profitable. The intervention of the law is needed to intimidate the druggists with respect to the one commodity that organized crime is trying to monopolize.

What about abortions? Why is it not "organized"? The answer is not easy, and there may be too many special characteristics of this market to permit a selection of the critical one. The consumer and the product have unusual characteristics. Nobody is a "regular" consumer the way a person may regularly gamble, drink, or take dope. (A woman may repeatedly need the services of an abortionist, but each occasion is once-for-all.) The consumers are more secret about dealing with this black market, secret among intimate friends and relations, than are the consumers of most banned commodities. It is a dirty business, and too many of the customers die; and while organized crime might drastically reduce fatalities, it may be afraid of getting involved with anything that kills and maims so many customers in a way that could be blamed on the criminal himself rather than just on the commodity that is sold.

## BLACK MARKETS AND COMPETITION
I have emphasized that a difference between black market crimes and most others, like racketeering and robbery, is that they are "crimes" only because we have legislated against the commodity they provide. We single out certain goods and services as harmful or sinful; for reasons of history and tradition, and for other reasons, we forbid dope but not tobacco, gambling in casinos but not on the stockmarket, extra-marital sex but not gluttony, erotic stories but not mystery stories. We do all this for reasons different from those behind the laws against robbery and tax evasion.

It is policy that determines the black markets. Cigarettes and firearms are borderline cases. We can, as a matter of policy, make the sales of guns and cigarettes illegal. We can also, as a matter of policy, make contraceptives and abortion illegal. Times change, policies change, and what was banned yesterday can become legitimate today; what was freely available yesterday, can be banned tomorrow. Evidently there are changes under way in policy on birth control; there may be changes on abortion and homosexuality, and there may be legislation restricting the sale of firearms.

The pure black markets reflect some moral tastes, economic principles, paternalistic interests, and notions of personal freedom in a way that the rackets do not. And these tastes and principles change. We can revise our policy on birth control (and we are changing it) in a way that we could not change our policy on armed robbery. The usury laws may to some extent be a holdover from medieval economics; and some of the laws on prostitution, abortion, and contraception were products of the Victorian era and reflect the political power of various church groups. One cannot even deduce from the existence of abortion laws that a majority of the voters, even a majority of enlightened voters, oppose abortion; and the wise money would probably bet that the things that we shall be forbidding in fifty years will differ substantially from the things we forbid now.

What happens when a forbidden industry is subjected to legitimate competition? Legalized gambling is a good example. What has ahppened to Las Vegas is hardly reassuring. On the other hand, the legalization of liquor in the early 1930's swamped the criminal liquor industry with competition.

safe, and able to corrupt public officials. In economic-development terms, these black markets may provide the central core (or "infra-structure") of underworld business.

A good economic history of prohibition in the 1920's has never been attempted, so far as I know. By all accounts, though, prohibition was a mistake. It merely turned the liquor industry over to organized crime. In the end we gave up, probably because not everybody agreed drinking was bad (or, if it was bad, that it was anybody's political business), but also because the attempt was an evident failure and a costly one in its social by-products. It may have propelled underworld business in the United States into what economic developers call the "take-off" into self-sustained growth.

## 42   WHITE COLLAR CRIME   EDWIN H. SUTHERLAND

Criminal statistics show unequivocally that crime, as popularly understood officially measured, has a high incidence in the lower socio-economic class and a low incidence in the upper socio-economic class. Crime, as thus understood, includes the ordinary violations of the penal code, such as murder, assault, burglary, robbery, larceny, sex offenses, and public intoxication, but does not include traffic violations. Persons who are accused or convicted of these ordinary crimes are dealt with by the police, juvenile or criminal courts, probation departments, and correctional institutions.

The concentration of crimes, as conventionally understood, in the lower socio-economic class has been demonstrated by two types of research studies. First, the analysis of case histories of offenders and of their parents shows a high incidence of poverty in such cases. Sheldon and Eleanor Glueck

Reprinted from *White Collar Crime*, by Edwin H. Sutherland pp. 3–13, 44–55, by permission of Holt, Rinehart and Winston, Inc. Copyright © 1961 by Holt, Rinehart and Winston, Inc.

studied one thousand juvenile delinquents who had appeared before the juvenile courts of Greater Boston, five hundred young-adult males who had been committed to the State Reformatory of Massachusetts, and five hundred women who had been committed to the Massachusetts Reformatory for Women. The economic status of the parents in these three series of offenders is presented in Table 1. This shows that 71.2 percent of the offenders in one series and 91.3 percent in the series at the other extreme were below the "level of comfort," which was defined as possession of sufficient surplus to enable a family to maintain itself for four months of unemployment without going on relief. Other data in these studies of the families of offenders show a high incidence of unemployment, of mothers engaged in remunerative occupations, of fathers in unskilled and semi-skilled occupations, and of parents who lacked formal education; they show, also, that a large proportion of the offenders left school at an early age to engage in gainful occupations.[1]

TABLE 1   *Percentage distribution of three series of offenders, by economic status of parental families*

| Parental economic status | 1,000 juvenile delinquents | 500 young-adult male delinquents | 500 female delinquents |
|---|---|---|---|
| Dependent | 8.1 | 14.8 | 13.3 |
| Marginal | 68.2 | 56.4 | 78.0 |
| Comfortable | 23.7 | 28.8 | 8.7 |

Criminals are alleged to have moved into church bingo, but they have never got much of a hold on the stockmarket. Evidently criminals cannot always survive competition, evidently sometimes they can.

The question is important in the field of narcotics. We could easily put insulin and antibiotics into the hands of organized crime by forbidding their sale; we could do the same with a dentist's novocaine. (We could, that is, if we could sufficiently enforce the prohibition. If we cannot enforce it, the black market would be too competitive for any organized monopoly to arise.) If narcotics were not illegal, there could be no black market and no monopoly profits; the interest in "pushing" it would not be much greater than the pharmaceutical interest in pills to reduce the symptoms of common colds. This argument cannot by itself settle the question of whether (and which) narcotics (or other evil commodities) ought to be banned, but it is an important consideration.

The greatest gambling enterprise in the United States has not been significantly touched by organized crime. That is the stock market. (There has been criminal activity in the stock market, but not monopoly by what we usually call "organized crime.") Nor has organized crime succeeded in controlling the foreign currency black markets around the world. The reason is that the market works too well. Federal control over the stock market, designed mainly to keep it honest and informative, and aimed at maximizing the competitiveness of the market and the information of the consumer, makes it a hard market to tamper with.

Ordinary gambling ought to be one of the hardest industries to monopolize. Almost anybody can compete, whether in taking bets or providing cards, dice, or racing information. "Wire services" could not stand the ordinary competition of radio and Western Union; bookmakers could hardly be intimidated if the police were not available to intimidate them. If ordinary brokerage firms were encouraged to take horse-racing accounts, and buy and sell bets by telephone for their customers, it is hard to see how racketeers could get any kind of grip on it. And when any restaurant, bar, country club or fraternity house can provide tables and sell fresh decks of cards, it is hard to see how gambling can be monopolized any more than the soft-drink or television business, or any other.

We can still think gambling is a sin, and try to eliminate it; but we should probably try not to use the argument that it would remain in the hands of criminals if we legalized it. Both reason and evidence seem to indicate the contrary.

The decisive question is whether the goal of somewhat reducing the consumption of narcotics, gambling, prostitution, abortion or anything else that is forced by law into the black market, is or is not outweighed by the costs to society of creating a criminal industry. The costs to society of creating these black markets are several.

1 It gives the criminal the same kind of protection that a tariff gives to a domestic monopoly. It guarantees the absence of competition from people who are unwilling to be criminal, and an advantage to those whose skill is in evading the law.

2 It provides a special incentive to corrupt the police, because the police not only may be susceptible to being bought off but can even be used to eliminate competition.

3 A large number of consumers who are probably not ordinary criminals—the conventioneers who visit prostitutes, the housewives who bet on horses, the women who seek abortions—are taught contempt, even enmity, for the law by being obliged to purchase particular commodities and services from criminals in an illegal transaction.

4 Dope addiction may so aggravate poverty for certain desperate people that they are induced to commit crimes, or can be urged to commit crimes, because the law arranges that the only (or main) source for what they desperately demand will be a criminal (high-priced) source.

5 These big black markets may guarantee enough incentive and enough profit for organized crime so that large-scale criminal organization comes into being and maintains itself. It may be—this is an important question for research—that without these important black markets, crime would be substantially decentralized, lacking the kind of organization that makes it enterprising,

The United States Bureau of the Census made an analysis of the economic status and earnings of persons committed to state and federal prisons and reformatories in 1923. The usual weekly earnings of these persons prior to commitment are shown in Table 2. This indicates that 60.1 percent of the males and 92.1 percent of the females who were committed to prisons in 1923, had previous weekly earnings of less than $30.[2] Other evidence in this report similarly supports the conclusion that crimes are concentrated in the lower economic class.

The second method of demonstrating the concentration of crimes in the lower socio-economic class is by statistical analysis of the residential areas of offenders; this is ordinarily called the "ecological distribution of offenders." Shaw and McKay have analyzed the data regarding the residences of juvenile delinquents and adult criminals in twenty cities in the United States. In each of these cities the offenders are concentrated in areas of poverty. In Chicago the correlation between boy delinquency cases and families on relief by square mile area is $+ .89 \pm .01$. Boy delinquency is positively correlated by high coefficients with unemployment and with buildings condemned as unsafe for residence, and negatively with rentals; also boy delinquency shows a high correlation with girl delinquency, with young-adult male delinquency, and with adult delinquency.[3]

The scholars who have stated general theories of criminal behavior have used statistics such as those outlined above and individual case histories from which these statistics are compiled. Since these cases are concentrated in the lower socio-economic class, the theories of criminal behavior have placed much emphasis on poverty as the cause of crime or on other social conditions and personal traits which are associated with poverty. The assumption in these theories is that criminal behavior can be explained only by pathological factors, either social or personal. The social pathologies which have been emphasized are poverty and, related to it, poor housing, lack of organized recreations, lack of education, and disruptions in family life. The personal pathologies which have been suggested as explanations of criminal behavior were, at first, biological abnormalities; when research studies threw doubt on the validity of these biological explanations, the next explanation was intellectual inferiority, and more recently emotional instability. Some of these scholars believed that the personal pathologies were inherited and were the cause of the poverty as well as of the criminal behavior, while others believed that the personal pathologies were produced by poverty or by the pathological conditions associated with poverty, and that this personal pathology contributed to the perpetuation of the poverty and of the related social pathologies.

The thesis of this book is that these social and personal pathologies are not an adequate explanation of criminal behavior. The general theories of criminal behavior which take their data from poverty and the conditions related to it are inadequate and invalid: first, because the theories do not consistently fit the data of criminal behavior; and second, because the cases on which these theories are based are a biased sample of all criminal acts. These two defects are elaborated in the following paragraphs.

First, many of the facts regarding criminal behavior cannot be explained by poverty and its related pathologies.

1 The statistics of juvenile courts show that at the present time in the United States approximately 85 percent of the juveniles adjudged delinquent are boys and only 15 percent girls. The proportion of girls in the United States who are in poverty is approximately the same as the proportion of boys; the two sexes come equally from

**TABLE 2**  *Percentage distribution of persons committed to state and federal prisons and reformatories in 1923, by sex of offenders and by usual weekly earnings*

| Weekly earnings | Male | Female |
|---|---|---|
| Under $10 | 4.6 | 27.3 |
| $10–19 | 25.0 | 53.0 |
| $20–29 | 30.5 | 11.8 |
| $30 and over | 39.9 | 7.9 |

homes with inadequate housing, are equally lacking in recreational facilities, are equal in intelligence tests and in emotional stability. With this approximate equality of the two sexes, poverty and its related pathologies obviously cannot explain the difference in the delinquency rates of the two sexes.

2 Many groups on the frontiers have been in extreme poverty but, nevertheless, have had low rates of juvenile delinquency and adult crime.

3 Many groups residing in slum areas of cities are in great poverty but have low rates of juvenile and adult delinquency, as illustrated by the Chinese colonies.

4 Certain immigrant groups have migrated from peasant communities in Europe, where they had low crime rates although living in poverty, to American cities, where they have high crime rates with perhaps less poverty than in their peasant communities.[4]

5 Studies of the relation between crime rates and the business cycle have shown no significant association or a very slight association between depressions and crime rates in general, and no significant association between depressions and the crimes against property.[5] These conclusions regarding crime and the business cycle, when considered in connection with the ecological studies, raise the question: Why does poverty, when distributed spatially by residential areas, show a strikingly uniform and high association with crime, but when distributed chronologically in business cycles, show a slight and inconsistent association with crime? The answer is that the causal factor is not poverty in the sense of economic need, but the social and interpersonal relations which are associated sometimes with poverty and sometimes with wealth.

Second, the conventional explanations of criminal behavior are invalid in that they are based on biased statistics. These statistics are biased in two respects:

1 Persons of the upper socio-economic class are more powerful politically and financially and escape arrest and conviction to a greater extent than persons who lack such power, even when equally guilty of crimes. Wealthy persons can employ skilled attorneys and in other ways influence the administration of justice in their own favor more effectively than can persons of the lower socio-economic class. Even professional criminals, who have financial and political power, escape arrest and conviction more effectively than amateur and occasional criminals who have little financial or political power.[6] This bias, while indubitable, is not of great importance from the point of view of criminological theory.

2 Much more important is the bias involved in the administration of criminal justice under laws which apply exclusively to business and the professions and which therefore involve only the upper socio-economic class. Persons who violate laws regarding restraint of trade, advertising, pure food and drugs are not arrested by uniformed policemen, are not often tried in criminal courts, and are not committed to prisons; their illegal behavior generally receives the attention of administrative commissions and of courts operating under civil or equity jurisdiction. For this reason such violations of law are not included in the criminal statistics nor are individual cases brought to the attention of the scholars who write the theories of criminal behavior. The sample of criminal behavior on which the theories are founded is biased as to socio-economic status, since it excludes these business and professional men. This bias is quite as certain as it would be if the scholars selected only red-haired criminals for study and reached the conclusion that redness of hair was the cause of crime.

The thesis of this book, stated positively, is that persons of the upper socio-economic class engage in much criminal behavior; that this criminal behavior differs from the criminal behavior of the lower socio-economic class principally in the administrative procedures which are used in dealing with the offenders; and that variations in administrative procedures are not significant from the point of view of causation of crime. Today tuberculosis is treated by streptomycin; but the causes of tuberculosis were no different when it was treated by poultices and blood-letting.

These violations of law by persons in the upper

socio-economic class are, for convenience, called "white collar crimes." This concept is not intended to be definitive, but merely to call attention to crimes which are not ordinarily included within the scope of criminology. White collar crime may be defined approximately as a crime committed by a person of respectability and high social status in the course of his occupation.[7] Consequently, it excludes many crimes of the upper class, such as most of their cases of murder, adultery, and intoxication, since these are not customarily a part of their occupational procedures. Also, it excludes the confidence games of wealthy members of the underworld, since they are not persons of respectability and high social status.

The significant thing about white collar crime is that it is not associated with poverty or with social and personal pathologies which accompany poverty. If it can be shown that white collar crimes are frequent, a general theory that crime is due to poverty and its related pathologies is shown to be invalid. Furthermore, the study of white collar crime may assist in locating those factors which, being common to the crimes of the rich and the poor, are most significant for a general theory of criminal behavior.

A great deal of scattered and unorganized material indicates that white collar crimes are very prevalent. The "robber barons" of the last half of the nineteenth century were white collar criminals, as practically everyone now agrees. Their behavior was illustrated by such statements as the following. Colonel Vanderbilt asked: "You don't suppose you can run a railway in accordance with the statutes, do you?" A. B. Stickney, a railroad president, said to sixteen other railroad presidents in the home of J. P. Morgan in 1890: "I have the utmost respect for you gentlemen individually, but as railroad presidents, I wouldn't trust you with my watch out of my sight." Charles Francis Adams said: "One difficulty in railroad management . . . lies in the covetousness, want of good faith, low moral tone of railway managers, in the complete absence of any high standard of commercial honesty." James M. Beck said in regard to the period 1905–1917: "Diogenes would have been hard put to it to find an honest man in the Wall Street which I knew as a corporation attorney."

The present-day white collar criminals are more suave and less forthright than the "robber barons" of last century but not less criminal. Criminality has been demonstrated again and again in investigations of land offices, railways, insurance, munitions, banking, public utilities, stock exchanges, the petroleum industry, the real estate industry, receiverships, bankruptcies, and politics. When the airmail contracts were canceled because of graft, Will Rogers said: "I hope they don't stop every industry where they find crookedness at the top"; and Elmer Davis said: "If they are going to stop every industry where they find crookedness at the top they will have to stop them all." The Federal Trade Commission reported in 1920 that commercial bribery was a prevalent and common practice in many industries. In certain chain stores the net shortage in weight was sufficient to pay 3.4 percent on the investment, while no net shortage in weights was found in independent stores and cooperative stores. The Comptroller of the Currency reported in 1908 that violations of banking laws were found in 75 percent of the banks examined in a three months' period. Lie-detector tests of all employees in certain Chicago banks, supported in almost all cases by subsequent confessions, showed that 20 percent of them had stolen bank property, and lie-detector tests of a cross-section sample of the employees of a chain store showed approximately 75 percent had stolen money or merchandise from the store.[8] Investigators for the *Readers Digest* in 1941 drove their car into many garages with a defect artificially produced for this experiment. A proper charge for attaching the wire which had been loosened might be twenty-five cents. But 75 percent of the garages misrepresented the defect and the work which was done; the average charge was $4 and some garages charged as much as $25. Similar frauds were found in the watch-repair, radio-repair, and typewriter-repair business.[9]

White collar crime in politics, which is popularly supposed to be very prevalent, has been used by some persons as a rough gauge by which to measure white collar crime in business. James A. Farley, who has had experience both in business and in politics, says: "The standards of conduct are as high among office-holders and politicians as they are in commercial life." Anton J. Cermak, once mayor of Chicago and a businessman, said: "There is less graft in politics than in business." John T. Flynn asserts: "The average politician is the merest amateur in the gentle art of graft compared with his brother in the field of business." And Walter Lippmann writes: "Poor as they are, the standards of public life are so much more social than those of business that financiers who enter politics regard themselves as philanthropists."

In the medical profession, which is used here as an example of the professions because it is probably less criminal than other professions, are found illegal sales of alcohol and narcotics, abortion, illegal services to underworld criminals, fraudulent reports and testimony in accident cases, fraud in income tax returns, extreme instances of unnecessary treatment and surgical operations, fake specialists, restriction of competition, and fee-splitting. Fee-splitting, for example, is a violation of a specific law in many states and a violation of the conditions of admission to the profession in all states. The physician who participates in fee-splitting tends to send his patients to the surgeon who will split the largest fee rather than to the surgeon who will do the best work. The report has been made that two-thirds of the surgeons in New York City split fees and that more than half of the physicians in a north central state who answered a questionnaire on this point favored fee-splitting.

The financial cost of white collar crime is probably several times as great as the financial cost of all the crimes which are customarily regarded as "the crime problem." An officer of a chain grocery store in one year embezzled $600,000, which was six times as much as the annual losses from five hundred burglaries and robberies of the stores in that chain. Public enemies number one to six secured $130,000 by burglary and robbery in 1938, while the sum stolen by Ivar Krueger is estimated at $250,000,000, or nearly two thousand

times as much. The *New York Times* in 1931 reported four cases of embezzlement in the United States with a loss of more than a million dollars each and a combined loss of nine million dollars. Although a million-dollar burglar or robber is practically unheard of, the million-dollar embezzler is a small-fry among white collar criminals. The estimated loss to investors in one investment trust from 1929 to 1935 was $580,000,000, due primarily to the fact that 75 percent of the values in the portfolio were in securities of affiliated companies, although this investment house advertised the importance of diversification in investments and its expert services in selecting safe investments. The claim was made in Chicago around 1930 that householders lost $54,000,000 in two years during the tenure of a city sealer who granted immunity from inspection to stores which provided Christmas baskets for his constituents. This financial loss from white collar crime, great as it is, is less important than the damage to social relations. White collar crimes violate trust and therefore create distrust; this lowers social morale and produces social disorganization. Many of the white collar crimes attack the fundamental principles of the American institutions. Ordinary crimes, on the other hand, produce little effect on social institutions or social organization.

Statements such as those made above do little more than provide a justification for further investigation. Obviously they are not precise. For that reason, a detailed investigation of violations of certain laws by a sample of the large corporations has been made and is reported in the following chapters.

White collar crime is similar to juvenile delinquency in respect to the stigma. In both cases the procedures of the criminal law are modified so that the stigma of crime will not attach to the offenders. The stigma of crime has been less completely eliminated from juvenile delinquency than from white collar crimes because the procedures for the former are a less complete departure from conventional criminal procedures, because most juvenile delinquents come from the lower class, and because the juveniles are not organized to protect their good names. Because these juvenile delinquents have not been successfully freed from the stigma of crime, they have been generally held to be within the scope of the theories of criminal behavior and in fact provide a large part of the data for criminology. Because the external symbols have been more completely eliminated from white collar crimes, these crimes have generally not been included within the scope of criminology. These procedural symbols, however, are not the essential elements in criminality, and white collar crime belongs logically within the scope of criminology, just as does juvenile delinquency.

Those who insist that moral culpability is a necessary element in crime argue that criminality is lacking in the violations of laws which have eliminated the stigma from crime. This involves the general question of the relation of criminal law to the mores. The laws with which we are here concerned are not arbitrary, as is the regulation that one must drive on the right side of the street. The Sherman Antitrust Law, for example, represents a settled tradition in favor of free competition and free enterprise. This ideology is obvious in the resentment against communism. A violation of the antitrust law is a violation of strongly entrenched moral sentiments. The value of these laws is questioned principally by persons who believe in a more collectivistic system, and these persons are limited to two principal groups, namely, the socialists and the leaders of Big Business. When the business leaders, through corporate activities, violate the antitrust law, they are violating the moral sentiments of practically all sections of the American public except the socialists.

The other laws for the regulation of business are similarly rooted in moral sentiments. Violations of these laws, to be sure, do not call forth as much resentment as do murder and rape, but not all laws in the penal code involve equal resentments by the public. We divide crimes into felonies, which elicit more resentment, and misdemeanors, which elicit less resentment. Within each of these classes, again, the several statutes may be arranged in order of the degree of atrocity of the behavior. White collar crimes, presumably, would be in the lower part of the range in this respect but not entirely out of the range. Moreover, very few of the ordinary crimes arouse much resentment in the ordinary citizen unless the crimes are very spectacular or unless he or his immediate friends are affected. The average citizen, reading in the morning newspaper that the home of an unknown person has been burglarized by another unknown person, has no appreciable increase in blood pressure. Fear and resentment develop in the modern city principally as the result of an accumulation of crimes, as depicted in crime rates or in general descriptions. Such resentment develops under those circumstances both as to white collar crimes and other crimes. Finally, not all parts of the society react in the same manner against the violations of a particular law. It is true that one's business associates do not regard a violation of a business regulation as atrocious. It is true, also, that people in certain slum areas do not regard larceny by their neighbors as atrocious, for they will ordinarily give assistance to these neighbors who are being pursued by the agents of criminal justice.

The differential implementation of the law as it applies to large corporations may be explained by three factors, namely, the status of the businessman, the trend away from punishment, and the relatively unorganized resentment of the public against white collar crimes. Each of these will be described.

First, the methods used in the enforcement of any law are an adaptation to the characteristics of the prospective violators of that law, as appraised by the legislators and the judicial and administrative personnel. The appraisals regarding businessmen, who are the prospective violators of the law now under consideration, include a combination of fear and admiration. Those who are responsible for the system of criminal justice are afraid to antagonize businessmen; among other consequences, such antagonism may result in a reduction in contributions to the campaign funds needed to win the next election. The amendment to the Pure Food and Drug Law of 1938 explicitly excludes from the penal provisions of that law the advertising agencies and media (that is, principally, newspapers and journals) which participate in the misrepresentation. Accessories to crimes are customarily included within the scope of the criminal law, but these accessories are very powerful and influential in the determination of public opinion and they are made immune. Probably much more important than fear, however, is the cultural homogeneity of legislators, judges, and administrators with businessmen. Legislators admire and respect businessmen and cannot conceive of them as criminals; businessmen do not conform to the popular stereotype of "the criminal." The legislators are confident that these respectable gentlemen will conform to the law as the result of very mild pressure. The most powerful group in medieval society secured relative immunity from punishment by "benefit of clergy," and now our most powerful group secures relative immunity by "benefit of business," or more generally by "high social status." The statement of Daniel Drew, a pious old fraud, describes the working of the criminal law with accuracy: "Law is like a cobweb; it's made for flies and the smaller kind of insects, so to speak, but lets the big bumblebees break through. When technicalities of the law stood in my way, I have always been able to brush them aside easy as anything."

This interpretation meets with considerable opposition from persons who insist that this is an egalitarian society in which all men are equal in the eyes of the law. It is not possible to give a complete demonstration of the validity of this interpretation of class differences, but four types of evidence are presented in the following paragraphs as partial demonstration.

The Department of Justice is authorized to use both criminal prosecutions and petitions in equity to enforce the Sherman Antitrust Law. The Department has selected the method of criminal prosecution in a larger proportion of cases against trade unions than of cases against corporations, although the law was enacted primarily because of fear of the corporations. From 1890 to 1929, the Department of Justice initiated 438 actions under this law with decisions favorable to the United

States. Of the actions against business firms and associations of business firms, 27 percent were criminal prosecutions, while of the actions against trade unions 71 percent were criminal prosecutions.[10] This shows that the Department of Justice has been more inclined to use a method which carries with it the stigma of crime against trade unions than against business firms.

The method of criminal prosecution in enforcement of the Sherman Antitrust Law has varied from one presidential administration to another. It was seldom used in the administrations of the presidents who are popularly appraised as friendly toward business, namely, McKinley, Harding, Coolidge, and Hoover.

Businessmen suffered their greatest loss of prestige in the depression which began in 1929. It was precisely in this period of low status of businessmen that the most strenuous efforts were made to enforce the old laws and enact new laws for the regulation of businessmen. The appropriations for this purpose were multiplied several times and persons were selected for their vigor in administration of the law, with the result that the number of decisions against the seventy corporations was quadrupled in the next decade.

The Federal Trade Commission Law states that a violation of the law by a corporation shall be deemed to be also a violation by the officers and directors of the corporation. Businessmen, however, are seldom convicted in criminal courts, and several cases have been reported, like the six percent case in the automobile industry, in which corporations were convicted while the persons who directed the corporations were acquitted. Executives of corporations are convicted in criminal courts principally when they use methods of crime similar to the methods of the lower socio-economic class.

A second factor in the explanation of the differential implementation of the law as applied to white collar criminals is the trend away from penal methods. This trend advanced more rapidly in the area of white collar crimes than that of other crimes. The trend is seen in general in the almost complete abandonment of the extreme penalties of death and physical torture; in the supplanting of conventional penal methods by non-penal methods such as probation and the case-work methods which accompany probation; and in the supplementing of penal methods by non-penal methods, as in the development of case work and educational policies in prisons. These decreases in penal methods are explained by a series of social changes: the increased power of the lower socio-economic class upon which previously most of the penalties were inflicted; the inclusion within the scope of the penal laws of a large part of the upper socio-economic class as illustrated by traffic regulations; the increased social interaction among the classes, which has resulted in increased understanding and sympathy; the failure of penal methods to make substantial reductions in crime rates; and the weakening hold on the legal profession and others of the individualistic and hedonistic psychology which had placed great emphasis on pain in the control of behavior. To some extent overlapping those just mentioned, is the fact that punishment, which was previously the chief reliance for control in the home, the school, and the church, has tended to disappear from those institutions, leaving the State without cultural support for its own penal methods.[11]

The third factor in the differential implementation of the law in the area of white collar crime is the relatively unorganized resentment of the public toward white collar crime. Three reasons for the different relation between law and mores in this area may be given.

1 The violations of law by businessmen are complex and their effects diffused. They are not simple and direct attacks by one person on another person, as is assault and battery. Many of the white collar crimes can be appreciated only by persons who are experts in the occupations in which they occur. A corporation often violates a law for a decade or longer before the administrative agencies or the public become aware of the violation. The effects of these crimes may be diffused over a long period of time and perhaps among millions of people, with no particular person suffering much at a particular time.

2 The public agencies of communication do not express the organized moral sentiments of the community as to white collar crimes, in part because the crimes are complicated and not easily presented as news, but probably in greater part because these agencies of communication are owned or controlled by businessmen and because these agencies are themselves involved in the violations of many of these laws. Public opinion in regard to picking pockets would not be well organized if most of the information regarding this crime came to the public directly from the pickpockets themselves. This failure of the public agencies may be illustrated by the almost complete lack of attention by newspapers to the evidence presented in the trial of A. B. Dick and other business machine companies that these companies maintained a sabotage school in Chicago in which their employees were trained to sabotage the machines of rival companies, and even machines of their own companies if the supplies of rival companies were being used.[12] Many newspapers did not even mention this decision, and those which did mention it placed a brief paragraph on an inner page. Analogous behavior of trade unions, with features as spectacular as in this case, would have been presented with large headlines in the front page of hundreds of newspapers.

3 These laws for the regulation of business belong to a relatively new and specialized part of the statutes. The old common law crimes, as continued in the regular penal codes, were generally limited to person-to-person attacks, which might have been committed by any person in any society.

In the more complex society of the present day, legislatures have felt compelled to regulate many special occupations and other special groups. The penal code of California, for instance, contains an index of penal provisions in the statutes outside of the penal code, which are designed to regulate barbers, plumbers, farmers, corporations, and other special groups. This index occupies 46 pages, and the complete statutes to which reference is made in the index occupy many hundreds of pages. This illustrates the great expansion of penal laws beyond the simple requirements of earlier societies. The teachers of criminal law, who generally confine their attention to the old penal code, miss the larger part of the penal law of the modern state. Similarly, the public is not generally aware of many of these specialized provisions, and consequently the resentment of the public is not organized.

For the three reasons which have been presented, the public does not have the same organized resentment against white collar crimes as against certain of the serious felonies. The relation between the law and mores, finally, tends to be circular. The laws, to a considerable extent, are crystallizations of the mores, and each act of enforcement of the laws tends to re-enforce the mores. The laws regarding white collar crimes, which conceal the criminality of the behavior, have been less effective than other criminal laws in re-enforcing the mores.

The answers to the questions posed at the beginning of this chapter may be summarized in the following propositions: First, the white collar crimes which are discussed in this book have the general criteria of criminal behavior, namely, legal definition of social injuries and legal provision of penal sanctions. They are therefore cognate with other crimes. Second, these white collar crimes have generally not been regarded by criminologists as cognate with other crimes and as within the scope of theories of criminal behavior because the administrative and judicial procedures have been different for these violations of criminal law than for other violations of criminal law. Third, this differential implementation of the criminal law as applied to businessmen, is explained by the status of the businessmen, the trend away from punitive methods, and the relatively unorganized resentment of the public toward white collar crimes.

Since this analysis is concerned with violations of laws by corporations, a brief description of the relation of the corporation to the criminal law is necessary. Three or four generations ago the courts with unanimity decided that corporations could not commit crimes. These decisions were based on one or more of the following principles. First, since the corporation is a legislative artifact and does not have a mind or soul, it cannot have criminal intent and therefore cannot commit a crime. Second, since a corporation is not authorized to do unlawful acts, the agents of a corporation are not authorized to do unlawful acts. If those agents commit unlawful acts, they do so in their personal capacity and not in their capacity as agents. They may be punished, therefore, as persons but not as agents. Third, with a few exceptions, the only penalties that can be imposed on corporations, if found guilty of crimes, are fines. These fines are injuries to stockholders rather than to the agents who are directly responsible for the violations of the laws. Therefore, as a matter of policy, the agents rather than the stockholders should be punished.

In contrast with earlier practice, corporations are now frequently convicted of crimes. Corporations have been convicted of larceny, manslaughter, keeping disorderly houses, breaking the Sabbath, destruction of property, and a variety of other crimes.[13] Such decisions involve reversal of the three principles on which the earlier decisions were based. First, the corporation is not merely a legislative artifact. Associations of persons existed prior to the law and some of these associations have been recognized as entities by legislatures. These corporations and other associations are instrumental in determining legislation. Consequently legislation is in part an artifact of corporations, just as corporations are in part an artifact of legislatures.[14] Second, the requirement that criminal intent be demonstrated has been eliminated from an increasing number of criminal laws, as has been described above. Third, the location of responsibility has been extremely difficult in many parts of modern society, and responsibility is certainly a much more complicated concept than is ordinarily believed. The old employers' liability laws, which were based on the principle of individual responsibility, broke down because responsibility for industrial accidents could not be located. Workmen's compensation laws were substituted, with their principle that the industrial establishment should bear the cost of industrial accidents. Some attention has been given to the location of responsiblity for decisions in the policies of large corporations.[15] Although responsibility for actions of particular types may be located, power to modify such actions lies also at various other points. Owing largely to the complexity of this concept, the question of individual responsibility is frequently waived and penalties are imposed on corporations. This does, to be sure, affect the stockholders who may have almost no power in making decisions as to policy; the same thing is true of other penalties which have been suggested as substitutes for fines on corporations, namely, dissolution of the corporation, suspension of business for a specified time, restriction of sphere of action of the corporation, confiscation of goods, publicity, surety for good behavior, and supervision by the court.

Two questions may be raised regarding the responsibility of corporations from the point of view of the statistical tabulation of violations of law presented in an earlier chapter. The first is whether a corporation should be held responsible for the action of a special department of the corporation. The advertising department, for example, may prepare and distribute advertisements which violate the law. The customary plea of the executives of the corporation is that they were ignorant of and not responsible for the action of the special department. This plea is akin to the alibi of the ordinary criminal and need not be taken seriously. The departments of a corporation know that their recognition by the executives of the corporation depends on results and that few questions will be asked if results are achieved. In the rare case in which the executives are not only unaware of but sincerely opposed to the policy of a particular department, the corporation is customarily held responsible by the court. That is the only question of interest in the present connection. Consequently, an illegal act is reported as the act of the corporation without consideration of the location of responsibility within the corporation.

The second question is concerned with the relation between the parent corporation and the subsidiaries. This relationship varies widely from one corporation to another and even within one corporate system. When subsidiaries are prosecuted for violations of law, the parent company gener-ally pleads ignorance of the methods which were used by the subsidiary. This, again, is customarily an alibi, although it may be true in some cases. For instance, the automobile corporations generally insist that the labor policy of each subsidiary is determined by that subsidiary and is not within the control of the parent company. However, when a labor controversy arose in a plant in Texas and a settlement was proposed by the labor leaders, the personnel department of that plant replied: "We must consult Detroit." They reported the following morning: "Detroit says 'no.' " For the present purpose, the corporation and its subsidiaries are treated as a unit, without regard to the location of responsibility within the unit.

## REFERENCES AND NOTES

1  Sheldon and Eleanor Glueck, *One Thousand Juvenile Delinquents*, Cambridge, Mass., 1934; *Five Hundred Criminal Careers*, New York, 1930; *Five Hundred Delinquent Women*, New York, 1934.

2  *The Prisoners' Antecedents*, Washington, D.C.: U.S. Bureau of the Census, 1923, p. 32.

3  Clifford R. Shaw and Henry D. McKay, *Juvenile Delinquency and Urban Areas*, Chicago, 1943.

4  An excellent analysis of a group of this nature is by Pauline V. Young, *The Pilgrims of Russian-Town*, Chicago, 1932.

5  These studies are summarized by Thorsten Sellin, *Research Memorandum on Crime in the Depression*, New York, 1937.

6  Edwin H. Sutherland, *The Professional Thief*, Chicago, 1937.

7  The term "white collar" is used here to refer principally to business managers and executives, in the sense in which it was used by a president of General Motors who wrote *An Autobiography of a White Collar Worker*.

8  F. P. McEvoy, "The Lie Detector Goes into Business," *Readers Digest*, February 1941, p. 69.

9  Roger W. Riis and John Patric, *The Repairman Will Get You If You Don't Look Out*, Garden City, N.Y., 1942.

10  Percentages compiled from cases listed in the report of the Department of Justice, *Federal Antitrust Laws, 1938*.

11  The trend away from penal methods suggests that the penal sanction may not be a completely adequate criterion in the definition of crime.

12  *New York Times*, March 26, 1948, pp. 31, 37.

13   George F. Canfield, "Corporate Responsibility for Crime," *Columbia Law Review*, vol. 14 (June 1941) pp. 469–481; Frederic P. Lee, "Corporate Liability," *Columbia Law Review*, vol. 28 (February 1928) pp. 1–28; Max Radin, "Endless Problem of Corporate Personality," *Columbia Law Review*, vol. 32 (April 1932) pp. 643–667.

14   For a summary of classical theories of corporate personality, see Frederick Hallis, *Corporate Personality*, London, 1930. See also Henri Lévy-Brühl, "Collective Personality in the Law," *Annales Sociologiques*, series C, no. 3 (1938).

15   Robert A. Gordon, *Business Leadership in the Large Corporation*, Washington, D.C., 1945.

## SUPPLEMENTAL READINGS

Cavan, Ruth Shonle: "The Concepts of Tolerance and Contraculture as Applied to Delinquency," *Sociological Quarterly*, vol. 2 (October 1961), pp. 243–258.

Clemmer, Donald: *The Prison Community*, New York: Holt, Rinehart and Winston, 1958.

Empey, LaMar: "Delinquency Theory and Recent Research," *Journal of Research in Crime and Delinquency*, vol. 4 (January 1967), pp. 28–42.

Enker, Arnold: "Perspectives on Plea Bargaining," *Task Force Report: The Courts*, President's Commission on Law Enforcement and Administration of Justice, Washington, D.C.: U.S. Government Printing Office, 1967, pp. 108–119.

Fuller, Lon L.: *Anatomy of the Law*, New York: Federick A. Praeger, Inc., 1968.

Giallombardo, Rose: *Society of Women: A Study of a Women's Prison*, New York: John Wiley & Sons, Inc., 1966.

Gibbons, Don C.: *Changing the Lawbreaker*, Englewood Cliffs, N.J.: Prentice-Hall, Inc., 1965.

Glaser, Daniel: "National Goals and Indicators for the Reduction of Crime and Delinquency," *The Annals*, vol. 371 (May 1967), pp. 105–126.

Goldstein, Abraham S.: *The Insanity Defense*, New Haven, Conn.: Yale University Press, 1967.

Kadish, Sanford H.: "The Crisis of Overcriminalization," *The Annals*, vol. 374 (November 1967), pp. 157–170.

Lemert, Edwin M.: "The Juvenile Court: Quest and Realities," *Task Force Report: Juvenile Delinquency and Youth Crime*, President's Commission on Law Enforcement and Administration of Justice, Washington, D.C.: U.S. Government Printing Office, 1967, pp. 91–106 (see also *In re Gault*, U.S. Supreme Court, May 15, 1967, pp. 57–76).

Matza, David: *Delinquency and Drift*, New York: John Wiley & Sons, Inc., 1964.

Schafer, Stephen: *The Victim and His Criminal*, New York: Random House, Inc., 1968.

Schur, Edwin M.: *Law and Society*, New York: Random House, Inc., 1967.

Short, James F., Jr., and Fred L. Strodtbeck: *Group Process and Gang Delinquency*, Chicago: The University of Chicago Press, 1965.

Skolnick, Jerome H.: *Justice without Trial: Law Enforcement in Demo-Society*, New York: John Wiley & Sons, Inc., 1966.

Sutherland, Edwin H.: *The Professional Thief*, Chicago: The University of Chicago Press, 1937.

Sykes, Gresham M.: *Crime and Society*, 2d ed., New York: Random House, Inc., 1967.

Wolfgang, Marvin E., and Franco Ferracuti: *The Subculture of Violence*, London: Social Science Paperbacks, 1967.

*The Challenge of Crime in a Free Society, President's Commission on Law Enforcement and Administration of Justice*, Washington, D.C.: U.S. Government Printing Office, 1967.

"The Police and the Community," *Task Force Report: The Police*, President's Commission on Law Enforcement and Administration of Justice, Washington, D.C.: U.S. Government Printing Office, 1967, pp. 144–207.

Rosett, Arthur: "The Negotiated Guilty Plea," *The Annals*, vol. 374 (November 1967), pp. 70–81.

Problems such as drug addiction, alcoholism, sex offenses, and mental illness are often considered more in terms of personality characteristics of the individual than in terms of social forces. Personality traits are usually not innate, but bear at least some relation to personal or social interaction and the prevailing sociocultural environment. Thus, although the basic dimensions of cause, diagnosis, and treatment from a medical standpoint are outside the province of sociology, the sociologist is interested in personality problems as manifestations of the existing social order, the public's reactions to the behavior deviations of others, the treatment of and probable outcome for persons considered to have problem status, and the functional aspects of such problems as they relate to society as a whole.

A few definitions are in order as a guide to our subsequent discussion. Personality refers to the integration of an individual's basic habits, attitudes, values, beliefs, and sentiments that are acquired through socialization and that affect the quality of his interaction with other persons. Personality deviation or disorganization is any enduring condition in which an individual is unable to integrate his perceived roles in a particular situation or group into an accepted societal pattern of behavior. For our purposes drug addiction is defined as the continual use of any habit-forming narcotic to the point of inability to discontinue further consumption. The primary characteristics, as specified by the World Health Organization, are (1) an overpowering compulsion to continue taking the drug, (2) a tendency to increase the amount, and (3) a psychological, and occasionally physical, dependence on the effects of the drug.

Prostitution and homosexuality are the sex offenses of greatest prevalence. Prostitution is defined as promiscuous sexual intercourse, with emotional indifference, for financial gain. The key sources of societal disapproval are the separation of the sexual act from the family and the element of promiscuity. Homosexuality is defined as sexual relations between persons of the same sex. The designation alcoholic should probably be reserved for those who have lost control of their drinking and are unable to regulate the amount of their intake. This category would therefore not include the heavy drinker who makes liquor a part of daily life.

The difficulty in drawing a sharp line between the deviant and nondeviant personality is particularly apparent in the area of mental disorder because of the influence of value judgments. For example, the variation among social classes in what is considered appropriate or acceptable behavior prevents a more specific definition of personality deviation than the one above. An operational distinction is often made in the degree of mental impairment by the terms "neurosis" and "psychosis." The psychoses (schizophrenia, paranoia, and the manic-depressive and organic psychoses) are delimited by a markedly impaired perception of reality, often with delusions, hallucinations, and disorientation, and they usually necessitate at least one period of institutionalization. The person subject to neurosis has found it difficult to adjust to his environment but retains at least a functional contact with reality and can be treated within the community.

Each of the personality problems merits consideration at length because of the public's tendency to express its great concern in oversimplified and stereotyped forms. Even the professional literature is too often handicapped by simplistic and biased analyses that are invalidated by more current data and theoretical formulations. Since an introductory passage cannot cover in detail even the limited number of personality disorders noted above, perhaps it will suffice to survey some of the misconceptions pertaining to these problems. Hopefully the student will wish to explore in depth the issues raised in the remainder of this introduction and in the readings.

The widespread misconceptions about the behavior and traits of offenders are well illustrated in the popular concept of the sex offender. Contrary to popular opinion, most sex offenses are not distinguished by violence, nor are the violators dangerous "sex fiends." In fact, the vast majority of rape cases consist of sexually normal behavior, since they are for statutory rape (usually intercourse without force with a female below the age of consent) rather than for forcible rape. Even in cases of forcible rape Menachem Amir found little support for the "sex-fiend" syndrome in an analysis of 646 cases that occurred in Philadelphia from 1958 to 1960. He also found that rape is an *intra*racial rather than an *inter*racial event, that in more than one-third of the cases the victim knew the offender quite well and the offense frequently took place in the residence of one of the parties, and that "over 50 percent of the victims failed to resist their attackers in any way."

It is also commonly believed that the drug addict experiences a wonderful euphoria when using drugs. Although this may be true initially, shortly thereafter the addict must continue simply to offset the effects of withdrawal or to bring himself to a state of normalcy. As Norman E. Zinberg has recommended, discussions of drug abuse should incorporate the distinction between the "oblivion-seekers" and the "experience-seekers." The former, who are primarily from the lower socioeconomic strata of the population, use drugs such as heroin to "escape from lives that seem unbearable and hopeless." It is this category that has been the focus of attention by official agencies over the years. Although not recognized as a real problem until recently, the experience seekers, who come from the middle or upper socioeconomic strata and who seek to expand their sensory capacities with drugs, may well constitute the essence of the drug problem in the near future. The article by Richard H. Blum, prepared for the President's Crime Commission, documents the conclusion that drug abuse is far wider in scope than addiction to narcotics.

The fact that none of us is immune to mental illness should suggest a revision in the typical views of the nature of mental impairment. Thomas Scheff's observation that many persons experience transitory mental disorders points to a difference in degree rather than kind. Alan Dershowitz, in a provocative article in the last chapter, discusses the current tendency to overpredict the likelihood of serious consequences if persons with impaired mental processes are not confined, and the balance of interests of the potential patient and society.

The above observations are not intended to minimize the extent of personality problems. The looseness in definitions makes accurate estimates impossible, but the best available projections are 60,000 to 100,000 active drug addicts, approximately 300,000 full-time prostitutes, some 3 million male and 1.5 million female true homosexuals (that is, on the basis of the Kinsey findings), and 5 million alcoholics. No estimates for mental disorders are feasible in light of the definitional handicaps noted earlier. The use of tranquilizers has facilitated a reduction of about 20 percent over the past decade in the number of patients in long-term mental hospitals to a total of approximately 450,000 in 1966; however, the total of all persons confined during the year is considerably higher as a result of patient movement in and out of these hospitals.

Discussions of the causes of personality problems are also clouded by stereotyped portrayals. Certainly one of the best illustrations is the belief that alcoholism is a disease of organic origin. The process leading to alcoholism is not fully understood, but the efforts to discover what variables determine susceptibility have generally eliminated both physiological and psychological factors, and sociocultural antecedents are increasingly the focus of attention. The conclusion is much the same for the etiology of drug addiction; it is seen as a socially engendered behavior that does not depend on the prior existence of a specific personality syndrome or genetic background. The key word here is "prior." Sociologists postulate that the personality traits associated with these problems are more likely to be a consequence of the deviant behavior than a cause of it. Thus, although potential addicts and alcoholics may manifest a wide variation in personality characteristics, career addicts or alcoholics show a marked similarity in traits.

Several of the more significant social factors thought to underlie mental disorders are social pressure to "succeed" without the means or ability to gain the goals defined as "success," conflict over which values to attain or which roles to enact, and primary emphasis on one role to the neglect or exclusion of other socially demanded roles. Thomas J. Scheff contends that even though the causes of "psychiatric symptoms" are not adequately understood at present, the sociologists can analyze significant issues without isolating the exact origins of mental illnesses. One illustration is provided by his discussion of "stable" mental disorders as a product, in large part, of labeling processes, which gain substantive content from the interplay of the beliefs of the mentally ill and those reacting to them. Elsewhere Scheff has suggested additional examples, including descriptions of behavior and the conditions for its recognition, treatment, and termination; conflicts between medical and legal institutions in connection with hospitalization, divorce, and criminal justice; and overall appraisals of the impact of such disorders on the community.

William Simon and John H. Gagnon are similarly disenchanted with the extreme emphasis placed on the etiology of homosexual behavior. As they note, "we have allowed the homosexual's sexual object choice to dominate and control our imagery of him and have let this aspect of his total life experience appear to determine all his products, concerns, and activities." Their formulation views homosexuality as a heterogeneous category based on the variety of homosexual and nonsexual roles the homosexual may adopt and emphasizes the ways in which nonsexual components (earning a living, maintaining a residence, relations with family, and religion) influence sexual roles and commitments.

It is often falsely assumed that we know how to stop the occurrence of these problems. Despite the desire expressed by Scheff and Simon and Gagnon to minimize the attention focused on the origins of disorders, effective prevention depends on a greater understanding of the causal nexuses than we now have. Intervention for preventive purposes is relatively meaningless unless it can be effectively concentrated. If the causes of alcoholism are not known, what should be the recommended drinking patterns for college students? What parental relationship will decrease the prospects of future homosexual behavior? What distinguishes the "pot" smoker who goes on to experiment with narcotics from those who are satisfied with the comparatively moderate potency of marihuana? Even if we had definitive answers to this question, we would have difficulty selecting from among such solutions to drug abuse as legalization of some drugs, licensing of some users, sponsoring Synanon programs, and developing drug antagonists.

The closest thing to a truism is that rigid control techniques are not the answer. Harsh legal penalties will not deter the alcoholic, the drug addict, or the compulsive sex offender. These are social-welfare, medical, or psychiatric problems that are not alleviated by the traditional legal processes. In this connection, the popular view that personality deviants have a low potential for rehabilitation is a serious overgeneralization. There is solid evidence for the adage "once an addict, always an addict" in the almost 100 percent relapse rate for all but very few of the present treatment programs; however, the small proportion of known addicts over the age of thirty-five requires some explanation. From a different perspective, it may be quite difficult to effect a "cure" for homosexuality, but a therapist may assist the individual in making an adequate personal adjustment to his own behavior; or if the general public were less prone to stigmatize the homosexual in nonsexual contexts, then his deviant behavior in one area would not have the negative consequences that flow from a generalized stereotype of psychopathology. The treatment prospects for a substantial portion of the mentally disordered are favorable if the present paucity of personnel and facilities is overcome and the chasm between lower-class patients and psychiatrists can be bridged. The former limitation has been partially alleviated by drug-therapy programs administered within the community.

In conclusion, probably the most significant misconception from the sociological frame of reference is the public's failure to recognize explicitly the functional aspects of deviant behavior.

The first article, by Lewis A. Coser, offers a provocative analysis of the positive contributions of deviance for the larger society. Coser's thesis is that deviance can be profitably examined as the inevitable outcome of the existing social arrangements, and he discusses in depth a number of the functional dimensions of deviance. Scheff presents a sociological theory of the development of stable patterns of mental disorders. Similarly, Simon and Gagnon advance an explanation of homosexuality that integrates the developmental processes of both deviant and nondeviant behaviors. The contribution by Egon Bittner, which describes police practices on skid row, focuses on the pragmatic aspects of the management of large numbers of deviants through procedures designed to minimize outbreaks of trouble. Richard H. Blum synthesizes and evaluates the available data on the relationship of selected mind-altering drugs (marihuana, hallucinogens, and tranquilizers) to dangerous behavior, with the goal of making recommendations for research, penal reform, control programs, and dissemination of information.

## 43   FUNCTIONS OF DEVIANT BEHAVIOR   LEWIS A. COSER

Most contemporary sociological theorizing about deviant behavior has tended to focus on mechanisms of social control. The analysis of instances in which behavior that violates institutional expectations may be considered functional for an ongoing social system has been largely neglected. This paper tries to highlight some functions of deviance for social structures. This does not deny, of course, the dysfunctions of deviance, but only suggests that an exclusive emphasis on these may result in inadequate and distorted analysis.

### CONSEQUENCES OF DEVIANCE FOR INTERNAL GROUP RELATIONS

We have known ever since Durkheim that crime alerts the common conscience and contributes to the revival and maintenance of common sentiments by arousing the community to the consequences of infringements of rules. "Crime," he wrote, "brings together upright consciences and concentrates them."[1] It will also be remembered that Mead wrote in a similar vein: "The criminal . . . is responsible for a sense of solidarity, aroused among those whose attitude would otherwise be

Reprinted from *The American Journal of Sociology,* vol. 68 (September 1962), pp. 172–182, by permission of the author and The University of Chicago Press. Copyright© 1962 by The University of Chicago Press.

This article was substantially completed during the author's stay at the Institute for Social Research, Oslo, Norway, under a Fulbright Senior Research Scholarship. I wish to express my appreciation to a number of European colleagues, too numerous to mention, whose critical reading of an earlier draft of this paper was most helpful. I owe a special debt to Johan Galtung, of the University of Oslo and the Institute for Social Research, Oslo, to Yrjö Littunen, School of Social Sciences, Tampere, Finland, and to Robert K. Merton, of Columbia University, who made a number of very valuable suggestions. Several propositions of this paper were adumbrated in the author's *The Functions of Social Conflict*, Glencoe, Ill.: The Free Press, 1956.

centered upon interests quite divergent from each other." "The attitude of hostility toward the lawbreaker has the unique advantage of uniting all members of the community."[2] Durkheim and Mead both state that, though an individual criminal act elicits negative sanctions, crime also has positive consequences for the society or group since the breach of a norm calls attention to its importance for the common weal. Like bodily pain serves as a danger signal, calling for the mobilization of energies against the source of disease, so crime, these writers argue, alerts the body social and leads to the mobilization of otherwise inactive defense mechanisms.

Durkheim and Mead are often quoted in current theorizing, yet their pertinent insight on the functions of crime has been somewhat neglected. Thus Parsons focuses attention on mechanisms of social control which serve to check deviant behavior but fails to consider possible contributions that deviance may make to the system in which it occurs. He distinguishes types of deviance that "fall within the range of permissiveness which should be considered normal to people under certain strains" and "a vicious circle of gratification of deviant wishes [leading to the] undermining of the main value system."[3] But he does not consider those deviant acts which, though not considered "normal to people under strain," reinforce rather than undermine the social system. We shall see in a later part of this paper that different types of deviant behavior must be discussed in terms of their differential impact. Even if we should agree, for the purpose of discussion, that deviants are always motivated to defy the group's norms, nothing requires us to assume that such acts may not have the unanticipated consequence of strengthening those norms.

Durkheim and Mead see the functional consequences of deviance in the strengthening of the group which results from the collective rejection of the deviant. This assumption is indeed borne out by much of small-group research. An article summarizing much of the research findings in this field states, for example: "When a member deviates markedly from a group standard, the remaining members of the group bring pressures to bear on the deviate to bring him back to conformity. If pressure is of no avail, the deviate is rejected and cast out of the group."[4] Statements such as these seem to imply, though the authors do not explicitly say so, that deviations from group standards lead to the mobilization of the group's energies. But small-group research has not adequately considered the possibility that the repression of deviance may not in all cases be functional for the group. Moreover, it has not been shown that all types of groups will reject deviance under all circumstances. These two variables—"strengthening of the group" and "rejection of the deviant"—call attention to four possible cases: (1) the deviant is opposed and the group is strengthened—the situation discussed by Durkheim and Mead; (2) the deviant is tolerated or even accepted and the group is strengthened; (3) the deviant is rejected and the group is weakened; and (4) the deviant is not rejected and the group is weakened. The last case is relatively unproblematical, but the other three have not been given sufficient systematic attention in sociological theorizing, although empirical evidence about them is available.

**1** *The deviant is opposed and the group is strengthened* In the process of uniting itself against deviance, the community not only revives and maintains common sentiments but creatively establishes moral rules and redefines "normal" behavior. "Each time the community brings sanctions against a detail of behavior . . . it sharpens the authority of the violated norm and redefines the boundaries within which the norm exercises its special jurisdiction."[5] Thus the criminal, the scapegoat, the mentally ill, in their diverse ways, allow the group to reaffirm not only its social but also its moral identity, for they establish signposts which serve as normative yardsticks.[6] Deviance "establishes the point beyond which behavior is no longer within acceptable reach of the norm, and in this way gives substance and authority to the norm itself."[7]

Thus, definition of what is considered normal in the group takes place with reference to what is considered deviant, and morality is given its content through the contrast provided by that which is not moral. We touch here upon a dialectical relation which Gestalt psychology has discussed in detail with respect to perception. Figures cannot be perceived except in relation to grounds setting them off. In the same way, normalcy can hardly be perceived except against the ground of deviance; to be "good" makes sense only in relation to being "bad."

It is with the body social as it is with individuals: moral indignation against deviants serves to purge the righteous from a sense of their own sins and unworthiness and helps sustain their moral identity. Such indignation may well serve as a reaction-forming, securing the ego against the repressed impulse to identify with the criminal.[8] It is against the ground of their deviance that the righteous achieve the comforting affirmation of their normality. Inasmuch as "our" innocence is contingent upon "their" guilt, dereliction by others provides occasion for self-congratulations.

But dereliction by others also provides occasion for self-examination. Thus, when a crime is committed in the community, religious leaders use the occasion to exhort the congregation to re-examine themselves and "purify their souls." Deviance is taken as a warning that there is something foul in the state of Denmark that needs correction—correction not only on the individual level but in the social realm as well. Thus, Stewart and Helen Perry have shown that in the mental hospitals deviant patients may, by their acting out, "act as a fire alarm for the ward." By upsetting the social equilibrium of the ward, the "fire-alarm patient" may highlight such defects as understaffing, staff overwork, and the like and thus dramatize the need for remedial action.[9] Bureaucratic organizations are familiar with similar situations in which the failure effectively to control behavior in terms of official goals will be used by practitioners as a convincing means for appealing for increased resources. Thus many organizations (as well as many role incumbents) have a vested interest, though rarely acknowledged, in the very deviant behavior which they are set up to combat, for deviance provides the reason for their existence: Increases in deviance may help them to highlight the need for strengthening the organization (or the department in the organization) to cope more effectively with disturbing behavior.

**2** What has been said so far about reactions to deviance—be it a spontaneous, that is, a non-deliberate "pulling together" of group members, or deliberate policy—refers to those instances in which deviant behavior leads to its rejection. The second case is that of *tolerance or acceptance of the deviant with concomitant strengthening of the group.* There are groups in which deviants provide the occasion for a reaffirmation of values without incurring rejection. Thus in a seminal paper, Dentler and Erikson give illustrations from Quaker work camps and Army Basic Training Squads where deviants do indeed "become critical referents for establishing the end points (of the range of possibilities judged permissible within the group's boundaries)"—the figure-ground effect discussed earlier —and where "the deviant is someone about whom something should be done, and the group, in expressing this concern, is able to affirm its essential cohesion and indicate what the group is and what it can do."[10] However, in these cases the occasion for affirmation of cohesion does not come from rejecting the deviant but rather from protecting him: he "becomes the ward of the group. . . . In a setting in which having buddies is highly valued, he is unlikely to receive any sociometric choices at all. But it would be quite unfortunate to assume that he is therefore isolated from the group or repudiated by it: an accurate sociogram would have the deviant individual encircled by the interlocking sociometric preferences, sheltered by the group structure."[11]

It would seem that in some groups tolerance of deviance is a function of a specific value system: among Quakers, "tolerance" is a salient component of the ideology. In tolerating or protecting a deviant, they practice what they publicly profess. (It may even be said that such groups do, in fact, need social objects upon whom "tolerance" can be exercised because they provide the occasion for testing and confirming their values.)

If it is objected that tolerance of deviance in army units is merely a manifestation of opposition to official army goals, that is, part of a collective effort to "get back" at army authority, this only confirms the analytical point: by setting itself off against an intolerant environment, the group exercises tolerance precisely with regard to those individuals who would otherwise be the victims of the very environment whose values the group rejects. In both cases—Quaker camps and army units— acceptance of deviance is contingent upon the value system of the group. What Kelley and Thibault say about the rejection of deviance applies to its tolerance as well: "Generally, the same factors responsible for the emergence of group standards will also in large measure be responsible for the motivations to enforce conformity to them."[12] Thus in the groups discussed by Dentler and Erikson, the practice of tolerance—whether positively stated as a "way of life" as among Quakers, or stated in opposition to the intolerance of army authorities as in army units—would seem to be a basis for the emergence or strengthening of group standards and would therefore be the guiding principle that motivates the responses of group members to non-conformity among them.

**3** So far, the assertion has been made that deviants offer to group members the opportunity to reaffirm common values, be it by providing an occasion to oppose them collectively (case 1), or by bringing about a situation in which their acceptance or tolerance serves as an affirmation of beliefs held in common (case 2). In these cases, the groups were strengthened. There are groups, however, for whom *rigid and repeated rejection of deviants has serious dysfunctional consequences* (case 3). Rigidly structured sects or radical political organizations of the sectarian type provide examples in point. Even a cursory perusal of the history of the Trotskyist movement leaves no doubt about the fact that the lack of ability to tolerate deviance led to further and further fragmentation of the movement. Religious sects provide similar examples.

To be sure, in such groups each single case of negative sanctions against deviant behavior led, at the moment the act of sanctioning occurred, to a reaffirmation of values among those who remained faithful. Yet, rejection of nonconformity as an ongoing organizational activity was disruptive as a *process* in that in the long run it weakened the group in relation to its external environment.

This calls attention to the need to consider the relation between the group within which deviance occurs and the external context.

### CONSEQUENCES OF DEVIANCE FOR GROUP RELATIONS WITH THE OUTSIDE

In the first two situations discussed—one of rejection and the other of tolerance of the deviant—our concern was with relationships within the group. It now turns out that what may be functional for the group in one respect—that is, the reaffirmation of its norms—may turn out to be detrimental in another respect, namely, in its relation to the outside. To consider only the internal consequences of deviance and of responses to it, that is, to limit analysis to the group processes within given subsystems without paying attention to the group's relations with the outside, is a common pitfall in sociological theorizing, especially in small-group research. In contrast to much of such research, Kelley and Shapiro set up an experimental group in a situation in which the group's norms were discordant with outside reality.[13] In this situation conformity to these norms tended to be detrimental to the success of the group. (Situations similar to those contrived in the laboratory are likely to occur when disparate rates of change impinge on a group and lead to cultural lags and dysfunctional resistances of vested interests.)

It turned out that in these experimental groups deviation from the norms did not call forth rejection. This case is, in this respect, more similar to case 2 discussed above, for here also deviance is accepted. While in the Quaker camps deviance may be *implicitly* welcomed as an occasion for group members to live up to professed values, in these experimental groups deviant behavior seems to have been *explicitly* welcomed as an occasion for better adaptability to outside reality. Indeed, it turned out that in these groups persons who deviated from the group's norms were also those who were judged to be highly acceptable as coworkers.

A consideration of the external environment for the understanding of internal dynamics of deviance and responses to it makes it possible to throw more light on the behavior of the Quaker camps and army units discussed earlier. There also the relation with the outside would seem to be one important determinant of inside responses: in Quaker groups and army camps alike, the norms that guide the behavior of members toward deviants seemed to consist in *countervalues* to patterns prevailing on the outside. Thus in Kelley and Thibault's groups, as in the groups studied by Dentler and Erikson, outside reality was an important determinant—whether as a spur for adaptation or for opposition to it—of the responses to deviant behavior within.

The evidence so far indicates that the widely accepted notion that groups always reject deviance is, at the least, open to question. To be sure, deviance may be *proscribed* as in the examples of criminal behavior used by Durkheim and Mead. Yet, a deviant redefinition of norms may be *permitted*, as when the value system of the group prescribes tolerance. It may be *preferred*, as when it is accepted as a means for better adaptability of the group.[14]

Deviant behavior may also be *prescribed*, as during periodic feasts when the participants are expected to infringe the norms of ordinary behavior.[15] These, however, are instances where it would be deviant not to deviate; that is, they are special instances of conformity which do not concern us here.

The recognition that departure from the norms may be preferred, permitted, or proscribed raises two related problems:

1 The license to deviate is differentially distrib-

uted among members of a group. For example, there is tolerance of deviance for special role incumbents such as the "star," the "stranger," or the "fool";[16] or there is some expectation of deviance for some group leaders who are supposed to be flexible and to depart from the norms to further the tasks of the group.

2 Another important problem raised by the differential response to deviance is the need to distinguish between different types of deviant behavior.

## DEVIANCE AND INNOVATION

So far the concept of deviance has been used here in accordance with it definition in most contemporary sociological work.[17] An overarching concept of this kind has the distinct merit of drawing attention to the structural similarities of a variety of behaviors which might otherwise seem but little related. Yet at the same time, it has the disadvantage of obscuring distinctions which might be crucial in certain contexts.[18] Thus Merton distinguishes nonconformity from such other kinds of deviant behavior as crime or juvenile delinquency. Criminal behavior is impelled by private and self-centered motives which are by definition antisocial. Innovating dissent of a nonconforming minority, on the other hand, may be manifestly intended to serve group interests in a more effective manner than the conforming majority. "These kinds of 'deviant behavior' differ structurally, culturally and functionally."[19]

While both the nonconformist and the criminal defy normative expectations, they are profoundly dissimilar: the nonconformist's dissent "is not a private dereliction, but a thrust toward a new morality (or a restoration of an old and almost forgotten morality) . . . ."[20] I have argued elsewhere in a similar vein that "When all forms of dissent are [considered] criminal by definition, we are in the presence of a system which is ill-equipped to reveal fully the extent to which nonconformity, as distinct from crime, involves the striving forward on an alternative moral basis rather than moral deviation."[21]

To be sure, the behavior of the nonconformist may bring forth community reactions similar to those occasioned by criminal violations of the norms, yet the innovations he proposes allegedly in the interest of the group's welfare are likely to be evaluated in their own right, if only by a minority. This is why, as distinct from the case of the criminal, there is likely to be buried under layers of hostility a certain measure of respect for the disinterested dissenter. Being oriented toward the collectivity, he is led to seek and to find an audience within it. The innovator sends a message intended to be picked up and diffused. His behavior proceeds, so to speak, in broad daylight in order to attract a maximum audience. While the criminal seeks to minimize the chances of detection, the innovator seeks maximum publicity for his message. One may argue with an innovator but hardly with a criminal.[22]

Just as with various types of deviance, the innovations which the nonconformist proposes for the consideration of the group may be prescribed or proscribed with various degrees of tolerance, depending on the structured and normative context. Moreover, they may be wittingly favored by the group or the group may unwittingly be favored by them.

When innovation is highly valued, as, for example, in scientific societies, innovating behavior must be considered a special type of conformity rather than deviation. In the context of the institution of science, innovations and discoveries, provided they satisfy the criteria of evidence, are highly valued variants that permit the goals of the group to be more adequately met—though even here the innovator may at first encounter the resistance of vested interests.[23]

On the other hand, in groups which place no value on innovation, an innovating response will be considered truly nonconformist. In contrast to the case of the criminal, however, at least some of the group's members might perceive that the innovator intends to perform a positive task for the group. This might then lead to a conflict within the group over the issue raised. If this happens, the innovator has transformed individual nonconformity into group conflict and has raised it from the idiosyncratic to the collective level.

Thus, pressures for innovation are likely to result in the emergence of social conflicts within a system. Such conflicts, as I have shown elsewhere, may be highly functional for that system.[24] Dewey has noted that "conflict shocks us out of sheep-like passivity, and sets us at noting and contriving . . . it is a *sine qua non* of reflection and ingenuity."[25] The innovator's behavior may serve to reduce the chances that adherence to the routines of yesterday render the group unable to meet the challenges of today. The innovator may thus be a pace-setter and a setter of new standards. By attacking vested interests in the habitual, the innovator helps insure that the group does not stifle in the deadening routines of ritualism.

What is said here of group process indeed applies to every fruitful interaction as well. Interaction does not merely consist of mutual filling of expectations but in ever renewed innovating contributions. In much current theorizing it is assumed that the equilibrium of a group is a function of the extent to which group members habitually conform to each other's expectations. The maintenance of complementarity between the interaction orientations of alter and ego is said to be the mark of a stable social system.[26] "This model seems to assume," Gouldner has noted, "that each of a sequence of identical conforming acts will yield either the same or an increasing degree of appreciation and satisfaction and will thus elicit the same or increasing amounts of reward."[27] Yet, "later conforming actions are worth less than earlier ones, in terms of the rewards or propensity to reciprocate which they elicit." When conformity is taken for granted, the propensity to reciprocate is weakened in the long run. Homans also states this principle of satiation, a version of marginal utility: "The more often a man has in the recent past received a rewarding activity from another, the less valuable any further unit of that activity becomes to him."[28]

The Finnish sociologist Yrjö Littunen has formulated an "optimal frustration" hypothesis: "Persons who have to maintain a monotonous interaction pattern for a long period of time tend to become bored with each other. This phenomenon of *social fatigue* may be understood as a situation where there is no excitement in the interaction to maintain the cohesiveness, to increase liking."[29] Although sustained conformity may bring the reward of smooth adjustment to expectations, it also brings the penalty of boredom. That is why apathy and monotony may lead a person to "seek a frustration which his energy potential can adequately balance and overcome."[30] This hypothesis, which Littunen developed on the basis of the psychological research of Hebb and Thompson,[31] gains added theoretical relevance with Gouldner's recognition that a system built upon the habituation of conforming responses may be said to contain built-in tendencies toward a high level of entropy. It is high social entropy that the innovator, as an agent of change, helps to prevent.

## NORMATIVE FLEXIBILITY AND INNOVATING ROLES

In monolithic structures role requirements may be so rigidly defined that only fully conforming role performance will be tolerated; in less rigid structures, on the other hand, a measure of diversity may be tolerated at various levels in the system.[32] For example, low-ranking deviants may perform important functions for the group. This was the case in the groups discussed earlier, about which Dentler and Erikson have argued that low-ranking members who deviate from the group's norms "become critical referents for establishing the end points" of the range of possibilities judged permissible within the group's boundaries.[33]

Such considerations direct attention to the relation between status, group structure, and the acceptance of innovation by the group.

Deviant behavior as well as innovation varies within different social structures. Furthermore, the social structure puts pressure on some of its status-occupants to engage in innovating rather than in conforming behavior.[34] For example, as Veblen and Simmel,[35] among others, have pointed out, marginal individuals are likely to be highly motivated to engage in innovating behavior because they are structurally induced to depart from prevailing social norms. "With the least opportunity for full participation in the most valued activities of their own society,"[36] they may be stimulated to make new responses which depart from the habitually required. Being less tied to the system of wont and use which regulates the lives of insiders, they may see alternatives of action that escape the latter's attention. The structural circumstance of their exclusion from some of the prized values of the group may make the marginal man more sensitive to the lacunae which may well remain hidden from "well-adjusted" members of the group. If he wishes to gain acceptance among insiders, he will be motivated to propose innovating means designed to allow the group to reach its goals more effectively than before.

There are also other positions in a group than those of marginal men that motivate innovating departures from the norms. For example, the status of leader requires the ability to adjust to new circumstances. The rank and file may take the customary for granted, but a break of wont and use may enhance the reputation of the leader. The flexibility required in leadership roles may entail greater or lesser departures from otherwise expected behavior so that a certain amount of license to deviate and to violate norms is built into the very definition of leadership.

Homans, who had argued in an earlier work that "the higher the rank (or status) of a person within a group, the more nearly his activities conform to the norms of the group,"[37] stated more recently, after discussing, among others, the above-quoted study by Kelley and Shapiro, that "we now have experimental evidence that it is not just the members of low status, but members of high status as well, who are prone at times to non-conformity."[38] It will be remembered that in these groups deviant behavior helped the group to adapt to the outside. This suggests that the pressure on the leader to engage in innovating behavior may derive from the structural circumstance that he is the group's representative to the outside. He stands at the point of interchange between in-group and out-group. A leader may be considered a special case of the marginal man: having the task to relate his group to the demands of the environment, he is oriented, at the same time as he is the group's representative, toward extra-group values.

In view of these requirements of leadership, it is not always clear whether the leader's innovation can be called "deviant" at all. Though it involves adoption of new procedures, innovation in this case still takes place within normative limits. Just as with groups in which innovation is highly prized, so in situations in which the leader's departure from institutionalized procedures is part of the system of expectations, what may be considered deviation from one point of view may well be considered conforming behavior from another.

Yet leaders are often also permitted some deviant behavior that neither increases the group's adaptation to the outside nor otherwise directly benefits the group in any way. Simply by virtue of otherwise showing prized qualities, a leader accumulates what Hollander has called "idiosyncrasy credit."[39]

One would assume that the more task-oriented a group, the less its tolerance of deviant behavior that interferes with the attainment of the group's goal. This may well be so, but if a leader is seen as important for the attainment of these goals, or even for their partial attainment, the group may tolerate individual deviation when it is seen as balanced by positive contributions. A man may lose credit for deviations, but only when his credit balance is exhausted will he be removed. If he continues to amass credit in the eyes of the members through group-approved activities, he attains a threshold permitting deviations from common expectations. This may explain, at least in part, why a leader may be given greater leeway for deviating behavior than his followers: his having accumulated highly visible merit gives him a leeway in behavior not granted to less meritorious members; the group will take from "him" what it will not take from "them." Task orientation and tolerance of deviance are therefore not necessarily mutually exclusive.

The term "idiosyncrasy credit" readily brings

to mind the image of a "would-be" innovator, who is tolerated because of other contributions, yet whose innovating message is largely ignored by the group. This is not necessarily so. "Idiosyncrasy credit" because of high achievement does not merely imply tolerance of otherwise unacceptable behavior; it also implies that members of the group will listen more readily.

## THE TIME DIMENSION OF INNOVATION

Innovations must not only be analyzed in terms of the structural circumstances under which they occur but also in terms of their impact over time. They must be located in social time as well as in social space.

A type of behavior which might at first be perceived by the group as an attack on its norms and values might at a later time be considered in a different light. If this happens during the lifetime of the innovator he is likely to experience a sharp change in status; he will then reap the rewards of an action which was at first negatively sanctioned. The innovator is then co-opted, perhaps even against his will, into the ranks of the upholders of conformity. If, on the other hand, he obtains recognition only after his death, the lifelong heretic becomes, in effect, a posthumous saint. The Catholic church, with its amazing flexibility, has been especially adept at this process of social transmutation in which, through a remarkable alchemy, its victims have been transformed into patron saints so that Joan of Arc in due time became Saint Joan. As Merton has observed: "In the history of every society . . . some of its cultural heroes have been regarded as heroic precisely because they have had the courage and the vision to depart from norms then obtaining in the group. As we all know, the rebel, revolutionary, nonconformist, individualist, heretic and renegade of an earlier time is often the culture hero of today."[40] The Jewish prophets, those holy demagogues, were feared, despised, and outcast by the religious and secular powers of their day. Yet, as Max Weber has noted, "it is completely inconceivable that without a profound experience of a confirmation of the pro-

phetic words of doom . . . the belief of the people was not only unbroken by the fearful political fate, but in a unique and quite unheard of historical paradox was definitely confirmed. The entire inner construction of the Old Testament is inconceivable without its orientation in terms of the oracles of the prophets. These giants cast their shadows through the millenia into the present."[41]

## REFERENCES AND NOTES

1  Emile Durkheim, *Division of Labor in Society*, Glencoe, Ill.: The Free Press, 1947, p. 102.

2  George Herbert Mead, "The Psychology of Punitive Justice," *American Journal of Sociology*, vol. 23 (1928), pp. 557–602, especially p. 591. See also Marx's parallel formulation: "The criminal produces an impression now moral, now tragic, and renders a 'service' by arousing the moral and aesthetic sentiments of the public." Quoted in Bottomore and Rubel (eds.), *Karl Marx*, London: Watts & Co., 1956, p. 159.

3  Talcott Parsons, *The Social System*, Glencoe, Ill.: The Free Press, 1951, p. 512.

4  Harold H. Kelley and John W. Thibault, "Experimental Studies of Group Problem Solving and Process" in Gardner Lindzey (ed.), *Handbook of Social Psychology*, Cambridge, Mass.: Addison-Wesley Publishing Co., Inc., 1954, vol. 2, p. 768.

5  Kai T. Erikson, "Social Margins: Some Notes on the Sociology of Deviance," paper read at the Fifty-fifth Annual Meeting of the American Sociological Association, New York, 1960.

6  W.E.H. Lecky wrote about the prostitute: "herself the supreme type of vice, she is ultimately the most efficient guardian of virtue." Quoted by Kingsley Davis, "Prostitution," in Robert K. Merton and Robert A. Nisbet (eds.), *Contemporary Social Problems*, New York: Harcourt, Brace & Co., 1961, pp. 262–288. Davis shows the close connection between prostitution and the maintenance of traditional family patterns.

7  Erikson, *op. cit.* See also V. W. Turner's parallel formulation: "The norm derives strength and definition from condemnation of its breach in the public situations of ritual and law. The deviant, the haphazard and the contingent can only be recognized to be such where consensus to what is typical, orthodox, regular exists. And vice versa." *Schism and Continuity in an African Society*, Manchester: Manchester University Press, 1957, p. 329. This is of course what Hegel meant when he asserted that "no step in philosophy was possible" unless it was recognized that

the positive and the negative gain their "truth only in their relation to each other so that each contains the other within it." Lasson (ed.), *Wissenschaft der Logik*, Leipzig: Felix Meiner, 1923, vol. 2, pp. 54–56.

8   See Anna Freud, *The Ego and the Mechanisms of Defense*, New York: International Universities Press, 1946, pp. 117ff.

9   Stewart E. Perry and Helen Swick Perry, "Deviant Behavior, Function and Dysfunction on the Psychiatric Ward," paper read at the Eastern Sociological Society Meetings, Boston, April 23–24, 1960.

10  Robert A. Dentler and Kai T. Erikson, "The Functions of Deviance in Groups," *Social Problems*, vol. 7, no. 2 (fall 1959), pp. 98–107.

11  *Ibid.*, p. 105.

12  Kelley and Thibault, *op. cit.*, p. 766.

13  Harold H. Kelley and Martin M. Shapiro, "An Experiment on Conformity to Group Norms Where Conformity Is Detrimental to Group Achievement," *American Sociological Review*, vol. 19 (1954), pp. 667–677.

14  These variations in social control have been identified and discussed by Robert K. Merton in "Social Structure and Anomie," *Social Theory and Social Structure*, rev. ed., Glencoe, Ill.: The Free Press, 1957, especially p. 133.

15  Roger Caillois, "Theory of the Festival," *Man and the Sacred*, Glencoe, Ill.: The Free Press, 1959.

16  Georg Simmel, "The Stranger," in Kurt H. Wolff (trans. and ed.), *The Sociology of Georg Simmel*, Glencoe, Ill.: The Free Press, 1950; and Orrin E. Klapp, "The Fool as a Social Type," *American Journal of Sociology, vol. 55 (1949), pp 157–162.*

17  See Albert K. Cohen, "The Study of Social Organization and Deviant Behavior," in Robert K. Merton *et al.* (eds.), *Sociology Today*, New York: Basic Books, Inc., 1959, pp. 461–484.

18  It was a distinct step forward to conceptualize the sick and the criminal as deviants from the institutionalized norms on the ground that both roles called forth social control mechanisms designed to restore "health." Nevertheless, as Vilhelm Aubert and Sheldon Messinger have recently argued ["The Criminal and the Sick," *Inquiry* (Oslo), vol. 1, no. 3 (fall 1958), pp. 137–160], these roles are also crucially dissimilar insofar as, among other things, the sick is conceived as one who cannot be held responsible for his failure to perform previously assumed roles, while the criminal is not perceived in terms of inability but rather as having been able to act differently had he chosen to do so.

19  Merton *op. cit.*, p. 360. See also Robert K. Merton, "Social Problems and Sociological Theory" in Merton and Nisbet, *op. cit.*, pp. 697–737.

20  Merton, *op. cit.*, p. 363 *et passim.*

21  Lewis A. Coser, "Durkheim's Conservatism and Its Implications for Sociological Theory," in Kurt H. Wolff (ed.), *Emile Durkheim*, Columbus, Ohio: Ohio State University Press, 1961, pp. 211–232. See also Roger Nett, "Conformity-Deviation and the Social Control Concept," *Ethics*, vol. 64 (1953), pp. 38–45.

22  Gandhi distinguished between criminal and civil disobedience in terms of the concept of publicity. Civil disobedience, to him, was by definition public action.

23  See Robert K. Merton, "Social Conformity, Deviation and Opportunity-structures," *American Sociological Review*, vol. 24, no. 2 (April 1959), pp. 177–189, especially p. 181. See also Herbert Menzel, "Innovation, Integration, and Marginality," *American Sociological Review*, vol. 25, no. 5 (October 1960), pp. 704–713.

24  Lewis A. Coser, "Social Conflict and the Theory of Social Change," *British Journal of Sociology*, vol. 8, no. 3 (September 1957), pp. 197–207.

25  John Dewey, *Human Nature and Conduct*, New York: Modern Library, 1930, p. 300.

26  Parsons, *op. cit.*, pp. 204–205 *et passim.*

27  Alvin M. Gouldner, "Organizational Analysis," in Merton *et al.*, *op. cit.*, pp. 423ff.

28  George Homans, *Social Behavior*, New York: Harcourt, Brace & Co., 1961, p. 55.

29  "Income-Security Values at Different Levels of Frustration," *Transactions of the Westermarck Society*, vol. 4, no. 4 (Copenhagen: Ejnar Munks-gaard, 1959), pp. 234–235ff. See also Goethe's "Nichts ist schwerer zu ertragen als eine Reihe von Schoenen Tagen."

30  Littunen, *op. cit.*, p. 224. See also Marx's statement: "The criminal interrupts the monotony and security of bourgeois life. Thus he protects it from Stagnation." In Bottomore and Ruben, *op. cit.*, p. 159.

31  D. O. Hebb and W. R. Thompson, "The Social Significance of Animal Studies," in Lindzey, *op. cit.*, vol. 1, pp. 532–561.

32  Daniel J. Levinson, "Role, Personality, and Social Structure in the Organizational Setting," *Journal of Abnormal and Social Psychology*, vol. 58 (1959), pp. 170–180. See also Erving Goffman's discussion of "Role Distance" in his *Encounters*, Indianapolis, Ind.: Bobbs, Merrill Company, Inc., 1961.

33  *Op. cit.* See also E. Paul Torrance, "Function of Expressed Disagreement in Small Group Processes" in A. Rubenstein and C. Haberstroh (eds.), *Some Theories of Organization*, Homewood, Ill.: The Dorsey Press, 1960, pp. 250–257.

34  Merton, "Social Structure and Anomie," *op. cit.*, pp. 131–160.

35    Simmel, "The Stranger," *op. cit.*; and Thorstein Veblen, "The Intellectual Preeminence of the Jews," *Essays in Our Changing Order*, pp. 219–231.

36    H. G. Barnett, *Innovation: the Basis of Cultural Change*, New York: McGraw-Hill Book Co., 1953, p. 404. See also Karl Mannheim, *Man and Society in an Age of Reconstruction*, London: Routledge & Kegan Paul, 1940, especially pp. 56–57, as well as Robert Park's "Introduction" to E. V. Stonequist, *The Marginal Man*, New York: Charles Scribner's Sons, 1937.

37    George Homans, *The Human Group*, New York: Harcourt, Brace & World, 1950, p. 141.

38    Homans, *Social Behavior*, *op. cit.*, p. 346. Recent experimental work throws doubt on the idea that the relation between status and conformity is ever a simple one. Dittes and Kelley showed, e.g., that individuals who felt acceptable in a group felt freer to express disagreements publicly, while those with a low sense of acceptance were much higher in their *public* than in the *private* conformity. J. E. Dittes and H. H. Kelley, "Effects of Different Conditions of Acceptance upon Conformity to Group Norms," *Journal of Abnormal and Social Psychology*, vol. 53, (1956) pp. 100–107. See also Herbert Menzel, "Public and Private Conformity under Different Conditions of Acceptance in the Group," *Journal of Abnormal and Social Psychology*, vol. 55 (1957), pp. 398–402.

39    E. P. Hollander, "Conformity, Status and Idiosyncrasy Credit," *Psychological Review*, vol. 65 (1958), pp. 117–127.

40    Merton, *Social Theory*, *op. cit.*, p. 183.

41    Max Weber, *Ancient Judaism* (trans. and ed.), Hans H. Gerth and Don Martindale, Glencoe, Ill.: The Free Press, 1952, p. 334.

# 44    DYNAMICS OF MENTAL DISORDER    THOMAS J. SCHEFF

Although the last two decades have seen a vast increase in the number of studies of functional mental disorder, there is as yet no substantial, verified body of knowledge in this area. A quotation from a recent symposium on schizophrenia summarizes the present situation:

> During the past decade, the problems of chronic schizophrenia have claimed the energy of workers in many fields. Despite significant contributions which reflect continuing progress, *we have yet to learn to ask ourselves the right questions.*[1]

Many investigators apparently agree; systematic studies have not only failed to provide answers to the problem of causation, but there is considerable feeling that the problem itself has not been formulated correctly.

Reprinted with the permission of the author and the publisher from "The Role of the Mentally Ill and the Dynamics of Mental Disorder," *Sociometry*, vol. 26 (December 1963), pp. 436–453. A more recent statement of this theory can be found in the author's *Being Mentally Ill*, Chicago: Aldine Publishing Co., 1966.

This project was supported in part by the Graduate Research Committee of the University of Wisconsin. The help of many persons, too numerous to list here, who criticized earlier drafts is gratefully acknowledged.

One frequently noted deficiency in psychiatric formulations of the problem is the failure to incorporate social processes into the dynamics of mental disorder. Although the importance of these processes is increasingly recognized by psychiatrists, the conceptual models used in formulating research questions are basically concerned with individual rather than social systems. Genetic, biochemical, and psychological investigations seek different causal agents, but utilize similar models: dynamic systems which are located within the individual. In these investigations, social processes tend to be relegated to a subsidiary role, because the model focuses attention on individual differences, rather than on the social system in which the individuals are involved.

Recently a number of writers have sought to develop an approach which would give more emphasis to social processes. Lemert, Erikson, Goffman, and Szasz have notably contributed to this approach.[2] Lemert, particularly, by rejecting the more conventional concern with the origins of mental deviance, and stressing instead the potential importance of the societal reaction in stabilizing deviance, focuses primarily on mechanisms of social control. The work of all of these authors suggests research avenues which are analytically separable from questions of individual systems and point, therefore, to a theory which would incorporate social processes.

The purpose of the present paper is to contribute to the formulation of such a theory by stating a set of nine propositions which make up basic assumptions for a social system model of mental disorder. This set is largely derived from the work of the authors listed above, all but two of the propositions (4 and 5) being suggested, with varying degrees of explicitness, in the cited references. By stating these propositions explicitly, this paper attempts to facilitate testing of basic assumptions, all of which are empirically unverified, or only partly verified. By stating these assumptions in terms of standard sociological concepts, this paper attempts to show the relevance to studies of mental disorder of findings from diverse areas of social science, such as race relations and prestige suggestion. This paper also delineates three problems which are crucial for a sociological theory of mental disorder: what are the conditions in a culture under which diverse kinds of deviance become stable and uniform; to what extent, in different phases of careers of mental patients, are symptoms of mental illness the result of conforming behavior; is there a general set of contingencies which lead to the definition of deviant behavior as a manifestation of mental illness? Finally, this paper attempts to formulate special conceptual tools to deal with these problems, which are directly linked to sociological theory. The social institution of insanity, residual deviance, the social role of the mentally ill, and the bifurcation of the societal reaction into the alternative reactions of denial and labeling, are examples of such conceptual tools.

These conceptual tools are utilized to construct a theory of mental disorder in which psychiatric symptoms are considered to be violations of social norms, and stable "mental illness" to be a social role. The validity of this theory depends upon verification of the nine propositions listed below in future studies, and should, therefore, be applied with caution, and with appreciation for its limitations. One such limitation is that the theory attempts to account for a much narrower class of phenomena than is usually found under the rubric of mental disorder; the discussion that follows will be focused exclusively on stable or recurring mental disorder, and does not explain the causes of single deviant episodes. A second major limitation is that the theory probably distorts the phenomena under discussion. Just as the individual system models under-stress social processes, the model presented here probably exaggerates their importance. The social system model "holds constant" individual differences, in order to articulate the relationship between society and mental disorder. Ultimately, a framework which encompassed both individual and social systems would be desirable. Given the present state of knowledge, however, this framework may prove useful by providing an explicit contrast to the more conventional medical and psychological approaches, and thus assisting in the formulation of sociological studies of mental disorder.

### THE SYMPTOMS OF "MENTAL ILLNESS" AS RESIDUALLY DEVIANT BEHAVIOR

One source of immediate embarrassment to any social theory of "mental illness" is that the terms used in referring to these phenomena in our society prejudge the issue. The medical metaphor "mental illness" suggests a determinate process which occurs within the individual: the unfolding and development of disease. It is convenient, therefore, to drop terms derived from the disease metaphor in favor of a standard sociological concept, deviant behavior, which signifies behavior that violates a social norm in a given society.

If the symptoms of mental illness are to be construed as violations of social norms, it is necessary to specify the type of norms involved. Most norm violations do not cause the violator to be labeled as mentally ill, but as ill-mannered, ignorant, sinful, criminal, or perhaps just harried, depending on the type of norm involved. There are innumerable norms, however, over which consensus is so complete that the members of a group appear to take them for granted. A host of such norms surround even the simplest conversation: a person engaged in conversation is expected to face toward his partner, rather than directly away from him; if his gaze is toward the partner, he is expected to look toward his eyes, rather than, say, toward his forehead; to stand at a proper conversational distance, neither one inch away nor across the room, and so on. A person who regularly violated these expectations probably would not be thought to be merely ill-bred, but as strange, bizarre, and frightening, because his behavior violates the assumptive world of the group, the world that is construed to be the only one that is natural, decent, and possible.

The culture of the group provides a vocabulary of terms for categorizing many norm violations: crime, perversion, drunkenness, and bad manners are familiar examples. Each of these terms is derived from the type of norm broken, and ultimately, from the type of behavior involved. After exhausting these categories, however, there is always a residue of the most diverse kinds of violations, for which the culture provides no explicit label. For example, although there is great cultural variation in what is defined as decent or real, each culture tends to reify its definition of decency and reality, and so provide no way of handling violations of its expectations in these areas. The typical norm governing decency or reality, therefore, literally "goes without saying" and its violation is unthinkable for most of its members. For the convenience of the society in construing those instances of unnamable deviance which are called to its attention, these violations may be lumped together into a residual category: witchcraft, spirit possession, or, in our own society, mental illness. In this paper, the diverse kinds of deviation for which our society provides no explicit label, and which, therefore, sometimes lead to the labeling of the violator as mentally ill, will be considered to be technically *residual deviance*.

## THE ORIGINS, PREVALENCE AND COURSE OF RESIDUAL DEVIANCE

The first proposition concerns the origins of residual deviance.

*Residual deviance arises from fundamentally diverse sources*

It has been demonstrated that some types of mental disorder are the result of organic causes. It appears likely, therefore, that there are genetic, biochemical or physiological origins for residual deviance. It also appears that residual deviance can arise from individual psychological peculiarities and from differences in upbringing and training. Residual deviance can also probably be produced by various kinds of external stress: the sustained fear and hardship of combat, and deprivation of food, sleep, and even sensory experience.[3] Residual deviance, finally, can be a volitional act of innovation or defiance. The kinds of behavior deemed typical of mental illness, such as hallucinations, delusions, depression, and mania, can all arise from these diverse sources.

The second proposition concerns the prevalence of residual deviance which is analogous to the "total" or "true" prevalence of mental disorder (in contrast to the "treated" prevalence).

*Relative to the rate of treated mental illness, the rate of unrecorded residual deviance is extremely high*

There is evidence that grossly deviant behavior is often not noticed or, if it is noticed, it is rationalized as eccentricity. Apparently, many persons who are extremely withdrawn, or who "fly off the handle" for extended periods of time, who imagine fantastic events, or who hear voices or see visions, are not labeled as insane either by themselves or others.[4] Their deviance, rather, is unrecognized, ignored, or rationalized. This pattern of inattention and rationalization will be called "denial."[5]

In addition to the kind of evidence cited above there are a number of epidemiological studies of total prevalence. There are numerous problems in interpreting the results of these studies; the major difficulty is that the definition of mental disorder is different in each study, as are the methods used to screen cases. These studies represent, however, the best available information and can be used to estimate total prevalence.

A convenient summary of findings is presented in Plunkett and Gordon.[6] This source compares the methods and populations used in eleven field studies, and lists rates of total prevalence (in percentages) as 1.7, 3.6, 4.5, 4.7, 5.3, 6.1, 10.9, 13.8, 23.2, 23.3, and 33.3.

How do these total rates compare with the rates of treated mental disorder? One of the studies cited by Plunkett and Gordon, the Baltimore study reported by Pasamanick, is useful in this regard since it includes both treated and untreated rates.[7] As compared with the untreated rate of 10.9 percent, the rate of treatment in state, VA, and private hospitals of Baltimore residents was .5 percent.[8] That is, for every mental patient there were approximately 20 untreated cases located by the survey. It is possible that the treated rate is too low, however, since patients treated by private physicians were not included. Judging from another study, the New Haven study of treated prevalence, the number of patients treated in private practice is small compared to those hospitalized: over 70 percent of the patients located in that study were hospitalized even though extensive case-finding techniques were employed. The overall treated prevalence in the New Haven study was reported as .8 percent, which is in good agreement with my estimate of .7 percent for the Baltimore study.[9] If we accept .8 percent as an estimate of the upper limit of treated prevalence for the Pasamanick study, the ratio of treated to untreated cases is 1/14. That is, for every treated patient we should expect to find 14 untreated cases in the community.

One interpretation of this finding is that the untreated patients in the community represent those cases with less severe disorders, while those patients with severe impairments all fall into the treated group. Some of the findings in the Pasamanick study point in this direction. Of the un-

treated patients, about half are classified as psychoneurotic. Of the psychoneurotics, in turn, about half again are classified as suffering from minimal impairment. At least a fourth of the untreated group, then, involved very mild disorders.[10]

The evidence from the group diagnosed as psychotic does not support this interpretation, however. Almost all of the cases diagnosed as psychotic were judged to involve severe impairment, yet half of the diagnoses of psychosis occurred in the untreated group. In other words, according to this study there were as many untreated as treated cases of psychoses.[11]

On the basis of the high total prevalence rates cited above and other evidence, it seems plausible that residual deviant behavior is usually transitory, which is the substance of the third proposition.

*Most residual deviance is "denied" and is transitory*

The high rates of total prevalence suggest that most residual deviancy is unrecognized or rationalized away. For this type of deviance, which is amorphous and uncrystallized, Lemert uses the term "primary deviation."[12] Balint describes similar behavior as "the unorganized phase of illness."[13] Although Balint assumes that patients in this phase ultimately "settle down" to an "organized illness," other outcomes are possible. A person in this stage may "organize" his deviance in other than illness terms, e.g., as eccentricity or genius, or the deviant acts may terminate when situational stress is removed.

The experience of battlefield psychiatrists can be interpreted to support the hypothesis that residual deviance is usually transitory. Glass reports that combat neurosis is often self-terminating if the soldier is kept with his unit and given only the most superficial medical attention.[14] Descriptions of child behavior can be interpreted in the same way. According to these reports, most children go through periods in which at least several of the following kinds of deviance may occur: temper tantrums, head banging, scratching, pinching, biting, fantasy playmates or pets, illusory physical complaints, and fears of sounds, shapes, colors, persons, animals, darkness, weather, ghosts, and so on.[15] In the vast majority of instances, however, these behavior patterns do not become stable.

If residual deviance is highly prevalent among ostensibly "normal" persons and is usually transitory, as suggested by the last two propositions, what accounts for the small percentage of residual deviants who go on to deviant careers? To put the question another way, under what conditions is residual deviance stabilized? The conventional hypothesis is that the answer lies in the deviant himself. The hypothesis suggested here is that the most important single factor (but not the only factor) in the stabilization of residual deviance is the societal reaction. Residual deviance may be stabilized if it is defined to be evidence of mental illness, and/or the deviant is placed in a deviant status, and begins to play the role of the mentally ill. In order to avoid the implication that mental disorder is merely role-playing and pretence, it is first necessary to discuss the social institution of insanity.

## SOCIAL CONTROL: INDIVIDUAL AND SOCIAL SYSTEMS OF BEHAVIOR

In *The Myth of Mental Illness*, Szasz proposes that mental disorder be viewed within the framework of "the game-playing model of human behavior." He then describes hysteria, schizophrenia, and other mental disorders as the "impersonation" of sick persons by those whose "real" problem concerns "problems of living." Although Szasz states that role-playing by mental patients may not be completely or even mostly voluntary, the implication is that mental disorders be viewed as a strategy chosen by the individual as a way of obtaining help from others. Thus, the term "impersonation" suggests calculated and deliberate shamming by the patient. In his comparisons of hysteria, malingering, and cheating, although he notes differences between these behavior patterns, he suggests that these differences may be mostly a matter of whose point of view is taken in describing the behavior.

The present paper also uses the role-playing model to analyze mental disorder, but places more emphasis on the involuntary aspects of role-playing than Szasz, who tends to treat role-playing as an individual system of behavior. In many social psychological discussions, however, role-playing is considered as a part of a social system. The individual plays his role by articulating his behavior with the cues and actions of other persons involved in the transaction. The proper performance of a role is dependent on having a cooperative audience. This proposition may also be reversed: having an audience which acts toward the individual in a uniform way may lead the actor to play the expected role even if he is not particularly interested in doing so. The "baby of the family" may come to find this role obnoxious, but the uniform pattern of cues and actions which confronts him in the family may lock in with his own vocabulary of responses so that it is inconvenient and difficult for him not to play the part expected of him. To the degree that alternative roles are closed off, the proffered role may come to be the only way the individual can cope with the situation.

One of Szasz's very apt formulations touches upon the social systemic aspects of role-playing. He draws an analogy between the role of the mentally ill and the "type-casting" of actors.[16] Some actors get a reputation for playing one type of role, and find it difficult to obtain other roles. Although they may be displeased, they may also come to incorporate aspects of the type-cast role into their self-conceptions, and ultimately into their behavior. Findings in several social psychological studies suggest that an individual's role behavior may be shaped by the kinds of "deference" that he regularly receives from others.[17]

One aspect of the voluntariness of role-playing is the extent to which the actor believes in the part he is playing. Although a role may be played cynically, with no belief, or completely sincerely, with whole-hearted belief, many roles are played on the basis of an intricate mixture of belief and disbelief. During the course of a study of a large public mental hospital, several patients told the author in confidence about their cynical use of their symptoms—to frighten new personnel, to escape from unpleasant work details, and so on. Yet these *same* patients, at other times, appear to have been sincere in their symptomatic behavior. Apparently it was sometimes difficult for them to tell whether they were playing the role or the role was playing them. Certain types of symptomatology are quite interesting in this connection. In simulation of previous psychotic states, and in the behavior pattern known to psychiatrists as the Ganser syndrome, it is apparently almost impossible for the observer to separate feigning of symptoms from involuntary acts with any degree of certainty.[18] In accordance with what has been said so far, the difficulty is probably that the patient is just as confused by his own behavior as is the observer.

This discussion suggests that a stable role performance may arise when the actor's role imagery locks in with the type of "deference" which he regularly receives. An extreme example of this process may be taken from anthropological and medical reports concerning the "dead role," as in deaths attributed to "bone-pointing." Death from bone-pointing appears to arise from the conjunction of two fundamental processes which characterize all social behavior. First, all individuals continually orient themselves by means of responses which are perceived in social interaction: the individual's identity and continuity of experience are dependent on these cues.[19] Secondly, the individual has his own vocabulary of expectations, which may in a particular situation either agree with or be in conflict with the sanctions to which he is exposed. Entry into a role may be complete when this role is part of the individual's expectations, and when these expectations are reaffirmed in social interaction. In the following pages this principle will be applied to the problem of the causation of mental disorder.

What are the beliefs and practices that constitute the social institution of insanity?[20] And how do they figure in the development of mental disorder? Two propositions concerning beliefs about mental disorder in the general public will now be considered.

*Stereotyped imagery of mental disorder is learned in early childhood*

Although there are no substantiating studies in this area, scattered observations lead the author to conclude that children learn a considerable amount of imagery concerning deviance very early, and that much of the imagery comes from their peers rather than from adults. The literal meaning of "crazy," a term now used in a wide variety of contexts, is probably grasped by children during the first years of elementary school. Since adults are often vague and evasive in their responses to questions in this area, an aura of mystery surrounds it. In this socialization the grossest stereotypes which are heir to childhood fears, e.g., of the "boogie man," survive. These conclusions are quite speculative, of course, and need to be investigated systematically, possibly with techniques similar to those used in studies of the early learning of racial sterotypes.

Assuming, however, that this hypothesis is sound, what effect does early learning have on the shared conceptions of insanity held in the community? There is much fallacious material learned in early childhood which is later discarded when more adequate information replaces it. This question leads to hypothesis 5.

*The stereotypes of insanity are continually reaffirmed, inadvertently, in ordinary social interaction*

Although many adults become acquainted with medical concepts of mental illness, the traditional stereotypes are not discarded, but continue to exist alongside the medical conceptions, because the stereotypes receive almost continual support from the mass media and in ordinary social discourse. In newspapers, it is a common practice to mention that a rapist or a murderer was once a mental patient. This negative information, however, is seldom offset by positive reports. An item like the following is almost inconceivable:

> Mrs. Ralph Jones, an ex-mental patient, was elected president of the Fairview Home and Garden Society in their meeting last Thursday.

Because of highly biased reporting, the reader is free to make the unwarranted inference that murder and rape occur more frequently among ex-mental patients than among the population at large. Actually, it has been demonstrated that the incidence of crimes of violence, or of any crime, is much lower among ex-mental patients than among the general population.[21] Yet, this is not the picture presented to the public.

Reaffirmation of the stereotype of insanity occurs not only in the mass media, but also in ordinary conversation, in jokes, anecdotes, and even in conventional phrases. Such phrases as "Are you crazy?", or "It would be a madhouse," "It's driving me out of my mind," or "It's driving me distracted," and hundreds of others occur frequently in informal conversations. In this usage insanity itself is seldom the topic of conversation; the phrases are so much a part of ordinary language that only the person who considers each word carefully can eliminate them from his speech. Through verbal usages the stereotypes of insanity are a relatively permanent part of the social structure.

In a recent study Nunnally demonstrated that reaffirmation of stereotypes occurs in the mass media. In a systematic and extensive content analysis of television, radio, newspapers and magazines, including "confession" magazines, they found an image of mental disorder presented which was overwhelmingly stereotyped.

> ... media presentations emphasized the bizarre symptoms of the mentally ill. For example, information relating to Factor I (the conception that mentally ill persons look and act different from "normal" people) was recorded 89 times. Of these, 88 affirmed the factor, that is, indicated or suggested that people with mental-health problems "look and act different": only one item denied Factor I. In television dramas, for example, the afflicted person often enters the scene staring glassy-eyed, with his mouth widely ajar, mumbling incoherent phrases or laughing uncontrollably. Even in what would be considered the milder disorders, neurotic phobias and obsessions, the afflicted person is presented as having bizarre facial expressions and actions.[22]

## DENIAL AND LABELING

According to the analysis presented here, the traditional stereotypes of mental disorder are solidly entrenched in the population because they are learned early in childhood and are continuously reaffirmed in the mass media in everyday conversation. How do these beliefs function in the processes leading to mental disorder? This question will be considered by first referring to the earlier discussion of the societal reaction to residual deviance.

It was stated that the usual reaction to residual deviance is denial, and that in these cases most residual deviance is transitory. The societal reaction to deviance is not always denial, however. In a small proportion of cases the reaction goes the other way, exaggerating and at times distorting the extent and degree of deviation. This pattern of exaggeration, which we will call "labeling," has been noted by Garfinkel in his discussion of the "degradation" of officially recognized criminals.[23] Goffman makes a similar point in his description of the "discrediting" of mental patients.[24] Apparently under some conditions the societal reaction to deviance is to seek out signs of abnormality in the deviant's history to show that he was always essentially a deviant.

The contrasting social reactions of denial and labeling provide a means of answering two fundamental questions. If deviance arises from diverse sources—physical, psychological, and situational—how does the uniformity of behavior that is associated with insanity develop? Secondly, if deviance is usually transitory, how does it become stabilized in those patients who become chronically deviant? To summarize, what are the sources of uniformity and stability of deviant behavior?

In the approach taken here the answer to this question is based on hypotheses Nos. 4 and 5, that the role imagery of insanity is learned in childhood, and is reaffirmed in social interaction. In a crisis, when the deviance of an individual becomes a public issue, the traditional stereotype of insanity becomes the guiding imagery for action, both for those reacting to the deviant and, at times, for the deviant himself. When societal agents and persons around the deviant react to him uniformly in terms of the traditional stereotypes of insanity, his amorphous and unstructured deviant behavior tends to crystallize in conformity to these expectations, thus becoming similar to the behavior of other deviants classified as mentally ill, and stable over time. The process of becoming uniform and stable is completed when the traditional imagery becomes a part of the deviant's orientation for guiding his own behavior.

The idea that cultural stereotypes may stabilize primary deviance, and tend to produce uniformity in symptoms, is supported by cross-cultural studies of mental disorder. Although some observers insist there are underlying similarities, most agree that there are enormous differences in the manifest symptoms of stable mental disorder *between* societies, and great similarity *within* societies.[25]

These considerations suggest that the labeling process is a crucial contingency in most careers of residual deviance. Thus Glass, who observed that neuropsychiatric casualties may not become mentally ill if they are kept with their unit, goes on to say that military experience with psychotherapy has been disappointing. Soldiers who are removed from their unit to a hospital, he states, often go on to become chronically impaired.[26] That is, their deviance is stabilized by the labeling process, which is implicit in their removal and hospitalization. A similar interpretation can be made by comparing the observations of childhood disorders among Mexican-Americans with those of "Anglo" children. Childhood disorders such as *susto* (an illness believed to result from fright) sometimes have damaging outcomes in Mexican-American children.[27] Yet the deviant behavior involved is very similar to that which seems to have high incidence among Anglo children, with permanent impairment virtually never occurring. Apparently through cues from his elders the Mexican-American child, behaving initially much like his Anglo counterpart, learns to enter the sick role, at times with serious consequences.[28]

## ACCEPTANCE OF THE DEVIANT ROLE

From this point of view, then, most mental disorder can be considered to be a social role. This social role complements and reflects the status of the insane in the social structure. It is through the social processes which maintain the status of the insane that the varied deviances from which mental disorder arises are made uniform and stable. The stabilization and uniformization of residual deviance are completed when the deviant accepts the role of the insane as the framework within which he organizes his own behavior. Three hypotheses are stated below which suggest some of the processes which cause the deviant to accept such a stigmatized role.

### Labeled deviants may be rewarded for playing the stereotyped deviant role

Ordinarily patients who display "insight" are rewarded by psychiatrists and other personnel. That is, patients who manage to find evidence of "their illness" in their past and present behavior, confirming the medical and societal diagnosis, receive benefits. This pattern of behavior is a special case of a more general pattern that has been called the "apostolic function" by Balint, in which the physician and others inadvertently cause the patient to display symptoms of the illness the physician thinks the patient has.[29] Not only physicians but other hospital personnel and even other patients, reward the deviant for conforming to the stereotypes.[30]

### Labeled deviants are punished when they attempt the return to conventional roles

The second process operative is the systematic blockage of entry to nondeviant roles once the label has been publicly applied. Thus the ex-mental patient, although he is urged to rehabilitate himself in the community, usually finds himself discriminated against in seeking to return to his old status, and on trying to find a new one in the occupational, marital, social, and other spheres.[31]

Thus, to a degree, the labeled deviant is rewarded for deviating, and punished for attempting to conform.

*In the crisis occurring when a primary deviant is publicly labeled, the deviant is highly suggestible, and may accept the proffered role of the insane as the only alternative*

When gross deviancy is publicly recognized and made an issue, the primary deviant may be profoundly confused, anxious, and ashamed. In this crisis it seems reasonable to assume that the deviant will be suggestible to the cues that he gets from the reactions of others toward him.[32] But those around him are also in a crisis; the incomprehensible nature of the deviance, and the seeming need for immediate action lead them to take collective action against the deviant on the basis of the attitude which all share—the traditional stereotypes of insanity. The deviant is sensitive to the cues provided by these others and begins to think of himself in terms of the stereotyped role of insanity, which is part of his own role vocabulary also, since he, like those reacting to him, learned it early in childhood. In this situation his behavior may begin to follow the pattern suggested by his own stereotypes and the reactions of others. That is, when a primary deviant organizes his behavior within the framework of mental disorder, and when his organization is validated by others, particularly prestigeful others such as physicians, he is "hooked" and will proceed on a career of chronic deviance.

The role of suggestion is noted by Warner in his description of bone-pointing magic:

The effect of (the suggestion of the entire community on the victim) is obviously drastic. An analogous situation in our society is hard to imagine. If all a man's near kin, his father, mother, brothers and sisters, wife, children, business associates, friends and all the other members of the society, should suddenly withdraw themselves because of some dramatic cir-

cumstance, refusing to take any attitude but one of taboo . . . and then perform over him a sacred ceremony . . . the enormous suggestive power of this movement . . . of the community after it has had its attitudes (toward the victim) crystallized can be somewhat understood by ourselves.[33]

If we substitute for black magic the taboo that usually accompanies mental disorder, and consider a commitment proceeding or even mental hospital admission as a sacred ceremony, the similarity between Warner's description and the typical events in the development of mental disorder is considerable.

The last three propositions suggest that once a person has been placed in a deviant status there are rewards for conforming to the deviant role, and punishments for not conforming to the deviant role. This is not to imply, however, that the symptomatic behavior of persons occupying a deviant status is always a manifestation of conforming behavior. To explain this point, some discussion of the process of self-control in "normals" is necessary.

In a recent discussion of the process of self-control, Shibutani notes that self-control is not automatic, but is an intricate and delicately balanced process, sustainable only under propitious circumstances.[34] He points out that fatigue, the reaction to narcotics, excessive excitement or tension (such as is generated in mobs), or a number of other conditions interfere with self-control; conversely, conditions which produce normal bodily states, and deliberative processes such as symbolization and imaginative rehearsal before action, facilitate it.

One might argue that a crucially important aspect of imaginative rehearsal is the image of himself that the actor projects into his future action. Certainly in American society, the cultural image of the "normal" adult is that of a person endowed with self-control ("will-power," "back-bone," "strength of character," etc.) For the person who sees himself as endowed with the trait of self-control, self-control is facilitated, since he can imagine himself enduring stress during his imaginative rehearsal, and also while under actual stress.

For a person who has acquired an image of himself as lacking the ability to control his own actions, the process of self-control is likely to break down under stress. Such a person may feel that he has reached his "breaking-point" under circumstances which would be endured by a person with a "normal" self-conception. This is to say, a greater lack of self-control than can be explained by stress tends to appear in those roles for which the culture transmits imagery which emphasizes lack of self-control. In American society such imagery is transmitted for the roles of the very young and very old, drunkards and drug addicts, gamblers, and the mentally ill.

Thus, the social role of the mentally ill has a different significance at different phases of residual deviance. When labeling first occurs, it merely gives a name to primary deviation which has other roots. When (and if) the primary deviance becomes an issue, and is not ignored or rationalized away, labeling may create a social type, a pattern of "symptomatic" behavior in conformity with the stereotyped expectations of others. Finally, to the extent that the deviant role becomes a part of the deviant's self-conception, his ability to control his own behavior may be impaired under stress, resulting in episodes of compulsive behavior.

The preceding eight hypotheses form the basis for the final causal hypothesis.

*Among residual deviants, labeling is the single most important cause of careers of residual deviance*

This hypothesis assumes that most residual deviance, if it does not become the basis for entry into the sick role, will not lead to a deviant career. Most deviant careers, according to this point of view, arise out of career contingencies, and are therefore not directly connected with the origins of the initial deviance.[35] Although there are a wide variety of contingencies which lead to labeling rather than denial, these contingencies can be usefully classified in terms of the nature of the deviant behavior, the person who commits the deviant acts, and the community in which the deviance occurs. Other things being equal, the severity of the societal reaction to deviance is a function of, first, the degree, amount, and visibility of the deviant behavior; second, the power of the deviant, and the social distance between the deviant and the agents of social control; and finally, the tolerance level of the community, and the availability in the culture of the community of alternative nondeviant roles.[36] Particularly crucial for future research is the importance of the first two contingencies (the amount and degree of deviance), which are characteristics of the deviant, relative to the remaining five contingencies, which are characteristics of the social system.[37] To the extent that these five factors are found empirically to be independent determinants of labeling and denial, the status of the mental patient can be considered a partly ascribed rather than a completely achieved status. The dynamics of treated mental illness could then be profitably studied quite apart from the individual dynamics of mental disorder.

### CONCLUSION

This paper has presented a sociological theory of the causation of stable mental disorder. Since the evidence advanced in support of the theory was scattered and fragmentary, it can only be suggested as a stimulus to further discussion and research. Among the areas pointed out for further investigation are field studies of the prevalence and duration of residual deviance; investigations of stereotypes of mental disorder in children, the mass media, and adult conversations; studies of the rewarding of stereotyped deviation, blockage of return to conventional roles, and of the suggestibility of primary deviants in crises. The final causal hypothesis suggests studies of the conditions under which denial and labeling of residual deviation occur. The variables which might effect the societal reaction concern the nature of the deviance, the deviant himself, and the community in which the deviation occurs. Although many of the hypotheses suggested are largely unverified, they suggest avenues for investigating mental disorder different than those that are usually followed, and the rudiments of a general theory of deviant behavior.

## REFERENCES AND NOTES

1  Nathaniel S. Apter, "Our Growing Restlessness with Problems of Chronic Schizophrenia," in Lawrence Appleby *et al., Chronic Schizophrenia,* Glencoe, Ill.: The Free Press, 1958.

2  Edwin M. Lemert, *Social Pathology,* New York: McGraw-Hill Book Co., 1951; Kai T. Erikson, "Patient Role and Social Uncertainty: A Dilemma of the Mentally Ill," *Psychiatry,* vol. 20 (August 1957), pp. 263–274; Erving Goffman, *Asylums,* New York: Doubleday & Company, Inc., 1961; Thomas S. Szasz, *The Myth of Mental Illness,* New York: Hoeber-Harper, 1961.

3  Philip Solomon *et al.* (eds.), *Sensory Deprivation* Cambridge, Mass.: Harvard University Press, 1961; E. L. Bliss *et al.,* "Studies of Sleep Deprivation: Relationship to Schizophrenia," *A.M.A. Archives of Neurology and Psychiatry,* vol. 81 (March 1959), pp. 348–359.

4  See, for example, John A. Clausen and Marian R. Yarrow, "Paths to the Mental Hospital," *Journal of Social Issues,* vol. 11 (December 1955), pp. 25–32; August B. Hollingshead and Frederick C. Redlich, *Social Class and Mental Illness,* New York: John Wiley & Sons, Inc., 1958, pp. 172–176; and Elaine Cumming and John Cumming, *Closed Ranks,* Cambridge, Mass.: Harvard University Press, 1957, pp. 92–103.

5  The term "denial" is used in the same sense as in Cumming and Cumming, *op. cit.,* chap. VII.

6  Richard J. Plunkett and John E. Gordon, *Epidemiology and Mental Illness,* New York: Basic Books, Inc., 1960.

7  Benjamin Pasamanick, "A Survey of Mental Disease in an Urban Population: IV, An Approach to Total Prevalence Rates," *Archives of General Psychiatry,* vol. 5 (August 1961), pp. 151–155.

8  *Ibid.,* p. 153.

9  Hollingshead and Redlich, *op. cit.,* p. 109.

10  Pasamanick, *op. cit.,* pp. 153–154.

11  *Ibid.*

12  Lemert, *op. cit.,* chap. 4.

13  Michael Balint, *The Doctor, His Patient, and the Illness,* New York: International Universities Press, 1957, p. 18.

14  Albert J. Glass, "Psychotherapy in the Combat Zone," in *Symposium on Stress,* Washington, D.C.: Army Medical Service Graduate School, 1953. *Cf.* Abraham Kardiner and H. Spiegel, *War Stress and Neurotic Illness,* New York: Hoeber, 1947, chaps. III–IV.

15  Frances L. Ilg and Louise B. Ames, *Child Behavior,* New York: Dell, 1960, pp. 138–188.

16  Szasz, *op. cit.,* p. 252. For a discussion of type-casting see Orrin E. Klapp, *Heroes, Villains and Fools,* Englewood Cliffs, N.J.: Prentice-Hall, Inc., 1962, pp. 5–8 *et passim.*

17  *Cf.* Zena S. Blau, "Changes in Status and Age Identification," *American Sociological Review,* vol. 21 (April 1956), pp. 198–203; James Benjamins, "Changes in Performance in Relation to Influences upon Self-conceptualization," *Journal of Abnormal and Social Psychology,* vol. 45 (July 1950), pp. 473–480; Albert Ellis, "The Sexual Psychology of Human Hermaphrodites," *Psychosomatic Medicine,* vol. 7 (March 1945), pp. 108–125; S. Liberman, "The Effect of Changes in Roles on the Attitudes of Role Occupants," *Human Relations,* vol. 9 (1956), pp. 385–402. For a review of experimental evidence, see John H. Mann, "Experimental Evaluations of Role Playing," *Psychological Bulletin,* vol. 53 (May 1956), pp. 227–234. For an interesting demonstration of the inter-relations between the symptoms of patients on the same ward, see Sheppard G. Kellam and J. B. Chassan, "Social Context and Symptom Fluctuation," *Psychiatry,* vol. 25 (November 1962), pp. 370–381.

18  Leo Sadow and Alvin Suslick, "Simulation of a Previous Psychotic State," *A.M.A. Archives of General Psychiatry,* vol. 4 (May 1961), pp. 452–458.

19  Generalizing from experimental findings, Blake and Mouton make this statement about the processes of conformity, resistance to influence, and conversion to a new role: ". . . an individual requires a stable framework, including salient and firm reference points, in order to orient himself and to regulate his interactions with others. This framework consists of external and internal anchorages available to the individual whether he is aware of them or not. With an acceptable framework he can resist giving or accepting information that is inconsistent with that framework or that requires him to relinquish it. In the absence of a stable framework he actively seeks to establish one through his own strivings by making use of significant and relevant information provided within the context of interaction. *By controlling the amount and kind of information available for orientation, he can be led to embrace conforming attitudes which are entirely foreign to his earlier ways of thinking.* Robert R. Blake and Jane S. Mouton, "Conformity, Resistance and Conversion," in Irwin A. Berg and Bernard M. Bass (eds.), *Conformity and*

*Deviation*, New York: Harper & Row, Publishers, 1961, pp. 1–2. For a recent and striking demonstration of the effect on social communication in defining internal stimuli, see Stanley Schachter and Jerome E. Singer, "Cognitive, Social, and Physiological Determinants of Emotional State," *Psychological Review*, vol. 69 (September 1962), pp. 379–399.

20  The Cummings describe the social institution of insanity (the "patterned response" to deviance) in terms of denial, isolation, and insulation. Cumming and Cumming, *loc. cit.*

21  Henry Brill and Benjamin Malzberg, "Statistical Report Based on the Arrest Record of 5354 Male Ex-patients Released from New York State Mental Hospitals during the Period 1946–48" (mimeographed); L. H. Cohen and H. Freeman, "How Dangerous to the Community are State Hospital Patients?", *Connecticut State Medical Journal*, vol. 9 (September 1945), pp. 697–701.

22  Jum C. Nunnally, Jr., *Popular Conceptions of Mental Health*, New York: Holt, Rinehart and Winston, 1961, p. 74.

23  Harold Garfinkel, "Conditions of Successful Degradation Ceremonies," *American Journal of Sociology*, vol. 61 (March 1956), pp. 420–424.

24  Goffman, *op. cit.*, pp. 125–171.

25  P. M. Yap, "Mental Diseases Peculiar to Certain Cultures: A Survey of Comparative Psychiatry," *Journal of Mental Science*, vol. 97 (April 1951), pp. 313–327; Paul E. Benedict and Irving Jacks, "Mental Illness in Primitive Societies," *Psychiatry*, vol. 17 (November 1954), pp. 377–389.

26  Glass, *op. cit.*

27  Lyle Saunders, *Cultural Differences and Medical Care*, New York: Russell Sage Foundation, 1954, p. 142.

28  For discussion, with many illustrative cases, of the process in which persons play the "dead role" and subsequently die, see Charles C. Herbert, "Life-influencing Interactions," in Alexander Simon *et al.* (eds.), *The Physiology of Emotions*, New York: Charles C. Thomas, 1961.

29  Balint, *op. cit.*, pp. 215–239. *Cf.* Thomas J. Scheff, "Decision Rules, Types of Error and Their Consequences in Medical Diagnosis," *Behavioral Science*, vol. 8 (April 1963), pp. 97–107.

30  William Caudill, F. C. Redlich, H. R. Gilmore, and E. B. Brody, "Social Structure and the Interaction Processes on a Psychiatric Ward," *American Journal of Orthopsychiatry*, vol. 22 (April 1952), pp. 314–334.

31  Lemert, *op. cit.*, pp. 434–440, provides an extensive discussion of this process under the heading "limitation of participation."

32  This proposition receives support from Erikson's observations: Erikson, *loc. cit.*

33  W. Lloyd Warner, *A Black Civilization*, rev. ed., New York: Harper & Brothers, 1958, p. 242.

34  T. Shibutani, *Society and Personality*, Englewood Cliffs, N.J.: Prentice-Hall, Inc., 1961, chap. 6, "Consciousness and Voluntary Conduct."

35  It should be noted, however, that these contingencies are causal only because they become part of a dynamic system: the reciprocal and cumulative interrelation between the deviant's behavior and the societal reaction. For example, the more the deviant enters the role of the mentally ill, the more he is defined by others as mentally ill; but the more he is defined as mentally ill, the more fully he enters the role, and so on. By representing this theory in the form of a flow chart, Walter Buckley pointed out that there are numerous such feedback loops implied here. For an explicit treatment of feedback, see Edwin M. Lemert, "Paranoia and the Dynamics of Exclusion," *Sociometry*, vol. 25 (March 1962), pp. 2–20.

36  *Cf.* Lemert, *op. cit.*, pp. 51–53, 55–68; Goffman, *op. cit.*, pp. 134–135; David Mechanic, "Some Factors in Identifying and Defining Mental Illness," *Mental Hygiene*, vol. 46 (January 1962), pp. 66–74. For a list of similar factors in the reaction to physical illness, see Earl L. Koos, *The Health of Regionville*, New York: Columbia University Press, 1954, pp. 30–38.

37  *Cf.* Thomas J. Scheff, "Psychiatric and Social Contingencies in the Release of Mental Patients in a Midwestern State," forthcoming; Simon Dinitz, Mark Lefton, Shirley Angrist, and Benjamin Pasamanick, "Psychiatric and Social Attributes as Predictors of Case Outcome in Mental Hospitalization," *Social Problems*, vol. 8 (spring 1961), pp. 322–328.

45    HOMOSEXUALITY    WILLIAM SIMON    JOHN H. GAGNON

The study of homosexuality today, except for a few rare and relatively recent examples, suffers from two major defects: it is ruled by a simplistic and homogeneous view of the psychological and social contents of the category "homosexual," and at the same time it is nearly exclusively interested in the most difficult and least rewarding of all questions, that of etiology. While some small exceptions are allowed for adolescent homosexual experimentation, the person with a major to nearly exclusive sexual interest in persons of the same sex is perceived as belonging to a uniform category whose adult behavior is a necessary outcome and, in a sense, reenactment of certain early and determining experiences. This is the prevailing image of the homosexual and the substantive concern of the literature in psychiatry and psychology today.[1]

In addition to the fact that sexual contact with persons of the same sex, even if over the age of consent, is against the law in 49 of the 50 states, the homosexual labors under another burden that is commonly the lot of the deviant in any society.[2] The process of labeling and stigmatizing behavior not only facilitates the work of legal agencies in creating a bounded category of deviant actors such as the "normal burglar" and the "normal child molester" as suggested by Sudnow, but it also creates an image of large classes of deviant actors all operating from the same motivations and for the same etiological reasons.[3] The homosexual, like most significantly labeled persons (whether the label be positive or negative), has *all* of his acts interpreted through the framework of his homosexuality.

Reprinted from *Journal of Health and Social Behavior*, vol. 8 (September 1967), pp. 177–185, by permission of the authors and the American Sociological Association.

A revised version of a paper presented at the Sixty-first Annual Meetings of the American Sociological Association in Miami, August–September 1966. This research was supported in part by USPHS MH grants #07742 and #12535.

Thus the creative activity of the playwright or painter who happens to be homosexual is interpreted in terms of his homosexuality rather than in terms of the artistic rules and conventions of the particular art form in which he works. The plays of the dramatist are scanned for the Albertine Ploy and the painter's paintings for an excessive or deficient use of phallic imagery or vaginal teeth.

It is this nearly obsessive concern with the ultimate causes of adult conditions that has played a major role in structuring our concerns about beliefs and attitudes toward the homosexual. Whatever the specific elements that make up an etiological theory, the search for etiology has its own consequences for research methodology and the construction of theories about behavior. In the case of homosexuality, if one moves beyond those explanations of homosexual behavior that are rooted in constitutional or biological characteristics—that is, something in the genes or in the hormonal system—one is left with etiological explanations located in the structure of the family and its malfunctions.[4] The most compelling of these theories are grounded ultimately in Freudian psychology, where the roots of this as well as the rest of human character structure is to be found in the pathological relationships between parents and their children.[5]

As a consequence of our preliminary work and the work of others, such as Hooker, Reiss, Leznoff and Westley, Achilles, and Schofield,[6] we would like to propose some alternative considerations in terms of the complexity of the life cycle of the homosexual, the roles that mark various stages of this cycle, and the kinds of forces, both sexual and nonsexual, that impinge on this individual actor. It is our current feeling that the problem of finding out how people become homosexual requires an adequate theory of how they become heterosexual; that is, one cannot explain homosexuality in one way and leave heterosexuality as a large residual category labeled "all other." Indeed, the explanation of homosexuality in this sense may await the explanation of the larger and more modal category of adjustment.

Further, from a sociological point of view, what the original causes were may not even be very important for the patterns of homosexuality observed in a society. Much as the medical student who comes to medicine for many reasons, and for whom the homogenous character of professional behavior arises from the experiences of medical school rather than from the root causes of his occupational choice, the patterns of adult homosexuality are consequent upon the social structures and values that surround the homosexual after he becomes, or conceives of himself as, homosexual rather than upon original and ultimate causes.[7]

What we are suggesting here is that we have allowed the homosexual's sexual object choice to dominate and control our imagery of him and have let this aspect of his total life experience appear to determine all his products, concerns, and activities. This prepossessing concern on the part of non-homosexuals with the purely sexual aspect of the homosexual's life is something we would not allow to occur if we were interested in the heterosexual. However, the mere presence of sexual deviation seems to give the sexual content of life an overwhelming significance. Homosexuals, moreover, vary profoundly in the degree to which their homosexual commitment and its facilitation becomes the organizing principle of their lives. Involved here is a complex outcome that is less likely to be explained by originating circumstances than by the consequences of the establishment of the commitment itself.

Even with the relatively recent shift in the normative framework available for considering homosexuality—that is, from a rhetoric of sin to a rhetoric of mental health—the preponderance of the sexual factor is evident. The change itself may have major significance in the ways homosexual persons are dealt with; at the same time, however, the mental health rhetoric seems equally wide of the mark in understanding homosexuality. One advance, however, is that in place of a language of

optimum man which characterized both the moral and the early mental health writings, we find a growing literature concerned with the psychological characteristics necessary for a person to survive in some manner within specific social systems and social situations.[8] In this post-Freudian world, major psychic wounds are increasingly viewed as par for the human condition and, as one major psychiatric theoretician observes, few survive the relationship with their parents without such wounding.[9] The problem becomes then, whether these wounds become exposed to social situations that render them either too costly to the individual or to the surrounding community. Accompanying this trend toward a reconceptualization of mental health has been a scaling-down of the goals set for men; instead of exceedingly vague and somewhat utopian goals, we tend to ask more pragmatic questions: Is the individual self-supporting? Does he manage to conduct his affairs without the intervention of the police or the growing number of mental health authorities? Does he have adequate sources of social support? A positively-balanced and adequately-developed repertoire for gratification? Has he learned to accept himself? These are questions we are learning to ask of nearly all men, but among the exceptions is found the homosexual. In practically all cases, the presence of homosexuality is seen as prima facie evidence of major psychopathology. When the heterosexual meets these minimal definitions of mental health, he is exculpated; the homosexual—no matter how good his adjustment in nonsexual areas of life—remains suspect.

Recent tabulations drawn from a group of 550 white males with extensive histories of homosexuality, interviewed outside institutions by Kinsey and his associates, suggest that most homosexuals cope fairly well, and even particularly well, when we consider the stigmatized and in fact criminal nature of their sexual interests.[10] Of this group, between 75 and 80 per cent reported having had no trouble with the police, the proportion varying by the exclusivity of their homosexual commitment and their educational attainment (see Table 1). Following this same pattern, trouble with their

TABLE 1    *Reported incidence of social difficulties by education and exclusivity of homosexual commitment*

| Trouble with | High school | | College | |
| --- | --- | --- | --- | --- |
| | Exclusive homosexual, % | Mixed homosexual and heterosexual, % | Exclusive homosexual, % | Mixed homosexual and heterosexual, % |
| Police | 31 | 22 | 24 | 17 |
| Family of origin | 25 | 16 | 19 | 11 |
| Occupation | 10 | 8 | 7 | 8 |
| N | (83) | (83) | (283) | (101) |

families of origin tended to occur in a joint relationship with level of education and degree of homosexual commitment, with the less educated and the more homosexual reporting a greater incidence of difficulties. Only about 10 per cent of the group reported trouble at work and less than five per cent at school as a result of their homosexuality. Of those who had military experience, only one fifth reported difficulties in that milieu. In the military, possibly more than in civilian life, homosexuality is a difficulty that obliterates all other evaluations made of the person.

We do not wish to say that homosexual life does not contain a great potential for demoralization, despair, and self-hatred. To the contrary, as in most deviant careers, there remains the potential for a significant escalation of individual psychopathology. This potential is suggested by some other aspects of these same data. About one half of these males reported that 60 per cent or more of their sexual partners were persons with whom they had sex only one time. Between 10 and 20 per cent report that they often picked up their sexual partners in public terminals, and an even larger proportion reported similar contacts in other public or semipublic locations. Between a quarter and a third reported having been robbed by a sexual partner, with a larger proportion characteristically having exclusively homosexual histories. Finally, between 10 and 15 per cent reported having been blackmailed because of their homosexuality (see Table 2).

There were further indicators of alienation and difficulty in the findings. For two fifths of the respondents the longest homosexual affair lasted less than one year, and for about one quarter

kissing occurred in one third or less of their sexual contacts. In addition, about 30 per cent reported never having had sex in their own homes. Accumulatively, such conditions add up to the two fifths of these men who indicated some serious feelings of regret about being homosexual, giving such reasons as fear of social disapproval or rejection, inability to experience a conventional family life, feelings of guilt or shame, or fear of potential trouble with the law. These figures require a more detailed analysis, and there are also uncertainties about sample bias that must be considered. However, it is our feeling that these proportions would not be substantially changed, given a more complete exploration of these factors. These data, then, suggest a depersonalized character, a driven or compulsive quality of the sexual activity of many homosexuals, which cannot be reckoned as anything but extremely costly to them.

Obviously, the satisfaction of a homosexual commitment—like most forms of deviance—makes social adjustment more problematic than it might be for members of a conventional population. What is important to understand is that consequences of these sexual practices are not necessarily direct functions of the nature of such practices. It is necessary to move away from an obsessive concern with the sexuality of the individual, and attempt to see the homosexual in terms of the broader attachments that he must make to live in the world around him. Like the heterosexual, the homosexual must come to terms with the problems that are attendant upon being a member of society: he must find a place to work, learn to live with or without his family, be involved or apathetic in political life, find a group of friends to

**TABLE 2** *Selected negative aspects of a homosexual career by education and exclusivity of homosexual commitment*

| Aspect | High school | | College | |
|---|---|---|---|---|
| | Exclusive homosexual, % | Mixed homosexual and heterosexual, % | Exclusive homosexual, % | Mixed homosexual and heterosexual, % |
| Proportion with 60% or more of sexual partners with whom had sex only once | 49 | 43 | 51 | 45 |
| Often pickup partners in public terminals | 19 | 18 | 17 | 7 |
| Ever been rolled | 37 | 26 | 34 | 29 |
| Ever been blackmailed | 16 | 6 | 12 | 15 |
| N | (83) | (83) | (283) | (101) |

talk to and live with, fill his leisure time usefully or frivolously, handle all of the common and uncommon problems of impulse control and personal gratification, and in some manner socialize his sexual interests.

There is a seldom-noticed diversity to be found in the life cycle of the homosexual, both in terms of solving general human problems and in terms of the particular characteristics of the life cycle itself. Not only are there as many ways of being homosexual as there are of being heterosexual, but the individual homosexual, in the course of his everyday life, encounters as many choices and as many crises as the heterosexual. It is much too easy to allow the label, once applied, to suggest that the complexities of role transition and identity crises are easily attributable to, or are a crucial exemplification of, some previously existing etiological defect.

An example of this is in the phase of homosexuality called "coming out," which is that point in time when there is self-recognition by the individual of his identity as a homosexual and the first major exploration of the homosexual community. At this point in time the removal of inhibiting doubts frequently releases a great deal of sexual energy. Sexual contacts during this period are often pursued nearly indiscriminately and with greater vigor than caution. This is very close to that period in the life of the heterosexual called the "honeymoon," when coitus is legitimate and is pursued with a substantial amount of energy. This

high rate of marital coitus, however, declines as demands are made on the young couple to take their place in the framework of the larger social system. In these same terms, during the homosexual "honeymoon" many individuals begin to learn ways of acting out a homosexual object choice that involve homosexual gratification, but that are not necessarily directly sexual and do not involve the genitalia.

It is during this period that many homosexuals go through a crisis of femininity; that is, they "act out" in relatively public places in a somewhat effeminate manner; and some, in a transitory fashion, wear female clothing, known in the homosexual argot as "going in drag." During this period one of the major confirming aspects of masculinity—that is, nonsexual reinforcement by females of masculine status—has been abandoned, and it is not surprising that the very core of masculine identity should not be seriously questioned. This crisis is partially structured by the already existing homosexual culture in which persons already in the crisis stage become models for those who are newer to their homosexual commitment. A few males retain this pseudofeminine commitment, a few others emerge masquerading as female prostitutes to males, and still others pursue careers as female impersonators. This adjustment might be more widely adapted if feminine behavior by men —except in sharply delimited occupational roles— was not negatively sanctioned. Thus the tendency is for this kind of behavior to be a transitional experiment for most homosexuals, an experiment that leaves vestiges of "camp" behavior, but traces more often expressive of the character of the cultural life of the homosexual community than of some overriding need of individual homosexuals. Since this period of personal disorganization and identity problems is at the same time highly visible to the broader community, this femininity is enlisted as evidence for theories of homosexuality that see, as a central component in its etiology, the failure of sexual identification. The homosexual at this point of his life cycle is more likely to be in psychotherapy, and this is often construed as evidence for a theory which is supported by a mis-sampling of the ways of being homosexual.

Another life cycle crisis that the homosexual shares with the heterosexual in this youth-oriented society is the crisis of aging. While American society places an inordinate positive emphasis on youth, the homosexual community, by and large, places a still greater emphasis on this fleeting characteristic. In general, the homosexual has fewer resources with which to meet this crisis. For the heterosexual there are his children whose careers assure a sense of the future and a wife whose sexual availability cushions the shock of declining sexual attractiveness. In addition, the crisis of aging comes later to the heterosexual, at an age when his sexual powers have declined and expectations concerning his sexuality are considerably lower. The management of aging by the homosexual is not well understood, but there are, at this point in his life, a series of behavioral manifestations (symptoms) attendant to this dramatic transition that are misread as global aspects of homosexuality. Here, as with "coming out," it is important to note that most homosexuals, even with fewer resources than their heterosexual counterparts, manage to weather the period with relative success.

A central concern underlying these options and the management of a homosexual career is the presence and complexity of a homosexual community, which serves most simply for some persons as a sexual market place, but for others as the locus of friendships, opportunities, recreation, and expansion of the base of social life. Such a community is filled with both formal and informal institutions for meeting others and for following, to the degree the individual wants, a homosexual life style. Minimally, the community provides a source of social support, for it is one of the few places where the homosexual may get positive validation of his own self-image. Though the community often provides more feminine or "camp" behavior than some individuals might desire, in a major sense "camp" behavior may well be an expression of aggregate community characteristics without an equal commitment to this behavior on the part of its members. Further, "camp" behavior may also be seen as a form of interpersonal communication characteristic of intracommunity behavior and significantly altered for most during interaction with the larger society. The community serves as a way of mediating sexuality by providing a situation in which one can know and evaluate peers and, in a significant sense, convert sexual behavior into sexual conduct.[11] Insofar as the community provides these relationships for the individual homosexual, it allows for the dilution of sexual drives by providing social gratification in ways that are not directly sexual. Consequently, the homosexual with access to the community is more protected from impulsive sexual "acting out" than the homosexual who has only his own fear and knowledge of the society's prohibitions to mediate his sexual impulses.

It should be pointed out that in contrast to ethnic and occupational subcultures the homosexual community, as well as other deviant subcommunities, has very limited content.[12] This derives from the fact that the community members often have only their sexual commitment in common. Thus, while the community may reduce the problems of access to sexual partners and reduce guilt by providing a structure of shared values, often the shared value structure is far too narrow to transcend other areas of value disagreement. The college-trained professional and the bus boy, the WASP and the Negro slum dweller, may meet in sexual congress, but the similarity of their sexual interests does not eliminate larger social and cultural barriers.[13] The important fact is that the homosexual community is in itself an impoverished cultural unit. This impoverishment, however, may be only partially limiting, since it constrains most members to participate in it on a limited basis, reducing their anxiety and conflicts in the sexual sphere and increasing the quality of their performance in other aspects of social life.

Earlier we briefly listed some of the general problems that the homosexual—in common with the heterosexual—must face; these included earning a living, maintaining a residence, relations with family, and so on. At this point we might consider some of these in greater detail.

First there is the most basic problem of all: earning a living. Initially, the variables that apply to all labor force participants generally apply to homosexuals also. In addition there are the special conditions imposed by the deviant definition of the homosexual commitment. What is important is that the occupational activity of homosexuals represents a fairly broad range. The differences in occupational activity can be conceptualized along a number of dimensions, some of which would be conventional concerns of occupational sociology, while others would reflect the special situation of the homosexual. For example, one element is the degree of occupational involvement, that is, the degree to which occupational activity, or activity ancillary to it, is defined as intrinsically gratifying. This would obviously vary from professional to ribbon clerk to factory laborer. A corollary to this is the degree to which the world of work penetrates other aspects of life. In terms of influence upon a homosexual career, occupational involvement very likely plays a constraining role during the acting-out phase associated with "coming out," as well as serving as an alternative source of investment during the "crisis of aging." Another aspect bears directly upon the issue of the consequences of having one's deviant commitment exposed. For some occupational roles disclosure would clearly be a disaster—the school teacher, the minister, and the politician, to mention just three. There are other occupations where the disclosure or assumption of homosexual interests is either of little consequence or—though relatively rare—has a

positive consequence. It should be evident that the crucial question of anxiety and depersonalization in the conduct of sexual activity can be linked to this variable in a rather direct way.

A second series of questions could deal with the effects of a deviant sexual commitment upon occupational activity itself. In some cases the effect may be extremely negative, since the pursuit of homosexual interests may generate irresponsibility and irregularity. Some part of this might flow from what we associate with bachelorhood generally: detachment from conventional families and, in terms of sex, constant striving for what is essentially regularized in marriage. Illustrations of these behaviors include too many late nights out, too much drinking in too many taverns, and unevenness in emotional condition. On the other hand, several positive effects can be observed. Detachment from the demands of domestic life not only frees one for greater dedication to the pursuit of sexual goals, but also for greater dedication to work. Also, the ability of some jobs to facilitate homosexual activity—such as certain marginal, low-paying, white-collar jobs—serves as compensation for low pay or limited opportunity for advancement. There may be few simple or consistent patterns emerging from this type of consideration, yet the overdetermination of the sexual element in the study of the homosexual rests in our prior reluctance to consider these questions which are both complex and pedestrian.

Similarly, just as most homosexuals have to earn a living, so must they come to terms with their immediate families. There is no substantial evidence to suggest that the proportion of homosexuals for whom relatives are significant persons differs from that of heterosexuals. The important differences rest in the way the relationships are managed and, again, the consequences they have for other aspects of life. Here also one could expect considerable variation containing patterns of rejection, continuing involvement without knowledge, ritualistically suppressed knowledge, and knowledge and acceptance. This becomes more complex because several patterns may be operative at the same time with different members of one's family constellation. Here again it is not unreasonable to assume a considerable degree of variation in the course of managing a homosexual commitment as this kind of factor varies. Yet the literature is almost totally without reference to this relationship. Curiously, in the psychiatric literature —where mother and father play crucial roles in the formation of a homosexual commitment—they tend to be significant by their absence in considerations of how homosexual careers are managed.

This order of discussion could be extended into a large number of areas. Let us consider just one more: religion. As a variable, religion (as both an identification and a quality of religiosity) manifests no indication that it plays an important role in the generation of homosexual commitments. However, it clearly does, or can, play a significant role in the management of that commitment. Here, as in other spheres of life, we must be prepared to deal with complex, interactive relations rather than fixed, static ones. Crucial to the homosexual's ability to "accept himself" is his ability to bring his own homosexuality within a sense of the moral order as it is projected by the institutions surrounding him as well as his own vision of this order. It may be that the issue of including homosexuality within a religious definition is the way the question should be framed only part of the time, and for only part of a homosexual population. At other times and for other homosexuals, to frame the question in terms of bringing religiosity within the homosexual definition might be more appropriate. The need for damnation (that rare sense of being genuinely evil) and the need for redemption (a sense of potentially being returned to the community in good standing) can be expected to vary, given different stages of the life cycle, different styles of being homosexual, and varying environments for enactment of the homosexual commitment. And our sense of the relation suggests that, more than asking about the homosexual's religious orientation and how it expresses his homosexuality, we must also learn to ask how his homosexuality expresses his commitment to the religious.

The aims, then, of a sociological approach to homosexuality are to begin to define the factors—both individual and situational—that predispose a homosexual to follow one homosexual path as against others; to spell out the contingencies that will shape the career that has been embarked upon; and to trace out the patterns of living in both their pedestrian and their seemingly exotic aspects. Only then will we begin to understand the homosexual. This pursuit must inevitably bring us —though from a particular angle—to those complex matrices wherein most human behavior is fashioned.

### REFERENCES AND NOTES

1   Irving Bieber *et al.*, *Homosexuality: A Psychoanalytic Study*, New York: Basic Books, Inc., 1962.

2   Sex law reform occurred in the state of Illinois as part of a general reform of the criminal code in 1961. For the manner in which the law's reform was translated for police officials, see Claude Sowle, *A Concise Explanation of the Illinois Criminal Code of 1961*, Chicago: B. Smith, 1961.

3   David Sudnow, "Normal Crimes," *Social Problems*, vol. 12 (winter 1965), pp. 255–276.

4   A. C. Kinsey, "Criteria for the Hormonal Explanation of the Homosexual," *Journal of Clinical Endocrinology*, vol. 1 (May 1941), pp. 424–428; F. J. Kallman, "Comparative Twin Study on the Genetic Aspects of Male Homosexuality," *Journal of Nervous and Mental Disorders*, vol. 115 (1952), pp. 283–298; F. J. Kallman, "Genetic Aspects of Sex Determination and Sexual Maturation Potentials in Man," in George Winokur (ed.), *Determinants of Human Sexual Behavior*, Springfield, Ill.: Charles C. Thomas, 1963, pp. 5–18; and John Money, "Factors in the Genesis of Homosexuality," in Winokur, *op. cit.*, pp. 19–43.

5   The work of Bieber, *op. cit.*, is the most recent of these analytic explorations, the central finding of which is that in a highly selected group of male homosexuals there was a larger proporation of males who had mothers who could be described as close-binding and intimate and fathers who were detached and hostile. The argument proceeds that the mother has selected this child for special overprotection and seductive care. In the process of childrearing, sexual interest is both elicited and then blocked by punishing its behavioral manifestations. As a result of the mother's special ties to the child, the father is alienated from familial interaction, is hostile to the child, and fails to become a source of masculine attachment.

Regardless of the rather engaging and persuasive character of the theory, there are substantial complications. It assumes that there is a necessary relationship between the development of masculinity and femininity and heterosexuality and homosexuality. There is the assumption that homosexuals play sexual roles that are explicitly modeled upon those of the heterosexual and that these roles are well-defined and widespread. This confusion of the dimensions of sexual object choice and masculinity and feminity is based on two complementary errors. The first is that the very physical sexual activities of the homosexual are often characterized as passive (to be read feminine) or active (to be read masculine) and that these physical activities are read as direct homologues of the complex matters of masculinity and femininity. The second source of the confusion lies in the two situations in which homosexuality can be most easily observed. One is the prison, where the characteristics of homosexuality do tend to model themselves more closely on the patterns of heterosexuality in the outside community, but where the sources and the character of behavior are in the service of different ends. The second situation is that of public homosexuality characterized by the flaunted female gesture which has become sterotypic of homosexuality. This is not to say that such beliefs about the nature of homosexuality on the part of the heterosexual majority do not influence the homosexual's behavior; however, just because stereotypes are held does not mean that they play a role in the etiology of the behavior that they purport to explain.

Another major problem that exists for etiological theories of homosexuality based on family structure is the difficulty one finds in all theories that depend on the individual's memories of his childhood and that call upon him for hearsay evidence not only about himself, but about his parents. We live in a post-Freudian world and the vocabulary of motives of the most psychologically illiterate is replete with the concepts of repression, inhibition, the oedipus complex, and castration fears. The rhetoric of psychoanalysis permeates the culture as a result of a process that might best be called the democratization of mental health. One of the lessons of existentialism is that our biographies are not fixed quantities but are subject to revision, elision, and other forms of subtle editing based on our place in the life cycle, our audience, and the mask that we are currently wearing. Indeed, for many persons the rehearsed past and the real past become so intermixed that there is only the present. Recent research in childrearing practices suggests that two years after the major events of childrearing, weaning, and toilet training, mothers fail to recall accurately their pre-

vious conduct and hence sound a good deal like Dr. Spock. An important footnote here is that persons do not always edit the past to improve their image in the conventional sense. Often the patient in psychotherapy works very hard to bring out more and more self-denigrating materials to assure the therapist that he, the patient, is really working hard and searching for his true motives.

6   Evelyn Hooker, "The Homosexual Community," in James C. Palmer and Michael J. Goldstein (eds.), *Perspectives in Psychopathology*, New York: Oxford University Press, 1966, pp. 354–364; Albert J. Reiss, "The Social Integration of Queers and Peers," *Social Problems*, vol. 9 (fall 1961), pp. 102–120; M. Leznoff and W. A. Westley, "The Homosexual Community," *Social Problems*, vol. 3 (April 1956), pp. 257–263; N. Achilles, "The Development of the Homosexual Bar as an Institution," in J. H. Gagnon and W. Simon (eds.), *Sexual Deviance*, New York: Harper and Row, Publishers, 1967; and Michael Schofield, *Sociological Aspects of Homosexuality*, Boston: Little, Brown and Company, 1965.

7   Howard S. Becker, "Change in Adult Life," *Sociometry*, vol. 27 (March 1964), pp. 40–53.
    Howard S. Becker, Blanche Geer, and Everett C. Hughes, *Boys in White: Student Culture in the Medical School*, Chicago: The University of Chicago Press, 1961.

8   Marie Jahoda, "Toward a Social Psychology of Mental Health" in Arnold M. Rose (ed.), *Mental Health and Mental Disorder*, New York: W. W. Norton and Co., 1955, pp. 556–577; F. C. Redlich, "The Concept of Health in Psychiatry," in A. H. Leighton, J. A. Clausen, and R. N. Wilson (eds.), *Explorations in Social Psychiatry*, New York: Basic Books, Inc., 1957, pp. 138–164.

9   Lawrence Kubie, "Social Forces and the Neurotic Process," in Leighton *et al., op. cit.*, pp. 77–104.

10  Extensive homosexuality is here defined as a minimum of 51 or more times and/or contact with 21 or more males.

11  Ernest W. Burgess makes this useful distinction in his article "The Sociologic Theory of Psychosexual Behavior," in Paul H. Hoch and Joseph Zubin (eds.), *Psychosexual Development in Health and Disease*, New York: Grune and Stratton, 1949, pp. 227–243. Burgess says, "Accurately speaking the various forms of sexual outlet for man are not behavior, they are conduct. Conduct is behavior as prescribed or evaluated by the group. It is not simply external observable behavior, but behavior that expresses a norm or evaluation."

12  For descriptions of the content of other deviant subcultures, see Harold Finestone, "Cats, Kicks and Color," *Social Problems*, vol. 5 (July 1957), pp.

3–13; Howard S. Becker, *The Outsiders*, New York: The Free Press, 1963; and James H. Bryan, "Apprenticeships in Prostitution," *Social Problems*, vol. 12 (winter 1965), pp. 278–297.

13  The homosexual community does provide for an easing of strain by training essentially lower class types in middle class life styles and even middle class occupational roles to a greater extent than most people realize. In contrast, for those for whom homosexuality becomes the salient organizing experience of their lives there may be a concomitant downward mobility as their ties with commitments to systems of roles that are larger than the homosexual community decrease.

## 46    THE POLICE ON SKID-ROW    EGON BITTNER

The prototype of modern police organization, the Metropolitan Police of London, was created to replace an antiquated and corrupt system of law enforcement. The early planners were motivated by the mixture of hardheaded business rationality and humane sentiment that characterized liberal British thought of the first half of the nineteenth century.[1] Partly to meet the objections of a parliamentary committee, which was opposed to the establishment of the police in England, and partly because it was in line with their own thinking, the planners sought to produce an instrument that could not readily be used in the play of internal power politics but which would, instead, advance and protect conditions favorable to industry and commerce and to urban civil life in general. These intentions were not very specific and had to be reconciled with the existing structures of governing, administering justice, and keeping the peace. Consequently, the locus and mandate of the police in the modern polity were ill-defined at the outset. On the one hand, the new institution was to be a part of the executive branch of government, organized, funded, and staffed in accordance with stan-

Reprinted with the permission of the author, the American Sociological Association, and the publisher, *American Sociological Review*, vol. 32 (October 1967), pp. 699–715.

This research was supported in part by Grant 64-1-35 from the California Department of Mental Hygiene. I gratefully acknowledge the help I received from Fred Davis, Sheldon Messinger, Leonard Schatzman, and Anselm Strauss in the preparation of this paper.

dards that were typical for the entire system of the executive. On the other hand, the duties that were given to the police organization brought it under direct control of the judiciary in its day-to-day operation.

The dual patronage of the police by the executive and the judiciary is characteristic for all democratically governed countries. Moreover, it is generally the case, or at least it is deemed desirable, that judges *rather than* executive officials have control over police use and procedures.[2] This preference is based on two considerations. First, in the tenets of the democratic creed, the possibility of direct control of the police by a government in power is repugnant.[3] Even when the specter of the police state in its more ominous forms is not a concern, close ties between those who govern and those who police are viewed as a sign of political corruption.[4] Hence, mayors, governors, and cabinet officers—although the nominal superiors of the police—tend to maintain, or to pretend, a hands-off policy. Second, it is commonly understood that the main function of the police is the control of crime. Since the concept of crime belongs wholly to the law, and its treatment is exhaustively based on considerations of legality, police procedure automatically stands under the same system of review that controls the administration of justice in general.

By nature, judicial control encompasses only those aspects of police activity that are directly related to full-dress legal prosecution of offenders. The judiciary has neither the authority nor the means to direct, supervise, and review those activities of the police that do not result in prosecution. Yet such other activities are unavoidable, frequent, and largely within the realm of public expectations. It might be assumed that in this domain of practice the police are under executive control. This is not the case, however, except in a marginal sense.[5] Not only are police departments generally free to determine what need be done and how, but aside from informal pressures they are given scant direction in these matters. Thus, there appear to exist two relatively independent domains of police activity. In one, their methods are constrained by the prospect of the future disposition of a case in the courts; in the other, they operate under some other consideration and largely with no structured and continuous outside constraint. Following the terminology suggested by Michael Banton, they may be said to function in the first instance as "law officers" and in the second instance as "peace officers."[6] It must be emphasized that the designation "peace officer" is a residual term, with only some vaguely presumptive content. The role, as Banton speaks of it, is supposed to encompass all occupational routines not directly related to making arrests, without, however, specifying what determines the limits of competence and availability of the police in such actions.

Efforts to characterize a large domain of activities of an important public agency have so far yielded only negative definitions. We know that they do not involve arrests; we also know that they do not stand under judicial control, and that they are not, in any important sense, determined by specific executive or legislative mandates. In police textbooks and manuals, these activities receive only casual attention, and the role of the "peace officer" is typically stated in terms suggesting that his work is governed mainly by the individual officer's personal wisdom, integrity, and altruism.[7] Police departments generally keep no records of procedures that do not involve making arrests. Policemen, when asked, insist that they merely use common sense when acting as "peace officers," though they tend to emphasize the elements of experience and practice in discharging

the role adequately. All this ambiguity is the more remarkable for the fact that peace keeping tasks, i.e., procedures not involving the formal legal remedy of arrest, were explicitly built into the program of the modern police from the outset.[8] The early executives of the London police saw with great clarity that their organization had a dual function. While it was to be an arm of the administration of justice, in respect of which it developed certain techniques for bringing offenders to trial, it was also expected to function apart from, and at times in lieu of, the employment of full-dress legal procedure. Despite its early origin, despite a great deal of public knowledge about it, despite the fact that it is routinely done by policemen, no one can say with any clarity what it means to do a good job of keeping the peace. To be sure, there is vague consensus that when policemen direct, aid, inform, pacify, warn, discipline, roust, and do whatever else they do without making arrests, they do this with some reference to the circumstances of the occasion and, thus, somehow contribute to the maintenance of the peace and order. Peace keeping appears to be a solution to an unknown problem arrived at by unknown means.

The following is an attempt to clarify conceptually the mandate and the practice of keeping the peace. The effort will be directed not to the formulation of a comprehensive solution of the problem but to a detailed consideration of some aspects of it. Only in order to place the particular into the overall domain to which it belongs will the structural determinants of keeping the peace in general be discussed. By structural determinants are meant the typical situations that policemen perceive as *demand conditions* for action without arrest. This will be followed by a description of peace keeping in skid-row districts, with the object of identifying those aspects of it that constitute a *practical skill*.

Since the major object of this paper is to elucidate peace keeping practice as a skilled performance, it is necessary to make clear how the use of the term is intended.

Practical skill will be used to refer to those methods of doing certain things, and to the information that underlies the use of the methods, that *practitioners themselves* view as proper and efficient. Skill is, therefore, a stable orientation to work tasks that is relatively independent of the personal feelings and judgments of those who employ it. Whether the exercise of this skilled performance is desirable or not, and whether it is based on correct information or not, are specifically outside the scope of interest of this presentation. The following is deliberately confined to a description of what police patrolmen consider to be the reality of their work circumstances, what they do, and what they feel they must do to do a good job. That the practice is thought to be determined by normative standards of skill minimizes but does not eliminate the factors of personal interest or inclination. Moreover, the distribution of skill varies among practitioners in the very standards they set for themselves. For example, we will show that patrolmen view a measure of rough informality as good practice vis-a-vis skid-row inhabitants. By this standard, patrolmen who are "not rough enough," or who are "too rough," or whose roughness is determined by personal feelings rather than by situational exigencies, are judged to be poor craftsmen.

The description and analysis are based on twelve months of field work with the police departments of two large cities west of the Mississippi. Eleven weeks of this time were spent in skid-row and skid-row-like districts. The observations were augmented by approximately one hundred interviews with police officers of all ranks. The formulations that will be proposed were discussed in these interviews. They were recognized by the respondents as elements of standard practice. The respondents' recognition was often accompanied by remarks indicating that they had never thought about things in this way and that they were not aware how standardized police work was.

### STRUCTURAL DEMAND CONDITIONS OF PEACE KEEPING

There exist at least five types of relatively distinct circumstances that produce police activities that do not involve invoking the law and that are only in a trivial sense determined by those considerations of legality that determine law enforcement. This does not mean that these activities are illegal but merely that there is no legal directive that informs the acting policeman whether what he does must be done or how it is to be done. In these circumstances, policemen act as all-purpose and terminal remedial agents, and the confronted problem is solved in the field. If these practices stand under any kind of review at all, and typically they do not, it is only through internal police department control.

1 Although the executive branch of government generally refrains from exercising a controlling influence over the direction of police interest, it manages to extract certain performances from it. Two important examples of this are the supervision of certain licensed services and premises and the regulation of traffic.[9] With respect to the first, the police tend to concentrate on what might be called the moral aspects of establishments rather than on questions relating to the technical adequacy of the service. This orientation is based on the assumption that certain types of businesses lend themselves to exploitation for undesirable and illegal purposes. Since this tendency cannot be fully controlled, it is only natural that the police will be inclined to favor licensees who are at least cooperative. This, however, transforms the task from the mere scrutiny of credentials and the passing of judgments, to the creation and maintenance of a network of connections that conveys influence, pressure, and information. The duty to inspect is the background of this network, but the resulting contacts acquire additional value for solving crimes and maintaining public order. Bartenders, shopkeepers, and hotel clerks become, for patrolmen, a resource that must be continuously serviced by visits and exchanges of favors. While it is apparent that this condition lends itself to corrupt exploitation by individual officers, even the most flawlessly honest policeman must participate in this network of exchanges if he is to function adequately. Thus, engaging in such exchanges be-

comes an occupational task that demands attention and time.

Regulation of traffic is considerably less complex. More than anything else, traffic control symbolizes the autonomous authority of policemen. Their commands generally are met with unquestioned compliance. Even when they issue citations, which seemingly refer the case to the courts, it is common practice for the accused to view the allegation as a finding against him and to pay the fine. Police officials emphasize that it is more important to be circumspect than legalistic in traffic control. Officers are often reminded that a large segment of the public has no other contacts with the police, and that the field lends itself to public relations work by the line personnel.[10]

2 Policemen often do not arrest persons who have committed minor offences in circumstances in which the arrest is technically possible. This practice has recently received considerable attention in legal and sociological literature. The studies were motivated by the realization that "police decisions not to invoke the criminal process determine the outer limits of law enforcement."[11] From these researches, it was learned that the police tend to impose more stringent criteria of law enforcement on certain segments of the community than on others.[12] It was also learned that, from the perspective of the administration of justice, the decisions not to make arrests often are based on compelling reasons.[13] It is less well appreciated that policemen often not only refrain from invoking the law formally but also employ alternative sanctions. For example, it is standard practice that violators are warned not to repeat the offense. This often leads to patrolmen's "keeping an eye" on certain persons. Less frequent, though not unusual, is the practice of direct disciplining of offenders, especially when they are juveniles, which occasionally involves inducing them to repair the damage occasioned by their misconduct.[14]

The power to arrest and the freedom not to arrest can be used in cases that do not involve patent offenses. An officer can say to a person whose behavior he wishes to control, "I'll let you go this time!" without indicating to him that he could not have been arrested in any case. Nor is this always deliberate misrepresentation, for in many cases the law is sufficiently ambiguous to allow alternative interpretations. In short, not to make an arrest is rarely, if ever, merely a decision not to act; it is most often a decision to act alternatively. In the case of minor offenses, to make an arrest often is merely one of several possible proper actions.

3 There exists a public demand for police intervention in matters that contain no criminal and often no legal aspects.[15] For example, it is commonly assumed that officers will be available to arbitrate quarrels, to pacify the unruly, and to help in keeping order. They are supposed also to aid people in trouble, and there is scarcely a human predicament imaginable for which police aid has not been solicited and obtained at one time or another. Most authors writing about the police consider such activities only marginally related to the police mandate. This view fails to reckon with the fact that the availability of these performances is taken for granted and the police assign a substantial amount of their resources to such work. Although this work cannot be subsumed under the concept of legal action, it does involve the exercise of a form of authority that most people associate with the police. In fact, no matter how trivial the occasion, the device of "calling the cops" transforms any problem. It implies that a situation is, or is getting, out of hand. Police responses to public demands are always oriented to this implication, and the risk of proliferation of troubles makes every call a potentially serious matter.[16]

4 Certain mass phenomena of either a regular or a spontaneous nature require direct monitoring. Most important is the controlling of crowds in incipient stages of disorder. The specter of mob violence frequently calls for measures that involve coercion, including the use of physical force. Legal theory allows, of course, that public officials are empowered to use coercion in situations of imminent danger.[17] Unfortunately, the doctrine is not

sufficiently specific to be of much help as a rule of practice. It is based on the assumption of the adventitiousness of danger, and thus does not lend itself readily to elaborations that could direct the routines of early detection and prevention of untoward developments. It is interesting that the objective of preventing riots by informal means posed one of the central organizational problems for the police in England during the era of the Chartists.[18]

5 The police have certain special duties with respect to persons who are viewed as less than fully accountable for their actions. Examples of those eligible for special consideration are those who are under age[19] and those who are mentally ill.[20] Although it is virtually never acknowledged explicitly, those receiving special treatment include people who do not lead "normal" lives and who occupy a pariah status in society. This group includes residents of ethnic ghettos, certain types of bohemians and vagabonds, and persons of known criminal background. The special treatment of children and of sick persons is permissively sanctioned by the law, but the special treatment of others is, in principle, opposed by the leading theme of legality and the tenets of the democratic faith.[21] The important point is not that such persons are arrested more often than others, which is quite true, but that they are perceived by the police as producing a special problem that necessitates continuous attention and the use of special procedures.

The five types of demand conditions do not exclude the possibility of invoking the criminal process. Indeed, arrests do occur quite frequently in all these circumstances. But the concerns generated in these areas cause activities that usually do not terminate in an arrest. When arrests are made, there exist, at least in the ideal, certain criteria by reference to which the arrest can be judged as having been made more or less properly, and there are some persons who, in the natural course of events, actually judge the performance.[22] But for actions not resulting in arrest there are no such criteria and no such judges. How, then, can one speak of

such actions as necessary and proper? Since there does not exist any offical answer to this query, and since policemen act in the role of "peace officers" pretty much without external direction or constraint, the question comes down to asking how the policeman himself knows whether he has any business with a person he does not arrest, and if so, what that business might be. Furthermore, if there exists a domain of concerns and activities that is largely independent of the law enforcement mandate, it is reasonable to assume that it will exercise some degree of influence on how and to what ends the law is invoked in cases of arrests.

Skid-row presents one excellent opportunity to study these problems. The area contains a heavy concentration of persons who do not live "normal" lives in terms of prevailing standards of middle-class morality. Since the police respond to this situation by intensive patrolling, the structure of peace keeping should be readily observable. Needless to say, the findings and conclusions will not be necessarily generalizable to other types of demand conditions.

## THE PROBLEM OF KEEPING THE PEACE IN SKID-ROW

Skid-row has always occupied a special place among the various forms of urban life. While other areas are perceived as being different in many ways, skid-row is seen as completely different. Though it is located in the heart of civilization, it is viewed as containing aspects of the primordial jungle, calling for missionary activities and offering opportunities for exotic adventure. While each inhabitant individually can be seen as tragically linked to the vicissitudes of "normal" life, allowing others to say "here but for the Grace of God go I," those who live there are believed to have repudiated the entire role-casting scheme of the majority and to live apart from normalcy. Accordingly, the traditional attitude of civic-mindedness toward skid-row has been dominated by the desire to contain it and to salvage souls from its clutches.[23] The specific task of containment has been left to the police. That this task pressed upon the police some rather special duties has never come under explicit consideration, either from the government that expects control or from the police departments that implement it. Instead, the prevailing method of carrying out the task is to assign patrolmen to the area on a fairly permanent basis and to allow them to work out their own ways of running things. External influence is confined largely to the supply of support and facilities, on the one hand, and to occasional expressions of criticism about the overall conditions, on the other. Within the limits of available resources and general expectations, patrolmen are supposed to know what to do and are free to do it.[24]

Patrolmen who are more or less permanently assigned to skid-row districts tend to develop a conception of the nature of their "domain" that is surprisingly uniform. Individual officers differ in many aspects of practice, emphasize different concerns, and maintain different contacts, but they are in fundamental agreement about the structure of skid-row life. This relatively uniform conception includes an implicit formulation of the problem of keeping the peace in skid-row.

In the view of experienced patrolmen, life on skid-row is fundamentally different from life in other parts of society. To be sure, they say, around its geographic limits the area tends to blend into the surrounding environment, and its population always encompasses some persons who are only transitionally associated with it. Basically, however, skid-row is perceived as the natural habitat of people who lack the capacities and commitments to live "normal" lives on a sustained basis. The presence of these people defines the nature of social reality in the area. In general, and especially in casual encounters, the presumption of incompetence of the disinclination to be "normal" is the leading theme for the interpretation of all actions and relations. Not only do people approach one another in this manner, but presumably they also expect to be approached in this way, and they conduct themselves accordingly.

In practice, the restriction of interactional possibilities that is based on the patrolman's stereotyped conception of skid-row residents is always subject to revision and modification toward particular individuals. Thus, it is entirely possible, and not unusual, for patrolmen to view certain skid-row inhabitants in terms that involve non-skid-row aspects of normality. Instances of such approaches and relationships invariably involve personal acquaintance and the knowledge of a good deal of individually qualifying information. Such instances are seen, despite their relative frequency, as exceptions to the rule. The awareness of the possibility of breakdown, frustration, and betrayal is ever-present, basic wariness is never wholly dissipated, and undaunted trust can never be fully reconciled with presence on skid-row.

What patrolmen view as normal on skid-row—and what they also think is taken for granted as "life as usual" by the inhabitants—is not easily summarized. It seems to focus on the idea that the dominant consideration governing all enterprise and association is directed to the occasion of the moment. Nothing is thought of as having a background that might have led up to the present in terms of some compelling moral or practical necessity. There are some exceptions to this rule, of course: the police themselves, and those who run certain establishments, are perceived as engaged in important and necessary activities. But in order to carry them out they, too, must be geared to the overall atmosphere of fortuitousness. In this atmosphere, the range of control that persons have over one another is exceedingly narrow. Good faith, even where it is valued, is seen merely as a personal matter. Its violations are the victim's own hard luck, rather than demonstrable violations of property. There is only a private sense of irony at having been victimized. The overall air is not so much one of active distrust as it is one of irrelevance of trust; as patrolmen often emphasize, the situation does not necessarily cause all relations to be predatory, but the possibility of exploitation if not checked by the expectation that it will not happen.

Just as the past is seen by the policeman as having only the most attenuated relevance to the present, so the future implications of present situations are said to be generally devoid of prospective coherence. No venture, especially no joint venture, can be said to have a strongly predictable future in line with its initial objectives. It is a matter of adventitious circumstance whether or not matters go as anticipated. That which is not within the grasp of momentary control is outside of practical social reality.

Though patrolmen see the temporal framework of the occasion of the moment mainly as a lack of trustworthiness, they also recognize that it involves more than merely the personal motives of individuals. In addition to the fact that everybody *feels* that things matter only at the moment, irresponsibility takes an *objectified* form on skid-row. The places the residents occupy, the social relations they entertain, and the activities that engage them are not meaningfully connected over time. Thus, for example, address, occupation, marital status, etc., matter much less on skid-row than in any other part of society. The fact that present whereabouts, activities, and affiliations imply neither continuity nor direction means that life on skid-row lacks a socially structured background of accountability. Of course, everybody's life contains some sequential incongruities, but in the life of a skid-row inhabitant every moment is an accident. That a man has no "address" in the future that could be in some way inferred from where he is and what he does makes him a person of *radically reduced visibility.* If he disappears from sight and one wishes to locate him, it is virtually impossible to systematize the search. All one can know with relative certainty is that he will be somewhere on some skid-row and the only thing one can do is to trace the factual contiguities of his whereabouts.

It is commonly known that the police are expert in finding people and that they have developed an exquisite technology involving special facilities and procedures of sleuthing. It is less well appreciated that all this technology builds upon those socially structured features of everyday life that render persons findable in the first place.

Under ordinary conditions, the query as to where a person is can be addressed, from the outset, to a restricted realm of possibilities that can be further narrowed by looking into certain places and asking certain persons. The map of whereabouts that normally competent persons use whenever they wish to locate someone is constituted by the basic facts of membership in society. Insofar as membership consists of status incumbencies, each of which has an adumbrated future that substantially reduces unpredictability, it is itself a guarantee of the order within which it is quite difficult to get lost. Membership is thus visible not only now but also as its own projection into the future. It is in terms of this prospective availability that the skid-row inhabitant is a person of reduced visibility. His membership is viewed as extraordinary because its extension into the future is *not* reduced to a restricted realm of possibilities. Neither his subjective dispositions, nor his circumstances, indicate that he is oriented to any particular long-range interests. But, as he may claim every contingent opportunity, his claims are always seen as based on slight merit or right, at least to the extent that interfering with them does not constitute a substantial denial of his freedom.

This, then, constitutes the problem of keeping the peace on skid-row. Considerations of momentary expediency are seen as having unqualified priority as maxims of conduct; consequently, the controlling influences of the pursuit of sustained interests are presumed to be absent.

### THE PRACTICES OF KEEPING THE PEACE IN SKID-ROW

From the perspective of society as a whole, skid-row inhabitants appear troublesome in a variety of ways. The uncommitted life attributed to them is perceived as inherently offensive; its very existence arouses indignation and contempt. More important, however, is the feeling that persons who have repudiated the entire role-status casting system of society, persons whose lives forever collapse into a succession of random moments, are seen as constituting a practical risk. As they have nothing to foresake, nothing is thought safe from them.[25]

The skid-row patrolman's concept of his mandate includes an awareness of this presumed risk.

He is constantly attuned to the possibility of violence, and he is convinced that things to which the inhabitants have free access are as good as lost. But his concern is directed toward the continuous condition of peril *in the area* rather than *for society in general*. While he is obviously conscious of the presence of many persons who have committed crimes outside of skid-row and will arrest them when they come to his attention, this is a peripheral part of his routine activities. In general, the skid-row patrolman and his superiors take for granted that his main business is to keep the peace and enforce the laws *on skid-row*, and that he is involved only incidentally in protecting society at large. Thus, his task is formulated basically as the protection of putative predators from one another. The maintenance of peace and safety is difficult because everyday life on skid-row is viewed as an open field for reciprocal exploitation. As the lives of the inhabitants lack the prospective coherence associated with status incumbency, the realization of self-interest does not produce order. Hence, mechanisms that control risk must work primarily from without.

External containment, to be effective, must be oriented to the realities of existence. Thus, the skid-row patrolman employs an approach that he views as appropriate to the *ad hoc* nature of skid-row life. The following are the three most prominent elements of this approach. First, the seasoned patrolman seeks to acquire a richly particularized knowledge of people and places in the area. Second, he gives the consideration of strict culpability a subordinate status among grounds for remedial sanction. Third, his use and choice of coercive interventions is determined mainly by exigencies of situations and with little regard for possible long range effects on individual persons.

THE PARTICULARIZATION OF KNOWLEDGE    The patrolman's orientation to people on skid-row is structured basically by the presupposition that if he does not know a man personally there is very little that he can assume about him. This rule determines his interaction with people who live on skid-row. Since the area also contains other types

of persons, however, its applicability is not universal. To some such persons it does not apply at all, and it has a somewhat mitigated significance with certain others. For example, some persons encountered on skid-row can be recognized immediately as outsiders. Among them are workers who are employed in commerical and industrial enterprises that abut the area, persons who come for the purpose of adventurous "slumming," and some patrons of second-hand stores and pawn shops. Even with very little experience, it is relatively easy to identify these people by appearance, demeanor, and the time and place of their presence. The patrolman maintains an impersonal attitude toward them, and they are, under ordinary circumstances, not the objects of his attention.[26]

Clearly set off from these outsiders are the residents and the entire corps of personnel that services skid-row. It would be fair to say that one of the main routine activities of patrolmen is the establishment and maintenance of familiar relationships with individual members of these groups. Officers emphasize their interest in this, and they maintain that their grasp of and control over skid-row is precisely commensurate with the extent to which they "know the people." By this they do not mean having a quasi-theoretical understanding of human nature but rather the common practice of individualized and reciprocal recognition. As this group encompasses both those who render services on skid-row and those who are serviced, individualized interest is not always based on the desire to overcome uncertainty. Instead, relations with service personnel become absorbed into the network of particularized attention. Ties between patrolmen, on the one hand, and businessmen, managers, and workers, on the other hand, are often defined in terms of shared or similar interests. It bears mentioning that many persons live *and* work on skid-row. Thus, the distinction between those who service and those who are serviced is not a clearcut dichotomy but a spectrum of affiliations.

As a general rule, the skid-row patrolman possesses an immensely detailed factual knowledge of his beat. He knows, and knows a great deal about, a large number of residents. He is likely to know every person who manages or works in the local bars, hotels, shops, stores, and missions. Moreover, he probably knows every public and private place inside and out. Finally, he ordinarily remembers countless events of the past which he can recount by citing names, dates and places with remarkable precision. Though there are always some threads missing in the fabric of information, it is continuously woven and mended even as it is being used. New facts, however, are added to the texture, not in terms of structured categories but in terms of adjoining known realities. In other words, the content and organization of the patrolman's knowledge is primarily ideographic and only vestigially, if at all, nomothetic.

Individual patrolmen vary in the extent to which they make themselves available or actively pursue personal acquaintances. But even the most aloof are continuously greeted and engaged in conversations that indicate a background of individualistic associations. While this scarcely has the appearance of work, because of its casual character, patrolmen do not view it as an optional activity. In the course of making their rounds, patrolmen seem to have access to every place, and their entry causes no surprise or consternation. Instead, the entry tends to lead to informal exchanges of small talk. At times the rounds include entering hotels and gaining access to rooms or dormitories, often for no other purpose than asking the occupants how things are going. In all this, patrolmen address innumerable persons by name and are in turn addressed by name. The conversational style that characterizes these exchanges is casual to an extent that by non-skid-row standards might suggest intimacy. Not only does the officer himself avoid all terms of deference and respect but he does not seem to expect or demand them. For example, a patrolman said to a man radiating an alcoholic glow on the street, "You've got enough of a heat on now; I'll give you ten minutes to get your ass off the street!" Without stopping, the man answered, "Oh, why don't you go and piss in your own pot!" The officer's only response was, "All right, in ten minutes you're either in bed or on your way to the can."

This kind of expressive freedom is an intricately limited privilege. Persons of acquaintance are entitled to it and appear to exercise it mainly in routinized encounters. But strangers, too, can use it with impunity. The safe way of gaining the privilege is to respond to the patrolman in ways that do not challenge his right to ask questions and issue commands. Once the concession is made that the officer is entitled to inquire into a man's background, business, and intentions, and that he is entitled to obedience, there opens a field of colloquial license. A patrolman seems to grant expressive freedom in recognition of a person's acceptance of his access to areas of life ordinarily defined as private and subject to coercive control only under special circumstances. While patrolmen accept and seemingly even cultivate the rough *quid pro quo* of informality, and while they do not expect sincerity, candor, or obedience in their dealings with the inhabitants, they do not allow the rejection of their approach.

The explicit refusal to answer questions of a personal nature and the demand to know why the questions are asked significantly enhances a person's chances of being arrested on some minor charge. While most patrolmen tend to be personally indignant about this kind of response and use the arrest to compose their own hurt feelings, this is merely a case of affect being in line with the method. There are other officers who proceed in the same manner without taking offense, or even with feelings of regret. Such patrolmen often maintain that their colleagues' affective involvement is a corruption of an essentially valid technique. The technique is oriented to the goal of maintaining operational control. The patrolman's conception of this goal places him hierarchically above whomever he approaches, and makes him the sole judge of the propriety of the occasion. As he alone is oriented to this goal, and as he seeks to attain it by means of individualized access to persons, those who frustrate him are seen as motivated at best by the desire to "give him a hard time" and at worst by some darkly devious purpose.

Officers are quite aware that the directness of their approach and the demands they make are difficult to reconcile with the doctrines of civil liberties, but they maintain that they are in accord with the general freedom of access that persons living on skid-row normally grant one another. That is, they believe that the imposition of personalized and far-reaching control is in tune with standard expectancies. In terms of these expectancies, people are not so much denied the right to privacy as they are seen as not having any privacy. Thus, officers seek to install themselves in the center of people's lives and let the consciousness of their presence play the part of conscience.

When talking about the practical necessity of an aggressively personal approach, officers do not refer merely to the need for maintaining control over lives that are open in the direction of the untoward. They also see it as the basis for the supply of certain valued services to inhabitants of skid-row. The coerced or conceded access to persons often imposes on the patrolman tasks that are, in the main, in line with these persons' expressed or implied interest. In asserting this connection, patrolmen note that they frequently help people to obtain meals, lodging, employment, that they direct them to welfare and health services, and that they aid them in various other ways. Though patrolmen tend to describe such services mainly as the product of their own altruism, they also say that their colleagues who avoid them are simply doing a poor job of patrolling. The acceptance of the need to help people is based on the realization that the hungry, the sick, and the troubled are a potential source of problems. Moreover, that patrolmen will help people is part of the background expectancies of life on skid-row. Hotel clerks normally call policemen when someone gets so sick as to need attention; merchants expect to be taxed, in a manner of speaking, to meet the pressing needs of certain persons; and the inhabitants do not hesitate to accept, solicit, and demand every kind of aid. The domain of the patrolman's service activity is virtually limitless, and it is no exaggeration to say that the solution of every conceivable problem has at one time or another been attempted by a police officer. In one observed instance, a patrolman unceremoniously entered the room of a man he had never seen before. The man, who gave no indication that he regarded the officer's entry and questions as anything but part of life as usual, related a story of having had his dentures stolen by his wife. In the course of the subsequent rounds, the patrolman sought to locate the woman and the dentures. This did not become the evening's project but was attended to while doing other things. In the densely matted activities of the patrolman, the questioning became one more strand, not so much to be pursued to its solution as a theme that organized the memory of one more man known individually. In all this, the officer followed the precept formulated by a somewhat more articulate patrolman:

> If I want to be in control of my work and keep the street relatively peaceful, I have to know the people. To know them I must gain their trust, which means that I have to be involved in their lives. But I can't be soft like a social worker because unlike him I cannot call the cops when things go wrong. I am the cops![27]

### THE RESTRICTED RELEVANCE OF CULPABILITY

It is well known that policemen exercise discretionary freedom in invoking the law. It is also conceded that, in some measure, the practice is unavoidable. This being so, the outstanding problem is whether or not the decisions are in line with the intent of the law. On skid-row, patrolmen often make decisions based on reasons that the law probably does not recognize as valid. The problem can best be introduced by citing an example.

A man in a relatively mild state of intoxication (by skid-row standards) approached a patrolman to tell him that he had a room in a hotel, to which the officer responded by urging him to go to bed instead of getting drunk. As the man walked off, the officer related the following thoughts: Here is a completely lost soul. Though he probably is no more than thirty-five years old, he looks to be in his fifties. He never works and he hardly ever has a place to stay. He has been on the street for several years and is known as "Dakota." During the past few days, "Dakota" has been seen in the company of "Big Jim." The latter is an invalid living on some sort of pension with which he pays for a room in the hotel to which "Dakota" referred and for four weekly meal tickets in one of the restaurants on the street. Whatever is left he spends on wine and beer. Occasionally, "Big Jim" goes on drinking sprees in the company of someone like "Dakota." Leaving aside the consideration that there is probably a homosexual background to the association, and that it is not right that "Big Jim" should have to support the drinking habit of someone else, there is the more important risk that if "Dakota" moves in with "Big Jim" he will very likely walk off with whatever the latter keeps in his room. "Big Jim" would never dream of reporting the theft; he would just beat the hell out of "Dakota" after he sobered up. When asked what could be done to prevent the theft and the subsequent recriminations, the patrolman proposed that in this particular case he would throw "Big Jim" into jail if he found him tonight and then tell the hotel clerk to throw "Dakota" out of the room. When asked why he did not arrest "Dakota," who was, after all, drunk enough to warrant an arrest, the officer explained that this would not solve anything. While "Dakota" was in jail "Big Jim" would continue drinking and would either strike up another liaison or embrace his old buddy after he had been released. The only thing to do was to get "Big Jim" to sober up, and the only sure way of doing this was to arrest him.

As it turned out, "Big Jim" was not located that evening. But had he been located and arrested on a drunk charge, the fact that he was intoxicated would not have been the real reason for proceeding against him, but merely the pretext. The point of the example is not that it illustrates the tendency of skid-row patrolmen to arrest persons who would not be arrested under conditions of full respect for their legal rights. To be sure, this too happens. In the majority of minor arrest cases, however, the criteria the law specifies are met. But it is the rare exception that the law is invoked merely because the specifications of the law are

met. That is, compliance with the law is merely the outward appearance of an intervention that is actually based on altogether different considerations. Thus, it could be said that patrolmen do not really enforce the law, even when they do invoke it, but merely use it as a resource to solve certain pressing practical problems in keeping the peace. This observation goes beyond the conclusion that many of the lesser norms of the criminal law are treated as defeasible in police work. It is patently not the case that skid-row patrolmen apply the legal norms while recognizing many exceptions to their applicability. Instead, the observation leads to the conclusion that in keeping the peace on skid-row, patrolmen encounter certain matters they attend to by means of coercive action, e.g., arrests. In doing this, they invoke legal norms that are available, and with some regard for substantive appropriateness. Hence, the problem patrolmen confront is not which drunks, beggars, or disturbers of the peace should be arrested and which can be let go as exceptions to the rule. Rather, the problem is whether, when someone "needs" to be arrested, he should be charged with drunkeness, begging, or disturbing the peace. Speculating further, one is almost compelled to infer that virtually any set of norms could be used in this manner, provided that they sanction relatively common forms of behavior.

The reduced relevance of culpability in peace keeping practice on skid-row is not readily visible. As mentioned, most arrested persons were actually found in the act, or in the state, alleged in the arrest record. It becomes partly visible when one views the treatment of persons who are not arrested even though all the legal grounds for an arrest are present. Whenever such persons are encountered and can be induced to leave, or taken to some shelter, or remanded to someone's care, then patrolmen feel, or at least maintain, that an arrest would serve no useful purpose. That is, whenever there exist means for controlling the troublesome aspects of some person's presence in some way alternative to an arrest, such means are preferentially employed, provided, of course, that the case at hand involves only a minor offense.[28]

The attenuation of the relevance of culpability is most visible when the presence of legal grounds for an arrest could be questioned, i.e., in cases that sometimes are euphemistically called "preventive arrests." In one observed instance, a man who attempted to trade a pocket knife came to the attention of a patrolman. The initial encounter was attended by a good deal of levity and the man willingly responded to the officer's inquiries about his identity and business. The man laughingly acknowledged that he needed some money to get drunk. In the course of the exchange it came to light that he had just arrived in town, traveling in his automobile. When confronted with the demand to lead the officer to the car, the man's expression became serious and he pointedly stated that he would not comply because this was none of the officer's business. After a bit more prodding, which the patrolman initially kept in the light mood, the man was arrested on a charge involving begging. In subsequent conversation the patrolman acknowledged that the charge was only speciously appropriate and mainly a pretext. Having committed himself to demanding information he could not accept defeat. When this incident was discussed with another patrolman, the second officer found fault not with the fact that the arrest was made on a pretext but with the first officer's own contribution to the creation of conditions that made it unavoidable. "You see," he continued, "there is always the risk that the man is testing you and you must let him know what is what. The best among us can usually keep the upper hand in such situations without making arrests. But when it comes down to the wire, then you can't let them get away with it."

Finally, it must be mentioned that the reduction of the significance of culpability is built into the normal order of skid-row life, as patrolmen see it. Officers almost unfailingly say, pointing to some particular person, "I know that he knows that I know that some of the things he 'owns' are stolen, and that nothing can be done about it." In saying this, they often claim to have knowledge of such a degree of certainty as would normally be sufficient for virtually any kind of action except

legal proceedings. Against this background, patrolmen adopt the view that the law is not merely imperfect and difficult to implement, but that on skid-row, at least, the association between delict and sanction is distinctly occasional. Thus, to implement the law naively, i.e., to arrest someone *merely* because he committed some minor offense, is perceived as containing elements of injustice.

Moreover, patrolmen often deal with situations in which questions of culpability are profoundly ambiguous. For example, an officer was called to help in settling a violent dispute in a hotel room. The object of the quarrel was a supposedly stolen pair of trousers. As the story unfolded in the conflicting versions of the participants, it was not possible to decide who was the complainant and who was alleged to be the thief, nor did it come to light who occupied the room in which the fracas took place, or whether the trousers were taken from the room or to the room. Though the officer did ask some questions, it seemed, and was confirmed in later conversation, that he was there not to solve the puzzle of the missing trousers but to keep the situation from getting out of hand. In the end, the exhausted participants dispersed, and this was the conclusion of the case. The patrolman maintained that no one could unravel mysteries of this sort because "these people take things from each other so often that no one could tell what 'belongs' to whom." In fact, he suggested, the terms owning, stealing, and swindling, in their strict sense, do not really belong on skid-row, and all efforts to distribute guilt and innocence according to some rational formula of justice are doomed to failure.

It could be said that the term "curb-stone justice" that is sometimes applied to the procedures of patrolmen in skid-rows contains a double irony. Not only is the procedure not legally authorized, which is the intended irony in the expression, but it does not even pretend to distribute deserts. The best among the patrolmen, according to their own standards, use the law to keep skid-row inhabitants from sinking deeper into the misery they already experience. The worst, in terms of these same standards, exploit the practice for personal aggrandizement or gain. Leaving motives aside, however, it is easy to see that if culpability is not the salient consideration leading to an arrest in cases where it is patently obvious, then the practical patrolman may not view it as being wholly out of line to make arrests lacking in formal legal justification. Conversely, he will come to view minor offense arrests made solely because legal standards are met as poor craftsmanship.

### THE BACKGROUND OF AD HOC DECISION MAKING

When skid-row patrolmen are pressed to explain their reasons for minor offense arrests, they most often mention that it is done for the protection of the arrested person. This, they maintain, is the case in virtually all drunk arrests, in the majority of arrests involving begging and other nuisance offenses, and in many cases involving acts of violence. When they are asked to explain further such arrests as the one cited earlier involving the man attempting to sell the pocket knife, who was certainly not arrested for his own protection, they cite the consideration that belligerent persons constitute a much greater menace on skid-row than any place else in the city. The reasons for this are twofold. First, many of the inhabitants are old, feeble, and not too smart, all of which makes them relatively defenseless. Second, many of the inhabitants are involved in illegal activities and are known as persons of bad character, which does not make them credible victims or witnesses. Potential predators realize that the resources society has mobilized to minimize the risk of criminal victimization do not protect the predator himself. Thus, reciprocal exploitation constitutes a preferred risk. The high vulnerability of everybody on skid-row is public knowledge and causes every seemingly aggressive act to be seen as a potentially grave risk.

When, in response to all this, patrolmen are confronted with the observation that many minor offense arrests they make do not seem to involve a careful evaluation of facts before acting, they give the following explanations: First, the two reasons of protection and prevention represent a global background, and in individual cases it may sometimes not be possible to produce adequate justification on these grounds. Nor is it thought to be a problem of great moment to estimate precisely whether someone is more likely to come to grief or to cause grief when the objective is to prevent the proliferation of troubles. Second, patrolmen maintain that some of the seemingly spur-of-the-moment decisions are actually made against a background of knowledge of facts that are not readily apparent in the situations. Since experience not only contains this information but also causes it to come to mind, patrolmen claim to have developed a special sensitivity for qualities of appearances that allow an intuitive grasp of probable tendencies. In this context, little things are said to have high informational value and lead to conclusions without the intervention of explicitly reasoned chains of inferences. Third, patrolmen readily admit that they do not adhere to high standards of adequacy of justification. They do not seek to defend the adequacy of their method against some abstract criteria of merit. Instead, when questioned, they assess their methods against the background of a whole system of *ad hoc* decision making, a system that encompasses the courts, correction facilities, the welfare establishment, and medical services. In fact, policemen generally maintain that their own procedures not only measure up to the workings of this system but exceed them in the attitude of carefulness.

In addition to these recognized reasons, there are two additional background factors that play a significant part in decisions to employ coercion. One has to do with the relevance of situational factors, and the other with the evaluation of coercion as relatively insignificant in the lives of the inhabitants.

There is no doubt that the nature of the circumstances often has decisive influence on what will be done. For example, the same patrolman who arrested the man trying to sell his pocket knife was observed dealing with a young couple. Though the officer was clearly angered by what he perceived as insolence and threatened the man with arrest, he merely ordered him and his companion to leave the street. He saw them walking away in a deliberately slow manner and when he noticed them a while later, still standing only a short distance away from the place of encounter, he did not respond to their presence. The difference between the two cases was that in the first there was a crowd of amused bystanders, while the latter case was not witnessed by anyone. In another instance, the patrolman was directed to a hotel and found a father and son fighting about money. The father occupied a room in the hotel and the son occasionally shared his quarters. There were two other men present, and they made it clear that their sympathies were with the older man. The son was whisked off to jail without much study of the relative merits of the conflicting claims. In yet another case, a middle-aged woman was forcefully evacuated from a bar even after the bartender explained that her loud behavior was merely a response to goading by some foul-mouth youth.

In all such circumstances, coercive control is exercised as a means of coming to grips with situational exigencies. Force is used against particular persons but is incidental to the task. An ideal of "economy of intervention" dictates in these and similar cases that the person whose presence is most likely to perpetuate the troublesome development be removed. Moreover, the decision as to who is to be removed is arrived at very quickly. Officers feel considerable pressure to act unhesitatingly, and many give accounts of situations that got out of hand because of desires to handle cases with careful consideration. However, even when there is no apparent risk of rapid proliferation of trouble, the tactic of removing one or two persons is used to control an undesirable situation. Thus, when a patrolman ran into a group of four men sharing a bottle of wine in an alley, he emptied the remaining contents of the bottle into the gutter, arrested one man—who was no more and no less drunk than the others—and let the others disperse in various directions.

The exigential nature of control is also evident in the handling of isolated drunks. Men are arrested because of where they happen to be encountered. In this, it matters not only whether a man is found in a conspicuous place or not, but also how far away he is from his domicile. The

further away he is, the less likely it is that he will make it to his room, and the more likely the arrest. Sometimes drunk arrests are made mainly because the police van is available. In one case a patrolman summoned the van to pick up an arrested man. As the van was pulling away from the curb the officer stopped the driver because he sighted another drunk stumbling across the street. The second man protested saying that he "wasn't even half drunk yet." The patrolman's response was "OK, I'll owe you half a drunk." In sum, the basic routine of keeping the peace on skid-row involves a process of matching the resources of control with situational exigencies. The overall objective is to reduce the total amount of risk in the area. In this, practicality plays a considerably more important role than legal norms. Precisely because patrolmen see legal reasons for coercive action much more widely distributed on skid-row than could ever be matched by interventions, they intervene not in the interest of law enforcement but in the interest of producing relative tranquility and order on the street.

Taking the perspective of the victim of coercive measures, one could ask why he, in particular, has to bear the cost of keeping the aggregate of troubles down while others, who are equally or perhaps even more implicated, go scot-free. Patrolmen maintain that the *ad hoc* selection of persons for attention must be viewed in the light of the following consideration: Arresting a person on skid-row on some minor charge may save him and others a lot of trouble, but it does not work any real hardships on the arrested person. It is difficult to overestimate the skid-row patrolman's feeling of certainty that his coercive and disciplinary actions toward the inhabitants have but the most passing significance in their lives. Sending a man to jail on some charge that will hold him for a couple of days is seen as a matter of such slight importance to the affected person that it could hardly give rise to scruples. Thus, every indication that a coercive measure should be taken is accompanied by the realization "I might as well, for all it matters to him." Certain realities of life on skid-row furnish the context for this belief in the attenuated relevance of coercion in the lives of the inhabitants. Foremost among them is that the use of police authority is seen as totally unremarkable by everybody on skid-row. Persons who live or work there are continuously exposed to it and take its existence for granted. Shopkeepers, hotel clerks, and bartenders call patrolmen to rid themselves of unwanted and troublesome patrons. Residents expect patrolmen to arbitrate their quarrels authoritatively. Men who receive orders, whether they obey them or not, treat them as part of life as usual. Moreover, patrolmen find that disciplinary and coercive actions apparently do not affect their friendly relations with the persons against whom these actions are taken. Those who greet and chat with them are the very same men who have been disciplined, arrested, and ordered around in the past, and who expect to be thus treated again in the future. From all this, officers gather that though the people on skid-row seek to evade police authority, they do not really object to it. Indeed, it happens quite frequently that officers encounter men who welcome being arrested and even actively ask for it. Finally, officers point out that sending someone to jail from skid-row does not upset his relatives or his family life, does not cause him to miss work or lose a job, does not lead to his being reproached by friends and associates, does not lead to failure to meet commitments or protect investments, and does not conflict with any but the most passing intentions of the arrested person. Seasoned patrolmen are not oblivious to the irony of the fact that measures intended as mechanisms for distributing deserts can be used freely because these measures are relatively impotent in their effects.

## SUMMARY AND CONCLUSIONS

It was the purpose of this paper to render an account of a domain of police practice that does not seem subject to any system of external control. Following the terminology suggested by Michael Banton, this practice was called keeping the peace. The procedures employed in keeping the peace are not determined by legal mandates but are, instead, responses to certain demand conditions. From among several demand conditions, we concentrated on the one produced by the concentration of certain types of persons in districts known as skid-row. Patrolmen maintain that the lives of the inhabitants of the area are lacking in prospective coherence. The consequent reduction in the temporal horizon of predictability constitutes the main problem of keeping the peace on skid-row.

Peace keeping procedure on skid-row consists of three elements. Patrolmen seek to acquire a rich body of concrete knowledge about people by cultivating personal acquaintance with as many residents as possible. They tend to proceed against persons mainly on the basis of perceived risk, rather than on the basis of culpability. And they are more interested in reducing the aggregate total of troubles in the area than in evaluating individual cases according to merit.

There may seem to be a discrepancy between the skid-row patrolman's objective of preventing disorder and his efforts to maintain personal acquaintance with as many persons as possible. But these efforts are principally a tactical device. By knowing someone individually the patrolman reduces ambiguity, extends trust and favors, but does not grant immunity. The informality of interaction on skid-row always contains some indications of the hierarchical superiority of the patrolman and the reality of his potential power lurks in the background of every encounter.

Though our interest was focused initially on those police procedures that did not involve invoking the law, we found that the two cannot be separated. The reason for the connection is not given in the circumstance that the roles of the "law officer" and of the "peace officer" are enacted by the same person and thus are contiguous. According to our observations, patrolmen do not act alternatively as one or the other, with certain actions being determined by the intended objective of keeping the peace and others being determined by the duty to enforce the law. Instead, we have found that *peace keeping occasionally acquires the external aspects of law enforcement*. This makes it specious to inquire whether or not police discretion in invoking the law conforms with the intention of some specific legal formula. The real reason behind an arrest is virtually always the actual state of particular social situations, or of the skid-row area in general.

We have concentrated on those procedures and considerations that skid-row patrolmen regard as necessary, proper, and efficient relative to the circumstances in which they are employed. In this way, we attempted to disclose the conception of the mandate to which the police feel summoned. It was entirely outside the scope of the presentation to review the merits of this conception and of the methods used to meet it. Only insofar as patrolmen themselves recognized instances and patterns of malpractice did we take note of them. Most of the criticism voiced by officers had to do with the use of undue harshness and with the indiscriminate use of arrest powers when these were based on personal feelings rather than the requirements of the situation. According to prevailing opinion, patrolmen guilty of such abuses make life unnecessarily difficult for themselves and for their co-workers. Despite disapproval of harshness, officers tend to be defensive about it. For example, one sergeant who was outspokenly critical of brutality, said that though in general brutal men create more problems than they solve, "they do a good job in some situations for which the better men have no stomach." Moreover, supervisory personnel exhibit a strong reluctance to direct their subordinates in the particulars of their work performance. According to our observations, control is exercised mainly through consultation with superiors, and directives take the form of requests rather than orders. In the background of all this is the belief that patrol work on skid-row requires a great deal of discretionary freedom. In the words of the same sergeant quoted above, "a good man has things worked out in his own ways on his beat and he doesn't need anybody to tell him what to do."

The virtual absence of disciplinary control and the demand for discretionary freedom are related to the idea that patrol work involves "playing by ear." For if it is true that peace keeping cannot be systematically generalized, then, of course, it cannot be organizationally constrained. What the seasoned patrolman means, however, in saying that he "plays by ear" is that he is making his decisions while being attuned to the realities of complex situations about which he has immensely detailed knowledge. This studied aspect of peace keeping generally is not made explicit, nor is the tyro or the outsider made aware of it. Quite to the contrary, the ability to discharge the duties associated with keeping the peace is viewed as a reflection of an innate talent of "getting along with people." Thus, the same demands are made of barely initiated officers as are made of experienced practitioners. Correspondingly, beginners tend to think that they can do as well as their more knowledgeable peers. As this leads to inevitable frustrations, they find themselves in a situation that is conducive to the development of a particular sense of "touchiness." Personal dispositions of individual officers are, of course, of great relevance. But the license of discretionary freedom and the expectation of success under conditions of autonomy, without any indication that the work of the successful craftsman is based on an acquired preparedness for the task, is ready-made for failure and malpractice. Moreover, it leads to slipshod practices of patrol that also infect the standards of the careful craftsman.

The uniformed patrol, and especially the foot patrol, has a low preferential value in the division of labor of police work. This is, in part, at least, due to the belief that "anyone could do it." In fact, this belief is thoroughly mistaken. At present, however, the recognition that the practice requires preparation, and the process of obtaining the preparation itself, is left entirely to the practitioner.

## REFERENCES AND NOTES

1   The bill for a Metropolitan Police was actually enacted under the sponsorship of Robert Peel, the Home Secretary in the Tory Government of the Duke of Wellington. There is, however, no doubt that it was one of the several reform tendencies that Peel assimilated into Tory politics in his long career. *Cf.* J. L. Lyman, "The Metropolitan Police Act of

1829," *Journal of Criminal Law, Criminology and Police Science*, vol. 55 (1964), pp. 141-154.

2   Jerome Hall, "Police and Law in a Democratic Society," *Indiana Law Journal*, vol. 28 (1953), pp. 133-177. Though other authors are less emphatic on this point, judicial control is generally taken for granted. The point has been made, however, that in modern times judicial control over the police has been asserted mainly because of the default of any other general controlling authority. *Cf.* E. L. Barrett, Jr., "Police Practice and the Law," *California Law Review*, vol. 50 (1962), pp. 11-55.

3   "One concept, in particular, should be kept in mind. A dictatorship can never exist unless the police system of the country is under the absolute control of the dictator. There is no other way to uphold a dictatorship except by terror, and the instrument of this total terror is the secret police, whatever its name. In every country where freedom has been lost, law enforcement has been a dominant instrument in destroying it." A. C. German, F. D. Day, and R.R.J. Gallati, *Introduction to Law Enforcement*, Springfield, Ill.: C. C. Thomas, 1966, p. 80.

4   The point is frequently made; *cf.* Raymond B. Fosdick, *American Police Systems*, New York: Century Company, 1920; Bruce Smith, *Police Systems in the United States*, 2d ed., New York: Harper & Row, Publishers, Inc., 1960.

5   The executive margin of control is set mainly in terms of budgetary determinations and the mapping of some formal aspects of the organization of departments.

6   Michael Banton, *The Policeman in the Community*, New York: Basic Books, Inc., 1964, pp. 6-7, 127ff.

7   R. Bruce Holmgren, *Primary Police Functions*, New York: William C. Copp, 1962.

8   *Cf.* Lyman, *op. cit.*, p. 153; F. C. Mather, *Public Order in the Age of the Chartists*, Manchester: Manchester University Press, 1959, chap. IV. See also Robert H. Bremer, "Police, Penal and Parole Policies in Cleveland and Toledo," *American Journal of Economics and Sociology*, vol. 14 (1955), pp. 387-398, for similar recognition in the United States at about the turn of this century.

9   Smith, *op. cit.*, pp. 15ff.

10  Orlando W. Wilson, "Police Authority in a Free Society," *Journal of Criminal Law, Criminology and Police Science*, vol. 54 (1964), pp. 175-177.

11  Joseph Goldstein, "Police Discretion Not to Invoke the Criminal Process," *Yale Law Journal*, vol. 69 (1960), p. 543.

12  Jerome Skolnick, *Justice without Trial*, New York: John Wiley & Sons, Inc., 1966.

13  Wayne LaFave, "The Police and Nonenforcement of the Law," *Wisconsin Law Review*, 1962, pp. 104-137, 179-239.

14  Nathan Goldman, *The Differential Selection of Juvenile Offenders for Court Appearance*, National Research and Information Center, National Council on Crime and Delinquency, 1963, pp. 114ff.

15  Elaine Cumming, Ian Cumming, and Laura Edell, "Policeman as Philosopher, Guide and Friend," *Social Problems*, vol. 12 (1965), pp. 276-286.

16  There is little doubt that many requests for service are turned down by the police, especially when they are made over the telephone or by mail; *cf.* LaFave, *op. cit.*, p. 212, no. 124. The uniformed patrolman, however, finds it virtually impossible to leave the scene without becoming involved in some way or another.

17  Hans Kelsen, *General Theory of Law and State*, New York: Russell & Russell, 1961, pp. 278-279; H. L. A. Hart, *The Concept of Law*, Oxford: Clarendon Press, 1961, pp. 20-21.

18  Mather, *op. cit.*; see also, Jenifer Hart, "Reform of the Borough Police, 1835-1856," *English History Review*, vol. 70 (1955), pp. 411-427.

19  Francis A. Allen, *The Borderland of Criminal Justice*, Chicago: The University of Chicago Press, 1964.

20  Egon Bittner, "Police Discretion in Emergency Apprehension of Mentally Ill Persons," *Social Problems*, vol. 14 (1967), pp. 278-292.

21  It bears mentioning, however, that differential treatment is not unique with the police, but is also in many ways representative for the administration of justice in general; *cf.* J. E. Carlin, Jan Howard and S. L. Messinger, "Civil Justice and the Poor," *Law and Society*, vol. 1 (1966), pp. 9-89; Jacobus tenBroek (ed.) *The Law of the Poor*, San Francisco, Calif.: Chandler Publishing Co., 1966.

22  This is, however, true only in the ideal. It is well known that a substantial number of persons who are arrested are subsequently released without every being charged and tried. *Cf.* Barret, *op. cit.*

23  The literature on skid-row is voluminous. The classic in the field is Nels Anderson, *The Hobo*, Chicago: The University of Chicago Press, 1923. Samuel E. Wallace, *Skid-row as a Way of Life*, Totowa, N.J.: The Bedminster Press, 1965, is a more recent descriptive account and contains a useful bibliography. Donald A. Bogue, *Skid-row in American Cities*, Chicago: University of Chicago, Community and Family Center, 1963, contains an exhaustive quantitative survey of Chicago skid-row.

24  One of the two cities described in this paper also employed the procedure of the "round-up" of drunks. In this, the police van toured the skid-row area twice daily, during the mid-afternoon and early evening hours, and the officers who manned it picked up drunks they sighted. A similar procedure is used in New York's Bowery and the officers who do it are called "condition men." *Cf. Bowery*

*Project*, Summary Report of a Study Undertaken under Contract Approved by the Board of Estimates, Columbia University Bureau of Applied Social Research, 1963, p. 11 (mimeographed).

25  An illuminating parallel to the perception of skid-row can be found in the more traditional concept of vagabondage. *Cf.* Alexandre Vexliard, *Introduction a la Sociologie du Vagabondage*, Paris: Libraire Marcel Riviere, 1956; and "La Disparition du Vagabondage comme Fleau Social Universel," *Revue de L'Instut de Sociologie*, 1963, pp. 53-79. The classic account of English conditions up to the 19th century is C. J. Ribton-Turner, *A History of Vagrants and Vagrancy and Beggars and Begging*, London: Chapman and Hall, 1887.

26  Several patrolmen complained about the influx of "tourists" into skid-row. Since such "tourists" are perceived as seeking illicit adventure, they receive little sympathy from patrolmen when the complain about being victimized.

27  The same officer commented further, "If a man looks for something, I might help him. But I don't stay with him till he finds what he is looking for. If I did, I would never get to do anything else. In the last analysis, I really never solve any problems. The best I can hope for is to keep things from getting worse."

28  When evidence is present to indicate that a serious crime has been committed, considerations of culpability acquire a position of priority. Two such arrests were observed, both involving check passers. The first offender was caught *in flagrante delicto*. In the second instance, the suspect attracted the attention of the patrolman because of his sickly appearance. In the ensuing conversation the man made some remarks that led the officer to place a call with the Warrant Division of his department. According to the information that was obtained by checking records, the man was a wanted checkpasser and was immediately arrested.

## 47   DANGEROUS DRUGS   RICHARD H. BLUM

It is the purpose of this report to present, in a preliminary fashion, the available facts about the relationship of certain mind-altering drugs to dangerous behavior, specifically to crimes, to vehicle accidents, and to suicide. It is also the purpose of this report to evaluate the data at hand and to make preliminary recommendations.

Our full report consists of several different papers, one on narcotics (opiates, synthetic opiates, and cocaine), one on alcohol, the present document which encompasses marihuana, hallucinogens, amphetamines, tranquilizers, barbiturates, and the volatile intoxicants, and one paper on drugs and social policy. There is an introduction only to

Reprinted with the permission of the author from *Task Force Report: Narcotics and Drug Abuse*, President's Commission on Law Enforcement and Administration of Justice, Washington, D.C.: U.S. Government Printing Office, 1967, pp. 21–39.

The papers on narcotics and on drugs and social policy also appear in this Task Force Report as appendix A-2 and appendix A-3. The paper on alcohol appears in the Task Force Report on drunkenness as appendix B.

the present document, consequently for the reader interested in all of the papers, it is best to read this introduction and the accompanying paper first and to read the social policy paper last.

The collection of papers which constitute the full report suffers a number of limitations some of which must be made explicit. Only a small budget was allocated for the work so that it has been necessary to restrict the literature review to published reports, most of these in English. Only 4 months were available for the preparation of all four papers; the deadlines for the work of the Commission being so critical that no further time could be allocated. None of the work was done on a full-time basis since neither the funds available nor the other obligations of the authors allowed a full-time effort. In consequence it must be recognized that the literature survey may be incomplete, and that supplemental unpublished data could not be incorporated. It will also be found that there is overlap between the papers with reference to discussion of fundamental issues. Part of that overlap can be attributed to the fact that at the time of the writing of the present document (perhaps best referred to as the "dangerous drugs" paper in spite of the inapplicability of that term—in regard to legal status—to marihuana and the volatile intoxicants), it was not known that the narcotics, alcohol, and social policy papers were to be prepared.

SCOPE OF THE FULL REPORT    Our task has been to concentrate on those drugs whose primary effects are mind altering and behavior changing—that is, they ordinarily affect moods, states of consciousness, levels of feeling and arousal and subsequent conduct. Sometimes called psychoactive or psychotropic drugs, these substances include preparations classified as opiates, stimulants, sedatives, intoxicants, tranquilizers, antidepressants, and hallucinogens. Among these the term "narcotic" is most often applied to opium, its derivatives and synthetic analogs Among intoxicants may be included alcohol, the volatile intoxicants such as some glues, gasoline, paint thinners, ether, etc., and, in another class, cannabis-derived preparations such as marihuana. As we shall shortly note, all classifications of drugs based on presumed behavior outcomes or on legal status are inadequate and confusing. Suffice it to note that ether is also an anesthetic, marihuana a narcotic or an hallucinogen, and alcohol a stimulant, depressant, or tranquilizer depending upon the circumstances of the discussion.

In our report we have excluded a number of substances which do affect consciousness and conduct. We have not discussed drugs which are used primarily in the medical treatment of physical illnesses but which may also have mind-altering side effects—cortisone and belladonna are examples. Some persons now use these substances for psychological rather than medical purposes. We have also excluded ordinary spices, foods and beverages which some persons can employ for mind-altering effects; nutmeg is an example. Finally, we have not attended to the mild stimulants such as caffeine (coffee, tea, some soft drinks), theobromine (from cacao beans and kola nuts, found in cocoa, chocolate, cola drinks), the mild pain killers (aspirin, etc.), and tobacco.

Our review has not focused on the outcomes of drug use that are primarily medical, that is, biochemical, physiological or anatomical; rather we have concentrated on human behavior associated with drug use. In attending to behavior, it has been necessary to consider a wide range of human activity associated with drug use but, for reporting purposes, we have restricted ourselves to behavior designated as criminal, suicidal, or associated with vehicle accidents (or industrial and other accidents when data is available).

We have been interested in several different kinds of data. We have sought "hard" experimental data which shows causal relationships between drug ingestion (under given dosage, routes of administration, settings, and kinds of persons) and dangerous behavior. We have been interested in data showing or suggesting correlations between several kinds of behavior, some of which involves drug use and some of which is dangerous, but where no causal links are demonstrated. We have been interested in clinical reports which observe individual reactions associated with drug ingestion or use overtime but where there have been no systematic scientific controls made in the observation. We have also been interested in popular beliefs, in the claims made by writers, witnesses and pressure groups, and in the opinions expressed by advocates of various kinds of drug distributing or drug controlling positions.

SOURCES REVIEWED    In our work to date we have reviewed the following reference sources: The abstract library of the Psychopharmacology Project at Stanford (consisting of some 1,600 article reviews derived from continuing scientific literature surveys), "Psychopharmacology Abstracts," "Psychological Abstracts," "Int. Bibliography on Crime and Delinquency," "Current Projects: Crime and Delinquency," "Readers Guide to Periodical Literature," "Excerpta Criminologica," "The Question of Cannabis," "A Bibliography" (U.N. Commission on Narcotic Drugs, 1965), "Smith, Kline, and French Drug Abuse Bibliography," "Drug Addiction," "A Bibliography" (Tompkins, Washington, D.C., 1960), and the "Classified Abstract Archives of the Alcohol Literature." We have also referred to other bibliographical compilations, to references in primary sources, and have, of course, read all the primary sources available. In addition, we have addressed inquiries to several dozens of investigators, institutions, and agencies interested in dangerous behavior and drug use and met with as many workers in the field as possible.

**SUMMARY OF CURRENT KNOWLEDGE**    It is best to begin with a few general statements designed to put drug use and drug effects in perspective. In the first place, it is clear that our interest should be not in what drugs as such do, but rather in what people do after they take drugs. Drugs may modify behavior but they do not create it. Our focus must remain on the persons taking drugs rather than on the pharmaceuticals alone. The second fact to bear in mind is that no mind-altering drug, taken with the range of dosage that allows the person taking the drug any choice of actions (when the dosage becomes so great that choice behavior is eliminated, the outcome is then usually stupor, coma, shock, psychosis or death), ever has a single uniformly predictable behavior outcome. The general classifications used for these drugs, for example "sedatives" or "stimulants" are misleading; these only describe probable outcomes for certain persons under certain conditions. Within normal dosage ranges there will be among a group of persons or even for the same person on different occasions a variety of behavior outcomes. These outcomes will be partly and sometimes largely determined by factors other than the pharmaceutical substance itself, for example by the person's expectations of what the drug should do, his current moods and motives, the social setting in which the drug is used, the tasks he is performing and so forth. Consequently one must be careful not to assume that the popular terminology employed for classes of drugs is an accurate description of their effect. For example, LSD is called a "hallucinogen" but the research to date shows that hallucinations are one of the infrequent experiences reported by persons taking LSD. Marihuana is classified as a "narcotic" under some laws; nevertheless, it seems more likely to produce intoxicating effects similar to alcohol. Because of the great variability in behavior under drugs it is also necessary to keep in mind that there can be considerable overlap among drug classes in terms of outcomes or, put differently, different kinds of drugs can produce similar behavior, for example an intoxicant (alcohol, marihuana), a sedative, and a tranquilizer may all appear to produce sleep in one subject under one circumstance (for example, at bedtime); these same drugs given to the same subject in a different setting (for example, a party) may all appear to produce stimulation.

A third general consideration is that the drugs under consideration in this report are commonly used outside of medical channels even when the law may stipulate, as in "dangerous drug" statutes, that use is to be limited to medically supervised circumstances. Their use may be "social" in the sense that the drugs are taken by people when they are together or "private" in that they are taken when a person is alone. The presumption is often made that nonmedical use implies both pleasure and risk and so it is that such drugs may be termed "pleasure-producing" or "euphoria-producing" drugs as well as being considered dangerous or illicit. It may also popularly be believed that the medical use of such substances is therapeutic and therefore not pleasurable and also that in medical use there is no social risk. It must be recognized that the foregoing are all assumptions and not facts. On the basis of available evidence it seems clear that the implication of "pleasure" is not a satisfactory explanation for much social and private (nonmedical) drug use, that the definition of some of these substances as "dangerous" in the social sense (crime, accidents, suicide) rests on very shaky grounds as opposed to clinical and medical dangers which are for the most part better documented, and that, in turn, the medically supervised use of drugs does not exclude social risks (crime, accidents, and suicide).

As a fourth consideration it is to be noted that

all of the drugs considered here have been described, by one or another source, as potentially "addicting" or "habit forming." Under the new terminology recommended by the World Health Organization the word "addiction" is to be dropped in favor of "dependency." In any event these drugs are described as substances to which persons become habituated so that they use them often and perhaps in increasing amounts and may, upon withdrawal, experience some form of distress. It is important to realize that although the probabilities of withdrawal symptoms (for example, pain, nausea, acute anxiety) as such do vary depending upon the drug's physiological effects, dependency potential itself seems very much to be linked to persons as much as to drugs. As yet not completely understood sociopsychological (and perhaps physiological and genetic) factors seem to predispose persons to become drug dependent; it is possible that the particular drug or groups of drugs (multihabituation) upon which they become dependent is incidental. In considering the behavioral consequences of drug use it is well to realize that habituation can exist without there being concomitant criminality. Whether habituation can exist without an increased risk of death or accidents remains to be established. Insofar as the use of a drug is itself illicit then there can be no drug use without criminality; if however one attends to crimes against person or property as opposed simply to the violation of law occurring because a drug is used, then the best evidence to date suggests that the drug-crime relationship depends upon the kinds of persons who choose to use drugs, the kinds of persons one meets as a drug user, and on the life circumstances both before drug use and those developing afterward by virtue of the individual's own (e.g., dependent or addictive) response and society's response to him (prohibition of use, arrest, and incarceration, etc.). In spite of popular beliefs to the contrary, one dare not assume that drug-dependency *qua* dependency leads inevitably to any particular type of social conduct, including criminality. Insofar as some activities are part of obtaining and using the drugs themselves, these will be repeated but these activities may or may not be criminal depending, as we have noted, on the laws and social circumstance of the person.

There is another fact to consider as part of the evaluation of drug use, drug abuse, and dangerous outcomes. Mind-altering drug use is common to mankind. Such drugs have been employed for millennia in almost all cultures. In our own work we have been able to identify only a few societies in the world today where no mind-altering drugs are used; these are small and isolated cultures. Our own society puts great stress on mind-altering drugs as desirable products which are used in many acceptable ways (under medical supervision, as part of family home remedies, in self-medication, in social use [alcohol, tea parties, coffee klatches, etc.] and in private use [cigarettes, etc.]). In terms of drug use the rarest or most abnormal form of behavior is not to take any mind-altering drugs at all. Most adult Americans are users of drugs, many are frequent users of a wide variety of them. If one is to use the term "drug user" it applies to nearly all of us. Given this fact, the frequently expressed concern about drug "use" might better be put in terms of drug "abuse." "Abuse" of course is also ill defined. Presumably judgments of abuse rest on such questions as (1) How much of the drug, or drug combinations, is taken and how is intake distributed? (2) Does the person take disapproved drugs? (for example, heroin instead of alcohol, marihuana instead of tranquilizers), (3) Does he take drugs in unapproved settings? (an adolescent drinking wine with a gang rather than at the family dinner table, an adult taking amphetamines without medical approval), (4) Does his behavior under drugs offer some real risk to himself or to others? (Our primary concern here: Crime, accidents, suicide, but also dependency, medical danger, etc.) There are, no doubt, other factors that would be revealed should one do a study of how people come to judge that drug "abuse" is occurring. The critical point for us is the realization that "use," "abuse," and "risk" are emotionally charged terms that may be based on hidden determinants or open assumptions that cannot be shown to have a factual basis.

To offer one conclusion at the outset, it is that current evaluations of drug use by the public, by the mass media, and by some officials, are often emotional. The programs, laws and recommendations that arise from these emotional responses may well be inappropriate if the steps taken do not match drug use realities. What those "realities" might be is most uncertain, for at the present time we know little about the extent of the use of any of the mind-altering drugs, about the characteristics of those using one or another "dangerous drug" (excluding alcohol and opiates), or about the kinds and frequencies of risks as a function of dosage, frequency, setting, and kinds of persons using any of these drugs. Consequently, we do not presently have enough knowledge at hand about persons, about conduct, about drugs per se, or about the effects of one or another programs of control or cure to make any recommendations for prevention, control, or cure where there can be certainty about the results even if those recommendations were to be fully implemented. The fact pervades policymaking with reference to mind-altering drugs.

## MARIHUANA

**DISTRIBUTION**    Nearly worldwide in both production and use.

**EXTENT OF USE IN THE UNITED STATES**    Only limited epidemiological data available. A few sociological studies of special using groups (musicians, professional people, slum Negroes, students.) Police statistics are an inadequate source of data because of apparent concentration of arrests in lower class groups and because marihuana arrests may be combined statistically with heroin and opium arrests. There is no current way of assessing the relationship of cases known to the authorities to actual prevalence of use in the population. Furthermore, fashions in drug use appear to be changing rapidly so that earlier data is likely to be inaccurate. One recent pilot study [Blum, Braunstein, and Stone, 1965, unpublished]* in two west coast

*References are listed at the end of the article.

metropolitan communities, the sample size too small to allow any assumption of accuracy of estimate, reported 9 percent of the adult population had tried marihuana and 2 percent were using it either occasionally or regularly. In one west coast university, a university health officer [Powelson, 1966; Corry, 1966] estimated 20 percent of the students were using marihuana; the police department [Berkeley Police Department, 1966] estimated only 1 percent use. Another unpublished student study (121 students in a west coast college) reported 11 percent experienced but none as regular users [Med. Soc. of New York, 1966]. Great Britain [Anon., 1964] reports sixfold increase in hashish smuggling from 1963 to 1964 and other British reports suggest, as do impressionistic United States reports, a continuing increase in use.

**CHARACTERISTICS OF USERS**    There are no epidemiological or "drug census" studies for the Nation as a whole. Descriptions made in the 1930's and 1940's found use was predominantly among minority group members and economically depressed urban youth, especially those judged as having inadequate personalities. Studies in Asia and Africa [Asuni, 1964; Chopra, 1939; Lambo, 1965; Watt, 1936] suggest use is concentrated among the young, urban poor and is associated with dissatisfaction, deprivation, and mobility. In India upper class and "respectable" use occurs [Chopra]. In the United States the impression, not supported by adequate studies, is that use ranges from young urban poor, including minorities, to disaffected "beatniks" through artistic and university communities to younger professional persons in metropolitan centers. Use appears to be concentrated in the 18 to 30 age group but reports of both downward (high school) and upward (over 30) diffusion are appearing. The best estimate is that experimentation is far more common than regular use and that heavy use (as occurs in Africa and Asia) is quite rare.

**REPORTED RISKS**    Some law enforcement officials and Federal Bureau of Narcotics personnel have held that marihuana leads to (1) criminal acts associated with impulsivity, recklessness, and violence, (2) distasteful behavior associated with disregard for cleanliness, unrestrained sexuality, rebelliousness, unpredictable relations with others, (3) risk of later heroin dependency because marihuana use creates interest in having drugs experiences which marihuana cannot produce and because it is obtained through illicit channels which also provide opportunities for access to heroin (and cocaine). Also reported [Watt; Asuni; Chopra; Murphy, 1963; Wendt, 1954] as risks are cannabis psychoses, cannabis dependency, decrements in work performance, and traffic accidents due to poor judgment and attention.

**VERIFIED RISKS**   Studies in India [Chopra] and North Africa [Asuni; Lambo] show that cannabis psychoses occur in association with heavy use of potent forms of cannabis. Dependency is also described, as is apathy, reduced work, and social effectiveness, etc. These effects may be due, in some measure, to the vulnerability of the using population (already hopeless, sick, hungry, etc.). In the United States neither cannabis psychosis nor cannabis dependency has been described, although marihuana may be one of a variety of drugs used in the multihabituation [Cohen and Ditman, 1962] pattern, where a person takes many different drugs and appears dependent, but not on any one of them. Case history material suggests that many identified heroin users have had earlier experiences with marihuana, but their "natural history" is also likely to include even earlier illicit use of cigarettes and alcohol. The evidence from our college students and utopiate and news articles is clear that many persons not in heroin-risk neighborhoods who experiment with marihuana do not "progress" to "hard" narcotics.

With regard to crime, other than the violation of law occurring by virtue of acquiring and possessing marihuana, there is no reliable evidence that marihuana "causes" crime. One Brazilian study [Andrade, 1964] observed 120 marihuana-using criminals and concluded their criminal actions were not a result of their drug use. A Nigerian study [Asuni] suggests that those who are at risk of hashish use are also at risk of criminality because of their primary social and psychological characteristics (being members of frustrated underprivileged groups living in urban areas with opportunities for committing crimes). In Nigerian hospitals with patients with histories of cannabis psychosis or use, there was no relationship of use to crime. In Indian studies [Chopra] a negative relationship has been suggested, for with heavy cannabis use stupor occurs during which the commission of crimes is unlikely. Among populations of students, artists, and other more "privileged" pot smokers in the United States there is no recent evidence of associated criminality; similarly in the famous "La Guardia Report" [1940] in New York City marihuana was not found to be either criminogenic or associated with criminal subgroups. With regard to traffic accidents, data is lacking. One study by Wendt [1954] in the United States using a cannabis-like compound suggested that motor performance was not impaired but that the ability to shift attention was reduced. Effects are no doubt related to dosage but no studies on varied dosage using driving tasks have been done.

**LEGAL CONTROLS AND THEIR EFFECTIVENESS**
Except for very limited research purposes, marihuana is not legally available. Its acquisition and/or possession are punishable by law in the United States. Both felony and misdemeanor charges may be levelled; we are not aware of any studies of actual charges and dispositions. In spite of legal controls marihuana is said to be obtainable in most metropolitan centers in the United States. It is not, however, readily available in the sense that a naive person has an easy opportunity to obtain it. Acquisition is dependent upon being a member of, or having access to, some social group where it is used. The penalty has clearly not prevented all marihuana use nor the reported recent upsurge in use. To what extent controls on availability and the penalty risks have reduced use cannot be said. If one were to argue by analogy, taking alcohol which is available without penalty as a comparison, then one would suggest that legal controls

have worked to suppress if not to prevent marihuana use. Some users interviewed recently argue that they have chosen to smoke "pot" because the laws are so patently inappropriate and they wish to signify their disapproval through direct disobedience. In California, a movement called LEMAR (legalize marihuana) is now collecting signatures for a referendum asking the voters to make the drug legally available. There is in addition sentiment among scholars and some liberal legislators not to legalize use but drastically to reduce the penalities now written in the law.

**OTHER CONTROLS**    In some States efforts are made to prevent marihuana use by means of education in elementary and high schools. Review of some of the text and pamphlet materials that have been employed in the past, and casual interviews with students, suggest that much of this material may be not only out of date and blatantly incorrect, but also conducive to ridicule and consequent counterreactions among the now often well-informed youngsters. Demands not to use marihuana based on arguments against sin or self-indulgence may not be appropriate to sophisticated and secular metropolitan areas. Arguments against use based on claims of dramatically deleterious effects which are contrary to what is known cannot command respect.

Studies on persuasion show that for an informed audience, the most successful persuasion is one which acknowledges both sides of an argument. So it is that if educational efforts are to be undertaken with respect to the prevention of marihuana use, it would appear wise to base these upon (1) a rational policy about use which is itself based on objective appraisals of the significance and risks of use, (2) educational materials which are appropriate to the facts and keyed to the contemporary state of student knowledge and interest, and (3) evaluations of the effects of educational efforts so that unsuccessful or "boomerang" programs can be abandoned.

Aside from laws regulating availability and prescribing penalties and aside from educational efforts in the schools, we are not aware of other formal marihuana use control programs. It is likely that informal social and moral standards are more powerful determinants of drug-using behavior than are either laws or school programs. If that is so, control of marihuana use is vested in the home and among youthful peer groups. It would be of interest to learn how parents and peers come to adopt standards about marihuana, and how these standards are applied, and what events produce change in views about drug use among parents and peer groups. No such studies have been done to date.

**COMMENT**    We have suggested that educational and legal efforts should reflect a rational policy about marihuana. We have further suggested that policy itself should be based on the facts. The inadequate data available today indicate that risk of crime, accidents, and suicide (and of undesirable physiological side effects) are not likely to be greater than those associated with alcohol (and may be less). If the equivalence between alcohol and marihuana is to be accepted as an operating assumption until more facts are at hand—and we think that is a prudent position to take—it then follows that a public debate is in order with regard to the best regulation of marihuana.

It must be acknowledged that there are other "facts" besides those of risk which will enter into policymaking. Perhaps the most significant of these is the widespread law enforcement and public belief that marihuana is as dangerous as heroin in terms of dependency-producing potential and that its use is associated with criminality. These beliefs, even if incorrect, are facts to which policy must address itself. Since there is no strong evidence (although there are some suggestions in the clinical literature) of the medical value of marihuana, there cannot be said to be any urgent reason to make it available, except for research purposes. Similarly if there is a parallel in kinds of outcomes between it and alcohol, there is clearly a risk of unknown proportion that increased marihuana availability, as for example with its legalization, might lead to increased dependency and dangerous outcomes of the sort associated with alcohol itself, the latter unquestionably being a "dangerous" drug in the social rather than legal sense. The recent experience of Asian and African countries is compatible with such a fear.

In the meantime there appears to be good reason to encourage research on marihuana which in turn requires increased ease of obtaining it and permission to employ it on human subjects for bona fide experiments. There also appears to be good reason to moderate present punitive legislation so that penalties are more in keeping with what is now known about risks; that is, they are not great. A revision of penal codes so that marihuana acquisition and possession becomes a misdemeanor only would not seem inappropriate. In addition, since the significance of marihuana use may well be for some persons that of rebellion or disrespect for law or tentative explorations in criminality, or it may portend developing dependency proneness on drugs as such, it would appear worthwhile for apprehended persons to undergo social and psychological (psychiatric) evaluations. If destructive tendencies (toward self or others) are found the person can then become the subject of nonpunitive rehabilitative or preventive efforts by welfare, medical, probation, or community psychiatric agencies.

In point of fact we do not know if such preventive or therapeutic efforts are of value; the hope is that they will be. We may at least expect them not to be harmful.

TENTATIVE RECOMMENDATION   In consultation with police, legal, and health personnel and with participation of research workers and interested citizen groups to formulate procedures (1) allowing for increased access to and human experimentation with marihuana by bona fide research workers, (2) to encourage funds for epidemiological research on drug use aimed at defining the characteristics of users and nonusers, their interests, conduct, health, etc., (3) to revise present penal codes so that marihuana acquisition and possession becomes a misdemeanor rather than a felony, (4) to support research and practical experiments in education, in schools and among parents and peers, focusing on conveying information about drugs

which encourages nondamaging conduct, (5) to assume a policy stance of flexibility and objectivity which will not only allow for but anticipate that changes in legislative, health, and educational programs will occur as new facts about drug use arise and as new public problems or benefits become apparent.

In addition to the immediate steps set forth above, there are several areas in which long-term endeavors may be envisioned. We conceive of these to involve planning and consultative efforts with law enforcement agencies, with health and behavioral scientists, and with legislators. Work with the public both in terms of assessment of views on drug use and on the determinants of those views and educational efforts designed to alter incorrect opinions might also be appropriate. It is premature to set forth in this paper the details of these efforts.

In general, the goal would be to provide a common base among informed and interested persons and institutions for planning—in concert—revisions in the law, in police procedures, and perhaps in public health and other medical-psychiatric practice so that marihuana and related drug use—and we must stress here that marihuana is frequently but one of a number of drugs being interchangeably used—can be handled with minimum cost to the taxpayer, minimum damage to the offender, with minimum strain on the police, and without creating anxiety among the public which in turn expresses itself as pressure on legislators for inappropriate laws. These goals, while sounding utopian, may very well be capable of at least partial achievement for of all the drugs considered in this report, marihuana is the one where there is the greatest discrepancy between public beliefs and probable drug effects, and between present versus reasonable legislation. The development of a moderate and consistent policy will much improve the present state of affairs.

## HALLUCINOGENS

A group of drugs whose effects often include imagery and changes in felt sensory intensity—less often hallucinations as such—including lysergic acid diethylamide, LSD-25, dimethyltriptamine, DMT, mescaline, peyote, and others.

**DISTRIBUTION**   Naturally occurring in many plants (mushrooms, cactus, tree barks, flower seeds, seaweed, etc.) and capable of being synthesized in laboratories, hallucinogens are widely distributed over the world.

**EXTENT OF USE**   Hallucinogen use has been restricted to relatively isolated nonliterate societies. Certain South and North American Indian groups and Siberian tribes have employed the hallucinogen historically. Within the last century the use of peyote by American Indians has spread widely and within the last decade the use of LSD, DMT, mescaline, and other products has been adopted in metropolitan areas of the Western countries, primarily in the United States.

**USE IN THE UNITED STATES**   No reliable epidemiological or "drug" census data exist. Use appears to be concentrated in young adults age 20 to 35 but there are signs of rather rapid diffusion to high school age levels and less rapidly to middle and older age adults. Employed in medical research, LSD has been given to small numbers of psychiatric patients, alcoholics, schizophrenic children and has been tested on terminal (dying) patients as a means of easing their distress. Employed in pharmacological and behavioral research, it has been given to volunteers, for the most part students. Employed by religious and philosophical seekers it has been given in institutions and centers, and other settings. These institutional uses account for only a fraction of current use; impressionistic but probably trustworthy reports indicate expanding social and private use of the drug derived from black market sources. Ease of transport and of synthesis make LSD distribution easy. The use of other hallucinogens, peyote for example [La Barre, 1938], has been fairly well confined to traditional (Indian) groups, but their use, too, is expanding to young urban people.

As has been the history with many mind-altering drugs, the pattern of LSD diffusion has been overtime from older prestigeful ones, also from institutionalized medical and religious (or pseudoreligious) settings to more secular use [Blum, 1966]. With secular use, a drug becomes "social," use is subject to less constraint, and greater variability in outcomes can be expected as a greater variety of personalities, settings, and expectations are involved. At the present time, it would be unwise to venture any estimate of the number of Americans who have tried one or another hallucinogen; any numerical estimates must be suspect. One may presume that given a condition of continued easy availability of the drug plus wide publicity about its favorable effects, use would expand rapidly; historically the epidemic spread of tobacco smoking, opium use, and distilled alcoholic beverages provide illustrations. What effect current legislation to control manufacture, distribution, sale—and in some States, possession—will have on LSD use cannot be said at this time. It has generally been the case that interest in drugs can be channeled but not repressed; so it is that the choice of available drugs may be limited, but not the practice of using one or another drug. Historical examples showing shifts are those of opium to heroin, hashish to alcohol, and more generally from naturally occurring milder drugs to synthetic stronger ones.

**CHARACTERISTICS OF USERS**   In the United States—as has been indicated—peyote use is concentrated among American Indians, but does not occur among all tribes. LSD, DMT, etc., were first confined to physicians and other research workers and then spread to their subjects, patients, families, and friends. Until a few years ago, LSD remained limited to an "elite" group of successful professionals, artists, and communications industry personnel, their families and friends. These same groups still appear to be using hallucinogens, but the concentration of use appears to have shifted to younger persons. Among teenagers, motorcycle club members, delinquents, urban poor and minorities, etc., there are reports [Senate Subcommittee on Government Reorganization, 1966] of spreading interest, suggesting the expected diffusion down the socioeconomic scale. No common psychological or sociological features may be expected among the users of any secular and social drug; different people take drugs for different reasons. Within groups sharing common sociological characteristics it is sometimes possible to differentiate drug-interested persons, regular users, heavy users, etc., on the basis of psychological or background factors. For example, among graduate students one study reports that LSD-interested persons are more introverted and at the same time more excitement seeking than disinterested persons [McGlothlin and Cohen, 1965; McGlothlin, Cohen, and McGlothlin, 1966]. Similar studies comparing psychological and background characteristics have identified certain differences among those trying (and not trying), continuing (and discontinuing) to use, and becoming dependent (and not becoming dependent upon) other drugs, for example, tobacco, heroin, alcohol [Blum and Associates, 1964].

**REPORTED RISKS**    Risks reported in popular articles include, especially for LSD, psychosis, suicide, continuing undesirable personality changes, release of sexual and aggressive impulses (leading to murder, rape, homosexual episodes, etc.), habituation, hallucinatory redintegration (return of the LSD state unasked and without taking the drug), development of interests in illicit drugs (marihuana, "goof balls," etc.), development of "cult" interests, and consequent warping of ordinary social outlooks, reduced work and social effectiveness, risk of divorce, increased accident risks when driving under drug influence, etc. Its exploitative use (control, seduction, purposeful production of psychoses) has also been reported.

**VERIFIED RISKS**    Psychosis following LSD is verified [Blum and Associates, 1964; Cohen, 1962; Downing, 1966]; there is no adequate estimate of the frequency of psychosis as a function of incidence of use. Mescaline psychoses are also verified. Some psychotic reactions are temporary, many are now "treated" at home by the subject's friends; counteracting tranquilizers (e.g., thorazine) are now sold on the black market as part of the LSD

"trip" equipment. Other psychotic reactions require long-term hospitalization. The most recent study available to us, that of Ungerleider, Fisher, and Fuller [1966] studied 70 post-LSD psychiatric admissions during a 6-month period in a Los Angeles medical center, these patients representing 12 percent of all admissions during that period. One-third of the LSD patients were psychotic on admission; two-thirds of the patients required more than 1 month of hospitalization. Recently reported in California [*San Francisco Chronicle*, 1966] is teenage use of jimsonweed (datura stramonium) a substance employed by Luiseno and Chumash Indians to achieve visions. Deaths among these Indians occurred following overdose [Harner, 1966] and overdose among contemporary youth may also be expected to lead to illness or death. Suicide attempts are hard to distinguish from bizarre behavior occurring under LSD, for example jumping from windows because "I can fly," so it is that although suicidal feelings are reported and clinical workers describe attempts, there is no sound data on the probability of suicide attempts as a function of dosage, setting, personality, incidence of use, etc.

Crime associated with hallucinogen use appears to have been minimal. Police reports before a California legislative committee emphasized disturbances of the peace (1965) rather than felonies. Occasional accounts of homicide [*New York Times*, June 5, 1966; Geert-Jorgensen, 1964], violence, resisting arrest, etc., have not been subject to followup case studies. It would appear that insofar as decent citizens take hallucinogens their behavior will remain lawful. We may expect that with the expansion of hallucinogen use to delinquent groups—and perhaps because it is now unlawful in some States, so that its use becomes criminal—a greater frequency of crime will be reported. A tangential remark is offered here. It is the person, not the drug, which is "responsible" for criminal acts. When an already delinquent youth takes LSD and commits yet another delinquent act, it may well be that the timing or expression of the delinquency is shaped by the drug-induced state of mind, but—as an example—aggression will not be a drug phenomenon. Generally speaking, one would expect (although the scientific evidence is far from adequate) that well-integrated people under heavy drug doses will not do things contrary to their ordinary conduct. Less mature, more neurotic or otherwise less well integrated persons would seem to be more vulnerable to the acting-out of impulses, the temporary expression of conflicts or of being persuaded by others to misbehave. Consequently, one's review of crimes reportedly committed under drug influence must attend to the prior criminal and sociopsychological history of the offender. It is also necessary to have regard for the role of clouded judgment or reduced muscular coordination in producing behavior (e.g., a traffic accident leading to manslaughter) that is criminal. There can also be long-run changes associated with drug use, as for example, the clouding of judgment associated with habituation and drug stupor or in psychotic personality change, where criminal acts may conceivably occur (e.g., smuggling marihuana, perjury, theft) as part of a poor judgment syndrome.

With regard to vehicle accidents and hallucinogens, there have been no studies and no verified reports in spite of some remarkable "I was there" accounts. Experimental work showing slowed responses and reduced information processing make it highly likely that accidents will occur when under hallucinogen influence. This expectation should be tested in laboratory studies.

With regard to the other claims about hallucinogens—dependency, social and work decrement, divorce, etc.—the scientific sources are reliable but samples are small and insufficient followup studies exist.

COMMENT    It is particularly difficult to assess either the significance or the social effects of the hallucinogens during the present period when there is such a widespread change in the pattern of use. The present LSD "epidemic" generates interest and alarm as well as social research; unfortunately, the research results take a while to be generated—by which time they may no longer be applicable. As a best estimate one may suggest that any powerful drug produces dangerous side effects and that any powerful mind-altering drug is likely to alter judgment and conduct, some of which alteration is likely to make trouble for someone. But the problem of trouble over frequency of drug use remains a critical one and until the facts are at hand any extreme programs—either for the use of the drug or for punishment of use—would appear precipitous. Indeed, the present spate of publicity, whether crying alarm or claiming untold delights, is likely to be highly undesirable in itself; creating interest in the use of potent substances among a number of young people or disturbed personalities who are clearly ill-equipped to handle an intense drug experience. Similarly, this same publicity creates fear in the public and generates pressures on legislators to pass premature punitive legislation. We agree with the present plans of the National Institutes of Health—notably spurred on by Senators Robert Kennedy and Abraham Ribicoff—to conduct epidemiological research on expanding American drug use and to finance further research on the hallucinogens. We also agree with the present policy of the Food and Drug Administration setting up controls over the manufacture and distribution of LSD but not making possession a law violation.

Precipitously, several States (California and Nevada) have made possession unlawful. Peace officers have pressed for such laws partly because of the difficulty they have in proving intent to sell in cases where persons possess drugs at the time of arrest, but where no long preparation of a case has taken place, so that a sale is witnessed by officers. The dilemma of the law enforcement people is genuine and arises out of pressures on them to "crack down" on sales alone, since the (mostly undercover) effort in such cases consumes an immense amount of time. The arrest and conviction of those possessing drugs is much easier. Since much police experience with narcotics suggests that those possessing and those selling will be one and the same (except at upper echelons of organization), the popular desire to "bear down heaviest" on drug sellers results in fact in bearing down on user-possessors. Whether or not the narcotics seller-user pattern will be repeated with LSD and the other "soft" drugs is not yet known. It remains likely that some of the best organized production and distribution will be by persons not users; whether or not they can be controlled by local police using ordinary procedures is a question beyond the scope of this report. In any event, it must be recognized that if the law does outlaw sale, but does not allow arrest for possession, whether this be for LSD, marihuana, or any other drug, the work of the police will be long and hard and the public must not expect large numbers of arrests. As a corollary it is quite possible that such a policy would, as many law enforcement persons might fear, result in less suppression of illicit drug traffic and subsequent greater use.

Should this prove to be the case—and an evaluative effort is most strongly recommended to find out—there are several alternatives. One is to accept some illicit use as a fact of modern life and to concentrate on its control through educational and social rather than legal means. Another is to retain the nonpunitive aspects of the law, but nevertheless to require mandatory examination of all illicit and dangerous drug user-possessors by health, psychiatric, and possibly welfare (or other sociocriminological) authorities. Any found to be ill, disturbed, or otherwise maladapted might be referred to outpatient clinics for care or, failing their appearance for treatment, be subject to hospitalization under public health rather than criminal codes. These suggestions are only tentative and can be seen to follow present developments in the treatment of alcoholics and narcotic users. They also introduce serious problems of civil rights in terms of deprivation of liberty by health officers without due process. Treatment programs of a mandatory nature cannot be defended until much needed evaluation takes place to assure us they do, in fact, have a possibility of working. Further consideration of these points is beyond the scope of this report.

**RECOMMENDATIONS** It is recommended that Federal agencies be encouraged to support clinical and experimental research on the hallucinogens and epidemiological studies of population drug use. It is recommended that current FDA codes on hallucinogens be accepted as adequate, at least until more is known, and that individual States be discouraged from making hallucinogen possession a felony. It is recommended that the difficulty of the police task in controlling illicit drug traffic be acknowledged, especially when arrest for possession is not possible. In consultation with persons and staff groups interested in the prevention of drug dependency and in rehabilitation it is further recommended that various plans and programs for nonpunitive handling of the user of illicit drugs be evaluated (for one such evaluation see Blum, Eva, and Blum, Richard, "Alcoholism: Psychological Approaches to Treatment," in press). It is apparent from our comments and recommendations that we do not consider hallucinogen use to be a phenomena divorced from other forms of drug use. We are aware that there is disagreement about whether or not a particular drug use (especially alcohol and LSD) is a special case rather than part of a generalized drug picture. On the basis of our assumption and because of the differing positions others hold, it is recommended that general studies be continued which attend to all aspects of drug use, seeking to define both similarities and differences by drug or classes of drug as well as by user or population use habit characteristics.

As a final recommendation we would request of the mass media an emphasis on less sensational reporting and feature writing in regard to LSD and other drugs, would invite the public to give their legislators a moratorium during which time knowledge can be evaluated and reasonable approaches proposed, and would generally suggest as a matter of school and public health education that an effort be made to admit to uncertainty and to restrain emotion in the consideration of drug effects and the changing pattern of drug use.

## STIMULANTS

**STIMULANTS** A variety of substances may act as stimulants in terms of elevating mood, preventing fatigue or leading to short-term improvement in performance. Placebos, alcohol, tea, coffee, cigarettes, are so employed. Our focus here is on the major stimulant employed pharmacologically, amphetamine.

**DISTRIBUTION**   The amphetamines are a manufactured product available in all countries where Western medicine is practiced. Their concentration appears to be the same as the concentration of medical care, general pharmaceuticals, etc., namely in metropolitan areas. Nations which have reported amphetamine abuse include the United States, Great Britain, and Japan.

**EXTENT OF USE IN THE UNITED STATES**   Amphetamines are widely prescribed by physicians in attempts to reduce weight, control fatigue, overcome minor depressions, and in psychiatric care, in the treatment of behavior disorders in youngsters. In addition to supervised medical use, amphetamines are apparently widely employed in self-medication by persons seeking to combat lethargy, overweight, and fatigue. In this latter context, use by students studying for exams, by truck drivers and by nightshift workers is described [Roose, 1966]. Social and private use is also reported for persons seeking excitement or mood changes in the sense of "kicks" or "highs." No drug census has been taken so it is not possible to describe the actual incidence of use by population groups for the Nation as a whole. Social, criminological, and legal studies have identified use among late adolescents, including delinquents but extending to others said to be "rebellious," "wild," or simply "party going." In the United States, entertainers, actors, and other show business people are said to be users. In Japan during their postwar epidemic of amphetamine use, users were described as artists, entertainers, waitresses, and delinquents [Ministry of Welfare, Japan, 1964]. Use was concentrated in the late teens and early twenties [Masaki, 1956]. An English study [Scott and Willcox, 1965] described young occasional or party users as in no way delinquent or psychopathological; chronic users were however youngsters with personality disorders who came from unfavorable home settings. Other data supports the view that amphetamine abusers and those prone to dependency are badly adjusted youngsters before they turn to amphetamine use.

Japanese statistics [Masaki] showed at the height of the epidemic 7 percent of the population were taking "wake-amines" and 2 percent were abusers. Among Japanese arrested for use, half were said to be dependent. An Indian study [Banerjee, 1963] among students found 11 percent using amphetamines for studying, but none abusing the drug. In the United States 75,000 pounds were produced in 1959, enough for 20 tablets per capita. In 1962 a survey of producers showed a minimal production of 4.5 billion tablets (10 mg. strength) or 25 tablets per person [Lewis Laster, 1964]. Half of that production was reported by FDA to be going into illicit distribution channels (for social and private use). Recent arrest data shows an increase in arrests for amphetamine use [San Diego Narcotics Detail report to Senate Hearings, 1962]. There is some evidence then that production and use (presumably medical, self-medicating and social) is increasing.

**REPORTED RISKS**   Habituation (dependency) including physiological addiction (withdrawal symptoms present), traffic and airplane accidents, psychosis, medical ill effects including shock, convulsions, coma and death, and violence are among the risks which have been reported. For example, claims before the U.S. Senate hearings included, "children or youths . . . prone to sexual offenses," "a law-abiding person may go berserk . . . may participate in mass violence . . . ," "extremely dangerous," "proven to be a major contributor to this Nation's crime problem," and "the use of these drugs has a direct causal relationship to crimes of violence." With reference to accidents, claims before the Senate subcommittee included, ". . . a considerable number of serious accidents on the highways and in the air were traced to the use of amphetamines by persons operating such vehicles."

**VERIFIED RISKS**   Research done to date directly contradicts the claims linking amphetamine use either to crimes of violence, sexual crimes, or to accidents. For example, a careful search of reports reveals no case of an airplane accident attributable to amphetamines. Truck accidents, commonly attributed to high rates of use by truckers, upon careful search reveal—using Senate hearing data as a base—that in 1957 (the year for which statistics were presented) of 40 truck accidents with amphetamine use by the driver implicated, only 13 were described as being due to driver-performance error presumably due to amphetamines. These 13 cases were out of 25,000 truck accidents filed for that year, .0005 percent [James Fort, 1964]. Experimental work leads to findings like those of Miller [1962] reporting no detrimental effect on driving within normal dosage ranges or Murray [1960] finding that driving skills may be improved, especially for fatigued persons or those with depressed performance due to other drugs (e.g., barbiturates, alcohol).

With regard to crime the San Diego Narcotics Detail in a background study of offenders found those arrested for dangerous drug violations (including amphetamines) had no history of other criminal violations. Scott and Wilcox [1965], in a very careful study compared amphetamine-using delinquents with nonusing delinquents in England and found no differences in overall delinquency rates. But there were no crimes of violence, no road accidents, and no firearm possession violations in the amphetamine-user sample. In another study amphetamines were given to delinquents as part of a treatment effort and under these drugs the boys were found to show better adjustment and better work compared to delinquents not so treated [Eisenberg, 1963; Pasamanick, 1951]. Regarding sexual offenses, an observational study [Scott and Wilcox] shows loss of sexual interest among amphetamine-using youngsters. A review of the literature and of all evidence submitted to Government hearings shows no verified case of sexual offenses arising out of amphetamine use. This does not exclude delinquent sexual behavior among youths who, as part of their pattern of maladapted behavior, also use amphetamines. There is some evidence that judgment can be impaired by

use in some cases and that risk-taking may increase; again the personality and social context are likely to be major factors influencing actual behavior.

With reference to dependency and physiological ill effects, the evidence supports their occurrence. Twenty percent of a sample of users studied showed dependency, but withdrawal symptoms (physical) occur rarely [Kiloh and Brandon, 1962]. In a Boston hospital study of drug abusers [Schremly and Solomon, 1964], the abuse (dependency) of amphetamines and barbiturates (the up-and-down cycle) was observed in a few cases. The suggestion is made that several drugs will be found to be used sequentially or in the "multihabituation" pattern whenever amphetamines are involved in dependency. One clinical study of three medically supervised patients using heavy amounts of amphetamines indicated that neither dependency nor behavior toxicity need occur. General observations on amphetamine use would confirm the view that dependency is by no means inevitable but rather appears to occur only when some prior personality disturbance is present. Further research is much needed to find out just what kinds of persons are at risk of becoming dependent on drugs. The work of Chein and his colleagues on heroin [1964] provides an excellent example of what can be done.

Psychosis is an outcome not often mentioned by those alarmed at amphetamine abuse. Nevertheless psychosis does occur and, unlike crime and accidents, seems to be a genuine risk. Breitner [1963] describes cases of psychoses after use of amphetamines prescribed for weight control and for mood elevation. He suggests, as does Brandon, and also Beamish and Kiloh [1960] that many cases admitted as paranoid psychoses may be unrecognized cases of toxic reactions to the amphetamines. A general assumption is made by many psychiatrists, one insufficiently unsubstantiated by research, that psychotic reactions to drugs occur only when there is recognizable prior personality disorder.

COMMENT     One serious risk that we have not

discussed arises from the fact that the nonmedical use of dangerous drugs, as with marihuana and narcotics, can lead to arrest and incarceration. Many sociologists and criminologists contend that arrest and subsequent experiences when one is treated as a criminal produce many injurious consequences and increase the likelihood of expanded rather than reduced criminal and socially maladaptive behavior. Especially in the field of drugs where use is a crime regardless of whether or not any other damaging behavior occurs has there been discussion of the undesirable features of "turning the person into a criminal" through treating him like one and exposing him to contact with "genuine" offenders. As an alternative it is often recommended that criminal prosecution be limited to criminal behavior as such (i.e., crimes against person and property) and that drug use be handled (1) as a normal phenomenon, since this is a drug-using society except (2) when dependency occurs or other behavioral toxicity (aberrant actions, suicidal impulses, psychosis, etc.) emerges at which time the person may be subject to medical-psychological-social rehabilitation efforts. The evidence for arrest and prosecution as methods more likely to create a criminal out of a drug abuser than to correct him remains very contradictory. The situation is complex and no simple predictions seem tenable. It is made more complicated, as we indicated in the marihuana discussion, by the lack of assurance that ordinarily psychiatric-social rehabilitation efforts will work either. Even so, it can be argued that on grounds of economics and humanity it may be better to handle any person abusing drugs (that is anyone dependent and acting in damaging ways) by other than criminal procedures. On the other hand, proponents for legal restraints call attention to the role of law as an educative device to warn persons of drug risks and as a means of controlling drug availability which is, without much doubt, an important factor in determining at least which drug a drug-interested or potentially drug-dependent person will try. Proponents of punishment also contend that the stance of the law does influence use among reasonable persons by making use itself risky and by setting

forth the general message, a social consensus, that drugs are to be handled with caution and that abuse is disapproved. Many citizens would subscribe to this view of laws as a means for expressing ideals, educational goals, and social consensus. Whether or not criminal codes constraining drug use itself do accomplish these ends, regardless of their apparent inability to prevent or correct some drug dependency, remains a question. It is beyond the scope of this report to consider these problems further. We do call attention to the debate which now occurs about ways and means of preventing and correcting drug abuse and to the possibility that revisions in current punitive approaches may be in order. We would also suggest that studies of what laws do accomplish in areas of drug use and vice are very much in order.

In the introduction to this report we said that abuse is itself an emotionally loaded word. What is said to be a risk may reflect fears rather than facts as well. In reviewing the claims made about the undesirable outcomes of amphetamine use (and of marihuana and opiate use as well), one is struck by the lack of support for the claims advanced by reputable and well-intentioned persons, including government officials, to the effect that these drugs cause crime and accidents. We have taken special care in reviewing the claims of risk to trace back reports to their sources. We have, for example, gone back to the original sources for the very important paper produced by WHO (World Health Organization) which concludes that amphetamine risks are high for accidents and implicate amphetamines in crime as well. Looking at the references cited in support of the statements in the WHO paper one finds, that in some cases, the reference has little relevance to the statement. In other cases, one finds that the reference itself is not a scientific report or other careful observation but only an impression or opinion written in as a letter or clinical note to one or another medical journal. Sometimes several references are cited which upon inspection are only quotes from an earlier source or simple repetitions of a claim. We find this distressing for several reasons. First, it suggests that scientific and official reporting about drug effects may itself be subject to strong bias and may reflect preconceived ideas rather than an adequate appraisal of the evidence. Second, it makes the job of layman, official, or scientist harder in the sense he cannot rely on reports by presumably objective agencies but must return to original sources and thus spend unnecessary time and effort. Third, it reflects what is seen daily in the popular press, what is heard in official hearings, and what we see and hear around us in social conversation to the effect that opinions and emotions about drug use and drug risks are strong but that the evidence may be weak.

We have also taken time to survey some of the recent popular articles about amphetamine abuse, tracing their development in magazines. One finds the evolution of alarm and a sense of crisis, one article expanding on the one before, elaborating claims, exaggerating unsubstantiated cases, and becoming more intense in the cry for legislative control. Sensationalism can only be part of the reason the public must be receptive to such snowballing appeals and such receptivity reflects, we believe, general public anxiety. This anxiety expresses itself about drug use and insofar as new drugs do present unknown dangers and known drugs clearly do have bad effects as well as benign ones, that anxiety is justified. Nevertheless the extreme feelings apparent, and the catering to bias in popular and purportedly authoritative publications, reflect more, we believe, than a reasonable worry about drugs. In keeping with the thesis in our introduction to this report we would propose that people are worried about people, not about drugs except as these are a mirror reflecting distress. What people are said to do because of drugs—to rob and steal and rape, to injure and kill one another on the highways, and to become dependent and psychotic—these are the things that people do and we—all of us—have good reason to be upset about them. But people do not need drugs to act in these frightening and damaging ways; and the general evidence is that drugs in fact play a very small part in the production of our overall rates of trouble. They do play some part of course and insofar as they do, they add to the already great social burden. What we suggest is that the worry about drugs is extreme because somehow these substances have come to be symptoms of individual uncertainty and distress and can be used as explanations of why bad things are happening. As an explanation of the otherwise inexplicable willingness—or compulsion—of humans to damage themselves and one another, drugs are scientifically insufficient, but in terms of a public explanation they seem to serve that purpose. Our speculation, and it is only speculation without one shred of evidence to support it, at least focuses on the irrationality of much that passes for fact about drug abuse. It also suggests that further lawmaking about drug use need attend to at least two matters: One is that a law which is not based on facts and which has an unknown effect as far as control is concerned—or in terms of making the problem worse—is not likely to solve real problems associated with drug use. The other matter is that the apparent satisfaction produced by passing a criminal law directed at drug users must have some social function, perhaps it does at least alleviate public anxiety or allow one to single out for punishment at least someone who represents the bad things happening. If that is the case, then any revisions in handling drug users which focused only on users and on the facts of risk, but which failed to realize the intensity of public worry, and perhaps satisfaction with punitive approaches, might well generate further troubles—this time not for drug users but for the public deprived of at least this form of expression. If any of these speculations are correct it would follow that public soundings, public education, and direct efforts to recognize and try to resolve relevant public distress over unacceptable deviation and criminality—which is in fact one task of the President's Commission—must precede and accompany all provisional efforts at handling drug abuse.

**RECOMMENDATIONS**    A general revision of criminal codes pertaining to illicit drugs should be undertaken. A reasonable change might eliminate criminal prosecution provisions for the possession of dangerous drugs including the amphetamines.

Consideration may also be given to reducing penalties for acquisition and perhaps for sales under certain circumstances. Such reforms, themselves to be provisional on the assumption that drug use patterns will continue to change, should be carefully planned in concert with interested groups. Extreme demands by interest groups must be muted by having available reliable scientific evidence on use, risks, and control-effort impact.

Studies of the assumptions which underlie demands for particular forms of drug legislation should also be undertaken including studies of public attitudes and emotions, of law enforcement and church groups, and of reformers as well.

It will be helpful if commissions or other bodies planning legislative changes have before them careful evaluations of the actual effects of dangerous drug and narcotic control laws. These effects should be defined not only in terms of impact on drug users and on drug-interested potential users, but in terms of public beliefs and emotions and in terms of the impact on interest groups "displaced" by reforms, as for example narcotics police, temperance groups, narcotic treatment institutions, and the like. Because drug users themselves do not constitute an effective "lobby" but must be represented by others, as for example the present Senate subcommittee concerned with Federal programs for the handicapped, the function of present laws and the impact of changes on other interest groups (lobbies) should be anticipated in advance. New legislation cannot be expected to satisfy everyone, nor should it attempt to, but it must base itself on the correction of current inconsistencies, on the anticipation of known effects, and can plan on meeting standards of economy, humanity, and good sense; standards now not always found in measures affecting drug use.

Other means of reducing drug risks aside from laws must be stressed. Expanded public education, direct efforts to correct social and personality disorders conducive to drug abuse, expanded education of physicians, druggists and other drug "gatekeepers" may well prove beneficial. As with most other public efforts directed to reduce social ills and mental disorders, it will be unwise to be overly optimistic about producing immediate change. It would also be unwise to expect specific programs to solve more general human problems. So it is that broad scale programs such as those envisioned in welfare, antipoverty, mental health, public health, and other progressive efforts can be expected to contribute to the control of if not to a reduction in drug abuse.

In planning any program aimed at preventing or correcting drug abuse, it is important to be realistic about the limitations of any effort. As a society in the habit of using drugs and with the approved expansion of pharmacological research and the medical application of drugs, and with the ever-present strain of technological life, there is reason to expect medical, social, and private drug use to expand. Much of this use is benign and without serious risk and no free modern society would seek to prohibit such use. Risks and some bad effects will be inevitable, at least within the present generation.

A quote from Dr. Maurice Seevers [1962], Professor of Pharmacology at the University of Michigan is appropriate:

> The obvious lesson of history is that a certain segment of the population, probably a much larger one than we would like to believe, must find release or relief in drugs. . . . It is up to society, therefore, to find the means by which this may be accomplished with minimal hazard to the individual and to itself.

## TRANQUILIZERS

**DRUG CLASS**  Tranquilizers include a variety of different products, including some drugs which act essentially as sedatives, designed to counteract anxiety and agitation, control psychotic behavior, and to energize seriously depressed persons. The modern chemical families of tranquilizers have been introduced into Western medical practice only in recent years. Tranquilizers are sometimes classified as strong and mild depending on their chemical structure and effects. In practice there is overlap between drug classes as sedatives and those considered tranquilizers.

**DISTRIBUTION**    As naturally occurring substances, tranquilizers have been employed in folk medicine in Asia and perhaps Africa and Europe for centuries. As prepared pharmaceuticals, their use is primarily in Western medical practice, not necessarily psychiatric practice alone. Distribution is probably associated with availability of medical care as well as with economic factors associated with therapeutic drug use.

**EXTENT OF USE IN THE UNITED STATES**    There have been studies of prescription practices showing that from 6 percent [Shapiro and Baron, 1961] to 10 percent [Baron and Fisher, n.d.] of all medical prescriptions contain tranquilizers. Production figures from the pharmaceutical industry indicate that in 1963 over 1 million pounds of tranquilizers were sold in the United States [U.S. Tariff Commission]. Unfortunately, studies of prescriptions and of production do not tell us about what kind of people take how much of a given tranquilizer how often. They do not tell us about how formal medical channels for prescription are converted into informal channels for distribution without medical supervision. There are enough tranquilizers available to allow every citizen to take them often; since this is probably not the case, the best estimate is that some citizens use them quite heavily.

**CHARACTERISTICS OF USERS**    Prescription studies show that women more often than men receive tranquilizers as patients [Shapiro and Baron; Baron and Fisher; Glatt, 1962]. A drinking survey shows that middle-aged people use tranquilizers more than other age groups [Cisin and Cahalan, 1966]. United Nations and WHO personnel estimate that tranquilizer users tend to be middle and upper class respectable persons.

**REPORTED RISKS**    Tranquilizers have been implicated in suicide [Senate Hearing, 1964], in drug dependency (including stuporous or slowed behavior [Senate Hearing]), in traffic accidents [New York Academy of Medicine, 1964], and, in one report, in aggressive behavior [WHO, 1965]. They are contraindicated for airplane pilots. Recent Food and Drug Administration Hearings [1966] have yielded testimony to the effect that one tranquilizer, meprobamate, leads to dependency. Lemere [FDA Hearings, 1966] contends that 1 percent nonalcoholic and 4 percent (former) alcoholic (addict) users are dependent on that drug. Physical addiction is also reported, animal studies showing [FDA Hearings] physical "abstinence" symptoms including death when meprobamate is withdrawn. A variety of medical risks have also been described, some so severe that particular products have been removed from the market.

**VERIFIED RISKS**    In a study of 1963 suicides, Berger [1966] found 12 percent used analgesics and soporifics. Of these, barbiturates accounted for 75 percent and tranquilizers an unknown portion of the remainder. It is clear that overdoses can lead to death and that purposefully or accidentally (as for example, in potentiation with alcohol), tranquilizers have been used in suicide, but would account for less than 2.5 percent of all suicides occurring in the United States. Given enough equivalence in overall production in tranquilizers as opposed to barbiturates so that both classes of drugs are readily available, it is clear that barbiturates are preferred over tranquilizers as suicide means. In a study of New York City adolescents the Poison Control Center found tranquilizers used in 12 percent of the attempts in which one or another chemical was employed [Jacobziner, 1965]. (Aspirin was used in 35 percent, barbiturates in 35 percent.)

Dependency data is spotty; clinical studies make it clear that withdrawal symptoms do occur, so that tranquilizers may be classified as physiologically addicting drugs [Ewing, 1958; Hollister, 1960]. Autopsies and clinical observations indicate that an unknown proportion of persons are habituated. In a careful study of Boston hospital patients [Schremly and Solomon, 1964] out of 100,000 admissions six cases of tranquilizer dependency were found. Admitted patients were lower class persons; a hospital serving a different social clientele might have yielded higher figures.

There is no reliable evidence to the effect that

tranquilizers are associated with antisocial behavior. Behavior may change and some observers may disapprove of changes, but crime itself has not been shown to occur. One may keep in mind Dr. Jonathan Cole's statement [1960] that "behavior toxicity, like beauty, may be chiefly in the observer's eye." Behavior toxicity is a broad term and can be used to describe any form of presumably deleterious conduct.

With regard to traffic accidents clinical descriptions have stated that librium is associated with accidents [Murray, 1960]. In simulated driving experiments contradictory findings emerge. Marquis [1957] found no impairment of driving ability, Loomis and West [1958] with a better experiment, found tranquilizers did impair performance, chlorpromazine for example by nearly 70 percent. Various doses of several different compounds given in test situations by Miller *et al.* [1962] showed some impairment with tranquilizers, but not judged to be serious for transient use. Chronic heavy dosage is thought to be a genuine hazard to driving. Frank [1966] has cited a study showing that a group of patients receiving a tranquilizer for 90 days had 10 times more traffic accidents than the population at large. In considering driving or other tasks where accidents can occur, one must note that the particular condition of the person as well as dosage and kind of drug play a role; "norms" or standards of acceptable driving skill are also but poorly established. For a nervous person a tranquilizer might improve performance over prior driving; old age appears to lead to considerably reduced driving skill, so that a good middle-aged driver on a tranquilizer might perform better than that same person at age 70 driving without any drugs. We have been unable to find simulated flight studies showing the effect of tranquilizers on flying skills.

CONTROL MEASURES   Available on medical prescription only, there is nevertheless considerable informal private use of tranquilizers without physician supervision due to the practice of prescribing large amounts which are refillable and can be distributed by patients. No black market distribution chains have come to our attention, but this does not rule out their existence. There is no public or official alarm over present use, even if it is acknowledged that behavior toxicity may occur. Consequently, present control measures have not been criticized.

RECOMMENDATION   There is a need for further work on tranquilizer effects on driving skills, but this might well be part of a sustained and large-scale study of driver performance under a variety of influences. Very considerable Federal encouragement and support for such traffic safety work and for later inevitable stronger controls on licensing and driving is recommended.

Suicide is another area deserving further attention through research; again, the emphasis should not be on which drug, but rather on the factors creating suicide risk and means to their control. The work of the Suicide Prevention Center (Los Angeles) and of the Poison Control Center (New York City) is exemplary.

If epidemiological work shows further expansion in public use without adequate medical supervision, or without patient or physician awareness of possible toxic somatic as well as behaviorally toxic effects, additional controls may be considered. These might well be in the form of physician and public education. Physicians, laboratory experimenters, and other "gatekeepers" (responsible people who introduce or "initiate" others into drug use), often seem unaware of the consequences of their well-intentioned acts. As a general policy, physicians and experimenters should be made more aware of the risk of continuing informal (unsupervised) drug use which follows introduction to *any* mind-altering substance. Professional schools and associations might well be asked to play a larger part in this education of gatekeepers.

## BARBITURATES

BARBITURATES AS A CLASS   A number of substances have been employed to produce sleep, but our focus here is limited to barbiturates which are the most frequently prescribed group of sedatives. Other prescription sedatives are referred to in research cited here. Some sedatives, for example certain antihistamines, are available without prescription.

DISTRIBUTION    Barbiturates are manufactured products, available wherever modern medicine is practiced and where manufactured pharmaceuticals are sold. For the most part these are the technologically advanced countries.

EXTENT OF USE IN THE UNITED STATES    No drug census or epidemiological study has been made so that there is little good information about which people use barbiturates and how often. In 1963, drug stores filled 47,795,000 barbiturate prescriptions (Berger citing Gosselin Prescription Audits) and nearly 61 million for tranquilizers, but one cannot say how many of these prescribed drugs were used over what time period by what number of patients. Abuse is likewise difficult to assess, especially since case finding procedures are subject to error. Schremley and Solomon [1964] found for example that of 82 cases of all drug abusers (including barbiturates) identified in a Boston hospital, only six had been officially reported to an agency. In public health work and in police records, the problem of unreported cases ("the dark number") in crime remains a critical area of ignorance.

CHARACTERISTICS OF USERS    Surveys of drinking practices suggest that women employ barbiturates more than men [Sotiroff, 1965; Baron and Fisher]. Prescription studies concur. One authority [Isbell, 1950] finds that barbiturate abusers are similar to alcoholics.

REPORTED RISK    Medical risks include convulsions, coma, and death; barbiturates are used in suicides. Accidental death occurs with particular risk when alcohol potentiates physiological depression. Traffic accidents and crimes have also been attributed to barbiturate use. Dependency including physiological addiction is reported.

VERIFIED RISKS    Barbiturate suicide is the most frequent suicide device used by women. Of all suicides in one county (Los Angeles) barbiturates accounted for about 20 percent (annual report of coroner of Los Angeles County, July 1955–1966).

A review of national statistics [Berger, 1963] shows drug suicides accounting for 12 percent of the annual total, 75 percent of these employing barbiturates. Suicide itself appears on the increase (about 16,000 in 1954 reported compared to about 21,000 in 1963—many are not reported at all) and drug suicides are becoming an increasing proportion of all suicides (5 percent in 1954, 12 percent in 1963). Barbiturates have risen in preference accordingly. Of attempted adolescent suicides in New York City, 33 percent used barbiturates [Jacobziner, 1962]. In addition, poisoning and accidental deaths occur, some of which cannot be distinguished from suicides. For example, in 1965 New York reported 3,000 deaths due either to accidental or intentional overdoses [Medical Society of New York County]. In 1958, over 1,100 cases of barbiturate poisoning were reported in New York City. Accidental overdose can occur [Joel Fort, 1964 b] because of sleepiness or confusion following an initial dose after which further doses may unwittingly be taken [Berger, 1966].

Other than arrests for dangerous drug use as such there are no verified cases (at least coming to our attention) of any crimes against person or property occurring because of barbiturate ingestion. Dangerous drug use and arrests for that use appear to be increasing [Fort, 1964].

Regarding accidents there is not yet sufficient knowledge about the barbiturate role. Neil [1962] notes that "statistics are not available on the effect of drugs (other than alcohol which is associated with up to 50 percent of fatal accidents) on the overall accident rate." Inferential experimental evidence strongly suggests impairment of functioning in response to barbiturate use [Von Felsinger, 1953]. For example Miller [1962] found marked decrease in reaction times; Loomis and West [1958] using simulated driving apparatus found that barbiturates produced impairment in driving skill. One hundred mg. twice daily produced impairment as great as that accompanying blood alcohol levels of 150 mg. ("drunk") usually associated with great performance decrement. California Highway Patrol researchers (1964) have sought further data on drug use and traffic fatality but found research difficulties in detecting barbiturates in hospital and accident settings. Quick and reliable determination methods would be useful. A German study [Wagner, 1961] of over 2,000 drunken drivers found that 11 percent admitted taking other drugs as well within the last 24 hours, mostly barbiturates. Sixty-seven percent of all the (drunken) drivers had had accidents; 70 percent of the alcohol plus other drug group had accidents, not a statistically significant difference. Concentrating on the alcohol plus sedative group (only 23), 77 percent had had accidents. The upward trend, even if not statistically significant, demands notice and is compatible with other studies on summation and potentiation with combined depressant drugs.

Dependency including physiological addiciton is clearly present in chronic barbiturate use. Isbell found that 0.8 g daily for 6 weeks or more will produce severe addiction and in 60 percent of the cases toxic psychosis or delirium. Withdrawal symptoms resemble those produced by alcohol abstinence; alcoholics sometimes substitute barbiturates when alcohol is not available. In a Lexington (USPH hospital) survey about 23 percent of the addicts there also were using barbiturates [Hamburger, 1964].

Among the nonbarbiturate sedatives from which one may expect increasing problems are glutethimide compounds (Doriden). Clinical reports of psychological distress, physiological dependency, neurological disorder and death are accumulating [Lingl, 1966]. Since psychotic reactions have been observed, the possibility of dangerous behavior occurring in connection with use or withdrawal from Doriden cannot be ignored. These findings lead to the general statement that many of the problems associated with barbiturates will occur with other sedatives.

COMMENT   Barbiturates are addicting, are used

for suicide, can produce poisoning and accidental death, appear further to endanger those who have been drinking alcohol, and are likely to play a role in traffic fatalities. They cannot be implicated in criminal acts apart from their illicit use. The problem of suicide is not, however, a problem in drug control. It is a social and psychological problem and must be studied and prevented as such. Similarly the rising traffic accident rate must be considered overall. Drug use certainly plays a role here; the question is can drug-using drivers be identified in advance of their dangerous behavior and somehow prevented from driving? A consideration of alcohol accident prevention programs in Europe will suggest possible control devices. To what extent physicians themselves can play a role in educating their patients, or in watching for dependency and overuse preceding toxic effects remains a question. One of the critical problems underlying each of these questions is that of identifying the potentially or already abusing or drug-endangered person prior to his killing himself, hurting another in an accident, or becoming addicted.

The problem is not dissimilar from other case-finding needs in public health, in criminology, or in psychiatry. It is not impossible that these needs to identify citizens before trouble occurs—or afterwards but before they are dead—can be combined in community programs. One important focus will obviously be on drug-use habits; the excessive use of drugs may well prove to be a sign of general distress as well as of potential danger. Bearing on this is a recent finding of ours to the effect that 4 percent of a sample of persons admitting varied and frequent drug use also admitted to having attempted suicide with drugs [Blum, Braunstein, and Stone, 1966]. This sample also expressed dissatisfaction with themselves and their lives. We think it is likely that if drug abuse is taken as a symptom of distress and community-wide identification programs undertaken that preventive and rehabilitative measures may wisely be employed.

RECOMMENDATIONS   As an immediate need, inexpensive and reliable techniques for establishing the presence of mind-altering drugs (other than alcohol) in persons arrested or in hospitals are much in order. These techniques available for field use by police officers and other emergency personnel would be most useful.

Large-scale studies of traffic accidents focusing on the bad driver are in order. Out of such studies —but not before them—one envisions programs arising for careful prelicensing examination, periodic reexamination, driver education, and perhaps stringent legislation pertaining to those driving after drug use.

Community-wide programs of case-finding which not only focus on drug use but which are coordinated with public health, psychiatric, suicide, and criminological "dark number" research workers can be envisioned. Pilot projects should be financed along with pilot studies of prevention and rehabilitation once cases of troubled, ill, or dangerous persons are identified.

Efforts to educate druggists, physicians, teachers, and others as case-finders for barbiturates and other drug abusers are in order. Procedures for referral which do not work hardships on the drug users can be established.

## VOLATILE INTOXICANT SNIFFING

**DRUG CLASS**    The class of volatile intoxicants includes all substances which when sniffed or inhaled produce altered states of consciousness (ether, nitrous oxide, paint thinner, some glues, gasoline, etc.).

**DISTRIBUTION**    As manufactured substances, these are available primarily in technologically advanced countries. As for sniffing as a means of drug ingestion, certain naturally occurring substances such as the hallucinogen parica are sniffed by South American Indians, while tobacco is sniffed as snuff. Opium and hashish may also be sniffed, but these are not primary routes of administration.

**EXTENT OF USE**    A New York City survey of identified cases in schools in 1962 revealed only 31 cases in 21 schools. Another simultaneous New York City study showed 46 cases in 31 schools. In the last 3 months of 1962 the New York City police reported 503 cases (87 reported by schools) and during the first quarter of 1963, 443 cases. Winick reports for New York City over 2,000 cases in 1963. Among 75,000 Stockholm schoolchildren, there were 20 paint thinner addicts identified during a 1-year period. From these figures, and others taken from Los Angeles, Denver, and Detroit, it appears that sniffing violatile intoxicants is a rare occurrence.

**CHARACTERISTICS OF USERS**    Most identified sniffers of volatile intoxicants in the United States have been children in urban areas. Studies of select groups show more males than females, and a median age of about 13. Minority group members may be overrepresented. A study of backgrounds reveals serious family problems including alcoholism in the homes of thinner sniffers. Winick describes glue sniffers as having low self-esteem, being anxious and passive, and having poor personality adjustment. Another study found sniffers to have delinquent histories prior to sniffing, to be poor students with school adjustment problems and unsatisfactory homelife. Not all sniffers are children; a Detroit study finds young adult "swingers" and the "gay crowd" to sniff nitrous oxide; some clinical observations have found anesthesiologists to be a high-risk group for anesthesia sniffing.

In our pilot study of a normal population, we found adults who had been sniffers as children to be in the heavy (or exotic) drug-use category in adult life.

**REPORTED RISKS**    Reported risks include death and physiological damage (liver), dependency, self-destructive acts, antisocial acts while under influence; use is also reported to lead to other drugs, including heroin.

**VERIFIED RISKS**    Although violence appears rare, some of the intoxicated children have been assaultive or suicidal. Physiological damage does occur. Hard core sniffers do appear to be troubled persons interested in drug use and susceptible to further drug experimentation on a road that may lead to further dependencies. Mild dependency to sniffing intoxicants may occur.

CONTROL MEASURES Attempts to identify sniffers and to refer them to psychiatric authorities are predominant. Police appear to refer cases to other agencies but a further study of actual dispositions and later outcomes would be useful.

COMMENT Intoxicant sniffing is, in itself, rare enough not to cause alarm. The identification of sniffers is, however, of great importance so that rehabilitative measures can be introduced to (1) prevent danger while intoxicated and (2) to forestall the otherwise very likely development of later dependency on other drugs and presumed criminogenic associations possibly arising out of interest in illicit drugs. It is clear from the present data that case-finding methods (through doctors, police, schools) may require elaboration. One recent effort has been attempts to reach patients through pamphlet materials. Since parents of the sniffers are apparently a less than satisfactory group, such direct education does not offer much help or hope.

RECOMMENDATIONS To encourage school and public health people to develop new methods for case finding for children engaged in sniffing volatile intoxicants; also to recommend that each school, health, and police agency participates in a community-wide program for the referral of such children to psychiatric personnel.

## REFERENCES AND NOTES

Ackerly, W. C., and G. Gibson, "Lighter Fluid Sniffing," *Am. J. Psychiat.*, vol. 120 (1964), pp. 1056-1061.

Andrade, O. M., "The Criminogenic Action of Cannabis (Marijuana) and Narcotics," *Bulletin of Narcotics*, vol. 14, no. 4 (1964), pp. 23-28.

Anon., "Hashish," *Brit. Med. J.*, vol. 5421 (1964), pp. 1348-1349.

Asuni, T., "Socio-psychiatric Problems of Cannabis in Nigeria," *Bulletin of Narcotics*, vol. 16, no. 2 (1964), pp. 17-28.

Bachrich, P. R., "New Drugs of Addiction," *Brit. Med. J.*, vol. 5386 (1964), pp. 834-835.

Banerjee, R. D., "Prevalence of Habit Forming Drugs and Smoking Among the College Students; A Survey," *Indian Med. J.*, vol. 57, no. 8 (1963), pp. 193-196.

Baron, S. H., and S. Fisher, *Psychotropic Drug Use in a General Medical Outpatient Population*, mimeographed report, n.d.

Bartholomew, Allen, "A Dramatic Side Effect of a New Drug Librium," *Med. J. Australia*, 1961, pp. 436-437.

Beamish, P., and L. Kiloh, "Psychoses Due to Amphetamine Consumption," *J. Ment. Sci.*, vol. 106 (1960), p. 337.

Berger, F. M., "Role of Drugs in Suicide," *Curr. Med. Digest*, vol. 33, no. 2 (1966), pp. 250-255.

Bindra, D., K. Nyman, and J. Wise, "Barbiturate-induced Disassociation of Acquisition and Extinction: Role of Movement-initiating Processes," *J. Comp. Physiol. Psychol.*, vol. 60 (1965), pp. 223-228.

Bloomberg, W., "The Results of Use of Large Doses of Amphetamine Sulphate over Prolonged Periods," *N. Eng. J. Med.*, vol. 222 (1940), pp. 946-948.

Blum, Eva M., and Richard H. Blum, *Alcoholism: Psychological Approaches to Treatment*, San Francisco: Jossey Bass Publishers, 1967.

Blum, Richard H., *et al.*, *Utopiates: A Study of the Use and Users of LSD 25*, New York: Atherton Press, 1964.

Blum, Richard H., "Users and Abusers of LSD," paper presented to the U.C. Symposium on LSD, June 1966, in press.

Blum, Richard H., "Social and Epidemiological Aspects of Psychopharmacology," in C.R.B. Joyce (ed.), *Psychopharmacology: The Present Status*, London, in press.

Blum, Richard H., and M. Crouse, "An Historical Study of Drug Diffusion," unpublished.

Blum, Richard H., and Mary Lou Funkhouser, "Legislators on Social Scientists and a Social Issue: A Report and Commentary on Some Discussions with Lawmakers about Drug Abuse," Stanford: Institute for the Study of Human Problems, reprinted from *J. Appl. Behav. Sci.*, vol. 1, no. 1 (1965).

Blum, R. H., and M. L. Funkhouser-Balbaky, "A Cross Cultural Study of Drug Use," unpublished.

Blum, Richard H., L. Braunstein, and A. Stone, "A Pilot Study of Normal Population Drug Use," unpublished.

Brandon, Sydney, "Addiction to Amphetamines," *Brit. Med. J.*, vol. 5366 (1963), p. 1204.

Breitner, Carl, "Appetite Suppressing Drugs as an Etiologic Factor in Mental Illness," *Psychosomatics*, vol. 4 (1963), pp. 327-333.

Bromberg, W., "Marijuana," *J.A.M.A.*, vol. 113, no. 1 (1939), pp. 4-12.

Brooke, E. M., and M. M. Glatt, "More and More Barbiturates," *Medicine, Science and the Law*, October 1964, pp. 227-282.

Breuner, H., *et al.*, "The Effect of Some Drugs Important to Traffic Medicine on the Human Capacity for Performance," *Arzneimittelforschung*, vol. 11 (1961), pp. 995-1000.

Chein, I., D. L. Gerard, R. S. Lee, and E. Rosenfeld, *The Road to H*, New York: Basic Books, Inc., 1964.

Cisin, I., and D. Cahalan, "Social Research Project: National Survey of Drinking," George Washington University, unpublished. See also, "American Drinking Practices," UCLA Symposium, 1966.

Chopra, R. N., and G. S. Chopra, "The Present Position of Hemp Drug Addiction in India," *India Med. Res. Memoirs*, vol. 31 (1939), pp. 1-119.

Cohen, S., and K. Ditman, "Complications Associated with LSD-25," *J.A.M.A.*, vol. 181 (1962), pp. 161-162.

Cohen, S., *et al.*, "Prolonged Adverse Reactions to LSD," *Arch. Gen. Psychiat.*, vol. 8 (1963), pp. 475-480.

Cohen, S., Calista V. Leonard, and N. L. Farberow, "Tranquilizers and Suicide in the Schizophrenic Patient," *Arch. Gen. Psychiat.*, vol. 11, no. 3 (1964), pp. 312-321.

Cole, Johnathon, "Behavioral Toxicity," in Leonard Uhr and James G. Miller (eds.), *Drugs and Behavior*, New York: John Wiley & Sons, Inc., 1960.

Conlon, Michael F., "Addiction to Chlorodyne," *Brit. Med. J.*, vol. 5366 (1963), pp. 1177-1178.

"Control of Psychotoxic Drugs." Hearings, Subcommittee on Health of the Committee on Labor and Public Welfare, U.S. Senate, 88th Cong., 2d Sess., on S. 2628, Aug. 3, 1964.

Corry, John, "Drugs a Growing Campus Problem," *New York Times*, Mar. 21, 1966.

Danto, B. L., "A Bag Full of Laughs," *Am. J. Psychiat.*, vol. 121 (1964), pp. 612-613.

Davidson, Henry A., "Confessions of a Goofball Addict," *Am. J. Psychiat.*, vol. 120 (1964), pp 750-756.

Dille, J. Robert, "Drugs and Flying Personnel," *GP*, vol. 30, no. 5 (1964), pp. 86-90.

Downing, J. J., Testimony before California Assembly Committee on Criminal Procedure, Sept. 8, 1966.

"Drugs and Driving," *Traffic Laws Commentary*, publication of the National Committee on Uniform Traffic Laws and Ordinances, No. 65-1. Washington, D.C., April 30, 1965.

Edwards, R. E., "Abuse of Central Nervous System Stimulants," *Am. J. Hospital Pharm.*, vol. 22 (1965), pp. 130-153.

Eisenberg, Leon, *et al.*, "A Psychopharmacological Experiment in a Training School for Delinquent Boys," *Am. J. Orthopsychiat.*, vol. 33 (1963), pp. 431-437.

Ewing, John, "A Controlled Study of the Habit Forming Propensities of Meprobamate," *Amer. J. Psychiat.*, vol. 114 (1958), p. 835.

FDA Commissioner Larrick, "Control of Psychotoxic Drugs," Hearings, Subcommittee on Health of the Committee on Labor and Public Welfare, U.S. Senate, 88th Cong., 2d Sess., on S. 2628, Aug. 3, 1964.

Fiddle, Seymour, "A User's View," presentation to the Conferees Attending the First National Institute on Amphetamine Abuse, Southern Illinois University, Feb. 21-25, 1966.

Fort, James F., statement before the Meeting of the American Trucking Association, Inc., Washington, D.C., 1964.

Fort, Joel, "Cultural Aspects of Alcohol (and Drug) Problems," paper presented at International Congress on Alcohol and Alcoholism at Frankfurt, September 1964 (*a*).

Fort, Joel, "The Problem of Barbiturates in the United States of America," *Bulletin Narcotics*, vol. 16, no. 1 (1964), pp. 17-35 (*b*).

Fort, Joel, "Trends in Drug Addiction in Asia in Recent Years," *WHO*, Feb. 9, 1964 (*c*).

Frank, J. K., "Galloping Technology: A New Social Disease," paper presented to the Society for the Psychological Study of Social Issues, Sept. 3, 1966.

Frosch, W. A., E. S. Robbins, and M. Stern, "Untoward Reactions to Lysergic Acid Diethylamide (LSD) Resulting in Hospitalization," *N. Eng. J. Med.*, vol. 273 (1965), pp. 1235-1236.

Geert-Jorgensen, E., "LSD: Treatment Experience Gained within a 3-year Period," *Acta Psychiat. Scand.*, 40th sup., vol. 180 (1964), p. 373.

Glatt, M. M., "Treatment for Addictions," *Lancet*, part 2, vol. 7254 (1962), pp. 504-505.

Glatt, M. M., and L. H. Koon, "Alcohol Addiction in England and Opium Addiction in Singapore: Some Differences and Similarities," *Psychiat. Quart.*, vol. 35 (1961), pp. 1-17.

Gleason, Marion, "A Limited Scale Questionnaire Study of Accident Cases," *Proc. Second Highway Safety Research Correlation Conf.*, Washington, D.C., April 5-6, 1954.

Hamburger, E., "Barbiturate Use in Narcotic Addicts," *J.A.M.A.*, vol. 189 (1964), pp. 366-368.

Hauty, G. T., and R. B. Payne, "The Effects of Dexedrine and Benadrylhyocine upon Judgment," *USAF Sch. Av. Med. Report No. 55-104*, Randolph AFB, Tex., November 1955.

Harner, M. J., "A Jimson Weed Warning," *San Francisco Chronicle*, Aug. 22, 1966.

Hollister, Leo, and F. Glazener, "Withdrawal Reactions from Meprobamate, Alone and Combined with Promazine: A Controlled Study," *Psychopharmacologia*, vol. 1 (1960), p. 336.

Huffman, W. J., *et al.*, "The Influence of Two Selected Tranquilizers on Driving Skills," *Amer. J. Pyschiat.*, vol. 119 (1963), pp. 885-886.

Hurst, Paul M., "The Effects of d-Amphetamine on Risk Taking," *Psychopharmacologia*, vol. 3 (1962), pp. 283-290.

Ingram, I., and G. Imburg, "Letter to the Journal," *Lancet*, vol. 2 (1960), p. 766.

Isbell, H., "Abuse of Barbiturates" (editorial), *Bulletin Narcotics*, vol. 9 (1957), p. 14.

Isbell, H., "Chronic Barbiturate Intoxication: An Experimental Study," *Arch. Neurol. Psychiat.*, vol. 64 (1950), pp. 1-28.

Isbell, H., and H. F. Fraser, "Addiction to Analgesics and Barbiturates," *Pharmacol. Rev.*, vol. 2 (1950), pp. 355-397.

"Issues and Answers: Tranquilizers and Operation of Automobiles," *J.A.M.A.*, vol. 164, (1957), p. 1171.

Jacobziner, Harold, "Attempted Suicides in Adolescence," *J.A.M.A.*, vol. 191 (1965), pp. 101-105.

Jacobziner, H., and H. W. Raybin, "Glue Sniffing," *N.Y. J. Med.*, vol. 63, no. 16 (1963), pp. 2415-2418.

Kiloh, L. G., and S. Brandon, "Habituation and Addiction to Amphetamines," *Brit. Med. J.*, vol. 2 (1962), pp. 40-43.

Kleber, H. D., "Student Use of Hallucinogens," Psychopharmacology Service Center, unpublished.

Kline, N. S., "Drugs and Community Mental Hygiene Clinics," *Am. J. Public Health*, Psychopharmacology and Community Health Services Supp., vol. 52 (1962), pp. 1–8.

Kopf, W. B., *et al.*, "A Method for Determining Some Epidemiological Aspects of Motor Vehicle Accidents," *Proc. Second Highway Safety Research Correlation Conf.*, Washington, D.C., April 5-6, 1954, pub. 328.

Krug, D. C., J. Sokol, and I. Nylander, "Inhalation of Commercial Solvents: A Form of Deviance among Adolescents," in Ernest Harms (ed.), *Drug Addiction in Youth*, New York: Pergamon Press, 1965.

LaBarre, Weston, *The Peyote Cult*, Yale University Publications in Anthropology, No. 19, New Haven, Conn.: Yale University Press, 1938.

Lambo, T. A., "Medical and Social Problems of Drug Addiction in West Africa," *Bull. Narcotics*, vol. 17 (1965), pp. 3-13.

Landis, Carney, "Comments on Effects of Certain Antihistamines," *Proc. Second Highway Safety Research Correlation Conf.*, Washington, D.C., April 5-6, 1954.

Laster, Lewis, "Survey of Producers of the Chemical Form of Amphetamines," Senate Hearings of the FDA, 1964.

Leake, Chauncey D., *The Amphetamines: Their Actions and Uses*, Springfield, Ill.: Charles C. Thomas, 1958.

Legge, D., and H. Steinberg, "Actions of a Mixture of Amphetamine and Barbiturate in Man," *Brit. J. Pharmacol. Chemotherapy*, vol. 18 (1962), pp. 490-500.

Lemere, F., "Habit Forming Properties of Meprobamate (Miltown or Equanil)," *Arch. Neurol.*, vol. 76 (1956), pp. 205-206.

Lemere, F., FDA Hearing, June 1966.

"Letter to Mr. John Lawrence," Managing Director of the American Trucking Association from Abe McGregor Goff, Interstate Commerce Commission, Washington, D.C., June 1964.

Lewin, Louis, *Phantastica: Narcotic and Stimulating Drugs, Their Use and Abuse*. New York: E. P. Dutton & Co., Inc., 1964.

Lingl, F. A., "Irreversible Effects of Glutethimide Addiction," *Am. J. Psychiat.*, vol. 123 (1966), pp. 349-351.

Loomis, T. A., and T. C. West, "Comparative Sedative Effects of a Barbiturate and Some Tranquilizer Drugs on Normal Subjects," *J. Pharmacol.*, vol. 122 (1958), pp. 525-531.

Los Angeles County Sheriff's Department, "Recent LSD Case Summaries Submitted to Senate Fact Finding Committee," 1965.

Ludwig, A. M., and J. Levine, "Patterns of Hallucinogenic Drug Abuse," *J.A.M.A.*, vol. 191 (1965), pp. 92-96.

Marquis, D. G., *et al.*, "Experimental Studies of Behavioral Effects of Meprobamate on Normal Subjects," *Ann. N.Y. Acad. Sci.*, vol. 67 (1957), pp. 701-711.

Masaki, T., "The Amphetamine Problem in Japan," *Sixth Report of the Expert Committee on Drugs Liable to Produce Addiction*, WHO Tech. Rept. Series, vol. 102 (1956), p. 14.

Master, Roshen S., "An Attempted Suicide with a Chlorpromazine Cocktail," *Am. J. Psychiat.*, vol. 120 (1964), pp. 1126-1128.

McCormick, T. C., Jr., "Toxic Reactions to the Amphetamines," *Dis. Nerv. Syst.*, vol. 23 (1962), pp. 219-224.

McGlothlin, W. H., S. Cohen, and M. McGlothlin, "Personality and Attitude Changes in Volunteer Subjects following Repeated Administration of LSD," paper presented before the Fifth International Congress, Collegium Neuro-psychopharmacologicum, March 1966.

McGlothlin, W. H., and S. Cohen, "The Use of Hallucinogenic Drugs Among College Students," *Am. J. Psychiat.*, vol. 122 (1965), pp. 572-574.

Medical Society of the County of New York, *Report of Deaths Due to Drugs*, New York, 1965.

Subcommittee on Narcotics Addiction, "The Dangerous Drug Problem," *New York Med.*, vol. 22 (1966), p. 93.

Miller, James, "Objective Measurements of the Effects of Drugs on Driver Behavior," *J.A.M.A.*, vol. 179, no. 12 (1962).

Ministry of Health and Welfare, Japan, "Brief Account on the Situation of the Control of the Dangerous Drugs in Japan," pamphlet, December 1964.

Mintz, M., *The Therapeutic Nightmare*, New York: Houghton Mifflin Co., 1965.

"Modern Life and Sedatives," *Living Age*, vol. 238 (1903), pp. 571-574.

Mouna, Donald B. (New York Med. Soc.), quoted in *Newsweek*, May 9, 1966, pp. 59-64. Also quoted in *Time*, April 22, 1966, p. 52.

Murphy, H.B.N., "The Cannabis Habit: A Review of Recent Psychiatric Literature," *Bull. Narcotics*, vol. 15 (1963), pp. 15-23.

Murray, Neville, "Methaminodiazopoxide," *J.A.M.A.*, vol. 173 (1960), pp. 1760-1761.

Neil, W. H., "Influence of Drugs on Driving," *Texas State Med. J.*, vol. 58 (1962), pp. 92-97.

New York City Mayor's Committee on Marihuana, *The Problem of Marihuana in the City of New York*, 1940.

*New York Times*, June 5, 1966.

Ong, Beale H., "Dextroamphetamine Poisoning," *N. Eng. J. Med.*, vol. 266 (1962), pp. 1321-1322.

Osterhaus, E., "Investigations on the Effect of Taking Sodium Barbiturate Alone or with Alcohol in Addition, and on the Excretion of Barbituric Acids," *Med. Welt.* (Stuttg.), vol. 44 (1964), pp. 2363-2368.

"On the Problem of the Chemical Detection of Drug-induced Driving Insecurity for Forensic Evaluation and to Establish Blame," *Arzneimittel forschung*, vol. 12 (1962), pp. 1079-1081.

Pasamanick, B., "Anticonvulsant Drug Therapy of Behavior Problem Children with Abnormal EEG," *Arch. Neurol. Psychol.*, vol. 65 (1951), p. 752.

Pearlman, Samuel, "Drug Experiences and Attitudes Among Seniors in a Liberal Arts College," unpublished.

"Pep pill menace," *Brit. Med. J.*, vol. 5386 (1964), p. 792.

Penick, S. B., and S. Fisher, "Drug-set Interaction: Psychological and Physiological Effects of Epinephrine under Differential Expectation," *Psychosomatic Med.*, vol. 27 (1965), pp. 177-182.

Powelson, Student Health Officer and Chief Narcotics Officer, University of California, Berkeley, Calif., personal interview.

Rawlin, John W., " 'Street Level' Abusage of Amphetamines," paper presented to the First National Institute on Amphetamine Abuse, Southern Illinois University, Feb. 21-25, 1966.

Roose, W. A., Chief of Drug Section, Division of Food and Drugs, Indiana State Board of Health, documents submitted to the Amphetamine Abuse Conference, 1966.

Rosenthal, S. H., "Persistent Hallucinosis following Repeated Administration of Hallucinogenic Drugs," *Am. J. Psychiat.*, vol. 121 (1964), pp. 238-244.

Russo, J. Robert, Delinquency Study and Youth Development Project, First National Institute on Amphetamine Abuse, 1966.

San Diego, Calif., Narcotics Detail, report to the Senate Hearings, 1962.

Satloff, A., "Patterns of Drug Usage in a Psychiatric Patient Population," *Am. J. Psychiat.*, vol. 121 (1964), pp. 382-384.

Schremly, J. A., and P. Solomon, "Drug Abuse and Addiction Reporting in a General Hospital," *J.A.M.A.*, vol. 189 (1964), pp. 512-514.

Scott, P. D., and D.R.C. Willcox, "Delinquency and Amphetamines," *Brit. J. Psychiat.*, vol. 3 (1965), pp. 865-875.

Seevers, Maurice H., "The Use, Misuse, and Abuse of Amphetamine-Type Drugs from the Medical Viewpoint," a presentation to the Conferees, First National Institute on Amphetamine Abuse, Southern Illinois University, Feb. 21-25, 1966.

"Medical Perspectives on Habituation and Addiction," *J.A.M.A.*, vol. 181 (1962), pp. 92-98.

Seidle, L. G., G. F. Thornton, and L. E. Cluff, "Epidemiological Studies of Adverse Drug Reactions," *Am. J. Public Health*, vol. 55 (1965), pp. 1170-1175.

Shapiro, S., and S. H. Baron, "Prescriptions for Psychotropic Drugs in a Noninstitutional Population," *Public Health Reports*, vol. 76 (1961), pp. 481–488.

Simon, A., *The Physiology of Emotions*, Springfield, Ill.: Charles C. Thomas, 1961.

Slater, B. J., and N. Francis, "Benadryl: A Contributing Cause of an Accident," *J.A.M.A.*, vol. 132 (1946), p. 212.

Sotiroff, "Barbiturates and Use by Females," personal communication, 1965.

Spelman, J. W., "Autopsies Find Excessive Drugs in Fourth of Cases," *Palo Alto Times*, Palo Alto, Calif., late October 1965.

State of California, California Highway Patrol research study, 1964.

Hearings of the Senate Juvenile Delinquency Subcommittee of California, May 1965.

Sterling, J. W., "A Comparative Examination of Two Modes of Intoxication: An Exploratory Study of Glue Sniffing," *J. Crim. Law, Criminology and Police Sci.*, vol. 55 (1964), pp. 94-99.

Straus, B., *et al.*, "Hypnotic Effects of an Antihistamine-methapyritene Hydrochloride," *Am. Intern. Med.*, vol. 42 (1955), pp. 574-582.

Swanton, Cedric, "Letter to the Journal," *Med. J. of Australia*, vol. 21 (1963), p. 795.

Szasz, T. S., "Some Observations on the Use of Tranquilizing Drugs," *AMA Arch. Neurol. and Psychiat.*, vol. 77 (1957), pp. 86-92.

Terry, Anthony, "Recent Increase in the Use of Marihuana among American Troops in Germany," London Sunday *Times*, cited in *San Francisco Chronicle*, Nov. 17, 1964, p. 49.

*The Medical Letter*, vol. 5 (1963), p. 93.

"Traffic Safety," hearing before a Subcommittee on Interstate and Foreign Commerce, House of Representatives, 84th Cong., 2d Sess. Washington, D.C.: U.S. Government Printing Office, 1956.

Ungerleider, J. T., D. Fisher, and M. Fuller, "The Dangers of LSD," *J.A.M.A.*, vol. 197 (1966), pp. 389-392.

United Nations Economic and Social Council, *The Cannabis Problem: A Note on the Problem and the History of International Action*, 1962.

"Effects of the Use and Abuse of Narcotic Drugs on Accidents in General and on Road Accidents in Particular," report prepared for the 20th Sess. of the Commission on Narcotic Drugs, Sept. 14, 1965.

United Nations, Commission on Narcotic Drugs, *The Question of Cannabis*, United Nations Economic and Social Council, 20th Sess., Sept. 15, 1965.

United States Tariff Commission, 1964.

Von Felsinger, J., L. Lasagna, and Beecher, "The Persistence of Mental Impairment following a Hypnotic Dose of a Barbiturate," *J. Pharm. and Exp. Therapy*, vol. 109 (1953), pp. 284-291.

Wagner, von Hans J., "Die Bedentung der Untersuchung von Blut-bzw: Marnproben auf arzneimothel nach Verkehrsunlallen auf grund der Uberprüfung von 2060 Personeu," *Arzneimittel Forschung*, vol. 11 (1961), p. 992.

Walton, Robert P., *Marihuana, America's New Drug Problem*, New York: J. P. Lippincott Company, 1938.

Watt, L. M., and Biandwijk Breyer, "Forensic and Sociological Aspects of the Dagga Problem in South Africa," *South African Med. J.*, vol. 10 (1936), pp. 573-579.

Wendt, G. R., "Effects of Certain Drugs Used in Self Medication in Relation to Driving Performance and Traffic Hazards," *Proc. Second Highway Safety Research Correlation Conf.*, Washington, D.C., April 5-6, 1954.

White House Conference on Narcotic and Drug Abuse, *Proceedings*, Washington, D.C., 1962.

White, James R., Jr., "Marihuana Puff-in," Petition in the Supreme Court of California *In re Eggemeier*, November 1964.

Winick, C., and J. Goldstein, *The Glue Sniffing Problem*, New York: American Social Health Association, n.d.

Winstanley, G. A., *Annual Report, Coroner of Los Angeles County, California*, July 1, 1955-June 30, 1956.

World Health Organization, "Psychoactive Drugs and Road Safety," report prepared for the 18th and 19th Sess. United Nations Commission on Narcotic Drugs, March 13, 1965.

Zirkle, G. A., "Chlorpramazine and Alcohol on Coordination and Judgment," *J.A.M.A.*, vol. 171 (1959), pp. 1496-1499.

## SUPPLEMENTAL READINGS

Angrist, Shirley S., *et al.: Women after Treatment*, New York: Appleton-Century-Crofts, Inc., 1968.

Becker, Howard S.: *Outsiders: Studies in the Sociology of Deviance*, New York: The Free Press, 1963.

Bittner, Egon: "Police Discretion in Emergency Apprehension of Mentally Ill Persons," *Social Problems*, vol. 14 (winter 1967), pp. 278-292.

Bryan, James H.: "Apprenticeships in Prostitution," *Social Problems*, vol. 12 (winter 1965), pp. 278-297.

Cohen, Albert K.: *Deviance and Control*, Englewood Cliffs, N.J.: Prentice-Hall, Inc., 1966.

Douglas, Jack D.: *The Social Meanings of Suicide*, Princeton, N.J.: Princeton University Press, 1967.

Erikson, Kai T.: *Wayward Puritans*, New York: John Wiley & Sons, Inc., 1966.

Gebhard, Paul H., *et. al.: Sex Offenders*, New York: Bantam Books, Inc., 1967.

Goffman, Erving: *Stigma: Notes on the Management of Spoiled Identity*, Englewood Cliffs, N.J.: Prentice-Hall, Inc., 1963.

Goldman, Nathan: "Social Breakdown," *The Annals*, vol. 373 (September 1967), pp. 157-179.

Lindesmith, Alfred R.: *Addiction and Opiates*, Chicago: Aldine Publishing Co., 1968.

Masters, William, and Virginia Johnson: *Human Sexual Response*, Boston: Little, Brown and Company, 1966.

Pasamanick, Benjamin, *et al.: Schizophrenics in the Community*, New York: Appleton-Century-Crofts, Inc., 1967.

Pittman, David J., and Charles R. Snyder (eds.): *Society, Culture, Drinking Patterns*, New York: John Wiley & Sons, Inc., 1962.

Reiss, Albert J., Jr.: "The Social Integration of Queers and Peers," *Social Problems*, vol. 9 (fall 1961), pp. 102-120.

Schatzman, Leonard, and Anselm Strauss: "A Sociology of Psychiatry," *Social Problems*, vol. 14 (summer 1966), pp. 3-16.

Schur, Edwin M.: *Crimes without Victims: Deviant Behavior and Public Policy*, Englewood Cliffs, N.J.: Prentice-Hall, Inc., 1965.

Yablonsky, Lewis: *Synanon: The Tunnel Back*, Baltimore: Penguin Books, Inc., 1965.

*Task Force Report: Drunkenness*, President's Commission on Law Enforcement and Administration of Justice, Washington, D.C.: U.S. Government Printing Office, 1967.

*Task Force Report: Narcotics and Drug Abuse*, President's Commission on Law Enforcement and Administration of Justice, Washington, D.C.: U.S. Government Printing Office, 1967.

PART FOUR

SOCIAL ACTION

Many social scientists believe that the search for solutions to social problems falls outside the legitimate purview of their professional activities. This position rests on the premise that the investigator's objectivity is impaired to the extent that he makes value judgments concerning existing conditions and that vested interests are developed in implementing recommended solutions. Moreover, since the scientific method does not allow for analysis of the relative merits of opposing values, social scientists possess no special insight in this realm of inquiry. An opposite position, which is not as widely accepted among specialists (although the number seems to be increasing rapidly) but holds considerable appeal for students, is that the representatives of academic disciplines should participate by applying their findings to the amelioration of social problems precisely because they are better informed than any other segment of the society.

As with most polemic controversies, the widest support is given to an alternative that incorporates the strengths of these divergent points of view. This alternative view is that the social scientist is under obligation to build as complete a fund of knowledge as possible, including information on the potential consequences of alternative courses of action, but his recommendation of any of these alternatives should be only on the basis of his nonprofessional capacity as a citizen. An example of this "middle-ground" tack is provided by Melvin M. Tumin, who believes that the social scientist should "go where the action is and tell it as it really is," that is, clarify and add to knowledge about the competing forces in crucial issues of public policy, without becoming partisan for any one element.

The academic approaches that emphasize abstinence from direct participation in the resolution of social problems stand in contrast to the general actionist orientation of the lay public. Despite the periodic sense of frustration over such issues as high taxes, lack of success in concluding the Vietnam War, racial disorders, and the problems of modern urban life, the typical response is that something can and should be done to cope with problems. The obvious question is why a nation such as the United States, with almost unlimited resources and an activist philosophy of life, seems unable to reduce the scope and impact of these undesired social conditions. The answers to this question repre-

*587*

sent the basis of the sociological orientation to the study of social problems.

In the first place, sociologists posit that social problems can be viewed most effectively as the natural, often inevitable, consequences of the patterns of social relations and cultural norms that are given general approval by society. Thus the population explosion in underdeveloped countries reflects in large part the widespread application of advances in medical science, with the resultant dramatic decreases in infant mortality. The increasing difficulties associated with the aged, particularly in terms of their lack of integration in the life of the community, may be traced to society's emphasis on a nuclear family, which in turn is most compatible with the requirements of an industrial economy. Many of the problems in education are a direct outgrowth of the commitment to provide education for all to the limit of their capacities.

A second, and closely related, postulate is that action to ameliorate current problems may lead to changes that become the basis of new problems. Population growth is one such example. As another example, many whites have expected blacks to be satisfied with the gains achieved during the past decade. Instead the aspirations of all minorities are now higher, and divisions among racial and ethnic groups are sharper. Still another illustration is the increasing influence of the federal government in the daily life of the individual. The fact that some level of government now intervenes in almost every conceivable activity is a consequence of previous pressures from almost every segment of the population to protect or promote their special interests. Even those who advocate less supervision and control by government do not indicate that the trend toward concentration at the national level will be reversed. In this connection the public tends toward greater apathy in those instances in which an unanticipated problem arises in the course of resolving one that is in direct conflict with the mores. For example, the view that during the tenure of Earl Warren as Chief Justice the United States Supreme Court improperly interpreted the Constitution in decisions pertaining to the legal rights of criminals and Communists, housing, school desegregation and the integration of public facilities, and the place of religion in public schools has resulted in strong pressure for legislative or initiative action that clearly violates constitutional provisions.

A third postulate is that different segments of a heterogeneous population are differently involved in and affected by the ramifications of existing social problems, and hence definitions of what is a social problem vary accordingly. Alan M. Dershowitz points out the conflicts between the legal and medical models in dealing with the issue of commitment of the mentally ill. Even the relatively unsuccessful ordinary thief, who spends much of his life behind bars, may justify his behavior on the basis that every man has his racket, with explicit reference to bribes paid to alter the legal process, and more generally, to illegal business and professional practices. The view that the Negro is biologically less advanced than the white has long been used to justify the discrepancy between society's practices and the professed ideals of the "American Creed."

Finally, the proposals and programs developed to solve social problems do not often receive unanimous support because, at the risk of an oversimplification, what is one man's solution may be another man's problem. A new freeway that cuts driving time in half may also cut a swath in a previously isolated residential area; expanded medical care for the aged and indigent may result in more detailed government supervision of doctors and hospitals; and automation may increase the affluence of the employed but also enlarge the proportion of the population subsisting at a poverty level.

In seeking to understand why social problems are so much a part of contemporary urban life, the frequently neglected functional aspects must also be examined. The selection by Lewis Coser in the previous chapter provides comprehensive coverage of this issue. In essence, Coser indicates that deviant behavior reaffirms basic values and definitions of "normal" behavior by establishing normative limits, contributes to a sense of self-righteousness and worthiness through the collective rejection of the deviant, calls attention to the need for remedial action, and stimulates innovations that may serve the group's welfare. Along a somewhat different, though no less important, line of analysis, deviant behavior represents a substantial vested interest to those whose employment and primary sources of income are tied directly or indirectly to its control and amelioration, or to those who stand to gain in some way from its perpetuation. These observations on the functional dimensions of deviant behavior are generally applicable to the broader spectrum of social problems.

Consideration of the actual efforts to correct unwanted conditions raises still further questions. For example, why is science unable to provide the solutions to chronic problems? One answer is indicated by Travis Hirschi and Hanan C. Selvin in a carefully reasoned statement which alerts us to the hazards of applying illegitimate criteria in analyzing the causes of social problems. If the results of scientific investigations are to furnish an effective basis for action programs, research designs must incorporate more precise statements of the problems, causal models with empirical referents that are subject to alteration in the context of everyday social behavior, more accurate measurement techniques, and more use of genuinely experimental methods.

A related issue is whether science either *will* or *can* advance the necessary means. The assumption that scientific knowledge is automatically applicable to social problems is rendered invalid by competing value positions. Even where scientific solutions are applicable, the questions of when and under what conditions must be clarified. For example, in considering problems of urban living we can distinguish between those features that are remediable (noise, dirt, traffic congestion, smog, and unpleasant working conditions) and those that are inherent to this form of social life (predominance of impersonal superficial relationships, a relaxed moral tone, and commercialism). Science plays a continuing role in reducing the former, but the latter are by nature essentially unsusceptible to change unless the city is replaced by a new form of social organization. Nevertheless, Robert E. Lane's thesis that we live in a "knowledgeable society" in which there is increased application of scientific criteria for policy decisions allows a more optimistic view of the probable impact of science in the amelioration of social problems. Lane is confident that as the state of our knowledge continues to improve, it will create pressures for change that are independent of political or ideological criteria.

Another question concerns the results achieved by action programs now under way. Obviously, the tremendous variation in objectives, resources, and scope precludes a single all-inclusive response, as illustrated by the numerous "solution-oriented" articles throughout this text, as well as the ones in this chapter. The reports by Charles C. Moskos, Jr., "Racial Integration in the Armed Forces," and by Rita Volkman and Donald R. Cressey, "Rehabilitation of Drug Addicts," represent those instances in which substantial gains have been realized. But the results, as should be expected, are mixed. Thus Moskos points out that, in contrast with on-duty integration, racial separatism is the general off-duty rule in both the United States and foreign locations. Although the comparatively high "reform" rates for drug addicts participating in Synanon programs contrast markedly with less favorable rates for institutions maintained by official agencies, the proportion of the total addict population who could succeed in a Synanon regime and subsequently return to the community is very small in absolute terms. In summary, it is probably fair to state that there has been comparatively little headway in developing programs that are sufficiently on target to solve a given problem condition with a nominal investment of resources. Hence we should not expect dramatic changes even with large-scale ameliorative and corrective programs. Most of the current action efforts are oriented to treatment rather than prevention, and they tend to focus on the rehabilitation of individuals on a case-by-case basis. As a consequence, the basic causes remain unchecked to create a continuous flow of new "patients." Successful cures for those alcoholics now undergoing some form of treatment will not decrease the alcoholic population in future generations.

These remarks are not intended to convey the impression that additional endeavors are futile. To what extent has our society devoted material resources to social problems? The Vietnam War has diverted large portions of tax funds that might normally be allocated for domestic problems. Yet our financial commitments to the poverty programs are still nominal in comparison to our expenditures for the development and marketing of new products, peacetime national defense, space programs, political campaigns, and leisure activities. Ironically, although financial support is increasing for needed research along both theoretical and applied lines, the lack of qualified personnel now limits progress. As a result, the public's willingness to extend its support may be negated by the marginal returns resulting from the inability to make effective use of present resources—a version of the "vicious circle" discussed in the chapter on race relations. These interconnected issues must be reconciled as a prerequisite for continued public interest.

Two final questions pave the way to our summary statement on the search for solutions. Does the discussion of social problems create new or more intense problems, as suggested by the principle of the "self-fulfilling prophecy"? Can the view of the activist orientation of our society be reconciled with frequently reported instances of public apathy? If we have succeeded in placing the nature, extent, and impact of social problems in perspective, then the answer to both questions should be affirmative. However, both questions point to the need for closer correlation between our aspirations and reality, perhaps the single most important theme of this book. Ultimate resolution of the present challenges to our social order depends on the origination of new expectations and norms that give explicit recognition to the unique character of contemporary urban life. Only then can we effectively direct our efforts to reducing the concomitant costs.

The numerous issues and conflicting views of the social scientist's role in alleviating social problems are subjected to a thorough analysis by Melvin M. Tumin. A sense of both the limitations and potentialities of the present scientific literature is conveyed by the next two articles: Lane stresses the development of a "knowledgeable society" and discusses historical trends that portend increased dependence on scientific criteria to determine public policy. Hirschi and Selvin demonstrate that widespread use of invalid criteria in causal analyses has prematurely negated the relevance of certain variables and has unnecessarily dampened interest in the study of causal relationships. In conclusion, Dershowitz highlights the unintended, and often negative, consequences that can emanate from indiscriminate application of a given solution—in this instance, one with general support by professionals and the lay public. The discussions by Volkman and Cressey of the Synanon program and by Moskos of racial integration of the military establishment delineate reasonably successful "action" programs based on sociological concepts.

48    IN DISPRAISE OF LOYALTY    MELVIN M. TUMIN

It is by now well understood that the application of such global terms as "modern" or "traditional" to societies or epochs is at best a modest linguistic convenience, to be indulged in only with the understanding that all societies and epochs are mixed and uneven in their characteristics and that, at any given time, numerous streams in social development, representing all shades of traditionalism and modernity, will be found running side by side.

One of the most fascinating of sociological enterprises is to attempt to chart the profiles of uneven development, noting what types of social sectors and institutions change and what types remain relatively stable; and to try to understand the interplay of these unevenly changing facets of society. Recent historical writings, for instance, have gone to considerable pains to point out that the Dark and the Middle Ages are not to be separated so neatly as our school history books have previously taught us to do, and that depending on whether it is painting or commerce or government of which one is speaking, and depending on which portion of the globe we refer to, the so-called distinctive characteristics of *numerous* historical epochs will be found not only in conjunction but often in a curious form of benign complementarity.

One should not expect today's social structures to be exceptions to the principles of uneven development. Nor is it to be supposed that ways of thinking shall develop any more evenly than do forms of social organization. And it is about the unevenness in certain intellectual orientations that I want to speak tonight.

I have in mind particularly the contrast between what may be called the secularization of the

Reprinted from *Social Problems* vol. 15 (winter 1968), pp. 267–279, by permission of the author and The American Academy of Political and Social Science.

Presidential address to the Society for the Study of Social Problems, San Francisco, August 1967.

modern mind, as prototypically evidenced, for instance, in those activities called science, on the one hand, and the persisting sacredness of thought, often by people called scientists, when the issues at stake may be called "moral."

Consider, at the outset, how we orient ourselves to moral issues; both from the point of view of moral philosophy and that of the sociology of morals. I think mainly now of the fact that we tend most often to treat the cardinal virtues, such as truth, honor, and loyalty, in much the same way as these have come down to us from sacred sources; and we therefore tend to be intellectually and sentimentally bound to these virtues in the same undifferentiated and uncritical ways that formerly made it possible for a priesthood of sacred and authoritarian officials to claim prepotence in moral interpretation, guidance, and sanction.

If for some years we have been operating under the assumption that morals have become secularized because secular philosophers of morals now do for us what sacred officials used to do, we are now being disembarrassed of this notion by the philosophers themselves, who are taking considerable pains to point out to us that there is no certifiable expertise among philosophers or in the discipline itself with regard to moral problems, and that such clarification of moral issues as philosophers sometimes attempt requires that they function as sociologists or anthropologists or social psychologists, when they are not playing at the game of linguistic analysis of moral claims. That is to say, the so-called philosopher-expert is expert in proportion to his competence, however acquired, as a sociologist or other form of social scientist. The expertise, in short, lies in the ability to clarify the sources, the distributions, the connections, and the consequences of various kinds of moral judgments. We would readily admit that, as described, this is a typical sociological enterprise.

Perhaps because we have assumed that the clarification of moral issues was a typically philosophical problem we have been derelict in addressing ourselves explicitly to such problems. At the same time it must be pointed out that we have often unwittingly engaged in this task when, for instance, we examine the distribution and consequences of various sets of attitudes toward issues of public policy. We may hesitate to dignify this apparently mundane enterprise with the term "the sociology of morals" but in fact that is what it is. Like M. Jourdain, many of us have been talking modern philosophical prose without knowing it.

We have been further derelict in failing to draw out and communicate the implications of our findings, however few they may be, regarding the distributions and consequences of moral sentiments.

These implications make crucial comments on the still widespread claims and beliefs regarding the sacredness of the cardinal virtues, their fixity, their indispensability, and their regnancy in the determination of behavior. Yet, we still allow the names of these virtues to carry immediately positive and sacredly sanctified connotations, and, by derivation, their opposites are immediately subject to invidious evaluation. Note, please, how unqualifiedly positive are the terms truth, honor, and loyalty, and how the addition of the denying prefixes, yielding the terms dishonor, untruth, and disloyalty, immediately evoke the feelings of anathema and condemnation, which only grow more intense when we substitute simple equivalents such as the terms "lying" and "treason." In short, the language of moral discourse is such that neutral sociological analysis is made extremely difficult at the outset.

As a result, we take lying, dishonor, and treason as problematic and troublesome, and feel compelled to account for them as forms of undesirable deviance, acting often as though they were not only statistically deviant (which in fact they may not be) but also as though they were inherently and normatively deviant and undesirable.

Too few of us have felt impelled to follow the lead offered by Durkheim in his assessment of the positive functions of criminal behavior. We have instead accepted the general public's so-called received wisdom in these matters, one which requires us to act as if the total elimination of such behavior would be the most salutary possible condition of life. As a corollary, we have failed to ask how much of what kinds of mixtures of honesty and dishonesty, truth and lying, honor and dishonor, loyalty and disloyalty might be useful for various conditions of social organization and various desired social outcomes. It is in this regard that we have remained essentially sacred and traditional and I venture that this has been damaging to all of us, generally, as a civilization, and particularly to us as a profession that prides itself on its deliberate posture of distance and disengagement from the moral assumptions of the populace under examination.

How can we account for the persisting sacredness of orientation to, and thought about, morality among otherwise secular persons, or at least among persons who pride themselves on their secularity and whose professional ideologies require such secularity?

As a first approximation, we probably must take account of the extent to which many if not most of us were conditioned in our childhood to deep beliefs in supernatural spirits and forces. We should not be expected to have overcome our beliefs in and fears of these forces any more than we have been cleared of our notions that mothers and fathers are sacred beings.

For those for whom this account is unsatisfactory, perhaps a more important factor is the deep-lying belief that the skepticism commanded by the philosophical position of moral relativism is itself weak and inept. As held by many self-proclaimed relativists, this position argues that man is the ultimate arbiter of moral doctrines and convictions, but "confesses" apologetically that man's authority is arbitrary, as though there were really some non-arbitrary source of moral enlightenment, and that, in fact, there are absolute virtues.

Still another possible reason for the persistence

of such a sacred type of thinking among secular men derives from the realization that the moral relativist position ultimately accepts the final role of force in settling otherwise irreconcilable moral positions (when either of the protagonists insists on pursuing his chosen course of conduct and in the process threatens the spiritual or physical welfare of his opposition). It seems anomalous that a doctrine which arises from the opposition of freedom to authoritarianism, and of individual enlightenment to priestly revelation, should be no better off, when the social chips are down, than the opposing doctrines that prevailed in the ages of priests and witchdoctors and that ultimately employed the auto-da-fe and the sword to decide competitions of ideas.

Perhaps another source of some of the unyielding sacredness of our feelings about cardinal virtues is our realization that secular men have captured the major social institutions of modern life and have been able to substitute, at least for the moment, their versions of truth, honor, and loyalty for those of the traditional opposition. To acknowledge the avowedly optional ground on which our moral positions are held would be to weaken the claim to legitimacy of secular rule. We do not trust, I believe it fair to say, in the peaceful interplay of democratic institutions which should, in principle, command the loyalty of all modern secular men.

A newer set of motives also probably obliges us to remain sacred in our orientations to cardinal virtues. There are many among us who have for some time identified with the underdogs and the disinherited in modern society, and we know as well as, if not better than, others how relatively high are their rates of violation of the cardinal virtues. We are therefore reluctant to push open the doors to genuinely free moral inquiry lest we be put into the position of openly defending treason, crime, lying, and cruelty, not to mention arson, pillage, rape, and looting. Our nearly open approval of the behavior of our clients among the disinherited often brings us perilously close to such a position. But we are understandably reluctant to be politically compromised by an open defense of such generally disapproved behavior.

The foregoing account of some sources of persisting sacredness in our moral orientations might seem quite satisfactory, taken together, and thus quiet any sense of need to pursue deeper and further. I venture the hypothesis, however, that there is a far simpler yet more fundamental reason than any given so far: that social scientists as a group simply believe deeply in the sacred virtues and in the associated pieties of posture and of action. And we do so, I believe, because our backgrounds as "people of the book"—under whatever denominational disguise—and our attendant sensitivity to the calling that attracted us and selectively culled us for the roles we occupy, are one of a piece with the belief in the essential character of virtue written large.

How else could we possibly account for our assuming professional roles as prophets, and seekers and disseminators of truth and justice, except as we believed in their unquestioned virtue, their universal and eternal importance, but also saw their fragility and hence the perils which would beset these norms of conduct had they no champions who would defend them against the philistines and barbarians? And wherein lies our personal safety if not in the universal adherence to these virtues?

Why, too, in the same vein, should we conduct copious studies designed to show the equality of all men, or find persuasive reasons why men are momentarily unequal, against all common opinion to the contrary, if we were not committed deep in our secret hearts to the belief in the virtue of equality? If we say it is because the evidence shows men to be equal, why, still we must ask, do we feel compelled to secure that evidence and propagate it?

Why, too, should we care about integration and alienation as central sociological constructs, and as guiding points of research and theory, if at bottom we are not deeply concerned with the disappearance of community, the fragmentation of personality, the breaking of the bonds that unite men? There is, after all, at least as much if not more solidarity and community than there is individuation and alienation. Why do we view alienation as problematic?

Why, too, should ours be the discipline par excellence that puts "fairness" and "justice" and "moral rectitude" at the center of our analyses of societies, and proclaims this to be the hallmark of a civilization that is modernizing? If you do not recognize the concept of fairness under the flimsy guise of the concept of universalism, then you have been a devotee of virtue in spite of yourself.

Why, too, should most of us see ourselves as teachers, pride ourselves on our capacity to teach, and feel within us the incapacity to function in any other central occupation? Teaching, after all, is a sacred occupation. It is presumably indifferent and alien to the main impulses of the market place which moves our neighbors and which make of them men of lesser virtue than we pride ourselves on being. We see ourselves as dedicated to service, to the shaping of the younger generation, to the propagation of the truth. These are the ideal terms of our self definition.

Perhaps now we can see more clearly how we have gotten into the position where just underneath the surface of all that we profess about how secular and detached we are from the sacred ties that bind other men we find ourselves just as attached, if not more, to ties that are just as sacred, though their points of anchorage may be somewhat different. Can it be that in this new combination of secular roofing upon sacred walls and foundations, we are implicitly trying to create a model for a new Universal Church to which we can pledge our dedication and commitment, and which will be as grand if not grander than the old church to which we can no longer ever belong?

Yet our secret dreams are probably for naught, for we insist, as we cannot avoid doing, on coming to such a church under impossible circumstances—namely, in full possession of our secular rationalities and of all the understanding which such an attitude toward ourselves and such a suspicion of churches gives us. We insist in short on being grown up, independent, unfettered by traditional faith, accepting nothing blindly, making no concessions to tribal sentiment, but only to the power

of proof and of reason. We know of course that these are impossible demands and terms, but we insist upon them.

We define not only our profession but our very manhood in terms of our freedom from narrow parochialisms; our capacities to transcend the enfeebling perspectives of men caught in the trap of limited vision and unquestioning conformity to their restricted and restrictive memberships. We argue that such transcendence marks whatever progress we are willing to affirm in the evolution of civilization: the evolution from men of the blood and soil to men of the book.

So we yearn for the pieties and verities, for community and fraternity, and truth, honor, and loyalty; but we feel compelled by our covenant with our images of ourselves as men of reason and intellect to turn our backs on these when they show themselves in their traditional forms. At the same time, we search for as yet uncreated and perhaps unimagined ways in which we might reconcile this duality in ourselves.

Nowhere is this duality and ambivalence more clearly *in view*, yet more confusing *in consequence*, than in the case of loyalty.

Note, first, that of all the sacred virtues we are perhaps most immediately sneering and contemptuous of the demand for loyalty. Some reasons are immediately apparent.

In the first instance, to applaud loyalty in the abstract seems meaningless on the face of things since loyalty always refers to loyalty about something or to something or someone. Loyalty is therefore always conditional. Such a conditionality does not at the outset seem to circumscribe truth and honor nearly as much. They seem by comparison to be much more self commending and intact at least on initial inspection, however much a bit of analysis will reveal them to be as fully conditional.

Secular man's doubts about loyalty are also increased by the frequency with which obvious enemies of secularism and freedom wave various flags and banners to which they demand unquestioned loyalty and adherence. Even the commanders of quasi-secular institutions, such as universities, seek to integrate their social control over the potentially dangerous free and independent thought of their employees by making institutional loyalty a prime requisite of institutional recognition and reward. Nor are matters helped by the obvious fact that such institutional commissars seem often to be deluded by a sense of the indispensability of their trivial institutions to the welfare of society in general, and of their own personal commandship to the welfare of their institution. Above all, in universities, where men are nominally recruited on the basis of the presumed excellence, and hence, the independence and creativity of their minds, the demand or institutional loyalty, superseding loyalty to the profession and its standards, is in principle intolerable.

Loyalty thus seems to us to demand the surrender of the very heart of our secularization; our new and barely won and only tentatively and imperfectly-rooted freedom from parochialism. We are not likely to pay much obeisance to such a so-called virtue nor to respect the touters thereof.

But there are other loyalties that do have a call on us however secular we fancy ourselves to be. These come out of our memberships in various social groups, categories, or even geo-social areas: memberships defined by age, or sex, or religion, or race, or ethnos, or region, whether local or national. These are not themselves status-structured roles in any formal sense. But they are surely as salient in shaping the courses of our lives as are our more formally structured major roles. They give special flavor, perspective, and even content to our roles. They are used partly to help explain why we behave in our roles the way we do, why we are the particular kinds of fathers or husbands or lovers or friends or colleagues others find us to be: why, in short, in addition to the expected and normal round of role obligations we discharge (which can be explained simply by presence in the role and its general dynamics), we also behave in ways quite different from others in the same roles. Identities then, are both aspects of roles, and independent units of social analysis.

However viewed they are potent factors in our behavior. For, they are really forms of primary groups, whether totally private or shared with others. They are often laden with affect, and even drenched with sentiment. Sometimes they are embodied and represented concretely by living persons whom we encounter face to face, or by our alter egos whom we meet coming and going. They are primordial in the force they exert for they represent the core ingredients of our definitions of ourselves. That is why a knowledge of our major social roles may tell other individuals what they may expect from us in general, but a knowledge of our real identities, of how we see ourselves, is more revealing of what one can really expect from us in any choice situation; where we will put our money and our resources; what will bring flashes of joy and shame to our cheeks; whom we will stand by and for, when battle lines have been drawn. Our loyalties are our ultimate prides and as such it is in terms of them that we can be most deeply offended and insulted by others, and it is common membership in them that narrows the circle of people from whom we will draw our friends and intimates. Moreover, in their finest moments, and their worst, they are the very sustenance from which we draw the vigor of life and the energy for action.

We know this in the intimacy of our own hearts, of course, when in painful moments of consciousness we find ourselves responding to the primitive demands of these memberships beyond any justification by reason. As sociologists, too, we give continuing recognition to these identities as basic sources and modifiers of behavior. They are the familiar so-called background variables that virtually every research design includes as possible first approximations in accounting for similarities and differences in the behavior of respondents.

Yet it is equally clear that both as individuals and as members of our profession we have militantly insisted that decent, acceptable, and mature citizenship demand indifference to these categories; that a sound society cannot afford to recognize them as respectable units of social distinction; and that the mature, free, secular, and just person is he who is blind to these characteristics in others, relating to these others without regard to sex or color or religion or nation.

Why should this be so? Why is it better to attempt to blur identities, and break down lines of distinction rather than solidify them, ritualize them, and make them basic principles of social organization? Everywhere the struggle now goes on between these two opposing sets of forces—those who seek to maintain and strengthen existing categorical distinctions and those who seek to obliterate them or make them inconsequential. This external social struggle is of course duplicated point for point within each of us. Why?

The answer—or an answer—is given unwittingly I believe in the programs of the numerous ecumenical movements—relevant not only to religion, but to race, sex, age, and region. All such movements start with the cognizance of the fact that if these categories are admittedly rallying points of affiliation, inclusion, and solidarity, they are by the same token the foci of divisiveness, exclusion, invidious comparisons, and harmful discriminations. Wherever these distinctions are found, they serve simultaneously as bases of hostility to others as well as sympathy to fellow members. In short, they seem inherently incapable of functioning as neutral principles of social organization. Everywhere they are the rationales for inequality—inequality that is considered unfair and undesirable by those who experience the short end—although it doesn't matter that sometimes the young are preferred to the old, sometimes the women to the men, sometimes the Southerners to the Northerners. The variability in the focus of discrimination and inequality does not alter the fact of inequality.

Because we see this, our efforts both individually and professionally have turned toward making these distinctions as inconsequential as possible. The truly secular man, with an image of himself as a man of no parochialisms, prides himself on being indifferent to these distinctions; he makes every effort to avoid responding in their terms; where possible he dissociates himself formally from such identities, though this has proven possible only in the case of formal religious membership. More than personal dissociation, it is modern secular

leadership which has brought into being both the social movements and the scientific researches aimed at removing the disabilities suffered by virtue of age, sex, race, religion, and nationality.

If one does not take very good inventory of gains and losses, it appears at first sight as though substantial changes have been wrought in the relations among such groups and categories. A form of ecumenicism *has* become the vogue. Cultural pluralism is the by-word of progressive thought. Equality for women and among races are worldwide slogans. Independence for ever younger age groups has become a rallying cry in all parts of the globe.

A more searching inventory will reveal, however, that here too development is most uneven. For everywhere we turn we find that these traditional and centuries-old bases of social distinction are vitally alive, and still function as bases of social distance, hostility and, where possible, discrimination and inequality.

There is, however, a substantial difference between today and yesterday. It consists in the fact that the captive groups—women, Negroes, children, small nations, despised regions and religions—are now discarding their traditional docility and are beginning to insist on the implementation of the new slogans and doctrines of equality which have become part and parcel of the ritual of public assembly throughout most of the globe.

Social scientists have become identified (whether for better or for worse we shall soon inquire), with the causes of the captive groups. Their researches have been taken to indicate the positive value of greater freedom and greater equality of power, privilege, and property for the underdog groups. But of course our researches cannot show any such thing, unless one *assumes* the preferability of those relationships which greater freedom and equality can bring. But no social science data can possibly support *that* assumption when it is taken as the ultimate value against which, then, the efficacy of intervening values is measured.

We face two problems here—one as individuals, for whom our roles as social scientists are but part of our total identity; and one as social functionaries, for whom no identity but that of social scientists should be given serious consideration or priority. The fact is unhappily clear that as a profession, and not just as individuals, we have become identified as the champions of Negroes, the youth, of underdeveloped nations, of the rights of women, of greater roles for the poor, of equal education for all. In short, we have become identified with every major social reform movement now being fought out in public. Whether we have wished our profession to become so value-identified or not, there is no doubt that it has so become. And we have been responsible for this identification because in fact in our public roles we *have* acted often as partisans. We have clearly indicated our preference for equality over inequality; for the irrelevance of distinctions by race and religion. We have done so by accepting the premises of, and by providing skilled services to, liberal change-minded governments, and to the social movements that give these governments impetus and guidance. We have accepted these change-oriented premises and have taken on the tasks of discovering, by such scientific analysis as we are capable of, what are the most effective ways to bring about the desired changes at the earliest possible moment.

The championing of the causes of the captive groups constitutes in effect a fundamental betrayal of certain basic loyalties. For most of us are solid establishmentarians: White, male, adult, well-to-do, educated, powerful, autonomous. Yet we serve Negroes rather than whites; women's equality rather than male dominance; the freedom and autonomy of youth rather than the rule of our own age group; the equality of all religions rather than the exclusive truth and power of our own; and even, from time to time, the cause of internationalism, and even of other nations, as against that of our own countries. Can it be that we feel that in betraying our own memberships we are thereby freeing ourselves from the parochial limits that loyalty to our own identities would impose upon us? Is it true, then, that our *latterly* acquired loyalties to our identities as secular men, as liberals or socialists, as universal men, as men of social justice—is it true that these have triumphed momentarily over

our more deeply laid down and earlier memberships in categories of race, religion, sex, age, and nation, and do we thereby testify eloquently to our dispraise of these loyalties?

Or have we in fact moved out of the restrictions of one set of loyalties only to be caught up in another? Have we perhaps used our hard-won freedom from the enmeshment of our own primary groups with all their irrationalities only to be adopted into the equally disenabling and restricting network of other primary group loyalties? And have we not in the process then fundamentally disserved our mission of rendering all such identifications irrelevant? For in serving as the champions of the new causes have we not thereby helped re-establish and re-affirm the significance of these other loyalties—and, by transfer, of primary group loyalty in general, albeit at a new point of equilibrium?

What else in fact are we doing when we champion black power against white power; youth power against adult power; sexual freedom against sexual restraint; deviance against conformity; the rights of small countries against those of large ones?

Can it be that we cannot bear to be without primary group loyalties, causes, and missions? Can it be, too, that we think we have found in these new causes the kind of power for our profession that we have felt denied to us heretofore? Are we not for the first time in our histories the most sought after professionals; the magic workers who have secret and mystical answers to the problems that perplex the populace? And if we have deserted our roles as social scientists in order to have this power, will we remain deliberately ignorant of the corruption inherent in power? Perhaps the terms should be reversed in order to understand what we have done, for it is now altogether clear that not only does power corrupt, but corruption brings power.

I believe we may be in for a serious comeuppance. For, if for a moment in historical time we seem, with our newly inverted loyalties, to be riding the crest of the dominant wave of events, there are now portents that we are likely to be betrayed by these newfound loyalties into ditches. A number of our causes have either turned upon us, or have become absurd caricatures of what we envisioned, or both, with the result that we are now being pressured into still other more extreme identifications and chauvinisms that are impossible to manage.

I refer here to the riots this summer, last summer, next summer, participated in by Negroes of all ages and classes including lumpen proletariat youth who make it clear that no white man is to be trusted, and especially not liberal whites, and most especially, not white Jewish liberals.

I refer also to the lines of solidarity which have formed among the youth so that no person past 25—is it 26 today or has it moved down to 24—is considered decent or capable of understanding; and to the failure of nerve and heart among these youth, as they choose to flee life, whether through pot, acid, or sex juice, or whatever today's form of sense-death and withdrawal may be.

I refer also to the destruction of genuine sexual freedom among these youth by the blurring both of sense aliveness and of distinct sex identity. I refer also to the deliberate and suicidal rejection of intellect and reason. I refer also to the absolute chaos which has been made of so-called international community by the acceptance of the formal right of every Pacific coral atoll to declare itself a nation and join as an equal partner in the United Nations.

Surely, too, we have been made absurd by our own government which—whatever its initially good intentions with regard to the poor, the Negroes, and the disadvantaged—has made mockeries of our researches and discoveries regarding needed investments in social rehabilitation, by diverting the largest part of our nation's resources to the conduct of an insane war.

The reactions of some to these absurdities and mockeries has been to court even further degradation. Instead of accepting the fundamental fact that you cannot with grace and decency pour new whims into old beatles—there are some among us who struggle against the unbeatable odds to act as if in fact we were young rather than old; beat rather than square; Negro rather than white; passionate rather than reflective.

In these ill-fitting new guises, some have come or been driven to applaud the riots because of their effectiveness as forms of communication of certain Negro feelings without taking into account the most significant communication that brings on the disastrous backlash, or the absolute impossibility of producing effective short-range measures to overcome the bitterness of the lumpen youth.

Some, too, have grown adamant in their defense of the youth who flee from life, by dignifying and gracing the flight with the terms rebellion and dissent. They have mistaken the unreasoning despair of the youth for a reasoned and initially productive program for the future. No such program is to be found in the injunction to tune out, turn on, and take off (this is my version—not Leary's; my version describes the "process" more accurately), or even in the sweet and gentle cult of love and horticulture.

The change of loyalty from primary membership groups to those attached to our identities as universal men of science and finders and speakers of truth has proven awkward and difficult enough for many of us. How much more difficult, not to mention unseemly and unbecoming, is it, therefore, for us to try to stand our former identities on their heads and view the world upside down?

Those who try it will surely fail, unless they are willing to give up their minds, their power as scientists, their hard won maturity, and their stakes in this system in which they have become solid, successful citizens. And who here is willing to do so? Minus such renunciation, how can genuine conversion into honorary membership among the disinherited, unpropertied, powerless, and alienated be accomplished? Are psychedelic movies, sounds, and clothes the functional equivalents of the *real* thing, whatever that is? To try to know and understand and tell others what is going on in the minds and hearts of the youth and Negroes is one thing. But to emulate them feebly and ludicrously—the new form of passing—and to be betrayed into applauding the suicidal impulses that well up out of their despair, whether genuine or false—that is quite another.

Perhaps it does not matter if selected individuals among us are embarked on this quixotic search for new identities, across lines of age, sex, color and nationality. In the last analysis that is their personal hang-up. Each man to his own *meshugas*, as my grandfather would say.

But it does matter to us collectively, as a people and particularly to us as a profession, if we indulge our personal hang-ups and search for new experience under the guise of the dictates of social science. We endanger that bit of dominance which reason, reflectiveness, secularity, and active intellect have managed for the moment to acquire. And we endanger and damage our profession beyond easy repair. For who will believe that what we have to say is anything more than a partisan plea for the welfare of one group against another if we continue to be identified as champions of these groups? In this light consider the hostilities currently being directed against social scientists for their denunciations of existing forms of social welfare and reform of which they or their immediate professional ancestors were the political exponents as well as the structural draftsmen.

It will not do, then, I think, to seek personal salvation, thrills, or power in the guise of social scientists. Let each one find his salvation where he can, on his own, devoid of the protection or the stigma of his guild membership. Nor will it do to switch from one set of sacred loyalties to another. Neither one is suited to us professionally. Nor will it do to try to build a house of secular communion on the foundations of these sacred commitments.

There is, however, one course of action that may yield treasures both personally and professionally, and that may serve almost all the purposes we seek as we try to find the way out of the muddle of our ambivalences. That course of action is to be found, strangely, in two injunctions first coined for us by youth and Negroes: namely, "go where the action is" and "tell it as it really is." For us these mean "be relevant in your concerns" and "tell the truth."

For our personal lives, we are thereby enjoined to take into the fullest account in our own personal behavior, in our relations with youth and Negroes and other newly risen captive groups, what we know about the conditions necessary for genuine equality and dignity and for motivation to participate in this life. We may not be able to rise over the encumbrances and temptations that our powers and comforts now give us. But at least we shall know how far and in what ways we fail. And we shall temper our excessive responses to the apparently outlandish behavior of the rising captives by our seeing these as expectable forms of reaction to publicly symbolized degradation and to the perception that all is vanity.

For our professional lives, we are enjoined to play a role that virtually no one else is capable of playing. For today nearly everyone's passions have been stirred; their tribal loyalties evoked; they are readying for pitched battle: parent against child, black against white, youth against adult, nation against nation, poor against rich, religion against religion. If they are not readying for active battle, then, just as bad, they are actively fleeing life.

That role for which we are eminently and uniquely suited is to keep alive the possibilities of rapprochement and return among the warring and fleeing parties before the alienation and bitterness grow so intense that the terms of ultimate peace and return will entail destruction of much that is valued by everyone concerned, or before a generation of youngsters literally destroy themselves, physically, psychologically, and socially.

And there is time and there is a place for this role, today, now. For most of the youth, most of the Negroes, most of the disaffected people throughout our nation and in the world would very much prefer to share in the world's possible joys than to destroy everything in sight, or flee from it all, if they thought those joys might be possible for them too.

To tell it as it really is, then, involves us in many urgent tasks. It is up to us to make each set of combatants know what is really in the hearts of the other. It is up to us to spell out the costs of return and rapprochement. It is up to us to discover the conditions under which we can, in decency and fairness to all, bridge the gap between the generations, the sexes, and the races and religions and nations—a gap now filled with loyalties and their attendant prides, fears, hates, and passions.

For the point is, is it not, that these basic identities are not going to disappear. We, as intellectuals and free men and women, may have disavowed them. But they are the heart of social organization everywhere and they are likely to be, at the least, enduring, if not permanent. They have heretofore served, as we know, primarily as bases of tribal allegiance, ethnocentrism, warfare, systematic exploitation, lines of allocation of joy and despair, of fundamental inequalities in power, property, and privilege.

Can they be converted, we must ask, so that they do not break the back of our civilization as they have done to others in the past and as they now threaten us? Can they be modified, attenuated, made less passionately significant? Are there countervailing forces that can be employed to reduce their impact? Are there perhaps new institutions and loyalties that can be fostered that will transcend and displace those which now serve as bases of outgroup hatreds?

No one else, I repeat, is in a better position than are we to penetrate these problems. Indeed, almost no one else is in any position at all to come at this problem as it must be come at, and to be able to command the proper attention. But we shall lose every bit of advantage we might now enjoy if we become identified simply as partisans of one tribe against another. All of us sometime, and most of us all the time, still act far more in accordance with our senses of tribal memberships and our sacred affiliations. Genuinely democratic pluralism proves simply too difficult for most of us to sustain especially when and if any of our sacred interests are threatened. The veneer of secular civilization is frighteningly thin. It no longer requires extreme circumstances for men who have been cajoled temporarily into secular, rational behavior to revert quickly and fully to tribal warriors, ready to take the blood of their enemies. Whatever salvation may be possible in this situation depends upon our knowing the conditions

that foster tribalism and those that strengthen the ever tentative commitment to a less-than-sacred world. When we know what will lead us to desire the destruction of others, and, in turn, to our own destruction, we have some chance, if we are so minded, to avert the disasters.

Only knowledge can yield the freedom we need: the freedom to serve our loyalties well, that is, to require our loyalties to serve us, rather than be disserved and dominated by them; the freedom to combine our sentiments and our rationalities in productive ways; the freedom and the power to chart the times and places when rational thought must rule and when it may be suspended; the knowledge of when it is best to lie and when to tell the truth; when to know and when to be ignorant; when to be passionate and when to pause and reflect.

That is the anomaly of the human condition: that only knowledge can declare when ignorance is best; only secularity can chart the times and places for the safe and productive enjoyment of sacred pieties; only rationality can specify the conditions of maximum enjoyment of sentiment; only self-conscious detachment can specify when unselfconscious spontaneity will yield its wonders of pleasure.

This is why, then, the preservation, nourishment, and increase of a cadre of dedicated social scientists is an absolute minimum requirement for that tiny bit of enlightened and humane social change that may be possible. Surely we must entertain doubts about how scientific even dedicated scientists can truly be. And surely we will all fail to some degree. But if we cease to strain toward the implementation of the ideals of science, we will have done ourselves in.

Many will see this as advocacy of withdrawal from the battlegrounds on which the crucial issues of public policy are today being contested. But this is a serious mistake. For in our scientific roles we are advocates and actors of high orders of political importance. No action is more crucial than that which clarifies the alternative possible politics of civilization and consciousness, and here science is intertwined beyond separability. So science is where the action is. And that is what knowledge is for.

Nature and society have favored us over many others in permitting us to occupy our very privileged places and to play our crucial roles on this scene. We are, I believe, under deep obligation to this identity we have assumed. It is one of the very few imaginable sources of light on the way out of the otherwise unending warfare that is chronically generated by acting out of loyalties to those tribal affiliations. I have spoken in serious dispraise of them, while recognizing their pernicious tenacity, and I speak in equally serious praise of our new identity as men of science and conscience, and of the loyalty to that identity that commands that we go where the action is and tell it as it really is.

## 49   A KNOWLEDGEABLE SOCIETY   ROBERT E. LANE

It has been a common thing to speak of a "democratic society," and recently of an "affluent society." Could one, in some analogous sense, speak of a "knowledgeable society," or perhaps historically of an "age of knowledge"? Good scholars are likely to be so aware of what they do not know to regard the term as pretentious, yet they are familiar with, and perhaps accept the implications of conventional statements on the "scientific age." The purpose of this piece is to explore the concept of a knowledgeable society, and to examine some of its political implications.

The strands of thinking which may be woven into such a conceptual fabric are many and varied and curiously isolated from one another. There are, in the first place, certain early sociological and anthropological thinkers, each with a somewhat different interpretation of the stages of development of knowledge.[1] The Marxian dialectic offers a further developmental analysis, in the tradition of the sociology of knowledge.[2] Students of social change,[3] historians of science,[4] and philosophers of science[5] add to the picture. Knowledge is cognition—psychologists dealing with cognitive processes and concept formation and thinking illuminate the microprocesses given greater emphasis in an age of knowledge.[6] Even economists have recently dealt with knowledge.[7] The organization and professionalization of knowledge is analyzed in the works of contemporary sociologists.[8] The relationship of science to government has many contemporary students, some of them gathered together in a recent collection.[9] Finally, the current controversies dealing with the "end of ideology" on the one hand, and the place of the intellectual in modern society on the other, bear on the matter.[10] Obviously the scope of the problem is large, the complexity great, and the various treatments disparate. Nevertheless in discussing the concept of a knowledgeable society, we have the help of many others.

"Knowledge," of course is a broad term and I mean to use it broadly. It includes both "the known" and "the state of knowing."[11] Thus a knowledgeable society would be one where there is much knowledge, and where many people go about the business of knowing in a proper fashion. As a first approximation to a definition, the knowledgeable society is one in which, more than in other societies, its members: (1) inquire into the basis of their beliefs about man, nature, and society; (2) are guided (perhaps unconsciously) by objective standards of veridical truth, and, at the upper levels of education, follow scientific rules of evidence and inference in inquiry; (3) devote considerable resources to this inquiry and thus have a large store of knowledge; (4) collect, organize, and

Reprinted with the permission of the author, the American Sociological Association, and the publisher from "The Decline of Politics and Ideology in a Knowledgeable Society," *American Sociological Review*, vol. 31 (October 1966), pp. 649–662.

interpret their knowledge in a constant effort to extract further meaning from it for the purposes at hand; (5) employ this knowledge to illuminate (and perhaps modify) their values and goals as well as to advance them. Just as the "democratic society" has a foundation in governmental and interpersonal relations, and "the affluent society" a foundation in economics, so the knowledgeable society has its roots in epistemology and the logic of inquiry.

In order to support such an epistemological effort, a society must be open, i.e., free discussion must be allowed on every topic, with the outer limit posed not by threats of social change, but by concern for survival as a society. It must be stable enough to maintain the order necessary for the process of inquiry, trusting enough to encourage cooperative effort and acceptance of each other's "findings,"[12] rich enough to educate its population in the modes of inquiry, dissatisfied or curious enough to want to know more.

Obviously this definition and these conditions raise more questions than can be answered easily: Who are these paragons? What power have they? What standards of knowledge qualify a man or a group or a society? How shall we deal with mystical and religious knowledge? With poetical and artistic knowledge? What about the basis for the epistemology itself—is not this the crudest act of faith? This is only an approximate definition of a model of a "knowledgeable society." The elements are present in some degree in every society; in the knowledgeable society they are present to the greatest degree.

## COMMENTS ON THE DEVELOPMENT OF THE KNOWLEDGEABLE SOCIETY

I have defined the knowledgeable society in terms of an epistemology, a search for and quantity of knowledge, and a pattern of use of that knowledge. Any effort to examine in detail how such a society developed leads into theories of social change. Let us briefly consider the problem of development, partly as a means of showing, for contrast, what the knowledgeable society is not.

THE GROWTH AND COMMUNICATION OF EXPERIENCE     Malinowski gives us a starting point: "every primitive community is in possession of a considerable store of knowledge, based on experience and fashioned by reason."[13] He is here arguing against the view that primitive men are irrational and mystical; his argument takes the form of identifying the "profane" domain of life where cause and effect and the effectiveness of skill and reason are clearly perceived, in short, where "scientific thought" is dominant. Wherever the relationships between action and results are obscure, magic and religion have their domain, but the two may be kept separate and the latter need not dominate the former.[14] The knowledgeable society develops by an extension of an understanding of the cause-and-effect relationships in everyday experience and the withering away of the supernatural. Two further points can be made. Following Sumner part way,[15] we propose that philosophy and ethics, and perhaps a kind of low-level science, come to be the generalized and rationalized versions of everyday experience. To some extent they are emergent from and dependent upon the codification of everyday experience. The interaction between science, or at least technology, and philosophy and religion, is an interaction between experience of the mass and the reflections of the elite. In making experience conscious, modern society may, quite apart from the apparatus of science, increase the knowledge applied to everyday acts and decrease their magical and religious components. When experience is "lost" or when it is unconscious and traditional, the opportunities to build a knowledgeable society at this level are wasted.

THE GROWTH OF CULTURE AND SCIENCE     In *Configurations of Culture Growth*,[16] Kroeber employs the notion of episodic cultural "flowering," of typical phases of early growth, pause, maturity, perhaps revival, and then exhaustion. The reference is to all phases of culture—art, music, architecture and philosophy, as well as science and invention. The flowering of one field of culture is, according to Kroeber, likely to be accompanied by the flowering of others, but there are no necessary associations. "Flowering" and "growth," identified by historical recognition of excellence, represent the selection of a dominant "pattern," reinforced (or at least not opposed) by other social forces or areas, and selectively exploited until the possibilities of this particular specialized way of looking at things is exhausted, ending either in repetition or in rebellion, perhaps with an occasional revival.[17] Science, it seems, is no different. "It is . . . specifically to be noted that continuity is a proper quality only of the results of scientific activity. The activity itself is discontinuous."[18] Following Kroeber's line of thought on general culture growth, a knowledgeable society might be in a period of special "flowering," to be followed by decline; there have been many such in history. But since we are interested in exactly those areas of knowledge that are cumulative (and we have reason to believe that the policy sciences are beginning to show this property) we consider a trend to be more reasonable than a cycle.

The concept of growth in knowledge together with irregular scientific "flowering" is partly at odds with Ogburn's concept of an exponential growth of invention, due to the ever-expanding number of "elements" in a culture. Invention, for Ogburn, is the recombination of these elements into a new pattern. Since the invention of printing, "elements" are unlikely to be lost, and the communication process promotes increased diffusion; the possibility of new combinations is cumulative, and restrained only by friction, lag and disturbance. Ogburn seems less concerned with the "quality" of the invention, a property central to Kroeber's ideas, than with the quantity and the accelerated rate of innovations of all kinds, and with their capacity for creating social change and social strain.[19] Thus, the knowledgeable society is a strained society.

Derek Price has made some relevant observations, by considering the numbers of scientific journals, abstracts in specific sciences, and trained scientists, over time. Price finds something similar to Ogburn's cumulative curve. He says:

It must be recognized that the growth of science is something very much more active, much vaster in its problems, than any other sort of growth happening in the world today. For one thing, it has been going on for a longer time and more steadily than most other things. More important, it is growing much more rapidly than anything else. All other things in population, economics, nonscientific culture, are growing so as to double in roughly every human generation or say thirty to fifty years. Science in America is growing so as to double in only ten years. . . . If you care to regard it this way, the density of science in our culture is quadrupling during each generation.[20]

But Price is explicit about the inhibition of science. Clearly such exponential growth cannot continue: "To go beyond the bounds of absurdity, another couple of centuries of normal growth of science would give us dozens of scientists per man, woman, child and dog of world population."[21]

According to Price, the curve of development is logistic in shape and we are nearing the point of deceleration of growth. One could then, at least on this quantitative basis, differentiate perhaps three periods: (1) accelerating rate of growth; (2) some intermediate constant rate; and (3) decelerating rate of growth. But this is still quantitative growth; it is at least possible that Kroeber's comments on "bursts" of greatness or eminence or quality apply. Nevertheless Kroeber's view that "there is no clear evidence of a tendency toward acceleration of growth as we pass from ancient to modern times"[22] seems to require reservations with respect to science.

Machlup is concerned with yet another kind of relevant data: the increase in personnel and expenditure on knowledge, and the implicit evaluation of worth by society relative to other pursuits. Machlup's concept of "the knowledge industry" is much broader than the focus on "science" or even "culture"; it includes those who distribute knowledge (in education and teaching) as well as those who produce it. He finds that knowledge-producing occupations have grown much more rapidly than others and that the salaries of knowledge-producers and distributors, relative to other occupations with equal education, have tended to increase. He also observes a changing emphasis within the knowledge industry: "While in the first part of this century growth was fastest in the clerical occupations, the lead was then taken by managerial and executive occupations, and more recently by professional and technical personnel."[23] The knowledgeable society encourages and rewards the "men of knowledge," compared to the "men of affairs."

The United States has been slow to recognize the importance of scientific knowledge, partly, as Machlup says, because of the "American idiosyncrasy in favor of the immediately practical and against the general-theoretical."[24] Although, in some ways, science grows out of technology,[25] it is often the other way around; even in technology the United States in the 19th Century tended to lag behind Europe.[26]

This is no longer so. Consider the following data on current American expansion in the sciences:

1    From 1940 to 1957, Federal government expenditures for research and development (excluding military pay) increased from $74 million to $2,835 million; from 1953 to 1963, total Federal expenditures for these purposes increased from $3 billion to $10 billion.[27]

2    In the ten-year period from 1953 to 1963, expenditures for research and development by colleges and universities increased from $420 million to $1,700 million.[28]

3    In the seven-year period from 1957 to 1964, the number of Ph.D.'s conferred annually increased as follows:[29] from 1,634 to 2,320 in the Life sciences; from 2,535 to 4,980 in the Physical sciences; and from 1,824 to 2,860 in the Social sciences.

4    In the period from 1950 to 1964 books in "science" published annually in the United States increased from 705 to 2,738 and books in "sociology, economics" from 515 to 3,272.[30]

The prodigious and increasing resources poured into research, the large and increasing numbers of trained people working on various natural and social "problems," and the expanding productivity resulting from this work, is, at least in size, a new factor in social, and (I shall argue) in political life. This "second scientific revolution," as it is sometimes called, reflects both a new appreciation of the role of scientific knowledge, and a new merger of western organizational and scientific skills.[31]

The knowledgeable society is a modern phenomenon; it has inherited a body of knowledge of man, nature, and society which has been continually created and reversed throughout a history of accelerating attention to systematic investigation, despite the irregularity of the production of "great" ideas. The scientific and technological component of culture is different from all other cultural products. Unlike "schools of art and literature," or religious movements, or political movements with their regional incidence, it is a worldwide phenomenon, with demonstrable success in implementing whatever purposes it is applied to.[32] All countries are devoting increasing resources to scientific investigation, and part of this increase is in the social or behavioral sciences. Like the rest of the "knowledge industry," to use Machlup's term, the social knowledge industry is expanding.

### THE THOUGHTWAYS OF A KNOWLEDGEABLE SOCIETY

The knowledgeable society is characterized by a relative emphasis upon certain ways of thinking, a certain epistemology, or, at the very least, a certain knowledge about knowledge. Is this epistemological skill more characteristic of modern, particularly American, society, than of societies in previous periods? It is possible to speak of the development of epistemology somewhat as one speaks of economic and political development, and to construct a sketch of the "thoughtways" of a knowledgeable society. The view that these qualities are more widely distributed today than ever before (one of the themes of Whitehead's *Science and the Modern World*), and are more thoroughly understood by a governing elite of professionals and managers, is reinforced by research showing the impact of modern education upon thinking processes.[33]

## ANTHROPOMORPHIC AND ANALOGICAL THINKING

The first stage of thought is labelling, i.e., assigning things to classes—a more complicated process than at first appears.[34] Durkheim and Mauss argue that primitive classification was first developed according to social categories: "the first classes of things were classes of men, into which things were integrated. It was because men were grouped, and thought of themselves in the form of groups, that in their ideas they grouped other things, and in the beginning the two modes of grouping were merged to the point of being indistinct." So, also, "the unity of knowledge is nothing else than the very unity of the collectivity. . . . Logical relations are thus, in a sense, domestic relations."[35] This view has been criticized in detail,[36] but the general point, seen in animistic thought everywhere, is valid: Men classified the unfamiliar in terms of the homely, familiar concepts developed in daily living. Even in the history of science the use of familiar analogies dominated thought. For example, it is said that Aristotle thought of causal effects in terms of a horse drawing a cart and that Galileo thought of heavenly bodies as something like ships moving in an ocean without friction.[37] The knowledgeable society is one where, by successive approximation, categories and classes of things move from the immediate, personal and familiar, to more abstract concepts with a better fit (more adequate to account for the properties of the phenomena observed).

## DIFFERENTIATION OF EGO FROM INNER WORLD AND FROM ENVIRONMENT

The more a person responds "unselfconsciously" to his inner moods and fantasy life, without conscious thought, or to the stimuli of his environment, reactively, the less able he is either to schedule his drives and maximize his purposes or to master and control the environment. Somehow he must be "separate" from his inner world and his outer world; he must have ego strength to think through his problems, synthesize his desires and control his behavior.

These qualities are said to be lacking in primitive man, as they are demonstrably lacking in a child. Indeed as one ascends the phylogenetic scale, the separation of ego from inner and outer worlds becomes more and more marked.[38] This is sometimes mistaken for alienation; in reality it is a necessary element in thought and a necessary ingredient of the knowledgeable society.

## IMAGINING SITUATIONS CONTRARY TO FACT OR BEYOND EXPERIENCE

In *The Passing of Traditional Society*, Daniel Lerner reports on surveys where Middle Eastern subjects are asked to imagine themselves as editors of a newspaper, Governor or President of their society, or residents in a foreign country. Those with the most limited experience and the most parochial orientations cannot do this; they boggle at the very thought. Lerner refers to this imagination of the self in the place of another as "empathy."[39] A more general notion is the "assumption of a mental set willfully and consciously," as distinguished from a capacity to respond only in terms of a given and familiar state of affairs and an inability to manipulate concepts in the mind so as to reconstruct them in an ungiven manner.[40] Any society which relies upon widely distributed initiative, ambition, and innovation must encourage these qualities of imagination: men must think of themselves and of elements of their situation as other than they are.

## HOLDING SIMULTANEOUSLY IN MIND VARIOUS ASPECTS OF A SITUATION

Primitive and uneducated people can learn a task, a creed, a message, a set of conventions, but it takes special qualities to grasp the "essential" parts, to see how they are put together, to compare them, in short, to analyze them. Comparison and contrast implies holding and bringing together at least two things at once.[41] Rote learning, as in many traditional schools, does not develop these special analytical qualities; it only teaches parts, or, perhaps, sequences. To analyze is to question, and questioning is regarded as dangerous.

**THE REFLECTIVE ABSTRACTION OF COMMON PROPERTIES AND THE FORMATION OF HIERARCHIC CONCEPTS**   The capacity to compare and analyze, to disintegrate a whole, is usually paired with the more difficult task of integrating and organizing parts into a new pattern: analysis and synthesis. In the most primitive societies, the concept of abstract numbers, in contrast to concrete instances, is sometimes missing.[42] Once possessed of the idea of, say, "fiveness" it is not difficult to assign groups with five discrete elements to this class; but to invent, from a multiplicity of objects, the concept of "five" or any other abstract number is the act of genius. The knowledgeable society is not only endowed with a great variety of useful concepts, it actively encourages concept formation to create classes and relationships which give a better account of observable phenomena. The preknowledgeable society employs the concepts given by tradition.

The qualities discussed above fall along a dimension of concreteness-abstraction. The concrete style of thinking is stimulus-bound, unreflective, unanalytic, unsynthetic, and unimaginative. Present in all societies, it is most evident in primitive societies. Harvey, Hunt and Schroder believe it has social consequences, which can be summarized in these ways:[43] Greater concreteness tends to be accompanied by absolutism, categorical thinking, and stereotyping; it is likely to be expressed in attribution of external causality and "oughtness" to rules; it disposes toward catechisms and word magic; it tends to be accompanied by negativism and resistance to suggestion; and it encourages ritualism. In these ways, as readers of *The Authoritarian Personality* and of *The Open and Closed Mind* will recognize, the dimension of concreteness-abstraction has political and social implications: concreteness is related to authoritariansim and to dogmatic, rigid, and opinionated thinking;[44] the democratic society in contrast is marked by abstract thinking.

**EMPLOYMENT OF OBJECTIVE TRUTH CRITERIA**   A knowledgeable society is not only one where more people value knowledge, but one where knowledge is more likely to be valued if it can be shown to be true by certain objective criteria. In the words of Ithiel Pool:

> To evaluate assertions primarily by a criterion of objective truth is not a natural human way of doing things; it is one of the peculiar features of the Graeco-Roman-Western tradition. . . . The Western criterion of truth-value . . . assumes that a statement has a validity or lack of it inherent in itself and quite independent of who says it and why. . . . In most societies facts must be validated by an in-group authority before they can be considered credible.[45]

In most societies, statements are true according to whether the spokesman is powerful and likely to dominate others, whether he is "one of us," whether it is expressed with appropriate politeness, and so forth. Moreover, in Eastern philosophies a thing can both be true and not true at the same time; there is no rule of the undistributed middle.[46]

In a sense, this is a facet of a much larger problem analyzed by Rokeach: the processing of information according to its "intrinsic merits." In his discussion of the open and closed mind, he says that the "basic characteristic that defines the extent to which a person's system is open or closed," is "the extent to which the person can receive, evaluate, and act on relevant information received from the outside on its own intrinsic merits, unencumbered by irrelevant factors in the situation arising from within the person or from the outside." By irrelevant internal pressures Rokeach means unconscious intruding habits and poses, irrational power needs or needs for self-aggrandizement, the need to allay anxiety, to create an impression, and so forth. The irrelevant outside factors are attitudes of dislike towards the source, conformity pressures, the rewards and punishments implied by acceptance and rejection.[47] The knowledgeable society screens out more of the irrelevant internal and external factors for more people.

**TOLERANCE OF DISSONANCE AND AMBIGUITY**   The authoritarian personality, according to Else

Frenkel-Brunswik, is intolerant of ambiguous stimuli; he needs quick, sharp resolution of his doubts. Thus he likes sharply defined art, quick (and usually easy) answers, people who are decisive.[48] The person with a closed mind, according to Rokeach, does not bring together conflicting elements of his belief system; rather he compartmentalizes them, linking them only through the authority of the dogma or the party line or the dominant spokesmen's view.[49] Similarly the capacity and inclination to hold simultaneously in view opinions or attitudes each of which "implies" the reverse of the other (a favored message from a hated source) varies greatly in the population, and generally forces various kinds of reconceptualization to reestablish a consonant emotional posture.[50] More than others, the members of a knowledgeable society are endowed with the capacity to tolerate ambiguity, conflict and dissonance.

### CHANGED VIEWS OF METAPHYSICS AND RELIGION

Comte, writing in the early nineteenth century, held that social progress was produced by a changing epistemology and metaphysics. Societies pass (necessarily, he thought) through certain stages marked by the dominance in modes of thought and emphasis first, of theology, then of metaphysics, and finally of science associated with industrial development, centrally planned and controlled with the help of extensive sociological studies which give the controllers knowledge of the laws of society.[51] The agency of change is, however, unclear; there is no epistemological dialectic. Yet one can at least accept the idea that in the knowledgeable society theological and metaphysical modes of thought shrink in contrast to scientific modes.

Within this framework, however, certain kinds of religious thought seem to have encouraged the growth of science. Merton expressed his position as follows: "It is the thesis of this study that the Puritan ethic, as an ideal-typical expression of the value-attitudes basic to ascetic Protestantism generally, so canalized the interests of seventeenth-century Englishmen as to constitute one important *element* in the enhanced cultivation of science.

The religious *interests* of the day demanded in their forceful implications the systematic, rational, and empirical study of Nature for the glorification of God in His works and for the control of the corrupt world."[52] A knowledgeable society, then, emerges from and is reinforced by religious beliefs which, however framed, focus attention upon this world, and allow for or encourage a scientific epistemology. Today, scientists and professional people are much less likely to be religious or believe in God than businessmen, bankers, and lawyers.[53]

### CHANGED PHILOSOPHY OF KNOWLEDGE

The mind vs. matter problem appears in many guises: as the contrast between "words and things", as rationalism vs. empiricism, as idealism vs. nominalism, and so forth. Whitehead considered that the great difference between the modern scientific age and all other periods was the wedding together of speculative and theoretical modes of thought with empirical and systematic modes of investigation.[54] Similarly Reichenbach has argued that the rise of scientific philosophy is grounded in a shift from "*transcendental* conception of knowledge, according to which knowledge transcends the observable things and depends upon the use of other sources than sense perception," to a "*functional* conception of knowledge, which regards knowledge as an instrument of prediction and for which sense observation is the only admissible criterion of nonempty truth."[55] There are not two worlds, an ideal and a real one, but one integrated world of thought and experience. The knowledgeable society is marked by an increased acceptance of this view. "The opium of the intellectuals" is not so much, as Raymond Aron thinks, Marxism,[56] as it is philosophical idealism.

One facet of this changed concept of knowledge has been an emphasis upon operationalism, *i.e.*, the position that concepts are related, however indirectly, to the operations which measure them, and by intersubjective testability. Knowledge in the knowledgeable society must be public, its sources indicated and its conceptual boundaries marked by something other than incommunicable experience.

**FROM SYMPTOMATOLOGY TO TAXONOMY TO EXPLANATION** The history of the biological and behavioral sciences reveals a tendency first to report observations on phenomena (the naturalist and the journalist), then, with greater care, to group these observations into classes and syndromes, and then, with experimental or controlled observational techniques, to attempt to understand causal relationships, to explain why the phenomena change as they do. When this latter phase is successful, control is more feasible and social policy is likely to be more adequate to the situation. In the knowledgeable society, the intellectual emphasis is more likely to be upon laws of behavior, change, and control. Attaching metrics to phenomena often improves our understanding and our control. The knowledgeable society increasingly employs mathematical modes of expression and thought.

**THE CONTRIBUTION OF THE PHILOSOPHY OF SCIENCE** We have been discussing the complex of attitudes and skills which equip men to deal realistically with the events which impinge upon their lives—policy-formation at the micro-level. This is related to but separate from the ways of thinking of scientists and philosophers who are interested in social policy. This history of social thought reveals the importance of analogical thinking: If geometry yields results from axiomatic methods, so should sociology; in an age of mechanics the model may be clockworks or hydraulics to some (cf. Freud); organismic theories dominate certain periods: a primitive set of anatomical analogies seems to have been prevalent in the Middle Ages.[57]

It seems to me that the emergence of a coherent philosophy of science or logic of inquiry represents a crucial change in this groping toward a method of studying society, particularly as it has matured and increased the scope given to imagination. If one goes back no further than the beginning of this century, with the rise of analytic philosophy in Austria (the Vienna Circle) and in England, the development of the "unified science" group at Chicago, perhaps the general systems theorists, and the widespread teaching of the

philosophy of science today, a change in intellectual posture toward man and society so great as to represent a watershed is evident. Other knowledgeable societies, marked by Kroeber's "bursts" of culture growth, have not sustained their performance. I believe the development and widespread acceptance of the philosophy of science as a basis for social inquiry represents a "take-off" phenomenon in social science, promising sustained growth in social interpretation.

## PROFESSIONALISM AND THE "PREFORMULATION" OF POLICY

The discussion so far has sought to illuminate the development of the knowledgeable society, and to show its characteristic thoughtways. Now we turn to the application of this knowledge to public policy. The people who make this application are, in the first instance the professionals, organized in their own associations, governing and staffing institutions devised to develop and teach the new knowledge and apply it to current problems. Within the professions there are tendencies to allocate responsibility for knowledge domains and hence responsibilities for working out "solutions" of social problems relevant to these domains. One aspect of professionalization is the establishment of standards of performance well above actual performance. The gap between the actual and the idea creates within the profession a kind of strain towards remedial action. The consciousness of meeting or failing to meet standards enlists professional ambition, reputation, credit and blame. Staff conferences, annual meetings, and new research studies set up strains for better performance, better instruments, better laws, and new agencies to meet the new standards. In the knowledgeable society, much policy is made first through professional intercourse, concerning what solutions to press upon the government and what men to advance to positions of influence as well as what standards to impose. In some ways this is only a change of venue for political maneuvering, but in an important sense it implies a change in criteria for decision-makers from immediate political advantage to something within the professionalized domain of knowledge.

## KNOWLEDGE IS ENCROACHING ON POLITICS

If one thinks of a domain of "pure politics" where decisions are determined by calculations of influence, power, or electoral advantage, and a domain of "pure knowledge" where decisions are determined by calculations of how to implement agreed-upon values with rationality and efficiency, it appears to me that the political domain is shrinking and the knowledge domain is growing, in terms of criteria for decisions, kinds of counsel sought, evidence adduced, and nature of the "rationality" employed. Some of the evidence for this direction of change may be suggested in the following sampling of recent events:

1   With due allowance for political slippage, there has been a gradual expansion of the civil service based on competitive examinations from 23 per cent of personnel employed in the executive branch of the Federal government in 1891, to 87 per cent in 1962.

2   The General Accounting Office, established in 1921, and the General Service Administration, established in 1949, supervise government business operations so as to encourage economic rather than political criteria.

3   The Council of Economic Advisers was set up in 1946, symbolizing the introduction of economic criteria into the monetary and fiscal operations of government.

4   The professionalization of the attack on poverty is illustrated by the contrast between the methods and programs of the Works Progress Administration (1933) and the Office of Economic Opportunity (1965).

5   The growing use of extra-governmental organizations, like Rand and the university research centers, to study social and technical problems and formulate policy proposals, introduces a variety of less political (if not value-free) criteria for policy-making.

6   Similarly the growing employment of

Presidential Commissions and Committees and White House Conferences changes the nature of the criteria employed in policy-making.

7   An enlarged governmental apparatus has been created to enlist scientific advice on a variety of topics (not just what is coming to be called the management of "science affairs"), as seen in the President's Scientific Advisory Committee and the Office of Science and Technology, and even the Office of Science Adviser to the Secretary of State.[58]

Moreover, the dominant scholarly interpretation of policy-making processes has changed in the direction of emphasizing the greater autonomy of political leaders and legislators: with respect to the role of pressure groups,[59] the power elite,[60] and the electorate.[61] If leaders and other legislators are less bound by the domain of pure politics than we had thought, then they are freer to be guided by the promptings of scientists and findings from the domain of knowledge.

Studies of the legislative process reinforce this view. A massive literature documents four relevant points: (1) the rising influence of the bureaucracy is based in large part on bureaucratic command over the sources of knowledge; (2) state and national legislators respond to the growing importance of technical knowledge both with increased standards for their own mastery of subject-matter fields and with demands for greater staff resources to help them meet the challenge; (3) there is an increased reliance on the kind of professional help enlisted by the executive; and (4) the power of the lobby is less likely to be based on electoral sanctions than upon specialized information helpful (however self-interested) in formulating policy change.[62]

## THE CHANGED APPROACH TO PROBLEMS

Of course there will always be politics; there will always be rationalized self-interest, mobilized by interest groups and articulated in political parties. But, if political criteria decline in importance relative to more universalistic scientific criteria, and if the professional problem-oriented scientists rather than laymen come to have more to say about social policy, the shift in perspective is likely to occasion some differences in policy itself. What would these be?

In the first place there is the question of the very *consciousness* of a problem. The man in the middle of the problem (sickness, poverty, waste and especially ignorance) often does not know there is anything problematic about his state. He may accept his condition as embodying the costs of living: if one accepts his lot in life, one accepts lesions, hunger, overwork and unemployment. For this reason such people are often hard to reach. As Harrington says, "First and foremost, any attempt to abolish poverty in the United States must seek to destroy the pessimism and fatalism that flourish in the other America," the America of the poor.[63] Often it takes years of dedicated agitation to make people aware that they live in the midst of a problem. The curious thing about modern times is the degree to which government itself undertakes to do what, in the past, has so often been the task of the agitator. The New Deal helped to organize labor, and the New Frontier and the Great Society help Negroes to demand more of society, and help organize the poor to pursue their own interests. Admittedly there are political benefits in these acts, and they can be attributed only in minor part to the growing insights into the nature of poverty and apathy. Yet consciousness of a problem may come *first* to the authorities, scientific and governmental. People may have to be told, not that they are miserable, but that the conditions of their lives are, in some sense, remediable.

Beyond consciousness is something else, the analysis of the nature of the trouble: its causes, and what should be done about it. Here the main point is the environmentalism of the authoritative scientific or governmental view, in contrast to the personalism of the man involved. The problem as it presents itself to these two attentive persons is in each case different. For the unemployed worker, his problem is to find a job; for the economist, the problem is to analyze the causes of unemployment and sometimes to suggest remedial action. To the worker the "cause" of his plight is that he

was let go; to the economist, the cause of the worker's plight may be insufficiency of demand due to higher interest rates and a budgetary surplus. What is cause to the worker is to the economist only a symptom, so different are their perspectives.

The view of a problem by scientific or governmental authorities is very often an analysis of the environment in which it occurs; the causes for the scientist are the factors which make the "problem" for the individual. In consequence, the political demands of the affected group and the demands of the professionals interested in the group's condition, may lead in different directions.

For people within a system (hospital, market, watershed, communication network), the boundaries and budgets seem fixed; they bargain for limited resources and more for them seems necessarily to imply less for someone else. An authoritative overview can change that perspective by introducing the possibility not of reallocating limited values but of generating an increase in values. Thus an economist today considers the problems of equity and efficiency in distribution in conjunction with the problem of growth. For the medical sociologist, the problem of the distribution of hospital facilities is paired with the problem of more and better facilities and better health; he is unsatisfied simply with a redistribution of untreated illness in a more equitable fashion. Political scientists have failed to understand this point, because their attention to "the authoritative allocation of values" has tended to obscure another facet of government: the generation of values.

## KNOWLEDGE IS ENCROACHING ON IDEOLOGY

If we employ the term "ideology" to mean a comprehensive, passionately believed, self-activating view of society, usually organized as a social movement, rather than a latent half-conscious belief system,[64] it makes sense to think of a domain of knowledge distinguishable from a domain of ideology, despite the extent to which they may overlap. Since knowledge and ideology serve somewhat as functional equivalents in orienting a person toward the problems he must face and the policies he must select, the growth of the domain of knowledge causes it to impinge on the domain of ideology.

Silvan Tomkins has developed a theory of a basic ideological left-right dimension in virtually all domains of life, turning on the questions, "Is man the measure, an end in himself, an active, creative, thinking, desiring, loving, force in nature? Or must man realize himself, attain his full stature only through struggle toward, participation in, conformity to, a norm, a measure, an ideal essence basically independent of man?"[65] He believes that arguments along these lines develop in passionate forms (in philosophy, mathematics, jurisprudence, etc., as well as in politics) wherever men are least certain of their ground. These arguments thrive on uncertainty and ignorance. "When the same ideas [that men have been arguing over in these ideological terms] are firmly established and incorporated into the fabric of a science or tested and found wanting, they cease to constitute an ideology in the sense in which we are using the term. At the growing edge of the frontier of all sciences there necessarily is a maximum of uncertainty, and what is lacking in evidence is filled by passion and faith and by hatred and scorn for the disbelievers. Science will never be free of ideology, though yesterday's ideology is today's fact or fiction."[66] The theory, then, is of an "ideo-affective" orientation toward the world directed towards subjects about which there is doubt. If the doubt is clarified by knowledge, this ideological orientation moves on to some other marginal and uncertain area. Increasing knowledge about man, nature, and society can be said to reduce the target area for ideological thinking.

A second way in which the characteristics of a knowledgeable society may be thought to reduce ideological thinking, is through the reduction of dogmatic thinking. Following Rokeach, we may conceive of dogmatic thinking as a selection and interpretation of information so as to reinforce a previously established creed, dogma, or political ideology. Information is used, not so much to understand the world as it really is, but as a means of defending against conflict and uncertainty.[67] The knowledgeable society is marked by a relatively greater stress on the use of information veridically, relying on its truth value and not on any adventitious defense, popularity, or reinforcement value. This should be associated with a decline in dogmatic thinking. The decline of dogmatism implies the decline of ideology, in the narrower sense of the term used here.

In the third place, consider the way in which knowledge may limit Mannheim's thesis that political thinking is inevitably biased. He says "all knowledge which is either political or which involves a world view is inevitably partisan"; and later "at the point where what is properly political begins, the evaluative element cannot easily be separated out," and still later, "the peculiar nature of political knowledge, as contrasted to the 'exact' sciences, arises out of the inseparability, in this realm, of knowledge from interest and motivation."[68] Mannheim has in view only the thinking of those who are themselves engaged in political strife; he does not envisage the possibility of such studies as *The Legislative System* and *The American Voter*,[69] which, although evaluative in many ways, nevertheless narrow the range of partisan, irrational and evaluative thought. Granting that interested parties form their ideas about politics into ideological constructs it seems likely that knowledge may constrict the scope of their ideology.

This narrowing effect was, in fact, experienced by the participants at the conference of the Congress for Cultural Freedom in Milan in 1955 out of which the theme of "the end of ideology" developed. These scholars and scientists came expecting, indeed inviting, a great confrontation of world views. Under the pressure of economic and social knowledge, a growing body of research, and the codified experience of society, ideological argument tended to give way to technical argument, apparently to the disappointment of some.[70] The debate remained evaluative and partisan, but the domain of ideology was shrunken by the dominance of knowledge.

## KNOWLEDGE AS DISEQUILIBRIUM

What happens when the scientific apparatus of the knowledgeable society produces some important findings: existential, causal, remedial, or whatever? Here are some examples from the social sciences:

Among the nations of the world, the United States ranked 16th in rate of infant mortality in 1961.[71]

To raise every individual and family in the nation now below a subsistence income to the subsistence level would cost about $10 billion a year. This is less than 2 per cent of the gross national product. It is less than 10 per cent of tax revenues. It is about one-fifth of the cost of national defense.[72]

The reinforcing experience for convicted criminals while in jail results in high rates of recidivism: about three-fourths of those entering jail have been there before. And the younger the person at the time of first offense, the higher the rate of recidivism and the sooner it occurs.[73]

Today, more American school children die of cancer than from any other disease. So serious has this situation become that Boston has established the first hospital in the United States devoted exclusively to the treatment of children with cancer. . . . One of the earliest pesticides associated with cancer is arsenic. . . . In the United States the arsenic-drenched soils of tobacco plantations, of many orchards in the Northwest, and of blueberry lands in the East easily lead to pollution of water supplies.[74]

The more an individual engages in personal interaction with persons of different race, religious, or national background, the lower is his general level of prejudice. This result holds not only for majority group prejudices but also for minority prejudices against the majority group and other minorities. It is true of youths as well as their elders. It has been confirmed in 14 different samples, involving about 6000 persons.[75]

Such knowledge—discovered, organized, and communicated by professional men—creates a pressure for policy change with a force all its own. Knowledge (and what is regarded as knowledge) is pressure even without pressure groups, and without reference to an articulated forensic ideology. If the reader of these statements experiences some kind of policy-oriented speculation, so, I believe, do policy-making officials. The source of the tension is not difficult to discover. In skeleton form, the sequence may be as follows:

1   A state of affairs as presented, conveying new or more precise information than that previously known (infants and children are dying at a "high" rate; poverty could be eliminated).

2   A value is engaged (early death is bad; poverty is worse than prosperity).

3   In some cases the information applies to particular groups whose needs and values are especially significant to an observer (Northwest apple growers, Southern Negroes and Whites, delinquent youth).

4   Remedial action may be suggested (subsidies to the poor, policing of pesticides, enforced integration).

5   Social, economic, and political costs are implied (taxation for subsidies to the poor, expensive re-education for prisoners, and opposition of tobacco growers).

6   Certain "pre-political ideological" positions on man and society are enlisted (Can man control his own fate? Is poverty "necessary"? Is human nature a constant?).

7   Certain ideological postures toward the business of government are enlisted (Is every increment of government a bad policy in itself? Is government too corrupt an instrument to employ in changing conditions? Are tax dollars better spent by private organizations and individuals?).

Let us suppose, as seems likely, that knowledge like that presented above sets up a kind of "disequilibrium" in a person's mind. The restoration of equilibrium, then, is the problem-solving process, perhaps by questioning the data or the source, perhaps by changing one's own priorities of action, perhaps by selective inattention, perhaps by delegation (real or symbolic), perhaps by purely expressive as opposed to instrumental behavior, perhaps by rationalization, perhaps by scapegoating, perhaps by advocating simplistic solutions, and so forth.[76] But the point is that knowledge, with little more, often sets up a disequilibrium or pressure which requires compensating thought or action.

## SUMMARY

In this article I have tried, first, to develop the idea of a knowledgeable society, with special attention to questions of growth and epistemology. Then, assuming that the concept applies to modern American society, I have suggested that the professionals and their associations have a role in the preformulation of policy, not all good, but generally responsive to the needs of society. Further, in comparing two "pure" domains, that of politics and that of knowledge, I have suggested that the criteria and scope of politics are shrinking while those of knowledge are growing. This has created a difference in perspectives of policy-makers: a different kind of consciousness, an environmentalist approach, and a concept of the generation of values. Like politics, ideology is declining as a *necessary* ingredient in change, partly because, given present values, knowledge sets up a powerful kind of attitudinal disequilibrium all its own.

## REFERENCES AND NOTES

1   See Auguste Comte, *A General View of Positivism*, trans. J. H. Bridges, Stanford, Calif.: Academic Reprints, 1958; and comments in Howard Becker and Harry Elmer Barnes, *Social Thought from Lore to Science*, 3d ed., vol. 2, New York: Dover Publications, Inc., 1961, pp. 573–574; Emile Durkheim and Marcel Mauss, *Primitive Classification*, trans. Rodney Needham, Chicago: The University of Chicago Press, 1963; Bronislaw Malinowski, *Magic, Science and Religion*, Garden City, N.Y.: Doubleday & Company, Inc., Anchor edition, 1955; A. L. Kroeber, *Configurations of Culture Growth*, Berkeley, Calif.: University of California Press, 1944.

2   See Marx's discussion of consciousness and of ideas as superstructures in his "Economic and Philosophi-

cal Manuscripts" and "German Ideology," in *Marx's Concept of Man*, edited Erich Fromm, New York: Ungar, 1961; Karl Mannheim, *Ideology and Utopia*, trans. Louis Wirth and Edward Shils, London: Routledge & Kegan Paul, 1949; Robert K. Merton, *Social Theory and Social Structure*, rev. ed., New York: The Free Press of Glencoe, 1957, parts 3 and 4.

3   See especially "Social Evolution Reconsidered" (1950), in *William F. Ogburn on Culture and Social Change*, ed. Otis D. Duncan, Chicago: The University of Chicago Press, 1964.

4   Derek J. de Sola Price, *Science Since Babylon*, New Haven: Yale University Press, 1961; Herbert Butterfield, *The Origins of Modern Science*, rev. ed., New York: The Macmillan Company, 1961.

5   Alfred N. Whitehead, *Science and the Modern World*, Cambridge: Cambridge University Press, 1933; Carl G. Hempel, *Fundamentals of Concept Formation*, Chicago: The University of Chicago Press, 1952, vol. 2, no. 7 of the *International Encyclopedia of Unified Science*; Hans Reichenbach, *The Rise of Scientific Philosophy*, Berkeley, Calif.: University of California Press, 1953.

6   For a general overview, see D. E. Berlyne, *Structure and Direction in Thinking*, New York: John Wiley & Sons, Inc., 1965; a developmental (individual and social) view is presented in O. J. Harvey, D. E. Hunt, and H. M. Schroder, *Conceptual Systems and Personality Organization*, New York: John Wiley & Sons, Inc., 1961; I have found Milton Rokeach's work especially helpful, *The Open and Closed Mind*, New York: Basic Books, Inc., 1960.

7   Fritz Machlup, *The Production and Distribution of Knowledge in the United States*, Princeton, N.J.: Princeton University Press, 1962.

8   Bernard Barber, *Science and the Social Order*, Glencoe, Ill.: The Free Press, 1952; Florian Znaniecki, *The Social Role of the Man of Knowledge*, New York: Columbia University Press, 1940; Everett C. Hughes, *Men and their Work*, Glencoe, Ill.: The Free Press, 1958; T. H. Marshall, *Class Citizenship and Social Development*, Garden City, N.Y.: Doubleday & Company, Inc., 1964, especially chap. VI; H. L. Wilensky, "The Professionalization of Everyone?" *American Journal of Sociology*, vol. 70 (1964), pp. 137–158.

9   Robert Gilpin and Christopher Wright (eds.), *Scientists and National Policy Making*, New York: Columbia University Press, 1964; Don K. Price, *Government and Science*, New York: New York University Press, 1954.

10  Daniel Bell, "The End of Ideology in the West" in *The End of Ideology*, Glencoe, Ill.: The Free Press, 1960; Edward Shils, "The End of Ideology?," *Encounter*, vol. 5 (November 1955), pp. 52–58; S. M.

Lipset, "The End of Ideology?," in *Political Man*, Garden City, N.Y.: Doubleday & Company, Inc., 1960.

11   Machlup, *op. cit.*, p. 13.

12   Ithiel Pool holds that acceptance of statements on grounds other than the status of the source implies "an unusually high degree of mutual trust in interpersonal relations." See "The Mass Media and Politics in the Modernization Process," in Lucien Pye (ed.), *Communications and Political Development*, Princeton, N.J.: Princeton University Press, 1963, p. 242.

13   Malinowski, *op. cit.*, p. 26.

14   *Ibid.*, pp. 26–36.

15   William Graham Sumner, *Folkways*, Boston: Ginn & Co., 1940, pp. 1–74.

16   See note 1. For a cyclical theory of cultural change, see P. A. Sorokin, *Social and Cultural Dynamics*, vols. I–IV, New York: American Book Company, 1937, 1941.

17   Kroeber, *op. cit.*, pp. 762–777.

18   *Ibid.*, p. 204.

19   Ogburn, *op. cit.*, pp. 17–32.

20   Price, *op. cit.*, pp. 107–108.

21   *Ibid.*, p. 113.

22   Kroeber, *op. cit.*, p. 842.

23   Machlup, *op. cit.*, p. 396.

24   *Ibid.*, p. 202.

25   See Derek Price's discussion of "Renaissance Roots of Yankee Ingenuity" in *Science Since Babylon*, pp. 45–67.

26   Eugene Ayres, "Social Attitudes toward Invention," *American Scientist*, vol. 43 (1955), pp. 533–535; quoted in Machlup, *op. cit.*, p. 202.

27   *Historical Statistics of the United States, Colonial Times to 1957* and *Continuation to 1962 and Revisions*, U.S. Bureau of the Census Series 79, 80, Washington, D.C.: U.S. Government Printing Office, 1960 and 1965.

28   *Statistical Abstract for the United States: 1965*, Washington D.C.: U.S. Government Printing Office, 1965, p. 545.

29   *Ibid.*, p. 551.

30   *Ibid.*, p. 527.

31   See John J. Beer and W. David Lewis, "Aspects of the Professionalization of Science," *Daedalus*, vol. 92, no. 4 (1963), pp. 764–784.

32   "The Reformation, for all its importance, may be considered as a domestic affair of the European races. . . . Modern science was born in Europe, but its home is the whole world." Whitehead, *op. cit.*, pp. 3–4.

33   See Harold Webster, Mervin B. Friedman, and Paul Heist, "Personality Changes in College Students," in Nevitt Sanford (ed.), *The American College*, New York: John Wiley & Sons, Inc., 1962, pp. 811–846.

34   See the discussion of "concept attainment" in Jerome S. Bruner, Jacqueline J. Goodnow, and George A. Austin, *A Study of Thinking*, New York: John Wiley & Sons, Inc., 1956.

35   *Primitive Classification*, pp. 82–84.

36   See Rodney Needham's excellent introduction to Durkheim and Mauss, *ibid.*, pp. vii–xlviii.

37   Stephen Toulmin, *Foresight and Understanding*, New York: Harper Torchbook, 1961, pp. 52, 54.

38   This point and several following are derived from Harvey, Hunt, and Schroder's explication and development of Goldstein and Scheerer's concept of a concrete-abstractness dimension of thought, originating from studies of children and brain-damaged patients. See Harvey *et al.*, *op. cit.*, pp. 24–49.

39   *The Passing of Traditional Society*, New York: The Free Press of Glencoe, 1958, pp. 47–52.

40   Harvey *et al.*, *op. cit.*, p. 29.

41   See the discussion of "conceptualizing in political discourse," in Robert E. Lane, *Political Ideology*, New York: The Free Press, 1962, pp. 346–363.

42   H. Werner, *Comparative Psychology of Mental Development*, rev. ed., New York: International Universities Press, 1957, quoted in Harvey *et al.*, *op. cit.*, p. 33.

43   Harvey *et al.*, *op. cit.*, pp. 36–46.

44   T. W. Adorno, Else Frenkel-Brunswik, Daniel J. Levinson, and R. Nevitt Sanford, *The Authoritarian Personality*, New York: Harper & Row, Publishers, 1950; Rokeach, *op. cit.*

45   Pool, *op. cit.*, p. 242.

46   *Ibid.*, pp. 242–244.

47   Rokeach, *op. cit.*, p. 57.

48   "Intolerance of Ambiguity as an Emotional and Perceptual Variable," *Journal of Personality*, vol. 18 (1949), pp. 108–143.

49   Rokeach, *op. cit.*, pp. 67–97.

50   I think the most useful short account of the general phenomenon of cognitive dissonance and cognitive balancing is in Milton Rosenberg *et al.*, *Attitude Organization and Change*, New Haven: Yale University Press, 1960, pp. 112–163.

51   Comte, *op. cit.*, *passim*.

52   Merton, *op. cit.*, pp. 574–575 (Merton's emphasis).

53   Lipset, *op. cit.*, p. 314.

54   *Science and the Modern World* p. 3.

55   *The Rise of Scientific Philosophy*, p. 252.

56   *The Opium of the Intellectuals*, trans. T. Kilmartin, New York: W. W. Norton and Co., 1957.

57   Karl Deutsch has an interesting discussion of these analogies in his *The Nerves of Government*, New York: The Free Press, 1963, pp. 24–38. The anatomical metaphor in medieval political thought is most explicit in Otto Gierke, *Political Theories of the Mid-*

dle Ages, trans. F. W. Maitland, Boston: Beacon Press, 1958.

58 Much of this is reported and commented upon in Gilpin and Wright, *Scientists and National Policy Making*. Here (p. 109) one will find Wallace Sayre making the point that "politics is inescapable." Nothing in this section should be read as implying anything contrary to this maxim.

59 E. E. Schattschneider, *Politics, Pressures and the Tariff*, New York: Prentice-Hall, Inc., 1935; Peter H. Odegard, *Pressure Politics*, New York, Columbia University Press, 1928; Raymond A. Bauer, Ithiel de S. Pool, and L. A. Dexter, *American Business and Public Policy*, New York: Atherton Press, 1963.

60 Floyd Hunter, *Community Power Structure*, Chapel Hill, N.C.: University of North Carolina Press, 1953; Robert A. Dahl, *Who Governs?*, New Haven, Conn.: Yale University Press, 1961.

61 "Toward a More Responsible Two-party System," Supplement to *American Political Science Review*, vol. 44, no. 3 (1950); and see, for example, Warren E. Miller and Donald E. Stokes, "Constituency Influence in Congress," *American Political Science Review*, vol. 57 (1963), pp. 45–56.

62 See, for example, John Wahlke, Heinz Eulau, *et. al.*, *The Legislative System*, New York: John Wiley & Sons, Inc., 1962; James D. Barber, *The Lawmaker*, New Haven, Conn.: Yale University Press, 1965; Bauer, Pool, and Dexter, *op. cit.*; Robert L. Peabody and Nelson W. Polsby (eds.), *New Perspectives on the House of Representatives*, Chicago: Rand McNally & Co., 1963; Donald R. Matthews, *U.S. Senators and Their World*, New York: Random House, Inc., Vintage edition, 1960.

63 Michael Harrington, *The Other America*, New York: The Macmillan Company, 1963, p. 163.

64 See Lane, *op. cit.*, pp. 13–16, and note 10 above. Of course there are many definitions of ideology referring to a wider range of "mental products."

65 "Left and Right: A Basic Dimension of Ideology and Personality," in Robert W. White (ed.), *The Study of Lives*, New York: Atherton Press, 1963, pp. 391–392.

66 *Ibid.*, p. 389.

67 Rokeach, *op. cit.*

68 "The Prospects of Scientific Politics," in *Ideology and Utopia*, pp. 132, 168, 170.

69 Angus Campbell, Philip E. Converse, Warren E. Miller, and Donald E. Stokes, *The American Voter*, New York: John Wiley & Sons, Inc., 1960.

70 Bell, *op. cit.*, Shils, *op. cit.*; and Lipset, *op. cit.*

71 *United Nations Statistical Yearbook, 1962*, New York: United Nations, 1963, p. 50.

72 James N. Morgan *et al., Income and Welfare in the United States*, New York: McGraw-Hill Book Co., 1962, pp. 3–4.

73 Bernard Berelson and Gary Steiner, *Human Behavior*, New York: Harcourt, Brace & Co., 1964, p. 630.

74 Rachel Carson, *Silent Spring*, Boston: Houghton Mifflin Co., 1962, pp. 221–223.

75 Robin M. Williams, quoted in Berelson and Steiner, *op. cit.*, p. 519.

76 Dan Berlyne's *Structure and Direction in Thinking* illuminates the processes of "problematicity" and problem-solving, especially pp. 236–293.

## 50 FALSE CRITERIA OF CAUSALITY

### TRAVIS HIRSCHI HANAN C. SELVIN

Smoking per se is not a cause of lung cancer. Evidence for this statement comes from the thousands of people who smoke and yet live normal, healthy lives. Lung cancer is simply unknown to the vast majority of smokers, even among those who smoke two or more packs a day. Whether smoking is a cause of lung cancer, then, depends upon the reaction of the lung

Reprinted from *Social Problems*, vol. 13 (winter 1966), pp. 254–268, by permission of the authors and The American Academy of Political and Social Science.

This is publication A-56 of the Survey Research Center, University of California, Berkeley. We are grateful to the Ford Foundation for financial support of the larger study from which this paper is drawn. An early account of this study, which does not include the present paper, is *The Methodological Adequacy of Delinquency Research*, Berkeley, Calif.: Survey Research Center, 1962. Ian Currie, John Lofland, Alan B. Wilson, and Herbert L. Costner made useful criticisms of previous versions of this article.

tissues to the smoke inhaled. The important thing is not whether a person smokes, but how his lungs react to the smoke inhaled. These facts point to the danger of imputing causal significance to superficial variables. In essence, it is not smoking as such, but the carcinogenic elements in tobacco smoke that are the real causes of lung cancer.[1]

The task of determining whether such variables as broken homes, gang membership, or anomie are "causes" of delinquency benefits from a comparison with the more familiar problem of deciding whether cigarette smoking "causes" cancer. In both fields many statistical studies have shown strong relations between these presumed causes and the observed effects, but the critics of these studies often attack them as "merely statistical." This phrase has two meanings. To some critics it stands for the belief that only with experimental manipulation of the independent variables is a satisfactory causal inference possible. To others it is a brief way of saying that observing a statistical association between two phenomena is only the first step in plausibly inferring causality. Since no one proposes trying to give people cancer or to make them delinquent, the fruitful way toward better causal analyses in these two fields is to concentrate on improving the statistical approach.

In setting this task for ourselves we can begin with one area of agreement: all statistical analyses of causal relations in delinquency rest on observed associations between the independent and dependent variables. Beyond this there is less agreement. Following Hyman's reasoning,[2] we believe that these two additional criteria are the minimum requirements for an adequate causal analysis: (1) the independent variable is causally prior to the dependent variable (we shall refer to this as the criterion of "causal order"), and (2) the original association does not disappear when the influences of other variables causally prior to both of the original variables are removed ("lack of spuriousness").[3]

The investigator who tries to meet these criteria does not have an easy time of it.[4] Our examination of statistical research on the causes of delinquency shows, however, that many investigators do not try to meet these criteria but instead invent one or another new criterion of causality—or, more often, of noncausality, perhaps because noncausality is easier to demonstrate. To establish causality one must forge a chain of three links (association, causal order, and lack of spuriousness), and the possibility that an antecedent variable not yet considered may account for the observed relation makes the third link inherently weak. To establish noncausality, one has only to break any one of these links.[5]

Despite the greater ease with which noncausality may be demonstrated, many assertions of noncausality in the delinquency literature turn out to be invalid. Some are invalid because the authors misuse statistical tools or misinterpret their findings. But many more are invalid because the authors invoke one or another false criterion of noncausality. Perhaps because assertions of noncausality are so easy to demonstrate, these invalid assertions have received a great deal of attention.

A clear assertion that certain variables long considered causes of delinquency are not really causes comes from a 1960 *Report to The Congress*:

> Many factors frequently cited as causes of delinquency are really only concomitants. They are not causes in the sense that if they were removed delinquency would decline. Among these factors are:
> Broken homes.
> Poverty.
> Poor housing.
> Lack of recreational facilities.
> Poor physical health.
> Race.
> Working mothers.[6]

According to this report, all of these variables are statistically associated with delinquency, i.e., they are all "concomitants." To prove that they are not causes of delinquency it is necessary either to show that their relations with delinquency are spurious or that they are effects of delinquency rather than causes. Since all of these presumptive causes appear to precede delinquency, the only legitimate way to prove noncausality is to find an antecedent variable that accounts for the observed relations. None of the studies cited in the *Report* does this.[7] Instead, the assertion that broken homes, poverty, lack of recreational facilities, race, and working mothers are not causes of delinquency appears to be based on one or more of the following false "criteria":[8]

1   Insofar as a relation between two variables is not *perfect*, the relation is not causal. (a) Insofar as a factor is not a *necessary condition* for delinquency, it is not a cause of delinquency. (b) Insofar as a factor is not a *sufficient condition* for delinquency, it is not a cause of delinquency.

2   Insofar as a factor is not *"characteristic"* of delinquents, it is not a cause of delinquency.

3   If a relation between an independent variable and delinquency is found for a *single value of a situational or contextual factor*, then the situational or contextual factor cannot be a cause of delinquency.

4   If a relation is observed between an independent variable and delinquency and if a psychological variable is suggested as *intervening* between these two variables, then the original relation is not causal.

5   *Measurable* variables are not causes.

6   If a relation between an independent variable and delinquency is *conditional* upon the value of other variables, the independent variable is not a cause of delinquency.[9]

In our opinion, all of these criteria of noncausality are illegitimate. If they were systematically applied to any field of research, no relation would survive the test. Some of them, however, have a superficial plausibility, both as stated or implied in the original works and as reformulated here. It will therefore be useful to consider in some detail just why these criteria are illegitimate and to see how they appear in delinquency research.

*False criterion 1   Insofar as a relation between two variables is not perfect, the relation is not causal*

Despite the preponderance of Negro delin-

quency, one must beware of imputing any causal significance to race per se. There is no *necessary* concomitance between the presence of Negroes and delinquency. In Census Tracts 9-1 and 20-2, with populations of 124 and 75 Negro juveniles, there were no recorded cases of delinquency during the study period. The rates of Negro delinquency also vary as widely as do the white rates indicating large differences in behavior patterns that are not a function or effect of race per se. It is also of interest to note that in at least 10% of the districts with substantial Negro juvenile populations, the Negro delinquency rate is lower than the corresponding white rate.[10]

There are three facts here: (1) not all Negroes are delinquents; (2) the rates of Negro delinquency vary from place to place; (3) in some circumstances, Negroes are less likely than whites to be delinquent. These facts lead Lander to conclude that race has no causal significance in delinquency.

In each case the reasoning is the same: each fact is another way of saying that the statistical relation between race and delinquency is not perfect, and this apparently is enough to disqualify race as a cause. To see why this reasoning is invalid one has only to ask for the conditions under which race *could be* a cause of delinquency if this criterion were accepted. Suppose that the contrary of the first fact above were true, that *all* Negroes are delinquent. It would then follow necessarily that Negro delinquency rates would not vary from place to place (fact 2) and that the white rate would never be greater than the Negro rate (fact 3). Thus in order for race to have "any" causal significance, all Negroes must be delinquents (or all whites non-delinquents). In short, race must be perfectly related to delinquency.[11]

Now if an independent variable and a dependent variable are perfectly associated,[12] no other independent variable is needed: that is, perfect association implies single causation, and less-than-perfect association implies multiple causation. Rejecting as causes of delinquency those variables whose association with delinquency is less than perfect thus implies rejecting the principle of multiple causation. Although there is nothing sacred about this principle, at least at the level of empirical research it is more viable than the principle of single causation. All studies show that more than one independent variable is needed to account for delinquency. In this field, as in others, perfect relations are virtually unknown. The researcher who finds a less-than-perfect relation between variable $X$ and delinquency should not conclude that $X$ is not a cause of delinquency, but merely that it is not the *only* cause.[13]

For example, suppose that tables like the following have been found for variables $A$, $B$, $C$, and $D$ as well as for $X$:

*Delinquency by X, where X is neither a necessary nor a sufficient condition for delinquency, but may be one of several causes*

|  | X | Not X |
|---|---|---|
| Delinquent | 40 | 20 |
| Nondelinquent | 60 | 80 |

The researcher using the perfect relation criterion would have to conclude that none of the causes of delinquency has yet been discovered. Indeed, this criterion would force him to conclude that there are *no causes* of delinquency except *the* cause. The far-from-perfect relation between variable $X$ and delinquency in the table above leads him to reject variable $X$ as a cause of delinquency. Since variables $A$, $B$, $C$, and $D$ are also far from perfectly related to delinquency, he must likewise reject them. Since it is unlikely that *the* cause of delinquency will ever be discovered by quantitative research, the researcher who accepts the perfect relation criterion should come to believe that such research is useless: all it can show is that there are *no* causes of delinquency.

*False criterion 1a   Insofar as a factor is not a necessary condition for delinquency, it is not a cause of delinquency*

The "not necessary" (and of course the "not sufficient") argument against causation is a variant of the "perfect relation" criterion. A factor is a necessary condition for delinquency if it must be present for delinquency to occur—e.g., knowledge of the operation of an automobile is a necessary condition for auto theft (although all individuals charged with auto theft need not know how to drive a car). In the following table the independent variable $X$ is a necessary (but not sufficient[14]) condition for delinquency.

*Delinquency by X, where X is a necessary but not sufficient condition for delinquency*

|  | X | Not X |
|---|---|---|
| Delinquent | 67 | 0 |
| Nondelinquent | 33 | 100 |

The strongest statement we can find in the work cited by the Children's Bureau in support of the contention that the broken home is not a cause of delinquency is the following:

> We can leave this phase of the subject by stating that the phenomenon of the physically broken home as a cause of delinquent behavior is, in itself, not so important as was once believed. In essence, it is not that the home is broken, but rather that the home is inadequate, that really matters.[15]

This statement suggests that the broken home is not a necessary condition for delinquency (delinquents may come from intact but "inadequate" homes). The variable with which the broken home is compared, inadequacy, has all the attributes of a necessary condition for delinquency: a home that is "adequate" with respect to the prevention of delinquency will obviously produce no delinquent children. If, as appears to be the case, the relation between inadequacy and delinquency is a matter of definition, the comparison of this relation with the relation between the broken home and delinquency is simply an application of the illegitimate "necessary conditions" criterion. Compared to a necessary condition, the broken home is "not so important." Compared to some (or some *other*) *measure* of inadequacy, however, the broken home may be very important. For that matter, once "inadequacy" is empirically defined, the broken home may turn out to be one of its important causes. Thus the fact that the broken home is not a necessary condition for delinquency does not justify the statement that the broken home is "not [a cause of delinquency] in the sense that if [it] were removed delinquency would decline."[16]

*False criterion 1b   Insofar as a factor is not a sufficient condition for delinquency, it is not a cause of delinquency*

A factor is a sufficient condition for delinquency if its presence is invariably followed by delinquency. Examples of sufficient conditions are hard to find in empirical research.[17] The nearest one comes to such conditions in delinquency research is in the use of predictive devices in which several factors taken together are virtually sufficient for delinquency.[18] (The fact that several variables are required even to approach sufficiency is of course one of the strongest arguments in favor of multiple causation.) Since sufficient conditions are rare, this unrealistic standard can be used against almost any imputation of causality.

First, however, let us make our position clear on the question. Poverty per se is not a cause of delinquency or criminal behavior; this statement is evidenced by the courage, fortitude, honesty, and moral stamina of thousands of parents who would rather starve than steal and who inculcate this attitude in their children. Even in the blighted neighborhoods of poverty and wretched housing conditions, crime and delinquency are simply nonexistent among most residents.[19]

Many mothers, and some fathers, who have lost their mates through separation, divorce, or death, are doing a splendid job of rearing their children.[20]

Our point of view is that the structure of the family *itself* does not cause delinquency. For example, the fact that a home is broken does not cause delinquency, but it is more difficult for a single parent to provide material needs, direct controls, and other important elements of family life.[21]

The error here lies in equating "not sufficient" with "not a cause." Even if every delinquent child were from an impoverished (or broken) home—that is, even if this factor were a necessary condition for delinquency—it would still be possible to show that poverty is not a sufficient condition for delinquency.

In order for the researcher to conclude that poverty is a cause of delinquency, it is not necessary that all or most of those who are poor become delinquent.[22] If it were, causal variables would be virtually impossible to find. From the standpoint of social action, this criterion can be particularly unfortunate. Suppose that poverty were a necessary but not sufficient condition for delinquency, as in the table on page 619. Advocates of the "not sufficient" criterion would be forced to conclude that, if poverty were removed, delinquency would not decline. As the table clearly shows, however, removal of poverty under these hypothetical conditions would *eliminate* delinquency!

To take another example, Wootton reports Carr-Saunders as finding that 28% of his delinquents and 16% of his controls came from broken homes and that this difference held in both London and the provinces. She quotes Carr-Saunders' "cautious" conclusion:

> We can only point out that the broken home may have some influence on delinquency, though since we get control cases coming from broken homes, we cannot assert that there is a direct link between this factor and delinquency.[23]

Carr-Saunders' caution apparently stems from the "not sufficient" criterion, for unless the broken home is a sufficient condition for delinquency, there must be control cases (nondelinquents) from broken homes.

In each of these examples the attack on causality rests on the numbers in a single table. Since all of these tables show a non-zero relation, it seems to us that these researchers have mininterpreted the platitude "correlation is not causation." To us, this platitude means that one must go beyond the observed fact of association in order to demonstrate causality. To those who employ one or another variant of the perfect relation criterion, it appears to mean that there is something suspect in any numerical demonstration of association. Instead of being the first evidence for causality, an observed association becomes evidence against causality.

*False criterion 2   Insofar as a factor is not "characteristic" of delinquents, it is not a cause of delinquency*

Many correlation studies in delinquency may conquer all these hurdles and still fail to satisfy the vigorous demands of scientific causation. Frequently a group of delinquents is found to differ in a statistically significant way from a nondelinquent control group with which it is compared. Nevertheless, the differentiating trait may not be at all characteristic of the delinquent group. Suppose, for example, that a researcher compares 100 delinquent girls with 100 nondelinquent girls with respect to broken homes. He finds, let us say, that 10% of the nondelinquent come from broken homes, whereas this is true of 30% of the delinquent girls. Although the difference between the two groups is significant, the researcher has not demonstrated that the broken home is characteristic of delinquents. The fact is that 70% of them come from unbroken homes. Again, ecological studies showing a high correlation between residence in interstitial areas and delinquency, as compared with lower rates of delinquency in other areas, overlook the fact that even in the most marked interstitial area nine tenths of the children do not become delinquent.[24]

This argument is superficially plausible. If a factor is not characteristic, then it is apparently not important. But does "characteristic" mean "important"? No. Importance refers to the variation accounted for, to the size of the association, while "being characteristic" refers to only one of the conditional distributions (rows or columns) in the table (in the table on page 619, X is characteristic of delinquents because more than half of the delinquents are X). This is not enough to infer association, any more than the statement that 95% of the Negroes in some sample are illiterate can be taken to say anything about the association between race and illiteracy in that sample without a corresponding statement about the whites. In the following table, although Negroes are predominantly ("characteristically") illiterate, race has no effect on literacy, for the whites are equally likely to be illiterate.

|            | *Negro* | *White* |
|------------|---------|---------|
| Literate   | 5       | 5       |
| Illiterate | 95      | 95      |

More generally, even if a trait characterizes a large proportion of delinquents and also characterizes a large proportion of nondelinquents, it may be less important as a cause of delinquency than a trait that characterizes a much smaller porportion of delinquents. The strength of the relation is what matters—that is, the *difference* between delinquents and nondelinquents in the proportion having the trait (in other words, the difference between the conditional distributions of the dependent variable). In the quotation from Barron at the beginning of this section, would it make any difference for the imputation of causality if the proportions coming from broken homes had been 40% for the nondelinquents and 60% for the delinquents, instead of 10 and 30%? Although broken homes would now be "characteristic" of delinquents, the percentage difference is the same as before. And the percentage difference would still be the same if the figures were 60 and 80%, but now broken homes would be characteristic of *both* nondelinquents and delinquents!

The "characteristic" criterion is thus statistically irrelevant to the task of assessing causality. It also appears to be inconsistent with the principle of multiple causation, to which Barron elsewhere subscribes.[25] If delinquency is really traceable to a plurality of causes, then some of these causes may well "characterize" a minority of delinquents. Furthermore, this "inconsistency" is empirical as well as logical: in survey data taken from ordinary populations it is rare to find that any group defined by more than three traits includes a majority of the cases.[26]

*False criterion 3   If a relation between an independent variable and delinquency is found for a single value of a situational or contextual factor, that situational or contextual factor cannot be a cause of delinquency*

No investigation can establish the causal importance of variables that do not vary. This obvious fact should be even more obvious when the design of the study restricts it to single values of certain variables. Thus the researcher who restricts his sample to white Mormon boys cannot use his data to determine the importance of race, religious affiliation, or sex as causes of delinquency. Nevertheless, students of delinquency who discover either from research or logical analysis that an independent variable is related to delinquency in certain situations or contexts often conlude that these situational or contextual variables are not important causes of delinquency. Since personality or perceptual variables are related to delinquency in most kinds of social situations, social variables have suffered most from the application of this criterion:

Let the reader assume that a boy is returning home from school and sees an unexpected group of people at his doorstep, including a policeman, several neighbors, and some strangers. He may suppose that they have gathered to welcome him and congratulate him as the winner of a nationwide contest he entered several months ago. On the other hand, his supposition may be that they have discovered that he was one of several boys who broke some windows in the neighborhood on Halloween. If his interpretation is that they are a welcoming group he will respond one way; but if he feels that they have come to "get" him, his response is likely to be quite different. In either case he may be entirely wrong in his interpretation. *The important point, however, is that the external sit-uation is relatively unimportant.* Rather, what the boy himself thinks of them [it] and how he interprets them [it] is the crucial factor in his response.[27]

There are at least three independent "variables" in this illustration: (1) the external situation—the group at the doorstep; (2) the boy's past behavior—entering a contest, breaking windows, etc.; (3) the boy's interpretation of the group's purpose. As Barron notes, variable 3 is obviously important in determining the boy's response. It does not follow from this, however, that variables 1 and 2 are unimportant. As a matter of fact, it is easy to see how variable 2, the boy's past behavior, could influence his interpretation of the group's purpose and thus affect his response. If he had not broken any windows in the neighborhood, for example, it is less likely that he would think that the group had come to "get" him, and it is therefore less likely that his response would be one of fear. Since Barron does not examine the relation between this situational variable and the response, he cannot make a legitimate statement about its causal importance.

Within the context of this illustration it is impossible to relate variable 1, the group at the doorstep, to the response. The reason for this is simple: this "variable" does not vary—it is fixed, given, constant. In order to assess the influence of a group at the doorstep (the external situation) on the response, it would be necessary to compare the effects of groups varying in size or composition. Suppose that there was no group at the doorstep. Presumably, if this were the case, the boy would feel neither fear nor joy. Barron restricts his examination of the relation between interpretation and response to a single situation, and on this basis concludes that what appears to be a necessary condition for the response is *relatively unimportant!*

In our opinion, it is sometimes better to say nothing about the effects of a variable whose range is restricted than to attempt to reach some idea of its importance with inadequate data. The first paragraph of the following statement suggests that its authors are completely aware of this problem.

Nevertheless, the concluding paragraphs are misleading:

We recognized that the Cambridge-Somerville area represented a fairly restricted socio-economic region. Although the bitter wave of the depression had passed, it had left in its wake large numbers of unemployed. Ten years after its onset, Cambridge and Somerville still showed the effects of the depression. Even the best neighborhoods in this study were lower middle class. Consequently, our results represent only a section of the class structure.

In our sample, however [*therefore*], there is not a *highly* significant relation between "delinquency areas," or subcultures, and crime. If we had predicted that every child who lived in the poorer Cambridge-Somerville areas would have committed a crime, we would have been more often wrong than right. Thus, current sociological theory, by itself, cannot explain why the majority of children, even those from the "worst" areas, never became delinquent.

*Social factors*, in our sample, were not strongly related to criminality. The fact that a child's neighborhood did not, by itself, exert an independently important influence may [*should not*] surprise social scientists. Undeniably, a slum neighborhood can mold a child's personality—but apparently only if other factors in his background make him susceptible to the sub-culture that surrounds him.[28]

*False criterion 4    If a relation is observed between an independent variable and delinquency and if a psychological variable is suggested as intervening between these two variables, then the original relation is not causal*

There appear to be two elements in this causal reasoning. One is the procedure of *conjectural interpretation*.[29] The other is the confusion between *explanation*, in which an antecedent variable "explains away" an observed relation, and *interpretation*, in which an intervening variable links more tightly the two variables of the original relation. In short, the vanishing of the partial relations is assumed, not demonstrated, and this assumed

statistical configuration is misconstrued.

This criterion is often encountered in a subtle form suggestive of social psychological theory:

The appropriate inference from the available data, on the basis of our present understanding of the nature of cause, is that whether poverty, broken homes, or working mothers are factors which cause delinquency depends upon the meaning the situation has for the child.[30]

It now appears that neither of these factors [the broken home and parental discipline] is so important in itself as is the child's reaction to them.[31]

A factor, whether personal or situational, does not become a cause unless and until it first becomes a motive.[32]

The appropriate inference about whether some factor is a cause of delinquency depends on the relation between that factor and delinquency (and possibly on other factors causally prior to both of these). All that can be determined about meanings, motives, or reactions that *follow from* the factor and *precede* delinquency can only strengthen the conclusion that the factor is a cause of delinquency, not weaken it.

A different example may make our argument clearer. *Given* the bombing of Pearl Harbor, the crucial factor in America's response to this situation was its interpretation of the meaning of this event. Is one to conclude, therefore, that the bombing of Pearl Harbor was relatively unimportant as a cause of America's entry into World War II? Intervening variables of this type are no less important than variables further removed from the dependent variable, but to limit analysis to them, to deny the importance of objective conditions, is to distort reality as much as do those who ignore intervening subjective states.[33]

This kind of mistaken causal inference can occur long after the original analysis of the data. A case in point is the inference in the *Report to The Congress*[34] that irregular employment of the mother does not cause delinquency. This inference appears to come from misreading

Maccoby's reanalysis of the Gluecks' results.

Maccoby begins by noting that "the association between irregular employment and delinquency suggests at the outset that it may not be the mother's absence from home per se which creates adjustment problems for the children. Rather, the cause may be found in the conditions of the mother's employment or the family characteristics leading a mother to undertake outside employment."[35] She then lists several characteristics of the sporadically working mothers that might account for the greater likelihood of their children becoming delinquent. For example, many had a history of delinquency themselves. In our opinion, such conjectural "explanations" are legitimate guides to further study but, as Maccoby says, they leave the causal problem unsettled:

> It is a moot question, therefore, whether it is the mother's sporadic employment as such which conduced to delinquency in the sons; equally tenable is the interpretation that the emotionally disturbed and antisocial characteristics of the parents produced both a sporadic work pattern on the part of the mother and delinquent tendencies in the son.[36]

Maccoby's final step, and the one of greatest interest here, is to examine simultaneously the effects of mother's employment and mother's supervision on delinquency. From this examination she concludes:

> It can be seen that, whether the mother is working or not, the quality of the supervision her child receives is paramount. If the mother remains at home but does not keep track of where her child is and what he is doing, he is far more likely to become a delinquent (within this highly selected sample), than if he is closely watched. Furthermore, if a mother who works does arrange adequate care for the child in her absence, he is no more likely to be delinquent . . . than the adequately supervised child of a mother who does not work. But there is one more lesson to be learned from the data: among the working mothers, a majority did not in fact

arrange adequate supervision for their children in their absence.[37]

It is clear, then, that regardless of the mother's employment status, supervision is related to delinquency. According to criterion 3, employment status is therefore not a cause of delinquency. It is also clear that when supervision is held relatively constant, the relation between employment status and delinquency disappears. According to criterion 4, employment status is therefore *not* a cause of delinquency. This appears to be the reasoning by which the authors of the *Report to The Congress* reject mother's employment as a cause of delinquency. But criterion 3 ignores the association between employment status and delinquency and is thus irrelevant. And criterion 4 treats what is probably best seen as an intervening variable as an antecedent variable and is thus a misconstruction of a legitimate criterion. Actually, the evidence that allows the user of criterion 4 to reach a conclusion of noncausality is, at least psychologically, evidence of *causality*. The disappearance of the relation between mother's employment and delinquency when supervision is held relatively constant makes the "How?" of the original relation clear: working mothers are less likely to provide adequate supervision for their children, and inadequately supervised children are more likely to become delinquent.

*False criterion 5    Measurable variables are not causes*

In tract 11-1, and to a lesser extent in tract 11-2, the actual rate [of delinquency] is lower than the predicted rate. We suggest that these deviations [of the actual delinquency rate from the rate predicted from home ownership] point up the danger of imputing a causal significance to an index, per se, despite its statistical significance in a prediction formula. It is fallacious to impute causal significance to home ownership as such. In the present study, the author hypothesizes that the extent of home ownership is probably highly correlated with, and hence constitutes a measure of community anomie.[38]

As a preventive, "keeping youth busy," whether through compulsory education, drafting for service in the armed forces, providing fun through recreation, or early employment, can, at best, only temporarily postpone behavior that is symptomatic of more deep-seated or culturally oriented factors. . . . Merely "keeping idle hands occupied" touches only surface symptoms and overlooks underlying factors known to generate norm-violating behavior patterns.[39]

The criterion of causation that, in effect, denies causal status to measurable variables occurs frequently in delinquency research. In the passages above, home ownership, compulsory education, military service, recreation, and early employment are all called into question as causes of delinquency. In their stead one finds as causes anomie and "deepseated or culturally oriented factors." The appeal to abstract as opposed to more directly measurable variables appears to be especially persuasive. Broad general concepts embrace such a variety of directly measurable variables that their causal efficacy becomes almost self evident. The broken home, for example, is no match for the "inadequate" home:

> [T]he physically broken home as a cause of delinquent behavior is, in itself, not so important as was once believed. In essence, it is not that the home is broken, but rather that the home is inadequate, that really matters.[40]

The persuasiveness of these arguments against the causal efficacy of measurable variables has two additional sources: (1) their logical form resembles that of the legitimate criterion "lack of spuriousness"; (2) they are based on the seemingly obvious fact that "operational indices" (measures) do not *cause* the variations in other operational indices. Both of the following arguments can thus be brought against the assertion that, for example, home ownership causes delinquency.

Anomie causes delinquency. Home ownership is a measure of anomie. Anomie is thus the "source of variation" in both home ownership and delinquency. If the effects of anomie were removed, the observed relation between home ownership and delinquency would disappear. This observed relation is thus causally spurious.

Home ownership is used as an indicator of anomie, just as responses to questionnaire items are used as indicators of such things as "authoritarianism," "achievement motivation," and "religiosity." No one will argue that the responses to items on a questionnaire *cause* race hatred, long years of self-denial, or attendance at religious services. For the same reason, it is erroneous to think that home ownership "causes" delinquency.

Both of these arguments beg the question. As mentioned earlier, conjectural explanations, although legitimate guides to further study, leave the causal problem unsettled. The proposed "antecedent variable" may or *may not* actually account for the observed relation.

Our argument assumes that the proposed antecedent variable is directly measurable. In the cases cited here it is not. If the antecedent variable logic is accepted as appropriate in these cases, all relations between measurable variables and delinquency may be said to be causally spurious. If anomie can "explain away" the relation between *one* of its indicators and delinquency, it can explain away the relations between *all* of its indicators and delinquency.[41] No matter how closely a given indicator measures anomie, the indicator is not anomie, and thus not a cause of delinquency. The difficulty with these conjectural explanations is thus not that they may be false, but that they are *non-falsifiable.*[42]

The second argument against the causality of measurable variables overlooks the following point: it is one thing to use a measurable variable as an indicator of another, not directly measurable, variable; it is something else again to assume that the measurable variable is *only* an indicator. Not owning one's home may indeed be a useful indicator of anomie; it may, at the same time, be a potent cause of delinquency in its own right.

The user of the "measurable variables are not causes" criterion treats measurable variables as epiphenomena. He strips these variables of all their causal efficacy (and of all their meaning) by treating them merely as indexes, and by using such words as *per se, as such*, and *in itself*.[43] In so doing, he begs rather than answers the important question: Are these measurable variables causes of delinquency?

*False criterion 6    If the relation between an independent variable and delinquency is conditional upon the value of other variables, the independent variable is not a cause of delinquency*

The rates of Negro delinquency also vary as widely as do the white rates indicating large differences in behavior patterns that are not a function or effect of rate per se. It is also of interest to note that in at least 10 percent of the districts with substantial Negro juvenile populations, the Negro delinquency rate is lower than the corresponding white rate.[44]

The appropriate inference from the available data, on the basis of our present understanding of the nature of cause, is that whether poverty, broken homes, or working mothers are factors which cause delinquency depends upon the meaning the situation has for the child.[45]

Both of these quotations make the same point: the association between an independent variable and delinquency depends on the value of a third variable. The original two-variable relation thus becomes a three-variable conditional relation. In the first quotation, the relation between race and delinquency is shown to depend on some (unspecified) property of census tracts. In the second quotation, each of three variables is said to "interact" with "the meaning of the situation" to cause delinquency.

One consequence of showing that certain variables are only conditionally related to delinquency is to invalidate what Albert K. Cohen has aptly named "the assumption of intrinsic pathogenic qualities"—the assumption that the causal efficacy of a variable is, or can be, independent of the value of other causal variables.[46] Invalidating this

assumption, which Cohen shows to be widespread in the literature on delinquency, is a step in the right direction. As many of the quotations in this paper suggest, however, the discovery that a variable has no *intrinsic* pathogenic qualities has often led to the conclusion that it has no pathogenic qualities at all. The consequences of accepting this conclusion can be shown for delinquency research and theory.

Cloward and Ohlin's theory that delinquency is the product of lack of access to legitimate means *and* the availability of illegitimate means assumes, as Palmore and Hammond have shown,[47] that each of these states is a necessary condition for the other—i.e., that lack of access to legitimate and access to illegitimate means "interact" to produce delinquency. Now, if "conditional relations" are non-causal, neither lack of access to legitimate nor the availability of illegitimate means is a cause of delinquency, and one could manipulate either without affecting the delinquency rate.

Similarly absurd conclusions could be drawn from the results of empirical research in delinquency, since all relations between independent variables and delinquency are at least conceivably conditional (the paucity of empirical generalizations produced by delinquency research as a whole shows that most of these relations have already actually been found to be conditional).[48]

Although conditional relations may be conceptually or statistically complicated and therefore psychologically unsatisfying, their discovery does not justify the conclusion that the variables involved are not causes of delinquency. In fact, the researcher who would grant causal status only to unconditional relations will end by granting it to none.

Any one of the criteria of causality discussed in this paper makes it possible to question the causality of most of the relations that have been or could be revealed by quantitative research. Some of these criteria stem from perfectionistic interpretations of legitimate criteria, others from misapplication of these legitimate criteria. Still others, especially the argument that a cause must be "characteristic" of delinquents, appear to result from practical considerations. (It would indeed be valuable to the practitioner if he could point to some easily identifiable trait as the "hallmark" of the delinquent.) Finally, one of these criteria is based on a mistaken notion of the relation between abstract concepts and measurable variables—a notion that only the former can be the causes of anything.

The implications of these standards of causality for practical efforts to reduce delinquency are devastating. Since nothing that can be pointed to in the practical world is a cause of delinquency (e.g., poverty, broken homes, lack of recreational facilities, working mothers), the practitioner is left with the task of combatting a nebulous "anomie" or an unmeasured "inadequacy of the home"; or else he must change the adolescent's interpretation of the "meaning" of events without at the same time changing the events themselves or the context in which they occur.

Mills has suggested that accepting the principle of multiple causation implies denying the possibility of radical change in the social structure.[49] Our analysis suggests that rejecting the principle of multiple causation implies denying the possibility of *any* change in the social structure—since, in this view, nothing causes anything.

## REFERENCES AND NOTES

1 This is a manufactured "quotation"; its source will become obvious shortly.

2 Herbert H. Hyman, *Survey Design and Analysis*, Glencoe, Ill.: The Free Press, 1955, chaps. 5-7.

3 Hyman appears to advocate another criterion as well: that a chain of intervening variables must link the independent and dependent variables of the original relation. We regard this as psychologically or theoretically desirable but not as part of the minimum methodological requirements for demonstrating causality in nonexperimental research.

4 Travis Hirschi and Hanan C. Selvin, *The Methodological Adequacy of Delinquency Research*, Berkeley, Calif.: Survey Research Center, 1962.

5 Popper calls this the asymmetry of verifiability and falsifiability. Karl R. Popper, *The Logic of Scientific Discovery*, New York: Basic Books Inc., 1959, especially pp. 27-48. For a fresh view of the verification-falsification controversy, see Thomas S. Kuhn, *The Structure of Scientific Revolutions*, Chicago:

The University of Chicago Press, 1962. Kuhn discusses Popper's views on pp. 145-146. Actually, it is harder to establish non-causality than our statement suggests, because of the possibility of "spurious independence." This problem is discussed in Hirschi and Selvin, *op. cit.*, pp. 38-45, as "elaboration of a zero relation."

6 U.S. Department of Health, Education, and Welfare, *Report to The Congress on Juvenile Delinquency*, Washington, D.C.: U.S. Government Printing Office, 1960, p. 21. The conclusion that "poor housing" is not a cause of delinquency is based on Mildred Hartsough, *The Relation between Housing and Delinquency*, Federal Emergency Administration of Public Works, Housing Division, 1936. The conclusion that "poor physical health" is not a cause is based on Edward Piper's "unpublished Children's Bureau manuscript summarizing the findings of numerous investigators on this subject." Since we have not examined these two works, the following conclusions do not apply to them.

7 The works cited are broken homes, Negly K. Teeters and John Otto Reinemann, *The Challenge of Delinquency*, New York: Prentice-Hall, Inc., 1950, pp. 149-154; poverty, Bernard Lander, *Toward an Understanding of Juvenile Delinquency*, New York: Columbia University Press, 1954; recreational facilities, Ethel Shanas and Catherine E. Dunning, *Recreation and Delinquency*, Chicago: Chicago Recreation Commission, 1942; race, Lander, *op. cit.*; working mothers, Eleanor E. Maccoby, "Children and Working Mothers," *Children*, vol. 5 (May-June, 1958), pp. 83-89.

8 It is not clear in every case that the researcher himself reached the conclusion of noncausality or, if he did, that this conclusion was based on the false criteria discussed below. Maccoby's article, for example, contains a "conjectural explanation" of the relation between mother's employment and delinquency (i.e., without presenting any statistical evidence she suggests that the original relation came about through some antecedent variable), but it appears that the conclusion of noncausality in the *Report* is based on other statements in her work.

9 All the foregoing criteria are related to the "perfect relation" criterion in that they all require variation in delinquency that is unexplained by the "noncausal" variable. A more general statement of criterion 3 would be: "if variable $X$ is related to delinquency when there is no variation in variable $T$, then variable $T$ is not a cause of delinquency." In order for this criterion to be applicable, there must be some residual variation in delinquency after $T$ has had its effect.

Although both forms of this criterion fairly represent the reasoning involved in some claims of non-causality, and although both are false, the less explicit version in the text is superficially more plausible. This inverse relation between explicitness and plausibility is one reason for the kind of methodological explication presented here.

10 Bernard Lander, *Towards an Understanding of Juvenile Delinquency*, New York: Columbia University Press, 1954, p. 32. Italics in original. An alternative interpretation of the assumptions implicit in this quotation is presented in the discussion of criterion 6, below.

11 Strictly speaking, in this quotation Lander does not demand that race be perfectly related to delinquency, but only that all Negroes be delinquents (the sufficient conditions of criterion 1*b*). Precedent for the "perfect relation" criterion of causality appears in a generally excellent critique of crime and delinquency research by Jerome Michael and Mortimer J. Adler published in 1933: "There is still another way of saying that none of the statistical findings derived from the quantitative data yields answers to etiological questions. The findings themselves show that every factor which can be seen to be in some way associated with criminality is also associated with non-criminality, and also that criminality is found in the absence of every factor with which it is also seen to be associated. In other words, what has been found is merely additional evidence of what we either knew or could have suspected, namely, that there is a plurality of related factors in this field." *Crime, Law and Social Science*, New York: Harcourt, Brace, & Co., p.53.

12 "Perfect association" here means that all of the cases fall into the main diagonal of the table, that (in the 2 × 2 table) the independent variable is both a necessary and a sufficient cause of the dependent variable. Less stringent definitions of perfect association are considered in the following paragraphs. Since Lander deals with ecological correlations, he could reject race as a cause of delinquency even if it were perfectly related to delinquency at the census tract level, since the ecological and the individual correlations are not identical.

13 We are assuming that the causal order and lack of spuriousness criteria are satisfied.

14 To say that $X$ is a necessary condition for delinquency means that all delinquents are $X$ (i.e., that the cell in the upper right of this table is zero); to say that $X$ is a sufficient condition for delinquency implies that all $X$'s are delinquent (i.e., that the cell in the lower left is zero); to say that $X$ is a necessary and sufficient condition for delinquency means that all $X$'s and no other persons are delinquent (i.e., that both cells in the minor diagonal of this table are zero).

15 Teeters and Reinemann, *op. cit.*, p. 154.

16 *Report to The Congress, op. cit.*, p. 21. Two additional illegitimate criteria of causality listed above are implicit in the quotation from Teeters and Reinemann. "Inadequacy of the home" could be treated as an intervening variable which interprets the relation between the broken home and delinquency (criterion 4) or as a theoretical variable of which the broken home is an indicator (criterion 5). These criteria are discussed below.

17 In his *Theory of Collective Behavior* (New York: The Free Press of Glencoe, 1963) Neil J. Smelser suggests sets of necessary conditions for riots, panics, and other forms of collective behavior; in this theory the entire set of necessary conditions for any one form of behavior is a sufficient condition for that form to occur.

18 In the Gluecks' prediction table, those with scores of 400 or more have a 98.1% chance of delinquency. However, as Reiss has pointed out, the Gluecks *start* with a sample that is 50% delinquent. Had they started with a sample in which only 10% were delinquent, it would obviously have been more difficult to approach sufficiency. Sheldon Glueck and Eleanor Glueck, *Unraveling Juvenile Delinquency*, Cambridge, Mass.: Harvard University Press, 1950, pp. 260–262; Albert J. Reiss, Jr., "Unraveling Juvenile Delinquency, II: An Appraisal of the Research Methods," *American Journal of Sociology*, vol. 57, no. 2 (1951), pp. 115–120.

19 Teeters and Reinemann, *op. cit.*, p. 127.

20 *Ibid.*, p. 154.

21 F. Ivan Nye, *Family Relationships and Delinquent Behavior*, New York: John Wiley & Sons, Inc., 1958, p. 34. Italics in original.

22 We are of course assuming throughout this discussion that the variables in question meet what we consider to be legitimate criteria of causality.

23 Barbara Wootton, *Social Science and Social Pathology*, New York: The Macmillan Company, 1959, p. 118.

24 Milton L. Barron, *The Juvenile in Delinquent Society*, New York: Alfred A. Knopf, Inc., 1954, pp. 86–87.

25 *Ibid.*, pp. 81–83.

26 There are two reasons for this: the less-than-perfect association between individual traits and the fact that few traits are simple dichotomies. Of course, it is always possible to take the logical complement of a set of traits describing a minority and thus arrive at a set of traits that does "characterize" a group, but such artificial combinations have too much internal heterogeneity to be meaningful. What, for example, can one say of the delinquents who share the following set of traits: not Catholic, not middle class, not of average intelligence?

The problem of "characteristic" traits arises only when the dependent variable is inherently categorical (Democratic; member of a gang, an athletic club, or neither) or is treated as one (performs none, a few, or many delinquent acts). In other words, this criterion arises only in tabular analysis, not where some summary measure is used to describe the association between variables.

27 Barron, *op. cit.*, pp. 87–88. Italics added.

28 William McCord and Joan McCord, *Origins of Crime*, New York: Columbia University Press, 1959, pp. 71, 167.

In a study restricted to "known *offenders*" in which the dependent variable is the *seriousness* of the *first offense* Richard S. Sterne concludes: "Delinquency cannot be fruitfully controlled through broad programs to prevent divorce or other breaks in family life. The prevention of these would certainly decrease unhappiness, but it would not help to relieve the problem of delinquency." Since the range of the dependent variable, delinquency, is seriously reduced in a study restricted to *offenders*, such conclusions can not follow from the data. Richard S. Sterne, *Delinquent Conduct and Broken Homes*, New Haven, Conn.: College and University Press, 1964, p. 96.

29 Like conjectural explanation, this is an argument, unsupported by statistical data, that the relation between two variables would vanish if the effects of a third variable were removed; here, however, the third variable "intervenes" causally between the original independent and dependent variables.

30 Sophia Robison, *Juvenile Delinquency*, New York: Holt, Rinehart and Winston, 1961, p. 116.

31 Paul W. Tappan, *Juvenile Delinquency*, New York: McGraw-Hill Book Co., 1949, p. 135.

32 Sheldon and Eleanor Glueck, *Family Environment and Delinquency*, Boston: Houghton Mifflin Co., 1962, p. 153. This statement is attributed to Bernard Glueck. No specific reference is provided.

33 "Write your own life history, showing the factors *really* operative in you coming to college, contrasted with the external social and cultural factors of your situation." Barron, *op. cit.*, p. 89.

34 *Op. cit.*, p. 21.

35 Eleanor E. Maccoby, "Effects upon Children of Their Mothers' Outside Employment," in Norman W. Bell and Ezra F. Vogel (eds.), *A Modern Introduction to The Family*, Glencoe, Ill.: The Free Press, 1960, p. 523. In fairness to the Children's Bureau report, it should be mentioned that Maccoby's argument against the causality of the relation between mother's employment and delinquency has a stronger tone in the article cited there (see note 7) than in the version we have used as a source of quotations.

36 *Ibid.*

37 *Ibid.*, p. 524.

38 Lander, *op. cit.*, p. 71.

39 William C. Kvaraceus and Walter B. Miller, *Delinquent Behavior: Culture and the Individual*, National Education Association, 1959, p. 39.

40 Teeters and Reinemann, *op. cit.*, p. 154.

41 As would be expected, Lander succeeds in disposing of all the variables in his study as causes of delinquency—even those he says at some points are "*fundamentally* related to delinquency."

42 While Lander throws out his measurable independent variables in favor of anomie, Kvaraceus and Miller throw out their measurable dependent variable in favor of "something else." "Series of norm-violating behaviors, which run counter to legal codes and which are engaged in by youngsters [delinquency], are [is] only symptomatic of something else in the personal make-up of the individual, in his home and family, or in his cultural milieu." Kvaraceus and Miller, *op. cit.*, p. 34. The result is the same, as the quotations suggest.

43 The appearance of these terms in the literature on delinquency almost invariably signals a logical difficulty.

44 Lander, *op. cit.*, p. 32. This statement is quoted more fully above (see note 10).

45 Robison, *op. cit.*, p. 116.

46 "Multiple Factor Approaches," in Marvin E. Wolfgang *et al.* (eds.), *The Sociology of Crime and Delinquency*, New York: John Wiley & Sons, Inc., 1962, pp. 78–79.

47 Erdman B. Palmore and Phillip E. Hammond, "Interacting Factors in Juvenile Delinquency," *American Sociological Review*, vol. 29 (December 1964), pp. 848–854.

48 After reviewing the findings of twenty-one studies as they bear on the relations between twelve commonly used independent variables and delinquency, Barbara Wootton concludes: "All in all, therefore, this collection of studies, although chosen for its comparative methodological merit, produces only the most meager, and dubiously supported generalizations." Wooton, *op. cit.*, p. 134.

49 C. Wright Mills, "The Professional Ideology of Social Pathologists," *American Journal of Sociology*, vol. 44 (September 1942), pp. 165–180, especially pp. 171–172.

## 51   PSYCHIATRY IN THE LEGAL PROCESS   ALAN M. DERSHOWITZ

In the trial scene from *Brothers Karamozov*, Dostoyevsky, speaking through the lips of the defense attorney, issued a stern warning to the legal profession: "Profound as psychology is, it's a knife that cuts both ways . . . . You can prove anything by it. I am speaking of the abuse of psychology, gentlemen." I will speak today about another knife that cuts two ways, psychiatry in the legal process. Much has been written about one cutting edge, the contributions made by psychiatry. I will focus on the other side of the blade, the social costs incurred by the increasing involvement of the psychiatrist in the administration of justice. An important, if subtle, consequence of psychiatric involvement has been the gradual introduction of a medical model in place of the laws' efforts to articulate legally relevant criteria. The cost of this substitution has been confusion of purpose, and in some instances, needless deprivation of liberty.

A brief look at the history of the insanity defense will serve to illustrate this process. The law had, for centuries, been groping for a rule which would express the deeply felt conviction that some people who commit condemnable acts are not themselves deserving of condemnation. In the seventeenth century, a person was held irresponsible if he "doth not know what he was doing, no more than an infant or a wild beast." There was an obvious relationship between this "wild beast" test and the rest of the criminal law: neither an infant nor a wild beast was held responsible, so why, it was asked, should an adult who was functionally similar. In the much villified *McNaughten* case, the House of Lords also analogized irrespons-

Reprinted with the permission of the author from "Psychiatry in the Legal Process: 'A Knife That Cuts Both Ways,' " a Sesquicentennial Address to the Harvard Law School, Cambridge, Mass.: Harvard University, Sept. 23, 1967.

ibility to a deeply rooted principle of the criminal law. It held that a man who suffers from delusions "must be considered in the same situation as to responsibility as if the facts with respect to which the delusion exists were real." This was a simple extension of the traditional mistake-of-fact defense to certain unreasonable mistakes. The Lords' attempt to generalize this principle under the rubric "know the nature and quality of the act," and know that it was "wrong," was surely not the clearest way of saying what they meant. But it *was* clear that they, like the framers of the "wild-beast" test, were setting down a *legal* rule designed to further *legal* policies; they were not attempting to identify and exculpate a particular psychiatric category of persons: the mentally ill, the insane, or the psychotic. Indeed, the ruling explicitly recognized the rather limited role of the psychiatrist in administering the insanity defense. Nevertheless, much of the criticism of McNaughten has been premised on the erroneous assumption that the purpose of that test *was* to describe a psychiatric entity. Thus Dr. Isaac Ray, an early psychiatric critic, called the McNaughten rule a "fallacious" test of criminal responsibility, arguing that "Insanity is a disease, and, as in the case with all other diseases, the fact of its existence is never established by a single diagnostic symptom," such as inability to distinguish right from wrong. But the Lords had focused on inability to distinguish right from wrong not because they thought it was a scientifically valid symptom of disease, but because they deemed it a just and useful legal criterion for distinguishing those who should be held responsible and punished from those who should be held irresponsible and hospitalized. Now, this criterion may be criticized as unjust or unworkable, but to say it is "fallacious" is to misunderstand the nature of legal rules. Ray was attempting to substitute a medical model of responsibility for the legal one; and the law was not engaging in a fallacy by insisting on asking its own questions and establishing criteria relevant to its own purposes.

This attempt to impose a medical model on the legal process of distinguishing the responsible from the irresponsible continued through the nineteenth century and into the twentieth. It culminated in the case of *Durham v. United States*, decided in 1954. The argument for the *Durham* rule was simple—if one accepted Ray's erroneous premise. For if McNaughten was simply an attempt to identify those persons considered mentally ill by psychiatrists, then why bother to go through the indirection of listing symptoms? Why not make the test the existence of mental illness itself? Abe Fortas, counsel for Durham and now Mr. Justice Fortas, argued that substitution of a new rule for *Mc-Naughten* would permit psychiatrists to testify in "the terms of their own discipline, and not in the terminology of an irrelevant formula." Why the "right-wrong" formula was irrelevant for legal purposes the court was never told, except that it did not permit psychiatrists to testify in terms of their own discipline. The possibility that the terms of their own discipline are not particularly relevant to a perfectly rational legal rule was never considered. The court was simply urged to adopt the psychiatrists' medical model of "insanity" and abandon any efforts of its own to articulate legally functional rules. The United States Court of Appeals for the District of Columbia accepted Fortas' arguments and adopted a rule framed in medical terms: "an accused is not responsible if his unlawful act was the product of a mental disease or defect." Although the author of *Durham*, Judge Bazelon, has always regarded that case as merely an opening wedge in a continuing search for just and workable criteria of responsibility, many psychiatrists interpreted *Durham* as an invitation for them to decide who should and who should not be held criminally responsible. Indeed, in one famous episode, the staff of a large mental hospital apparently took a vote to determine whether or not sociopathic personality was to be regarded as a mental disease.

The issue of criminal responsibility was finally where Isaac Ray thought it belonged: in the therapeutic hands of the psychiatrist.

This then is a capsule history of one encounter between law and psychiatry. It is not a complete history. There have been judicial adumbrations of disillusionment with the medical model. But it is a discouraging history of usurpation and abdication: of an expert being summoned for a limited purpose, assuming his own indispensibility, and then persuading the law to ask the critical questions in terms which make him more comfortable and his testimony more relevant. The upshot has been to make the psychiatrist's testimony more relevant to the questions posed, but to make the questions themselves less relevant to the purpose of the law.

This history has been repeated in other areas of the law, less well known than the insanity defense. Let me now turn to one in which psychiatric involvement has incurred even higher social costs, costs measured in years of needless and unjustified deprivation of liberty. I speak of the process known as civil commitment of the mentally ill, whereby almost 1 million persons are today confined behind the locked doors of state mental hospitals, though never convicted of crime.

Not in every society and not in every age were the insane confined by the state. The building of asylums on a wide scale did not begin until the seventeenth century. Such confinement, like the defense of insanity, was originally designed to further vaguely articulated legal goals. In the eighteenth and early nineteenth centuries these laws were part of a larger tapestry which included "suppression of Rogues, vagabonds, Common Beggers, and other idle, disorderly, and lewd persons." The legislative purpose seems clear: to isolate those persons who—for whatever reason—were regarded as intolerably obnoxious to the community. Medical testimony had little to offer in making this judgment; the people knew whom they regarded as obnoxious. By the middle of the nineteenth century—again through the influence of Dr. Isaac Ray—madness was becoming widely regarded as a disease which should be treated by physicians with little, or no, interference by courts. The present situation comes close to reflecting that view; the criteria for confinement are so vague that courts sit—when they sit at all—merely to review decisions made by psychiatrists. Indeed, the typical criteria are so meaningless as even to preclude effective review. In Connecticut, for example, the court is supposed to commit any person whom a doctor reasonably finds is "mentally ill and a fit subject for treatment in a hospital for mental illness, or that he ought to be confined." This circularity is typical of the criteria, or lack thereof, in about half of our states. Even in those jurisdictions with legal-sounding criteria—such as the District of Columbia, where the committed person must be mentally ill and likely to injure himself or others— the operative phrases are so vague that courts rarely upset psychiatric determinations.

The distorting effect of this medical model of confinement may be illustrated by comparing two recent cases from the District of Columbia. One involved Bong Yol Yang, an American of Korean origin who appeared at the White House gate asking to see the President about people who were following him and "revealing his subconscious thoughts." He also wondered whether his talents as an artist could be put to some use by the government. The gate officer had him committed to a mental hospital. Yang demanded a jury trial, at which a psychiatrist testified that he was mentally ill, a paranoid schizophrenic, and that although there was no "evidence of his ever attacking anyone so far," there is always a possibility that "if his frustrations . . . became great enough, he may potentially attack someone . . . ." On the basis of this diagnosis and prediction, the judge permitted a jury to commit Yang to a mental hospital until he is no longer mentally ill and likely to injure himself or others.

The other case involved a man named Dallas Williams, who at age 39 spent half his life in jail for seven convictions of assult with a deadly weapon and one conviction of manslaughter. Just before his scheduled release from jail, the government petitioned for his civil commitment. Two psychiatrists testified that although "at the present time [he] shows no evidence of active mental illness . . . he is potentially dangerous to others and if released is likely to repeat his patterns of criminal behavior, and might commit homicide." The judge, in denying the government's petition and ordering Williams' release, observed that "the courts have no legal basis for ordering confinement on mere apprehension of future unlawful acts. They must wait until another crime is committed or the person is found insane." Within months of his release, Williams lived up to the prediction of the psychiatrists and shot two men to death in an unprovoked attack.

Are there any distinctions between the Williams and Yang cases which justify the release of the former and the incarceration of the latter? There was no evidence that Yang was more dangerous, more amenable to treatment, or less competent than Williams. But Yang was diagnosed mentally ill and thus within the medical model, whereas Williams was not so diagnosed. Although there was nothing about Yang's mental illness which made him a more appropriate subject for involuntary confinement than Williams, the law attributed conclusive significance to its existence *vel non*. The outcomes in these cases, which make little sense when evaluated against any rational criteria for confinement, are typical under the present civil-commitment process. And this will continue, as long as the law continues to ask the dispositive questions in medical rather than legally functional terms, because the medical model does not ask the proper questions, or asks them in meaningless vague terms. Is the person mentally ill? Is he dangerous to himself or others? Is he in need of care or treatment?

Nor is this the only way to ask the questions to which the civil-commitment process is responsive. It will be instructive to restate the problem of civil commitment without employing medical terms and see whether the answers suggested differ from those now given.

There are in every society people who may cause trouble if not confined. The trouble may be serious (such as homicide), trivial (making of offensive remarks), or somewhere in between (forging checks). The trouble may be directed at others, at the person himself, or at both. It may be very likely that he will cause trouble, or fairly likely, or farily unlikely. In some instances this likelihood may be considerably reduced by a relatively short period of involuntary confinement; in others, a longer period may be required, with no assurances of reduced risk; while in still others, the likelihood can never be significantly reduced. Some people will have fairly good insight into the risks they pose and the costs entailed by an effort to reduce those risks; others will have poor insight into these factors.

When the issues are put this way, there begin to emerge a series of meaningful questions capable of traditional legal analyses: What sorts of anticipated harm warrant involuntary confinement? How likely must it be that the harm will occur? Must there be a significant component of harm to others, or may the harm be to self alone? If harm to self is sufficient, must the person also be incapable, because he lacks insight, of weighing the risks to himself against the costs of confinement? How long a period of involuntary confinement is justified to prevent which sorts of harms? Must the likelihood of the harm increase as its severity decreases? Or as the component of harm to others decreases?

These questions are complex, but this is as it should be, for the business of balancing the liberty of the individual against the risks a free society must tolerate is very complex. That is the business of the law, and these are the questions which need asking and answering before liberty is denied, but they are obscured when the issue is phrased in medical terms which frighten, or bore, lawyers away. Nor have I simply manufactured these questions. They are the very questions which are being implicitly answered every day by psychiatrists, but they are not being openly asked, and many psychiatrists do not realize that they are, in fact, answering them.

Let us consider two of these questions and compare how they are being dealt with—or not dealt with—under the present system with how they might be handled under functional, nonmedical criteria. The initial and fundamental question

which must be asked by any system authorizing incarceration is which harms are sufficiently serious to justify resort to this rather severe sanction. This question is asked and answered in the criminal law by the substantive definitions of crime. Thus homicide is a harm which justifies the sanction of imprisonment; miscegenation does not; and adultery is a close case about which reasonable people may, and do, disagree. It is difficult to conceive of a criminal process which did not make some effort at articulating these distinctions. Imagine, for example, a penal code which simply made it an imprisonable crime to cause injury to self or others, without defining injury. It is also difficult to conceive of a criminal process, at least in jurisdictions with an Anglo-American tradition, in which these distinctions were not drawn by the legislature or courts. It would seem beyond dispute that the question of which harms do and which do not justify incarceration is a legal, indeed a political, decision, to be made not by experts, but by the constitutionally authorized agents of the people. Again, try to imagine a penal code which authorized incarceration for anyone who performed an act regarded as injurious by a designated expert, say a psychiatrist or penologist.

To be sure, there are differences between the crininal- and the civil-commitment processes; the criminal law is supposed to punish people for having committed harmful acts in the past, whereas, civil commitment is supposed to prevent people from committing harmful acts in the future. While this difference may have important implications in some contexts, it would seem entirely irrelevant in deciding which acts are sufficiently harmful to justify incarceration, either as an after-the-fact punitive sanction or as a before-the-fact preventive sanction. The considerations which require clear definition of such harms in the criminal process would seem to be fully applicable to the civil-commitment process.

Yet the situation which I said would be hard to imagine in the criminal law is precisely the one which prevails with civil commitment. The statutes authorize preventive incarceration of mentally ill persons who are likely to injure themselves or others. Generally "injure" is not further defined in the statutes or in the case law, and the critical decision, whether a predicted pattern of behavior is sufficiently injurious to warrant incarceration, is relegated to the unarticulated judgments of the psychiatrist.

Some psychiatrists are perfectly willing to provide their own personal opinions—often falsely disguised as expert opinions—about which harms are sufficiently serious. One psychiatrist recently told a meeting of the American Psychiatric Association that "you—[the psychiatrist]—have to define for yourself the word danger, and then having decided that in your mind . . . look for it with every conceivable means. . . ."

My own conversations with psychiatrists reveal wide differences in opinion over what sorts of harms justify incarceration. As one would expect, some psychiatrists are political conservatives, while others are liberals; some place a greater premium on safety, and others on liberty. Their opinions about which harms do and which do not justify confinement probably cover the range of opinions one would expect to encounter in any educated segment of the public. But they are opinions about matters which each of us is as qualified to make as they are. Thus this most fundamental decision, which harms justify confinement, is almost never made by the legislature or the courts; often it is never explicitly made by anybody; and when it is explicitly made, it is by an unelected and unappointed expert operating outside the area of his expertise.

Consider, for example, the age-old philosophical dispute about the government's authority to incarcerate someone for his own good. The classic statement denying such authority was made by John Stewart Mill in his treatise *On Liberty*. He deemed it fundamental

> . . . that the only purpose for which power can be rightfully exercised against any member of a civilized community, against his will, is to prevent harm to others. He cannot rightfully be compelled to do or forbear because it will be better for him to do so, because it will make

him happier, because . . . to do so would be wise or even right. . . .

The most eloquent presentation of the other view was made by the poet John Donne in a famous stanza from his "Devotions":

> No man is an island, entire of itself;
> Every man is a piece of the continent,
> A part of the main;
> If a clod be washed away from the sea,
> Europe is the less . . . ;
> Any man's death diminishes me, because I am involved in mankind;
> And therefore never send to know for whom the bell tolls;
> It tolls for thee.

These statements, eloquent as they are, are far too polarized for useful discourse. In our complex and interdependent society there is hardly a harm to one man which does not have radiations beyond the island of his person. But this observation does not, in itself, destroy the thrust of Mills' argument. Society may still have less justification for incarcerating a person to prevent a harm to himself which contains only a slight component of harm to others than if it contained a large component of such harm.

Compare, for example, a recent case which arose under the civil-commitment process with a similar fact situation which produced no case at all. Mrs. Lake, a 62-year old woman, suffers from arteriosclerosis which causes periods of confusion interspersed with periods of relative rationality. One day she was found wandering around downtown Washington looking confused but bothering no one, whereupon she was committed to a mental hospital. She petitioned for release and at her trial testified, during a period of apparent rationality, that she was aware of her problem, that she knew that her periods of confusion endangered her health and even her life, but that she had experienced the mental hospital and preferred to assume the risk of living, and perhaps dying, outside its walls. Her petition was denied, and despite continued litigation, she is still involuntarily confined in the closed ward of the mental hospital.

Compare Mrs. Lake's decision to one made by Supreme Court Justice Jackson, who at the same age of 62 suffered a severe heart attack while serving on the Supreme Court. As Solicitor-General Sobeloff recalled in his memorial tribute, Jackson's "doctors gave him the choice between years of comparative inactivity or a continuation of his normal activity at the risk of death at any time." Characteristically, he chose the second alternative, and suffered a fatal heart attack shortly thereafter. No court interfered with his risky decision. A similar decision, though in a lighter vein, is described in a limerick entitled "The Lament of a Coronary Patient:"

> My doctor has made a prognosis
> That intercourse fosters thrombosis
> But I'd rather expire
> Fulfilling desire
> Than abstain, and develop neurosis.

Few courts, I suspect, would interfere with that decision.

Why, then, do courts respond so differently to what appear to be essentially similar decisions by Mrs. Lake, Justice Jackson, and the coronary patient? Because these similarities are obscured by the medical model imposed upon Mrs. Lake's case but not upon the other two. Most courts would distinguish the cases by simply saying that Mrs. Lake is mentally ill, while Jackson and the coronary patient are not, without pausing to ask whether there is anything about her "mental illness" which makes her case functionally different from the others. To be sure, there are some mentally ill people whose decisions are different from those made by Justice Jackson and the coronary patient. Some mentally ill people have little insight into their condition, the risks it poses, and the possibility of change. Their capacity for choosing between the risks of liberty and the security of incarceration may be substantially impaired. And in some cases, perhaps the state ought to act in *parens patriae* make the decision for them. But not all persons so diagnosed are incapable of weighing risks and making important decisions. This has

been recognized by some of the very psychiatrists who advocate the medical model most forcefully. Dr. Jack Ewalt, Chairman of the Department of Psychiatry at Harvard, recently offered the following observation to a Senate Subcommittee:

> The mentally sick patient may be disoriented, but he is not a fool. He has read the newspapers about overcrowded and understaffed hospitals. He is alert to the tough time he will have getting a job when he gets out, if he gets out. He knows that there lurks in the minds of his former friends the suspicion that he is a dangerous fellow. He is sensitive that a mother may recoil in fright if he stops to give her child a pat on the head.

But Dr. Ewalt uses this observation not as an argument in favor of self-determination by the mentally ill, but rather as showing the need for medical commitment without judicial interference.

The appropriateness and limitations of such benevolent compulsion are in the forefront of our concerns in the criminal law (witness the wide attention received by the Hart-Devlin debate). Although there is as much reason for concern about these issues in the civil-commitment context, they are being ignored, because the law has inadvertantly relegated them to the unarticulated value judgments of the expert psychiatrist.

This is equally true of another important question which rarely gets asked in the civil-commitment process: How likely should the predicted event have to be to justify preventive incarceration? Even if it is agreed, for example, that preventing a serious physical assault would justify incarceration, an important question still remains: How likely should it have to be that the person will assault before incarceration is justified? If the likelihood is very high, say 90 percent, then a strong argument can be made for some incarceration. If the likelihood is very small, say 5 percent, then it would be hard to justify confinement. Here, unlike the process of defining harm, little guidance can be obtained from the criminal law, for there are only a few occasions where the criminal law is explicitly predictive, and no judicial or legislative guidelines have been developed for determining the degree of likelihood required.

But someone is deciding what degree of likelihood should be required in every case. Today the psychiatrist makes that important decision. He is asked whether a given harm is likely, and he generally answers yes or no. He may, in his own mind, be defining "likely" to mean anything from virtual certainty to slightly above chance. And his definition will not be a reflection of any expertise, but again of his own personal preference for safety or liberty. Not only do psychiatrists determine the degree of likelihood which should be required for incarceration, they are also the ones who decide whether that degree of likelihood exists in any particular case.

Now this, you say may be thinking, is surely an appropriate role for the expert psychiatrist. But just how expert are psychiatrists in making the sorts of predictions upon which incarceration is presently based? Considering the heavy, indeed exclusive, reliance the law places on psychiatric predictions, one would expect there to be numerous follow-up studies establishing their accuracy. Over this past year, with the help of two researchers, I conducted a thorough survey of all the published literature on the prediction of antisocial conduct. We read and summarized many hundreds of articles, monographs, and books. Surprisingly enough, we were able to discover fewer than a dozen studies which followed up psychiatric predictions of antisocial conduct. And even more surprisingly, these few studies strongly suggest that psychiatrists are rather inaccurate predictors—inaccurate in an absolute sense, and even less accurate in comparison with other professionals, such as psychologists, social workers, and correctional officials, and in comparison with actuarial devices, such as prediction or experience tables. Even more significantly for legal purposes, it seems that psychiatrists are particularly prone to one type of error—overprediction. In other words, they tend to predict antisocial conduct in many instances where it would not, in fact, occur. Indeed, our research suggests that for every correct psychiatric prediction of violence, there are numerous erroneous predic-

tions. That is, among every group of inmates presently confined on the basis of psychiatric predictions of violence, there are only a few who would, and many more who would not, actually engage in such conduct if released.

One reason for this overprediction is that a psychiatrist almost never learns about his erroneous predictions of violence, for predicted assailants are generally incarcerated and have little opportunity to prove or disprove the prediction; but he always learns about his erroneous predictions of nonviolence, often from newspaper headlines announcing the crime. This higher visability of erroneous predictions of nonviolence inclines him, whether consciously or unconsciously, to overpredict rather than underpredict violent behavior.

What, then, have been the effects of virtually turning over to the psychiatrists the civil-commitment process? We have accepted a legal policy, never approved by any authorized decision maker, which permits significant overprediction—in effect, a rule that it is better to confine ten men who would not assault than to let go free one man who would. We have defined danger to include all sorts of minor social disruptions. We have equated harm to self with harm to others, without recognizing the debatable nature of that equation.

Now it may well be that if we substitute functional legal criteria for the medical model, we would still accept many of the answers we accept today. Perhaps our society is willing to tolerate significant overprediction. Perhaps we do want incarceration to prevent minor social harms. Perhaps we do want to protect people from themselves as much as from others. But we will never learn the answers to these questions unless they are exposed and openly debated. And such open debate is discouraged, indeed made impossible, when the questions are disguised in medical jargon against which the lawyer, and the citizen, feels helpless.

The lesson of this experience, and our similar if less costly one with the insanity defense, is that no legal rule should ever be phrased in medical terms, that no legal decision should ever be turned over to the psychiatrist, that there is no such thing as a legal problem which cannot or should not be phrased in terms familiar to lawyers. And civil commitment of the mentally ill is a legal problem. Whenever compulsion is used or freedom denied—whether by the state, the church, the union, the university, or the psychiatrist—the issue becomes a legal one; and lawyers must be quick to immerse themselves in it. The words of Brandeis ring as true today as they did in 1927, and are as applicable to the psychiatrist as to the wiretapper:

Experience should teach us to be most on our guard to protect liberty when the Government's purposes are beneficient. Men born to freedom are naturally alert to repel invasion of their liberty by evil-minded rulers. The greatest dangers to liberty lurk in insidious encroachment by men of zeal, well-meaning but without understanding.

## 52    RACIAL INTEGRATION IN THE ARMED FORCES
### CHARLES C. MOSKOS, JR.

On July 28, 1948, President Truman issued an executive order abolishing racial segregation in the armed forces of the United States. By the middle 1950's this policy was an accomplished fact. The lessons of the racial integration of the military are many. Within a remarkably short period the make-up of a major American institution underwent a far-reaching transformation. At the same time, the desegregation of the military can be used to trace

Reprinted from *The American Journal of Sociology*, vol. 72 (September 1966) pp. 132–148, by permission of the author and The University of Chicago Press. Copyright © 1966 by The University of Chicago Press.

Many persons have given the writer invaluable assistance during his collection and analysis of the materials for this paper. I would especially like to thank Lieutenant Colonel Roger W. Little, U.S. Military Academy, John B. Spore, editor of *Army* magazine, Philip M. Timpane, staff assistant for civil rights, Department of Defense, and Morris Janowitz, University of Chicago. Also, the author's access to military personnel at all levels was made possible by the more than perfunctory co-operation of numerous military information officers, men who perform a difficult task with both efficiency and good humor. Financial support was given by the Inter-University Seminar on Armed Forces and Society sponsored by the Russell Sage Foundation. Additional funds for travel were made available by the University of Michigan, and the Council for Intersocietal Studies of Northwestern University. It must be stressed, however, that the usual caveat that the author alone accepts responsibility for the interpretations and conclusions is especially relevant here.

some of the mutual permeations between the internal organization of the military establishment and the racial and social cleavages found in the larger setting of American society. Further, because of the favorable contrast in the military performance of integrated Negro servicemen with that of all-Negro units, the integration of the armed services is a demonstration of how changes in social organization can bring about a marked and rapid improvement in individual and group achievement. The desegregated military, moreover, offers itself as a graphic example of the abilities of both whites and Negroes to adjust to egalitarian racial relations with surprisingly little strain. Also, an examination of the racial situation in the contemporary military establishment can serve as a partial guideline as to what one might expect in a racially integrated America. It is to these and related issues that this article is addressed.[1]

### DESEGREGATING THE MILITARY[2]

Negroes have taken part in all of this country's wars. An estimated 5,000 Negroes, some scattered as individuals and others in segregated units, fought on the American side in the War of Independence. Several thousand Negroes saw service in the War of 1812. During the Civil War 180,000 Negroes were recruited into the Union army and served in segregated regiments.[3] Following the Civil War four Negro regiments were established and were active in the Indian wars on the Western frontier and later fought with distinction in Cuba during the Spanish-American War. In the early twentieth century, however, owing to a general rise in American racial tensions and specific outbreaks of violence between Negro troops and whites, opinion began to turn against the use of Negro soldiers. Evaluation of Negro soldiers was further lowered by events in World War I. The combat performance of the all-Negro 92nd Infantry, one of its regiments having fled in the German offensive at Meuse-Argonne, came under heavy criticism. Yet it was also observed that Negro units operating under French command, in a more racially tolerant situation, performed well.

In the interval between the two world wars, the Army not only remained segregated but also adopted a policy of a Negro quota that was to keep the number of Negroes in the Army proportionate to the total population. Never in the pre-World War II period, however, did the number of Negroes approach this quota. On the eve of Pearl Harbor, Negroes constituted 5.9 per cent of the Army; and there were only five Negro officers, three of whom were chaplains. During World War II Negroes entered the Army in larger numbers, but at no time did they exceed 10 per cent of total personnel. Negro soldiers remained in segregated units, and approximately three-quarters served in the quartermaster, engineer, and transportation corps. To make matters worse from the viewpoint of "the right to fight," a slogan loudly echoed by Negro organizations in the United States, even Negro combat units were frequently used for heavy-duty labor. This was highlighted when the 2nd Cavalry was broken up into service units owing to command apprehension over the combat qualities, even though untested, of this all-Negro division. The record of those Negro units that did see combat in World War II was mixed. The performance of the 92nd Infantry Division again came under heavy criticism, this time for alleged unreliability in the Italian campaign.

An important exception to the general pattern

of utilization of Negro troops in World War II occurred in the winter months of 1944-45 in the Ardennes battle. Desperate shortages of combat personnel resulted in the Army asking for Negro volunteers. The plan was to have platoons (approximately 40 men) of Negroes serve in companies (approximately 200 men) previously all-white. Some 2,500 Negroes volunteered for this assignment. Both in terms of Negro combat performance and white soldiers' reactions, the Ardennes experiment was an unqualified success. This incident would later be used to support arguments for integration.

After World War II, pressure from Negro and liberal groups coupled with an acknowledgment that Negro soldiers were being poorly utilized led the Army to re-examine its racial policies. A report by an Army board in 1945, while holding racial integration to be a desirable goal and while making recommendations to improve Negro opportunity in the Army, concluded that practical considerations required a maintenance of segregation and the quota system. In light of World War II experiences, the report further recommended that Negro personnel be exclusively assigned to support rather than combat units. Another Army board report came out in 1950 with essentially the same conclusions.[4] Both reports placed heavy stress on the supervisory and disciplinary problems resulting from the disproportionate number of Negroes, as established by Army examinations, found in the lower mental and aptitude classification levels. In 1950, for example, 60 per cent of the Negro personnel fell into the Army's lowest categories compared with 29 per cent of the white soldiers. From the standpoint of the performance requirements of the military, such facts could not be lightly dismissed.

After the Truman desegregation order of 1948, however, the die was cast. The President followed his edict by setting up a committee, chaired by Charles Fahy, to pursue the implementation of equal treatment and opportunity for armed forces personnel. Under the impetus of the Fahy committee, the Army abolished the quota system in 1950, and was beginning to integrate some training camps when the conflict in Korea broke out. The Korean War was the coup de grâce for segregation in the Army. Manpower requirements in the field for combat soldiers resulted in many instances of *ad hoc* integration. As was true in the Ardennes experience, Negro soldiers in previously all-white units performed well in combat. As integration in Korea became more standard, observers consistently noted that the fighting abilities of Negroes differed little from those of whites.[5] This contrasted with the blemished record of the all-Negro 24th Infantry Regiment.[6] Its performance in the Korean War was judged to be so poor that its divisional commander recommended the unit be dissolved as quickly as possible. Concurrent with events in Korea, integration was introduced in the United States. By 1956, three years after the end of the Korean War, the remnants of Army Jim Crow disappeared at home and in overseas installations. At the time of the Truman order, Negroes constituted 8.8 per cent of Army personnel. In 1964 the figure was 12.3 per cent.

In each of the other services, the history of desegregation varied from the Army pattern. The Army Air Force, like its parent body, generally assigned Negroes to segregated support units. (However, a unique military venture taken during the war was the formation of three all-Negro, including officers, air combat units.) At the end of World War II the proportion of Negroes in the Army Air Force was only 4 per cent, less than half what it was in the Army. Upon its establishment as an independent service in 1947, the Air Force began to take steps toward integration even before the Truman order. By the time of the Fahy committee report in 1950, the Air Force was already largely integrated. Since integration there has been a substantial increase in the proportion of Negroes serving in the Air Force, from less than 5 per cent in 1949 to 8.6 per cent in 1964.

Although large numbers of Negroes had served in the Navy during the Civil War and for some period afterward, restrictive policies were introduced in the early 1900's and by the end of World War I only about 1 per cent of Navy personnel were Negroes. In 1920 the Navy adopted a policy of total racial exclusion and barred all Negro enlistments. This policy was changed in 1932 when Negroes, along with Filipinos, were again allowed to join the Navy but only as stewards in the messman's branch. Further modifications were made in Navy policy in 1942 when some openings in general service for Negroes were created. Negro sailors in these positions, however, were limited to segregated harbor and shore assignments.[7] In 1944, in the first effort toward desegregation in any of the armed services, a small number of Negro sailors in general service were integrated on ocean-going vessels. After the end of World War II the Navy, again ahead of the other services, began to take major steps toward elimination of racial barriers. Even in the integrated Navy of today, however, approximately a quarter of Negro personnel still serve as stewards. Also, despite the early steps toward integration taken by the Navy, the proportion of Negro sailors has remained fairly constant over the past two decades, averaging around 5 per cent.

The Marine Corps has gone from a policy of exclusion to segregation to integration. Before World War II there were no Negro marines. In 1942 Negroes were accepted into the Marine Corps but assigned to segregated units where they were heavy-duty laborers, ammunition handlers, and anti-aircraft gunners. After the war small-scale integration of Negro marines into white units was begun. In 1949 and 1950 Marine Corps training units were integrated, and by 1954 the color line was largely erased throughout the Corps. Since integration began, the proportion of Negroes has increased markedly. In 1949 less than 2 per cent of all marines were Negroes compared with 8.2 per cent in 1964.

Although the various military services are all similar in being integrated today, they differ in their proportion of Negroes. As shown in Table 1, the Negro distribution in the total armed forces in 1962 and 1964, respectively, was 8.2 per cent and 9.0 per cent, lower than the 11-12 per cent constituting the Negro proportion in the total population. It is virtually certain, however, that among those *eligible*, a higher proportion of Negroes than whites enter the armed forces. That is, a much

**TABLE 1**    *Negroes in the armed forces and each service as a percentage of total personnel, 1962 and 1964*

| Service | 1962 | 1964 |
|---|---|---|
| Army | 11.1 | 12.3 |
| Air Force | 7.8 | 8.6 |
| Navy | 4.7 | 5.1 |
| Marine Corps | 7.0 | 8.2 |
| Total armed forces | 8.2 | 9.0 |

Source: U.S. Commission on Civil Rights, "The Negro in The Armed Forces," *Civil Rights '63*, Washington, D.C.: U.S. Government Printing Office, 1963, p. 218; U.S. Department of Defense statistics.

larger number of Negroes do not meet the entrance standards required by the military services. In 1962, for example, 56.1 per cent of Negroes did not pass the preinduction mental examinations given to draftees, almost four times the 15.4 per cent of whites who failed these same tests.[8] Because of the relatively low number of Negroes obtaining student or occupational deferments, however, it is the Army drawing upon the draft that is the only military service where the percentage of Negroes approximates the national proportion. Thus, despite the high number of Negroes who fail to meet induction standards, Army statistics for 1960-65 show Negroes constituted about 15 per cent of those drafted.

Even if one takes account of the Army's reliance on the selective service for much of its personnel, the most recent figures still show important differences in the number of Negroes in those services meeting their manpower requirements solely through voluntary enlistments; the 5.1 per cent Negro in the Navy is lower than the 8.2 per cent for the Marine Corps or the 8.6 per cent for the Air Force. Moreover, the Army, besides its drawing upon the draft, also has the highest Negro initial enlistment rate of any of the services. As reported in Table 2, we find in 1964 that the Army drew 14.1 per cent of its volunteer incoming personnel from Negroes as compared with 13.1 per cent for the Air Force, 8.4 per cent for the Marine Corps, and 5.8 per cent for the Navy. As also

shown in Table 2, there has been a very sizable increase in Negro enlistments from 1961 to 1965 in all four of the armed services.

There are also diverse patterns between the individual services as to the rank or grade distribution of Negroes. Looking at Table 3, we find the ratio of Negro to white officers is roughly 1 to 30 in the Army, 1 to 70 in the Air Force, 1 to 250 in the Marine Corps, and 1 to 300 in the Navy. Among enlisted men, Negroes are underrepresented in the top three enlisted ranks in the Army and the top four ranks in the other three services. We also find a disproportionate concentration of Negroes in the lower non-commissioned officer ranks in all of the armed forces, but especially so in the Army. An assessment of these data reveals that the Army, followed by the Air Force, has not only the largest proportion of Negroes in its total personnel, but also the most equitable distribution of Negroes throughout its ranks. Although the Navy was the first service to integrate and the Army the last, in a kind of tortoise and hare fashion, it is the Army that has become the most representative service for Negroes.

## CHANGING MILITARY REQUIREMENTS AND NEGRO OPPORTUNITIES

A pervasive trend within the military establishment singled out by students of this institution is the long-term direction toward greater technical complexity and narrowing of civilian-military occupational skills.[9] An indicator, albeit a crude one, of this trend toward "professionalization" of mili-

**TABLE 2**    *Negroes in each of the armed services as a percentage of initial enlistments, 1961, 1963, and 1965*

| Year | Army | Air Force | Navy | Marine Corps |
|---|---|---|---|---|
| 1961 | 8.2 | 9.5 | 2.9 | 5.9 |
| 1963 | 11.2 | 10.5 | 4.3 | 5.5 |
| 1965 | 14.1 | 13.1 | 5.8 | 8.4 |

Source: U.S. Department of Defense statistics.

TABLE 3    *Negroes as a percentage of total personnel in each grade for each service, 1964*

| Grade | Army | Air Force | Navy | Marine Corps |
|---|---|---|---|---|
| **Officers** | | | | |
| Generals/admirals | . . . | 0.2 | . . . | . . . |
| Colonels/captains | 0.2 | 0.2 | . . . | . . . |
| Lt. cols./commanders | 1.1 | 0.5 | 0.6 | . . . |
| Majors/lt. commanders | 3.6 | 0.8 | 0.3 | 0.3 |
| Captains/lieutenants | 5.4 | 2.0 | 0.5 | 0.4 |
| 1st lieutenants/lts. (j.g.) | 3.8 | 1.8 | 0.2 | 0.4 |
| 2d lieutenants/ensigns | 2.7 | 2.5 | 0.7 | 0.3 |
| **Total officers** | 3.4 | 1.5 | 0.3 | 0.4 |
| **Enlisted*** | | | | |
| E-9 (sgt. major) | 3.5 | 1.2 | 1.5 | 0.8 |
| E-8 (master sgt.) | 6.1 | 2.2 | 1.9 | 1.2 |
| E-7 (sgt. 1st class) | 8.5 | 3.2 | 2.9 | 2.3 |
| E-6 (staff sgt.) | 13.9 | 5.3 | 4.7 | 5.0 |
| E-5 (sgt.) | 17.4 | 10.8 | 6.6 | 11.2 |
| E-4 (corp.) | 14.2 | 12.7 | 5.9 | 10.4 |
| E-3 (pvt. 1st class) | 13.6 | 9.7 | 6.6 | 7.8 |
| E-2 (private) | 13.1 | 11.7 | 5.7 | 9.5 |
| E-1 (recruit) | 6.8 | 14.4 | 7.1 | 9.1 |
| **Total enlisted men** | 13.4 | 10.0 | 5.8 | 8.7 |

*Army and Marine Corps enlisted titles indicated in parentheses have equivalent pay grades in Navy and Air Force.

Source: U.S. Department of Defense statistics.

tary roles is the changing proportion of men assigned to combat arms. Given in Table 4, along with concomitant white-Negro distributions, are figures comparing the percentage of Army enlisted personnel in combat arms (e.g., infantry, armor, artillery) for the years 1945 and 1962. We find that the proportion of men in combat arms—that is, traditional military specialties—dropped from 44.5 per cent in 1945 to 26.0 per cent in 1962. Also, the percentage of white personnel in traditional military specialties approximates the total proportional decrease in the combat arms over the seventeen-year period.

For Negro soldiers, however, a different picture emerges. While the percentage of Negro enlisted men in the Army increased only slightly between 1945 and 1962, the likelihood of a Negro serving in a combat arm is almost three times greater in 1962 than it was at the end of World War II. Fur-

ther, when comparisons are made between military specialties *within* the combat arms, the Negro proportion is noticeably higher in line rather than staff assignments. This is especially the case in airborne and marine units. Put in another way, the direction in assignment of Negro soldiers in the desegregated military is testimony to the continuing consequences of differential Negro opportunity originating in the larger society. That is, even though integration of the military has led to great improvement in the performance of Negro servicemen, the social and particularly educational deprivations suffered by the Negro in American society can be mitigated but not entirely eliminated by the racial egalitarianism existing within the armed forces.[10] These findings need not be interpreted as a decline in the "status" of the Negro in the integrated military. Actually there is evidence that higher prestige—but not envy—is accorded combat

**TABLE 4** *Total Negro army enlisted personnel and white and Negro enlisted personnel in combat arms, 1945 and 1962*

| Category | 1945* | 1962 |
|---|---|---|
| Negroes as percentage of total personnel | 10.5 | 12.2 |
| Percentage of total personnel in combat arms | 44.5 | 26.0 |
| Percentage of total white personnel in combat arms | 48.2 | 24.9 |
| Percentage of total Negro personnel in combat arms | 12.1 | 33.4 |

*Excludes Army Air Force.

Source: *Project Clear: The Utilization of Negro Manpower in the Army*, Chevy Chase, Md.: Operations Research Office, Johns Hopkins University, April 1955, pp. 563–64; U.S. Civil Rights Commission, "The Negro in The Armed Forces," *Civil Rights '63*, Washington, D.C.: U.S. Government Printing Office, 1963, pp. 219–22.

personnel by those in non-combat activities within the military.[11] And taken within the historical context of "the right to fight," the Negro's overrepresentation in the combat arms is a kind of ironic step forward.[12]

Moreover, the military at the enlisted ranks has become a major avenue of career mobility for many Negro men.[13] As shown earlier in Table 3, in all four services, and especially in the Army, there is some overrepresentation of Negroes at the junior NCO levels (pay grades E-4–E-6). The disproportionate concentration of Negroes at these levels implies a higher than average re-enlistment as these grades are not normally attained until after a second enlistment. This assumption is supported by the data given in Table 5. We find that in 1965 for all four services the Negro re-enlistment rate is approximately twice that of white servicemen. Indeed, about half of all first-term Negro servicemen chose to remain in the armed forces for at least a second term. The greater likelihood of Negroes to select a service career suggests that the military establishment is undergoing a significant change in its NCO core. Such an outcome would reflect not only the "pull" of the appeals offered by a racially egalitarian institution, but also the "push" gener-

ated by the plight of the Negro in the American economy.[14] At the minimum, it is very probable that as the present cohort of Negro junior NCO's attains seniority there will be a greater representation of Negroes in the advanced NCO grades. The expansion of the armed forces arising from the war in Viet Nam and the resulting opening up of "rank" will accelerate this development.

## ATTITUDES OF SOLDIERS

So far the discussion has sought to document the degree of penetration and the kind of distribution characterizing Negro servicemen in the integrated military establishment. We now introduce certain survey and interview data dealing more directly with the question of soldiers' attitudes toward military desegregation. Commenting on the difficulties of social analysis, the authors of *The American Soldier* wrote that few problems are "more formidable than that of obtaining dependable records of attitudes toward racial separation in the Army."[15] Without underestimating the continuing difficulty of this problem, an opportunity exists to compare attitudes toward racial integration held by American soldiers in two different periods. This is done by contrasting responses to equivalent items given in World War II as reported in *The American Soldier* with those reported in Project Clear, a study sponsored by the Defense Department during the Korean War.[16]

In both *The American Soldier* and Project Clear (the surveys under consideration were conducted in 1943 and 1951, respectively) large samples of

**TABLE 5** *First-term re-enlistment rates in the armed forces and each service by race in 1965, per cent*

| Race | Total armed forces | Army | Air Force | Navy | Marine Corps |
|---|---|---|---|---|---|
| White | 21.6 | 18.5 | 27.4 | 21.6 | 12.9 |
| Negro | 46.6 | 49.3 | 50.3 | 41.3 | 50.3 |

Source: U.S. Department of Defense statistics.

Army personnel in segregated military settings were categorized as to whether they were favorable, indifferent, or opposed to racial integration in Army units. We find, as presented in Table 6, massive shifts in soldiers' attitudes over the eight-year period, shifts showing a much more positive disposition toward racial integration among both whites and Negroes in the later year. A look at the distribution of attitudes held by white soldiers reveals opposition to integration goes from 84 per cent in 1943 to less than half in 1951. That such a change could occur in less than a decade counters viewpoints that see basic social attitudes in large populations being prone to glacial-like changes. Yet, an even more remarkable change is found among the Negro soldiers. Where in 1945, favorable, indifferent, or opposing attitudes were roughly equally distributed among the Negro soldiers, by 1951 opposition or indifference to racial integration had become negligible. Such a finding is strongly indicative of a reformation in Negro public opinion from traditional acquiescence to Jim Crow to the ground swell that laid the basis for the subsequent civil rights movement.

While the data on Negro attitudes toward integration given in Table 6 were elicited during the segregated military of 1943 and 1951, we also

**TABLE 6**  *Attitudes of white and Negro soldiers toward racial integration in the segregated Army, 1943 and 1951*

| Attitude toward integration | White soldiers, % | | Negro soldiers, % | |
|---|---|---|---|---|
| | 1943 | 1951 | 1943 | 1951 |
| Favorable | 12 | 25 | 37 | 90 |
| Indifferent | 4 | 31 | 27 | 6 |
| Opposed | 84 | 44 | 36 | 4 |
| Number | (4,800) | (1,983) | (3,000) | (1,384) |

Source: Stouffer, *The American Soldier: Adjustment during Army Life*, vol. I, Princeton, N.J.: Princeton University Press, 1949, p. 568; *Project Clear: The Utilization of Negro Manpower in the Army*, Chevy Chase, Md.: Operations Research Office, Johns Hopkins University, April 1955, pp. 322, 433.

**TABLE 7**  *Attitudes of Negro soldiers in 1965 comparing racial equality in military and civilian life, total and by home region, per cent*

| Where more racial equality | Total | Home region | |
|---|---|---|---|
| | | North | South |
| Military life | 84 | 75 | 93 |
| Civilian life | 3 | 6 | 0 |
| No difference | 13 | 19 | 7 |
| Number | (67) | (36) | (31) |

have evidence on how Negro soldiers react to military integration in the contemporary setting. As reported in Table 7, the Army is overwhelmingly thought to be more racially egalitarian than civilian life. Only 16 per cent of sixty-seven Negro soldiers interviewed in 1965 said civilian life was more racially equal or no different than the Army. By region, as might be expected, we find southern Negroes more likely than northern Negroes to take a benign view of racial relations in the Army when these are compared to civilian life. The data in Table 7 support the proposition that, despite existing deviations from military policy at the level of informal discrimination, the military establishment stands in sharp and favorable contrast to the racial relations prevalent in the larger American society.

One of the most celebrated findings of *The American Soldier* was the discovery that the more contact white soldiers had with Negro troops, the more favorable was their reaction toward racial integration.[17] This conclusion is consistently supported in the surveys conducted by Project Clear. Again and again, comparisons of white soldiers in integrated units with those in segregated units show the former to be more supportive of desegregation. Illustrative of this pattern are the data shown in Table 8. Among combat infantrymen in Korea, 51 per cent in all-white units say outfits are better segregated as compared to 31 per cent in integrated units. For enlisted personnel stationed in the United States, strong objection to integration characterizes 44 per cent serving in segregated units while less than one-fifth of the men in inte-

TABLE 8   *Racial attitudes of white soldiers in segregated and integrated settings, 1951*

| Racial Attitudes | All-white units | | Integrated units | |
|---|---|---|---|---|
| | % | No. | % | No. |
| Combat infantrymen in Korea saying segregated outfits better | 51 | (195) | 31 | (1,024) |
| Enlisted personnel in the U.S. strongly objecting to racial integration | 44 | (1,983) | 17 | (1,683) |
| Officers rating Negroes worse than white soldiers | 79 | (233) | 28 | (385) |

Source: *Project Clear: The Utilization of Negro Manpower in the Army*, Chevy Chase, Md.: Operations Research Office, Johns Hopkins University, April 1955, pp. 141, 322, 333, 356.

grated units feel the same way. Seventy-nine per cent of officers on segregated posts rate Negroes worse than white soldiers as compared with 28 per cent holding similar beliefs on integrated posts.

## OFFICIAL POLICY AND ACTUAL PRACTICE

For the man newly entering the armed forces, it is hard to conceive that the military was one of America's most segregated institutions less than two decades ago. For today color barriers at the formal level are absent throughout the military establishment. Equal treatment regardless of race is official policy in such non-duty facilities as swimming pools, chapels, barbershops, post exchanges, movie theaters, snack bars, and dependents' housing as well as in the more strictly military endeavors involved in the assignment, promotion, and living conditions of members of the armed services.[18] Moreover, white personnel are often commanded by Negro superiors, a situation rarely obtained in civilian life. Recently the military has sought to implement its policy of equal opportunity by exerting pressure on local communities where segregated patterns affect military personnel. This policy deserves careful examination owing to its ramifications on the traditional separation of civilian and military spheres in American society. A measure of the extent and thoroughness of military desegregation is found in comparing the 1950 President's committee report dealing with racial integration and the 1963 and 1964 reports of a second President's committee. Where

the earlier report dealt entirely with internal military organization, the recent reports address themselves primarily to the National Guard and off-base discrimination.[19] Along this same line, Congressman Adam Clayton Powell has said that up to the middle 1950's he used to receive 5,000 letters a year from Negro servicemen complaining of discrimination in the military. In recent years, he receives less than 1,500 such letters annually and these largely pertain to off-base problems.[20] In brief, military life is characterized by an interracial equalitarianism of a quantity and of a kind that is seldom found in the other major institutions of American society.

In their performance of military duties, whites and Negroes work together with little display of racial tension. This is not to say racial animosity is absent in the military. Racial incidents do occur, but these are reduced by the severe sanctions imposed by the military for such acts. Such confrontations are almost always off-duty, if not off-base. In no sense, however, is the military sitting on top of a racial volcano, a state of affairs differing from the frequent clashes between the races that were a feature of the military in the segregated era. Additionally, it must be stressed that conflict situations stemming from non-racial causes characterize most sources of friction in the military establishment, for example, enlisted men versus officers, lower-ranking enlisted men versus non-commissioned officers, soldiers of middle-class background versus those of the working-class, conscriptees versus volunteers, line units versus staff units, rear echelon versus front echelon, combat units versus non-combat units, newly arrived units versus earlier stationed units, etc.

Yet the fact remains that the general pattern of day-to-day relationships *off the job* is usually one of mutual racial exclusivism. As one Negro soldier put it, "A man can be my best buddy in the Army, but he won't ask me to go to town with him." Closest friendships normally develop within races between individuals of similar educational background. Beyond one's hard core of friends there exists a level of friendly acquaintants. Here the pattern seems to be one of educational similarities overriding racial differences. On the whole, racial integration at informal as well as formal levels works best on-duty vis-à-vis off-duty, on-base vis-à-vis off-base, basic training and maneuvers vis-à-vis garrison, sea vis-à-vis shore duty, and combat vis-à-vis non-combat. In other words, the behavior of servicemen resembles the racial (and class) separatism of the larger American society, the more they are removed from the military environment.

For nearly all white soldiers the military is a first experience with close and equal contact with a large group of Negroes. There has developed what has become practically a military custom: the look over the shoulder, upon the telling of a racial joke, to see if there are any Negroes in hearing distance. Some racial animosity is reflected in accusations that Negro soldiers use the defense of racial discrimination to avoid disciplinary action. Many white soldiers claim they like Negroes as individuals but "can't stand them in bunches." In a few extreme cases, white married personnel may even live off the military base and pay higher rents rather than live in integrated military housing. On the whole, however, the segregationist-inclined white soldier regards racial integration as something to be accepted pragmatically, if not enthusiastically, as are so many situations in military life.

The most overt source of racial unrest in the military community centers in dancing situations. A commentary on American mores is a finding reported in Project Clear: three-quarters of a large sample of white soldiers said they would not mind Negro couples on the same dance floor, but approximately the same number disapproved of Negro soldiers dancing with white girls.[21] In many non-commissioned officer (NCO) clubs, the likelihood of interracial dancing partners is a constant producer of tension. In fact, the only major exception to integration within the military community is on a number of large posts where there are two or more NCO clubs. In such situations one of the clubs usually becomes tacitly designated as the Negro club.

Although there is almost universal support for racial integration by Negro soldiers, some strains are also evident among Negro personnel in the military. There seems to be a tendency among lower-ranking Negro enlisted men, especially conscriptees, to view Negro NCO's as "Uncle Toms" or "handkerchief heads." Negro NCO's are alleged to pick on Negroes when it comes time to assign men unpleasant duties. Negro officers are sometimes seen as being too strict or "chicken" when it comes to enforcing military discipline on Negro soldiers. As one Negro serviceman said, "I'm proud when I see a Negro officer, but not in my company."

One Negro writer, who served in the segregated Army and now has two sons in the integrated military, has proposed that what was thought by soldiers in all-Negro units to be racial discrimination was sometimes nothing more than harassment of lower-ranking enlisted personnel.[22] In fact, the analogy between enlisted men vis-à-vis officers in the military and Negroes vis-à-vis whites in the larger society has often been noted.[23] It has been less frequently observed, however, that enlisted men's behavior is often similar to many of the stereotypes associated with Negroes, for example, laziness, boisterousness, emphasis on sexual prowess, consciously acting stupid, obsequiousness in front of superiors combined with ridicule of absent superiors, etc. Placement of white adult males in a subordinate position within a rigidly stratified system, that is, appears to produce behavior not all that different from the so-called personality traits commonly held to be an outcome of cultural or psychological patterns unique to Negro life. Indeed, it might be argued that relatively little adjustment on the part of the command structure was required when the infusion of Negroes into the enlisted ranks occurred as the military establishment was desegregated. It is suggested, in other words, one factor contributing to the generally smooth racial integration of the military might be due to the standard treatment—"like Negroes" in a sense—accorded to all lower-ranking enlisted personnel.

Looking at changes in Negro behavior in the integrated military we find other indications of the immediate effects of social organization on individual behavior. Even though I am fully cognizant of the almost insurmountable difficulties involved in comparing crime statistics, the fact remains that students of the problem agree Negro crime is far higher than white crime.[24] There is no consensus, however, on what amount of the difference is due, on the one hand, to Negro cultural or psychological conditions or, on the other, to structural and class variables. Presented here, in a very preliminary fashion, is some evidence bearing on the consequences arising from changes in social organization on Negro crime. Reported by Project Clear are Negro-white crime differentials for three segregated posts in 1950. Proportionately, Negro soldiers committed four times more crime than white soldiers.[25] In 1964, in the integrated military, statistics of a major Army Command in Europe show Negroes accounting for 21 per cent of the crime while constituting 16 per cent of the total personnel. In a large combat unit in Viet Nam, for a three-month period in the summer of 1965, Negroes received 19 per cent of the disciplinary reports but made up 22 per cent of the troop assignment. These are the only Negro-white crime ratios in the integrated military that the writer has seen.[26] Although these findings, of course, are incomplete, they do point to a marked drop in Negro crime as compared with both the earlier segregated military as well as contemporary civilian life.[27]

## THE NEGRO SOLDIER OVERSEAS

Some special remarks are needed concerning Negro servicemen overseas. Suffice it to say for prefatory purposes, the American soldier, be he either white or Negro, is usually in a place where he does not understand the language, is received with mixed feelings by the local population, spends the greater part of his time in a transplanted American environment, sometimes plays the role of tourist, is relatively affluent in relation to the local economy, takes advantage and is at the mercy of a *comprador* class, and in comparison with his counterpart at home is more heavily involved in military duties.

In general, the pattern of racial relations observed in the United States—integration in the military setting and racial exclusivism off-duty—prevails in overseas assignments as well. This norm is reflected in one of the most characteristic features of American military life overseas, a bifurcation of the vice structure into groups that pander almost exclusively (or assert they do) to only one of the races. A frequent claim of local bar owners is that they discourage racially mixed trade because of the demands of their G.I. clientele. And, indeed, many of the establishments catering to American personnel that ring most military installations are segregated in practice. To a similar degree this is true of shore towns where Navy personnel take liberty. Violation of these implicit taboos can lead to physical threat if not violence.

The pattern of off-duty racial separatism is most pronounced in Japan and Germany, and less so in Korea. A major exception to this norm is found in the Dominican Republic. There all troops are restricted and leaving the military compound necessitates soldiers collaborating if they are not to be detected; such ventures are often as not interracial. In certain off-duty areas on Okinawa, on the other hand, racial separatism is complicated by interservice rivalries and a fourfold ecological pattern shows up: white-Army, Negro-Army, white-Marine Corps, and Negro-Marine Corps. Combat conditions in Viet Nam make the issue of off-duty racial relations academic for those troops in the field. In the cities, however, racial separatism off-duty is already apparent. It is said that the riverfront district in Saigon, Kanh Hoi, frequented by American Negro soldiers was formerly patronized by Senegalese troops during the French occupation.

In Germany one impact of that country's economic boom has been to depress the relative position of the American soldier vis-à-vis the German working man. In the Germany of ten or fifteen years ago (or the Korea of today) all American military personnel were affluent by local standards with all that implied. This was (and is in Korea) an especially novel experience for the Negro soldier. The status drop of American soldiers stationed in Germany has particularly affected the Negro serviceman, who has the additional handicap of being black in a country where there are no Negro girls. The old "good duty" days for Negro soldiers in Germany are now coming to an end as he finds his previous access to girls other than prostitutes severely reduced. The German economic boom has affected Negro soldiers in another way. In recent years there has been some friction between foreign laborers (mostly Mediterranean) and Negro soldiers. Both groups of men apparently are competing for the same girls. At the same time, the foreign workers have little contact with white American soldiers who move in a different segment of the vice structure.

Nonetheless, overseas duty for the Negro serviceman, in Germany as well as the Far East, gives him an opportunity, even if peripheral, to witness societies where racial discrimination is less practiced than it is in his home country. Although the level of Negro acceptance in societies other than America is usually exaggerated, the Negro soldier is hard put not to make invidious comparisons with the American scene.[28] In interviews conducted with Negro servicemen in Germany, 64 per cent said there was more racial equality in Germany than America, 30 per cent saw little difference between the two countries, and only 6 per cent believed Negroes were treated better in the United States.

Observers of overseas American personnel have told the writer that Negro soldiers are more likely than whites to learn local languages (though for both groups of servicemen this is a very small number). Evidence for this supposition is given in Table 9. Three German-national barbers, who were permanently hired to cut the hair of all the men in

**TABLE 9**   *Command of German language by white and Negro soldiers in a German-based U.S. Army battalion in 1965, per cent*

| Command of German* | White soldiers, % | Negro soldiers, % |
|---|---|---|
| Conversational | 1.4 | 7.4 |
| Some | 3.0 | 7.4 |
| Little or none | 95.6 | 85.2 |
| Number | (629) | (98) |

*Based on evaluations of German-national battalion employees.

one battalion, were asked by the writer to evaluate the German language proficiency of the individual personnel in that battalion.[29] When these evaluations were correlated with race, it was found that Negro soldiers were five times more likely to know "conversational" German, and three times more likely to know "some" German than were white soldiers.[30] Actually, the likelihood of Negro soldiers compared to whites in learning the language of the country in which they are stationed may be even greater than indicated in Table 9. Several of the German-speaking white soldiers were of German ethnic background and acquired some knowledge of the language in their home environments back in the United States. These data testify, then, that the Negro soldiers overseas, perhaps because of the more favorable racial climate, are more willing to take advantage of participation at informal levels with local populations.[31]

## CIVIL RIGHTS AT HOME AND WAR ABROAD

It is important to remember that the military establishment was desegregated before the current civil rights drive gained momentum. In the segregated military, embroilments between Negro units and whites were an ever present problem. In the light of subsequent developments in the domestic racial picture, it is likely that severe disciplinary problems would have occurred had military integration not come about when it did. The timing of desegregation in the military defused an ingredient—

all-Negro military units—that would have been potentially explosive in this nation's current racial strife.[32]

It is also probable, however, that military experience contributes to an activist posture on the part of Negro servicemen returning to civilian life. The Negro ex-serviceman, that is, may be less willing to accommodate himself to second-class citizenship after participation in the racially egalitarian military establishment. Further, especially in situations where Negroes are intimidated by physical threat or force, techniques of violence and organizational skill acquired in military service may be a new factor in the Negro's quest for equality. Robert F. Williams, the leading advocate of armed self-defense for Negroes, explicitly states that his Marine Corps experience led to his beliefs.[33] It also seems more than coincidence that the ten founders of the Deacons for Defense and Justice, a paramilitary group organized in 1964 to counter Ku Klux Klan terrorism, were all veterans of Korea or World War II.[34]

One must also take into account the possible consequences of the civil rights movement on Negro military behavior. Much attention has been given to a convergence of an important segment of the civil rights movement with the movement against the war in Viet Nam. The Student Nonviolent Coordinating Committee has formally denounced American action in Viet Nam as aggression. Civil rights organizers claim they find Negroes who do not want to fight "whitey's war." A Negro is barred from taking his seat in the Georgia legislature because he condones violations of the draft law. Rumors are heard of isolated incidents of Negro insubordination in the armed services. Despite this chain of events, however, the main stream of the civil rights drive has remained largely removed from those groups highly critical of this country's recent military policies. Indeed, the antiwar movement will likely aggravate an already existing cleavage between moderate and radical leaders—between those who accept versus those who reject the legitimacy of the American political system—in the civil rights movement itself. The more pertinent question at this time appears to be

not what are the implications of the civil rights movement for the military establishment, but what will be the effects of the Viet Nam war on the civil rights movement itself. Although it would be premature to offer a definitive statement on any future interpenetrations between the civil rights and antiwar movements, a major turning away of Negroes per se from military commitment is viewed as highly doubtful. Most likely, and somewhat paradoxically, we will witness more vocal antiwar sentiment within certain civil rights organizations at the same time that the military is becoming an avenue of career opportunity for many Negro men.

Nevertheless, there has usually been and is today a presumption on the part of America's military opponents that Negroes should be less committed soldiers than whites. Whether for tactical or ideological reasons, the Negro serviceman has been frequently defined as a special target for propaganda by forces opposing America in military conflicts. In World War II the Japanese directed radio appeals specifically to Negro servicemen in the Pacific theater. The Chinese in the Korean War used racial arguments on Negro prisoners of war. Yet a careful study of American POW behavior in Korea made no mention of differences in Negro and white behavior except to note that the segregation of Negro POW's by the Chinese had a boomerang effect on Communist indoctrination methods.[35]

The current military involvement of the United States on the international scene raises again the question of the motivation and performance of Negro soldiers in combat. A spokesman for the National Liberation Front of South Viet Nam has recently asserted that "liberation forces have a special attitude toward American soldiers who happen to be Negroes."[36] Up to now at least, however, efforts to test the loyalty of Negro soldiers have not met with success. This writer, as well as others, detected no differences in white or Negro combat performance in Viet Nam.[37] In the Dominican Republic, where the proportion of Negroes in line units run as high as 40 per cent, a pamphlet was distributed to Negro soldiers exhorting them to "turn your guns on your white oppressors and join your Dominican brothers."[38] Again, personal observation buttressed by comments from Dominicans revealed no significant differences between white and Negro military performance.[39]

The writer's appraisal is that among officers and NCO's there is no discernible difference between the races concerning military commitment in either the Dominican Republic or Viet Nam. Among Negro soldiers in the lower enlisted ranks, however, there is somewhat greater disenchantment compared to whites as to the merits of America's current military ventures. Such unease, however, has little effect on military performance, most especially in the actual combat situation. The evidence strongly suggests that the racial integration of the armed forces, coming about when it did, effectively precluded any potential success on the part of America's military opponents to differentiate Negro from white soldiers.

### CONCLUSION

Although the military was until recent times one of America's most segregated institutions, it has leaped into the forefront of racial equality in the past decade. What features of the military establishment can account for this about-face? There is a combination of mutually supporting factors that operate in the successful racial integration of the armed forces. For one thing, the military—an institution revolving around techniques of violence—is to an important degree discontinuous from other areas of social life. And this apartness served to allow, once the course had been decided, a rapid and complete racial integration. The path of desegregation was further made easier by characteristics peculiar or at least more pronounced in the military compared to other institutions. With its hierarchical power structure, predicated on stable and patterned relationships, decisions need take relatively little account of the personal desires of service personnel. Additionally, because roles and activities are more defined and specific in the military than in most other social arenas, conflicts that might have ensued within a more diffuse and ambiguous setting were largely absent. Likewise, desegregation was facilitated by the pervasiveness in the military of a bureaucratic ethos, with its concomitant formality and high social distance, that mitigated tensions arising from individual or personal feelings.

At the same time it must also be remembered that the military establishment has means of coercion not readily available in most civilian pursuits. Violations of norms are both more visible and subject to quicker sanctions. The military is premised, moreover, on the accountability of its members for effective performance. Owing to the aptly termed "chain of command," failures in policy implementation can be pinpointed. This in turn means that satisfactory carrying out of stated policy advances one's own position. In other words, it is to each individual's personal interest, if he anticipates receiving the rewards of a military career, to insure that decisions going through him are executed with minimum difficulty. Or put in another way, whatever the internal policy decided upon, racial integration being a paramount but only one example, the military establishment is uniquely suited to realize its implementation.

What implications does the military integration experience have for civilian society? Although it is certainly true that the means by which desegregation was accomplished in the military establishment are not easily translated to the civilian community, the end result of integration in the contemporary armed forces can suggest some qualities of what—if it came about—an integrated American society would be *within the context of the prevailing structural and value system.* Equality of treatment would be the rule in formal and task-specific relationships. Racial animosity would diminish but not disappear. We would expect a sharp improvement in Negro mobility and performance in the occupational sphere even taking into consideration on-going social and educational handicaps arising from existing inequities. Yet, because of these inequities, Negroes would still be overconcentrated in less skilled positions. We would also expect primary group ties and informal associations to remain largely within one's own racial group. But even at primary group levels, the integrated society would exhibit a much higher interracial intimacy than exists in the non-integrated society.

Such a description of the racially integrated society is, of course, what one finds in today's military establishment. Although the advent of the integrated society in this country is yet to occur, the desegregation of the armed forces has served to bring that day closer.

## REFERENCES AND NOTES

1   The information on which the observations presented in this article are based is of a varied sort. A primary source are Department of Defense statistics and those United States government reports dealing with racial relations in the armed forces: President's Committee on Equality of Treatment and Opportunity in the Armed Forces ("Fahy Committee"), *Freedom to Serve: Equality of Treatment and Opportunity in the Armed Forces*, Washington, D.C.: U.S. Government Printing Office, 1950; U.S. Commission on Civil Rights, "The Negro in the Armed Forces," *Civil Rights '63*, Washington D.C.: U.S. Government Printing Office, 1963, pp. 169–224; President's Committee on Equal Opportunity in the Armed Forces ("Gesell Committee"), "Initial Report: Equality of Treatment and Opportunity for Negro Personnel Stationed within the United States," June 1963 (mimeographed); "Final Report: Military Personnel Stationed Overseas and Membership and Participation in the National Guard," November 1964, (mimeographed). Also, participant observations were made by the author while on active duty in the Army and during field trips to military installations in Germany, Viet Nam, and Korea in the summer of 1965 and in the Dominican Republic in the spring of 1966. Additionally, during the field trip in Germany, sixty-seven formal interviews were conducted with soldiers who made up nearly all of the total Negro enlisted personnel in two Army companies. Another source of data is found in *Project Clear: The Utilization of Negro Manpower in the Army*, Chevy Chase, Md.: Operations Research Office, Johns Hopkins University, April 1955. The ORO surveys queried several thousand servicemen during the Korean War on a variety of items relating to attitudes toward racial integration in the Army. The findings of Project Clear, heretofore classified, have now been made available for professional scrutiny. Some comparable data were

obtained from the section dealing with Negro soldiers in Samuel A. Stouffer *et al.*, *The American Soldier: Adjustment during Army Life*, vol. I, Princeton, N.J.: Princeton University Press, 1949, pp. 486–599.

2   This background of the Negro's role in the American military is derived, in addition to the sources cited in note 1, from Seymour J. Schoenfeld, *The Negro in the Armed Forces*, Washington, D.C.: Associated Publishers, 1945; Paul C. Davis, "The Negro in the Armed Services," *Virginia Quarterly*, vol. 24 (fall 1948), pp. 499–520; Herbert Aptheker, *Essays in the History of the American Negro*, New York: International Publishers, 1945; Arnold M. Rose, "Army Policies toward Negro Soldiers," *Annals of the American Academy of Political and Social Science*, vol. 244 (March 1946), pp. 90–94; Eli Ginzburg, "The Negro Soldier," *The Negro Potential*, New York: Columbia University Press, 1956, pp. 61–91; David G. Mandelbaum, *Soldiers' Groups and Negro Soldiers*, Berkeley, Calif.: University of California Press, 1952; and Benjamin Quarles, *The Negro in the Making of America*, New York: Collier Books, 1964, *passim*. A good account of the early days of military desegregation is Lee Nichols, *Breakthrough on the Color Front*, New York: Random House, Inc., 1954.

Though the last several years have seen little social science research on racial relations in the armed forces, there has recently been a spate of novels dealing with this theme. See, e.g., John Oliver Killens, *And Then We Heard the Thunder*, New York: Alfred A. Knopf, Inc., 1963; James Drought, *Mover*, New York: Avon Books, 1963; Webb Beech, *Article 92*, Greenwich, Conn.: Gold Medal Books, 1964; Gene L. Coon, *The Short End*, New York: Dell Publishing Co., 1964; Hari Rhodes, *A Chosen Few*, New York: Bantam Books, Inc., 1965; and Jack Pearl, *Stockade*, New York: Pocket Books, 1965.

It should be noted that Negroes have not been the only ethnic or racial group to occupy a unique position in the American military. Indians served in separate battalions in the Civil War and were used as scouts in the frontier wars. Filipinos have long been a major source of recruitment for stewards in the Navy. The much decorated 442nd ("Go for Broke") Infantry Regiment of World War II was composed entirely of Japanese-Americans. Also in World War II, a separate battalion of Norwegian-Americans was drawn up for intended service in Scandinavia. The participation of Puerto Ricans in the American military deserves special attention. A recent case of large-scale use of non-American soldiers are the Korean fillers or "Katusas" (from Korean Augmentation to the U.S. Army) who make up roughly one-sixth of the current personnel of the Eighth Army.

3   A particularly insightful contemporary report on Negro soldiers in the Civil War is Thomas Wentworth Higgins, *Army Life in a Black Regiment*, New York: Collier Books, 1962.

4   The 1945 and 1950 Army board reports are commonly referred to by the names of the officers who headed these boards: respectively, Lieutenant General Alvan C. Gillem, Jr., and Lieutenant General S. J. Chamberlin.

5   These evaluations are summarized in *Project Clear*, *op. cit.*, pp. 16–19, 47–105, 582–583.

6   The notoriety of the 24th Infantry Regiment was aggravated by a song—"The Bug-out Boogie"—attributed to it: "When them Chinese mortars begin to thud / The old Deuce-Four begin to bug / When they started falling 'round the CP [command post] tent / Everybody wonder where the high brass went / They were buggin' out / Just movin' on."

7   A lesson in the rewriting of history is gained from the movie *PT-109*, a dramatization of John Kennedy's war exploits. In this film, released in the early 1960's, the Navy is portrayed as racially integrated in World War II.

8   *The Negro Family: The Case for National Action*, the Moynihan Report, Washington, D.C.: U.S. Government Printing Office, 1965, p. 75.

9   Morris Janowitz with Roger Little, *Sociology and the Military Establishment*, New York: Russell Sage Foundation, 1965, pp. 17–49; and Kurt Lang, "Technology and Career Management in the Military Establishment," in Morris Janowitz (ed.), *The New Military: Changing Patterns of Organization*, New York: Russell Sage Foundation, 1964, pp. 39–81.

10  World War II evidence shows that much of the incidence of psychoneurotic breakdown among Negro soldiers, compared to whites, was associated with psychological handicaps originating before entrance into military service. Arnold M. Rose, "Psychoneurotic Breakdown among Negro Soldiers," *Phylon*, vol. 17, no. 1 (1956), pp. 61–73.

11  Stouffer *et al.*, *op. cit.*, vol. II, pp. 242–289; Raymond W. Mack, "The Prestige System of an Air Base: Squadron Rankings and Morale," *American Sociological Review*, vol. 19 (June 1954), pp. 281–287; Morris Janowitz, *The Professional Soldier*, Glencoe, Ill.: The Free Press, 1960, pp. 31–36.

12  There are, as should be expected, differences among Negro soldiers as to their desire to see combat. From data not shown here, interviews with Negro soldiers stationed in Germany revealed reluctance to go to Viet Nam was greatest among those with high-school education or better and northern home residence. This is in direct contrast with the findings reported in *The American Soldier*. In the segregated Army of World War II, northern and more highly educated Negro soldiers were most likely to want to get into combat, an outcome of the onus of inferiority felt to accompany service in support units. Stouffer *et al.*, *op. cit.*, vol. I, pp. 523–524.

13  The emphasis on academic education for officer careers effectively limits most Negro opportunity to the enlisted levels. Lang, *op. cit.*, p. 62.

14  Documentation shows the gap between Negro and white job opportunities has not diminished appreciably, if at all, in the past twenty years. *The Negro Family*, *op. cit.*, pp. 19–21; Thomas F. Pettigrew, *A Profile of the Negro American*, Princeton, N.J.: D. Van Nostrand Company, Inc., 1964, pp. 168–174.

15  Stouffer *et al.*, *op. cit.*, p. 566.

16  What methodological bias exists is that the Korean War question was a stronger description of racial integration than the item used in World War II. Compare "What is your feeling about serving in a platoon containing both whites and colored soldiers, all working and training together, sleeping in the same barracks and eating in the same mess hall?" with "Do you think white and Negro soldiers should be in separate outfits or should they be together in the same outfits?" (respectively, *Project Clear*, *op. cit.*, p. 453, and Stouffer *et al.*, *op. cit.*, p. 568).

17  *Ibid.*, p. 594.

18  The comprehensive scope of military integration is found in the official guidelines set forth under "Equal Opportunity and Treatment of Military Personnel," in *Army Regulation 600-21*, *Air Force Regulations 35-78*, and *Secretary of the Navy Instruction 5350.6*.

19  Compare the Fahy Committee report (1950) with the Gesell Committee reports (1963 and 1964). The Moynihan Report comments, "Service in the United States Armed Forces is the only experience open to the Negro American in which he is truly treated as an equal. . . . If this is a statement of the ideal rather than reality, it is an ideal that is close to realization." *The Negro Family*, *op. cit.*, p. 42.

20  In an interview with the *Overseas Weekly*, a newspaper published in Germany with a large readership among American servicemen. Personal communication with staff members.

21  *Project Clear*, *op. cit.*, p. 388.

22  James Anderson, "Fathers and Sons: An Evaluation of Military Racial Relations in Two Generations," term paper, University of Michigan, December 1965.

23  Stouffer and his associates, for example, report enlisted men as compared to officers, as Negro soldiers to white soldiers, were more prone to have "low spirits," to be less desirous of entering combat, and to be more dissatisfied than perceived by others.

Stouffer *et al., op. cit.*, vol. II, p. 345, vol. I, pp. 392–394, 506, 521, 538.

24  Marvin E. Wolfgang, *Crime and Race*, New York: Institute of Human Relations Press, 1964; and *The Negro Family, op. cit.*, pp. 38–40.

25  *Project Clear, op. cit.*, p. 354.

26  The data reported here are from offices of the Military Police, private communication.

27  A caution to be introduced in assessing these findings is that the Army discharged many personnel of limited potential as determined by aptitude tests in 1957-58. Negroes were disproportionately represented in the released personnel. U.S. Commission on Civil Rights, *op. cit.*, pp. 176–177. Although Negroes are still overrepresented in the lower classification levels, there are probably proportionately fewer in these categories today than in 1950, and this most likely has some effect on the drop in Negro crime in the Army.

28  A social-distance study conducted among Korean college students found the following placement, from near to far: Chinese, Europeans and white Americans, Filipinos, Indians (from India), and Negroes. Man Gap Lee, Seoul National University, personal communication.

29  These barbers were focal points of much of the battalion's gossip and between themselves saw every man in the battalion on the average of at least twice a month.

30  The same data, in tables not shown here, reveal that there is an *inverse* correlation between formal education (as ascertained from battalion personnel records) and likelihood of learning German! This reflects the greater likelihood of Negro soldiers, compared to whites, to learn German while averaging fewer years of formal education.

31  In 1965 a widely seen German television commercial portrayed two American soldiers, one white and the other Negro. Only the Negro soldier spoke German.

32  Although non-violence is the hallmark of the main thrust of the modern civil rights movement, there is, nevertheless, the leitmotiv of a Negro insurrection in the thinking of such Negro figures as James Baldwin, Malcolm X, William Epton, Warren Miller, and LeRoi Jones. Congruent with the idea of armed conflict between the races are the gothic endings—whites and Negro soldiers engaging in a bloodbath—in recent Negro-authored novels. See Killens, *op. cit.*, and Rhodes, *op. cit.*

33  Robert F. Williams, *Negroes with Guns*, New York: Marzani & Munsell, 1962.

34  *The Militant*, Nov. 22, 1965, p. 1.

35  Albert D. Biderman, *March to Calumny*, New York: The Macmillan Company, 1964, p. 60.

36  *The Minority of One*, October 1965, p. 9.

37  "Only One Color," *Newsweek*, Dec. 6, 1965, pp. 42–43; Robin Moore, *The Green Berets*, New York: Avon Books, 1965, *passim*; and Herbert Mitgang, "Looking for a War," *New York Times Magazine*, May 22, 1966, pp. 114–115.

38  A copy of the entire pamphlet is reproduced in the Dominican news magazine *Ahora*, no. 108 (Sept. 18, 1965). Although many whites were unaware of the pamphlet's existence, virtually every Negro soldier the writer talked to in Santo Domingo said he had seen the pamphlet. The effectiveness of the pamphlet on Negro soldiers was minimal, among other reasons, because it claimed Negro equality existed in the Dominican Republic, a statement belied by brief observation of the Dominican social scene.

39  Similarly in an interview with a Negro reporter, the commandant of "constitutionalist rebel" forces in Santo Domingo stated that to his dismay Negro American soldiers fought no differently from whites. Laurence Harvey, "Report from the Dominican Republic," *Realist*, June 1965, p. 18.

# 53  REHABILITATION OF DRUG ADDICTS

### RITA VOLKMAN    DONALD R. CRESSEY

In 1955 Cressey listed five principles for applying Edwin Sutherland's theory of differential association to the rehabilitation of criminals.[1] While this

Reprinted from *The American Journal of Sociology*, vol. 69 (September 1963), pp. 129–143, by permission of the authors and The University of Chicago Press. Copyright © 1963 by the University of Chicago Press.

article is now frequently cited in the sociological literature dealing with group therapy, "therapeutic communities," and "total institutions," we know of no program of rehabilitation that has been explicitly based on the principles. The major point of Cressey's article, which referred to criminals, not addicts, is similar to the following recommendation by the Chief of the United States Narcotics Division: "The community should restore the former addict to his proper place in society and help him avoid associations that would influence him to return to the use of drugs."[2]

Cressey gives five rules (to be reviewed below) for implementing this directive to "restore," "help," and "influence" the addict. These rules, derived from the sociological and social-psychological literature on social movements, crime prevention, group therapy, communications, personality change, and social change, were designed to show that sociology has distinctive, nonpsychiatric, theory that can be used effectively by practitioners seeking to prevent crime and change criminals. Sutherland also had this as a principle objective when he formulated his theory of differential association.[3]

Assuming, as we do, that Cressey's principles are consistent with Sutherland's theory and that his theory, in turn, is consistent with more general sociological theory, a test of the principles would be a test of the more general formulations. Ideally, such a test would involve careful study of the results of a program rationally designed to utilize the principles to change criminals. To our knowledge, such a test has not been made.[4] As a "next best" test, we may study rehabilitation programs that use the principles, however unwittingly. Such a program has been in operation since 1958. Insofar as it is remarkably similar to any program that could have been designed to implement the principles, the results over the years can be viewed as at least a crude test of the principles. Since the principles are interrelated, the parts of any program implementing them must necessarily overlap.

"Synanon," an organization of former drug addicts, was founded in May, 1958, by a member of Alcoholics Anonymous with the assistance of an alcoholic and a drug addict. In December, 1958, Volkman (a non-addict) heard about the two dozen ex-addicts living together in an abandoned store, and she obtained permission of the Synanon Board of Directors[5] to visit the group daily and to live in during the weekends. In July, 1959, she moved into the girls' dormitory of the group's

new, larger quarters and continued to reside at Synanon House until June, 1960. Cressey (also a non-addict) visited the House at Volkman's invitation in the spring of 1960; for one year, beginning in July, 1960, he visited the organization on the average of at least once a week. He deliberately refrained from trying to influence policy or program, and his theory about the effects of group relationships on rehabilitation were unknown to the group. Most of the interview material and statistical data reported below were collected by Volkman during her 1959-60 period of residence and were used in the thesis for her Master's degree, prepared under the direction of C. Wayne Gordon.[6] As both a full-fledged member of Synanon and as a participant observer, Volkman attended about three hundred group sessions, a few of which were recorded. She was accorded the same work responsibilities, rights, and privileges as any other member, and she was considered one of Synanon's first "graduates."

### THE SUBJECTS

Background data were available on only the first fifty-two persons entering Synanon after July, 1958. These records were prepared by a resident who in July, 1959, took it upon himself to interview and compile the information. We have no way of determining whether these fifty-two persons are representative of all addicts. However, we believe they are similar to the 215 persons who have resided at Synanon for at least one month.

Age and sex distributions are shown in Table 1: 44 percent of the fifty-two were Protestant, 35 percent Catholic, 8 percent Jewish.[7] Racially, 27 percent were Negro, and there were no Orientals; 19 percent of the Caucasians were of Mexican origin and 13 percent were of Italian origin. Educational attainment is shown in Table 2. Although the data on early family life are poor because the resident simply asked "What was your family like?" it may be noted that only five of the fifty-two indicated satisfaction with the home. Words and phrases such as "tension," "arguing," "bickering," "violence," "lack of warmth," "went back

**TABLE 1** *Age and sex\**

| Age, years | Males No. | % | Females No. | % | Total No. | % |
|---|---|---|---|---|---|---|
| 18–20 | 0 | 0 | 1 | 7 | 1 | 2 |
| 21–30 | 17 | 44 | 11 | 79 | 28 | 54 |
| 31–40 | 18 | 48 | 2 | 14 | 20 | 38 |
| 41–50 | 1 | 3 | 0 | 0 | 1 | 2 |
| 51–60 | 2 | 5 | 0 | 0 | 2 | 4 |
| Total | 38 | 100 | 14 | 100 | 52 | 100 |

*\*Median ages: males, 31.0; females, 27.5.*

and forth," and "nagged" were common.[8]

The sporadic and tenuous occupational ties held by the group are indicated in Table 3. This table supports the notion that addicts cannot maintain steady jobs because their addiction interferes with the work routine; it suggests also that these members had few lasting peer group contacts or ties, at least so far as work associations go. In view of their poor employment records, it might be asked how the addicts supported their addictions, which cost from $30 to $50 a day and sometimes ran to $100 a day. Only four of the men reported that they obtained their incomes by legitimate work alone; thirty (79 percent) were engaged in illegitimate activities, with theft, burglary, armed robbery, shoplifting, and pimping leading the list. One man and seven women were supplied with either drugs or money by their mates or families, and five of these females supplemented this source by prostitution or other illegitimate work. Five of the fourteen women had no income except that from illegitimate activities, and none of the women supported themselves by legitimate work only.

**TABLE 2** *Educational attainment*

| | No. | Percent |
|---|---|---|
| Part grade school | 1 | 2 |
| Completed grade school | 3 | 6 |
| Part high school | 24 | 46 |
| Completed high school | 11 | 21 |
| Part college | 13 | 25 |
| Completed college | 0 | 0 |
| Total | 52 | 100 |

**TABLE 3** *Length and continuity of employment*

| No. of years on one job | Unsteady (discontinuous or sporadic) | Steady (continuous) | Total |
|---|---|---|---|
| Under 1 | 36\* | 4 | 40 |
| 2–3 | 3 | 2 | 5 |
| 4–5 | 1 | 3 | 4 |
| 6 or over | 2 | 1 | 3 |
| Total | 42 | 10 | 52 |

*\*Of this category 67 percent defined their work as "for short periods only."*

Institutional histories and military service histories are consistent with the work and educational histories, indicating that the fifty-two members were not somehow inadvertently selected as "easy" rehabilitation cases. The fifty-two had been in and out of prisons, jails, and hospitals all over the United States. Table 4 shows that ten men and one woman had been confined seven or more times; the mean number of confinements for males was 5.5 and for females 3.9. The table seems to indicate that whatever value confinement in institutions might have had for this group, it clearly did not prevent further confinements.

In sum, the pre-Synanon experiences of the fifty-two residents seems to indicate nonidentification with pro-legal activities and norms. Neither the home, the armed services, the occupational world, schools, prisons, nor hospitals served as links with the larger and more socially acceptable community. This, then, is the kind of "raw material" with which Synanon has been working.[9]

**TABLE 4** *Confinements in institutions*

| No. of confinements | Male | Female | Total\* |
|---|---|---|---|
| 1–3 | 9 | 6 | 15 |
| 4–6 | 12 | 7 | 19 |
| 7–9 | 8 | 0 | 8 |
| 10–12 | 8 | 1 | 1 |
| 13–15 | 2 | 0 | 2 |
| Total | 166 | 59 | 225 |

*\*Three males indicated "numerous arrests," and four supplied no information. These seven were not included in the tally.*

## THE PROGRAM

**ADMISSION**    Not every addict who knocks on the door of Synanon is given admission. Nevertheless, the only admission criterion we have been able to find is *expressed willingness* to submit one's self to a group that hates drug addiction. Use of this criterion has unwittingly implemented one of Cressey's principles:

> If criminals are to be changed, they must be assimilated into groups which emphasize values conducive to law-abiding behavior and, concurrently, alienated from groups emphasizing values conducive to criminality. Since our experience has been that the majority of criminals experience great difficulty in securing intimate contacts in ordinary groups, special groups whose major common goal is the reformation of criminals must be created.

This process of assimilation and alienation begins the moment an addict arrives at Synanon, and it continues throughout his stay. The following are two leaders' comments on admission interviews; they are consistent with our own observations of about twenty such interviews.

When a new guy comes in we want to find out whether a person has one inkling of seriousness. Everybody who comes here is what we call a psychopathic liar. We don't take them all, either. We work off the top spontaneously, in terms of feeling. We use a sort of intuitive faculty. You know he's lying, but you figure, "Well, maybe if you get a halfway positive feeling that he'll stay. . . ." We ask him things like "What do you want from us?" "Don't you think you're an idiot or insane?" "Doesn't it sound insane for you to be running around the alleys stealing money from others so's you can go and stick something up your arm?" "Does this sound sane to you?" "Have you got family and friends outside?" We might tell him to go do his business now and come back when he's ready to do business with us. We tell him, "We don't need you." "You need *us*." And if we figure he's only halfway with us, we'll chop off his hair.

It's all in the *attitude*. It's got to be positive. We don't want their money. But we may just tell him to bring back some dough next week. If he pleads and begs—the money's not important. If he shows he really cares. If his attitude is good. It's all in the attitude.

Mostly, if people don't have a family outside, with no business to take care of, they're ready to stay. They ain't going to have much time to think about themselves otherwise. . . . Now, when he's got problems, when he's got things outside, if he's got mickey mouse objections, like when you ask him "How do you feel about staying here for a year?" and he's got to bargain with you, like he needs to stay with his wife or his sick mother—then we tell him to get lost. If he can't listen to a few harsh words thrown at him, he's not ready. Sometimes we yell at him, "You're a goddamned liar!" If he's serious he'll take it. He'll do anything if he's serious.

But each guy's different. If he sounds sincere, we're not so hard. If he's sick of running the rat race out there, or afraid of going to the penitentiary, he's ready to do anything. Then we let him right in. . . .

This admission process seems to have two principal functions. First, it forces the newcomer to admit, at least on a verbal level, that he is willing to try to conform to the norms of the group, whose members will not tolerate any liking for drugs or drug addicts. From the minute he enters the door, his expressed desire to join the group is tested by giving him difficult orders—to have his hair cut off, to give up all his money, to sever all family ties, to come back in ten days or even thirty days. He is given expert help and explicit but simple criteria for separating the "good guys" from the "bad guys"—the latter shoot dope. Second, the admission process weeds out men and women who simply want to lie down for a few days to rest, to obtain free room and board, or to stay out of the hands of the police. In the terms used by Lindesmith, and also in the terms used at Synanon, the person must want to give up drug *addiction*, not just the drug *habit*.[10] This means that he must at least *say* that he wants to quit using drugs once and for all, in order to realize his potentials as an adult; he must not indicate that he merely wants a convenient place in which to go through withdrawal distress so that he can be rid of his habit for a short time because he has lost his connection, or for some other reason. He must be willing to give up all ambitions, desires, and social interactions that might prevent the group from assimilating him completely.

If he says he just wants to kick, he's no good. Out with him. Now we know nine out of ten lie, but we don't care. We'd rather have him make an attempt and *lie* and then get him in there for thirty days or so—then he might stick. It takes months to decide to stay.

Most fish [newcomers] don't take us seriously. We know what they want, out in front. A dope fiend wants dope, nothing else. All the rest is garbage. We've even taken that ugly thing called money. This shows that they're serious. Now this guy today was sincere. We told him we didn't want money. We could see he would at least give the place a try. We have to find out if he's sincere. Is he willing to have us cut off his curly locks? I imagine cutting his hair off makes him take us seriously. . . .

Although it is impossible to say whether Synanon's selective admission process inadvertently admits those addicts who are most amenable to change, no addict has been refused admission on the ground that his case is "hopeless" or "difficult" or that he is "unreachable." On the contrary, before coming to Synanon, twenty-nine of the fifty-two addicts had been on drugs for at least ten years. Two of these were addicted for over forty years, and had been in and out of institutions during that period. The average length of time on drugs for the fifty-two was eleven years, and 56 percent reported less than one month as the longest period of time voluntarily free of drugs after addiction and prior to Synanon.

**INDOCTRINATION**    In the admission process, and throughout his residence, the addict discovers over and over again that the group to which he is submitting is antidrug, anticrime, and antialcohol. At least a dozen times a day he hears someone tell him that he can remain at Synanon only as long as he "stays clean," that is, stays away from crime, alcohol, and drugs. This emphasis is an unwitting implementation of Cressey's second principle:

*The more relevant the common purpose of the group to the reformation of criminals, the greater will be its influence on the criminal members' attitudes and values. Just as a labor union exerts strong influence over its members' attitudes toward management but less influence on their attitudes toward say, Negroes, so a group organized for recreation or welfare purposes will have less success in influencing criminalistic attitudes and values than will one whose explicit purpose is to change criminals.*

Indoctrination makes clear the notion that Synanon exists in order to keep addicts off drugs, not for purposes of recreation, vocational education, etc. Within a week after admission, each newcomer participates in an indoctrination session by a spontaneous group made up of four or five older members. Ordinarily, at least one member of the Board of Directors is present, and he acts as leader. The following are excerpts from one such session with a woman addict. The rules indicate the extreme extent to which it is necessary for the individual to subvert his personal desires and ambitions to the antidrug, anticrime group.

Remember, we told you not to go outside by yourself. Whenever anybody leaves this building they have to check in and out at the desk. For a while, stay in the living room. Don't take showers alone or even go to the bathroom alone, see. While you're kicking, somebody will be with you all the time. And stay away from newcomers. You got nothing to talk to them about, except street talk, and before you know it you'll be splitting [leaving] to take a fix together. Stay out of the streets, mentally and physically, or get lost now.

No phone calls or letters for a while—if you get one, you'll read it in front of us. We'll be monitoring all your phone calls for a while. You see, you got no ties, no business out there any more. You don't need them. You never could handle them before, so don't start thinking you can do it now. All you knew how to do was shoot dope and go to prison.

You could never take care of your daughter before. You didn't know how to be a mother. It's garbage. All a dope fiend knows how to do is shoot dope. Forget it.

There are two obvious illustrations of the anti-drug and anticrime nature of the group's subculture. First, there is a strong taboo against what is called "street talk." Discussion of how it feels to take a fix, who one's connection was, where one took his shot, the crimes one has committed, or who one associated with is severely censured. One's best friend and confidant at Synanon might well be the person that administers a tongue lashing for street talk, and the person who calls your undesirable behavior to the attention of the entire group during a general meeting.

Second, a member must never, in any circumstances, identify with the "code of the streets," which says that a criminal is supposed to keep quiet about the criminal activities of his peers. Even calling an ordinary citizen "square" is likely to stimulate a spontaneous lecture, in heated and colorful terms, on the notion that the people who are *really* square are those that go around as bums sticking needles in their arms. A person who, as a criminal, learned to hate stool pigeons and finks with a passion must now turn even his closest friend over to the authorities, the older members of Synanon, if the friend shows any signs of non-conformity. If he should find that a member is considering "sneaking off to a fix somewhere," has kept pills, drugs, or an "outfit" with him when he joined the organization, or even has violated rules such as that prohibiting walking alone on the beach, he must by Synanon's code relinquish his emotional ties with the violator and expose the matter to another member or even to the total

membership at a general meeting. If he does not do so, more pressure is put upon him than upon the violator, for he is expected to have "known better." Thus, for perhaps the first time in his life he will be censured for *not* "squealing" rather than for "squealing."[11] He must identify with the law and not with the criminal intent or act.

The sanctions enforcing this norm are severe, for its violation threatens the very existence of the group. "Guilt by association" is the rule. In several instances, during a general meeting the entire group spontaneously voted to "throw out" both a member who had used drugs and a member who had known of this use but had not informed the group. Banishment from the group is considered the worst possible punishment, for it is stressed over and over again that life in the streets "in your condition" can only mean imprisonment or death.

That the group's purpose is keeping addicts off drugs is given emphasis in formal and informal sessions—called "haircuts" or "pull ups"—as well as in spontaneous denunciations, and in denunciations at general meetings. The "synanon," discussed below, also serves this purpose. A "haircut" is a deliberately contrived device for minimizing the importance of the individual and maximizing the importance of the group, and for defining the group's basic purpose—keeping addicts off drugs and crime. The following is the response of a leader to the questions, "What's a haircut? What's its purpose?"

When you are pointing out what a guy is doing. We do this through mechanisms of exaggeration. We blow up an incident so he can really get a look at it. The Coordinators [a coordinator resembles an officer of the day] and the Board members and sometimes an old timer may sit in on it. We do this when we see a person's attitude becoming negative in some area.

For a *real* haircut, I'll give you myself. I was in a tender trap. My girl split. She called me on the job three days in a row. I made a date with her. We kept the date and I stayed out all night with her. Now, she was loaded [using drugs]. I neglected—or I refused—to call the house. By doing this I ranked everybody. You know doing something like that was no good. They were all concerned. They sent three or four autos looking for me because I didn't come back from work. You see, I was in Stage II.

X found me and he made me feel real lousy, because I knew he worked and was concerned. Here he was out looking for me and he had to get up in the morning.

Well, I called the house the next morning and came back. I got called in for a haircut.

I sat down with three Board members in the office. They stopped everything to give the haircut. That impressed me. Both Y and Z, they pointed out my absurd and ridiculous behavior by saying things like this—though I did not get loaded, I associated with a broad I was emotionally involved with who was using junk. I jeopardized my *own* existence by doing this. So they told me, "Well, you fool, you might as well have shot dope by associating with a using addict." I was given an ultimatum. If I called her again or got in touch with her I would be thrown out.

("Why?")

Because continued correspondence with a using dope fiend is a crime against *me*—it hurts *me*. It was also pointed out how rank I was to people who are concerned with me. I didn't seem to care about people who were trying to help me. I'm inconsiderate to folks who've wiped my nose, fed me, clothed me. I'm like a child, I guess. I bite the hand that feeds me.

To top that off, I had to call a general meeting and I told everybody in the building what a jerk I was and I was sorry for acting like a little punk. I just sort of tore myself down. Told everyone what a phony I had been. And then the ridiculing questions began. Everybody started in. Like, "Where do you get off doing that to us?" That kind of stuff. When I was getting the treatment they asked me what I'd do—whether I would continue the relationship, whether I'd cut it off, or if I really wanted to stay at Synanon and do something about myself and my problem. But I made the decision before I even went in that I'd stay and cut the broad loose. I had enough time under my belt to know enough to make that decision before I even came back to the house. . . .

GROUP COHESION    The daily program at Synanon is consistent with Cressey's third principle, and appears to be an unwitting attempt to implement that principle:

*The more cohesive the group, the greater the members' readiness to influence others and the more relevant the problem of conformity to group norms. The criminals who are to be reformed and the persons expected to effect the change must, then, have a strong sense of belonging to one group: between them there must be a genuine "we" feeling. The reformers, consequently should not be identifiable as correctional workers, probation or parole officers, or social workers.*

Cohesion is maximized by a "family" analogy and by the fact that all but some "third-stage" members live and work together. The daily program has been deliberately designed to throw members into continuous mutual activity. In addition to the free, unrestricted interaction in small groups called "synanons," the members meet as a group at least twice each day. After breakfast, someone is called upon to read the "Synanon Philosophy," which is a kind of declaration of principles, the day's work schedule is discussed, bits of gossip are publicly shared, the group or individual members are spontaneously praised or scolded by older members. Following a morning of work activities, members meet in the dining room after lunch to discuss some concept or quotation that has been written on a blackboard. Stress is on participation and expression; quotations are selected by Board members to provoke controversy and examination of the meaning, or lack of meaning, or words. Discussion sometimes continues informally during the afternoon work period and in "synanons," which are held after dinner (see below). In addition, lectures and classes, conducted by any member or outside speaker who will take on the responsibility, are held several times a week for all members who feel a need for them. Topics have included "semantics," "group dynamics," "meaning of truth," and "Oedipus complex."

There are weekend recreational activities, and holidays, wedding anniversaries, and birthdays are celebrated. Each member is urged: "Be yourself," "Speak the truth," "Be honest," and this kind of action in an atmosphere that is informal and open quickly gives participants a strong sense of "belonging." Since many of the members have been homeless drifters, it is not surprising to hear frequent repetition of some comment to the effect that "This is the first home I ever had."

Also of direct relevance to the third principle is the *voluntary* character of Synanon. Any member can walk out at any time; at night the doors are locked against persons who might want to enter, but not against persons who might want to leave. Many do leave.

Holding addicts in the house once they have been allowed to enter is a strong appeal to ideas such as "We have all been in the shape you are now in," or "Mike was on heroin for twenty years and *he's* off." It is significant, in this connection, that addicts who "kick" (go through withdrawal distress) at Synanon universally report that the sickness is not as severe as it is in involuntary organizations, such as jails and mental hospitals. One important variable here, we believe, is the practice of not giving "kicking dope fiends" special quarters. A newcomer kicks on a davenport in the center of the large living room, not in a special isolation room or quarantine room. Life goes on around him. Although a member will be assigned to watch him, he soon learns that his sickness is not important to men and women who have themselves kicked the habit. In the living room, one or two couples might be dancing, five or six people may be arguing, a man may be practicing the guitar, and a girl may be ironing. The kicking addict learns his lesson: These others have made it. This subtle device is supplemented by explicit comments from various members as they walk by or as they drop in to chat with him. We have heard the following comments, and many similar ones, made to new addicts lying sick from withdrawal. It should be noted that none of the comments could reasonably have been made by a rehabilitation official or a professional therapist.

"It's OK boy. We've all been through it before."

"For once you're with people like us. You've got everything to gain here and nothing to lose."

"You think you're tough. Listen, we've got guys in here who could run circles around you, so quit your bull ——."

"You're one of us now, so keep your eyes open, your mouth shut and try to listen for a while. Maybe you'll learn a few things."

"Hang tough, baby. We won't let you die."

STATUS ASCRIPTION    Cressey's fourth principle is:

*Both reformers and those to be reformed must achieve status within the group by exhibition of "pro-reform" or anti-criminal values and behavior patterns. As a novitiate . . . he is a therapeutic parasite and not actually a member until he accepts the group's own system for assigning status.*

This is the crucial point in Cressey's formula, and it is on this point that Synanon seems most effective. The house has an explicit program for distributing status symbols to members in return for staying off the drug and, later, for actually displaying antidrug attitudes. The resident, no longer restricted to the status of "inmate" or "patient" as in a prison or hospital, can achieve any staff position in the status hierarchy.

The Synanon experience is organized into a career of roles that represent stages of graded competence, at whose end are roles that might later be used in the broader community. Figure 1 shows the status system in terms of occupational roles, each box signifying a stratum. Such cliques as exist at Synanon tend to be among persons of the same stratum. Significantly, obtaining jobs of increased

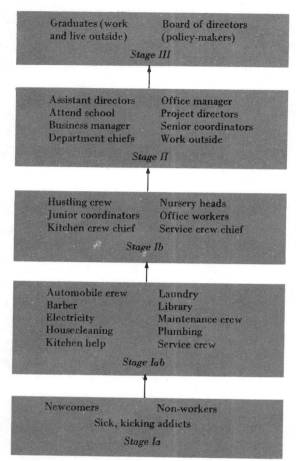

**FIGURE 1** *Division of labor and stratification system, Synanon, June, 1962.*

responsibility and status is almost completely dependent upon one's attitudes toward crime and the use of drugs. To obtain a job such as Senior Coordinator, for example, the member must have demonstrated that he can remain free of drugs, crime, and alcohol for at least three to six months. Equally important, he must show that he can function without drugs in situations where he might have used drugs before he came to Synanon. Since he is believed to have avoided positions of responsibility by taking drugs, he must gradually take on positions of responsibility without the use of drugs. Thus, he cannot go up the status ladder unless his "attitudes" are right, no matter what degree of skill he might have as a workman. Evaluation is rather casual, but it is evaluation nevertheless—he will not be given a decent job in the organization unless he relinquishes the role of the "con artist" and answers questions honestly, expresses emotions freely, co-operates in group activities, and demonstrates leadership. In a letter to a public official in May, 1960, the founder explained the system as follows:

> Continued residence [at Synanon], which we feel to be necessary to work out the problem of interpersonal relationships which underlie the addiction symptom is based on adherence by the individual to standards of behavior, thinking, and feeling acceptable to our culture. There is much work to be done here, as we have no paid help, and each person must assume his share of the burden. Increased levels of responsibility are sought and the experience of self-satisfaction comes with seeking and assuming these higher levels and seems to be an extremely important part of emotional growth.[12]

An analogy with a family and the development of a child also is used. Officially, every member is expected to go through three "stages of growth," indicated by Roman numerals in Figure 1. Stage I has two phases, "infancy" and "adolescence." In the "infancy" phase (Ia) the member behaves like an infant and is treated as one; as he kicks the habit "cold turkey" (without the aid of drugs) in the living room, he is dependent on the others, and he is supervised and watched at all times. When he is physically and mentally able, he performs menial tasks such as dishwashing and sweeping in a kind of "preadolescent" stage (Iab) and then takes on more responsible positions (Ib). In this "adolescence" phase he takes on responsibility for maintenance work, participates actively in group meetings, demonstrates a concern for "emotional growth," mingles with newcomers and visitors, and accepts responsibilities for dealing with them. In work activities, for example, he might drive the group's delivery truck alone, watch over a sick addict, supervise the dishwashing or cleanup crews, or meet strangers at the door.

Stage II is called the "young adult stage." Here, the member is in a position to choose between making Synanon a "career," attending school, or going to work at least part time. If he works for Synanon, his position is complex and involves enforcing policy over a wide range of members. In Stage III, "adult," he moves up to a policy-making position in the Board of Directors or moves out of Synanon but returns with his friends and family for occasional visits. He can apparently resist the urge to resort to drugs in times of crisis without the direct help of Synanon members. One man described this stage by saying, "They go out, get jobs, lose jobs, get married, get divorced, get married again, just like everyone else." However, the group does maintain a degree of control. Graduates are never supposed to cut off their ties with their Synanon "family," and they are expected to return frequently to display themselves as "a dope fiend made good."

From Table 5 it is apparent that seniority in the form of length of residence (equivalent to the number of "clean" days) is an important determinant of status. As time of residence increases, responsibilities to the group, in the forms of work and leadership, tend to increase. In June, 1962,

**TABLE 5**   *Length of residence and "stage" of members, June 1962*

| Length of residence, months | Stages | | | No. | Percent |
|---|---|---|---|---|---|
| | I | II | III | | |
| 1–3 | 20 | 0 | 0 | 20 | 19 |
| 4–6 | 15 | 0 | 0 | 15 | 14 |
| 7–9 | 7 | 3 | 0 | 10 | 9 |
| 10–12 | 2 | 0 | 0 | 2 | 2 |
| 13–15 | 3 | 4 | 0 | 7 | 7 |
| 16–18 | 3 | 0 | 2 | 5 | 5 |
| 19–21 | 4 | 1 | 0 | 5 | 5 |
| 22–24 | 0 | 4 | 1 | 5 | 5 |
| 25 and over | 0 | 12 | 24 | 36 | 34 |
| Total | 54 | 24 | 27 | 105 | 100 |

twenty-seven of the 105 members of Synanon were in Stage III. It should be noted that while stage is associated with length of residence, advancement through the stages is not automatic. The longer one lives at Synanon, the "cleaner" he is, the more diffuse the roles he performs, and the higher his status.

It is also important to note that high status does not depend entirely upon one's conduct within the house. Before he graduates to Stage III a member must in some way be accorded an increase in status by the legitimate outside community. This is further insurance that status will be conferred for activities that are antidrug in character. In early 1960, the members began to take an active part in legitimate community activities, mostly in the form of lectures and discussion groups. Since Synanon's inception, more than 350 service groups, church groups, political groups, school and college classes, etc., have been addressed by speakers from Synanon. Such speeches and discussions gain community support for the organization, but they further function to give members a feeling of being important enough to be honored by an invitation to speak before community groups. Similarly, members are proud of those individuals who have "made good" in the outside community by becoming board members of the P.T.A., Sunday-school teachers, college students, and members of civic and service organizations. Over thirty-five Synanon members are now working full or part-time in the community, holding a wide range of unskilled (janitor, parking attendant), skilled (truck driver, carpenter, electrician), white-collar (secretary, photographer), and executive (purchasing agent) posts.

Further, the legitimate status of the *group* has increasingly risen during the last two years. Since the summer of 1960, an average of 100-150 guests have attended open-house meetings, and the guests have included distinguished persons from all walks of legitimate life. Well-known psychiatrists, correctional workers, businessmen, newspapermen, and politicians have publicly praised the work of the group. There have been requests for Synanon houses and for Synanon groups from several communities, and Synanon projects are now being conducted at Terminal Island Federal Prison and the Nevada State Prison. Recently, the group has been featured in films, on television and radio shows, and in national magazines. At least two books and a movie are being written about it. Over five hundred citizens have formed an organization called "Sponsors of Synanon." Even strong attacks from some members of the local community and complicated legal battles about zoning ordinances have served principally to unite the group and maximize the *espirit de corps.*

**THE "SYNANON"** Synanon got its name from an addict who was trying to say "seminar." The term "Synanon" is used to refer to the entire organization, but when it is spelled with a lower-case *s* it refers only to the meetings occurring in the evenings among small groups of six to ten members. Each evening, all members are assigned to such groups, and membership in the groups is rotated so that one does not regularly interact with the same six or ten persons. The announced aim of these meetings is to "trigger feelings" and to allow what some members refer to as "a catharsis." The sessions are not "group therapy" in the usual sense, for no trained therapist is present. Moreover, the emphasis is on enforcing anticriminal and antidrug norms, as well as upon emotional adjustment.[13] These sessions, like the entire program, constitute a system for implementing Cressey's fifth principle, although they were not designed to do so.

*The most effective mechanism for exerting group pressure on members will be found in groups so organized that criminals are induced to join with noncriminals for the purpose of changing other criminals. A group in which criminal A joins with some noncriminals to change criminal B is probably most effective in changing criminal A, not B; in order to change criminal B, criminal A must necessarily share the values of the anticriminal members.*

In the house, the behavior of all members is visible to all others. What a member is seen to do at the breakfast table, for example, might well be scrutinized and discussed at his synanon that evening. The synanon sessions differ from everyday honesty by virtue of the fact that in these discussions one is expected to *insist on* the truth as well as to tell the truth. Any weapon, such as ridicule, cross-examination, or hostile attack, is both permissible and expected. The sessions seem to provide an atmosphere of truth-seeking that is reflected in the rest of the social life within the household so that a simple question like "How are you?" is likely to be answered by a five-minute discourse in which the respondent searches for the truth. The following discussion is from a tape recording of a synanon session held in June, 1961. It should be noted that an "innocent" question about appearance, asked by an older member who has become a non-criminal and a non-addict, led to an opportunity to emphasize the importance of loyalty to the antidrug, anticrime group.

"What are you doing about losing weight?"

"Why? Is that your business?"

"I asked you a question."

"I don't intend to answer it. It's not your business."

"Why do you want to lose weight?"

"I don't intend to answer it."

"Why?"

"Because it's an irrelevant and meaningless question. You know I had a baby only three weeks ago, and you've been attacking me about my weight. It's none of your business."

"Why did you call your doctor?"

"Why? Because I'm on a diet."

"What did he prescribe for you?"

"I don't know. I didn't ask him."

"What did you ask for?"

"I didn't. I don't know what he gave me."

"Come on now. What kind of pills are they?"

"I don't know. I'm not a chemist. Look the doctor knows I'm an addict. He knows I live at Synanon. He knows a whole lot about me."

"Yeah, well, I heard you also talking to him on the phone, and you sounded just like any other addict trying to cop a doctor out of pills."

"You're a goddamned liar!"

"Yeah, well X was sitting right there. Look, does the doctor know and does the Board know?"

"I spoke to Y [Board member]. It's all been verified."

"What did Y say?"

"I was talking to. . ."

"What did Y say?"

"Well, will you wait just a minute?"

"What did Y say?"

"Well, let her talk."

"I don't want to hear no stories."

"I'm not telling stories."

"What did Y say?"

"That it was harmless. The doctor said he'd give me nothing that would affect me. There's nothing in it. He knows it all. I told Y."

"Oh, you're all like a pack of wolves. You don't need to yell and scream at her."

"Look, I heard her on the phone and the way she talked she was trying to manipulate the doctor."

"Do you resent the fact that she's still acting like a dope fiend and she still sounds like she's conning the doctor out of something? She's a dope fiend. Maybe she can't talk to a doctor any differently."

"Look, I called the doctor today. He said I should call him if I need him. He gave me vitamins and lots of other things."

"Now wait a minute. You called to find out if you could get some more pills."

"Besides, it's the attitude they heard over the phone. That's the main thing."

"Yeah, well they probably projected it onto me."

"Then how come you don't like anyone listening to your phone calls?"

"Are you feeling guilty?"

"Who said?"

"Me. That's who. You even got sore when you found out X and me heard you on the phone, didn't you? You didn't like that at all, did you?"

"Is that so?"

(*Silence*)

"I don't think her old man wants her back."

"Well, who would? An old fat slob like that."

"Sure, that's probably why she's thinking of leaving all the time and ordering pills."

"Sure."

(*Silence*)

"My appearance is none of your business."

"Everything here is our business."

"Look, when a woman has a baby you can't understand she can't go back to normal weight in a day."

"Now *you* look. We're really not interested in your weight problem now. Not really. We just want to know why you've got to have pills to solve the problem. We're going to talk about that if we want to. That's what we're here for."

"Look, something's bugging you. We all know that. I even noticed it in your attitude toward me."

"Yeah, I don't care about those pills. I want to know how you're feeling. What's behind all this? Something's wrong. What is it?"

(*Silence*)

"Have you asked your old man if you could come home yet?"

(*Softly*) "Yes."

"What did he say?"

(*Softly*) "He asked me how I felt. Wanted to know why I felt I was ready to come home. . . ."

(*Silence*)

(*Softly*) "I did it out of anger. I wasn't very happy. (*Pause*) A day before I tried [telephoning him] and he wasn't there. (*Pause*) Just this funny feeling about my husband being there and me here. My other kid's there and this one's here. (*Pause*) A mixed-up family."

"Why do you want to stay then? Do you want to be here?"

"No. I don't want to be here. That's exactly why I'm staying. I need to stay till I'm ready."

"Look, you've got to cut them loose for a while. You may not be ready for the rest of your life. You may not ever be able to be with those people."

(*Tears*)

"I know. . . ."

After the synanon sessions, the house is always noisy and lively. We have seen members sulk, cry, shout, and threaten to leave the group, as a result of conversation in the synanon. The following comments, every one of which represents the expression of a pro-reform attitude by the speaker, were heard after one session. It is our hypothesis that such expressions are the important ones, for they indicate that the speaker has become a reformer and, thus, is reinforcing his own pro-reform attitudes every time he tries to comfort or reform another.

> "Were they hard on you?"
> "I really let him have it tonight."
> "I couldn't get to her. She's so damned blocked she couldn't even hear what I was trying to tell her."
> "Hang tough, man; it gets easier."
> "One of these days he'll drop those defenses of his and start getting honest."
> "Don't leave. We all love you and want you to get well."

At Synanon, disassociating with former friends, avoiding street talk, and becoming disloyal to criminals are emphasized at the same time that loyalty to non-criminals, telling the truth to authority figures, and legitimate work are stressed. We have no direct evidence that haircuts, synanons, and both formal and spontaneous denunciations of street talk and the code of the streets have important rehabilitative effects on the actor, as well as (or, perhaps even "rather than") on the victim. It seems rather apparent, however, that an individual's own behavior must be dramatically influenced when he acts in the role of a moral policeman and "takes apart" another member. It is significant that older members of Synanon like to point out that the "real Synanon" began on "the night of the big cop out" (confession). In its earliest days, Synanon had neither the group cohesiveness nor the degree of control it now has. Some participants remained as addicts while proclaiming their loyalty to the principle of antiaddiction, and other participants knew of this condition. One evening in a general meeting a man spontaneously stood up and confessed ("copped out") that he had sneaked out for a shot. One by one, with no prompting, the others present rose to confess either their own violations or their knowledge of the violations of their friends. From that moment, the Board of Directors believe, the organization became a truly antidrug group; there has been no problem of drug use since.

## THE RESULTS

Of the fifty-two residents described earlier, four are "graduates" of Synanon, are living in the community, and are not using alcohol or drugs. Twenty-three (44.2 percent) are still in residence and are not using alcohol or drugs. Two of these are on the Board of Directors and eleven are working part or full time. The remaining twenty-five left Synanon against the advice of the Board and the older members.

Information regarding the longest period of voluntary abstinence from drugs after the onset of addiction but prior to entering Synanon was obtained on forty-eight of the fifty-two persons. Eleven reported that they were "never" clean, six said they were continuously clean for less than one week, ten were continuously clean for less than one month. Thirty-nine (81 percent) said they had been continuously clean for less than six months, and only two had been clean for as long as a one-year period. Twenty-seven (52 percent) of the fifty-two residents have now abstained for at least six months; twelve of these have been clean for at least two years and two have been off drugs continually for over three years.

Between May, 1958 (when Synanon started), and May, 1961, 263 persons were admitted or readmitted to Synanon. Of these, 190 (72 percent) left Synanon against the advice of the Board of Directors and the older members. Significantly, 59 percent of all dropouts occurred within the first month of residence, 90 percent within the first three months. Synanon is not adverse to giving a person a second chance, or even a third or fourth chance: of the 190 persons dropping out, eighty-three (44 percent) were persons who had been readmitted. The dropout behavior of persons who were readmitted was, in general, similar to first admissions; 64 percent of their dropouts occurred within the first month, 93 percent within the first three months after readmission.

Of all the Synanon enrolees up to August, 1962, 108 out of 372 (29 percent) are known to be off drugs. More significantly, of the 215 persons who have remained at Synanon for at least one month, 103 (48 percent) are still off drugs; of the 143 who have remained for at least three months, 95 (66 percent) are still non-users; of the 87 who have remained at least seven months, 75 (86 percent) are non-users. These statistics seem to us to be most relevant, for they indicate that once an addict actually becomes a member of the anti-drug community (as indicated by three to six months of participation), the probability that he will leave and revert to the use of drugs is low.

## CONCLUSIONS

Synanon's leaders do not claim to "cure" drug addicts. They are prone to measure success by pointing to the fact that the organization now includes the membership of forty-five persons who were heroin addicts for at least ten years. Two of these were addicted for more than thirty years and spent those thirty years going in and out of prisons, jails, the U.S. Public Service Hospital, and similar institutions. The leaders have rather inadvertently used a theory of rehabilitation that implies that it is as ridiculous to try to "cure" a man of drug addiction as it is to try to "cure" him of sexual intercourse. A man can be helped to stay away from drugs, however, and this seems to be the contribution Synanon is making. In this regard, its "success" rate is higher than that of those institutions officially designated by society as places for the confinement and "reform" of drug addicts. Such a comparison is not fair, however, both because it is not known whether the subjects in Synanon are comparable to those confined in institutions, and because many official institutions do not concentrate on trying to keep addicts off drugs, being content to withdraw the drug, build

up the addicts physically, strengthen vocational skills, and eliminate gaps in educational backgrounds.[14]

We cannot be certain that it is the group relationships at Synanon, rather than something else, that is keeping addicts away from crime and drugs. However, both the times at which dropouts occur and the increasing antidrug attitudes displayed with increasing length of residence tend to substantiate Sutherland's theory of differential association and Cressey's notion that modifying social relationships is an effective supplement to the clinical handling of convicted criminals. Drug addiction is, in fact, a severe test of Sutherland's sociological theory and Cressey's sociological principles, for addicts have the double problem of criminality and the drug habit. The statistics on dropouts suggest that the group relations method of rehabilitation does not begin to have its effects until newcomers are truly integrated into the antidrug, anticrime group that is Synanon.

## REFERENCES AND NOTES

1   Donald R. Cressey, "Changing Criminals: The Application of the Theory of Differential Association," *American Journal of Sociology*, vol. 61 (September 1955), pp. 116–120; see also Cressey, "Contradictory Theories in Correctional Group Therapy Programs," *Federal Probation*, vol. 18 (June 1954), pp. 20–26.
2   Harry J. Anslinger, "Drug Addiction," *Encyclopaedia Britannica*, vol. VII, 1960, pp. 667–679.
3   Edwin H. Sutherland and Donald R. Cressey, *Principles of Criminology* 6th ed., Philadelphia: J. B. Lippincott Company, 1960, pp. 74–80.
4   See, however, Joseph A. Cook and Gilbert Geis, "Forum Anonymous: The Techniques of Alcoholics Anonymous Applied to Prison Therapy," *Journal of Social Therapy*, vol. 3 (first quarter 1957), pp. 9–13.
5   The Board at first was composed of the three original members. It is now made up of the founder (an ex-alcoholic but a non-addict) and seven long-term residents who have remained off drugs and who have demonstrated their strict loyalty to the group and its principles.
6   Rita Volkman, "A Descriptive Case Study of Synanon as a Primary Group Organization," unpublished master's thesis, University of California, Department of Education, Los Angeles, 1961.

7  In May 1961 20 percent of the residents were Jewish.

8  *Cf. Family Background as an Etiological Factor in Personality Predisposition to Heroin Addiction*, New York: New York University Research Center for Human Relations, 1956.

9  Of the fifty-two members, 60 percent first heard about Synanon from addicts on the street or in jails, prisons, or hospitals; about a fourth heard about it on television or read about it in a magazine; and the remainder were told of it by members or past members.

10  Alfred R. Lindesmith, *Opiate Addiction*, Bloomington, Ind.: Principia Press, 1947, pp. 44–66.

11  See Lewis Yablonsky, "The Anti-criminal Society: Synanon," *Federal Probation*, vol. 26 (September 1962), pp. 50–57; and Lewis Yablonsky, *The Violent Gang*, New York: The Macmillan Company, 1962, pp. 252–263.

12  See Volkman, *op. cit.*, pp. 90–96.

13  See Cressey, "Contradictory Theories in Correctional Group Therapy Programs," *op. cit.*

14  *Cf.* Harrison M. Trice, "Alcoholism: Group Factors in Etiology and Therapy," *Human Organization*, vol. 15 (summer 1956), pp. 33–40; see also Donald R. Cressey, "The Nature and Effectiveness of Correctional Techniques," *Law and Contemporary Problems*, vol. 23 (fall 1958), pp. 754–771.

## SUPPLEMENTAL READINGS

Bauer, Raymond A.: "Societal Feedback," *The Annals*, vol. 373 (September 1967), pp. 181–192.

Becker, Howard S.: "Whose Side Are We On?," *Social Problems*, vol. 14 (winter 1967), pp. 239–247.

Bell, Daniel: *The End of Ideology*, New York: P. F. Collier & Sons, Corporation, 1961.

Cain, Arthur: "Alcoholics Anonymous: Cult or Cure?," *Harper's Magazine*, vol. 226 (February 1963), pp. 48–52.

Clinard, Marshall B.: *Slums and Community Development: Experiments in Self-help*, New York: The Free Press, 1966.

Empey, LaMar T., and Jerome Rabow: "The Provo Experiment in Delinquency Rehabilitation," *American Sociological Review*, vol. 26 (October 1961), pp. 679–695.

Etzioni, Amitai, and Edward W. Lehman: "Some Dangers in 'Valid' Social Measurement," *The Annals*, vol. 373 (September 1967), pp. 2–15.

Gardner, John W.: *No Easy Victories*, New York: Harper & Row, Publishers, 1968.

Hammond, Philip E. (ed.): *Sociologists at Work*, New York: Basic Books, Inc., 1964.

Hammond, Philip E., and Robert E. Mitchell: "Segmentation of Radicalism: The Case of the Protestant Campus Minister," *American Journal of Sociology*, vol. 71 (September 1965), pp. 133–143.

Haurek, Edward W., and John P. Clark: "Variants of Integration of Social Control Agencies," *Social Problems*, vol. 15 (summer 1967), pp. 46–60.

Horowitz, Irving L.: *The Rise and Fall of Project Camelot: Studies in* the Relationship between Social Science and Practical Politics, Cambridge, Mass.: The M.I.T. Press, 1967.

Keyserling, Leon H.: "Employment and the 'New Economics,' " *The Annals*, vol. 373 (September 1967), pp. 103–119.

Rainwater, Lee, and David J. Pittman: "Ethical Problems in Studying a Politically Sensitive and Deviant Community," *Social Problems*, vol. 14 (spring 1967), pp. 358–366.

Rose, Arnold: "School Desegregation," *Law and Society Review*, vol. 2 (November 1967) pp. 125–140.

Silverman, Charles E.: "Up from Apathy: The Woodlawn Experiment," *Commentary*, vol. 37 (May 1964), pp. 51–58.

Theobald, Robert: " 'Abundance' in Perspective: Should Men Compete with Machines?," *Nation*, vol. 202 (May 9, 1966), pp. 544–550.

Waitzkin, Howard: "Truth's Search for Power: The Dilemmas of the Social Sciences," *Social Problems*, vol. 15 (spring 1968), pp. 408–419.

Westin, Alan F.: "Science, Privacy, and Freedom," *Columbia Law Review*, vol. 67 (February 1967).